The Modern Theologians

An Introduction to Christian Theology since 1918

Third Edition

Edited by

David F. Ford
University of Cambridge

With

Rachel Muers
University of Exeter

Blackwell
Publishing

BLACKWELL PUBLISHING
350 Main Street, Malden, MA 02148-5020, USA
9600 Garsington Road, Oxford OX4 2DQ, UK
550 Swanston Street, Carlton, Victoria 3053, Australia

First published 2005 by Blackwell Publishing Ltd

9   2015

Library of Congress Cataloging-in-Publication Data

The modern theologians : an introduction to Christian theology since 1918.— 3rd ed. /
edited by David F. Ford with Rachel Muers.
   p. cm—(The great theologians)
  Includes bibliographical references and index.
  ISBN 978-1-4051-0276-6 (hard cover : alk. paper)
  ISBN 978-1-4051-0277-3 (pbk. : alk. paper)
  1. Theology, Doctrinal—History—20th century. 2. Theology, Doctrinal—History—21st
century. I. Ford, David, 1948– II. Muers, Rachel. III. Series.

  BT28.M59 2005
  230′.09′04—dc22

          2004029751

A catalogue record for this title is available from the British Library.

Set in 10/12pt Galliard
by Graphicraft Limited, Hong Kong

For further information on
Blackwell Publishing, visit our website:
www.blackwellpublishing.com

The Modern Theologians

The Great Theologians

A comprehensive series devoted to highlighting the major theologians of different periods. Each theologian is presented by a world-renowned scholar.

Published

The Modern Theologians, Third Edition
An Introduction to Christian Theology since 1918
David F. Ford with Rachel Muers

The Medieval Theologians
An Introduction to Theology in the Medieval Period
G. R. Evans

The Reformation Theologians
An Introduction to Theology in the Early Modern Period
Carter Lindberg

The First Christian Theologians
An Introduction to Theology in the Early Church
G. R. Evans

The Pietist Theologians
An Introduction to Theology in the Seventeenth and Eighteenth Centuries
Carter Lindberg

Contents

Preface

The main aim of this volume is to introduce the thought of most leading Christian theologians and movements in theology since the end of World War I (1914–18). Two criteria of selection were that the theologians should have written constructively on a broad range of theological issues, and that they should be widely studied at present, especially in universities, seminaries, and by others at the third level. There were also the more controversial criteria of quality and significance, and in some cases these have been decisive for inclusion.

The contributors are mostly based in Europe or North America and come from a wide range of institutions, denominational backgrounds, and countries. Most are themselves constructively engaged in modern theology, and their purpose has been both to produce a scholarly account of their subject and also to carry further the theological dialogue in each case. So the aim has been partly "historical theology" but also the sort of engaged discussion that comes from those who are practitioners in the field. We have been acutely aware of the impossibility of trying to look at this vast field from every angle and of the limitations in our chosen way of trying to do some justice to it.

The chapters try to help readers to think in a way appropriate to a theologian or movement while also encouraging dialogue and argument. The only way this can happen adequately is by close study of a theologian's writings, and it is to these above all that we aim to introduce readers. The main intended use of this volume is therefore to prepare for, accompany, and aid reflection on the study of texts. Yet few will be able to read all these theologies, so the complementary intention is to give some grasp of the rest of the field, beyond what any particular person has read.

There is a common pattern followed by most of the contributors: introduction, survey, content (concentrating on the main issues of a theology, or on particular members of movements), the debate about the content, an assessment of the theology's influence, achievement, and agenda for the future, and a short bibliography. Yet contributors have been allowed considerable freedom to adapt this pattern to their topic. In addition, each part of the book has a brief introduction. At the end of the volume there is a glossary of key words and phrases which a student entering the field might not have met already.

The grouping of theologians and movements into parts and sections should not have too much read into it. The arrangement has not been arrived at easily, because other schemes had almost equal advantages, and students of the two previous editions will notice the changes. Our brief introductions try to explain the selections, but the overriding concern has been for the particularity of each theology as understood by another theologian.

Part 1 concentrates on six theologians who are considered as classics of the twentieth century: Barth, Bonhoeffer, Tillich, de Lubac, Rahner, and Balthasar. (Bultmann probably deserves a place here too, but he is discussed under the heading of biblical interpretation in chapter 17.) None of those chosen is now living, three are Protestant, three Roman Catholic, and all except de Lubac are from German-speaking Europe (three Germans, two Swiss). That German-language tradition of academic theology perhaps deserves its prominence in this volume because, for all its problems and peculiarities, it is, as the Introduction explains, the most sustained and intensive example of engagement in the enterprise of modern theology in the nineteenth and twentieth centuries. To know that tradition is to be acquainted with a range of paradigmatic attempts to tackle key issues of modernity and religion in theology. It is not by any means all-inclusive, but it has the diversity, the coherence, and the thinkers of genius that make it educationally the best single tradition through which to be introduced to what it means to do Christian theology in intelligent engagement with modern disciplines, societies, churches, and traumatic events.

Part II on Theological Responses to Modernity in Europe and the USA shows how theology in those regions continues to be deeply indebted to the modern German-language tradition. In addition, it includes not only very different traditions rooted in Britain and the US (and there are others too, such as the Dutch and Scandinavian, not covered here) but also a range of new theological initiatives around which a good deal of early twenty-first century discussion revolves. Two innovations in this edition are the magisterial accounts of philosophical theology and of Roman Catholic theology after Vatican II.

Part III expands the treatment of theology's engagement with the natural sciences, in light of the enormous impact of recent developments, particularly in the biological sciences. Part IV on Theology, Prayer, and Practice is entirely new, reflecting both the huge interest in spirituality and pastoral practice and also the maturing of theological engagement with them in academic settings.

Part V on Particularizing Theology engages more extensively than the second edition with some of the deepest and most controversial issues of our times – race, gender, colonialism, liberation – and also with the continents of Latin America, Africa, and Asia. Distinctive theologies have been developing there that are closely involved with a huge variety of peoples, cultures, and religions but are often underrepresented in academic discussion outside their local contexts.

Part VI on Global Engagements looks at the theology of the ecumenical movement that so transformed twentieth-century relations between many churches, and also at the thinking going on within three of the most numerous strands of Christianity: Eastern Orthodoxy, Pentecostalism, and Evangelicalism. Pentecostalism, which has perhaps become the largest religious movement in history, is new to this edition.

Part VII on Theology Between Faiths has also moved beyond the second edition to include Islam and Buddhism as well as Judaism. It may well be that the peace of the twenty-first century depends more on relations between religions (and, inseparably, between religions and secular forces) than anything else, yet there is a sense of it being still "early days" in theological engagement with this sphere.

Finally, Part VIII on Theology in Many Media has added film to the visual arts and music, including a globally controversial film about the passion of Christ as a symbol both of the broad significance of this medium at present and also of its capacity to provoke intensive theological discussion.

In studying these 42 chapters one can glimpse the global scope of Christian theology, its diversity amounting often to fragmentation, and the immense intellectual energy with which it has accompanied or challenged or been knitted into major Christian, interreligious, and secular movements. At every point we have been painfully aware of having to omit theologies which would, given more space, have merited inclusion. Whole regions with rich theological traditions have been passed over. The scope for further "Theology and . . ." studies is limitless – we have added biological sciences, spirituality, Islam, Buddhism, and film, but the list of desirable candidates is far longer, including psychology, information technology, economics, management, social anthropology, medicine, education, criminology, and architecture.

Nevertheless, we hope that the changes in this volume are an improvement on the first two editions. They are in large part a response to many comments from readers and from fellow academics whose courses require an expanded coverage, and we are grateful to the respondents to a survey conducted by Blackwell among those using the second edition. For those accustomed to the second edition, the main differences (including those mentioned above) are: new chapters (some on topics treated in other ways in previous editions) on de Lubac, T. F. Torrance, Anglican Theology, H. Richard Niebuhr, Reinhold Niebuhr, Systematic Theology after Barth, Roman Catholic Theology after Vatican II, Philosophical Theology, Theology and the Biological Sciences, Theology and Spirituality, Pastoral Theology, Feminism, Gender and Theology, Theologies of South and of East Asia, Postcolonial Biblical Interpretation, Pentecostal Theology, Islam and Christian Theology, Buddhism and Christian Theology, and Theology and Film; new authors of previous chapters on Barth, Bonhoeffer, Rahner, Postliberal Theology, Theology and the Physical Sciences, Black Theology, African Theology, Ecumenical Theology, and Theology and the Visual Arts; no separate chapters on Bultmann (see chapter 17), Jüngel (see chapter 15), French Theology (see chapter 4), Schillebeeckx (see chapter 16), Küng (see chapter 16), British theologies (see chapters 9, 10, 14, 15, 16, 18, 19, and Parts 3, 4, 5, 6, 7, 8), Theological Ethics in the USA (see chapters 11, 12, 14), Black, Hispanic/Latino, and Native American Theologies in the USA (see chapters 25, 26), Feminist and Womanist Theologies in the USA (see chapter 25), Asian Theology (see chapters 29, 30), Theology of Mission (see chapters 34, 35), and transregional feminist theology (see chapter 25). Many chapters whose titles and authors remain the same or similar have undergone substantial revision since the second edition.

Finally, the Epilogue risks offering some theses that add up to a manifesto for Christian theology in the twenty-first century.

David F. Ford
Cambridge
Rachel Muers
Exeter
September 2004

Acknowledgments

Editing this volume for the third time has been immeasurably more enjoyable and less work because the labor has been shared with a fellow editor, Rachel Muers. My gratitude to her is immense, not only for the many hours she has put in, but also for her tracking of the various aspects of a considerably larger edition, and above all for her wise advice and judgment. She has accompanied this edition from its inception, and it has been a continual stimulation to look at *The Modern Theologians* through her eyes, and to discuss each contribution, her own not least.

The other people who have helped with this edition are numerous. First, there is each contributor. It seems amazing to us that all 42 chapters were actually produced, and I know that for many it was a considerable extra demand in already busy lives. I am most grateful for the quality of what has been written and for the patience shown to the editors when they demanded sometimes extensive changes. Then there is Ben Fulford, who has done such a thorough job on revising and updating the glossary. A special word of thanks is due to those who collaborated with contributors to previous editions who could not revise their contributions themselves: Ethna Regan, A. M. Allchin, and Peter C. Bouteneff. Rebecca Harkin, Laura Barry, Sophie Gibson, and others at Blackwell have been continually helpful and responded promptly to inquiries. There have been valuable conversations with a large number of colleagues in this fascinating field. Doreen Kunze has been a source of unfailing and encouragingly cheerful assistance in the office of the Faculty of Divinity in Cambridge. And the debts of gratitude to my family and friends continue to mount: to my wife Deborah, my mother Phyllis Ford, Dan and Perrin Hardy, my brother Alan Ford, Ben Quash, and Micheal O'Siadhail.

The first edition was dedicated to the memory of Hans W. Frei, teacher and friend to me and many others. The second edition was dedicated to my friend, co-author, and colleague for many years, Frances Young, Edward Cadbury Professor of Theology at the University of Birmingham. During the course of preparing this edition, Colin Gunton, who had agreed to contribute the chapter on T. F. Torrance, died suddenly. It is hard to do justice to what Colin meant to generations of theologians in Britain (and increasingly from abroad, too). John Webster was, at the time of Colin's death, already writing chapter 15 of this edition, in which his work is discussed and his considerable achievement acknowledged. The chapter on Torrance was taken over by Dan Hardy, my friend, father-in-law, and collaborator in much writing and other activity. Dan was a friend of Colin over several decades, and has contributed pervasively to all three editions of *The Modern Theologians* – the first edition was inspired largely by the course on modern theological thought that Dan devised and later co-taught with me at the University of Birmingham. So it seems deeply appropriate to dedicate this edition jointly to both Colin Gunton and Dan Hardy.

David F. Ford

Notes on Contributors

Allan Anderson is Reader in Pentecostal Studies in the Department of Theology at the University of Birmingham. He has a D.Th. from the University of South Africa, where he worked for 23 years as a Pentecostal/Charismatic minister and theological educator. He has written numerous articles and five books on African Pentecostalism and Independentism and has edited two books on global Pentecostalism. His latest books are *African Reformation* (2001) and *An Introduction to Pentecostalism* (2004).

Richard Bauckham is Professor of New Testament Studies and Bishop Wardlaw Professor at the University of St. Andrews. He was born and educated in England. His many publications include *Moltmann: Messianic Theology in the Making* (1987), *The Bible in Politics: How to Read the Bible Politically* (1990), *The Theology of Jürgen Moltmann* (1995), *God and the Crisis of Freedom: Biblical and Contemporary Perspectives* (2002), *Bible and Mission: Christian Witness in a Postmodern World* (2003), and (with Trevor Hart) *Hope against Hope: Christian Eschatology at the Turn of the Millennium* (1999).

Jeremy S. Begbie is Associate Principal of Ridley Hall, Cambridge, Honorary Professor at the University of St. Andrews, and an Affiliated Lecturer in the Faculty of Divinity, University of Cambridge. He directs an international research project, "Theology Through the Arts," and his publications include *Music in God's Purposes* (1988), *Voicing Creation's Praise: Towards a Theology of the Arts* (1991), *Theology, Music and Time* (2000), and (ed.) *Sounding the Depths: Theology Through the Arts* (2002).

James J. Buckley is Professor of Theology and Dean of the College of Arts and Sciences at Loyola College, Baltimore. He was born and educated in the United States, with his doctorate in religious studies from Yale University. He has written *Seeking the Humanity of God: Practices, Doctrines, and Catholic Theology* (1992) as well as articles in contemporary theology. He is on the editorial boards of *Modern Theology* and *Pro Ecclesia*.

Rebecca S. Chopp is President of Colgate University, having previously served as Dean of Yale Divinity School and taught theology at Emory and Chicago. She is a past president of the American Academy of Religion. Her publications include *Saving Work: Feminist Practices of Theological Education* (1995), *The Power to Speak: Feminism, Language, God* (1989), and *The Praxis of Suffering: An Interpretation of Liberation and Political Theologies* (1986).

Philip Clayton is Professor of Theology at the Claremont School of Theology and Professor of Philosophy and Religion at the Claremont Graduate University. He holds a PhD in both Philosophy and Religious Studies from Yale University and has held Humboldt, Fulbright, and visiting professorships at the University of Munich and Harvard Divinity School. He is the author or editor of 12 books, including *The Problem of God in Modern Thought* (2000), *God and Contemporary Science* (1998), *Evolution and Ethics* (2004), *In Whom We Live and Move and Have Our Being* (2004), and *Science and the Spiritual Quest* (2002). His work on the theology of emergence, *The Emergence of Spirit*, was published in 2004.

Ingolf U. Dalferth is Director of the Institute for Hermeneutics and Philosophy of Religion in Zurich, where he lectures in systematic theology and the philosophy of religion. He was educated in Tübingen, Edinburgh, Vienna, and Cambridge. His publications include *Der auferweckte Gekreuzigte. Zur Grammatik der Christologie* (1994), *Gedeutete Gegenwart. Zur Wahrnehmung Gottes in den Erfahrungen der Zeit* (1997), *Theology and Philosophy* (2002), and *Die Wirklichkeit des Möglichen. Hermeneutische Religionsphilosophie* (2003).

Gavin D'Costa is Reader and Head of Department in the Department of Theology and Religious Studies at the University of Bristol. He is an Indian Roman Catholic who was educated at the Universities of Birmingham and Cambridge. His publications include *Theology and Religious Pluralism* (1986), *The Meeting of Religions and the Trinity* (2000), *Sexing the Trinity* (2000), and *The Virtue of Theology in a Secular Society* (2004). He is involved in interfaith dialogue and is an advisor to the Catholic Bishops of England and Wales and a consultant to the Pontifical Commission for Interreligious Dialogue.

Celia Deane-Drummond qualified originally as a plant scientist, and held several research and teaching posts in that field. She later studied theology at Manchester University, and is now Professor of Theology and the Biological Sciences at Chester College. Her publications include *A Handbook in Theology and Ecology* (1996), *Theology and Biotechnology: Implications for a New Science* (1997), *Creation Through Wisdom: Theology and the New Biology* (2000), *Biology and Theology Today: Exploring the Boundaries* (2001), and *The Ethics of Nature* (2003).

Wayne Whitson Floyd is the General Editor and Project Director of the Dietrich Bonhoeffer Works, English edition (DBWE). He is the former Canon Theologian of the Cathedral Church of St. Stephen in Harrisburg, PA, and later of the Episcopal Diocese of Southern Virginia, where he also served as founder and director of the

Anglican Center for Theology and Spirituality. Besides serving as editor for two DBWE volumes – *Act and Being* and *Letters and Papers from Prison* – he is the author of *Theology and the Dialectics of Otherness: On Reading Bonhoeffer and Adorno* (1988) and *The Wisdom and Witness of Dietrich Bonhoeffer* (2000), and the editor (with Charles Marsh) of *Theology and the Practice of Responsibility: Essays on Dietrich Bonhoeffer* (1994).

James Fodor is Associate Professor of Theological Ethics/Moral Theology at St. Bonaventure University. He is the author of *Christian Hermeneutics: Paul Ricoeur and the Refiguring of Theology* (1995) and is co-editor of the journal *Modern Theology*.

David F. Ford is Regius Professor of Divinity at the University of Cambridge. He is the author of *Theology: A Very Short Introduction* (2000), *Self and Salvation: Being Transformed* (1999), *The Shape of Living* (1997), *Meaning and Truth in 2 Corinthians* (1988, with Frances M. Young), *Jubilate: Theology in Praise* (1984, with Daniel W. Hardy), and *Barth and God's Story: Biblical Narrative and the Theological Method of Karl Barth in the Church Dogmatics* (1981). He also directs the Cambridge Interfaith Programme and is a member of the editorial board of a number of journals, including *Modern Theology* and *Scottish Journal of Theology*.

John W. de Gruchy, educated in South Africa and the USA, taught for thirty years at the University of Cape Town, where he was the first incumbent of the Robert Selby Taylor Chair of Christian Studies. He was the founder of the *Journal of Theology for Southern Africa*. His many books include *Christianity, Art and Transformation: Theological Aesthetics in the Struggle for Justice* (2001), *Reconciliation: Restoring Justice* (2003), *Theology and Ministry in Context and Crisis: A South African Perspective* (1987), and (edited with Ralf K. Wustenberg and Lyn Holness) *Theology in Dialogue: The Impact of the Arts, Humanities and Science on Contemporary Religious Thought* (2002).

Daniel W. Hardy is a senior member of the Faculty of Divinity in the University of Cambridge, having previously been Van Mildert Professor of Divinity at Durham and the Director of the Center of Theological Inquiry at Princeton. His publications include *God's Ways With the World: Thinking and Practicing Christian Faith* (1996), *Finding the Church: The Dynamic Truth of Anglicanism* (2001), and *Jubilate: Theology as Praise* (with David F. Ford, 1984).

Stanley Hauerwas is Gilbert T. Rowe Professor of Theological Ethics at Duke University. Among his many publications are *The Peaceable Kingdom: A Primer in Christian Ethics* (2003), *Character and the Christian Life: A Study in Theological Ethics* (1994), and *Sanctify Them in the Truth: Holiness Exemplified* (1998). His 2000–1 Gifford lectures were published as *With the Grain of the Universe* (2001).

Dwight N. Hopkins, Professor of Theology at the University of Chicago Divinity School, received a PhD from Union Theological Seminary (New York) and a second PhD from the University of Cape Town. His works include *Shoes That Fit Our*

Feet: Sources for a Constructive Black Theology (1994), *Down, Up and Over: Slave Religion and Black Theology* (2000), *Introducing Black Theology of Liberation* (1999), *Heart and Head: Black Theology Past, Present and Future* (2003), and *On Being Human: Black Theology Looks at Culture, Self, and Race* (2004).

Paul O. Ingram is Professor of Religion at Pacific Lutheran University. He has published widely in the field of history of religions, focusing on Japanese religious history, as well as Buddhist–Christian dialogue. His most recent books are *The Modern Buddhist–Christian Dialogue* (1988) and *Wrestling With the Ox: A Theology of Religious Experience* (1997). His current research interest and publications are in the area of interreligious dialogue with the natural sciences.

David H. Kelsey is Luther Weigle Professor of Theology at Yale Divinity School. He studied philosophy and theology at Haverford and Yale. His many books include *The Fabric of Paul Tillich's Theology* (1967), *The Uses of Scripture in Recent Theology* (1975), and *Between Athens and Berlin: The Theological Education Debate* (1993).

Karen Kilby is Lecturer in Systematic Theology at the University of Nottingham, having studied theology at Yale and held posts at St. Andrews and Birmingham. She is the author of *Karl Rahner: Theology and Philosophy* (2004) and *Karl Rahner* (1987), as well as of numerous articles and reviews in systematic theology.

Archie Chi Chung Lee is Professor in the Department of Cultural and Religious Studies, the Chinese University of Hong Kong. His main research interests are the Hebrew Bible and Christianity in Asia. He has published widely in these areas, as well as in cross-textual hermeneutics and Chinese classics. His publications include *Discourse and Identity: A Study of the Hebrew Megilloth* (in Chinese). He is one of the associate editors of the *Global Bible Commentary*.

Gordon Lynch is Lecturer in Practical Theology in the Department of Theology at the University of Birmingham. His recent publications include *After Religion: "Generation X" and the Search for Meaning* (2002) and *Pastoral Care and Counselling* (2002). He is currently working on practical theological engagements with popular culture.

Mark A. McIntosh, Associate Professor of Theology at Loyola University Chicago, is an Episcopal priest, currently serving as Chaplain to the House of Bishops of the Episcopal Church and Canon Theologian to the Presiding Bishop and Primate. He holds degrees in history and theology from Yale, Oxford, and the University of Chicago, and has published several works at the intersection of theology and spirituality, most recently *Discerning Truth: The Spirituality and Theology of Knowledge* (2004), and the *Blackwell Guide to Christian Theology* (2006).

Tinyiko Sam Maluleke holds the Chair of Black and African Theology in the departments of Missiology and Systematic Theology at the Pretoria-based University of South Africa. He is currently serving as Deputy Executive Dean (College of Human Sciences) at the same university. He has published more than sixty book chapters and scientific essays in the area of African studies, missiology, African theology, and Black theology. He is a frequent theological consultant and speaker at the All Africa Conference of Churches, the World Council of Churches, and the South African Council of Churches, and is the current General Secretary of the Southern Africa Missiological Society.

John Milbank is Professor of Religion, Politics and Ethics at the University of Nottingham, having previously held posts at the Universities of Lancaster, Cambridge, and Virginia. He was educated at Oxford, Cambridge, and Birmingham. His books include *Theology and Social Theory: Beyond Secular Reason* (1990), *The Word Made Strange* (1997), *Being Reconciled: Ontology and Pardon* (2002), and (co-edited with Graham Ward and Catherine Pickstock) *Radical Orthodoxy: A New Theology* (1999).

Jolyon Mitchell is Senior Lecturer at New College, Edinburgh University, and also a life member of Clare Hall, Cambridge University. He was educated at Cambridge, Durham, and Edinburgh Universities. He is the author of *Visually Speaking: Radio and the Renaissance of Preaching* (1999) and co-editor of *Mediating Religion: Conversations in Media, Religion and Culture* (2003). He was formerly a producer and journalist with the BBC World Service, and is currently working on *Media and Christian Ethics* (forthcoming).

Rachel Muers is Lecturer in Theology at the University of Exeter. She was educated at Cambridge and held a research fellowship at Girton College. She is the author of *Keeping God's Silence: Towards a Theological Ethics of Communication* (2004), and of several articles and reviews in feminist theology and theological ethics.

Paul D. Murray is Lecturer in Systematic Theology at the University of Durham. He has previously held lecturing posts at St. Cuthbert's Seminary, Ushaw College, Durham, and Newman College of Higher Education, Birmingham and has worked as an Adult Christian Educator within the Department of Pastoral Formation of the Archdiocese of Liverpool. He is the author of *Reason, Truth and Theology in Pragmatist Perspective* (2004) and of several articles and essays in the areas of science and theology and philosophical theology.

Peter Ochs is the Edgar Bronfman Professor of Modern Judaic Studies at the University of Virginia and co-founder of the Society for Textual Reasoning, the Society for Scriptural Reasoning, and the Children of Abraham Institute. He was co-author/editor of "Dabru Emet (A Jewish Statement on Christians and Christianity)" and the accompanying book *Christianity in Jewish Terms* (2002). Among his books are *Peirce, Pragmatism and the Logic of Scripture* (1998), *Reasoning after Revelation: Dialogues in Postmodern Jewish Philosophy* (with Robert Gibbs and Steven Kepnes, 1998), and *Textual Reasonings* (edited with Nancy Levene, 2002).

Stephen Pattison is head of the School of Religious and Theological Studies at Cardiff University and was formerly a senior lecturer in the School of Health and Social Welfare at the Open University. Educated at Cambridge, Edinburgh, Birmingham, and Open Universities, he is the author of *Pastoral Care and Liberation Theology* (1997), *The Faith of the Managers* (1997), *A Critique of Pastoral Care* (2000), and *Shame: Theory, Therapy, Theology* (2000) and editor, with others, of *The Blackwell Reader in Pastoral and Practical Theology* (2000) and *Values in Professional Practice* (2004).

Ben Quash is Dean and Fellow of Peterhouse and teaches Christian theology in the Faculty of Divinity at the University of Cambridge. He has been a visiting lecturer at the University of Tübingen. He is co-author (with Lucy Gardner, David Moss, and Graham Ward) of *Balthasar at the End of Modernity* (1999), and his publications include contributions to *Conversing With Barth* (2004, ed. John C. McDowell and Mike Higton), *The Cambridge Companion to Hans Urs von Balthasar* (2004, ed. David Moss and Edward T. Oakes), and *Sounding the Depths: Theology Through the Arts* (2002, ed. Jeremy Begbie).

Ethna Regan is Lecturer in Theology at the University of the West Indies, Trinidad, and Chair of the Credo Foundation for Justice in Port of Spain. She was born in Ireland and educated in Dublin, at Fordham University, and at the University of Cambridge. A Holy Faith Sister, she has worked in Samoa and the Caribbean.

Richard H. Roberts is Professor Emeritus of Religious Studies at Lancaster University and Honorary Professor of Religious Studies at the University of Stirling. He studied at the universities of Lancaster, Cambridge, Edinburgh, and Tübingen. He was Professor of Divinity at the University of St. Andrews and then held a Chair in Religious Studies at Lancaster University. He has written or edited books on Karl Barth, Ernst Bloch, rhetoric and interdisciplinarity, religion and the transformations of capitalism, time and value, contemporary "nature religion," and space and time in the modern/postmodern matrix. His most recent book is *Religion, Theology and the Human Sciences* (2002).

Christoph Schwöbel is Professor of Systematic Theology and Philosophy of Religion, and Director of the Institute of Hermeneutics, at the University of Tübingen. He was born and educated in Germany, and has held posts at King's College London, the University of Kiel, and the University of Heidelberg, where he was Director of the Ecumenical Institute. He is the author of *Martin Rade* (1980), *God, Action, and Revelation* (1992), *Gott in Beziehung* (2002), and *Christlicher Glaube im Pluralismus* (2003).

Peter Sedgwick is Principal of St. Michael's College, Llandaff, Wales. Until 2004 he was Policy Officer on Criminal Justice for the Church of England Public Affairs Unit. He previously lectured in modern theology and Christian ethics at the Universities of Hull and Birmingham. He has degrees in theology and history from the University of Cambridge and a doctorate in Anglican historical theology from the University of Durham. He is the author of several works in social ethics, including *Economic Theory and Christian Belief* (with Andrew Britton, 2003), *The Market Economy and Christian Ethics* (1999), and *The Enterprise Culture* (1992), and has edited *The Future of Criminal Justice* (with C. Jones, 2002), *God in the City* (1996), and *The Weight of Glory: The Future of Liberal Theology* (with D. W. Hardy, 1992).

Ataullah Siddiqui is a Senior Research Fellow at the Islamic Foundation, Leicester and Assistant Director of the Markfield Institute of Higher Education. He is also Visiting Fellow in the Centre for the History of Religious and Political Pluralism, University of Leicester, and co-editor of *Encounters: Journal of Inter-Cultural Perspectives*. His publications include *Christian–Muslim Dialogue in the Twentieth Century* (1997), *Islam and Other Faiths*, a collection of Ismail Raji Al Faruqi's articles (1998), and *Christians and Muslims in the Commonwealth: A Dynamic Role in the Future* (co-edited, 2001).

R. S. Sugirtharajah is Professor of Biblical Hermeneutics, University of Birmingham. He was born in Sri Lanka and was educated in Bangalore and Birmingham. His publications include *Postcolonial Reconfigurations: An Alternative Way of Reading the Bible and Doing Theology* (2003), *Postcolonial Criticism and Biblical Interpretation* (2002), and *The Bible and the Third World: Precolonial, Colonial and Postcolonial Encounters* (2001).

Mary Tanner taught Hebrew and Old Testament for twenty years in the Universities of Hull and Bristol and at Westcott House, Cambridge. In 1982 she joined the staff of the Board for Mission and Unity of the General Synod of the Church of England and when the Board divided became the first General Secretary of the Council for Christian Unity. She served on the Faith and Order Commission of the World Council of Churches and was its Moderator from 1991 to 1998. She served on the International Anglican–Roman Catholic Commission and is currently a member of the Special Commission on Orthodox Relations set up by the World Council of Churches.

Anthony C. Thiselton is Emeritus Professor of Christian Theology at the University of Nottingham, Research Professor at University College Chester, and Canon Theologian of Leicester Cathedral and of Southwell Minster. He has a PhD from the University of Sheffield and honorary doctorates from Durham and from the Archbishop of Canterbury. He has published over seventy articles and books, including *The First Epistle to the Corinthians: A Commentary on the Greek Text* (2000), *Interpreting God and the Postmodern Self* (1995), *New Horizons in Hermeneutics* (1992), and *The Two Horizons* (1980).

Graham Ward is Professor of Contextual Theology at the University of Manchester, and was previously Dean of Peterhouse, Cambridge. His books include *Theology and Contemporary Critical Theory* (1996), *Cities of God* (2000), and *True Religion* (2002), and he edited the *Blackwell Companion to Postmodern Theology* (2001). He is editor of the journal *Literature and Theology*.

John Webster is Professor of Systematic Theology at the University of Aberdeen. He is the author of *Barth's Ethics of Reconciliation* (1995), *Barth's Moral Theology* (1998), and *Barth* (2000), and he edited *The Cambridge Companion to Karl Barth*

(2000). More recently he has written *Word and Church* (2001), *Holiness* (2002), and *Holy Scripture* (2003).

David F. Wells is the Andrew Mutch Distinguished Professor of Historical and Systematic Theology at Gordon-Conwell Theological Seminary in Massachusetts. He was born in Rhodesia, now Zimbabwe, and was educated at the Universities of Cape Town, London, and Manchester and was a post-doctoral fellow at Yale. His publications include *The Person of Christ: A Biblical and Historical Analysis of the Incarnation* (1984), *No Place for Truth: Or, Whatever Happened to Evangelical Theology?* (1993), *God in the Wasteland: The Reality of Truth in a World of Fading Dreams* (1994), and *Above All Earthly Pow'rs: Christ in a Postmodern World* (2004).

William Werpehowski is Professor of Christian Ethics at Villanova University, and also Director of Villanova's Center for Peace and Justice Education. He studied theology and religious ethics at Princeton and Yale. He has published *American Protestant Ethics and the Legacy of H. Richard Niebuhr* (2003).

Felix Wilfred is Professor and Head of the Department of Christian Studies at the University of Madras, Chennai. He has been President of the Indian Theological Association and a member of the Vatican's International Theological Commission, and is a member of the board of directors of *Concilium*. His publications include *Leave the Temple: Indian Paths to Human Liberation* (1992), *On the Banks of Ganges: Doing Contextual Theology* (2002), and *Beyond Settled Foundations: The Journey of Indian Theology* (1993).

Rowan Williams is Archbishop of Canterbury. Born in Wales, he studied theology at Cambridge and Oxford. His previous positions include Lady Margaret Professor of Divinity at Oxford and Dean of Clare College, Cambridge. He became Archbishop of Wales in 2000 and Archbishop of Canterbury in 2002. A Fellow of the British Academy, he has published widely; his books include *Arius: Heresy and Tradition* (second edition 2001), *Sergei Bulgakov* (1999), and *On Christian Theology* (2000).

Introduction to Modern Christian Theology

David F. Ford

Christian theology since 1918 has been immensely varied. This has not just been a matter of diverse approaches and conclusions, but also of fundamental differences about what theology is, what modernity is, and what Christianity is, and which questions within these areas are to be given priority. This makes an overview difficult, all the more so because many of the theologians are still alive and producing new works, and some of the movements are still young. This introduction attempts to give, not an integrating picture, but sufficient background and general understanding of the field to help readers approaching it for the first time to find their bearings, and to assist more experienced readers to explore it further. The Epilogue gives a more forward-looking set of theses for the start of the twenty-first century.

What Sort of Subject is Modern Christian Theology?

Between the European Middle Ages and the end of the nineteenth century there were many major events and transformations of life and thought, often originating in Europe but with global consequences. Chief among these have been the Renaissance and Reformation, the colonization of the Americas, the Enlightenment, the American and French Revolutions, the rise of nationalism, the Industrial Revolution, and the development of the natural sciences, technologies, medical science, and the human sciences. There has also been the combined impact of bureaucracies, constitutional democracy, new means of warfare and of communication, mass education and public health programs, and new movements in the arts and in philosophy and religion. Theologians have been members of societies, churches, and academic institutions through this innovative, traumatic period, and their theology has inevitably been influenced by it. That is how, in a minimal sense, their theology is modern: by taking account of such developments, even if sometimes in order to dismiss, criticize, resist, or try to reverse them.

Some may wish to repeat a past theology, but this is not possible. The context has changed, and what is actually communicated and understood today can be very far from the original meaning. Yet Christian theology always requires some continuity with the past, so the question is how there can be appropriate continuity without simple repetition.

What is the significance of modernity for the content and method of theology? What is the importance of Christianity for a proper appreciation and response to modernity? And might it be that a religion with the discontinuity of the crucifixion at its heart enables a creative way of coping with the novelty and disruption of modernity? Such questions, which are broadly in the area of interpretation or hermeneutics, are inextricable from others about the nature of Christianity and of theology. All the theologians treated in this volume have to handle them, and it might be helpful to note some of the main strategies they use.

Imagine a line punctuated by five types of theology.[1] At one end, the first type is the attempt to repeat a traditional theology or version of Christianity and see all reality in its own terms, with no recognition of the significance for it of other perspectives or of all that has happened in recent centuries. At the other extreme, the fifth type gives complete priority to some modern secular philosophy or worldview, and Christianity in its own terms is only valid insofar as it fits in with that. So, for this fifth type, parts of Christian faith and practice may be found true or acceptable, but the assessment is always made according to criteria which are external to Christian understanding and which claim superiority to it. Neither of these extremes is represented among the theologians studied in this book, the first because it is hardly modern in the sense intended, the fifth because it is hardly Christian.

That leaves three types in between. Type two gives priority to the self-description of the Christian community (which is, of course, by no means uncontroversial) and might be characterized by Anselm of Canterbury's motto, "faith seeking understanding." It insists that Christian identity is primary and that all other reality needs to be construed in relation to it, but also that Christianity itself needs continually to be rethought and that theology must engage seriously with the modern world in its quest for understanding. Karl Barth is a leading representative of this approach, though this typecasting by no means exhausts his theology – and the same is true of attempts to pigeonhole most of the other theologians. Daniel Hardy's essay (chapter 1) describes this theology in its development and content, and traces its remarkable fruitfulness in the work of other leading theologians. Further examples of this type are Bonhoeffer (though some would dispute this, especially as regards his latest letters and papers), de Lubac, Balthasar, Torrance, MacKinnon, Ramsey, Williams, most postliberals, Jüngel, Jenson, Gunton, John Paul II, Lash, those called conservative postmoderns in chapter 19, and much ecumenical, Eastern Orthodox, Evangelical, and Pentecostal theology. Peter Ochs in chapter 37 offers an analysis of how this type especially relates to Judaism and Jewish theologies.

Type three comes exactly at the middle of the line. It is a theology of correlation. It brings traditional Christian faith and understanding into dialogue with modernity, and tries to correlate the two in a wide variety of ways. It does not claim any overarching integration of Christianity and modernity – neither one that would subsume modernity within Christian terms nor one that would exhaustively present Christianity in specifically modern terms. In its classic modern representative, Paul Tillich, it takes the form of the basic questions raised in contemporary life and thought being correlated with answers developed through interpretation of key Christian symbols. In a period of fragmentation and pluralism the method of correlation is especially attractive as a way of keeping going a range of open dialogues. It is a component in most theologies and is particularly important in Schillebeeckx, Küng, some of those theologies labeled "particularizing" in Part V, and many of those in North America who could be called revisionist. James Buckley in chapter 13 defines revisionists as those "devoted to shaping Christian practices and teachings in dialogue with modern philosophies, cultures, and social practices."

The fourth type uses a particular (or sometimes more than one) modern philosophy, conceptuality, or problem as a way of integrating Christianity with an understanding of modernity. It wants to do justice to both and sees the best way of doing this to be the consistent reinterpretation of Christianity in terms of some contemporary idiom or concern. Examples of this fourth type might be Pannenberg, those Buckley describes as liberals, and some leading representatives of particularizing theologies which propose issues of gender, race, political liberation, regional context, or historical experience as the decisive integrators. Rudolf Bultmann in chapter 17 can also be seen in these terms, using existentialism as the key to interpreting the New Testament.

Such a scheme is too neat to fit the whole of any major theology, but it helps in mapping some of the main possibilities in relation to a central and unavoidable matter, the interaction of Christianity with modernity. It also enables us to notice some theologians in whom apparently no one type is dominant. Karl Rahner (chapter 5) is irreducibly pluralist, even though many standard readings of him make him seem, in his use of a particular philosophical anthropology, to fit the fourth type. It can be immensely significant for a theologian's reputation and reception to liberate him or her from inadequate typing, as Karen Kilby does with Rahner, and when a particular theology seems to fit well into one type there must be a special effort to discern the ways in which the type is also transcended. Christoph Schwöbel's description of Pannenberg in chapter 7 does this for him. It may also be that, whatever one's own preferred type, the quality of one's theology is still linked to the depth of engagement with those who might be categorized under other types. Hans Frei, who developed the typology on which mine is based, saw himself doing theology between the second and third types, while intellectually and aesthetically participating in all five.

This leads into a final observation that some of the deepest differences about important matters, and even whole ways of doing theology, cut across the above types. This applies, for example, to the role of practice or of decision in Christianity, and to some conceptions of human freedom, divine action, the shape of the church, the significance of gender, and much else. One way of both enriching and relativizing any typology is to compare and contrast it with others. Within this volume there is a fascinating range of typologies used (see, for example, chapters 16, 18, 19, 20, 22, 25, 28, 32, 35, and Parts VII and VIII). Yet there is no substitute for engaging with issues of content, and often in the intensive grappling with key questions the rather formal and abstract concern about mapping the types is swallowed up in the adventure of a particular intellectual, spiritual, and practical journey.

Key Modern Issues

What have been the main issues in theology since 1918? The following five sections explore what has been characteristic: the continuing importance of the inherited agenda of doctrines, the problem of how to integrate a theology, the recovery and criticism of the past, the special significance of the nineteenth century, and the conditioning of theologies by their contexts and interests.

The systematic agenda

The traditional topics of what is variously called systematic theology, Christian doctrine, dogmatic theology, or constructive theology are: God and revelation, pre-destination (or election), creation and providence, human being, sin and evil, Jesus Christ, atonement (or redemption or salvation), the Holy Spirit (or grace), and Christian living (including justification, sanctification, vocation, ethics, and politics), the church, ministry and sacraments, and eschatology. These doctrines (or dogmas or loci) can be seen as a concentration of the main events and issues in the Christian overarching story from before creation until after the consummation of history. They continue to be important for modern theology, and even when a theologian has a very different framework the questions raised by these doctrines will have to be answered. Among those topics, there have been some characteristic modern emphases. At least until the 1960s the distinctive contributions of twentieth-century thinkers were in the areas of God (especially the reconception of the Trinity and the relationship of suffering to God), revelation (very different approaches, represented for example by Barth, Tillich, Rahner, Pannenberg, and Bultmann), Jesus Christ and salvation in history (closely tied to the previous two issues), human being, and eschatology.

Eschatology deserves special mention. The twentieth century opened with the rediscovery by academic theology of its importance in the New Testament. Secular eschatologies (of progress, socialist revolution, empire, or race) have had immense influence in modern times, but mainstream Christianity had largely ignored the eschatological dimension of its own origins. When it was widely recognized, partly under the pressure of secular alternatives and the crisis of European culture and society manifest in World War I, then it gave a new standpoint for thinking through Christianity. There was a great variety of eschatologies, and the unavoidability of the question has been one of the distinctive marks of twentieth-century – in contrast with nineteenth-century – theology.

It becomes increasingly difficult to generalize or have any adequate perspective on more recent years. Any neglect of sin and evil (especially in the aftermath of the Holocaust and other genocides, the Gulag, and Hiroshima) is being corrected in recent theology. As the Pentecostal movement has spread, not only in new inde-pendent churches but also through millions in the traditional denominations, the Holy Spirit has also been a major topic, though some would see this as a variation on the typically modern preoccupation with subjectivity and immediate experience. Christian living and the church have also had increasing attention, in line with emphases on praxis and community. The earlier concern with eschatology has been somewhat overshadowed by a (not unrelated) focus on creation and ecological matters. Some of the additions to this third edition tell their own story about recent doctrinal concerns: Jenson, Gunton, John Paul II, philosophical theology, theology and spirituality, pastoral theology, and Pentecostal theology.

Integrations

How is a theologian to relate these various topics to each other? One tendency (corresponding to the second type described above) is to see Christianity as having a certain coherence in itself. The doctrines together are the intellectual description of this. So Lindbeck (see chapter 14) compares doctrines to the statement of the basic grammar or rules showing how a language or culture hangs together. This makes the Christian community the main home of Christian theology (cf. Barth's *Church Dogmatics*) and asserts the priority of a distinctive Christian identity, as expressed above all in the Bible. The way theology is integrated in such an approach is through something internal to the tradition, usually the Bible or one or more key doctrines. Other worldviews and disciplines are discussed and may contribute, but not as equals or superiors.

Other theologians (in the third correlating type, and the fourth type that integrates around some modern conceptuality or concern) see integration with modernity as more important and even as essential to a modern theology. Typical concerns are to work out a theological method comparable with other disciplines, often trying to show that theology can justify its claims to rationality and knowledge (see Pannenberg, revisionists and liberals, and many participants in the debates about theology and the sciences outlined in Part III), or to affirm the relevance of Christian faith by reinterpreting it in relation to a modern philosophy (see Dalferth's survey of philosophical theology in chapter 18) or urgent issues (oppression, gender, race, nuclear war, ecology, relations between religions).

Overall, these theologies display a tension between the identity of Christianity and its relevance to modernity. At the international and institutional levels this has in the twentieth century been dramatized most publicly in ecumenical theology, and it has been built into the World Council of Churches' twin focus on Faith and Order and Life and Work. But Christianity in the twentieth century has also added hundreds of millions to its numbers in many parts of the world, and here the tensions of identity and relevance are often extreme. Many theologies of Africa, Asia, and Pentecostalism illustrate this.

Recovering and criticizing the past

A major feature of modernity has been its concern with history. Underlying this is a heightened awareness of change and innovation. The tools that have served this are new methods of research and new criteria for historical reliability. These, together with the greatly increased scale of historical study and research, have had the most obvious effects on theology. The Bible (see especially chapters 17 and 31) and the rest of the Christian heritage have been examined afresh and traditional opinions often challenged. But that has been just one manifestation of a more comprehensive problem.

Modern historical consciousness recognizes that meaning is closely bound up with changing contexts and that today we are also conditioned by many factors as we try to understand the past. Is the whole enterprise of "true" interpretation possible?

For Christian theologians, it has seemed unavoidable to attempt it, and the most fundamental reason for this is that Christianity (and it is not alone in this) cannot do without the authority of the past in some form. So a great deal of attention has been paid to what is often called hermeneutics, the art and theory of interpretation (chapter 17). How do we cope with the "hermeneutical circle," the problem that in understanding the past we tend to draw conclusions based on our own presuppositions, interests, and involvements? Is the meaning or truth of a text such as a gospel necessarily bound up with its being historically factual? There are very broad questions about language and self in relation to reality (there has been a great deal of reflection on metaphor, narrative, objectivity, and subjectivity), and other questions about genre, the intention of the author, or the relative roles of disciplines such as philology, literary criticism, sociology, psychology, comparative religion, philosophy, and history. And often there is a divergence between those who see much of the Christian past as on the whole worth recovering, and others who see it more as something from which liberation is needed and who use a "hermeneutic of suspicion" to do so.

The themes of suspicion, doubt, and radical critique are constantly present in modern thought, raising most sharply the issues of authority and reliability. For many, the very discipline of theology has disintegrated and lost its intellectual integrity in the face of all this. So most theologians discussed in these volumes are engaged in a recovery of Christianity in the face of unprecedented devastating, sophisticated, and widely disseminated dismissals of both Christianity and theology. That, at least, is the situation in the West and in those influenced by it. But some, such as Latin American liberation theologies (chapter 27), try to redefine the concerns and context of theology so that the confrontation with doubt, agnosticism, atheism, and the intellectual world of the modern West takes second place to serving a praxis of liberation.

In addition (and sometimes, as with Marx, accompanying a fundamental strategy of suspicion) there has been the challenge from modern overviews of history as alternatives to the much-criticized traditional Christian story stretching from creation to consummation. Does Christian theology need a renewed overarching conception of history? Pannenberg and Rahner would say so, but Bultmann would see such an idea as dangerously mythological, and many others too have serious reservations.

That and all the issues mentioned thus far can be seen as aspects of a pivotal modern theological concern: the relationship of faith and history. In continental European Protestant theology this was a fundamental matter dividing Barth and Bultmann. When they were found wanting by successors such as Pannenberg and Moltmann it was again this issue that was central. It has likewise been a dominant concern in much British, North American, and Evangelical theology, and many new challenges in theology also focus on it in their own ways. It is perhaps in Roman Catholic theology that the implications of modern thinking about faith and history are most sharply underlined. This is partly because it was only in the third quarter of the twentieth century that Roman Catholic theologians could use modern historical methods without official disapproval. So, since World War II, there has been a hectic period of assimilation, reinterpretation, and controversy. It is symbolized in Schillebeeckx's journey from a tradition in which philosophy, not history, was the main partner of doctrine, through *ressourcement* and hermeneutics to a massive and controversial treatment of the main topic in the nineteenth- and twentieth-century debate about faith and history: Jesus Christ.

The nineteenth century: Creativity and crisis

In the recovery and criticism of the past a theologian frequently gives a special place to particular periods or contributions. It is often more true to say that a theologian seems gripped in this way, and is immersed in texts and debates which have an authority that permeates his or her theology. The Bible is most widely treated in this way, and the patristic period is likewise usually privileged. The other two main reference points before the modern period are medieval theology and the Reformation. Periods, traditions, and theologies interanimate each other in subtle ways, and it is often crude to draw clear lines of influence. Yet it remains important to understand with whom a theologian finds dialogue most worthwhile.

One period, however, stands out as the most helpful in understanding what it means for theology since 1918 to be specifically modern: the nineteenth century (which I will consider as extending to 1918). That was the century in which the issues of modernity were tackled comprehensively for the first time, and most of the main Christian responses to them explored. So it is not surprising that the main dialogue partners for twentieth-century theologians (especially those in the West or educated in the West) outside their own period tend to be either nineteenth-century figures or movements of thought which were shaped then. Even though most theologies are, of course, deeply indebted to other periods as well, in their under-standing of them the philosophical and historical habits of nineteenth-century thought are usually very influential. Barth, for example, who wanted to break with much of what he saw as characteristic of nineteenth-century theology, was steeped in it and has to be understood in relationship to it. The cost of ignoring the nineteenth century is often paid in energetically repeating the exploration of options which were developed and thoroughly discussed then, and most twentieth-century theologians know this.

It is therefore worth surveying the nineteenth century in its importance for this volume. The brevity of this can best be expanded through two capable treatments of this field, one by Claude Welch and the other edited by Ninian Smart and others.[2] There were three thrusts in nineteenth-century thought which especially need to be appreciated in relation to twentieth-century theologians. The first was the rethinking of knowledge and rationality, and the accompanying need to reconceive theology. This will be treated below through Kant, Schleiermacher, and Hegel. The second was the development of a new historical consciousness joined with the application of critical historical methods to religion. This will be traced through Hegel and Strauss. The third was the challenge of alternative explanations of religion, as seen in Feuerbach, Marx, Durkheim, and others. In the middle comes the awkward figure of Kierkegaard, and at the end the summing up of many of the issues in Troeltsch.

Immanuel Kant (1724–1804) died just inside the nineteenth century and is the crucial figure linking it to the eighteenth century, especially its rationalist tradition. He offered an account of knowledge, and especially of the human knower in inter-action with the object of knowledge, according to which claims to knowledge by both "natural theology" and "revelation" were disallowed. In place of his denial of knowledge he affirmed a faith which was practical and moral rather than theoretical, and which was not especially religious. The central notion is that of freedom. Its reality cannot be either proved or disproved by "pure reason," but it is reasonable to postulate it in order to make sense of human action and morality. This is the realm of "practical reason," through which Kant argues for the rationality not only of freedom but also of God and immortality. His own main theological work, *Religion within the Limits of Reason Alone,* is a thorough "moralization" of religion, and in its pruning of Christianity to fit his philosophy is a good example of the fifth type of theology described above.[3] Yet he is decisively theistic, with an austere conception of God as the "unconditioned" or "absolute," whose reality is beyond all knowledge or experience but is mediated through our sense of moral obligation. We see in Kant the most influential statement of the modern tendency to distinguish fact (pure reason) from value (practical reason) and to categorize religion and morality together under the latter. We see also the emphasis, typical of so many modern theologies, on the practical or ethical content of Christianity, especially the centrality of freedom. Sometimes this is developed focusing on personal freedom and intersubjectivity, as in existentialism's concern for encounter and decision. In others, such as Moltmann and liberation theologies, the practicality takes a social and political form and is more affected by post-Kantian ideas of history and society.

It is worth reflecting on why Kant's stress on the ethical, practical, and intersubjective in religion continued to be attractive. Partly it is because Kant shared common roots with many theologians in a Lutheran faith constituted by a dynamic interactive relationship between the believer and God. For those who came later, it also represented an appealing response to the most dangerous threats which modernity posed, not only to theology but also to the whole realm of value, ethics, and the personal. These were the challenges of naturalistic and other "reductionist" explanations of religion, morality, and humanity which by the end of the century had been built up to massive proportions by such figures as Strauss (critical history), Feuerbach (philosophy), Marx (politics and economics), Durkheim and Weber (sociology), Frazer (comparative religion), William James (psychology), Darwin (evolutionary biology), and Nietzsche (philosophy). These have decisively shaped the "common sense" of many twentieth-century educated Western people about religion, and in the face of them the claim of Kant that the realm of freedom and practicality could not be reduced to any "objective" explanation offered theologians something which was both widely appealing beyond Christianity and a medium through which to express Christianity.

Kant's ethical interpretation was challenged by two major alternative ways of conceiving Christianity and theology in the early nineteenth century, those of Hegel and Schleiermacher. Friedrich Schleiermacher (1768–1834) is usually regarded as the outstanding theologian of the century. At the root of his achievement was a reconception of religion. For him, it is primarily neither morality nor belief (knowledge) but is an immediate self-consciousness or feeling of absolute dependence on God. So the roots of faith are pre-moral and pre-cognitive, and this religious consciousness is common to all people, though very variously recognized and expressed. While, in Kant, God (the absolute or unconditioned) is present through our sense of moral obligation, in Schleiermacher, God is present in an immediate dynamic relationship that grasps our whole being. Christianity is the specific form of this God-consciousness shaped through Jesus Christ and the community of faith in him. This was a view of religion which had an integrity of its own in the subjective realm of feeling or consciousness, but which yet could be reflected upon and discussed intellectually in theology and could inform the whole of practical living. It offered an idiom through which all of Christian doctrine could be expressed afresh. *The Christian Faith* is his culminating work, offering a method of theology which relates it to other disciplines and working out the content of faith with central reference to Jesus Christ and the experience of those with faith in him.[4]

Schleiermacher's influence has been immense. Besides his powerful account of religion's validity rooted in the dynamics of awareness of God, he pioneered modern hermeneutics; he maintained the importance of aesthetics in theology; he offered a "noninterventionist" account of God's relation to the world, which included a critique of religious language; he suggested a restructuring of the whole theological enterprise which was, due to his advocacy, partly embodied in the new University of Berlin; and in his public ecclesiastical, cultural, and political life he represented a lively and effective integration of modernity and Christian faith. All this was seen by him as in continuity with the Protestant Reformation and its evangelical tradition.

The post-World War I twentieth century began with a reaction against him led by Barth, who yet always acknowledged his greatness. Schleiermacher is the grandfather of those who attempt to correlate or integrate faith with modernity, and particularly of those who see the point of contact in human interiority – Tillich's "ultimate concern." He is the principal creative sponsor of the whole revisionist and liberal enterprise, but he himself constantly eludes simple categories: in those used above he seems, according to interpretation, to oscillate between the third and fourth types.

The second major early nineteenth-century challenge to Kant came from G. W. F. Hegel (1770–1831). He criticized both Kant and Schleiermacher for having an inadequate notion of rationality. Both of them had left the concept of God (the absolute, or unconditioned) relatively untouched. Hegel developed a system in which the absolute was conceived as rational and dynamic, realizing itself through a dialectical process in history. He saw the Trinity as the supreme reality, in which God differentiates himself and becomes actual in Jesus Christ and enters into suffering and death on the way to the ultimate reconciliation of all in the Spirit. The system thus had a dialectical logic embracing history with its developments and conflicts, and Hegel surveyed all of history, including the religions, in order to show the basic forms of life, society, and religion in their evolution. He also saw himself as a Christian, Lutheran philosopher recovering the truth of the basic doctrines of Trinity, creation, fall, incarnation, reconciliation, and the Holy Spirit. For him, Christianity was religion in its absolute expression, but, while its content could not be surpassed, philosophy could give a more adequate conceptual expression of it as truth, uniting it with all other truth.

The nineteenth-century shift toward more historical, process-oriented ways of understanding reality was profoundly affected by Hegel. Kant had separated the self from other reality: Hegel offered a comprehensive, historical integration of subjectivity and objectivity in which reason and even logic took on dynamic form, and Kant's restriction of theoretical reason in knowing God was overcome. Hegel daringly reconceived the idea of God and his involvement with the world (sometimes described as a type of "panentheism"); he placed the issue of truth, not religion, at the top of the agenda; and he encouraged rational and historical reconsideration of key doctrines.

The twentieth-century theologians who have wrestled most thoroughly with Hegel have often emerged deeply ambiguous about him as a Christian thinker – this is true in various ways of Barth, Jüngel, Rahner, Pannenberg, Balthasar, and Küng. One reason may be that, insofar as he can be related to our types, he, like Schleiermacher, oscillates according to the interpretation. However, with him it is between the fourth and fifth types: some see him offering an appropriate modern conception of Christianity, others as absorbing it into his system on his own alien terms. But both by setting an agenda and in his contribution on specific issues (a way of conceiving the integration of history in the Trinity in Barth, Rahner, Pannenberg, and Moltmann; the death of God in Jüngel and Moltmann; Rahner's way of affirming reality as rational; Balthasar's genres of epic, lyric, and drama, Pannenberg's concepts of rationality and universal history; Küng's approach to incarnation) he is still shaping theological debate.

In addition, the reactions provoked by Hegel resonate through the rest of the nineteenth century and into our own. One of the most passionate, that of the Dane Søren Kierkegaard (1813–58), went virtually unnoticed in his own time, but exploded in early twentieth-century existentialism and especially influenced Barth, Bultmann, and Tillich. Kierkegaard rejected Hegel's rational integration, accusing him especially of failing to take account of the existing, deciding individual, and he put forward a radical concept of Christian subjectivity which was not dependent on rational or historical justification. We live life forwards, with no neutral or overarching standpoints. We are faced with decisions and have to choose without any guarantees that we are right. We are constituted by such decisions and through them become different in ourselves. All ethical and religious existence is participated in in such self-involving and self-transforming ways. The gospel faces us with the most radical decision of all; which probes us to the depths and challenges us to go the paradoxical way of the cross. In this Kierkegaard is expanding the practical side of Kant and giving it more full-blooded Christian content. He denies both Kant's and Hegel's versions of how reason relates to faith and sees instead the paradoxical reality of incarnation and cross eliciting the leap of radical faith.

More typical of the nineteenth century was the development of Hegel's stress on history, but rejecting his tendency to give ideas and concepts primacy over empirical research. David Friedrich Strauss (1808–74) was the most controversial figure in this. He applied historical critical methods to the accounts of the life of Jesus, found a great deal that he called "mythical" (that is, religious ideas given in the form of historical accounts), and decided that there was little reliable factual information about Jesus.

The issue of the historical Jesus in relation to the Christ of faith was now firmly on the theological agenda. The rest of the nineteenth century saw many other developments in historical study which are part of the essential background to the twentieth century, especially in the fields of history of dogma and (more widely) historical theology (outstanding figures being Ferdinand Christian Baur and Adolf von Harnack), but the controversial center of the field remained the figure of Jesus, a focus which has been a legacy to many theologians treated in this volume.

The middle third of the nineteenth century saw many attempts to rethink and restore orthodox Christianity in Germany, Britain, the United States, and elsewhere, and many of these have continued to be influential, generally within particular churches or traditions (for example, biblical fundamentalism, Anglo-Catholicism, various types of confessionalism). It was also the time when new critiques of religion, such as those proposed by Ludwig Feuerbach (1804–72), began to be developed. They multiplied as the century went on, as religion was scrutinized through the disciplines of history, literature, philosophy, geology, biology, physics, psychology, sociology, politics, economics, and comparative religion. These, as mentioned above, were to help cause a major intellectual and cultural crisis in Western Christianity after 1918, but they have also been engaged in a variety of ways by theologians, and the critical dialogues with them are a major theme running through theologies in the late nineteenth and twentieth centuries – for example, Bonhoeffer with sociology; Tillich with socialism, depth psychology, and much else; Balthasar with aesthetics and drama; Pannenberg, Moltmann, Küng, and Tracy with almost every area; Teilhard de Chardin and process thought with evolutionary biology; Moltmann and liberation theologies with Marxism; Torrance and those discussed in Part III with the physical, biological, and human sciences; postmodern theology with Nietzsche; and theology of religions with comparative religion.

Finally, overlapping the two centuries is Ernst Troeltsch (1865–1923), who in many ways summed up the nineteenth century and is the indispensable background for the twentieth. He saw the Enlightenment, not the Reformation, as the genesis of modernity, and the main nineteenth-century development as that of a comprehensive historical consciousness. So, while constantly in dialogue with the theology of Schleiermacher and the philosophies of Kant and Hegel, he saw them all as needing to be criticized through a more thoroughly historical method. He was immersed in late nineteenth-century history of religions and sociology, and wrestled with the enduring problems raised by them, such as the absoluteness of Christianity, the role of the historical Jesus in Christian faith, and the inseparability of all religion from its social and historical context. He arrived at a complex critical and constructive position: resisting naturalistic, reductionist explanations of religion; emphasizing Christianity's distinctive values worked out through the centuries in interaction with different situations, and calling for a fresh, creative social embodiment of those values in twentieth-century Europe; and stressing the ambiguities of both Christianity and modernity. After World War I, the dialectical theologians, especially Barth, tended to see Troeltsch's main achievement as negative, showing the cul-de-sac arrived at when theology tries to move from human experience, history, and religion to God. But Troeltsch has also been continually influential, as in the historical critical and sociological approaches to the Bible, the later Tillich's method in dealing with historical patterns and the world religions, Pannenberg's conception of a theology that is consistently and critically historical, North American attempts to work out a practical and sociologically aware theology in a pluralist society, the widespread move to take local contexts more fully into account in doing theology, and the discussion in theology of religions about the uniqueness of Christianity.

The above account of the nineteenth century as it has affected theologians writing after 1918 has been largely centered on Germany and on those most influenced by German-language theology and philosophy. This is because that German tradition, while having many limitations, is the most sustained and intensive example of engagement in the enterprise of modern theology, as already defined, and is the most direct way of introducing historically the typical problems of modernity, such as knowledge and rationality, historical consciousness, and alternative explanations of religion. Other parts of this volume portray traditions which often approach theology very differently and in some cases are in critical confrontation with the methods and habits of the German academy. A striking development in the last twenty years of the twentieth century was a surge in theological creativity and productivity in other languages, notably English and Spanish, and the German theological tradition at the start of the twenty-first century is facing a critical challenge as to whether its previous two centuries of achievement can be sustained.

Contexts and interests

The nineteenth- and twentieth-century historical and sociological insights urge theologians to take fuller account of the situation in which theology is done and for whom and by whom it is done. The history of ideas is not enough. Theology needs to be seen in relation to many forces and events helping to shape it through the centuries. The twentieth century has added its own conditioning, such as the Holocaust and concentration camps; the unprecedented scale of mass killing of fellow human beings in wars; the Russian, Chinese, and Iranian revolutions; the emergence of new, postcolonial societies; the collapse of Soviet and European communism; the spread of mass communications, business corporations, technology, and science of many sorts; an unprecedented dialectic of the local and the global, especially in economics and culture; struggles against fascism, racism, and sexism; the ecological crisis; and a vast expansion of professions and academic disciplines and institutions. More specific to religion have been the Pentecostal movement, Christian and interreligious ecumenism, the World Council of Churches, the Second Vatican Council, the spread of Islam and Christianity (especially in Africa), many armed conflicts with significant religious elements, an immense amount of religious persecution and martyrdom, new religious movements outside the main world religions, the multiplication of "basic communities," liturgical reforms in Christian churches, and new translations of the Bible. Most of these feature in the theologies of this volume, though many are only implicit, or are ignored by theologians in ways that call for more explicit recognition.

More narrowly, there is the significance of the social and institutional context in which theology is produced. All of the nineteenth-century theologies mentioned above and most of the theologies in this volume, as well as the essays on them, were written in universities or, to a lesser extent, seminaries. They are therefore at home in an academic, largely middle-class "high culture," which, in its main centers in continental Europe, Britain, and the United States, has been remarkably stable through a century of traumas. One of the main tensions in Christian theology has been between its participation in this wider academic culture and its relationship to the Christian community. That has been sharpened by the growing professionalization of the clergy. In German-speaking countries academic theology and clergy education has long been integrated in state-financed universities, so that theology has been drawn both toward being an academic discipline on a par with others and toward serving the needs of a profession. These two easily conflict, and the results for theology are symbolized in the debate about the Jesus of history (academic emphasis) and the Christ of faith (clerical requirement).[5]

In the United States the separation of church and state tied theology more exclusively to seminaries and divinity schools and therefore to the clerical profession. This has tended to polarize "theology" and "religious studies," often in different institutions. It has also contributed to the present situation in which religion is widely practiced and influential but theology tends to be seen as a specialized professional discipline and is marginal within both academic and wider culture. In Britain many universities have departments of "theology and religious studies," often accompanied by institutional links with seminaries, thus developing a third option between the German confessional model and the American polarization.

The marginalizing of theology is not only an American phenomenon but has also happened in varying degrees in Britain, Germany, and elsewhere. It poses a problem for most of the traditions of theology dealt with in this volume: given the largely academic setting, together with the academic marginalization of theology, what sort of academic discipline is it? The main temptation within academic life is clearly to become increasingly specialized and allied with other specialized disciplines. That is just the temptation to which the sort of theology covered in this volume cannot completely succumb, because it is about major issues and their interrelation, and inevitably crosses disciplines. But if theology does not fragment into specialties or become absorbed into other disciplines, how does it understand itself? Other related hard questions follow. What is theology's relation to religious communities and their need not only for professional training but also for critical and constructive thinking? How should it handle its own "ideological" tendency to serve the interests of a particular group, culture, class, religion, or profession? Does theology abandon or compromise or fulfill its academic commitments by fuller involvement in practical social and political matters, whether radical, moderate, or conservative?

Another way of looking at such questions is to ask how theology relates to its three main "publics": the academy, the churches, and society.[6] Most of the theologians who are the subjects of this volume are members of all three but concentrate mainly on addressing two of them, usually academy and church. Yet many (especially in the particularizing theology of Part V) question this in favor of more attention to addressing and changing society. But such an overview needs to be made more complex by noting major contemporary features of each public. The academy has become more pluralist and self-critical and, at the same time (especially in the West), more subject to pressures to serve the economy in short-term and direct ways. The pluralism of methods appropriate to different disciplines and the increasing awareness by other disciplines of their own often ideological character have somewhat undermined the self-confident positivism and secularism that contributed to theology being marginalized; while economic and political pressures have put many other disciplines in both humanities and sciences in a marginal position.

As for the public in the mainstream churches, there has been more corporate social and political controversy and involvement this century, especially in liberal and radical causes – two major instances are the World Council of Churches and post-Vatican II Roman Catholicism. In this context it has become harder for a "church" theologian to cover the major areas of Christian thought without grappling with social and political issues. For the "public," that is society around the world, matters of religion or quasi-religion have been (often tragically) prominent in recent decades, as with the September 11, 2001 attack on the World Trade Center in New York and the Pentagon in Washington, DC this century. It has become less easy with integrity to privatize or cordon off religion and reduce its public significance. The interrelation of religious and secular aspects of society has rightly attracted a great deal of attention. It has been increasingly recognized, both by those who identify with or participate in religious traditions and those who do not, that the world is complexly both religious and secular, and that the flourishing of the world in the twenty-first century depends to a considerable extent on how various religious and secular forces learn to live together.

For these and other reasons it has become in some ways easier to make the case for the need for high quality public discourse within and between religions as well as about them. The theologians treated in *The Modern Theologians* try to provide such discourse. They have worked at the leading edge of Christianity since 1918 and have contributed to the making of its history. They are of interest both as a "religious study" of twentieth-century Christian thought and also as examples and partners for those who follow them in their discipline or try, without claiming to be theologians, to think through questions of meaning, truth, practice, and beauty in relation to God and the purposes of God. The coverage is not complete but, even including the omissions that had to be made in order that this book not be too large, it is worth remembering that the field of such theology is even wider. A great deal of theology is done by those who write little or who may not write it down at all. A lifetime's theological wisdom may be channeled into prayer, politics, family life, coping with suffering, teaching or other activity, and may have no written expression. That sort of theology cannot be treated directly here, but it helps to keep the whole enterprise in perspective to remember that at the origins of the two traditions most influential on the theologies of this volume are Socrates and Jesus, neither of whom left us any writings.

Notes

1 The typology that follows draws on the work of Hans W. Frei in *Types of Christian Theology*, though numbering the types in reverse order to that used by him. For a brief account and discussion of Frei's typology, see my review article, "On Being Theologically Hospitable to Jesus Christ: Hans Frei's Achievement," in *Journal of Theological Studies* NS 46 (October 1995), pp. 532–46.

2 C. Welch, *Protestant Thought in the Nineteenth Century*, and N. Smart et al., *Nineteenth Century Religious Thought in the West*.

3 Immanuel Kant, *Religion within the Limits of Reason Alone*, first published 1793.

4 Friedrich Schleiermacher, *The Christian Faith* (Edinburgh, 1928; New York, 1948).

5 Cf. Hans W. Frei, *Types of Christian Theology*.

6 See David Tracy, *The Analogical Imagination*, ch. 1.

Bibliography

Primary

Cunliffe-Jones, H., *A History of Christian Doctrine* (Edinburgh, 1978).

Frei, H. W., *Types of Christian Theology*, ed. George Hunsinger and William C. Placher (New Haven, CT, 1992).

Gunton, C. (ed.), *The Cambridge Companion to Christian Doctrine* (Cambridge, 1997).

Heron, A. I. C., *A Century of Protestant Theology* (Cambridge, 1980).

Hodgson, P. and King. R. H., *Christian Theology: An Introduction to its Traditions and Tasks* (London, 1983).

Kelsey, D. H., *Between Athens and Jerusalem: The Theological Education Debate* (Grand Rapids, MI, 1993).

Küng, H., *Great Christian Thinkers* (London, 1994).

Pelikan, J., *The Christian Tradition: A History of the Development of Doctrine*, 5 vols. (Chicago, 1989).

Schoof, T. M., *A Survey of Catholic Theology 1800–1970* (New York, 1970).

Smart, N., Clayton, J., Katz, S., and Sherry, P. (eds.), *Nineteenth Century Religious Thought in the West*, 3 vols. (Cambridge, 1985).

Soskice, J. M. and Lipton, D. (eds.), *Feminism and Theology* (Oxford, 2003).

Welch, C., *Protestant Thought in the Nineteenth Century*, 2 vols. (New Haven, CT, 1972–85).

Secondary

Bediako, K., *Christianity in Africa: The Renewal of a Non-Western Religion* (Maryknoll, NY, 1995).

Feuerbach, L., *The Essence of Christianity* (New York, 1957).

Ford, D. F., *Theology: A Very Short Introduction* (Oxford, 2000).

Gunton, C., *The Christian Faith* (Oxford, 2001).

Kant, I., *Religion within the Limits of Reason Alone* (New York, 1960).

Lindbeck, G., *The Nature of Doctrine: Religion and Theology in a Postliberal Age* (Philadelphia, PA, 1994).

Lonergan, B., *Method in Theology* (New York, 1972).

Moltmann, J., *Theology Today* (London, 1988).

Parsons, S. (ed.), *The Cambridge Companion to Feminist Theology* (Cambridge, 2002).

Schleiermacher, F., *Brief Outline on the Study of Theology* (Richmond, 1966) [first published 1810; 2nd edn. 1830].

Song, C. S., *Third-Eye Theology: Theology in Formation in Asian Setting* (Maryknoll, NY, 1979).

Sykes, S. W., *The Identity of Christianity* (London, 1984).

Tracy, D., *The Analogical Imagination* (London, 1982).

Troeltsch, E., *Protestantism and Progress: The Significance of Protestantism for the Rise of the Modern World* (Philadelphia, PA, 1986).

Classics of the Twentieth Century

World War I (1914–18) brought about a major crisis in European culture and society. This was the context for Karl Barth's *The Epistle to the Romans* and the explosion of dialectical theology, followed by Barth's attempt to rethink the whole enterprise of modern theology. Daniel Hardy describes Barth's development and the theology of his massive *Church Dogmatics*, traces the variety of responses by other theologians, and addresses probing questions to him.

Barth is an unquestionable name on any list of twentieth-century classics. Dietrich Bonhoeffer's lifetime was less than half that of Barth, and for nearly twelve of his thirty-nine years he was caught up in resistance to the Nazis and did his theology piecemeal outside the university. Yet the publication of seventeen volumes of his collected works has shown the scale of his achievement. Wayne Whitson Floyd (editor of the English edition) shows not only why Bonhoeffer merits classic status, but also his significance for the present century.

Paul Tillich, after his exile from Hitler's Germany, became perhaps the most celebrated theologian in post-World War II USA. David Kelsey describes Tillich's lifelong concern for Christianity and culture, and his method of flexibly, openly, and creatively correlating the two. His central achievement is his three-volume *Systematic Theology*, the conceptual coherence and main content of which is laid out by Kelsey. Tillich's reputation suffered something of an eclipse after his death, but his work is now being freshly appreciated and stands as the leading twentieth-century classic in what the Introduction to this volume calls "type three" theology of correlation.

Henri de Lubac is unique among the classics selected here in doing his most significant work as historical theology. There is of course much else in his *oeuvre*, but John Milbank's vigorous exposition shows him identifying the prophetically crucial importance of questions surrounding nature, grace, and the vision of God, and bringing his massive learning and theological acuity to bear in demonstrating how their historical forms are relevant to key current issues. De Lubac is probably the least recognized of our classics, and Milbank's assessment of him challenges the "canon."

Karl Rahner is another theologian whose reputation declined somewhat after his death, especially in his own Roman Catholic Church. Chapter 16 in Part II of this volume illuminates some of the reasons for this decline, connected with the course of Catholic theology under Pope John Paul II. In chapter 5, Karen Kilby is more concerned to correct interpretations of aspects of his theology (and especially the relationship of philosophy to his theology) that allowed some to dismiss him too easily. She retrieves the breadth, variety, and richness of his vast *oeuvre*, while also asking some hard questions of it.

Finally, the work of Hans Urs von Balthasar came into its own in the aftermath of his death, as one of the theologians most favored by Pope John Paul II. Ben Quash follows the contours of his massive achievement and also opens up a range of critical engagements with it.

One of the marks of a classic is that repeated engagement with it is fruitful. Looking through other parts of this volume it is possible to see how each is affected by these six classics. As might be expected, all are influential in Part II's theologies of Europe and the USA. They are least significant for theology and the sciences in Part III (though note the contribution of Bonhoeffer to theology and social science), and for most of the global engagements of Part VI (the exception being ecumenical theology). Many particularizing theologies (Part V) have criticized them and called attention to their limitations. But this too is the mark of a classic – that it is unavoidable, even if one wants to reject it. Part I represents the editors' attempt to select those twentieth-century theologians with whom twenty-first century theologians and others should not avoid wrestling.

Karl Barth

Daniel W. Hardy

Approaching Karl Barth

Karl Barth (1886–1968) was undoubtedly one of the most significant figures in post-Reformation Protestant theology, perhaps even more so than Friedrich Schleiermacher a century before; and his importance reaches well beyond that tradition. In the context of nineteenth and twentieth-century theology, he – more than any other – restored Christian theology to strength. Although himself at first deeply immersed in the "modern theology" which had begun with the Enlightenment, Barth became the pivotal figure in the transformation of theology during the early twentieth century. He found a critical basis – the "theological object" – by which to respond to the previous era: ever-renewed engagement with this, and from it the building of a comprehensive account of Christian theology, became his main achievements.

His progress with the task advanced through several stages. At first, he issued a call for radical correction; and later he moved toward, and eventually provided, a remarkably full account of the scope of Christian belief which showed the marks of his continuing struggle for truth. Its sharpness on the one hand, and its comprehensiveness on the other, turned the tide of conviction about what Christian theology should now be.

Commensurate with its importance, Barth's theology has drawn wide comment, but often of such a kind as to content itself with interpreting him without moving far forward with the "further work which is needed today."[1] In any case, as with the most valuable theology, it is better to read Barth's own writing. And it needs to be encountered with the utmost seriousness, as testing all aspects of belief and life. That is not to suggest that it cannot, or should not, be questioned: the reader needs also to reach through the particular notions and words used by Barth to recall us to the "theological object" which so much concerned him, the dynamic relation of the divine and the human, and to ask whether he has discerned this fully or appropriately. The very task of "finding the 'theological object'" presumes that Barth and his reader will test each other. What we will therefore attempt to provide here is an introduction to the most central aspects of Barth's theology in which this mutual testing needs to go on, together with suggestions as to where critical examination might lead.

Biography

Heir to two Reformed theological dynasties, Sartorius and Barth, Karl Barth was the first son of Johann Friedrich Barth, a pastor from the conservative wing of his church and lecturer at the ten-year-old College of Preachers in Basel, Switzerland, who three years later became professor in early and modern church history at the University of Berne. Raised and schooled in the strong affirmations of Christian faith, Barth studied philosophy and theology at the leading universities of Germany: deterred by his father from the pursuit of the liberal theology then prevalent, he began his studies at Berne, but soon went on to Berlin, Tübingen, and Marburg, and studied under those most influential at the time: Adolf von Harnack, whose disciple Barth claimed to be at that point, Julius Kaftan, Hermann Gunkel, Wilhelm Herrmann, and Adolf Schlatter. Despite his father's commitment to "positive theology," the young Barth became a disciple of the "modern school" of theology that – like so many who followed the adaptation of Christianity to the philosophy of Immanuel Kant, other idealists, and the modern preoccupation with history – correlated the history of Christian religion with the human experience of the divine. Under the shadow of von Harnack, this was an uneasy combination, which often made the truth of faith fully dependent on historical research; but Barth worked all his life with the tools of historical criticism, while wanting to surpass it by standing before "the mystery of the *subject matter*" not merely the mystery of the *document*. He followed the liberal Wilhelm Herrmann in considering the inward certainty of faith as normative for ethical life.

Following his final theological examinations in 1908, Barth was ordained a pastor in the Bern Münster church, and served briefly as a pastor in the Jura Mountains before staying with Martin Rade and working for two terms as his editorial assistant in Marburg for the influential *Die Christliche Welt*, then for two years an assistant pastor in Geneva, where he first met leaders of the ecumenical movement. It was in Geneva that he met his future wife, Nelly Hoffmann (they had one daughter and four sons). In July 1911, he became pastor of Safenwil, a farming and industrial area near Zurich, where he remained for ten years; his friend and theological partner Eduard Thurneysen was nearby.

Confronted there by the misery of working people, he found himself responsible for preaching the gospel to them, but his theology proved unequal to the task. Joining the religious Social Democratic Party (led by Ragaz and Kutter), much involved in the labor movement, and deeply disturbed, at the outbreak of World War I, to find that his teachers were among those supporting the Kaiser in making war, he found how bankrupt the theology he had learned was, and how close it was to the ideology of the "cultivated" Europe then tearing itself apart. As a result he broke with the theology in which he had been trained, and rejected any easy linking of social action with the Kingdom of God; now *theologically realistic* hope for the Kingdom of God became central to his thinking. Finding a new theological basis became a matter of urgency; and he sought to engage with historical criticism while yet looking through it and allowing the Word of God in scripture to come afresh to him, free – he hoped – of accommodation to the culture of the day.

The outward story of his next years is multifaceted but straightforward, though its significance is much debated. It had two decisive strands, the theological and the political, both of them important throughout his life, although we can only consider the theological here. His early public opposition to the prevailing theology, in lectures and papers,[2] and also in a *Commentary on Romans* at first published in Berne (1919) but soon much more widely distributed by a prominent Munich publisher, brought him notoriety and an invitation to an honorary professorship of Reformed theology at Göttingen to begin in October 1921. A group sympathetic to the "dialectical theology" Barth advocated also founded a journal, *Zwischen den Zeiten* (*Between the Times*); it included Barth, Eduard Thurneysen, and Friedrich Gogarten, with Georg Merz (of Christian Kaiser Verlag) as editor.

When Barth went to Göttingen, without advanced study in theology, he was unprepared for his teaching responsibilities in Reformed confession, doctrine, and church life. He began a time of intensive research into figures he had barely read previously, concentrating on Calvin and Zwingli, Schleiermacher and Feuerbach, Anselm and Aquinas. The task was daunting, but as he faced it Barth began the extended series of engagements with theological tradition that was to be a hallmark of his subsequent theology, a "third party" in Barth's engagement with the Bible. It was in Göttingen that he also started explicitly dogmatic work, in his case a dialectical re-reading of the Reformed tradition; it began his steady effort to replace the defective theology he was dismantling with a better one.[3]

In 1925 he became professor of dogmatics and New Testament exegesis at Münster, where he was in close contact with philosophy and Catholicism. There, Barth set about writing what was to be a multi-volume *Christian Dogmatics*, but only the first volume appeared in 1927; and – closely linked – there were lectures on ethics in 1928.[4] In 1930, as the West sank into recession, and amid a social and political crisis in Germany, he came to the chair of systematic theology at Bonn, immediately attracting crowds of students. Although he was distracted by intensifying disagreement with the others involved in *Zwischen den Zeiten*, which eventually brought about its discontinuance, his lecturing continued along the same lines as at Münster. When the full implications of Hitler's policies became apparent in the early 1930s, his trenchant stand on the predicament of theology, which was simultaneously a political stand, a plea for going "to the heart of the matter," was widely known; and Barth largely drafted the Theological Declaration of the "Confessing Church" declaring its opposition to the German Church assimilated to Hitler's policies. In the end, his refusal to take an oath of unconditional loyalty to Hitler resulted in disciplinary proceedings, dismissal, and an appeal after which he was "pensioned off"; further publications by him were banned in Germany. He was called to a chair at Basel, where he wrote his major multi-volume work *Church Dogmatics*, and from where he actively engaged with the world of theology and society. When in 1962 he retired from the teaching which had given him the contact with students through which all the previous material had been refined, that ended an "essential part of the impulse" of his work. He went on a tour of America, but afterward was hospitalized for some time. Furthermore, he was now without the assistance of the woman who had been his close collaborator through the whole project, Charlotte von Kirschbaum, herself seriously ill. Within the limits of his health, he remained active until his death in 1968.

Content: Barth's Major Works

Barth himself recognized that his work passed through several major stages, each culminating in a particularly important book: (1) Beginnings, to the first version of the *Commentary on Romans* in 1919; (2) Dialectical theology, to *Christian Dogmatics in Outline*, 1927; (3) Dogmatic theology, principally the vast *Church Dogmatics* (four volumes, 13 parts in all, the last only a fragment [Volume 5, The Doctrine of Redemption, was never written]).

Much attention has been given to the continuities and discontinuities evident in Barth's lifework, especially the suggestion by the Roman Catholic theologian Hans Urs von Balthasar[5] that Barth had shifted from dialectical to analogical theology. Suffice it to say that Barth's theology never lost its dialectical edge while he also found a full basis for dogmatics of a certain kind, through his theological actualism. His locating of the possibility of theology in the dialectical relation of God and humanity in which the two were united through the actualization of the Word of God, Jesus Christ, received in faith by the grace of the Holy Spirit, precluded conventional views of analogy.

Beginnings, to the 1919 Commentary on Romans

What is heard in the 1919 *Commentary on Romans* is a passionate and vivid cry – in the form of a careful paraphrase of Paul's letter – to start all theology from the Reality of God, "complete and whole in itself apart from and prior to the knowing activity of human individuals,"[6] dialectically distinct from the reality of the world: "World remains world. But God is God." That required the subordination of all worldly human possibilities – history, ideas, distinctions, and relations, including religion – to the sovereign God as sure and certain reality above them all. But how, if the object of theology was so sharply distinct from the world, was there a relation between these two realities? The answer offered was that through *divine decision* they coincide in God's cosmically reconciling activity present in a particular historical event where this world is made new – Jesus Christ and his Cross – in which God's reign has dawned. There the movement of God in history is actualized, in such a way as to be accessible through participatory, personal knowledge, but beyond access by historical investigation.

Dialectical theology to Christian Dogmatics in Outline, *1927*

No doubt the cry expressed in the 1919 *Commentary on Romans* captured the imagination of a generation confused, empty, and dismayed by the horror of World War I, the Bolshevik Revolution in 1917, rampant inflation, political uncertainties, and immensely difficult living conditions in the traumas during and after the war.

But it was also undeveloped theologically, and Barth soon began again, rewriting *Romans* between late 1920 and mid-1921 before leaving for Göttingen.[7] His principal question was: "how can God make Himself known to human beings without ceasing . . . to be the *Subject* of revelation,"[8] that is ceasing to be God by subjecting himself to human control. And Barth's modes of expression were now different – anger, indirect and paradoxical speech – reflecting the condition of crisis, almost tangible at the time. But the actuality of full relationship with God remained, through belonging to Christ as the decisive occurrence of grace for historical human beings as they were enabled to receive it by the Holy Spirit.[9] The occurrence places human beings in "a final, unavoidable KRISIS": "there is only life under His judgment and under His promise; there is only life characterized by death but qualified, through the death of Christ, as the hope of life eternal.[10]

Although such views were intelligible enough when juxtaposed with biblical texts, they also invoked some of the key questions of philosophy and theology, especially the relation between eternity and time, and the placing of eschatology. Renewed study led Barth to see in the historical figure of Jesus Christ God's eternal act in him; hence he "dehistoricized" eschatology in order to avoid confusing God's act of self-revelation with history.[11] The key issue for Barth was Søren Kierkegaard's "infinite qualitative distinction between time and eternity," between the sphere of humanity and that of God.[12] This "dialectical" phase of Barth's thinking found that the only basis for Christian faith was in the contrast between the Holy God and sinful humanity, Creator and creature, revelation and religion, gospel and church, sacred history and profane history, in each case the contrast between the free grace of God in Jesus Christ and that which resists it and therefore stands under judgment. At the same time, Barth struggled to free "dialectical method" from its associations with nineteenth-century idealism. His notion of dialectic was of a particular kind, and derived from ethical and theological considerations.

When Barth arrived in Göttingen, and found himself engaging not only with the scriptures but also with the history of the Reformed tradition,[13] and with Orthodox, scholastic, and patristic theology, he began to see theology as a science serving the church – an "ecclesiastical science" – and to see the value of sustained theological exposition. The result was three cycles of lecturing and writing on dogmatics, at Göttingen, and later at Münster and Bonn. This was dogmatics not as a theoretical science detached from its expression in preaching and ethical practice – in the fashion common in English-speaking countries – but as a science whose discipline establishes true believing and true living in the life of the church.[14] This was its logic, but theology needed continually to modify, correct, refine, and develop its vision; in that sense, the theologian is free to experiment with what is best, and to engage anew with centuries of tradition.

In Barth's first cycle of dogmatics, this dialectic continues throughout, holding in tension the hiddenness and the communication of God. The center-point is now, however, not in dialectic as such, but in Christology. Here is a major step forward, the placing of the incarnate Mediator *within* the "infinite qualitative distinction" between God and humanity, within the veiling and unveiling of God. The divine Yes in the union of divine and human natures in Christ, in which the dialectic of the incomprehensible and comprehensible is focused, freed Barth from the dialectic of eternity and time (which had encumbered his previous work) and became the prototype of every relationship of God and creature. This move was important: the radicality of Barth's earlier theology remained, but now became the beginning of dogmatics. It opened up the possibility of much fuller treatment of the person and work of Jesus Christ as informing all of dogmatics and its implications for the here and now.

Barth's brief time in Münster, in a small Protestant theological faculty in a predominantly Roman Catholic city, concentrated his attention on Catholicism as a conversation partner instead of neoliberalism. In a Catholic context, Barth consistently found himself addressing the same realities – dogmatics and church – but within a different frame of reference from Catholics: the issue was the "distinction . . . to be made between the direct authority of Christ and his mediated authority which he granted to the Church."[15]

The same issue was at stake in conceptions of analogy. For Catholics as he understood them, God's creation endowed the creature with the capacity to "establish and survey (for example, in a scheme of the unity of like and unlike) his relation to God, and thereby interpret himself as 'open upwards,'" placing God's revealedness as "within the compass of his own understanding by itself."[16] Barth saw things otherwise: if created reality is posited by God, with a reality distinct from but next to God's *by virtue of God's love*, then the uncreated cannot be revealed to, cannot belong to, the creature except through the Creator's *relating to* the creature – as a "second miracle" of God's love and gift. Barth's use of analogy was not analogical in the sense then accepted by Catholics; it was always a notion of analogy which derived from God's renewal of the graceful gift of the relation which human beings have with God.

Dogmatic theology and the Church Dogmatics

A new beginning?

In significant respects, Barth had established the pattern of his future work by the time he arrived at Bonn in March 1930. Yet many claim that his book on Anselm was a new beginning. He had taught Anselm in 1926, and written of him in the *Christian Dogmatics* of 1927, but now he did return to him in a seminar in the summer of 1930. The issue which especially concerned him was how human reason functioned in relation to the reality of God. For Anselm, he finds, *intelligere* is desired by faith, and when the *ratio* of faith is shown, results in joy. Furthermore, "this reason, which the *intelligere* seeks and finds, possesses in itself not only *utilitas* . . . but also *pulchritudo*."[17] So the source of the search for reason is within faith itself: believing – not a human striving toward God, but a striving *into*, and *creaturely participation in* God's mode of Being – brings the desire for *intelligere*. We are to think in/after (*nach-denken*) faith, rationally acknowledging what has occurred in faith.[18] In this book on Anselm, Barth extends his earlier work into the central issues of cognition and the heartlands of philosophy.

Meanwhile, he was turning away from his previous attempt – in *Die christliche Dogmatik* – to a new project, the *Church Dogmatics*. Why? It seems a familiar predicament: in the attempt to complete the former, the latter simply took shape; and it was not the same project! And as the new work developed, it assumed massive proportions, in which there were not only continuities but also transformations. The project – integrating scripture, historical theology, dogmatics, and ethics – occupied Barth for the remainder of his life, and even then was never completed.

Approaching the *Church Dogmatics*

Before we look more closely at the content of the *Church Dogmatics*, we need to notice some of its distinctive features.

1   The first is the manner of its presentation. Each part-volume is presented in three levels, (a) dogmatic theses or propositions (printed in bold type), (b) dogmatic presentation (in ordinary type), and (c) "interposed sections in small print" where attention is given to "biblico-theological presuppositions and the historico-dogmatic and polemical relations of my statements."[19] In practice, the levels are not so easily separated: understanding the first requires consideration of the second, and thorough attention calls the reader to engage with the third. For students of scripture and historical doctrine, the last is the most concrete and interesting of all, but relegating these to small print tends to favor dogmatic statements, and to deemphasize them.
2   It is very long and comprehensive, and the text is – as some have said – like "iron." As such, it tends to "haunt and comfort the rest of us" (Hans Frei). Despite what is often said, that Barth uses too many words and talks around topics, his prose is terse and demands the reader's full concentration.
3   Despite its division into four major doctrines – the Word of God, God, Creation, and Reconciliation (one on Redemption was never written) – the *Church Dogmatics* is a continuous whole; the chapters are consecutively numbered throughout (I to XVI). Later ones trace what is implicit in earlier ones, but also significantly enlarge – and sometimes change the balance of – what precedes. Volume 4, for example, changes the exclusive preoccupation with deity in the earlier volumes for greater concern for the humanity of Jesus in God's reconciling work.[20]
4   It maintains remarkable pungency: it is marked by a strong sense of the contingency of everything on the action of God, yet it also finds the fullest coherence in what God does. Two recurring notions support this contingency:[21] (a) the "actualism" of God's acting to be God, as God in active and actual relatedness in himself and with man; God is sovereign in his freedom and love, both within himself and for humanity, as distinct from more "fixed" conceptions describing these things as "states" of being or relation, whether for God or for human beings; and (b) the "particularity" of proclamation, whose "content must be found each time in the middle space between the particular text in the context of the whole Bible and the particular situation of the changing moment."[22]
5   In its unity, it is "richly dynamic, endlessly surprising, and deeply mysterious.[23] Not only does Barth – like his beloved Mozart – love thematic interplay, he also concentrates on particular themes, bringing them elegantly into new combinations and contrapositions "within an ever forward spiraling theological whole."[24] Although, as we will see, there is only one entrance point, that allows us to be led into everything. It is the task of theology, not to employ systematization as

such, but "to describe as carefully as possible, from many different angles, the network of interconnections which constitute the great crystal in its totality."

6　It is coherent: (a) although dependent on God's act, theological language is used analogically; it refers to its object reliably and self-involvingly, with sufficient certainty, in a use which is neither literal nor expressive, and which – in broader contexts like history – forms narrative and legend, as distinct from fact or myth; (b) as befits "scientific theology," God's self-relation in God's relation to the creature is "objective reality" which makes knowledge available in faith, the one through the other, outside of which there is only "unreality"; and (c) God's encounter with humanity as mediated by Jesus Christ is personal, which binds Jesus deeply to the subjectivity of human beings, incorporating them in him and making it possible for them to share in the intimacy of the triune God.

7　Both pungency and coherence appear in the patterns which operate in the *Church Dogmatics*. (a) There are genuine knowledge and grounds for belief, but they derive *from faith* which rests on the *grace* of God. (b) At another – ontological – level, there is a repeated asking of what are the *operative conditions* for what is given to faith: what makes this actuality actual? It is, Barth says, not necessarily the case, but is *made* the case – actualized – by God, ultimately because of the freedom by which God chose to be this way and not another: "all actualities ultimately find their possibility (however variously) as grounded in that freedom."[25] (c) Here, it seems, is a dialectic, in which what is "natural" is distinct from – even opposed to – what is "God's," but one transcended by the free grace of God giving the condition for the one to be actually related to the other. "Nature" and "grace" are in dialectical opposition, but this opposition is surpassed by a relation of the two actualized by the triune God.

The logic of dogmatics

From the outset, Barth focuses not on humanity or the church as such but on what is deemed central to church life: proclamation. The purpose is to identify the *operative condition* by which it *is* proclamation (or the church *is* the church) as distinct from something else, that is the *Word of God* as attested in the preached, written, and revealed Word of God. Next, we find that the Word of God thus found has its *operative condition* in that it is God's *actual speech* to humanity; and the *operative condition* for that is then also found, etc. This "chain" of "operative conditions" is at the heart of this *Dogmatics*. Dogmatics, as a theological science distinct from testimony and service, is to be the self-examination of the church to find whether, at each level of assertion, its operative condition is in place. To put it differently, Dogmatics is to examine the agreement of human speech or concept with its operative condition: uncovering truth as the agreement of the two is the task of theology. But if the *operative condition* for human speech is other than Word of God/God's Speech/God's Self-Revelation/etc. – as appropriate to the level of examination – then whatever is said is simply human speech or concept and, from a theological viewpoint, untrue.

　　Here we begin to see the pattern of the *Church Dogmatics* as a whole. It is, it seems, a chain of dialectical unities: if it is to be more than human practice or concept, the "lower" in each case must rest on the *operative condition* of the "higher," without which it falls out of its relation to God into the kind of "distance" of which Barth spoke so passionately in his commentaries on the Epistle to the Romans. But if it does indeed rest on the operative condition thus identified, it is indeed the speaking of God, the God who is free to be – and to reveal himself in – Jesus Christ. With this in mind, we need to trace the chain of connections in the subject-matter of the different volumes in the *Church Dogmatics.*

The Church Dogmatics

The *Church Dogmatics* is self-consciously addressed to a familiar audience, those unconcerned with the connectedness of their life and behavior with the things of God, who "have no more urgent wish than to give as little heed as possible to the doctrine of the Church."[26] Reestablishing that "connectedness" is the major issue, and Barth sets about it in a particular way.

Volume 1: *The Doctrine of the Word of God*

Introduction (§§1–2): The Task and Position of Dogmatics and Prolegomena
What makes *human speech* in the church *proclamation* is the question, then; *testing the connection* – evaluating proclamation by the norm under which it stands, revelation – is the task of dogmatics; dogmatics itself "does not seek to give a positive, stimulating and edifying presentation." (Barth's approach resembles Kant's exhaustive search in the *Critiques* for what makes "knowledge" *knowledge* and "good" *good*.)

Chapter I (§§3–5): The Word of God as Criterion
The *operative condition* that makes human speech and life *actually proclamation and church* is the *Word of God*. This is what operates within the ambivalence and opposition of humanity to God, and visibly awakens, separates, and gathers people into the church where "God Himself speaks like a king through the mouth of his herald."[27] Barth pursues this *operative condition* in each of the three forms characteristic of the church's life:

- In preaching, "the *Word of God* is the [actualizing] event through which proclamation becomes real proclamation."[28]
- In the written word which carries past revelation toward the future, holy scripture is normative (a) for memory (it "shuts out Platonic *anamnesis*"), (b) because "the prophetic and apostolic word [is] the necessary rule of every word that is valid in the Church,"[29] and (c) because it summons and directs the church to its empowering by the *Word of God* revealed. Scripture is "an event, and . . . to be understood only as an event . . . in this event the Bible is God's Word."
- While the Bible is not as such seen as God's revelation, it serves past revelation; in order to be considered revelation, it must become the place where there occurs "an event through which, by the act of God, the Word is revealed."[30]

Hence, every one of the three – preached, written, and revealed – as well as their unity, rests on an *operative condition*, the event in which God's Word happens through them. When seen in this way, they as "objective" have only one subject, the triunity of God, as Father, Son, and Holy Spirit. Tracing them thus was one of the first great achievements of Barth's dogmatics.

Everything therefore rests on the Word of God as God's speech to humanity. Although the nature of this Word might appear to be "natural" or "historical," "this is something God Himself must constantly tell us afresh," encountering us but not in such a way as to be assumed into man's knowing. The divine telling is always primary. As embodied in God's Son, it is speech in which – as a rational and personal event – God's reason and person communicates with the human reason and person, lifting the human being out of autonomous self-reference and demanding hearing and obedience in which the relation of Creator to creature is renewed. As the act of God in the Word, however, it is always both itself and also particular to the time in which it is heard, proclaimed, and obeyed: it is therefore *contingently contemporaneous* and decisive there.[31] Whose decisive act is this? It remains God's, not the God of the philosophers but God according to God's self-conception, beyond comparison with anything else, and ultimately mysterious as a Word of grace incarnate in the world. In God's unveiling of himself in his Word, we must also acknowledge his veiling of himself.

In that sense, there is no further grounding for the Word of God than itself; and "the possibility of knowledge of God's Word lies in God's Word and nowhere else."[32] Hence we cannot ask how human beings know the Word, and we do not simply presuppose it; we know it only by acknowledging it, when we are turned away from ourselves and are oriented to it. Where faith is put into effect by the Word of God, a faith that makes knowledge possible, there is an *analogia fidei*. Likewise, when we refer to the Word, the Word makes this reference actual, and thereby determines and renews both our talking of God and our human existence as *imago dei*; outside of that there is no way of referring to God or truly existing.

These are the criteria administered by dogmatics as it tests the connection and agreement between human proclamation or relationships and the revelation by which they are proclamation and church. Nothing can replace the active Word of God as the concrete independent criterion; it is not a mere idea, not subsumable under other criteria, not provable, does not produce dogmas (unlike dogmatics in the Roman Catholic Church), but is the Word that *actually encounters* the church and by whose encounter in proclamation and church their connection with revelation is tested. In that way, dogmatics becomes scientific, by finding the agreement of proclamation and church with the revelation of the Word attested in scripture. Alternatives – humanistic theology or in our day religious studies – are to be regarded as corruptions.

Chapter II: The Revelation of God
Part I (§§8–12): The Triune God
God's Word has as its operative condition God himself in his revelation. And scripture signifies that the God thus revealed is Lord, unimpaired in unity and distinction as Revealer, Revelation, and Revealedness. Unlike the experiential and historical approaches dominant in his time, Barth places the Trinity at the forefront: the Father is Lord of our existence (Creator), the Son is Lord in our enmity towards him and as he sets us free (Reconciler), and the Holy Spirit sets us free to respond

to our God. Why such a complex operative condition? It is because the fullness of God's Lordship – in the three aspects – is witnessed to in the scriptures, but is antecedently within God and so apparent in God's relation to us in our existence, reconciliation, and freedom.

Part II (§§13–15): The Incarnation of the Word

Here Barth traces how God moves freely toward humanity, in a meeting of divine and human time, in the mystery of revelation. He equates God's revelation with the reality of the event in which the Word of God becomes human in Jesus Christ, and a human being thereby becomes God's Word: here Jesus Christ is the *objective reality* of revelation which provides its *objective possibility*. This implies the *temporal particularity* of God's revelation where "it must signify that revelation becomes history, but not that history becomes revelation."[33] God's time and our time are fulfilled in the event of Jesus Christ, where Old Testament expectation and New Testament recollection meet in the fulfilled time "in the midst of the times." And yet this brings us to the heart of the mystery of Christ: Jesus Christ is "very God and very Man," a dogma describing the "necessary" mystery of revelation seen in the miracle of Christmas.

Part III (§§16–18): The Outpouring of the Holy Spirit

The focus turns to life in the Holy Spirit, considering the gifts of the Spirit, the "religious" ways in which they are avoided, and what is the true life of the children of God. The outpouring of the Holy Spirit – as the *subjective reality* of revelation – *really* enlightens us for knowledge of the Word, gives the freedom to be who we are in true freedom for God, and reverses alternatives – autonomous religious competence, experience and activity (all are conducive to unbelief) – so that human beings can live as children of God in a church which has its origin in Christ. This church is therefore enfleshed; its purpose is to live life for Christ's sake; its common life is dependent on the Incarnate Word; and it is therefore both divine/eternal/ invisible and human/temporal/visible. Here people are in their appropriate relation to God of knowledge, love, and praise. And here is the only "religion," where there is an actuality "called and dedicated to the declaration of the name of Jesus Christ.[34]

Chapter III (§§19–21): Holy Scripture

The issue here is how the Word of God operates for the church, as its only authority and the only basis for its freedom. Because the Word of God is God himself who once spoke to Moses, the prophets, the evangelists, and apostles, he now speaks through their written word as Lord to the church as – by the Holy Spirit – it became and will become a witness to divine revelation. It is in obedience to the Word in scripture that the church has its only authority, which – though only indirect and relative and formal – also provides and limits the freedom of the church.

Chapter IV (§§22–24): The Proclamation of the Church

When God himself speaks in the Word of God in the proclamation of the church of Christ, there is a commission for the church to speak of him; when it does, God himself declares his revelation in his witnesses, and this proclamation is pure doctrine when it confirms the biblical witness and brings obedience to the Word. Dogmatics is the means by which the church learns to hear and teach truly.

Volume II: *The Doctrine of God*

In a volume written during the violent years of Nazism during the 1930s, Barth focuses on how God is God *for us*: "God's free grace is God Himself in His most inner and essential nature, God Himself as He is."[35] This is recognition that the reality of God is known through his own graceful self-determination and self-demonstration, not an independent demonstration of the existence of God. God *determines* himself by his *determination of us* and the conditions of our existence, electing, creating, rescuing, and glorifying human covenant partners for himself. This doctrine of God is "at one and the same time a classic treatment of divine sovereignty and Christian humanism."[36]

Chapter V (§§25–27): The Knowledge of God
Unlike other anthropological attempts to resolve the problem of relating the object-ive reality of God and the human subject, Barth maintains that the knowledge of God occurs – not possibly but actually, not through an independent epistemology but by God's act – in the *fulfillment* of revelation in the Word and the Holy Spirit, in the reality of faith and obedience. This is a knowledge which has its *operative condition* in the truth of God given to be known as truth in the Word of God by the Holy Spirit, in which human beings participate in God's truth, not independently but only insofar as our ways of doing so are adopted by God in grace. (This was a point famously dividing Barth from Emil Brunner.) This fulfillment is intensely real (as we might say) because it is based in the existence of God.

Chapter VI (§§28–31): The Reality of God
In the act of God's revelation we find who God is: God is One who seeks and creates fellowship with us in love. Even without us, he is free to have this life in himself as Father, Son, and Holy Spirit, since he lives perfectly in the abundance of many distinct perfections (a word Barth prefers to "attributes") as loving in free-dom. Here is a rich description of the two primary characteristics of God as gracious and holy love and yet constant and eternal in his freedom to be so.

Chapter VII (§§32–35): The Election of God
Barth's redevelopment of Calvin's notion of predestination is sometimes called his greatest achievement. He discusses the way God is in his freedom in his relatedness: God freely "determines" himself as God who loves in freedom. In knowing Jesus Christ, we find the "electing God" and the "elected human being" in one, wherein God predestines himself in predestining humanity; this testifies to the "eternal, free and unchanging grace" of God, who freely determines himself for sinful humanity, and sinful humanity for himself, and therefore takes upon himself the rejection of humanity, electing humanity to participate in his glory. From this comes the eternal election of the community of witness by which every rejection is voided by Jesus Christ and every member is elected as bearer of witness to the whole world. In this

context, we see the place of ethics as divine command originating in the claim, decision, and judgment of God.

Chapter VIII (§§36–39): The Command of God

Here, the implications of the electing God for humanity are shown, as grace by which God savingly engages us, claiming our obedience as we live in the decision of God which is our beginning and our goal, and – by judgment in Christ's death – pronouncing us righteous and freeing us for everlasting life under the lordship of God.

Volume III: *The Doctrine of Creation*

Unlike most modern theological work on creation, Barth's approach focuses on what is known through the revealed Word of God: on God's side, creation is the creating and seeking of a distinct reality with which to share his life and glory; on the human side, it is an existence in grace; and both anticipate their completion in redemption.

Chapter IX (§§40–42): The Work of Creation

Only by faith in response to the divine self-witness in Jesus Christ, not by human self-explanation or through the insights of other techniques and disciplines, do people discover the source of their existence and form, and that of the reality in which they are set. In faith they know that God is creator and that the world *is*. And this faith derives from knowledge of Jesus – in the unity of Creator and creature actualized in him, in life as mediated by him, and in the goodness found in him – by the Holy Spirit. This immediately associates the meaning of creation (whose history eludes all observation and explanation, and is expressed as *saga*) with God's purposes for its goodness enacted in the history of the covenant by which human fellowship with God has its beginning, center, and culmination in Jesus Christ. The history of the covenant is the goal of creation, and creation its beginning. So we know the work of the Creator as benefit, which within the limits of creatureliness, is actualized for goodness.

Chapter X (§§43–47): The Creature

The human being is in a central position, as the creature whose relation to God is revealed in the Word of God. This does not yield a specific cosmology (which always tends to displace attention from the Word of God), but only the indissoluble connection of creation with covenant, of "nature" with the history of personal responsibility and its fulfillment. In the man Jesus Christ – "the one in whose identity with himself we must recognize at once the identity of God with Himself"[37] – we know what created humanity properly is, as elected and called to responsibility by God, and capable of fulfilling it. To be a human being is to be with God, and the glory of Christ is that he is both a real creature and "stands so utterly in the service of God."[38] The humanity thus seen is co-humanity, being in concrete encounter, *being for others*, singularity in duality. Evidently learning from Dietrich Bonhoeffer, Barth describes the creatureliness of humanity as the encounter of man and woman, in which humanity learns its likeness to – and its hope in – its Creator. And through the Spirit, human beings know themselves as subjects and souls in inseparable unity with their bodies; and they live their span of life always circumscribed by the eternal God who is their creator, covenant partner, and the hope for their temporal life.

Chapter XI (§§48–51): Creator and Creature

Having correlated creation with covenant, "nature" with this "history," Barth shows how this covenant history has an "external basis" in "the sway of divine providence."[39] In some of the most strikingly original parts of his work, Barth takes up questions associated with the divine rule in the *history* of created being: it is under the comprehensively graceful providential care of the Creator, whose will is accomplished in covenant history and complete in Jesus Christ. This care is as embracing – preserving, accompanying, and ruling – as is the Lordship of God. And it is by the free love of God that creation receives its *telos* and character, not from its own contribution. Everything in its particular existence, in which God rejoices, is also ordered by God: "Both in general and in particular God Himself fixes for the creature its goals, that is, the goals it will actually attain . . . ultimately [to] realize the divine decree."[40] A major issue occurs here, however: the inherent opposition and resistance of creation to God's world dominion, the intrusion of an "alien factor" termed "nothingness." In one of the most important sections of the *Church Dogmatics*, Barth delineates the "ontic peculiarity" of nothingness as evil, which arises from refusal of and resistance to God's grace, evil and human sin as the privation of grace which are – when seen retrospectively from Christ's resurrection and coming again – consigned to the past.[41] These insights are mirrored in Barth's reassertion of the finality of the Lordship of God in Jesus Christ in the kingdom of heaven, and from there the sending of "pure witnesses" (angels) who come with God as he acts in the world with those who witness to him and vanquish the power of evil there.

Chapter XII (§§52–55): The Command of God the Creator

Throughout volume 3, Barth is concerned with creation and covenant, nature and providential history, and he turns now to their ethical counterparts, command and freedom in the spheres discussed previously: encounter, life, and limitation. Like God, created being is providential act: "true humanity is characterized by action, by good action, as the true God is characterized by action, by good action."[42] In a discussion of the general form, spheres, and relations of ethics, not of particular decisions or situations, we find that the Word of God in Christian proclamation takes the form of God's gracious command of what is good in human action, from which the human being is to act concretely. Both God's command and human action are "historically articulated," and have different elements, but the triune God nonetheless meets humanity as the Creator and Commander who has already sanctified creaturely activity in Jesus Christ. The issue then considered is how God's call to responsibility is fulfilled through human freedom before God (in Sabbath worship, freedom and joy, and in confession and petition), human freedom in fellowship (families and neighbors affirm, honor, and enjoy each other), freedom for life (the calling to turn to fellow human beings); in all cases, the question is how people are to respect and protect all life, within the intention, temporal limit, vocation, and honor set by God for humanity as Creator and Lord.

Volume IV: *The Christian Doctrine of Reconciliation*

Barth now turns to the dynamic of the Word of God which is specific to reconciliation. He deploys the Christology he had set out in *Church Dogmatics* I/2, but now incorporates in a single *historical* narrative the person, office, and way of Jesus Christ, sin, judgment, and justification, sanctification, vocation, community, and individual within a dynamic of the Son in our place "going into the far country," his "homecoming" and his unity of the two. It shows a Christology – with both noetic and ontological implications – in which Jesus Christ manifests his divinity in his humiliation, his humanity in his exaltation, and the unity of the "God-man" in his self-manifestation as the mediator. As such it is a remarkable recapitulation and revision of what had preceded it, which has provided for many readers an alternative access to the *Church Dogmatics*: "Barth intensifies his previous anti-metaphysical, trinitarian formulation of the concept of God by identifying Christ's humiliation and obedience unto death as a movement in God's being," correcting his earlier tendencies to "abstract theomonism" by a "theanthropology."[43] Within this, old doctrinal themes are rearranged and reformed.

Chapter XIII (§§57–58): Subject-Matter, Problems, and Survey
Here, after the "heart of the Christian message," is presented the knowledge of Jesus Christ who is "very God, very man," and (in the unity of the two) guarantor of our atonement. The free act of the faithfulness of God in Jesus Christ is seen to *include* (a) the knowledge of self-ruined humanity (pride, sloth, and falsehood); (b) the knowledge of reconciliation (justification, sanctification, and calling); (c) the knowledge of the work of the Holy Spirit (the gathering, upbuilding, and sending of the community); and (d) the being of Christians in Jesus Christ (in faith, love, and hope). The movement by which these occur is shown in the three chapters that follow.

Chapter XIV (§§59–63): Jesus Christ, the Lord as Servant
Here is where the movement of Jesus Christ as true God – by which humanity is reconciled – begins to be seen. In God's majesty the eternal Son of the eternal Father became obedient for us by offering and humbling himself to be brother to the transgressor, judging him by judging himself and dying in his place, to be raised by the Father as a satisfaction for us. In this it is seen what is the condition of the human being as sinner, how he is justified, and how – by the Holy Spirit – he is awakened and gathered in a new community.

Chapter XV (§§64–68): Jesus Christ, the Servant as Lord
The Son of God thus humbled to serve humankind is also exalted to be the Lord, the new and true "royal man" who fully participates in the being, life, and Lordship of God for all other human beings as their Representative and Savior, and the content of the divine direction in the Holy Spirit. This in turn brings to light other aspects: of human sin (refusal of freedom and miserably self-enclosed being), of salvation (a new form of existence as covenant partner, awakening and conversion), and of the Holy Spirit's work to quicken Christianity in the world as his earthly historical body and also Christians to witness.

Chapter XVI (§§69–73)

As seen in holy scripture, the movements just described testify to Jesus as the one Word of God who is to be heard, trusted, and obeyed in life and in death. They are the effecting of the promise of God as it encounters humanity in the resurrection of Jesus Christ. As such they show a further aspect of human sin (that humanity is bound within false self-assertion, perversion, and inevitable perishing), of salvation (the creative call for the awakening of human beings to active knowledge of the truth and the new standing – in Jesus Christ – of the Christian, fellowship with God, and prophetic witness and service), and of the Holy Spirit's work to become one of his community of hope (anticipating the new coming to consummate the revelation and will of God fulfilled in Jesus Christ).

Hence, in this volume, we see a threefold movement, each involving a range of different themes and aspects: (1) the *person* of Jesus Christ as God, as human being, and as true witness: his *office* as priest, king, and prophet, his *way* as self-emptying, exalted, and Light; (2) *human sin* as pride and fall, sloth and misery, and falsehood and condemnation; *salvation* as judgment and justification, direction and sanctification, and promise and vocation; (3) the *work of the Holy Spirit* in *community* as gathering, upbuilding, and sending, and in the *individual* as faith, hope, and love. In short, Jesus Christ follows the dialectical self-distancing of humanity to its eventuality in death, but in doing so reverses it and brings people to life in God.

Volume IV, Part 4 (Fragment): *The Christian Life*

Barth intended this part to show "the free and active answer of the human being to the divine work and word of grace," and to explain how the recollection of the divine gift makes the Christian life possible. Within this, the means by which such memory is enacted in the church – baptism, prayer, and the Lord's Supper – were of pivotal importance; and Barth intended at each point to show these as God's work and human work. The surviving fragment on baptism is distinctive for its emphasis on the priority of the Kingdom of God now made actual, in which the freedom of the gracious God – and nothing else – brings a true change in a human being. True change by divine judgment to be free to become what one was not before, to be faithful to God, is only accomplished where "man himself, in his most proper subjectivity, ceases to stand without as a stranger . . . approaches and comes inside to the place where all things are ready for him specifically." Here the power of God in his freedom – in the history of Jesus Christ, and by the Holy Spirit – is such that a person is enabled to participate actively in God's grace. This "baptism of the Spirit" becomes the epitome of the beginning of the Christian life, when someone – in co-confession with the Christian community – asks for and receives Christian baptism by water, which is directed through the Holy Spirit toward a "future thing." Barth's view thus abandons the "sacramental" view of baptism, and provides a positive alternative.

Debate

Karl Barth's lifelong search was to establish a strong position for orthodox Christian faith in a world in which it had been marginalized, and which had been seriously

corrupted as a result. This "world" was not of recent origin: it included the subversive tendencies found throughout the history of Christianity as well as in the present
day, many of which he confronted throughout the *Church Dogmatics*. These tendencies can be seen as counterparts of the reductive ways of the theology in which
Barth had been educated, a combination of Kantianism, Hegelianism, Schleiermacher,
Von Harnack, and others, and in the approaches advocated by some of his contemporaries. The hydra-headed monster – largely a compound of history and philosophy
– with which he was struggling, both in the past and in the present, was a real
threat, and it survives in assumptions commonly made today. Barth, however, was
not intimidated, largely because he found it possible to trace the actuality of God's
self-revelation.

Much of his achievement lies in his capacity to combine what can be called "depth
analysis" – by which he located the strengths and weaknesses of historical and
contemporary theology – with the critical reconstruction of Reformed Christianity.
By comparison, many other theologians of the twentieth century seem very limited
in their attempts to do either the one or the other. His close conjunction of
historical analysis and reconstruction means that his adjudication of the value of
other positions is directly related to the constructive position by which he judges
them. If there is a problem in the one, then there will be a problem in the other.
Early in his *Church Dogmatics* he states that dogmatics is to test the church and its
proclamation, and he frequently returns to this critical task, but then he also reconstructs the content of Christian theology. How are the two to be related in what we
now do in theology?

Broadly speaking, his ways of dealing with many of the central aspects of Christian
theology are agreed – often without tracing them to him – among many Christians
today, but Barth's own conclusions about how God is known are more severe and
stringent than the ways in which many now suppose that such knowledge occurs.
Putting it in different words, he finds that the truth of God presents itself as the
pure intensive event of the Word of God known through faith by God's grace,
which is comprehensively important for our understanding of God, creation, and
reconciliation. More recent notions are often less precise and much milder, that
faith is more like "experience" and the rest of theology like human apprehensions of
meaning. One of the chief lessons of Barth's theology lies in the sustained sharpness
of its insight, both in the demands of faith as such and also in the range of its
implications for all created and redeemed being and activity. That should not be
avoided in favor of milder and less carefully thought alternatives. Yet Barth is not an
easy companion: he resists any symbiosis of God's word and systems of human
experience, and supposes that the Word of God as he finds it is normative for all
human life and understanding.

This immediately projects us into major issues about his theology. The basis of
Barth's theology is in God's self-initiated relation to humanity in the world, God's
active self-revelation in the Word of God, by which he interprets the scriptures and
through which all else about God, the world, and humanity is known. This particular act, by which God chooses to be himself, both inwardly and outwardly as
Trinity, electing in the Son to be both electing God and elected human being,
Creator and covenant partner, providential and reconciling, even to the point of the
fullest outward movement by which to redeem and glorify humanity, is that on

which all else hangs. Easy as it is to describe it as "actualism," in Barth's case this is *God's sovereign act*, not a general philosophical position.

For all the virtues of this way of construing God's self-relation to the world, not least its (modern) clarity and discreteness, it is a particular way of identifying God, seeing the identity of God (being) in its relation (intersubjective action).[44] Whether the complex biblical witness, in which the infinitely intense identity of the Lord is conferred through the identification of Israel and through the "I am" of Jesus, is adequately caught by Barth's way of construing both God and his relation to all else, is a matter of question. It is attractive because it allows full scope for the sovereign freedom of God's choice in all matters, including direct correlation with the Word of God in Jesus Christ, the establishing of what are truth and goodness, and – in effect – the controlling of all that is, or is true, or is good. But it may also unduly clarify what remains historical, complex, particular, and mysterious, despite Barth's latter-day (and limited) allowances for these.

Such a way of proceeding allows theology also to focus regularly on the pivotal moments of decision, in which the standards of right and wrong conduct are chosen for us, and we must choose accordingly. At least in the later parts of the *Church Dogmatics*, Barth makes it clear that these – like the contingent contemporaneity of the Word of God – are general, and do not prejudice the particularity of human beings and their situations. But it remains the case that God's choices are decisive, and so must ours be. And this forces us to ask whether all things are constituted in such decisive ways, to which the answer seems to be: sometimes yes, and sometimes no. Even Barth focuses on the major points at which there are pivotal decisions, and we can readily imagine that our lives too must be decisive in major ways. Whether this is so helpful in the myriad of small ways in which we live is more a question. Perhaps they are suitable for the transcendent; are they for the immanent complexity of life?

Such issues become very difficult where human words and actions are involved. For one thing, how is the purity of God's purposes evident in his Word, when used as dogmatic criterion, actually found in scripture, church, and proclamation? Does it authorize us to search within *scripture*, not only for the Word but also for clear doctrinal criteria and statements? That runs the danger of *merging* scripture and doctrine, the latter finding the inner logical patterns of the former, and the former to be the exemplifications – perhaps very nuanced ones – of doctrinal points. Shouldn't scripture – while maintaining its contingency upon revelation and its position as the normative carrier for memory – and doctrine be more carefully distinguished? Secondly, so far as the *church* is concerned, is such purity, even when constantly refreshed in encounter with God, best shown in the summoning and separating of people into the church, from which they must proclaim to the "outside" world? Or are the boundaries of the church, as Bonhoeffer found, less well-defined, there being a real question about whether revelation in the social reality of the church is so sharply distinct from social reality in general? Thirdly, does such strong emphasis on the purity of proclamation not refine its position almost to the vanishing point of those events in which – *per impossibile* – it happens? The result is to de-sacramentalize the preached Word.

There are comparable questions in the notions of the Trinity developed in the earlier parts of the *Church Dogmatics*. At first, Barth's "pure theology of the Word" safeguards the Trinity, but does so as a "vertical" unity in distinction: the God who is thus revealed is Lord, in unimpaired unity in unimpaired distinction as Revealer, Revelation, and Revealedness. Even the very rich elucidations that follow in the volumes dedicated to God and creation, leave the Trinity in the position of a *summation* of God's work in the world, where God is seen as Lord of our existence, Lord in our enmity towards him and liberator from it, and Lord who frees us to respond. And even where (in volume 4) Barth appears most free of the constraints of such "vertical" logic, the "spiral" downward–upward unity he finds in God's reconciling work still shows the residuum of such thinking. Does he, when he deals with the explicitly historical – that is in covenant history, providence, and reconciliation – ever fully allow history *per se* to modify this logic? He does go much farther in that direction than he is usually given credit for, and does acknowledge the particularity of created existence much more fully. But even there God is seen primarily as setting the character, order, and *telos* of created existence, whose fullest expressions are seen in the Lordship of Jesus Christ in the Kingdom of God. But does this allow for the fullest participation of God in the history and struggles of human beings? Or does it, as is so often suggested, leave Barth with a Word of God whose form is too general to allow the fullest engagement by God in the particularities – spatial and temporal – of the human situation? In other words, even where Barth turns to a "history of truth" in volume 4, it is embraced within the definitive work of God as previously stated, and history plays a small role.

As has occasionally been suggested (by Jüngel, for example), the root problem may be that – for all its pungency, range, and brilliance – Barth's theology may be too much confined by a few structural assumptions to match the more complex needs of today. To say that, however, is not to deny its lasting significance as a gauge for Christian belief.

Influence, Achievement, and Agenda

The influence of Karl Barth has been so extensive as to be virtually coterminous with the history of theology during and since his lifetime. Since his work was both so decisive in its method and so comprehensive in its scope, we continue to meet it both in those whose approaches coincide with his, in those who argue – against him – for other ways, and also in those who extend the topics with which he was concerned within and outside his frame of reference. So much did he reconstitute and consolidate the state of Christian theology for the twentieth century that he is always a point of departure for others. Nonetheless, broadly speaking, we can identify particular types of his influence, and a selection of those influenced.

There are those who stay almost entirely within his construction of the appropriate frame of reference for theology today, tracing, interpreting, and confirming its importance (e.g., Bruce McCormack, George Hunsinger, John Webster). Others stay within his frame of reference, but extend it into areas with which Barth himself was not directly concerned (e.g., Thomas Torrance, Alan Torrance, Timothy Gorringe).

There are those who agree with Barth's theology in significant respects, and do him justice by using other frames of reference by which to enlarge the significance of what he did (e.g., Dietrich Bonhoeffer, Donald Mackinnon, Hans Frei, Eberhard

Jüngel, Robert Jenson, Stephen Sykes, Oliver O'Donovan, Colin Gunton, David Ford, Rowan Williams, Stanley Hauerwas). Others depart critically from his frame of reference and transpose his concerns into other ones (e.g., Wolfhart Pannenberg, Jürgen Moltmann, Hans Küng, Hans Urs von Balthasar, Graham Ward).

Such a sketch still understates the disseminated influence of Barth, however. If we consider the ways in which doctrinal theology is pursued today, Barth's treatments of particular topics – revelation, Christology, Trinity, creation, evil, redemption – are tacitly accepted as the formulations from which further discussions begin. In one sense, this piecemeal use of Barth often does not spring from, or produce, thorough understanding of his theology; but in another sense, it testifies to the importance it has had for subsequent theology.

If we consider Barth's place in the wider scene of theology today, however, we find that his theology is now seen as the chief example of a particular option – what can be called the "traditional doctrinal" – as one who shows how to refound, consolidate, and strengthen it. As we have seen, he does this by establishing the normative standing of a theology whose method and content are interwoven, whose epistemology is built on the actuality of the event of revelation in Jesus Christ, the Word of God through whom God constitutes himself triunely in the creation and redemption of the world, and all that can be concluded therefrom. Today, however, Barth's work seems more a splendidly worked example of "traditional doctrine" – intense, rich, and provocative – of what can be achieved within the parameters he established, and sustained through a remarkable purity of form (which is what makes its adaptation very difficult). Even to suggest that is to recognize the contingency of Barth's approach: not simply that it is – as he claims it should be – contingent upon the act of God, but that it is also contingent, even in its method and content, upon the ultimate outworking of the Kingdom of God. If that is so, then the certainty which Barth's theology yields, albeit a very restricted form of certainty, is transposed into a historical–eschatological frame of reference which will require it – and all its features – to be opened for fresh exploration. But, as we have seen, the close interweaving of method and content in his theology makes this very difficult: it resists acknowledgment of its own historical contingency, which is perhaps why Barth so often found himself starting afresh and why so many of Barth's interpreters stay within the "traditional doctrinal" option in the use they make of him.

Notes

1 Karl Barth, *Letters 1961–1968*, Grand Rapids, MI: William B. Eerdmans, 1981, p. 203.
2 These are collected in *The Word of God and the Word of Man*, trans. Douglas Horton, New York: Harper & Brothers, 1957.
3 Karl Barth, *The Göttingen Dogmatics*, trans. Geoffrey W. Bromiley, Grand Rapids, MI: William B. Eerdmans, 1991.
4 Barth was unwilling to have these published, although they were later published as *Eth-*

ics, ed. Dietrich Braun, 1973, 1978, trans. Geoffrey W. Bromiley, Edinburgh: T. & T. Clark, 1981.
5 Hans Urs von Balthasar, *The Theology of Karl Barth*, trans. John Drury, New York: Holt, Rinehart, and Winston, 1971.
6 McCormack, p. 129.
7 Published in 1922. It was the sixth edition of this commentary that was translated into English by Edwin Hoskyns and published in 1933.

8   McCormack, p. 207.

9   "Spirit means the eternal decision by which God decides for men and men for God. Spirit is the pleasure which God has in men and the goodwill which men have towards God. Spirit means to belong to Christ, to participate in His question and, consequently, in His answer; in His sin and, consequently, in His righteousness; in His 'No' and, consequently, in His 'Yes'; in His death and, consequently, in His life. The Spirit is existential meaning and sense. It makes and creates sense." Karl Barth, *The Epistle to the Romans*, 6th edn., trans. Edwyn C. Hoskyns, Oxford: Oxford University Press, 1933, p. 283.

10 Ibid, p. 512.

11 Of Paul, Franz Overbeck, Plato, and Kant, some of the writings of Søren Kierkegaard (only then achieving prominence) and Dostoyevsky, in particular.

12 Karl Barth, *Commentary on the Epistle to the Romans*, preface to the second edition, p. 10.

13 His lectures have been published as Karl Barth, *The Theology of the Reformed Confessions 1923*, trans. Darrell L. Guder and Judith J. Guder, Louisville, KY: Westminster John Knox Press, 2002.

14 It had "no absolute supposition apart from the Word of God in which dogmas are grounded and from which they necessarily follow." Karl Barth, *The Göttingen Dogmatics: Instruction in the Christian Religion*, ed. Hannelotte Reiffen, trans. Geoffrey W. Bromiley, Grand Rapids, MI: William B. Eerdmans, 1991, Vol. 1, p. 13.

15 Karl Barth, "Church and Theology" in *Theology and Church: Shorter Writings 1920–1928*, Munich 1928, trans. Louise Pettibone Smith, London: SCM Press, 1962, p. 295.

16 Karl Barth, *The Holy Ghost and the Christian Life (1929)*, trans. R. Birch Hoyle, London: Frederick Muller, 1938, p. 15.

17 Karl Barth, *Anselm: Fides Quaerens Intellectum*, 2nd edn. 1958, trans. Ian W. Robertson, London: SCM Press, 1960, p. 15.

18 Cf. McCormack, p. 425.

19 Karl Barth, *Church Dogmatics*, Edinburgh: T. & T. Clark, 1936–77, ET of *Kirchliche Dogmatik, 1932–1970*, I/1, p. xii. Hereafter, "CD."

20 This was indicated in a lecture delivered in 1956. "What began forcibly to press itself upon us about forty years ago was not so much the humanity of God as His *deity* – a God absolutely unique in His relation to man and the world, overpoweringly lofty and distant, strange, yes even wholly other . . . the *humanity* of God at that time moved from the center to the periphery." "All this, however well it may have been meant and however much it may have mattered, was nevertheless said somewhat severely and brutally, and moreover – at least according to the other side – in part heretically." "The Humanity of God," trans. John Newton Thomas in Karl Barth, *The Humanity of God*, Richmond, VI: John Knox Press, 1960, pp. 38, 43.

21 These "motifs," as he calls them, are well described in Hunsinger, *How to Read Karl Barth*, ch. 1, but they are not arranged as here.

22 CD I/1, p. 79.

23 Ibid, p. 29.

24 Hunsinger, p. 28.

25 Hunsinger, p. 58. The same can be found at every level of the *Church Dogmatics*. In each case we move from the proximate to what gives it its actuality, but then we also move beyond this "what" – as proximate – to that which makes it what it is, and eventually to the source of all determination in the being of the God who acts as this God does.

26 CD I/1, p. xii.

27 CD I/1, p. 52.

28 CD I/1, p. 94.

29 CD I/1, p. 104.

30 CD I/1, p. 113.

31 CD I/1, p. 145.

32 CD I/1, p. 222.

33 CD I/2, p. 58.

34 CD I/2, p. 359.

35 Karl Barth, "The Proclamation of God's Free Grace" in *God Here and Now*, trans. Paul M. van Buren, London: Routledge, 2003, pp. 36ff.

36 John Webster, *Karl Barth*, London: Continuum, 2000, pp. 76ff.

37 CD III/2, p. 68.

38 CD III/2, p. 64.

39 CD III/3, p. 7.

40 CD III/3, p. 167.

41 CD III/3, p. 353.
42 CD III/4, p. 3.
43 Jüngel, p. 46.

44 There may be overtones of modern post-Kantian idealism (e.g., Croce and Gentile) here.

Bibliography

Primary

The Word of God and the Word of Man (New York, 1957).
The Epistle to the Romans (London, 1933).
Anselm: Fides Quaerens Intellectum (London, 1960).
The German Church Conflict (London, 1965).
Church Dogmatics (Edinburgh, 1936–69).
Protestant Theology in the Nineteenth Century (London 1952, 1972).
God Here and Now (New York, 1964).
Wolfgang Amadeus Mozart (Grand Rapids, MI, 1986).

Secondary

Busch, Eberhard, *Karl Barth: His Life from Letters and Autobiographical Texts* (London, 1976).

Ford, David F., *Barth and God's Story* (Frankfurt, 1981).
Hunsinger, George, *How to Read Karl Barth: The Shape of His Theology* (New York, 1991).
Jehle, Frank, *Ever Against the Stream: The Politics of Karl Barth, 1906–1968* (Grand Rapids, MI, 2002).
Jenson, Robert W., *God After God* (New York, 1969).
Jüngel, Eberhard, *Karl Barth: A Theological Legacy* (Philadelphia, PA, 1986).
McCormack, Bruce L., *Karl Barth's Critically Realistic Dialectical Theology: Its Genesis and Development* (Oxford, 1995).
Torrance, Thomas F., *Karl Barth, Biblical and Evangelical Theologian* (Edinburgh, 1990).

Dietrich Bonhoeffer

Wayne Whitson Floyd

Introduction

Dietrich Bonhoeffer has remained a partner in theological conversation just long enough to have been both lauded as the quintessence of modern theology and derided as approaching obsolescence precisely because, too long after the postmodern turn, his voice remains hopelessly mired in that same antiquated modernity. Dyed-in-the-wool liberals as well as reactionary conservatives, Catholics and Protestants, the European and American mainstream as well as voices for liberation in the Global South – all have seen in him a foreshadowing or inspiration for their own theological commitments. Harvey Cox's quip remains as true now as it did when he made it four decades ago, that Bonhoeffer has served as a veritable Rorschach test for modern theology.

"Discovered" in British and American circles primarily through his misidentification as a "radical secularist," Bonhoeffer must once and for all be disengaged from the clutches of the "death of God" movement.[1] Contrariwise, despite his own broad comfort zone with a traditional biblical and theological lexicon and its themes, Bonhoeffer cannot be shoehorned into anything resembling a simplistic conservative-evangelical mold.[2]

Bonhoeffer's phrases and themes, once having entered the modern Christian theological canon, have by their very familiarity tended to domesticate their counter-cultural origins, which had been based upon sensibilities that had set Bonhoeffer apart from his own peers. Especially in academia, a "Bonhoeffer orthodoxy" has emerged that assumes to know all too well what he can and cannot be understood to have said and meant, to the point that few any longer expect to be sharply discomfited by anything in his literary legacy and seldom find themselves existentially challenged by Bonhoeffer's intended challenges to the status quo – socially, politically, and theologically.

The completion at last of an entire critical edition of his writings,[3] and the emergence of its English edition counterpart,[4] reveal a wealth of previously unavailable letters, essays, sermons, novel fragments, poems, spiritual writings, and philosophical musings – including finished books published in Bonhoeffer's own lifetime, and other works left in uncompleted and fragmentary form at his untimely death. He has left "the coming generation" with a nuanced, sometimes unnerving, and yet eminently concrete and pastorally practical spirituality, that is at once intimately personal and publicly challenging in its unabashedly worldly implications. Bonhoeffer remains evocative, as well as provocative, not just because his life and words provide some fresh ways of approaching the perennial questions of Christianity, but because they renew the very spirit of inquiry and decision that has always shaped the landscape of Christian faithfulness. Bonhoeffer is a "modern" theologian who has a future richer even than his past, seventy years now since the start of his vocation of resistance, which first brought him to the attention of scholars and laity alike.

Biography and Context

There is a profound congruence between Bonhoeffer's life and times and thought. The telling of his story here will indeed attempt to supply the necessary context for understanding his contributions to religious thought and life, but without pretending that knowing the biography is a sufficient rendering of the remarkable contributions of Dietrich Bonhoeffer to modern theology and practice.

Born on February 4, 1906, Dietrich was the sixth of eight siblings, including his twin sister Sabine, all born in the space of ten years. One brother, Walter, did not survive World War I; another brother, Klaus, was to be executed for his own participation in the July 20, 1944 plot to assassinate Hitler. Dietrich himself did not live until his fortieth birthday, as he was hanged by the Gestapo at Flossenbürg concentration camp on April 9, 1945 for his own acts of resistance against Nazism.[5] Dietrich's father, Karl Bonhoeffer, was a noted neurologist and professor of psychiatry at the Friedrich Wilhelm University in Berlin. Dietrich's mother, Paula – herself a university graduate and a descendent of a long line of pastors, theologians, and musicians – home-schooled her children.

Out of this family (along with Klaus and Dietrich), Rüdiger Schleicher, the husband of Dietrich's sister Ursula, and Hans von Dohnanyi, the husband of Dietrich's sister Christine, would later be executed for their parts in the resistance. Other surviving siblings included his brother, Karl-Friedrich, a physicist, and a sister Susanne.

In the calm before the storm of Nazism, the Bonhoeffers were a family, as Eberhard and Renate Bethge have described them, with "a deep-rooted sense of obligation, the awareness of being guardian of a great historical heritage and cultural tradition."[6] Visitors in the Bonhoeffer home included academics and professionals from the university. Evenings found the family gathered for musical performances, with Dietrich playing the piano, which at one time he considered pursuing as a career.

At an early age Dietrich excelled in sports, and then later in music and in his facility with learning foreign languages (especially Latin, Hebrew, and Greek). As a teenage student his broader intellectual precociousness became evident. Barely 17 when he completed his Gymnasium studies in Berlin, Dietrich began his degree at Tübingen University, where he studied in 1923–4, the year of the Munich Putsch. While Adolf Hitler was writing *Mein Kampf* in prison, Dietrich was immersed in Kant's *Critique of Pure Reason* ("I liked it a lot").

Just turned 18, Bonhoeffer spent April 3 to June 4, 1924 on an extended trip to Rome and North Africa with his brother Klaus. His diary from the journey reveals the young Protestant's first concrete encounter with the Catholic Church. He was not too impressed with his audience with Pope Pius XI ("Great expectations dashed"). But upon seeing St. Peter's he remarked: "You are immediately overwhelmed." And his experience of the liturgies of Holy Week in Rome was a memorable, indeed transformative, encounter with Christianity's universality: "I believe I am beginning to understand the concept of 'church.'"[7]

Back at the University of Berlin, where he was a student from 1924 to 1927, Bonhoeffer read Max Weber and Ernst Troeltsch, Edmund Husserl and Friedrich Schleiermacher. He was part of one of Adolf von Harnack's seminars, and that same year also first encountered the writings of Karl Barth. The confluence of the latter's Christocentrism and the former's concern to show the relevance of Christianity to the modern world would have an indelible effect on Bonhoeffer's approach to theology.

In Berlin, Bonhoeffer studied Luther with Karl Holl, systematic theology and ethics with Reinhold Seeberg, epistemology with Heinrich Maier, and practical theology and catechetics with Friedrich Mahling. He received his licentiate in theology in December 1927, upon the successful defense under Reinhold Seeberg of his doctoral dissertation, *The Communion of Saints*, which Karl Barth later described as a "theological miracle."

In January 1928 Bonhoeffer passed his first set of theological examinations and was accepted as a candidate for ordination. He then spent February 1928 to February 1929 as assistant pastor in the German-speaking Lutheran congregation in Barcelona. "Bonhoeffer was increasingly aware of the international financial crisis of the late 1920s and the resulting social chaos in Europe. One wonders about the reaction of his prosperous congregation members when Bonhoeffer preached to them about their difficulty in connecting the gospel with the increasingly evident needs of the world around them. 'God wanders among us in human form,' one sermon said, 'speaking to us in those who cross our paths, be they stranger, beggar, sick, or even in those nearest to us in everyday life, becoming Christ's demand on our faith in him.'"[8]

Bonhoeffer returned to the University of Berlin in 1929 to serve as an assistant to Wilhelm Lütgert, a specialist in German idealism, presenting his first lectures in the summer of 1929. There he secured his credentials to teach in the university by writing his *Habilitationsschrift*, *Act and Being*, which was accepted on July 18, 1930. Thus qualified as a university teacher, his official inaugural lecture, "Humanity in Contemporary Philosophy and Theology," was presented two weeks later.

On September 5, 1930, he traveled to New York as a postgraduate Sloane Fellow at Union Theological Seminary. His German arrogance flashed in his early estimations of his faculty and fellow students: "There is no theology here."[9] Still, there were life-changing friendships to be made, for example with Frank Fisher, an African-American student at Union who took Bonhoeffer to Harlem to Abyssinian Baptist Church, where Bonhoeffer taught a Sunday School class, but perhaps more importantly learned lessons about American racism that he was to take home to Germany and apply to anti-Semitism there. There he met Erwin Sutz, the Swiss student who shared with Bonhoeffer a love of the piano, and who became a confidant and contact later during the war years; and Jean Lassere, the French pacifist whose influence can be seen throughout Bonhoeffer's writings about peace and loving one's enemies all through the 1930s; and Paul and Marion Lehmann, who gave Bonhoeffer a home away from home in New York, and who with Reinhold Niebuhr made the last-gasp effort later in 1939 to convince Bonhoeffer to remain in New York in the face of the looming prospect of war.

For a place with "no theology," New York provided Bonhoeffer a life-altering laboratory for learning about the demands of the world on the life of the church. Perhaps these were the "first impressions abroad" to which Bonhoeffer referred later in a letter from April 22, 1944, to Bethge, the point at which Bonhoeffer said: "I turned from phraseology to reality."[10] One thing is sure, after New York he would never be the same.

Bonhoeffer returned to Germany in July 1931 facing a dramatically changed academic, political, social, and economic environment. Full of enthusiasm from his first personal meeting with Karl Barth at the University of Bonn earlier that month, Bonhoeffer in August joined the theological faculty at Berlin as *Privatdozent* or unpaid assistant lecturer, a position he continued through the summer semester of 1933. His *Habilitationsschrift, Act and Being*, was published two months later. A promising academic career was underway, and over the next year he taught courses on the history of twentieth-century systematic theology, the nature of the church, and Christian ethics.

And yet a larger world and the practical affairs of the church beckoned, as well. In August and September 1931 Bonhoeffer had attended conferences of the World Alliance for Promoting International Friendship through the Churches, principally in Cambridge; this was his first formal involvement in the ecumenical movement and his first trip to England. That November 15, at the age of 25, he was ordained at St. Matthias Church, Berlin, and began his duties as a chaplain at the Technical College at Charlottenburg, where he also served until 1933. His ecumenical travels continued during July and August 1932, when he attended ecumenical gatherings at Geneva and Gland, as well as a Youth Peace Conference in Ciernohorské Kúpele, Czechoslovakia.

But when on January 30, 1933 Adolf Hitler became the Chancellor of Germany, all of Bonhoeffer's plans for a routine academic, as well as ecclesiastical, life were irrevocably altered. While Bonhoeffer's letters from the end of 1932 often still arose from his fresh new interest in ecumenical activities – and include Bonhoeffer's earliest surviving letter to Karl Barth, dated Christmas eve 1932 – those from early 1933 begin to be haunted by more ominous possibilities, reflected in letters to friends such as Anneliese Schnurmann, who was being forced to leave Germany because of her Jewish background, or one to Reinhold Niebuhr the week after Hitler became chancellor.

His 1932–3 winter-semester course "Creation and Sin," published in 1933 as *Creation and Fall*, and the summer-semester 1933 courses "Christology" and "The Philosophy of Hegel," were to be his last offerings before leaving the University of Berlin. Already it was clear that his energies and commitments were leading him elsewhere. As he watched the National Socialists sign the Concordat with the papacy on July 20, 1933, and reeled from the crisis brought on by the German Christians' winning up to 70 percent of church posts in Protestant church elections on July 23, he began to understand that the church in Germany – indeed, among Christians anywhere – had reached a *status confessionis*, a moment of decision when it must either submit to the claim upon it by the gospel, or the counterclaim being made by Nazi authoritarianism. With his colleague Martin Niemöller, Bonhoeffer helped form the Pastor's Emergency League in September 1933, a forerunner to the Confessing Church that was to be organized in May 1934 as a protest against National Socialism's deepening control over Christianity in Germany.

Bonhoeffer's patience and energy had by this time worn thin. He needed, he wrote Karl Barth, "time to go for a while into the desert." And so in October 1933 Bonhoeffer moved to London to begin serving pastorates at the German Evangelical Church, Sydenham, and the Reformed Church of St. Paul, London. In London, Bonhoeffer made one of the two most significant friendships that were to shape his path through the last dozen years of his life: George Bell, formerly Dean of Canterbury Cathedral and, when Bonhoeffer knew him, Anglican Bishop of Chichester.[11] Bell and Bonhoeffer first met in person in November 1933, soon learning that they shared the same birthday, a love of music and the arts, and a commitment to ecumenism. During this time Bonhoeffer traveled to Fanø, Denmark, to attend the World Alliance for Promoting International Friendship through the Churches, making there a plea on behalf of the Confessing Church. "The hour is late," Bonhoeffer wrote to his ecumenical colleagues. "The world is choked with weapons, and dreadful is the distrust which looks out of all men's eyes. The trumpets of war may blow tomorrow. For what are we waiting?"[12] Bonhoeffer was frustrated that even his more progressive friends in the ecumenical movement seemed so prone to indecisiveness: "People have to make up their minds and cannot keep waiting for ever for a sign from heaven, for a solution to the difficulty suddenly to fall into their laps. The ecumenical movement must decide too . . . Postponed or belated decisions can be more sinful than wrong decisions made in faith and love . . . To believe means to decide."[13]

Bonhoeffer was divided about whether to study in India under Gandhi or to return to Germany. In the end Bonhoeffer chose to go home, perhaps remembering Karl Barth's sharp rebuke in November 1933 for fleeing Germany in the first place: "The building of your church is burning . . . come home on the next ship!"[14] On April 29, 1935 Bonhoeffer returned to Germany and became director of the underground seminary just founded at Zingst on the Baltic coast of Pomerania and then moved in June to Finkenwalde. Back home, Bonhoeffer continued to use his contacts in the ecumenical movement, particularly his deep friendship with George Bell, to garner support for the Confessing Church's opposition to Nazism. Meanwhile, Bonhoeffer's authorization to teach at the University of Berlin was revoked in August 1936, and the Finkenwalde seminary was itself finally closed by order of the Gestapo in September 1937, after two years of illegal operation.

Having been forbidden to work in Berlin after January 1938, Bonhoeffer was among those who refused in April 1938 to take the oath of allegiance to Hitler in commemoration of Hitler's fiftieth birthday. Over the next two years Bonhoeffer continued a clandestine ministry through the so-called "collective pastorates" through which he and his former Finkenwalde students continued their work underground in Köslin, Schlawe (later moved to Sigurdshof), and Gross-Schlönwitz.

Bonhoeffer traveled to New York a second time from June 2 to July 27, 1939, at the invitation of Reinhold Niebuhr and other friends who hoped Bonhoeffer might choose to remain there. But in July 1939 Bonhoeffer chose to return to Germany to share in the fate of his country. The collective pastorates, too, were closed in 1940, and by September 1940 Bonhoeffer was prohibited from speaking in public and was required to report regularly to the authorities about his activities. That November he was assigned to the Abwehr (or Military Intelligence Office) staff in Munich, in which was working the conspirators' group – led by his brother-in-law, Hans von Dohnanyi, Admiral Wilhelm Canaris, Major General Hans Oster, and Col. General Ludwig Beck – planning to assassinate Hitler.

Stationed in Munich, Bonhoeffer lived from November 1940 to February 1941 at the Benedictine Abbey in Ettal, near Munich. Through this position and his contacts in the ecumenical movement, Bonhoeffer continued to be able to travel during 1941 and 1942, making contacts for the resistance movement in Switzerland, Norway, Sweden, and Italy. Bonhoeffer took part that October in "Operation 7," an Abwehr-based enterprise which successfully smuggled 14 Jews into Switzerland.

On April 5, 1943, less than three months after his engagement to Maria von Wedemeyer, Bonhoeffer was arrested because of the increasing suspicions about the nature of his travels outside Germany and about his participation in the Operation 7 rescue of Jews. He was sent to the military interrogation prison in Berlin, first to the third floor, then to a 6′ × 9′ cell (no. 92) on the first floor, with a plank bed, shelf, stool, and bucket, where he was to remain for 18 months. It was from Tegel Prison that Bonhoeffer wrote the letters to his fiancé, family, and his friend, Eberhard Bethge, collected in the *Letters and Papers from Prison*.

The failed attempt on Hitler's life on July 20, 1944, by Count Klaus von Stauffenberg, and the discovery of incriminating Abwehr files concerning the Bonhoeffer family, led to deepening suspicion that Bonhoeffer himself was more broadly involved in the work of the resistance movement. In October 1944 his brother Klaus, and Rüdiger Schleicher, were arrested by the Gestapo. On October 8, 1944 Bonhoeffer was moved to the Gestapo prison at Prinz-Albrecht-Strasse in Berlin, and the letters to Bethge, which had lasted barely a year, came to an end. From February 7 to April 3, 1945 Bonhoeffer was moved to Buchenwald, then in April to Regensburg, then to Schönberg, and finally to Flossenbürg concentration camp. There, along with other members of the resistance movement, he was hanged on April 9, 1945, by order of Himmler. That same day at Sachsenhausen, Hans von Dohnanyi was executed. In the night of April 22–23, 1945 Dietrich's brother Klaus and his brother-in-law Rüdiger Schleicher were shot by the SS, the day the Red Army reached Berlin. A week later, on April 30, Hitler committed suicide. On May 7, 1945 the war in Europe ended.

Major Writings

Of Bonhoeffer's major writings, the two dissertations – *Sanctorum Communio* and *Act and Being* – plus *Creation and Fall, Christ the Center*,[15] *Life Together*, and *Discipleship* were published during his lifetime. *Creation and Fall* and *Christ the Center*[16] originated as lectures at the University of Berlin; *Life Together* and *Discipleship* were based on Bonhoeffer's experiences at Finkenwalde and his presentations to his students there. At the time of Bonhoeffer's arrest in April 1943, *Ethics*[17] was left in manuscript form, with parts still in preliminary drafts, which were published only after the war. The *Letters and Papers*[18] themselves survived only due to the help of friendly prison guards, the diligence of Eberhard Bethge and his family, and not a small bit of luck.[19]

Sanctorum Communio

Bonhoeffer's practical pastoral concerns and his philosophical–theological explorations and interests were but the warp and woof of a conceptual fabric to be woven over his lifetime. *Sanctorum Communio*, written under the direction of Reinhold Seeberg when Bonhoeffer was twenty-one, provides one bookend to his literary legacy. In his first dissertation, Bonhoeffer treats not just the social philosophy of Plato, Aristotle, Thomas Hobbes, Hegel, and Max Schuller, but also the social–theoretical writings of Max Weber, Emil Durkheim, Theodor Litt, Georg Simmel, Alfred Vierkandt, and Ferdinand Tönnies. His dialogical–personalist approach has affinities to Martin Buber's *Ich und Du* (1920) and to others who had discussed the relationship between the "I" and the "Other" or "Thou" during the 1920s – Hans Ehrenberg, Ferdinand Ebner, and Franz Rosenzweig. The "other" was in the air, and Bonhoeffer breathed it deeply, writing about the nature of community – the ways in which the sociality, or interrelatedness, of persons is at the heart of the very way we understand God, ourselves, and one another. "It is in relation to persons and community that the concept of God is formed," Bonhoeffer writes, and he wishes to explore "the social intention of all the basic Christian concepts."[20]

I and You – the very relationships that are the basis of human community – are for Bonhoeffer always to be understood as providing an ethical boundary for one another, not merely a conceptual challenge. The other person is indeed to be encountered as a limit beyond which responsible behavior cannot transgress. The result is that sin is understood to be not so much a basic as a derived theological category, the breaking of the very relationships with God and one another that constitute who we are. Sin is the violation of a limit, the transgression of a boundary, the denial of the freedom of the "other" person to "be" who they are so that we might enter into relationship with them, the desire to make the "other" into just an image of myself.

The quintessence of our sociality is what Bonhoeffer termed *Stellvertretung*, or "vicarious representative action" – the willingness not merely to allow the other to exist, but the choice to bear the claim of the other person on me, to take them on as an obligation, to allow the other to place upon me the burden of their freedom to be who they are. Such "taking on of the burden of the other" was for Bonhoeffer at the center of Christ's messianic vocation.[21] Yet Bonhoeffer did not see such radical existing-for-the-sake-of-the-other as restricted to the figure of Christ. It is, rather, to be seen in every human act in which selfish egoism is overcome and in which "readiness to do and bear everything in the neighbor's place, indeed, if necessary, to sacrifice myself, standing as a substitute for my neighbor" claims the center of my moral attention. Bonhoeffer begins here a lifelong preoccupation with his conviction that the church "is" its sociality – that community which, as he will later put the matter from prison, radically "exists for others." The church "is" "Christ existing as such community."

Act and Being

Act and Being, Bonhoeffer's second dissertation, turned to the Christian theological category of revelation in order to articulate the very sense of boundary and "Otherness" which he thought that idealist philosophy had posed, but had been unable adequately to answer. Drawing upon resources as diverse as Luther's commentary on Galatians and Heidegger's *Being and Time*, Bonhoeffer engaged in a critique of the moral process of knowledge itself, which idealism had construed as a matter of the subject's power and control over the possibility of any authentic otherness of its object. Building upon Luther's "insights about the origin of human sinfulness in the *cor curvum in se* – the heart turned in upon itself and thus open neither to the revelation of God, nor to the encounter with the neighbor"[22] – *Act and Being* mounts a sustained critique of all totalizing thinking and action. Sin itself is to be understood, after all, as the violent imposition of one's own totalizing desire to define the being of the other, deciding even whether or not the other has the right to exist at all.[23]

Creation and Fall

Bonhoeffer's winter semester 1932–3 lectures "Schöpfung und Sünde," "Creation and sin," were published as his third book, *Schöpfung und Fall, Creation and Fall*.[24] This is not exegesis, but theological interpretation. In *Creation and Fall* Bonhoeffer succinctly and coherently relates the interdependency among the recurring constellation of themes: community, creation, Christology, and the costliness of discipleship. The *imago dei*, the image of God, and "the likeness, the analogy of the human to God" is best understood, Bonhoeffer writes, not by comparing ourselves to God's *being* (*analogia entis*) but by analogy between our relationship with God (and one another) and God's own inter-trinitarian relationship as Father, Son, and Holy Spirit – an analogy of *relationship* (*analogia relationis*). "The creatureliness of humans . . . is to be defined . . . as absolutely nothing other than the relations of human beings with one another."[25] Indeed, "the fall" is for Bonhoeffer the Promethean attempt to play God, to exist *sicut deus*, to become limitless, all-powerful, one whose very existence comes to be defined by the violent transgression of the limit of the Other. The Cain and Abel story, Bonhoeffer realizes, is really the conclusion of the creation–fall narrative in Genesis, for at this point one of the first two human siblings renounces his own creatureliness by playing God and taking the life of his brother.

Christology

Following the "Creation and Sin" lectures, Bonhoeffer turned his attention in the summer of 1933 to a course on "Christology."[26] In *Christ the Center* Bonhoeffer refuses to engage in a speculative conjecture about "how" or "why" God chooses to become human. Rather, what is crucial for Bonhoeffer is the question "who" the church claims Christ to be. And, for Bonhoeffer, the answer is plain: Jesus is the person *par excellence*, the sought-for limit to human pretensions, the center of human existence, history, and nature. "Jesus Christ is the unveiled image of God." Jesus's messianic act is not merely to come into the midst of the world, thereby showing creation to be God's proper place to be. The messianic event consists in the fact that Jesus brings into our midst God-who-is-our-boundary, the creative limit that allows humanity to be authentically human, rather than a demonic usurper of divine power. God lets violence be done to God's very self, so that an authentic limit or boundary – the absolute futility of human power and domination – might be encountered in all its concreteness. Therefore, Bonhoeffer concludes: "If Jesus Christ is to be described as God, we may not speak of this divine being, nor of his omnipotence, nor his omniscience; but we must speak of this weak man among sinners, of his manger and his cross. If we are to deal with the deity of Jesus, we must speak of his weakness."[27] As he would later put it in one of the prison letters: "Only the suffering God can help."

Discipleship

Originally published in November 1937, just after the closing of Finkenwalde, *Discipleship* developed a theology of Christian vocation in dialogue with Jesus's Sermon on the Mount from the Gospel of Matthew. The tone is eschatological, the urgency palpable. The church, Bonhoeffer charges, has become the purveyor of "cheap grace" – "grace without discipleship, grace without the cross, grace without Jesus Christ, living and incarnate" – and remains unwilling to pay the "cost" of the loss of its power, its privilege, its domination of one another. In its support of warfare, and in its refusal to protest the vengeful urge towards genocide, the church has forgotten that "the brother's life is a boundary which we dare not pass."[28]

The church has forgotten the "costliness" of God's bearing our flesh, bearing the burden of our sinfulness. And so we have forgotten how to live with one another. We have forgotten that "as Christ bears our burdens, so ought we to bear the burdens of other human beings . . . not only the Other's outward lot . . . but quite literally the Other's sin. And the only way to bear that sin is by forgiving it in the power of the cross of Christ in which I now share . . . Forgiveness is the Christlike suffering which it is the Christian's duty to bear."[29]

In *Discipleship* Bonhoeffer made a most remarkable case for claiming that the thing that makes Christians *distinct*, indeed what is *extraordinary* about being a Christian at all, is Christ's costly command to love our enemies. Loving one's enemies is what distinguishes *not* just the most saintly of the followers of Christ, but *any* Christian precisely *as* a Christian at all. Without it, for Bonhoeffer, we are no different from the unbelievers, who also love their family and friends, while for Jesus, "love is defined in uncompromising terms, as the love of our enemies."[30]

During the 1930s this theme of the love of one's enemies became more and more prominent in Bonhoeffer's writings. He leaves no room for ambiguity: "Christian love draws no distinction between one enemy and another, except that the more bitter our enemy's hatred, the greater our enemy's need of love . . . No sacrifice which a lover would make for their beloved is too great for us to make for our enemy."[31] Bonhoeffer concluded in moving, and measured words: "Giving up our desire to take revenge," he told his listeners, is "a hard sacrifice, perhaps the hardest, which Christ requires of us."[32] Take heed of the fact, he concluded, that "The first person born on this earth to humankind murdered his brother . . . 'Never be conceited' – lest you become murderers of your brothers."[33]

Life Together

In March 1935 Bonhoeffer had spent a week at the Anglican Community of the Resurrection in Mirfield, a monastic community for whom the gospel speaks "of a Christ who took on flesh, became human, lived with the poor, the outcast and died the death of a criminal." Mirfield's own history thus describes its founders: "So they came to grimy, smoky, industrial Yorkshire to live the monastic life."[34] This was one model Bonhoeffer drew upon when he arrived at Finkenwalde a few months later, particularly for the "community of brothers" that he formed there as he undertook a decidedly un-Lutheran experiment in "monastic" community.

Life Together recollects the daily life at Finkenwalde and the theology of community undergirding it.[35] This is no monastic retreat from the world, nor does it imply a turn away from the costliness of grace demanded by *The Cost of Discipleship*. Rather, here Bonhoeffer had the chance to live out in intentional community his theology of sociality, putting into practice, like the community at Mirfield, a "worldly" and engaged spirituality, belief hand-in-glove with obedience.

"To learn not merely to tolerate, but to delight in, the freedom of the other," Bonhoeffer wrote in *Life Together*,

> is not the maximal requirement for the Christian. It is a minimal description of our utter faith in God's ways . . . It means the recognition, indeed our delight, that God did not make others as I would have made them. God did not give them to me so that I could dominate and control them, but so that I might find the Creator by means of them . . . God does not want me to mold others into the image that seems good to me, that is, into my own image. Instead, in their freedom from me God made other people in God's own image.[36]

And it is the supreme expression of God's love for us that

> when God's son took on flesh, he truly and bodily, out of pure grace, took on our being, our nature, ourselves . . . Now we are in him. Wherever he is, he bears our flesh, he bears us. And, where he is, there we are too – in the incarnation, on the cross, and in his resurrection. We belong to him because we are in him. That is why the scriptures call us the body of Christ.[37]

Ethics

When Bonhoeffer was arrested and imprisoned in the spring of 1943, he was still writing drafts of his *Ethics*. What might have been his magnum opus as a result remains a series of 13 manuscripts that Bonhoeffer himself had not yet arranged in any final form before his death. Themes joust with one another for prominence. A few, however, stand out, both for their distinctiveness and for their extension and development of conversations already begun.

One is the process of "formation" of Christians in community, that is to say, the conformation of Christians with Christ – incarnate, crucified, and risen. God's claim on creation is not partial – there is not one sphere of reality that belongs to God and another that does not. Rather, Christ was God's embrace of the entirety of created-and-fallen reality, reconciling the world to God despite anything that humanity may try to do to choose otherwise. We were created in and for relationship – with God and one another.[38] Formation means to be molded into what we were made to be.

The church is to be the *Stellvertreter* for the world – taking on the guilt not just for its individual sins, but for those of a broken world, bearing them as its own. The church has failed to be the church whenever it has denied compassion to the outcast. In Bonhoeffer's words, "the church was mute when it should have cried out, because the blood of the innocent cried out to heaven." The church has sinned against God each time it "has looked on while injustice and violence have been done, under the cover of the name of Christ." In its vocation of confessing and bearing the sins of the world, we hear not a statement of the heroic and saintly maximum that is required only in the extraordinary situation; it is a statement of the bare minimum of what is required in order to make one a Christian at all.

Previous themes from throughout his theological career reappear, now to be connected in new constellations of significance, each transformed into a more mature theological statement. "Christ existing as church community" becomes the church understood as that "section of humanity in which Christ has really taken form." The theme of creation, about which Bonhoeffer had maintained a "qualified silence" for almost a decade, due to the cooptation by "German Christians" of the language of "orders of creation" in order to give credence to its racist points of view, now reemerges under the heading of "Das natürliche Leben," "natural life." The "divine mandates" are heir to Bonhoeffer's concept of the "orders of preservation." And the concept of *Stellvertretung*, vicarious representative action, reappears as the heart of "the structure of responsible life."

Letters and Papers from Prison

The decade leading up to his imprisonment, Bonhoeffer wrote to his friends and co-conspirators at Christmas 1942, had been a time when "evil appear[ed] in the form of light, beneficence, loyalty and renewal" of blood and soil, nationalism and strength. "Every available alternative seemed equally intolerable, repugnant, and futile."[39] This essay, "After Ten Years," still stands as the gateway to the *Letters and Papers from Prison*, rooted firmly in the recent past and present for Bonhoeffer. Some of his words sear us: "There is hardly one of us who has not known what it is to be betrayed." Others haunt us now because of our recognition of the personal agonies they so thinly masked: "Civil courage . . . depends on a God who demands responsible action in a bold venture of faith, and who promises forgiveness and consolation to the [person] who becomes a sinner in that venture."[40] Having seen for once in his life "the great events of world history from below, from the perspective of the outcast, the suspects, the maltreated, the powerless, the oppressed, the reviled – in short, from the perspective of those who suffer," Bonhoeffer asks, "are we still of any use?"

The texture of the letters is visible only to the peripheral vision of our minds; awareness of it demands that we notice what is said between the lines, as it were. As Christian Gremmels, the editor of the new *Dietrich Bonhoeffer Werke* redaction of the letters, has pointed out, Bonhoeffer "takes his temporal orientation from the church year, as shown by the Latin designations for Sunday accompanying the dates on his letters. And as shown by the musical notation Bonhoeffer wrote down from memory, the world of music is also present at Tegel, linked to the church year by the music of Advent, Christmas, and Easter, and by the compositions of Heinrich Schütz, and yet also far transcending the sacral sphere."[41] Also included are poignant pieces such as his "Thoughts on the Day of the Baptism of Dietrich Wilhelm Rüdiger Bethge" from May 1944, which remind us how anchored in family and friends Bonhoeffer remained throughout his imprisonment, as well as the letters he wrote both in his own defense and to cover up the participation in conspiracy by others, and then the letters he wrote anxiously awaiting a trial date.

During this time Bonhoeffer was also writing a drama and a novel, sizeable fragments of which are published as *Fiction from Tegel Prison*.[42] These thinly veiled biographical fictions give us insight into the Bonhoeffer family and its friends, their world and outlook, or as Bonhoeffer put it in a contemporary letter to Bethge, "middle-class life as we know it in our own families, and especially in the light of Christianity."[43]

And there is the enigmatic "Outline for a Book," leading toward a church understood as a servant community which "must share in the secular problems of ordinary human life, not dominating, but helping and serving . . . [and telling persons] of every calling what it means to live in Christ, to exist for others."[44] There are also a number of pieces of poetry in the *Letters and Papers from Prison*, such as "Who Am I?" and "Night Voices in Tegel," reflecting on prison life. Others, such as "Christians and Pagans," "Jonah," and "Powers of Good," are overtly theological, extensions of the reflections in the later letters themselves. Still others, such as "Stations on the Road to Freedom," convey the development of Bonhoeffer's theological interpretation of his own plight. And "The Friend" is a deeply personal meditation on his relationship with Bethge.

The attention, indeed the notoriety, that the letters have commanded, however, comes not from any of this, but rather from a brief series of letters to Eberhard Bethge which begin rather suddenly on April 30, 1944 – the so-called "theological letters." For a generation of students of Bonhoeffer in the 1960s and 1970s, these seemed to stand traditional theology on its ear. Indeed, when his contemporaries read the post-April 30th letters many were shocked, with some like Karl Barth warning against them, saying, in Bethge's words, that "the lonely prisoner might possibly have 'peeped around some corner' and seen something that was true, but that it was too 'enigmatic' and that it was better to stick to the early Bonhoeffer"![45] Yet even Bonhoeffer seemed aware that there was something about these letters worth revisiting, although his own response was somewhat droll: "By the way," he wrote Bethge, "it would be very nice if you didn't throw away my theological letters . . . Perhaps I might want to read them again later for my work"![46]

When we do read them again now for our own work in theology and spirituality, we must hear in the striking language especially of the "theological letters" not only the polyphony of all the Bonhoefferian themes that came before, but the fragmentariness of the "not yet" that is open to a future yet unrealized. This was, after all, the way that Bonhoeffer's *Act and Being* concluded at the start of his career, when he wrote:

> This is the new creation of the new human being of the future, . . . of those who no longer look back upon themselves, but only away from themselves . . . to Christ. This is the new creation of those born from out of the world's confines into the wideness of heaven, becoming what they were or never were, a creature of God, a child.[47]

In his "Nachwort" to the new German edition of *Widerstand und Ergebung*, Christian Gremmels had argued persuasively that "Bonhoeffer's theme is *not* really the 'coming of age,' 'this-worldliness,' and 'religionlessness' of the modern world," which had been the catchwords of the interpretation of Bonhoeffer as a "radical" or "secular" theologian in the 1960s. "As plausible and impressive as these expressions are, theologically they function only as auxiliary concepts facilitating the task of witnessing the presence of Jesus Christ in the present: 'What is bothering me incessantly is the question what Christianity really is, or indeed who Christ [653] really is, for us today.'" Bonhoeffer addresses "this-worldliness," "worldliness," and "autonomy" thematically precisely because the real theme is "the claim of a world that has come of age by Jesus Christ."[48]

What is "radical" about Bonhoeffer are the radical implications he sees in the peculiar Christian confluence of Christology, creation, community, and costly discipleship. The "church existing for others," sharing in the "secular problems of ordinary life," being "Christ for others," is a church which is now "certain that our joy is hidden in suffering, and our life in death; it is certain that in all this we are in a fellowship that sustains us," that "in Jesus God has said Yes and Amen to it all." This is what it means to rediscover redemption in the center of life, not beyond it. This is what it means to have faith – to trust that "pain and joy are also part of life's polyphony."[49] This is what Bonhoeffer meant when he wrote:

> It is only by living completely in this world that one learns to have faith . . . By this-worldliness I mean living unreservedly in life's duties, problems, successes and failures, experiences and perplexities. In so doing we throw ourselves completely into the arms of God, taking seriously, not our own sufferings, but those of God in the world . . . That, I think, is faith; that is *metanoia*; and that is how one becomes a human being and a Christian.[50]

Debate and Agenda

In Bonhoeffer's theology we don't see the development of a methodically consistent system, but the emerging coherence of a constellation of issues and themes that dominated his writing almost from the beginning: community, creation, Christology, and the costliness of discipleship. We *are* our relationships, Bonhoeffer was convinced, for we were *created* for community, brought into being reflecting the image of a God who is the relationship of Father, Son, and Holy Spirit. In Christ, whom Paul called "the second Adam," we see both what *God* is like and who *we* are as well, and the God-human reveals that it is God's nature as well as our own to be *free for* encounter with an authentic "other," desiring out of love to be loved in return, freely and without coercion or constraint. Any and everything that counters this is sin; to be redeemed is to be fully reconciled with God and one another.

Bonhoeffer is a thinker who defies easy categorization. He is not just unsystematic in his approach to theology, but opposes all theological system on principle. Thus, it is not enough to decide whether his writings demonstrate a continuity or discontinuity of thought; more importantly we need to discover more clearly how to frame him as a religious thinker and writer at all. Thus, it remains far more difficult to summarize his thought than to offer an invitation into conversation with the themes and perspectives that defined him.

Because of his own use of metaphors of the incompleteness and fragmentariness of life, it has been all too easy to think that his own lack of systematization reflects chiefly the lack of opportunity for it – that finitude and fate merely got in the way. There is much to suggest, however, that Bonhoeffer's writing can best be encountered as the "spirituality" of the "pastor" as much as the "theology" of the "professor." That is to say, he is as concerned to articulate a "pastoral" theology of vocation as to state any systematic "answers" to the mysteries of faith. He is best understood as himself a perpetual pilgrim – for whom being a Christian was a *task* rather than an *accomplishment* – who as a theologian longed to provide that grammar of faith capable of putting into play all the grand voices of the theological greats before him – and more importantly, capable of giving voice to the transformative capacity of the gospel to remake life anew.

As Douglas John Hall has noted:

> Comparing and contrasting Bonhoeffer's sojourn with that of Paul Tillich, Bethge notes that while Tillich came from the church and discovered the world, Bonhoeffer came from the world and discovered the church; and "having discovered the Church, Bonhoeffer took her more seriously than she was accustomed to being taken and never ceased to appeal for more appropriate forms of life and witness to replace perverted ones."[51]

The result is a disconcerting *naïveté* to much of Bonhoeffer's use of the vocabulary of the traditional theological loci, coming not from a thoughtless familiarity from overuse, but from his uncovering the radical possibilities of language that might not yet have had its day.

Bonhoeffer frustrates us, too, because so often in theological debate he refuses to choose sides, to view theology as an either/or enterprise, but rather finds in conversation, in dialogue – in the mystery of the encounter with what comes to us as authentically "other" – a both/and approach that can infuriate as well as inspire. During the Finkenwalde experiment, to name just one episode in his theological development, Bonhoeffer did not ask his students or readers to choose between emphasizing the goodness of creation-in-the-image-of-God or the depth of human sinfulness – or between incarnation or redemption, the manger or the cross – or between justification and sanctification[52] (and formation) – or between person and community – or between belief and active obedience – or between a recognition of Christ's unique messianic vocation as reconciler of the world and our own participation in Christ's ministry of *Stellvertretung* as we confess, and take on guilt for, the sins of the world.

Bonhoeffer's thought is perhaps most fertile when it is allowed to act as a catalyst for the theological work of others. The greatest care needs to be taken not to domesticate – and render inert – the "radicality" of his vision that first enthralled his readers. Of course, this is, too, the source of the "creative misuses" of Bonhoeffer against which Harvey Cox railed four decades ago, for such interpretations may serve as a Trojan horse by means of which to sneak in the self-serving ideologies of others. Yet it is clear that Bonhoeffer himself, for example, realized that something "new" and distinctive was happening in the "theological letters" from prison beginning April 30, 1944. For this reason, there may always be a dialectic between the historical–biographical dimension of Bonhoeffer studies and the "creative misuses" of his theology that allow it to escape the clutches of "mere history" and come to life again as constructive thought. The one impulse is as necessary as the other, with the "misuses" providing the spark of interest that leads to closer reexaminations of his thought and rediscoveries of the peculiar historical circumstances of its genesis. The surprise in reading Bonhoeffer almost always comes in the fact that his "radicality" turns out to be different than we had anticipated.

Of course, Bonhoeffer also had his blind spots that we have an obligation to see through and move beyond. Perhaps the most significant is the fact that "Much of his theological work reflected traditional Christian attitudes toward Judaism. Like most Christians of his generation, Bonhoeffer believed that God's special destiny for the Jewish people included their eventual acceptance of Jesus as the Messiah."[53] Awareness of this anti-Jewish (but not anti-Semitic) thematic not only has contributed to discomfort in the Jewish community about what to make, finally, of Bonhoeffer (witness the protracted debate at Yad Vashem about whether or not to honor Bonhoeffer as a "Righteous Gentile"), but has also kept post-Auschwitz Christians alert to the need to resist martyr hagiography with Bonhoeffer, and instead engage in a more nuanced and self-critical reading of not just his theology but his biography as well.[54]

What then to make of Bonhoeffer seventy years now after the rise of Nazism and the beginnings of the Church Struggle which came to define him? If "modernity" is but what Wolfgang Huber described as "a limited epoch in history, now behind us,"[55] then to speak of Bonhoeffer as a "modern theologian" is already to have framed everything else that can be said of him. He is then principally a figure slipping slowly, but inexorably, into the past; and soon his biography alone will define his significance for us. If, on the other hand, "modernity" speaks of a broader impulse of freedom and responsibility, critique and revisioning, then Bonhoeffer may have a future at least as bright as his past. And if, as the *Ethics* and *Letters and Papers from Prison* both suggest, "modernity" was something that Bonhoeffer himself was already looking beyond – if his can justifiably be understood as a proto-postmodern perspective – then we must be careful not to condemn him to the dustbin of a past that was never able completely to define him even when he was alive.[56]

Bonhoeffer's theology and spirituality brought into our very definitions of "modernity" something new, inspiring, and disturbing at the same time. Perhaps its radicality in the end is that he discomfits not only those who come after him, but the whole order of what we understood "theology" and "spirituality" to be before him, as well. T.S. Eliot put it this way in *The Sacred Wood*:

> What happens when a new work of art is created is something that happens simultaneously to all the works of art which preceded it. The existing monuments form an ideal order among themselves, which is modified by the introduction of the new (the really new) work of art among them. The existing order is complete before the new work arrives; for order to persist after the supervention of novelty, the *whole* existing order must be, if ever so slightly, altered; and so the relations, proportions, values of each work of art toward the whole are readjusted; and this is conformity between the old and the new.

Among the "modern" theologians, Bonhoeffer's radicality is that he not only opened a different future for the lived theologies of Christianity, but that he reopened for us the past, as well, making us adjust ever so slightly our perspective on all that has come before us, opening us to more faithful encounter with the themes of community, creation, Christology, and costliness – as part of the living grammar of faith.

Notes

1   See John A. T. Robinson's electric 1963 book, *Honest to God*. Surprisingly, he still is allowed to be so construed by the publisher of the English edition of his works – see *Fortress Introduction to Contemporary Theologies* (1998).

2   The first work to do so at length was Georg Huntemann's *The Other Bonhoeffer: An Evangelical Reassessment of Dietrich Bonhoeffer* (1993).

3   *Dietrich Bonhoeffer Werke*, 16 volumes; henceforth, "DBW."

4   *Dietrich Bonhoeffer Works*, henceforth, "DBWE."

5   See Eberhard Bethge, *Dietrich Bonhoeffer: Man of Vision, Man of Courage*, trans. Eric Mosbacher, Peter and Betty Ross, Frank Clarke, and William Glen-Doepel (New York: Harper & Row, 1967). A wholly revised and newly edited translation was published by Fortress Press in 2000, revised and edited by Victoria J. Barnett. See also Leibholz-Bonhoeffer, *The Bonhoeffers: Portrait of a Faimily*.

6   Eberhard Bethge, Renate Bethge, and Christian Gremmels, eds., *Dietrich Bonhoeffer: A Life in Pictures* (Philadelphia, PA: Fortress Press, 1986), p. 12.

7   DBWE 9: 107, 83, 88, 89.

8   DBW 10: 472–3. Translation from *A Testament to Freedom*, revd. edn., p. 8, ed. Geffrey B. Kelly and F. Burton Nelson (San Francisco: Harper San Francisco, 1995).

9   DBW 10: 220.

10 *Letters and Papers from Prison*, p. 275; henceforth, "LPP."

11 Bell has been called "the finest Archbishop of Canterbury that never was"; some feel that it was his close friendships and alliances with members of the German resistance, such as Dietrich Bonhoeffer, as well as Bell's protests against indiscriminate Allied bombing of German civilians, that cost him his rightful accession as ecclesiastical leader of the Anglican Communion.

12 DBW 13: 304.

13 Letter of April 7, 1934 to Henry L. Henriod; quoted in Bethge, Bethge, and Gremmels, *Dietrich Bonhoeffer: A Life in Pictures*, p. 116.

14 Ibid, p. 33.

15 Published as *Christology* in the UK and *Christ the Center* in the USA.

16 Published in 1933.

17 Written between 1940 and 1943.

18 Written between 1943 and 1944.

19 Bethge, "How the Prison Letters Survived." In Eberhard Bethge, *Friendship and Resistance: Essays on Dietrich Bonhoeffer* (Geneva: WCC Publications; Grand Rapids, MI: William B. Eerdmans, 1995).

20 *Sanctorum Communio* 22, 21; henceforth, "SC."

21 DBW 1: 75, 91ff., 99ff., 121ff., 125, 166, 260, 262. Many readers encounter *Stellvertretung* first in his *Ethik* (DBW 6: 234, 256–8, 289, 392–3, 408) and assume this to be an expression of his late, rather than his early, theology.

22 DBWE 2: 7; also see Wayne Whitson Floyd, *Theology and the Dialectics of Otherness: On Reading Bonhoeffer and Adorno* (Lanham, MD: University Press of America, 1988).

23 See Wayne Whitson Floyd, "Transcendence in the Light of Redemption: Adorno and the Legacy of Rosenzweig and Benjamin."

24 DBWE 3: *Creation and Fall*, ed. John de Gruchy, trans. Douglas Bax (Minneapolis, MN: Fortress Press, 1997).

25 Ibid, 114.

26 The Christology lectures survived only as a reconstruction of student notes; an entirely new reconstruction, based on a single set of student notes, is found in DBW 12: 279–348.

27 Ibid, 104.

28 *The Cost of Discipleship* (New York: Macmillan, 1963), p. 47, trans. altered.

29 Ibid, 100, trans. altered.

30 DBWE 4: 162.

31 Geffrey B. Kelly and F. Burton Nelson (eds.), *A Testament to Freedom: The Essential Writings of Dietrich Bonhoeffer* (San Francisco, 1995), 164, 165.

32 Ibid, 287.

33 Ibid, 285.

34 From the website of the Community of the Resurrection, Mirfield.

35 Also from Finkenwalde come Bonhoeffer's homiletics lectures, "Vorlesung über Homiletik" (DBW 14: 478–527); examples of sermons, meditations, and Bible studies (DBW 14: 849–988); catechetical lectures, "Vorlesung über Katechetik"

(DBW 14: 530–54); and the lectures on pastoral care, "Vorlesung über Seelsorge" (DBW 14: 554–91).

36 *Life Together*, 95.

37 Ibid, 33; emphasis added.

38 DBWE 6: 92ff.

39 LPP 3.

40 LPP 6, 11–12.

41 DBW 8: 639.

42 DBWE 7.

43 LPP 129–30.

44 LPP 282–3.

45 Bethge, *Dietrich Bonhoeffer*, p. 889.

46 July 8, 1943; LPP 347.

47 DBWE 2: 161.

48 Christian Gremmels, "Nachwort der Herausgeber," DBW 8: 652–3; quoting LPP.

49 LPP 382ff., 381ff., 391, 336ff., 305.

50 LPP 370, trans. altered.

51 Douglas John Hall, in Floyd and Marsh, *Theology and the Practice of Responsibility*, p. 65.

52 Cf. Eastern Orthodox *theosis*.

53 Victoria Barnett, online exhibit on the website of the United States Holocaust Memorial Museum.

54 On the question of Bonhoeffer and the Jews, see Bethge's "Dietrich Bonhoeffer and the Jews," in John Godsey and Geffrey B. Kelly, eds., *Ethical Responsibility: Bonhoeffer's Legacy to the Churches* (New York: Edwin Mellen Press, 1981), pp. 43–96; also see the University of Heidelberg dissertation by Christine-Ruth Müller, *Dietrich Bonhoeffers Kampf gegen die nationalsozialistische Verfolgung und Vernichtung der Juden*, 1986; and William Peck, "From Cain to the Death Camps: An Essay on Bonhoeffer and Judaism," *Union Seminary Quarterly Review* 28, no. 2 (winter, 1973): 158–76 (also published as "Bonhoeffer's View of Judaism," *Christian Attitudes on Jews and Judaism* 31–2 (August–October 1973).

55 Floyd and Marsh, *Theology and the Practice of Responsibility*, p. 5.

56 On Bonhoeffer the proto-deconstructionist, see Walter J. Lowe, "Bonhoeffer and Deconstruction: Toward a Theology of the Crucified Logos," in Floyd and Marsh, *Theology and the Practice of Responsibility*, pp. 207–21.

Bibliography

Primary

Act and Being: Transcendental Philosophy and Ontology in Systematic Theology. Edited by Wayne Whitson Floyd Jr. Translated by Martin Rumscheidt. Minneapolis, MN: Fortress Press, 1996.

Christ the Center. Translated by Edwin Robertson. San Francisco: Harper & Row, 1978.

Creation and Fall: A Theological Exposition of Genesis 1–3. Edited by John W. de Gruchy. Translated by Douglas Stephen Bax. Minneapolis, MN: Fortress Press, 1996.

Dietrich Bonhoeffer Werke [DBW], 17 vols. Edited by Eberhard Bethge et al. Munich and Gütersloh: Chr. Kaiser/Gütersloher Verlagshaus, 1986–99. English translation: *Dietrich Bonhoeffer Works* [DBWE], 17 vols. Wayne Whitson Floyd Jr., General Editor. Minneapolis, MN: Fortress Press, 1996–.

Discipleship. Edited by Geffrey B. Kelly and John D. Godsey. Translated by Barbara Green and Reinhard Krauss. Minneapolis, MN: Fortress Press, 2001.

Ethics. Edited by Clifford J. Green. Translated by Reinhard Krauss, Charles C. West, and Douglas W. Stott. Minneapolis, MN: Fortress Press, 2005.

Fiction from Tegel Prison. Edited by Clifford J. Green. Translated by Nancy Lukens. Minneapolis, MN: Fortress Press, 2000.

Letters and Papers from Prison [LPP]. Edited by Eberhard Bethge. New York: Simon & Schuster, 1997.

Life Together and *Prayerbook of the Bible.* Edited by Geffrey B. Kelly. Translated by Daniel W. Bloesch and James H. Burtness. Minneapolis, MN: Fortress Press, 1996.

Sanctorum Communio: A Theological Study of the Sociology of the Church [SC]. Edited by Clifford J. Green. Translated by Reinhard Krauss and Nancy Lukens. Minneapolis, MN: Fortress Press, 1998.

Bonhoeffer, Dietrich, and Maria von Wedemeyer. *Love Letters from Cell 92: The Correspondence between Dietrich Bonhoeffer and Maria von Wedemeyer, 1943–1945.* Translated by John Brownjohn. Nashville, TN: Abingdon Press, 1995.

Secondary

Bethge, Eberhard. *Dietrich Bonhoeffer: A Biography.* Revised and edited by Victoria J. Barnett. Minneapolis, MN: Fortress Press, 2000.

De Gruchy, John W., ed. *Bonhoeffer for a New Day: Theology in a Time of Transition.* Grand Rapids, MI: William B. Eerdmans, 1997.

—— *The Cambridge Companion to Dietrich Bonhoeffer.* Cambridge: Cambridge University Press, 1999.

Floyd, Wayne W. *The Wisdom and Witness of Dietrich Bonhoeffer.* Minneapolis, MN: Fortress Press, 2000.

Floyd, Wayne W. and Clifford J. Green, eds. *Bonhoeffer Bibliography: Primary Sources and Secondary Literature in English.* Evanston, IL: American Theological Library Association, 1992.

Floyd, Wayne W. and Charles Marsh. *Theology and the Practice of Responsibility.* Valley Forge, PA: Trinity Press, 1994.

Hauerwas, Stanley M. *Performing the Faith: Bonhoeffer and the Practice of Nonviolence.* Grand Rapids, MI: Brazos Press, 2004.

Haynes, Stephen R. *The Bonhoeffer Phenomenon: Portraits of a Protestant Saint.* Minneapolis, MN: Fortress Press, 2004.

Kelly, Geffrey B. and Burton Nelson. *The Cost of Moral Leadership: The Spirituality of Dietrich Bonhoeffer.* Grand Rapids, MI: William B. Eerdmans, 2002.

Kelly, Geffrey B. and C. John Weborg. *Reflections on Bonhoeffer: Essays in Honor of F. Burton Nelson.* Chicago: Covenant, 1999.

Kleinhans, Theodore J. *Till the Night Be Past: The Life and Times of Dietrich Bonhoeffer.* St. Louis, MO: Concordia Publishing House, 2002.

Lange, Fritz de. *Waiting for the Word: Dietrich Bonhoeffer on Speaking about God.* Grand Rapids, MI: William B. Eerdmans, 1995.

Leibholz-Bonhoeffer, Sabine. *The Bonhoeffers: Portrait of a Family.* Chicago: Covenant, 1994.

Marsh, Charles. *Reclaiming Dietrich Bonhoeffer: The Promise of His Theology.* Oxford: Oxford University Press, 1994.

Pangritz, Andreas. *Karl Barth in the Theology of Dietrich Bonhoeffer.* Grand Rapids, MI: William B. Eerdmans, 2000.

Plant, Stephen. *Bonhoeffer*. London: Continuum, 2004.

Slane, Craig J. *Bonhoeffer as Martyr: Social Responsibility and Modern Christian Commitment*. Grand Rapids, MI: Brazos Press, 2004.

Young, Josiah Ulysses, III. *No Difference in the Fare: Dietrich Bonhoeffer and the Problem of Racism*. Grand Rapids, MI: William B. Eerdmans, 1998.

Paul Tillich

David H. Kelsey

Introduction: Life

Paul Tillich's principal goal was to make Christianity understandable and persuasive to religiously skeptical people, modern in culture and secular in sensibility. He came to be extraordinarily effective in that role; getting there involved two wrenching turns in his life.

The first was World War I. When he entered the German Army in 1914 as a chaplain, Tillich's life had been fairly sheltered and his views, except in theology, were conventionally conservative. Born in 1886, he was raised in a conservative Lutheran pastor's home. He studied at the universities of Berlin, Tübingen, and Halle. In 1910 he received a PhD from the University of Breslau for a thesis on the nineteenth-century philosopher Frederick Schelling, whose thought was to remain deeply influential on Tillich. He was then ordained and served a few years as an assistant pastor. However, four years spent sharing the carnage and suffering of war with working-class men utterly transformed him. As his biographers, Wilhelm and Marion Pauck put it, by the time he left the army in 1918, "the traditional monarchist had become a religious socialist, the Christian believer a cultural pessimist, and the repressed puritanical boy a 'wild man.' These years represented *the* turning point of Paul Tillich's life."[1]

That experience gave focus to his vocation. The title of his first public lecture in Berlin following the war named the topic that was to remain central to his theology for the rest of his life: "On the Idea of a Theology of Culture." The Berlin to which he returned in 1919 to begin his academic career was a major center for radical politics and avant-garde art. His fairly chaotic personal life while teaching theology at the University of Berlin was deeply involved in a bohemian world of artists and political agitators. Thereafter, with the exception of three apparently unhappy terms at the University of Marburg (1924–5), Tillich's appointments were not to theological faculties but to "religious studies" (at the Dresden Institute of Technology, 1925–9) or in philosophy (at the University of Frankfurt, 1929–33). In both cases he rejoiced at being "on the boundary," at the point of intersection between a religious tradition and major movements in secular culture. In his years at Frankfurt

Tillich became nationally known in German academic circles. There, at the height of his powers, a second wrenching turn was forced on to his life.

In 1933 the Nazi authorities suspended Tillich from his academic position at Frankfurt because his book *The Socialist Decision* attacked Nazi ideology. When it became clear that Tillich had to flee Germany, American friends arranged an appointment to the faculty of Union Theological Seminary in New York City. In the fall of 1933, at the age of 47, Tillich began a second academic career in a culture and language with which he was entirely unfamiliar.

For the next 15 years Tillich taught at Union in relative obscurity, which was not much dispelled by the publication in 1936 of autobiographical reflections, *On the Boundary*. He was widely respected within small circles of academic theologians, but few of his writings were available in English. He came to write effectively in English, but he spoke in so heavy an accent that he was difficult to understand. Then, in 1948, a small volume of sermons he had preached in the seminary chapel was published as *The Shaking of the Foundations* and, against all expectations, it became a bestseller. Three years later the first volume of his *Systematic Theology* was published. It immediately became the subject of vigorous discussion in both academic and church circles. The press gave him considerable coverage, and suddenly this relentlessly complex Germanic thinker became something of an intellectual superstar in America. Tillich retired from Union in 1955, accepting the post of University Professor at Harvard University. There he published the second volume of the *Systematic Theology* in 1957. In 1962 he accepted a second post-retirement appointment at the University of Chicago, where the third volume of the *Systematic Theology* was published in 1963. Tillich died in 1965, perhaps the most widely known theologian in American history. In the years since his death there has been a vigorous rediscovery of Tillich in German theological circles.

Survey: Work, Approach, and Themes

Of more than 500 works in Tillich's bibliography, the writings available in English fall into four rough groups: (1) the three volumes of his *Systematic Theology*; (2) writings outside the system dealing with individual topics that are also discussed within the system, notably *Biblical Religion and the Search for Ultimate Reality*; *Love, Power and Justice*; *The Protestant Era*; and *Theology of Culture*; (3) three volumes of sermons, *The Shaking of the Foundations*; *The New Being*; *The Eternal Now*; and (4) essays in the philosophy of religion, notably *The Courage to Be*. In our discussion of Tillich's theology we shall focus on the *Systematic Theology*. All of these writings may be viewed as variations on the same theological strategy: to *mediate* between contemporary culture and historical Christianity, to show that faith need not be unacceptable to contemporary culture and that contemporary culture need not be unacceptable to faith. That is, they are exercises in the theology of culture. For Tillich, that means that making a case for Christianity ("apologetics") is not a specialized branch of theology but rather is one dimension of every subsection of theology.[2]

In his *Systematic Theology* Tillich undertakes this mediating task by exhibiting a *correlation* between religion and culture. The relation between the two, he suggests, is like the correlation between "questioning" and "answering" in a conversation. Or it is like the correlation between "form" and "content" (or "substance") in a work of art. Indeed, it is possible to correlate them because in concrete reality "religion" and "culture" are always a single whole of which "the form of religion is culture and the substance of culture is religion."[3]

Tillich suggests that the human condition always raises fundamental questions which human cultures express in various ways in the dominant styles of their works of art, and to which religious traditions offer answers expressed in religious symbols. Accordingly, he organizes his *Systematic Theology* into five parts. In each part a major biblical religious symbol is correlated as "answer" to a major human question as expressed by modern culture. Part I correlates the symbol "Logos" with modern culture's form of the skeptical question: "How can we know with certainty any humanly important truth?" Part II correlates the symbol "God as Creator" with modern culture's expressions of the question of finitude: "How can we withstand the destructive forces that threaten to disintegrate our lives?" Part III correlates the symbol "Jesus as the Christ" with modern culture's secular expressions of the question of estrangement: "How can we find healing of the alienation we experience from ourselves and from our neighbors?" Part IV correlates the symbol "Spirit" with modern culture's expressions of the question of ambiguity: "How can our lives be authentic when our morality, religious practices, and cultural self-expressions are so thoroughly ambiguous?" And Part V correlates the symbol "Kingdom of God" with the question: "Has history any meaning?"

Content: Essential nature, existential disruption, and actuality

These five pairs of correlated questions and answers are the main themes in Tillich's theology. They resolve into three major subdivisions that deal with what he abstractly calls, respectively, the "essential nature," the "existential disruption," and the "actuality" of our lives and of every reality. We will follow this trinitarian structure in our discussion of the content of Tillich's theology.

Essential nature

The first two parts of the system deal with questions concerning our "essential nature." "Essence" refers to what something most fundamentally is. In Tillich's view, anything whatever that is actual (as opposed to merely ideal) exhibits three very general features: (1) it is itself an integral whole, perhaps we might say, a "system"; (2) it is part of more inclusive wholes with whose other members it is engaged in various kinds of transactions; (3) it is "finite," that is, inherently vulnerable to disintegration of itself and to separation from the whole to which it belongs. Tillich analyzes these three features of our essential nature in considerable detail at a high level of abstraction. Part I deals with our essential nature as "knowers." Part II deals with our essential nature as "creatures." It may make his analysis clearer if we take these two parts of the system in reverse order.

Part II addresses the question raised by experience of the threatenedness of our lives. (Incidentally, taking this as his central focus, and drawing on Kierkegaard and

Nietzsche, earned Tillich the label "existentialist.") There are moments when we experience our lives on the edge of being overwhelmed by meaninglessness, guilt, and death. Put abstractly, "being" is threatened by "non-being." What is equally important for Tillich is that we also have the experience of continually resisting this threat. Put abstractly, we experience the presence of the "power of being." Out of this rises the question, "Whence comes the power to resist the threat of non-being?" The answer is provided by the Christian symbol "God as Creator."

Before we can get clear about that, Tillich thinks, we need to ask what it is about us that leaves us so vulnerable to the threat of "non-being." Here we encounter Tillich's celebrated ontology. "Ontology" is thought [in Greek: *logos*] about what it is to be [in Greek: *on* gen. *ontos*]. It is a topic many philosophers have taken up. Tillich borrows from a great many of them and was perhaps especially influenced by Martin Heiddeger. Note that while some philosophers hold that from a careful analysis of what it is "to be" one can demonstrate the reality of God, Tillich is not among them. His ontological analysis is confined to showing our *finitude* (i.e., that we are inherently threatened by non-being and that we are not ourselves the source of the power of being which resists the threat). Tillich suggests that all our interactions with the world exhibit the same basic structure. The structure consists of three pairs of "polar elements." In every transaction with the world we have to strike a balance between "individualization" and "participation," between preserving and nurturing our own individuality and sharing in community and communion with others. The balance is not a given. We have to strike it again and again, and it is always possible that we shall fail. Obviously, many psychological and social problems can be understood as situations in which these two poles come into conflict with each other. In every transaction, secondly, we have to keep a balance between "dynamics" and "form." Without rules (form), interactions become unreliable and chaotic. But without creativity and novelty (dynamics), they become rigid. Many political revolutions can be understood as situations in which these two poles have come into conflict with one another. Finally, in every transaction we have to keep "freedom" and "destiny" balanced. At the moment of any transaction with the world we are deeply conditioned by the immediate context and by the entire history of what we have done and undergone to that point. That is our "destiny," determining who we are at that moment and setting us on a certain trajectory into the future. At the same time we must exercise our freedom, deciding what to do and taking responsibility for it. On this analysis, then, to *be* is necessarily to be *finite*. It is to be inherently, not just accidentally, vulnerable to interaction with the world in which individualization separates from participation, dynamics separates from form, destiny separates from freedom, and, one pole in each pair dominating who we are in the interaction, our ontological integrity begins to disintegrate.

Yet we never totally fall apart. Whence comes the power to resist the threats of non-being? That is the question about our "ultimate concern." Whatever concerns us ultimately, says Tillich, is our "god." So this is a question about god. The answer is provided by Christian symbols of God. They are images and stories about God, especially as Creator, that express the experience of the presence of the power of being in a specially appropriate way. "Creator" does not name a theory about the origin of things. Rather, "God is creator" expresses an experience of a state of affairs: the power of being present actively ("God lives"), continuously ("God sustains"), grounding our being in the very midst of the threat of non-being ("God creates out of chaos"). At the same time the symbol is nuanced to express another feature of the experience: the presence of the power is experienced as "inexplicable and uncanny" ("God is holy"). As the ontological analysis has confirmed, this power is not an element in the structure of being. It is not just another name for the structure of being taken as a whole (i.e., the structure consisting of the tensed polarities individualization/participation, dynamics/form, destiny/freedom). Tillich rejects that as a type of pantheism. Nor can this power be a "supreme being" for, by definition, *any* entity is finite. Hence, Tillich refuses to speak of the "existence" of God. No, the power of being or "ground of being" is "being-itself," utterly unconditioned by anything else – while being present to everything ("God is Lord").

Part I of the system applies this same pattern of analysis to one type of transaction with the world: cognition. It addresses the skeptical question raised by our persistent frustrations in trying to know humanly important truth. Tillich adopts a very rich concept of knowledge. Knowing covers every type of transaction with the world in which we both grasp and shape it. Our capacity to do this is the structure of the mind, which Tillich calls "ontological reason." It is much richer than mere "technical reason" or problem-solving capacities. We constantly find our efforts to grasp and shape reality threatened either with meaninglessness or with uncertainty. And yet we do know enough to live on. The question is, "How can it be that the threat is overcome?" The answer is provided by the Christian symbol "Logos."

We need to ask why our efforts to know are threatened before we can get clear how "Logos" addresses our skepticism. Our rational efforts are threatened, of course, because ontological reason is finite. Three pairs of polar elements must be kept in balance in our grasping and shaping of reality, and they threaten to conflict. Rational grasp of reality involves both formal and emotional dimensions. However, the formal and emotional roles of our cognitive transactions with the world threaten to conflict and we yearn for some kind of knowing in which they are united. Rational grasp of reality must also hold static and dynamic aspects in balance. These aspects constantly threaten to conflict. One-sided stress on static principles looks from the other perspective like conservative "absolutism"; one-sided stress on concrete changes looks from the other perspective like rootless "relativism." The tension between "absolutists" and "relativists" is common enough. We yearn for some kind of knowing in which absolute and concrete are held together.

There is a third tension in ontological reason that makes it inherently vulnerable to skepticism. We experience a conflict between relying on ourselves as the final authority in cognition ("autonomy": self [Greek: *autos*] as law [Greek: *nomos*]) and relying on another, perhaps a tradition or an established "authority figure" ("heteronomy": other [Greek: *heteros*] as law). The conflict is rooted in a polarity between what Tillich calls the "structure" and the "depth" of reason. The "structure" of reason is that which makes it possible for us to grasp and shape reality. But grasping and shaping always involve making judgments about what is more (or less) true, good, or beautiful than something else. In making such judgments we employ standards. Furthermore, Tillich holds (borrowing, he thinks, from Plato) we must all, at least implicitly and unselfconsciously, rely on the same ultimate standards or we should never agree that there is such a thing as "more true, good, or beautiful."[4] The "depth" of reason refers to the fact that we engage in rational transactions in the light of these standards even when we are unaware of doing so. The presence to reason of these ultimate standards ("truth-itself"; "beauty-itself"; "goodness-itself") *is* the presence of the power of being ("being-itself") to the mind. Because we are unaware of its presence, however, we alternate between relying on something outside us (a tradition or powerful personality) and relying on ourselves. Neither is adequate and we yearn for some kind of knowing in which the standards are not simply dependent on our own opinion and yet are not imposed on us as something alien to us. In short, in the very possibility of there being reliable meaning in our lives seems to depend on some type of knowing which is at once formal and emotional, absolute and concrete, and in which the structure and depth of reason are united. Where do we ever know in that way?

That, says Tillich, is a question about "revelation." The answer is to be correlated with the Christian symbol, Jesus as the "Logos."[5] It is a question about revelation because it is a question about disclosure of our ultimate concern: that which grounds meaning in life. The disclosure is a revelatory event with two sides. The "receiving" side is a group of persons who are totally grasped by the event, emotions and intellect united in integral wholeness. To be in this state is to be in "faith." Tillich also calls it "ecstasy." It is a state in which reason transcends itself in a *self-conscious* grasp of the depth of reason, the ground of meaning. The "giving" side of the revelatory event Tillich calls "miracle." It is some particular concrete object, event, or person that functions as a sign-event or religious symbol *through which* the ground of meaning in life makes itself present to persons. In the world's religions various sorts of things have filled the role of medium. For Jesus' disciples it was Jesus himself who was "miracle" or symbol mediating the ground of meaning to the disciples who received it in their ecstasy or faith. That was what Tillich calls an "original" revelatory event. The disciples *expressed* the fact that it had occurred by using a variety of stories and verbal images for Jesus which are preserved in New Testament writings. Central to them is the image "Jesus is the Logos." "Logos" (Greek: reason, word) expresses Jesus' function as concrete instantiation of the presence of the ground of meaning in life.

But just what is known in a revelatory event? Ontological analysis of finite reason has shown independently that the ground of meaning is *constantly* present to all human reason as its "depth," just as the ground of being is constantly present to every life as its "power of being." Just as the power of being is not simply one more item in the world which it grounds, so the ground of meaning is not one more object to be known. It transcends the structure of finite reason. It is inherently "mystery." It cannot cease to be mystery even in revelation. What then can be known of it through Jesus? Tillich stresses that, while the ground of meaning may be present to reason constantly, in fact we are not aware of it apart from revelation. The concreteness of the medium (for Christians, the man Jesus) makes self-consciousness possible about the presence of the absolute or unconditioned ground of meaning.

It is crucially important that the mystery whose presence is mediated should not be confused with the finite medium itself. To confuse them is idolatry, treating something finite as though it were itself ultimate. We may rank the central symbols of various religions with respect to how clearly they make this distinction. Tillich holds that on such a scale Jesus is "final revelation," the standard by which all others must be measured, because central to Jesus' functioning as mediator of the ground of meaning is his absolute transparency to the unconditioned. His total self-emptying, as expressed in the crucifixion, is a built-in reminder that he is not what is to be known, but only its medium. What is known of mystery through Jesus is, first, its reality and, second, in the midst of our unawareness, that we are indeed related to it. In short, the revelatory event in which the man Jesus is "the Logos" is a "knowing" that answers our skeptical question. It is awareness of the unity of the structure and depth of reason that overcomes the tension between autonomy and heteronomy. In its receiving side, or faith, emotional and formal are united, overcoming their tension. In its giving side, or miracle, the concrete and absolute are united without being confused, thereby overcoming the tension between relativism and absolutism.

Existential disruption

Part III deals with the questions arising from our "existential disruption." Existence means "standing out of" non-being. For Tillich, the "non-being" out of which each of us stands is our potentiality which, until it is realized, is simply a possibility. It is our essential nature. To exist is to be distanced, standing out from our essence. Hence, for Tillich, "existence" and "existential" usually have the sense of "estranged from essence."[6] Our existential situation is a state of estrangement from ourselves, others, and the power of being. Ontological analysis of our essential nature shows why we are inherently threatened by non-being. Description of our existential situation shows that the threat is actively being actualized. Estranged from the power of being, we are in fact unable to hold individualization and participation, dynamics and form, destiny and freedom, in balance in our transactions with our world. As a result, our transactions with others break down and our "world" becomes progressively chaotic. At the same time, our relations with ourselves are disrupted, and we become progressively disintegrated.

We experience all of this as a diffuse guilt, loneliness, and meaninglessness. The Christian symbols for this situation are "Fall" and "Sin." The story of the "Fall" of Adam and Eve is not an account of an event long ago. Rather, it expresses how the transition from essential nature to existential disruption is a result of our freedom and our destiny. On the one hand, the transition is not a natural or rational development. It is an absurd discontinuity, an inexplicable leap which freedom makes possible. It is actualized by each individual person. "Sin" is the religious symbol that expresses this personal responsibility for estrangement. On the other hand, each person does this as a participant in a society of persons who are already estranged. Fallenness is our destiny. Out of this arises the question, "Where can we find power for new being?" The Christian symbol for this "where" is "Messiah" or "Christ" (both mean "the anointed one"). Both symbols express the filling of a *function*: the one who functions to represent or manifest the power of being to finite human essential nature in the midst of its estrangement. The question about the power of new being is a question about the "Christ."

The answer to be correlated with this question is expressed by the Christian symbol "Jesus as the Christ as the power of New Being." Here, Tillich develops his Christology. Explanation of who Jesus is follows from explanation of what he did to "save" us. Furthermore, "salvation" and "revelation" name two aspects of the same reality. "Salvation" means "healing." Healing of existential estrangement comes by reconciliation with the power of being and, along with that, reconciliation with others and oneself. That is precisely what happens in a revelatory situation. The power of meaning that is given through Jesus as the Logos is, of course, none other than the power of being.

As the ontological analysis showed, the presence of the power of being is inexplicable. It is gift or "grace." It is the presence of the power of New Being in the midst of our estrangement from it. God participates *in* our existential situation of disruption. The power of New Being is supremely present in Jesus precisely because Jesus' crucifixion concretely manifests the presence of this power in the midst of an event of the most profound estrangement of persons from one another and from God. Jesus' death is not substitutionary punishment of human sin in the name of divine justice, but rather a manifestation of divine love. Divine removal of our guilt and punishment is not accomplished by God overlooking their depth, but by God entering into them in love so deeply as to transform us.

Our reception, in faith, of the power of New Being is a moment of insight in which one experiences one's unity with the depth of reason, that is, with the unconditioned mystery that is the ground of meaning and being. As in the moment of therapeutic insight in psychoanalysis, in that insight one is healed of one's ontological disintegratedness. It is only a momentary event, fragmentary and ambiguous. It does not eliminate the situation of existential disruptions. What is mediated through Jesus is the power of New Being in the midst of continuing estrangement. The event of mediation always needs to be repeated. But for that moment of the event it is genuine. Participation in the power of New Being is "new birth" or "regeneration." In one way this is our being accepted by the power of being ("God") despite or in the midst of our estrangement, or "justification"; in another way this is our transformation by the power of being, or "sanctification." These are simply different aspects of reconciliation with "God," or "atonement" (that is, at-one-ment; reunion).

Who Jesus is follows from what he did. What traditional Christology expressed by talking about the human and divine "natures" of Jesus Christ needs, in Tillich's view, to be reformulated today in order to make basically the same points but in less misleading ways. To say that Jesus is "human" is to say that the entire analysis of "essential nature" applies to him too, including vulnerability to disintegration and its underlying estrangement. To say that Jesus is "divine" is to say that the power of being which is constantly present to all persons is mediated to others through him as the power of New Being in the midst of estrangement from essential nature. To say that they are one in Jesus is to say that this one life actualized without existential disruption (i.e., without "sin") the eternal God-man-unity which characterizes our essential nature too (recall the ontological analysis' exhibition of the inexplicable but universal presence of the power of being to finite lives; recall the analysis of reason's unity of "structure" and "depth"). Faith thus has a large stake in the historical facticity of Jesus' life. Only if existential disruption is overcome in *one* point – a personal life, representing existence as a whole – is it conquered in principle, which means in "beginning and in power." Our question about where we can find the power to heal our existential disruption is answered by pointing to the particular man Jesus who actualized essential human nature but without existential disruption, and hence can mediate to us the power of New Being that heals or saves.

Actuality

The final two parts of the system deal with questions concerning our "actuality." "Actuality" is Tillich's technical ontological concept of concrete life – "life is the 'actuality of being.'" "Essence" designates one main qualification of being, taken in abstraction from any particular life in its concreteness. "Existence" designates the other main qualification, also taken in abstraction. "Actuality" refers to your life precisely *in* its concrete uniting of "essence" and "existence."[7] This is a key point. "Uniting" is a *process*, the process of actualizing potentiality or "essential nature" (here Tillich borrows from Aristotle). It is the dynamic process-character of "actuality" that makes it alive, a life. Beyond its organic and inorganic dimensions, human life has the dimension of "spirit." The word "spirit" denotes "the unity of life-power and life in meanings." In addition to sheer vitality ("life-power"), human life involves capacities to regulate ourselves according to ideas, purposes, and plans ("meanings") which we intensely love and freely choose for ourselves. The spiritual dimension of human actuality includes not only reason but also "eros, passions, imagination."[8]

With this brace of observations in place, Tillich can offer an ontological analysis of the process that constitutes life with a spiritual dimension. Such life has three functions. Your life involves *self-integration*, a circular movement out from what you have been into new experiences and back to integrate them into your centered self. You engage in self-integration in "moral" life. Here, "moral" is not used in contrast to "immoral." Rather, it is used to stress the fact that as self-integrating you are inescapably morally accountable both for integrating yourself as "centered" and for your choice of norms and goals to guide your interactions with others. However, the moral life is thoroughly ambiguous. No matter how "moral" an act may seem in some respects, we are aware that it cost the sacrifice of other acts through which we might have been more richly integrated, and that it involved some loss to some other person. Because our lives inherently drive toward self-integration, we ask whether there is any way to achieve it through unambiguous morality.

Second, your life process involves *self-creation*, a horizontal movement through time as you constantly make yourself up and deeply change. We engage in self-creation in work that produces meaningful artifacts, symbols, and styles of both art and behavior which comprise a culture and are significant because they express "meanings" in which a human life "participates." However, we experience ambiguity in all elements of culture, from individual artifacts to the way a society is organized and led, finding them both nurturing new life and oppressing it. Because our lives inherently drive toward self-creation, we ask whether there is any way to achieve it through an unambiguous culture.

Third, your life process involves *self-transcendence*, a vertical movement in which one is "driving toward the sublime." You engage in self-transcendence in religious activity. This function intersects and unites the other two. It is always moral and culturally creative lives that self-transcend. Hence, there is a religious dimension inherent in all moral and cultural acts. However, the ways in which the drive for self-transcendence expresses itself in ritual, myth, and institutional structures are inherently ambiguous. They are all finite things, functioning religiously to express the unconditioned, that toward which one "transcends" oneself. At the same time, they invite for themselves the ultimate concern appropriate only to the unconditioned. Thereby they become "demonic," powerfully destructive of the life trying to "transcend" itself. Because our lives inherently drive toward self-transcendence, we ask whether there is any way to achieve self-transcendence through unambiguous religion.

The answers to be correlated with the questions about unambiguous morality, culture, and religion are expressed in two Christian symbols. In Part IV Tillich correlates the symbol "Spiritual Presence" with the question of the ambiguity of every society synchronically. In Part V he correlates the symbol "Kingdom of God" with the question of ambiguity diachronically in the entire history of morality, culture, and religion.

In Part IV, "Spiritual Presence" is the Christian symbol expressive of the "revelatory experience of 'God present'" in life lived in the dimension of spirit (i.e., human life).[9] "Spirit" (with upper-case S) is the most completely adequate symbol for the unconditioned, because it expresses that the unconditioned power of being is *living*. "God as creator" expresses the presence of the unconditioned power of being to us in regard to our essential finitude, and "Jesus the Christ as the power of New Being" expresses its presence to us in our existential estrangement, but "Spirit" expresses its presence to us precisely in our concrete reality as spiritual (lower-cases) lives actualizing our potentiality. In our self-transcendence we reach for this presence. But we cannot grasp it, unless we are first grasped by it. When it does grasp us, we are drawn into its "transcendent unity of ambiguous life" and it creates unambiguous life in us.[10] In this experience of "the reunion of essential and existential being, ambiguous life is raised above itself to a transcendence that it could not achieve by its own power."[11]

Tillich stresses that such experiences are always social and fragmentary. To be sure, they have a subjective dimension which Tillich calls "mystical."[12] As the state of being *grasped by* the "transcendent unity of an unambiguous life," it is called the state of "faith." As the state of being *taken into* that transcendent unity, is called the state of "love." However, this always occurs in a communal setting, creating what Tillich calls a "Spiritual Community."[13] It is not identical with Christian churches. The Spiritual Community is not one group beside others. It is "a power and structure inherent" in some groups, making them religious groups. Spiritual Community is real but immanent in many "secular" communities outside the church and it is manifest explicitly sometimes in the churches. Now, given the ontological analysis of life, this means that when Spiritual Community "happens" the ambiguity of our religious enactments of self-transcending has been overcome. Because the ambiguity of self-integration and self-creation follows from the ambiguity of self-transcendence, this means that the experience symbolized by "Spiritual Presence" is also a moment of unambiguous cultural self-creativity and unambiguous moral self-integration. In those moments, cultural and moral activity themselves become self-transcending, that is, religious. Here, Tillich's theology of culture has its theological center and context. Tillich calls such moments "theonomous"[14] – living social moments whose norm (nomos) comes, not from ourselves nor from an alien "other," but from the "transcendent unity of unambiguous life" (theos), which precisely in its transcendence is nonetheless immediately present to us. "Spiritual Presence" expresses those moments when our questions about the possibility of unambiguous religion, culture, and morality are answered. Tillich insists that such moments in social life are fragmentary and paradoxical, but actually do occur in all societies. His favorite examples come from medieval European culture.

"Kingdom of God" is the religious symbol expressive of Christian answers to the question central to Part V about the possibility of unambiguous life in a historical rather than social dimension: "Is there any meaning to history?"[15] In Tillich's view groups, not individuals, are the bearers of history. The three movements comprising any life comprise history also: history drives self-integratingly toward the centeredness of groups in a harmony of justice and power, self-creatively toward the creation of new and unambiguous states of affairs, and self-transcendingly toward unambiguous fulfillment of potential being. "Kingdom of God" expresses the occurrence of this in two ways: as an inner-historical movement and as a transhistorical movement.[16]

In one way, "Kingdom of God" expresses the occurrence *in* the life of any one group which is the decisive and normative instance of "Spiritual Presence" in the group's history. It is the event which serves the group as the "center of history," the one particular point in history which is of universal significance for all groups at all times because it is the *most* adequate overcoming of the ambiguities of human life. In its inner-historical sense, the symbol "Kingdom of God" expresses the occurrence of this event. Tillich calls such a moment the *kairos* (Greek: "fulfillment of time"). In such moments a group's experience of unambiguous self-integration, self-creativity, and self-transcendence in a *kairos*, is its experience of the meaning, the point of history.[17]

"Kingdom of God" also expresses a transhistorical actualization of unambiguous historical life. Here it correlates with the question, "Is there anything of permanent value or meaning in the flow of history?" The same question is often expressed personally as a question about immortality: "Will anything of me survive this life?" Ontologically, this is a question about the relation of time to eternity. "Kingdom of God" expresses how the "inner aim" of created time is the elevating of the finite into the eternal.[18] Thus, there are two distinct themes in Tillich's explication of the transhistorical sense of the symbol "Kingdom of God." For the creature, the symbol expresses the insight that "nothing which has been created in history is lost, but it is liberated from the negative element with which it is entangled within its existence." Following Schelling, Tillich calls this "essentialization." It amounts to an unambiguous and *permanent* participation of finite life in the very life of Divine Spirit, for which the Christian symbol is "Eternal Life." Tillich says that this is not a dateable temporal event but rather what is going on all the time.[19] On the other hand, viewed as it were from God's perspective, the symbol gives expression to a cosmic process. Tillich calls that process "eschatological pan-en-theism."[20] In it, Divine Life realizes itself by a movement through self-alienation and engagement in creaturely existential disruption and then back to self-reconciliation, bringing the creaturely realm with it so that, fully reconciled, the creaturely realm is at the end ("eschatologically") wholly "within" the Divine Life (pan – "everything" – *en theos* – "within God").

Influence and Controversies

Tillich has had continuing influence on discussion of several theological issues. He has shaped the way the concepts of religion and the religious are widely understood in terms of "ultimate concern." Indeed, in coining the expression "ultimate concern" he introduced a new phrase into the English language to define religion. It even came to have standing in American law. His related theory of symbols, and of religious symbols in particular, has had similar continuing influence. In general, his theory of religion stimulated continuing discussions in two theological areas. It continues to be influential on theorizing about the relation between religion and the visual arts and religion and literature. And it continues to shape theological reflection on the phenomenon of religious pluralism and questions about how to understand the relations among the world's major religions.

A related theme in Tillich's theology of culture continues to influence American pastoral theology. When he taught and wrote in Germany, Tillich's reflections on the theology of culture tended to focus on social theory and politics. This side of his early interests has generated scholarly interest in a time when liberationist and political theologies are vital movements.[21] However, when he moved to the United States and to an unfamiliar political scene, Tillich's interests focused on the relation between religion and psychology. The way in which he explicated the theological concepts of sin and redemption dynamically in terms of "estrangement" and "reconciliation" has suggested the possibility of integrating theological notions with the various types of dynamic psychology that have shaped the practice of counseling and pastoral care.

Perhaps because of his effort to think theological and ontological lines of thought into each other, Tillich's theology has been of continuing interest to Roman Catholic theologians, prompting ecumenical theological scholarship. It has not been uncritical attention, and it would be difficult to show any broad "Tillichian" influence on Roman Catholic theology. Nonetheless, he has been found a fruitful subject of study in regard to the nature of the church, and in relation to both Thomist and Franciscan traditions of philosophical theology.[22]

The tradition of Tillich's philosophical theology has continuing influence on several Protestant theologians who find traditional theistic doctrines of God unacceptable. For example, theologians like Langdon Gilkey and Schubert Ogden, who find it difficult to make sense of the idea of God "acting," indeed to make sense of the idea of God as "a person," have found resources for alternative doctrines of God in Tillich's ontology and his emphatic insistence that God is not a "person."[23]

Indeed, Tillich's philosophical theology has in certain respects been surprisingly developed in a postmodernist direction, for example by Charles Winquist.[24] I say "surprising" because looked at one way many themes in Tillich look like classic evidence of a "modernist" orientation. The notion of the depth of reason looks like the basis of a claim that human consciousness has immediate and indubitable cognitive access to transcendence that serves as the foundation of all other theological claims, which postmodern thought rejects in its "non-foundationalist" theories of knowledge. The construal of God as "ground of being" immediately present in the power of being exercised by every finite life looks like an instance of the intellectual tradition of "onto-theology" critiqued by postmodern thought. The story in Part V of God actualizing Godself in a process that culminates in an eschatological panentheism looks like an instance of the "totalizing metanarratives" that postmodernist thought critiques. Finally, Tillich's doctrine of revelation and theory of religious symbols look like an example of an "emotive–expressivist" theory of religion that conservative postmodernists critique as cognitively empty and inadequate to the phenomena of historical Christianity. Yet Tillich's limiting of ontology to analysis of finite lives, his insistence that there is no universal or world history but only the histories of groups, his appropriation of Kierkegaard's insistence that existence is not a system and cannot be captured in a single story, and his stress on the way the unconditioned power of being escapes all articulation can all be developed in ways that point toward postmodernist themes.

On the other hand, certain doctrines in Tillich's system have been the subject of sustained controversy. His non-theist doctrine of God has left him open to the charge of finally being an atheist.[25] His Christology has been criticized on the grounds that it systematically makes the historical facticity of Jesus irrelevant to theological claims about Jesus' significance.[26] Finally, his method of correlation as the way in which to mediate between faith and culture has been controversial.[27] The controversy turns on whether such "correlation" does not finally result in translating the content of Christian faith without remainder into the deepest convictions of the secular culture it attempts to address. Theologians who have been influenced by Søren Kierkegaard or by Karl Barth charge that that is the outcome.[28] Conversely, many theologians influential in the United States, such as Gilkey and David Tracy,[29] are persuaded that Tillich was right and develop theological projects that employ some variant of Tillich's method.

Notes

1 Wilhelm and Marion Pauck, *Paul Tillich: His Life and Thought* (Chicago, 1976), vol. 1, p. 41.
2 Paul Tillich, *Systematic Theology* (Chicago, 1951), vol. 1, pp. 59–66.
3 Ibid, pp. 63–8.
4 *Theology of Culture* (New York, 1959), pp. 10–30.
5 *Systematic Theology* (New York, 1957), vol. 2, pp. 106–59.
6 Ibid, pp. 97–180.
7 *Systematic Theology* (Chicago, 1963), vol. 3, pp. 11–12; also vol. 2, p. 28.
8 Ibid, p. 31.
9 Ibid, p. 111.
10 Ibid, p. 112.
11 Ibid, p. 129.
12 Ibid, p. 242.
13 Ibid, p. 149ff.
14 Ibid, p. 266.
15 Ibid, p. 349.
16 Ibid, p. 357.
17 Ibid, p. 369.
18 Ibid, pp. 397, 399.
19 Ibid, pp. 399–400.
20 Ibid, pp. 421–2.

21 See Ronald P. Stone, *Paul Tillich's Radical Social Thought* (Atlanta, GA, 1980); A. James Reimer, *The Emanuel Hirsch and Paul Tillich Debate* (Lewiston, ME, 1989).
22 See Monica Hellwig (ed.), *Paul Tillich* (Collegeville, MN, 1994); Ronald Modres, *Paul Tillich's Theology of the Church* (Detroit, MI, 1976); Robert Barron, *A Study of the De Potentia of Thomas Aquinas in the Light of the Dogmatics of Paul Tillich* (San Francisco, 1993); John P. Dourley, *Paul Tillich and Bonaventure* (Leiden, 1975).
23 Langdon Gilkey, *Naming the Whirlwind* (Indianapolis, IN, 1969) and *Reaping the Whirlwind* (New York, 1976); Schubert Ogden, *The Point of Christology* (New York, 1982).
24 Charles E. Winquist, "Heterology and Ontology in the Thought of Paul Tillich," in *God and Being* (Berlin, 1989); "Untimely History" in *Truth and History – A Dialogue with Paul Tillich*, Gert Hummel (ed.) (Berlin, 1998).
25 See Leonard F. Wheat, *Paul Tillich's Dialectical Humanism: Unmasking the God above God* (Baltimore, MD, 1970).

26 See John Clayton and Robert Morgan, *Christ, Faith and History* (Cambridge, 1972); David Kelsey, *The Fabric of Paul Tillich's Theology* (New Haven, CT, 1967).

27 See John Clayton, *The Concept of Correlation* (Berlin, 1980).

28 See Kenneth Hamilton, *System and the Gospel* (New York, 1963); Alexander McKelway, *The Systematic Theology of Paul Tillich* (Detroit, MI, 1964).

29 David Tracy, *Blessed Rage for Order* (New York, 1988).

Bibliography

Primary

The Shaking of the Foundations (New York, 1948).

The Protestant Era (Chicago, 1948).

Systematic Theology, Vol. 1 (Chicago, 1951).

Love, Power and Justice (New York, 1955).

The New Being (New York, 1955).

Biblical Religion and the Search for Ultimate Reality (Chicago, 1956).

Eternal Now (New York, 1956).

Systematic Theology, Vol. 2 (Chicago, 1957).

Dynamics of Faith (New York, 1957).

Theology of Culture (New York, 1959).

Systematic Theology, Vol. 3 (Chicago, 1963).

On Art and Architecture (New York, 1986).

Secondary

Barron, Robert, *A Study of the De Potentia of Thomas Aquinas in the Light of the Dogmatic of Paul Tillich* (San Francisco, 1993).

Clayton, John P., *The Concept of Correlation* (Berlin, 1980).

Clayton, John P. and Morgan, Robert, *Christ, Faith and History* (Cambridge, 1972).

Dourley, John P., *Paul Tillich and Bonaventure* (Leiden, 1975).

Gilkey, Langdon, *Gilkey on Tillich* (New York, 1990).

—— *Naming the Whirlwind* (Indianapolis, IN, 1969).

—— *Reaping the Whirlwind* (New York, 1976).

Hamilton, Kenneth, *System and the Gospel* (New York, 1963).

Hellwig, Monica (ed.), *Paul Tillich: A New Roman Catholic Assessment* (Collegeville, MN, 1994).

Hook, Sidney (ed.), *Religious Experience and Truth* (New York, 1961).

Kelsey, David H., *The Fabric of Paul Tillich's Theology* (New Haven, CT, 1967).

McKelway, Alexander, *The Systematic Theology of Paul Tillich* (Detroit, MI, 1964).

Modres, Ronald, *Paul Tillich's Theology of the Church: A Catholic Appraisal* (Detroit, MI, 1976).

Ogden, Schubert, *The Point of Christology* (New York, 1982).

Pauck, Wilhelm and Pauk, Marion, *Paul Tillich: His Life and Thought*, Vol. 1 (Chicago, 1976).

Reimer, A. James, *The Emmanuel Hirsch and Paul Tillich Debate: A Study in the Political Ramifications of Theology* (Lewiston, ME, 1989).

Rowe, William, *Religious Symbols and God* (Chicago, 1976).

Wheat, Leonard F., *Paul Tillich's Dialectical Humanism: Unmasking the God above God* (Baltimore, MD, 1970).

Henri de Lubac

John Milbank

Introduction

> For what we do by means of our friends, is done in a sense, by ourselves. (Aristotle, cited by Aquinas, regarding the paradox of grace and the natural human orientation to the supernatural)[1]

> Moreover, this concept of a pure nature runs into great difficulties, the principal one of which seems to me to be the following: How can a conscious spirit be anything other than an absolute desire for God? (Henri de Lubac in a letter to Maurice Blondel, April 3, 1932)[2]

> Others destroy the gratuity of the supernatural order, since God, they say, cannot create intellectual beings without ordering and calling them to the beatific vision. (*Humani Generis*, August 12, 1950)[3]

> Le Surnaturel, c'est du réel précis. (Robert Bresson, film director)[4]

The above sequence of quotations traces in outline the theological and human drama of the life of Henri de Lubac. In the first, we have the patristic and High Medieval paradox of the supernatural which de Lubac sought to recover: what is wholly done for us by God, namely deification by grace, is yet also our highest act and as such properly our own – even that which is most properly our own.

The second encapsulates Henri du Lubac's core theological belief, based upon this paradox, here clearly stated in private, but almost never so clearly stated in public, namely that there *is* no spiritual, intelligent being (angelic or human) that is not ordered by grace to the beatific vision: that is, to be deified.

The third, with equal clarity, shows the papal suspicion of such a lurking view in de Lubac and many others. The opinion is roundly rejected. Defenders of de Lubac who deny that he was implicated in this rejection by Pius XII are surely wrong, and critics who insist that he was, are surely correct. Yet this of course leaves the theological issue open: it is hard to read de Lubac's penultimate book, *Pic de la Mirandole*, written when he was 80, without reaching the conclusion that he covertly rejected this paragraph of the encyclical to the end of his life.

The fourth, and most profound and comprehensive, reminds us that de Lubac's opinion, however controversial, informed a new sensibility which stood at the heart of the Catholic cultural revival in the twentieth century.

The Life and Writings of Henri de Lubac

Henri de Lubac was a Jesuit theologian who was educated at Jesuit centers in France and England before World War I. (Unlike some of his *confrères*, he received no other formal academic training.) In that war he was badly wounded in the head, a wound which affected him somewhat throughout his long life. In the interwar years, he was the central but sometimes shadowy figure of a diverse new theological tendency in France which demanded a rejection of neoscholasticism and a qualification of the scholastic stress upon speculation with a renewed interest in history, biblical exegesis, typology, art, literature, and mysticism. (Other important names are Jean Daniélou, M.-D. Chenu, Henry Bouillard, Yves Congar, and Gaston Fessard.) The initial aim was *ressourcement* – a recovery of the riches of Christian tradition, especially prior to 1300. The eventual aim though, was a renewal of speculative theology in a new mode that would restore its closeness to the exegetical, mystical, and liturgical reading of revealed signs. With *Catholicisme* in 1938, de Lubac produced one of the key texts of this tendency: the book stressed the social character of the church as the true universal community in embryo, rather than as a mere external machinery for the saving of individual souls.[5] It accordingly encouraged an open yet critical engagement with the world. Already, here, one of the "paradoxical" axes of de Lubac's thought was apparent: "Catholic" means a reach of divine grace that is all-encompassing – to the entire past and future and all of space, worldly and cosmic, extending beyond the explicit profession of Christianity. Yet, at the same time, "Catholic" means a universality whose grammar is only fully spelt out in the life of the incarnate Logos. Within this harmonious tension, the sway of de Lubac's first and last master – Origen of Alexandria – is always apparent. Likewise evident is the practical missionary concern fused with intellectual rigor and non-compromising in essentials of a Jesuit Father.

If this follower of St. Ignatius was at all a saint, it was in a wholly militant mode. For all his reticence, his writings often exhibit a withering aristocratic disdain of philistine opponents, and for all the commitment to patient and exhaustive scholarship, his deliberate selection of august targets and coordination of intellectual strategy is often to the fore. Twice he was involved in secular warfare: once, as noted, under the drastic aegis of the French Republic which made no exemptions from military service for religious (a fellow Jesuit, and enormous intellectual influence, Pierre Rousselot, was killed in the trenches); secondly, on the run from the Vichy regime and later the Gestapo during World War II. At the time that he was composing his *Surnaturel* (arguably the key theological text of the twentieth century) he was also in touch, along with his fellow Jesuits of the School at Lyon, with the Gaullist resistance.[6] His *confrère* and intellectual collaborator Yves de Montcheuil was captured and martyred by the Gestapo. And it is vital to grasp that de Lubac and de Montcheuil's Catholic Rightist opponents supporting the Vichy regime and collaborating with the occupying Germans were also their *theological* opponents – reporting their dubious theological opinions as well as their dubious secular involvements back up the chains of Jesuit and Dominican command to Rome itself. (It should be stressed though, that de Lubac's enemies in the French Catholic hierarchy were often well to the right of Pius XII and his advisors in the Vatican.)

Surnaturel was a body blow aimed at the neoscholastic understandings of reason and grace, of philosophy, theology, and the relation between them. It was not that it advocated a particular view on a particular theological topic: it was rather than it implicitly (indeed, in an almost coded fashion) dismantled the entire set of reigning Catholic (and perhaps Protestant) assumptions about the character of Christian intellectual reflection. Moreover, it did so not in the name of innovation, but of an authentic tradition which it sought to recover.

Most of de Lubac's other writing, which in a sense works out the thesis of *Surnaturel* in relation to ecclesiology, exegesis, interreligious dialogue, and secular social and scientific thought, is of a similar character. It does not often contribute directly to the detailed development of doctrine. Nor, on the other hand, does it directly contribute to a metaphysical or a foundational theology. Rather, it offers something like a "grammar" of Christian understanding and practice, both for the individual and the community. I think that the word "grammar" is appropriate, yet it poses a trap for the Anglo-Saxon reader. In keeping with his double Jesuit vocation to the practical and the theoretical–contemplative, and in line with his immediate intellectual precursor, Maurice Blondel, de Lubac's pragmatic bent – his as it were "directions for the regulation of Christian ingenuity" (to echo Descartes) – was entirely bound up with an equal measure of visionary *élan*. The grammar of Christian life was reenvisaged along with a reenvisaging of ontology itself.

This absolutely fundamental aspect of his work can, however, elude the reader. After all, have I not just said that de Lubac did *not* ever construct a metaphysic, nor pursue a speculative dogmatics? So what room for ontology is there here, if he offered neither a philosophical metaphysics, nor a revisionary one based upon faith? The answer is that he implicitly proposed a new sort of ontology – indeed, in a sense a "non-ontology," articulated *between* the discourses of philosophy and theology, fracturing their respective autonomies, but tying them loosely and yet firmly together. (The expression "non-ontology" seems required because, strictly speaking, the word "ontology" was first used in the early seventeenth century to denote a purely philosophical classification of being, cognitively prior to a consideration of the divine.)

This "non-ontology" de Lubac saw as the return of authentic Christian discourse, which could be indifferently described as "Christian philosophy" or as "sacred doctrine." By "non-ontology" (my term) I must stress that I do not mean that de Lubac refused ontology; rather, I mean that he articulated an ontology between the field of pure immanent being proper to philosophy on the one hand, and the field of the revelatory event proper to theology on the other.

This new ontological discourse concerned the paradoxical definition of human nature as intrinsically raised above itself to the "super-nature" of divinity. Since, as we shall see, for de Lubac, all created nature was in some sense oriented to human nature, this paradoxical structure even extended to the constitution of all finite beings as such.

This enigma always ran for de Lubac equally in two opposite directions. The extra-ordinary, the supernatural, which is always manifest within the Creation, is present at the heart of the ordinary: it is "precisely the real," as Bresson put it. On the other hand, the ordinary and given always at its heart points beyond itself, and in spiritual nature aspires upwards to the highest. Grace is always kenotic; the natural is always elevated but not destroyed. Yet, by a symmetrical paradox, the "more" that is demanded by nature can only be received from God as a gift.

After World War II de Lubac further worked out this twofold paradox of grace in the realms of ecclesiology and sacramental theology (*Corpus mysticum*, 1944), biblical exegesis (*Exégèse médiévale*, 1959–64),[7] and in reflection on the evolutionary theory of his friend Teilhard de Chardin. One of the most attractive aspects of de Lubac's personality was the way in which he defended and sought to deepen the position of Teilhard, even though he thought that it at times verged on heresy. This same sympathy for marginal Christian or non-Christian thinkers who might be more profoundly near the heart of Christian truth than more "orthodox" ones, de Lubac applied also to thinkers of the past – to Origen himself, to Pico, to Proudhon, and to Buddhist philosophers.

In the postwar years the battle with the Christian political right had been won, but not that with ecclesiastical conservatism. After initial papal sympathy, neoscholastic forces in his own order brought him under papal suspicion, and following upon the publication of the papal encyclical *Humani Generis* he was forbidden to teach or publish for several years. Gradually, however, he and fellow exponents of what was now dubbed by their enemies the *nouvelle théologie* moved back not simply into favor but into the vanguard. De Lubac played a role in Vatican II, though scholarship now sees its pronouncements as reflecting the unresolved battles and partial compromises among the *nouvelle théologie*, neothomism, and a liberal accommodation to modernity.

Indeed, soon after the council, de Lubac was once more out of favor, this time for his criticism of the bureaucratic diminution of the authority of local bishops.[8] He was only made a cardinal near the end of his life. After *Humani Generis*, outside his historical work, de Lubac comes across as a stuttering, somewhat traumatized theologian, only able to articulate himself in somewhat oblique fragments. He failed to write his proposed Bérulle-like theological–historical–mystical treatise on Christ, and his projected history of mysticism. These two books, supposed to be his central works, are missing from the heart of his *oeuvre*. He himself disarmingly said that some sort of spiritual failing rendered him only able to express his views through the interpretation of those of others.

Yet it is clear that this incapacity became more chronic after *Humani Generis*. De Lubac *did* continue to express certain views in his own voice, yet unlike the earlier case of *Catholicism*, his *crucial* views were now always expressed indirectly through historical interpretations. His reaction to the encyclical remains highly controverted in its significance and (as we shall see below) it is arguable that it involved him in severe theoretical incoherence. Sections of the *Surnaturel* were reworked as *Augustinisme et théologie moderne* and *Le Mystère du surnaturel* (both 1965).[9] In these works, de Lubac, in response to *Humani Generis*, makes certain crucial qualifications to his understanding of the supernatural, most notably in relation to the question of whether there could be a spiritual nature *not* oriented towards grace. He now allows that, formally speaking, there could be. However, the view that this betokens any real shift in opinion is unconvincing. In its general implications this can be summed up as "Christianity is a humanism, else it is misunderstood. On the other hand, secular humanism is the absolute antithesis of the gospel." De Lubac's late work *Pic de la Mirandole* gives the sharpest account of this tension and in its deepened advocacy of a Christian humanism shows no sign whatsoever of a conservative dotage that would stress the ecclesiastical transmission of faith, as opposed to its cultural embeddedness.

De Lubac's increasing indirection reflected both a continuing trauma after 1950, and a continued need for caution, even into his old age, and despite his resonance with some "conservative" ecclesiastical themes: opposition to a debased liturgy, to bureaucratic rule, to obeisance before secular norms.

Yet perhaps there is also a deeper reason for de Lubac's failure (if it is counted such) often to write in his own voice. In effect, the *surnaturel* thesis *deconstructs* the possibility of dogmatic theology as previously understood in modern times, just as it equally deconstructs the possibility of philosophical theology or even of a clearly autonomous philosophy *tout court*. For now, on the one hand, doctrine remains "extrinsic," arbitrary, and incomprehensible unless interpreted in accordance with an innate, radically given human nature. The positive foundations of theology (its *topoi*) are no longer sufficient to determine the range of its conclusions. On the other hand, this "given" human nature is only given to philosophy as paradoxically exceeding itself, and later de Lubac denied that it is ever given at all, with any clarity, for reason alone. Philosophy then appears to require the transcendent supplement of theology, yet theology equally requires the (consequently non-available) foundation of philosophy. As the new-Thomist critics understandably bewailed, de Lubac's paradox looks less like paradox than irresolvable *aporia*. With great accuracy, von Balthasar described de Lubac's writing as occupying a problematic "suspended middle."[10]

Arguably, his literary production reflects this *aporia* in its expansion and untidiness. De Lubac elaborated a "discourse of the supernatural" that was neither dogmatics nor philosophical theology – although he would have insisted that this was a restoration of an Augustinian "Christian philosophy" or a Thomist *Sacra Doctrina*. This usually took the (partially only apparent) form of a historical theology. Such a form was inevitable insofar as a combination of event and sign in continuous process would seem to be the only possible ground that de Lubac's paradoxical discourse can occupy. De Lubac indeed declared that theology should be a mysticism and that mysticism was essentially a reading of signs. In the 1960s he even appealed to the semiotic vogue against humanism: since we are ruled by signs it is as rational to read, with Origen, St. Luke's publicans as angels, as suspiciously to read the angels as publicans – as humanist modernity would encourage. On the other hand, the relative absence of dogmatics and metaphysics in de Lubac also reflects a confinement to *ressourcement* and a failure to proceed to a newly enhanced "speculation" on the part of a thinker at once traumatized and forced to speak always with caution.

The Surnaturel *of 1946*

De Lubac's most famous and controversial book was a somewhat *ad hoc* jamming together of several earlier long articles which nonetheless converged upon a single thesis. Tracing the origin of the terms *hyperphues* and *supernaturalis*, de Lubac shows that, following pagan antiquity, they had first of all simply denoted the realm of the divine above that of known *physis*. The Christian usage referring to an intrusion of the divine within the cosmos and an elevation of humanity was cognate both with a new sense of *pneuma* (after Paul and Origen) to mean the deepest part of the human being that retains a profound ontological kinship with the divine origin, and with an understanding of salvation as deification, or ontological transformation into as close a likeness with God as is consistent with a persisting created status. These conceptual affinities are important, because they show that de Lubac, like Jean Daniélou, wished to stress that the original and authentic Latin understanding of the operation of grace (especially that of Augustine) was not essentially different from the Greek notion of deification.

For de Lubac, a break with such an understanding had only occurred in late medieval and early modern scholasticism: first with Denys the Carthusian and then decisively with Cajetan. The latter inaugurated (for de Lubac) a new reading of Aquinas on grace which has come to dominate all later theology. According to this reading, when Aquinas speaks, in several passages, of a *desiderium naturale* or even a *desiderium naturae* (as de Lubac stresses, against neothomism) in angels and humans for God, this does not denote an "innate" desire in us for the beatific vision, a kind of deep ontological thrust, prior to any reflection. Instead, it merely denotes an "elicited" desire, which is *purely of the will*, although occasioned by a curiosity proper to the intellect. We behold the effects of creation and desire by a mere vague *velleity* fully to know what has caused them. Thus we in no way remotely anticipate, by a sort of ineradicable mystical bias, the true substance of the beatific vision.

But more precisely, Cajetan dealt with Thomas' "natural desire for the supernatural" by an intellectual dividing and ruling. On the one hand, before the call of grace, besides the "elicited" natural desire, there is a mere *potentia obedientiae* of the human to the divine will. On the other hand, an authentic natural desire for the supernatural arises only with the grant of grace – which, it is important to stress, was, even for Cajetan, in *actuality* always present, both before the fall and after it.

Nevertheless, for Cajetan, Aquinas had to be rendered consistent by elaborating a doctrine of "pure nature" which would alone do justice both to his doctrine of the gratuity of grace and his repeated distinction between what is due to humanity by nature and what accrues to him by free supernatural addition. Thus Cajetan, unlike Aquinas, explicitly says that human nature *in actuality* is fully definable in merely natural terms. This means that there can be an entirely natural and adequate ethics, politics, and philosophy and so forth. Man might even offend the moral law, and yet not be directly guilty of sin.

All later scholasticism rang changes upon these themes, with no essential dissent, right down to the early twentieth century. De Lubac, however, along with several others at the time, denied in *Surnaturel* that this was a true reading of Aquinas. The angelic doctor's position on this issue remains today an interpretive crux, for no merely adventitious reasons – as will presently be explained.

In his historical tracing of the meaning of the word "supernatural," de Lubac further noted that, despite the specifically Christian shift in its range of implication, the essential contrast, up until the High Middle Ages, remained one between *natural* and *moral* and not *natural* and *supernatural*. The former usage though, de Lubac argued, itself reflected the authentic new Christian sense of the notion of the super-natural. For on the one hand there was created *nature*; on the other hand there was created *spirit*, which was free, and intellectually reflexive ("personal"). This "moral" realm was in some sense not just created; it bore a more radical imprint of divinity: the *imago dei*.

For de Lubac, what undoubtedly upset the reign of the natural/moral schema was the irruption of Aristotelianism. Whereas neoplatonism itself in its own way explored a complex boundary between supernatural deity and material nature and so had been readily Christianized by the church fathers, Aristotelianism, even in its Arabic neoplatonized forms (because these were specifically philosophical, not theological), tended to insist that human nature could be adequately grasped as belonging to a natural cosmos, and with the help of a strictly analytic rather than intuitive reason. Even where rational contemplation passed over into an intuitive grasp of the unity of all, this remained a cosmic and unassisted vision, not a supernatural raising into identity with the first cause.

The question then becomes, was Aquinas able to assimilate the Arabic Aristotle while retaining the older concepts of the supernatural?

For de Lubac, the distinct Aristotelian moment in Aquinas remains subordinate to an Augustinianism blended with Procleanism (mediated by Dionysius and the Arabs). De Lubac explicitly endorses mid-century readings of Aquinas stressing the neoplatonic and Augustinian dimension, while at the same time his *Augustine* is much more humanist and "Thomistic" than the previous run of French tradition.

However, for the alternative neoscholastic construal of the "natural desire of the supernatural," Aquinas represented much more of a watershed and indeed the be-ginning of proper scientific (as opposed to a semi-narrative and rhetorical) theology. For the first time, supposedly, it is clearly allowed by Aquinas and his contempor-aries that there is an autonomous natural sphere comprising all of human activity outside the order of salvation. In this way, intrinsic human dignity and autonomy is allowed to emerge, while conversely and concomitantly the true gratuity of grace stands out along with the unnatural wonder of works of self-forgetting mercy inspired by our gracious elevation into friendship with God. De Lubac's reading seemed, for this outlook, simultaneously to compromise the legitimate domain of the secular *and* the contrasting surprisingness and gratuitousness of the divine works of freedom.

Put this way, it should be clear that, while "neoscholastic" suggests the fusty and obscurantist, this point of view – just because it is so modern and indeed the parent of modernity – runs far more with average contemporary common sense than does the difficult (but paleo-Christian) position of de Lubac.

For the latter, neither humanist autonomy nor sheer external gratuity is desirable. There was a double danger: pure humanism without reference beyond humanity and of the illusory piety of a religion without humanity produced by the neoscholastic understanding of grace. Quite apart from the question of the correct reading of Aquinas, it would be possible to argue that he is accurate in his understanding of the loss of the older Greek/Latin understanding of salvation and grace. It might be held that the attempt to incorporate Aristotle was simply a disaster. Why then did Aquinas matter for de Lubac?

The answer is, in part, that for de Lubac, Aquinas represented the possibility of an East–West synthesis (Augustine plus the Dionysius/Damascene legacy) and even more crucially that the attempt to incorporate Aristotle *was* positive insofar as it meant a deeper reckoning with reflection upon the operations of nature and of this-worldly human behavior. Here again, de Lubac's "paradoxical" doctrine of the supernatural cuts both ways at once. The older sense that *everything* must be viewed in an elevated light loses all cogency and depth if this light cannot ceaselessly shine within dark corners of finite existence newly explored. Without this continued deepening, the elevation would itself lapse back into the extrinsic.

For just this reason, de Lubac ceaselessly favored "science" and theological dialogue with science. This is in part why he liked Origen: he admired his literal concern with place, time, season, and measurement. This is also why he later celebrated Cusa and Bérulle's attempt spiritually to respond to the new heliocentric cosmology; it is finally why he spent so much time reflecting, alongside Teilhard, on the import of evolutionary theory.

And it is for this reason that the compatibility of the older sense of the supernatural with the new incorporation of Aristotle mattered for de Lubac. It is as if for him (and quite legitimately) Aquinas was an early Renaissance as much as he was a medieval figure: concerned to integrate into the Christian synthesis a new interest in nature and in urban civilization.

Somewhat conflating de Lubac with Henri Bouillard, whose work he knew well, one can summarize his view of Aquinas on the supernatural as follows. First of all, as we have seen, grace for Aquinas was not extrinsic, since it was not a *miracle*: as such it neither interrupted nor simply added to the order of nature; rather, it intrinsically completed it. Secondly, neither for angels nor men was there any stage of nature that might be qualified as impervious to sin, as incapable of this condition (as the neoscholastics often thought, especially for angels) or, at the opposite extreme, *if* involved in sin, then totally destroyed by it – as if to be "natural" equated with "being sinless." All of spiritual nature is permeated by *freedom*, and freedom as such is a relation to divine law and the ultimate divine end. Thirdly, the natural desire of the supernatural in us cannot be merely elicited, because Aquinas says in the *Summa contra Gentiles* that we are drawn to the beatific vision in *exactly the same way* that every creature is moved by God towards some sort of unity with God. It is simply that we as *intellectual* creatures are moved in an intellectual way towards an intellectual union. Angels and humans *as spirits* are innately called to the beatific vision. The curiosity instigated by created effects is itself an erotic curiosity; while inversely the "elicited" desire to know God is itself a cognitive desire. De Lubac always insisted that the "will" in humanity was no faculty, but an integral expression of personhood: of will, intellect, and feeling.[11]

According to this conception of spirit, God, for Aquinas, is in the soul as the object of an (ontological) operation is in the operator. The natural orientation to the supernatural therefore indicates the presence of the divine to us always in the depths: our latent mystical condition. This is so proper to our nature that de Lubac asked, in the fourth place, why, if grace is a kind of superadded extra and there can be nature without sin, a knowing refusal of grace should, for the entire tradition, incur the *poena damni*?

In the fifth and final place, de Lubac argued that, for Aquinas, the natural desire for the supernatural could not, in divine justice, be disappointed, without violating the Aristotelian principle that a natural impulse to an end cannot (unless abnormally) be frustrated: *Desiderium naturale nequit esse inane.*

Just as de Lubac linked the loss of the true account of the supernatural to the loss of teleology, so he also linked it to the rise of a univocal ontology and a merely semantic account of analogy sundered from a metaphysic of existential participation. De Lubac insisted that analogy concerned the range of *judgment* of a soul participating in divine spirit, not simply the range in meaning of a linguistic concept.

This link to debates concerning analogy is not accidental. In his book on Barth, von Balthasar brought together de Lubac's account of the supernatural with Erich Przywara's restoration of the *analogia entis* against both a liberal theology starting from a human foundation below, and a Barthian commencement with a revelation over-against a nature at once utterly depraved and merely passively open to the divine (in the sense of a passivity "opposed" to human activity, not a radical passivity with respect to God in the heart of the active itself).[12] In the case of both refusals, one has to do with a "suspended middle" and a non-ontology, since both analogy and the supernatural belong neither to natural theology nor to doctrine, while at the same time they belong to both and encompass both. Natural analogies for God remotely anticipate even the divine essence, while the discourse of grace must perforce still deploy natural analogues.

Nevertheless, considerable obscurities remain. Is the natural desire of the supernatural *already* the working of grace? In that case, why is it a natural desire? But if it is not already grace at work, is there not an *exigency* for grace on the part of human nature, which suggests that it unfolds as if from a seed, rather than arriving from without? And if the cosmos returns to God more fully through spirits, did God *have* to create spirits? Is it truly inevitable that the latter are oriented to the beatific vision, given the continuity of intellect with the function of the animal soul after Aristotle? Finally, if the orientation to grace is simply the mode taken by createdness in the intellectual creature, what becomes of the distinction between the *datum optimum* of creation on the one hand, and the *donum perfectum* of grace on the other?

All these questions continued to haunt de Lubac for long after he had seen the back of the Gestapo and the secular power of his Catholic Rightist opponents.

Around Humani Generis

De Lubac had to clarify, at one end of his problematic, the relation between the natural desire for the supernatural and the actual historical offer of grace (even if he took this, with the tradition, as always already begun – as the uninterrupted mode of divine action – immediately after the fall and as mediated to all humans by typological anticipation).[13] But at the other end, he also had to clarify the issues of *natura pura*. As we have seen from the quotation in the introduction, *Humani Generis* challenged him to explain whether or not there could really be *no* spiritual existence outside the destiny of supernatural beatitude. Already, in the essay "The Mystery of the Supernatural" written before the encyclical (but perhaps anticipating its imminence), de Lubac conceded (or alternatively made explicit) that in theory God could have created a cosmos without spiritual creatures; that he could have created spiritual creatures without a natural orientation to the supernatural; and finally that the latter in no way obligates grace.

It is clear (despite all round evasion of the point) that *Humani Generis did* entertain the notion of an identifiable pure nature. For its claim is that only the supposition of the possibility of the creation of purely natural spirits preserves the gratuity of grace – as opposed to what belongs intrinsically to human nature. For de Lubac, the supposition was weakly regulative in the sense that it guarantees that God is not by alien necessity the God of grace. But, for Pius XII, it was more strongly regulative in that it serves to distinguish God's gracious action from his creative action. Grace is gratuitous because it gives to us what by no means belongs to us by nature – nature here including such things as the capacity to walk, the power of speech, and the tendency to political organization which we can readily identify as innate and universal.

De Lubac denies that the thesis of pure nature can guarantee the gratuity of grace. In one of the most crucial passages in his entire *oeuvre* he deals, in the original essay (which is superior), with this point in terms of the logic of the *gift* and relates this directly to the Heideggerean–Gilsonian question of the logic of *existence*.[14]

The neothomists, de Lubac implies, think in terms of God and creatures as individual beings on the same plane, either competitively jostling with each other or forming compacts to specify respective spheres of influence. They forget (as Gilson has now reminded them) that God is *esse* itself, not an *ens* but the eminent reality of all *entia*.[15] As such he never properly speaking interacts with creatures. But this has implications for the logic of the gift. We imagine that the gratuitous needs to be contrasted with the obligatory or the inherent; yet this only applies to the inter-actions between beings in the ontic realm. In the realm of the ontological difference, of the creative emergence of *entia* from *esse*, gratuity arises before necessity or obligation and does not even require this contrast in order to be comprehensible. The creature as creature is not the recipient of a gift; it *is* this gift. The same applies to a spiritual creature: as spirit, he does not receive a gift; he is this gift of spirit. Since there is no preceding recipient, the spirit is the gift of a gift to a gift and the gift of giving oneself to oneself, which is the only way consciously to *live being a gift* and so to be spirit. To receive spirit, according to de Lubac, is always to be con-scious of partial reception: one knows that one is not all of possible knowing and willing and feeling and moreover that, since our share of these things *is* what we are, we do not really command them, after the mode of a recipient of possessions. Hence to will, know, and feel is to render gratitude, else we would refuse ourselves as constituted as gift. Such gratitude to an implied infinite source can only be, as gratitude, openness to an unlimited reception from this source, which is tantamount to a desire to know the giver. In this way, for de Lubac, the opening to the question of being of the intellectual creature (what Heidegger called *Dasein*) is at the same time the gratitude of spirit to the unknown giver, the desire further to understand this giver and thereby to comprehend and receive better his mysterious gift. In *Les Chemins de Dieu*, de Lubac summed up his linking of the Gilsonian problematic of *esse* with his own problematic of the *surnaturel* (or of *espirit*) as follows: "Intelligence is the faculty of being because spirit is the genuine capacity for God."[16]

Hence, for de Lubac – and those who have elaborated him on this point, especially Claude Bruaire – the logic of spirit as gift governs both the realm of nature and the realm of grace and the hinge between them that is the mystery of the supernatural. Were one, says de Lubac, to allow the thesis of pure nature, no gratuity of grace would thereby be established, but only the kind of gratuity proper to a this-worldly ontic gift offered to an already present and "ungiven" recipient. This model, however, cannot reach radical divine ontological gratuity.

The supposition of an actual identifiable pure nature in fact ruins the articulation of divine gratuity and can historically be shown to have done so. The gift of deification is guaranteed by *no* contrast, not even with Creation, never mind nature. How could it be, since like the Creation, it is the gift of a gift to a gift which, in this spiritual instance, gift then gives to itself in order to sustain its only nature? How could it be guaranteed by contrast, since the gift of deification is so much in excess of Creation that it entirely includes it? In the ultimate experience of the supernatural which orients it, namely the beatific vision, our entire being is transfigured by the divine light. Here we *become* the reception of this light and there is no longer any "natural" recipient of this reception. But this ensures, and does not destroy, radical gratuity. This is perhaps the subtle heart of de Lubac's theology. In these *loci*, de Lubac inaugurated a new discourse of the spirit as gift which he may well have seen as more satisfactory than the older language of the supernatural (he at least once indicated that this could not really do justice to the paradox of grace).[17] This discourse, if it deals with the middle that is suspended between nature and grace, does not itself belong either to philosophy or theology (as Bruaire's work tends to show). In accordance with this, de Lubac stated in *The Mystery of the Supernatural* that the natural desire for the supernatural could itself, though "natural," only fully be recognized by faith and not by reason alone.[18]

The supernatural in relation to de Lubac's other theological thematics

De Lubac's other significant theological writings on other topics bear out the idea that he saw the paradox of grace as equally the paradox of culture and of human history. We can see this in three specific instances: evolution, scriptural exegesis, and ecclesiology.

In all three cases, as von Balthasar well points out, de Lubac follows the logic of a later and essential addition that nonetheless arrives from above as a gift and does not unfold ineluctably from below. So, in the first instance, with Teilhard, he reads the early stages of evolution not so much as teleologically directed to the later ones but rather as "typologically" foreshadowing them. What to atheist eyes might then seem the merely chance and adventitious in later "random" mutation, is rather to the theologian the sign of a completion in some sense "required" by what went before, but nonetheless supplied as a surprising gift.[19]

The same logic governs the traditional "fourfold" exegesis, beginning with Origen.[20] Literal meanings foreshadow, but do not logically entail, higher "mystical" meanings or later "eschatological" ones. In insisting upon traditional allegory, de Lubac continued his battle against extrinsicism. Christ's human nature could not exhibit through divine personification the divine idiom unless the literal events of his life were doubled by an allegorical summation of all of the Old Testament and indeed all foregoing reality.[21] Only the metanarrative level of allegory, which links events beyond causal connection, sustains the narrative coherence relevant to and constitutive of Christianity as such. (This is one reason why de Lubac exalts the allegorizing Erasmus above Luther and Calvin.) This allegorical narrative situates us within the world text (not, as for much Protestantism, hermeneutically outside it as "interpreters"), which we must continue to write through moral tropological performance, whose reaction to evil is only sustained in its goodness by a transmoral looking towards an anagogic plenitude of meaning beyond good and evil (because purely good) that is at once personal and mystical and collective and eschatological. (The assertion of the primacy of the mystical over the moral is exhibited elsewhere to be de Lubac's creative reaction to Nietzsche and to Buddhism.)[22]

On the other hand, in accordance with the paradox of the supernatural, the movement of inspired reading is not entirely spiritual, or forwards and upwards. To suppose this would be to commit the Joachite error of spirit escaping from historical form: an error which de Lubac deemed to be especially heinous.[23] Every allegorizing exegesis also points backwards: if baptism "fulfills" the crossing of the Red Sea it does not *supersede* the latter, but in part can *only* be expounded in terms of the latter. For allegory to work and be renewed we are always returned to the literal – just as, for the mystical path to be taken, we are always returned to the social, political, and ecclesial. In the literal resides the springs of spiritual plenitude, even though there is no exigency for the latter, just as the supernatural always eventuates as the fulfillment of the natural. The more exceeding the height, the greater the echo of the resounding deeps.

De Lubac confirms that his attitude here is that of the tradition by showing that, from Origen onwards, a "scientific" interest in the history of the Bible – in date, time, place, authorship, etc. – could naturally go along with, and even reinforce, the interest in spiritual meaning. Accordingly, de Lubac hoped for a new future synthesis of biblical criticism with literary sensibility. The same structure – down-to-up-and-down-again, back-to-forward-and-back-again – is seen in de Lubac's ecclesiology, which is almost as central to his *opus* as the *surnaturel* thematic. Crucial to the linkage of the two is de Lubac's denial that an Augustinian integration of nature and grace encouraged any drift towards papalist theocracy and politicization of the spiritual in the later Middle Ages. To the contrary, de Lubac shows that Giles of Rome's advocacy of papal coercive power was linked with an Averroism that construed even spiritual power in quasi-physical terms of a more intense literal force. By contrast, the Augustinian perspective saw the power of the church as strictly spiritual and suasive, not as having any even indirect authority to intervene in civil coercive legality – for example to depose a head of state and promulgate a civil law. (De Lubac arguably exaggerates this, and certainly – in understandable reaction to the Catholic right-wing *intégristes* – fails fully to grasp the notion of the church as a replete society in Augustine's *Civitas Dei*.) However, even though the church's authority was spiritual, its relevance stretched everywhere and it could have a view on even the smallest particulars. This, for de Lubac, distinguishes Augustinian integration from later notions of an autonomous secular sphere where ecclesial interference might extend only to the laying down of general principles.

Here then also, human social nature in its entirety can only be judged rightly in the light of the supernatural, but the latter is not a sort of additional "something" operating a theocratic usurpation of natural human debate and action.

Nor is the authority of grace within the church something extrinsic and invisible, in contrast to visible church structures which can be justified on merely rational principles (often a post-Tridentine view). Instead, it arrives intrinsically, in the symbolism and liturgy of the Eucharist which "makes" the church. Once again, authority here only arises from above (whether the Episcopal hierarchy or the scriptures) and the future by returning us also to the below and to the past for legitimation.

The Eucharist, up to 1300 or so, remained, according to de Lubac, less a derivation from clerical power and a present miraculous spectacle than a re-presentation of the historical body of Christ.[24] The supernaturally spiritual was here not temporally prior, but rather first arose in the temporal mirror of individual spiritual digestion of eucharistic meaning. And again, this elevated moment was not for now to be persisted in, as its "mysticism" only foreshadowed the collective mystical *eschaton*. After internal absorption comes once again the external, this time in the mode of the meritorious building up of the body of Christ which further realizes the eucharistic repetition of Christ's literal historicity. Authority in the church is therefore a hierarchical flow through time, not an alien imposition from a removed space in the present – whether this be the Counter-Reformation papacy or the typed, bound, and sealed scriptures, bare of all commentary, promulgated by the Reformers.

The Limit and the Renown of Henri de Lubac

The drastic implications of Henri de Lubac's thought have only gradually come to light. Despite the indirectness and fragmentary character of his work, despite even his failure "to do theology" or "to do philosophy," his influence has now outlasted that of many once-famous names. Arguably, he is, along with Sergei Bulgakov, one of the two truly great theologians of the twentieth century.

Yet the lacunae in his work were partly shaped by his battles with authority. Is there not some contradiction here between his and von Balthasar's formal capitulation to papal authority on the one hand, and their ecclesiology on the other, which stressed the primacy of the sacramental influence of the bishops as eucharistic mediators? Also with de Lubac's acknowledgment that papal power in the Middle Ages was falsely and permanently directed into an overly judicial and non-spiritual direction? And is there not some link to be made here with a failure to tackle the question of patriarchy and the rule of a male hierarchy? This question is not raised extrinsically, out of mere obeisance to fashion.

For latterly, both thinkers were wont to link the questions of the laity and of the church with the question of the "feminine." Both of them adopted dualist models of the church, distinguishing between a lay, receptive, mystical, cultural "Marian" aspect and a more legal, regulative, intellectual, abstract, "Petrine" aspect.

Does not this duality ruin the inner structure of de Lubac's fundamental thought regarding the supernatural? If "the eternal feminine" is close to the natural desire for the supernatural, then it should be something paradoxically passive–active, and radically passive only in the sense that the most active human action is passive in relation to God. The Petrine function should also be, *as such*, Marian, in that, at the heart of its shaping activity, it is also to do with a receptive giving birth again to Christ in the Eucharist, from whence (according to de Lubac) flows the body of the church. If there is, indeed, a sheerly "seminal" aspect, then this has more to do with non-human word and sacrament "flowing into" the church and informing all levels of its hierarchy, which are in various degrees and at various times passive–active. A distinct "passive" dimension to the church sounds all too like a kind of collective "supernatural existential" awaiting the extrinsic impact of male seminal authority.

If, for de Lubac, the supernatural is ultimately the "eternal feminine" and the aporetic heart of creation itself as not God/created God, then it should follow that that which is Marian is not simply receptive, but "actively receptive," just as the Mary of traditional annunciation pictures receiving the angel is also the Mary actively interpreting the scriptures which she peruses. Moreover, this aporetic heart is itself the showing forth outside of God of the heart of God as the interplay of donative difference. This interplay, this essence, is also the active/passive (infinitely dynamic yet infinitely replete) *Sophia* which names the Christian Godhead (in its unified essence) as "goddess."

De Lubac belonged to a particular generation and within that generation he was incomparable. Yet this generation scarcely prepared him to deal with all the many dimensions of patriarchal authority that I have indicated above. Nevertheless, the radicalism of his own account of the supernatural suggests that it must be faced more critically than he ever imagined.

This issue aside, it is fair to say that contemporary Catholic theology, if it is to avoid both a liberalism and a conservatism that are predicated on the idea of an autonomous pure nature, needs to recover the authentic and more radical account of the natural desire of the supernatural as offered by de Lubac, both early and late in his career.

Notes

1 Aristotle, *Ethics* iii. 3, cited by Aquinas at *Summa Theologiae* 1–11 Q.5 a4 ad 1.

2 Cited by Lawrence Feingold, *The Natural Desire to see God according to St. Thomas and His Interpreters* (Rome: Apollinare Studi, 2001), p. 628.

3 *Humani Generis* in *The Papal Encyclicals 1939–58*, ed. Claudia Carlen (Raleigh, NC: McGrath, 1981), pp. 175–85, 26.

4 Cited by P. Georges Chantraine, SJ in his article "Le Surnaturel: discernement de la pensée catholique selon Henri de Lubac" in *Revue Thomiste, Surnaturel* special issue, Jan.–June 2001, 31–50.

5 *Catholicism: Christ and the Common Destiny of Man*, trans. Lancelot C. Sheppard (London: Burns and Oates, 1937).

6 Henri de Lubac, *Surnaturel: études historiques* (Paris: Desclée de Brouwer, 1991).

7 Henri de Lubac, *Corpus mysticum: l'eucharistie et l'eglise au moyen age* (Paris: Aubier-Montaigne, 1949). A translation of this work into English is in progress. Henri de Lubac, *Exégèse médiévale: les quatres sens de l'écriture* (Paris: Aubier, 1940). This is in four volumes. The first two volumes have been translated into English (with the other two projected) as *Medieval Exegesis: The Four Senses of Scripture*, trans. Mark Sebanc, Vols. 1 and 2 (Grand Rapids, MI/Edinburgh: Eerdmans/T. and T. Clark, 1998 and 2000).

8 Von Balthasar, *The Theology of Henri de Lubac: An Overview* (San Francisco: Ignatius, 1991), pp. 113–14.

9 Henri de Lubac, *Augustinianism and Modern Theology*, trans. Rosemary Sheed (London: Geoffrey Chapman, 1967).

10 Von Balthasar, *The Theology of Henri de Lubac*, p. 15. Von Balthasar's summary here is wonderfully accurate: "De Lubac soon realized that his position moved into a suspended middle in which he could not practice any philosophy without its transcendence into theology, but also any theology without its essential inner structure of philosophy." The question is, did von Balthasar himself to some degree see such suspension as an *aporia* that froze all discourse? Does he always remain in this suspension, or does he himself practice some philosophy before theology and some theology in a "mythical" mode beyond philosophy? See the discussion below.

11 Henri de Lubac, *Pic de la Mirandole* (Paris: Aubier-Montaigne, 1974), p. 171. De Lubac says here, admiringly, that for Pico freedom was "the deep substance of humanity" rather than a faculty and that his radical sense of human liberty was in no way akin to that of late scholastic voluntarism.

12 Hans Urs von Balthasar, *The Theology of Karl Barth*, trans. John Drury (New York: Holt, Rinehart, and Winston, 1971).

13 *Catholicism*, 194. Unbelievers "will be able . . . to obtain . . . salvation by virtue of the mysterious bonds that unite them to believers." See also John Milbank and Catherine Pickstock, *Truth in Aquinas* (London: Routledge, 2001), p. 39.

14 *The Mystery of the Supernatural*, trans. Rosemary Sheed (New York: Crossroads/Herder and Herder, 1998), pp. 218–99.

15 See Etienne Gilson, *Letters to Henri de Lubac* (San Francisco: Ignatius, 1986).

16 *The Discovery of God*, trans. Alexander Dru (New York: P. J. Kennedy, 1960), p. 75.

17 Henri de Lubac, *Atheisme et sens de l'homme* (Paris: Aubier-Montaigne, 1968), p. 95; von Balthasar, *Henri de Lubac*, p. 68.

18 *The Mystery of the Supernatural*, pp. 274–5.

19 *Teilhard de Chardin: The Man and his Meaning*, trans. René Hague (New York: Hawthorn, 1965).

20 See *Medieval Exegesis*. For a summation, see Henri de Lubac, *Scripture in the Tradition*, trans. Luke O'Neill (New York: Herder and Herder, 1968).

21 *Medieval Exegesis*, Vol. 2, 41–7.

22 See, for this thematic, "Tripartite Anthropology" in *Theology in History* (San Francisco: Ignatius, 1996).

23 Henri de Lubac, *La Posterité spirituelle de Joachim de Flore*, 2 vols. (Paris: Aubier-Montaigne, 1979–81). De Lubac's last work, written in his eighties, therefore concerned the danger of detaching *espirit* from both nature and the word. The simultaneous attack upon secular utopianism and over-spiritualizing pietism sustains his central paradox to the end. It also complements his genealogy of the pernicious effects of "pure nature" with a complementary genealogy of the equally deleterious consequences of "pure spirit."

24 See *Corpus mysticum*.

Bibliography

Primary

Augustinianism and Modern Theology, trans. Rosemary Sheed (London: Geoffrey Chapman, 1967).

Catholicism: Christ and the Common Destiny of Man, trans. Lancelot C. Sheppard (London: Burns and Oates, 1937).

Corpus mysticum: l'eucharistie et l'eglise au moyen âge (Paris: Aubier: Montaigne, 1949).

The Discovery of God [Les Chemins de dieu], trans. Alexander Dru (New York: P. J. Kennedy, 1960).

The Drama of Atheist Humanism, trans A. M. Riley et al. (San Francisco: Ignatius, 1995).

The Eternal Feminine, trans René Hague (London: Collins, 1971).

Exégèse médièvale: les quatres sens de l'écriture, 4 vols. (Paris: Aubier, 1940). The first two volumes are translated into English as *Medieval Exegesis: The Four Senses of Scripture*, trans. Marc Sebanc (Edinburgh: T. and T. Clark, 1998, 2000).

The Mystery of the Supernatural, trans. Rosemary Sheed (New York: Crossroads/Herder and Herder, 1998).

"Nature and Grace" in *The Word in History: The St. Xavier Symposium*, ed. T. Patrick Burke (London: Collins, 1968).

Paradoxes et mystères de l'église (Paris: Aubier-Montaigne, 1967).

Pic de la Mirandole (Paris: Aubier-Montaigne, 1974).

La Posterité spirituelle de Joachim de Flore, 2 vols. (Paris: Aubier-Montaigne, 1979–81).

Surnaturel: études historiques (Paris: Désclée de Brouwer, 1991).

Teilhard de Chardin: The Man and his Meaning, trans. René Hague (New York: Hawthorn, 1965).

Théologies d'occasion (Paris: Desclée de Brouwer, 1984). This volume contains in particular "Autorité de l'église en matière temporelle" (pp. 217–40).

Theology in History, foreword by Michael Sales (San Francisco: Ignatius, 1996). This volume contains in particular "The Mystery of the Supernatural" (pp. 281–317) and "Tripartite Anthropology" (pp. 117–223).

Secondary

Balthasar, Hans urs von, *The Theology of Henri de Lubac: An Overview* (San Francisco: Ignatius, 1991).

Bouillard, Henri, *Conversion et grace chez Thomas d'Aquin* (Paris: Aubier-Montaigne, 1964).

Boulnois, Olivier, "Surnaturel" in *Dictionnaire critique de théologie*, ed. J.-Y. Lacoste (Paris: PUF, 1998).

Bruaire, Claude, *L'Être et l'ésprit* (Paris: PUF, 1983).

Carlen, Claudia (ed.), "Humani Generis" in *The Papal Encyclicals 1939–58* (Raleigh, NC: McGrath, 1981), pp. 175–85.

Feingold, Lawrence, *The Natural Desire to See God According to St. Thomas and his Interpreters* (Rome: Apollinare Studi, 2001).

Gilson, Etienne, *Letters to Henri de Lubac* (San Francisco: Ignatius, 1986).

Kerr, Fergus, *Immortal Longings* (Notre Dame, IN: Notre Dame University Press, 1997).

—— *After Aquinas: Versions of Thomism* (Oxford: Blackwell, 2002).

Milbank, John and Pickstock, Catherine, *Truth in Aquinas* (London: Routledge, 2001).

Revue Thomiste, special issue *Surnaturel*, Jan.–June 2001.

Rowlands, Tracey, *Culture and the Thomist Tradition after Vatican II* (London: Routledge, 2003).

Karl Rahner

Karen Kilby

Introduction: Life

Karl Rahner is one of the giants of twentieth-century theology. He wrote prolifically, lectured widely, and exerted a major influence on theology within and beyond
the Roman Catholic Church. He had a tremendous intellectual reach, writing on
the full range of theological topics and a good deal more, and produced a body of
work consistently marked by a distinctive and often highly creative combination of
fidelity to the church and honest engagement with modern thought.

Rahner's life was, on his own account, rather dull. He was born in Freiburg im
Breisgau in Germany, into a middle-class Roman Catholic family, one of seven
children. Upon finishing his schooling at 18, he entered the Jesuit order, and
remained a Jesuit until his death in 1984. Whereas for some joining a religious order
has been a radical act (Thomas Aquinas' family is said to have imprisoned him for a
year in an attempt to dissuade him from becoming a Dominican), for Rahner it was
undramatic: he was following in the footsteps of his elder brother Hugo, and later in
life claimed not to remember the precise reasons he took this step.

After completing the Jesuit novitiate in 1924, Rahner spent most of the next 12
years studying philosophy and theology, and then more philosophy and more theology. Following the usual Jesuit pattern, he began with three years of philosophical
study and then, after a two-year period teaching Latin, did four years of theology.
The theology that Rahner learned during these years was the neoscholasticism
dominating Roman Catholic seminaries of the time, and one can go a long way
towards understanding him by understanding the critical and complex relationship
he retained to this system of thought throughout much of his career. After these
years of theology there followed a year of tertianship – the final year of a Jesuit's
formation – and then Rahner was sent back to Freiburg, the place of his birth, to do
a PhD in philosophy.

The intention of Rahner's superiors, in sending him for the PhD, was to prepare
him to teach the history of philosophy to Jesuits in training. Accordingly, Rahner
wrote a thesis, eventually published as *Spirit in the World*, on an aspect of the
thought of Thomas Aquinas. His official supervisor was Martin Honecker, but a

more significant influence was Martin Heidegger, to whose seminar Rahner belonged during his time in Freiburg (1934–6). The thesis, which interpreted Aquinas through the lens of Kant and post-Kantian thinkers, and which showed some influence from Heidegger, was failed by Honecker. Rahner's future had however already been rethought by his superiors, who wished him to replace a retiring Jesuit and teach theology at the University of Innsbruck. Here, within the year, he produced a successful PhD in theology, and in 1937 began teaching.

The arrival of the Nazis in Austria in 1938 disrupted teaching in Innsbruck, however. Rahner spent a number of years in Vienna, working in the diocesan Pastoral Institute, and the final year of the war as the parish priest of a Bavarian village. In 1948 he returned to Innsbruck, and there began a period of great theological productivity. This was also a time during which Rahner's theology came under official suspicion at a number of points. He was refused permission to publish a long book on Mary in 1951, forbidden to discuss the issue of concelebration in 1954, and told in 1962 that all his writings would have to be read by a Roman censor.

The opening of the Second Vatican Council later in 1962 marked a kind of turning point in Rahner's career, at least as regards his standing in the church. Rahner was brought to the Council as a private advisor of Cardinal König of Vienna, and given the official role of *periti*, theological expert. All talk of a special censor for his writings ceased. He was tremendously active during the period of the Council, and is generally regarded as having had a significant influence on many of its documents. This is difficult to measure precisely, given the complexity of the process by which these documents emerged, and given that elements from Rahner's theology which make an appearance in them can often also be traced to other sources. Rahner himself was agnostic about the exact nature of his impact on the Council. Nevertheless, by the end of the Second Vatican Council Rahner had undeniably emerged as a major theologian, and he had moved from the position of a somewhat suspect theological figure to become the leading representative of what was (at least for a time) a new mainstream.

In 1964, during the period of the Council, Rahner left Innsbruck to take up a chair in Christianity and the Philosophy of Religion in the philosophy faculty of the University of Munich. He moved again in 1967 to the University of Münster, where he remained until his retirement in 1971. He continued to lecture and write over the next 13 years, and died in 1984.

In many cases one can go a long way towards understanding a thinker's work by explaining its relationship to one or two other figures, whether these serve as the source of inspiration or as that which must be reacted against (or both). One thinks of Kierkegaard in relation to Hegel, for instance, or Barth in relation to Schleiermacher, or Balthasar in relation to Barth. For Rahner, however, there is no particular intellectual predecessor who serves either as an obvious foil or as a chief inspiration. Rahner was, as we have seen, a student of Heidegger for a time, and one can find a certain amount of Heideggerian language and concepts and even some Heideggerian strategies in his work. But these are best seen as relatively *ad hoc* borrowings rather than as a systematic adaptation of Heidegger's thought (in any of its periods) for theology. It is true, again, that lying behind *Spirit in the World*, Rahner's first major work and his most philosophical effort, is the influence of Joseph Maréchal, a Belgian Jesuit philosopher of the previous generation. From Maréchal, who has come to be known as the father of Transcendental Thomism, Rahner learned to read Aquinas through the lens of Kant and post-Kantian philosophy, but it would be a mistake to draw the conclusion that the influence of Maréchal was decisive for Rahner's thought taken as a whole. One can place *Spirit in the World* alongside a number of other works of the so-called Transcendental Thomists, and see them as developing in different ways the project of Maréchal, but one has to be careful about assuming that this is therefore an adequate characterization of all of the subsequent work of a man who would later insist that he was not a philosopher and had no philosophy.

There are a number of intellectual figures who played a role in the development of Rahner's thought, then – Aquinas, Kant, Maréchal, Heidegger – but no one who can be singled out as really decisive. Indeed, if one is to point to a single "other" who has shaped Rahner and against whom he struggles, it should perhaps not be any individual, but, as we hinted above, the neoscholasticism that predominated during his years of formation.[1] Neoscholasticism was an intellectual system which claimed allegiance to the thought of the Middle Ages, and of Thomas Aquinas in particular. It was fundamentally hostile towards modern (Kantian and post-Kantian) movements in philosophy. In the second half of the nineteenth century neo-scholasticism had succeeded in defeating its rivals and establishing its hegemony as *the* accepted form of Roman Catholic thought. It remained in the ascendency for several generations, and became a comprehensive and quite tidy philosophical and theological scheme, where the questions were well defined and well understood, the range of acceptable answers could be specified, and the manner in which the answers were to be supported and defended was clear.

Rahner was not alone in having objections to this self-enclosed system of philosophy and theology. A number of thinkers in the previous generation had in various ways struggled against it, though they had yet to make a large impact. Hans Urs von Balthasar, Rahner's contemporary, complained that this theology was dry as dust and was *reported* to have stopped up his ears during lectures in order to read Augustine unhindered. What is significant about Rahner, however, is that he did not, like Balthasar, simply set aside neoscholasticism in order to do theology in a different way. Instead, Rahner worked to a large extent with the system, probing and questioning it, seeking to bring it into contact with modern philosophy, and to open it up from within to the modern world.

Survey

Rahner's first major publication was *Spirit in the World*, the product of his doctoral work in philosophy and a ferociously difficult piece of writing.[2] His next book, based on lectures given in 1937, was *Hearer of the Word*; here, Rahner outlined an understanding of philosophy of religion as the study of the conditions of the possibility of the reception of revelation – what must be true about us if we are to be beings capable of hearing a possible revelation from God? These two works are often taken to provide the "philosophical foundations" of all that follows, though Rahner himself distanced himself from them to some degree (he referred to them in an interview, for instance, as "lop-sided works of my youth"). If, as a number of commentators have done, one understands *Spirit in the World* and *Hearer of the*

Word as the basis upon which the later work is built, and as therefore to a large degree determining the shape of Rahner's theology, one has a quick way of getting a handle on Rahner, but one also runs the risk of reading him reductively, of missing the real interest of much of his work. Certainly, many of the same instincts and concerns that are to be found in Rahner's later theology make an appearance in these philosophical works, and certainly Rahner will later make use of some of the philosophical material he has developed in *Spirit in the World*, but it is inadvisable to read the theology as founded upon or in any simple way flowing from the philosophy.

Rahner's characteristic approach as a theologian was not to write large tomes setting out comprehensive treatments of theology as a whole, nor even to attempt to treat individual doctrines exhaustively. Instead, he wrote primarily, and was at his best in the writing of, relatively short essays, essays probing particular questions from particular angles. For this reason the single most important place to look for Rahner's theology is in the *Theological Investigations*, a collection of essays running to 23 volumes in English. Rahner's output was not however exhausted by these 23 volumes. Some of his essays in pastoral theology are collected in *Mission and Grace*, which appears in three volumes in English. In addition, Rahner wrote eight volumes of his own and eight volumes with a co-author in a series entitled *Quaestiones Disputatae*. *Quaestiones Disputatae* was a series which Rahner himself was involved in founding and editing, a series aimed at renewing the tradition of vigorous debate within Roman Catholic theology, and Rahner's own contributions, though a little longer than the characteristic essay of the *Theological Investigations*, are once again probing explorations of particular questions, rather than exhaustive treatments of historical or dogmatic themes.

One exception to this general pattern is *Foundations of Christian Faith* – here, in a volume published when Rahner was in his early seventies, he comes the closest to summarizing his theology as a whole. Even here, however, there is a particular context and a specific purpose to the work. *Foundations of Christian Faith*, which is subtitled "An Introduction to the Idea of Christianity," offers itself as "a first level of reflection," prior to the division of theology into all of its sub-specialisms, which will enable the student and the reflective Christian to give an intellectually honest justification of their faith. What Rahner is intending to offer here, then, is not a systematic summation of all his theology – though he does draw on, and in some cases simply repeats, a good deal of material that he had developed in other contexts – but a particular experiment in a new genre of theological writing.

In addition to his prolific writing, Rahner did an enormous amount of work as an editor. The *Quaestiones Disputatae* series was only one of a number of major projects he was involved with. In some cases he took over the responsibility for new editions of existing works: in the 1950s he brought out several editions of Denzinger's *Enchiridion Symbolorum*, which contains the texts of official church teaching, and between 1957 and 1965 together with a co-editor he published a new edition of Herder's *Lexicon für Theologie und Kirche*. He also undertook, usually in conjunction with others, major new projects: he was for instance an editor of *Sacramentum Mundi*, and of the *Handbuch der Pastoraltheologie*, and together with Edward Schillebeeckx and others he founded the international journal *Concilium*.

Rahner's bibliography is not only long, it is also wide. Rahner wrote on an enormous number, and an almost whimsical range, of topics. There are few subjects into which he did not stray. Rahner's works include – to mention some themes almost at random – essays on the Trinity, the Incarnation, the church, the sacraments, Mary, angels, indulgences, heresy, the development of doctrine, the diaconate, concupiscence, poetry, childhood, power, leisure, sleep, pluralism, mystery, symbol, old age, death, devotion to the sacred heart of Jesus, devotion to the saints, asceticism, prayer, theological education, eucharistic devotion, Ignatian mysticism, the relationship of Christianity to Marxism, to evolutionary theory, and to psychotherapy, the relationship between nature and grace, between scripture and tradition, between exegesis and theology, between the papacy and the episcopate, and between the Mass and television.

Rahner sometimes liked to describe himself as a theological dilettante, and this was not sheer modesty. It conveys some sense of the freedom of his theological work, and of the fact that he did not usually follow a model of scholarship in which one works in a well-defined field and expounds the whole history of an issue before making one's own contribution. Rahner was also not, essentially, a "systematic" theologian. It is true that his thought has a kind of center – a few interlocking themes to which he returns again and again – and it is true that if one read only *Foundations of Christian Faith* one might be forgiven for supposing he was a highly systematic thinker. But Rahner's essays on particular topics ought not to be read as part of a process of working out a larger system; the essays were occasioned by contemporary theological debates or contemporary pastoral problems, by new pronouncements of church authorities, by invitations to give lectures, lead retreats, or participate in conferences, or simply by Rahner's teaching duties.

Overall, Rahner is a challenging figure to come to terms with: there is the great quantity of his writings, the fact that he wrote across such a broad spectrum of issues, and also the sheer difficulty of his works. In interviews, published prayers, and the writings in his later years, he is more accessible, but on the whole he is among the most daunting of modern theologians to read. The mixture of scholastic categories and the language of modern German philosophy is one reason for this. Another factor is the ecclesial context of his writings. Rahner was a creative and daring thinker. He almost never simply reasserted the common wisdom of his period, and he often challenged the received view. In doing this in a potentially hostile ecclesial environment, he needed to exhibit the orthodoxy of his proposals. So he drew on an immense knowledge of the tradition and of official church teaching to support, hedge, and qualify his assertions. This resulted in rich and nuanced, but also complex, sometimes labyrinthine, sentences and paragraphs.

In spite of the difficulty of his work, it is important to realize that Rahner's fundamental orientation is not abstract or academic, but pastoral. There is a narrow sense of "pastoral" which would describe only some of Rahner's theology – that which is concerned with the specific work a pastor does, with how to organize a parish, preach sermons, counsel individuals, and so on. But there is a broader sense of the word in which almost all of Rahner's theology, even when it is concerned with the Trinity, the Incarnation, the notion of heresy, or the significance for theology of the theory of evolution, is pastoral. A recurring concern of Rahner's work is to confront the ways in which modern people, including "good Catholics," can find Christianity alien, something foreign, something that they cannot make sense of, something which they perhaps accept but which has little to do with them, and to seek to understand anew Christian doctrines and the Christian faith so as to overcome this felt foreignness.

If openness to the world, honesty in confronting difficulties in belief, and the desire to reconceive the Christian faith for the contemporary world sound like the typical virtues and characteristics of a theological liberal, it is important to keep in mind that in Rahner's case these are found in a person profoundly steeped in the tradition, and absolutely committed to being faithful to the teachings of the Roman Catholic Church.

Content

Although Rahner is not fundamentally a system builder, there are certain recurrent, and to some degree interlocking, elements in his thinking. To understand them is to be well equipped for the reading of many of Rahner's essays, though one should beware of the danger of taking these notions, abstracted from particular concrete contexts, as a simple summary of Rahner's theology.

Two closely related ideas that weave their way in and out of many of Rahner's writings are the *Vorgriff auf esse* (often translated as "pre-apprehension of being") and the supernatural existential. Rahner maintains that in every human act of knowing and willing there is a pre-apprehension of infinite being, and therefore of God. God cannot be known directly: God is never the object of an act of knowledge in the way that chairs and tables can be; but when the mind knows some particular object, or wills some finite value, it never *merely* knows or chooses the particular, but is always at the same time reaching beyond it, towards the whole of being, and therefore towards God. The relationship of this *Vorgriff* to the knowledge of particular objects can be conceived with the help of an image drawn from Heidegger – we are aware of infinite being as the *horizon* for our knowledge of particular things – or one drawn from Aquinas – the *Vorgriff* is the *light* which in illumining the individual objects allows our intellect to grasp them. It can also be understood with the help of Kantian terminology: the *Vorgriff* is, according to Rahner, a transcendental condition of the possibility of knowing and willing. Just as for Kant we do not come across time, space, and the categories of the understanding in the world, do not deduce them from experience, but necessarily bring them to experience, so for Rahner we do not discover infinite being in the world nor subsequently deduce it from what we learn of the world; rather, we are unable to have anything to do with the world at all except against the background of this pre-apprehension.

The *Vorgriff* is argued for at some length in *Spirit in the World*, and Rahner makes use of it (sometimes under other names) in a variety of ways in his theological writings. The assertion that there is a *Vorgriff* is clearly a bold one: if Rahner is right, then everyone, whether they describe themselves as agnostic or atheist or indifferent, is actually on some level aware of God. Though Rahner is not involved in proving the existence of God, if he is right no such proof is necessary, since anyone who tries to deny the existence of God is in fact in contradiction with herself.

The "supernatural existential" is closely related, but distinguished from the *Vorgriff* at least in principle. Just as there is (according to Rahner) a universal apprehension of God, so there is also, he holds, a universal experience of grace, or at least of grace as offered.[3]

"Existential" is a term Rahner borrowed from Heidegger; it refers to a fundamental element in human existence, something which is a feature of all our experience rather than one object of experience or one experience among others. This, according to Rahner, is the fundamental character of grace. It is not, or not primarily, something given now and then – the forgiveness of a particular sin, the sudden capacity to overcome a temptation, a particular help in a particular situation, a definitive response to prayer; it is instead an ever-present gift offered to us at such a fundamental and central level that it affects all that we are, and know, and do: "grace . . . always surrounds man, even the sinner and the unbeliever, as the inescapable setting of his existence."[4]

The supernatural existential is *supernatural* in that it takes human beings beyond their nature. It is not something which is an intrinsic part of what it is to be a human being, not something which humanity can claim as its right. This is a rather delicate point, since on Rahner's account human nature has never in fact existed without this supernatural elevation. Human beings *could*, however, have existed on a merely natural level, and so the supernatural existential is genuinely gratuitous, a gift from God beyond the basic gift of creation.

Rahner regards the *Vorgriff*, by contrast, as built into our nature as such – not just built into the way we actually find ourselves to be, our concrete nature, but built into human nature in the abstract theological sense: it is a condition of the possibility of our experience, and without it we would not be human beings at all. The supernatural existential can be thought of as affecting the way in which the *Vorgriff* is experienced – it alters our relation to our horizon. Because of the supernatural existential, God is not just the infinitely distant goal of all our striving, but the goal which, Rahner says, "draws near" and "gives itself." (The images here, it should perhaps be noted, are not easily pinned down: though the goal may give itself, it does not become something *possessed* in our experience, something we can grasp and understand and manipulate like anything else we know. The horizon, even if it draws near, remains the horizon.)

It is worth making clear that in speaking of a universal elevation of human nature, Rahner is not declaring that all are in a state of sanctifying grace and therefore justified. He wants to steer a delicate course, in fact, between maintaining that sanctifying grace is universally present, and everyone is in a state of grace (which would be to say too much), and maintaining that sanctifying grace is universally offered, but *given* only to those who accept the offer (which would be to say too little). His solution is to describe grace as universally present, but present *as offered*. It is, one might say, "there" in all of us, but we have a role in that we accept or reject it, and only if we accept it can we be said to be in a state of sanctifying grace, justified, saved.[5]

It is important to realize that both the supernatural existential itself and its acceptance (or rejection) are according to Rahner "pre-thematic." The supernatural existential can be present without one being reflexively aware of it – this is, one might say, because it lies so deep within us, because it is an existential, not one distinguishable bit of experience among others, but ever-present, impossible to pin down, easily missable. Rahner suggests that his readers should perhaps be able to recognize in their own experience what he is talking about: "If this theological and dogmatic interpretation of [a person's] transcendental experience is offered to him by the history of revelation and by Christianity he can recognize his own experience in it."[6] This is, however, very carefully qualified – the experience itself remains ambiguous and introspection on its own would not enable a person to come to such a conclusion.

Quite closely related to the ideas of the *Vorgriff* and the supernatural existential is the notion of "transcendental experience." To transcend means simply to go beyond: transcendental experience is the experience of going beyond all the things we know and choose and love, even as we are knowing and choosing and loving them – and when we go beyond all particular things, what we go towards is, on Rahner's account, God.

Just as the awareness of God given in the *Vorgriff* is not ever had on its own, apart from our dealings with the world, and just as the experience of grace is not a separate experience among others but an existential, so transcendental experience is not something occurring in isolation. It is always given only in an experience of the concrete, the particular, the finite. Rahner characteristically expresses this point by pairing "the transcendental" with either "the categorical" (the realm of that which can be put into categories, that which can be pinned down and grasped by concepts) or "the historical."

The relationship between the transcendental and the categorical is a recurring theme for Rahner, and two points need to be noted concerning it. First, transcendental experience is not merely an accompaniment to the historical and the categorical. It does not merely happen to be there, riding along the top of our ordinary experience, but is according to Rahner what makes this "ordinary" experience possible in the first place. (This is essentially a transposition into different language of the claim that the *Vorgriff auf esse* is a condition of the possibility of our knowing and willing.) Secondly, Rahner maintains that the transcendental always needs somehow to articulate itself, to express itself, in the categorical. By definition, of course, transcendental experience is that realm of experience where language fails: we have language for objects, for distinguishing one thing from another, for putting things in categories, but not for that which cannot in principle be an object, for that which is beyond all categories, for the infinite horizon within which the distinguishing takes place. And yet transcendental experience cannot simply remain inarticulate, but always seeks expression in the realm of the categorial. The expression will never be wholly adequate, will always in some way fail, but it must always nevertheless be attempted.

The *Vorgriff* and the supernatural existential are also closely related to Rahner's Christology, or at least to some aspects of it. In a discussion of the Incarnation, for instance, Rahner suggests it is possible to go some way towards expressing what is meant by the statement "the Word of God became a human being" by thinking carefully about the meaning of "human being." If it is the nature of the human being to be a kind of infinite openness, always in the encounter with the finite to be striving beyond it towards the infinite, always to be "beings who are referred to the incomprehensible God,"[7] then the normally paradoxical Chalcedonian doctrine comes to seem not quite so difficult. Christ can be seen, on Rahner's account, as the radicalization, the supreme case, of what is true of all human beings. To be human is to transcend all things, to "go beyond" all things towards God: when this transcendence, this "going beyond," is carried to its single, highest, and most radical instance, then in that case to be human simply is to be God. The divinity of Christ, then, can be conceived not as the contradiction of his humanity, but as its ultimate fulfillment.

Rahner's single most famous proposal is that those of other faiths, or of no faith at all, may be considered "anonymous Christians," and his development of this notion also has connections to the ideas of the *Vorgriff* and particularly the supernatural existential. He begins from the fact that Christians believe in the universal salvific will of God on the one hand, and in the necessity of faith in Christ and membership of the church for salvation on the other. How can these be reconciled? If church membership is necessary for salvation then, reasons Rahner, it must be a possibility for all people, and if an explicit church membership is not a real possibility for some people then it follows that there must be some other kind of church membership. Similarly, if faith in Christ is necessary for salvation but explicit, professed faith is not a real possibility for all, then there simply must be something which is *not* explicit and professed and yet which still is faith in Christ. It is when it comes to suggesting how what *must* be the case *can* be the case that Rahner draws on the notion of the supernatural existential. Rahner proposes that individuals who are not professed Christians, who may never have come across Christianity, are nevertheless offered the grace of Christ in the depths of their experience, and may, without ever recognizing it to *be* that, accept it. These then are anonymous Christians.

If the *Vorgriff* and the supernatural existential provide one starting point for exploring a number of Rahner's proposals, his theology of the symbol offers another. A symbol – a real symbol, in any case – is not merely an external sign, according to Rahner: it is intrinsically related to what it symbolizes. One might think of the example (though this is not one that Rahner gives) of a kiss. The kiss as a symbol of love is not simply a pointer, standing in for something essentially different from it, but is intrinsically related to the love; the love expresses itself, and becomes more fully itself, in the kiss. Rahner in fact thinks that all of reality is symbolic, that all being necessarily expresses itself in an "other," and in fact only fully becomes itself, only "comes to itself," in thus expressing itself.

One obvious place where this notion of symbol is useful, and on which in fact it is at least in part based, is the theology of the Trinity. The traditional understanding of the relation of the first and second persons of the Trinity – of the Father to the Son – can be translated neatly into the statement that the Son is the symbol of the Father. Just as a symbol is neither identical with nor simply different from that which it symbolizes, so the Son is distinct from and yet one with the Father. Just as a symbol expresses what it symbolizes, so the "Word" is the self-expression of the Father. And just as a being becomes itself through expressing itself in its symbol, so the Father would not be the Father without the Son, but "is himself by the very fact that he opposes to himself the image which is of the same essence as himself, as the person who is other than himself."[8]

The Incarnation too can be understood in symbolic terms. In the Incarnation God expressed himself exteriorly, and more particularly, expressed "what God wished to be, in free grace, to the world."[9] There can be a tendency, Rahner suggests, to think of the humanity of Christ as a mere instrument of God, a tool which the second person of the Trinity takes up in order to convey a message to the world. In fact, however, Christ's humanity is not just a sign arbitrarily chosen to indicate the presence of God, but a real symbol of God. And it is because of this that Jesus himself (and not just what Jesus says or does) can genuinely be the revelation of God – because the humanity is a symbol of the divinity, Christians can say that in Christ they do not just find some pointer to God, but actually encounter God himself. The fact that the humanity of Christ is the real symbol of God also has profound significance for how we are to think about humanity: human beings are not just something that God happened to choose to create; humanity is "that which 'appears' when in his self-exteriorization [God] goes out of himself into that which is other than he."[10]

Rahner has many things to say about the church – in fact, over half of his publications are on eccelesiology[11] – but one central and significant theme here too draws on the theology of the symbol. The church is itself a symbol: it is the "symbolic reality of the presence of Christ, of his definite work of salvation in the world.[12] The role of the church is to continue over time and in a social form the function of the Incarnation, of making grace tangible and historically definitive, of symbolizing grace. This is what it means to call the church the "body of Christ." The grace which enters history in a definite way and becomes incarnate in Christ in turn needs to be made concrete in a socially organized community. The church is thus, according to Rahner, the fundamental sacrament. Sacraments in the ordinary sense of the word, the seven sacraments, are also of course to be understood symbolically, and they are to be understood as flowing from the nature of the church as sacrament. The sacraments in the ordinary sense of the word are the particular acts in which the primary sacrament, the church, concretely expresses itself. When the church does what is its business to do, namely to make grace concrete and present, to symbolize grace, and when it does this as fully and as formally as possible, then there occurs a sacrament in the usual sense of the word.

Debate

A persistent worry about Rahner is that in his efforts to open up Roman Catholic theology to both modern philosophy and the modern world, and to reformulate Christian doctrine in a way that will make sense to the contemporary person, he runs the risk of losing sight of the particularity, the historical rootedness, and the concrete shape of Christianity, and forcing it into the procrustean bed of an *a priori* anthropology.

This worry lies behind objections on a number of different levels. There has been a good deal of criticism of *Spirit in the World*, Rahner's first book and his major piece of philosophical writing. The legitimacy of Rahner's interpretation of Aquinas has been called into question a number of times, and the arguments of *Spirit in the World*, viewed as philosophical arguments in their own right, have also failed to persuade in a number of quarters. Because many have seen *Spirit in the World* as a "foundational" work, it is often assumed that if Rahner has gone wrong at this point, all of his subsequent theology will be called into question. If one takes a more cautious and complex view of the relationship of this youthful work to Rahner's later essays, however, it is not so clear that philosophical or interpretive weaknesses of *Spirit in the World* need be of such overwhelming significance for his theology.

The same worry has sometimes been expressed as an unease with Rahner's "transcendental method" or transcendental approach to theology: by insisting upon the introduction of a Kantian turn to the subject within theology, Rahner is felt to be pursuing an ultimately reductive project. Though it is in fact not possible to find any one method or technique which unifies all, or even most, of Rahner's writings, Rahner does at times make programmatic statements, insisting for instance that "theology today must be theological anthropology,"[13] and discussing a "method" of transcendental theology.[14] One of the points at which he himself seems to be closest to following this method (the method which, "regardless of the particular area of subject matter in which it is applied ... raises the question of the conditions in which knowledge of a specific subject is possible in the knowing subject himself")[15] is in his proposal of a "transcendental Christology," and this has come under particular criticism.[16] Rahner here begins by asking what must be true about human beings if they are to be capable of hearing of Christ and having faith in Christ – "what are the *a priori* possibilities in man which make the coming of the message of Christ possible." It is in our very nature, he argues, to be searching through history for an "absolute savior." Thus, when we do in fact hear of Christ, we are hearing not of something that is utterly strange to us, that seems to have nothing to do with us. Rahner seems to think one can reconstruct the broad outlines of a Christology in this transcendental mode, including the Chalcedonian formula, and that without such a transcendental Christology traditional Christological formulae are in danger of appearing mythological.[17]

How much weight one gives to worries about the reductive tendencies of Rahner's transcendental approach will be bound up once again with the question of how one construes the overall shape of his *oeuvre*. If one sees it as, in spite of all its variety, essentially promoting *a* vision and *a* system of theology, whose essence is captured by the notion of a transcendental method, and whose apogee is reached in a rendition of Christ as essentially knowable in advance, then the problem of reductionism, of the loss of the concrete and historical particularities of the Christian faith, is likely to seem acute.[18] But, as we have already seen, there is another possibility. Rahner's discussion of transcendental Christology can be viewed simply as one among a number of suggestions he had to make in the area of Christology, and not necessarily the most persuasive; Rahner's comments on the transcendental and anthropological nature of theology are taken to point to *some* of his interests in the particular context of the need to get away from the dry formality and "extrinsicism" of neoscholasticism. Reductionism in this case may still be seen as a danger which Rahner courts from time to time, but not as the fundamental character of a theology which in fact repeatedly begins, not from its own first principles, but from what is concretely given in the faith of the church.

What Rahner has most frequently been criticized for is the theory of the anonymous Christian, and some of these criticisms, particularly insofar as they have come from thinkers such as Henri de Lubac and Hans Urs von Balthasar, reflect once again the concern that Rahner's thought is reductionist. If Christianity can be spoken of as existing in a person apart from any explicit reference to Christ and his cross, then surely it has been evacuated of content: the notion of the anonymous Christian, as Balthasar sees it, undermines Christianity as a distinctive, particular form of life which exists as a response to the distinctiveness of Christ's love. Insofar as the theory of the anonymous Christian has also been taken up as the classic example of "inclusivism," however, it has come in for a number of other criticisms. Rahner has been accused of failing to allow for the real "otherness" of other religions, and of being patronizing, thinking he knows better than those of other faiths what they "really" believe, finding a way to bring into the fold those who do not want to be brought in. To some extent at least these latter criticisms are based on taking Rahner's theory out of its context, and misconstruing his purpose in proposing it.[19]

A criticism from a somewhat different direction has to do with the individualism of Rahner's thought. With the notions of *Vorgriff* and the supernatural existential, Rahner envisages human relationship to God primarily as an individual matter, taking place in the depths of each person's consciousness. He does insist on the importance and necessity of the church, and more generally the social and historical nature of human beings and the consequent necessity of transcendental experience expressing itself in social form. And he did himself operate very much as a theologian working within and for the church. Nevertheless, it is hard to avoid the impression that as he typically envisaged it, the relationship with God originally and fundamentally occurs on the level of the individual's transcendental experience, and only subsequently finds expression in social form. This is a point on which Rahner has been criticized from a Wittgensteinian point of view by Fergus Kerr,[20] and also a point on which Latin American liberation theologians, who in many cases were influenced by Rahner, differ notably from him.

Influence, Achievement, and Agenda

The significance of Rahner's work can be considered on two levels: there is the question of his immediate influence in the Roman Catholic Church, the impact of his writings upon and their place within the ebb and flow of ecclesiastical politics; and there is the slightly different question of his lasting achievement.

Rahner's immediate influence was considerable. As we have seen, his was among – and perhaps preeminent among – the theological voices that shaped to a considerable degree the outcome of the Second Vatican Council. His teaching and his writings also did much to form the thought of the next generation of theologians in the United States, of theologians and bishops in Germany, and to some degree of emerging theological movements such as Latin American liberation theology. On the other hand fashions, in ecclesiastical politics as elsewhere, change. In terms of ecclesiastical cachet, Rahner's standing was at a high point in the period immediately following the Council, but in recent years one is more likely to hear overtones of the thought of Hans Urs von Balthasar (who had been out of favor during the years of the Council) in documents coming from Rome.

Rahner and Balthasar are in fact often presented as two distinct roads down which Roman Catholic theology can go. With each is associated a journal (*Concilium* in Rahner's case, *Communio* in Balthasar's), a style of doing theology, and a distinctive attitude towards the church–world relationship. The contrast with Balthasar, however, interesting though it is in other ways, does not provide a good basis on which to assess the lasting achievement of Rahner; there is a danger of an excessive identification of Rahner's work with the particular features Balthasar (not always fairly) criticized. Balthasar objected to what he took to be the influence of German idealism on Rahner's philosophy (and the philosophy he took to be the starting point of all of Rahner's thought), to the anthropological turn and the limitations of a transcendental approach, to a loss and distortion of content that he believed resulted from trying to translate the Christian faith into something that makes sense to the modern world, and to the theory of anonymous Christianity as the culmination of all this. Now, if Rahner is read as offering a grand system of theology, which beginning from an idealist-inspired philosophy methodically applies an anthropological turn and a transcendental method to the various questions of theology – if Rahner is seen in other words as systematically adopting the presuppositions of modernity in order to make Christianity presentable to the modern world – then it is not unreasonable to regard him as in danger of seeming, once the word "postmodern" comes to be mentioned, passé.

What is most significant about Rahner, however, is not in fact any systematic application of a transcendental method or anthropological turn, but instead the way in which he demonstrated the possibility of a theology which is simultaneously faithful and creative, a theology which is genuinely immersed in the tradition and also genuinely open to the difficulties and insights of the contemporary world. Rahner showed that this kind of theology is possible, not by working out in principle how it should be done, but simply in the doing of it, repeatedly, across a vast range of subjects.

Notes

1   Another approach would be to look, not to explicitly intellectual influences, but to the influence of the spiritual exercises of Ignatius of Loyola. Rahner himself, especially towards the end of his life, pointed to Ignatius, the founder of the Jesuits, as a decisively important influence on him. See Philip Endean, *Karl Rahner and Ignatian Spirituality* (Oxford: Oxford University Press, 2001) for an interesting and full attempt to explore the significance of such claims.

2   *Spirit in the World* is Rahner's first *major* work, but not his first work: he had already published a number of articles on the history of spirituality.

3   The account of the supernatural existential given here is based on some of Rahner's later writings. In an earlier version of the notion, presented in "Concerning the relationship between nature and grace" (*Theological Investigations* 1), the supernatural existential appeared not as grace nor even its offer, but as the desire for, and the orientation towards, grace and the beatific vision.

4   *Theological Investigations* 4, p. 181.
5   Even this acceptance of grace, Rahner is careful to insist, is "borne" by God, made possible by grace itself. This may seem to confuse the issue, but if Rahner did not insist on this point he would be courting accusations of semi-Pelagianism.
6   *Foundations of Christian Faith*, p. 131.
7   *Theological Investigations* 4, p. 108.
8   Ibid, p. 236.
9   Ibid, p. 237.
10   Ibid, p. 239.
11   See Richard Lennan, *The Ecclesiology of Karl Rahner* (Oxford: Clarendon Press, 1995).
12   *Theological Investigations* 4, p. 241.
13   "Theology and anthropology," *Theological Investigations* 9, pp. 28, 29.
14   In, for instance, the second part of "Reflections on methodology in theology," *Theological Investigations* 11 (London: Darton, Longman, and Todd, 1974).
15   Ibid, p. 87. This is of course broadly speaking a Kantian use of the term "transcendental," though it is worth noting that Rahner deviates from Kant's usage in cer-

tain ways: in particular, what is to be investigated according to Rahner is not, as with
Kant, the conditions of the possibility of
knowledge or experience as such, but
instead the conditions of the possibility of
some quite delimited kind of knowledge –
for instance, knowledge of some one particular dogma.

16 This has been criticized by Balthasar at various points, and in particular by Bruce
Marshall in *Christology in Conflict: The Identity of a Saviour in Rahner and Barth* (Oxford: Blackwell, 1987).

17 Rahner also notes, however, that it is not
possible to clearly and explicitly formulate
such a transcendental Christology until after the fact, until after a relationship with

the actual Jesus Christ is already present
(*Foundations of Christian Faith*, p. 207).
Transcendental Christology is *a priori* only
in principle: in actuality it is a retracing of
what is already concretely known.

18 If this is the way one envisions Rahner's
work, the fact that he frequently insists that
the historical as well as the transcendental
side of theology must be acknowledged will
fail to reassure.

19 See chapter 7 of Karen Kilby, *Karl Rahner:
Theology and Philosophy* (New York:
Routledge, 2004) for a fuller discussion
of the debate surrounding anonymous
Christianity.

20 See Fergus Kerr, *Theology after Wittgenstein*
(London: SPCK, 1997).

Bibliography

Primary

Theological Investigations, 23 vols (Baltimore,
MD, 1961–9; New York, 1971–92).
Foundations of Christian Faith, trans. William
Dych (New York, 1989).
*The Practice of Faith: A Handbook of Contem-
porary Spirituality*, ed. Karl Lehmann and Karl
Raffelt (New York, 1992).
Hearer of the Word, trans. Joseph Donceel (New
York, 1994).
Spirit in the World, trans. William V. Dych (New
York, 1994).

Secondary

Patrick Burke, *Reinterpreting Rahner: A Critical
Study of his Major Themes* (New York, 2002).
William Dych, *Karl Rahner* (Collegeville, MN,
1992).
Philip Endean, *Karl Rahner and Ignatian Spir-
ituality* (Oxford, 2001).
Karen Kilby, *Karl Rahner: Theology and Philo-
sophy* (New York, 2004).
Richard Lennan, *The Ecclesiology of Karl Rahner*
(Oxford, 1995).
Leo O'Donovan, ed. *A World of Grace: An Intro-
duction to the Themes and Foundations of Karl
Rahner's Theology* (Washington, DC, 1995).
Herbert Vorgrimler, *Understanding Karl Rahner*
(New York, 1986).

Hans Urs von Balthasar

Ben Quash

Introduction and Survey

To describe Hans Urs von Balthasar's theology as an "academic theology" is to fail to capture its distinctive character. While there is no denying how formidably learned his writings are, the fact remains that Balthasar never held a university post, and the circle which surrounded him was drawn as much from the church and the literary world as from that of academia. In his own view the most important influence on him during his active life was that of a medical doctor and mystic, Adrienne von Speyr. His own time, since 1948, was divided between running a publishing house, writing, translating and editing, and being chaplain to a new form of religious order, a secular institute, which he founded with Adrienne. His theology springs from a sense of his own commission (*Auftrag*), which has linked him to the development of new forms of life in the church with their roots in the Johannine/Ignatian tradition of spirituality.

Born in 1905 in Lucerne, Balthasar was educated first by the Benedictines at Engelberg, then by the Jesuits in Feldkirch. In 1923 he enrolled in the university of Zurich. His studies in philosophy and German literature led him to Vienna and Berlin and culminated in his doctoral work on German idealism, subsequently published in three volumes as *Apokalypse der deutschen Seele* (1937–9). At this point, 1929, he entered the Society of Jesus. Three years' philosophy at Pullach near Munich brought him into contact with Erich Przywara, whose work on *analogia entis* (the analogy of being) had a foundational influence on him. For his theological studies he went to the Jesuit school at Lyons. Here he encountered Daniélou, Fessard, and Henri de Lubac, who gave him his enduring love of the church fathers, which was to lead to his studies of Maximus, *Kosmische Liturgie* (1941), and Gregory of Nyssa, *Présence et pensée* (1942). It was here too that he met the French Catholic poet Paul Claudel, whose works he was to translate into German. Lyons was the center of the *nouvelle théologie* which raised deep questions about the neoscholastic doctrine of grace and nature, with its suggestion that human nature could be conceived of in isolation from its relation to the vision of God. Hence the appeal to the fathers with their conviction that communion with God is of the essence of humanity.[1] Hence, too, Balthasar's own conviction that nowhere is humanity ever wholly bereft of the grace of God – and his lifetime search for the fruits of such openness in the works of philosophers and poets outside the Christian tradition, notably in the grand tradition of classical antiquity.

Balthasar also found in the patristic writers (as Nichols puts it) "mystical warmth" and "rhetorical power,"[2] and no fear of paradox. He found a genuinely prayerful theology; a reverent relationship to God and a sense of his dynamism and freedom. He found an interest in the whole cosmos as it related to Christ. He did not find anything like a historical–critical reductionism where the Bible was concerned. He found an openness to the full dimensions of God's revelation. He found passion in the doing of theology. In all this, he was inspired by the theologians of the patristic *ressourcement*, and Henri de Lubac in particular.

After his studies at Lyons he was briefly in Munich as editor of *Stimmen der Zeit*. There then followed a period of eight years as student chaplain at Basel which shaped the pattern of the rest of his life. Here he met Adrienne von Speyr and received her into the Catholic Church. Together, they conceived the idea of a new form of religious order whose members would continue to exercise their normal professions and occupations in the world. It was on the occasion of the first retreat which Balthasar conducted for this *Johannes-Gemeinschaft*, that Adrienne experienced the first of the visions which were to accompany her for the rest of her life and to provide the central themes of Balthasar's own writing (documented in *First Glance at Adrienne von Speyr* and in the many published transcripts of her meditations and experiences, which Balthasar himself made). And it was in Basel that Balthasar turned his attention to the work of Karl Barth, which gave him "the vision of a comprehensive biblical theology."[3] His relationship with Barth, at first enthusiastic and friendly, may arguably have cooled, but Barth's theology remained for Balthasar one of the fixed points by which he set the course of his own work. Though he filtered it through a thoroughly Catholic ecclesiology, he took from Barth a firm insistence on the seriousness of the Christian revelation's call to a radical newness of faith and life, and consequently the disturbing and challenging character of the Christian presence in the world. Moreover, he found Barth's emphasis on, so to speak, the "priority" of God (and on the divine freedom) reinforcing the insights he had gained from his Jesuit mentor Erich Przywara. He concurred with – indeed, was profoundly influenced by – Barth's affirmation of the utter sovereignty of the divine initiative. And for him, as for Barth, the reality of God preceding all human doing and knowing was a *personal* reality – that is to say, intrinsically relational, free, and loving; not an "It" but a "Thou." Barth's theology saw itself as in the kind of responsive relationship to its "object" that Balthasar would go on to characterize as fundamentally dramatic, and he saw Barth's theology doing what his own aimed to do also: to "draw all intraworldly being and essence . . . to the concrete, personal and historical Logos."[4]

In 1950 Balthasar left the Society of Jesus, which would not allow him to remain a member while he was developing his work with the secular institutes. For a long time he was in the ecclesiastical wilderness, yet it was during this period of isolation and disfavor that his major writings were produced or conceived. He published important studies of literary figures (Bernanos, Schneider) and the saints (Thérèse of Lisieux and Elisabeth of Dijon) and it was at this time that the first volumes of his great trilogy (*The Glory of the Lord*, *Theo-Drama*, and *Theo-Logic*) began to appear. His restoration to favor came in the wake of Vatican II. In 1967 he was appointed to the Papal Theological Commission and began now to gain the reputation of a conservative theologian, not least for his pronouncements on the ordination of women and on his fellow Swiss, Hans Küng. However inadequate such a tag may be, there was nevertheless a growing rift between Balthasar and the circles around Rahner, Küng, and Schillebeeckx which came to the fore in Balthasar's attack on Rahner's notion of "anonymous Christians" in *Cordula* (1966) and his own part in the establishment of a rival periodical to *Concilium* entitled *Communio*. Although it has gained increasing influence on contemporary Catholic thought – especially in Europe and the United States – and although it has commanded the very public respect of leading Catholic teachers such as Joseph Ratzinger and John Paul II, Balthasar's work remains suspect to this day in the eyes of many progressive Catholic theologians. And yet there is much that each side could learn from the other.

Balthasar died in 1988, a few days before he was due to become a cardinal.

Content

Analogy

Balthasar outlines his approach in the following terms: faithfulness to Christ must be at the center of all theological endeavor, but this "Christian 'exclusivity' demands precisely the inclusion of all human thinking." Human nature "in all its forms is understood as the essential language of the *Logos*."[5] Here, initially, we catch sight of the deep concern in Balthasar's thought to sustain an openness to the world. Such concern arises from a commitment, formed along with de Lubac, to raze the bastions of fear which had kept the church isolated from its cultural and philosophical environment, and had thereby prevented it from engaging freely and redemptively with the world. Balthasar sets out with the bold and consciously "catholic" desire to embrace "all human thinking," and to trace "human nature" through the diverse forms in which it comes to expression.

Nevertheless, there is an important qualification that Balthasar is keen to make – and this qualification comes increasingly to reflect his anxiety over developments in progressive Roman Catholic circles where openness to the world, the readiness to baptize secular and religious movements outside the church as examples of "anonymous Christianity," might lead to a loss of identity, of consciousness of the specifically Christian call and witness. For Balthasar, there are definite terms on which "the inclusion of all human thinking" by "the Christian 'exclusivity'" can take place. Human thinking is included "as something judged (*gerichtetes*), . . . 'broken,' realigned, and reset (*ab- aus-, und eingerichtet*)."[6]

Already, the guiding concerns of Balthasar's theology are before us. There is (1) a respect for the way that human life and thought find expression in a great variety of *forms*. There is (2) a desire to see theology treating these forms with seriousness, as having some conceivable *relation* to the revelation centered in Christ. Alongside this desire, at every stage, there is (3) a belief that the relation is grounded not straightforwardly in similarity, but simultaneously in *dissimilarity*: that this dissimilarity has the power to judge and to break worldly forms. And yet beyond this judgment there is (4) the suggestion of a new ("supra-") form, in which, as we shall see, some kind of "reset" *harmony* between the divine and the human can be intuited by the faithful believer; a "supra-form" which is the free gift of God and quite underivable from its worldly analogues.[7]

Thus, on the one hand, we find in Balthasar's work a deep concern with the themes which have given form and continuity to Western metaphysics (the perception of unity in diversity; of beauty, goodness, and truth) as proper to our "natural" knowledge of the order which God has created. In support of this, Balthasar stresses a common ground between God and the world which is founded in creation and cannot entirely be destroyed: "Every real 'contra' presupposes a constantly to be understood relationship and thus at least a minimal community in order to be really a 'contra' and not a totally unrelated 'other.'"[8] On the other hand, he holds fast to the belief that it is only in Jesus Christ that this relation is established, brought to its perfection, and truly revealed to the eyes of faith. The order of creation may only be interpreted properly when it is interpreted in its union with the order of salvation, which shows that community with God (that which is common both to God and to the creature) is pure gift, undeserved and impossible to predict in advance (however much convergence on the form of Christ we may see with hindsight in the ancients, in the Old Testament, in literature, and in the metaphysical tradition).

This presents Balthasar with the challenge of how properly to relate the many competing movements of the human spirit to the central "revelation-figure" of Christ. How to do justice to the unity and diversity not only of the Christian tradition, with its various mediations of the glory at its Christological center, but also of the richness of perceptions of beauty, goodness, and truth which are to be met with outside that tradition, in the poets, the philosophers, and the myth-makers? How to avoid reducing the originality and freshness of such perceptions simply to inadequate copies of the Christian revelation itself? Such concerns characterize Balthasar's engagement with Barth throughout the first part of his trilogy, *The Glory of the Lord*, and his standpoint finds articulation in summary form in *Love Alone*. What emerges (and what binds together the three panels of Balthasar's great theological triptych) is a distinctive form of analogical thinking, which owes its character both to Przywara's thought and to the debates Balthasar had with Barth.

Balthasar's use of analogy is not so much a method (it is too *ad hoc* to be that) as a broad, guiding principle. It continues to leave room for fascination with and insights from outside a narrowly defined Christian tradition, at the same time as it stresses the free, transcendent, and finally truth-imparting character of the Christian revelation. Analogy is, for Balthasar, a means of recognizing the relation within difference, and the similarity within ever-greater dissimilarity (*maior dissimilitudo*), of human life and thought (on the one hand) and the divine revelation (on the other). The touchstone for Balthasar here (as for Przywara) is the famous text from the Fourth Lateran Council (1215): "As great as may be the similarity, so much greater must the dissimilarity between creator and creature be preserved." Whether operating between aesthetic beauty and revealed glory, between human drama and the all-encompassing theo-drama, or between the inquiries of philosophy and the obedient reflection of prayerful faith, analogy works to achieve the mediation upon which Balthasar's theology depends.

Though involving some finely tuned intellectual discussion, Balthasar's thought in this area is actually drawing heavily on a devotional tradition: the Ignatian one in which he was trained as a Jesuit. The "definition" of the *maior dissimilitudo* by the Fourth Lateran Council appeals so much to von Balthasar, and has such prominence in his theology, partly because it expresses what Ignatius taught about life before God: that love is caught up in ever-increasing awe. And it is out of this vision of analogical relation, in which similarity between the creaturely form and the divine revelation is suspended but preserved in ever-greater dissimilarity, that Balthasar's contemplative, eclectic, and enormously wide-ranging theology is born. In each part of his trilogy he will contemplate particular forms of human expression and experience. In *The Glory of the Lord*, the forms of beauty and its perception; in *Theo-Drama*, the forms of human action as depicted and interpreted in history and in literature; in *Theo-Logic*, the forms of philosophical insight. The very fact that the trilogy is constructed so as to answer the ancient concern with beauty, goodness, and truth as manifested in all Being shows Balthasar's respect for the "form" which metaphysical reflection has traditionally taken. Balthasar's theology seeks to attend to such worldly forms in a way that will draw on a Christologically centered and ecclesially learned "sensorium" for the revelation form (the *Gestalt Christi*, or "form of Christ") in which all other forms find their true center and ground.[9]

Of course, the tension between similarity and dissimilarity, form and supra-form, is a difficult one to sustain, and this difficulty in Balthasar's thought will become more apparent as we proceed.

Beauty and the glory of God

The truth of God takes form for us in the world. This form, according to Balthasar, is self-disclosing and enrapturing, and the conditions for the perception of this form (which is the *Gestalt Christi*) are given with and in it. We are not to pick it apart with tools derived from elsewhere, making it so much an object of *our* inquiry that we are never confronted and shaped by *it*; never *its* objects.

Balthasar's approach to the question of God's self-disclosure is contemplative as opposed to critical; it is concrete rather than abstract. Much of Balthasar's work in the first volume of *The Glory of the Lord* is concerned with the notion of the light of faith, with the way of perceiving its object which is peculiar to faith. The biblical writers, Paul and John at least, speak of faith, not simply in terms of modifications of the believers' own self-understanding, but as a particular mode of apprehending and entering into relationship with the object of faith: God in Christ. In polemical terms this brings Balthasar into sharp conflict with all those who have turned away from contemplation of the object of theological reflection, God in his self-revelation, to a consideration of the conditions of human subjectivity and the manner of our apprehension of that revelation. And this distinguishes his approach as much from Bultmann's program of existential interpretation as from Catholic transcendental theology. What Balthasar particularly singles out in Bultmann is the combination of critical historical study with an anthropological reduction of faith to the moment of decision. For Balthasar, Bultmann's demythologization and reductive explanations of the origins of mythological concepts in the biblical texts, together with his existential interpretation of those texts, both serve equally to dispel the object of faith, leaving only an existential moralism.[10] And there is a recurring polemic throughout Balthasar's writings against those who choose reductive explanations, historical, psychological or whatever, and thereby fail to do justice to the object of their study.[11]

It is in defense of this concentration on the object in *The Glory of the Lord* that we find Balthasar deploying analogy in a characteristic way. He turns to analogies from the world of aesthetic appreciation to demonstrate that in artistic terms, too, the object of perception has priority. For Balthasar, to perceive beauty is to perceive the manner of manifestation of a thing as it reveals its being, its reality. To be sure, where a work of art is concerned, we may profit from an understanding of its constituent parts, of the influences and circumstances of the artist, of preliminary sketches and of contemporary developments in the medium; but none of that will of itself bring understanding unless it enables us to see the work as a whole, to perceive, as Hopkins would have said, its "inscape."[12] Understanding of this kind comes with practised contemplation, a cultivation of one's appreciation.

On another front, Balthasar rejects, quite justifiably, the charge that such a concern with form and beauty is Platonist. It is not that he wishes to penetrate behind the appearances of things to the enduring, eternal ideas of which they are manifestations only. He refuses to denigrate the differentiated diversity of material things, for they are capable of a mediation that is almost sacramental in character, enabling one to see the luminosity or "splendor" of being in a way that would be impossible in abstraction from actual, finite particulars. He will not accept any version of the view that "the material is the dispensable shell, and can be left behind by those with advanced spiritual vision once they have penetrated to the pure spiritual core."[13] On the contrary, as Kevin Mongrain summarizes the matter, Balthasar believes "every particular finite reality can be a communication of spirit and the absolute truth of being."[14]

Cultivation of the capacity to perceive artistic beauty is analogous to the contemplative discipline of the saints, who act as a model for our own reception of the form that comes to us (volumes 2 and 3 of *The Glory of the Lord* are given over to studies of saints and contemplative theologians, clerical and lay). Such saints rekindle in an all too functionalist world our sense of the graciousness of things as they give themselves for our beholding. Balthasar's debt here is again to Ignatius, whose *Spiritual Exercises* he conducted some hundred times, to the Society of Jesus and to his own *Johannes-Gemeinschaft*; above all to Adrienne, "who showed the way in which Ignatius is fulfilled by John, and therewith laid the basis for most of what I have published since 1940. Her work and mine are neither psychologically nor philologically to be separated: two halves of a single whole, which has at its center a unique foundation."[15] The work and insights of contemplative sanctity stand over against those Western theological and philosophical developments (largely post-Reformation, says Balthasar)[16] that have lost sight of the sacramental revelation-figure in which the divine glory is seen.[17] Theology of such a kind can listen only to the echoes of the divine word in its own self-consciousness; it loses its power to attract and to convince; it ceases to be concrete and concerns itself with the abstract, that which is perceived as the condition of the possibility of any perception at all. By contrast, the example of the saints – and, indeed, of Balthasar's theological aesthetics as a whole (influenced as it is by Adrienne) – recalls us to the nurture of our perception and understanding in the face of God's glory.

In the concluding volumes of *The Glory of the Lord* (on the Old and New Covenants) it becomes clear that for Balthasar all worldly forms, words and thoughts – those of the Old Testament included – are measured by that which they exist to serve: the Christological *deus dixit* (God has spoken) which is presented to us in the underlying unity of the scriptural *Gestalt*. It is largely to Barth that Balthasar owes this vision of a comprehensive biblical theology. The biblical Word – the Word of grace and promise – has its own unique *Gestalt* or form, in which human words and concepts are given their true sense as they are pressed into the service of the "new" creation in Christ. No demythologization of the New Testament is required by this, but rather a discovery of how all myths have been rescued and transformed in the witness of the Word to itself.

Thus far, the outline of the analogical framework (with its *maior dissimilitudo*) is apparent. Beauty is not strictly the same thing as glory. The "glorious" form of Christ is marred as well as beautiful. But contemplative perception of the beautiful nevertheless finds itself preserved as an analogue of our infinitely rich contemplation of God's glory, which only the approach of that glory (reinforcing its sovereign distinctiveness and freedom by its very approach) makes possible.

Drama and the Christ-event

As the church's obedient receptivity gives birth to discipleship, after the manner of the transition in Ignatian spirituality from contemplation to mission, so *The Glory of the Lord* gives birth to *Theo-Drama*. It is out of believers' obedience to the one divine Word that the richness and diversity of the many aspects of the Christian church's life are born. Hence the lives of the saints and the classical Christian theologians are not to be seen as pale copies which obstruct our view of the unchangeable reality of the biblical Word. Rather, because it is in the nature of the Word to generate new forms of life insofar as people are obedient and faithful to it, so too we may learn in the study of such lives and theologies to catch sight of the divine glory as it has transformed their lives and in so doing to discipline ourselves in the same obedience. The saints – and most of all Mary as (for Balthasar) the archetype of the believing church – constellate around the form of Christ which their lives represent and mediate, and this ecclesial constellation thereby participates in the fullness of the *Gestalt Christi*. Put another way, the forms of life which take shape in the church (in response to the generative Word) participate in an overall event of revelation. And for Balthasar, this event of revelation has all the dimensions of an actual drama between God and his creatures.

Drama, then, is the field of analogy which informs *Theo-Drama*. And, in characteristic fashion, Balthasar refuses to contemplate the specifically ecclesial experiences and the specifically theological representations of the drama between God and his creatures in isolation from all the analogous dramatic representations that are available for contemplation in literature and the theatre. Just as *The Glory of the Lord* began with a consideration of the experience of beauty (and related theories of aesthetic apprehension), so *Theo-Drama* begins with a consideration of a great (though almost exclusively Western) tradition of drama. Drama is the medium in which human beings address questions about agency and event at the widest level, and attempt to do full justice to acting subjects, their freedom and their inter-relations. Drama, from Aeschylus to Brecht and Ionesco, represents a cavalcade of human self-interpretation, and its value for Balthasar, following the pattern of *The Glory of the Lord*, is linked to the degree to which it shows itself related to a higher, Christological, meaning (sometimes negatively, through its fragmentation and its need to be judged and reset – "*ab- aus-, und eingerichtet*").

Balthasar's assumption is that all drama points to a Christian horizon on which is situated the ultimately dramatic (the theodramatic), which is to say that which safeguards but transforms the humanly dramatic. Starting with the Christological reflections of *Heart of the World*, and running via his reflections on the *triduum mortis* (Good Friday, Holy Saturday, Easter Sunday) in *Mysterium Paschale*, Balthasar presses on towards his sustained meditation in *Theo-Drama* on the central mystery of the Christian faith: the drama of the passion of the eternal Son (with the cry from the cross sounding at its heart); the Son's subsequent descent into Hell; and his entry into resurrection life. It is in these events that both human action, and the inner life of the Trinity which is the condition for all creaturely freedom, are displayed in the full depth of their interrelation.

Vital things come to light here about Balthasar's doctrine of the person and work of Christ, and the way that his dramatic perspective recasts and reenlivens them. Like Barth, Balthasar asserts an identity between Christology and soteriology: they are not to be separated. In drama, characters are associated with their roles in the overall movement of the play, but there is always a residual distance which persists between the actor and the role. (This is true for Balthasar at a more general level, too, in society and in social "role-playing.") The theological analogue of the notion of role, which overcomes this residual distance, is the Ignatian/Johannine notion of "mission" (*Sendung*). And it is in *Christ's* mission, in which human beings have the possibility of sharing, that there is a perfect coincidence of person and work. Christ's person is wholly invested in his work. Balthasar likes to name him, in strongly Johannine fashion, the "One Sent," thus specifying his core identity in terms of his core task. And it is in the nature of the work of salvation – which involves the bearing of the totality of the world's sin in order to initiate and maintain the New Covenant between God and humanity – that it cannot be undertaken unless a "person" is offered in and with the task. The person of Christ alone can accomplish this, because his human life is so wholly lent to the divine movement of love and self-donation. Thus Balthasar is prevented from lapsing into "the kind of purely extrahistorical, static, 'essence' Christology that sees itself as a complete and rounded 'part one,' smoothly unfolding into a soteriological 'part two' . . . the question of [Christ's] work implies the question of his person: Who *must* he be, to behave and act in this way?"[18]

As the "One Sent" – or, as elsewhere, the "Beloved Son" (Matthew 3: 17 and par) – Jesus is the actively obedient one, the perfection of whose obedience is the expression and ground of his personal and immediate relation to the Father, as well as of his human faithfulness. Being the Son is not being in a static state; it is being engaged in a personal relationship. "Every worldly dramatic production," says Balthasar, "must take its bearings from, and be judged by, the ideal nature of this [Christological] coincidence of freedom and obedience or of self-being and consciously acknowledged dependence."[19] Balthasar sees in this complete availability to the will of the Father, as mediated by the Spirit, the ground of what theology calls the "hypostatic union": the union of the two natures of Christ, divine and human. The procession of the Logos from the Father and the "sent-ness" of the earthly Son are one and the same movement, constitutive of Jesus Christ's very being. He thus takes a doctrine that is often handled in an "essentialist" way (in discussion of essences or natures) and transforms it by handling it in an "actualist" way. The ground of the hypostatic union is not the conjunction of two sorts of "stuff"; it is the conjunction of two "movements" in a single filial dynamic.

Meanwhile, the doctrine of salvation is developed by Balthasar in a way that has both substitutionary (or representative) and participatory aspects. Because of the condition of sin that prevails after the fall (a negative condition of distance-as-alienation which has overtaken and vitiated the positive condition of distance-as-difference that properly holds between Creator and creature), Christ must act *for us*. No one other than Christ can traverse the abyss that sin has opened up, thus demonstrating the limitless reach of the divine love. But having done this, a possibility is opened up for the human creature to enter *into* the movement of Christ's mission (the "acting area"). The believer can be brought right into the heart of the drama that Christ acts out in history; the "filial dynamic" of Christ's life, death, and resurrection becomes shareable. The effect of such a mode of life is to take human persons in their defensiveness and self-enclosure, and to set them in motion towards God and others: such a person "feels himself breaking out of his own private world."[20] This is what traditional theological language calls becoming united with Christ, or being part of his body, and it offers the possibility of participating in something of the relational character of the divine persons. By handing oneself over, one can be drawn into God's own mutuality, exchange, and love: a wholly new and liberating possibility for the human creature.

It is apparent once again how dramatic concerns enliven the picture – particularly here in relation to Balthasar's soteriology. And again, it is something inescapably *personal* that is going on. It is as the person he is that Jesus has the mission he has, with its soteriological goal and eschatological reach. And his saving work can continue to take effect in the present, because he continues to be operative in the personal mode in the *Spirit*, still encountering others and drawing them into dramatic relationship with him. Thus the drama is transposed into the life of the church, within which – and in relation to which – human beings find themselves challenged to have their lives shaped after the pattern of Christ, finding their own genuine personhood as a consequence.

On Balthasar's account, the great inclusive drama of Christ's work (whose full ramifications are only to be worked out eschatologically, in the Battle of the Logos)[21] reveals that the yardstick of all truly dramatic action lies in the supra-drama of the trinitarian God of love. But Balthasar's insistence on the fact and continued possibility of the transposition of this pattern of divine self-donation and mutual receptivity into human lives and communities shows his conviction that the supra-drama respects the value of the ordinary dramas of human encounter which can point to it. He is anxious to hold on to this. The outline of the supra-drama, the measure of all drama, can be traced by the eyes of faith in any giving and rendering back of freedom (of love and obedience; generosity and surrender) between a "Thou" and an "I":

[The Christian's] faith teaches him to see within the most seemingly unimportant interpersonal relation the making present and the "sacrament" of the eternal I–Thou relation which is the ground of the free Creation and again the reason why God the Father yields His Son to the death of darkness for the salvation of every Thou.[22]

We should pause at this point to consider Balthasar's treatment of the "death of darkness" as signaled in this quotation, because it provides the core of his most original theological reflection. The Son descends into Hell, into the absolute God-forsakenness of the dead. He takes upon himself the fate (not only the substance but the condition) of sinful humanity, drinks its cup to the lees, and so embraces that which is wholly opposed to God – and yet remains God. The exploration of this theological motif which has rarely attracted much attention proves surprisingly fruitful. It is a very distinctive development of the concerns of kenotic Christology. The kenosis of the Son, for Balthasar, finds its fullest expression precisely in his willingness to take upon himself the whole condition of sinful human nature, in order to "live it round." The full meaning of the burden which he assumes is glimpsed only when we realize that it means the bearing, not only of the pains of dying but of the state of being dead itself. Balthasar draws here on the tradition of Virgil and Dante, more closely on the mystical experience of Adrienne. The passing into the realm of the dead is a passing into the place that is cut off from God, which is beyond hope, where the dead are confronted with the reality of that which is wholly opposed to God. This is the measure then of the Son's obedience to the Father: that he goes into the realm of that which is at enmity with him in order to bring it back under his rule. The momentum of his obedience carries him into this abyss.

And yet it is *God* who enters into the realm of that which is opposed to himself – and he remains God. Such presence of the divine in the God-forsakenness of Hell is possible only on the basis of the trinitarian distinction between the Father and the Son.

This opposition between God, the creative origin (the "Father"), and the man who, faithful to the mission of the origin, ventures on into ultimate perdition (the "son"), this bond stretched to breaking point does not break because the same Spirit of absolute love (the "spirit") informs both the one who sends and the one sent. God causes God to go into abandonment by God while accompanying him on the way with his Spirit.[23]

Balthasar has managed, like Moltmann, to recast the traditional doctrine of the immutability of God in a way that brings out the full trinitarian implications of the death of the Son. But he does not make the doctrine of the divine immutability the object of sustained criticism as a result. This is not his main concern or focus. Rather, as we have seen, he stresses those aspects of the divine sending and the divine obedience that are the loving, inner-trinitarian *supra*-conditions within God's freedom for the suffering into which the Son enters. Christ's action, as Balthasar says, indicates "a drama in the very heart of God."[24] "The dramatic dimension that is part of the definition of the person of Jesus does not belong exclusively to the worldly side of his being: its ultimate presuppositions lie in the divine life itself."[25]

Balthasar's worry, as Mongrain has pointed out, is that Moltmann "runs the risk of identifying the inner-trinitarian suffering and alienation of God with the suffering and tragedies within the temporal order of creation," thus tangling the divine life up with the unfolding of world process. He fears that Moltmann's Trinity needs the world in order to be itself; needs the world in order to *actualize* itself. His own view, by contrast, is that the space required for the world to be itself is freely, and not *necessarily*, generated by this trinitarian dynamism. All the alienation manifest within world process is held within a greater *diastasis*, which is the perfect and self-sufficient condition of relationality between the persons of the Trinity. The "incomprehensible and unique 'separation' of God from himself" is a supra-event that "*includes* and grounds every other separation – be it never so dark and bitter."[26] It is the highest pitch of the "eternal, absolute self-surrender"[27] which is between Father and Son in the Holy Spirit, and which belongs to God's absolute love.

Here we glimpse Balthasar's vision of the utter perichoretic self-donation (and simultaneous mutual constitution) of the trinitarian persons in the perfection of their love. Beginning from the events and actions of Jesus' life, and thinking outwards from those, he extrapolates a radically dramatic picture of the complete mutual outpouring of the persons of the Trinity, without reserve. Yet it is not one that compromises the doctrine of divine immutability. Certainly, according to Balthasar, even the Father surrenders himself without remainder, imparting to the Son all that is his; yet *because* this handing over is complete and mutual (*because* the Son offers everything back to the Father), the whole divine life remains in complete, dynamic perfection. The self-bestowal of the persons one to another is simultaneously their self-constitution in an eternal triune event of love.

How is Balthasar's use of analogy at work in all of this? Well, the relation of all human action to the supra-drama of the Christian God is a relation of similarity suspended in ever greater dissimilarity. Worldly dramas can, of course, give insight into the constitutive receptivity and relationality of human life. But the trinitarian self-giving and yet perpetual fullness which are revealed to us in the perfect generosity and perfect obedience (or self-abandonment) of Jesus Christ remain in significant measure beyond our grasp. No one worldly drama can be adequate to the representation of this truth.

Nevertheless, as we have seen, Balthasar *is* prepared to allow a privileged form of participative, mediating representation of this truth to take shape in the church, and above all in Mary, in whose will there is no tension with regard to the theodramatic *telos*; no resistance. Her own self-abandonment, though formally dependent on Christ's, is the quality the human participants in the Theo-Drama are most encouraged to emulate.[28] Her receptivity brings about her fulfillment.

There are ambiguities in Balthasar's thought here. Noel O'Donoghue has pointed out that Balthasar is suspended between conceiving the obedience of faith as pure passivity ("Barthian 'monergism'") and as a creative response to the enabling divine grace (the synergic theology of Scheeben, Adam, Guardini, and Przywara).[29] As Balthasar characterizes it, the response of Mary, the type of the human believer, wavers between these poles, and Balthasar's particular applications of dramatic metaphor do not resolve the ambiguities in any decisive way.

Debate

Balthasar's theology, as we have seen, is biblical and expository. Much of it has been done in and through a sustained engagement with others' work, among them many of his contemporaries in Protestant as well as Catholic theology.

Although Balthasar's desire is not to construct a philosophical or natural theology as a framework around which to erect a "revealed" theology (he begins from the revealed form of Jesus Christ in scripture, sacraments, and church teaching), nevertheless he does not wish to deny all validity to the long history of human search for truth and life outside the Christian faith. His distinctive argument is that the revealed Word is the "apex" inserted into the world *from above*, such that "the revelation of God in Christ and its proclamation is not derivable from the 'base' of cosmic and human nature but can be what it is only as the apex of the base."[30] This is an argument grounded in belief in the identity of the revealed Word and the Creator. Precisely because of this identity, Balthasar maintains, the revelation does not simply cut across the world's attempts to come at the truth but both judges and fulfills them.

Barth was never entirely convinced by this, nor happy with Balthasar's claim in the preface to the second edition of *The Theology of Karl Barth* that the dispute between them had been resolved. He remained deeply suspicious of the dangers of a natural theology which would ultimately control a theology of revelation, a suspicion greatly fueled by his battles with theologians like Brunner and Althaus who advocated a doctrine of orders of creation.

Yet Balthasar himself was fully alive to such dangers in the debates he conducted elsewhere. He was to live to see the way in which the opening up of the church to the world which he and others had fought for could easily lead to the erosion of that which was distinctively Christian. Hence his fierce reaction, notably in *Cordula*,[31] to Rahner's development of the notion of "anonymous Christians." What Balthasar attacked in *Cordula* was Rahner's emphasis on the sense in which men and women are by virtue of their own inherent spiritual dynamism capable of apprehending the divine, of believing, hoping, and loving. If elsewhere Balthasar was sympathetic to Blondel's "méthode de l'immanence," which attempted to demonstrate from a study of human dynamism the need for divine revelation, he saw in Rahner's identification of such natural spiritual dynamism with the life of faith a fatal blurring of the distinction between men and women's apprehension of the divine and the divine self-revelation. To speak thus was, in Balthasar's terms, to confuse the natural searching of men and women for the truth with that ultimate vision of God which both fulfills and transcends those intimations of the divine which he had himself treated so sensitively in *The Glory of the Lord: The Realm of Metaphysics*. It was above all to lose sight of the way in which true Christian belief flourishes as a response to the encounter with the revelation *Gestalt* of Christ. Hence his emphasis on the place of martyrdom and witness in the Christian life. Christian faith is a faith "to die for."[32]

In a different field of debate – that of biblical theology and its proper method – it is this same stress on the revelation form and its normative power that makes Balthasar's approach so distinct from that of Bultmann. As we noticed, Balthasar objected first to Bultmann's reduction of the Christological and soteriological elements in the New Testament to their sources in first-century mythology, and second to his anthropological reduction of faith to the sightless decision whereby "my" existence is transformed. The combined result of these reductions is that the Christ of faith becomes an incognito Christ grasped only in the *pro me* of "the process of the upturning of all man's natural aims in life."[33] They are two very different kinds of reduction, as John Riches has shown. In the first case we have an *explanatory* reduction whereby, true to the program of the History of Religions School, religious beliefs are explained "out of," that is to say in terms of, their sources in other contemporary – or near contemporary – religious beliefs and systems. In the second we have a *conceptual* reduction: what is being affirmed is that what may have been thought of as statements about the manner of God's action in the world, in certain events in human history, *are really* statements about the manner in which I may experience a change in my existence.

Now it is perfectly true that there is a neat fit between these two reductionisms in Bultmann's historical and theological method. Nevertheless there is a less than adequate acknowledgment in his work of the sense in which he passes from historical exposition of, say, John's Gospel to rational, theological reconstruction of it. What Balthasar wants to affirm is equally two things. First, it is that a proper exposition of such texts must pay due attention, not only to the historical sources of particular doctrines but also to the integrity of the synthesis which is achieved by the author when he or she puts such ideas to work. This seems to be a wholly necessary corrective to much of the work which, directly or indirectly, stems from the History of Religions School. The second point is quite different: it is that in reading such texts we should be attempting to see the way in which they mediate to us the revelation-*Gestalt*, in which that is to say there appears in them the divine glory for those who have eyes to see. This is properly contentious. Indeed, it is an open question as to whether Bultmann is right in his claim that the only way in which we can understand such texts is insofar as they confront us with an existential decision. He might even be right to rejoin that there is no conceptual reduction involved in reading them in this way; that this was indeed how they were meant to be understood by Paul and John.

To whatever degree Balthasar's *Gestalt* theology is seen as a valuable corrective in the area of biblical study, there remains a question about whether this same *Gestalt* theology can be used too overbearingly by Balthasar to suppress the crucial role of the *maior dissimilitudo* in the context of his analogical framework. Is the *maior dissimilitudo* always strong enough to prevent supra-form or supra-drama from becoming just very large and very comprehensive versions of worldly form and worldly drama? For where similarity is not properly suspended in dissimilarity, seeing things whole can sometimes appear to entail the excessive tidying up of loose ends. In relation to his theological aesthetics, Balthasar's intermittent reliance on metaphors of *harmony* and interweaving *concord*, though qualified, is often read by his interpreters as the unqualified key to his theological vision, and Balthasar himself often fails to take the necessary precautions to defend against such interpretation. Similarly, in relation to his theological dramatic theory, the "shape" which Balthasar imputes to Theo-Drama can seem insufficiently distinct from the famously "shaped" model of drama presented in the dramatic theory of Hegel (whose influence on

Balthasar in this area is profound). Balthasar's emphasis on the integrating power of dramatic form (even a theodramatic supra-form) makes it hard for him to distance himself from Hegel's belief that achieving a clear resolution is the one thing of overriding importance in a drama, and that, if necessary, the "pathos" of each individual protagonist must be sacrificed to this end. The theological question that needs to be put both to an aesthetics that is inclined to speak in terms of harmony and a dramatics that is inclined to look for clear resolution, is whether it is proper for any disciple of the Crucified to intuit such things too readily.[34]

The inclination to see clear resolution is linked with the Marian dimension of Balthasar's theology. Balthasar writes that "to the extent that the Church is Marian, she is a pure form which is immediately legible and comprehensible."[35] This Marian form of the church, which includes the ecclesial constellation of saints and their exemplary interrelations,[36] seems to intrude into the area of the *maior dissimilitudo* by means of a privileged mediation of the supra-form. Marian self-abandonment (echoing the Hegelian call for a sacrifice of the individual "pathos") stands as the analogical counterpart of divine self-giving or kenosis, and archetypally represents the human role in Theo-Drama. But does this analogy (between Marian self-abandonment and divine self-giving) become too uncritical and too unreserved a mediation between divine and creaturely action? All analogical apprehensions of the divine–human relation are strictly provisional – even, presumably, those intuited in the story of Mary. This is so, however tempting it might be to set her up as the embodiment of timeless virtue (and in Balthasar's case, primarily the virtue of obedience). So there is a question here about the legitimacy of a theology of what Balthasar calls the *Ecclesia Immaculata*, as focused in Mary, and has parallels with the Barthian challenge to analogy more generally.

But there is also a question of great importance about whether in such approaches Balthasar side-steps or downplays history as having no real consequence for theological insight. His tendency seems often to be to intuit super-historical forms, forms that are wholly invulnerable to contradiction in the light of historical experience, and in no need of enrichment or supplementation, provided they are understood in the light of Catholic teaching. Such a betrayal of history would be a betrayal of some of his own dearly held commitments to show Christian truth in terms of an unfolding drama.

Apparently undeterred by the risks, however, Balthasar seems content to rest a lot of theological weight on the analogy between Marian receptivity and divine kenosis, and one realizes that beneath this analogy there lies a further (and equally suspect) typology of what constitutes the male–female relation, whose suitability as an analogue of the Creator–creature relation may need more critical caution to be applied than is apparently the case. Here, too, a notion of "form" plays too readily into the hands of an over-resolved patterning of "types," which suppresses the provisionality that ought to accompany our sense of the *maior dissimilitudo*, as when Balthasar states "the active potency of the bearing, giving birth, and nourishing female organism . . . makes the creature as such appear essentially female over against the creating God."[37]

Meanwhile, Balthasar orders a more extended typology of saints around the Marian archetype, in which for instance John (with Mary) represents "love," Peter "office," and Paul and James alongside them make up a fourfold structure on which the church and its theology rest.[38] While consonant with the trends of Balthasar's more general approach to scripture, this is a manifestation of *Gestalt* theology which depends on some decidedly speculative interpretations of biblical passages. The fact, for example, that Peter and John run together to the tomb of Jesus is taken as evidence of the birth of "a Church with two poles: the Church of office and the Church of love, with a harmonious [!] tension between them."[39]

It must be acknowledged that Balthasar attempts to counterbalance his theology of the *Ecclesia Immaculata* with a powerful recognition of the marred and sinful aspects of the church: the wound of the Reformation, the division from Israel, the atrocities and corruptions of the church's history.[40] This more tragic vision should not be underestimated in his theology. In conjunction with his theology of Holy Saturday it expresses an acute sensitivity to the concrete reality of death, of betrayal, and of the weight and consequence of sin. Balthasar clearly resists anything like a Barthian doctrine of the unreality of evil.[41] His outlook owes itself at least in part to the contribution that Adrienne von Speyr's mystical experience of Hell (documented most notably in *Kreuz und Hölle*) has made to his theology. Indeed, it can be argued that his distinctive development of the theology of divine kenosis (as found in the witness of Paul and, even more notably, John) to include a concentrated meditation on Hell is undertaken precisely to emphasize the fact that unless the divine act of salvation embraces the reality of Hell there remains that of human evil which is for ever past redemption; that in which Christ cannot be made legible.

This emphasis helps explain Donald MacKinnon's admiration for Balthasar. MacKinnon wrote that it is a test of any contemporary theology that it should refuse to turn aside from the overwhelming, pervasive reality of evil, which was manifested in the deliberate murder of six million Jews in the years between 1933 and 1945. In Balthasar's meditations on Holy Saturday, and also on the Stations of the Cross,[42] he wrestles with the enormity of that history and the ultimate question of its redemption. Balthasar, for MacKinnon, shows signs of that "remorseless emphasis on the concrete"[43] which resists all harmonious and systematizing visions of worldly relationship to the divine purpose.

Yet subsequent commentators have questioned quite how remorseless this emphasis on the concrete really is. For Balthasar's emphasis on the *triduum mortis* (three days of death) and specifically the *descensus* (descent into Hell) is most concrete at the point at which it is also most mythological. It seems to divert attention from the struggles and sufferings that characterize the social and material aspects of human history, and to demonstrate an avoidance of the structural and political aspects of sin, in favor of a realm in which the trinitarian relations are acted out for us and for our salvation *beyond* or *outside* historical time. This has led Gerard O'Hanlon to remark that "from one who is so conscious of the reality of evil there is a curious lack of engagement with the great modern structural evils."[44]

Achievement and Agenda

Balthasar is not an *argumentative* theologian. His theology seeks less to analyze, or to construct and systematize a theology on the basis of rational argument, than to give creative, imaginative expression to Christian truth. He wants to articulate a vision of the Christian mystery that is in the end *attractive*, and persuasive for *that* reason. Persuasive because it is allowed to exert its own compelling power rather than because of mere force of argument; and attractive not in a superficial "aestheticized" sense, but because of a capacity to accommodate (and often interrelate) the tensions and intensities of human life and thought in all their variety.

The overriding task he sets himself is to articulate a vision of the Christian mystery which draws on the great riches of the Christian tradition as that comes again to life in the meditations of Adrienne, but which above all is rooted and grounded in the language and imagery of the Bible. His achievement is to hold together his love of European culture and letters, his searching study of scripture and tradition, his debt to Adrienne's mysticism, and his own sense of vocation in developing with Adrienne the work of the secular institute, and to make of them something that is deeply ecclesial theology. The intellectual rigor of his work is joined to the fact that his is self-confessedly a theology done "kneeling":[45] a theology with its roots in meditation and prayer, and above all in the spirituality of Ignatius.

Balthasar's comprehensive vision of the Christian mystery bequeathes to those who come after him the perennial task of any church theology: how, as someone who is set in a particular time and culture, to create a theology which is truly catholic, truly universal? Balthasar's context is clearly a fundamental influence in his theology, though it is a context very different from that of the church theologians in Latin America, Africa, and elsewhere; and different again from the academic context to which much Western theology has had to answer. Yet, as John Riches has said, Balthasar clearly believes that in the measure that one is obedient to the particular vocation that one receives – whatever the context – one is drawn into the paschal mystery and enabled to see the glory of the Lord: and it is this vision which enables one in turn to see the world, with all its *grandeurs et misères*, as never without grace, though always in need of reconciliation and transformation. Catholic in this sense means perceiving the inexhaustible fullness of the revealed glory, not reducing or foreshortening it. It means then constantly working to recover those aspects of the tradition which have been lost and obscured. And it means ever greater openness to the world, to its beauties and consolations, its terrors and *longueurs*. In this sense the task of theology is never done. It needs constantly to battle against the tendency to foreclose: to absolutize its own particularities.

We have seen that Balthasar's theology of an enrapturing, dramatic, and eventful trinitarian God has the resources to sustain such openness. Indeed, as O'Hanlon has intimated, it has the resources for its own development beyond the realms of art, music, drama, and philosophy, perhaps in order to engage with the realms of economics and politics as well (if such a development is left as a latent potentiality by Balthasar himself then it can be part of the task taken up by those who follow him). As Balthasar depicts them, the central mysteries of the cross and resurrection, of the bearing and overcoming of human enmity by the Lord of glory, claim and challenge all theologies in every context, from the theologies of revolutionary Latin America, to those of the Western universities. And for as long as this divine drama exerts its claim, Balthasar's meditations will have strange and compelling insights to offer.

Acknowledgment

This chapter has evolved from the earlier chapter coauthored by John Riches, and is substantially indebted to him.

Notes

1 See Kevin Mongrain, *The Systematic Thought of Hans Urs von Balthasar: An Irenaean Retrieval* (New York: Herder and Herder, 2002). Mongrain argues for the particular structuring influence of Irenaeus' thought on von Balthasar's theology, and the especial importance of his doxological understanding of the mutual (though asymmetrical) ordering of God and humanity: each is oriented towards the glorification of the other, though there is a fundamental ontological distinction between the creaturely and the divine.

2 Aidan Nichols, *The Word Has Been Abroad: A Guide Through Balthasar's Aesthetics* (Edinburgh: T. & T. Clark, 1998), p. xv.

3 Balthasar, "In Retrospect," in J. Riches (ed.), *The Analogy of Beauty: The theology of Hans Urs von Balthasar* (Edinburgh, 1986), p. 220.

4 Hans Urs von Balthasar, *The Theology of Karl Barth: Exposition and Interpretation* (San Francisco: Ignatius Press, 1992), p. 341.

5 Ibid, p. 204.

6 Ibid.

7 "Supra-" is a translation of the German prefix "*Über-*," which is used with great frequency in Balthasar's work. As an example of its use, see *The Glory of the Lord*, Vol. 1, p. 602.

8 Balthasar, "Analogie und Dialektik," in *Divus Thomas* 22 (1944), p. 196; cited in Medard Kehl, "Hans Urs von Balthasar: A Portrait" in *The Von Balthasar Reader*, ed. Medard Kehl and Werner Löser (Edinburgh, 1982), p. 23.

9 See Balthasar, *The Glory of the Lord*, Vol. 1, p. 253.

10 Ibid, pp. 44ff., 52, 56.

11 See, for example, Balthasar's essay in *Elucidations*, "A Verse of Matthias Claudius."

12 See Balthasar's own study in *The Glory of the Lord*, Vol. 3.

13 Balthasar, *The Glory of the Lord*, Vol. 4, p. 437.

14 Mongrain, *The Systematic Thought of Hans Urs von Balthasar*, p. 62.

15 Riches, *The Analogy of Beauty*, p. 220.

16 Balthasar, *The Glory of the Lord*, Vol. I, pp. 45–79.

17 Volumes 4 and 5 of *The Glory of the Lord* trace the fate of the perception of Being (in its openness to divine glory) through the whole history of Western metaphysics, ancient and modern. The story of modern metaphysics as Balthasar tells it is a story about the danger (exemplified by Hegel) of closing off the realm of the sovereign transcendence in the light of which alone Being can be perceived for what it is (the gift of God).

18 Balthasar, *Theo-Drama*, Vol. 3, p. 149.

19 Balthasar, *Theo-Drama*, Vol. 2, p. 268.

20 Balthasar, *Prayer*, trans. A. V. Littledale (New York: Paulist Press, 1967), p. 104.

21 See Balthasar, *Theo-Drama*, Vol. 4.

22 Balthasar, *The Glory of the Lord*, Vol. 5, p. 649.

23 Balthasar, *Elucidations*, p. 51.

24 Balthasar, *Theo-Drama*, Vol. 3, p. 119.

25 Ibid, p. 159.

26 Ibid, p. 325.

27 Balthasar, *Theo-Drama*, Vol. 4, p. 323.

28 See, for instance, the ideal of creaturely cooperation as presented in Balthasar, *The Glory of the Lord*, Vol. 5, p. 105, and its exemplification in Mary (e.g., in Balthasar, *First Glance at Adrienne von Speyr*, p. 52).

29 Riches, *The Analogy of Beauty*, p. 4.

30 Balthasar, "Christlicher Universalismus," in *Verbum Caro* (Einsiedeln, 1960), p. 262.

31 English translation, *The Moment of Christian Witness*.

32 Philip Endean, "Von Balthasar, Rahner, and the Commissar" in *New Blackfriars* 79: 923 (1998), p. 34.

33 R. Bultmann, *The Gospel of John* (Oxford, 1971), p. 69.

34 For an example of the tendency to see clear resolution in drama, see Balthasar on Shakespeare in *Theo-Drama*, Vol. 1, p. 478. It is questionable whether the darker ambiguities of this most subtle of playwrights allow one to say with Balthasar that "all the time he is utterly certain that the highest good is to be found in forgiveness."

35 Balthasar, *The Glory of the Lord*, Vol. 1, p. 562.

36 Cf. Balthasar's speculations about the quasi-mathematical structure of the communion of saints and its capacity to configure the fullness of the church's sanctity in *First Glance*, pp. 82–5.

37 Kehl and Löser, *The Von Balthasar Reader*, p. 233; taken from Balthasar, *Neue Klarstellungen*.

38 Cf., for example, Balthasar, *The Glory of the Lord*, Vol. 7, p. 111.

39 Balthasar, *Mysterium Paschale*, p. 259.

40 Cf. especially Balthasar, "Tragedy and Christian Faith" in *Creator Spirit: Explorations in Theology III* (San Francisco, 1994).

41 Balthasar, "Christlicher Universalismus," p. 269.

42 Balthasar, *The Way of the Cross*.

43 Riches, *The Analogy of Beauty*, p. 167.

44 O'Hanlon, "Theological Dramatics" in B. McGregor and T. Norris (eds.), *The Beauty of Christ: An Introduction to the Theology of Hans Urs von Balthasar* (Edinburgh, T. & T. Clark, 1994), p. 109.

45 Jakob Laubach, "Hans Urs von Balthasar" in *Theologians of Our Time*, ed. Leonhard Reinisch (Notre Dame, IN, 1964), pp. 146–7.

Bibliography

Primary

Heart of the World (San Francisco, 1979; first published 1945).

The Theology of Karl Barth (San Francisco, 1992; first published 1951).

A Theology of History (New York, 1963; first published 1959).

The Glory of the Lord, 7 vols. (Edinburgh, 1982–91; first published 1961–9).

Love Alone: The Way of Revelation (London, 1968; first published 1963).

The Way of the Cross (London, 1969; first published 1964).

The Moment of Christian Witness (New York, 1968; first published 1966).

First Glance at Adrienne von Speyr (San Francisco, 1981; first published 1968).

Mysterium Paschale (Edinburgh, 1990; first published 1970).

Elucidations (London, 1975; first published 1971).

Theo-Drama, 5 vols. (San Francisco, 1988–98; first published 1973–83).

The Christian State of Life (San Francisco, 1984; first published 1977).

Secondary

McGregor, B. and Norris, T. (eds.), *The Beauty of Christ: An Introduction to the Theology of Hans Urs von Balthasar* (Edinburgh, 1994).

Mongrain, K., *The Systematic Thought of Hans Urs von Balthasar: An Irenaean Retrieval* (New York, 2002).

Moss, D. and Oakes, E. T., *The Cambridge Companion to Hans Urs von Balthasar* (Cambridge, 2004).

Nichols, A., *The Word Has Been Abroad: A Guide Through Balthasar's Aesthetics* (Edinburgh, 1998).

—— *No Bloodless Myth: A Guide Through Balthasar's Dramatics* (Edinburgh, 2000).

—— *Say It Is Pentecost: A Guide Through Balthasar's Logic* (Edinburgh, 2001).

Oakes, E. T., *Pattern of Redemption: The Theology of Hans Urs von Balthasar* (New York, 1994).

O'Donnell, J., *Hans Urs von Balthasar* (London, 1992).

O'Hanlon, G. F., *The Immutability of God in the Theology of Hans Urs von Balthasar* (Cambridge, 1990).

Riches, J. (ed.), *The Analogy of Beauty: The Theology of Hans Urs von Balthasar* (Edinburgh, 1986).

Theological Responses to Modernity in Europe and the USA

Europe and the USA have been central to the complex set of developments described in the Introduction as modernity. The most thorough attempt to wrestle with modernity in theology has been in the German-language theological tradition beginning with Schleiermacher and the University of Berlin. Part II shows the continuing importance of this tradition into the twenty-first century.

In Germany itself, apart from those treated in Part I, the leading figures of the second half of the twentieth century have been Wolfhart Pannenberg (chapter 7), Jürgen Moltmann (chapter 8), and Eberhard Jüngel (chapter 15), and the first two have had broad involvement with theology elsewhere in the world. Beyond Germany, Thomas F. Torrance (chapter 9), the Anglican theologians Michael Ramsey, Donald MacKinnon, Stephen Sykes, and Daniel Hardy (chapter 10), the German-American Niebuhr brothers (chapters 11 and 12), leading revisionists, liberals, and postliberals (chapters 13 and 14), Robert Jenson in America (chapter 15), Colin Gunton in England (chapter 15), Roman Catholics Hans Küng, Edward Schillebeeckx, and Nicholas Lash (chapter 16), most biblical and hermeneutical theologians (chapter 17), and a good deal of philosophical theology (chapter 18) are all deeply indebted to that German tradition with its scholarship, its philosophy, and its theology.

Yet Part II gives a different picture if Europe and the USA are seen synchronically at the start of the twenty-first century. Some of the most creative recent developments have had other sources of inspiration – see especially the Anglicans, postliberals, philosophical theologians, hermeneutical thinkers such as Paul Ricoeur, and postmoderns. Both the content and genres of theology are at issue, with systematic theology far less in favor. It appears that in most of Europe and the USA the new century's theologians are being apprenticed in ways that are unlikely to lead to more Pannenbergs. To some this is a matter of regret, and there are some energetic attempts to continue the classic German systematic tradition. To others it is something of a liberation, not necessarily *from* that tradition (it is usually granted that it still has a great deal to teach) as *for* a variety of other genres and ways of conceiving theology. The German heartland itself has been suffering from declining student numbers, cutbacks in posts, ecclesiastical pressure for "safe" appointments, and dissatisfaction at its confessional limitation to Protestant and Roman Catholic. Elsewhere, new sorts of theology are being nurtured in different institutional settings, students from many parts of the world come for higher degrees with a considerable effect on thinking, and the prospect for the twenty-first century in Europe and the USA is that of a lively bazaar of theologies in conversation (often electronically as well as in print and face to face) with no single tradition dominant as in the nineteenth and twentieth centuries.

One challenge is to refine and mature different genres of theology, nurturing traditions of high-quality thought, expression, and debate to set alongside the best in classic theological traditions. Part II shows this already being faced in Europe and the USA, and this is even more apparent when the European and American elements in later parts of this volume are noted. Much of the vibrancy of current theology is found in intensive engagement with particular issues or contexts, or in conversation about or with sciences, practices, other religious traditions, the arts, and other media.

Wolfhart Pannenberg

Christoph Schwöbel

Introduction

In 1961 a slim volume of essays published by a group of younger academics created a considerable sensation in the somewhat static situation of Protestant theology in Germany. The title of the collection, *Offenbarung als Geschichte* (*Revelation as History*), was correctly understood by the theological public as the programmatic statement of a new theological conception. The group of essayists soon became known under the name of their editor as the Pannenberg Circle.[1] It was Wolfhart Pannenberg, the systematic theologian of the group, whose "Dogmatic Theses on the Doctrine of Revelation" contributed significantly to the programmatic character of the volume, who was soon identified with this theological conception that was widely considered to be a genuinely new approach to fundamental issues of modern theology.

Revelation as History did not only provide the basis from which Pannenberg developed his systematic conception; it can also be regarded as the provisional conclusion of his earlier development in which he gradually achieved an independent position. Born in 1928 in Stettin (now Poland), Pannenberg grew up in the atmosphere of the totalitarian regime of National Socialism, before he began his studies after the war at the University of Berlin.[2] After spending some time in Göttingen and after a short interlude in Basel where he encountered Karl Barth, Pannenberg continued his theological studies at the University of Heidelberg. There he wrote his doctoral dissertation *Die Prädestinationslehre des Duns Skotus* (published in 1954) under the supervision of the Lutheran Barthian Edmund Schlink, and in 1955 completed his *Habilitationsschrift* with an analysis of the role of analogy in Western thought up to Thomas Aquinas. After a few years of academic teaching at Heidelberg as *Privatdozent*, in which he discovered the significance of Hegel's thought for the formation of modern theology, Pannenberg was called to become professor at the *Kirchliche Hochschule* in Wuppertal where Jürgen Moltmann was his colleague. In 1961 he was appointed to the chair in systematic theology at the University of Mainz.

It is perhaps justified to say that Pannenberg's own theological conception developed in his attempt to hammer out the full implications of the basic ideas contained in *Revelation as History* and to find sufficient strategies for substantiating its claims in response to its critics. The "working circle" discontinued its regular meetings in 1969 and since then other members have presented theological conceptions, whether in biblical or in systematic theology, which are notably different from that of Pannenberg.

Pannenberg's encounter with North American theology is one of the factors that has shaped the systematic elaboration of his thought. Beginning with an invitation as a guest professor to the University of Chicago in 1963, Pannenberg has lectured widely at most centers of theological learning in the United States, and his continuing dialogue with the leading exponents of process thought has contributed significantly to the development of his theology. He is today at least as widely recognized as a leading contemporary theologian in the United States as in Germany. Pannenberg's involvement in ecumenical theology, which acquired increasing importance after his move in 1967 to the chair in systematic theology at the University of Munich where he was also director of the Ecumenical Institute until 1993, has led to new areas of theological reflection in which he attempts to demonstrate the relevance and comprehensiveness of his theological approach. From 1988 to 1993 Pannenberg published the three volumes of his *Systematische Theologie*, which presents the synthesis of the various strands of his theological development in a comprehensive dogmatic conception.

Survey

In his analysis of the structure of the concept of revelation in *Revelation and History*, Pannenberg starts from the assertion that revelation cannot be adequately understood as the disclosure of truths about God. It has to be interpreted strictly as the self-revelation of God.[3] Divine self-revelation entails – and in this Pannenberg agrees with Barth – that if there is only one God there can only be a single and unique revelation in which God is at the same time author and medium of revelation. It constitutes genuine, though not necessarily exhaustive, knowledge of God. The next step – and here Pannenberg parts company with Barth – is the thesis that according to the biblical traditions God does not reveal himself directly (e.g., in his "Word"), but *indirectly* through his acts in history. On the basis of the strict understanding of revelation as God's self-revelation this cannot refer to specific historical events or series of events. It can only be applied to the end of history from which every preceding event and, indeed, the whole of reality, is illuminated. This eschatological perspective constitutes the universality of revelation.

It is for Pannenberg the distinctive claim of Christian faith that God's eschatological self-demonstration is proleptically actualized in the destiny of Jesus of Nazareth; more precisely, in his resurrection. The preceding history of Israel has to be understood as a gradual universalization of the understanding of God's action in history, reaching its final stage in Jewish Apocalypticism where the end of history is expected as the complete revelation of God. From the end the course of history – now understood in its entirety – can be seen as God's indirect self-revelation, which, in principle, can be recognized by all who have eyes to see.

The crucial point of this rudimentary program is the claim that the end of history as the final self-revelation of God is proleptically realized in the resurrection of

Jesus. Pannenberg tackled the task of substantiating this claim in a comprehensive Christological conception published in 1964 as *Grundzüge der Christologie* (translated in 1968 as *Jesus – God and Man.*) The distinctive and much debated feature of this Christological conception is its methodology, which follows from Pannenberg's understanding of the task of Christology as that of *establishing* the true significance of Jesus as the Christ of God from his history. For this reason – Pannenberg claims – Christological reflection must go back behind the New Testament kerygma to the historical reality of Jesus himself and start "from below." Pannenberg uses this somewhat ambiguous metaphor to designate the difference of his method from the approach "from above," starting with the incarnation of the second person of the Trinity, which presupposes what it seeks to establish (i.e., the divinity of Jesus Christ). In Pannenberg's view it also neglects the historical particularity of the man Jesus in the religious and cultural context of his time and adopts a humanly impossible epistemic stance. Furthermore, Pannenberg rejects the approach to Christology from the question of the significance of Jesus Christ for us, which, in his view, implies that Christology becomes, in effect, a "function of soteriology" (Tillich). This procedure runs the risk of being dominated by soteriological interests which all too easily turn into the Christological projection of human desires for salvation. What Jesus *means* for us must be grounded in what he is, and what he *is* can only be established by starting from the past reality of the historical Jesus.

The starting point "from below" does not, however, mean that Pannenberg's Christology remains below. Knowledge of the divinity of Jesus is grounded in the resurrection in which his unity with God is established in such a way that the claim implied in his pre-Easter appearance is vindicated. Only on the presupposition that the resurrection is understood against the background of apocalyptic expectation as the proleptic actualization of the end of history is it possible to see Jesus in his person as God's self-revelation, because the vindication of his unity with God in the resurrection extends retroactively to the pre-Easter life of Jesus. This does not mean that the distinction between Jesus and God the Father is blurred at any point in this conception. In the framework of the revelational unity of God and Jesus the divinity of Jesus has to be understood as the unity of the Son with the Father which leads directly to the Christian understanding of God as Trinity. More recently Pannenberg has worked out in detail what this self-differentiation in the triune life of God, implied in the cross and resurrection of Jesus, would suggest for a fully-fledged doctrine of the Trinity.

The resurrection, which Pannenberg attempts to establish as a historical event whose probability is stronger than any alternative explanation, is not only the crucial point for the validation of the claims of Jesus' divinity; it is also the foundation for understanding the true humanity of Jesus as the fulfillment of human destiny. Pannenberg explores the possibility of asserting that the identity of Jesus with the Son of God is established indirectly through his relationship of absolute obedience to God the Father. In this sense, Jesus' eternal Sonship is interpreted as dialectically identical with his humanity, insofar as the relationship of Jesus to God the Father in the historical aspect of his existence mediates the relationship of the eternal Son to the Father.

At a number of crucial points the validity of this Christological conception rests on the justifiability of its *anthropological* presuppositions. Pannenberg's thesis that the identity of Jesus and the eternal Son is established indirectly through his humanity presupposes that the openness for God which is the hallmark of Jesus' obedience to the Father is the determinative feature of the human condition. In his writings on theological anthropology, beginning with a published series of radio talks (*What is Man?*, 1970; German edition, 1962) and coming to a preliminary conclusion in his magisterial work *Anthropology in Theological Perspective* (1985; German edition, 1983), Pannenberg has combined the more specific aim of providing the foundational principles for his exposition of Christian faith with the general task of elucidating the anthropological foundation for Christian truth-claims. After the atheistic critique of religion in the modern era anthropology has become for him the battlefield on which theology has to demonstrate the validity of its claims to universality.

The decisive thesis which has been extensively developed over a period of more than twenty years is already introduced in the first chapter of *What is Man?* The fundamental openness to the world which has been interpreted by modern philosophical anthropology as the key to the understanding of what it means to be human has to be interpreted as a fundamental openness for God. God is the infinite horizon which is implicitly presupposed in every act of human self-transcendence. This fundamental relatedness to God constitutes the irreducible dimension of human religiousness which, according to Pannenberg, underlies all structures of human culture.

In contrast to actual human existence, which is characterized by the egocentricity of sin which denies the fundamental exocentricity of human life, what it means to be human has to be understood as the destiny of humanity, which was essentially realized in Jesus but is not yet effectively actualized for all humankind. The term "human nature" should therefore be understood as designating the history of the realization of the human destiny.[4] On this basis Pannenberg offers a theological explanation of the reality of freedom as well as of the communal destiny of humanity. Jesus' resurrection as the foundation of our future resurrection is seen as the warrant for the conviction that the individual human person, as the obedient object of God's love, has infinite value and dignity. This is the ground of freedom which cannot be inferred from the actual existence of humanity. It can only be communicated by reconciliation with God in Christ. On the other hand, Christ's sacrificial devotion to God in giving himself to the world, which is vindicated in the resurrection, pre-actualizes the communal destiny of humanity in the Kingdom of God which finds its anticipatory actualization and symbolic representation in the church, expressed most cogently in the Eucharist.[5] With this attempt Pannenberg tries to point to the mediation of freedom and community in the Kingdom of God and develops on this basis the constructive task of the church in representing the true "global village" of the Kingdom of God and its critical task of resisting every denial of freedom in the name of penultimate communities and authorities. This perspective not only provides a basis for the description of the role of the church in society, it also illuminates the motivation for Pannenberg's ecumenical activity. If the symbolic representation of the community of humankind in God's kingdom is the primary character of the church from which all other tasks are to be determined, the separation of the churches must seem theologically scandalous.[6] The awakening of a new eucharistic piety appears from this viewpoint as the most decisive sign of hope for ecumenism.

The way in which Pannenberg has tried from the outset to integrate different theological disciplines and to relate theological reflection to various non-theological sciences raises many questions concerning the scientific status of theology and its methodology. Pannenberg addressed these questions in his *Theology and the Philosophy of Science* (1976; German edition, 1973) against the backdrop of a detailed description of the development of the philosophy of science and of an exposition of the different historical attempts to determine the scientific character of theology.

In all of Pannenberg's writings there is a thorough-going engagement with the classical themes and theories of the Western philosophical tradition. His theology has also often been criticized as the theological articulation of an underlying philosophical theory, such as the Hegelian metaphysics of history. Pannenberg has consistently rejected such criticisms while insisting that Christian theology must engage with philosophical reflection in order to secure its intelligibility and give a rational account of its claims to universality. In the same year when the first volume of the *Systematic Theology* appeared, Pannenberg also published a book on *Metaphysics and the Idea of God* (1988, Eng. trans. 1990). Pannenberg argues that, historically, philosophy developed from a critique of the gods of Greek religion in their depiction by the poets. Systematically, he claims, there will always be a convergence of themes between philosophy and theology, if philosophy transcends the natural consciousness of our everyday experience and raises questions about the totality and unity of our pluriform experience of the world and of ourselves. Conversely, theology will always have to engage with philosophical thinking if it attempts to validate its claims that the one God is the ultimate horizon for the unity of the world and our experiences of it.

Pannenberg investigates this convergence further in an analysis of the problem of the Absolute. A truly monotheistic conception of God must understand God as being both transcendent and immanent in relation to the world. Hegel attempted to bring these aspects together in the concept of the Spirit. For Pannenberg, Hegel's view of the Spirit and his conception of the Trinity remains, in spite of all its achievements, theologically insufficient, because it does not succeed in offering a complete conceptualization of the representation of the religious consciousness. This shows for Pannenberg that the philosophical conception of the Absolute can offer criteria for the interpretation of the understanding of God in the Christian religious tradition, but it cannot replace a theological concept of God.

In his considerations on the relationship between consciousness and subjectivity Pannenberg follows suggestions made by William James and developed by George Herbert Mead and Erik H. Erikson that the consciousness of the unity of the ego is mediated through our experience of the world so that the self can be understood as constituted in social and spiritual interaction. Pannenberg then presents it as one of the tasks of a renewed metaphysics of the Absolute to show that both the experience of the world and self-consciousness in their mutual relationship have their foundation in the relationship to the Absolute. Drawing on such diverse sources as Plotinus, Dilthey and Heidegger, and correcting what he sees as their shortcomings, Pannenberg argues that the totality of finite being should be thought of as participation in eternity so that the future is conceived as the origin of the totality of finite beings and their being understood as the anticipation of their future.

All concepts are for Pannenberg anticipations of the reality they denote; all factual statements anticipate the appearance of the state of affairs they express. Furthermore, the conceptual anticipation is *not yet* identical with the reality it anticipates. However, since this reality will be fully disclosed in the future, it is *already*, albeit fragmentarily, present in its conceptual anticipation. Ontologically and epistemologically, Pannenberg's philosophy can be characterized as a *realism of anticipation* which corresponds to and is part of the *eschatological realism* of his theology. Philosophical reflection has in his view primarily not a foundational but a criteriological function for theology. However, it is theology which is based on the revelation of God in history that completes the philosophical enterprise of grasping the unity of reality in the One by presenting all reality as grounded in the reality of God. That is the unifying theme of the three volumes of his *Systematic Theology*.

In his publications after the conclusion of the *Systematic Theology* Pannenberg has concentrated on three main areas of his theological reflection: (1) the relationship between theology and philosophy, (2) the questions of a theology of nature developed in dialogue with the natural sciences, and (3) the issues of ecumenism. The first area is represented by the book *Theologie und Philosophie. Ihr Verhältnis im Lichte ihrer gemeinsamen Geschichte* (1996), devoted to a historical and systematic elucidation of the relationship between theology and philosophy. This is also one of the main themes of Pannenberg's history of modern theology, published under the title *Problemgeschichte der neueren evangelischen Theologie in Deutschland. Von Schleiermacher bis Barth und Tillich* (1997). This area is also the thematic focus of the first volume in Pannenberg's new series of collected papers called *Beiträge zur Systematischen Theologie*, where the contribution to the relationship between theology and philosophy is summarized under the title "Philosophie, Religion, Offenbarung" (1999). The second area, Pannenberg's dialogue with the natural sciences, is a conversation conducted on the field of philosophy, which is seen as the area of convergence between theology and the sciences. It is represented by the book *Toward a Theology of Nature: Essays on Science and Faith* (1993). A more comprehensive collection of Pannenberg's writings in this area is found in volume 2 of the *Beiträge*, bearing the title "Natur und Mensch – und die Zukunft der Schöpfung" (2000). The third area, Pannenberg's concern for ecumenism, especially the dialogue with Roman Catholicism, has grown out of his participation in ecumenical dialogue groups. In addition to being part of the conversations of *Faith and Order* in the World Council of Churches, Pannenberg was a member of the *Arbeitskreis evangelischer und Römisch-katholischer Theologen*. The work of this group, founded in the aftermath of World War II by Lorenz Cardinal Jaeger and the Lutheran theologian Wilhelm Stählin, focused since the 1970s on a reexamination of the mutual anathemas between the Roman Catholic Church and the Lutheran churches in the light of current doctrinal teaching in both churches. This reexamination, which had come to the conclusion that the anathemas of the sixteenth century do not apply to the current teaching of the Roman Catholic Church and the Lutheran churches, formed the background to the hotly debated "Joint Declaration on the Doctrine of Justification" (1998), trying to formulate a "differentiated consensus" in the teaching of both churches. This area is represented in the third volume of the *Beiträge*, "Kirche und Ökumene" (2000). If one asked what could be the underlying common theme that finds its expression in all three areas, one would have to point to Pannenberg's concern for the unity of truth which forms the background of his notion of a universal history and of the totality of meaning which can only be fully grasped if the course of time is completed in eternity. This unity is not an attribute of truth *per se* and it is certainly not a self-evident attribute of history. It can only be appropriately considered if the unity of God and God's action is seen as the foundation of all unity and totality in creation, be it the unity of truth or the totality of meaning and being. Because in God unity is the unity-in-difference which characterizes the trinitarian being of God, this theological foundation protects the concern for unity from becoming monistic and the engagement with totality from becoming totalitarian.

Systematic Theology

In the spring of 1988 Pannenberg published the first volume of his *Systematische Theologie*, comprising the prolegomena to dogmatics and the doctrine of God. The second and third volumes followed in 1991 and 1993. Compared to Pannenberg's earlier writings one distinctive difference becomes immediately obvious. While the earlier works can be seen as successive steps in the development of the theological conception that was programmatically introduced in *Revelation as History*, this conception is now presented in its full systematic *Gestalt*.

Truth and God

Pannenberg starts with a discussion of the truth of Christian doctrine as the organizing theme of systematic theology. First of all, Pannenberg rejects the notion that theology can be adequately understood as the expression of human notions about the divine. It must be grounded in the divine mediation of God in revelation. This implies, secondly, understanding dogma not primarily as an expression of the consensus of the church, but as an "eschatological concept" (Barth), referring to the final disclosure of truth at the end of history, which is nevertheless proleptically present in God's self-revelation in Christ as it is presented in scripture. It follows, thirdly, that dogmatic theology has to presuppose the truth of the tradition of faith grounded in revelation without claiming that this is an already established and self-evident truth. In order to overcome this apparent dilemma, Pannenberg suggests that the fact that God's reality and the truth of his revelation remains contentious before the *eschaton* must itself be understood as grounded in God, if God is indeed the creator of heaven and earth. The metaphysical concept of God functions as a general condition for understanding Christian God-talk. It has to be presupposed in order to assert the claim that the God of the philosophers really exists as the God of the Bible.

For Pannenberg, there is a *cognitio Dei naturalis insita*, an innate knowledge of God in human beings. The claim to such awareness of God can in his view be substantiated from anthropology, and is discussed in the history of religious thought with reference to concepts such as "conscience," "immediate awareness," and "basic trust." These notions express, according to Pannenberg, the fact that human beings live in virtue of the "excentric openness" of their existence in an unthematic awareness of their own life as being posited into the whole of reality and dependent on the divine ground of reality. Although this awareness is unthematic and can only be identified as awareness of God from the perspective of a reflective interpretive framework, it is nevertheless not a human possibility that awaits actualization; it is fully actual in the very fact of human existence.

However, Pannenberg emphasizes the very attempt at finding a universal foundation for religious claims has to be based on the interpretation of reality in the concrete religions. Therefore, Pannenberg interprets the history of religions as the history of the appearance of the unity of God. In Pannenberg's view, Israel's understanding of history as the sphere of the appearance of God's unity provides the key for the theological interpretation of the history of religions because the mediation of particularity and universality is an essential characteristic of divine self-demonstration in history itself. Within the framework of this conception the concept of revelation denotes the origin and basic criterion of knowledge of God.

Pannenberg's analysis of revelation is in many ways the center of the exposition in the first volume of the *Systematische Theologie*. First of all, it is the place where it has to be shown that human knowledge of God has its origin and foundation in God's self-disclosure. Secondly, it has to be demonstrated how the unthematic awareness of the divine ground of reality receives a definite content in revelation. And thirdly, it is here that the justification of the claim that the notion of God's self-demonstration in history can mediate particularity and universality in the history of religions has to be developed. At the same time, these considerations are also the turning point for the structure of the argument in the *Systematische Theologie*. Pannenberg turns from the external perspective, where the conception of God and the claims of the history of religions are phenomenologically introduced and analyzed with regard to their function for the view of reality, to the internal perspective of Christian revelation from which a systematic reconstruction of Christian doctrine is developed.

Pannenberg's conception of the doctrine of the Trinity is perhaps the most interesting aspect of his dogmatic synthesis, since he introduces trinitarian reflection as a new approach to the solution of some of the crucial problems of the traditional conception of the doctrine of God. The result is a reversal of the traditional structure for the exposition of the doctrine of God, which started from the existence of God, proceeded to the discussion of the essence and attributes of the one God, and then added the doctrine of the Trinity. Instead, Pannenberg starts from the doctrine of the Trinity and employs this as the interpretive key for the conception of the being and attributes of the triune God.

Pannenberg's proposal is to develop the doctrine of the Trinity from the way in which the relationship of Father, Son, and Spirit is disclosed in revelation.[7] Therefore, the mutual self-differentiation of Father, Son, and Spirit in the divine economy must be seen as the concrete form of the immanent trinitarian relations. The key to an adequate description of these relations is for Pannenberg the fact that Jesus distinguishes himself clearly from the God he calls Father, but in renouncing himself completely he makes room for the action of the Father and the coming of his kingdom. In this way, God, as he eternally is, discloses himself in his relationship to Jesus, and this reveals an "aspect" in the humanity of Jesus which is the eternal correlate to the Fatherhood of God: the eternal Son. The self-differentiation of the Son from the Father corresponds to the self-differentiation of the Father from the Son, which consists in the fact that the Son receives all power in heaven and on earth from the Father (Matthew 28: 18) until God's rule has become universally victorious, when the Son will return the power to the Father (cf. 1 Corinthians 15: 24, 28).

The resurrection is in Pannenberg's view the access to an adequate understanding of the Third Person, because it depicts the dependence of the Father and the Son on the Spirit as the medium of their community. And from this perspective the whole work of the Son in the glorification of the Father can be assessed on the basis of his dependence on the Spirit. From this approach it is not surprising that Pannenberg rejects the addition of the *filioque* to the Nicene–Constantinopolitan Creed by the Western church. The reason is not simply that this one-sided step was uncanonical, but more importantly, that it rests on the mistaken Augustinian view of all relations of the Trinity as originating relations, which overlooks the pluriform character of the trinitarian relations and cannot do justice to the Spirit as the medium of the community of the Father and the Son.

The conception of the Trinity that is developed in this way implies that the three persons have to be understood as three centers of activity, and each of them is a focus of a network of relationships. The mutuality of their active relationships implies for Pannenberg furthermore that the *monarchia* of the Father has to be understood as the result of the cooperation of all three persons. The full realization of the *monarchia* of the Father is the kingdom. From this perspective the world as a whole can be seen as the history in which it will be finally demonstrated that the trinitarian God is the only true God.

In the last chapter of the first volume of the *Systematic Theology* Pannenberg turns to the issues of the unity of the divine essence and the divine attributes. Pannenberg connects the trinitarian question of the unity of the divine essence with the fundamental questions about God's existence and attributes that are commonly treated before the doctrine of the Trinity. His reformulation of the traditional problem of the relationship of God's *essentia* and his *existentia* forms the background for Pannenberg's reflections on the doctrine of the divine attributes. Pannenberg sees many of the difficulties in this field rooted in the underlying understanding of God as *nous* and he attempts to solve these problems by pointing to the analogies of the biblical notions of God as Spirit with the scientific concept of a universal field of force that is manifested in particular corpuscular constellations. This move enables Pannenberg to retain the notions of energy, dynamic effects, and life without ascribing them to a self-conscious subject. His bold proposal is to understand the divine essence and life on the analogy of the field model and not in terms of the *nous* model. The Godhead is in this way understood as the divine Spirit or life that is manifested in the three persons of Father, Son, and Spirit. Since the three persons have to be seen as the forms of existence of the one divine life, they are eternally constituted and correlated by its overflowing energy, which is mediated through the inner-trinitarian relations.

On the basis of this view, Pannenberg explains the relationship between the immanent and the economic Trinity by stating that in their active presence to the world as Father, Son, and Spirit the persons of the Trinity also relate to themselves. Pannenberg interprets the unity of God's action by relating the *monarchia* of the Father to the Kingdom of God as the ultimate "objective" of God's action. This *monarchia* is mediated through the Son, who becomes incarnate to make the participation of God's creatures in the kingdom possible and through the Spirit who enables them to participate in the relationship of Father and Son. The *monarchia* of the Father in the kingdom is the unitary focus of all divine activity in creation, redemption, and salvation and of the interrelationship of the three trinitarian persons.

The divine attributes are divided into two groups by Pannenberg: the first set comprises those attributes (like infinity, eternity, omnipotence, and omnipresence) that identify the being who is the subject of further predications. Their function is to make sure that these attributes are indeed attributes of *God*. The attributes of the second set (like righteousness, faithfulness, wisdom, mercy, patience, etc.) are predicated of the being that conforms to the minimal conditions for talking about God laid down by the first set of attributes. The concept of the Infinite is presented as the fundamental notion that regulates the entire conception of the divine attributes. The truly Infinite, Pannenberg insists, must comprehend everything finite within itself without blurring the initial contrast of infinity and finitude. In order to underline the religious significance of such a conception of God as infinite, Pannenberg refers to the biblical understanding of God's holiness, which sees holiness as opposed to the profane, but also comprehends the profane through its inclusion into the sanctifying dynamic of God's truly infinite holiness.

This pattern of opposition and inclusion also determines the conception of the other divine attributes. God's eternity cannot only be understood in contrast to time; it must also be thought of as including time in its totality. In contrast to his temporal creatures, God is his own future and this implies perfect freedom, a freedom that is not restricted by being bound to a temporally limited present.

Omnipresence is a condition for divine omnipotence. Perfect omnipotence can only be predicated of God the creator. Seeing God as the creator implies that God's omnipotence cannot be understood as opposed to the being of his creation. The perfect exercise of omnipotence therefore consists – according to Pannenberg – in the divine activity that overcomes the alienation between the creator and his creation. For this reason the incarnation of the Son must be understood as the highest expression of God's omnipotence.

This thought leads already to the treatment of the divine attributes that are predicated of God on the basis of his trinitarian action. Here the notion of divine love has the same integrative and regulative function as the notion of the Infinite for the "metaphysical" attributes of God. On the basis of God's revelation in the story of Jesus, love has to be understood as the concrete form of the unity of the divine essence, which is manifested in the relationship of the trinitarian persons. Pannenberg therefore presents God's goodness, grace, mercy, righteousness, faithfulness, patience, and wisdom as aspects of the all-encompassing reality of divine love. In this way the trinitarian conception of love becomes the coping-stone of Pannenberg's dogmatic synthesis.

Pannenberg's exposition of the divine economy in the subsequent two volumes of the *Systematic Theology* presents the unfolding of his conception of God as trinitarian love in the history of salvation, which concludes with the ultimate revelation of God's love in the Kingdom of God.[8] It is one of the major achievements of Pannenberg's *Systematic Theology* that it is a consistently trinitarian theology in which everything that can be said in dogmatics must be seen in the framework of an understanding of God as Trinity.

Creation and Christ

The theological possibilities that are opened up by such a consistently trinitarian account are clearly demonstrated in Pannenberg's exposition of the doctrine of creation.[9] It follows from this approach that the relationship of God to what is not God is seen as rooted in the immanent relations of the Trinity. Pannenberg follows the Western trinitarian tradition of describing the immanent Trinity in terms of immanent *actions*, which are the ground of God's action in relation to the world. It is the emphasis of God's creating as a free and sovereign act which leads in Pannenberg's view to the understanding of creation as *creatio ex nihilo*. God's freedom in creating, however, must be understood as the freedom of love, which includes difference and communion, if God grants creation its own relatively independent being and its own relative permanence. Like Hegel, Pannenberg sees the Son as the principle of difference in the Trinity and so as the generative principle of created reality existing in relative independence from God. Unlike Hegel, Pannenberg does not interpret the Son as a logically necessary stage in the history of the Absolute, but sees the free self-distinction of Jesus from the Father as the *ratio cognoscendi*, the foundation of knowing, of the eternal Sonship of Jesus, and this as the basis for the claim that the corresponding eternal self-distinction of the Son from the Father is the *ratio essendi*, the ground of being, for the existence of creation. The Son is therefore the structural archetype of the destiny of creation to achieve communion with God. This, however, can only be achieved through the Spirit, who is the principle of communion in the immanent Trinity and so the medium of the participation of created life in the divine trinitarian life.

It is for Pannenberg an essential aspect of the task of a theology of creation to relate its assertions to the findings of the scientific investigation of the world. His own proposals for a dialogue between theology and the sciences concentrate on his understanding of the Spirit and the Spirit's activity in terms of a field of force, but others include his notion of "beginning" in relation to eschatology, which he works out in dialogue with scientific cosmology.

The trinitarian framework also shapes Pannenberg's anthropological reflections. In contrast to the mainstream of tradition which identified *pneuma* with *nous*, Pannenberg distinguishes them. This means that human reason just as much as the material existence of humans depends on the life-giving Spirit. While reason, with its capacity for discerning differences, reflects the self-differentiation of the Son from the Father as the ground of all difference, the unity of consciousness, located in the imagination, and the unity of personhood, the disclosure of the totality of a personal life in its existence, are both mediated by the Spirit, the principle of unity in its eschatological fulfillment. Rejecting both the notion of an original perfection of humans and of the fall as the loss of the image of God, Pannenberg interprets the image of God as a dynamic notion for the human destiny to live in communion with God, which is realized in the Incarnation. However, human beings can only achieve their destiny in conformity with the self-distinction of the Son from the Father. Sin is therefore defined as the refusal of humans to accept their created finitude by distinguishing themselves explicitly from God. In this way they attempt to assume the place of God.

In his Christology in the *Systematic Theology*,[10] Pannenberg offers an extensive discussion of the relationship of a Christology "from below" to a Christology "from above." In the context of the *Systematic Theology*, which interprets the history and destiny of Jesus as the action of the trinitarian God for the salvation of humankind, Christology "from below" and "from above" are complementary insofar as the former offers a reconstruction of the foundation of the statements the latter develops systematically. The starting point of Christology is, for Pannenberg, the distinctive humanity of Christ in which the destiny of humanity to live in communion with God becomes reality in Jesus' filial relationship to God. Rooted in his self-distinction from the Father by becoming obedient to him, the divinity of Jesus is therefore not a foreign element added to the reality of Jesus' humanity, but the reflection from Jesus' relationship to the Father on his being and on the eternal being of God. The resurrection is in Pannenberg's interpretation the justification of Jesus' claim to filial authority by God the Father and in this way validates Jesus' message. This implies that God is eternally as Jesus proclaimed God to be: God is eternally the Father revealed in the Son and therefore the Son is eternally in relation with the Father and in this sense preexistent.

In this trinitarian framework humanity is conceived to be essentially in relation to God because it is a specific expression of the Son as the generative principle of difference and of created independence. It therefore has the capacity of becoming the medium for expressing the self-distinction of the Son from the Father and so their communion-in-difference. Since living in communion with God is the created destiny of humanity from the beginning, the Incarnation is not an alien intrusion into humanity but the actualization of its destiny. However, this is only possible where the Spirit elevates humanity ecstatically above its finitude and so enables it to accept its finitude and so to become the medium of the expression of the relationship of Father and Son. Conversely, the Incarnation is the self-actualization or self-fulfillment of God in his relationship to the world, though not – and here Pannenberg differs from Barth – in the eternal immanent trinitarian relations.

For Pannenberg, soteriology is a function of Christology. The reconciliation of God and the world in Christ is exclusively God's work. Nevertheless, it has the "form" of representation, since humanity participates in this process by being represented in Christ. Jesus' death discloses this representation, since he dies for those who condemned him and so brought God's judgment upon themselves. Jesus' representation of humanity, not only through the cross but also in his whole history and destiny, has an inclusive significance for all humankind, though only in an anticipatory sense which is worked out through the apostolic ministry of the church. Therefore, Pannenberg discusses the theological significance of the gospel and the doctrine of the inspiration of scripture in the context of the doctrine of reconciliation.

The church and the Kingdom of God

The third volume of the *Systematic Theology* comprises Pannenberg's ecclesiology and his eschatology. His treatment of the church documents his commitment to the ecumenical process. His specific aim is to offer a reassessment of the doctrinal differences between Protestantism and Roman Catholicism in order to examine and, if possible, to overcome the doctrinal obstacles for achieving greater visible unity of the church. This ecumenical emphasis follows from Pannenberg's view that the church is to be interpreted as the anticipation and sign of the community of human-kind in the Kingdom of God. This eschatological horizon for discussing the church as the "sacrament of the Kingdom"[11] relativizes all exclusive claims that might be made for any historical ecclesial community, and it forms the background for Pannenberg's ecumenical hermeneutic for ecclesiology, which is designed to show that apparently contradictory doctrinal positions can be seen as complementary aspects of a more comprehensive truth.

Pannenberg combines traditional Western and Eastern emphases by arguing that the church is constituted by the Son and the Spirit together. This trinitarian approach also shapes the systematic structure of Pannenberg's ecclesiology. Pannenberg gives priority neither to the appropriation of salvation by the individual believer nor to the communion of saints. Both are integrated in an ecclesiological perspective which sees individual and communal aspects of salvation as related dimensions of the work of the Spirit. The personal communion of believers is mediated through participa-tion in the sacraments as the means of grace. Eucharistic communion demonstrates that for Pannenberg most clearly: membership in the body binds the relationship of believers with Christ inextricably together with their relationship with one another. The Spirit is interpreted in this way as the focus of various relationships that make up the church, enabling the immediacy of every individual Christian to God and joining them together in the communion of the body of Christ, where they receive in the Spirit their fundamental orientation towards the Kingdom of God.

Pannenberg's discussion of the doctrine of justification is shaped by the ecumen-ical intention of his ecclesiology. Over against an exclusively forensic understanding of justification, Pannenberg argues that the Pauline treatment of the notion of righteousness of faith shows that being declared righteous must have its basis in the righteousness of faith, it does not constitute it. Righteousness of faith, he argues, is to be understood as living in communion with Christ by participating in his death and resurrection through baptism. From this perspective the doctrinal differences in the treatment of justification between the Reformers and the Council of Trent can no longer be seen as fundamental differences that could be allowed to serve as a justification for the continuing division between the Protestant churches and the Roman Catholic Church.

With his interpretation of justification Pannenberg has brought baptism and justi-fication closely together. The point of baptism is to be found in the participation of the believer in the death and resurrection of Christ. The celebration of the Eucharist is, for Pannenberg, the symbolic anticipation of the coming reign of God in the presence of the risen Lord. This is the basis for asserting the ecclesiological primacy of the local church: wherever the Eucharist is celebrated, there is the church. Pannenberg follows the approach of recent ecumenical eucharistic theology by stressing that the real presence of Christ cannot be exclusively located in the elements of bread and wine. It must be seen as being mediated in the whole act of eucharistic worship. The link between anamnesis and epiclesis requires a consistently trinitarian interpretation. The Spirit as the transforming power of the world is at work where we are drawn into the movement of Christ's self-giving love. Because the sacraments are indications of the mystery of salvation in Christ, and since the sign indicates the presence of the reality signified, Pannenberg can argue for a wide notion of sacramentality. If the character of a sacrament depends exclusively on whether something can be shown to be included in or ordered towards the mystery of salvation in Christ, as Pannenberg argues, it follows that the files on the case of the recognition of the seven sacraments of the Roman Catholic Church by the Protestant churches must be reopened.

A similar ecumenical thrust can be found in Pannenberg's discussion of church leadership. Church leadership in all its forms is in his view rooted in the notion of apostolic leadership, which is called to serve the unity of the church. Since unity is for Pannenberg the first and foremost of the essential attributes of the church, he attempts to correlate different levels of leadership with different levels of church unity, from the local church to the worldwide church. It is consistent with this approach that Pannenberg's reflections conclude with a call for the recognition of the historic function of the bishop of Rome to act as the representative for the whole of Christianity. However, this is for Pannenberg not to be justified by appealing to divine right. It is a matter of historic authority.

The doctrine of election is according to Pannenberg the link between ecclesiology and eschatology. For him, the biblical image of the "people of God" is the central term of the doctrine of election. It is systematically displaced, he finds, if it is employed only in the context of the church. The notion of the people of God helps to see election in its concrete historical circumstances as God's call to particular people to be the church and so to be an anticipatory representation of the universal character of God's will of salvation for the whole of humankind. Pannenberg sees this mediation of particularity and universality as the basis for a comprehensive theology of history which attempts to develop a theological interpretation of church history.

The *Systematic Theology* concludes with a discussion on "the perfection of creation in the Kingdom of God." The Kingdom of God is, first of all, the consummation of the community of humankind, and this, radically conceived, includes the resurrection of the dead. Secondly, it is the end of history which in the context of Christian faith cannot mean its abolition and transition into nothingness, but can only mean the inclusion of history in God's eternity. Therefore, the Kingdom of God is, thirdly, the entering of eternity into time. This last aspect has central significance for Pannenberg: everything in eschatology revolves around the relationship of time and eternity. If eternity is understood as the future of perfection of everything, then this future is present in the processes occurring in time as the aim of these processes. Everything that occurs and perishes in time, Pannenberg claims, is preserved in God's eternity, which includes all temporal events. The identity of every created being is preserved by their being included into God's eternity and it is reconstituted after their death in the resurrection.

The metaphor of the "Last Judgment" in Pannenberg's interpretation expresses that the participation of created beings in God's eternity requires their radical transformation. The point of divine judgment is therefore not the annihilation of the world but its purification by the light of God's glory to enable its participation in God's eternal life.

Eschatology is also the place in the systematic structure of a Christian theology where the question of theodicy must be answered.[12] Pannenberg emphasizes with

Hegel that all theoretical attempts at offering justification of God in view of the evil in the world remain pointless unless there is a real history of reconciliation, of the overcoming of evil by the rule of God. This history of reconciliation culminates in the eschatological perfection of creation. However, the ultimate perfection of creation is for Pannenberg already present in the time of creation, because the whole of the divine economy reflects the self-prevenience of the future of God in the time of creation.

In this way divine love is seen by Pannenberg as the ground for the distinction of the immanent and the economic trinity and the foundation of their unity. God's love goes beyond the immanent trinitarian life to recreate, to reconcile, and to bring the created world to perfection. Conversely, in the economy of salvation, the created world is taken beyond itself in order to be included in the unity of God's own trinitarian life. The distinction and the unity of the immanent and the economic Trinity, which will be fully disclosed in the *eschaton*, is therefore for Pannenberg the heartbeat of divine love, the ground and destiny of the created world.

Achievement and Debate

When one attempts to summarize the achievements of Pannenberg's theological conception three characteristics seem to be most notable. First of all, Pannenberg's theology is an attempt to meet the challenge of the atheistic critique of religion in the modern era without seeking refuge in strategies of intellectual immunization, and on the reflective level that is required by the intellectual standard of the critique and by its pervasive influence in contemporary culture. Secondly, Pannenberg seeks to realize this aim by developing his theology in close contact with the findings of biblical exegesis and against the background of a comprehensive analysis of the Christian tradition. Thirdly, one of the distinctive marks of Pannenberg's theological reflection is the awareness of the necessity for interdisciplinary cooperation with the human sciences and, to a certain extent, with natural science, in which Christian theology interacts with the intellectual efforts of its time. All three characteristics illustrate the conviction underlying Pannenberg's entire conception that Christian theology will only be able to fulfill its task adequately if it develops a comprehensive view of reality that is authentically Christian as well as intellectually plausible and that provides ethical orientation in the complexities of the modern situation.

It is precisely this view of the task of theology which can provoke a number of critical questions with regard to the conceptual framework in terms of which Pannenberg attempts its execution. The development of a comprehensive view of reality in Christian theology seems to require some kind of ontology which explains what there is and how it is to be interpreted. If the activity of determining how something is to be interpreted is to be capable of resulting in genuine truth-claims, it is necessary to establish that it can correspond to the determination of what there is. Especially in Pannenberg's earlier writings, we encounter at this point a twofold *indeterminacy* in Pannenberg's conception: what something *is* is only established in what it *becomes* in the future; and every act of determining how what there is is to be interpreted has an irreducibly hypothetical status. Is this a necessary corollary of Christian eschatology or does it introduce an unnecessary element of indeterminacy into the Christian view of reality, which would have to be seen as self-defeating? This problem is further illustrated by Pannenberg's proposal of comprehending both God's creation and his self-revelation in the concept of the futurity of God. If the existence and nature of God are finally determined and made evident only in the eschatological self-demonstration of his kingdom, it would seem that God's relation to the world remains – at least penultimately – indeterminate.

The *Systematic Theology* does not only document Pannenberg's awareness of these difficulties, it also demonstrates his attempt to overcome its problematical consequences. This is illustrated by the determinative role of the doctrine of the Trinity not only for the understanding of God, but also for the entire dogmatic conception. If everything that is is ultimately grounded in God's trinitarian relation to his creation, and if God's relation to the world is the repetition or reenactment of his eternal being as Father, Son, and Spirit, then the apparent indeterminacy has its limit precisely in the eternal identity of the triune God.

This leads to the second problem that seems to underlie many of the crucial and much debated features of Pannenberg's theological methodology. Pannenberg has from the outset attempted to find a middle way between the Scylla of a "dogmatic" exposition of Christian doctrine based on revelation, which fails to offer sufficient reasons for its assertions, and the Charybdis of a "rationalist" treatment of theology which only allows such statements that can be justified by means of reason alone. The *Systematic Theology* presents his most developed attempt to mediate between the internal perspective of faith and the external perspective of reason. His approach to start from the description of religious and theological claims and to identify within this framework the concept of revelation as the irreplaceable foundation of all theological claims from which the reconstruction of the contents of revelation can then proceed, is certainly one of the most interesting proposals for the solution of this thorny problem in modern theology. It documents Pannenberg's insistence that faith is not grounded in itself and can therefore not be treated as self-justifying, and it illustrates the determined effort to give reasons for the assertions of faith that are intelligible and rationally plausible within the framework of reason. But at least some would disagree with the conclusions which Pannenberg draws from this for the conception of Christian theology. For Pannenberg, it is essential that the theologian can establish certain foundational principles outside the perspective of faith that would support the claims to universality made within that framework. Therefore, he attempts to reconstitute the traditional insights of natural theology in his conception of the non-thematic awareness of the Infinite that is given in the factual constitution of humanity. The use of anthropological and epistemological reflections as a modern *praeambula fidei* would seem to provoke the danger that these considerations are made subject to far-ranging theological reinterpretations that would reduce philosophy to an ancillary role for the constructive theological task. It would also appear that if the theologian employs non-theological considerations as foundational principles for theology, the categories developed from the perspective of reason would have a determinative effect for the conception the theologian develops in the reconstruction of the contents of faith from the perspective of faith.

The problems of Pannenberg's attempt at combining the perspective of reason and the perspective of faith in his theological conception could be summarized in the following question: is it necessary to try to establish the basis for the claims to universality in Christian faith from the perspective of reason, before one turns to the explication of the contents of faith as they are grounded in revelation, or would it be more adequate to treat the universality of theological truth-claims as an implication of the Christian revelation that can only be developed in terms of a rational reconstruction of its contents from the perspective of faith?

Is Pannenberg's theology the type of theology that will determine the future of theology? With regard to its conception of the task of theology in presenting an authentically Christian and intellectually plausible view of reality, developed in intradisciplinary theological cooperation and tested in interdisciplinary dialogue with other sciences, it is to be hoped that many theologians will follow the inspiration of Pannenberg's enterprise. The intellectual rigor of Pannenberg's theological thinking and the willingness, documented in the development of his thought, to subject his arguments to constant reexamination, require to be taken so seriously that one should not hesitate to criticize the execution of this program in Pannenberg's own work. However, Pannenberg's work has set standards which also his critics should attempt to meet.

Notes

1 The original group of Rolf Rendtorff and Klaus Koch (Old Testament) and Ulrich Wilckens and Dietrich Rössler (New Testament), which was later joined by Martin Elze (church history) and Trutz Rendtorff (social ethics), represented together with Pannenberg almost a complete faculty, and this interdisciplinary cooperation constituted an effective counter-move against the growing alienation of dogmatic, exegetical, and historical theology.

2 For a biographical portrait, see R. J. Neuhaus, "Pannenberg: Profile of a Theologian," in Pannenberg, *Theology and the Kingdom of God*, pp. 9–50. See also Wenz, *Wolfhart Pannenbergs Systematische Theologie*, pp. 9–14. Pannenberg's own account can be found in Braaten and Clayton, *The Theology of Wolfhart Pannenberg*, pp. 11–18.

3 Cf. "Dogmatic Theses on the Doctrine of Revelation" in *Revelation as History*, pp. 125–58.

4 Cf. *Human Nature*, p. 24.

5 Cf. "Eucharistic Piety: A New Experience of Christian Community," in *Christian Spirituality and Sacramental Community*, pp. 31–49, esp. 38ff.

6 See also "The Kingdom of God and the Church," in *Theology and the Kingdom of God*, pp. 72–101.

7 Cf. ibid, pp. 331ff. Pannenberg criticizes Barth (who argued programmatically for the same approach) for not following his own program, since he develops the doctrine of the Trinity from the formal notion of revelation as expressed in the statement "God reveals himself as the Lord." With this approach, Barth renews Hegel's conception of describing the three persons of the Trinity as "moments" or "states" of the divine self-consciousness by talking about "modes of being" in the one divine subjectivity. Pannenberg interprets this strategy as a renaissance of Augustine's psychological theory of the *vestigia trinitatis* (which Barth had explicitly rejected), since its interpretive key is the *imago trinitatis* in the human soul. Instead of starting from the formal notion of revelation, Pannenberg proposes to develop his trinitarian conception from the content of God's revelation in Christ.

8 Cf. Vol. 3, pp. 689–94.

9 Cf. Vol. 2, pp. 15–201.

10 Cf. ibid, pp. 315–439.

11 Cf. Vol. 3, p. 59.

12 The problem is raised in the context of belief in God the creator; cf. Vol. 2, pp. 189–201. It is only possible to attempt an answer in the context of eschatology; cf. Vol. 3, pp. 679–89.

Bibliography

A complete bibliography of primary and secondary works up to the year 1988 can be found in *Vernunft des Glaubens. Wissenschaftliche Theologie und kirchliche Lehre.* Festschrift zum 60. Geburtstag von Wolfhart Pannenberg. Mit einem bibliographischen Anhang herausgegeben von Jan Rohls und Gunther Wenz (Göttingen: Vandenhoeck & Ruprecht, 1988), pp. 693–718. This bibliography has been continued by Friderike Nüssel in the journal *Kerygma und Dogma* 43 (1999), 143–54. Pannenberg's writings from 1998 to 2002 are listed in Wenz, *Wolfhart Pannenbergs Systematische Theologie*, pp. 296–300.

Primary

"Dogmatic Theses on the Doctrine of Revelation," in Wolfhart Pannenberg (ed.), *Revelation as History* (New York, 1968); also in *Human Nature, Election and History* (Philadelphia, PA, 1977).

Jesus – God and Man (London, 1968).

Theology and the Kingdom of God, ed. R. J. Neuhaus (Philadelphia, PA, 1969).

Basic Questions in Theology: Collected Essays, 3 vols. (London, 1970, 1971, 1973). (Volume 3 is also published under the title *The Idea of God and Human Freedom*, Philadelphia, PA, 1973.)

What Is Man? Contemporary Anthropology in Theological Perspective (Philadelphia, PA, 1970).

The Apostles' Creed: In the Light of Today's Questions (Philadelphia, PA, 1972).

Theology and the Philosophy of Science (London, 1976).

Reality and Faith (Philadelphia, PA, 1977).

Christian Spirituality and Sacramental Community (London, 1984).

Anthropology in Theological Perspective (Edinburgh, 1985).

Metaphysics and the Idea of God (Edinburgh, 1990).

Systematic Theology Vols. 1–3 (Edinburgh, 1991, 1994, 1998).

An Introduction to Systematic Theology (Edinburgh, 1991).

Toward a Theology of Nature: Essays on Science and Faith (Louisville, KY, 1993).

Grundlagen der Ethik. Philosophisch-theologische Perspektiven (Göttingen, 1996).

Theologie und Philosophie. Ihr Verhältnis im Lichte ihrer gemeinsamen Geschichte (Göttingen, 1996).

Problemgeschichte der neueren evangelischen Theologie in Deutschland. Von Schleiermacher zu Barth und Tillich (Göttingen, 1997).

Beiträge zur Systematischen Theologie: Band 1: Philosophie, Religion, Offenbarung (Göttingen, 1999). *Band 2: Natur und Mensch – und die Zukunft der Schöpfung* (Göttingen, 2000). *Band 3: Kirche und Ökumene* (Göttingen, 2000).

Secondary

Carl E. Braaten and Philip Clayton (eds.), *The Theology of Wolfhart Pannenberg: Twelve American Critiques, with an Autobiographical Essay and Response* (Minneapolis, MN, 1988). This contains an excellent bibliography.

D. McKenzie, *Wolfhart Pannenberg and Religious Philosophy* (Washington, DC, 1980).

E. F. Tupper, *The Theology of Wolfhart Pannenberg*, postscript by Wolfhart Pannenberg (London, 1974).

Gunther Wenz, *Wolfhart Pannenbergs Systematische Theologie. Ein einführender Bericht* (Göttingen, 2003).

Jürgen Moltmann

Richard Bauckham

Introduction: Life and Influences

Jürgen Moltmann, born in 1926, and from 1967 to 1994 professor of systematic theology at Tübingen, is one of the most influential of contemporary German Protestant theologians, in the non-Western as well as the Western world, and in wider church circles as well as in academic theology.

Moltmann himself finds the initial source of his theology in his first experience of the reality of God when he was a prisoner of war in the period 1945–8. This was an experience both of God as the power of hope and of God's presence in suffering: the two themes which were to form the two complementary sides of his theology in the 1960s and early 1970s. Moreover, his sense of involvement, during and after the war, in the collective suffering and guilt of the German nation, set him on the road to his later theological involvement with public and political issues, not least the legacy of Auschwitz.

As a student at Göttingen after the war, Moltmann imbibed the theology of Karl Barth and it was some time before he saw any need to move beyond it. The new directions in which he was to move were inspired in the first place by his teachers at Göttingen: Otto Weber, Ernst Wolf, Hans Joachim Iwand, Gerhard von Rad, and Ernst Käsemann. From Weber and the Dutch "apostolate theology" of A. A. van Ruler and J. C. Hoekendijk, he gained the eschatological perspective of the church's universal mission toward the coming Kingdom of God. Moltmann was one of the first theologians seriously to study Bonhoeffer's work, from which, as well as from Wolf, he developed his concern for social ethics and the church's involvement in secular society. Both Hegel and Iwand contributed significantly to the development of his dialectical interpretation of the cross and the resurrection. Finally, von Rad and Käsemann helped to give his early theology its grounding in biblical theology.

The catalyst which finally brought together these converging influences and concerns in Moltmann's theology of hope was the work of the Jewish Marxist philosopher Ernst Bloch. Moltmann conceived his *Theology of Hope* as a kind of theological parallel to Bloch's philosophy of hope, and has kept up a continuing dialogue with

Bloch throughout his career. Since it was possible for Moltmann to see Bloch's work as a kind of Marxist inheritance of Jewish messianism, it is not surprising that several subsequent influences on Moltmann's thought from outside Christian theology were Marxist and Jewish. In the 1960s he was involved in the Christian–Marxist dialogue and, especially in the early 1970s, he took up important concepts from the critical theory of the Frankfurt School. The influence of Jewish theologians such as Franz Rosenzweig and Abraham Heschel can be found at many points in his work. The influence of Marxism later gave way to other political concerns, such as the peace movement and the Green movement.

While Moltmann remains a recognizably Protestant theologian writing in the German context, his work has become increasingly open to other traditions and movements: Roman Catholic theology, Orthodox theology, and the liberation theologies of the Third World. His experience of the worldwide church – including the sufferings, the charismatic worship, and the political commitment of churches in many parts of the world – affected his ecclesiology in particular.

Survey: Works, Key Ideas, Method

Moltmann's major works comprise two distinct series. In the first place, there is the early trilogy: *Theology of Hope* (1964), *The Crucified God* (1972), and *The Church in the Power of the Spirit* (1975). These represent three complementary perspectives on Christian theology. *Theology of Hope* is not a study of eschatology so much as a study of the eschatological orientation of the whole of theology. *The Crucified God* is a "theology of the cross" in Luther's sense: an attempt to see the crucified Christ as the criterion of Christian theology. *The Church in the Power of the Spirit* complements these two angles of approach with an ecclesiological and pneumatological perspective. The three volumes can be read as complementary perspectives in a single theological vision.

Moltmann regards this trilogy as preparatory studies for his second series of major works. This comprises studies of particular Christian doctrines in a planned order. Although they resemble a "dogmatics," Moltmann prefers to call them a series of "contributions" to theological discussion. There are six volumes: *The Trinity and the Kingdom of God* (1980); *God in Creation* (1985); *The Way of Jesus Christ* (1989); *The Spirit of Life* (1991); *The Coming of God* (1996); and *Experiences in Theology* (2000).

The most important controlling theological idea in Moltmann's early work is his dialectical interpretation of the cross and the resurrection of Jesus, which is then subsumed into the particular form of trinitarianism that becomes the overarching theological principle of his later work. Moltmann's dialectic of cross and resurrection is an interpretation of the cross and resurrection together that underlies the arguments of both *Theology of Hope* and *The Crucified God*. The cross and the resurrection are taken to represent opposites: death and life, the absence of God and the presence of God. Yet the crucified and risen Jesus is the same Jesus in this total contradiction. By raising the crucified Jesus to new life, God created continuity in radical discontinuity. Furthermore, the contradiction of cross and resurrection corresponds to the contradiction between what reality is now and what God promises to make it. In his cross Jesus was identified with the present reality of the world in all its negativity: its subjection to sin, suffering, and death, or what Moltmann calls its godlessness, godforsakenness, and transitoriness. But since the same Jesus was raised, his resurrection constitutes God's promise of new creation for the whole of the reality which the crucified Jesus represents. Moltmann's first two major books work in two complementary directions from this fundamental concept. In *Theology of Hope* the *resurrection* of the crucified Christ is understood in eschatological perspective and interpreted by the themes of dialectical promise, hope, and mission, while in *The Crucified God* the *cross* of the risen Christ is understood from the perspective of the theodicy problem and interpreted by the themes of dialectical love, suffering, and solidarity. (These themes will be explained below.) Finally, it is possible to see *The Church in the Power of the Spirit* as completing this scheme: the Spirit, whose mission derives from the event of the cross and resurrection, moves reality toward the resolution of the dialectic, filling the godforsaken world with God's presence and preparing for the coming kingdom in which the whole world will be transformed in correspondence to the resurrection of Jesus.

The dialectic of cross and resurrection gave Moltmann's theology a strongly Christological center in the particular history of Jesus and at the same time a universal direction. The resurrection as eschatological promise opens theology and the church to the whole world and to its future, while the cross as God's identification in love with the godless and the godforsaken requires solidarity with them on the part of theology and the church.

In *The Crucified God* Moltmann's theology became strongly trinitarian, since he interpreted the cross as a trinitarian event between the Father and the Son. From this point he developed an understanding of the *trinitarian history* of God with the world, in which the mutual involvement of God and the world is increasingly stressed. God experiences a history with the world in which he both affects and is affected by the world, and which is also the history of his own trinitarian relationships as a community of divine Persons who include the world within their love. This trinitarian doctrine dominates Moltmann's later work, in which the mutual relationships of the three Persons as a perichoretic, social Trinity are the context for understanding the reciprocal relationships of God and the world. The dialectic of cross and resurrection, developed in a fully trinitarian way, now becomes the decisive moment within this broader trinitarian history, which retains the eschatological direction of *Theology of Hope* and *The Crucified God*'s suffering solidarity with the world, but also goes further in taking the whole of creation and history within the divine experience. Increasingly, Moltmann has sought to overcome the subordination of pneumatology to Christology, and instead to develop both Christology and pneumatology in mutual relationship within a trinitarian framework.

Although Moltmann addresses issues of theological method at various points in his work, he characteristically focuses on content rather than method, which he often leaves implicit rather than explicit. His last major work, *Experiences in Theology*, partly makes up for this by reflecting retrospectively on methodology.

Three key methodological principles of Moltmann's theology should be mentioned. The first, which is entailed by the key ideas we have just outlined, is that theology is always "public theology" or "theology for the Kingdom of God," addressing not only the church but also the world beyond the church and carried on in a pluralistic context of common concern for and dialogue about the world.

While this is as clear in Moltmann's early as in his later work, his early work soon moved beyond an exclusive emphasis on praxis. Hence the second methodological principle to be noted is the orientation of theology both to praxis and to doxology. Already with *Theology and Joy* (1971) he became dissatisfied with seeing theology purely as "a theory of a practice," and began to inject elements of contemplation, celebration, and doxology. Praxis itself is distorted into activism unless there is also enjoyment of being and praise of God, not only for what God has done but also for what God is. And if praxis is inspired and required by the eschatological hope of new creation, contemplation anticipates the goal of new creation: enjoyment of God and participation in God's pleasure in his creation. This rejection of the *exclusive* claims of praxis in theology enables Moltmann also, in his later work, to distinguish theological knowledge from the pragmatic thinking of the modern world in which the knowing subject masters its object in order to dominate it, and to reinstate that participatory knowledge in which the subject opens herself to the other in wonder and love, perceives herself in mutual relationship with the other, and so can be changed. Such an emphasis fits easily within Moltmann's later trinitarianism, in which reality is characterized by mutual, non-hierarchical relationships – within the Trinity, between the Trinity and creation, and within creation. Closely related is Moltmann's refusal to polarize revelation and experience, as well as his recognition that a theologian's biography is integrally related to his theology. Theology combines "biographical subjectivity and self-forgetting objectivity" (*Experiences in Theology*, p. xix).

Thirdly, Moltmann's theology is characterized by its openness to dialogue. He resists the idea of creating a theological "system" and stresses the provisionality of all theological work and the ability of one theologian only to contribute to the continuing discussion within an ecumenical community of theologians, which itself must be in touch with the wider life and thinking of the churches and the sufferings and hopes of the world. His theology is also open to dialogue with other academic disciplines, including especially the sciences. This openness is a *structural* openness inherent in his theology from the beginning, since it results from the eschatological perspective of his theology of hope. Theology is in the service of the church's mission as, from its starting point in the cross and resurrection of Jesus, it relates to the world for the sake of the future of the world. The genuine openness of this future ensures that theology does not already know all the answers but can learn from others and other approaches to reality. At the same time the Christological starting point, in the light of which the future is the future of Jesus Christ, keeps Christian theology faithful to its own truth and so allows it to question other approaches and enter *critical* dialogue with them. In later work, this structural openness is reinforced by the principle of relationality that becomes increasingly important to Moltmann: to recognize that one's own standpoint is *relative* to others can lead not to relativism but to productive relationship. In biographical terms, this openness to dialogue has made Moltmann's theological development a journey into unknown and often surprising territory.

Content

Eschatology

One of the most important achievements of Moltmann's early theology was to rehabilitate future eschatology. This was in part a response to the demonstration by biblical scholarship that future eschatology is of determinative significance for biblical faith. Whereas Schweitzer, Bultmann, and others had thought biblical eschatology unacceptable to the modern mind unless stripped of reference to the real temporal future of the world, Moltmann, along with some other German theologians in the 1960s, saw in future eschatology precisely the way to make Christian faith relevant in the modern world. He wished to show how the modern experience of history as a process of constant change, in hopeful search of a new future, need not be rejected by the church, as though Christianity stood for reactionary traditionalism or withdrawal from the world. Rather, the orientation of biblical faith toward the future of the world requires the church to engage with the possibilities for change in the modern world, to promote them against tendencies to stagnation, and to direct them toward the coming Kingdom of God. The gospel proves relevant and credible today precisely through the eschatological faith that truth lies in the future and proves itself in changing the present in the direction of the future.

Christian hope, for Moltmann, is thoroughly Christological, since it arises from the resurrection of Jesus. His famous claim that "from first to last, and not merely in the epilogue, Christianity is eschatology, is hope" (*Theology of Hope*, p. 16) was possible only because it was a claim about the meaning of the resurrection of Jesus. Since the God of Israel had revealed himself to Israel by making promises which opened up the future, his act of raising the crucified Jesus to new life is to be understood as the culminating and definitive event of divine promise. In it God promises the resurrection of all the dead, the new creation of all reality, and the coming of his kingdom of righteousness and glory, and he guarantees this promise by enacting it in Jesus' person. Jesus' resurrection entails the eschatological future of all reality.

When this concept of the resurrection as promise is related to Moltmann's dialectic of cross and resurrection (see above), important aspects of his eschatology emerge. In the first place, the *contradiction* between the cross and the resurrection creates a *dialectical* eschatology, in which the promise contradicts present reality. The eschatological kingdom is no mere fulfillment of the immanent possibilities of the present, but represents a radically new future: life for the dead, righteousness for the unrighteous, new creation for a creation subject to evil and death. But secondly, the *identity* of Jesus in the total contradiction of cross and resurrection is also important. The resurrection was not the survival of some aspect of Jesus which was not subject to death: Jesus was *wholly* dead and *wholly* raised by God. The continuity was given in God's act of new creation. Similarly, God's promise is not for *another* world, but for the new creation of *this* world, in all its material and worldly reality. The whole of creation, subject as it is to sin and suffering and death, will be transformed in God's new creation.

Christian eschatology is therefore the hope that the world will be different. It is aroused by a promise whose fulfillment can come only from God's eschatological action transcending all the possibilities of history, since it involves the end of all evil, suffering, and death in the glory of the divine presence indwelling all things. But it is not therefore without effect in the present. On the contrary, Jesus' resurrection set in motion a historical process in which the promise already affects the world and moves it in the direction of its future transformation. This process is the universal mission of the church. This is the point at which Moltmann's *Theology of Hope* opened the church to the world as well as to the future. Authentic Christian hope is not that purely other-worldly expectation that is resigned to the unalterability of affairs in this world. Rather, because it is hope for the future of this world, its effect is to show present reality to be *not yet* what it can and will be. The world is transformable in the direction of the promised future. In this way believers are liberated from accommodation to the status quo and set critically against it. They suffer the contradiction between what is and what is promised. But this critical distance also enables them to seek and to activate those present possibilities of world history that lead in the direction of the eschatological future. Thus, by arousing *active* hope, the promise creates anticipations of the future kingdom within history.

While *Theology of Hope* was more about the eschatological orientation of theology than the content of eschatological hope, *The Coming of God* is a systematic eschatology, a detailed exposition of the Christian hope in personal, historical, cosmic, and divine aspects. A notable feature is Moltmann's now much more critical attitude to the progressivism of the modern West, which projects the future only as the processive completion of history, rather than also as the messianic redemption of history. Moltmann sees the liberating potential of the modern West compromised by its justification of domination as progress.

Theodicy

From the beginning, Moltmann's theology gave prominence to the question of God's righteousness in the face of the suffering and evil of the world. In the first phase of his response to the problem, in *Theology of Hope*, he proposed an eschatological theodicy. Innocent and involuntary suffering must not be justified, as it would be if it were explained as contributing to the divine purpose. The promise given in the resurrection of Jesus gives no explanation of suffering, but it does provide hope for God's final triumph over all evil and suffering, and thereby also an initiative for Christian praxis in overcoming suffering now.

In *The Crucified God* this approach to the problem is deepened by the additional theme of God's loving solidarity with the world in its suffering. When Moltmann turned from his focus on the resurrection to a complementary focus on the cross, he was concerned to extend the traditional soteriological interest in the cross to embrace "both the question of human guilt and man's liberation from it, and also the question of human suffering and man's liberation from it" (*The Crucified God*, p. 134). He uses the expression "the godless and the godforsaken" to refer to the plight both of sinners who suffer their own turning away from God and of those who are the innocent victims of pointless suffering. This is the plight of the world, in the absence of divine righteousness, with which Jesus was identified on the cross.

As Moltmann's thinking moved back from the resurrection as the event of divine promise to the cross as the event of divine love, he was asking the question: How does the promise reach those to whom it is addressed, the godless and the godforsaken? His answer is that it reaches them through Jesus' *identification* with them, in their condition, on the cross. His resurrection represents salvation *for them* only because he dies for them, identified with them in their suffering of God's absence. The central concept of *The Crucified God* is love, which suffers in solidarity with those who suffer. This is love which meets the involuntary suffering of the godforsaken with another kind of suffering: voluntary fellow-suffering.

To see the cross as God's act of loving solidarity with all who suffer apparently abandoned by God requires an incarnational and trinitarian theology of the cross. By recognizing God's presence, as the incarnate Son of God, in the abandonment of the cross, Moltmann brings the dialectic of cross and resurrection within God's own experience. The cross and resurrection represent the opposition between a reality which does not correspond to God – the world subject to sin, suffering, and death – and the promise of a reality which does correspond to God – the new creation which will reflect God's glory. But if God is present in the cross he is present in his own contradiction. God's love is such that it embraces the godforsaken reality that does not correspond to him, and so God suffers. God's love is not simply active benevolence towards humanity. It is dialectical love which in embracing its own contradiction must suffer. Of course, it does so in order to overcome the contradiction: to deliver from sin, suffering, and death.

If Jesus the divine Son suffers the abandonment of the godforsaken, as the cry of desolation shows, the cross must be a trinitarian event between the incarnate Son and his Father who leaves him to die. It is an event of divine suffering in which Jesus suffers dying in abandonment by his Father and the Father suffers in grief the death of his Son. As such it is the act of divine solidarity with the godforsaken world, in which the Son willingly surrenders himself in love for the world and the Father willingly surrenders his Son in love for the world. Because at the point of their deepest separation, the Father and the Son are united in their love for the world, the event that separates them is salvific. The love between them now spans the gulf that separates the godless and the godforsaken from God and overcomes it.

In Moltmann's understanding, the cross does not solve the problem of suffering, but meets it with the voluntary fellow-suffering of love. Solidarity in suffering – in the first place, the crucified God's solidarity with all who suffer, and then also his followers' identification with them – does not abolish suffering, but it overcomes what Moltmann calls "the suffering in suffering": the lack of love, the abandonment in suffering. Moreover, such solidarity, so far from promoting fatalistic submission to suffering, necessarily includes love's protest against the infliction of suffering on those it loves. It leads believers through their solidarity with the suffering into liberating praxis on their behalf.

The church

Moltmann describes his ecclesiology alternatively as "messianic ecclesiology" or "relational ecclesiology." Both terms serve to situate the church within God's trinitarian history with the world, more specifically within the missions of the Son and the Spirit on their way to the eschatological kingdom. In the first place, Moltmann's ecclesiology is rooted in his eschatological Christology. The church lives between the past history of Jesus and the universal future in which that history will reach its fulfillment: the former directs it in mission toward the latter. But this also means that Moltmann's ecclesiology is strongly pneumatological. For, in Moltmann's understanding of the trinitarian history, it is the Holy Spirit who now, between the history of Jesus and the coming of the kingdom, mediates the eschatological future to the world. If the church is an anticipation of the messianic kingdom, it is so because it is created by and participates in the mission of the Spirit. Its defining characteristics are not therefore its own, but those of the presence and activity of Christ and the Spirit. At every point ecclesiology must be determined by the church's role as a movement within the trinitarian history of God with the world.

If "messianic ecclesiology" characterizes the church as oriented by the missions of Christ and the Spirit toward their eschatological goal, "relational ecclesiology" indicates that, because of its place within the trinitarian history, the church does not exist in, of, or for itself, but only in relationship and can only be understood in its relationships. It participates in the messianic history of Jesus, it lives in the presence and powers of the Spirit, and it exists as a provisional reality for the sake of the universal kingdom of the future. Since the mission of the Spirit on the way to the kingdom includes but is not confined to the church, the church cannot absolutize itself, but must fulfill its own messianic role in open and critical relationship with other realities, its partners in history, notably Israel, the other world religions, and the secular order.

Within this context, the church can only adequately fulfill its vocation if it becomes a "messianic fellowship" of mature and responsible disciples. Here Moltmann, with his eye especially on the German Protestant scene, proposes radical reform and renewal of the church. His criticism is of the extent to which the church is still the civil religion of society, a pastoral church *for* all the people, unable to take up a critical stance in relation to society, unable to foster real community and active Christian commitment. The ideal is a church *of* the people, a fellowship of committed disciples called to responsible participation in messianic mission. Membership of the church must therefore be voluntary (from this follows Moltmann's critique of infant baptism) and characterized not only by faith but also by discipleship and a distinctive lifestyle. The messianic fellowship will also be a free society of equals, since the Spirit frees and empowers all Christians for messianic service (from this follows Moltmann's critique of traditional doctrines of the ministry). Its life of loving acceptance of the other, however different, Moltmann is fond of characterizing as "open friendship," since friendship is a relationship of freedom and the church's life of friendly relationships is always essentially open to others. Finally, the church's open friendship must be modeled on that of Jesus and therefore take the form especially of solidarity with the poor. Unlike the pastoral church, with its tendency to accept the status quo in society, the church as a voluntary fellowship of committed disciples is free to be a socially critical church, identified with the most marginalized and needy.

Doctrine of God

Moltmann's mature doctrine of God could be said to hinge on a concept of dynamic relationality. It understands the trinitarian God as three divine subjects in mutual loving relationship, and God's relationship to the world as a reciprocal relationship in which God in his love for the world not only affects the world but is also affected by it. God relates to the world as Trinity, experiencing the world within his own trinitarian experience, and so God's changing experience of the world is also a changing experience of himself. The trinitarian history of God's relationship with the world is thus a real history for God as well as for the world: it is the history in which God includes the world within his own trinitarian relationships. All this Moltmann takes to be the meaning of the Christian claim that God is love.

Moltmann's distinctive development of the doctrine of God was initiated by his interpretation of the cross in *The Crucified God*. There he took three crucial steps. In the first place, as an event between the Father and the Son, in which God suffers the godforsakenness that separates the Son from the Father, the cross required trinitarian language of a kind which emphasized intersubjective relationship between the divine persons. (The Spirit, however, is less clearly personal at this stage.) Secondly, it also necessitated a doctrine of divine passibility, not only in the narrow sense that God can suffer pain, but in the broader sense that God can be affected by his creation. In rejecting the traditional doctrine of divine impassibility, Moltmann is careful to make clear that not every kind of suffering can be attributed, even analogically, to God. But suffering which is freely undertaken in love for those who suffer Moltmann claims to be required by God's nature as love. Divine love is a genuinely two-way relationship in which God is so involved with his creation as to be affected by it.

The third step follows: Moltmann abandons the traditional distinction between the immanent and the economic trinities, between what God eternally is in himself and how he acts outside himself in the world. The cross (and, by extension, the rest of God's history with the world) is *internal* to the divine trinitarian experience. Because God is love, what he is for us he is also for himself. The doctrine of the Trinity is thus not an extrapolation from the history of Jesus and the Spirit: it actually is the history of Jesus and the Spirit in its theological interpretation. It can really only take narrative form as a history of God's changing trinitarian relationships in himself and simultaneously with the world. In his later work Moltmann elaborates this narrative in various forms, eventually including creation.

In all this, Moltmann found himself talking of God's experience. If it is as love that we experience God, then in some sense in experiencing God we also experience God's experience of us, and if it is as trinitarian love that we experience God, then in some sense we experience even God's threefold experience of himself in our history. On this basis Moltmann developed his fully social doctrine of the Trinity. For this to be possible, Moltmann had to recognize an activity of the Spirit in which the Spirit acts as subject in relation to the Father and the Son: this is the Spirit's work of glorifying the Father and the Son. This makes it clear that the divine persons are all subjects in relation to each other. It also makes clear that there is no fixed order in the Trinity: the traditional, "descending" order Father–Son–Spirit is only one of the changing patterns of trinitarian relationship in God's history with the world. Behind and within these changing relationships is the enduring trinitarian fellowship, in which there is no subordination, only mutual love in freedom.

Moltmann constantly opposes any "monotheistic" or "monarchical" doctrine of God that would reduce the real subjectivity of the persons. Instead, he insists that God's unity is the unity of persons in relationship. Three points can be made about this. First, it is in their relationships to each other that the three are persons. They are both three and one in their mutual indwelling (perichoresis). Secondly, since the unity of God is thus defined in terms of love, as perichoresis, it is a unity which can open itself to and include the world within itself. The goal of the trinitarian history of God is the uniting of all things with God and in God: a trinitarian and eschatological panentheism. Thirdly, Moltmann sees "monotheism" as legitimating "monarchical" relationships of domination and subjection, whereas social trinitarianism grounds relationships of freedom and equality. In himself, God is not rule but a fellowship of love; in his relationship with the world it is not so much lordship as loving fellowship that God seeks; and in God's "kingdom" it is relationships of free friendship that most adequately reflect and participate in the trinitarian life.

Creation

The doctrine of creation, relatively neglected in Moltmann's earlier work, receives full attention in *God in Creation*. Its explicit context is the ecological crisis, a crisis in the human relationship to nature that requires, in Moltmann's view, a renewed understanding of nature and humanity as God's creation and of God's relationship to the world as his creation.

The kind of human relationship to nature that has created the crisis is that of exploitative domination. In its place, Moltmann advocates a sense of human community with nature, respecting nature's independence and participating in mutual relationships with it. Humans, as the image of God, have a distinctive place within nature, but they are not the owners or rulers of nature: they belong with nature in a community of creation that, as *creation*, is not anthropocentric but theocentric. In order to ground theologically this emphasis on mutual relationships in creation, Moltmann appeals to his doctrine of God, whose own trinitarian community provides the model for the life of his creation as a community of reciprocal relationships.

Not only is the trinitarian God a perichoretic community and his creation a perichoretic community, but also God's relationship to the creation is one of mutual indwelling. Because God is transcendent beyond the world, it dwells in God, but because, as the Spirit, God is also immanent within the world, God dwells in it. This notion of the Spirit in creation enables Moltmann also to take the non-human creation into his general concept of the trinitarian history. The whole of creation from the beginning has a messianic orientation toward a future goal: its glorification through divine indwelling. The Spirit in creation co-suffers with creation in its bondage to decay, keeping it open to God and its future with God. Humanity's eschatological goal does not lift us out of the material creation but confirms our solidarity and relatedness with it. In all of this Moltmann achieves a strong continuity between creation and redemption, and between the creative and salvific activities of the Spirit.

Political theology

Moltmann has never reduced the gospel to its political aspect, but he has consistently emphasized it. In the years immediately after *Theology of Hope* he developed his thought into an explicitly political theology, in the sense in which that term came into use in Germany at that time (i.e., a politically critical theology aiming at radical change in society). Moltmann's praxis-oriented dialectical eschatology was not difficult to translate into an imperative for radical political change, though what appealed to him in Marxism was its vision of a new society of freedom, rather than its economic analysis or its strategy for revolution.

Moltmann's turn to the cross brought with it the requirement of a political praxis of solidarity with the victims, which deepens the praxis of hope. The latter was rescued from the danger of a rather romantic vision of revolution or of confusion with the ideological optimism of the affluent by the requirement that desire for radical change must result from real solidarity with the victims of society and be rooted in their actual interests.

Political concerns continue to feature in his later theology. For example, social trinitarianism provides a theological basis for democratic freedom in society (see above). Another important development was the prominence of the notion of human rights, which Moltmann grounds in the created dignity and eschatological destiny of humanity as the image of God. It is by means of the concept of human rights that Moltmann's political theology is able to formulate specific political goals. The two earlier themes of revolutionary hope and solidarity with victims gain concreteness especially in this form. Eschatological hope finds its immediate application in striving for the realization of human rights – new dimensions of which can constantly come to light in the movement of history toward the fulfillment of human destiny in the Kingdom of God. Solidarity with victims takes political effect in the attempt to secure their rights and dignity as full members of the human community. The concept of human rights is a way of specifying the concrete implications of political theology, and a way of doing so that makes contact with non-Christian political goals, thus enabling Christians to join with others in a common struggle for liberation. With Moltmann's growing concern with Green issues he also complemented the idea of human rights with that of animal rights and the rights of all creation.

Christology

In *The Way of Jesus Christ* Moltmann returned to the Christological center of his early work, and was now able to develop a more comprehensive Christology. The dialectic of cross and resurrection is retained from the early work, as is the stress on the Old Testament/Jewish framework of theological interpretation for the history of Jesus. The latter is now developed in a more distinctively messianic rather than simply eschatological form: the Christian dialogue with Judaism must keep Christology messianic, looking not only to Jesus' past but also to his future, which is the messianic future of the as yet still unredeemed world. Whereas Moltmann's early theology focused on the way the resurrection of Jesus opened up the eschatological future for the world, but did not stress the parousia of Jesus himself, the range of Moltmann's Christology now extends to the coming Christ. The metaphor of Jesus Christ "on his way" indicates, among other things, that he is on his way to the messianic future. Christology therefore is necessarily *Christologia viae*, not fixed and static, but provisional and open to the future.

As well as this more explicit development of the eschatological aspect of Christology, there is also much more attention to the earthly life and ministry of Jesus than in Moltmann's previous work – more, indeed, than in most Christologies. This has at least two important consequences. First, Moltmann develops a Spirit Christology, which stresses that the life and ministry of Jesus, as the messianic prophet, take place in the power of the Spirit. This emphasis belongs within Moltmann's mature view of the trinitarian history of God with the world, in which the trinitarian persons inter-relate in changing and reciprocal ways. The history of Jesus is not to be understood in a narrowly Christological but rather in a fully trinitarian way, in which Jesus lives in relation to his Father and the Spirit. The uniqueness of Jesus' trinitarian relationship to the Father and the Spirit prevents this Spirit Christology from being a mere "degree Christology," as other forms of Spirit Christology have often been. Secondly, Moltmann highlights, unusually in a Christology, the distinctive ethical way of life that Jesus taught his disciples. Christology, he claims, is inextricably related not only to soteriology, but also to Christian ethics; Christology must be done in close conjunction with "Christopraxis"; and the "total, holistic knowledge of Christ" entails a life of following his way, in the community of his disciples, in fellowship with him.

Finally, holistic Christology requires holistic soteriology: a view of salvation that encompasses body and soul, individual and community, humanity and the rest of nature, in a vision of the universal abolition of transience and death and the new creation of all things. This is not new in Moltmann's theology, but the explicit development of the universal aspect of Christology and soteriology as involving the non-human creation results from Moltmann's perception of the universal peril in which all creation on this planet now stands. In the situation of nuclear threat and ecological destruction, the world is now in a literally "end-time" situation, in which "the great apocalyptic dying, the death of all things" looms – not, of course, as a fatalistic prophecy, but as an unprecedented peril that puts humanity and the rest of nature in a common danger. In this apocalyptically understood context, Moltmann is able to open up new dimensions of the eschatological dialectic of the cross and the resurrection. In his cross, Jesus enters and suffers vicariously the end-time sufferings that threaten the whole creation. He identifies with dying nature as well as with abandoned humans. He undergoes the birth pangs of the new creation, and his resurrection is the eschatological springtime of all nature.

Pneumatology

Moltmann's theology has become more and more strongly pneumatological, a development that culminates in *The Spirit of Life*. This is in part a consequence of his trinitarian doctrine, which stresses the reciprocal and changing relationships of the three persons, and rejects the subordination of pneumatology to Christology. The principle for both pneumatology and Christology is that they must be understood in relation to each other within an overall trinitarian framework, rather than that pneumatology should be developed exclusively from Christology. This allows Moltmann to give more attention to the Spirit's role for its own sake than the Western theological tradition has often done. His attention to pneumatology also, however, corresponds to his growing stress on the immanence of God in creation, as his eschatological panentheism (the hope that God will indwell all things in the new creation) has been increasingly accompanied by a stress on the coinherence of God and the world already. As the Spirit, God is already present in his creation, both in suffering the transience and evil of the world and in anticipating the eschatological rebirth of all things.

Moltmann's developed pneumatology understands the Holy Spirit primarily as the divine source of *life*: "the eternal Spirit is the divine wellspring of life – the source of life created, life preserved and life daily renewed, and finally the source of eternal life of all created being" (*The Spirit of Life*, p. 82). This emphasis serves a number of important purposes. First, it breaks out of the narrow association of the Spirit with revelation, which was characteristic of Barth's theology, and so enables Moltmann, in one of his more emphatic rejections of Barthian positions, to give *experience* – the experience of God in the whole of life and of all things in God – a place in theology, not as alternative to but in correlation with the revelatory word of God. The Spirit of life is God experienced in the profundity and vitality of life lived in God. As the Spirit is the wellspring of all life, so all experience can be a discovery of this living source in God.

Secondly, a "holistic pneumatology" corresponds to Moltmann's holistic Christology and soteriology. As the Spirit of life, the Spirit is not related to the "spiritual" as opposed to the bodily and material, or to the individual as opposed to the social, or to the human as opposed to the rest of creation. The Spirit is the source of the whole of life in bodiliness and community. Life in the Spirit is not a life of withdrawal from the world into God, but the "vitality of a creative life out of God," which is characterized by love of life and affirmation of all life. This is a relatively new form of Moltmann's characteristic concern for a theology of positive involvement in God's world.

Thirdly, the notion of the Spirit as the divine source of all life highlights both the continuity of God's life and the life of his creation, such that the creatures are not distant from God but live out of his life, and also the continuity of creation and salvation, in that the Spirit is the source both of the transient life that ends in death and of the eternal life of the new creation. The Spirit gives life to all things, sustains all things in life, and brings all things to rebirth beyond death and beyond the reach of death. But finally, this continuity of creation and new creation is not to be understood as excluding the eschatological dualism that has always been a key to Moltmann's thought. Creation is subject to the powers of death and destruction, and the Spirit is the power of the liberating struggle of life against death, the source of life renewed out of death. The continuity of creation and new creation is created by the Spirit's act of restoring the old creation in the eschatologically transcendent new creation. The Christological center of Moltmann's theology – the dialectic in which the Spirit raises the crucified Jesus to eschatological life – still holds.

Debate

Some of the issues that have been raised in criticism of Moltmann's work are as follows.

Critics of Moltmann's early work frequently complained of one-sided emphasis on some theological themes at the expense of others. This was said especially of the emphasis on the future in *Theology of Hope*, which appeared to deny all present experience of God. However, in retrospect, this one-sidedness can be seen to be a result of Moltmann's method, in the early works, of taking up *in turn* a number of complementary perspectives on theology. In the context of the whole trilogy, the one-sidedness of each book is balanced by the others. Present experience of God, polemically played down in *Theology of Hope*, is fully acknowledged in later work, but given an eschatological orientation which preserves the intention of *Theology of Hope*.

Much criticism focused on the political implications of *Theology of Hope*, though not always with due attention to the subsequent essays in which these were fully developed. From the liberation theologians of Latin America came the criticism that the eschatological transcendence of the kingdom beyond all its present anticipations sanctions the typical European theologian's detachment from concrete political movements and objectives. From some more conservative theologians comes the opposite complaint that Moltmann reduces eschatology to human political achievements. Both criticisms miss the careful way in which Moltmann relates the eschatological kingdom to its anticipations in history, though there is something in the liberationists' charge that Moltmann's political theology is *relatively* lacking in concrete proposals.

Various criticisms of Moltmann's doctrine of God have been offered. Some have suggested that, in rejecting the traditional doctrines of divine aseity and impassibility, Moltmann compromises the freedom of God and falls into the "Hegelian" mistake of making world history the process by which God realizes himself. To some extent such criticisms provoked Moltmann, after *The Crucified God*, into clarifying his view. He does not dissolve God into world history, but he does intend a real interaction between God and the world. The problem of divine freedom leads him to deny the reality of the contrast between necessity and freedom of choice in God. Because God's freedom is the freedom of his love, he cannot choose not to love and as love he is intrinsically related to the world.

A closely related line of critique alleges that Moltmann's later emphasis on the mutual perichoresis of God and the world comes close to pantheism. But it is important to recognize that, in Moltmann's "trinitarian panentheism," perichoresis is a movement of relationship in *differentiation*.

A third kind of criticism of Moltmann's doctrine of God finds it hard to distinguish his social trinitarianism from tritheism, a charge that careful reading of his later trinitarian work fails to support. The fundamental point – that the trinitarian persons relate to each other as personal subjects – has, in fact, more claim to represent the mainstream Christian theological tradition than the modern tendency to conceive God as the supreme individual.

Many critics, especially in the Anglo-Saxon tradition, find Moltmann's work lacking in philosophical analysis and logical rigor. This is a question of theological style, and Moltmann's way of doing theology has other merits, such as breadth of vision, that more analytical treatments lack. But it is true that it sometimes obscures conceptual problems in his work that could otherwise come to light and be overcome more quickly. Related to this criticism is the charge that Moltmann is insufficiently aware of the necessarily analogical nature of talk about God, so that his discussion of the divine experience too often becomes unconsciously mythological.

Moltmann's biblical hermeneutics are a problematic area that has not received much attention. Whereas his earlier work was carefully rooted in current biblical scholarship, his use of biblical material in the later work often ignores historical–critical interpretation and leaves his hermeneutical principles dangerously unclear. His own explanation is that increasingly he found the divergent critical discussions a hindrance to actually listening to the biblical texts, and so instead he found himself adopting a more direct and naive relationship to the texts.

Achievement

Perhaps Moltmann's greatest achievement in the earlier works was to open up hermeneutical structures for relating biblical faith to the modern world. The strength and appropriateness of these structures lie in their biblical basis, their Christological center, and their eschatological openness. They give Moltmann's theology a relevance to the modern world that is achieved not only without surrendering the central features of biblical and historic Christian faith, but much more positively by probing the theological meaning of these in relation to contemporary realities and concerns. By recovering a Christological center that is both dialectical and eschatological, Moltmann's theology acquired an openness to the world which is not in tension with the Christological center but is actually required by the Christological center, and which is not an accommodation to conservative, liberal, or radical values, but has a critical edge and a consistent solidarity with the most marginalized members of society.

His later work continues to bring both the biblical history and the central themes of the Christian theological tradition into productive relationship with the contemporary context. In doing so, he has become the contemporary theologian who has perhaps most successfully transcended the dominant (theological and non-theological) paradigm of reality as human history, recognized in this a reflex of the modern ideology of domination, and attempted to enter theologically into the reciprocity of human history and the rest of nature as the history of God's creation. That he has been able to do so by developing and expanding the structures of his earlier thought, rather than rejecting and replacing them, demonstrates the hermeneutical fecundity of his theological vision and its ability to relate illuminatingly to fresh situations and insights.

A very notable feature of the later work is Moltmann's sustained attempt to reconceive the doctrine of God in order to do better justice than the tradition to the Christian perception of God as trinitarian love. In a period when many major theologians, questioning the axioms of metaphysical theism, have recognized the need to envisage God as receptive and suffering as well as active, and have also rediscovered the potential of thorough-going trinitarianism, Moltmann's has been one of the boldest and fullest explorations of such a doctrine of God. Its merits lie in the attempt to take utterly seriously those claims about God that lie at the heart of the Christian revelation. The attempt has its problems, but the issues are indisputably important for the credibility of the God of Christian faith today.

Bibliography

A bibliography of Moltmann's works up to 1987 is in D. Ising, *Bibliographie Jürgen Moltmann* (Munich, 1987), and a further bibliography of Moltmann's works in English translation (together with secondary literature) is in R. Bauckham, *The Theology of Jürgen Moltmann* (Edinburgh, 1995).

Primary

Theology of Hope (London, 1967).
Theology and Joy (London, 1973).
The Crucified God (London, 1974).
The Church in the Power of the Spirit (London, 1975).
The Trinity and the Kingdom of God (London, 1981).
On Human Dignity (London, 1984).
God in Creation (London, 1985).
The Way of Jesus Christ (London, 1989).

The Spirit of Life (London, 1991).
History and the Triune God (London, 1991).
The Coming of God (London, 1996).
Experiences in Theology (London, 2000).

Secondary

Bauckham, R., *Moltmann: Messianic Theology in the Making* (Basingstoke, 1987).
——— *The Theology of Jürgen Moltmann* (Edinburgh, 1995).
——— (ed.), *God Will be All in All: The Eschatology of Jürgen Moltmann* (Edinburgh, 1999).
Conyers, A. J., *God, Hope, and History* (Macon, GA, 1988).
Meeks, M. D., *Origins of the Theology of Hope* (Philadelphia, PA, 1974).
Müller-Fahrenholz, G., *The Kingdom and the Power* (London, 2000).

T. F. Torrance

Daniel W. Hardy

Introduction

Thomas Torrance was born in West China on August 30, 1913, the second of six children of "loving and godly parents"[1] who served a number of Bible societies in China, his father a Church of Scotland missionary and his mother an Anglican one. Reared in their deeply personal and Word-centered encounter with the living God, he went to a Canadian school in China and afterward (from 1927) to a school at Bellshill, Scotland, before studying classics and philosophy at Edinburgh University (1931–4), among others with two authorities in ancient and modern philosophy, A. E. Taylor and Norman Kemp Smith. Scotland was hard-hit by unemployment at the time, and despite his interest in philosophy, he needed to complete his degree in three years (not the usual four) and move to the Faculty of Divinity (New College). His interest in theology was not a detached one; he was active in evangelism and intended to become a missionary. In the then-usual British fashion, he concentrated first on Greek and Hebrew and biblical studies; only afterwards did he specialize in systematic theology. In this, two more conservative teachers influenced him particularly: H. R. Mackintosh (through whom he became interested in Karl Barth) and Daniel Lamont, who brought a scientific background to the relation of theology and modern science, and taught apologetics. At the conclusion of his undergraduate studies in 1937, Torrance was licensed as a probationer minister in the Church of Scotland.

A scholarship allowed Torrance three years of postgraduate study in Basel with Karl Barth. Barth discouraged him, however, from attempting a dissertation on his chosen topic (the scientific structure of Christian dogmatics), suggesting instead that he write on the doctrine of grace in the second-century church fathers; his completion of the thesis was long delayed: in 1938 by a period teaching theology at Auburn Seminary in upstate New York (when he was offered two other posts, at McCormick Seminary in Chicago and at Princeton University); in 1939 by a year at Oriel College Oxford; in 1940–3 by his ordination and ministry in a Perthshire parish, and finally (as he had always wished) by service as a chaplain in North Africa, the Middle East, and Italy (he was awarded the MBE for bravery) and his return to his parish – until it was submitted and defended in May 1946. Later that year, he married Margaret Spear; they have two sons and a daughter, Thomas, Iain, and Alison.

In November 1947, he began three years of ministry in Beechgrove Church in Aberdeen, publishing *Calvin's Doctrine of Man* (1949), before being elected to the Chair of Church History at Edinburgh, and moving from parish minister straight to university professor. Although this allowed him to teach historical theology (e.g., Calvin, Knox, etc.), when it became possible he changed to the Chair of Christian Dogmatics, which he occupied from 1952 until his "retirement" in 1979.

His position at New College was not so straightforward as it might seem, because "divinity" – taught by John Baillie – was taken as what was elsewhere called "philosophical theology," and included the doctrine of God (and the Trinity), while "Christian dogmatics" – taught by Torrance – included the field of systematic theology. This division also represented a considerable difference of outlook between Baillie and Torrance as to how theology should be approached; and the difference became stronger when Baillie's place was taken by John McIntyre and the College moved away from its traditional focus on dogmatics. Such things had long-term consequences, in effect confining Torrance to "evangelical" topics: Christology and soteriology, church, ministry and sacraments, an undergraduate seminar on patristic texts, and postgraduate seminars on Barth's theology and theology and science.

During his earlier years at New College, Torrance's interest in early church theology and Calvin and the Reformers made him a significant spokesman for the Reformed tradition in the World Council of Churches (Amsterdam 1948, Lund 1952, and Evanston in 1954, and in the Faith and Order Commission 1952–62), and in bilateral dialogues and consultations: Church of Scotland–Church of England, Reformed–Roman Catholic (on the Eucharist), and Reformed–Orthodox (on the doctrine of the Trinity). In each case, his contributions were important: he was intent on recovering the Reformation emphasis on eschatology – disallowing the identification of particular features of the church with the future Kingdom of God – in the context of discussions with Anglicans and Roman Catholics. His interest in the Eastern church fathers was much appreciated by the Greek Orthodox Church, which made him a presbyter and gave him the honorary title of protopresbyter. Later, his advocacy of the Reformed tradition within the Church of Scotland brought him to the position of Moderator of the General Assembly in 1976–7.

Torrance's contribution was much wider than such activities. He established or renewed societies and institutions (including universities) for good theology, and also initiated translations of major works – Calvin and Barth – not otherwise available. In the late 1960s, as his philosophical and scientific interests came more to the foreground, he took part in the Académie Internationale des Sciences Religieuses and the Académie Internationale de Philosophie des Sciences. In 1979 he became a fellow of the Royal Society of Edinburgh, and in 1982 a fellow of the British Academy. His achievements in theology and science brought him the celebrated Templeton Prize for Progress in Religion in 1978.

A Survey of Torrance's Work

Torrance's research, teaching, speaking, and writing have always been driven by strong convictions. His personal faith, his evangelical and Reformed concerns, his development of the insights of Karl Barth's approach to theology, his work on the relation of theology and science, and the strength of his personality, have been powerfully evident, eliciting both strong support and opposition. His passion has been in the way in which faith and theology are rightly pursued, and many of his books have been attempts to restore and reshape theology as a whole. The issues at stake were fundamental ones: he was thought by liberals to be too confident about the possibility of knowledge of God and about Christ and salvation, and by conservatives as emphasizing too much the freedom of God's unconditional grace in the person and work of Jesus Christ. In Torrance, therefore, we meet a theologian who stands powerfully astride divergent tendencies in theology, both liberal and conservative, and does so with the armory of a theology refined by the consideration of scientific realism.

His writings are vast (more than 600 in number); even his books are a shelf-full. Many are addresses and essays for particular occasions, and range extraordinarily widely, from God in Christ to God's work in the natural world, from the engagement of orthodoxy with philosophy and the sciences in different eras, from those supportive of Reformed Christianity in ecumenical encounter to those – the greatest number – developing the place of theology among the sciences. And at no point are they less than thorough: his theology is always an engagement with the Bible, the history of Christian thought, the Reformed tradition, and the possibilities subsequently offered for communicating the gospel; and it is always also an attempt to correct falsehood or limitation in theology and church. The result is a range of writings very difficult to present in any systematic fashion. And Torrance has not provided a comprehensive statement of theology as such, even if one is implied in what he has written.[2] He has concentrated instead on two things: (1) the central truths of Christian faith, consistently refining their presentation and showing how they differ from persistent errors; and (2) theology as a science.

His theology is therefore what can be called a *declarative* one, identifying and presenting core Christian truth as it has developed in seminal periods and people, and a *relational* one, showing its distinctive place among the sciences. These two are never altogether separate in his work: they interact with each other in the fashion of a spiral, with one receiving special attention, enriching the other, and then receding as the other takes its place. The result is a gradual flowering in his presentation of the depth and intelligibility of Christian truth.

Content

A declarative theology

As we have seen, Torrance had strong convictions from the beginning: evangelical, ecclesial, and reformed in the Scottish tradition, and missionary. His convictions were, it seems, sharpened by the pervasive presence of the liberalism into which – as he thought – Scottish theology had sunk, even in the place where he studied and became professor, New College at the University of Edinburgh, personified there by John Baillie. In his resistance to these tendencies, Torrance's principal allies were H. R. Mackintosh (his earlier mentor who had introduced the study of Barth at Edinburgh in the 1930s) and his *doktorvater* Karl Barth, and later, as he dealt with the sciences, the example of Michael Polanyi was also very important.

Torrance's convictions are a constant presence through his work. His central and comprehensive insight was (in my words) that "the true object – God – gracefully objectifies all else." God is *per se* the central and comprehensive reality, which constitutes all other reality. Yet that does not mean that God is known from creation (the presumption of natural theology). God confers knowledge of God for those who are otherwise blind to God. Like Barth, Torrance insists that this occurs only through God's act, "an *act* in which *His act and Person* are *identical*, in which God's presence, personal presence, is present in His act, in which the act is the Person and the Person is the Act."[3] This is an act which occurs as God becomes human in Jesus Christ, through whom human life, culture, and language are constituted as what they should be.

Accordingly, Torrance – like Barth – saw the *homoousion* as pivotal for knowledge of God: God's Word is *God himself* incarnate in Jesus in the world, there revealing and recreating human being. The Word of God in Jesus is not, as so many suppose, only symbolic of God. Nor does this mean that Jesus is less than fully human:

> Jesus steps into the actual situation where we are summoned to have faith in God, to believe and trust in him, and he acts in our place and in our stead from within the depths of our unfaithfulness and provides us freely with a faithfulness in which we may share.[4]

This decisively defeats the dualism – between God and the world, and between God and revelation – with which Christian thought has often been infected.

The same emphasis on the *homoousion* leads Torrance to see that God's grace is personally and freely given in Christ to human beings for their salvation. The implications are profound: there is the closest possible relation between God, incarnation, atonement, and Spirit, and the freedom of God is in the Incarnation, where human beings are incorporated into Christ, and God acts in the place of all human beings for their redemption; the relation of giver, gift, and recipients is *internal* to each; this falsifies the (dualistic) divisions Torrance finds characteristic of so much Western theology.

What Torrance thus unearths is what he maintains is the *inner logic* of Christian faith. It is correlative with the account he offers of the history of this truth as distilled from the New Testament witness and grasped in seminal periods and figures such as the Eastern Fathers (especially Athanasius), Calvin, Mackintosh, and Barth.

> The incarnation of the eternal Word of God made flesh in Jesus Christ . . . prescribes for us in Christian theology both its proper matter and form, so that whether in its activity as a whole or in the formulation of a doctrine in any part, it is the Christological pattern that will appear throughout the whole body of Christian dogmatics . . . While the Lord Jesus Christ constitutes the pivotal center of our knowledge of God, God's distinctive self-revelation as Holy Trinity, One Being, Three Persons, creates the overall framework within which all Christian theology is to be formulated.[5]

This "revolution in our knowledge of God" is what comprises the "classical theology" of the church, and enables it to be distinguished from aberrations throughout the history of human understanding.

In the extensive critical attention he accords to such sources throughout his writing,[6] Torrance finds them united by their scientific theological engagement with the reality of God, that is by their success in investigating and conceptualizing God in a manner appropriate to God's own nature. From what God is toward us and for us in our history, they discern what/who God is antecedently, inherently, and internally. In other words, the "evangelical Trinity" – "the truth content of the Gospel as it is revealed to us through the incarnate or human economy . . . which Christ undertook toward us" corresponds to the *theological Trinity*, "the truth of the eternal Being and Activity of God" as God.[7]

Scientific theology and the sciences

Theology as knowledge

In the context of the positivism which dominated the British academic scene during the 1940s and after, the question of whether theology is indeed a form of knowledge at all was of overwhelming importance. In *Theological Science* (1969), based on lectures given in the USA in 1959, Torrance gave a full response. It was both a very personal one and also a philosophical–theological one: "I find the presence and being of God bearing upon my experience and thought so powerfully that I cannot but be convinced of His overwhelming reality and rationality . . . Scientific theology is active engagement in that cognitive relation to God in obedience to the demands of his reality and self-giving."[8] He finds the same to be true of natural scientific inquiry wherever undertaken: the intelligible provides the possibility of intelligent engagement with it.[9] Both alike rest on the given, either the self-presentation of divine reality for theology, or the given of contingent reality for the natural sciences. In his view, therefore, theological science and natural science are *a posteriori* activities, conditioned by the reality grasped in each, and not based on *a priori*, surface impressions or conventional conceptions. These activities are to probe as deeply as possible into the constitutive factors of these realities, to discover what makes each what it is and how the two are related. This agenda shows itself in two "sides" of his work, a pursuit of the *substance* of evangelical theology and of modern science, and a search for the *means* by which each must be pursued.

Two things need to be noticed. First, Torrance is convinced that there can be no sharp distinction between what we have called "substance" and "means." The *means to understanding* must be in accordance with the *substance of what is sought*; epistemology must follow ontology, just as form and being are inseparable in what is known. Second, for Torrance, there is no ultimate distinction between theology and the natural sciences, even if each has its own distinguishable subject matter; the two are ultimately to be coordinated in a unified view: a truly Christian notion of reality supports the natural-scientific notion of reality, and the latter presumes (but does not attempt) the former. How?

1 Investigation of the intelligible reality of the triune God in his creation of the contingent and orderly universe, and in the depth of his relation to the universe in his Son, provides for the natural sciences the vertical and horizontal coordinates for the integration of the universe.[10]

2   The work of the natural sciences enables theology to understand the nature of scientific method, a method which in many respects is the same even if the demands of their respective subject matter make their work distinctive.

3   The natural sciences enlarge understanding of the structures of created reality, the spatiotemporal world with which God is so directly involved in his creative and redemptive work.

4   The more profound scientific inquiry into the universe becomes, the more it faces cosmological questions and is forced to adopt a fundamental attitude to the universe as a whole.[11]

These conclusions result from Torrance's concern to "evangelize the foundations . . . of scientific culture" in such a way "that dogmatics can take root in that kind of structure."[12]

History of theology and history of science

Torrance is convinced that an intelligent grasp of the reality with which theology and the natural sciences are concerned has been achieved in the decisive periods of theological and natural-scientific advance. He proceeds by *reflecting critically* upon the knowledge which has been achieved in the past and the means by which it has been achieved, in order to discriminate between achievements and distortions in the work of past centuries. Moreover, his reflection is guided by the positive position which he develops and employs; the two – positive position and historical reflection – are subtly interrelated: his positive position is established by reference to his historical work, while he judges what history is important, and interprets it, with criteria which employ his positive position.

The circularity thus apparent in his approach is not a naive one. It is directed to the discovery of the active truth of God present in history through human under-standing past and present. The theories found in history are properly "transparent 'disclosure-models' through which . . . the truth in the creation as it has come from God . . . shine[s] through."[13] Such theories need therefore to show their truth again, to be coordinated with other theories of later times, in which the truth also shines forth, in a unitary view of truth. The approach thus undertaken is in self-conscious opposition to most modern biblical and historical interpretation, which tends to suppose that theories are the product of autonomous human grasping for truth in a fashion which is relative to their culture.

Realism in theology and science: Conformity to the given

Torrance sees reality as disclosing itself to the various sciences, theological and natural, in such a way as to make human beings capable of understanding. Hence, the way forward is to start from the self-presentation of reality, as reality makes itself known to us, recognizing that theology and science are always *a posteriori* and *realistic*: their business is to think the reality which presents itself as known, and to find the deep order intrinsic to that.[14] This is no easy achievement, and it must not be confused with substitutes. What is required is a trust in reality as it presents itself, joined to a continuing struggle to allow thought to be conformed to this reality and to find its inner relations.

It is possible to *know* such things because the nature of the reality prescribes the mode of rationality which is appropriate to it.[15] God is the paramount case of this reality: both by having created us and also by his oneness with us through Christ in our created existence, he sustains our knowing of him. But this is also true of contingent reality, because it has been given its intelligibility by God. It is for this reason that the term "realist" must be used with some caution for Torrance. If realism means a *necessary* correspondence between reality and thought, such as medieval theology asserted by the "analogy of being," he is not a realist. But, in another and quite precise sense, he is. His realism suggests that there is an *actual* correspondence between reality and thought or language *if* the thinker is conformed to the mode of rationality afforded by reality. Scientific knowledge might therefore be described as proceeding within a "double activity," wherein reality actively gives itself – together with the appropriate mode of knowing it – and we actively respond by knowing it in this mode. Only under such circumstances is there a genuine correspondence (or transparence) between reality and thought or language.

Scientific intuition: Human response to the given

Just as intelligible reality meets us and confers a suitable mode of knowing it, so the human response required is *openness to this gift*. Knowledge does not arise *a priori* outside the relation to the reality being confronted, but through an insight which takes shape in our understanding under the imprint of the internal structure of that into which we inquire, and develops within the structural kinship that arises between our knowing and what we know as we indwell it and gain access to its meaning. Not an *a priori* conception or preconception, the foreknowledge with which scientific inquiry operates is an *intuitive anticipation* of a hitherto unknown pattern which arises compellingly in our minds under the intrinsic claim of the subject matter.[16] It is at this point that Torrance finds Michael Polanyi's understanding of the logic of discovery helpful.[17]

Polanyi analyzed the "tacit power" of the human mind to discern *Gestalten* or patterns in experience through a heuristic leap from parts to a whole in which patterns of coherence are seen. What enables us to move from a jumble of discrete bits of experience to their fusion in an integrated whole is an intuitive leap in which "clues" are united in a single pattern. Polanyi likened it to looking at a pair of stereoscopic pictures; seeing the two slightly different pictures in a viewer produces a single three-dimensional picture. Like this, "foreknowledge" or "scientific intuition" forms disparate elements into an interrelated whole through a *personal* and *informal* integrative process of insight. Such insight persists in scientific work and – through its alternation with analytic and deductive procedures – produces a deepening awareness of the object.

Reality, realism, and belief

Where others may proceed with scientific knowledge in a more pragmatic fashion, sustained by the conviction that "it works," Torrance suggests that the basis of scientific activity, whether theological or natural, is actually *belief*.

There is a sense in which the structure of belief duplicates that of natural scientific activity; in the case of the latter, *reality* gives the modes by which we know it, where in the case of the former, the *object of belief* commands our belief, which is "a prescientific but fundamental act of acknowledgment of some significant aspect of the nature of things . . . without which scientific inquiry would not be possible."[18] Such belief is integral to knowledge and its establishment, and is not to be *contrasted* with knowledge, as if belief requires rational demonstration. A belief is actually irrefutable and unprovable: any attempt to prove or disprove belief would have to invoke belief, but belief cannot be put into a form by which it could be proved or disproved. In other words, faith is integral to reason; faith is the very mode of rationality adopted by the reason as it seeks to understand, and as such, faith constitutes the most basic form of knowledge upon which all subsequent rational inquiry proceeds.[19] And beliefs are proportional to the *nature of the truth* to which they are directed, ranging from God's truth, to the truth of natural things, to the truth of human knowledge. A mismatch of beliefs and truths begets idolatry, by which disproportionate importance is accorded to what is lesser.

Belief/faith may seem – as for Locke – a maximal act of human judgment or the ultimate resort of the desire to sustain the possibility of knowledge. For Torrance, it is more like an act of repose, "the resting of our mind upon objective reality . . . that which really is, the nature and truth of things."[20] This is not "subjective" in the usual modern sense, but a personal recognition of what is objective. There are different *kinds of objectivity*, ranging from the objectivity of God, to the objectivity of natural things, to the objectivity of human beings, and appropriate beliefs sustain our dialogical relation to such objectivities. The objectivity of God's truth for humanity in Jesus Christ sustains scientific theological activity; and the objectivity of the truth of nature sustains natural science.

If beliefs differ in such a way, there may be no unity of the theological and natural sciences after all. Certainly, no such unity is available within the natural sciences, even if there may be some forms of unity available within them. However, ultimately, there is a *theological basis* for a unity of the theological and natural sciences: the different "levels" of truth and objectivity, divine and natural, are both differentiated and unified by God's self-giving action in creation and Jesus Christ. And the belief which responds to this is one which derives from God's action in the Holy Spirit.

Insofar as they are personal in their believing, human beings are also responding to an objectivity which constitutes their personhood. The God to whom their belief is ultimately directed is "a coinherence of . . . three divine Persons in the one identical being of God."[21] And this not only unifies their believing, but also personalizes it and them. The personalization of their believing is not a pragmatic construct of theirs, but is derived from God's own nature as Trinity.

What then is to be made of differences in personal believing? Torrance's view of beliefs allows for the deep difference between people's beliefs or "fiduciary frameworks." Since such frameworks are implicated in the lives of the believers, differences between them cannot be overcome by compulsion; they can only be changed by persuasion resulting in a radical conversion (*metanoia*) from old frameworks and reconciliation to the new. That is not simply a human persuasion from one set of human beliefs to another, however; properly it occurs under the claim of divine truth.

The "new objectivity" of science

Torrance is encouraged in his views by what he finds happening in modern science. Einsteinian physical science has, he says, rediscovered what we may call the "sovereign" character of reality, one which transcends all human concepts. The universe is now seen as *intelligible* but *mysterious*, with an infinite depth of comprehensibility which precludes any final notion of physical reality of the sort claimed by physicists at the turn of the century. The intelligibility found by the physical and natural sciences also stretches out beyond what we can comprehend. "There now opens up a dynamic, open-structured universe, in which the human spirit is liberated from its captivity in closed deterministic systems of cause and effect, and a correspondingly free and open-structured society is struggling to emerge."[22] "Einstein's own theory of relativity means that the more profoundly we penetrate into the ultimate invariances in the space-time structures of the universe, we reach objectivity in our basic description of the universe only so far as relativity is conferred upon the domain of our immediate observations."[23]

Belief in an orderly universe and a contingent universe are the two main "ultimates" which are employed in the natural sciences. And with them, the natural sciences are concerned with the investigation both of the ordered and the contingent world, the structures which determine its order and the vectorial character of its change, including its ultimate origins and ultimate ends. It is no part of their purpose, however, to establish the source of contingent order, or the rational basis of these "ultimates." There are theoretical and empirical limits to the enterprise of science; and these are necessary for science to be what it is.

The source of order and contingency in God's creation

With such a transformation in the scientific understanding of reality, there comes to light "a hidden traffic between theological and scientific ideas of the most far-reaching significance for both theology and science . . . where [they] are found to have deep mutual relations."[24] It is clear that there is a very close link between the new objectivity of the natural sciences, with the beliefs which sustain it, and the truth and objectivity of the Judeo-Christian tradition, its ultimate beliefs.

By contrast with the Greek philosophical tradition, the Judeo-Christian view combines many elements within one view to provide a more suitable basis for the new understanding we find in the natural sciences today:

1 The Old Testament view of the transcendent Lord God who freely created a world distinct from himself and constituted its order and the place of human beings as distinct from, but related to, him.

2 The recognition that the Lord is faithful in his creative act, and thus unceasingly operative in preserving and regulating his world.

3 The still more radical understanding of the world, both its matter and its form, "as equally created out of nothing and as inseparably unified in one pervasive contingent rational order in the universe".[25]

4 The Christian understanding of the Incarnation of the Son of God, as showing the full relation of God to the natural world, how the self-giving action of God differentiates and unifies divine and natural order, and how deep is God's relation to the actual spatiotemporal structure and dynamic of the existent universe.

5 The Incarnation as revealing the depth of the relation between the inner constitution of the trinitarian God and the inner constitution of the world, and how God continually sustains the order and contingency of the world.

All of this adds up to a "peculiar" interlocking of the independence of the world from God with its dependence upon him, an independence which gives the world its nature and movement (and requires the self-contained attempt of natural science to know it) and yet refers the nature of the world (and natural-scientific understanding) beyond itself to its freely intelligent and creative source (which requires scientific –theological understanding).[26] This has the effect of directing each to its proper object: natural science to the contingent order of the universe, thereby to grasp its fundamental structure, and theological science to the source of the contingent order of the universe in the self-presentation of the triune God.

Debate

Torrance's work constitutes a powerfully integrated combination of theology, science, and history in response to current suppositions about the realities with which theology deals and its capacity for knowledge of them. He aims to distill and demonstrate central Christian beliefs, identifying what is their inner logic and showing how they correlate with the nature of scientific understanding. For all its brilliance, insight, and persuasiveness, his approach raises a number of important questions.

Torrance's approach draws heavily on a certain kind of physical science philosophically analyzed. Even if we set aside the question of whether he is not taking the implications of this physical science beyond what its practitioners would wish (and there are varieties of view today about how modern physical science yields knowledge), there is still the wider issue of whether physical science can be representative of all "the natural sciences." At the least, such an approach leaves undecided the question of the value of the biological and social sciences for the natural sciences and for theology; it also allows Torrance to sidestep difficult questions about the diversity of creation, which appear when one considers the implications of the biological sciences, or those which appear in the social sciences.

Perhaps because it is narrowly based both in physics and a theory of correspondence between reality and knowledge often found there, Torrance's position is the strongest version of realism, the realism both of scientific activity and of scientific belief, which is available in (and perhaps outside) theology today. If it has not made as wide an impact as one might expect, this may be due to questions about realism in Christian theology and in physics.

On the one hand, Christian theologians most inclined to realist views (those who adopt a conservative position) rarely give high priority to "creation" or "nature," or the need to incorporate them in an intellectual vision of faith. On the other hand, those theologians who are interested in a rational response to the scientific context prefer a "soft" version of science which accounts for scientific activity by reference to "paradigms" and for scientific development by social explanations. For different reasons, these two groups are unlikely to consider Torrance's severely realist approach as seriously as it deserves.

A further issue about Torrance's thought is raised by his constant emphasis on the need to distill the relations and dynamics of theological and scientific understanding. This raises three difficulties, two substantial and one presentational.

First, it leads him to focus on the *outcomes* of what are often complex historical, theological, or scientific processes, as distinct from the means by which they are reached, or on the univocal meaning of complex sources. For example, even for those who accept the normative position of (say) patristic doctrine, is it sufficient to concentrate on such "distillations" without greater attention to the polyvalence of the scriptures – and the dynamics of doctrine and history – in Christian theology?

Second, he often employs second-order conceptualizations for things which are deep and complex, whether historical, theological, or scientific, and also uses concepts as if they themselves are primary rather than pointers to what is deeper. For example, Torrance – like Barth – moves decisively beyond the limitations of overly logical systematizations of Calvin, and appropriates the possibilities of both Calvin and Barth for the intellectual vision of God demanded by Christian faith in a free scientific–theological response to God, but his own work still emphasizes close and well-defined logical connections. Perhaps this is an understandable result of his anxiety to move beyond the "soft" indefiniteness of liberalism, but it quickly produces the opposite extreme. His procedure raises an important question about the goal of theology: should it approximate to close logical statement or to the form of wisdom?

Third, although there is genuine struggle involved in the comprehensive scientific–theological–historical task which he attempts, and in communicating the results to diverse audiences, his accounts of positions – his own and others – and their relations are terse to the point of unintelligibility, even for those who appreciate succinctness and know the importance of theory in and beyond theology. There are many times when the ideas which he cites need more elucidation and support. But so vast is the terrain upon which he works, so anxious is he to interconnect ideas, and so intent on enabling others to see these relations, that he often lapses into such terseness.

It may also be that Torrance's difficulty in communicating his position is connected with the nature of the position he adopts, which verges on the private and publicly inexpressible. His concern is to make the *actuality* – in the sense of an occurrence of empirical–theoretical knowledge of and from reality – *transparent* to others. (The empirical–theoretical knowledge with which he is concerned is to suit the internal correspondences of reality, such as those of being and form. He thereby avoids the *naïveté* of those who disjoin the two; he is rightly alarmed by those who try to deduce theories from observation or experience, as when people deduce a doctrine of the Incarnation from observational data.) What *actually* occurs in knowledge is that reality actualizes itself in our empirical–theoretical understanding, and that is the way in which we participate in the self-knowing of God through and in the natural world. Furthermore, we are sustained in that actuality by *belief* that truth and objectivity meet us in that way. But the relation of knower and known, of empirical–theoretical knowledge and the being and form of the known, cannot be verified outside the fact that it actually occurs. In other words, it is known to occur by those to whom it occurs. And the best they can do for others is to speak in such a way that their words and ideas are transparencies through which others may see.

The means by which Torrance speaks is to call attention to structures of reality and belief, and their validation of the relation between knower and known, to show that the world *is* ordered this way. And that, in turn, is validated by another structural relationship, that which is made by God, as it is seen in his active deeds of self-giving in creation and Incarnation.

The problem which arises from this is a tendency to remain at the level of what we could call "factuality" (which is, to be sure, the factuality of a dynamic), remaining content with the *fact* that these relations occur. Torrance's great contribution lies in his extremely careful statement, supported by evidence drawn from Christian and natural-scientific views, of the fact that it occurs in theology and the natural sciences, and occurs in such a way as to have brought knowledge of the reality with which they are concerned. That, in the end, is what distinguishes his position from those much less certain that it occurs or occurs in such a way as to yield knowledge. Compare his position with (say) existentialists who at the most will admit that "something salvific" happened, but not in such a way as to provide knowledge; for them, there is no "factuality of relation" and no authorization of knowledge, only "something" and human "interpretations." Maintaining the occurrence of this "fact" enables a full appreciation of the positive achievements of the theology and natural science of the past and present, which the others are inclined to treat either negatively or much more tentatively. As was indicated much earlier, he finds depths and correspondences, both in traditional and modern material and between theology and the "hard" sciences, which other more skeptical people do not find.

Within the struggle to stay within the "fact" of knowledge (which, for Torrance, is a struggle to purify available knowledge by probing its inner structure), there are three other issues. One is the privileged position which it accords to those who live in the "fact," the meta-science by which they understand their position, the knowledge which they achieve, and their belief that this is "fact." Of course, the privilege which is theirs is not, in a sense, theirs at all. It is the product of the deep relation in which they participate; they and the statements by which they express the fruits of this relation are "transparencies." Nonetheless, in the history of theology or science, they are taken to provide true knowledge. But, even with all the safeguards which Torrance builds in to prevent intellectual pride, can they be taken so unquestioningly as the bearers of knowledge? There are times when it seems in Torrance's view that human beings are given such a high "intuitive intellectual judgment"[27] as to be put in the place of angels. That is precisely the question which many would raise about such realism today.

Remaining within the factuality of knowledge provided by reality also makes for an exclusivist and occasionalist tendency in Torrance's theology, which he shares with the actualist ontology of Karl Barth. In most of his work, there is a very sharp distinction between those who respond properly to truth and those who do not, between when they do and when they do not. On the one hand, in the "fact" of proper response to truth, human beings achieve knowledge. On the other hand, outside the "fact" of proper response to truth are those who impose "self-willed," "distorting idealizations[s]"[28] on reality. That seems to exclude all but that which conforms very strictly and unswervingly to the conditions of the reality which provides the rationality by which it is known.

In Torrance's later work, there is more recognition of the contingency of knowledge, though still within the "fact" of proper response to truth: "multidimensionality" is conferred upon us by the "range of intelligible structures which spread out before us," and we rise through the "levels of organized concepts."[29] This welcome emphasis on the richness of reality and conceptualities opens the way for a more positive notion of ideas and practices which the earlier view seemed to eliminate. It is not less exclusivist; what is permissible is wider, but it must – and must always be – authorized by reality. This leaves the question of whether the many mundane devices which human beings use in their life and work, from sacraments to technology, are not still too much discounted; contingent structures though they are, they may constitute proper response to an ineffable reality.

There is one final issue which arises from Torrance's concentration on the "fact" of the relationship between truth and knowledge; it concentrates so much on the occurrence of empirico-theoretical knowledge that it produces a restricted view of history. It is admirable to defend and explain the position of space and time in relation to God, and therefore to recognize the contingency of human knowledge, whether theological or natural scientific. But while this justifies some of the categories which will be useful in considering history, it is not sufficient for the task of providing an historical account of theology. As we have seen, Torrance has produced fascinating accounts of the history of theology and natural science, evaluating the basic decisions taken by major figures in the past and present as correct responses to truth, but it remains a question whether his is a fully historical account. The truth of history is certainly more than the achievement of correct accounts of truth.

Achievement, Influence, Agenda

Torrance has been a major proponent of Christian dogmatics in a situation in which it has been deeply undermined by "accommodationist" patterns of thought, those embracing less cognitive approaches. His synthesis of historical, scientific, and systematic theology came at a time when theology was regarded as incapable of providing knowledge in any strong sense, and was seen – at most – through empirical–historical, literary, or cultural lenses. And it represented a very strong alternative, which was profoundly influential among those who sought something stronger than the prevailing "liberal" approaches, even if they did not follow the details of his argument. And it seems again to be gaining new influence, though in different ways.

Ten years ago, there was relatively little direct response to Torrance's work. Now, thankfully, the situation is different. Although one does not find his work being taught as such, it has attracted a number of careful studies. Most come from those who are predisposed to systematic theology and primarily consider his contribution to the content of theology; of these, most are descriptive and analytical, and do not challenge his ways and conclusions; only a few go further to probe and challenge his work. Almost no one has engaged with Torrance's major contribution, which was in a carefully integrated case for a scientific approach through which the substance and method of theology and the natural sciences are unified.

We await someone who can, as Torrance did with Barth, stand on Torrance's shoulders and provide the cognitive account of the bases of Christian theology which he attempted, which is responsive to the changing understanding both of the sciences and of theology.

Notes

1 David W. Torrance in *The Promise of Trinitarian Theology*, ed. E. M. Colyer (Oxford, 2001), p. 2.

2 Following Torrance's statement that it is "in its *doctrine of God* that the really fundamental character of any church tradition becomes revealed" (*Incarnational Ministry*, ed. C. D. Kettler and T. H. Speidell [Colorado Springs, 1990, p. 2]). There are, however, two books which present the core of Christian belief in systematic fashion: *The Trinitarian Faith* (Edinburgh, 1988) and *The Christian Doctrine of God: One Being, Three Persons* (Edinburgh, 1996).

3 Quoted in A. E. McGrath, *T. F. Torrance: An Intellectual Biography* (Edinburgh, 1999), p. 149.

4 *The Mediation of Christ* (Exeter, 1983), p. 69.

5 *The Christian Doctrine of God*, pp. 1–2.

6 His writings are studded with cameo portraits, but the most comprehensive studies are *The Hermeneutics of John Calvin* (Edinburgh, 1988) and *Divine Meaning: Studies in Patristic Hermeneutics* (Edinburgh, 1995), which were intended as parts of an uncompleted three-volume work on the history of hermeneutical thought.

7 *The Christian Doctrine of God*, p. 7.

8 *Theological Science* (Oxford, 1969), p. ix.

9 *Reality and Scientific Theology* (Edinburgh, 1985), p. xiii.

10 *Divine and Contingent Order* (Oxford, 1981), p. 24.

11 Ibid, p. 1.

12 "A Pilgrimage in the School of Christ – An Interview with T. F. Torrance, by I. John Hesselink," *Reformed Review*, Autumn 1984, Vol. 38, No. 1, p. 59.

13 Ibid, p. 63.

14 *Theological Science*, p. 186.

15 Ibid, p. 9.

16 *Transformation and Convergence in the Frame of Knowledge* (Belfast, 1984), pp. 113ff.

17 As found particularly in *Personal Knowledge, Science, Faith and Society, The Tacit Dimension*, and *Knowing and Being*.

18 *Transformation and Convergence in the Frame of Knowledge*, p. 195.

19 Ibid, p. 194.

20 Ibid, p. 195.

21 *The Trinitarian Faith*, p. 199.

22 *Reality and Scientific Theology*, p. ix.

23 Ibid, p. 136.

24 Ibid, pp. ix–x.

25 *Divine and Contingent Order*, p. 31.

26 These are matters to which *Space, Time and Incarnation* (1969) and *Space, Time and Resurrection* (1976) are devoted.

27 R. Hooker, *Of the Laws of Ecclesiastical Polity* (London, 1977), p. 84.

28 "Divine and Contingent Order" in A. R. Peacocke (ed.), *The Sciences and Theology in the Twentieth Century* (Notre Dame, IN, 1981), p. 93.

29 *Divine and Contingent Order*, pp. 27ff.

Bibliography

Primary

Royal Priesthood (Edinburgh, 1955).
Theology in Reconstruction (London, 1965).
Theological Science (Oxford, 1969).
Space, Time and Incarnation (Oxford, 1969).
Space, Time and Resurrection (Edinburgh, 1969).
Theology in Reconciliation (London, 1975).
The Ground and Grammar of Theology (Belfast, 1980).
Christian Theology and Scientific Culture (New York, 1980).
Divine and Contingent Order (Oxford, 1981).
Reality and Evangelical Theology (Philadelphia, PA, 1982).
Transformation and Convergence in the Frame of Knowledge (Belfast, 1984).
Reality and Scientific Theology (Edinburgh, 1985).

The Trinitarian Faith (Edinburgh, 1988).
The Christian Doctrine of God: One Being, Three Persons (Edinburgh, 1996).

Secondary

Colyer, E. M., *How to Read T. F. Torrance* (Downers Grove, 2000).
—— (ed.), *The Promise of Trinitarian Theology* (Lanham, MD, 2001).
Luoma, T., *Incarnation and Physics: Natural Science in the Theology of Thomas F. Torrance* (Oxford, 2002).
McGrath, A. E., *T. F. Torrance: An Intellectual Biography* (Edinburgh, 1999).
Morrison, J. D., *Knowledge of the Self-Revealing God in the Thought of Thomas Forsyth Torrance* (New York, 1997).

Anglican Theology

Peter Sedgwick

Introduction

Anglican theology in England began the twentieth century in a paradoxical situation. On the one hand, there was a widespread intellectual and cultural crisis in England which pervaded much of society. There was also deep seated poverty and class division in the midst of huge wealth. Anglican theology consciously sought to respond to this crisis through such publications as the collection of essays written in 1891 by a group of liberal Anglicans of High Church persuasion based in Oxford and entitled *Lux Mundi* (1891).[1] Such theology argued for an incarnational, kenotic identification of God with human suffering which enabled the Anglican church to identify with the contemporary cultural and social crisis. On the other hand, Anglican theology was part of the self-understanding of the Church of England, and this church was not only established but also enjoyed unparalleled influence in a country that ruled a worldwide empire.

The twentieth century saw not only the dissolution of this empire but also the transformation of English society in ways that were unprecedented, resulting in what is now arguably one of the most secularized countries in the Western world. Anglican theology initially responded to these changes in ways that were gradualist, and suffered from cultural isolation from German and North American theology, until the fateful year of 1940.[2] In this year Michael Ramsey, who had just been appointed professor of theology at Durham University at the age of 36, and Donald MacKinnon began to appreciate the crisis of thought and culture that was affecting Europe.[3] MacKinnon was then a young man teaching theology and philosophy in Oxford, but his response was very different from *Lux Mundi* fifty years earlier.

MacKinnon, Ramsey, and a third Anglican theologian, Austin Farrer, did not create a school of English Anglican theology, either individually or collectively, but they did begin to shape the manner of theological response to national life. Another paradox follows. When the later cultural changes of the 1960s took place in an English society which was very different from that which experienced the political crisis of 1940, the response of much English Anglican theology was to embrace a wholesale liberalism (John Macquarrie, Peter Baelz, Ian Ramsey, Maurice Wiles,

Dennis Nineham, and Don Cupitt) which paralleled other non-Anglican theologians such as John Hick.[4] This was not, however, to be the approach of the theologians previously mentioned. In particular, Donald MacKinnon adopted his own exploration of tragedy and political activity from a rigorous philosophical base. In turn, he (and to some extent Michael Ramsey and Austin Farrer) shaped a new generation of theologians who outlived the liberalism of the 1960s. Stephen Sykes, Daniel Hardy, and (from a younger generation) Rowan Williams became the dominant voices of English Anglican theology as the twentieth century ended.

What then was the response to modernity by these theologians in this deeply secular nation where churchgoing was a minority pursuit? It has been characterized as the search for a "wisdom theology" where prayer and spirituality were of the greatest importance, and where finding the right path (wisdom) to respond to national culture was crucial.[5] Such a theology no longer suffered from the cultural isolation of the first four decades of the twentieth century, and it is significant that Hardy is from the United States. All these theologians have spent much of their working life in dialogue with North American and German theologians. Yet this theology resists the systematization of German thought: there are no fully developed English, Anglican systematic theologies, for instance, and the characteristic style is that of the essay or article. There is a profound appreciation of both the riches of Anglican thought in the centuries after the Reformation and the whole Christian tradition before modernity. This would be especially true of Williams, with his interest in patristics as well as spirituality across the history of Christianity.

The greatest challenge that this group of theologians now confronts is the place of theology in English cultural and intellectual life. Their influence on English theology has been considerable, and to a lesser extent on the life of both their own church and of other denominations. However, as in 1900, there is a profound, if differently articulated, sense of dislocation in English cultural life. It is not clear whether this long engagement with the society around them, articulated in many different forms of dialogue from intellectual, through the cultural and political, to the pastoral, will ultimately end in the marginalization of theology. For theology, this represents the difficult challenge of public intelligibility.

Survey

Theology in English universities up to the 1960s was taught in a way that reflected the institutional basis of the subject. Although most of the teachers in the universities of Oxford, Cambridge, and Durham, where theology was predominantly taught, were in Anglican orders, nevertheless there was no particular theological method in the syllabus of these faculties. From the beginning of the twentieth century, however, the Anglican monopoly on the ancient universities was broken. This led to a concern for denominational neutrality and courses were developed from the early decades of the century which reflected English empiricism, in historical, linguistic, and textual areas of study.[6]

Systematic theology was ignored and in its place there was the study of biblical texts and church history. However in the twentieth century there came a variety of substitutes for systematics, such as biblical, dogmatic, and philosophical theology.

Biblical theology traced the underlying themes in scripture, and was highly influential in the 1960s and 1970s. Dogmatic theology examined the dogmas of the early church. Philosophical theology was developed throughout the twentieth century and especially appealed to those of a liberal persuasion. It studied the relationship of God and creation (including humanity), including freedom, immortality, and providence, but not eschatology or redemption. It was not until the last three decades of the twentieth century that systematic theology began to be written in English universities by Anglicans (Sykes, Hardy, Williams, McFadyen). When it did begin to be written it was in a characteristic Anglican form, without a concern for cognitive certainty or comprehensiveness. The systematic theology found in Torrance or Gunton would be very different. Anglican systematic theology at the end of the century has been called a "wisdom theology," as noted above. However, Ramsey highlighted the importance of the two concepts of "truth" and "wisdom" as long ago as 1936 in his first major work, *The Gospel and the Catholic Church*.

There is also a distinctive attitude in contemporary Anglican theology to modernity which denies that there is a massive gulf between premodernity and the present. Indeed, the awareness of the long history of English culture can sometimes obscure how great the disruption of modernity has been, and the Anglican fascination with patristics (especially found in Ramsey and Williams) means that there is a constant engagement with premodern thought forms.

A final aspect of this theology is its concern with the well-being of society and culture, whether in the 1930s in Ramsey or at the start of the twenty-first century almost seventy years later in Williams. It is never a theology indifferent to the place of the church in English society, or of society *per se*, even if this does not become a confessional study. The health of civilization was of importance, and this encompassed literature, the history of the nation, and a social life where the church was in critical solidarity with the state. Indeed, this could be a reason for writing a theology, as it clearly is in the opening pages of Ramsey's *Gospel*. Christian faith was never opposed to the forces of civilization.

The Church of England did develop its own independent theological colleges or seminaries, where liturgy and pastoral studies were taught. So too did Roman Catholic and Protestant colleges. It is significant that Ramsey's first book was written when he was teaching in Lincoln Theological College, an Anglican foundation with a tradition of a daily Eucharist. It is also noteworthy that Farrer's work on biblical imagery in the 1940s took biblical theology in a direction that anticipated the concern of systematics with textual reasoning at the end of the twentieth century, even if this was not developed for many decades in the ways that it might have been.

There was another reason for the delay in establishing systematics in the syllabus and that was the impact of logical positivism. This philosophy was opposed to the truth-claims of theology, but it did not impact on English theology until the 1940s. Due to the onslaught of logical positivism, especially in the works of A. J. Ayer and the early Wittgenstein, Anglican theology often became apologetic and wary of positive claims. The prevailing philosophical skepticism to any propositions which could not be verified by sense experience in principle, meant that English theology adopted a defensive air. The fact that Ramsey left university life for an episcopal role at the early age of 48 also meant that his positive influence was much reduced in intellectual life.

It was to be the major work of Donald MacKinnon and Austin Farrer to develop a theology of transcendence which denied the force of the claims of logical positivism. One of the few Anglican major theological works which faced it early on was Austin Farrer's *Finite and Infinite*. Others tended to try to mediate between skeptical philosophy and the claims of theology. One mediating theologian was Ian Ramsey in the 1960s, with his philosophical account of "cosmic disclosure." Another was Basil Mitchell, also an Anglican, who worked with Farrer and others in a group at Oxford called the Metaphysicals, and who sought to develop a defense of faith independent of the strictures of logical positivism. Faith, for Mitchell, had empirical implications, but its truth-claims were independent of empiricism.[7]

Michael Ramsey

Ramsey had been educated at Cambridge in the 1920s in a theology faculty that was deeply hostile to traditional forms of Christian orthodoxy. Its primary figure was J. F. Bethune-Baker, who advocated an English version of Harnack's liberal modernism. He emphasized moral values and a deist cosmology which rejected miracles out of hand as a supernaturalist theology. His Christology saw Christ as different from humanity only in degree. Bethune-Baker achieved his greatest prominence at the 1921 Cambridge conference on modernism. Science had disproved the beliefs of Christianity on divine action, and the modernists were attempting to save what could be salvaged in a post-Hegelian immanentism.

Ramsey found this deeply uncongenial and was influenced by a young theologian, Edwyn Hoskyns, whose article on Christology in 1926 argued that the gospels were formed by Christ's own interpretation of himself, rather than being shaped by early Christian responses to Middle Eastern philosophies, cults, and religions. Hoskyns introduced Ramsey to Barth's theology, but so great was the hostility to Barth, and indeed to Hoskyns by his colleagues, that Ramsey was rejected when he applied for a research post at his own faculty. Instead, Ramsey, after a spell of parish work, went to a theological college at Lincoln for six years. Such was the impact of his major work, *The Gospel and the Catholic Church*, written there in 1936 at the age of 32, that within four years he was offered the chair of theology at Durham. The chair at Cambridge then followed before he left university life for good, aged 48.

What was it about *The Gospel and the Catholic Church* which made such an impact? Ramsey rejected the idea that the relevance of the church was found in its "ability to take the lead in social and international politics."[8] Instead, there is a stress on judgment, and a repeated reference to the scandal of the church. The scandalous nature of its existence lies in its witness to the resurrection and to the way that the passion of Christ is known there. Ramsey sees the church as pointing beyond both theology and philanthropy. The church is the corporate expression of the atoning death of Christ and the controlling categories of interpretation for both doctrine and history in the understanding of the church must be cross and resurrection. The power of evil in the world is broken by the death of Christ and this establishes the Kingdom of God. Death has both a moral meaning and a redemptive power. In language reminiscent of dialectical theology in Germany, Ramsey speaks of man as a "dying creature," confronted with both the boundary of his life and the fear of death. The purpose of the Incarnation was the death of Christ ("he came in order to die, so as to be man, in man, of man")[9] and this death contains within it the fact of the church by Christ's baptism into humanity and by his negation of the rights of self before God. Ramsey emphasizes far more than Farrer does the necessity of the death of Christ as the central meaning of the Incarnation. However, any exposition of the death of Christ must always be followed by the fact of the resurrection.

Both events pierce into the order of time, and also become part of the disciples who followed Christ. At this point Ramsey introduces a far more pneumatological dimension, seeing the church as constituted by the koinonia of the Spirit which is the Spirit of him who died. Apostolicity and Catholicity are aspects of this pneumatological reality and in so doing the outward order of the church tells of the gospel. All sacramental order points to the inward truth of the historical Jesus, and his passion. Ramsey appreciated Barth's appeal to the unity of divine action behind the historical record, and his belief that such action was determinative of human history. However, he felt that Barth accepted too easily the belief that the truth of this insight could not be embodied in organic structures. The church is not an institution but an organic reality which is "part of the utterance of God's redemptive love."[10]

Ramsey justifies his theology by appealing to the importance of truth and wisdom in the theological task. Citing Barth in *Romans*, he equated truth not with human thought but with divine action. Such truth is learnt in Christian discipleship and the learning of that truth leads to the recognition of the wisdom of God working through all of created life.

It might be asked how this exposition of redemption and ecclesiology as a single whole related to British society. Ramsey's mother had been a passionate supporter of the Labour Party until her early death in a car accident, and Ramsey had met many of the leading socialist politicians as a boy. As an undergraduate he was active in politics. What happened to this political interest? Was it simply swallowed up in the fascination of creating a theology that combined aspects of Barth's soteriology with Catholic ecclesiology?

The answer is both yes and no. It is certainly true that it is difficult to read *The Gospel and the Catholic Church* and find much sense of how the rest of human society is to be affected by the reality of the church, although Ramsey never denied natural theology and recognized in his first work the importance of finding people of good will to collaborate with. His academic work after *The Gospel and the Catholic Church* consisted of a study of glory and transfiguration (an interest in imagery which Farrer was to take much further) and a work on *The Resurrection of Christ*. This did not take Ramsey's concern for society much further.

Yet it would be wrong to dismiss Ramsey as having no social theology. He knew that the theology of Maurice, Gore, and Westcott was at a discount.[11] The incarnational theology of the period 1890–1940 has passed away and in its place there is a much harsher existence. What he sought was to bring the social insights of William Temple (whom he always revered)[12] into alliance with a refashioned theology of redemption. But this was expressed episodically and in fragments of short essays and addresses. It was left to MacKinnon, and the later generation of Anglican theologians (especially Hardy), to develop his theology of catholicity into one of sociality which could engage more fully with the social order. Ramsey laid the groundwork, but did no more.

Austin Farrer

Farrer and Ramsey were close friends: they met at Cuddesdon Theological College outside Oxford in 1926 on their first day there, and remained both personally and theologically indebted to each other for the rest of their lives. Both saw liberal modernism as an inadequate response to modernity, although Ramsey was more concerned with rehabilitating the scandal of the soteriological work of Christ expressed in the being of the church. Farrer, who worked virtually all his life at Oxford University, preferred to demonstrate the rationality of the Christian faith, but also paradoxically explored the revelatory power of images and textual reasoning. Each saw their work as complementary to the other, and both found the revival of liberalism in the 1960s uncongenial to their theological worldview.

Farrer's theology was certainly highly rational, including the grounds of theistic belief but also the nature of freedom and evil. Within this exposition, however, he developed a remarkable theology of imagery, in which he anticipated the interest in textual reasoning by several decades. A third interest of his, though far less extensive, is his doctrinal writing, especially on Christology. His rational theology included his major work, *Finite and Infinite*, published in 1943. He analyzed the experience of finitude, especially causality, and sought to find within the nature of change, motion and contingency, an indirect knowledge of the infinite as the revelation of God's own being. Within this defense of theism he also included a strong belief in the freedom of the will, which was to be the subject of a later book with that title, written in 1958, and containing his Gifford lectures. Farrer was concerned to examine how theological statements were used, but he also sought to find the nature of God who both exists in himself and yet is our creator.

In *The Glass of Vision*, written in 1948, Farrer changed direction dramatically. His rational theology was not repudiated for a moment, but it was now seen to be the prolegomena to an investigation of biblical symbolism and imagery. He turned his attention to the revelation of St. John the Divine and its imagery, which he explored in great detail: "The interpretive work of the apostles must be understood as participation in the mind of Christ, through the Holy Ghost. They are the members, upon whom inflows the life of the Head."[13] Images set forth the supernatural mystery at the heart of Christ's teaching. There is a duality of event and interpretation, and only through this is revelation accomplished. "The stuff of inspiration is living images. Theology is the analysis and criticism of the revealed image."[14] Each image has its own conceptual conventions proper to the figure it embodies. This revelation is an objective reality which is not to be reduced to a subjective form of religious experience, or to biblical formulae. The supernatural act in man is a foretaste of the whole substance of the saving mystery, and he will behold it in the beatific vision, but it is no more than a foretaste. The theologian cannot judge the images according to their adequacy to the object they describe. All he can do is confront one image with another, although rational theology (in the same way as the apostles) can regulate the overall vision which the images present to the believer. The Incarnation is the rebirth of imagery, prefigured in the Israelite prophets: "Poetry and divine inspiration have this in common, that both are projected in images which cannot be decoded, but must be allowed to signify what they signify of the reality beyond them."[15] Between the sober analogies of metaphysical discourse and the free irresponsibility of poetical images there stands divine inspiration. In a later work, *A Rebirth of Images*, also on the Johannine Apocalypse, he wrote of human imagination, its relationship to the divine power, and the mediating category of images. Such imagery flows into the mind of the individual at a subconscious level, drawing from the society in which she is placed, and acting upon the will of the person. Religion transforms itself, and the society where it is embodied, by the transfiguration of its language through its imagery. Christ is the archetypal transformer of such imagery, but he does so because he is divine, and not the other way around.

Farrer saw Christology as deeply contingent: rational theology cannot show how God works by grace. God's action is to bring us into a personal union with himself, and he speculates that the Incarnation would have happened even without human sin: "Surely he would still have come . . . to transform human hope and to bring men into a more privileged association with their creator than they could otherwise enjoy. For it is by the descent of God into man that the life of God takes on a form with which we have direct sympathy and personal union."[16] Nevertheless the mystery of the Incarnation remains. Above all it is in the light of trinitarian doctrine that Farrer sees the Incarnation. In his sermons Farrer emphasizes that the Son is derived from the Father in the Trinity and in Jesus' reference to the Father who sent him the same response is made in the Incarnation.

Donald MacKinnon

MacKinnon was the one layman in this group of Anglican theologians. He was born and brought up in Scotland, and never forgot his Scottish ancestry, finally retiring to live there until his death in 1994. Equally, he was the most philosophically acute of their number. However, his interest lies in the way he bridged the two eras of Anglican theology. He was a devout Anglo-Catholic who discovered Karl Barth early on. In this respect he was little different from Michael Ramsey, whom he greatly admired.[17] But whereas Ramsey abandoned academic life in 1952 at the age of 48, when he was persuaded to accept the offer of the see of Durham, MacKinnon remained involved in academic scholarship right up to his death. He was therefore a teaching colleague of Stephen Sykes, but he also taught and profoundly influenced Rowan Williams. He is therefore of interest in two ways. On the one hand, there is his own unique and deeply idiosyncratic combination of philosophical rigor, interest in biblical and systematic studies, awareness of the dimension of tragedy in literature and human life, and an active membership of the British Labour Party. On the other hand, in a long life with an abiding interest in the personalities of those who had been his theological colleagues over many generations, he united the world of the 1930s and 1940s (when Barth was first being understood in England, Ramsey was beginning to publish, and the struggle against fascism was at its height) with the 1970s and 1980s, when a reaction began to set in against the liberalism of those like Nineham and Macquarrie. MacKinnon was hostile to the theology of those who found in human beings' search for selfhood, united with what was left of scripture after the historical–critical method had done its work, the future direction of theological scholarship. He felt that such apologists lacked the intellectual rigor of those of his atheist colleagues in philosophy who had rejected religion as meaningless, were often politically rather complacent of social injustice, and failed to see the moral power of continental theologians in their struggle with the truth of Christ's passion. MacKinnon was drawn both to continental Catholic theologians such as von Balthasar and also to the German Protestant tradition of dialectical theology.

His concern was with the controversy between realism and idealism, to which he often returned. He sought a metaphysics which would thrust against the limits of language and to find in the facticity of the universe something more than the logical empiricism of the 1950s would allow. However, this did not mean abandoning a dialogue with positivism, for in idealism he felt that there could be an escape from the harsh reality of existence. In cognition, in moral choice, and in parabolic drama MacKinnon sought to fashion a world that was more open textured than many would allow. Public life illustrated the dilemmas of existence in which the *mysterium Christi* bore down upon statesmen as they wrestled with difficult ethical problems. Neither ethical naturalism nor liberal theology was adequate to these claims. MacKinnon translates the theology of Ramsey and Barth into the world of history and public life, but he does so not simply to construct arguments about moral problems. Rather, he sought to refashion the metaphysical debate in the light of moral existence. His concern remained metaphysical rather than ethical. This gave his theology a tentative, exploratory feel, where he rebuked idealists such as Bultmann for "supposing that one can translate propositions concerning actual historical transactions into propositions relating to the spiritual lives of individuals and of groups."[18] He could certainly argue that an awareness of silence before God was necessary if theology was to retain credibility with the world, but it was in the silence that the possibility of speech (fragmented, broken, and unsystematic discourse) became a reality.

MacKinnon wrote a great deal about the reality of power politics and religious faith, remaining a stern critic of ecclesiastical self-absorption. "There is something almost pathetic (if it were not also so coldly cruel in its manifestations) about the ways in which ecclesiastical authority seeks to retain the styles of a past age."[19] However, his desire to break the establishment of the Church of England, seen most clearly in the 1968 Gore memorial lecture, *Kenosis and Establishment*, never departed far from the familiar Anglican issues of Christology and kenosis. Equally, he returned repeatedly to the issue of biblical language, and in particular to the nature of the parables as displaying a realism which enables us to explore the nature of the divine. The parables, and the nature of the Eucharist as a parabolic action as well as inaugurating liturgical tradition, took MacKinnon back to the necessity of a rigorous involvement with philosophical and theological issues of transcendence. In turn, the question of trinitarian relationships is considered because of the self-limitation of God in his self-transformation in the Incarnation. MacKinnon, like his pupil Rowan Williams, was concerned about the abuse of kenosis as a theological term. This questioning, philosophical mode of doing theology deeply influenced his students, many of whom now occupy senior positions in English theology.

Stephen Sykes

Sykes began writing his contribution to English, Anglican theology after a period in which he became very familiar with historical and contemporary German Protestant theology. This marked his writings, and much of his work can be seen as an attempt to persuade his contemporaries to adopt the intellectual rigor and self-awareness found in Schleiermacher and Barth. Sykes sought to persuade English Anglican theology that it lacked integrity because it failed to be sufficiently rigorous about its own self-definition. His target was not only the state of Anglican theology but also of the Church of England, which he belonged to and in which he eventually held episcopal office. He was appreciative of the creativity of preeminent Anglican theologians of previous generations, such as F. D. Maurice and Michael Ramsey, recognizing that they held a profound commitment to incarnational theology, but he was concerned at Ramsey's celebration of what he felt was theological incoherence in its methodology. The concept of Anglican comprehensiveness, developed by F. D. Maurice in the nineteenth century, was also subject to extensive criticism: "Is there an Anglican theology, a proposal many have denied? Is there an Anglican method in theology, which some have affirmed while denying that there is an Anglican theology? And what in any case is the present state of the Anglican study of the church?"[20]

His first book, *The Integrity of Anglicanism*, was designed to make the case for a theological method in Anglicanism, where systematic theology was defined in functional terms as "that constructive discipline which presents the substance of the Christian faith with a claim on the minds of men."[21] But this quest also led him to consider the nature of conflict and doctrinal speculation, and to see liturgy as the means by which a church may preserve its own identity. How the liturgy was transmitted from one generation to another, and how this liturgy and ecclesiastical order defined a church's self-understanding over the speculations of theologians became the central topic for Sykes. Conflict was inherent in theology partly because of the tension between the outward and inward expressions of Christianity, and partly because of the inevitable imprecision of words and the necessity of doctrinal reformulation over time. In his view, Christianity was an "essentially contested" concept. Theological debate has not produced an agreed definition of Christianity, despite attempts to discern an "essence of Christianity." Sykes gave a historical survey of the conflicts in modern theological thought, especially in its attempt to evaluate the search for truth by theologians as diverse as Schleiermacher, Newman, Harnack, and Barth. In particular there was endemic conflict in English Anglicanism:

> The Anglican Church, which has developed, under the impact of modern liberal theology, a breadth of doctrinal tolerance of doubt and internal contradiction unparalleled by that of other Episcopal churches, has an urgent responsibility to articulate what it stands for as an institution in its liturgy and canon law, and to subject that content to rigorous criticism.[22]

The theory of the comprehensiveness of Anglican theology, which held together diverse truth-claims, failed to justify why conflicting truth-claims should coexist in the same church. However, internal conflict cannot be regarded with equanimity. Conflict without limit would destroy the integrity of a religious tradition such as Anglicanism. Disagreements can be clarified by the precision of doctrinal formulation, but ultimately there is an issue about the compatibility of the diversity of theological speculation with denominational integrity. The liturgy and canon law of the church expressed this integrity, and so it was here that the power of the church was located: "Only in the phenomenon of Christian worship could the conditions of vigorous argument be regarded as a constructive contribution to the performance of Christian identity in the modern world."[23]

This meant that the theology of power was raised for the first time in English Anglicanism as a major topic, using the extensive sociological interest in this concept as well as the notion of routinization, whereby charismatic influences are incorporated into the regular life of the church. Theologians exercise power by their interventions in the life of the church. The true achievement of the Christian religion at its origin was to create a normative, transcendent community rather than (as Troeltsch had argued) to offer a spiritual alternative to a material world. Such a community can only be maintained by allowing the organization to articulate rules as to who shall be authentically part of it, and by giving to its hierarchy the power to reform itself. In his own life, Sykes played such a role as an Anglican bishop.

There was also a prophetic element in Sykes' writing. He recognized the growing threat which Western culture posed to the practice of the faith. The internalized imperatives of destructive individualism in the realms of power, sex, and money amounted to a form of enslavement. Liberation was possible when local churches embodied a life of grace and fellowship analogous to their life in the Greco-Roman world. In a nation where the Christian faith was rapidly losing credibility there had to be a clarity about what individual Christians believed if the arguments of the secular world were to be resisted. This could be achieved by the role of worship in the life of the believer and the Christian community. The nature of modern society is irreducibly pluralistic and here the variety of roles open to an individual weakens religious commitment, especially in Protestantism with its relatively slight interest in external rituals and consequent loss of coherence. This is then expressed in behavior which is at odds with Christian discipleship, whether in personal or social forms of life. Worship is the antidote to this philosophy of liberal individualism, as Alistair MacIntyre has described it. It presents the disciple with the demands of Christianity, where the texts of communal worship contextualize the necessarily provisional conclusions of doctrinal investigations.

Daniel W. Hardy

Daniel Hardy (b. 1930) is an American who spent most of his working life in England. He studied in Oxford, taught in Birmingham University, and was Van Mildert Professor of Divinity in the University of Durham. He served as Director of the Princeton Center of Theological Inquiry for five years, before returning to an active retirement based in the Faculty of Divinity in the University of Cambridge.

It is a striking fact that Hardy expounded one of his most penetrating accounts of sociality (the concept of human beings' fundamental interrelatedness) in a lecture in honor of Michael Ramsey. Hardy develops his thought considerably beyond Ramsey's reflections on human fellowship, but it nevertheless shows how much the English, Anglican school of theology has an essential coherence. Hardy develops his theology into an account of how cognition is founded in worship, since the movement of

God towards humanity enables a response to be made which creates the possibility of a formed Christian character. Worship is the recognition of the dynamic relationality of God in his being towards humanity which structures all our knowledge and relationships. God as an energy event enacts his sociality in such a way that human beings also find the possibility of their sociality enlarged. Thus, ethics flow out of cognition and both have their foundation in worship and the self-movement of God towards the world he creates, nurtures, and loves. "As God extends his sociality into relationship with a universe which is social, that sociality is ramified in an increasingly complex sociality."[24]

Social structures have, however, become polarized in recent centuries and this is directly related to their instrumentality in which the fundamental nature of such structures is their ability to be managed so as to produce wealth, or other forms of social control. The complexity of the large-scale formal organization is juxtaposed with the fragmented and informal, and the prevailing view in society is that there are no intrinsic forms of social relationships: all such relationships are externally constructed. This loss of true social coherence is directly related to the displacement of the presence of God in society, and the consequent tendency to see God (if seen at all) in deist terms. Hardy resists this, since a proper trinitarian vision would see "an energetic unity" (the Spirit) "true to its initial conditions" (the Father) through "ordering its interactions" (the Son).[25]

This leads him into a consideration of how Christianity in general, and Anglicanism in particular, can contribute to the well-being of society and enter into dialogue with other disciplines in universities. For Hardy, it is imperative that communication with cultural norms be kept open so that such practices can be recalled to their full richness in God. In his later collection of essays, *Finding the Church*, he reflects the sustained work which he has carried out on behalf of the Anglican Communion worldwide. This is, however, earthed in his work on sociality. Two such essays may be mentioned. "The Sociality of Evangelical Catholicity" is an essay given in honor of Michael Ramsey, sixty years after the publication of *The Gospel and the Catholic Church*. The logic of the mission of the church is threefold. First, there is a concern for the sociality of human relationships. Second, there is the embodiment of this in the sacraments of the church, which exemplify God's healing of the nations. Third, there are the structures of the church, which disseminate responsibility for the world and its good order within them. "Its order must always be directed to the exemplification of God's abundantly compassionate healing of the world within the world."[26]

A later essay expresses this in terms of contemporary debates in the church.[27] Here, Hardy expounds Coleridge's analysis of society in his work *On the Constitution of Church and State*. Is the true end for society a transcendental notion, discernible to reason, serving as a standard of reference in human affairs? Is it a purely theological actuality, arising from the being and activity of God among human beings? Or is it a substantive condition under which the good of all citizens is subsumed? Anglicanism answers such questions both from its ancient heritage and in its ecclesial form. By fulfilling its marks of holiness and catholicity the church represents the true possibility for society of all humankind. The nature of the Church of England disallows an introverted view of catholicity. However, Hardy is critical of Temple's view of the relationship of church and state: "The underlying supposition is that there are moral principles and ideals followed by the state which are derived from theological propositions, and applied in particular cases, as if there were a linear relation between theology and state which is mediated by the Church."[28]

Hardy thinks this is inadequate. Government has not only marginalized other institutions, but also there is little capacity in any institution to recognize the need of true sociality. As a response to this situation there is now a prophetic dimension in English Anglicanism which begins with the reality of division and seeks a new interpersonal community.

> This way to the true possibility of society is far from the view that the true possibility of social life is best served by interactive, mutually correcting institutions by which human beings are raised to true society through dynamic provision for their mutual needs and by cultivating them in the cultured civility which society requires, these in turn corrected and raised by the Church of Christ.[29]

Anglicanism is now made up of a vigorous dialogue between the constitutional and prophetic elements, which both renews its sense of purpose and its comment on society. This contingency, if not crisis, within Anglicanism leads Hardy to reflect that renewed attention needs to be given to the ontological basis of social institutions in the trinitarian being of God. This is best described as an "ordered energy" by which the "coherence of abundance" engenders the contingency of social life and forms in the world through the action of the spirit. The practical outcomes of this polity are a renewed vision of the life of the people over against a "now-rampant statism" in terms of social interaction, economic distribution, cultural life, and social vision.

Rowan Williams

Rowan Williams (b. 1950) studied and also held academic posts in both Oxford and Cambridge before becoming a bishop in the Church in Wales and later Archbishop of Canterbury.

The diversity of Williams' writing is remarkable. He has written studies of Christian spirituality, patristic theology, sermons, and a major work of theological essays. This latter work, *On Christian Theology*, has a systematic internal coherence about its argument. The essays range over ontology and the Trinity, pluralism, methodology Christology, the sacraments, ethics, and social theology. Written in the decade up to 1998, they represent a sustained wrestling with contemporary theology from the standpoint of both an academic and a bishop.

Williams developed a clear philosophical position, deeply indebted both to Donald MacKinnon whose name occurs repeatedly in his writings, and to a much younger philosopher, Gillian Rose, who died in 1995 at the age of 48. Rose was baptized into the Church of England on her deathbed. Williams had a close relationship with her and he cited her posthumous collection of essays *Mourning Becomes the Law: Philosophy and Representation* when considering how Christianity might express itself in the secular society that is contemporary English life. Her understanding of the political cut across communitarianism and liberalism. Liberalism is enslaved to an atomized view of the individual with his or her given agenda, while communitarianism has a static account of the community. Both are complicit in the other, based on the failure to relate law and self-understanding. Instead, Rose offers a Hegelian account of how we educate each other by participation in political life through imagination and education, or *Bildung*. "The law therefore in its actuality means full mutual recognition, 'spirit' or ethical life."[30] In historical practice, the process of public debate exposes our failures of mutual recognition and moves us toward authentically moral behavior. Liberalism, which is the dominant ideology of English political and social life, reaches fundamental consensus on social goods on only one thing. This is the facilitating of individual autonomy by the mechanics of public agreement. But this cannot be a substantive good. An uncritical narrativist appeal to Christian identity can become complicit in this misrecognition of the other. Law, for Rose (and Williams), is a synonym for a wide range of social practices and discourses in community. However, as the process of mutual self-recognition reveals the complementarity of the other (Williams notes how Rose is uneasy with Levinas' political ethics here), a narrative is projected in which there is space for theological insight:

> It must also be a narrative in which the common enterprise of humanity is essentially something that is being continually learned . . . This assembly (the Church) exists not to make political policy or to witness to an abstract universal justice or emancipation, but to speak of and enact the patterns of self-displacing and self-risking invited by the story of the self-displacing God, who elects to live in the light of the other (contingent and historical humanity, mortal vulnerability).[31]

Williams rejects the idea of the Christian narrative being an illustrative gloss on ideals of universal kinship. He prefers to speak of the narrative encompassing tragedy and irony (a clear echo of MacKinnon) and also of the narrative grounding the possibility of human self-recognition (through the doctrine of creation in the Word) and refashioning (again dependent on divine self-loss consummated in the cross). Secularism is a mirror image of fundamentalism.

How then are these general remarks about the relationship of philosophy to theology taken into a self-understanding that will enable Williams to set forth his own theology? Williams speaks of three modes of theology, which are the celebratory, the communicative, and the critical. Celebratory theology "evokes a fullness of vision" which displays "the fullest possible range of significance in the language used." Communicative theology experiments with dialogue with an uncommitted environment such as feminism or Marxism. Critical theology engages in an internal critique of theology, including philosophical theology, but also mystical theology and the apophatic tradition. Williams works with all of them, engaging in a constant dialogue with history and social practice.

It is, however, a theological practice that is critical of some Anglican practice in the past, especially *Lux Mundi*. In his 1989 Gore lecture in Westminster Abbey Williams exposed the "incarnational consensus"[32] to stringent criticism. Williams saw this theology as indebted to F. D. Maurice, a mid-nineteenth century theologian who celebrated the dual theological principle of Anglicanism. This was God's raising of human nature in the Incarnation and the establishing as abiding tokens of God's presence certain material acts and objects ("sacraments"). Such theology could also be seen in Moltmann's writings in a different but analogous form ("human forms of relatedness are to be judged yet also transfigured by the solidarity of God with human beings"), which explained the great impact of Moltmann in the Church of England in past decades. Moltmann, indeed, explicitly took up Anglican Christian Socialist theology in *The Trinity and the Kingdom of God*.

Williams dissents from this theology. It tends to sacralize the present social order unhelpfully and it abstracts too much from the contingent reality of the story of Jesus. This story is marked by conflict with social forms of belonging such as family, status, even membership of the Abrahamic community. The isolation of Jesus on the cross poses sharp questions to incarnational theology.[33]

In trinitarian terms, Williams is equally skeptical of any conception of kenosis as the process by which God becomes human. Kenosis is the pattern of Jesus in his historical life, but Williams seeks to avoid presenting the human Jesus as a static icon of the divine. Williams returns to the importance of questioning, of freedom, of historical practice. In the words of Lossky, whom Williams studied for his doctorate, tradition is what keeps the church free to question its traditions, and to give us some part in the freedom of God as it is lived out in Jesus. There is no contradiction between Catholic order and Protestant freedom: both (as Ramsey had argued decades before) are derived from the passion of the cross.

Agenda

English Anglican theology became far more sophisticated, self-aware, and rigorous between the 1930s and the present day. It engaged with other theological disciplines (and its current major challenge is of course the dialogue with other faiths) and became more philosophically rigorous. The attitude to the surrounding culture varied. However, a prevailing norm among contemporary English, Anglican theologians is that Western Christianity has entered a period of profound unease with the surrounding materialism in our society and that it is necessary to rediscover a prophetic edge to the Christian faith. The excision of memory in English culture much described by sociologists of religion[34] has led to a rapid decline in churchgoing unparalleled in English history. The note of judgment articulated by Michael Ramsey in 1936 has come back to English theology as the century ends. Nevertheless that would not be the only note to be struck. In a volume published in 2003, *Anglicanism: The Answer to Modernity*,[35] there is an attempt to engage with modernity in a confident spirit. If modernity is a set of questions, then Anglicanism is an attempt to enter a conversation with that culture. This dialogue is neither defensive nor ill-equipped in terms of theology's engagement with other disciplines. It remains to be seen how this dialogue is to be continued in a search for wisdom that unites prayer, intellectual discipline, and pastoral concern for the society in which it is set. What is most striking, though, is the continuity in Anglican theology over the last seventy years, as it sought to respond to modernity in an attitude of "critical solidarity." There seems little sign that even in a society where religious practice has diminished to an enormous extent that English Anglican theology will change its overall direction.

Notes

1 On the philosophical background, see "Some Aspects of the Treatment of Christianity by the British Idealists" in D. M. MacKinnon, *Themes in Theology*, p. 51.
2 See A. M. Ramsey, *From Gore to Temple*.
3 See A. Hastings, *A History of English Christianity 1920–1990*, pp. 259–61 (on Ramsey) and p. 397 (on the 1941 Malvern Conference attended by Temple, and MacKinnon). See also O. Chadwick, *Michael Ramsey*, on Ramsey's meeting with Reinhold Niebuhr, Emil Brunner, and William Temple in 1936 when Ramsey was 32.
4 See the surveys of these theologians in D. W. Hardy, "Theology through Philosophy," in D. F. Ford (ed.), *The Modern Theologians* (2nd edn., Oxford, 1997; 1st edn., Oxford, 1991: the different editions contain surveys of different theologians). See also the survey of English biblical theologians and historians in the same period by S. W. Sykes, "Theology through History," in the same volumes.
5 D. F. Ford, "Theological Wisdom, British Style," *Christian Century*, April 5, 2000: 12, 19.
6 S. W. Sykes, *The Integrity of Anglicanism*, surveys the teaching of theology in the first part of the twentieth century.
7 B. Mitchell, *The Justification of Religious Belief* (London, 1973).
8 *The Gospel and the Catholic Church*, p. 3.
9 Ibid, p. 23.
10 Ibid, p. 66.
11 Ramsey, *Durham Essays and Addresses*, p. 43.
12 See Ramsey's tribute to Temple on the centenary of his birth (October 15, 1881) in *The Times* of October 10, 1981. See also Ken Leech, *The Social Theology of Michael Ramsey* (London, 1988).
13 Farrer, *The Glass of Vision*, p. 4.
14 Ibid, p. 44.

15 Ibid, p. 148.
16 See the essay "The Doctrine of the Incarnation in the thought of Austin Farrer" in B. Hebblethwaite, *The Incarnation* (Cambridge, 1987), p. 114, quoting Farrer's *Saving Belief*, pp. 111–12.
17 See his tribute to Ramsey for his 1952 review of the book edited by MacKinnon, *Christian Faith and Communist Faith*. The tribute is given in MacKinnon, *Explorations in Theology 5*, p. 24.
18 MacKinnon, *Borderlands of Theology and Other Essays*, p. 88.
19 *The Stripping of the Altars*, p. 59.
20 Sykes, *The Integrity of Anglicanism*, p. 5.
21 Ibid, p. ix.
22 Ibid, p. 51.
23 Sykes, *The Identity of Christianity*, p. 265.
24 Hardy, *God's Ways With The World*, p. 29.
25 Ibid, p. 186.
26 Hardy, *Finding the Church*, p. 94.
27 Unpublished paper, "An Anglican View of the Common Good."
28 Ibid, p. 11.
29 Ibid, p. 15.
30 Williams, "Beyond Liberalism," in *Political Theology*, 3.1, November 2001, citing Gillian Rose, *Mourning Becomes the Law: Philosophy and Representation* (Cambridge, 1996), p. 76.
31 Ibid, p. 71.
32 Williams, *On Christian Theology*, p. 227.
33 Ibid, p. 229.
34 Grace Davie, *Religion in Britain since 1945*: *Believing without Belonging* (Oxford, 1994); *Religion in Modern Europe: A Memory Mutates* (Oxford, 2000); *Europe: The Exceptional Case. Parameters of Faith in the Modern World* (London, 2002).
35 D. Dormor, J. McDonald, and J. Caddick, *Anglicanism: The Answer to Modernity* (London, 2003).

Bibliography

Primary

Farrer, A. M., *Finite and Infinite* (London, 1943).
—— *The Glass of Vision* (London, 1948).

—— *A Rebirth of Images: The Making of St. John's Apocalypse* (London, 1949).
—— *The Freedom of the Will* (London, 1957).

—— *Love Almighty and Ills Unlimited* (London, 1962).

—— *The End of Man* (London, 1973).

—— *Saving Belief* (London, 1994).

Hardy, D. W., *God's Ways With The World: Thinking and Practicing Christian Faith* (Edinburgh, 1996).

—— *Finding the Church* (London, 2001).

MacKinnon, D. M., *A Study in Ethical Theory* (London, 1957).

—— *Borderlands of Theology and Other Essays* (London, 1968).

—— *The Stripping of the Altars* (London, 1969).

—— *The Problem of Metaphysics* (Cambridge, 1974).

—— *Explorations in Theology 5: Donald MacKinnon* (London, 1979).

—— *Themes in Theology* (Edinburgh, 1987).

Ramsey, A. M., *The Gospel and the Catholic Church* (London, 1936).

—— *The Resurrection of Christ* (London, 1945).

—— *The Glory of God and the Transfiguration of Christ* (London, 1949).

—— *Durham Essays and Addresses* (London, 1956).

—— *From Gore to Temple* (London, 1960).

—— *God, Christ and the World* (London, 1969).

Sykes, S. W., *The Integrity of Anglicanism* (London, 1978).

—— *The Identity of Christianity* (London, 1984).

—— *Unashamed Anglicanism* (London, 1995).

Williams, R. D., *The Wound of Knowledge* (London, 1979).

—— *Resurrection: Interpreting the Easter Gospel* (London, 1982).

—— *Arius* (London, 1987).

—— *Open to Judgement* (London, 1994).

—— *Lost Icons* (London, 2000).

—— *On Christian Theology* (London, 2000).

—— *The Poems of Rowan Williams* (London, 2002).

Secondary

Chadwick, O., *Michael Ramsey* (Oxford, 1990).

Ford, D. F. and Stamps, D. L. (eds.), *Essentials of Christian Community: Essays for Daniel W. Hardy* (Edinburgh, 1996).

Hastings, A. *A History of English Christianity 1920–1990*, 3rd edn. (London, 1991).

Hebblethwaite, B., "The Doctrine of the Incarnation in the thought of Austin Farrer," in *The Incarnation* (Cambridge, 1987).

Hebblethwaite, B. and Sutherland, S. (eds.), *The Philosophical Frontiers of Christian Theology: Essays presented to D. M. MacKinnon* (Cambridge, 1982).

Higton, Mike, *Difficult Gospel: The Theology of Rowan Williams* (London, 2004).

Surin, K. (ed.), *Christ, Ethics and Tragedy: Essays in Honour of Donald MacKinnon* (Cambridge, 1989).

USA

H. Richard Niebuhr

Stanley Hauerwas

Introduction

H. Richard Niebuhr's fate was and continues to be known as the "not as well known" brother of Reinhold Niebuhr. H. Richard Niebuhr would not have complained that he was so fated, not only because he admired his brother, but also because coming to terms with fate was a major trend in his work. Fate was the word Niebuhr used to remind us that we cannot escape the history in which we find ourselves. Thus, in the prologue to *The Responsible Self*, Niebuhr confesses "to be a Christian is simply part of my fate."[1] This leads some to wonder, given Spinoza's influence on Niebuhr, if he finally does not give us a Stoicized account of Christianity.

Reinhold Niebuhr may remain better known than H. Richard Niebuhr, but it is arguable that H. Richard Niebuhr's work has had a more lasting impact on contemporary theology. For example, the theological developments associated with the so called "Yale school" of theology are better understood against the background of H. Richard Niebuhr's work. H. Richard no doubt would have thought Hans Frei's work too influenced by Karl Barth, but the influence of Barth on Frei was at least partly the result of what Frei had learned from H. Richard Niebuhr.[2] Niebuhr's analysis of the "responsible self," moreover, provided the background necessary for the recovery of the importance of the virtues for any account of the moral life. Niebuhr also anticipated the focus on "narrative" and the correlative understanding of the storied character of the church in Christian theology and ethics.

H. Richard Niebuhr was born in Wright City, Missouri in 1884, two years after Reinhold had been born.[3] Their father, Gustav Niebuhr, was a pastor in the German Evangelical Synod. Not only was German the first language Reinhold and H. Richard learned, but they were also introduced to their father's critical reception of German theological figures such as Harnack. H. Richard followed Reinhold's educational path, going to Elmhurst College (1908–12) and then to Eden Theological Seminary (1912–15) in St. Louis. Elmhurst and Eden were the denominational schools of the Evangelical Synod whose primary purpose was to train young men for the ministry. H. Richard Niebuhr was accordingly ordained in 1916 to be the minister of Walnut Park Evangelical Church in St. Louis.

In contrast to the frantic pace of Reinhold's life, H. Richard's life was that of a teacher. He was called back to teach at Eden in 1919, but in 1922 he left to do graduate work at Yale Divinity School. However, before going to Yale he completed an MA at Washington University in St. Louis in German. He wrote on Richard Dehmel, the German poet. Before going to Yale, he took courses at Union Theological Seminary as well as the University of Chicago. His work at Chicago with G. H. Mead, the pragmatist philosopher and social psychologist, was particularly important as Mead's influence on Niebuhr is apparent from the beginning to the end of Niebuhr's work. He went to Yale Divinity School in 1922, where he received both his BD and PhD in 1924. After finishing his degrees at Yale, he became president of Elmhurst College until 1927, when he became the academic dean at Eden Seminary. Returning from a sabbatical to Germany in 1930, he received an invitation to teach at Yale Divinity School, where he taught until his retirement and death in 1962.

During his life, H. Richard Niebuhr published "only" six books, but his influence on American theology was immense. He became the teacher of teachers who would determine the main directions in theology and ethics in the second half of the twentieth century. Waldo Beach, Paul Ramsey, and James Gustafson were his students in Christian ethics, but Niebuhr also had a lasting influence on Gordon Kaufman and Van Harvey, as well as his own son, Richard Reinhold Niebuhr. A continuing theme in Niebuhr's work is his criticism of what he called the ethics of defense or survival, through which we attempt to protect ourselves against the threat of the other, and particularly the other called death, by defending the status quo. His teaching reflected his determination not to protect himself, his students, the church, or theology from criticism. As a result, students – whether those that he actually taught or those he taught through his writing – seemed to sense that here was a man that could be trusted to think hard and honestly about God and our relationship to God. Whatever the questions one may have about Niebuhr's "orthodoxy," and I certainly think Niebuhr is vulnerable to criticism from that direction, it is undeniable that in his person as well as in his work Niebuhr was a God-intoxicated man.

Background and Development

Niebuhr wrote his dissertation on the philosophical theology of Ernst Troeltsch.[4] To understand Niebuhr's project it is important to note that Niebuhr was primarily interested in Troeltsch's attempt to provide a response to relativism and historicism. In the acknowledgments that prefaced Niebuhr's most famous book, *Christ and Culture*, Niebuhr acknowledges his debt to Troeltsch. Niebuhr observes that Troeltsch taught him to respect "the multiformity and individuality of men and movements in Christian history, to be loath to force this rich variety into prefashioned, conceptual molds, and yet to seek *logos* in *mythos*, reason in history, essence in existence."[5] According to Niebuhr, Troeltsch helped him to accept the relativity not only of historical objects but also, even more important, the relativity of the historical subject, the observer, and interpreter. Niebuhr notes if he does "correct" Troeltsch, it is only because he tries to understand "historical relativism in the light of theological and theocentric relativism." He does so because all attempts to absolutize the finite are an aberration of faith as well as reason, and a denial of the governance of the absolute God.[6]

God's absolute sovereignty is the heart of Niebuhr's life and work. His rejection of any ethic that tempts us to live and think defensively is but a correlative of his insistence that "radical monotheism" is the determinative characteristic of the Christian faith. When Christians fail to acknowledge God's absolute sovereignty, they sinfully accommodate the church to the world. Such an accommodation was the subject of Niebuhr's biting critique in his first book, *The Social Sources of Denominationalism.* In fact, Niebuhr's critique of how the church in America was determined by economic class and nationalism in many ways provided the necessary background for his discovery of the significance of God's sovereignty. *The Social Sources of Denominationalism,* however, was a book shaped more by categories that reflected the influence of the social gospel movement than Niebuhr's later emphasis on God's sovereignty. For example, Niebuhr asserted in *The Social Sources of Denominationalism* that the purpose of Christianity is not the establishment of an ecclesiastical institution or the proclamation of a metaphysical creed, but its "purpose is the revelation to men of their potential childhood to the Father and their possible brotherhood with each other."[7]

Niebuhr's more mature theological position, his emphasis on God's sovereignty, does not mean he became less concerned about the accommodation of the church to the world. Indeed, in the famous exchange between H. Richard and Reinhold concerning how the United States should respond to the Japanese invasion of Manchuria in 1931, H. Richard argued that the "nothing" Christians should do in the face of such aggression is not quietism. Rather, Christians "can build cells of those within each nation who, divorcing themselves from the program of nationalism and of capitalism, unite in a higher loyalty which transcends national and class lines of division and prepare for the future. There is no such Christian international today because radical Christianity has not arrived as yet at a program and a philosophy of history, but such cells are forming."[8]

The book that not only established H. Richard Niebuhr as a force in American theology but also reflected his mature position was *The Kingdom of God in America.*[9] Niebuhr, drawing on what he had learned from Troeltsch, argues that there can be no easy separation of theology from history, particularly if we are to understand American culture. Accordingly, Niebuhr argues that America represents the experiment in constructive Protestantism originating with the Puritan acknowledgment of God's sovereignty which was, through developments in the eighteenth century, transformed into the belief that Christ's kingdom could be realized on earth. The Social Gospel became the exemplification of the domestication of God's sovereignty that finally results in the secularization of Christianity. Niebuhr characterized this development with the memorable sentence: "A God without wrath brought men without sin into a kingdom without judgment through the ministrations of a Christ without a cross."[10]

Niebuhr's stress on God's sovereignty as well as his criticism of liberal Christianity in *The Kingdom of God in America* seemed to put him on the side of the ill-defined "neo-orthodox" developments in theology. This impression was only strengthened by his claim in the preface to his book *The Meaning of Revelation* that he was attempting to combine the critical thought of Troeltsch with the constructive work of Karl Barth.[11] In *The Meaning of Revelation* Niebuhr argued "revelation cannot mean history, if it also means God."[12] Yet Christian theology has no way to think about God other than through our existence as historic and communal beings. At best, therefore, Christian theology cannot aspire to be anything more than confessional, that is, the self-critical exercise by which faith seeks to understand itself. According to Niebuhr, therefore, revelation names the special occasion by which images or symbols are provided that make it possible for communities and individuals to tell an intelligible story about their lives. Such a unity is the "inner history" that faith and repentance, that is, the confession of sin, makes possible.

The tensions entailed by Niebuhr's attempt to combine Troeltsch and Barth make *The Meaning of Revelation* an extraordinarily interesting and suggestive book. However, Niebuhr became increasingly critical of what he characterized, no doubt with Barth in mind, as Christomonism. In the final chapter of *The Meaning of Revelation* Niebuhr draws out the implication of his claim that revelation cannot mean history if it means God with the declaration that revelation must point to that which is more certain than Jesus.[13] In the collection of his essays entitled *Radical Monotheism and Western Culture*, Niebuhr clearly draws out the implications of his understanding of radical monotheism, observing: "we may use the theological word 'incarnation' in speaking of the coming of radically monotheistic faith into our history, meaning by it the concrete expression in a total human life of radical trust in the One and of universal loyalty to the realm of being."[14] For Niebuhr, Christians do not so much place their faith in Jesus Christ, as model their faith on the radical monotheistic faith of Christ. Accordingly, he criticizes liberal theologies that make love the primary attribute of Jesus' life, noting that "it was not love but God that filled his soul."[15]

H. Richard Niebuhr's "Ethics"

H. Richard Niebuhr is usually regarded as one of – if not *the* – most important Christian ethicist of the second half of the twentieth century.[16] Niebuhr's work, however, defies any strong distinction between theology and ethics. His theology shaped how he thought about the moral life and how he thought about the moral life was reflected in his theology. That his theology so determined his work is not always obvious. For example, most readers of his book *Christ and Culture* accept Niebuhr's claim in the last chapter, "A 'Concluding Unscientific Postscript,'" that it would be a mistake to regard any one of the "types" – Christ against culture, Christ of culture, Christ above culture, Christ and culture in paradox, Christ the transformer of culture – as the "Christian answer."[17] To do so would, as James Gustafson insists, mistakenly turn the typological method Niebuhr had learned from Weber and Troeltsch into a normative recommendation.[18]

There is no question, however, that *Christ and Culture* became the framework by which various ethical alternatives were evaluated. Niebuhr may have genuinely believed that each of the five types was an authentic expression of the social implications of the gospel, but "Christ the transformer of culture" was assumed by most readers of the book to be the most attractive position. That Niebuhr did not end his chapter on "Christ the transformer" with criticisms, as he had in his discussion of the other types, provides some warrant for the assumption by many that Niebuhr was in fact recommending the "transforming" type.

Niebuhr's criticisms of the other types is extremely interesting because his criticisms expose his understanding of the Trinity. Niebuhr often made reference to the Trinity, but he seldom used the language of Father, Son, and Holy Spirit. For Niebuhr, the Trinity primarily helps Christians delineate God's work as creator, governor, and redeemer. Accordingly, he criticized representatives of the "Christ against culture" type (Tertullian, Tolstoy, and Mennonites) for failing to acknowledge that God is not only the redeemer, but God also is the creator. Niebuhr, therefore, argued that representatives of the "against culture" type fail to give an account of the social and political institutions that make life possible.[19]

Niebuhr's stress on "radical monotheism" was combined with a passion for the importance and significance of the church. He assumed, with Troeltsch, that the sociological character of the church is the crucial indicator for understanding the content and shape of theological convictions. Accordingly, in stark contrast with Reinhold Niebuhr, H. Richard Niebuhr often directed his attention to what the church should be and do if it was to be faithful to its calling. In 1954 Niebuhr directed, along with Daniel Day Williams and James Gustafson, a major study of theological education in North America. His book, *The Purpose of the Church and Its Ministry*, is the outgrowth of that study. According to Niebuhr, the church's task is nothing less than the "increase among men of the love of God and neighbor."[20] Niebuhr elaborates that purpose in one of the great passages on love in contemporary theology, noting that by love he means the ability to rejoice in the sheer presence of the beloved, to give thanks for the presence of the beloved without seeking equality, to revere the beloved by keeping our distance even as she/he draws near, and in a loyalty that may well let the self be destroyed rather than for the beloved to cease to be.[21]

Niebuhr's most important book, *The Responsible Self: An Essay in Christian Moral Philosophy*, was published posthumously. We can have confidence, however, that the book reflects Niebuhr's most developed position not only because the book reflects the lectures he gave in the first part of his Christian ethics course he taught for many years at Yale, but also because the work is comprised of the Robertson lectures he gave at Glasgow in 1960 and the Earl lectures at the Pacific School of Religion in 1962. Moreover, not only do the dominant motifs of his previous work continue to be present in *The Responsible Self*, but also their systematic development in this book makes clear how Niebuhr understood how "it all fits together."

Niebuhr describes *The Responsible Self* as a work in Christian moral philosophy. By that he means no more than the book should be read as written by a Christian who seeks "to understand the mode of his existence and that of his fellow human beings as human agents."[22] Accordingly, Niebuhr's primary purpose in *The Responsible Self* is to provide a phenomenology of our moral experience that does justice not only to the character of our lives but also to the character of our relationship with God. He argues that the image of "man the responder" more adequately reflects who we are as human beings as well as Christians than the images of man the citizen or man the maker. Those who consistently think of man the maker subordinate the giving of laws to that of goals in the future; whereas those who think of our existence with the aid of the image of the citizen subordinate the good to the right.[23] Each of these images has corresponding accounts of God as the giver of the law or the One good to which all other goods are to be judged.

In contrast, the image of responsibility focuses our attention not by asking, "What does the law require?" or "What is the good to be done?" but rather by asking, "What is going on?" Therefore, Niebuhr suggests, the image of man the responder more adequately helps comprehend that, just as importantly as what we do is what we suffer. From such a perspective ethics is not so much about helping us to discern what should and should not be done, but is an exercise in understanding. To understand our lives as responders is to see ourselves as agents who exist in response to other agents in accordance with our interpretation of their actions in anticipation of their response to our response and all of this as part of a continuing community of agents.[24] The narrative character of our existence is unavoidable once we understand our lives from the perspective of responsibility. To be responsible we do not ask what is the good or the right, but rather what is the fitting. The fitting is determined by the ongoing narratives that shape the patterns of interpretation in which we find ourselves.

Having developed the typology of man the citizen, maker, and responder, Niebuhr then tests the adequacy of each in relation to the self in society, in time and history, in absolute dependence, and finally in relation to sin and salvation. The first two images, Niebuhr suggests, fail to do justice to the social character of our existence; nor can the images of man the citizen or maker account for our being in time or, more important, how time is in us. Moreover, ethics shaped by the images of citizen and maker tempt us to deny our dependency, leading us to live defensively, fearing the chaos that seems to make it impossible to live coherent lives.

By focusing our attention on the image of responsibility we can see clearly why living responsibly is so difficult. Niebuhr asks: "How is it possible to be *one* self in the multiplicity of events and of one's interpretations of them? How does the self as such become responsible instead of remaining a concatenation of responsive systems, fitting their actions now into this, now into that series of events?"[25] What ties all these responsibilities together so that there is a responsible *self* amid the many roles we may inhabit? Niebuhr answers these questions by returning to his claim in *The Meaning of Revelation*, that is: "To be a self is to have a god; to have a god is to have a history, that is, events connected in a meaningful pattern; to have one god is to have one history. God and the history of selves in community belong together in inseparable union."[26] To be responsible, therefore, requires we affirm: "God is acting in all actions upon you. So respond to all actions upon you as to respond to his actions."[27]

Niebuhr was well aware that to respond to all actions on us as God's action is as frightening as it is necessary. It should never be forgotten that the Niebuhr who wrote *The Responsible Self* is the same Niebuhr who wrote essays entitled "War as the Judgment of God" and "War as Crucifixion" during World War II.[28] For Niebuhr, therefore, the great moral challenge is how to live, particularly in the face of death, in a manner that we will be delivered from the deep distrust of the One on whom we depend. Christians believe that in the figure of Jesus Christ they have found the assurance that makes possible "the reinterpretation of all our interpretations of life and death. Death no less than life appears to us as an act of mercy, not of mercy to us only, but in the great vicariousness of responsive and responsible existence, as mercy to those in whom, with whom, and for whom we live."[29]

Niebuhr's "ethics" is bound to leave dissatisfied any who think ethics should provide guidance about what they should do in this or that circumstance. Niebuhr's image of responsibility is not meant to be a decision procedure, but rather to suggest how we should understand what it means to be "a self." According to James Gustafson, Niebuhr's favorite way of describing his work, a description borrowed from F. D. Maurice, was that of "digging."[30] Accordingly, Niebuhr did not seek to provide a comprehensive account of Christian ethics, but rather to provide a rich phenomenological account of human existence in order to spell out the implications of a radical monotheistic faith. At the end of *The Responsible Self*, Niebuhr observes he does not know whether to call the self-interpretation he thinks is required if we are to live responsibly Christian or simply human. Yet he is sure that – though Christians believe that the reinterpretation of existence has come into the world – it is equally the case that such a reinterpretation "is not confined to those who say, 'Lord, Lord,' nor even necessarily best represented by them."[31]

Responding to H. R. Niebuhr

Niebuhr was not a polemical thinker, which makes those who criticize him appear less than charitable. He commended J. S. Mill's view that men were generally right in what they affirmed and wrong in what they denied.[32] However, I believe that John Howard Yoder is right to criticize *Christ and Culture* for the assumed objective stance Niebuhr takes when in fact he uses that book to advance his theological agenda. Yoder's criticisms are not only right about *Christ and Culture*, but also apply to Niebuhr's overall position. For example, Yoder observes that the intention of the post-Nicene accounts of the Trinity was to deny what Niebuhr seems to want, that is, to deny that we receive different revelations from each person of the Trinity.[33] Of course, Niebuhr can rightly respond that he feels under no obligation to adhere to Nicean orthodoxy. But then he needs to say why he thinks he can use and exploit Christian language without acknowledging any responsibility to the Christian tradition.

Yoder also criticizes Niebuhr for assuming a monolithic concept of culture, but Yoder observes that Niebuhr's account of culture is but the reflection of his account of Jesus as the exemplification of a radically monotheistic faith. Jesus, so understood, simply becomes an empty cipher to remind us to never place our faith in anything other than the One that makes the finite finite. Because Niebuhr assumes a monolithic account of culture his criticism of the "Christ against culture" for allegedly denying the goodness of God's creation is but a truism. Yet, Yoder argues, the representatives Niebuhr names as exemplifications of the "Christ against culture" type never argued that culture must be accepted or rejected as a whole.[34] Indeed, Niebuhr seems to have forgotten that in his early work he thought the church should be a sociological unit distinguishable from the rest of the society as well as constituting an option to the culture in which it finds itself.[35]

Yoder's criticisms of *Christ and Culture* are but indications of the theological difficulty created by Niebuhr's account of "radical monotheism." For a position that centers on the absolute transcendence of God, Niebuhr's theology is primarily an anthropocentric account of why some understanding of faith is unavoidable.[36] To be sure, his phenomenological account of human existence can be quite suggestive, but it is by no means clear why Niebuhr seems to have thought his understanding of the human situation made it necessary to distance himself from central affirmations of the Christian faith. Niebuhr often provided insightful assessments of other theological alternatives as well as of the work of theology in modernity; but he used his account of Divine transcendence too easily to call into question truth claims made on behalf of other alternatives, with the effect of validating his own account of why all is relative.[37]

Yet I believe it would be a profound mistake for H. Richard Niebuhr to be ignored or dismissed because he fits so uneasily in categories used to type theologians as liberal or conservative. Niebuhr struggled to find the theological expression that could help Christian and non-Christian alike not to be determined by the temptation to live defensively. Niebuhr was convinced that we should and could live lives of trust and openness, and he struggled mightily to help us see how we could so live. We still have much to learn from his "digging."

Notes

1 H. Richard Niebuhr, *The Responsible Self: An Essay in Christian Moral Philosophy* (New York, 1963), pp. x, 43. For Niebuhr's more extensive account of fate, see pp. 112–26.

2 Hans Frei wrote two very important articles on Niebuhr. The first was for Niebuhr's *festschrift*, but was therefore early in Frei's academic work. The second was the last thing Frei wrote before he died. Indeed, he died before he was able to read the paper at a conference on Niebuhr at Harvard. See Hans Frei, "Niebuhr's Theological Background," in *Faith and Ethics: The Theology of H. Richard Niebuhr*, ed. Paul Ramsey (New York, 1957), pp. 9–118 and "H. Richard Niebuhr on History, Church, and Nation," in *The Legacy of H. Richard Niebuhr*, ed. Ronald Thieman (Minneapolis, MN, 1991), pp. 1–23.

3 Jon Diefenthaler's *H. Richard Niebuhr: A Lifetime of Reflections on the Church and the World* (Macon, GA, 1986) provides the best overview of Niebuhr's life we have.

4 H. Richard Niebuhr, *Ernst Troeltsch's Philosophy of Religion* (New Haven, CT, 1924).

5 H. Richard Niebuhr, *Christ and Culture*, preface by James Gustafson (San Francisco, 2001), p. xii.

6 Ibid, p. xii.

7 H. Richard Niebuhr, *The Social Sources of Denominationalism* (New York, 1957),

p. 278. The original publication date was 1927. Niebuhr does say in the same passage that Christianity does seek "the formation of a divine society and presupposes the metaphysics of a Christlike God."

8 H. Richard Niebuhr, "The Grace of Doing Nothing," in *War in the Twentieth Century: Sources in Theological Ethics*, ed. Richard Miller (Louisville, KY, 1992), p. 10. Miller's book also includes Reinhold's response to his brother, as well as H. Richard's reply. H. Richard had sounded this theme as early as 1925, in an article entitled "Back to Benedict," *Christian Century* 42 (July 2, 1925), pp. 860–1.

9 H. Richard Niebuhr, *The Kingdom of God in America* (New York, 1957). The book was originally published in 1937.

10 Ibid, p. 193.

11 H. Richard Niebuhr, *The Meaning of Revelation* (New York, 1970), p. xi. The book was originally published in 1941.

12 Ibid, p. 40.

13 Ibid, p. 111.

14 H. Richard Niebuhr, *Radical Monotheism and Western Culture, with Supplementary Essays* (Louisville, KY, 1970), p. 40. The book was originally published in 1943.

15 H. Richard Niebuhr, *Christ and Culture*, p. 19.

16 For an extremely informative account of Niebuhr's influence for the development

of Christian theology and ethics, see William Werpehowski, *American Protestant Ethics and the Legacy of H. Richard Niebuhr* (Washington, DC, 2002).

17 H. Richard Niebuhr, *Christ and Culture*, p. 232.

18 James Gustafson, "Preface: An Appreciative Interpretation," in H. Richard Niebuhr, *Christ and Culture*, pp. xiii–xxxv.

19 H. Richard Niebuhr, *Christ and Culture*, pp. 76–82.

20 H. Richard Niebuhr, *The Purpose of the Church and Its Ministry* (New York, 1956), p. 31.

21 Ibid, p. 35. Josiah Royce, and in particular Royce's account of loyalty, was a decisive influence on Niebuhr.

22 H. Richard Niebuhr, *The Responsible Self*, p. 42.

23 Ibid, p. 55.

24 Ibid, p. 65. Niebuhr credits G. H. Mead's continuing influence for shaping this understanding of responsibility, but he also refers to Adam Smith's understanding of the "impartial spectator" for helping us understand why we rightly think our moral behavior requires an account of disinterestedness.

25 Ibid, p. 121.

26 H. Richard Niebuhr, *The Meaning of Revelation*, p. 59.

27 Ibid, p. 126.

28 Both essays can be found in Miller, *War in the Twentieth Century*, pp. 47–55, 63–70.

29 Ibid, pp. 143–4.

30 Gustafson, introduction to H. Richard Niebuhr, *The Responsible Self*, p. 14.

31 H. Richard Niebuhr, *The Responsible Self*, p. 144.

32 H. Richard Niebuhr, *Christ and Culture*, p. 238.

33 Yoder, "How H. Richard Niebuhr Reasoned: A Critique of *Christ and Culture*," in Glen Stassen, D. M. Yeager, and John Howard Yoder, *Authentic Transformation: A New Vision of Christ and Culture* (Nashville, TN, 1996), p. 62.

34 Ibid, pp. 52–61.

35 Ibid, p. 75. In 1935 Niebuhr, along with Wilhelm Pauck and Francis Miller, wrote a book entitled *The Church Against the World* (Chicago, 1935). The last chapter of the book was written by Niebuhr and entitled "Toward the Independence of the Church."

36 Niebuhr translated as well as wrote an appreciative introduction to Paul Tillich's *The Religious Situation* (New York, 1956). It is hard not to read H. Richard's, as well as Reinhold's, theological project as exemplifications of Tillich's method of correlation. Niebuhr's most extensive account of faith is to be found in manuscripts discovered after his death by his son, Richard Reinhold Niebuhr. They are now published as *Faith on Earth: An Inquiry into the Structure of Human Faith*, ed. Richard Reinhold Niebuhr (New Haven, CT, 1989).

37 Yoder, "How H. Richard Niebuhr Reasoned: A Critique of *Christ and Culture*," p. 82. Some of Niebuhr's important occasional essays on other theologians as well as American democracy have been published in *Theology, History, and Culture*, ed. William Stacy Johnson (New Haven, CT, 1996).

Bibliography

Primary

Niebuhr, H. Richard, "Back to Benedict?" *Christian Century* 42 (July 2, 1925): pp. 860–1.
—— *Christ and Culture*. With a preface by James Gustafson. San Francisco, 2001.
—— *Ernst Troeltsch's Philosophy of Religion*. New Haven, CT, 1924.
—— *Faith on Earth: An Inquiry into the Structure of Human Faith*. Edited by Richard Reinhold Niebuhr. New Haven, CT, 1989.

—— "The Grace of Doing Nothing." In *War in the Twentieth Century*, edited by Richard Miller, pp. 6–11. Louisville, KY, 1992.
—— Introduction to *The Religious Situation*, by Paul Tillich. Translated by H. Richard Niebuhr. New York, 1956.
—— *The Kingdom of God in America*. New York, 1959.
—— *The Meaning of Revelation*. New York, 1970.
—— *The Purpose of the Church and Its Ministry*. New York, 1956.

—— *Radical Monotheism and Western Culture, with Supplementary Essays*. Louisville, KY, 1993.

—— *The Responsible Self: An Essay in Christian Moral Philosophy*. With an introduction by James Gustafson. New York, 1978.

—— *The Social Sources of Denominationalism*. New York, 1972.

—— *Theology, History, and Culture*. Edited by William Stacy Johnson. New Haven, CT, 1996.

—— "War as Crucifixion." In *War in the Twentieth Century*, edited by Richard Miller, pp. 63–70. Louisville, KY, 1992.

—— "War as the Judgment of God." In *War in the Twentieth Century*, edited by Richard Miller, pp. 47–55. Louisville, KY, 1992.

Niebuhr, H. Richard, Wilhelm Pauck, and Francis Miller, *The Church Against the World*. New York, 1935.

Secondary

Diefenthaler, Jon, *H. Richard Niebuhr: A Lifetime of Reflections on the Church and the World*. Macon, GA, 1986.

Frei, Hans, "H. Richard Niebuhr on History, Church, and Nation." In *The Legacy of H. Richard Niebuhr*, edited by Ronald Thieman, pp. 1–24. Minneapolis, MN, 1991.

—— "Niebuhr's Theological Background." In *Faith and Ethics: The Theology of H. Richard Niebuhr*, edited by Paul Ramsey, pp. 9–118. New York, 1957.

Werpehowski, William, *American Protestant Ethics and the Legacy of H. Richard Niebuhr*. Washington, DC, 2002.

Reinhold Niebuhr

William Werpehowski

Introduction

Christian theological ethics is an intellectual discipline that gives an account of the experience of the reality of God, as decisively disclosed in Jesus Christ, for the purpose of critically describing and commending the kinds of human character and conduct that would bear faithful witness to and/or participate in the life of that reality. It is a discipline situated primarily in and for the Christian community. This orientation is not exclusive, however, given the universal Lord to whom this community answers and the corresponding responsibilities of its members. The "practical import" of theological ethics "is to aid the community and its members in discerning what God is enabling and requiring them to be and to do."[1]

Among the several concerns that occupy the discipline of Christian ethics, five stand out for the purposes of this chapter. First, the content of theological ethics needs to engage the whole reality of God, the unity and distinction of God's creative, judging, governing, redemptive, and eschatological work. Second, the method of theological ethics should reflect this content in a fundamental respect. The God in whom Christians believe is disclosed in a particular narrative, the biblical story of Israel and Jesus Christ; yet this very God is trusted as governing and sustaining all of creation and with transcendent authority. Hence, theological ethics must honor its distinctively storied character while also affirming its universal reach and significance. Attempting neither a narrow fideism nor a futile rationalism, Christian ethicists must consider both the integral witness and discourse of Christian faith and speak with broader "public" or "universal" purpose.

The last three concerns establish tests for the strategic adequacy of Christian ethics as conceived above. So, third, an ethical account ought to avoid both a sentimental idealism that passes over the facts of human sin in history, and a cynicism that gives up on the objectively binding character of moral norms for the good in social life. Closely related to that, and fourth, practical reflection on what God is enabling and requiring us to do needs to steer clear of an idolatrous placement of ultimate faith in any good short of God, and a despair that finds no genuine good to be finally loved and trusted in hope as the meaning of human life in history.

Fifth, an ethics of the Christian church is to resist a strictly subordinate accommodation to this or that cultural ethos, and a categorical withdrawal from cultural life in the world. The church's particular historical situation may require a measured identification or a measured withdrawal from a cultural life of unbelief still governed by God; but in principle the church is to be neither strictly "worldly" nor "isolated."

Reinhold Niebuhr's critical attention to the whole reality of God stressed the possibilities and limits of history in terms of creaturely finitude and freedom, human fallenness and divine judgment upon it, and redemption through the *Agape* of Christ. He attacked what he often called "orthodox" and "liberal" versions of Christianity for their dogmatic insularity and rationalist universalism, respectively, and presented a theological ethic of his own that sought to interpret and partially "validate" "biblical faith" through reflection on the nature and experience of the human subject. His ethic of "public theology" came to have remarkable influence and significance in American political life.[2]

Niebuhr insisted on the intractability of sinful self-seeking in human affairs over against sentimentalism, and on self-giving love as the final norm of human existence to counter cynics. He worked out these two themes to protect against idolatry and despair in a view of moral agency that pursues justice in human communities in keeping with "the 'foolishness of God,' as revealed in the absurdity of the Cross, and in contrast to the 'wisdom of the world.'"

The failure of the wisdom of the world to discern the final source and end of life is due on the one hand to the fact that it seeks God too simply as the truth which supplements historic truth but does not stand in contradiction to it; which completes human virtue but does not judge it; and which guarantees some historic form of justice and does not anticipate its doom. On the other hand, the wisdom of the world may be so impressed by the fragmentary character of human virtue and knowledge and so overpowered by the tragedies and antinomies of life that it sinks into despair, finding no meaning in life and history at all.[3]

The social reality of this agency would be a church that remains ever critical of programs and policies in political affairs but is never purely "isolated" from the "world."

The adequacy of Niebuhr's Christian ethics may be considered to depend on how successfully he specifically addressed the five concerns.

Survey

Reinhold Niebuhr (1892–1971) was born in Wright City, Missouri, and raised in the German Evangelical Synod (later the Evangelical and Reformed Church). After two years studying at Yale, his work as a pastor in Detroit from 1915 to 1928 exposed him to the burdens and injustices of urban industrial life. He was forced to face the evident irrelevance of his "simple little moral homilies" to these circumstances.[4] *Leaves from the Notebook of a Tamed Cynic* vividly recounts the Detroit experience, which, Niebuhr says, "determined my development more than any books which I may have read."[5] He set off next for Union Theological Seminary in New York City, teaching there until his retirement in 1960.

In the 1930s Niebuhr criticized the "Social Gospel" vision of Washington Glad-den, Walter Rauschenbusch, and others. Recognizing the limits of the individualism of nineteenth-century Protestant ethics for responding to the social brutalities of the Industrial Revolution, the Social Gospel theologians countered with the ethic of Jesus as normative for personal and institutional life. The key here was a doctrine of the Kingdom of God, which was deemed in a fashion to be a historical possibility marked by social unity and the overturning of personal and structural assaults on the dignity of persons created by God. Niebuhr thought that the Social Gospel courted sentimentality and irrelevance because it presented "the law of love as a simple solution for every social problem."[6] In contrast to the moralistic tendency to see the church's ministry "to make selfish people unselfish, at least sufficiently unselfish to permit the creation of justice without conflict,"[7] Niebuhr held that an adequate theology of the Kingdom of God cannot be removed from an appreciation of the universality of sin in history and of God's thoroughgoing judgment of human vice and pretension. We may strive for the kingdom, "but we do not expect its full realization . . . The Kingdom of God always remains fragmentary and corrupted in history,"[8] since the latter is characterized by inordinately self-interested conflicts over power, and because "self-interest and power must be harnessed and beguiled rather than eliminated. In other words, forces which are morally dangerous must be used despite their peril."[9] Note the critical dialectic. We take responsibility for political goals that are always patient of criticism in terms of an ever transcending ideal. Overly "idealistic" efforts ignorant of sin corrupt realistic responsibility, and yet that responsibility still aspires to the ideal of the kingdom in (still "realistic") ways that forestall premature closure.

Niebuhr refined this dialectic in a large body of writing on political, moral, and theological issues, and in extensive lecture and consulting activity. *Moral Man and Immoral Society* (1932) relied in no small part on Marxian criticism of economic realities, and seemed to fit well with the general challenge to liberal sentimentalism and individualism; but Niebuhr later concluded that the book failed to recognize "the ultimate similarities, despite immediate differences, between liberal and Marxist utopianism."[10] In *An Interpretation of Christian Ethics* (1935) he argued for a prophetic Christian faith in which the Kingdom of God is both possible in history, because "its heights of pure love are organically related to the experience of love in all human life,"[11] and beyond every historical achievement, since the full eradication of egoism and attainment of disinterestedness is impossible. *The Nature and Destiny of Man* (1941, 1943), Niebuhr's Gifford lectures, compared Christian, classical, and modern conceptions of human nature and history in a manner that embodied the central theological and ethical insight that human political agency ought rightly to be set in a context of both contrition and trusting commitment to justice under God, and hence "in terms of the experience of justification by faith . . . We will know that we cannot purge ourselves of sin and guilt in which we are involved in the ambiguities of politics without also disavowing responsibility for the creative possibilities of justice."[12] The vision of *Nature and Destiny* is central to Niebuhr's subsequent work, including notably *The Children of Light and the Children of Dark-ness* (1944), *Faith and History* (1949), *The Self and the Dramas of History* (1955), and *Man's Nature and His Communities* (1965).

Content

Niebuhr's mature theological ethics carried forward his response to the idealism of the Social Gospel through a sustained analysis of human nature and its predicament that owed much to the ideas of Augustine, Pascal, and Kierkegaard. The point of departure for this analysis is a conception of the human creature as both finite and free. As finite, he or she is dependent upon nature, upon other persons, and above all upon God. As free, the human creature is capable of transcending his or her natural and interpersonal environment, so as to evaluate and transform it. The coincidence of finitude and freedom is the condition for the possibility of history; but this also generates in creatures anxiety in the form of uncertainty and insecurity about their dependence and vulnerability. Aware of their freedom, they would be tempted to deny their limitation and dependence through acts of inordinate self-assertion, seeking to set themselves up as laws sufficient unto themselves. When persons sin, their "fall," therefore, is inevitable but not necessary.[13] Thus, human history is broken with the activities of prideful persons who seek their own interests excessively. The basis of their self-elevation is an insecurity that stems from unbelief or the absence of trust in God.

Niebuhr affirms that the law or norm of human existence is the disinterested love of God and neighbor, for only in such love can self-transcendence complete itself. Individual persons retain a capacity for transcending their self-interest in loving regard for the welfare of others. The prospects for large-scale political and economic groups to do the same, however, are comparatively restricted. The causes and ideals of these groups readily become idols for their members, whose moral sensitivities are blunted by their appreciation of the power they hold from interests and resources held in common. They tend to cloak their claims with self-righteous rationales that contain "ideological taint," smugly shielding themselves and their ideals from criticism.[14] Since inordinate self-assertion is magnified in the lives of groups making competing claims upon one another, coercion becomes an irremovable feature of human social life, necessary for preserving order and restraining egoism. Still and all, from the standpoint of history, "mutual love is the highest good. Only in mutual love, in which the concern of one person for the interests of another prompts and elicits a reciprocal response, are the social demands of historical existence satisfied."[15]

Niebuhr interprets the cross of Jesus Christ to express the merciful love of God in relation to human sin. In perfectly self-giving and suffering love for the sake of others, Jesus refused to participate in the historical patterns of competing and self-interested claim and counterclaim. The love of Jesus Christ was an "impossible possibility" that can never finally be vindicated in history; its historical consequence is a life of self-sacrifice that ends tragically. Nevertheless, the love "which could not maintain itself in history becomes the symbol both of the new beginning which a man could make if he subjected his life to the judgment of Christ, and of the mercy of God which alone could overcome the fateful impotence of man ever to achieve so perfect a love."[16] As both the revelation of divine forgiveness and the norm of a new life, *agape* or the self-giving love of the Cross *completes* the incompleteness of mutuality or reciprocity. One can set no fixed limits to the latter given human self-transcendence, and no fixed limits to the former perfecting human relations through the curbing of self-interested calculation. Thus "even the purest form of *agape*, the love of the enemy and the forgiveness toward the evildoer, do not stand in contradiction to historical possibilities." There may always be some "admixture" of this love with real concerns for order and justice in a world of self-interest, coercion, and violence. Short of abandoning outright a sense of historical possibility, there is no limit to love's proportion within the admixture. Now this perfecting love also *clarifies* and *limits* what is possible in history. It opposes the "pathetic illusions" of "sectarian" and "secularized" Christian perfectionists, and encourages a needed resistance to pleas for collective self-sacrifice that amount to unjust betrayal of a group's interests.[17] Finally, the perfection of the Cross *corrects* or *judges* all arrangements for a tolerable social life. Any admixture of self-assertion and love is, of course, always also a *sinful* admixture. No (forgiving) remedial justice is not also vindictive, no communal fellowship is immune to imperialism, and no employment of power for impartial justice is not itself partial. This last point is an instance of Niebuhr's insistence on an "equality of sin" in human affairs.

But Niebuhr also insists on "an inequality of guilt," where guilt is the consequence of sin in injustice. There are *real moral differences* between different social and political programs to the extent that they embody, for example, the secure achievement of equality of conditions of life for human creatures. "Equality as a pinnacle of the ideal of justice implicitly points toward love as the final norm of justice; for equal justice is the approximation of brotherhood under the conditions of sin. A higher justice always means a more equal justice." That claims for and against equality carry an "ideological taint" (in one case, stressing its absolute validity without attending to differences of social need or function; in the other, focusing too much on the impossibility of its attainment) does not overcome this fact.[18] And the mere fact hardly overcomes the aforementioned corruptions, and hence their liability to criticism.

The quest for justice in the social order stands in tension with the demands for the preservation of order and the maintaining of freedom. Given the inevitable conjoining of justice and power, moreover, that quest must include the realistic conviction that the power of some must be checked by that of others. Niebuhr's argument for democratic dispersal and balance of political power relied on this last point. "Man's capacity for justice makes democracy possible; but man's inclination to injustice makes democracy necessary . . . If men are inclined to deal unjustly with their fellows, the possession of power aggravates this inclination. That is why irresponsible and uncontrolled power is the greatest source of injustice."[19] Even in this case Niebuhr warned against identifying our democratic ideals with the ultimate values of life.

The "Christian realist" attack on unchastened idealism was unrelenting, but almost as persistent was his attack on any ethic that would jettison moral values from the sphere of political life. He made much of the necessity of taking on moral responsibilities in history, and chided those who, by his lights, evaded them in the vain and futile quest to maintain moral purity. His challenge to many Christian pacifists followed this anti-perfectionist line, which he joined to his familiar charges of irrelevant idealism and the failure to take sin seriously. These pacifists merely assert that if only men loved one another, all the complex, and sometimes horrible realities of the political order could be dispensed with. They do not see that their "if" begs the most basic problem of human history. It is because men are sinners that justice can be achieved only by a certain degree of coercion on the one hand, and by resistance to coercion and tyranny on the other.[20]

Debate

We can organize some noteworthy criticisms of Reinhold Niebuhr with reference to the five issues posed at the beginning of this chapter. Regarding the whole reality of God's work, Paul Lehmann argues Niebuhr's Christology is "almost totally pre-occupied with the relations between the Father and the Son to the exclusion of the relations between the Son and the Spirit." The Cross is taken to be the *basis* of a new wisdom and power for life in history without corresponding regard for the way these are and must be *operative*; for sin "is overcome not merely 'in principle' but also 'in fact.' Justification is not only a principle of meaning and historical possibility. People are 'in fact' justified, and the fruits of faith in sanctification, however tenuous, are actual human and historical realities."[21] Niebuhr thus fails sufficiently to work from and work out of the *fact* that God's rule in Jesus Christ makes present a new life given and promised to the world and distinctively confessed in the church, a new life that involves more than repentant self-criticism in service of moral action amid the ambiguities and corruptions of history.

Niebuhr intends to take the truth of the gospel, apprehended in faith and repentance, and correlate it "to truths about life and history gained generally in experience." Correlation validates the truth of faith "insofar as it proves it to be a source and center of an interpretation of life, more adequate than alternative interpretations, because it comprehends all of life's antinomies and contradictions into a system of meaning and is conducive to a renewal of life."[22] The notorious danger in such a procedure is the reduction of theology to anthropology, "in which the moment of divine revelation is no more than a self-positing move . . . in which the mind imagines or sets over against itself a transcendent 'other' for its own regulating and constructing purposes."[23] In Niebuhr's case, the story would go, Christian faith as he develops it is but a resource for enabling finite, free, anxious, and inevitably corrupt persons to sustain a meaningful project of responsible moral existence in the world.[24]

The story continues. "Disinterested love," the *Agape* of Christ, becomes a critical principle that counters sentimental perfectionists and the havoc they can wreak. It is also a critical prod for expanding community beyond self-limiting calculations for reciprocal exchange. What is lacking in Niebuhr's work is close consideration of the social embodiment of *Agape* among disciples in the church, the specific practices and virtues that define life in Christ. Without this, his ethic can appear to be not so much a direction for existence before God as it is adherence to a moral principle that "realistically" seeks justice in a fallen world without complacency. Similarly, overcoming idolatry and despair equips persons with a sense of meaning (love as the law of human existence) without the pride which would glorify any group, nation, or state. Isolated from an eschatological view to God's actual governance in history, a governance which stands even over against our humble and repentant moral efforts, the quest for justice has seemed to some critics to involve a compromising accommodation to the worldly struggle of assertion and counter-assertion. "Justification by faith" fuels political agency for secure balances of power on these terms, rather than for a "reconstruction of habits" transformed by God's active and effective call for repentance, forgiveness, and reconciliation.[25] This interpretation of Niebuhr draws near to a perspective which John Howard Yoder, Stanley Hauerwas and others sharply reject, "the identification of the church's mission and the meaning of history with the function of the state in organizing sinful society."[26]

One may question such a reading at a number of points. Concerning Niebuhr's method of correlation, one can deny that it is reductionistic,[27] and affirm, with Robin Lovin, that theological apologetics are possible and necessary.

> Those who hold to the Christian faith do not live only in Barth's "strange new world of the Bible," but also in the modern world whose assumptions have made the Bible strange to us . . . Unless we can explain the Bible, at least provisionally, in terms that are coherent with the rest of what we know and believe, we will never know what its strangeness means for us.[28]

Niebuhr's relative neglect of the relation between Christian ethics and the practices of the church, moreover, ought not lead us to overlook his hope that, ideally, "the Christian community is the 'saving remnant' which calls nations to repentance and renewal and without the false belief that any nation or culture could finally fulfill the meaning of life or complete the purpose of history."[29] What remains in question, and in line with Lehmann's analysis, is whether and how, for Niebuhr, the resurrection and resurrection life stand in history, "that through Jesus Christ triumphant faith in God has been introduced into the world."[30]

Influence, Achievement, Agenda

Recall that for Reinhold Niebuhr an implication of the experience of justification by faith is our knowledge "that we cannot purge ourselves of sin and guilt in which we are involved in the ambiguities of politics without also disavowing responsibility for the creative possibilities of justice." One finds a measure of his enormous influence in the way in which this dictum liberated many twentieth-century Christians from an experience of moral confusion generated by varieties of unchastened idealism on the one hand and cynicism on the other.[31] His alternative of Christian realism, according to Robin Lovin, fit a century that needed it, "if its leaders were to escape moral pretensions that would tempt them to crusades, and if its people were to resist concealed powers that threatened to put their lives at the service of other people's interests."[32] In a contemporary American context, his political dialectic can be seen still to set the terms of debate between advocates of the use of power to defend and extend freedom and democracy and critics who see in such advocacy national hubris and imperial ambition.[33] A different sort of influence is present in circles of Christian ethics, where pacifists *resist* the terms of debate Niebuhr proposed for reflection on the meaning of a responsible Christian witness to the state and offer provocative and impressive responses.[34]

Whatever the theoretical merits or flaws ingredient in Niebuhr's theological apologetics, it is undeniable that he offered a powerful interpretation of distinctively Christian themes and dispositions that, accordingly, redescribed the world he inhabited and actions within it. This practice of "intratextuality," of supplying "the interpretive framework within which believers seek to live their lives or understand reality," is a considerable if controversial achievement. It is not alien to the spirit of Augustine, in many ways Niebuhr's theological beacon, "who struggled to insert everything from Platonism and the Pelagian problem to the fall of Rome into the world of the Bible."[35] Niebuhr's Christian critics can improve upon him by taking up this specific feature of his project and doing it better in the light of the reality of God in Jesus Christ. The agenda for theological advance includes (1) a more thorough treatment of God's work of redemption, as it is reflected in the practices of a church founded not only in contrition and hope, but also in reconciliation and the Peace given to it; and (2) an integrally connected account of what God is doing in the world in calling political agencies to repentance and conversion for the sake of that Peace.[36]

Notes

1   James Gustafson, *Can Ethics Be Christian?* (Chicago, 1975), p. 179.
2   See M. Himes and K. Himes, *Fullness of Faith* (New York, 1993), pp. 18–19.
3   *Faith and History* (New York, 1949), p. 152.
4   "Intellectual Autobiography of Reinhold Niebuhr," in C. W. Kegley and R. W. Bretall (eds.), *Reinhold Niebuhr: His Religious, Social, and Political Thought* (New York, 1961), p. 8.
5   *Leaves from the Notebooks of a Tamed Cynic* (New York, 1960), p. 5.
6   *Love and Justice*, ed. D. B. Robertson (Gloucester, MA, 1976), p. 25.
7   Ibid, p. 41.
8   *Reinhold Niebuhr: Theologian of Public Life*, ed. L. Rasmussen (Minneapolis, MN, 1991), p. 134.
9   *Love and Justice*, p. 59.
10 "Intellectual Autobiography," p. 8.
11 *An Interpretation of Christian Ethics* (New York, 1935), p. 19.
12 *The Nature and Destiny of Man, Vol. 2: Human Destiny* (New York, 1964), p. 284.
13 *The Nature and Destiny of Man, Vol. 1: Human Nature* (New York, 1964), p. 251.
14 Ibid, p. 182.
15 *Human Destiny*, p. 69.
16 *Faith and History*, pp. 143–4.
17 *Human Destiny*, pp. 85–6, 88.
18 Ibid, pp. 254–5.
19 *The Children of Light and the Children of Darkness* (New York, 1944), pp. xii–xiv.
20 *Reinhold Niebuhr: Theologian of Public Life*, pp. 243–4.
21 Paul Lehmann, "The Christology of Reinhold Niebuhr," in C. W. Kegley and R. W. Bretall (eds.), *Reinhold Niebuhr: His Religious, Social, and Political Thought* (New York, 1961), pp. 277, 279.
22 *Faith and History*, p. 165.
23 Hans Frei, *Theology and Narrative*, ed. G. Hunsinger and W. C. Placher (New York, 1993), p. 224.
24 Stanley Hauerwas, *With the Grain of the Universe* (Grand Rapids, MI, 2001), pp. 113–40.
25 H. Richard Niebuhr, "A Communication: The Only Way Into the Kingdom of God," in R. B. Miller (ed.), *War in the Twentieth Century* (Louisville, KY, 1992), pp. 19–21.
26 John Howard Yoder, *The Royal Priesthood*, ed. M. G. Cartwright (Grand Rapids, MI, 1994), p. 163.
27 As does Langdon Gilkey, *On Niebuhr* (Chicago, 2001), pp. 16–28, 53–77.
28 Robin, W. Lovin, *Reinhold Niebuhr and Christian Realism* (Cambridge, 1995), pp. 243–4.

29 *Faith and History*, p. 230.
30 H. Richard Niebuhr, *Theology, History, and Culture*, ed. W. S. Johnson (New Haven, CT, 1996), p. 99.
31 See Gilkey, *On Niebuhr*, pp. 3–15.
32 Lovin, *Reinhold Niebuhr*, p. 235.
33 See David Brooks, "A Man on a Grey Horse," www.theatlantic.com/issues2002// 09/brooks.htm (2002).
34 See, for example, John Howard Yoder, *The Christian Witness to the State* (Newton, KA, 1964).

35 George Lindbeck, *The Nature of Doctrine* (Philadelphia, PA, 1984), pp. 124, 117.
36 For more on this see William Werpehowski, "Reinhold Niebuhr and the Question of Free Political Responsibility," in Peter Scott and William T. Cavanaugh (eds.), *The Blackwell Companion to Political Theology* (Oxford, 2003).

Bibliography

Primary

Reinhold Niebuhr: Theologian of Public Life, ed. L. Rasmussen (Minneapolis, MN, 1991).
An Interpretation of Christian Ethics (New York, 1979).
Love and Justice, ed. D. B. Robertson (Gloucester, MA, 1976).
Man's Nature and His Communities (New York, 1965).
The Nature and Destiny of Man, Volume 1: Human Nature (New York, 1964).
The Nature and Destiny of Man, Volume 2: Human Destiny (New York, 1964).
Leaves from the Notebooks of a Tamed Cynic (New York, 1960).
"Intellectual Autobiography of Reinhold Niebuhr," in C. W. Kegley and R. W. Bretall (eds.), *Reinhold Niebuhr: His Religious, Social, and Political Thought* (New York, 1961).
The Self and the Dramas of History (New York, 1955).
Faith and History (New York, 1949).
The Children of Light and the Children of Darkness (New York, 1944).
An Interpretation of Christian Ethics (New York, 1935).
Moral Man and Immoral Society (New York, 1932).

Secondary

Frei, Hans, *Theology and Narrative*, ed. G. Hunsinger and W. C. Placher (New York, 1993).

Gilkey, Langdon, *On Niebuhr* (Chicago, 2001).
Gustafson, James M., *Can Ethics Be Christian?* (Chicago, 1975).
Hauerwas, Stanley, *With the Grain of the Universe* (Grand Rapids, MI, 2001).
Himes, M. and Himes, K., *Fullness of Faith* (New York, 1993).
Lehmann, Paul, "The Christology of Reinhold Niebuhr," in C. W. Kegley and R. W. Bretall (eds.), *Reinhold Niebuhr: His Religious, Social, and Political Thought* (New York, 1961).
Lovin, Robin W., *Reinhold Niebuhr and Christian Realism* (Cambridge, 1995).
Niebuhr, H. Richard, *Theology, History, and Culture*, ed. W. S. Johnson (New Haven, CT, 1996).
—— "A Communication: The Only Way Into the Kingdom of God," in R. B. Miller (ed.), *War in the Twentieth Century* (Louisville, KY, 1992).
Werpehowski, William, "Reinhold Niebuhr and the Question of Free Political Responsibility," in Peter Scott and William T. Cavanaugh (eds.), *The Blackwell Companion to Political Theology* (Oxford, 2003).
Yoder, John Howard, *For the Nations* (Grand Rapids, MI, 1997).
—— *The Royal Priesthood*, ed. M. G. Cartwright (Grand Rapids, MI, 1994).
—— *The Priestly Kingdom* (Notre Dame, IN, 1987).
—— *The Christian Witness to the State* (Newton, KA, 1964).

Revisionists and Liberals

James J. Buckley

Introduction, History, and Influences

Revisionists and liberals are a tradition (or so I shall stipulate) of theologians devoted to shaping Christian practices and teachings in dialogue with (revisionists) or on the basis of (liberals) modern philosophies, cultures, and social practices. However, almost all Christian theologians aim to "revise" their Christian heritage in some respects or "liberate it" from its foibles and sin; from this point of view, the labels "Revisionist" and "liberal" do not help us carefully discriminate among modern Christian theologians. There is an important lesson here. "Any philosophy [or theology] that can be put in a nutshell," it has been said, "deserves to be there."[1] The labels "revisionist" and "liberal" (like all theological labels) are only useful for some sharply circumscribed purposes.

This essay will concentrate less on the history of the labels "revisionist" or "liberal" than on the stands four representative theologians, Edward Farley (1929–), Gordon Kaufman (1925–), Schubert Ogden (1928–), and David Tracy (1939–), and one representative movement (process theology) take on four particular issues (truth, God, persons, and Jesus Christ). But readers should know that many figures and movements discussed elsewhere in this volume could also be taken as revisionist or liberal – Tillich, Rahner, and Schillebeeckx as well as many of the newer challenges in theology. Further, the nexus of influences on the theologians selected is quite different and will constantly jeopardize efforts to embrace them under a single label or as a single tradition. They are "Christian," but in very diverse ways: Farley is a Presbyterian retired at Vanderbilt Divinity School, Kaufman a Mennonite at Harvard Divinity School, Ogden a Methodist and emeritus professor at Southern Methodist University, and Tracy a Roman Catholic at the University of Chicago Divinity School. Process theology, originally centered at the University of Chicago Divinity School and now also at Claremont Graduate School in California, also has representatives from these and other churches and communities. All are committed to liberating Christian tradition or mediating Christian practices and teachings to modern culture, but they focus on different features of modernity. All are committed to critical revisions of this Christian fact and this modern culture, but each locates the key items up for revision in different ways. The following effort to sketch these revisionary and liberal proposals is made even more complicated by the fact that these individual theologians and movements will publish still other works over the next decades. All this suggests just a few of the limits of this effort to sift their proposals. As we work our way through some representative revisionist and liberal theologies, the central aim will be to clarify their theologies, the better to understand their internal debates as well as their external critics.

One crucial issue raised by revisionist and liberal theologies is the character of the story that needs to be told to suggest the need for revisions of the Christian tradition in modernity. On one version, challenged by the rise of modern philosophies and sciences and histories, Christian theologians were pressed to give a new account of the hope that was in them. From one side, orthodox fundamentalists and pietists perceived modernity as a massive threat; from the other side, Christians variously called liberal or modernist endeavored to show that Christian teachings and/or practices were the fulfillment of autonomous humanity. "Mediating theologians" positioned themselves on the boundary of such extremes, arguing Christian faith and modernity can and should live together in peace. Thus, for example, while a "liberal" like G. W. F. Hegel could argue that a faith focused on Jesus Christ could be shown to be "a demonstrable part" of modern science, a "revisionary" mediator like Friedrich Schleiermacher could suggest that the latter "does not contradict" the former.[2] In contrast to these early nineteenth-century European examples, similar examples could be given from England and North America – although the "Golden Age of Liberal Theology" in the United States was in the late nineteenth and early twentieth centuries.[3]

However, arguments among liberals and mediators were often overshadowed around the turn of the century by a sort of second stage in modern theology. In the face of cultures largely post-theistic, several novel (neo-) reaffirmations of classic Christianity ("-orthodoxy") were recovered or constructed (e.g., neothomism, Karl Barth). In fact, one rough way to distinguish revisionist and liberal narratives of modernity is whether they take this second, "neo-orthodox" stage as making a permanent (revisionist) or transient (liberal) contribution to contemporary theology. Today's revisionaries aim to resolve problems left by the second stage precisely by creating a third stage which sublates the first two. On this reading, neo-Marxists, existential phenomenologists, liberation theologians, and others in the 1970s and 1980s "resume the immanentist, humanist trend of nineteenth-century theology, after its interruption by the Barthian period in Protestantism and the Thomist revival in Catholicism."[4] I will not dwell on the early writings of Farley, Kaufman, Ogden, and Tracy,[5] but it is important to note that they include a critique of the internal inconsistency of some phase of neo-orthodoxy; in the fourth section below, we shall see Barth and Thomas return, this time as allies, at the end of the twentieth century.

Survey

We might characterize the Golden Age of Liberal Theology in the United States as the age of "naturalism," a broad academic and cultural movement to overcome peculiarly modern bifurcations between nature and spirit, materialism and idealism on modernity's own terms.[6] While it is deceptive to isolate any single academic figure of this era, one of the most important was the British mathematician and philosopher, Alfred North Whitehead (1861–1947). And one way to find a grip on Whitehead's thought is to consider his proposal that "the true method of discovery" is like the flight of an airplane: it begins from the ground of experience, takes off into "the thin air of imaginative generalization," and "again lands for renewed observation rendered acute by rational observation."[7] The theological runway whence Whitehead's plane takes off is a story of the need for a "new reformation" of a theological tradition. A revolution began with Plato (particularly his notion of the divine as persuasive rather than coercive) and early Christianity (particularly the humble power of "the bare manger" and later interpretations of this as the "mutual immanence" of God and world to each other). But this revolution (Whitehead said) failed in its medieval, Protestant, or Catholic forms. God remained too much like an Egyptian or Mesopotamian king, "internally complete."[8] What is the alternative?

Whitehead's personal sympathies were Unitarian.[9] The highest flight of his philosophical airplane into the airs of imaginative generalization was his construction of a "categorial scheme." In this scheme, "God is not to be treated as an exception to all metaphysical principles, invoked to save their collapse. He is their chief exemplification." For example, "analogously to all actual entities, the nature of God is dipolar. He has a primordial nature and a consequent nature." If God is analogous to other actual entities, God must be both similar to and different from them. "Actual entities" (Whitehead stipulates) are the entities that constitute the actual world; "the actual world is a process, and that process is the becoming of actual entities." Further, actual entities have "physical and mental poles." Crudely put, their "physical" pole is how they relate to ("prehend") other actual entities, while their "conceptual" pole is how they relate to that which is not (or not yet) actual (i.e., "eternal objects").[10]

God too is an actual entity, related to other actual entities and eternal objects. Thus, God too has a physical and conceptual pole. God's relationship to other actual entities is internal rather than external to God's identity. "It is as true to say that God transcends the World, as that the World transcends God. It is as true to say that God creates the World, as that the World creates God. God and the World are the contrasted opposites in terms of which Creativity achieves its supreme task." And yet it is also important that there are differences between God and other actual entities. Most importantly, God's conceptual pole (unlike that of other actual entities) is "primordial" (e.g., is prior to God's "physical" pole). "The given course of history presupposes [God's] primordial nature, but his primordial nature does not presuppose it." God's "primordial nature" is conceptual, while God's "consequent nature is the weaving of God's physical feelings upon his primordial concepts."

When Whitehead lands this airplane of imaginative generalization on the ground, the result is the "mutual immanence" of God and the world his "new reformation" sought. "By reason of this reciprocal relation, the love of the world passes into the love in heaven, and floods back again into the world. In this sense, God is the great companion – the fellow-sufferer who understands."[11]

The next generation of liberals included theologians in direct dialogue with Whitehead, as we shall see in the next section. But most of this next generation also carved out its own niche quite distinct from what would become "process theology."

The following paragraphs suggest how four common themes are dealt with in different ways by our four individual representatives: Farley, Kaufman, Ogden, and Tracy.

First, all four theologians agree that Christian theology makes truth-claims and provides reasons for its claims. Thus, all reject both the notion that Christian theology makes no truth-claims and simple appeals to "the house of authority" (Farley) to back up the truth-claims they do make. But how can *Christian* theology make *truth*-claims? Here they begin to diverge. Tracy, following Paul Tillich, uses what he sometimes calls a "method of correlation." The point of theology is to correlate our tradition and our situation in ways that are "mutually critical," careful to give neither pole (our tradition or our situation) unequivocal precedence and constantly searching for disclosures of theological truth.[12]

Ogden also speaks of theology as a sort of "correlation of the Christian witness of faith and human existence" subject to "the two criteria of appropriateness [Is x appropriate to normative Christian witness?] and credibility [Does x meet 'the relevant conditions of truth universally established with human existence?']." But Ogden also emphasizes that, since these dual criteria govern distinct aspects of Christian witness, it makes little sense to speak about "correlating" two poles.[13] Perhaps more than Tracy, Farley, or Kaufman, Ogden distinguishes Christian faith and theology (the latter a distinct act of critical reflection and validation).

Farley and Kaufman (for reasons we shall see) resist any talk of correlation or dual criteria, but share with Ogden and Tracy a concern with showing that Christian teachings are not only "Christian" but also "true." Farley proposes that the problem of truth is at once "the problem of reality" ("how reality comes forth, occurs, is manifest") and "the problem of criteria" ("how the reality manifesting grounding rises into the judgment"). Because the former is a faith-apprehension of reality, Farley insists that judgments about the latter are "not members of a more general class"; he calls the latter "ecclesial universals" to highlight the way they are different from and similar to more generic universals.[14] For Kaufman, "only criteria of coherence and pragmatic usefulness to human life are relevant and applicable" to large concepts like "world" and "God." He rejects "one-dimensional," authoritarian as well as "two-dimensional," correlational theologies in favor of his "holistic" theology, i.e., one that is a conversation about "the source and ground and meaning of *all that is*"; "(religious) truth should be understood to be specifically dialogical (and thus pluralistic) in character."[15]

Second, all four are concerned with human beings as free *subjects* embedded in a physical and social and historical world, radically threatened by ambiguity and suffering and evil, and seeking ways to overcome this situation. For Tracy, the self is "radical agapic self-transcendence." There are "real and perhaps even irreconcilable ideals of the self," but the self is subject-in-process, "never substance but subject, affected by and affecting both God and the world." The freedom of the Christian, Tracy suggests, is "the real but limited freedom of the prophetic-mystical subject-as-agent-in-process."[16] For Farley, faith-apprehensions "occur pre-reflectively and by means of an enduring participation in a form of corporate historical existence which we are calling ecclesia." Our subjectivity is always a "determinate intersubjectivity" expressed in stories and images, myths and doctrines – the "face" of "the interhuman."[17]

Ogden weaves together the diverse construals of subjectivity (Tracy) and intersubjectivity (Farley) in Wesley, Bultmann, and even liberation theology under a kind of process philosophy for which the self is aware of and responsible for itself as continually becoming, internally related to time and others, an essential fragment of "the integral whole of reality."[18] For Kaufman, human beings are "'biohistorical' beings," organically related to other life-forms and self-reflexive, corrupted by individual anxiety and guilt as well as societal oppression and disorder, and yet somehow participants in "directional movements in a serendipitous universe."[19]

Third, all agree that the monarchical God of classic theism (who acts in history in ways that jeopardize or destroy human subjectivity in nature and history) must be replaced by a God (or other ultimate reality) related to human, religious, or specifically Christian experience. Ogden[20] and Tracy[21] argue on behalf of the God whom we meet in the limit-questions of our experience and who, as soul of the world, is both in and beyond that world. This position is sometimes called panentheism (e.g., God is in everything, and everything is in God), although Tracy also insists that "no *ism* . . . is ever adequate for naming and thinking God."[22]

Farley argues for faith's indirect apprehension of God – not a God "represented mythically as thinking, willing, reflecting, and accomplishing in the mode of an in-the-world-being who intervenes selectively in world process," nor simply a general religious "transcendent," but a God for whom "ecclesial process as such *is* the salvific work of God in history."[23] Kaufman argues that "the image/concept of God serves as a focus or center for devotion and orientation" – a focus which must be represented "on a continuum running from highly mythical and symbolical images – God as a personal being who loves and cares – to the more abstract notion of the cosmic ground of all humanity."[24]

Fourth, all agree that life and thought in relationship to the specific figure of Jesus are shaped by the previous issues, although they diverge on exactly how. Of our four figures, Tracy and Farley are the most sympathetic to what Farley calls a kind of "primacy of Christology." For Tracy, the event and person of Jesus Christ – in the immediacy of experience mediated by the tradition (which is normed by the expressions of scripture), developed and corrected by historical and literary and social criticisms, and correlated with our present situation – is the prime analogue for theological imagination.[25] For Farley, Jesus of Nazareth is "appresented" as historical redeemer in ecclesial existence. One of the tasks, "perhaps the central one," of what Farley calls theological portraiture is inquiry into the Jesus of Nazareth "proclaimed as the redemption-effecting person" – "not simply the past Jesus but the present Christ."[26]

But, if Tracy and Farley are the most sympathetic to the primacy of Christology, Ogden has devoted the most care to articulating a "revisionary Christology." Ogden argues that "the Christological question is an existential–historical question about the meaning of Jesus for us." Further, "the subject of the Christological assertion is not Jesus in his being in himself, but rather Jesus in his meaning for us"; any appropriate Christological predicate is that Jesus Christ is the "decisive re-presentation of God for us" – a re-presentation of something that was there all along and now "becomes fully explicit."[27]

Of our four figures, Kaufman is most critical of traditional Christology, although he insists that "the picture and story of Jesus" provides "qualities and potentialities" "normative for human life." The category of Christ qualifies "in a definitive way" other theological concepts; "Christ crucified" is an appropriate image for a God who "suffers crucifixion in the hope of the resurrection of a new community called to non-violence."[28]

Representatives

Describing our representatives individually will suggest the differences that accompany their common ground on select issues. Whitehead was not a theologian. The theological features of his writing (surveyed above) are fragmentary, leaving a host of unanswered questions (e.g., what is the relation between God and Creativity? Is God dispensable to the categorial scheme? How does God relate to complex societies of actual entities like human beings?). Representatives of what came to be called process theology take up these and other issues left by the movement of "naturalism" of which Whitehead was a part.

Process theologians do not agree on how to describe the differences among themselves.[29] In some respects, process theology after Whitehead is like the history of German philosophy after Hegel, dividing into right wing (revisionary) and left wing (liberal) branches. I will focus on two central issues in the divide. First, can more (or less) of the Christian tradition be retrieved than Whitehead thought? Second, is Whitehead's "method of discovery" (the metaphor of the airplane's flight) rational or empirical?

Theologians like John B. Cobb (1925–) focus on reinterpreting Christian theology in dialogue with Whitehead. Cobb's *A Christian Natural Theology* (1964) does this most explicitly, arguing that a Christian theology ought to assess philosophies not only by their "intrinsic excellence" but also by whether they are or are not "hostile to Christian faith." "The quest for total consensus is an illusion." This "inner tension of Christianity, between its particularism and its universalism" characterizes Cobb's early writing. Despite criticisms, he has tried to maintain this tension as he explores "creative transformation" in Christ, Buddhist–Christian dialogue, and his more recent writing on public policy.[30] Cobb has shaped the version of process theology at Claremont Graduate School, along with David Griffin and Margorie Suchocki.[31]

On the other hand, Bernard Loomer (1912–85) was one of the shapers of a different reading of Whitehead at the University of Chicago Divinity School. He proposed that the consistent carrying out of Whitehead's "method of discovery" would yield a "God identified with the totality of the [world]" – a totality which is ambiguous. "An ambiguous God is of greater stature than an unambiguous deity."[32] Henry Nelson Wieman also came to propose radical reinterpretations of both Whitehead and Christianity.[33] If Cobb thinks that more of the Christian tradition can be retrieved than Whitehead thought, Loomer and Wieman think that less can – much less.

Whether these theologians revise Christian theology in light of something like Whitehead's brand of naturalism or Whitehead in light of Christian theology, a second difference emerges in how they go about doing this. Charles Hartshorne (1897–) was also at the University of Chicago Divinity School for many years. He shares Whitehead's skepticism on traditional claims about God and Jesus Christ – but he also differs from Whitehead on a number of points. For example, whereas Whitehead thought of God as an actual entity, Hartshorne thinks of God as a series of actual occasions – like a divine person, perfect in transcendence and immanence. He has said that "the whole point of my natural theology is that God is as literally infinite as finite, and vice versa, the union of these contraries . . . being the essence of 'process theology.'"[34] Hartshorne is also known for a version of the ontological argument for the existence of God, arguing that God's existence is logically necessary. On the other hand, process theologians like Henry Nelson Wieman and Bernard Loomer argue that this is a "rationalism" which undercuts the priority of Whitehead's Creativity (briefly mentioned in the previous section). Ogden has his criticisms of Hartshorne's philosophical theology; but he (like Cobb) has also spent more time than Hartshorne working not simply on theology's philosophical credibility but also its "appropriateness" to the apostolic witness of scripture.[35]

It is easier to summarize the particularities of our four other representatives of revisionist and liberal theology. Farley is writing a multivolume interpretation of the major themes of the Christian mythos. The first two volumes are prolegomena. *Ecclesial Man: A Social Phenomenology of Faith and Reality* is an analysis of faith's given apprehensions of reality, which occur "in a form of corporate, historical existence which we are calling ecclesia." *Ecclesial Reflection: An Anatomy of Theological Method* internally deconstructs various levels of the "house of authority." Ecclesial reflection is (roughly) an inquiry with three moments: historical and biblical ("theological portraiture"), philosophical and systematic, and practical. Farley has moved from such proposals about theology to his interpretation of the "Christian paradigm," construed as focusing on three themes: redeemed human being, God, and the historical mediations of redemption (Messiah and church). The first installment begins with a "reflective ontology," *Good and Evil: Interpreting a Human Condition*, in "three spheres of human reality: [individual, personal] agency, the interhuman, and the social." He makes the case that, although each of the three spheres has its own importance, "the interhuman is primary both to agents and the social because it is the sphere that engenders the criterion, the face (Emmanuel Levinas), for the workings of the other spheres." The final volume of Farley's central project is *Divine Empathy*. Here, Farley aims to adjudicate the theism of classic Catholic theology and the anti-theism of twentieth-century deconstructive theologies, as well as Jewish philosophy, climaxing in "divine empathy," a metaphorical description of the God who transcends the world, including our best metaphors. We find these ideas applied to theological education in Farley's *Theologia*, where theology is described as a particular sort of *habitus* in the context of ecclesiality. The broad and deep aesthetic sensibilities at work throughout Farley's theology are manifest in his *Faith and Beauty* as well as *Deep Symbols*.[36]

Gordon Kaufman's *Systematic Theology: An Historicist Perspective* sought to meet the problem of the irrelevance of Christian faith "by giving at every point a radically *historicist* view of the Christian." The collection of essays in *God the Problem* deconstructed the concept of God partly begun and partly presupposed in earlier writing, leading Kaufman later to propose a notion of theological method as the "activity of *construction* (and reconstruction) not of description or exposition." Kaufman's later essays develop and apply this new method to a range of topics. In *Nonresistance and Responsibility, and Other Mennonite Essays*, Kaufman displays the ways he has over the years sought "an understanding of Christian faith which is Mennonite but not authoritarian" – which, for all its technical changes, has remained "concerned primarily with forming persons and communities devoted to redemptive love." *In Face of Mystery: A Constructive Theology* is Kaufman's most thorough articulation of his position. Faith proceeds (Kaufman says) by several "small steps." Beginning with a sort of faith that God can be reflected upon in worthwhile ways, theology proceeds to excavate, critically examine, and imaginatively construct this faith by "sketching a picture of the world, and of humanity within the world, based largely on widely accepted modern knowledges and on the modes of experience that ground these knowledges." Theology then proceeds to construct the concept or image of God before re-visioning humanity and world and God in the light of the Christ.[37]

Schubert Ogden's own work reflects his description of theology as critical reflection on Christian witness (see above). The critical reflection initially took the form of a critique of the internal inconsistency of Bultmann's claims that Jesus Christ is act of God and his demand for existential demythologization. *The Reality of God and Other Essays* develops an alternative, using linguistic analysis (Toulmin) and process philosophy (Whitehead and Hartshorne) to support Christian claims about divine agency. *Faith and Freedom: Toward a Theology of Liberation* is a move from the issues raised by Bultmann's existentialism, process thought, and linguistic analysis to the challenge of liberation theologies on issues of "justice and action." *Is There Only One True Religion or Are There Many?* moves into the world of various religions, arguing against three standard ways of treating religions (exclusivism, inclusivism, and pluralism) in favor of "pluralistic inclusivism."[38]

David Tracy's main project may eventually yield a trilogy on fundamental, systematic, and practical theology. The first volume, *Blessed Rage for Order*, applies a method of correlation to issues of religion, God, and life. *The Analogical Imagination* turns to systematic theology. Systematic theology is hermeneutical, i.e., the interpretation (not repetition) of a tradition given us by our historicity and finitude. The key examples are "classics," especially religious classics. The *Christian* classic is "the event and person of Jesus Christ." *Analogical Imagination* is a paradigm of an analogical imagination which works by picking a primary analogue, showing the unity-in-difference within and between analogues (their order, perhaps harmony, their variety and intensity, including dialectical negations), and risking the self-exposure of putting these similarities and differences in the public forum. More recently, Tracy has "reconceived" (without abandoning) his revisionary methods, arguing that such revisionary methods "must be continually open to critique and revision." More particularly, he has reconceived his method in the light of the neoplatonic traditions (from Pseudo-Dionysius to Eckhart and especially Ruuysbroec), radical postmodern thought on negativity and difference (Derrida and Deleuze), and Buddhist – more exactly, Kyoto Mayahana Buddhist – thought. Tracy is currently completing a major project on the doctrine of God.[39]

The Debate

A full description of the debates over revisionary and liberal theologies would require locating these theologians in relationship to all the other chapters of this volume. Here we must be satisfied with more modest remarks. I will distinguish debates "internal" to the revisionist and liberal project and those "external" to the project.

The internal debate is shaped by a sense that the differences override the common ground. This applies to the debate among process theologians already sketched – that is, the debates between those who wish to retrieve more or less of the Christian tradition as well as between those who think Whitehead's airplane is most helpful on the "empirical" ground or in the "rational" and speculative air. But it applies even more to the forms of revisionist and liberal theologies more prominent in the second half of the twentieth century, for they are much more philosophically eclectic than the naturalism which initially spawned process theology. Farley is shaped by Husserl's phenomenology, Ogden by linguistic analysis and Bultmann's Heidegger (as well as Hartshorne), Kaufman by Kant, David Tracy by Lonergan and Ricoeur.[40]

This sense that the differences override the common ground also accounts for the fragmentary and even infrequently polemical nature of the debate among our four individual figures (e.g., Tracy accusing Kaufman of an uncritical acceptance of modernity, Farley accusing Tracy of pre-revisionary conservativism, and Kaufman accusing both of not carrying through their revisionary proposals to their practical conclusions.)[41]

Readers should not let this internal debate fool them into thinking that the differences among our representatives outweigh their common grounds; intra-familial debates, to use common wisdom, are often more intense than inter-familial arguments. In any case, these discussions offer clues to the larger controversies. Take, for example, the debate over the possibility and actuality of Christian truth-claims. One way to understand this debate is to range their positions on a spectrum from Farley's claim that faith-apprehension yields ecclesial universals, through Tracy's method of correlation and Ogden's "dual criteria," to Kaufman's ultimately pragmatic and humanistic test for truth. (Among process theologians, Cobb and Griffin would stand closer to Farley and Tracy on this issue, while Hartshorne and Wieman would stand closer to Ogden and Kaufman.)

This spectrum suggests a logic behind the remarks each has made about the others. Thus, Kaufman thinks that Farley's faith-apprehension retains too many vestiges of "objectivist thinking" and is a "version of confessionalism," while Farley wonders how Kaufman's critique of traditional correspondence theories of truth can lead us beyond subjectivism. Farley, let us say, uses a *general* phenomenological framework to show that Christian truth-claims are *specific* to particular communities, while Kaufman requires that specifically Christian claims conform to his pragmatic framework. Tracy and Ogden propose subtle correlations of generality and specificity (and hence belong in the middle of the spectrum). However, both Farley and Kaufman are suspicious of methods of correlation or "dual criteria" because they can threaten Christian particularity (Farley), because they leave Christian particularity "substantially unquestioned" (Kaufman), or because it is hard to tell whether their revisionary force is central or marginal. The spectrum places Tracy closer to Farley because Farley's "theological portraiture" and Tracy's hermeneutical conversation are more analogous to each other than either is to Ogden or Kaufman. Also, Farley and Kaufman seem less suspicious of Ogden's dual criteria than of Tracy's locating the correlational task in a philosophically eclectic "hermeneutical" context; Farley and Kaufman worry that Tracy's hermeneutical disclosure experiences avoid rather than confront hard questions about truth (as Farley and Kaufman variously define it). Tracy in turn worries that Ogden does not take into account the "poetic" character of the religious conversation, that Kaufman is too uncritical of modernity, and Farley only implicitly critical. Again, these oppositions should not make us forget their common ground.

The external debate is shaped by a sense that the common ground among revisionists and liberals overrides the differences they perceive among each other. For example, there are both theological and philosophical challenges to revisionist and liberal notions of truth. Thus, Ronald Thiemann proposes a notion of revelation which enables him to criticize Kaufman (for simply exchanging a divine foundation for a human one) as well as Tracy and Ogden (for steering an unstable middle course between revelation and human imagination).[42] Thiemann's criticisms of Kaufman are similar to Farley and Tracy's – and his criticisms of Tracy are similar to Farley and Kaufman's. More importantly, in at least some respects, Thiemann's proposal is an internal critique of Karl Barth's theology – a "critique" because Thiemann elucidates promissory revelation using Anglo-American "non-foundationalist" philosophy; "internal" because of Thiemann's Barth-like insistence on God's "prevenience" – God has loved us first, prior to our airplane ever arriving on the ground, taking off, or landing.[43]

A philosophical challenge comes from those philosophers of religions less interested in making or justifying Christian truth-claims than in studying them as doctrines of religious communities. Thus, William Christian has argued that there are fewer problems with a community taking its authentic doctrines to be true (Farley) than taking every truth to be a doctrine of their community (Kaufman) – or than "correlating" their own and other truth-claims (Tracy). Christian's stand is more like Farley's than Kaufman's or Ogden's or Tracy's, but his appeal is to the practices and teachings of *particular* communities rather than to Farley's *general* phenomenology (even though Farley's is a phenomenology which centers on faith's positivity and particularity).[44]

Alasdair MacIntyre goes even further in the direction of particularity, contrasting the encyclopedia (especially the "liberal" authors of the ninth edition of the *Encyclopedia Britannica*), the genealogy (Nietzsche), and tradition (Leo XIII) as different and opposed contexts for pursuing rational inquiry. He argues that liberal encyclopedists have not taken seriously the Nietzschean genealogical critique of modernity; this liberal–nihilist impasse generates MacIntyre's re-reading of Thomas Aquinas on the rationality of tradition for the pursuit of the true and the good.[45]

Achievement and Questions for the Future

The key achievement of revisionists and liberals has been to challenge our received practices and teachings about truth, human beings, God, and Christ. The key (if not only) questions for the future have to do with the alternatives revisionaries and liberals propose. On this score, certainly revisionists and liberals ought to continue to address the issues raised by the debate over "truth" (e.g., is truth correspondence to reality, pragmatic effectiveness, disclosure? Do we need a theory of truth, and method?). But both internal and external critics should not permit this issue to dominate the future agenda; settling issues of truth will not settle issues of who we are, who God is, or who Christ is.

For example, a major achievement of revisionary and liberal visions of humanity (our own and others) is the insistence on the way we are free subjects embedded in a physical, social, and historical world. Yet revisionists and liberals are divided among themselves as to how to do this. Can a categorial scheme applicable to the whole cosmos (like Whitehead's or Hartshorne's or Kaufman's) do justice to the particular joys and griefs of our human subjectivities? Can probing analyses of the heights and depths of our subjectivities (like Farley's *Good and Evil*) keep us embedded in our physical, social, and historical world? Does Tracy's mystical–political option show a way out, or does it just redescribe the problem? Internal critics of revisionist and liberal theologies offer different answers to such questions.[46] External critics have focused on the secular politics that arises out of revisionist and liberal theologies, arguing from the right or the left that liberal politics is dead. But a different group of external critics (including those dubbed "postliberal" in this volume) has argued that only a church constituted as the Other City can provide the counter-history, the counter-ethics, and the counter-ontology needed to reconcile our violent world.[47]

Another achievement of revisionary and liberal theologies is their insistence that our claims about God be related to the broader world of human religiosity. However, they have thus far paid more attention to the general features of the religious world than to its particularities. For example, all share a great deal if we focus on Kaufman's "formal" notion of God, Ogden's early use of God in a "completely general sense," or Tracy's case for Ultimate Reality.[48] Yet when it comes to identifying this God, Farley appeals to determinate divine activity, Ogden and Tracy to process theism modified by trinitarian theology, and Kaufman to a non-agential cosmic ground. These are the makings of different religions rather than of a common revisionary or liberal theological project.[49]

Admittedly, revisionists and liberals have entered into careful conversations with Buddhists. Cobb finds Christianity and some kinds of Buddhism complementary, if they can be "mutually transformed." Kaufman seems to go further, finding that a kenotic God (Phillipians 2: 7) is "moving toward" the Buddhist teaching that "everything ought to be understood in terms of 'emptiness.'" On the other hand, Tracy says that Buddhists have helped him understand Christian mystics like Meister Eckhart, although Tracy ultimately stands with Christian trinitarian mystics like Ruuysbroec rather than Eckhart. Ogden, while finding common ground as well as much that is difficult to understand in Buddhism, finds that arguments for analogies between Buddhist emptiness and the kenotic God assume that God can only be "infinitely related" and not also "infinitely unrelated," whereas Christians ought to confess both.[50] Are these different and opposed views of Christian relations with Buddhists symptoms of deep disagreements over Christian theology, or are they simply the result of the young stage of Buddhist–Christian dialogue? Besides Buddhists who might have such questions, another group of external critics of liberals and revisionists on the identity of God includes those who argue that the doctrine of trinitarian *hypostases* is no less unintelligible or inapplicable than dipolar theism, and that the Trinity is the best way to account for the transcendence and immanence of God in Christ, church, and world.[51]

Finally, a key debate between liberals and revisionists is whether to continue (like the revisionary tradition from Schleiermacher through Tracy) or discontinue (like the liberal tradition from Whitehead to Kaufman) a broadly Christocentric reading of life.

"Broadly" is important, for a central challenge to revisionist as well as liberal Christologies comes from those like Karl Barth who insist that "there is no question of placing Christ within some allegedly more comprehensive context. Christ *is* the adequate context of Christian theology."[52] Our representatives disagree over what the context ought to be: faith-apprehensions, conversations over texts, the modern world in its historicist–pragmatic complexity, etc. And it is more accurate to describe the revisionary (in contrast to liberal) task as one of relating "context" and "Christ" rather than giving absolute priority to the "event" or "person" (the "context" or "Christ") of Jesus Christ. But *that* the particular figure Jesus requires some prior context to be applicable or intelligible, all agree. From this point of view, while revisionists and liberals have made considerable advances over the anthropologies and cosmologies and epistemologies of their mediating predecessors, the Christological issue remains much the same.

The comprehensiveness of the revisionist and liberal agenda ensures that it will be subject to piecemeal critiques on each issue – and that it will withstand them for some time to come.

Notes

1 Bernard M. Loomer, "Process Theology: Origins, Strengths, Weaknesses," *Process Studies*, 16 (1987), pp. 245–54 (quoting Sidney Harris).

2 John P. Clayton, *The Concept of Correlation: Paul Tillich and the Possibility of a Mediating Theology* (New York: Walter DeGruyter, 1980), pp. 7–9; Hans Frei, "David Friedrich Strauss," in Ninian Smart, John Clayton, Steven Katz, and Patrick Sherry (eds.), *Nineteenth Century Religious Thought in the West*, Vol. 1 (Cambridge: Cambridge University Press, 1985), p. 221.

3 Syndey E. Ahlstrom, *A Religious History of the American People* (New Haven, CT, 1972), p. 763. See also Gary Dorrien's projected encyclopedic three volume history, *The Making of American Liberal Theology: Imagining Progressive Religion, 1805–1900* (Louisville, KY, 2001); *The Making of American Liberal Theology: Idealism, Realism, and Modernity* (Louisville, KY, 2003), including other ways of articulating the divide between what I here call liberals and revisionists.

4 John Macquarrie, *Twentieth Century Religious Thought: The Frontiers of Philosophy and Theology, 1900–1980*, revd. edn. (New York, 1981), pp. 380, 410.

5 Edward Farley, *The Transcendence of God: A Study in Contemporary Philosophical Theology* (Philadelphia, PA, 1960) and *Requiem for a Lost Piety: The Contemporary Search for the Christian Life* (Philadelphia, PA, 1966); Gordan Kaufman, *Relativism, Knowledge, and Faith* (Chicago, 1960) and *The Context of Decision* (New York, 1961); Schubert Ogden, *Christ without Myth: A Study Based on the Theology of Rudolph Bultmann* (Dallas, TX, 1979 [original 1962]); David Tracy, *The Achievement of Bernard Lonergan* (New York, 1970).

6 Bernard M. Loomer, "Process Theology: Origins, Strengths, Weaknesses," *Process Studies*, 16 (1987), pp. 245–54.

7 Alfred North Whitehead, *Process and Reality: An Essay in Cosmology*. Gifford lectures 1927–8. Corrected edition by David Ray Griffin and Donald W. Sherburne (London, 1978 [originally published 1929]), p. 5.

8 Alfred North Whitehead, *Adventures of Ideas* (New York, 1967 [originally published 1933]), pp. 167–8; *Process and Reality*, p. 342.

9 Victor Lowe, *Alfred North Whitehead*, ed. J. B. Schneewind (Baltimore, MD, 1990), ch. 9.

10 *Process and Reality*, pp. 18–30, 343, 345, 22, 239.

11 Ibid, pp. 31–2, 44, 75, 87, 345, 348, 351.

12 David Tracy, *The Analogical Imagination* (New York, 1981), pp. 59–62, 88 [note 44]; *On Naming the Present* (New York, 1995), p. 75.

13 Schubert M. Ogden, *On Theology* (Dallas, 1992), p. 3; "Doing Theology Today," in John D. Woodbridge and Thomas Edward McComiskey (eds.), *Doing Theology in Today's World* (Grand Rapids, MI, 1991), p. 424; Review of Hans Frei's *Types of Christian Theology* in *Modern Theology* 9 (1993), p. 214.

14 Edward Farley, *Ecclesial Reflection: An Anatomy of Theological Method* (Philadelphia, PA, 1982), pp. xiii, 304–5, 310, 338, 343; *Good and Evil: Interpreting a Human Condition* (Minneapolis, MN, 1990), p. 3; "Truth and the Wisdom of Enduring" in Daniel Guerriere (ed.), *Phenomenology of the Truth Proper to Religion* (Albany, NY, 1990).

15 Gordan Kaufman, *Relativism, Knowledge, and Faith* (Chicago, 1960), p. 94; *An Essay on Theological Method* (Missoula, MT, 1979), p. 75; *In Face of Mystery: A Constructive Theology* (Cambridge, MA, 1993), pp. 29, 467 [note 6].

16 Tracy, *The Analogical Imagination*, pp. 435–6: *Dialogue with the Other* (Grand Rapids, MI, 1990), pp. 118, 102.

17 Edward Farley, *Ecclesial Man: A Social Phenomenology of Faith and Reality* (Philadelphia, PA, 1975), pp. 127, xiii, 86, 93, 150, 158; *Good and Evil*, chs. 1, 13, and 16.

18 Schubert Ogden, "Process Theology and the Wesleyan Witness," *Perkins School of Theology Journal* 37 (1984), pp. 18–33.

19 Gordan Kaufman, *In Face of Mystery*, esp. chs. 8, 15, and 20.

20 Schubert Ogden, *The Reality of God and Other Essays* (Dallas, 1992).

21 David Tracy, *Blessed Rage for Order* (New York, 1975).

22 David Tracy, "Approaching the Christian Understanding of God" in Francis Schüssler Fiorenza and John P. Galvin (eds.), *Systematic Theology: Roman Catholic Perspectives* (Minneapolis, MN, 1991), pp. 131–48; "Literary Theory and the Return of the Forms for Naming and Thinking God in Theology," *Journal of Religion* 74 (1994), pp. 308–9; *On Naming the Present* (Maryknoll, NY, 1995), p. 18.

23 Edward Farley, *Ecclesial Man*, pp. 13, 224, 226; *Ecclesial Reflection*, pp. 156–7; with Peter C. Hodgson, "Scripture and Tradition" in Peter Hodgson and Robert King (eds.), *Christian Theology* (Philadelphia, PA, 1985), ch. 2.

24 Gordan Kaufman, *The Theological Imagination* (Philadelphia, PA, 1981), p. 32; *Theology for a Nuclear Age* (Manchester, 1985), ch. 3; *In Face of Mystery*, esp. part 4 and ch. 27.

25 Tracy, *The Analogical Imagination*, pp. 233–41; *On Naming the Present*, pp. 31, 37, 67, 79, 124–5.

26 Edward Farley, *Ecclesial Man*, pp. 217–19; *Ecclesial Reflection*, pp. xvii, 209, 225.

27 Schubert Ogden, *The Point of Christology* (Dallas, 1992), pp. 41, 62, 82.

28 Gordan Kaufmann, *The Theological Imagination*, pp. 116, 189–90; *Theology for a Nuclear Age*, ch. 4; *In Face of Mystery*, chs. 7, 25, 26.

29 Loomer reports that Hartschorne credited him with inventing the label "process theology" – and says that, if so, he repents of it as "a sin of my youth" ("Process Theology," p. 245). See also Delwin Brown, Ralph E. James, Jr., and Gene Reeves (eds.), *Process Philosophy and Christian Thought* (Indianapolis, IN, 1971); John B. Cobb and David Ray Griffin, *Process Theology: An Introductory Exposition* (Philadelphia, PA, 1976); Kenneth Surin, "Process Theology" in David Ford (ed.), *The Modern Theologians*, Vol. 2 (Oxford, 1989), pp. 103–14; Delwin Brown and Sheila Graves Davaney, "Methodological Alternatives in Process Theology," *Process Studies* 19 (1990), pp. 75–84; Denis Hurtubise, "One, Two, or Three Concepts of God in Alfred North Whitehead's *Process and Reality*," *Process Studies* 30 (2001), pp. 78–100.

30 John B. Cobb, Jr., *A Christian Natural Theology* (Philadelphia, PA, 1964); *Christ in a Pluralistic Age* (Philadelphia, PA, 1975); *Beyond Dialogue: Toward a Mutual Transformation of Christianity and Buddhism* (Philadelphia, PA, 1982); *Sustainability* (Maryknoll, NY, 1992); *Transforming Christianity and the World: A Way beyond Absolutism and Relativism* (Maryknoll, NY, 1999); *Postmodernism and Public Policy: Reframing Religion, Culture, Education,*

Sexuality, Class, Race (Albany, NY, 2002). See also David Ray Griffin and Thomas J. J. Altizer (eds.), *John Cobb's Theology in Process* (Philadelphia, PA, 1977); David Ray Griffin and Joseph C. Hough (eds.), *Theology and the University: Essays in Honor of John B. Cobb, Jr.* (Albany, NY, 1991).

31 David Griffin, *A Process Christology* (Philadelphia, PA, 1973); "Process Theology and the Christian Good News: A Response to Classical Free Will Theism," in John B. Cobb, Jr. and Clark H. Pinnock (eds.), *Searching for an Adequate God: A Dialogue between Process and Free Will Theists* (Grand Rapids, MI, 2000); *Religion and Scientific Naturalism* (Albany, NY, 2000); *Reenchantment without Supernaturalism: A Process Philosophy of Religion* (Ithaca, NY, 2001); "Being Bold: Anticipating a Whiteheadean Century," *Process Studies* 31 (2002), pp. 3–15. Margorie Hewitt Suchocki, *The End of Evil: Process Eschatology in Historical Context* (Albany, NY, 1988); *God, Christ, Church: A Practical Guide to Process Theology*, revd. edn. (New York, 1989); *Divinity and Diversity: A Christian Affirmation of Religious Pluralism* (Nashville, TN, 2003).

32 Bernard Loomer, "Process Theology," pp. 20–1; see W. Dean and L. E. Axel (eds.), *The Size of God: The Theology of Bernard Loomer* (Macon, GA, 1987).

33 Cobb and Griffin, *Process Theology*, pp. 177–8.

34 Charles Hartshorne, *The Darkness and the Light* (New York, 1990), p. 227; *Man's Vision of God and the Logic of Theism* (Hampden, CT, 1941); *The Divine Relativity* (New Haven, CT, 1948); *The Logic of Perfection, and Other Essays in Neoclassical Metaphysics* (LaSalle, IL, 1962); *Anselm's Discovery* (LaSalle, IL, 1965); *Creative Synthesis and Philosophical Method* (La Salle, IL, 1970); see also Lewis Ford (ed.), *Two Process Philosophers: Hartshorne's Encounter with Whitehead* (Talahassee, FL, 1973). For bibliography and further studies on Hartshorne, see the entire issue of *Process Studies* 30 (No. 2, winter, 2001).

35 Schubert Ogden, "The Experience of God: Critical Reflections on Hartshorne's Theory of Analogy," in John B. Cobb, Jr. and Franklin I. Gamwell (eds.), *Existence and Actuality: Conversations with Charles Hartshorne* (Chicago, 1984).

36 Farley, *Ecclesial Man*, pp. 127, 29, 57; *Ecclesial Reflection*, p. 190; *Good and Evil*, pp. xv–xvi, 28–9, 117–18, 287–92; *Divine Empathy: A Theology of God* (Minneapolis, MN, 1996). See also *Theologia* (Philadelphia, PA, 1983); *The Fragility of Knowledge* (Minneapolis, MN, 1988); *Deep Symbols: Their Postmodern Effacement and Reclamation* (Harrisburg, PA, 1996); *Faith and Beauty: A Theological Aesthetic* (Aldershot, 2001); and Robert R. Williams (ed.), *Theology and the Interhuman: Essays in Honor of Edward Farley* (Valley Forge, PA, 1995).

37 Kaufman, *Systematic Theology* (New York, 1978), p. 9; *God the Problem* (Cambridge, 1972); *An Essay on Theological Method*, pp. x, 46; *The Theological Imagination*, p. 102; *Nonresistance and Responsibility, and Other Mennonite Essays* (Newton, KS, 1979), pp. 9–10; *In Face of Mystery*, esp. chs. 17 and 29. See also *Mennonite Theology in Face of Modernity: Essays in Honor of Gordan D. Kaufman* (North Newton, KS, 1996).

38 Ogden, "Faith and Freedom," in James M. Wall (ed.), *Theologians in Transition* (*Christian Century* "How My Mind Has Changed" series) (New York, 1981); *Christ without Myth: A Study Based on the Theology of Rudolph Bultmann* (Dallas, TX, 1962); *Faith and Freedom: Toward a Theology of Liberation* (Nashville, TN, 1989); *Is There Only One True Religion or Are There Many?* (Dallas, TX, 1992). For an Ogden bibiliography, see Philip E. Devenish and George L. Goodwin (eds.), *Witness and Existence: Essays in Honor of Schubert M. Ogden* (Chicago, 1989).

39 Tracy, "Defending the Public Character of Theology," in James M. Wall (ed.), *Theologians in Transition* (*Christian Century* "How My Mind Has Changed" series) (New York, 1981), pp. 113–24; "Theological Method," in Peter Hodgson and Robert King (eds.), *Christian Theology* (Philadelphia, PA, 1985), pp. 35–60; *Plurality and Ambiguity* (San Francisco, 1987); "The Uneasy Alliance Reconceived: Catholic Theological Method, Modernity, and Postmodernity," *Theological Studies* 50 (1989), pp. 548–70; *Dialogue with the*

Other (Grand Rapids, MI, 1990); "Kenosis, Sunyata, and Trinity: A Dialogue with Masao Abe," in John B. Cobb and Christopher Ives (eds.), *The Emptying God: A Buddhist–Jewish–Christian Conversation* (Maryknoll, NY, 1990), pp. 135–54; "Approaching the Christian Understanding of God," in Francis Schüssler Fiorenza and John P. Galvin (eds.), *Systematic Theology: Roman Catholic Perspectives* (Minneapolis, MN, 1991); *The Fascination of Evil* (London, 1998). See also Steven Webb's bibliography in Werner G. Jeanrond and Jennifer L. Rike, *Radical Pluralism and Truth: David Tracy and the Hermeneutics of Religion* (New York, 1991).

40 For critical appreciations of process theology by this generation, see Ogden, "The Experience of God"; Tracy, "Theological Method" and "Kenosis, Sunyata, and Trinity," pp. 136–8; Farley, "Theocentric Ethics as a Genetic Argument," in Harlan R. Beckley and Charles M. Swezey (eds.), *James M. Gustafson's Theocentric Ethics* (Macon, GA, 1988), pp. 39–62 and *Good and Evil*, p. xx; Devaney's and Cobb's reviews of Kaufmann's *In Face of Mystery* in *Religious Studies Review* 20 (1994), pp. 171–81.

41 This and the next paragraphs are a summary of discussions and (more often) allusions our representatives make to each other in the texts cited above, reviews, and a set of unpublished responses of Farley and Kaufman and Tracy to each others' work at a 1982 meeting of the American Academy of Religion. The reviews include Edward Farley, "A Revisionist Model [on Tracy]," *Christian Century* 93 (1976), pp. 371–3; Gordan D. Kaufman [Review of Farley's *Ecclesial Man* and Tracy's *Blessed Rage for Order*], *Religious Studies Review* 2 (1976), pp. 7–12; "Conceptualizing Diversity Theologically [A review of Tracy's *The Analogical Imagination*]," *Journal of Religion* 62 (1982), pp. 392–401; *In Face of Mystery*, name index under Farley, Ogden, Tracy, and Whitehead. See also the essays in Sheila Greeve Devaney (ed.), *Theology at the End of Modernity: Essays in Honor of Gordon D. Kaufman* (Philadelphia, PA, 1991); Devenish and Goodwin, *Witness and Existence*; Jeanrond and Rike, *Radical Pluralism and Truth*.

42 Ronald F. Thiemann, *Revelation and Theology* (Notre Dame, IN, 1985).

43 For the renewed importance of Barth to the debate with liberals and revisionists, see Colin Gunton, *Becoming and Being: The Doctrine of God in Charles Hartshorne and Karl Barth* (New York, 1978); Sheila G. Devaney, *Divine Power: A Study of Karl Barth and Charles Hartshorne* (Philadelphia, PA, 1986); Michael Welker, "Barth's Theology and Process Theology," *Theology Today* 43 (No. 3, October, 1986), pp. 383–97; and *Universalität Gottes und Relativität der Welt. Theologische Cosmologie im Dialog mit dem amerikanische Theologie nach Whitehead* (2nd edn. Newkirchen-Vluyn, 1988).

44 William A. Christian, Sr., *Doctrines of Religious Communities* (New Haven, CT, 1987).

45 Alasdair MacIntyre, *Three Rival Versions of Moral Enquiry: Encyclopedia, Genealogy, and Tradition.* Gifford lectures 1988 (Notre Dame, IN, 1990). For more directly theological criticisms of process theology from a "Thomist" perspective, see David Burrell, *Aquinas: God and Action* (Notre Dame, IN, 1979), ch. 6; W. Norris Clarke, *The Philosophical Approach to God: A Neo-Thomist Perspective* (Winston-Salem, NC, 1979), ch. 3; and "Charles Hartshorne's Philosophy of God: A Thomistic Critique," in Santiago Sia (ed.), *Charles Hartshorne's Concept of God* (Dordrecht, 1990), ch. 7.

46 David Kelsey, "Human Being," in Peter Hodgson and Robert King (eds.), *Christian Theology* (Philadelphia, PA, 1985), ch. 6; Fergus Kerr, *Theology After Wittgenstein* (Oxford, 1986); Charles Taylor, *Sources of the Self: The Making of the Modern Identity* (Cambridge, MA, 1989).

47 John Milbank, *Theology and Social Theory: Beyond Secular Reason* (Oxford, 1990).

48 Kaufman, *Theology for a Nuclear Age*, p. 32; Ogden, *The Reality of God*, p. 10; Tracy, *Plurality and Ambiguity*, ch. 5.

49 See Thomas F. Tracy, "Enacting History: Ogden and Kaufman on God's Mighty Acts," *Journal of Religion* 64 (1984), pp. 20–36; Kathryn Tanner, Review of Edward Farley, *Divine Empathy*, *Modern Theology* 14 (1998), pp. 555–61 ("Farley's effort is less a mediating one than simply a development of classical theism").

50 Cobb, *Beyond Dialogue*; Kaufmann, "God and Emptiness," *Buddhist–Christian Studies* 9 (1989), pp. 175–87; Tracy, "Kenosis, Sunyata, and Trinity"; Ogden, "Faith in God and the Realization of Emptiness," in John B. Cobb and Christopher Ives (eds.), *The Emptying God: A Buddhist–Jewish–Christian Conversation* (Maryknoll, NY, 1990), pp. 125–42.

51 For example, William Hill, *The Three-Personed God* (Washington, DC, 1982). For a critique of liberal and revisionist proposals in relation to the classic doctrine of the Trinity and truth, see Bruce C. Marshall, *Trinity and Truth* (Cambridge, 2000).

52 Walter Lowe, "Christ and Salvation," in Peter Hodgson and Robert King (eds.), *Christian Theology* (Philadelphia, PA, 1985), ch. 8; Bruce Marshall, *Christology in Conflict: The Identity of a Saviour in Rahner and Barth* (Oxford, 1987).

Bibliography

Primary

Cobb, John B., Jr., *A Christian Natural Theology* (Philadelphia, PA, 1964).
—— *Christ in a Pluralistic Age* (Philadelphia, PA, 1975).
Farley, Edward, *Ecclesial Reflection: An Anatomy of Theological Method* (Philadelphia, PA, 1982).
—— *Divine Empathy: A Theology of God* (Minneapolis, MN, 1996).
Hartshorne, Charles, *The Divine Relativity* (New Haven, CT, 1948).
—— *The Darkness and the Light* (New York, 1990).
Kaufman, Gordon, *Theology for a Nuclear Age* (Philadelphia, PA, 1985).
—— *In Face of Mystery: A Constructive Theology* (Cambridge, MA, 1993).
Ogden, Schubert M., *The Reality of God and Other Essays* (Dallas, TX, 1992).
—— *On Theology* (Dallas, TX, 1992).
Tracy, David, *The Analogical Imagination* (New York, 1981).
—— *Plurality and Ambiguity* (San Francisco, 1987).
Whitehead, Alfred North, *Religion in the Making* (New York, 1926).
—— *Adventures of Ideas* (New York, 1967).

Secondary

There is an abundance of good secondary literature, so that even introductory recommendations are rather arbitrary. There are ongoing discussions and reviews of the above authors in *Religious Studies Review, Journal of Religion, Process Studies*, and *Theological Studies.*
Ahlstrom, Sydney E., *A Religious History of the American People* (New Haven, CT, 1972).
Cobb, John B. and Griffin, David Ray, *Process Theology: An Introductory Exposition* (Philadelphia, PA, 1976).
Dorrien, Gary, *The Making of American Liberal Theology: Idealism, Realism, and Modernity* (Louisville, KY, 2003).
Hodgson, Peter and King, Robert (eds.), *Christian Theology: An Introduction to Its Traditions and Tasks*, 2nd edn. (Philadelphia, PA, 1985).
Macquarrie, John, *Twentieth-Century Religious Thought* (New York, 1981).

THE CONTEMPORARY SCENE:
REAPPROPRIATING TRADITIONS

Postliberal Theology

James Fodor

Introduction

Postliberal theology names an internally highly differentiated movement in contemporary English-speaking theology (primarily in North America and Britain) whose aims are chiefly (1) faithful yet creative retrieval of the Christian tradition; (2) ecumenically open renewal of the church; and (3) compassionate healing and repair of the world. George Lindbeck and Hans Frei are the two seminal figures of this distinctive kind of theological engagement. Other exponents – and this is a representative not an exhaustive list – include Stanley Hauerwas, Ronald Thiemann, James Buckley, Joseph DiNoia, Garrett Green, George Hunsinger, William Werpehowski, Bruce Marshall, William Placher, Kathryn Greene-McCreight, Serene Jones, Joseph Mangina, Eugene Rogers, and Kathryn Tanner. In its more recent developments and permutations the list may be extended to include, on the one hand, figures like John Milbank, Catherine Pickstock, and Graham Ward and, on the other, Peter Ochs,[1] David Ford, and Daniel Hardy. To be sure, not all of the above would feel entirely comfortable accepting the appellation "postliberal" as a self-description, nor would they necessarily see themselves being classified together, let alone advancing a common cause. Exponents of postliberal theology are thus not finally reducible to "postliberalism" – which is to underscore its character as "a radical movement within a larger tradition."[2] As a term of art, "postliberal theology" surfaced soon after the appearance of Lindbeck's *The Nature of Doctrine: Religion and Theology in a Postliberal Age* (1984) and has since steadily gained in currency.

The intellectual influences shaping and informing postliberal theology are as diverse and varied as are its practitioners. Major impetuses include but are not limited to: the theology of Karl Barth; new appropriations of Martin Luther and Thomas Aquinas (principally inspired by the *nouvelle théologie* – a renewal within the Catholic Church to return critically to the sources of the faith in scripture and premodern tradition in light of contemporary needs); developments in the philosophy of science, especially the work of Thomas Kuhn and Michael Polanyi; new directions in philosophy of language indebted to Ludwig Wittgenstein and Gilbert

Ryle; an appreciation of recent sociological analyses and insights, principally those of Peter Berger and Robert Bellah; advances in the field of anthropology, specifically Clifford Geertz; recent work in narrative and narrative analysis from literary (Eric Auerbach, Frank Kermode), biblical (Michael Fishbane, Moshe Greenberg), and philosophical (Alasdair MacIntyre) perspectives.

Postliberal theology is occasionally referred to as intratextual or narrative theology, given its crucial emphasis on biblical narrative. It is also sometimes called the Yale school or the new Yale school of theology – historically signaling one of its important wellsprings: Yale University Divinity School. Postliberal theology's rapidly widening reception, but also its own internal evolution and transformation, means that it is now less directly affiliated with Yale, even though it continues to acknowledge many debts to that legacy. Whatever unity and cohesiveness postliberal theology possesses is achieved more by way of family resemblances than by a single feature or agenda. Postliberal theology is more accurately construed as a movement rather than a school, since much of its work proceeds by means of collaborative engagements in interrelated projects of doctrinal construction rather than through individual, "autonomous" scholarship.

Survey

In brief:

1   Postliberal theology represents a postcritical "journey to regain an inheritance" (i.e., a retrieval and redeployment of premodern sources in characteristically "unmodern" ways to meet today's challenges).
2   It self-consciously engages and reflects upon theology's tasks in relation to its ecclesial settings (borrowing but also adapting previously unavailable conceptual tools from the social sciences, especially in their descriptive aspects, to articulate how texts and readers interact).
3   It deploys narrative as a key category, promoting thereby a distinctively Christian form of intratextuality and a hermeneutics of social, ecclesial embodiment in service to the practical tasks of living the Christian life. Concretely embodying scripture in ecclesially appropriate ways stands in contrast to theologies which attempt to "lift" from the text certain teachings or moral truths in a manner that leaves the Bible behind, albeit as a necessary but finally dispensable resource, on the way to the "true meaning" of faith.
4   It emphasizes the peculiar grammar of Christian faith, concentrating on its scriptural logic and the regulative role of doctrine with a view to sustaining communities of "native speakers" facing diverse pressures (internal and external) that would weaken that competency, threaten the church's identity or otherwise distract it from its central mission as one of communal witness and service.
5   It allocates to theology a primarily corrective rather than constitutive function. Theology's aim is to repair, correct, and sustain rather than constitute Christian language-games. Its aim is not fundamentally to alter the ways or modes in which scripture is read and appropriated, but instead "to identify and correct errors by first-order interpretation's own implicit standards."[3] Much like a linguist

would study a natural language with a view to articulating its grammar and formulating rules of good or "proper" usage, so too the theologian investigates the first-order use of scripture in the faith community (in worship, prayer, preaching, catechesis, piety, and life) in order to generate "second-order concepts and theories which make maximum sense of these actual practices."[4]

6 It exhibits a distinctively Protestant flavor that yet is open to Catholic, Anglican, and Orthodox inflections in ways that promote comparative work of a reconciling, ecumenical nature within Christianity but also among the Abrahamic traditions.

7 It espouses a non-essentialist approach to religions (the belief that there is no universal "core" or "essence" that all religions share). Affirming and attending to the material specificities and irreducible differences among religions, rather than trying to "dissolve" them into a single commonality, helps check, on the one hand, proclivities toward supersessionism (the view that Christianity "fulfills" and thus surpasses and supplants Judaism by rendering it obsolete) and encourages, on the other, genuine interchange and mutual understanding. For instance, appreciating the ongoing differences between Judaism and Christianity, despite their joint witness to the one God, helps Christian theologians better understand not only the possibility but also the necessity of developing an Israel-like understanding of the church.

8 It adopts a non-foundational epistemological posture, committing itself to offering pragmatically superior and theologically fructifying conceptual redescriptions of the Christian faith, instead of attempting to ground those claims on purportedly universal principles or structures that can be accessed in a "neutral" and "objective" (i.e., framework-independent) manner. Taking Matthew 7: 16 ("By their fruits you will know them") as a guiding insight means that the rational coherence and credibility of faith exhibits itself more in terms of good performance and competent execution – as might be discerned, for example, in the gifted actor, the skilled craftsman, or the adept writer – than by conformity to independently formulated criteria. Because faith's rational qualities are more akin to tacit, unformalizable skills whose norms are too rich and subtle to be exhaustively specified in any general theory of reason or knowledge, religions' intellectual content calls out for practical display (how effectively they contribute to the gathering and up-building of communities of faith) rather than speculative "resolution."[5]

9 It sees its primary task as descriptive rather than apologetic. Energies are concentrated more on explicating the internal structures and logic of Christian life than on translating them into contemporary idioms and thought patterns, especially if the aim of translation is to solicit approval and/or legitimation. Whenever apologetic engagements are pursued, they are done in a non-systematic, *ad hoc* fashion – as the occasion arises, in connection with a particular issue, relative to a specific context, with respect to particular interlocutors.

George Lindbeck

Perhaps the most widely read and cited account of this distinctive type of theological engagement is Lindbeck's *The Nature of Doctrine*. To herald this work as a manifesto or the Magna Carta of postliberal theology, as some have done, is both unwarranted and misleading. At most it outlines a limited "programmatic proposal" concerning specific methodological ("pretheological") issues. Originally conceived as "a prolegomenon to a more substantive study" in comparative dogmatics,[6] this slim volume is set squarely within an ecumenical matrix and emerges, after long gestation, out of Lindbeck's growing dissatisfaction with the received ways of conceiving Christian doctrine. Doctrinal reconciliation of historically divided Christian confessions is clearly Lindbeck's chief motivating interest; nevertheless, the book appeals to a much wider audience principally because of the deep structural similarities drawn between theories of doctrine and theories of religion. At the risk of oversimplifying a highly complex array of views both within and without Christianity, Lindbeck ventures a threefold typology, each type of which endeavors to explain how religious doctrines actually work.

Two approaches that dominate modernity are the "propositionalist" and the "experiential–expressivist" models, respectively. According to the former, doctrines function as "informative propositions or truth-claims about objective realities." A doctrine's truth or falsity can thus be measured, independently of the subjective dispositions of those uttering it, by reference to certain facts or states of affairs. The "experiential–expressivist" model, by contrast, interprets doctrines entirely in subjectivist terms as "non-informative and non-discursive symbols of inner feelings, attitudes, or existential orientations." On Lindbeck's own preferred "cultural–linguistic" model, a doctrine's primary (only?) function is to articulate "communally authoritative rules of discourse, attitude, and action."[7]

Consider the Christian claim "Jesus is Lord." On Lindbeck's cultural–linguistic model this doctrinal affirmation operates as a rule, a second-order directive guiding and informing Christian practice – specifically, how rightly to speak, think, feel, and act in ways that cohere and are consistent with Christian convictions as a whole. "Always align whatever you desire, say, and do such that your life conforms to the mind of Christ" might be one way to articulate that rule. Notice that here the claim "Jesus is Lord" is not interpreted, as in the other models, as a first-order statement about objective facts (the "propositionalist") or subjective feelings (the "experiential–expressivist"), although it clearly entails both. Any attempt, therefore, to determine the veracity of "Jesus is Lord" by investigating its cognitive/ propositional content or by surveying those uttering it to see how well it captures their interior feelings or dispositions, is logically and conceptually confused. Making true or false assertions about God and his relations to ourselves or the world is not doctrine's chief function, but to offer direction and guidance regarding our dispositions, actions, and speech about God – including how to repair and/or correct past Christian abuses of the rule. Hence, the Christian crusader's use of "Jesus is Lord" "to authorize cleaving the skull of the infidel" proves false because deployed in a manner that "contradicts the Christian understanding of Lordship as embodying . . . suffering servanthood."[8]

Propositionalists can easily account for doctrinal constancy, but not doctrinal change; experiential–expressivists face the opposite problem: they can readily account for change, but are at a loss to explain doctrinal constancy. The superiority of a cultural–linguistic or rule-governed approach shows itself in several respects:

1   It does greater justice to the permanency and normativity intrinsic to authoritative church teaching by differentiating between what changes and what remains the same in doctrinal matters.

2   It encourages a certain pragmatic tentativeness in the use of philosophical concepts to explicate faith, since rule-following does not compel allegiance to any particular metaphysical outlook or allegiance to particular ontological beliefs, thereby honoring and upholding God's mystery.

3   It better accounts for the phenomena of doctrinal development (how new doctrines can arise over time), devolution (how old doctrines can become marginalized or forgotten altogether), and ecumenical reconciliation (how doctrines that once contradicted each other can be reconciled and yet retain their identity).

There is, on the cultural–linguistic account, no *direct* way to judge religious claims "true" or "false." Unlike other perspectives, the cultural–linguistic approach proposes no common framework within which to compare religions or distinct positions within a religion. One can only judge the truth of religious statements *indirectly* and *holistically* according to a pragmatic criterion of "fruitfulness." The "categorial adequacy" of a religious language must be complemented by the "intrasystemic coherence" as exhibited by its correlative forms of life. Given the fact that these criteria are both preconditions and tests for truth, determining the adequacy of these criteria is at once a linguistic and a practical undertaking. Does the grammar and vocabulary of this religion in the long run open the community to a richer, more abundant life of faithfulness to God? Or does it lead to a life increasingly self-centered, constricted, and mendacious?

To be sure, the intrasystemic truth of religious utterances does have ontological import; religious utterances do in fact "refer" and "correspond to" reality. But the character of that correspondence results not from features intrinsic to religious statements considered in and of themselves; that would be to espouse a vulgar, rationalistic sense of correspondence reducible to propositions. Correspondence is better construed in terms of the roles religious statements play in "constituting a form of life, a way of being in the world, which itself corresponds to the Most Important, the Ultimately Real."[9] Lindbeck's cultural–linguistic model, then, does make room for (although it does not require) a modest cognitive realism, a view of truth as an "adequation of the mind to the thing." But it does so with the proviso that the isomorphism between the statement and the reality is fundamentally performatory in nature and thus "must be pictured as part and parcel of a wider conformity of the self to God."[10] Truth as correspondence thus retains its significance for a cultural–linguistic model despite that model's understanding of truth as primarily categorial rather than propositional.

The upshot is that on a cultural–linguistic model, which construes religions as narratively embodied "comprehensive interpretive schemes," assessing truth-claims invariably and unavoidably occurs within the orbit of specific scriptural texts. Scripture structures and shapes "the entirety of life and thought,"[11] which means that the one and only true world for Christians can be none other than the world of the Bible. Moreover, since there can be no reality antecedent to the reality presented by the scriptural text, the task of theology remains "intratextual": it "redescribes reality within the scriptural framework rather than translating scripture into extrascriptural categories. It is the text, so to speak, which absorbs the world, rather than the world the text."[12] Christian faith's comprehensiveness, central importance, and unsurpassability – formal features characteristic of traditional conceptions of truth – are thus congruent with the pan-absorbing power of the scriptural text. At this juncture, Lindbeck's work draws significantly on Hans Frei, his longtime colleague and conversation partner.

Hans Frei

Hans Frei's contributions to postliberal theology are incontestably enormous. Two of the most central are his work in recovering the importance of scriptural narrative for theology and, concurrently, acknowledging in Christology "identity" over "presence."

In *The Eclipse of Biblical Narrative* (1974), Frei maps out in rich detail how a subtle yet profound transformation in historical consciousness over the last three hundred years has led to the concealment, if not the utter effacement, of scriptural narrative. The predominant way Christians acquired their self-understanding prior to the developments in eighteenth and nineteenth-century theology – which for Frei represents the high-water mark in this extraordinary sea-change – was by locating themselves within the overarching story of the Bible. It was the Bible's grand sweep – beginning with creation, moving through a long convoluted history of redemption, and culminating in the final consummation – that provided the church with its basic frame of reference but also the indispensable resources (conceptual, logical, symbolic, and imaginative) by which to live out its life in the world. Throughout most of the church's history, the Bible was regarded as offering "a coherent world of discourse in its own right, whose depictions and teachings had a reality of their own"; it was a world into which everything, in one way or another, was made to fit.[13] Christian life thus unfolded "within a story" and the Bible was read – literally, but also figurally and typologically – as a self-interpreting text.

Frei contends that the Bible is best read as "realistic narrative," to borrow a category from Eric Auerbach (*Mimesis*, 1953). On this account, narrative form and meaning are inseparable, such that whatever the Bible means emerges as "a function of the interaction of character and circumstances."[14] The meaning *is* the story itself – which is another way of asserting that the narrative structure of scripture is never superfluous or ancillary; it is not merely *illustrative* of "an intellectually presubsisting or preconceived archetype or ideal essence."[15] Its meaning, rather, is "*constituted* through the mutual, specific determination of agents, speech, social context, and circumstances that form the indispensable narrative web."[16] The Bible's narrative shape is thus integral to and indispensable for faith. "Realistic and figural reading . . . [allows] the reader to be incorporated and thus located in the world made accessible by the narration."[17] To be sure, scripture's meaning includes, even though it is not reducible to, its historical referents. Moreover, while the language of the Bible is certainly translatable into other idioms, the transposition of scripture's meaning into an alien conceptual scheme cannot be made without significant loss and/or distortion.

Regardless of their preferred interpretive strategies, modern theology invariably ends up encompassing scripture within a "larger framework or category of explanation."[18] For example, liberal theologians seek the "real" meaning of the Bible in transcendent truths about God and humanity, while conservative and fundamentalist theologians search for scripture's "real" meaning in its ostensive, factual referents. Either way, the world in which we now exist is no longer the biblical stories' world. A "great reversal" has thus taken place all across the theological spectrum: interpretation has become "a matter of fitting the biblical story in to another story."[19] Accommodating the Bible to a more determinative framework effectively robs scripture of its own reality-constituting powers, either by transforming it into a *source* for historical reconstruction of past events or reducing it to simply one more *instantiation* of timeless, universal symbols or general qualities of human experience. A theology that remains scripturally faithful, by contrast, is one which recognizes the Bible as "a world with its own linguistic integrity, much as a literary art work is a consistent world in its own right," but with one important proviso: "unlike any other depicted world [scripture] is the one common world in which we all live and move and have our being."[20]

Taking seriously scripture's reality-constituting powers also has deep implications for Christology. Frei demonstrates in *The Identity of Jesus Christ* (1975) how following scripture's logic in its narrative depiction of Jesus Christ accedes a certain priority to *identity* over *presence*. The order is crucial. For beginning, as many Christologies do, with "the often nagging and worrisome questions of *how* Christ is present to us and *how* we can believe in his presence," effectively ensnarls Christians in fruitless debates about how best to establish (i.e., mythically or historically) Jesus' "presence." Such foundational epistemological preoccupations are not only misleading, they also abdicate scripture's authority and allow other outlooks – idealist, phenomenological, etc. – to set the terms of Christian self-understanding.[21] Christians must instead attend first of all to the intention–action/subject–manifestation patterns (Gilbert Ryle) of the gospel narratives through which Jesus' presence is rendered. Only then can they ascertain, theologically and biblically, what Jesus Christ's presence "in" the church and "in" the world means.

Christians affirm that Jesus *is* the presence of God, but just as insistently that knowing Jesus' identity is the *same* as having him present or being in his presence.[22] Ascertaining Jesus' identity is thus identical with his being present – and this is uniquely the case, Frei argues, with respect to Jesus and the gospels. In a variation of Anselm's ontological argument, where if the definition of God is intelligible, then God must exist (since existence is necessary to God's definition), Frei contends that if the gospel stories are intelligible, then the one whose identity they render (Jesus) must also live.

Whether in matters of Christology or scriptural interpretation generally, Frei promotes habits of textual fidelity that reeducate and retrain Christians to think of the Bible less as a source to be used and more as a text to be indwelt. "Living in the world of the Bible" means assimilating extra-biblical realities into that world: scripturally encoding or textualizing the cosmos rather than somehow beginning independently with "reality" and then trying to make the Bible conform to it. Measuring scripture's veracity by its internal criteria as realistic narrative, not by criteria externally and "objectively" established, is not to eradicate the distinction between the biblical narrative and the "positioning perspective" of the interpreter. Rather, it is to refuse to concede any autonomous status to the latter. The text is logically distinct from its interpretation, but they are not separately available.

Lest one think Frei's argument divides into two antithetical options – indwelling the scriptural text or using it instrumentally to derive truths about a reality independently established – it must be remembered that the last decade of his life was spent trying to do justice to the complex overlappings and intersections of various theologies right across the theological gamut. Refusing to settle for an uncomplicated "either/or" between those who conceived of theology as a purely academic discipline and those who viewed it as an activity wholly internal to the Christian faith, Frei set forth a fivefold typology (from Gordon Kaufman and like-minded Kantians on one end, to D. Z. Philips and other "Wittgensteinian fideists" on the other).[23] Throughout Christian tradition the kinds of theology most faithful to scripture were those that variously combined and balanced the demands of the academy with those of the church. Frei's own approach, unsurprisingly, aligns with that of Barth, who accords a modest priority to theology's role in Christian community and whenever making forays into apologetics does so always in an *ad hoc* and never a systematic manner. Two of the more surprising features of Frei's typology, however, are how, first, the theological spectrum turns out to be more circular than linear and, second, how positions customarily seen as polar opposites turn out to be, in fact, proximate neighbors. For example, on Frei's typology, Kantians and Wittgensteinians come remarkably close, inasmuch as both proffer arguments why theology need not pay attention to philosophy. Likewise, of all the types identified, Schleiermachians and Barthians present, despite their historical divergences, the most promising second-order restatements of the Christian tradition. One of the indirect consequences of Frei's novel typologies is that they help locate important theologians (John Howard Yoder and P. T. Forsyth are but two examples) who do not otherwise appear on current intellectual maps.

Stanley Hauerwas

Postliberal theology is indebted to Stanley Hauerwas for helping work out some of its fundamental ethical and political implications. Taking up Frei's concentration on the primacy of scriptural narrative in determining Jesus' identity, Hauerwas extends this analysis to the church's self-understanding as a kind of prolongation of Christ's presence in the world. Embodying Christ in the world means that Christian identity *is* activity (not a mere precondition for it). That identity, moreover, is neither simple nor singular, but a communal accomplishment discovered and fashioned within the complex historical contingencies of an ongoing "story" of which Christians are clearly *not* the authors but to whose unfolding they nonetheless genuinely contribute.

Christian identity clearly requires narrative display, but this does not demand defending generalized claims about narrative beyond those specific to scripture. The first *scripture-specific* reason for narrative's importance is that apart from scripture's narratives it would be impossible to lead a life of Christian discipleship and virtue. Drawing on Alasdair MacIntyre's account of how "the Enlightenment project" has convinced us that jettisoning tradition is a necessary prerequisite if we are to be sovereign in our moral choices, Hauerwas contends that mainstream Christian theology has accepted modern liberalism's alluring but false story that we no longer have or need a determinative tradition.[24] Liberalism's story that we have no story is deceptively pernicious because in the name of liberation it severs the church's vital connections to resources indispensable for living the Christian moral life. Divorced from the wealth of logical, conceptual, symbolic, and imaginative reserves that is a community's tradition, moral agents find themselves deprived of the content but also the criteria necessary to make genuine moral decisions. Far from imprisoning Christians, shackling them in unfreedom by disallowing the exercise of full rational moral choices, tradition provides the essential conditions for the exercise of moral freedom rightly so called.

Second, narrative is crucial for the moral life because without it Christian character lacks a means of display, development, or correction. Deprived of scriptural narrative one is at a loss to understand how such virtues as constancy, patience, obedience, courage, and hope might be exhibited within the church or before a watching world.[25] Just as Christian preaching, catechesis, worship, and praise remain unintelligible aside from a storied world, so too Christian moral life lacks content, direction, and purpose if divested of its indispensable narrative qualities and structures. What Christians can best offer to the world in service to the God who has called them in Christ, therefore, is not to try to change it but to be the church. For only by being true itself in faith does the world stand a chance of recognizing itself as the world – which is the hope of salvation for both. Christians are called to live in the world and for the world, but without becoming the world.

Debate

Debates within and over postliberal theology are so complex as to defy any easy sorting out. Postliberal theology has clearly been subjected to vigorous opposition; what is not always apparent is whether these criticisms reflect real disagreement or simply misunderstanding. In some instances, critique has led to further clarification where postliberals disagree among themselves or have not yet worked out sufficiently the implications of their views. In others, dispute has generated more heat than light. Without pretending to do justice to the entire range of criticism, it is sufficient for present purposes to note some areas where energies are especially concentrated or where debate holds most promise of constructive developments.

Narrative

Virtually all exponents of postliberal theology emphasize the primacy of scriptural narrative for theology. While articulate and persuasive about scriptural narrative's fundamental importance, postliberals are not always as clear as they might be in (1) differentiating its properly cognitive significance from its pedagogical or aesthetic merits; (2) discriminating among the several ways the Bible constitutes a "habitable" or "followable" text, a guide to the faith community, and the sense in which narrative (as a literary form) constitutes the primary mode of this guidance; (3)

specifying how faith communities learn to indwell or inhabit the scriptural texts;[26] and (4) demarcating narrative's limits as well as its strengths.[27]

While rightly eschewing an unqualified endorsement of narrative *per se* (the idea that narrative form itself has special cognitive significance), postliberal theologians still need to account for the role of systematic discourse in theology without lessening their insistence on the indispensability of scriptural narrative. To be sure, scriptural narrative is capable of representing things that can be effectively represented in no other way, but this is not yet an argument for scriptural narrative's all-sufficiency. Even the catechetical (and perhaps also the apologetical) needs of the church require a kind and level of precision and systematization that narrative alone (as a literary form) is incapable of supplying. The tension thus generated between narrative and systematic discourse is something that postliberals need to expend more energies in sustaining. Because Christian faith makes claims of universal import (i.e., true always and everywhere – "non-temporally indexed," to use Griffiths' phrase), theology must be able to deploy "the abstract and denaturalized schemata of systematic discourse" as well as "the unsubstitutable specificities of narrative discourse" without interpreting the former as merely epiphenomenal of the latter.[28] Lindbeck's proposal that doctrine be limited to an *exclusively* regulative function may be seen as an attempt to reconstrue the church's need to address questions of a properly metaphysical sort as derivative of and thus subservient to its overarching narrative. Rejecting foundationalism, however, need not issue in a retreat from the deployment of systematic discourse, nor an evasion of the metaphysical questions spawned by that deployment. Because treatments of metaphysical questions are constitutive of theology, conceding that a cultural–linguistic approach *allows* for but does not *require* a modest cognitive realism may not entirely suffice. Postliberal theology needs to be more forthcoming, offering constructive suggestions about what such a cognitive, theological realism entails.

A related challenge concerns how the world of the Bible relates to other worlds. While postliberal theologians have made a very convincing case for the need to revive and sustain a scriptural imagination capable of deploying Christianity's most determinate narratives to make sense of the world, there is no clear consensus about how this "strange new world of the Bible" (Barth) relates to other worlds. How does the scriptural narrative impinge on what is "outside" it? Does the biblical narrative entirely supplant the contemporary world? Does it illuminate and transform it from within? Or does the encounter/confrontation between these worlds also raise prospects of mutual judgment and correction?

That the scriptural world "absorbs" all other worlds is, on one level, entirely understandable and unavoidable if Christianity is to retain its distinctive identity.[29] But the territorial and implicitly static cast of the controlling image of a framework into which all else must be "absorbed" or "inserted," not to mention the *unilinear direction* of that takeover, is worrying. Whenever the church attempts to interpret the world within its own scriptural framework – "absorb" it into itself, so to speak – there is, hopefully, a moment of critical self-discovery. "In judging the world, by its confrontation of the world with its own dramatic script, the church also judges itself: in attempting to show the world a critical truth, it shows itself to itself as church also."[30] The church can do no other than interpret the world in terms of its own foundational narratives; but what is often overlooked is the way that the very act of interpreting affects the narratives as well as the world.[31] Postliberal theology must do greater justice in future to characterizing this reciprocity and mutual correction. Unless postliberal theologians articulate with greater specificity how the scriptural world is not also judged and "corrected" by that encounter with the world it attempts to absorb, and if it does not accord a central place to the church's mission as one of *diakonia* (service) – service that takes the form of engagement and solidarity, a willingness to listen and respond, even and especially if that response be one of repentance – then the movement is in danger of betraying its own best insights.

The moments of critical self-discovery that arise when the church attempts to "absorb" the world into its own scriptural framework, is not the only benefit the church receives. Positively and constructively, these occasions of "world absorption" also exercise and enlarge the church's virtues of generosity and hospitality. Allowing one's own world to be tested by another in part involves discerning whether and to what extent other discourses can be at home in one's own theology. Cultivating a convivial disposition, fostering habits of hospitality and generosity, are thus ingredients to postliberal theology. The experience of "being returned to the scriptural text afresh by its own legacy as appropriated outside the theological community"[32] is one to which Christian theology must constantly remain open. Here, Christian virtues of patience and forgiveness, espoused by Hauerwas and others, but also a Spirit-guided reticence about forcing "the language and behavior of others into Christian categories prematurely, remembering that our own understanding of those categories themselves is still growing and changing," is especially appropriate.[33] Absent the exercise of such virtues, the assimilative powers of the scriptural narrative predominate, such that the manner of "absorption" becomes uncritical, wholesale, and hostile.

This complaint has been registered against Radical Orthodoxy, a movement recently (1997) spear-headed by John Milbank, Catherine Pickstock, and Graham Ward, that shares postliberal theology's non-foundational approach and stress on the unsurpassability of scriptural narrative, but which differentiates itself from postliberal theology by its peculiar mixture of premodern theology, postmodern philosophy, and radical ("left-wing") politics. When the assimilative powers of the scriptural text become *the* measure of its "reasonableness," and when the "reasonableness" is rhetorically recast in terms of the scriptural world's unchallengeable capacity to "out-narrate" or "out-wit" all other worlds, then, critics claim, little place is left in which to register resistance or exhibit repentance, let alone receive the benefits of mutual judgment and correction.

Texts and/or communities of readers?

How does Frei's early insistence that the biblical *text* be read as "realistic narrative" relate to his avowal, later in life, that the most faithful way of reading scripture is to be had only in *community* (i.e., a "literal reading" consistent with long-established ecclesial practice)? Are authoritative readings of scripture more a function of some feature(s) of the texts themselves or of how its principal community of its readers has more or less consistently understood them over time? If the latter, which church community, exactly, do postliberals have in mind? Lindbeck seems to emphasize that it is "the historically mainline churches" who are "the ecclesial bearers of the great tradition."[34] What contributions, if any, might historically marginalized Christian communities contribute to the "literal reading" of scripture? The relative coherence of narrative presents a separate but related issue. Deconstructionist and postmodern approaches emphasize the instability and indeterminacy of texts, challenging all grand narratives and raising doubts about appeals to *the* biblical narrative. Explicating more fully narrative's "concordant discordance" or "discordant concordance" (Paul Ricoeur) – both as a literary genre and as an internally plural and differentiated sociality – remains an ongoing challenge to postliberal theology.

Truth

The question of truth looms large in postliberal theology. To be sure, much of postliberal theology's polemic against existing theories of truth serves a wider agenda of correction, reform, and repair – which does *not* include setting up an alternative account of theological truth. Nevertheless, it is incumbent upon postliberals to become clearer on these matters than they have sometimes been. Frei in particular readily acknowledged the validity of asking of the gospels historical questions involving ontological reference such as, "What actually happened at Jesus' resurrection?," even though he was convinced that a historical answer could not fully account for the resurrection. Similarly, Lindbeck willingly recognizes the ontological import of Christian doctrinal truth-claims and the need to make room for a "modest cognitivism" – one offering a *limited or qualified* correspondence notion of truth as inspired by Aquinas' distinction between the signified (*significatum*) and the human mode of signifying (*modus significandi*). As a whole, postliberals have been less than forthcoming on what a more full-bodied, *theological* account of truth looks like.

A major step in this direction has recently been made in Bruce Marshall's *Trinity and Truth*, which sets forth a constitutively Christological and propositional account of truth from a postliberal perspective. Marshall shows how Christians can confidently draw upon and learn from the best of pagan thought (analytical philosophical tradition, in this instance) with the hope that such thought will find "completion" by Christian concepts and categories. For Marshall, such completion is achieved, first of all, by showing how embracing distinctively Christian criteria for truth does not inexorably end in fideism (the view that a web of beliefs comprising a given religion cannot be tested by criteria external to itself). To the contrary, Christian criteria for truth and justification *enjoin* rather than simply *permit* engagement with alien claims, the very success of that engagement being evidenced in the way Christianity has, over its long history, deployed those categories and criteria, assimilating and learning from them. Constructively, Marshall argues for the epistemic role of the Holy Spirit, through whom Christians are empowered to understand but also give assent to the beliefs that have for them "unrestricted epistemic primacy." Marshall's theologically disciplined and trinitarian-shaped account of truth persuasively integrates the fundamental Christian conviction that truth is a person (Jesus) with a philosophically sound theory of truth.

John Milbank and Catherine Pickstock (*Truth in Aquinas*) challenge Marshall's account, but at the same time develop further the liturgical and aesthetic dimensions of truth Christianly conceived. Unlike Marshall, Milbank and Pickstock are not convinced that retrieving correspondence theories from secular theorists (Tarski/ Davidson) best serves a Christian account of truth. Instead, they re-read Aquinas within an Augustinian/Platonic framework where divine illumination and discursive argumentation serve as registers of different "intensities" on a single faith/ reason continuum. The result is an entirely different approach to truth, perhaps the most distinguishing feature of which is the way it "requires a completion of the theoretical ascent to truth with a meeting of the divine descent in liturgical practice." Participating in God's truth means that human ascent and divine descent meet preeminently in Eucharist whereby we, "as it were, unwittingly, through our artistic and liturgical attempts to praise the divine," construct God's truth. Following Aquinas, truth as adequation is a real relation, a proportion or harmony, that introduces an aesthetic dimension that is concurrently teleological, practical, and theoretical.[35]

Sectarianism or sharing Israelhood?

Failure to differentiate adequately the church's fundamental theological existence from its pragmatic or sociological efficacy frequently triggers heated and largely futile debates about the "sectarian" bias in postliberal theology. Critics often interpret Hauerwas' claim about the epistemological priority of the church[36] or Lindbeck's contention that in a radically de-Christianized world the church must become sharply distinguished from the society at large (sociologically sectarian) if it is to preserve its identity against "alien forces,"[37] as endorsing a kind of cultural isolationism and political quietism whereby the church effectively abdicates its social responsibility. The preservation of ecclesial identity is fine, critics concede, but loss of social relevance and political influence is simply too high a price to pay.

The theological issue here is finally about election and the scandal of Christian particularity. While the church's "separated" life is logically entailed in an intratextual, cultural–linguistic account of religion with its stress on particularity, the theological nub of the debate centers on God's jealous, elective love as enfleshed in Israel and the church. Christians see themselves within the Hebrew Bible (which, read Christologically, is the church's basic ecclesiological textbook) as "the messianic pilgrim people of God typologically shaped by Israel's story."[38] Together with Judaism, Christianity is part of "God's people who have been chosen for service, not preferment, bound together in a historically and sociologically continuous community that God refuses to disown."[39] The challenge for the church, then, is "to be comparably tenacious and flexible in maintaining its identity as a people irresistibly called (and ineluctably failing) to witness by selfless service of all humankind to the universal yet thoroughly particular God of Abraham, Isaac, Jacob, and Jesus."[40] Stripping itself of its supersessionist proclivities even as it appropriates or retrieves from Judaism a sense of Israelhood is thus an indispensable requirement of the postliberal church.[41]

Recasting the debate in terms of election and appropriated Israelhood may not alleviate all the worries of critics like James Gustafson, who persistently question the "tribalistic," "fideistic," and "sectarian" tendencies of postliberal ecclesiologies, but it has distinct benefits, the first of which is to clarify the character of Christian sectarianism *vis-à-vis* the church's theological servanthood. Given its status as God's elect people – and thus its mission (along with Judaism) of bearing corporate witness to the God who promises to bless through their seed all humankind – the church can give itself wholly to its "separated life" knowing that it is not pursued for its own sake, let alone in isolation, but for the world. Thus imbued with a spirit of service, the church is free to advance a sectarianism that is "Catholic" or "ecumenical" in character, rather than one that is narrowly self-centered, divisive, and schismatic.

The church's "separated life" is not unrelated to its diaspora status – which is, Christianity's long history notwithstanding, the rule rather than the exception. "The Bible does not anticipate that the church will ever be anything except a little flock until the end of time. From this point of view, majority rather than minority existence is anomalous for Christians."[42] Whether or not present circumstances makes "diaspora" existence more or less probable, or even necessary, it nonetheless ever remains an *open possibility* for the church (a prospect that critics are surprisingly unwilling to entertain). Postliberal theologians note how the passing of Christendom (where Christianity's hegemonic control of cultural and social power no longer obtains) constitutes a reminder that Christendom itself was an unintended consequence of the early church's success in attending to its own communal life and language, and that recovering the latter may well be possible only if it is concretely re-learned in diaspora. However, re-learning is not simply retrieving earlier lessons; for "only if a precritical interpretation of scripture can be postcritically appropriated in a non-supersessionist form will it be useful in contemporary pluralistic settings."[43] Learning again – and yet, peculiarly, for the first time – Israel's story as ingredient to the gospel, may make it "increasingly important for the churches to turn for instruction to Judaism, for Jews learned much about faithful survival in hostile societies during the long *galut*; Christians need comparable lessons now that they are themselves becoming a worldwide diaspora."[44]

In re-learning these important lessons, Christianity may also, hopefully, recover corrective, critical voices by engaging other religious traditions. Indeed, one of the distinct advantages of making analogical comparisons among the Abrahamic traditions (Judaism and Christianity in this case), is that in retrieving an Old Testament understanding of itself as a shared Israelhood, the church becomes cognizant of but also, indirectly, equipped to challenge "the Christian tendency to polarize collectivism and individualism, this-worldliness and other-worldliness, extramural concern for humanity as a whole and intramural attention to the elect community."[45] Gustafson and other critics may not be fully satisfied with the "critical edge" thus gained to challenge Christianity's tendency to dichotomize "extramural concern for humanity as a whole and intramural attention to the elect community." Nonetheless, such engagement effectively exposes the terms of the discussion Gustafson simply assumes as normative; namely, a monistic political liberalism that purports to inhabit a vantage point outside any and every particular way of life or religious tradition. Assuming that adjudicating such polarities is done *only* from such a perspective minimizes and discredits the standards of judgment and discernment internal to religious traditions, on the one hand, and valorizes, on the other, those of another tradition (political liberalism), albeit not recognized as such.

Unencumbered by the need to ensure its own survival because God's elect, the church is, thirdly, liberated from pressures to justify itself to the world *on the world's terms*. To be sure, effecting change by virtue of majoritarian status or cultural prestige may be one way of advancing God's kingdom and/or measuring Christianity's social relevance and political influence. But it is not the only or perhaps even the best way in present circumstances. Furthering concrete, material changes for the good (justice, peace, and freedom for all) clearly matters in the church's mission, but as "out-workings" rather than "preconditions" of its fidelity. This is to construe the church's mission in terms of a communal analogue of justification by faith rather than to cede to political liberalism's utilitarian calculus of social effectiveness. It is as true for religious communities as it is for individuals that salvation is "not by works, nor is it faith for the sake of practical efficacy, and yet good works of unforeseeable kinds flow from faithfulness."[46] It is not part of the church's mission as servant-witness to guarantee the yield. Some cultivate, others plant, still others water; but God alone in his time "grants the increase."

Sponsoring a focally theological account of the church's "separated life" is not to preclude a sociological understanding; rather, it is to reposition it within a broader and more determinative theological vision. Still, the task of how best to deploy the church's social ethic in today's world remains, for postliberal theology, an ongoing challenge.

Achievement, Influence, and Agenda

Postliberal theology's contributions are best understood in terms of retrieval, repair, and renewal. Like the early Reformers, postliberals do not view themselves as carving out an alternative "school," but as a reforming movement in service to a wider theological enterprise. Its aims are principally corrective and ecumenically regenerative; its intention is to repair and upbuild, not replace and start afresh. Whether or not its account of foundationalism or its typologies ("propositionalist" and "experiential–expressivist") fully do justice to their opponents' positions, postliberals have nonetheless succeeded in raising awareness of the dangers of appealing to universal religious experience, but also the distortions accompanying accounts of Christian self-understanding based on foundational propositions.

Postliberal theology has contributed enormously to the reinvigoration of Christian ethics. Through its reaffirmation of scriptural narrative as integral to the church's self-identity; its redescription of doctrine as skill-based intelligibility acquired communally via apprenticeship to wise and virtuous exemplars, especially as that formation occurs within liturgical contexts; and its postcritical retrieval of premodern sources (Aquinas in particular), the language of "virtue," "character," and "narrative" are increasingly prominent in a discipline that has for the last several hundred years been thoroughly dominated by utilitarian and deontological outlooks.

Postliberal theology encourages a certain "generous orthodoxy" by underscoring the primarily corrective rather than constructive role of Christian doctrine. A cultural–linguistic, rule-governed approach to doctrine fosters a spacious, hospitable orthodoxy by opening up new ways for the church to retell in uncharted territory the self-same story of God's redemption. It permits multiple, distinct (sometimes irreconcilably distinct) "performance interpretations of scripture" without allowing diversity to fracture unity (i.e., turning differences into church-rupturing divisions). Attending carefully to the grammar of Christian communal discourse (past and present) enables postliberal theologians to identify doctrinal patterns that are distorting, misleading, or incoherent. Removing or otherwise attenuating these impediments that "the church has errantly let stand in the way of the reformational reading of scripture within the life of each Christian community" helps "release the mediating presence of God in the scriptural Word."[47]

The generosity exhibited by postliberal theology extends in principle and in practice beyond the church to other religions. Explicating the distinctive grammar of each religion, understanding it on its own terms rather than contorting and distorting it to fit the constraints of a purportedly universal idiom, encourages a certain "modesty and openness to dialogue, rather than proselytizing of, other religions."[48] Instead of translating each religion into a lowest common denominator as would be required by an "essentialist" view, energies are expended in renewing the grammatical faithfulness and intratextual integrity of each religion's discourse. Adherents are thereby better equipped to make fruitful analogical comparisons between their own and other religions with a view to mutual correction and illumination. Moreover, reciprocal benefit and correction need not come at the price of relinquishing a religion's claim to ultimate centrality, comprehensiveness, and unsurpassability. What is peculiar to postliberal theology, however, is not its concession that there may be important truths and realities "of which Christianity as yet knows nothing and by which it could be greatly enriched," but the scriptural reasoning through which those truths and realities are displayed.[49]

In retrieving the centrality of scripture for theology, postliberal theology has not restored the status quo ante – repristinating the historical Christian position where theologians were also *doctores sacrae paginae* (doctors of Holy Writ) prior to modernity's cordoning off of theology from the Bible into a separate guild. Rather, the restoration of scripture's centrality is accompanied by an extension that includes the Abrahamic traditions as a whole. The Society of Scriptural Reasoning – Jewish, Christian, and Muslim scholars reading together texts from their respective scriptural traditions – owes its vision and energies in large part to postliberal theology and represents a key development that has profoundly altered the character of the debate within Christian theology, not only about the role of other religions, but also its own self-understanding as always, already from the very outset, engaging other religions.

Postliberal theology helps overcome some of the polarities characteristic of modernity. Its "premodern yet postcritical" reading of scripture effects a *gestalt* shift that, simultaneously moving both backward and forward, advances theology beyond the liberal–conservative polarities of the last several hundred years.[50] That God alone is able to mediate the binaries and dualisms that typify modernity thus stands as one of postliberal theology's most abiding methodological insights.[51] That the "left" and the "right" alike struggle to make sense of postliberal theology's adoption and adaptation of avant-garde conceptualities along with a commitment to historic Christian faith, is indicative of how both remain entrapped within modernity's debilitating binaries (testimony, perhaps, to the accuracy of postliberalism's diagnosis if not its prescribed cure).

Postliberal theology further helps overcome the polarities of modernity as evidenced by the unhappy relationship between church and academy. The impasse between exponents of secular, academic study of religion and confessional, church-based study of theology is better tackled by challenging the common binarism resident in both cultures. Whether it is the churches' polarizing tendencies towards either liberal or anti-liberal Christianities, or the academy's struggle between foundationalist, positivistic rationalisms and anti-realist relativisms, the same agonistic dialectic animates both. The unending struggle between Enlightenment rationalism and romantic expressivism only serves to deepen rather than displace the dichotomy of "head" vs. "heart," reason vs. feeling, instinct and emotion. Postliberal theology attempts to do justice to the rational and the affective/conative dimensions of faith by affirming "the pneumatological grounding of the priority of practice."[52] Such a realignment is effected by shifting focus from a preoccupation with apologetics to a greater concentration on description, thereby meeting theology's academic as well as pastoral responsibilities. To the former, it pays tribute to theology's commitment as an academic discipline to the depiction of the normative "grammar" of the faith; to the latter, it recognizes theology's primary obligation as a pastoral practice to exercise fidelity to the Holy Spirit's guidance for upbuilding the churches' life.[53] Postliberal theology represents a methodological "third way" whereby "both church and academy can receive without abandoning their separate identities and inner disciplines."[54]

Extension and Supplementation of Postliberal Theology

One of the most promising indications of postliberal theology's continuing fruitfulness is its openness to developments that extend or supplement some of its enduring insights. For example, the Wittgensteinian-like construal of Christian doctrine as a set of cultural–linguistic, rule-governed practices correlative with peculiar forms of life stands in need of supplementation by a Peircean-type logic.[55] The latter assists in overcoming modernity's incapacitating polarities by articulating a form of scriptural reasoning that more fully explains how the church's historic practice of figural interpretation (including typology, metaphor, and the skilled use of analogical extensions – see David Burrell, Nicholas Lash, and David Dawson) both unifies and extends the plain sense of scripture. But the plain sense cannot be determined prior to the event of reading. "In Peirce's logical terms, the biblical plain sense is not fully determined, but remains intrinsically vague, which means that it displays its potential series of particular meanings, each of whose precise characterizations will become clear only on some future occasion."[56] "The strictly intratextual meaning of the cross, for example, is indefinite or vague (in Charles Peirce's sense of the term) until it is completed by such social–ritual–experiential enactments as taking up the cross, or bearing the cross, or being baptized into Christ's death so that we might rise with him."[57]

A second way that postliberal theology opens itself to supplementation is with regard to the development of forms of Spirit-guided, scriptural wisdom and discrimination placed in service to society and the needs of humanity. One step in this direction is David Ford's attempt to sketch the contours of a wisdom theology. By nature relational and communal (since acquired through apprenticeship to the wise within a transgenerational community), wisdom represents a distinctively premodern yet postcritically retrieved form of rationality or intelligibility. It is especially amenable to postliberal theology's emphasis on inhabiting the scriptural texts, but presses the issue further by asking how the scriptural world absorbs all other worlds. This process calls for a great deal of wisdom in practice, involving both "an intensive dimension" (longevity and durability) and "an extensive dimension" (adaptability, flexibility, and alertness to contingencies and change).[58] In many ways, postliberal theology's promise to engage in a deeper and more lively way with scripture as the church's primary premodern resource awaits fulfillment. One of the most promising trajectories is the attempt to describe how the institutional embodiment of wisdom in universities, colleges, and other social structures either fosters or impedes a certain kind of theological collegiality capable of reconnecting fundamental desires, dispositions, and methods of discernment *vis-à-vis* modernity and postmodernity.

Assessing postliberal theology's contributions, making full determination of its final yield, can only be made retrospectively and eschatologically. Nonetheless, several provisional signs of its early fruits (as outlined above) are encouraging and give reason for hope. Indeed, if success is measured less in terms of resolving theological problems and more in terms of generating productive tensions, the prospects of postliberal theology rendering service to a wider theological discussion into the foreseeable future remain strong.[59]

Notes

1   Ochs is an important postliberal Jewish voice with deep interests both in Frei and Lindbeck, but also in Peircean logic, the confluence of which has generated a fertile venture in scriptural reasoning.
2   Buckley, "Introduction," in Lindbeck, *The Church in a Postliberal Age*, viii.
3   Lindbeck, "Atonement and the Hermeneutics of Intratextual Social Embodiment," in Phillips and Okholm, *The Nature of Confession*, 224.
4   Ibid, 222.
5   Lindbeck, *The Church in a Postliberal Age*, 190.
6   Ibid, 197.
7   Lindbeck, *The Nature of Doctrine*, 16, 18, 19.
8   Ibid, 64.
9   Ibid, 65.
10 Ibid, 65.
11 Ibid, 32, 33.
12 Ibid, 118.
13 Frei, *The Eclipse of Biblical Narrative*, 90.
14 Ibid, 280.
15 Ibid, 280.
16 Ibid, 280.
17 Ibid, 199.
18 Ibid, 220.
19 Ibid, 130.
20 Frei, *Types of Christian Theology*, 161.
21 Frei, *The Identity of Jesus Christ*, 4.
22 Ibid, vii.
23 Frei, *Types of Christian Theology*, 1–7.
24 Hauerwas, in Berkman and Cartwright (eds.), *The Hauerwas Reader*, 250–1.
25 Hauerwas and Pinches, *Christians Among the Virtues*.
26 Nicholas Wolterstorff, "Living Within a Text," in Yandell, *Faith and Narrative*, 202–13.
27 Griffiths, "The Limits of Narrative Theology," in Yandell, *Faith and Narrative*, 217–36.
28 Ibid, 230.
29 Bruce Marshall, "Absorbing the World: Christianity and the Universe of Truths," in *Theology and Dialogue*, 69–102.
30 Rowan Williams, "Postmodern Theology and the Judgment of the World," in Burnham, *Postmodern Theology*, 95.

31 Ibid.
32 Ibid, 111, n. 2.
33 Ibid, 106.
34 Lindbeck, *The Church in a Postliberal Age*, 226.
35 Milbank and Pickstock, *Truth in Aquinas*, xiii, xiv, 5.
36 Hauerwas, in Berkman and Cartwright (eds.), *The Hauerwas Reader*, 90–110.
37 Lindbeck, *The Church in a Postliberal Age*, 97.
38 Ibid, 145.
39 Ibid, 8.
40 Ibid, 156.
41 Lindbeck, "What of the Future? A Christian Response," in Signer, *Christianity in Jewish Terms*, 357–66.
42 Lindbeck, *The Church in a Postliberal Age*, 94.
43 Ibid, 225.
44 Lindbeck, "What of the Future?" 365.
45 Ibid, 363.
46 Lindbeck, *The Church in a Postliberal Age*, 187–8.
47 Ochs, *Another Reformation*.
48 Lindbeck, *The Church in a Postliberal Age*, 81.
49 Ibid, 85.
50 Lindbeck, "Atonement," 240.
51 Ochs, *Another Reformation*.
52 Lindbeck, "Atonement," 225.
53 Ibid, 226.
54 Ochs, *Another Reformation*.
55 See Ochs, *Peirce, Pragmatism and the Logic of Scripture*.
56 Ochs, *Another Reformation*.
57 Lindbeck, "Atonement," 227.
58 David F. Ford, "The Blessing of Theology: God, Wisdom, and the Shaping of Christian Thought and Teaching in the Twenty-first Century." Opening lecture delivered at the "Practicing Theology Conference," Yale Divinity School, New Haven, CT, April 3–5, 2003.
59 Buckley, "Postliberal Theology: A Catholic Reading," 96.

Bibliography

Primary

Berkman, John and Michael Cartwright (eds.), *The Hauerwas Reader* (Durham, NC, 2001).
Frei, Hans W., *The Eclipse of Biblical Narrative* (New Haven, CT, 1974).
—— *The Identity of Jesus Christ* (Philadelphia, PA, 1975).
—— *Types of Christian Theology* (New Haven, CT, 1992).
—— *Theology and Narrative* (New York, 1993).
Hauerwas, Stanley and Charles Pinches, *Christians Among the Virtues* (Notre Dame, IN, 1997).
Lindbeck, George A., *The Church in a Postliberal Age*, James J. Buckley, ed. (Grand Rapids, MI, 2002).
—— *The Nature of Doctrine* (Philadelphia, PA, 1984).

Secondary

Buckley, James J., "Postliberal Theology: A Catholic Reading" in *Introduction to Christian Theology*, Roger A. Badham, ed. (Louisville, KY, 1996).
Burnham, Frederic B. (ed.), *Postmodern Theology: Christian Faith in a Pluralist World* (San Francisco, 1989).
Dawson, John David, *Christian Figural Reading and the Fashioning of Identity* (Berkeley, CA, 2002).
Frymer-Kensky, Tikva et. al. (eds.), *Christianity in Jewish Terms* (Boulder, CO, 2000).
Green, Garrett (ed.), *Scriptural Authority and Narrative Interpretation* (Philadelphia, PA, 1987).
Griffiths, Paul J., *Problems of Religious Diversity* (Oxford, 2001).
Journal of Scriptural Reasoning, www.etext.lib.virginia.edu/journals/ssr/.
Marshall, Bruce D. (ed.), *Theology and Dialogue* (Notre Dame, IN, 1990).
—— *Trinity and Truth* (Cambridge, 2000).
Milbank, John and Catherine Pickstock, *Truth in Aquinas* (Oxford, 2000).
Ochs, Peter. *Peirce, Pragmatism and the Logic of Scripture* (Cambridge, 1998).

—— *Another Reformation: Christian Postliberalism and the Jews* (forthcoming).

Phillips, Timothy R. and Dennis L. Okholm (eds.), *The Nature of Confession: Evangelicals and Postliberals in Conversation* (Downers Grove, IL, 1996).

Signer, Michael A. (ed.), *Christianity in Jewish Terms* (Boulder, CO: Westview Press, 2000).

Webster, John and George P. Schner (eds.), *Theology after Liberalism* (Oxford, 2000).

Yandell, Keith E. (ed.), *Faith and Narrative* (Oxford, 2001).

Systematic Theology after Barth: Jüngel, Jenson, and Gunton

John Webster

Introduction: The Legacy of Barth

From the late 1920s to the late 1960s, Barth was the commanding figure of European Protestant divinity. Since his death in 1968, his writings (bulked out over the years by a substantial body of posthumous material) have become the most considerable literary expression of Protestant dogmatic thought since the Enlightenment. Little wonder, then, that his thought has become epochal, such that his successors, even when they leave him behind, do their work "after Barth." Much would need to be discussed to explain how Barth came to acquire such stature. Among the factors would be: the way in which Barth's unique intellectual gifts and personal energies came to maturity in the early 1920s at a decisive moment of change in German-speaking Protestant theology and church life; his ability to interpret and direct that change through appeal to the doctrinal heritage of Reformed Christianity, and so to transform a gesture of defiance into an opportunity for construction; the sheer scale of his work, and the seemingly inexhaustible powers of description which he brought to it, most of all in the *Church Dogmatics*; the fact that his work rests on some theological principles of remarkable explanatory power, deeply pondered, fiercely defended, and relentlessly pursued (often against himself); a freedom to rethink doctrinal traditions from the ground up, yet to handle them with utter seriousness, generosity, and affection; a capacity to integrate biblical, historical, and dogmatic analysis with both the churchly and spiritual and the political and humane; and, not least, Barth's public presence in many of the major events of European Christianity in the period of his ascendancy. For these and other reasons, Barth was able to shape Protestant (and not only Protestant) theology and church life in its German-speaking heartlands and elsewhere, directly through his teaching and writings, indirectly through the influence of his thought on generations of theologians and pastors.

As is often the case with persons of considerable stature, the momentous character of Barth's achievement has meant that doing systematic theology in his wake has not proved an easy business. The discipline, of course, continues unabated in German Protestantism, where it retains a place of pride in the theological curriculum: the years since Barth's death have seen the publication of at least two dozen high-level comprehensive systematic theologies, Lutheran and Reformed. But Barth staked out the field with such decisiveness and expounded his views so authoritatively that those who follow him have had to discover ways of emerging from his shadow. Sometimes this has been accomplished by leaving behind Barth's rather traditionally nineteenth-century style of churchly systematic theology with a strong exegetical and historical component, and orienting theology to a different set of concerns (eschatological politics in the case of Moltmann, the hermeneutics of faith in the case of Ebeling). Sometimes resources have been found by working in a large and durable tradition in which Barth is only one feature (a notable example is Schlink's ecumenical dogmatics). Or, for those who have retained Barth's kind of church dogmatics, it has been necessary to work with a very different configuration of sources and norms and of doctrinal content: this last possibility is exemplified in Pannenberg's *Systematic Theology*, surely the most consequential Protestant account since Barth. Examination of any of these figures would be instructive in tracing the career of German Protestant divinity in the years after Barth's death (some are the subject of other chapters in this book). Here we look at the work of the Lutheran systematic and philosophical theologian Eberhard Jüngel, an eclectic thinker who both extends some of Barth's concerns and moves in some highly original directions.

Recent English-language systematic theology has been less overshadowed by Barth. The dominant conventions of mainstream academic theology in both the UK and North America have generally had a stronger interest in the experiential, practical, and intellectual phenomena of religion, have been more hospitable than Barth was to non-theological disciplines such as philosophy or religious studies, and have been more preoccupied with the explanatory and critical modes of theology than with the confessional or dogmatic. Moreover, the widespread prestige of critical social theory in North American religious academia and its derivatives has led many to set Barth to one side as probably the most consistent modern example of what is wrong with classical Christian doctrine. Further, the particular career of evangelical theology, both in North America and in Britain, especially its absorption with certain issues about the nature and authority of the Bible, has meant that Barth has not found a home in that strand of theology and church life to which he might naturally be thought to be companionable. It has thus proved easier for English-language systematic theology to work in relative independence from Barth's corpus. Nevertheless, Barth has exercised considerable influence on English-language Reformed theology (notably in Scotland and the US), and has been read with appreciation by those from a range of traditions who are concerned to promote a broadly orthodox and ecclesial theology, even when they have sought to move beyond his work. In this connection we consider two English-language systematic theologians for whom critical engagement with Barth has been formative: the American Lutheran Robert Jenson, and the English Reformed theologian Colin Gunton.

Eberhard Jüngel

Until recently Professor of Systematic Theology and Philosophy of Religion in the Protestant Theological Faculty in Tübingen, Jüngel was raised in the Stalinist GDR, studied under some of the leading figures of German theology in the 1950s, and taught in East Berlin and Zurich before moving to Tübingen. He has written extensively in many areas: New Testament, Christian doctrine and ethics, the theologies of Luther and Barth, and the history of philosophy. He is a renowned preacher and commentator on church and public life. His main contributions to date are in the areas of the doctrines of the Trinity and the work of Christ, and in the theology of justification. Jüngel is perhaps best considered as an informal systematic theologian. He has not published either a full dogmatics or studies which survey individual dogmatic articles. His approach is, rather, to develop themes from systematic theology, usually in relation to aspects of modern intellectual and moral culture. His account of the Christian faith is somewhat eclectic, and not derived simply from the topics, categories, or terms of classical dogmatics; in this, he differs from Barth, whose mind was profoundly shaped by those topics, categories, and terms, even when he deployed them with considerable freedom.

Jüngel is often considered to be a follower of Barth, and his interpretations of Barth's writings are justly admired. An early book, *God's Being is in Becoming*, remains a remarkably penetrating study of aspects of Barth's trinitarian theology, and subsequent studies did much to explain the deep theological concerns of Barth's late sacramental and ethical theology. Moreover, Barth has been a determinative influence on much of Jüngel's thought. Most of all, he finds in Barth a conception of Christian theology as a distinct field with its own integrity and proper modes of inquiry, and which does not require grounding in anything other than divine revelation. Formally, this presses Jüngel to resist any kind of theological idealism, in which conditions within the knower precede the object known; materially, it means the ordering of all Christian theology around the doctrine of God as its center. Further, again like Barth, Jüngel is insistent that the distinctive character of Christian beliefs about God, namely their trinitarian and incarnational content, must at all times be borne in mind in determining the nature of the divine being. He has learned much in this respect from Barth's emphasis that the essence of God is known in God's acts, for such an emphasis constitutes a blockage against speculation about the being of God underived from the economy of God's works, above all at the cross of Christ. And – particularly from Barth's later work – Jüngel has learned considerable resistance to anything which might suggest commonality of being between God and the world, since such assertions undermine the integrity of both God and creation. In all this, Barth's work has helped Jüngel frame the questions which he judges to be important, and has constituted a very major resource in answering them.

Yet Jüngel's project is by no means a simple continuation or adaptation of Barth. He has considerable independence of mind, and over the years has evolved a theological stance with a quite distinct character. In part, this results from his immersion in two other clusters of issues which have opened up for him areas of reflection beyond Barth. The first of these is the legacy of existential Lutheranism. Jüngel's first area of specialization was in New Testament studies and he was trained in the school of Bultmann, mediated to him through his *doktorvater* Ernst Fuchs. Fuchs took up Bultmann's theology of Christ's kerygmatic presence as Word and wedded it to a theory of language drawn from the later work of the philosopher Martin Heidegger. In this theory, language is not so much a symbol of reality but its real presence, an ontological happening or "speech event." Jüngel adopted this view, and, though he has refined it in later work, it remains a basic element of his thinking. Alongside this, he has been much impressed by the historical and systematic work of Gerhard Ebeling. Ebeling not only shared many of Fuchs' hermeneutical concerns, but also offered a restatement of Lutheran Christianity centered on the justifying Word of God and its effect in generating faith. Backed up by Ebeling's monumental labors as an interpreter of Luther, this bequeathed to Jüngel a fascination with a complex of themes: Word (the proclamation of Christ crucified in eschatological speech events); justification (expounded anthropologically as a declaration in which the being of the sinner is recreated); faith (understood as passive reception of the Word's saving effect). Such themes surface frequently in Jüngel's existential soteriology and anthropology, which, consequently, have a rather different character from Barth's more classically Reformed treatment, with its decidedly moral overtones.

Second, Jüngel has devoted considerable attention to the alienation of theology from modern philosophical culture, most of all in his magnum opus *God as the Mystery of the World*. In part, that work is devoted to showing how the incoherence of Christian response to philosophical challenge results from a theological failure to marshal the internal resources of Christian thought (above all, trinitarian resources) to meet its opponents. In this, Jüngel continues Barth's concern for theological integrity in extramural conversation, but with an important difference. Jüngel's history of modern culture is largely adopted from Heidegger, who provides him with the key episodes and figures (Descartes, German idealism, Nietzsche) to which theology must attend. Heidegger's interpretation of modernity is tragic, the story of the eclipse of truth which leaves modern culture in a deeply perilous situation; and Jüngel's account shares some of this anguish. Barth, on the other hand, was an immensely confident theologian who considered modernity as an episode – an important one, certainly, and one which adversely affected Christian theology, but only an episode, and not a determining condition. Barth could relativize modernity in this way because he thought of the texts and ideas of premodern Christianity not as a ruined past but as contemporary, and so he did not feel a strong necessity to preface constructive theological work by sorting out theology's relation to modern thought. Jüngel's particular configuration of interests is such that he feels the tug of modernity more sharply. Yet – like Barth – he resists apologetics, and is keen to demonstrate that the deity generated in the course of defending theistic belief is the problem, not the solution.

From the great variety of Jüngel's interests, three representative concerns can be identified: revelation and the theology of the word; the cross and the doctrine of the Trinity; and justification in relation to theological anthropology.

Jüngel's is a theology of the revelatory word, both in the formal sense that he considers human thinking and speaking about God to depend upon a prior divine act of communication, and in the material sense that the relations between creator and creation are centered on divine speech and human hearing. As in Barth, "word" refers most generally to revelation. However, for Jüngel, the precise referent of the term "word" is rather more restricted than in Barth's usage. For Barth, the "word" of revelation is God's communicative presence and activity encountered in the entire sweep of the work of the triune God in creation, reconciliation, and redemption. Revelation is the personal, dramatic act and speech through which the creation is

called to life and brought to perfection. For Jüngel, the range of reference is narrower, for two reasons. First, he maximizes the Christological component: Jesus is
constitutive of God's word, and little space is given to discussing the history of Israel
or of the church as part of the word's fullness. Second, Jüngel is fascinated by the
linguistic character of revelation as word, and has devoted a good deal of thought to
articulating how revelation is a divine linguistic performance.

His early attempts to do this – notably in *Paulus und Jesus* – appeal to the notion
of God's "coming-to-speech" in a highly eschatological manner. The parables of
Jesus are viewed as strangely intrusive speech-events which break into worldly reality
from outside, tearing apart linguistic and temporal continuities and making God
present in a wholly miraculous, discontinuous fashion. Later essays on metaphor and
anthropomorphism, as well as the treatment of the "analogy of advent" in *God as the
Mystery of the World*, soften the early contradiction into a distinction-in-relation.
Metaphorical language, for example, brings together two frames of reference, and so
testifies to the *historical* character of language as a process in which new realities are
evoked rather than as a signifier of fixed referential relations.

As with much of Jüngel's work, what he has to say is suggestive rather than fully
worked out. It can be seen to best advantage in its application to theological anthropology, where it offers Jüngel an idiom through which to describe the transformative
potency of divine revelation. Thus, he often explores such themes as temporality,
freedom, peace, or self-realization in relation to his understanding of the word as the
elemental interruption of human self-identity, through which persons are liberated
into receptivity. Nevertheless, Jüngel's commitment to this view of language introduces certain constrictions into his theology. It identifies normative Christian speech
with one mode of language (tropic, eschatological, interruptive); an immediate
effect of this is that Jüngel's work is undertaken at a curious distance from descriptive exegesis of the biblical canon in its full scope, and tends to be attracted to only
a few (synoptic and Pauline) high points. There are, furthermore, some Christological
and pneumatological questions raised by Jüngel's theology of language. The theology of the word tends to attribute to language the regenerative power more
normally reserved for Christ and Spirit. This may be the result of Jüngel's reticence
in developing an operative account of Christ's risen presence or of the Sprit's
agency; he shares this feature with much theology in the tradition of Bultmann. It is
also connected to the curious absence of a theology of God's historical action:
revelation is more a set of rhetorical episodes than an unfolding drama, and so can
have a slightly docetic air, with God and the created order joined by a slender thread
of eschatological speech.

Jüngel has taken to heart Barth's insistence on the Christological derivation of the
Christian doctrine of God, and has pressed it further by urging that it is the death of
Christ which forms the center of Christology and so of the doctrine of the Trinity.
In its doctrine of God, Christian theology does not presuppose a general conception
of deity as a maximally perfect being, characterized by infinity and its entailments
such as impassibility and omnipresence. Rather, the doctrine of God arises from
reflection upon God's self-identification with the crucified Jesus. In *God's Being is in
Becoming*, Jüngel shows how this rehearses a familiar Barthian move: God's essence
is determined by attention to his works, and so his being is itself in identification
with the contingent history of Jesus and its end at the cross. *God as the Mystery of the*

World, similarly, contains a lengthy treatment of the "death of God," arguing that it is not to be understood as an event in cultural history, but as a way of specifying God's being with reference to the cross. Consequently, Jüngel affirms that God can suffer, though his interest in doing so is not to set out a theodicy but to articulate "the peculiar ontological character of the divine being." That character is expressed, not denied, at the cross; but Calvary is not divine self-abandonment, for in the death of Christ there is actualized the sovereign freedom of God to be as he wills, even in the death of Christ. Christ's death thus becomes a mode of God's livingness. Much of Jüngel's best work is devoted to fashioning ontological categories to state how the life of God can be identified with the crucified: presence-in-absence, the struggle between being and non-being, the unity of life and death in favor of life. In this, the doctrine of the Trinity is given a major share of the work, since it indicates that God is in himself sovereign self-fulfillment and living self-gift, free in the act of self-surrender and so existing *a se in nihilum*, from himself in nothingness.

Jüngel's work on the doctrine of God, usually expressed with great rhetorical charge, brings together aspects of Barth's Christocentrism with strands of the Lutheran tradition, in particular the early Luther's theology of the divine passion, and a strong doctrine of the communication of attributes between the humanity and deity of Christ, on the basis of which Jesus' death can be attributed without residue to God. In a full systematic account, more would need to be spelled out. For example, Jüngel often speaks of God's relation to the crucified as one of "identification," a term which needs more explication before it can provide a metaphysics of incarnation of the sort furnished by the earlier language of substance. Or again, Jüngel's trinitarian theology is largely silent about the Holy Spirit, whether in the ministry of Jesus or in the creaturely realm; as with other theopaschite accounts, there is a distinct tug towards binitarianism. But the undoubted strength of Jüngel's case remains his use of the theology of the cross to mark out the difference of Christian faith from both theism and its atheistic shadow.

Jüngel has always regarded the doctrine of justification by faith as the basis of a distinctive Christian ontology of the human person. In some remarkably authoritative essays from the 1960s he explored the ontology of justification through a pointed contrast between self-realization through acts and the passive reception of the possibility of being. Later writings on anthropology lay considerable emphasis upon the theme of "living out of righteousness" as fundamental to the good ordering of human life in the light of the gospel of justification. This has often led to polemic against the primacy of practical reason in modern culture and theology. At times, this fiercely indicative theology of grace is balanced by what Jüngel has learned from Barth's moral theology, especially about the "correspondence" between divine and human action; but the primary anthropological motif is acquittal from self-realization. A book from the late 1990s, *Justification*, gives an exceptionally clear and potent presentation of these matters, centered on four exclusives: Christ alone, grace alone, word alone, faith alone. The precipating cause of the book was Roman Catholic–Lutheran *rapprochement* on the doctrine of justification, which became the occasion for one of his most lively and controversial pieces of theological writing in which his very basic commitments in soteriology, anthropology, ecclesiology, and sacramental theology are expounded with zest. The book's forcefulness derives from the vigor with which it pursues the theme of the proper distinction between God and the world, a distinction which is present in all Jüngel's writings. Barth shared the conviction that that distinction had to be maintained to prevent Christian theology and practice from drifting into moral immanentism. But his rich theology of election, incarnation, and the church gave him a more shapely, less episodic, sense of human historical being and action and of the ways of God in the world. This Jüngel lacks in some measure, having a rather muted theology of creation and temporality, a lack which can prove inhibiting in the development of a systematic theology of grace. Jüngel's achievements, however, lie elsewhere: in relentless theological interrogation of philosophical themes and texts; in his exposition of one version of Lutheran soteriology and anthropology; in some superlative studies of Barth; and in pursuing "positive" theology without the defensiveness, rancor, or closure which have sometimes afflicted Barth's lesser followers.

Robert Jenson

Raised in Midwest Lutheranism and educated at Luther College and Luther Seminary, Jenson wrote a doctorate in Heidelberg on Barth, giving a critically sympathetic reading of his doctrine of election and some of its entailments. He taught first at Luther College, then at Mansfield College, Oxford, returning to the US to the faculty of Luther Seminary in Gettysburg, where he established a considerable reputation as an authoritative systematician. In 1988 he began a decade of teaching at St. Olaf College; since then he has been associated with the Center of Theological Inquiry in Princeton. In addition to his work as reinterpreter of the Lutheran tradition, he has been a leading proponent of a set of radical ecumenical convictions, and his theology in its entirety is directed towards the renewal of the church as both evangelical and catholic. He exercises wide influence on North American theology and church life, in part though his work with the Center for Catholic and Evangelical Theology and its journal *Pro Ecclesia*. In 1997–9 he published a two-volume *Systematic Theology*.

Like Jüngel, Jenson's theological work has been nourished by the conversation between Luther and Barth (though Jenson has also immersed himself in the classics of Western Catholicism and Eastern Orthodoxy). From Heidelberg teachers like Peter Brunner and Edmund Schlink, Jenson grasped the possibility of genuine interchange between the Lutheran and the Reformed traditions, beyond the acrimonious debates in the unhappy years of the 1930s and 1940s. Jenson's particular perspective on both Luther and Barth can be appreciated by contrasting it with that of Jüngel. Jenson is very far from the anthropological reading of the doctrine of justification which Jüngel has learned from Ebeling, and does not share Jüngel's focus upon the "word of the cross" as constitutive for Christology and the doctrine of God. This is because on Jenson's account such emphases indicate a deep flaw in the developed Lutheran tradition, which it shares with other modern Western forms of Christian faith, namely, a failure to relate the eschatological reality of salvation to creaturely forms, and the consequent bifurcation of the gospel from the visible, public life of the ecclesial community. Where the existential tradition in Lutheranism has been deeply suspicious of "Catholicizing" accounts of the church, has strongly resisted ecumenical convergence in such matters as sacramental theology and soteriology, and has characteristically interpreted the salvific *pro me* individualist-ically, Jenson has sought to think through in a fundamental way the implications of the gospel's embodiment in dogma, community, and sacrament. In this, his work converges with thinkers in the recent Finnish school of Lutheran research, who have found in Luther a way of escape from the polarities of grace and creatureliness, divine work and human communion.

On Jenson's account, the ecclesiological antitheses in Lutheran and other post-Reformation forms of Christianity are symptomatic of a deep disorder in the way in which God and God's relation to the created realm are conceived. In a good deal of his writing, the attempt to expose and eradicate this disorder is at or near the surface. His initial map of the issues was drawn in the course of conversation with Barth, most of all in *Alpha and Omega* and *God after God*. Barth's momentous achievement, he argues, is that, by rooting the doctrine of the incarnation of the Word in the being of God, he is able to affirm God's temporality, and so to begin to overcome the metaphysical alienation of the divine and creaturely characteristic of some salient trends of Western philosophical and theological culture. But Barth's work is only a beginning, and remains overshadowed by some inherited disjunctions. The shadows are especially present in Barth's doctrine of election: the eternal decree of God is given such weight that the earthly history of reconciliation in the career of Jesus of Nazareth threatens to be resolved into a divine pretemporal decision of which it is an external actualization. "Is there not a danger that in Barth's hands Christ's history threatens to turn into something mightily resembling a metaphysical idea? Despite Barth's intent and protestations?" (*Alpha and Omega*, pp. 167ff.). Barth's emphasis on the transcendent, all-determining origin of created time gives inadequate space to the contingent, temporal character of the outworking of God's eternal will; put more dogmatically, it lacks a functional eschatology and a pneu-matology (themes which, as we shall see, Gunton develops further).

For Jenson, then, doing theology "after" Barth involves articulating a dogmatics of the gospel which both steers away from some of the structural flaws in Barth's conception of Christianity and radicalizes some of his dogmatic instincts in order to prise Christian theology free from the constrictions imposed by its alliance with the philosophical thought generated by antique Greek religion. The most important areas where there is work to be accomplished are the doctrines of the Trinity and of the church. On the first, Jenson wrote a startlingly original and programmatic book, *The Triune Identity*, on the second, an equally agenda-setting study of sacramental theology, *Visible Words* (material from both was included in a two-volume multi-author systematics which Jenson co-edited with long-time colleague Carl Braaten, *Christian Dogmatics*). Here, however, we concentrate on his handling of these topics in his *Systematic Theology*. Though there is, of course, much more than these two themes in the work, theology proper and ecclesiology together constitute its core. Indeed, the doctrine of the Trinity, which takes up the whole of the first volume, includes within its scope Christology, soteriology, and pneumatology, and in the second volume the doctrines of creation and the consummation of all things in the final kingdom form the frame for the central doctrine of the church. Achiev-ing rightly ordered doctrines of the Trinity and the church is thus fundamental to the project of allowing the gospel to break down the contradictions which have proved so unserviceable in the modern career of theology.

Systematic Theology is a disarming work. Its stylishly spare, often oblique prose suggests a great deal more than is explicit on the surface of the text; its historical judgments are characteristically summary, and rarely occasions for extended argument. Moreover, although it insists that the gospel is irreducibly narrative or dramatic, the genre of the work's presentation is most often analytic rather than descriptive (a feature which is reinforced by the relative brevity of exegetical comment). What is most striking is the sheer conceptual daring of the account, its confidence in espousing unconventional views and in setting them to work without much by way of qualification or apology.

The doctrine of the Trinity (in Jenson's extended understanding of the doctrine, which includes not only the being and relations of the triune persons but also their works) is built around two fundamental assertions. First, God's identity is triune. The task of a doctrine of God is analysis of the divine identity, that is, the formulation of an answer to the question "Who is God?" God's identity is triune in the sense that "the phrase 'Father, Son, and Holy Spirit' is simultaneously a very compressed telling of the total narrative by which scripture identifies God and a personal name for the God so specified" (*Systematic Theology*, I: 46) This is close to Barth's fundamental intentions, shorn of their remarkable descriptive expansion. Second, more controversially, the triune identity of God is actual in his history with the human creation:

> Presumably God could have been himself on different terms, established in his identity without reference to us or the time he makes for us, and so without confronting the death which closes our stories in that time . . . As it is, God's story is committed as a story with creatures. And so he too, as it is, can have no identity except as he meets the temporal end toward which creatures live. (*Systematic Theology*, I: 65)

What Jenson seeks to resist is the identification of divine reality with supra-temporal freedom to be other than or to exist independently of his relation to creation. Critics have been quick to point out that, without a more extended account of the sovereign will of God, this might lead to the collapse of the divine being into historical process, such that God *realizes* rather than *reveals* himself in temporality. On Jenson's account, the criticism simply rehearses a deep unease about the nature of the God of Israel and the church, who is not the antithesis of dramatic movement towards the future but rather has his identity in this drama. The "persons" of the Trinity are not anterior to the gospel events, but are rather "*dramatis dei personae*, 'characters in the drama of God'" (*Systematic Theology*, I: 75).

If the triune God is such that he cannot be identified apart from his external relations, the question of the nature of the church acquires considerable profile. The deficiency of a good deal of Protestant ecclesiology lies in its highly competitive assumption about the relation of divine grace to human creatureliness. Jenson's correction of the tradition is displayed most clearly in his reflections on the relation between the risen Christ and the church. "The church is ontologically the risen Christ's human body" (*Systematic Theology*, II: 213), and so it is as the church assembly that the risen Christ is available to the world. There are important qualifications, notably that Christ is available not only *as* his body but also *to* his body, so that seamless identity of Christ and community is avoided. But Christ's presence cannot be disembodied, since it is as human that he is risen and so is himself. "The church with her sacraments is truly Christ's availability to us just because Christ takes her as his availability to himself. Where does the risen Christ turn to find himself? To the sacramental gathering of believers" (*Systematic Theology*, II: 214). One way of understanding this affirmation is to see it as an ecclesiological extension of the Lutheran doctrine of the communication of properties. Jüngel appealed to that doctrine to overcome the disjunction between God and the crucified Christ, which was introduced by the notion of divine impassibility. Jenson presses the point much further: "the church is the risen Christ's Ego" (*Systematic Theology*, II: 215). Such a claim ought not to be construed simply as giving Christological warrants to certain ideas about, for example, the nature of the Eucharist or ministerial order; it is, rather, an attempt to carry through the gospel's drastic revision of metaphysical categories which have inhibited rather than enabled its expression.

Reception of the *Systematic Theology* is still in its early stages; it is almost certain to prove the most striking and ecumenically potent English-language statement of Christian theology of the last fifty years. Even given the compressed state of some of its passages of argument, its innovative character is unmistakable. Four areas might be noted as of decisive significance for the assessment of the work. First, does the presentation of God's relation to creaturely space and time imperil divine freedom? Second, can sufficient theological warrant be offered for some of the book's conceptual material, notably its ontology of personhood? Third, what are the gains and losses associated with the particular configuration of doctrines which Jenson adopts? Do certain doctrines (such as that of the immanent Trinity) drift to the margins? Fourth – and perhaps most important – can the book's theology of the gospel prove itself fruitful as a guide to the biblical drama of God's dealings with creatures?

Colin Gunton

At the time of his sudden death in 2003, Colin Gunton was Professor of Christian Doctrine at King's College, London, where he had taught since 1969. Educated at Oxford, where he wrote a doctorate on Barth (initially under Jenson), he was one of the key figures in the renewal of systematic theology in Britain in the last thirty years of the twentieth century. He wrote prolifically on many themes in constructive Christian theology, especially on the way in which trinitarian teaching impacts conceptions of God's relation to creation. At his death he left behind a draft of the first volume of a projected systematic theology, which would have been the first complete account from an English theologian since John Macquarrie's *Principles of Christian Theology* from the mid-1960s; a sketch of Gunton's project had been published a little earlier as *The Christian Faith*.

Gunton was deeply impressed by Barth's dogmatic achievement, and shared many of his instincts; but he was troubled by what he came to think of as imbalances in Barth's overall conception of Christian doctrine. *Becoming and Being*, his revised doctoral thesis, compares Barth to the process philosopher Hartshorne. Like Jüngel in *God's Being is in Becoming*, Gunton finds in Barth's actualism an alternative to both transcendentalist theologies of substance and immanentist metaphysics of the world process. From Jenson, however, Gunton adopts the criticism that Barth's notion of pretemporal divine election subtracts from the genuinely historical character of the world and of God's action in the world: divine history appears to be finished in advance, and so the eschatological movement of creation to its perfection is compromised as the past is allowed to become the center of gravity in God's dealings with the world. In effect, divine pretemporality threatens genuine creaturely temporality. This worry will surface often in subsequent writing on Barth, and the task of finding a more satisfactory way of relating God and creation will be a (perhaps *the*) major preoccupation of Gunton's mature constructive work. The core of his anxiety about Barth is trinitarian: Barth adheres too closely to an Augustinian conception of the Trinity which, it is argued, subordinates the particular intratrinitarian identities and economic acts of the persons to the underlying divine unity. The doctrine of the Spirit is an acute register of the problems. On Gunton's account, Barth limits the Spirit's work to that of subjective application of the saving benefits secured by the Son; but this restricted pneumatology gives little weight to the Spirit's distinctiveness as the agent of creaturely identity and integrity, and, moreover, orients pneumatology to the past (the Son's finished work, applied by the Spirit) and not to the future (the Spirit-generated history of creation moving to its eschatological perfection). This is connected to a Christological problem, namely an underdeveloped theology of the humanity of Christ. Gunton believed that Barth's treatment of Jesus' ministry, as well as of such topics as the Virgin Birth, the ascension, and the heavenly priesthood of Christ, was overly concerned with his deity. The reason for the imbalance is, once again, a thin pneumatology: Barth's trinitarian theology holds him back from attributing agency to the Holy Spirit in sustaining Jesus' genuine humanity. The result is that Jesus can sometimes seem to function as a Platonic form, absorbing all into itself but lacking historical determinateness. None of this suggests that Barth was for Gunton anything other than a theologian of enduring greatness; but as he develops his own configuration of systematic theology, Gunton will increasingly look to sources other than Barth (Irenaeus, the Cappadocians, Owen, Coleridge) whom he judges more adequate in deploying the range of trinitarian teaching.

Gunton was a major figure in retrieving the theology of the Trinity from the periphery and returning it to the center of British theology. He did this by demonstrating across a wide spread of doctrinal loci the difference which could be made by an operative doctrine of the Trinity. Above all, he urged (the word is not too strong) that trinitarian conceptions of the being and action of God must lie at the heart of a properly Christian construal of God's relation to the created order. Accounts of God's presence and action in material and historical reality are not independent of accounts of God's being, and Christian authenticity requires that both be determined by trinitarian considerations. The point is made polemically and constructively. In the polemic, Gunton's target is the – somewhat monolithically conceived – Western theological tradition, whose fount is Augustine and whose last great representative is (despite everything) Barth. In this tradition, the mutually determinative personal relations of Father, Son, and Spirit are not allowed to be constitutive of the being of God, which is thought to underlie God's triunity as its ontological ground. As a reading of Augustine and others, this is certainly sketchy; but it is best appreciated as a foil to a constructive doctrine of the Trinity as a communion of persons. If Augustine represents the intrusion of monism into Christian theology proper, a suitably trinitarian construal may most clearly be found exemplified in the Cappadocian fathers, especially as their thought has been synthesized in the work of the modern Orthodox theologian John Zizioulas. The "Cappadocian" doctrine not only furnishes a fully relational account of God's triune being (sometimes dubbed "social trinitarianism," though the term is not helpful, and Gunton distances himself from it), but also forms the basis for corollary teaching about the nature and ends of creaturely being and history.

There are thus two assertions at the heart of the model which Gunton develops. First, the deity of the three divine persons is fundamental and not derivative. God's unity is not the substrate of his triunity, but is the concrete unity of relation-in-difference, or communion, between Father, Son, and Spirit. This, in turn, is inseparable from a conception of "person" as "person-in-relation" rather than as individual substance – the latter idea, of Augustinian provenance, proved especially porous to Cartesian conceptions of persons as unrelated minds. Second, the three persons are agents of distinct, though related, modes of action in relation to the creation. On this account, the adage of Western trinitarianism – the external works of the Trinity are indivisible – indicates a serious reluctance to allow that appropriation of particular modes of action to particular persons is rooted in the inner being of God. For Gunton, on the other hand, divine simplicity is best conceived, not as underlying unity, but as the event of communion between agents in relation.

This leads to a specific account of God's action in the world. "All of God's acts take their beginning in the Father, are put into effect through the Son and reach their completion in the Spirit. Put otherwise, God's actions are *mediated*: he brings about his purposes towards and in the world by the mediating actions of the Son and the Spirit, his 'two hands'" (*Act and Being*, p. 77). Particularly in later work, the concept of "mediation" played a leading role, even though Gunton did not give a sustained analysis of what is involved. Generally speaking, "mediation" functions in two contexts for Gunton. First, in the doctrine of God it indicates the relation of Son and Spirit to the Father who is the fount of the Holy Trinity's acts. Rather than arranging God's economic acts serially (the Father creates, the Son reconciles, the Spirit sanctifies), Gunton prefers to speak of all God's acts as acts of the Father, but of the Father's acts as undertaken through the mediating activity of the other two persons. The differences are thus not those between discrete acts but between "forms" of action: the Son acts "immanently," within created reality, the Spirit acts "transcendentally" or "eschatologically," bringing creation to its end.

A second use of "mediation" indicates how the triune God acts in the world through creaturely media. This emphasis takes up Gunton's early criticism of Barth's dialectic of time and eternity: Gunton came to think that this dialectic, endemic in Western divinity, originated in Augustine's truce with neoplatonic thought, which protected God's immateriality by interposing a hierarchy of intermediate realities between God and creation, thereby throwing the doctrine of God back on itself in timeless transcendence. The alternative tradition which Gunton constructs (its figurehead is Irenaeus) finds the clue to resolving the problem in the doctrines of Christ and the Spirit. Gunton's Christology is perhaps the least "Reformed" aspect of his theology, in that he does not follow the characteristic Calvinist trend of assigning the lead to the deity in an account of the two natures of the incarnate one. Rather, he is emphatic that any theology of incarnation must safeguard the full integrity of Christ's humanity and that this can only be achieved through pneuma-tological teaching. Docetic Christologies assume a dualistic account of God's rela-tion to creatures, and so can make little sense of Jesus' humanity as itself the mediation of God's act. In a pneumatological Christology, on the other hand, the Spirit constitutes Jesus as the human person and agent in and as whom God's acts are undertaken without compromise to his human authenticity.

Before moving on to some ramifications of this theology of God's triune being and action, it is worth noting that, though he expounded it in many contexts, Gunton never achieved a fully articulated account of the matter. Along with "medi-ation," terms such as "communion," "person," and "relation" are used with great suggestiveness but not always accorded thorough analytical treatment; when coupled with a somewhat broad-brush presentation of the doctrine's history, they suggest that too much ground is covered too quickly. This may be the case; but two other factors should be borne in mind. One is that Gunton's trinitarian theology has to be viewed against the background of the instinctive deism of the leading British theologians from the 1950s on, in comparison with which Gunton's work has far greater depth and richness. In addition, the fertility of Gunton's trinitarian theology has to be seen in his application of it to the construction of Christian doctrine in other areas, particularly in the doctrines of creation and in the formulation of a Christian metaphysic and theory of culture.

Along with T. F. Torrance, Gunton was one of the few theologians in Barth's tradition to devote serious thought to theological description of the created order, and to believe that any such description must be undergirded by trinitarian teaching. On his account, doctrines of creation tend to be dominated either by the idiom of emanation (thereby eroding the integrity of both God and creation) or by that of causality. The latter has held pride of place in modern Western theology, and is judged ruinous because it quickly becomes an assertion of God as impersonal force, a will acting upon creation in an unmediated way and undermining a proper sense of the relative autonomy of creaturely reality. Over against causality, Gunton proposes an incarnational model of God's free personal relation to the world, and a pneuma-tological model in which the Spirit is the "perfecting cause" of creaturely being.

> The point of stressing a trinitarian way of construing the relation of Creator and creation is that it enables us to understand both the past and the continuing creative divine agency toward the world without closing the space between God and the created order. The doctrine of creation . . . has to do with the establishment of the other in its own distinctive reality: not divine self-communication, but divine constituting the world to be truly other, and so itself. (*The Doctrine of Creation*, pp. 81ff.)

This concern to develop a theological account of how the creation has its own identity in otherness from God is central in Gunton's most ambitious book, *The One, The Three and the Many*, which arose from his 1992 Bampton lectures. Like Jüngel's *God as the Mystery of the World*, the book is in part a theological diagnosis of salient aspects of modern culture (though it covers a much greater range of cultural expressions); and also like Jüngel, Gunton argues that an alternative Chris-tian vision must take its cues from trinitarian theology. The core of Gunton's pathology is that the West's monistic theology of God lies behind the loss of relationality in modern thought and cultural practice. Appealing to Coleridge, he argues that "the Trinity is the idea of ideas, in some way at once the clue to all thought and to all reality" (*The One, The Three and the Many*, p. 211). On this basis he constructs a trinitarian metaphysic of culture, drawing from the doctrine some transcendental structures of created being which echo the reality of God. In particular, he generates a theology of creaturely particularity in which the one and the many are held together in a perichoretic unity grounded in the triune communion of the being of God.

Gunton considered his work a set of essays in Christian ontology – an attempt to explicate the kind of being God is in order to explicate creaturely being. He undertook the task not so much descriptively as argumentatively (the idiom of his writing is usually second-order, not first-order). In approaching an area of doctrinal reflection, he characteristically asked how a proper distribution of weight could be maintained among the elements of Christian teaching, and sought to identify and excise developments in theology whose origin lay in metaphysical schemes uncorrected by the gospel (something he shares with both Jüngel and Jenson). He had a highly developed sense of the scope of dogmatics and of the integral importance of each of its parts, even though his writing in Christology and soteriology can be curiously flat. When his theology does not persuade, it is usually because he does not pause sufficiently long over exegetical or historical description, or because he assumes the viability of his presuppositions and presses ahead to draw corollaries. Like Jüngel, he was deeply concerned to deploy theological resources in the analysis of modern thought, though he brought a rather broader range of doctrinal material to the table, and a wider sweep of Christian history. Although his work was broken off before he gave a fully achieved account of his thought, his independence of mind, restlessly probing intelligence, and his acute dogmatic judgment put him among the handful of British systematicians of the last century whose work is of enduring value.

Conclusion

In what sense, then, are the theologies of Jüngel, Jenson, and Gunton "after" Barth? None of them is to be thought of as an imitator; but each in his own way is addressing questions, which have often absorbed those who take Barth very seriously, concerning the relation of divine grace to creatureliness. Jüngel's work often revolves around how eschatological divine action relates to created agency. But because he is substantially indebted to the tradition of Bultmann, he is less concerned than either Jenson or Gunton to explore the issues through a spacious doctrine of creation; indeed, his style of existential, word-centered Lutheranism tends to pull him away not only from them but also from elements of Barth's dogmatics of the biblical drama of the covenant between God and creatures. Jenson and Gunton, on the other hand, though they believe Barth correct to insist that the integrity of creation must be grounded in the antecedent reality of God, remain uneasy with the trinitarian teaching which Barth took to working out this conviction, since to them it often issues in the opposite of what it intends, namely in an insecure sense of creaturely substance. Where Jüngel presses for an account of God and the world centered on an interventionist eschatology of divine speech, Jenson and Gunton offer a more historically extended theology of created history in which eschatology is not the interruption of the world but rather its perfection through time.

Jüngel, Jenson, and Gunton are all in their different ways theologians of revelation, though for none of them is "revelation" primarily a term for a mysterious noetic transaction so much as a way of speaking of how God's presence and activity in the world conditions and directs the work of theological reason. All, therefore, are theological realists, in that they do not consider theology a work of poetic reason, but a "positive" science whose primary task is receiving the instruction proffered by God's given reality. All are church theologians, not only in the sense that all have had impact on the affairs of their church communities, but also because none of them considers that theological reason can operate in isolation from the practices of the church. All of them, further, do their work on the assumption that the church's confession of the gospel, most of all in its teaching about the Trinity and the Incarnation, precedes theological reflection, and does not have to wait for theological warrant before it can proceed. And all of them are concerned to explore how the gospel which is confessed by the church generates a distinctive Christian ontology. All this sets them firmly in the family of Protestant theology of which Barth remains the consummate twentieth-century example.

Bibliography

Gunton, Colin, *Enlightenment and Alienation: An Essay Towards a Trinitarian Theology* (London, 1985).

—— *The Actuality of Atonement* (Edinburgh, 1989).

—— *Christ and Creation* (Carlisle, 1993).

—— *The One, the Three, and the Many* (Cambridge, 1993).

—— *A Brief Theology of Revelation* (Edinburgh, 1995).

—— *Theology through the Theologians* (Edinburgh, 1996).

—— *The Promise of Trinitarian Theology* (Edinburgh, 1997).

—— *Yesterday and Today: A Study of Continuities in Christology* (London, 1997).

—— *The Triune Creator* (Edinburgh, 1998).

—— *Intellect and Action: Elucidations on Christian Theology and the Life of Faith* (Edinburgh, 2000).

—— *Becoming and Being: The Doctrine of God in Charles Hartshorne and Karl Barth* (London, 2001).

—— *The Christian Faith* (Oxford, 2001).

—— *Act and Being: Toward a Theology of the Divine Attributes* (London, 2002).

—— *Father, Son and Holy Spirit* (London, 2003).

Jenson, Robert, *Alpha and Omega: A Study in the Theology of Karl Barth* (New York, 1963).

—— *God after God: The God of the Past and the God of the Future Seen in the Work of Karl Barth* (New York, 1969).

—— *The Knowledge of Things Hoped For* (Oxford, 1969).

—— *Visible Words: The Interpretation and Practice of Christian Sacraments* (Philadelphia, PA, 1978).

—— *The Triune Identity: God According to the Gospel* (Philadelphia, PA, 1982).

—— *America's Theologian: A Recommendation of Jonathan Edwards* (Oxford, 1988).

—— *Unbaptized God: The Basic Flaw in Ecumenical Theology* (Minneapolis, MN, 1992).

—— *Systematic Theology*, 2 vols. (Oxford, 1997, 1999).

Jenson, Robert, and C. Braaten (eds.), *Christian Dogmatics*, 2 vols. (Philadelphia, PA, 1984).

Jüngel, Eberhard, *Paulus und Jesus* (Tübingen, 1962).

—— **Unterwegs zur Sache. Theologische Bemerkungen* (Munich, 1972).

—— *Gottes Sein ist im Werden* (Tübingen, 1975) [ET *God's Being is in Becoming* (Edinburgh, 2001)].

—— *Tod* (Stuttgart, 1971) [ET *Death* (Edinburgh, 1975)].

—— *Gott als Geheimnis der Welt* (Tübingen, 1977) [ET *God as the Mystery of the World* (Edinburgh, 1983).

—— ** Entsprechungen: Gott – Wahrheit – Mensch* (Munich, 1980).

—— *Barth-Studien* (Gütersloh, 1982) [partial ET: *Karl Barth: A Theological Legacy* (Philadelphia, PA, 1986)].

—— ** Wertlose Wahrheit* (Munich, 1990).

—— ** Indikative der Gnade–Imperative der Freiheit* (Tübingen, 2000).

—— *Das Evangelium von der Rechtfertigung des Gottlosen als Zentrum des christlichen Glaubens* (Tübingen, 1998) [ET *Justification* (Edinburgh, 2001)].

—— *Beziehungsreich. Perspektiven des Glaubens* (Stuttgart, 2002).

—— ** Ganz werden. Theologische Erörterungen V* (Tübingen, 2003).

Much of Jüngel's best work is contained in the five volumes of essays (* above) which collect the writings of the previous decade; selections from the first three volumes are published as *Theological Essays I* and *II* (Edinburgh, 1989, 1994).

Roman Catholic Theology after Vatican II

Paul D. Murray

Introduction

This volume already contains essays on three classics of twentieth-century Roman Catholic theology: Henri de Lubac, Karl Rahner, and Hans Urs von Balthasar. David Tracy, Michel de Certeau, and Jean-Luc Marion are also treated extensively in the chapters on "Revisionists and Liberals" and "Postmodern Theology," respectively. Beyond this, many other significant Catholic theologians feature throughout the other chapters.

Rather, therefore, than risk a superficial and repetitive summary of the relevant material in these other chapters, this chapter makes no attempt at a comprehensive review of all the significant individuals and movements of thought that comprise the world of Roman Catholic theology after Vatican II. The more modest aim is to explore the key factors, debates, and diverse – even conflicting – theological instincts and approaches that have shaped the story of European and North American Roman Catholic theology in this period. With this, the aim also is to identify what continues to be of real significance and, likewise, where the live issues are for contemporary Catholic theology.

The first main section explores something of the complexity surrounding the diverse ways in which the story of modern Catholicism can be told. Following this the heart of the chapter consists in a series of three interrelated surveys of key dimensions of change and development in Catholic theology after the Council. The first focuses upon some notable changes in the institutional context of Catholic theology. The second deals with various crucial developments in relation to its perceived task, scope, methods, and sources. In turn, the third explores a number of the most significant substantive changes in recent Catholic theological understanding. The concluding section draws all of this together by reflecting on what appropriate structures might enable Catholicism to negotiate most fruitfully the continuing task of discerning the living truth of God in Christ and the Spirit.

While many characters feature in the story here told, particularly frequent mention is made of five who do not receive extensive treatment elsewhere in this volume and whose work collectively (though diversely) is representative of much that is significant in the story of European and North American Roman Catholic theology after Vatican II. They are the Canadian Jesuit Bernard Lonergan (1904–84), the Belgian Dominican Edward Schillebeeckx (1914–), the Swiss diocesan priest Hans Küng (1928–), the Polish pope Karol Wojtyla/John Paul II (1920–2005), and the English lay theologian Nicholas Lash (1934–).

To some extent the entirety of Lonergan's work, culminating in his monumental 1957 text *Insight: A Study of Human Understanding* and his 1972 work *Method in Theology*, can be taken as representative of the concern to open up from within the neoscholastic system that so shaped Catholic understanding in the early part of the twentieth century, while preserving the role of philosophy as the privileged medium of theological analysis. In Lonergan's case his close analyses of the writings of Thomas Aquinas were informed in particular by transcendental philosophy, cognitional theory, and the philosophy of science.[1] Drawing upon such resources he integrated a considerably greater sense of dynamism and historicity into his work than had been typical of an earlier generation. Judging, however, by the industry of interpretation and application surrounding his work it seems that, for some, part of the attraction lies in the perception of finding here a system of thought as total and all-sufficient as the one Lonergan had sought to refresh.

From early in his training, Edward Schillebeeckx also was immersed in the concern to pursue a constructive appropriation of the neoscholastic inheritance. In Schillebeeckx's case, however, the influence of Dominic de Petter's phenomenological interests, while studying at Louvain, combined with the dual close attention given to historical particularity and contemporary social reality at Le Saulchoir, the Dominican house of graduate studies, instilled in him a sustained concern to think through the specificities of the complex relationship between Christian tradition and human experience. Informed both by historical–critical analyses of scripture and tradition on the one hand and social theoretical forms of analysis on the other, Schillebeeckx's major writings since the Council have characteristically taken the form of intensive, critical-cum-constructive studies of key doctrinal loci in relation to contemporary Christian thought and practice.[2]

Perhaps more clearly than any other contemporary Catholic theologian, Hans Küng symbolizes both the revisionist, progressivist spirit that came to prominence in the years immediately following Vatican II and the inevitable associated tensions concerning the appropriate relationship between academic and ecclesial authority.[3] When Küng appeared to be questioning the church's ability to discern aright the identifying rules of Catholic practice and belief in his 1971 work *Infallible? An Enquiry*, Karl Rahner was moved to liken the implications of Küng's position to that of a liberal Protestant who had relinquished the commitment to working within a received tradition of faith, accountable to the discerned mind of the church. Küng, for his part, rejected this interpretation.[4] Since that point, having written major studies of many of the key loci of Christian belief, Küng has turned his attention more recently to the broader ecumenical issue of interfaith dialogue and cooperation, particularly with a view to working together for a just global order.[5]

While it is somewhat unusual to treat a Roman pontiff as a theologian among theologians, there would be something incomplete about any telling of the story of Catholic theology after Vatican II that did not make mention of Karol Wojtyla/John Paul II. Not only was he a significant voice in his own right prior to his accession to the papacy, but since then the many writings bearing his authorization, together with the policies promoted by the various Roman curial bodies acting under his authority, have been decisive in determining the course and character of contemporary Catholic theology. Where the aforementioned figures were each variously formed in a Western Catholicism seeking to negotiate an opening to modern values and modes of understanding, Wojtyla studied for the priesthood in an underground seminary during Nazi occupation in a country intimately acquainted with the horrors of the Holocaust and the subsequent repression and state-sponsored atheism of the Soviet system.[6] It is, then, hardly surprising that Wojtyla/John Paul II's thought should be shaped, as was evident in his first encyclical *Redemptor Hominis* (1979) and consistently since, by a heightened sensitivity to the need for the "cultures of death" that masquerade as enlightened modernity to be confronted by the transformative power of the gospel, witnessed to in lives of holy, hope-filled contradiction. Moreover, his conviction is that this is not simply the calling of a prophetic minority subculture on the margins of the church, but the calling of the entire church militant. To this end he has sought to impose the discipline deemed necessary to equip the church for mission.

Although situated within the more rarefied atmosphere of the English academic establishment, Nicholas Lash's work also is marked by a consistent questioning of typically "modern" understandings of human rationality, with their strict bifurcation of fact and value and associated atomistic, reductionist accounts of human life and created reality more generally. Allied with this, again, is a fine-tuned critical stance toward any aspects of social, political, and economic reality that fail to observe the demands of human solidarity. While sharing, however, in the "postliberal" questioning of modern self-understanding and of theological liberalism in particular, Lash clearly continues with the basic liberal value of rigorous self-critique.[7] For Lash, an essential aspect of the theological task is to act as the uneasy conscience of faith, concerned to hold theological construction and church life and structure to account at the bar of critical reason.[8] Where John Paul II perceives a need to inspire and marshal a disciplined, vigorous force for change, Lash recognizes that the church's own polity must bespeak the proclaimed civilization of love if it is not to fall into serious performative contradiction.

The Stories of Modern Catholicism

As the above suggests, the story of modern Catholicism is considerably more complex than has sometimes been recognized. For a time it was typically told as a drama of two acts, unequal in length and strikingly different in their respective moods, with the Second Vatican Council (meeting in four sessions between 1962 and 1965) depicted as *the* great scene change and dramatic pivot.[9]

In such tellings Catholicism prior to Vatican II had become defined by a series of increasingly oppositional stances, first against the challenge of Protestantism from the sixteenth century, then against what was perceived as the irredeemably anti-Christian spirit of modern liberalism. As the last thesis of the 1864 "Syllabus of Errors" expresses it, "If anyone thinks that . . . the Roman pontiff can and should reconcile and harmonize himself with progress, with liberalism, and with recent civilization . . .

let him be anathema."[10] In each case the counter-move took the form of heightened emphases upon distinctively Catholic practices and beliefs and upon the Catholic Church's uniquely privileged ability to read reality aright, culminating in the proclamation of papal infallibility in 1870 during the final session of the curtailed First Vatican Council. Within Catholicism such defensiveness was felt most sharply through the policy promoted by Pope Pius X (1903–14) of rooting out and suppressing any scholars deemed to be infected by the ills of "modernist" commitment, the repressive after-effects of which policy continued long after its actual promotion.[11]

When set alongside this synopsis of modern Catholicism's supposed first act, Pope John XXIII's surprise announcement on January 25, 1959 of a Second Vatican Council concerned to renew Catholicism in the context of the modern world appears as a somewhat discontinuous turn of events. Indeed, if the final thesis of the *Syllabus* is emblematic of the "first act" of modern Catholicism so construed, equally so for the "second" are the opening words of *Gaudium et Spes* ("Pastoral Constitution on the Church in the Modern World," December 7, 1965): "The joy and hope, the grief and anguish of the men of our time . . . are the joy and hope, the grief and anguish of the followers of Christ as well. Nothing that is human fails to find an echo in their hearts."[12] In this spirit of passionate solidarity, generous hospitality, and confident trust in the prevenient ubiquity of God's gracious presence lies, for this telling of the story at least, the great, lasting legacy of Vatican II.

Since the election of Karol Wojtyla as Pope John Paul II in 1978, however, it has been necessary to tell a more complicated tale, one requiring, at the very least, a third controverted act or supplementary epilogue.[13] For some, despite his acknowledged development of Catholic social thought, John Paul II's papacy essentially represents a violent reversal of the central movement of Vatican II. For others, it represents a necessary corrective to a disastrous misappropriation of the Council influential in the years following it, driven by a naively optimistic embrace of modern liberal values at the very point at which they were beginning to be widely challenged.[14] These differing assessments of John Paul II and of the appropriate reception of Vatican II show that the binary two-phase narrative of modern Catholicism requires significant qualification.[15]

In general, it is as inaccurate to suggest that Pius IX's *Syllabus* and Pius X's anti-modernist campaign expressed the state of universal opinion in the pre-Vatican II church as it is to suggest that at Vatican II the bishops were in unanimous agreement on the wording and interpretation of the various documents endorsed. As regards the former, the Catholic Tübingen school requires particular mention, as do John Henry Newman and Friedrich von Hügel in England and Antonio Rosmini in Italy. Again, in the early to middle part of the twentieth century, despite the continuing reverberations of Pius X's anti-modernist campaign, there were many Catholic intellectuals who courageously, patiently, and imaginatively devoted themselves to seeking to give richer, more vital expression to the faith than the dominant neoscholastic categories allowed – Karl Adam, Romano Guardini, Marie-Dominique Chenu, Yves Congar, Henri de Lubac, Jean Daniélou, and Karl Rahner, to name but a few. Indeed, it was the very work of *ressourcement* upon which many of them were engaged – of returning behind the formulas of neoscholastic manuals to the great historic sources and expressions of Christian faith – that tilled the ground for what came to fruition in the Council.[16]

Equally, these renewed ways of thinking did not meet with universal approval during the Council any more than beforehand. A fluctuating minority remained opposed throughout and the final form of the documents reflects the compromises that had to be struck. Even among the approving majority there were differences between those who saw the task of renewal or *aggiornamento* as being limited to the time of the Council – with the post-conciliar task viewed purely in terms of consolidation and application – and those who regarded it as a necessarily continuing aspect of Catholicism.

Such tensions became significant well in advance of the accession of Wojtyla to the papacy, as symbolized by the break-away in 1972 of the *Communio* group of theologians (notably Balthasar, Ratzinger, de Lubac, and Kasper) from those associated with the journal *Concilium* (notably Rahner, Congar, Schillebeeckx, and Küng), which explicitly sought to extend the work of the Council. This tension continues as a defining force in European and North American Catholic theology.

It is simplistically wrongheaded to construe this as a tension between opposing stances of openness to and withdrawal from the world. As the topics covered in the respective journals indicate, the difference is less one of range than of tone and approach. It relates to the relative emphasis given to the possibility of Catholicism's learning from extra-ecclesial resources in its ongoing discernment of God's living truth and to the need for the world's sin-dimmed perception of half-truths to be judged and read aright in the light of Catholic Christian tradition. Alternatively stated, it concerns the balance to be maintained between the need to renew Catholic faith in the light of what can be appropriately learned from the world and the need to offer back a richer understanding than the world can achieve of its own resources. Also relevant, however, is the degree to which the church itself is viewed, in the terms of Vatican II's *Lumen Gentium* ("Dogmatic Constitution on the Church," November 21, 1964), as being in need of reform and renewal rather than as the perfect antidote to the world's ills.[17]

A better, although still imperfect, analogy for the relationship between "*Concilium*" and "*Communio*" tendencies is the potentially creative tension between revisionist and postliberal instincts in Christian theology more generally.[18] In this regard the comparison sometimes drawn between Rahner as a Catholic Schleiermacher and Balthasar as a Catholic Barth is not entirely without merit. The view espoused here is that the unfortunate ecclesial–political capital frequently made of the supposed irreconcilability of these two instincts would be better invested in viewing them as two sides of a healthy dialectical tension and this while recognizing with Lash the need to attend to matters of unequal power distribution.[19] As the Catholic convert philosopher Alasdair MacIntyre recognizes, "Traditions, when vital, embody continuities of conflict."[20]

As such, the real problem with the binary, two-act presentation of modern Catholicism is not that it is utterly devoid of truth. Whatever one makes of it, Vatican II was an event of extraordinary significance. Nor is it simply that completeness requires a third act, or epilogue, recounting a more recent postliberal reaction to the dramatic events of the second. The real problem is with its linear, neatly phased telling of a story considerably more complex in reality, with diverse, even conflicting, dimensions, pressures, and drives throughout. The instincts of the reactionary conservative, the progressive reformer, the creative retriever, the cautious consolidator, and the counter-cultural critic exist as differing yet overlapping parameters of concern. They constitute the diverse keys within which the music of Catholicism has been and is being variously performed with the possibility of both harmony and dissonance. The story of Catholic theology after Vatican II is the story or, more accurately, the story of the stories of these various performances.

Survey 1: Changes in the Institutional Context of Catholic Theology Since Vatican II

Mindful of Johnann-Baptist Metz's stipulation that the "important questions to be asked by theology" are "Who should do theology and where, in whose interest and for whom?"[21] the ambiguity of the phrase "Catholic theologian" should be noted. Officially, it refers only to theologians working on behalf of the Magisterium (understood here as the pope and the bishops) and/or holding a formal mandate to teach within a Catholic institution.[22] In a broader empirical fashion, however, it more naturally refers to any practicing Catholic engaged in theological work, regardless of context.

In the former sense the degree of change in the institutional context of Catholic theology has been relatively slight but nevertheless significant. While official Catholic theology continues to be located in the pontifical universities, the seminaries, and the various ecclesial bureaucratic bodies, and continues, in the main, to be pursued by ordained male celibates, it has become increasingly common for lay men and women to be coopted into such activities. Whether, however, the extension of perspective and concern this affords is proportionately contributing to the ongoing shaping of Catholic theology is questionable. Only those in full sympathy with existing teaching generally receive such access, with anything less being regarded as damaging "dissent" rather than constructive contribution.[23]

If the picture at the official level is one of relative stability, at the unofficial level it is one of tremendous vitality and diversity, at least in certain regions. With regards to the British context, for example, from local catechetical groups, diocesan programs of lay formation, the massively increased availability of degrees in theology in a wide range of institutions, through to the higher echelons of research in major international universities, there has been a genuine flowering of lay Catholic theology since the Council, in turn influential beyond Roman Catholicism.[24]

Particularly significant is the number of Catholic women who, having acquired theological training, have proceeded on to employment in pastoral ministry and theological education and research. Given that some, judging it to be irredeemably patriarchal, have subsequently passed beyond any form of Christian commitment, while others have moved into a space of prophetic opposition to the church as currently configured, all the more notable is the considerable number of feminist theologians who continue to find their home and calling within Catholicism.[25] Instances of women of feminist sympathy converting *into* Catholicism should also be noted.[26]

In this as in many other respects the vitality and range of unofficial Catholic theology, operating in myriad different contexts and with a breadth of experience generally unavailable at the official level, represents a potentially rich resource. Again, however, how to link the official and unofficial in appropriate conversation and structures of discernment remains a real challenge for contemporary Catholicism. The adage "the church is not a democracy" is inappropriately intoned when used to legitimate the church being something less rather than something more than a democracy. While competitive power-play and majority voting might be thought of as having only a limited role, at best, in the church's collective discerning (*sensus fidelium*), all with relevant experience and expertise should surely be able to participate by right rather than by concession in this process.

Survey 2: Changes in Understanding of the Task, Scope, Methods, and Sources of Catholic Theology Since Vatican II

As noted earlier, the neoscholastic concern for the orderly presentation and defense of Catholic belief in Aristotelian categories, dominant since the latter half of the nineteenth century, had already come under considerable strain prior to the Council. Taking their lead from Leo XIII's earlier promotion of Aquinas as the Catholic theologian *par excellence*, historical scholars such as Étienne Gilson and Marie-Dominique Chenu had recovered Aquinas' distinctiveness compared both with his contemporaries and later scholastic interpreters.[27] Perhaps most significant here was the recovery, variously performed by de Lubac, Rahner, and others, of a view of created reality as intrinsically oriented to God as its source, sustainer, and con-summation, in contrast to the "extrinsicist" tendency to view grace and nature, the sacred and the profane, as utterly distinct.[28]

More generally, studies in historical theology, most notably by Congar, combined with Pius XII's opening of Catholicism to modern modes of biblical study in his 1943 encyclical *Divino Afflante Spiritu*, had begun to show the need for increased hermeneutical sophistication *vis-à-vis* the historic sources of the tradition. Likewise, liturgical, patristic, and scriptural scholarship had served to give greater emphasis to the lived, ecclesial dimensions of faith and theology as complement to the cognitive, philosophical dimensions dominant within neoscholasticism. In turn, modern philosophical thought had already been used to give fresh articulation to the Thomistic inheritance. Particularly notable here is Joseph Maréchal's Kantian-influenced transcendental Thomism, in turn extended in different ways by, among others, Lonergan and Rahner. Also significant is Teilhard de Chardin's engagement with the human and natural sciences in his reflections on theological anthropology and created process and the diverse influence of phenomenological ideas on thinkers as otherwise different as Schillebeeckx and Wojtyla.[29]

Against this background, John XXIII's calling of the Council for purposes of pastoral reflection and ecclesial renewal rather than dogmatic definition, together with the bishops' rejection of the draft documents in favor of documents more scripturally rooted and pastoral in tone, gave official sanction to the move beyond neoscholasticism as the only valid mode of Catholic theological reflection.[30] At work in the resulting documents, preeminently so in *Gaudium et Spes*, is a recovery of the grand vision of Catholic theology as concerned to understand the significance of all particular things in relation to God's self-revelation in Christ and as correlatively open to the contributions of the diverse forms of analysis this requires.[31] It is this vision of rooted, practically engaged, disciplinary pluriform theological analysis and reflection that has continued to characterize Catholic theology after Vatican II, in turn reinforced by the shift in consciousness initiated there to being what Rahner referred to as a truly world church.[32]

While a range of appropriations of the Thomist tradition, from analytic and personalist to more self-consciously historical readings, still features as an important part of the contemporary Catholic theological scene, they now feature precisely as a part – and an internally differentiated part – rather than as the whole.[33] Informing them are diverse other modes of theologizing, typically shaped by similarly close engagement with other significant streams in the broad expanse of Christian tradition and one or more of the natural and social sciences, the various contemporary modes of analysis operative in the humanities and the practices and understanding of other faith traditions and non-European cultural contexts. Suffice to say that the work of Catholic theologians features significantly in each major example of contemporary theology in critical–constructive, expansive, interrogative mode.[34]

This shift is particularly clear in fundamental theology, which has progressed from the attempt to present tight proofs of Catholic belief modeled on deductive modes of reasoning to the utilization of a broad range of hermeneutical tools in service of more modest attempts to demonstrate its reasonableness and continuing relevance.[35] Reinforcing this move has been the assimilation into theology of post-foundationalist understandings of human rationality,[36] a development in some ways anticipated if not consistently carried through by Lonergan in the central role he accorded to "conversion" in theological understanding.

While this proliferation of methodologies and analytical tools has greatly enriched Catholic theology, it has become increasingly difficult to hold it in gathered, cross-boundary, mutually constructive conversation.[37] It is, consequently, as vital to Catholicism's health to develop and to sustain spaces for richly textured conversation between theologians of varying persuasions and differing expertise as it is to nurture the opportunities for similar conversations between theologians and the hierarchy.

Survey 3: Changes in Substantive Theological Understanding Since Vatican II

No aspect of Catholic thought and practice is untouched by the combined effects of the spirit of *ressourcement* and renewal, the new-found openness to the world, the increased sense of being a genuinely world church, the proliferation of theological approaches and resources, and the multiplication of contexts and perspectives that have together characterized Catholic theology after Vatican II. Reflecting the pastoral, ecclesial orientation of Vatican II and the fact that the specifically doctrinal tensions that have emerged since have frequently been indicative of prior ecclesiological concerns, these various aspects are here treated in the order *Church, Ecumenism, Ministry, Spirituality, Moral Theology, Political Theology, Revelation and Fundamental Christology, Trinity and Soteriology.*

Church

Clearly, there is a great deal more to say regarding the characteristic sense and practice of Catholicism than can be conveyed by focusing on institutional factors alone. Nevertheless, going right to the core of the notion of Catholicity, with profound implications both for the shaping of Catholicism's own internal structures and for the formal, institutional dimension of its witness to the world, are ongoing debates concerning the appropriate relationship between episcopal collegiality and Roman primacy or, alternatively expressed, between the various local churches that together constitute the universal church and the particular local church of Rome as the symbolic and structural organ of the church's unity.[38] In practical terms the change has been minimal. While a strong theology of the episcopate was included in *Lumen Gentium* as a counterbalance to the unqualified papal monarchianism of Vatican I, the precise relationship between the college of bishops and the pope was left unresolved. This, combined with the lack of any legislative requirement for the reform of the Roman Curia, has meant the balance of power has continued to be disproportionately weighted in favor of Rome, with the episcopacy effectively confined to the ranks of subalterns.

The centrality of this issue to the performance of Catholicism has, nevertheless, served to keep it a focus of attention at the highest levels. Compare here the published disputation between Cardinals Ratzinger and Kasper concerning the relationship between the universal church and the local churches, with Ratzinger arguing for the ontological priority of the former over the latter and Kasper arguing for their simultaneity and necessary reciprocity.[39] Quite apart from its role in shaping assumptions at every level of Catholic life concerning appropriate governance and authority, this issue raises in structural form the key question as to the quality of the unity the church is called to reflect – whether one of centralized, acontextual uniformity or one of internally differentiated, contextually specific communion.[40]

Ecumenism

Clearly related to the preceding discussion is the ecumenical issue placed so firmly on the Catholic agenda by the groundbreaking Council document *Unitatis Redintegratio*.[41] Particular highpoints since have been the recognition of the degree of communion that already exists between the divided churches, the progress made in various bilateral discussions (most notably the ARCIC (Anglican–Roman Catholic International Commission) process and the joint Roman Catholic–Lutheran declaration on justification), and the positive exploration of the idea of "reconciled diversity." With this also is John Paul II's affirming inventory in his 1995 encyclical *Ut Unum Sint* ("On Commitment to Ecumenism") of the significant progress made since Vatican II, culminating in his remarkable invitation to church leaders and theologians in other Christian traditions to help with the task of reimagining the Petrine office and its associated structures so that it might again become a perceptible resource for Christian unity rather than the continuing significant cause of division it currently is. Persistent tensions have also been in evidence, however, as came to a head in 2000 with the publication by the Congregation for the Doctrine of the Faith of *Dominus Iesus*. Its tone, particularly when read together with a note to bishops banning the use of the phrase "Sister churches" in reference to other Christian bodies, led many to infer that Roman policy was in reverse. It is to be hoped that it is the more constructive spirit of receptive ecumenism evinced by *Ut Unum Sint* that will prevail.

Ministry

Another key focus of attention in the years since Vatican II has been the relationship between the dignity, vocation, and ministry of the laity and the clergy. If the context for such discussions has been the massive development of lay ministry since the Council, framing them has been an apparent tension within *Lumen Gentium* where, despite structural precedence being given to the common baptismal dignity and priesthood of all over the hierarchical character of the church, it is, nevertheless, held that the specific priesthood of the ordained is essentially different to that of the laity.[42] Schillebeeckx, Küng, and others have charged that any such notion of an essential or ontological distinction between lay and ordained supports the perpetuation of a separate clerical caste by failing to give due recognition to the Spirit-indwelled, charism-endowed, priestly character of the entire "people of God."[43] In response it has been maintained that it is only by viewing ordained priesthood as a fundamentally different exercise of ministry to that of the laity that one avoids suggesting that the first is a better, more intense version of the same thing. Together with this is the recognition that the primacy and dynamism of grace requires ordination to be viewed as pertaining to the priest's vocation and being before God and not just the things he does.

The ecclesial political dimension that is a factor in all theological debate has been a particularly complicating factor here, with strong values such as the desire for a more collaborative, transparent, and accountable church and the concern to articulate a rich, sustaining theology of ordained ministry frequently finding themselves in conflict.[44] There is, consequently, an outstanding need within contemporary Catholicism for an integrated, non-competitively articulated theology of lay and ordained ministry capable of generating a working consensus.

A possible way forward here is to view the "sacramentality" of ordained priesthood as consisting in the public, officially authenticated, representative performance of the God-given ministry pertaining to the entire Spirit-filled People of God.[45] As such, the distinctiveness of ordained priesthood would be held to lie neither in it being an essentially different kind of priesthood to that of the laity, nor in it being a higher quality version of the same priesthood. Rather, its distinctiveness would lie in it being a fundamentally different mode of exercise (public, official, representative) of the one priesthood of Christ in which all the baptized share; a different mode of exercise, moreover, that defines the specific vocation of the ordained.

One implication is that for the sake of its own authenticity this distinctive exercise of ministry must be performed in genuine service of and accountability to the ministry of the entire church. A further implication might be that if the distinctive sacramentality of ordained ministry consists precisely in its being *representative* of the Spirit-filled, charism-endowed Body of Christ, then the regulations concerning eligibility for ordination should be altered so as to reflect the actual composition of that Body. In this regard the Council's decision to admit mature married men to the diaconate – one of the very few structural changes actually made at the Council – might be seen as a modest yet significant step in this direction.

Spirituality

Stimulated in part by the Council's recommendation that religious orders should reconnect with the charisms of their respective founders; in part by *Lumen Gentium*'s emphasis on the calling of the entire pilgrim people of God to holiness; in part by the increased emphasis placed on the need for prayerful reflection on the word of scripture; in part by the influence involvement in charismatic renewal has had on a good number of Catholics, both lay and ordained; in part by what Rahner recognized as the need for contemporary Christians to have an experiential dimension to their faith if they are to be sustained in a secularized context; and in part also, no doubt, by generally increased Western expectations of personal fulfillment, the net result is that growth towards Christian spiritual maturity is no longer viewed simply as an esoteric pursuit of the few, but as the normal path of Catholic life.

In terms of formal theology this shift is reflected in three ways. First is the growth of scholarship in the classics of spiritual theology and contemporary disciplines that has led to the emergence of spirituality as an academic subject area in its own right.[46] Second is the phenomenon of theologians whose writings, at least in part, take the explicit form of high-level meditative reflection-cum-spiritual counsel oriented toward the dramatic shaping of Christian life.[47] Third is an increasing concern to view theologians of even the most rigorously philosophical of appearances as seeking to articulate, in a fashion somewhat secondary to the living of Christian faith, good habits of thought in the service of Christian discipleship and the life of the church.[48] It is, perhaps, the second and third of these points in particular that help explain the significant interest now frequently shown in notable Catholic theologians by theologians in other Christian traditions.[49]

Moral theology

Reflecting in some ways an implicit tension between the ahistorical, universalist essentialism of neoscholastic natural law theory and the emphasis placed upon the role of the informed conscience in Vatican II teaching, much subsequent Catholic moral theology has been characterized by a profound disagreement between those of an "absolutist" commitment and those influenced by "proportionalist" ways of thinking.[50] It would be inaccurate to view this as a difference between Christocentric and personalist commitments. Catholic absolutists are as concerned for the flourishing of the person as Catholic proportionalists and the proportionalists are as concerned to articulate an ethic that reflects the discerned patterns of God's self-revelation in the incarnate Christ as the absolutists, albeit construed in different ways in each instance.

The difference relates more to whether human nature and the teleology of human acts are understood in fixed, essentialist terms or in historically particular and, hence, intrinsically plural terms requiring discerning judgment in the specificities of particular lives. Where absolutists judge proportionalists as guilty of an indulgent relativism, proportionalists judge absolutists as operating with an outmoded anthropology, particularly regarding human sexuality, that does not reflect the realities of created human life and renders Catholic moral teaching inflexible, incredible, and damaging to faith.[51]

The symbolic benchmark has taken the form of defense of or dissent from the 1968 encyclical *Humanae Vitae* in which, against the majority decision of the consultative commission but supported by the then Archbishop Karol Wojtyla, Pope Paul VI reaffirmed the traditional ban on so-called "artificial" means of contraception.[52] This has led to an unfortunate climate in which criticism of *Humanae Vitae* is generally but inaccurately read as a rejection of moral absolutism *per se*.

The renewed appeal to a Thomist-inspired virtue ethic might be assumed to offer a way of overcoming this stand-off. Here the emphasis is neither simply upon the observance of rules rightly viewed as absolute, nor upon the requirement that judgments always be made in proportion to one's perceived needs and circumstances. Rather, the emphasis is upon becoming sufficiently skilled in the habits of virtue, through disciplined practice among those already proficient in playing according to the rules, as to be able to make appropriately prudent judgments in the particularities of life.[53] In this understanding, unabrogable defining rules and creative play are not antitheses but necessary correlates of sound ethical apprenticeship in genuine Christian autonomy.

The disagreement between absolutist and supposedly proportionalist stances can be restated more precisely, then, in terms of the need for the formal Magisterium to examine whether the various positions it currently holds indiscriminately as absolutely binding laws are indeed all appropriately so regarded.[54] For all the energetically executed counter-moves of John Paul II, the Catholic Church still finds itself in a dysfunctional situation where the prayerfully discerned judgment of many playing members is at odds with the judgment of those controlling the revision of the rule book. Consequently, if the mantra once offered to Catholic laity was "Pay, pray, and obey," for many it has now become "It pays to pray about what it means to obey." Quite apart from its negative impact on Catholic ecclesial life, the danger for Catholicism's viability as a school of virtue is that, if left unrepaired, this crisis of authority will lead to more wholesale dismissals of the binding force of Catholic moral teaching and so further the kinds of uninformed autonomy it seeks to counter.

Political theology

The altered common sense that *Gaudium et Spes* and the subsequent emergence of Latin American liberation theology promoted is reflected most broadly in an increased concern to treat the various dimensions of Catholic faith in a way that draws out their social and political freight.[55] Significant in a more specific way are the contributions made by Catholics in the many contextual, or issue-based, theologies now generally covered by the phrase "political theology" – eco-theology, black theology, hispanic theology, gay theology and, as already noted, feminist theology

– with the latter itself now more appropriately subcategorized in terms of feminist, womanist, and mujerista theologies. In turn, for those whose specific focus is upon the explicitly economic dimensions of the political, the collapse of state communism in the former Soviet-bloc countries in 1989 and the subsequent globalization of the market economy is requiring a process of fresh thinking.

Although a desire lingers on in Catholic left circles, fired by a vision of the church as a prophetic community of resistance and counter-anticipation, to adopt a stance of fundamental opposition to the capitalist system, the increasing realization of our common implication in and dependence upon the global economy is leading to more subtle negotiations.[56] Of continuing importance here is the recognition of the "preferential option for the poor" as *the* vital lens through which to judge the grossly unjust and dehumanizing failings of the present system and, complementing this, the need for imaginatively enacted, evangelically inspired anticipations – lived parables, as it were – of a transformed order.[57] It is now more commonly appreciated, however, that equally important is the need to apply intelligence and vision to identifying integral ways in which the existing global system can be made more just, and correlative acumen and pressure to achieving these.[58] Given that the extent of theologians' engagement with economic theory is generally relatively slight – Lonergan and, more recently, Küng being notable exceptions[59] – there is a sense in which much of the most important work in Catholic political theology is now being carried out by theologically informed analysts, advocates, and campaign organizers within the Catholic aid and development agencies.

Revelation and fundamental Christology

Intertwined with the various substantive developments thus far reviewed have been a number of key shifts in specifically doctrinal understanding. Issuing, for example, from Vatican II's *Dei Verbum* ("Dogmatic Constitution on Divine Revelation," November 18, 1965), has been a more dynamic, pneumatologically governed understanding of revelation and tradition that has prompted a fresh emphasis upon the historicity of Christian life in much subsequent Catholic theology.[60] In this way of thinking it is inadequate simply to apply the inherited form of Catholic understanding to the specificities of contemporary experience in a secondary manner. Even allowing for Lindbeck's influential critique of the role of experience in theology, the intrinsic dynamism of Christian tradition itself requires a process of integral discerning of genuinely fresh yet authentic articulations in the new circumstances encountered.[61]

These fundamental shifts in perspective, combined with the further encouragement given in *Dei Verbum* to the use of critical methods of scripture study, prompted massive efforts of doctrinal reformulation, in some ways paralleling the process that Protestant theology had been working through since the nineteenth century.[62] As in that context a key concern has been how historical–critical methods of analyzing the gospels and other relevant documents are to be reconciled with the traditional doctrine of Christ and appropriately assimilated into its contemporary articulation.

For a period, the dominant approach, motivated both by apologetic concern and by the conviction that it supported significantly fresh understandings of God's self-revelation in Jesus, was to adopt a view, as it were, "from below," and to seek thereby to move inductively on the basis of historical analysis to an account of Jesus who became recognized as the Christ.[63] Typically accorded a fulcrum role in this process are traces in the New Testament writings of experiences of encounter with the saving, transforming reality of God in the risen Jesus and the Spirit.[64] In reaction, however, to what was felt to be the relative fragility and theologically thin texture of the resulting reconstructions, a renewed concern emerged, exemplified by Balthasar in Catholic theology, as previously by Barth in Protestant, to read the gospel accounts in a manner explicitly informed by traditional credal understanding of the identity of their central character.[65] For their part, the most astute interpreters recognized that, as befits the duality that is at issue in Christian understanding of the person of Jesus, both approaches are in fact necessary, each tending toward imbalance without the other.[66]

Indeed, in mainstream Catholic theology – within which both *Concilium* and *Communio* currents can be viewed as flowing – there is an important sense in which any notion of a supposedly irreconcilable tension between these approaches is somewhat artificial. For the vast majority of Catholic scholars adopting an approach "from below," liturgically informed credal faith can be assumed to provide an implicit prior frame of understanding, such that historical–critical methods are all along at the service of seeking to understand the character of God's self-revelation in the incarnate Word, Jesus of Nazareth, even when the explicit form and sequence of their writings does not suggest as much. Equally, historical analyses represent a vital ancillary resource both for the *ad hoc* testing and potential enrichment of more dogmatically driven Christologies and for helping guard against the dangers of indulgent fantasy and constriction of vision.

This Christologically focused issue can, then, be viewed as a particular instance of the broader issue, implicit in the work of Roman Catholic scripture scholars such as Raymond Brown, of how to integrate the various critical modes of scriptural analysis within what *Dei Verbum* recognized to be the continuing need for explicitly tradition-informed, canonical readings thereof.[67] In this regard Lash's espousal of a practically engaged, existentially rooted postliberalism that determinedly maintains the need for theology to engage with the full range of critical resources is suggestive of rich possibilities.[68]

Trinity and soteriology

Not unnaturally, accompanying these developments in fundamental Christology have been related developments in the theology of the Trinity and soteriology. With regard to the Trinity, particularly notable is the influence jointly exerted by Rahner's principle of the identity of the "economic Trinity" (the Trinity as disclosed in the economy of salvation) and the "immanent Trinity" (the inner trinitarian life of God) and the related traditional principle of the interrelated unity in act of the three distinct eternal modes of God's being.[69] Together, these principles have promoted a heightened concern to treat as genuinely disclosive of how God is what can be discerned of the patterns, actions, and commitments that characterized the life, death, and resurrection of Jesus and continued to characterize early Christian life in the Spirit.[70] Equally, viewed from a different angle, they have promoted dogmatically intensified readings of these patterns and commitments as the enactment in finite temporal reality of the dynamics that *are* the eternal being in act of God.[71]

More recently, such understandings of the being of God and, specifically, of the role of the Spirit, have been put to work in the context of seeking to articulate a theology of religious pluralism that can genuinely maintain the reality of God's presence and action in the distinct particularities of other faith traditions – and in ways from which Christians can learn – while also maintaining the traditional claim that there is nothing that can be known of God that will not cohere with what is shown in Jesus, the incarnate Word.[72] Particularly notable here is the move from viewing the covenant in Christ as dissolving the covenant with the Jewish people, as was standard in much pre-Vatican II understanding, to viewing the latter as of permanent validity.[73] This is of significance to all ecumenical and interfaith theological reflection, as it requires a considerably more subtle and sophisticated theology of divine providence and call than is implied by supercessionist accounts of the relationship between the Jewish and Christian covenants.

Turning to matters soteriological, the recurrent tension in recent Catholic theology between more world-receptive and more world-judging tendencies has been played out here in some interesting if unhelpful ways. According to the caricature, from the more world-receptive perspective, the world-judging tendency lacks due appreciation for the intrinsic goodness of God's grace-indwelled creation as brought to fulfillment in the Incarnation and so tends towards a form of sub-Christian dualism.[74] Equally, from the more world-judging perspective, the world-receptive tendency lacks a realistic understanding of the radical extent and disfiguring effects of sin and the consequent need for its unmasking and redemption in the cross and resurrection.[75] In reality the differences between these two emphases neither are, nor ever could be, as radically opposed as this suggests.

Rahner, for example, does, in a sense, view the Incarnation itself as the achievement of human salvation in as much as it represents the absolute self-communication of God being met with absolute responsive openness in a way that recapitulates, fulfills, and redeems the story of creation, grace, and sin.[76] He does not, however, take this as a merely static fact, but as a dynamic reality characterizing Jesus' entire life, climactically so in his death, and a movement, moreover, into which others are in turn drawn. Equally, for all Balthasar's concern to depict the contrast between the disorder of sin and the order of grace in starker terms than he finds in Rahner and, with this, to view God's judgment on sin in Jesus' crucifixion as an event of inner-trinitarian alienation, he also views the total event of the Incarnation as the crowning and fulfillment of creation. Again, despite their apparent greater sympathy with a Rahnerian rather than a Balthasarian/*Communio* orientation, it is a real concern also for politically conscious theologians such as Metz and Schillebeeckx that due emphasis be given to the counter-cultural, transformative dynamic at the heart of Jesus' life, death, and resurrection.

Further, it is possible to integrate this emphasis on the political/cultural dimensions of the soteriological significance of the Jesus event with a robust understanding of the trinitarian reality of God. In this way of thinking, the counter-cultural, transformative dynamic that shapes the particular story of Jesus is to be viewed as the dramatic performance within the conditions of temporal human life of the dynamic of life-enabling self-giving that *is* the eternal being of God. In turn, if this creative–

transforming dynamic constitutes the "objective" dimension to God's saving act in Christ and the Spirit, the "subjective" dimension consists in being drawn to participate in it and to grow into it even while continuing to exist in a world marked by the contrary self-serving dynamic of sin.[77] In such a perspective the primary calling of the church is to bear convincing, attractive witness to the counter-cultural, transforming action of God known in the church as at work in the world. Correlatively, it is in light of this that all aspects of church life and structure, both local and universal, need to be held open to judgment and potential reconfiguration lest they themselves become counter-signs of that which they proclaim. It is hardly surprising that this indicates the locus for many of the continuing challenges within contemporary Catholic theology.

Assessment and Conclusion: Anticipating the Future

The institutional (Survey 1), methodological (Survey 2), and substantive (Survey 3) developments that have occurred in Catholic theology since Vatican II each variously reflect the shift to being a truly world church, both one and universal. The fundamental issue of how to handle unity in diversity, how to hold plurality in appropriate communion, is raised in one way by the proliferation of specific theological commitments, methods, and resources and in a more pervasive way by an increased appreciation for the irreducible historicity and particularity of Christian life.

On the one hand, the proliferation of specialisms highlights the dual need to view theology as a collaborative exercise and to nurture structures that promote critically constructive conversation across specialisms and diverse perspectives. On the other hand, increased sensitivity to the historicity of Christian life highlights the need for mutual critically constructive interchange between the official and unofficial levels of Catholic theology in the dual process of sieving and retrieving the historic tradition and discerning its appropriate performance today. Each of these points, particularly the second, in turn requires that explicit attention be paid to core issues concerning the appropriate structures of governance and exercise of authority at the various levels of Catholic life.

Closely related to this is the need to move towards a more collegial and reciprocal and less monarchical exercise of the Petrine office and associated curial bureaucracy *vis-à-vis* the Catholic episcopate.[78] Quite apart from its bearing on the integrity, initiative, and potential contributions of the local churches, this issue is of enormous symbolic significance. It serves to shape the broader Catholic common sense as to the appropriate exercise of the dual ministry of authority and communion in its many other forms, whether episcopal, priestly, or lay. Again, it also bears directly on the ecumenical context, as John Paul II recognized in *Ut Unum Sint*. Interwoven with this, in turn, is the question of whether Catholicism can be genuinely receptive to what can be learned from the alternative ecclesial forms, structures, and practices of the other Christian traditions and so be held open to its own potential expansion and renewal.[79] Two particular cases in point here are the Anglican experience of synodical structures and the connexional ethos that is so deeply ingrained in Methodism, together with the associated role of Conference in decision making.

Alert to the institutional inertia and self-protection generated by long-established bureaucratic systems and, hence, of the likely inability of the Roman Curia to reform itself, Lash proposes as a way forward the establishment of a papal commission comprising "perhaps forty or fifty diocesan bishops, drawn from every corner of the world" with both curial officials and "historians, theologians and canon lawyers from outside Rome" acting as advisors. The brief would be "to draw up proposals for the transfer of governance in the Church from pope and Curia to pope and bishops, through the establishment of a standing synod, whose members would be diocesan bishops and whose work would be assisted by the offices of a curia so reformed as to function, not as an instrument of governance, but as a service of administration."[80]

Were such a significant shift in the culture of Catholic governance to take place in combination with the articulation of the non-competitive theology of lay and ordained ministry sketched earlier, the result could, as Lash hopes, be a "cascade of subsidiarity." Correlatively, this could create a climate in which it would appear simply nonsensical to handle contentious issues in the life of the church either by refusing to allow them to be discussed or by excluding all but those with sworn allegiance to the current state of official understanding from participation. On the contrary, while duly respecting the decision-making responsibility of those in authority in any given context, the assumed common sense would move towards recognizing the need to make appropriate spaces at both the local and universal levels of church life for theologians of differing perspectives and areas of expertise to meet with members of the hierarchy, ecclesial bureaucrats, and others, in order to work together at discerning the good of the Body.[81] The officially sponsored emergence of such structures for genuine, critically constructive conversation in service of the church's continued learning would represent a significant new phase in the institutional reception of Vatican II. Rather than difference and debate being viewed as its problematic inheritance, they would then both be valued as normal and necessary to the health of the whole. This would really be to do Catholic theology after Vatican II for, as Congar noted, its legacy lies in no small part in the way in which its very occurrence granted legitimacy to the fact of debate in the church and to the associated need for appropriate structures and practices of shared discernment by retrieving the ancient conciliar dimension of Catholic life.[82]

Acknowledgments

Grateful thanks are due to a number of friends and colleagues for their comments on earlier drafts of this chapter. Of these, particular mention must be made of Karen Kilby, Nicholas Lash, Patricia McDonald SHCJ, David McLoughlin, Paul McPartlan, Walter Moberly, and Janet Martin Soskice.

Notes

1 For Lonergan, see H. Meynell, "Bernard Lonergan," in D. F. Ford (ed.), *The Modern Theologians*, 1st edn. (Oxford, 1989), pp. 205–16; also F. E. Crowe, *Lonergan* (London, 1992).

2 For Schillebeeckx, see R. J. Schreiter, "Edward Schillebeeckx," in D. F. Ford (ed.), *The Modern Theologians*, 2nd edn. (Oxford, 1997), pp. 152–61; also P. Kennedy, *Schillebeeckx* (London, 1993).

3 For Küng, see W. G. Jeanrond, "Hans Küng," in D. F. Ford (ed.), *The Modern Theologians*, 2nd edn. (Oxford, 1997), pp. 162–78; also H. Häring and K.-J. Kuschel (eds.), *Hans Küng: New Horizons for Faith and Thought* (London, 1993).

4 See K. Rahner, "A Critique of Hans Küng: Concerning the Infallibility of Theological Propositions," *Homiletic and Pastoral Review*, 71 (1971), 10–26 (13); compare Rahner and Küng, "A 'Working Agreement' to Disagree," *America*, 129 (July 7, 1973), 11–12.

5 Küng, *Global Responsibility: In Search for a New World Ethic* (New York, 1991).

6 For a magisterial treatment of Wojtyla/John Paul II's life and thought, see G. Weigel, *Witness to Hope: The Biography of John Paul II* (London, 2001).

7 Cf. P. D. Murray, "A Liberal Helping of Postliberalism Please," in M. D. Chapman (ed.), *The Future of Liberal Theology* (Aldershot, 2002), pp. 208–18.

8 For Lash, see D. W. Hardy, "Theology Through Philosophy," in D. F. Ford (ed.), *The Modern Theologians*, 2nd edn. (Oxford, 1997), pp. 252–85; also P. D. Murray, " 'Theology Under the Lash': Theology as Idolatry-Critique in the Work of Nicholas Lash," in S. C. Barton (ed.), *Idolatry* (London, 2005).

9 For sophisticated versions of this telling, see E. Schillebeeckx, *Vatican II: The Real Achievement* (London, 1967); L. Gilkey, *Catholicism Confronts Modernity: A Protestant View* (New York, 1975); and for a sociologically informed account, B. McSweeney, *Roman Catholicism: The Search for Relevance* (Oxford, 1980).

10 Published alongside Pope Pius IX's encyclical *Quanta Cura*.

11 The "modernist" position condemned in Pius X's 1907 encyclical *Pascendi Dominici Gregis* was a synthetic construct of various of the ideas entertained by Catholic intellectuals exploring how Catholic faith might be integrated with modern thought; see Lash, "Modernism, Aggiornamento and the Night Battle," in A. Hastings (ed.), *Bishops and Writers: Aspects of the Evolution of Modern English Catholicism* (Wheathamstead, 1977), pp. 51–79.

12 A. Flannery (ed.), *Vatican Council II: The Conciliar and Post Conciliar Documents* (New York, 1981), pp. 903–1001.

13 See A. Hastings, "Catholic History from Vatican I to John Paul II," in A. Hastings (ed.), *Modern Catholicism: Vatican II and After* (London, 1991), pp. 1–13; McSweeney, *Roman Catholicism*, pp. 256–61.

14 For the first, negative assessment, see P. Hebblethwaite, "John Paul II," in A. Hastings (ed.), *Modern Catholicism: Vatican II and After* (London, 1991), pp. 447–56. For the second, more positive appraisal, see Weigel, *Witness to Hope*, pp. 486–90, 502–5, 846–7; T. Rowland, *Culture and the Thomist Tradition After Vatican II* (New York, 2003), pp. 11–50.

15 See J. Komonchak, "Vatican II as an 'Event,'" *Theology Digest*, 46 (1999), 337–52. I am grateful to Philip Caldwell for recommending this essay. Also G. Alberigo, J. P. Jossua, and J. Komonchak (eds.), *The Reception of Vatican II* (Washington, DC, 1987); G. Alberigo and J. Komonchak (eds.), *History of Vatican II*, Vols. 1–5 (New York, 1996–2004).

16 See M. Schoof, *Breakthrough: Beginnings of the New Catholic Theology* (Dublin, 1970).

17 See Flannery, *Vatican Council II*, pp. 350–423. Here, a fascinating cross-type discussion is to be found in N. M. Healy, *Church, World and Christian Life: Practical–Prophetic Ecclesiology* (Cambridge, 2000).

18 See J. Buckley, "Revisionists and Liberals," chapter 13 above; also J. Fodor, "Postliberal Theology," chapter 14 above.

19 See Lash, "Theologies at the Service of a Common Tradition," in C. Geffré, G. Gutiérrez, and V. Elizondo (eds.), *Concilium. Different Theologies, Common Responsibility: Babel or Pentecost?* (Edinburgh, 1984), pp. 74–83.

20 A. MacIntyre, *After Virtue: A Study in Moral Theory*, 2nd edn. (London, 1985), p. 222.

21 J.-B. Metz, *Faith in History and Society: Toward a Practical Fundamental Theology* (London, 1980), p. 58.

22 See Congregation for the Doctrine of the Faith (CDF), *Donum Veritatis*, Instruction

"On the Ecclesial Vocation of the Theologian" (Vatican City, 1990).

23 See John Paul II, *Veritatis Splendor*, Encyclical Letter "On the Church's Moral Teaching" (London, 1993), n. 113.

24 See J. Milbank, C. Pickstock, and G. Ward (eds.), *Radical Orthodoxy: A New Theology* (London, 1999); compare L. P. Hemming (ed.), *Radical Orthodoxy? A Catholic Enquiry* (Aldershot, 2000).

25 In the latter regard, Anne Carr, Mary Grey, Elizabeth Johnson, Catherine Mowry LaCugna, and Sandra M. Schneiders are particularly significant.

26 For example, in the British context, Janet Martin Soskice of the University of Cambridge, Tina Beattie of the Roehampton Institute, Sarah Boss of the Marian Studies Institute, Lampeter, and Susan Parsons of the Margaret Beaufort Institute, Cambridge.

27 See E. Gilson, *The Philosophy of Saint Thomas Aquinas*, 2nd edn. (New York, 1929); M.-D. Chenu, *Aquinas and His Role in Theology* (Collegeville, 2002), first published in French in 1959.

28 See S. J. Duffy, *The Graced Horizon: Nature and Grace in Modern Catholic Thought* (Collegeville, 1992).

29 For Teilhard, see C. Deane-Drummond, "Theology and the Biological Sciences," ch. 21 below. For the influence of Scheler's personalist phenomenology on Wojtyla, see R. Buttiglione, *Karol Wojtyla: The Thought of the Man Who Became Pope John Paul II* (Grand Rapids, MI, 1997), pp. 117–76 (first published in Italian).

30 See K. Rahner, "The Abiding Significance of Vatican II," *Theological Investigations XX* (London, 1981), pp. 90–102; B. J. F. Lonergan, "Theology in Its New Context" (1968), in W. F. J. Ryan and B. J. Tyrrell (eds.), *A Second Collection* (London, 1974), pp. 55–67; and in the same volume, "The Transition from a Classicist Worldview to Historical-Mindedness" (1967), pp. 1–9.

31 See Aquinas, *Summa Theologiae*, Ia.I, 7; compare *Gaudium et Spes*, n. 22.

32 See Rahner, "The Abiding Significance of Vatican II," pp. 91–2; also "Basic Theological Interpretation of the Second Vatican Council," *Theological Investigations XX*, pp. 77–89.

33 See G. McCool, *From Unity to Pluralism: The Internal Evolution of Thomism* (New York, 1987); F. Kerr, *After Aquinas: Versions of Thomism* (Oxford, 2002); F. Kerr (ed.), *Contemplating Aquinas* (London, 2003).

34 Note should also be made of the significance of fresh retrievals of the tradition within historical theology, preeminently so recent revisionist readings of the Reformations; see E. Duffy, *The Stripping of the Altars: Traditional Religion in England, c.1400–c.1580* (New Haven, CT, 1992) and *The Voices of Morebath: Reformation and Rebellion in an English Village* (New Haven, CT, 2001). I am grateful to Janet Martin Soskice for reminding me of this.

35 See G. O'Collins, *Fundamental Theology* (New York, 1981); L. J. O'Donovan and T. H. Sanks (eds.), *Faithful Witness: Foundations of Theology for Today's Church* (London, 1989); R. Latourelle and R. Fisichella (eds.), *Dictionary of Fundamental Theology* (New York, 1994).

36 See F. S. Fiorenza, *Foundational Theology: Jesus and the Church* (New York, 1984); A. Dulles, *The Craft of Theology: From Symbol to System* (Dublin, 1996), pp. 3–15, 53–68; also P. D. Murray, *Reason, Truth and Theology in Pragmatist Perspective* (Leuven, 2004).

37 See K. Rahner, "Reflections on Methodology in Theology," *Theological Investigations XI* (London, 1974), pp. 68–114.

38 See *Lumen Gentium*, nos. 21–7, in Flannery, *Vatican Council II*, pp. 372–84; also A. Dulles, *The Catholicity of the Church* (Oxford, 1985), pp. 106–46; H. Küng, *Structures of the Church* (New York, 1964), pp. 201–304, and *The Church* (Tunbridge Wells, 1968), pp. 444–80; compare H. U. von Balthasar, *The Office of Peter and the Structure of the Church* (San Francisco, 1986).

39 See W. Kasper, "On the Church," *The Tablet* (June 23, 2001), 927–30; J. Ratzinger, "The Local Church and the Universal Church: A Response to Walter Kasper," *America* (November 19, 2001), 7–11.

40 See B. Hoose (ed.), *Authority in the Roman Catholic Church: Theory and Practice* (Aldershot, 2002); K. Rahner, "Unity of the

Church – Unity of Mankind," *Theological Investigations XX*, pp. 154–72; also R. J. Schreiter, *The New Catholicity: Theology Between the Global and the Local* (Maryknoll, NY, 1997).

41 "Decree on Ecumenism," November 21, 1964, in Flannery, *Vatican Council II*, pp. 452–70.

42 See *Lumen Gentium*, n. 10.

43 See H. Küng, *Why Priests? A Proposal for a New Ministry* (London, 1972); E. Schillebeeckx, *Ministry: A Case for Change* (London, 1981).

44 For the latter concern, see John Paul II, *Letters to My Brother Priests: Holy Thursday (1979–1994)*, ed. J. P. Socias (Princeton, NJ, 1994); also CDF, Instruction "On Certain Questions Regarding the Collaboration of the Non-ordained Faithful in the Sacred Ministry of Priests" (Vatican City, 1997).

45 For a significant study in this regard, see R. Murray, "Christianity's 'Yes' to Priesthood," in N. Lash and J. Rhymer (eds.), *The Christian Priesthood* (London, 1970), pp. 16–39, particularly pp. 25–8, 37–9. I am grateful to Nicholas Lash for drawing my attention to this essay.

46 See S. M. Schneiders, "Spirituality in the Academy," *Theological Studies*, 50 (1989), 676–97.

47 The most obvious example here is Hans Urs von Balthasar. Notable also are the encyclical teachings of John Paul II.

48 See N. M. Healy, "Indirect Methods in Theology: Karl Rahner as an Ad Hoc Theologian," *Thomist*, 56 (1992), 613–34; P. Endean, *Karl Rahner and Ignatian Spirituality* (Oxford, 2001); also N. M. Healy, *Thomas Aquinas: Theologian of the Christian Life* (Aldershot, 2003).

49 For example, L. Gardner et al., *Balthasar at the End of Modernity* (Edinburgh, 1999); J. Milbank and C. Pickstock, *Truth in Aquinas* (New York, 2001).

50 Of the first group, Germain Grisez, John Finnis, John Ford, and John Paul II are the outstanding figures. Of the second, Bernard Häring, Joseph Fuchs, and Charles Curran have had particular influence. See R. A. McCormick, "Moral Theology 1940–1989: An Overview," *Theological Studies*, 50 (1989), 3–24; P. I. Odozor, *Moral*

Theology in an Age of Renewal: A Study of the Catholic Tradition Since Vatican II (Notre Dame, IN, 2003).

51 See John Paul II, *Veritatis Splendor*, nn. 28–83; cf. C. Curran, *Toward an American Catholic Moral Theology* (Notre Dame, IN, 1987).

52 See J. Komonchak, "*Humanae Vitae* and its Reception: Ecclesiological Reflections," *Theological Studies*, 39 (1978), 221–57; J. Ford and G. Grisez, "Contraception and the Infallibility of the Ordinary Magisterium," *Theological Studies*, 39 (1978), 258–312; compare John Paul II, *Veritatis Splendor*, n. 80; also *Familiaris Consortio*, Apostolic Exhortation "On the Role of the Christian Family in the Modern World" (London, 1981).

53 See H. McCabe, "Manuals and Rule Books," in J. Wilkins (ed.), *Understanding Veritatis Splendor* (London, 1994), pp. 61–8.

54 See R. A. McCormick, "Killing the Patient," in J. Wilkins (ed.), *Understanding Veritatis Splendor* (London, 1994), pp. 14–20.

55 See, for example, E. Schillebeeckx, *Christ: The Christian Experience in the Modern World* (London, 1977); N. Lash, *A Matter of Hope: A Theologian's Reflections on the Thought of Karl Marx* (London, 1981); N. Lash, *Believing Three Ways in One God: A Reading of the Apostles' Creed* (London, 1992); N. Lash, *Holiness, Speech and Silence* (Ashgate, 2004).

56 See Metz, *Faith in History and Society*, pp. 88–99, 200–4; cf. N. P. Boyle, *Who Are We Now? Christian Humanism and the Global Market from Hegel to Heaney* (Edinburgh, 1998).

57 See John Paul II, *Sollicitudo Rei Socialis*, Encyclical Letter "On the Twentieth Anniversary of *Populorum Progressio*" (London, 1987); *Tertio Millennio Adveniente*, Apostolic Letter "Towards the Third Millennium" (London, 1994).

58 See M. Khor, *Rethinking Globalization: Critical Issues and Policy Choices* (New York, 2001).

59 See H. Küng, *A Global Ethic for Global Politics and Economics* (London, 1997); B. J. F. Lonergan, *Collected Works of Bernard Lonergan, Vol. 15: Macroeconomic Dynamics: An Essay in Circulation Analysis*, ed. F.

G. Lawrence, P. H. Byrne, and C. C. Hefling (Toronto, 1999); *Collected Works of Bernard Lonergan, Vol. 21: For a New Political Economy*, ed. P. J. McShane (Toronto, 1998).

60 See Flannery, *Vatican Council II*, pp. 750–65; cf. Y. Congar, "The Pneumatology of Vatican II," in *I Believe in the Holy Spirit* (London, 1983), pp. 167–73, and "Part One: The Spirit Animates the Church," in *I Believe in the Holy Spirit*, pp. 3–64; G. O'Collins, *Retrieving Fundamental Theology: The Three Styles of Contemporary Theology* (London, 1993).

61 See G. Lindbeck, *The Nature of Doctrine: Religion and Theology in a Postliberal Age* (London, 1984); cf. Murray, "A Liberal Helping of Postliberalism Please."

62 See F. S. Fiorenza and J. P. Galvin (eds.), *Systematic Theology: Roman Catholic Perspectives* (New York, 1992).

63 See W. Kasper, *Jesus the Christ* (London, 1976); H. Küng, *On Being a Christian* (London, 1978); K. Rahner and W. Thüsing, *A New Christology* (London, 1980); E. Schillebeeckx, *Jesus, an Experiment in Christology* (London, 1979); also R. Brown, *An Introduction to New Testament Christology* (New York, 1994).

64 See Schillebeeckx, *Jesus*, pp. 320–571, esp. pp. 379–97.

65 Compare G. Loughlin, *Telling God's Story: Bible, Church and Narrative Theology* (Cambridge, 1996).

66 See N. Lash, "Up and Down in Christology," in S. W. Sykes and D. Holmes (eds.), *New Studies in Theology 1* (London, 1980), pp. 31–46.

67 See *Dei Verbum*, n. 12, in Flannery, *Vatican Council II*, p. 758; also the Pontifical Biblical Commission, "The Interpretation of the Bible in the Church" (Vatican City, 1994); cf. S. M. Schneiders, *The Revelatory Text: Interpreting the New Testament as Sacred Scripture*, 2nd edn. (Collegeville, 1999); L. T. Johnson and W. S. Kurz, *The Future of Catholic Biblical Scholarship: A Constructive Conversation* (Grand Rapids, MI, 2002).

68 See, for example, N. Lash, "Performing the Scriptures," in *Theology on the Way to Emmaus* (London, 1986), pp. 37–46; cf. W. G. Jeanrond, *Theological Hermeneutics:*

Development and Significance (London, 1991), pp. 172–80.

69 See K. Rahner, *The Trinity* (Tunbridge Wells, 1970), pp. 21–4, 34–8, 45–6, 68–73, 76–7; also W. Kasper, *The God of Jesus Christ* (London, 1983); Lash, *Believing Three Ways in One God*, pp. 30–3.

70 See C. M. LaCugna, *God For Us* (New York, 1991), pp. 21–52, 209–41, 377–417; also Lash, *Believing Three Ways in One God*.

71 Compare H. U. von Balthasar, *Mysterium Paschale* (Edinburgh, 1990), originally published in German in 1970.

72 See G. D'Costa, *The Meeting of Religions and the Trinity* (Edinburgh, 2000); J. Dupuis, *Toward a Christian Theology of Religious Pluralism*, 2nd edn. (Maryknoll, NY, 2001); M. Barnes, *Theology and the Dialogue of Religions* (Cambridge, 2002); cf. CDF, *Dominus Iesus*, Declaration "On the Unicity and Salvific Universality of Jesus Christ and the Church" (Vatican City, 2000).

73 See Vatican II, *Nostra Aetate* ("Declaration on the Relation of the Church to Non-Christian Religions," October 28, 1965), n. 4, in Flannery, *Vatican Council II*, pp. 738–42; Pontifical Biblical Commission, *The Jewish People and Their Sacred Scriptures in the Christian Bible* (Vatican City, 2002).

74 Cf. E. Schillebeeckx, *God Among Us: The Gospel Proclaimed* (New York, 1983), pp. 91–6.

75 See H. U. von Balthasar, *The Moment of Christian Witness* (San Francisco, 1994), first published in German in 1966.

76 From among many possible references, see K. Rahner, "Current Problems in Christology," *Theological Investigations I* (London, 1965), pp. 149–200; "Christology Within an Evolutionary View of the World," *Theological Investigations V* (London, 1966), pp. 157–92, esp. pp. 160–1, 174–5; *Foundations of Christian Faith: An Introduction to the Idea of Christianity* (London, 1978), pp. 181, 197.

77 Compare F. J. van Beeck, "Trinitarian Theology as Participation," in S. T. Davis, D. Kendall, and G. O'Collins (eds.), *The Trinity* (New York, 1999), pp. 295–325.

78 See also M. J. Buckley, *Papal Primacy and the Episcopate: Towards a Relational Understanding* (New York, 1998).

79 Compare W. Kasper, "The Future of Ecumenism," *Theology Digest*, 49 (2002), 203–10; "Ecumenism: The Way Ahead," *The Tablet* (May 24, 2003), 32–4.

80 N. Lash, "Vatican II: Of Happy Memory – and Hope?" in A. Ivereigh (ed.), *Unfinished Journey: The Church 40 Years after Vatican II* (New York, 2003), pp. 13–31. This represents a refinement of a related suggestion of Archbishop John Quinn, in *The Reform of the Papacy* (New York, 1999).

81 The Catholic Common Ground Initiative, set up in 1996 by the late Cardinal Bernardin of Chicago, might provide a role model here. See Joseph Cardinal Bernardin, *Common Ground* (National Pastoral Life Center, New York, August 12, 1996); compare T. P. Rausch, "Towards Common Ground in Theology," in *Reconciling Faith and Reason: Apologists, Evangelists, and Theologians in a Divided Church* (Collegeville, 2000), pp. 115–26.

82 See Congar, "A Last Look at the Council," in A. Stacpoole (ed.), *Vatican II: By Those Who Were There* (London, 1986), pp. 337–58. I am grateful to Paul McPartlan for reminding me of this essay.

Bibliography

Primary

Flannery, A. (ed.), *Vatican Council II: The Conciliar and Post Conciliar Documents* (New York, 1981).

John Paul II, Pope, *Redemptor Hominis*, Encyclical Letter "Redeemer of Humankind" (London, 1979).

—— *Crossing the Threshold of Hope*, ed. M. V. Vittorio (London, 1994).

—— *Ut Unum Sint*, Encyclical Letter "On Commitment to Ecumenism" (London, 1995).

Küng, H., *The Church* (Tunbridge Wells, 1968).

—— *On Being a Christian* (London, 1978).

—— *Theology for the Third Millennium: An Ecumenical View* (London, 1991).

Lash, N., *Believing Three Ways in One God: A Reading of the Apostles' Creed* (London, 1992).

—— *The Beginning and the End of 'Religion'* (Cambridge, 1996).

—— *Holiness, Speech and Silence* (Ashgate, 2004).

Lonergan, B. J. F., *Method in Theology* (London, 1972).

—— *A Second Collection*, ed. W. F. J. Ryan and B. J. Tyrrell (London, 1974).

Schillebeeckx, E., *Christ: The Christian Experience in the Modern World* (London, 1977).

—— *Jesus, an Experiment in Christology* (London, 1979).

—— *Church: The Human Story of God* (London, 1990).

Secondary

Alberigo, G. and Komonchak, J. A. (eds.), *History of Vatican II*, Vols. 1–5 (New York, 1996–2004).

Hastings, A. (ed.), *Modern Catholicism: Vatican II and After* (London, 1991).

Latourelle, R., *Vatican II: Assessment and Perspectives, Twenty-Five Years After (1962–1987)*, Vols. 1–3 (New York, 1988–9).

McBrien, Richard P., *The Harper Collins Encyclopedia of Catholicism* (New York, 1995).

Stacpoole, A. (ed.), *Vatican II: By Those Who Were There* (London, 1986).

Tracy, D., Küng, H., and Metz, J. B. (eds.), *Toward Vatican III: The Work That Needs to Be Done* (Dublin, 1978).

Vorgrimler, H. (ed.), *Commentary on the Documents of Vatican II*, Vols. 1–5 (New York, 1967–9).

TEXTS, TRUTH, AND SIGNIFICATION

Biblical Interpretation

Anthony C. Thiselton

Introduction: Context and Influences

Over the two centuries from about 1750 to 1950 no issue of method was more central to biblical interpretation in the universities than that of how biblical specialists were to respond to the impact of the Enlightenment. Some streams of thought retained affinities with English deism, and interpreted the Bible on the basis of excluding any appeal to divine providence, "miracle," or a theistic worldview. Other streams of thought attempted to hold together a tradition which, following John Locke, gave privilege to "reason" and "reasonableness" as a primary criterion of judgment, but within a broadly theistic theology. A third stream, especially among some American conservatives, resisted aspects of the Enlightenment mindset, although arguably where in some cases they saw the Bible as a quasi-scientific set of propositions they did not escape a residual rationalism. All streams of thought struggled to ascertain the appropriate roles of historical description and theological inquiry.

The often over-used term "*the* historical–critical method" (misleadingly as if to suggest that these were only one) denotes a concern with historical inquiry and with the use of critical judgment designed to perform two major tasks. On one side it sought to free biblical interpretation from the prior imposition of theological categories and constraints drawn from ecclesial traditions or from individual religious conviction. On the other side it sought to accord primacy within the task of interpretation to the particularities of the specific historical situations out of which, and for which, biblical books and passages were written. Interpretation began with what the authors of biblical texts sought to convey to the addressees of their own day. Many biblical specialists excluded from their agenda whether this produced resonances for readers of later generations.

The nature of historical–critical methods may be illustrated initially from the two writers who are often regarded as the founders of modern biblical criticism, Semler and Michaelis. Johann S. Semler (1725–91) had religious roots in German pietism, but was also influenced by English deism and especially Enlightenment rationalism. His was not, however, an anti-theist rationalism, but more akin to John Locke's appeal to "reasonableness" within a theistic worldview. Reason provided a defense against religious fancies, for mere intensity of religious conviction is no guarantee of truth. Semler was professor in the University of Halle, and produced a four-volume treatise on the "free" investigation of the canon (*Abhandlung von Freier Untersuchung des Canons*, 1771–5). He perceived the shaping of the biblical canon as a long process of human responses to contingent, historical situations, rather than as the direct product of divine providence or divine intervention. What came to count as "scripture" became a purely *historical* question.

Semler insisted upon a so-called objective interpretation of the Bible, freed from theological assumptions brought to the text. The New Testament is to be understood in the context of its own times. However, the *historically given* biblical text is not to be equated with "the word of God" as a *theological* reality.

Semler's contemporary J. D. Michaelis (1717–91) was professor at Göttingen, and in his *Introduction to the New Testament* (1750; 4th edition 1791) he also stressed the *historical* dimension of biblical studies. Arguably, it represented the first of a new genre of works by biblical specialists, namely an "introduction" that set out issues of authorship, date, purpose, historical sitting, integrity, literary genre, and the situation and identity of the addressees. Michaelis tied issues of canonicity closely to that of authorship. Michaelis became influential also outside Germany.

In these early years Johann P. Gabler (1753–1826) even subsumed "true" (*wahre*) biblical theology under the rubric of *historical description* alone, even if he also allowed a place for "pure" (*reine*) biblical theology as a more theological area of inquiry. Yet some of his assumptions and areas of work might not seem to qualify as sheer value-neutral "description" today. Together with J. G. Eichhorn (1753–1826), he made much of the alleged "primitive oriental mentality" of the Hebrew writers. A "true" account of Genesis 2–3 supposedly narrated a couple's becoming aware of sexual difference; being driven from a protective oasis by a violent storm; and inferring from this the notion of divine judgment upon their fallenness. By the mid-nineteenth century, David F. Strauss (1808–74) had drawn upon Hegel's contrast between the religious language of "representation" (*Vorstellung*) and the "higher" critical conceptual language (*Begriff*) of philosophy. Strauss understood Hebrew "myth" to portray *ideas* in the guise of historical *narrative*. Partly anticipating Rudolf Bultmann (1884–1976), Strauss initiated what amounted to a "demythologizing" of New Testament texts.

However, Strauss stands in a quasi-secular tradition far removed from that of Semler and Michaelis, and also from Bultmann. Semler believed that a more rational and historical approach to biblical interpretation genuinely served the Christian faith. It would fall to Friedrich Schleiermacher of Berlin (1758–1834) to show in his hermeneutics that such historical disciplines as "Introduction to the New Testament," far from being antiquarian and relegating texts only to the past, in fact provided part (although not all) of the road to a present encounter and active engagement with biblical texts in the present. We shall return to Schleiermacher's important work later.

Meanwhile, two trends continued during the nineteenth century that provided, respectively, two turning points in twentieth-century biblical interpretation. First, the impact of the contrast between "mythological" language in biblical texts and supposedly central "ideas" nurtured a liberal theology that reached its peak in the first two decades of the twentieth century. The climax of "liberal" biblical interpretation came with the liberal theology of Adolf von Harnack (1851–1930). Harnack believed that Jesus of Nazareth taught a minimal core of central ideas, which defined the "essence" of the teaching of Jesus, and hence, of Christianity. These were: the fatherhood of God, the brotherhood of humankind, and the infinite value of human soul. It was Paul and the hellenistic church who transposed these "simple" core ideas into a complex system of doctrine. The simple gospel became distorted by interaction with Greek metaphysics. Harnack popularized this thesis in lectures of 1899–1900, published as *The Essence of Christianity*, but translated into English under the title *What is Christianity?* (1900). This had an enormous influence.

Karl Barth (1886–1968) strongly and vehemently reacted against this liberal view of Jesus as a teacher of ideas: Jesus was the *Proclaimer* of an *eventful, active, divine word of grace* and *judgment*. Rudolf Bultmann also stressed that Jesus preached for a personal decision and response. Barth initiated a program of biblical interpretation that perceived biblical texts as mediating the Word of God in life-changing challenge and grace. Bultmann, from a very different theological perspective linked with existentialist insights, also rejected "value-neutral" reading. It is when the Bible engages with the questions that a reader brings to the text that scripture as divine Word springs into action.

The second turning point within twentieth-century biblical interpretation cannot be identified with a single date. However, from the 1950s to the present, the dominance of historical–critical methods of the kind described began to fragment into a more diversified and complex set of models and methods. Certainly, historical criticism continued to generate debate and struggle about the respective roles of historical and theological inquiry. Heikki Räisänen (b. 1941) of Helsinki has forcefully renewed this debate. He not only insists "there is no direct path from historical study to present application" (2001: 230), but also adds that all biblical interpretation should be strictly "historical." Räisänen cites with approval the claim of W. Wrede in 1897 that so-called "New Testament theology" can never be other than "the history of early Christian religion" (*Beyond New Testament Theology*, 1990). "Exegesis cannot provide theology with criteria that could determine the content of contemporary theological affirmations" (Räisänen 2001: 246; from "The New Testament in Theology," 1995).

At the same time, other writers fiercely contest this assumption. Peter Balla's *Challenge to New Testament Theology* (1997) offers detailed criticisms of Räisänen's claims. Christopher Seitz, R. Walter L. Moberly, N. T. Wright, and many mentioned below, hold together responsible interpretation of biblical material with critiques of exclusively developmental approaches or fragmented exegesis, and retain a central concern for the positive significance of the Bible for Christian theology today.

Furthermore, a new emphasis since the late 1960s and 1970s has nurtured interdisciplinary approaches to biblical interpretation. This has been nourished by the philosophical hermeneutics of Hans-Georg Gadamer (1900–2002); by the work of James Barr (b. 1924) and George B. Caird (1917–84) in linguistics and semantics; by the impact of literary theory, especially in American biblical interpretation; and most conspicuously by the creative and seminal work of Paul Ricoeur (b. 1913), who has taught in Paris and North America. Ricoeur breathed new life into biblical hermeneutics by drawing upon a variety of intellectual disciplines.

Survey: Biblical Interpretation in Theologians of the Word after 1919

Barth

Part I of this volume has already introduced Karl Barth. Nevertheless, a further short discussion of his biblical interpretation is called for here. Barth regards scripture as part of the threefold form of the Word of God. Some 1,400 pages of his *Church Dogmatics* bear the title "The Doctrine of the Word of God" (*Church Dogmatics* I: 1 and I: 2; i.e., in English the first two of thirteen (or fourteen) volumes). In section 4, Barth distinguishes between "The Word of God Preached" (Proclamation), "The Word of God Written" (Scripture), and "The Word of God Revealed" (the Person of Jesus Christ). Fundamentally, "Revelation . . . does not differ from the person of Jesus Christ nor from the reconciliation accomplished in Him" (p. 119). Yet, in a particular sense, the Word of God remains "one and the same whether we understand it as revelation, Bible, or proclamation" (p. 120).

This may seem to place the Bible in a different realm of discourse or "world" from that of mainline biblical criticism since Semler, and Barth acknowledged this. His preparation for ordination as a pastor at Safenwil, Switzerland, had been conducted under the guidance of such biblical teachers as W. Herrmann and Adolf von Harnack, whose approach we described above. Barth reflects: "In the end I failed as pastor at Safenwil." With Edward Thurneysen, he agonized about the causes of his "failure." Eventually, he came to believe that "we must begin all over again with a new orientation." In one of his earliest works, Barth wrote: "It is not right thoughts about God which form the content of the Bible, but the right divine thoughts about men" (Barth 1928: 43). "A new world projects itself into our old, ordinary, world" (p. 41). This "new world" centers on the sovereign grace of God, who creates out of nothing; it is not the history of humankind, but the "history of God" (p. 45).

The defense of Germany's role in World War I by 93 intellectuals who included "almost all of my German teachers" strained Barth's sympathies with them further. He declared: "A whole world of exegesis, dogmatics, and preaching, was shaken to the foundations." "Human independence is weighed in the balance and found wanting." At the age of 30 Barth began to "read [Romans] as though I had never read it before . . . I read and read and wrote and wrote." He found there a "new world" of divine grace and divine judgment that relativized all degrees of supposed human achievement, where "the world is the world: but God is God." The gospel is not "teaching," but *new creation*. In 1919 Barth published the first edition of his epoch-making commentary on Romans. At the same time, in addition to saturating himself in Paul, he also discovered the writings of the Danish thinker Søren Kierkegaard (1813–55), focusing on Kierkegaard's notion of the infinite qualitative difference between God and humankind. In 1922 a second edition of *Romans* appeared, with a yet stronger emphasis upon divine hiddenness, otherness, judgment, and holy transcendence. *Either* Christianity is a matter of human discovery, development, and "religious" capacities, *or* it is a matter of God's free, sovereign, transcendent, transforming, creative grace. Romans and the Bible, Barth declared, affirmed only the latter of these.

Barth's *Romans* made a huge impact on all sides. Many New Testament scholars in Germany rejected its failure to practice rigorous historical–critical exegesis. Bultmann was a major exception. He shared Barth's view that the Christian gospel offers not primarily "teaching," but a challenge to decision. Although he differed at crucial points from Barth, Bultmann agreed that interpreters cannot "understand" the Bible if they seek merely value-neutral information. With Paul, Barth and Bultmann perceive "the proclamation of the cross" as "an affront" to unbelievers (1 Corinthians 1: 18–25). This conviction characterizes their "Theology of the Word."

We cannot expand here on Barth's thought from his short prophetic commentary *The Resurrection of the Dead* (1924), through the period of *Anselm: Fides Quaerens Intellectum* (193–1), to his development through the *Church Dogmatics* (1936–67). In *The Resurrection of the Dead* he observes that the error at Corinth was to ground faith "not in God, but in their own belief in God and in particular leaders." The "secret nerve" of much of 1 Corinthians was "this 'of God' [1 Corinthians 4: 5]" (Barth 1933: 17, 18). In the *Dogmatics* (I: 1) the Bible is not *identical* with the Word of God, since *Christ* is primarily God's fullest Word. Nevertheless, the Bible witnesses to revelation and is inseparable from the divine Word, for God's Word is his own action and presence. God "speaks" when, where, and how it pleases God to speak (sect. 3). "God may speak to us through . . . a blossoming shrub or a dead dog" (p. 55). To open a Bible cannot force God to speak. Nevertheless, the Bible is the foundation that "impresses itself" upon the church and continuously constitutes it as church. "The canonical text has the character of a free power" that is to be distinguished from human commentary or preaching. What makes it the canon? "It is the Canon because it imposed itself upon the Church as such, and continually does so" (sect. 4, p. 107). The church did not *decide* what writings were canonical, but *recognized* where the Word of God made, and continued to make, a Christ-centered impact. Such an approach clearly differs from Semler's.

Barth places his view of the Bible as *divine address* within a framework of trinitarian doctrine and Christology. The incarnate Christ witnesses to the Godhood of the Father; the Bible witnesses to Christ; the Holy Spirit activates and actualizes scripture to mediate God's presence and promise. "The Word of God is God Himself in Holy Scripture . . . Scripture is holy and the Word of God because by the Holy Spirit it became and will become . . . a witness to divine revelation" (II: 2, sect. 19, p. 457). The church no more "controls" this word than it controls the sacraments; it draws its life from them. Humankind is not "autonomous."

Bultmann

Rudolf Bultmann (1884–1976) studied at Tübingen, Berlin, and Marburg. Hermann Gunkel (1862–1932) taught him Old Testament at Berlin, and introduced him to the method of form criticism. At Marburg, his teachers included W. Herrmann (1846–1922). Herrmann emphasized religious experience and relationship rather than doctrine, and held to a neo-Kantian disjunction between mere "facts" and the realm of "value." In conjunction with a nineteenth-century version of Lutheran pietism this neo-Kantian epistemology permitted Bultmann to relegate "history" to the realm of contingent facts, while faith belonged to the realm of value. Bultmann could thus write in 1941: "To believe in the cross of Christ does not mean to concern ourselves . . . with an objective event [*ein objektiv anschaubares Ereignis*] . . . but rather to make the cross of Christ our own, to undergo crucifixion with him" (Bultmann 1964: 36).

Bultmann's approach to New Testament interpretation both embraces historical–critical methods and simultaneously presupposes their inadequacy for Christian faith. He employs radical criteria for the task of historical reconstruction, as we clearly see in *The History of the Synoptic Tradition* (1921) and in *Jesus* (1926; English, *Jesus and the Word*). Bultmann's form criticism reflects the argument of W. Wrede's *The Messianic Secret* (1901) that much of the material in the gospels is not history, but theological expressions of the faith of early Christian communities.

Bultmann believes Albert Schweitzer's exposure of "failed" quests in his *Quest of the Historical Jesus* (1906) confirms this. He declares, "Interest in the personality of Jesus is excluded . . . We can now know almost nothing concerning the personality of Jesus, since the early Christian sources show interest in neither" (Bultmann 1958: 13–14). Bultmann does not reject *all* historical knowledge of Jesus. History does testify to "the that" (*das Dass*) of Jesus. Jesus called his disciples to follow him and proclaimed the Kingdom of God. However, Paul and the Synoptic traditions are not concerned with "the what" (*das Was*) of the character of Jesus, as if Jesus were a "phenomenon within the world" (Bultmann 1969: 239).

Bultmann insists that the concepts and language of value-neutral "facts" cannot be appropriate as a medium for understanding the Word of God, for God is "beyond" the world. In New Testament hermeneutics, "The most subjective [*subjektivste*] interpretation is . . . the most objective [*objektivste*], that is, only those who are stirred by the question of their own existence can hear the claim that the text makes" (Bultmann 1955: 256). Bultmann takes up the notion of "pre-understanding" [*Vorverständnis*] from Schleiermacher, Dilthey, and Heidegger: understanding "is constantly orientated to a particular formulation of a question [*Fragestellung*] . . . always *governed by a prior understanding of the subject*" (Bultmann 1955: 239; his italics). Biblical interpretation will never even *begin* if it is purely "objectivist" (i.e., without personal engagement). How could we *begin* to understand a musical or mathematical text, if we were first to *suppress all that we knew* about music or mathematics?

This view of hermeneutics and of different conceptual schemes (*Begrifflichkeit*) closely resonates with the philosophy of Martin Heidegger (1889–1976), Bultmann's contemporary, with whom he collaborated at Marburg. A third colleague, Hans Jonas, also argued that much of the language of second-century gnosticism was not "objective," but expressed *attitudes* under the guise of *appearing to describe states of affairs*, typically in gnosticism as astrological states of affairs.

All this sets the stage for Bultmann's influential essay "New Testament and Mythology" (1941). He writes, "Mythology is the use of imagery to express the other-worldly in terms of this world . . . For instance, divine transcendence is expressed as spatial distance" (Bultmann 1962: 11). More to the point, "The real purpose of myth is not to present an objective picture of the world as it is . . . Myth should be interpreted not cosmologically, but . . . existentially" (p. 11). Bultmann's proposal to "demythologize" the New Testament is thus largely a program of *de-objectification*.

It is unfortunate that several distinct issues now become confused, even conflated, as if they were one. The notion of myth as *analogy* (the normal vehicle of language in religion) becomes confused not only with "objectification," but also with a "history-of-religions" notion of myth as a conceptualization of divine action in the world as *supernatural miracle*. This last supposedly provokes a clash with "modernity." For "the idea of miracle has become impossible for us today . . . we understand nature as 'law-ful' occurrence" (p. 63).

It is not surprising that many misunderstand Bultmann's motivation here. His underlying concern is that the New Testament itself demands the interpretation of myth, since the "point" of the text is not to inform about the world, but to challenge and change human attitudes. Yet the intrusion of issues about miracles and a "three-decker universe" makes him appear to share the classical liberal concern about what "modern man" can or cannot believe. Bultmann rejects this kind of liberalism. Harnack and the liberals "wrongly reduced the gospel to a few basic principles of religion and ethics." In this case, "the kerygma has ceased to be kerygma" (p. 13); "the purpose of demythologizing is not to make religion more receptable to modern man . . . but to make clearer what the Christian faith is" (Bultmann 1964: 182–3). At its very best, Bultmann seeks to rediscover "the point" of New Testament texts in such a way as to remove false stumbling-blocks, to leave exposed only the genuine stumbling-block of the proclamation of the cross (1 Corinthians 1: 18–25).

Nevertheless, whatever his intentions, Bultmann leaves insuperable problems. The "givenness" of the Holy Spirit, for example, cannot be translated *without remainder* as "the possibility of a new life" or as openness to the future. The Lordship of Christ is not only an existential attitude of trust and obedience on the part of believers, but also an ontological status conferred by God (Romans 1: 3, 4). Bultmann offers an illuminating reply to a question from the World Council of Churches about whether "Jesus is God." He poses the question: "Does he help me because he is God's Son, or is he Son of God because he helps me?" (Bultmann 1955: 280). For him, it is decisively the latter: Christology does not offer "objectivizing propositions" (p. 281). To say "Jesus is God" means only "that God is to be encountered in him and only in him" (p. 274).

Similarly, to believe in the efficacy of the cross "does not mean to concern ourselves with a mythical process wrought outside of us" (Bultmann 1962: 36). The resurrection of Christ is "not an event of the past." "Faith in the resurrection is really the same thing as faith in the saving efficacy of the cross" (p. 39). As Barth observes, the resurrection is now no longer the foundation of Christian faith, but that which comes into being with the emergence of faith. The resurrection is "nothing other than the rise of faith in the risen one" (p. 42).

Bultmann disparages the attempts of conservative colleagues to defend the historicity of New Testament texts. This, he argues, leads to a false security. Faith should be directed not to arguments about historicity, but solely to the bare Word of God. Thus he regards his program of demythologizing as "a perfect parallel" to the Pauline and Lutheran doctrine of justification by grace through faith alone. Bultmann wants to reclaim the New Testament as *address from God* to influence the present; not as information *about* God, or merely *about* the past.

However, does Bultmann pay too heavy a price for this otherwise valid refocusing of perspective, and is this price necessary? I have argued elsewhere that an appeal to the Austinian or Anglo-American "logic of self-involvement" would have served his concern for reader-involvement, not in spite of a historical dimension, but precisely upon a basis of states of affairs or ontology (Thiselton 1992: 272–312). Bultmann's *Theology of the New Testament* (German, 1948–53) reflects this two-sided strength and weakness. He unfolds an existential or self-involving account of Pauline theology, but at the price of interpreting human existence as Paul's central theme. There is little on Paul's Christology or his theology of God.

Developing the Cambridge Tradition: British Exegetical Scholarship

The German agenda had been shaped by the legacy of Kant and such thinkers as Semler and Gabler, as well as Hegel and Strauss. However, apart from the brief influence of English deism, British scholars in the nineteenth century drew upon historical methods with less disjunction between the respective roles of history and theology. One example is the "Cambridge triumvirate" of B. F. Westcott (1825–1901), J. B. Lightfoot (1828–89), and F. J. A. Hort (1828–92). All three produced meticulous textual research; all were concerned to do justice to the particularities of historical background and context; and all aimed at exegetical precision. Nevertheless, they carried out their research as Cambridge professors with an eye to its theological significance for the church.

Hort rejected the "absolute infallibility" of the biblical text, but in collaboration with Westcott worked on the minutiae of the New Testament texts. He produced commentaries on the Greek text of 1 Peter (to 2: 17) and James (to 4: 7), and interpreted the heart of the fourth gospel in terms of revelation and incarnation (*The Way, The Truth, and The Life*, Hulsean lectures, 1871, published in 1908). In *The Christian Ecclesia* (1897) he traced the New Testament doctrine of the church to its background in the Old Testament notion of "assembly" (*qāhāl*), and its culmination as "universal" and "apostolic" in the later epistles.

Westcott wrote on the Gospel and Epistles of John, on the Epistle to the Hebrews, and on the canon. The Johannine Logos comes not from Alexandrian influences, but from a Jewish and Aramaic background including a Targumic interpretation of Genesis 1: 1. "The Word becomes flesh" (1: 14) implies the miraculous conception of Jesus Christ.

Lightfoot produced careful exegetical commentaries on Galatians and Philippians (1865 and 1868), of which the latter included a dissertation, "The Christian Ministry" (also published separately). He used this historical research to make a theological point: bishops were originally local presbyters, emerging from the presbyterate rather than from a continuing apostolate. Lightfoot's commentary on Colossians (1875) explicitly expounds a theological Christology, as well as preserving careful exegesis. His *Apostolic Fathers* (1890), also a model of historical research, served to cast doubt on the radical theories of F. C. Baur about Pauline and Jewish–Christian "parties" in the New Testament era. Lightfoot, and then Westcott, became successive bishops of Durham.

William Baird regards these scholars as founders of a "British Empire in NT study," and as being "equal in stature to the tallest of the Germans . . . [They] were servants of the church, dedicated to the relevance of the Bible for faith and life" (Baird 2003: 54, 83). They offered a model that remains a continuing component in much British biblical scholarship. Arguably Dodd, Caird, Moule, Barrett, Bruce, and more recently Dunn, Barton, and N. T. Wright, continue to reflect such a model. They permit critical questions to challenge religious assumptions, but ask critical questions from within the framework of Christian theism and they respect earlier traditions.

Charles H. Dodd (1884–1973) was professor successively at Manchester and Cambridge. Like the Cambridge three, he retained a consistent eye to the meaning of the New Testament for today, as his first book, *The Meaning of Paul for Today* (1920) indicates. His book *The Authority of the Bible* (1928) combines a commitment to the unique authority of the biblical writings as the primary witnesses to the faith of the apostolic age with an acceptance of "moderate" biblical criticism and a rejection of an "oracular" view of biblical inspiration. His *According to the Scriptures* (1952) strengthens these positive claims by defending the coherence with which the New Testament writers appealed to the Old Testament. Dodd's most widely known works are probably *The Parables of the Kingdom* (1935; also 1961 edn.), *The Epistle to the Romans* (1932), and *The Interpretation of the Fourth Gospel* (1953), as well as *Historical Tradition in the Fourth Gospel* (1963). These reflected Dodd's emphasis upon "realized" eschatology. The Kingdom of God, he urged, was *present* and not simply future for Jesus, because it was manifested in Jesus himself. A widespread consensus over the years suggests that this emphasis was helpful up to a point, but that Dodd overpressed it, thereby obscuring a theology of hope.

George B. Caird (1917–84) became Dean Ireland's Professor at Oxford. He produced a succinct historical study of the early church, *The Apostolic Age* (1955), and commentaries on *St. Luke*, (1963), *The Revelation of St. John the Divine* (1966; 2nd edn. 1985), and Paul's *Letters from Prison* (1976). Caird showed enormous sensitivity to issues of language and literature. Conversations with his colleague in semantics, Stephen Ullmann, led Caird into a deeper appreciation of biblical metaphor. He expounded this in lectures (1965) later published as *The Language and Imagery of the Bible* (1980, 1997). Caird insisted that to claim that Jesus was "mistaken" about the timing of a future "coming" was to confuse literal language with multi-level metaphor. He also worked on Septuagintal lexicography, and on a *New Testament Theology* (completed by L. D. Hurst, 1994).

Charles Kingsley Barrett (b. 1917) was Lecturer and then Professor of Divinity (1958) at Durham. His work is perhaps primarily exegetical, linguistic, and historical. His influential *The Gospel according to St. John* (1955; 2nd edn. 1978) was followed by *John and Judaism* (1975) and *Essays on John* (1982). His series of commentaries on Paul include *The Epistle to the Romans* (1957; 2nd edn. 1991), *The First Epistle to the Corinthians* (1968; 2nd edn. 1971), *The Second Epistle to the Corinthians* (1973), and *Freedom and Obligation* (1985, on Galatians). In recent years he has written especially on the Acts of the Apostles (volume 1 in the *International Critical Commentary* series, 1994). Barrett combines academic rigor with a personal ministry of preaching and teaching. Allusion to the traditions of the Cambridge triumvirate here is not arbitrary, for Barrett has also written *Westcott as a Communicator* (1959) and work on Lightfoot as a commentator (1992).

F. F. Bruce (1910–91) began as a classicist, became Professor of Biblical History and Literature at Sheffield, and then Rylands Professor of Biblical Criticism at

Manchester. Bruce wrote exegetical commentaries on almost every book of the New Testament, including all of the Pauline epistles, Acts, and Hebrews. His *New Testament History* (1969) and *Paul* (1977) have been influential textbooks. Bruce claimed that he did not alter his approach whether he was lecturing or preaching, and aimed to breathe life into the figures and events of the New Testament.

It is not the case that all British biblical scholarship followed this tradition. In Old Testament studies, Philip E. Davies of Sheffield (b. 1945) and Robert P. Carroll of Glasgow (b. 1941) urge the disengagement of biblical interpretation from Christian theology and the church. David J. A. Clines of Sheffield (b. 1938) has moved increasingly to a radically postmodern approach, in which no particular interpretation could claim privilege over another, except in relation to some predetermined context of inquiry. However, the approach of such "moderate" critical theistic scholars as John Barton of Oxford (b. 1948) might be said to represent British Old Testament scholarship more characteristically.

James Barr (b. 1924) deserves special note in a category of his own. He taught at Edinburgh, Princeton Theological Seminary, Manchester, and Oxford, and since 1989 at Vanderbilt. In addition to his work on Hebrew and Old Testament studies, Barr has written extensively on the nature of the Bible and its place in the church. He has sharply criticized fundamentalism, and attacked the assumptions of the so-called biblical theology movement.

In *The Semantics of Biblical Language* (1961) Barr aims "to criticize certain methods in the handling of linguistic evidence in theological discussion" (p. 6). In particular, he attacks the following:

1 The exaggerated contrast between "Greek" and "Hebrew" or "Israelite" thought that he finds, for example, in T. Boman and in the earlier volumes of Kittel's *Theological Dictionary of the New Testament*. It is not the case that Greek thought is always static, abstract, and dualistic, while Hebrew thought always is dynamic, concrete, and aspective.
2 The "one-word/one-concept" fallacy that confuses the lexicography of *words* with thematic discussions of *concepts*. (This partly parallels Wittgenstein's distinction between the "surface grammar" of words and the "depth-grammar" of word-uses.)
3 What he terms the practice of "illegitimate totality transfer" (p. 218). This process first identifies meanings of words in a *specific* passage; then, second, adds this meaning to a succession of cumulative meanings gathered from an array of quite different passages; finally, third, it "reads back" this "whole conception" into each *individual* passage.
4 Confusions between word-meaning and word-history. "Etymology" does not necessarily yield meanings for a later time: it is a diachronic account of word-history, not a synchronic account of meanings.

Like Caird, Barr sees the value of interdisciplinary research. Some claim that his incisiveness characterizes only his negative criticisms of others. However, his more recent *The Garden of Eden and the Hope of Immortality* (1992) shows positively that the notion of immortality is less rare in Israelite thought than many believe. Nevertheless, Barr's most forceful attacks occur in his *Fundamentalism* (1977) and *Beyond*

Fundamentalism (1984), where he seeks to demolish a conservative intellectual tradition in which he himself had formerly been involved in his own early student years. He believes that this theoretical intellectual framework is destructive, and that it contradicts the very ways in which moderate conservative scholars actually go about interpretation.

The "Cambridge" tradition continues to flourish. Graham N. Stanton (b. 1940), formerly of King's College, London, and now Cambridge, placed a question mark against Bultmann's assumption that the earliest Christians were uninterested in the person or basic history of Jesus, in his early *Jesus of Nazareth in New Testament Preaching* (1974). His more recent studies include *The Gospels and Jesus* (1989; 2nd edn. 2001) and *Matthew* (1994). James D. G. Dunn (b. 1939), Lightfoot Professor at Durham, has produced careful exegetical commentaries on the Greek text with an eye to theological meaning, including *Romans* (2 vols., 1998) and *Colossians and Philemon* (1996). Such works as *Unity and Diversity in the New Testament* (1977; 2nd edn. 1990), *Christology in the Making* (1980; 2nd edn. 1989), *The Theology of Paul the Apostle* (1998), and *Jesus Remembered* (2003) address broader theological and historical issues.

N. T. Wright (b. 1948) studied at Oxford under Caird, taught at Oxford, Cambridge, and McGill, and has produced an impressive series of incisive books, including *The New Testament and the People of God* (1992), *Jesus and the Victory of God* (1993), *The Climax of the Covenant* (1993), *The Meaning of Jesus* (1999), and *The Resurrection of the Son of God* (2003). However, he has also provided numerous commentaries at a popular level for the church. In a documented interview (1999) he observed: "The Bible is the book of my life. It is the book I live with, the book I live by, the book I want to die by." He added, however: "To get overprotective about particular readings of the Bible is always in danger of idolatry." Wright brings together history and theology, the academic and the church. In the tradition of Lightfoot and Westcott, he became Bishop of Durham (2003).

Re-enter Hermeneutics: Gadamer, Ricoeur, and American Literary Approaches

At the beginning of this chapter only pressures of space led to the omission of Schleiermacher alongside Semler, Michaelis, and Gabler. Friedrich Schleiermacher (1768–1834) was professor in the University of Berlin, but also preached almost every Sunday in Trinity Church, Berlin. Of his thirty published volumes, ten concern theology, ten concern philosophy, and ten, preaching. He agreed with Michaelis about the importance of "New Testament Introduction," but only for the sake of recovering accurate meanings for the present, not for more historical information as such.

Although Schleiermacher is popularly associated with an emphasis on "feeling," this may mislead us without careful qualification. He sought a balance between what he called the "feminine" dimension of intuitive, personal, "divinatory" understanding (like understanding a friend), and the "masculine" dimension of comparative, critical, rational, explanation (like scientific method). He valued the rational concerns of the Enlightenment, but he remained at heart a Christian pietist. Hermeneutics is not merely a matter of "rules," but an "art." "The divinatory method seeks to give an immediate comprehension of the author as an individual. The comparative method proceeds by subsuming the author under a general type" (Schleiermacher 1977: 150). Ahead of his time, he sees that understanding involves apprehending *both* "the content of the text *and* the range of effects" (p. 151, my italics). Without historical discipline the interpreter becomes a "nebulist"; but if historical inquiry alone is in view, the interpreter betrays "pedantry" (p. 205).

Schleiermacher's work is complex and subtle. Yet apart from work in philosophy from Dilthey to Heidegger his hermeneutics have been largely neglected. However, in the twentieth century, Hans-Georg Gadamer (1900–2002) placed the whole hermeneutical tradition on the agenda. Gadamer studied under Heidegger and published work on Plato in the 1930s. After difficult war years he became professor at Frankfurt and Heidelberg. His monumental *Truth and Method* (1960; 4th edn., 1975; English translation from 5th edn., 1989) has entirely reshaped twentieth-century hermeneutics. It led to reappraisals of reason in philosophy, of texts in theology and literary theory, and of understanding in social sciences. His *Collected Works* amount to ten volumes in German.

Gadamer sees "method" as standing in contrast to truth. Replicating the generalizing techniques of science, "method" tends to determine in advance the terms on which truth should be grasped. Deceived by "successful" methods in science, an interpreter tries to "master" texts, life, or art, rather than letting them confront him or her on their own terms. Except for his correct exemption of morality, Descartes in effect promoted "the total reconstruction of all truths by reason" (Gadamer 1989: 279). But Enlightenment "method" is misconceived. We must return with Vico to "old truths . . . to the *sensus communis* . . . to elements present in the classical concept of wisdom" (p. 19). Wisdom goes deeper than knowledge and draws on tradition for transmitting reinterpretations and actualizations of truth in events. It does not merely "subsume the individual under a universal category" (p. 21).

Like a game, or like a work of art, truth becomes disclosed through eventful, contingent, "performances," none of which is identical with another, or it would not be a game or performance as an art. Art is never "exhausted" by cashing it out as a series of "aesthetic concepts." In play, the game projects a "world" which enfolds the player in its own network of objectives and criteria of success. It provides the horizons within which players think and act. Here we see "the primacy of play over the consciousness of the player" (p. 102). Against the false trail initiated by Enlightenment rationalism, Gadamer traces the hermeneutical tradition from Schleiermacher through Dilthey, Husserl, and Yorck, to Heidegger.

In Heidegger, the horizon of a pre-given "world" provides the starting point for understanding. However, Gadamer has a more positive view of tradition and its "history of effects" (*Wirkungsgeschichte*) than Heidegger. A tradition which, along with its prejudices, also transmits wisdom, allows for a "formation" (*Bildung*) which "builds." In particular, this process is achieved through a mutual respect between those who stand within different horizons, through a genuine "listening," each to the other, in dialogue. If neither tries simply to impose assertions onto the other, "something *new*" may "emerge," in which truth becomes "actualized" in an event of meeting. The key is not "asserting one's view," but "being transformed . . . We do not remain what we were" (p. 379).

In theology this invites a renewed understanding of what it is to listen to the text and to listen to others (or to God) without imposing our own terms as the "grid" or "method" which we ourselves choose to use. In German New Testament scholarship, Ernst Fuchs (1903–83) explored this angle of approach, although not explicitly in dependence upon Gadamer. Fuchs taught New Testament at Tübingen and Marburg, but also served as a pastor. He asks: "What do we have to do at our desks if we want later to set the text in front of us in the pulpit?" (Fuchs 1964: 8). Like Schleiermacher and Gadamer, Fuchs insists that interpretation must not be reduced to a set of rules; the central aim involves rapport, resonance, or "common understanding" or "empathy" (*Einverständnis*) with what we seek to understand (Fuchs 1968: 171–81, 239–43). From the earlier Heidegger, Fuchs (like Gadamer) explores the notion of entering a "world" projected by the text. In particular, the parables of Jesus project a world which constitutes a "place of meeting." Jesus in his love does not "blurt out" a series of propositions, but projects a parable-"world" that "grips" the hearer so that "he is drawn over to God's side and learns to see with God's eyes" (Fuchs 1964: 155). "Is not his the way of true love? Love does not just blurt out. Instead, it provides in advance the sphere in which meeting takes place" (p. 129). The term "the new hermeneutic" was often used to denote the approach of Fuchs and his collaborator, Gerhard Ebeling.

A number of American biblical interpreters explore this angle of approach further. Robert Funk (b. 1926) of the University of Montana acknowledges that Fuchs provides the "hidden springs" that nourish his own dialogue with literary theory and theology in *Language, Hermeneutic and Word of God* (1966). He applies this hermeneutic to the parable of the prodigal son (Luke 15: 11–32). The "righteous" find themselves in the "world" of the elder brother. "The word of grace . . . divide(s) the audience into younger sons and elder sons – into sinners and Pharisees. This is what Ernst Fuchs means when he says that one does not interpret the parables; *the parables interpret him*" (p. 16; his italics). The judges find themselves judged. The direction of the flow between subject and object has been reversed. Thus, in 1 Corinthians 2: 6–16, "Paul is laboring to hear the word anew for himself and the Corinthians" (p. 276). There are also resonances with hermeneutical perspectives in Walter Wink (b. 1935) and with John Dominic Crossan (b. 1934) and Dan Otto Via (b. 1928).

Paul Ricoeur (b. 1913) deserves no less respect than Gadamer for his hermeneutics, and he has made a more direct impact on biblical interpretation and theology. He studied at the Sorbonne with Marcel, and has been a professor at Strasbourg, Paris, and Chicago. His earlier works on the human will (1950) and human fallibility (1960) reflect Marcel's interest in human personhood. During the years of war in which he was a prisoner in Germany, Ricoeur studied Jaspers, Husserl, and Heidegger more closely. Jaspers' dual interest in philosophy and psychiatry informed Ricoeur's work in *The Symbolism of Evil* (1960; English trans. 1969). Sharing Jaspers' positive view of symbols, Ricoeur argued that symbols operate with power not least because they embrace two levels of meaning. Guilt, for example, draws on the "double meaning" of burden, bondage, and stain. Far from being derivative from conceptual thought, "the symbol gives rise to thought."

Some French intellectual life initially cultivated structuralism and then in the wake of its own self-critique, poststructuralism. Ricoeur cautiously utilized aspects of these approaches for "explanation" or "critique," as a check against uncritical "under-standing." His "double" hermeneutic of critical "suspicion" and postcritical "retrieval" comes in *Freud and Philosophy* (1965; English trans. 1970). He explores "relations between desire and language." Freud had shown that dreams could be expressions of hidden desire, but were "disguised . . . expressions" (p. 5). Deception and disguise operate at several levels. Even the self is deceived about its true wishes. People "tell" dreams (the "dream-text") which differ from the dream-content ("dream-thoughts"). The interpreter needs "a hermeneutic of suspicion" to understand them. In a key comment, Ricoeur asserts: "Hermeneutics seems to me to be animated by this double motivation: willingness to suspect, willingness to listen; vow of rigor, vow of obedience" (p. 27). He concludes: "*The idols must die – so that symbols may live*" (p. 531; his italics).

Ricoeur pays particular attention to metaphor, where he draws on the interactive theory of Max Black. "Intensive" double-meaning expressions entail "split refer-ence" and operate with creative force. Probably the most creative of all Ricoeur's works is his three-volume *Time and Narrative* (1983–5; English trans. 1984–8), together with *Oneself as Another* (1990; English trans. 1992). *Time and Narrative* begins with Augustine's reflections on time. The human experience of time makes possible a differentiation into expectation (future), attention (present), and memory (past). Hence, "through the experience of human time we come to understand the world and our own present" (Ricoeur 1984–8, I: 16). "Temporality" (in Heidegger's sense of ground for "human" time) constitutes the necessary condition for narrative and for the *intelligibility* of texts and life.

Ricoeur complements this with Aristotle's theory of "plot" (*muthos*). "Plot" organizes narrative events into a coherent whole, through *poieis* (French, *faire*). "To make up a plot is, to make the intelligible spring from the accidental, the universal from the singular" (p. 22). This readily applies to biblical texts. The Gospel of Mark, some biblical interpreters argue, uses changes in the speed of "human time" as "narrative time" to depict "plot" that "organizes temporal action" to depict a hastening toward the goal of the passion, which is then portrayed as if in slow motion.

Ricoeur's complex volume *Oneself as Another* may exceed even *Time and Narrat-ive* in depth and power. He draws on earlier themes to vindicate a concept of per-sonhood as identity-within-temporal-change that does much to restore the notion of a stable human selfhood within change against the skepticism, not only of Hume and positivism, but more especially of the shifting quicksands of postmodernity.

In America, arguably the beginnings of literary reflection in biblical studies might be traced back to Horace Bushnell (1802–76). Bushnell is often regarded as the founder of American liberal theology. He rejected the notion that revelation com-municates cognitive quasi-scientific propositions, and rejected a penal substitutionary theology of the atonement. Much of his argument depended upon the recognition of metaphor. Jesus was a "sacrifice" only in the same metaphorical sense as Jesus was a "lamb." Charles Hodge (1797–1878) represented conservative biblical scholarship in America, and insisted that the Bible was a "storehouse of facts." Umberto Eco would later call such an approach an "engineering" or "handbook" model, rather than a literary or creative model. With hindsight it is unfortunate that the conservative–liberal debate in America became misdirected into an agenda where Bushnell could claim worthy predecessors on "literary" issues; but they did not tie them to "liberal" theology.

These unfortunate effects live on. Even from the late 1960s there was a tendency to leave "literary" exploration to such biblical scholars as Funk and Crossan, while more conservative scholars remained wedded to a strictly "historical" approach. Nevertheless, such a picture cannot be clear-cut, and many American scholars adopted a "historical" approach that was more firmly integrated with theology. Some still inclined toward the "biblical theology" movement of the 1950s and 1960s, associated with Oscar Cullmann (b. 1902) in Europe. George E. Ladd (1911–82), W. Albright (1891–1971), and notably George Ernest Wright (1909–74) represented this approach in America. Wright's classic "biblical theology" approach was *God who Acts* (1952). Biblical theology is "the confessional recital of the redemptive acts of God in a particular history, because history is the chief medium of salvation." Wright stressed the distinctiveness of the Old Testament, and (with Cullmann and Ladd) the categories of promise and fulfillment.

The work of Brevard Childs of Yale (b. 1923) has variously been described as "canonical criticism" and "kerygmatic," or as "postcritical." This last term resonates with Paul Ricoeur's emphasis upon postcritical reading. Childs explicitly engages with hermeneutical issues. Even in his early book *Myth and Reality in the Old Testament* (1960) he rightly distinguished between the form and function of myths, proposing the category of "broken myth" for much of the once-mythological imagery of the Old Testament. Further, he engaged with *traditions* of biblical interpretation in the church. In his commentary *The Book of Exodus* (1974) he provided what was perhaps the first "post-history," *Wirkungsgeschichte*, or Reception History, of the text, anticipating the work of Ulrich Luz on Matthew.

Childs' attention to the interplay of textual traditions and their subsequent post-history in tradition led him to refocus attention away from the developmental *pre*-history of history, to their inner relationships and effects in their "canonical context." This canonical context affords a genuine and creative hermeneutical resonance. His *Introduction to the Old Testament as Scripture* (1979), and subsequently *The New Testament as Canon* (1984), illustrate this approach. Childs was perhaps unfairly criticized as having an obsession with "the final form of the text," and he refined his views in *Old Testament Theology as a Canonical Context* (1985) and *Biblical Theology of the Old and New Testaments* (1993). Like Barth, Childs stresses the shaping power of scripture for life. This resonates with Gadamer's view of *Bildung* and the role of tradition.

Meanwhile, several other American writers explore hermeneutical and literary approaches. John Dominic Crossan (b. 1934) convincingly expounded a hermeneutic of the parables of reversal in the gospels. He writes: "Myth establishes world. Apologia defends world . . . Satire attacks world. Parable subverts world" (Crossan 1975: 59). The very notion of a "good" Samaritan subverts assumptions both about Samaritans and human "goodness" (pp. 106–7). Crossan's work, however, betrays an increasing shift to a purely intralinguistic and deconstructive hermeneutic. In *Raid on the Articulate* (1976) "reality" becomes a linguistic phenomenon, while in *Cliffs of Fall* (1980) Crossan expounds a clearly postmodern perspective in which "reflexivity" replaces "reflection." Parables becomes "metaparables": a parable mirrors not the world or hints of divine transcendence, but "itself." With Derrida, he becomes skeptical about textual determinacy and referential representation, at least in literary language.

Walter Brueggemann (b. 1932) draws on Paul Ricoeur. Like Ricoeur's hermeneutic of suspicion and retrieval, Brueggemann holds together a dialectic of historical discipline and living testimony or confession. His hermeneutic of suspicion draws at times on Norman Gottwald's work on the social "interests" of power structures. He also allows, also with Ricoeur, for tensions, conflicts, and pluralities in interpretation, but within an overarching stable unity. In Ricoeur this relates to human selfhood, in Brueggemann, to the role of canon. Brueggemann similarly draws on multidisciplinary resources, especially on literary and social-world perspectives, and theology.

Achievements, Agenda, and Debate

We have consciously omitted several movements which are included elsewhere in this volume. We should otherwise attempt to include Latin American liberation interpretation, feminist and womanist theology, interpretation in black theology, and "Social World" and postcolonial biblical interpretation (see Part V of this volume; also "Eastern Orthodox Theology" and "Pentecostal and Charismatic Theology" in Part VI). We have also omitted, because of pressures of space, discussions of the major "theologies" of the Old and New Testaments that featured in the previous (second) edition of this volume. Cullmann's work on time and on eschatology discussed there still repays study, but we have noted that the "biblical theology" movement ceased to remain a vital force on the agenda from around 1970.

Nevertheless, the issue of the unity of the New Testament remains a live issue. Heikki Räisänen claims that the lack of such "unity" is a major reason why we cannot base a Christian theology upon the biblical writings. The core of Räisänen's thesis is that "if biblical studies are taken really seriously, traditional ways of using the Bible in theology . . . become unviable," largely because of "the non-historicity of crucial events," but also because "the New Testament has turned out to be filled with theological contradictions" (Räisänen 2001: 227, 229).

Räisänen finds Dunn's identification of a theological unity in "the unity of the historical Jesus and the exalted Christ" to be at best "a thin and elusive bond," while "exegesis discloses the contradictory diversity of the New Testament." "There is no direct path from historical study to present-day application," and the work of conservative theologians (Childs and Stuhlmacher) runs counter to the rules of sound scholarship. There are no "insights about living" (pp. 230, 231). Movements such as liberation theology always appeal to *selected* traditions within the Bible, which are contradicted by others. Räisänen cites the conflicts over interpretations of New Testament eschatology and apocalyptic as a conclusive argument. He holds some common ground with Robert P. Carroll of Glasgow in his *Wolf in the Sheepfold: The Bible as a Problem for Christianity* (1991). He also attacks appeals to the notion of *Wirkungsgeschichte* or the history of effects of texts. He points to instances where some traditions are suppressed or distorted, and also to effects outside the church that generate unbelief rather than faith.

If Räisänen is right, we may wonder about how the "Cambridge tradition" could be sustained through such thinkers as Dodd, Caird, Barrett, Bruce, Dunn, and N. T.

Wright, with their common concern to combine critical rigor with theological construction. Numerous German and Swiss scholars write within broadly comparable traditions. We need only mention, for example, Ulrich Luz (b. 1938), Wolfgang Schrage (b. 1928), and Christian Wolff (b. 1943), as well as such distinguished American Catholic biblical scholars as Joseph Fitzmyer (b. 1920) and Raymond Brown (b. 1928). Moreover, writers such as Francis Watson (implicitly) and Peter Balla (explicitly) question many assumptions on which Räisänen appears to rely. This issue also touches upon the broader, continuing, "history versus theology" debate. Dunn, Stanton, N. T. Wright, and many others have striven to expose many of the artificial assumptions that underlie much of this debate, even if in Christology more may still need to be said. Hermeneutical inquiry and literary theory may yet shed more creative light on these issues, although the "literary paradigm" is not a competitor for the "historical paradigm," as Robert Morgan comes near to implying in his *Biblical Interpretation* (1988).

A debate about the value of reception history, or the history of effects of texts, is beginning to command attention. Räisänen is right, however, to include the history of effects outside the church, even if his are not fresh arguments for doing so. Theologians have long been aware of Friedrich Nietzsche's arguments that Christians can manipulate texts as well as anyone for self-interest and power. This relates closely, yet again, to postmodern and deconstructionist approaches in biblical interpretation.

In turn, this raises issues about the ethics of interpretation, on which a growing literature is now emerging. The current trend to draw upon wide resources of interdisciplinary study cannot but enrich interpretation. The Roman Catholic Pontifical Biblical Commission's report *The Interpretation of the Bible in the Church*, with a commendation from Pope John Paul II (1994), underlines this. The report commends rhetorical, narrative, semiotic, and canonical approaches (pp. 41–53), the study of the history of effects (pp. 55–7), sociological approaches (pp. 57–61), and hermeneutics (pp. 73–7). It expresses reservations only over "fundamentalism." In the twenty-first century it is likely that all of these disciplines will play an increasing and constructive part in biblical interpretation. The respective roles of historical and theological inquiry may remain controversial for some, but for the present writer both remain indispensable. Attention to Christian theological traditions broadens, rather than narrows, the task of interpretation.

Bibliography

Primary

Balla, Peter, *Challenges to New Testament Theology* (Peabody, MA, 1997).

Barr, James, *The Semantics of Biblical Language* (Oxford, 1961).

—— *Holy Scripture: Canon, Authority, Criticism* (Oxford, 1983).

Barth, Karl, "The Strange New World within the Bible." In *The Word of God and Word of Man* (London, 1928), pp. 28–50.

—— *The Resurrection of the Dead* (London, 1933).

—— *Church Dogmatics* I. 2: *The Doctrine of the Word of God* (Edinburgh, 1956).

—— *Epistle to the Romans* (Oxford, 1975).

Bultmann, Rudolf, *Theology of the New Testament*, 2 vols. (London, 1952–5).

—— *Essays Philosophical and Theological* [German, *Glauben und Verstehen*, Vol. 2] (London, 1955).

—— *Jesus and the Word* (London, 1958).

—— "New Testament and Mythology." In Hans-Werner Bartsch (ed.), *Kerygma and Myth*, 2 vols. (London, 1962, 1964).

—— *The History of the Synoptic Tradition* (Oxford, 1963).

—— *Faith and Understanding I* [German, *Glauben und Verstehen*, Vol. 1] (London, 1969).

Childs, Brevard, *Biblical Theology of the Old and New Testaments: Theological Reflections on the Christian Bible* (Minneapolis, MN, 1993).

Crossan, John D., *In Parables: The Challenge of the Historical Jesus* (New York, 1973).

—— *The Dark Interval* (Niles, 1975).

Fuchs, Ernst, *Studies of the Historical Jesus* (London, 1964).

—— *Marburger Hermeneutik* (Tübingen, 1968).

Funk, Robert, *Language, Hermeneutic and Word of God* (New York, 1966).

Gadamer, H.-G., *Truth and Method*, 2nd edn. (London, 1989).

Moberly, R. W. L., *The Bible, Theology and Faith* (Cambridge, 2000).

Räisänen, Heikki, *Challenges to Biblical Interpretation: Collected Essays 1991–2001* (Leiden, 2001).

Ricoeur, Paul, *Freud and Philosophy* (New Haven, CT, 1970).

—— *Essays on Biblical Interpretation* (London, 1981).

—— *Time and Narrative*, 3 vols. (Chicago, 1984–8).

Schleiermacher, F., *Hermeneutics: The Handwritten Manuscripts* (Missoula, MO, 1977).

Seitz, Christopher R., *Figured Out: Typology and Providence in Christian Scripture* (Louisville, KY, 2001).

Watson, Francis, *Text, Church and World: Biblical Interpretation in Theological Perspective* (Edinburgh, 1994).

Secondary

Baird, William, *History of New Testament Research, Vol. 2: From Jonathan Edwards to Rudolf Bultmann* (Minneapolis, MN, 2003).

Barton, John (ed.), *The Cambridge Companion to Biblical Interpretation* (Cambridge, 1998).

Morgan, Robert, *Biblical Interpretation* (Oxford, 1988).

Thiselton, A. C., *New Horizons in Hermeneutics* (London, 1992).

—— "New Testament in Historical Perspective." In Joel B. Green (ed.), *Hearing the New Testament: Strategies for Interpretation* (Grand Rapids, MI, 1995), pp. 10–36.

Philosophical Theology

Ingolf U. Dalferth

Introduction

There is not a single or simple definition of philosophical theology (PT). Sometimes the term is used to refer to the theology of the philosophers as opposed to, for example, the mythical theology of the poets or the political theology of cities and states in antiquity, or to the theology of Jews, Christians, or Muslims in more recent times. Or PT is marked off not from other forms of theology but other branches or disciplines of philosophy, for example, from philosophical psychology or cosmology in seventeenth and eighteenth-century rationalism. Or it refers to philosophical rather than biblical, historical, moral, etc. problems or topics or disciplines in (Christian) theology. Or it is used to distinguish a particular philosophical way of doing theology from other ways, for example, theology practiced in prayer and mediation, or confessional theology based on the faith of a particular religious community and tradition. Or it marks the particular philosophical "place" or setting of (doing) theology, either in the conceptual scheme of intellectual activities in a tradition or society, or in the institutional settings in which these have been incorporated.

All these various meanings cannot be harmonized or organized into a single pattern or a coherent definition of PT. Instead of defining the term, I shall describe PT as a range of reflective activities in philosophy and/or theology that have been practiced as distinct philosophical approaches to a distinct set of theological problems in modernity. Philosophical reflection aims at clarifying problems and puzzles in all areas of human life and thought, and it does so by exploring possibilities, elucidating conceptual options, and testing the coherence of views and positions in the area under discussion by all sorts of analysis and argumentation accepted in philosophy and the sciences. PT shares this approach with respect to problems and puzzles posed by belief in God, and it tackles them against the background of the sciences and the culture of the day. But there was a time when PT in this sense did not yet exist, even though very similar theological problems were discussed; and although PT is still with us in multiform ways, it was largely replaced some time ago by philosophy of religion. Thus the beginnings of PT are marked by the rise of modern science in the seventeenth century, and the end of PT was rung in with the arrival of philosophy of religion on the scene around the turn of the nineteenth century; and this is true even though PT has not only continued to be practiced to the present day but also in fact was provoked to react to the change of situation by new forms and programs.

Survey

PT began its modern career as a distinct philosophical project, and this it has largely remained. With some notable exceptions, it has not been understood and practiced as a branch of Christian theology but as a philosophical enterprise based not on faith and religion but on reason and reflection and/or nature, experience, and science. However, it has never been a monolithic endeavor. Its shape, content, and agenda vary widely with different philosophical approaches. And its impact on Christian thinking has been constructive as well as critical or even destructive.

Its prehistory, which is sometimes mistakenly taken to be part of it, includes such diverse factors as Platonist dualism, the Aristotelian pattern of causality, Stoic immanentism, Philonean personalism, neoplatonist negative theology, and Socinian antitrinitarianism. From its most ancient roots the theology of the philosophers in the Western tradition was intimately bound up with the rise of reason and science in ancient Greece. When the gods ceased to be part of the furniture of the world, God (the divine) became an explanatory principle based not on the traditional mythological tales but on cosmological science, astronomical speculation, and metaphysical reflection. Its idea of God involved the ideas of *divine singularity* (there is only one God), *divine transcendence* (God is neither part nor the whole of the world) and *divine immanence* (God's active presence can be discerned in the order, regularity, and beauty of the cosmos). And even though it took a long time to grasp those differences clearly, the *monotheistic difference* between gods and God, the *cosmological difference* between God and the world, and the *metaphysical difference* between the transcendence and immanence of God have remained central to the intellectual enterprise of theological reflection in philosophy.

Later, the medieval synthesis of reason and faith collapsed, on the one hand, with the differentiation of Christian theology into different confessional traditions since the Reformation and, on the other, with the rise of modern philosophy and empirical science. This fundamentally changed the situation for PT and marked the decisive step from its prehistory to its history. Philosophical reflection no longer served as a preliminary introduction to revealed knowledge of God. Rather, it began to establish itself in its own right independent of any reference to a particular religious (Christian, Jewish, Islamic) tradition, and this for mainly two reasons. In reaction to the theological polemic of opposing confessional parties and their inherently contentious interpretations of Christian beliefs and practices, PT attempted to formulate a framework of rational consensus about fundamental beliefs common to all parties that was based on grounds that were not in dispute between the confessional parties. And in response to the rise and challenge of modern atheism, fueled not only by the confessional conflicts but also by the atheistic implications of modern mechanical and mathematical science, it accepted the modern standards of reason, rationality, and knowledge to rebut atheism on its own ground. It was not very long before PT claimed, instead of waiting for being perfected by Christian theology, to be indispensable for grounding it: revelation may be the only secure way to divine truth, but reason is the only sure way to know whether something can legitimately lay claim to being revelation.

Thus the history of PT begins with Bacon's scientific methodology, Galileo's scientific discoveries, and Descartes' search for epistemic certainty. They all argue that complex problems must be broken down into basic units which are certain beyond doubt because they are known *clare et distincte*; and they conceive God either to be one of these fundamentally clear ideas (Descartes) or to be inferable from them. It reaches a first peak with Newton's scientific achievements and their theistic interpretations in the early eighteenth century, and then again, in a similar climate of debate with science (cosmology, biology), in the second half of the twentieth century with an amazing series of technically highly accomplished new versions of traditional (cosmological, ontological, teleological), neoclassical (process philosophy), and probabilistic (Swinburne) arguments for the existence of God.

It begins to decline with the philosophical critiques of Hume and Kant, and the rise of philosophy of religion and the onto-theological alternatives of Hegel and Schelling. Notwithstanding its continuation and even revival in the analytic theism of the second half of the twentieth century, it appears to many to be religiously barren and not a viable account of religious life and practice. It forfeits its scientific attractiveness by the shift from physics and astronomy to biology and the life sciences as the leading sciences of the day; its point through the demise of Cartesianism and transcendentalism, the discontent with mere epistemology, and the growing prominence of phenomenological and hermeneutical philosophies of life in contemporary philosophy; its philosophical persuasiveness by the insight that religious belief is warranted within a religious practice rather than in need of justification by a decontextualized PT; its apologetic value due to its failure to communicate to an increasingly uninterested public a philosophically mediated understanding of Christian faith; and its public function by undermining the autonomy of morality, by being stripped of its claim to be an unavoidable truth for all reasonable persons, and by the plausible charge that its arguments further the very skepticism in religion which they seek to combat.[1]

But all this is at most a partial truth about PT, and not the whole story. Not only is it well and alive, albeit in very different versions, in England (as *theism*), the United States (*realist metaphysical theologies*), or on the Continent (*subjective transcendentalism*), but its actual history is also much more diverse. The different versions of PT practiced in the twentieth century belong to different programs with common roots and a common crisis, but shaped by their very diverse ways of reacting to this crisis. Since the crisis culminated in the refutation of the decontextualized account of God in natural and rational PT, the two ways open to PT to overcome the crisis were either to refute the refutation or to react with a recontextualization or programmatic reembedding of its philosophical account of God. Both strategies were followed in various ways in the past two centuries and account for the different programs of modern PT after the collapse of natural and rational theology.

Now the decontextualized account of God in the early Enlightenment was not accidental. Its very point was to offer a philosophical theory of God, independent of the controversial forms of belief in God in the confessional traditions of seventeenth-century Christianity and able to rebut the attacks of modern atheism on its own grounds. To this effect it had to conceive God in a way that transcended the particularities of the different confessional traditions by concentrating on what it took to be the uncontroversial and common core of them, and it had to base its arguments for God on the very foundations on which the atheist critique rested (i.e., on natural reason and rational argument alone). The result was philosophical theism (or dogmatic philosophical theology) whose conception of God represented, in effect, an abstract and decontextualized version of selected aspects of the Christian concept of God, whereas its arguments for God were based on universal reason and common experience (i.e., the kind of reason and experience that is universal to humanity), and on the argumentative procedures of mathematical and mechanical rationality (i.e., the epistemological strategies of valid argument in science and mathematics).

However, when this decontextualizing approach to God collapsed under Hume and Kant's criticisms of natural and rational theology, this did not end the history of PT, but marked a new beginning, and the range of reactions to this crisis in effect defines the history of modern PT. We can distinguish at least five major developments or programs of PT after the demise of Enlightenment theism, still operative in the twentieth century: (1) dogmatic PT (philosophical theism); (2) critical PT (philosophical theology); (3) idealist PT (transcendental theism); (4) realist PT (speculative theism); and (5) (more indirectly and succeeding PT) philosophy of religion. They are not merely variations of the same, but transformations into something new. But whereas *dogmatic* PT in effect continues the decontextualizing program of PT by trying to refute its refutations, the other four represent different attempts at recontextualization: in the practical contexts of the religious life of individuals or particular religious communities (*critical* PT); in the foundationalist contexts of transcendental idealism (*idealist* PT); in the ontological or cosmological contexts of speculative panentheism (*realist* PT), and in the manifold contexts of empirical and historical religions (philosophy of religion).

Each of them exists in a variety of versions, and each has provoked critical and skeptical reactions that form part of their history. *Dogmatic* PT has been criticized by philosophical skeptics and proponents of scientism as being either false or unfounded, given our scientific knowledge of the universe, but it has also been dismissed as not false but meaningless by empiricists and logical positivists who held, as A. J. Ayer and Bertrand Russell did, that "the only propositions which are meaningful are those which can (in some sense) be verified by observation"; and this didn't leave much chance to PT's propositions about God. *Critical* PT, on the other hand, has been attacked by philosophical theists and transcendental idealists alike for its programmatic refusal to provide rational foundations for Christian faith and belief in God. *Idealist* PT, again, has been criticized by phenomenological and hermeneutical philosophers for moving within the narrow bounds of an abstract epistemological paradigm ("transcendental subjectivity") that ignores the constitutive role of the others (Buber, Rosenzweig, Levinas), of language (Heidegger, Gadamer, Wittgenstein, Ricoeur), of history (Dilthey, Blumenberg), and of the rich contexts of actual life (pragmatist philosophers from James to Rorty). *Realist* PT, finally, has been questioned by analytical philosophers for an ontological abuse of logic; by existential and existentialist thinkers such as Kierkegaard for unduly playing down the irreplaceable individuality of the subject or individual; by phenomenological critics such as Derrida for a misguided logocentric metaphysics of presence with no regard for the traces of God's absence in our experience (negative theology) or, in the phenomenological counter-move of Marion, for unduly objectifying and idolizing God rather than being open for his sacramental presence and self-giving; and finally by postmodernists in the wake of Nietzsche for presenting a far too inclusive and comprehensive mega-story which does not seriously engage with the ruptures, failures, breakdowns, fragility, and incompatibilities of human life as actually lived and experienced.

So in discussing PT at least five stories need to be told. They all start with the theistic project (i.e., natural and rational theology as purely philosophical accounts of God based on grounds independent of Christian theology and the traditions of faith). They all run into the fundamental crises of philosophical theism in the wake of Hume and Kant. But then, in reacting differently to this crisis, they develop different programs, which in their pros and cons still define the range of positions in PT at the beginning of the twenty-first century.

Content, Agendas, and Debates

Dogmatic philosophical theology or philosophical theism

Dogmatic PT (DPT) or philosophical theism begins as natural and rational theology (i.e., as the philosophical reaction to the atheist denials of traditional religion and, at the same time, as a philosophical alternative to the confessional theologies of the time). It disintegrates in the wake of Hume and Kant's refutations of its concept of God as incoherent, its arguments for God's existence as invalid, and its claims to provide an ultimate explanation of the universe superior to all alternatives as unfounded.

In the continental traditions the quest for ultimate explanation finds its place in the philosophical attempts of a transcendental foundation of human subjectivity (Fichte), or in philosophical (dialectical) materialism. In the Anglophone world, however, the situation is very different. Not only is DPT continued as unimpressed and undisturbed by those refutations as William Paley's *Natural Theology* was by Hume's critical arguments. It also stays a live option and major battleground for philosophers of religion, even though it failed long ago to achieve its original end of providing a common theistic consensus for modern pluralist society (Jefferson). It is sometimes restated by distinguishing between a *natural* theology that is based only on premises accessible to observation and reason, and a *philosophical* theology that also accepts doctrinal propositions among its premises as assumptions.[2] And it has even experienced a quite spectacular revival in the second half of the twentieth century in *analytical theism*, which has produced more and subtler versions of the traditional arguments for God's existence than at any time before. However, it is a philosophers' theoretical theism whose unending debate of the pros and cons of the theistic arguments, for all their technical excellence and subtle engagement with the latest niceties of logic, is of little or no avail to a general religious public or the believers of traditional religions. It defends, or attacks, a decontextualized concept of God as a personal, spiritual, eternal, free, omnipotent, omniscient, and benevolent being, but hardly stops to think whether what it defends or attacks is worth defending or attacking. For even where it succeeds, it only shows the tradition-free Enlightenment concept of God to be coherent. And even where it can show a version of the theistic arguments to be valid, it can do so only in a purely formal way (i.e., within a particular system of logic or set of rules and assumptions.)[3]

So the story of PT along these lines moves from foundationalism to formalism: what began its career as the foundationalist project of natural and rational theology, is transformed into the formalism of arguments that are only valid within certain logical systems whose rules as well as the assumptions of the arguments formulated in their terms may or may not be accepted. The arguments become explorations of possibilities in specific logical systems, but they no longer can claim to refute the atheist by "proving" God's existence beyond doubt to any rational person.

What may look like a loss to the rational foundationalist opened up new avenues for PT and allowed various confessional versions of DPT to develop. If the concept of God used in the theistic arguments is not that of tradition-free natural or rational theology, but taken from a particular religious or theological tradition (Thomism, for example, or Calvinism, or a combination of both as in Reformed Epistemology),[4] then what began as PT independent of, if not contrary to, confessional Christian theology is now transformed into a philosophical reflection and restatement of a particular confessional tradition (Anglican, Reformed, or Roman Catholic, but in principle open to Jewish or Islamic versions as well). The story now moves from foundationalism through formalism to confessionalism, and PT becomes virtually indistinguishable from (a philosophically restricted version of) confessional systematic theology.

Since DPT has served as the paradigm of PT, especially in Britain throughout the nineteenth and twentieth centuries, it deserves a closer analysis. Originally, it arose in reaction to modern atheism whose basic tenets were: (1) the incoherence of the concept of God; (2) the doubt or negation of the existence of God, and the denial of a universe ordered by a caring mind or intelligence and not merely by natural laws; and (3) the affirmation of inexplicable evil and unjust suffering in the world as fundamental reasons against all belief in God. Each of these became, and has remained, a major concern and philosophical preoccupation of DPT.

DPT defends a concept of God succinctly summarized by Swinburne: by "God" theists understand something like a "person without a body (i.e., a spirit) who is eternal, free, able to do anything, knows everything, is perfectly good, is the proper object of human worship and obedience, the creator and sustainer of the universe."[5] This concept of God results from three basic motifs of theism, two of which are directed against the tenets of atheism, the third against the particularity of opposing religious traditions. First, there is the cosmological motif, which makes God, not matter-in-motion as in Hobbes, or energy, or some other natural force, but the ultimate cause and explanation of the world. Second, there is the religious motif, which takes God to be not coextensive with the universe but transcendent, a personal being worthy of worship, able to act not only in creating the world but also in the created world, and hence free to respond to prayers.[6] Finally, there is the philosophical motif of concentrating the conception of God on those aspects of belief in God on which Jews, Christians, and Muslims cannot agree to differ without falling into self-contradiction. All three motifs combine in conceptualizing God and

God's relationship to the world by using certain models of thought (e.g. *Personal Explanation* in terms of actions and intentions; *Mind and Body, Mind; Subject;* the *Elusive Self or Soul; Personal Agency,* or *Personal Communicator*). The models used determine the divine properties attributed to God, such as infinity, eternity, freedom, omniscience, omnipotence, benevolence, creative activity, incorporeality. These motifs, and the models of God based on them, are usually combined, and hence the analogy between human persons as finite, but free and creative moral agents, and God as the Supreme Creative and Beneficent Agent becomes the key element in this conception of God.

The coherence of this concept of God is required for the second major component of DPT: its arguments for the existence of God. To show a Supreme Creative and Beneficent Agent to be possible is not enough; there must be good reasons for asserting the existence of such a being. Thus, arguments for and against the existence of God, in particular ontological and cosmological arguments, as well as arguments from design, have been, and still are, a major topic of DPT. In their different ways they all argue that the concept of God is coherent and the existence of such a supreme being is possible (arguments for the possibility of God); that such a being actually exists, either because it absolutely must (ontological arguments for the necessity of God) or has to, given the existence and character of the world (cosmological arguments and arguments from design for the actuality of God); that there can only be one such being, because the unity and singularity of the world allows for only one creator and providential lord of nature and history (arguments for the singularity of God).

The three sets of problems of the *possibility, necessity* and/or *actuality,* and *singularity* of God are central to DPT and have remained the focus of its debates until the present day.[7] For the question of the possibility of God implies fundamental questions about meaning, the coherence of concepts, and the use of words; the question of the necessity and/or actuality of God fundamental questions about logic, ontology, cosmology, and the character of the world; and the question of the singularity of God raises fundamental questions about the unity and plurality of worlds, the difference between actual and possible worlds, and the identity of individuals in different worlds. Thus, DPT places its construction of God at the center of philosophical debate with intimate links to virtually every philosophical topic.[8]

Recently, Reformed epistemologists such as Alvin Plantinga have combined the Calvinist *sensus divinitatis* tradition with the commonsense realism of Thomas Reid and argued that belief in God is a properly basic belief that may be part of the foundation of a person's noetic structure. According to Plantinga, (Christian) belief in God is rational, reasonable, justifiable, and ultimately warranted to accept, because humans not only have natural cognitive faculties, such as perception, memory, or reflection that allow us to gather knowledge about objects, but also a natural cognitive faculty that enables us to form basic beliefs about God.[9] And as long as the concept of God is not shown to be incoherent, or belief in God to be without warrant or deficient in some other respect because it is not formed by properly functioning cognitive faculties, believers should be judged according to the forensic principle "innocent until proven guilty": "Our beliefs are rational unless we have reasons for refraining; they are not non-rational unless we have reasons *for* believing."[10]

The problem of evil in the specific form of theodicy is one of the preoccupations of DPT. Horrendous evil, pain, suffering, and injustice in the world constitute a fundamental threat and insurmountable stumbling block for DPT because they lead us to question the nature and reality of God. In Epicurus' old questions rephrased by Hume: "Is God willing to prevent evil, but not able? Then he is impotent. Is he able, but not willing? Then he is malevolent. Is he both able and willing? Whence then is evil?"[11] Posed in this way the problem of evil is transformed into a problem of the logical compatibility of certain beliefs about God and the world; that is, the beliefs that:

(a)   God exists.
(b)   God is omnipotent.
(c)   God is omniscient.
(d)   God is wholly good.
(e)   There exists evil in the world.

This is a theoretical problem, and it has a number of theoretical solutions.[12] If we drop (a) or (e), the problem does not arise; if we give up the idea of infinity in (b) to (d), the problem disappears. Less radical solutions attempt to reject the alleged incompatibility in various ways. Thus, Plantinga has argued that beliefs (a) to (d) do not entail that God does not create, or has no reason to create, beings who perform evil deeds, and he takes this to be a *defense* of God (i.e., of the compatibility of the view of God outlined with the reality of evil in the world), but not a *theodicy* (i.e., an explanation of the fact and amount of evil in the actual world created by God).[13] Others argue that the existence of some evil is necessary for the existence of certain sorts of values and second-order goods; that the existence of morally free agents necessarily entails the possibility of moral evil ("Free Will Defence"); or that an infinite number of actions and interactions, both between agents in the world and between worldly agents and God, necessarily produces effects beyond the control of any individual agent, including God (Hartshorne).

None of these solutions is uncontested, but the theoretical way the problem is posed leaves all the suggested solutions with a ring of practical insignificance: even if belief in God in the face of evil and suffering could be made plausible, it would still not tell the believer how to cope with evil, or how to establish the truth of (a) through (d). All theoretical reflection can hope to show is "that no amount of evil will contradict the existence of a perfect God, as long as the requirement is met, that it is necessarily implied in the existence of a world which leads to overwhelming good."[14] But our actual experience gives little reason to suppose that this is the case. If we had reason to believe in the existence, power, wisdom, and goodness of God, we could agree with Leibniz that this is compatible with the evil and suffering in the world. But Hume has shown that we have little or no reason to infer these beliefs from our ambiguous experiences of the world, and Kant has shown that (a) through (d) are not the sort of beliefs whose truth could even in principle be established by theoretical reason.

So DPT indeed faces a dilemma. The compatibility of belief in God with our experience of the world is not enough to justify belief in God: we need independent arguments to sustain this belief. But the arguments of rational and natural theology for the existence of God do not stand up to examination. The *a posteriori* arguments of natural theology from the actual world to God cannot justify asserting the perfect existence, power, wisdom, and goodness of God in the face of evil, pain, and suffering. Therefore, the argument from design, based on our experience of order and disorder in our world, participates in the ambiguity of the world; and the cosmological argument cannot justify the assumed intelligibility of the world independently of its inference to a self-explanatory being who makes it intelligible. The *a priori* arguments of rational theology, which conceive God to be either impossible or necessary, either cannot justify why they assume the possibility of God's existence rather than of God's non-existence, and thus can no more prove the necessary existence of God than they can prove his necessary non-existence; or, they too must rely on *a posteriori* arguments for assuming the first rather than the second, but since all the evidence available is as compatible with the second view as it is with the first, this only manifests a question-begging religious perspective on the world. In short, without convincing arguments for the existence of God, DPT fails. Natural theology breaks down because, given the facts of evil, it cannot prove that our world is intelligible in a way that unambiguously points to God, and rational theology breaks down because it cannot make plausible why God should necessarily exist rather than necessarily not exist.

DPT stands or falls with its arguments for the existence of God. But even where it presents valid arguments in a given system of logic, it cannot succeed because of its decontextualized conception of God. To conceptualize beliefs about God irrespective of their experiential and doctrinal contexts can only result in misconceptions. This is borne out by DPT's arguments for the existence of God, which represent, under misleading disguises, isolated aspects of the Christian understanding of God, but distort the overall picture. For instance, the ontological argument represents the Christian experience of the reality, singularity, and unsurpassable sovereignty of God in terms of ontological necessity, but it breaks down because (among other things) it fails to provide adequate means for determining God's identity in the sense of bringing us to know who God is.[15] The cosmological argument represents the Christian experience of total dependence on the sovereign will of God as the metaphysical dependence of the contingent on the necessary, but it breaks down because it confuses different understandings of contingency.[16] Finally, the argument from design represents the Christian experience of the caring guidance of God as an underlying purposive order of nature and history, but it breaks down because all this can be explained without reference to God.[17] In short, DPT fails because it begins with abstractions and ends by committing what Whitehead has called the "fallacy of misplaced concreteness."

It is not enough, therefore, for the defenders of DPT to refute the philosophical criticisms of its arguments by ever-refined logical reconstructions. What is needed is rather to stop the decontextualizing approach of DPT and recontextualize its arguments in the context of, for example, specific religious traditions.

Critical philosophical theology

Critical PT (CPT) is Kant's constructive alternative to DPT after the collapse of natural and rational theology. In contrast to the "biblical theology" of the "scholar of scripture" (*Schriftgelehrte*), which is based on the statutory faith of the church

(*Kirchenglauben*), the CPT of the "scholar of reason" (*Vernunftgelehrte*) deals with "religious faith proper" (*Religionsglauben*) that is based on the "interior moral laws which can be derived from the [practical] reason of every human being." Whereas the *Kirchenglaube* is always contingent, particular, and plural, the *Religionsglaube* is necessarily universal and unique: one reason, one idea of God, one religion.[18] So Kant replaces DPT by a CPT that is recontextualized in the moral life of individuals in their inescapable need of intellectual, moral, and religious orientation. Kant's CPT is not merely meant to criticize the pitfalls of traditional philosophical and "ecclesiastical" theologies but also to provide the individual with moral arguments for religion – or rather, a religious enforcement of morality – without, however, interfering with the public practice of the accepted religion. Based on the distinction between private and public religion, it is aimed at helping the individual to decide for himself or herself what to think of religion, and whether or not to participate in the public practice of religion.

A generation later, Schleiermacher gives Kant's CPT a constructive twist and new application. In his *Brief Outline on the Study of Theology*, he organizes the study of theology into three branches: philosophical, historical, and practical theology. Schleiermacher recontextualized CPT within Protestant theology by proposing that it should be conceived as a theological discipline alongside historical and practical theology. Although he did not really succeed with respect to the syllabus of theological education, the line of thought opened up in this way developed into a practice of philosophical reflection *in* theology (sometimes called "fundamental theology") whose point is a twofold task: it explores and unfolds the internal grammar and plausibility-structures of a particular tradition of Christian life, faith, and practice (e.g., Protestantism), and it relates it to the wider cultural and/or scientific context of its time. This can be done either from the inside or the outside (i.e., be practiced as a philosophical *theology* or as a *philosophical* theology). The former is a theological enterprise that is located within a particular communal tradition of faith and explicates its grammar in terms that are accessible to those who do not belong to and participate in it. The latter is a philosophical enterprise that views it from the outside (i.e., without necessarily participating in it), describes and analyzes its "grammatical" structures and conceptual options, and relates them to the cultural context of this religious practice. The first route is typically taken by confessional versions of CPT, the second route by liberal versions. Between them they cover the majority of philosophers of religion and theologians in the twentieth century who have offered versions of CPT, from Tillich or Nygren, to MacKinnon, Kaufmann, Tracy, Lash, or Brümmer, to name but a few. They all have practiced versions of this approach, albeit in very different ways, some more constructive (Tillich, Kaufmann, Brümmer), others in a more tentative and explorative way (MacKinnon). So the story of CPT runs from the breakdown of dogmatic foundationalism through individualist moralism and communitarian confessionalism to a reflected theological culturalism. The function of CPT is not merely to provide the individual believer with a critical religious enforcement of his or her moral orientation (as in Kant), nor is it simply a way of unfolding the internal structure of a confessional tradition from within in philosophical terms, but a philosophical account of the place of religion and theology in a specific cultural matrix, and an exploration of the options in that matrix that can be accepted without contradiction.

Idealist philosophical theology or transcendental theism

Kant redefined the agenda of PT in more than one way. By showing the traditional onto-, cosmo-, and teleological arguments for the existence of God to be inconclusive, inconsistent, or based on untenable premises, he opened the door not only to CPT, but also to a critical transcendentalism that became the starting point of various idealist and speculative versions of PT; and he paved the way towards modern philosophy of religion, which no longer concentrates on God but on religion.

Idealist or subjectivist PT (IPT) combines Kant's criticism of Enlightenment DPT with a continuation of its quest for ultimate explanation in the context of a philosophy of transcendental subjectivity (Fichte). It accepts Kant's move from the empirical I to the transcendental I in his critical refocusing of philosophy from metaphysical *de facto* questions to transcendental *de jure* questions; it also follows him in conceiving God to be neither a *datum* nor a *dabile* of experience but a *cogitabile* that plays an indispensable unifying role in human knowledge; it also accepts the primacy of practical over theoretical reason; but it goes beyond Kant in taking the transcendental I as the creative center of all human activity and, as such, the autonomous unifying ground of all human knowing and doing; and it offers not only a performative account of the transcendental I but an idealist rereading of Kant's critical differentiation of various types of reason (theoretical, practical, aesthetical).

The upshot is an IPT that restricts what is legitimate in theology to that which can be shown to be certain in terms of transcendental subjectivity: truth is replaced by certainty, and certainty is restricted to that which can in principle be made, and hence known how to be made, by ourselves and which is necessarily presupposed in all our making, viz. God, the necessary condition of all our acting, thinking, and believing. Since nothing that we believe is such that it might not have been the case that we believe it, not what we believe but only how we believe can stand the test of transcendental subjectivity. Certainty in religious and all other matters is restricted to how we believe, not what we believe: all that matters is our *belief* in God, not our belief *in* God. So all theistic arguments for the existence of God are taken to be simply beside the point. What needs to be shown is not whether God exists (or that "God exists" is true), but rather that we are justified in *believing* – not in believing *something* (some contingent or even some necessary truth), but in believing *tout court*. The I is the rock on which everything is to be built, as so widely different thinkers as Fichte, Hirsch, Lonergan, Rahner, Verweyen, Barth, or Müller claim in their different ways.[19]

Realist or speculative philosophical theology

Realist or speculative PT (RPT) is a realist reaction to the idealist philosophy of transcendental subjectivity. It attempts to integrate the theistic quest for ultimate explanations in terms of God, the critique of natural and rational theology, and the epistemological insights of IPT into a more comprehensive realist approach. God is not conceived, as in IPT, as (intentional) object of human consciousness or necessary condition of the possibility of human knowledge and certainty. Rather, God is the ultimate or absolute subject that makes itself conceived by human consciousness through creating what can be conceived (the possible), what is conceived (the actual), and the very process of its conceiving in a progressive dialectical integration of everything true, good, and beautiful into a final synthesis of subject and object, God as knowing us and God as known by us. Only, as Hegel put it, if God is conceived not merely as substance (object) but as the true subject of all knowledge, including all knowledge of God, God is really appreciated as a *living* God and not merely as a possible or necessary object of human thought.[20] RPT, in short, is not a continuation of IPT (as often mistakenly thought), but its realist critique and correction.

This realist program has been worked out most prominently in Hegel's dialectical process ontology of the progressive self-realization of the Absolute in the history of the world; in Schelling's philosophy of revelation as God's development from abstract existence to concrete reality in the evolution of the world; or, in the twentieth century, in Whitehead and Hartshorne's process cosmologies. They all aim, in their different ways, at a realist and all-inclusive account of God's relations to the world and the world's relations to God. They all belong to a speculative program of PT whose story runs from realist reactions to idealist replacements of DPT by transcendental and subjectivist IPT to an all-inclusive panentheism. And both in its ontological (Hegel, Schelling) and cosmological (Whitehead, Hartshorne) versions this is achieved by the highly problematic move of basing RPT on a realist or ontological interpretation of a given form of logic. Thus, Hegel arrives at his dialectical ontology by a realist reading of the *syllogistic pattern* of concept, judgment, and inference. He interprets the transmission of truth from true premises to a true conclusion in a valid deductive argument as a real movement of truth from thesis through antithesis to synthesis in which the truth of the conclusion is constituted by integrating the partial truths of the major and minor premises. Whitehead, on the other hand, derives his process metaphysics from a realist interpretation of the *logic of relations* of the *Principia Mathematica* in that his actual entities are construed as self-realizing relations in which "the many become one, and are increased by one."[21] And Hartshorne, finally, interprets the relativity of God and world or the dependence of the world on God realistically as "the ontological correlate of the logical relation of entailment."[22] Whereas Wittgenstein rightly insisted in the *Tractatus* that logical signs, constants, or connectives do not represent anything (4.0312) (i.e., are not to be understood semantically or ontologically but only pragmatically as indicating operations that can be performed with propositions), Hartshorne's neoclassical PT is based on an ontological reading of *logical entailment*. God's existence is logically entailed by every actual existence: if anything exists at all, then God exists.

This raises at least two problems. The first is that the force of this kind of argument depends on the truth of the premise that God's existence is possible. But why assume the possibility of God's existence rather than the possibility of God's non-existence? Without being antecedently persuaded of the existence of God in one way or another RPT's arguments for God's necessary existence do not get off the ground.[23]

There is also a second problem. Since the necessary does not entail the contingent, God cannot be merely necessary if he is to explain the universe; but neither can he be merely contingent if he is to be distinguished from the world. So God must be in some respects both necessary and contingent.[24] Whitehead and Hartshorne try to capture this idea in a dipolar conception of God. In his "primordial nature" God is the necessary, changeless, and eternal realm of potentiality, the totality of unrealized possibilities. In his "consequent nature" he is the changing realm of actuality, the all-inclusive container of the real. God's two natures are related not directly, but indirectly through the world-process. This, however, risks reducing God to an *aliquid mundi*, a mere abstract structure of a world-process that permanently provides the possibilities for the creative advance into novelty and permanently integrates what has become actual into the unity of his being.

Ward therefore suggested a different solution. God is not a dipolar correlation of necessity and contingency but, rather, "the one self-existent being in whom creation and necessity originate and in whom they are reconciled."[25] Swinburne, on the other hand, starts *a posteriori* from the contingent world which requires, if anything, a contingent explanation. He therefore gives the contingent primacy over the necessary in God. "God exists" is a contingent proposition: to "say that 'God exists' is necessary is . . . to say that the existence of God is a brute fact which is inexplicable."[26] For Swinburne, God is the ultimate contingency even though his essence is an eternal essence, so that "if he exists at any time he exists at all times" – what we may call a "factually necessary existence."[27]

However, given all our ordinary information about the world, the idea of a personal explanation of it has little initial probability, as Mackie has pointed out.[28] And even if we accept it as the only possible ultimate explanation, why should we not then conceive the world itself in personal terms? The issue turns on our model of the world, which is not something given in experience, but the idea of the totality of interacting realities that can be experienced. We can use a number of models, including that of a person, to conceptualize this idea. Not all such models are compatible with a Christian understanding of creation, of course. But this is not the idea that RPT seeks to conceptualize.

Philosophy of religion

Philosophy of religion (PR), finally, has been the most promising and productive heir to DPT, but one that can only be hinted at here since it in fact supersedes the history of PT as conceived. Its basic move has been to refocus philosophical reflection from *God* to *religion* (i.e., recontextualize the notion of God in the religious practices in which it is incorporated), and this has opened up a whole new agenda for philosophy. There is no direct philosophical (rational or natural) access to God in isolation (i.e., apart from being the object of worship and religious belief). Therefore, philosophical reflection must start from religion (i.e., the communal practice of belief in God) and not from a decontextualized concept of God that is abstracted from the doctrinal scheme of Christian theology and used in philosophical attempts at "ultimate explanation" that disregard the manifold ways in which concepts, pictures, and metaphors of God function in religious practices to provide orientation in life. But elucidating this life-orienting capacity of religious belief and practice is the central task of PT/PR, as such seminal thinkers as Pascal, Kierkegaard,[29] and Wittgenstein have shown. So PR, construed in their way, can be seen as an attempt to recontextualize the whole agenda of PT in the actual life of religions, and this seems to be the really promising route to take for PT after the collapse of DPT.

However, PR has also been understood and practiced in different ways, and in a sense all the problems that arose in PT recur in a new guise. Indeed, some of those listed under the previous programs can also be interpreted as contributors to PR. To mention but some of the most important developments or programs of PR in the period under discussion: it concentrates on religion understood as a universal human phenomenon, or as a specific form of human culture, or as a particular historical religion, or as the actual and irreducible plurality of religions, approached either normatively or descriptively.

The story of PR ranges from subjectivist through culturalist, confessional and pluralist to criteriological or grammatical versions; that is, from concern with a universal concept of religion as the fundamental relation of finite to infinite that is seen to lie at the root of all religions (Barth);[30] or concern for religion as a particular form of common life in the wider context of human culture (Cassirer, Nygren);[31] through inquiries into the internal rationality of a particular religious practice and tradition (Judaism in Rosenzweig or Buber, Roman Catholicism in Newman or Lonergan, Anglicanism in Farrer, Reformed Christianity in Plantinga); to cognitive accounts of the plurality of religions as different phenomenal ways of referring to the same noumenal "Real" (Hick);[32] or descriptive approaches to the various ways and plural aspects of religious beliefs and practices to provide the orientation in life that characterizes a given religion (a contemplative PR in the tradition of Wittgenstein, Rhees, and Phillips).[33] The reflections of such PR are not themselves religious reflections, nor are they normally based on particular religious convictions (though they may be); but they are always located within a religious practice and tradition, and they view other religious orientations, not from nowhere or anywhere, but from that perspective.

A Future Agenda?

It is the task of philosophical reflection to explore possibilities of orientation ("life options") in the face of puzzles and problems that arise in life; and it is the task of philosophy of religion to explore possibilities of religious orientation ("religious options") in the face of puzzles and problems that arise in, or with respect to, specific religious beliefs and practices. But it is not its task to provide religious orientation itself or mistake its own philosophical (descriptive) role with that of theological (normative) reflection in a particular religious tradition. Philosophical reflection is not directive or foundational, but descriptive and orienting, and it orients *in thinking* by exploring options and possibilities, and not *in life* by providing direction and giving advice. Its task is not that of religion or theology, but of philosophical reflection in and about religion. Theology misses its point by not being normative, philosophy, on the other hand, by trying to be so.

In many versions, PT has been practiced as the mistaken attempt to provide religious orientation itself – a better, more comprehensive, more rational, better justified orientation than a particular religious tradition of lived and practiced communal faith is allegedly supposed to do. That is true of the foundationalist versions of philosophical theism (DPT), subjective transcendentalism (IPT), realist panentheism (RPT), as well as the directive versions of philosophy of religion. However, only a PT along the lines of a philosophy of religion that understands its task to be the descriptive and contemplative exploration of the grammar of a particular religious practice in the context of the wider culture of today will be able to provide the orientation in thought about religious orientation in life that will be helpful to overcome puzzles and confusions by showing possible ways out of practical confusions. Only in this religiously embedded way will PT have a future. Otherwise, it will either become indistinguishable from systematic or dogmatic theology, or remain a self-contained intellectual endeavor without a particular import either for those who live and participate in a common religious life, or for those who do not.

Notes

1   See L. Ashdown, *Anonymous Skeptics: Swinburne, Hick and Alston*, Tübingen, 2002.

2   N. Kretzmann, *Our Knowledge of God: Essays on Natural and Philosophical Theology*, ed. K. Clark, Dordrecht, 1992.

3   For example, Plantinga's "Victorious Modal Version" of the ontological argument, which accepts as premise that "it is possible that maximal greatness is exemplified," not only can be shown to be valid only in S_5 but not in other systems of modal logic, but also assumes without further argument that one should accept the former premise rather than "it is *not* possible that maximal greatness is exemplified," which would also produce as valid an argument in S_5 but with the opposite conclusion.

4   See A. Plantinga, *Warranted Christian Belief*, New York, 2000, pp. 167–98.

5   R. Swinburne, *The Coherence of Theism*, Oxford, 1977, p. 1.

6   V. Brümmer, *What Are We Doing When We Pray? A Philosophical Inquiry*, London, 1984.

7   See R. Swinburne, *The Existence of God*, Oxford, 1979; J. Mackie, *The Miracle of Theism*, Oxford, 1982; R. Gale, *On the Nature and Existence of God*, Cambridge, 1991; C. Taliaferro (ed.), *Contemporary Philosophy of Religion*, Oxford, 1998.

8   I. U. Dalferth, *Die Wirklichkeit des Möglichen*, Tübingen, 2003, pp. 257–335.

9   Plantinga, *Warranted Christian Belief*, pp. 167–353.

10 N. Wolterstorff, "Can Belief in God Be Rational If It Has No Foundations?" In A. Plantinga and N. Wolterstorff (eds.), *Faith and Rationality: Reason and Belief in God*, Notre Dame, IN, 1983, pp. 135–86.

11 D. Hume, *Dialogues Concerning Natural Religion* (1779), ed. N. K. Smith, London, 1947, p. 147, pt. X.

12 See I. U. Dalferth, *Religiöse Rede von Gott*, Munich, 1981, pp. 538ff.

13 A. Plantinga, "The Free Will Defence." In M. Black (ed.), *Philosophy in America*, London, 1965, pp. 204–20; *God and Other Minds: A Study of the Rational Justification of Belief in God*, Ithaca, NY, 1967, chs. 5 and 6; *The Nature of Necessity*, Oxford, 1974, ch. 9; *God, Freedom and Evil*, London, 1975.

14 K. Ward, *Rational Theology and the Creativity of God*, Oxford, 1982, pp. 206ff.

15 See J. Hintikka, "Kant on Existence, Predication, and the Ontological Argument." In S. Knuuttila and J. Hintikka (eds.), *The Logic of Being: Historical Studies*, Dordrecht, 1986, pp. 249–67.

16 J. L. Mackie, *The Miracle of Theism: Arguments For and Against the Existence of God*, Oxford, 1982, p. 84.

17 Dalferth, *Religiöse Rede von Gott*, pp. 532ff.

18 I. Kant, *The Conflict of the Faculties*, in P. Guyer and A. W. Wood (eds.), *The Cambridge Edition of the Works of Immanuel Kant*, Cambridge, 1996, A43–6.

19 For a critical discussion of these views, see Dalferth, *Die Wirklichkeit des Möglichen*, pp. 336–430.

20 See I. U. Dalferth, *Theology and Philosophy*, Oxford, 1988, pp. 177–82.

21 A. N. Whitehead, *Process and Reality*, corrected edn., ed. D. R. Griffin and D. W. Sherburne, London, 1978, p. 21.
22 C. Hartshorne, *The Divine Relativity: A Social Conception of God*, New Haven, CT, 1964, p. 9.
23 I. U. Dalferth, *Gott. Philosophisch-theologische Denkversuche*, Tübingen, 1992, pp. 192–212.
24 Ward, *Rational Theology*, p. 8.
25 Ibid, p. 3.
26 Swinburne, *The Existence of God*, p. 92.
27 Ibid, p. 93.
28 Mackie, *The Miracle of Theism*, pp. 100ff.
29 For an excellent analysis of Kierkegaard's subtle ways of doing this in his *Works of Love*, see M. J. Ferreira, *Love's Grateful Striving: A Commentary on Kierkegaard's Works of Love*, Oxford, 2001.
30 U. Barth, *Religion in der Moderne. Systematische und problemgeschichtliche Studien*, Tübingen, 2003.
31 C. Richter, *Die Religion in der Sprache der Kultur. Die theologische Bedeutung von Ernst Cassirers Philosophie der symbolischen Formen*, Tübingen, 2004.
32 J. Hick, *An Interpretation of Religion*, New Haven, CT, 1989.
33 R. Rhees, *On Religion and Philosophy*, Cambridge, 1997; *Wittgenstein and the Possibility of Discourse*, Cambridge, 1998. Cf. D. Z. Phillips, *Religion Without Explanation*, Oxford, 1976; *Faith after Foundationalism*, London, 1988; *Religion and the Hermeneutics of Contemplation*, Cambridge, 2001.

Bibliography

Primary

W. P. Alston, *Perceiving God: The Epistemology of Religious Experience*, Ithaca, NY, 1991.
V. Brümmer, *Speaking of a Personal God: An Essay in Philosophical Theology*, Cambridge, 1992.
I. U. Dalferth, *Die Wirklichkeit des Möglichen. Hermeneutische Religionsphilosophie*, Tübingen, 2003.
A. M. Farrer, *Finite and Infinite*, London, 1959.
C. Hartshorne, *The Logic of Perfection*, La Salle, IL, 1962.
—— *The Divine Relativity: A Social Conception of God*, New Haven, CT, 1964.
—— *A Natural Theology for Our Time*, La Salle, IL, 1967.
J. Hick, *Arguments for the Existence of God*, London, 1979.
—— *An Interpretation of Religion*, New Haven, CT, 1989.
D. Z. Phillips, *Religion Without Explanation*, Oxford, 1976.
—— *Faith after Foundationalism*, London, 1988.
—— *Religion and the Hermeneutics of Contemplation*, Cambridge, 2001.
A. Plantinga, *The Nature of Necessity*, Oxford, 1974.
—— *God, Freedom and Evil*, London, 1975.
—— *Warranted Christian Belief*, New York, 2000.

A. Plantinga and N. Wolterstorff (eds.), *Faith and Rationality: Reason and Belief in God*, Notre Dame, IN, 1983.
R. Rhees, *On Religion and Philosophy*, Cambridge, 1997.
—— *Wittgenstein and the Possibility of Discourse*, Cambridge, 1998.
R. Swinburne, *The Existence of God*, Oxford, 1979.
—— *Faith and Reason*, Oxford, 1981.
—— *The Coherence of Theism*, revd. edn., Oxford, 1993.
—— *Providence and the Problem of Evil*, Oxford, 1998.
F. Wagner, *Was ist Religion? Studien zu ihrem Begriff und Thema in Geschichte und Gegenwart*, Gütersloh, 1986.
K. Ward, *Rational Theology and the Creativity of God*, Oxford, 1982.
A. N. Whitehead, *Process and Reality*, corrected edn., ed. D. R. Griffin and D. W. Sherburne, London, 1978.

Secondary

L. Ashdown, *Anonymous Skeptics: Swinburne, Hick and Alston*, Tübingen, 2002.
I. U. Dalferth, *Religiöse Rede von Gott*, Munich, 1981.
—— *Gott. Philosophisch-theologische Denkversuche*, Tübingen, 1992.

—— *Theology and Philosophy*, Eugene, OR, 2001.

R. Gale, *On the Nature and Existence of God*, Cambridge, 1991.

J. Greisch, *Le Buisson ardent et les lumières de la raison: l'invention de la philosophie de la religion*, 2 vols., Paris, 2002.

J. L. Mackie, *The Miracle of Theism: Arguments For and Against the Existence of God*, Oxford, 1982.

J. Rohls, *Philosophie und Theologie in Geschichte und Gegenwart*, Tübingen, 2002.

E. Stump and M. Murray (eds.), *Philosophy of Religion: The Big Questions*, Oxford, 1999.

C. Taliaferro and P. J. Griffiths (eds.), *Philosophy of Religion: An Anthology*, Oxford, 2003.

H. de Vries, *Philosophy and the Turn to Religion*, Baltimore, MD, 1999.

Postmodern Theology

Graham Ward

Varieties of Postmodernism

If thinking in modernity (a period roughly inaugurated by the rapid development of capitalism, technology, and the cult of the individual in the late sixteenth century) is dominated by highly determined forms such as the circle, the cube, the spiral, even the double helix, then postmodernity (not a period, as we shall see, but more a condition) finds expression in indeterminate forms such as Deleuze and Guattari's thinking about the rhizome. As a form, the "rhizome is reducible neither to the One nor the multiple . . . It is composed not of units but of dimensions, or rather directions in motion. It has neither beginning nor end, but always a middle [*milieu*] from which it grows and which it overspills."[1] The dreams of order – Newtonian, Leibnizian – the economies of evolutionary progress – Hegelian and Darwinian – the aesthetics of pure color and geometrical forms – in Kandinsky and the Bauhaus – collapse into the subterranean complexity of the rhizome: a root-stock growing in no particular direction and without detectable regularity. Words like development, progression, advancement, meaning, profundity, and depths are supplanted by other words like dissemination, indeterminacy, deferral, *aporia*, seduction, and surface. Meaning is local, community is tribal, society is pluralistic, and economics is the pragmatics of the marketplace. This is the age of the sign.

In such a cultural space it is to be expected that there is not one postmodernism. There is the eclecticism of postmodern architecture in which classical columns and architraves are mixed with multicolored bricks or polychromatic ironwork. The building for the Judge Institute of Managerial Science, in Trumpington Street, Cambridge, is a good example of such architecture. Then there is the ironization of the aesthetic medium in the paintings of Anselm Kiefer, who employs materials like sand, earth, ash, straw, and charred photographs in compositions which play on a tension between spatial emptiness, burnt edges, blistered textures, and religious titles. A series of 16 paintings of stark desert landscapes made up of multilayered images is entitled *Departure from Egypt*.[2] There is a similar ironization (and irony is always iconoclastic) in the novels of Thomas Pynchon, in which characters are flat and cartoon-like and the narration endlessly turns in upon itself in a self-conscious "this-fiction-writer-is-writing-fiction" gesture. Obsessed to the point of paranoia by a symbol of a horn and the company WASTE for which it is the logo, one Oedipa Mass in Pynchon's *The Crying of Lot 49* attempts to decipher the gathering heaps of hieroglyphics around her by visiting Mr. Thoth. Mr. Thoth shows her a ring cut by his grandfather from the hand of a man disguised as an Indian who had attacked him one night. On the ring is the symbol of WASTE. Surprised, once again, Oedipa

> looked around, spooked at the sunlight pouring in all the windows, as if she had been trapped at the center of some intricate crystal, and said, "My God."
> "And I feel him, certain days, days of a certain temperature," said Mr. Thoth, "and barometric pressure. Did you know that? I feel him close to me."
> "Your grandfather?"
> "No, my God."[3]

Then there are the French intellectuals – Foucault, Lacan, Derrida, Levinas, Baudrillard, among others – whose work details radical critiques of history, rationality, representation, and self. Frequently, the poststructuralism and deconstruction they represent is seen as a post-1968 phenomenon. But several of these popular thinkers – like Blanchot, Bataille, Lacan, and Levinas – produced significant critical work much earlier.[4] All these postmodern projects are not easily made analogous. Besides, art theorists like Charles Jencks, Clement Greenberg, and Rosalind E. Krauss, philosophers like Jürgen Habermas, Jean-François Lyotard, and Gianni Vattimo, and social theorists like Zygmunt Bauman and Frederic Jameson still argue (frequently with each other) about the characteristics of various shades of modernism (in itself and then prefixed with "late" or "post").[5] In the *Zeitgeist* of postmodernity, there can only be postmodernisms.

Similarly, there is not one postmodern theology; there are (to quote the title of one of David Ray Griffin's books) *Varieties of Postmodern Theology.*[6] Even so this essay, while outlining this variety, nevertheless would wish to argue that some of these theologies are more thoroughly postmodern than others. It will argue for a distinction to be drawn between liberal and conservative postmodern theologies, pointing out that early espousals of postmodernism were simply continuing liberal theology's concerns with apologetics, correlation, and local expressions of a universal condition. Some practitioners of postmodern theology are therefore seen to be dreaming of a bacchanalian nihilism in what George Steiner terms the garden of liberal culture.[7] These thinkers can only advocate freedom through abandoning oneself to the effervescent flux because of the leisure society to which they belong (and which provides them with employment and an income). If liberalism promotes the politics and economics of *laissez-faire*, then their work is an expression of such a culture, not a critique of it.[8] Of course, among these theologians, some are more liberal than others, but all of them are idealists (and to use what is now a quaint term, bourgeois). As for the conservative postmodern theologians, they tend to employ the insights and analyses of postmodern thought to re-read foundational theological texts and, with reference to the scripture, liturgies, and creeds, construct new theologies in, through, and at the margins of postmodernism. Increasingly, these theologies are not simply Christian. There is a growing body of Jewish postmodern theology.[9] These theologians locate themselves in the place of faith and the tradition prior to the secondary, postmodern reflections upon that tradition which their work explores. Rather than interpreting poststructuralism or deconstruction as the final nail in theology's coffin, the work of these theologians opens up the theological horizons within postmodern thought itself. These theologians also recognize that postmodernism does not delineate an epoch at the end of modernism, beginning in the 1960s, say. Rather, postmodernism is a moment within modernism; the moment modernism pushes into the margins and represses in order to construct its circles of development, its linear progressions, and its harmonies of part and whole. In this sense, postmodernism, described in terms of Freudian psychoanalysis, marks the return of the repressed. It is the repressed "other" of modernism. This is postmodernism as understood and described by Jean-François Lyotard: "postmodernism is not modernism at its end, but in a nascent state, and this state is recurrent."[10]

> The postmodern would be that which in the modern invokes the unpresentable in presentation itself, that which refuses the consolation of correct forms, refuses the consensus of taste permitting a common experience of nostalgia for the impossible, and inquires into new presentations – not to take pleasure in them, but to better produce the feeling that there is something unpresentable . . . *Postmodern* would be understanding according to the paradox of the future (*post*) anterior (*modo*).[11]

Postmodern fosters a post-secular condition.[12]

The postmodern moment, then, is composed of that which is excluded from or excess to the discourses of knowledge or the orders governing various sciences, and the authorities which police them. The university, with its *Geist-* and *Naturwissenschaften* and the division of faculties, is one example of authority. In this way postmodern thinking forces open a new space for theological thinking by paying attention to the preemptive foreclosures of systems (philosophical, institutional, and political). With profound philosophical and psychological investigations into an unerasable instability, uncertainty, agnosticism, skepticism, even nihilism, theological questions have begun again to surface and permeate contemporary thought. It is not surprising then to find Derrida writing eloquently about Eckhart and negative theology in relation to his own notion of *différance*.[13] Not only does Kristeva distinguish the critical difference "love" in Christian discourses makes to primary narcissism in psychoanalytic discourses, but also a *theologia crucis* operates at the center of her thinking on the need to reintegrate the abjected, chaotic other, what she terms the *khora*.[14] Levinas, as a Jewish philosopher working out of the tradition which produced Hermann Cohen and Franz Rosenzweig, cannot separate God from his account of our primordial responsibility for the wholly other, what he terms *illeity*. The Good, the ethical God, lies beyond Being, but elects us all to an endless responsibility for the other.[15] Irigaray's work on sexual difference has repeatedly called for a feminine symbolics of the divine and a more developed notion of what it is to be incarnate ("bringing the god to life through us, in a resurrection or transfiguration of blood and flesh").[16] In Lyotard's more recent work, his concern with waging war on totality and bearing witness to the unpresentable has drawn him into detailed analyses of the sublime, its experience, its characterization.[17] Cixous has advocated we rethink our understanding of "soul," announces a radical ethics of love and kenosis, and refers throughout her work to the face of God, the Bible, and our immortality.[18]

Three particular theological (and ethical) horizons are opened up by this postmodern thinking. First, the role of the unsayable and unpresentable as it both constitutes and ruptures all that is said and presented. Secondly, the self as divided, multiple, or even abyssal, and therefore never self-enclosed but always open onto that which transcends its own self-understanding (rather than simply being an agent and a *cogito*). Thirdly, the movement of desire initiated and fostered by the other, that which lies outside and for future possession, the other which is also prior and cannot be gathered into the rational folds of present consciousness. The place in which these three horizons interlace is the "body." That is, these horizons can never be abstracted from the texts, the social practices, and the institutions which configure or give expression to them. As such, postmodernism's critique of body/soul, body/mind, form/contents, sign/signified divisions demands new understandings and imaginings of what it is to be embodied, incarnate. And although "the cross," "resurrection," the "soul," "immortality," and the "divine" are always employed rhetorically in these philosophical discourses, nevertheless they show themselves profoundly indebted to (if not heavily dependent upon) the Judeo-Christian tradition. Furthermore, they would question what is being meant when theologians seek for these words a literal reference. It is on the basis of these horizons that the sociologist Zygmunt Bauman has emphasized how "postmodernity can be seen as restoring to the world what modernity, presumptuously, had taken away; as a *re-enchantment* of the world that modernity tried hard to *disenchant*."[19]

Liberal Postmodern Theologies

Until recently, postmodern theology's most popular and well-known exponents in North America were Mark C. Taylor, Thomas J. J. Altizer, Robert P. Scharlemann, Charles Winquist, and David Ray Griffin. Its most popular and well-known exponent in Britain was Don Cupitt. Significantly, for all these writers, their projects issue from a radicalization of an older liberal theology that previously engaged them. The existential concerns of Paul Tillich and Rudolf Bultmann and the process philosophy of Alfred Whitehead remain as important as Nietzsche's pronouncements about the death of God and truth as a mobile army of metaphors. The projects of these postmodern theologians are not identical.

David Ray Griffin has been concerned to re-read process theology in the light of certain characteristics of postmodernity – particularly the critique of Enlightenment rationalism and the decentering of the Cartesian *cogito*. He develops, through an examination of quantum mechanics, a notion of postmodern animism in which everything in the world – from rocks to human beings – embodies creative energies. A postmodern naturalistic theism emerges.[20] There are certain aspects of this project which connect with the more recent work of Don Cupitt, who, in outlining the philosophy which informs his thinking, describes it as a *Lebensphilosophie*. Cupitt, too, is arguing for an "outlook that is monistic and naturalistic"[21] and appeals to the flux of life which is both biological and sociocultural. Where Cupitt differs from Griffin (and draws closer to Mark C. Taylor and Charles Winquist) is in the support he elicits from French postmodern philosophers like Jacques Derrida, Michel Foucault, and Gilles Deleuze. The writings of these thinkers provide the philosophical analysis and argument for the anti-foundationalism and the anti-realism that Cupitt and Taylor both wish to endorse and the bases for the a/theology they both advocate. In particular, the work of Cupitt and Taylor develops the consequences for theology of a linguistic idealism they believe Derrida and others expound.[22] The burden of Taylor's apocalyptic chapter "The Empty Mirror" (in his book *Deconstructing Theology*) is that we do not *find* but *construct* reality. We are not only caught up within but also constituted by nets of shifting signifiers endlessly deferring identity. We deal not with meaning but with interpretations. He, like Cupitt, encourages us to enjoy the cavalcade of tropes and metaphors, the endless stream of simulacra, which represent to us our world. We are advised to stop mourning for defunct authorities (the authority of God, Truth, and Self) and embrace the creativity of play and plurality. For "one who has gazed into the empty mirror can never regard God or self as he did before."[23] The death of God is the death of a transcendental signifier stabilizing identity and truth. It is the death of identity, *telos*, and therefore meaning in anything but a local and pragmatic sense. That death has led to a new emphasis upon the immanent flux, the material, the body and its desires – all of which deny there is anything "higher" or "out there." With Griffin, Cupitt, and Taylor, whatever is religious issues from a profoundly nihilistic ontology.

It is with the consequences of the death of God that Thomas Altizer's project is concerned, which, in the wake of Tillich, examines the relationship between contemporary culture and the Christian faith. Subsequently, Altizer reverses Tillich's priorities – judging God in the darkness of modern culture rather than culture by the ultimate revelation of God. Tillich and the death of God are also important orientating foci in the theological project of the late Charles Winquist. In one of his books, *Desiring Theology*, he speaks explicitly about extending rather than abandoning the theological work of Tillich.[24] Winquist's project is indebted to Altizer's. He considers Altizer to have made one of the most important statements of what it means to think theologically in the closing years of the twentieth century.[25] To a large extent, Winquist's form of deconstructing the pretensions of theology by reminding theologians they are only writing, is providing the fundamental theology Altizer's project lacks. For Winquist's work draws attention to the textual body of theology: to language as a dialectic of meaning and desire; to the endless deferral of truth that issues from theology's necessary dependence upon representation and tropes; to the wounds and fissures in logical argumentation which proliferate rather than delimit ambiguity and hinder rational progression. His is a navel-gazing theological investigation. He does not think theologically himself, rather (as he himself observes) "deconstruction in theology resembles a second-order critique looking for the conditions that make theological thinking possible."[26] Nevertheless, though the textual surface of theological discourse is broken up and raked, the Tillichian and liberal emphasis upon the primacy of "religous experience" remains. The gaps and *aporias* – what remains unsaid and unthought in what is said and thought in the textual body of theological discourse – point to "epiphanies of darkness" and the God of the gaps.

It is significant, with respect to the distinction drawn between liberal and conservative postmodern theology, that these theologians understand their French philosophical support to be advocating absence, non-identity, and the unbearable lightness of a being in which all is rhetoric and surface. It is also important that the relationship of postmodern philosophy to the projects of these radical theologians is epiphenomenal. Their work does not issue from postmodern philosophy, its insights and methodologies; postmodern philosophy (as they interpret it) substantiates their theses concerning contemporary culture. Altizer's theological project, for example, and Cupitt's, were underway several years before Derrida or Foucault, Lyotard or Deleuze were writing their poststructural philosophies. Nevertheless, if these thinkers represent for Mark C. Taylor and others the postmodern experience they wish theology to address and they are not representatives and purveyors of nihilism in the way Taylor and others believe, liberal postmodern theology may have to think again. For the moment it is sufficient to outline that all these postmodern theological projects are united in attempting to construct, in Taylor's words, "a radically new theology, a secular, post-ecclesiastical theology."²⁷ Each is aware that, in doing this, theology and anthropology become indistinguishable, religious studies becomes a subset of cultural studies, even aesthetics, and transcendence issues only within immanence. Hence Taylor's neologism: "a/theology."

While these theologians dissolve the specificity of Christianity into a world-spirit, the work of Robert P. Scharlemann does not go so far. Scharlemann's theology is still trading off the inheritance of Schleiermacher, Tillich, and Bultmann, but for him the specificity of the Christ-event remains uniquely paradigmatic. His work relies heavily on the existential analyses of Martin Heidegger. Soteriology is worked out in terms of selfhood, in terms, that is, of developing the notion of the "exstantial I." This I is the resurrected I, the I which is drawn out of the interiority of the *cogito* by the process of what Scharlemann calls "acoluthetic reason" – reason which follows after, follows in the wake of Christ. Christ himself instantiates, as archetypal example, the exstantial I as someone living beyond himself for the other, emptying himself out for the other.²⁸ As Scharlemann writes: "If the exstantial I is a symbol of God . . . then it is *as* that exstantial I that God (who is not I and not the world but not nothing either) exists. The exstantial I is not *what* God is but *where* God is."²⁹

Scharlemann's work is densely analytical and philosophical, and he permits (possibly like Winquist) a transcendence missing from Taylor, Altizer, and Cupitt. His is a repristination of Logos Christology and his central appeal to the ethics and theology of discipleship gives weight to ecclesiology. But his analyses and philosophy owe much to the projects of modernity rather than postmodernity. He, more than the others, illustrates the fact that these "postmodern theologians" are really theologians of modernity. Their work is not the deconstruction of the liberal tradition (however much they employ the term "deconstruction"), it is the apotheosis of the liberal tradition. Most of these figures have, at times, wished to emphasize they are not postmodern all the way; but the work of all of them has been characterized by a preoccupation with that most postmodern of all themes, the crisis of representation.

We need to return to the liberal roots of these theologies for a moment and reflect upon them in the context of the poststructural and deconstructive philosophies to which they frequently appeal. Each theologian, in his way, is continuing to write theological apologetics based upon the liberal notions of correlation, a primary monism, and the exponential pursuit of human emancipation. For what each assumes is a major cultural shift, what Altizer describes as the dawn of "a wholly new historical era,"³⁰ that can be described as "postmodern" and, like their liberal forebears, it is with relation to this new culture that theology must radically transform itself. What is significant is that the epithet "postmodern" is here being used as a period concept, frequently an apocalyptic concept denoting a culture at the "end of history," "the end of the autonomous person," the "end of representation," and the mortal wounding of rational argumentation. Altizer makes this explicit in his book *History as Apocalypse*. Our postmodern culture, he argues, is what the development of history has brought us to. Hence our new situation calls for a revolution in our thinking. The old texts have to be rewritten for them to speak again in contemporary society. Postmodernism, as such, becomes interchangeable with postmodernity (i.e., the sociological concept describing the character of the age in which we live). But as Lyotard has pointed out concerning this use of "post" in postmodernism, "this idea of a linear chronology is itself perfectly 'modern.'"[31] Connotations of "progress," "development," and "evolution" – the basis for the liberal dream for the emancipation of humanity – lie concealed about the body of "post"modernism as it is employed by these theologians. Let me delineate this further, for it is central to my argument. These theologians, in fact, are continuing the crisis of theology characteristic of "modernism," where it was believed that a clean break from theology's past was possible and necessary for a new liberation and new humanism. Their iconoclasm is only in the name of a more foundational monism – what Altizer terms a "new totality of bliss."[32] They are indissolubly linked, therefore, to a certain conception of history (a profoundly unpostmodern part-and-whole metanarrative). And this is the direct legacy of the historicism, romantic idealism, and neo-empiricism of the nineteenth century. Altizer writes: "Contemporary radical theologians inherit the nineteenth-century Catholic and Protestant theological conceptions of the evolutionary development of Christianity, but recognizing that the forward historical movement of Christianity has led to the eclipse or silence of God."[33]

There is, significantly for these liberal theologies, a difference between *deus absconditus* and *deus mortuus*. It is the death of God in history, not (as with Karl Barth and Hans Urs von Balthasar) God's hiddenness that is being foregrounded in their work. The death of God, as such, is part of the ever-deepening movement of the Incarnation. Hegel and a kenotic Christology emphasizing negativity and emptying are fundamental reference points. Christ merges with creation. As Altizer puts it: "The movement of secularization is finally a consequence of faith, and of faith in the Christ who lies in our future, the radical theologian is concerned with opening the corporate and communal body of faith to the new and more universal body of Christ."[34] Creation, not the church, is now the body of Christ. Institutions such as the church, bodies of historical tradition like its teaching and liturgies, find no room in such liberal "postmodern" theologies. The more profound the death of God, the more Christ is broken and poured out to perfume the mundane. The theological, stripped of any transcendence, becomes the incarnational to the point at which a Christian atheism emerges.

My question is whether this work can accurately be described as postmodern theology at all. To varying degrees each of these thinkers appeals to sets of ideas associated with postmodernism. We can distinguish five such sets. The first (and of primary importance to Cupitt, Taylor, and Winquist) is the way the linguistic turn in the early decades of the twentieth century has been transformed into the extended surface of ubiquitous textuality. On to this crisis of representation are grafted four other crises: the end of metaphysics, the end of history, the end of the subject, and the end of humanism. But significantly, with these five postmodern crises the end of liberalism itself is forcefully announced. Fundamentalism and postliberalism characterize the splintered culture of postmodernism. The isolation and construction of local, non-apologetic identities, of faiths radically opposed to Western globalization – these are the characteristics of postmodernity emphasized by sociologists such as Manuel Castells, Ernest Gellner, and Akbar S. Ahmed.[35] Hence, there are cultural (if not ethnographic) and philosophical tensions between these self-ascribed postmodern theologies and postmodernism itself. Each theology aims to eradicate difference or otherness because of the philosophical monism of their commitment to a general "life-force."[36] They each interpret Nietzsche's Eternal Recurrence as the dissolution of identity and difference[37] and this flies in the face of postmodernism, where difference is lionized. Nihilism, as such, is indifference; and joyful affirmation for these theologians issues from embracing the sheer contingent meaninglessness of existence.

Where do we look then for "postmodern theology" if the work of self-described postmodern theologians is not postmodern at all? We have seen that one possibility is to reject postmodernism as a period concept. Another is to recognize that for these theologians postmodernism is a given and emphatically a secular given. In other words, these thinkers do not examine the theological horizons of postmodernism, but rather the secular implications (in terms of critique) such postmodernism will have for the task of theology. Again, the "modern" character of their projects becomes increasingly manifest. For the various projects of Feuerbach, Durkheim, and Freud were all involved in the same program – the secularization of theology by means of developing more rational and comprehensive explanations: neo-Kantian anthropology, sociology, and psychology, respectively. As such, "postmodernism" provides these theologians with yet another grand explanatory narrative within the framework of which theology has to defend and adjust its thesis. And what happens is that theology, as such, is made bankrupt, its metaphors dispersed, its sacred space converted into a theme-park. But we can reverse the logic of this liberal analysis. Rather than postmodernism summoning theology to its judgment seat, we can explore the limits of the philosophical and the limits of explanatory narratives to which postmodernism draws attention. Theology then summons postmodernism to declare its own theological character. In fact, the theological horizons beyond philosophy (which postmodernism opens up) can be read as the theological fissuring and refiguring of the human, the mundane, and the metaphysical which it has consistently been the task of theology to investigate. What is then brought to our attention in the work of Derrida, Kristeva, Irigaray, Levinas, Lacan, and others can be read back into the theological tradition, beginning with such readings as their own. It is here that we can locate conservative postmodern theologies, which, I suggest, are more accurately entitled postmodern.

Conservative Postmodern Theologies

Among Anglo-American works, we could list here the postliberalism of George Lindbeck's influential volume *The Nature of Doctrine*,[38] building as it does on a cultural–linguistic model of religion owing much to the social anthropology of Clifford Geertz and Wittgenstein's notion of meaning issuing from specific linguistic practices or games. More recently, there has been the work produced in the series *Radical Orthodoxy*, in particular the postmodern Augustinianism of John Milbank and Catherine Pickstock.[39] The task of theology is rendered more questioning and complex by Rowan Williams,[40] Edith Wyschogrod's work on sainthood,[41] and my own postmodern Barthianism.[42] But conservative postmodern theologies are much more developed by French thinkers indebted to the Catholic heritage this century of Étienne Gilson, Henri de Lubac, and Jean Daniélou, and indebted also, more directly, to poststructural and deconstructive philosophies as they issued out of existential phenomenology. Of these theologies two names are becoming increasingly prominent in English and North American theological academies: Jean-Luc Marion and Michel de Certeau. Much of de Certeau's important work is now translated and, following in the wake of the intellectual stir caused by the translation of Marion's *God Without Being*, most of Marion's books are now translated into English. It is with the work of these theologians that a more "authentic" postmodern theology appears.[43]

Jean-Luc Marion

Jean-Luc Marion, a professor of philosophy at the University of Nanterre, established his academic reputation on analyses of Descartes' work. With Marion, a more nuanced Descartes emerges than the philosopher frequently cited as one of the primary craftsmen of modernity. Seen as the harbinger of our modern world, what is emphasized in Descartes' work is his notion of the self-determining *cogito*, the I which determines the nature of any object through its consciousness and the creation of ideas. As such, we are on the road to anthropology via atheism. But Marion's Descartes is haunted by questions of God and eternal truths. Marion's work points out that the gaze of the *cogito* in Descartes exists both in harmony and in conflict with a second gaze – the gaze of God. In harmony, the *cogito* is a reflection of *causa sive ratio* of God. In conflict, it is independent. An irreducible ambivalence emerges in Descartes' analysis of the *cogito*, for Descartes refuses to reduce the operation of consciousness upon the world either to anthropology or theology. Descartes, then, opens up *the question* of epistemological and ontological foundations, "a question concerning infinity and the unknown."[44]

It seems that Marion's project is to return to the philosophical origins of modernity and point up its ambivalences. Like his friend and colleague, the philosopher Jean-François Courtine, Marion has wished to distinguish between theological and metaphysical thinking. Metaphysical thinking about God is recognized as a product of modernity, issuing from the work of the Spanish Renaissance philosopher Francisco Suarez on Aristotle. With Suarez, God, Being, and Reason are conflated, leading to the project of onto-theology as it subsequently developed through Leibniz, Hegel, and finally Heidegger. What has been forgotten here – which was never forgotten by Anselm and Aquinas, for all their emphasis upon theology as seeking understanding – is the priority of faith and a God beyond both Being and human reason. Marion reaffirms that theological thinking proceeds along a different track and according to another logic. It is the logic of theology beyond the logic of philosophy which Marion attempts to elucidate in his theological books.[45] Marion was engaging with theology prior to and throughout his early researches into Cartesianism. His first published works were articles on Bultmann and Augustine, Maximus the Confessor and Pseudo-Dionysius, revelation and liturgy for the conservative French Catholic journal *Résurrection*. He was to go on to become a regular contributor to the *Revue catholique internationale Communio*.

In his theological researches, Marion draws heavily upon patristic thinkers. He is following here in the footsteps of those Catholic neo-patristic theologians Jean Daniélou, Henri de Lubac, and Hans Urs von Balthasar. He refers repeatedly to the work of Pseudo-Dionysius and the Cappadocian Fathers. He has, on the basis of his philosophical interest in consciousness and the construction of the object, consistently attempted a phenomenology of the icon, or more generally, visibility.[46] On the basis of this phenomenology he then proceeds to the theological implications of what he discerns as a gift of the invisible in the visible. The nature of this gift and this giving has continually interested him.[47]

We can observe the intellectual moves he makes in *God Without Being*. In that book he begins by sketching phenomenological accounts of the idol (which simply reflects its creator and is self-determinately visible) and the icon which provokes a vision of the invisible and infinite (whose visibility is a gift of the other). This gift or revelation of the infinite as it crosses through the finite and visible Marion reads as cutting across the metaphysics of modernity. We are drawn by the icon beyond a world created in the human consciousness by human ideas corresponding to the condition of reality "out there." The icon presents a different mode of being which stands in antithesis to the way human consciousness makes the world present to itself. An ontological difference is opened up by this crossing of the finite by the infinite. Here, Marion is indebted to Heidegger; though he believes his own work goes much further than Heidegger's.[48] This radical difference is read theologically. The gift crossing Being is the crucifixion of the Word in the world. The Cross is read as the unperceived watermark of the real. In the crisis of representation, when idolatry is struck through by the iconic, the visible by the invisible, there issues a revelation of divine distance, a revelation beyond Being and philosophy of consciousness. Marion reads this mode of revelation as having its origin in the Son's self-abandonment on the Cross. With the crucifixion of Christ there opens up in the world the space for seeing the kenotic love of the Father revealed in the Son. The crucifixion becomes the site for God's revelation of Himself. Marion develops his theological understanding of this crossing through Being and finitude – and the agapaic giving it reveals – through biblical exegesis of passages in the Old and New Testaments in which Being is recognized as questioned by the God beyond Being, the God who loves. "Only love does not have to be. And God loves without being."[49] Ecclesiastically, the Eucharist becomes the privileged site for Marion's theology of the icon – the site where God gives Himself and where the Word is therefore spoken in the breaking of the visible elements. Rather ironically, given that Marion is not a cleric, he advocates that the priest and bishop are the primary expositors of such a theology insofar as they participate in the sacramental practice as icons of Christ themselves.

The postmodernism of such a theology lies both in its ecclesiological conservatism and in its theological exploration of such postmodern themes as the crisis of representation and identity, the other, the unnameable, the aporetic, and the decon-struction of metaphysics. In the five essays that comprise an early volume called *L'Idole et la distance*, Marion advances his thesis of the principle of love (*charité*)[50] and the kenotic, unthinkable abandonment of the Father through the Son, on the basis of Heidegger's concept of *Ereignis* and withdrawal, Levinas' analysis of the infinite distance which both surpasses and provides the condition for Being, and Derrida's notion of *différance*, which sketches the economy of a trace beyond absence and presence. Marion's thesis situates his own project in relation to these postmodern thinkers, positing the trinitarian God as conceived by certain patristic writers, in the distance, the absence, the *aporia*, the anarchy which other postmodern thinkers have read as nihilism (though not Levinas or Derrida and, possibly, not Heidegger either). Postmodern critique therefore provides access to or is framed by a Christian faith which is never argued for; it is assumed. In *God Without Being*, on the basis of a distinction (first declared by Heidegger) that the logic of philosophy and the logic of faith are irreconcilable, Marion simply affirms "the field of revela-tion that the Johannine *Logos* opens to faith"[51] with the Bible and the Eucharist as the two sites in which this revelation manifests itself. Postmodern insights and approaches are employed within theological discussions concerning ontology and analogy.

Michel de Certeau

Like Marion in his early work on Descartes, Michel de Certeau returns us to the instauration of the modern in the sixteenth and seventeenth centuries.[52] As a Christian thinker concerned with history and the forces which create and sustain particular communities, de Certeau analyzes the mystical writings of that Counter-Reformation period in terms of the way in which the West opened itself (through travel and the economies of empire-building) to what was foreign or other only to colonize it. He points to disruptions, ambiguities, and the excesses of otherness as they infest the early evolution of modern thinking and rationalism. These were all eventually to be suppressed by a developing scientism and the politicization of the religious in the name of an economic, technological, and political progress: "a capitalist and conquering society."[53] With a rather idealistic notion of the medieval period, de Certeau observes that in the seventeenth century the churches began to receive "their models and their rights from the monarchies, even if they represent a 'religiousness' that legitimizes the temporal powers."[54] As the seventeenth and eight-eenth centuries develop, the temporal powers gradually transfer to their own account the religious values, kudos, and mystique that were once the exclusive property of the church. It is with this transference that secular reason announces itself. A new spatialization appears – the spatialization of knowledge with the advance of the different sciences, a spatialization of the world with cartography. This spatialization – corresponding to the new colonialism and imperialism of the West – aims at the conquest and subjugation of what is other. This spatialization in terms of the developing bodies of knowledge is founded upon the proliferation of writing (and texts). Modernity, for de Certeau, is the "scriptural age," the age of writing. Prior to this age the sacred text is a voice and so "this writing (Holy Scripture) speaks."[55] The modern age is formed by discovering "this Spoken Word is no longer heard, that it has been altered by textual corruptions and avatars of history."[56] Now, hearing and assimilation become working and the will to power. De Certeau recognizes that "the only force opposed to this passion to be a sign is the cry, a deviation or an ecstasy, a revolt or flight of that which, within the body, escapes the law of the named."[57] This deviation or rupture of the logic of the written is the postmodernist moment which, for de Certeau, is paradigmatically evident in the mystical manner of speaking.

In the closing pages of de Certeau's last work, *The Mystic Fable* (first published in 1982, four years before his death in 1986), we find: "We must, then, move through *mystics* once more, no longer exploring the language it invents but the 'body' that speaks therein: the social (or political) body, the lived (erotic and/or pathological) body, the scriptural body (like a biblical tattoo), the narrative body (a tale of passion), the poetic body (the 'glorious body'). Inventions of bodies for the Other."[58] With these words the distinctive characteristics and significance of de Certeau's work are evident. They announce what he himself calls "a poetics of the body."[59] The body here is not an object out there, nor the subject possessing his or her own body. Any body is disseminated across several fields (religious, psychological, socio-anthropological, political, ecclesiastical, literary, liturgical). Each field traffics in symbols and patrols its own self-legitimating discourse. For de Certeau, the fields of these discourses gravitate around desiring to locate the impossible body of the Other, impossible because always the Other is absent, excluded, abjected from the symbolic code constructed to describe and define it, which, in effect, substitutes for it. *Mystics* (understood not as a collection of spiritual people, but as a collection of spiritual texts displaying a new epistemological form and announcing a new field of knowledge),[60] reveal for de Certeau "how that 'difference' manifests itself socially, and also how it sallies forth from its repression to go elsewhere."[61] He is concerned in his work to excavate, not only what is believed, but also how what is believed becomes believable. Therefore, he examines the relationship between religious representations and the organization of society which gives or denies them credence. The theological (and ecclesiological) examination is undertaken by means of a hybrid methodology which draws the psychoanalysis of Freud and Lacan into the orbit of Bourdieu's social anthropology and Foucault's analyses of the politics of knowledge. He will also, though not uncritically, adopt some of the insights on the philosophical character of the spoken and the written developed in the early work of Derrida. On the basis of the critical histories which emerge, de Certeau then constructs a picture of the differences and gaps between beliefs and doctrines, experience and institutions. "Reference to what is *experienced* (illuminating or devastating) endlessly opens up the problem of its relation to what is *represented* (official, received, or imposed)."[62]

The experience of the divine Other is at the heart of de Certeau's understanding of language as the product and promoter of desire. The Other calls. It "echoes in the body like an inner voice that one cannot specify by name but that transforms one's use of words."[63] For de Certeau the Jesuit, "vocation" and "obedience" are as important for him as they are for that other Jesuit theologian, von Balthasar. He traces the linguistics and politics of vocation in what constitutes a theology of the Spirit, a pneumatology read through psychoanalytical accounts of desire. "Whoever is 'seized' or 'possessed' by it begins to speak in a haunted tongue. The music, come from an unknown quarter, inaugurates a new rhythm of existence . . . It simultaneously captivates an attentiveness from within, disturbs the orderly flow of thought, and opens up or frees new spaces. There is no *mystics* without it."[64] Mystic utterance becomes paradigmatic of an Other, an Unnameable, which appears in language which is consciously attempting to subvert its own logic. "Mystics is the anti-Babel, the quest for a common speech after its breakdown, the invention of a language 'of God' or 'of the angels' that would compensate for the dispersal of human language."[65] As such, knowledge is a product of language as desire. True knowledge of the other (which, after Lacan, de Certeau calls the *réel*) is, following Augustine and Anselm, situated in the field of prayer. Mystics speak from a different place and attempt to translate this into an acceptable parlance. The means by which that parlance is acceptable, while not completely domesticating the otherness from whence it receives its authority, involves it in a cultural politics, a writing and therefore a history. The body, therefore, any body of knowledge, every social institution, is "informed" by this call of the Other which it either suppresses or encourages. The body of Christ as the church has to weave a problematic way between its founding experience and its social reality, but there is a *sacramentum mundi* for those able to read it. Incarnation is a love song established by the call of the Other as the initiator of desire. And yet what de Certeau, the historian, charts is the policing of this Other throughout the development of modernity. He explores the borderlands of the sixteenth and seventeenth centuries as new sciences and knowledges establish themselves independent of the "unitary architecture of theology" in the medieval period.[66] Hence, the "vital role mysticism plays in the historian's relation with writing."[67] For with mysticism the hegemony of a specific culture is critiqued.

Historiography here is operating within a developed and explicit theology of history. But it is not a unified history, a Hegelian notion of history in which all time is swept up into the grand expression of the Absolute *Geist*. This is a broken history, a history of resistances to what is uniform and global, a history opening up to us other pasts, other options concerning the meaning of history. It is based not in chains of causes and effects, but in the fields of symbolic production and the relations of power which operate between and within these fields. *Aporias* are opened in theories of history. Events, which preoccupy the science of history, are understood as inextricably caught up in our projections, politics, and ideologies. They take place within fields of symbolic relations. Events are therefore highly coded texts which frame and obscure what psychoanalysis terms "the other scene." The scene of the other is Lacan's *réel* – the world unmediated by representations, that which is the raw material of experience prior to being filtered through systems of knowledge. This "scene of the other" can be glimpsed when the cultural is ruptured, and this occurs when the Spirit speaks. Mystic discourse is forever asking the question who is speaking and from whence.[68] The glimpse of the *réel* in the everyday, de Certeau calls *ravissement*. This is a word with mystical connotations, but which also has many affinities with Barthes' poststructural "bliss" and the *jouissance* of Lacan, Foucault, Irigaray, and Kristeva. There are affinities here also with Lyotard's analysis of the sublime.[69]

The postmodernism of de Certeau's theological project lies again in developing the horizons of the Other, examining what Derrida described as "a certain aporetic experience of the impossible."[70] In doing this he employs the postmodern methodologies of Lacan, Bourdieu, and Foucault to advocate a neo-medieval ecclesiology. As he emphasizes in his lecture "How is Christianity Thinkable Today?": "The Christian faith has no security other than the *living* God discovered by communities which are alive and which undergo the experience of *losing* objective securities . . . That is the first question: no longer to know whether God exists, but to *exist* as Christian communities."[71] From this emphasis de Certeau develops a theology of desire and praxis, a pneumatology, based in the mystical experience. If Marion's postmodern theology can be termed a fundamental theology (in the Catholic sense of a theology embracing both dogmatics and the philosophy of religion), de Certeau's work inscribes a historical theology which does not simply handle religious practices and religious societies as subjects for historiography, but also develops a theology of history. The text of history is a complex mapping and movement of praxes which no one explanatory principle can embrace. The meaning of history therefore must always remain open, excessive, to the writing of history. Like de Certeau's description of *Abbas* Daniel in the street of sixth-century Alexandria, "This seems to be his 'theological' task: to trace, in the symbolic institutions, an otherness already known to the crowd and that they are always 'forgetting.'"[72]

Conclusion

Postmodernism has been thought by some to be profoundly anti-religious. Partly, this is based upon a misreading of postmodern concerns with the deferral of meaning and the endless plurality of forces, political, cultural, physiological, economic, and psychological. Postmodernism popularly invokes fears of relativism, nihilism, and linguistic idealism (there is nothing that is not the construct of language). Liberal postmodern a/theologies do nothing to counter this popular conception. In fact, they have helped create it with their own emphases upon the death of God, an ontology of violence, and the untameable flux of existence. With Marion and de Certeau, postmodern theology portrays how religious questions are opened up (not closed down or annihilated) by postmodern thought. The postmodern God is emphatically the God of love, and the economy of love is kenotic. Desire, only possible through difference, alterity, and distance, is the substructure of creation. It makes transcendence both possible and necessary. In specific Christian communities – communities defined and created by the narratives of Christ's life and work, the creedal teachings of the church and liturgical practices – the operation of this love provides a redescription of the trinitarian God and the economy of salvation. Postmodernism, read theologically, is not the erasure of the divine. Rather, it defines the space within which the divine demands to be taken into account. The divine arrives with the endless institution of the question – Levinas' "enigma," Cixous's "mystery." Hélène Cixous, Jewish by origin, pupil of Derrida, co-founder of *Écriture féminine*,[73] confesses: "When I have finished writing, when I am a hundred and ten, all I will have done will have been to attempt a portrait of God. Of the God. Of what escapes us and makes us wonder. Of what we do not know but feel. Of what makes us live."[74]

Notes

1 Gilles Deleuze and Félix Guattari, *A Thousand Plateaus: Capitalism and Schizophrenia*, trans. Brian Massumi (Minneapolis, MN, 1987), p. 21.

2 See Mark C. Taylor's essay "Reframing Postmodernism" in Philippa Berry and Andrew Wernick (eds.), *Shadow of Spirit: Postmodernism and Religion* (London, 1992), pp. 11–29.

3 Thomas Pynchon, *The Crying of Lot 49* (London, 1979), p. 64.

4 Jacques Lacan's *Écrits* was first published in 1966 and consists of lectures given between 1948 and 1960; Emmanuel Levinas' *Totality and Infinity* was published in 1969; Thomas Pynchon's *The Crying of Lot 49* was first published in 1966.

5 For an excellent summary of the arguments waged among theorists and art critics over what postmodernism is and its relationship to modernism and high modernism, see Ingeborg Hoesterey (ed.), *Zeitgeist in Babel: The Postmodernist Controversy* (Bloomington, IN, 1991).

6 The range of postmodern theologies can be appreciated by examining the contents of my edited volume, *The Blackwell Companion to Postmodern Theology* (Oxford, 2001).

7 George Steiner, *In Bluebeard's Castle: Some Notes Towards a Redefinition of Culture* (London, 1971), p. 14.

8 For the association of liberalism with the doctrines of *laissez-faire*, see David Thomson's account of the development of the ideas of Adam Smith and Jeremy Bentham in Victorian Britain, in *England in the Nineteenth Century* (London, 1950).

9 See the work of Robert Gibbs, Stephen Kepnes, Elliot R. Wolfson, and Edith Wyschogrod.

10 Jean-François Lyotard, *The Postmodern Explained*, trans. Don Barry et al. (Minneapolis, MN, 1993), p. 13.

11 Ibid, p. 15.

12 We must not, though, mistake post-secularism as a positive return to religion. It is actually more the commodification of religion. See my *True Religion* (Oxford, 2003).

13 See "How to Avoid Speaking: Denials," trans. Ken Frieden. In Stanley Budick and Wolfgang Iser (eds.), *Languages of the Unsayable: The Play of Negativity in Literature and Literary Theory* (New York, 1989), pp. 3–70.

14 See Kristeva's books *Tales of Love*, trans. Leon Roudiez (New York, 1987) and *In the Beginning Was Love*, trans. Arthur Goldhammer (New York, 1988).

15 Levinas' epic works are *Totality and Infinity: Essay on Exteriority*, trans. A. Lingis (Pittsburgh, PA, 1969) and *Otherwise than Being or Beyond Essence*, trans. A. Lingis (The Hague, 1981).

16 See Irigaray's books *An Ethics of Sexual Difference*, trans. Carolyn Burke and Gillian C. Gill (London, 1993) and *Sexes and Genealogies*, trans. Gillian C. Gill (New York, 1993).

17 See Lyotard's books *The Inhuman*, trans. Geoffrey Bennington and Rachel Bowlby (Cambridge, 1993) and *Lessons on the Analytic of the Sublime*, trans. Elizabeth Rottenberg (Stanford, CA, 1994).

18 See Cixous' books *"Coming to Writing" and Other Essays*, trans. Sarah Cornell et al., ed. Deborah Jenson (Cambridge, MA, 1991) and *Reading with Clarice Lispector*, trans. Verena Andermatt Conley (Hemel Hempstead, 1990).

19 Zygmunt Bauman, *Intimations of Postmodernity* (London, 1992), p. x. Bauman is arguing for postmodernity as a sociological movement away from what Max Weber saw as the disenchantment of the world.

20 David Ray Griffin, *God and Religion in the Postmodern World: Essays in Postmodern Theology* (Albany, NY, 1989).

21 Don Cupitt, *The Last Philosophy* (London, 1995), p. 63.

22 Derrida himself has always countered the idea that he is advocating linguistic idealism. See here his interview entitled "Afterword" in *Limited Inc.*, trans. Samuel Weber (Evanston, IL, 1988), pp. 111–54, and my book *Barth, Derrida and the Language of Theology* (Cambridge, 1995).

23 Mark C. Taylor, *Deconstructing Theology* (Chicago, 1982), p. 103.

24 Charles Winquist, *Desiring Theology* (Chicago, 1995), p. 63.

25 Ibid, p. 108.

26 Ibid, p. xi.

27 Taylor, *Deconstructing Theology*, p. xix.

28 The concept of kenosis has an important place in death-of-God theologies. It is the concept rather than the traditional doctrine based upon the *carmen Christi* of Paul's Letter to the Philippians which is reworked. God's complete absence from the world is understood in terms of Christ's final identification with the world, which has been worked over through the historical development of Christianity as a religion. Christianity itself dissolves here. Kenosis is employed as a metaphor for this historical development and final eclipse of Christianity and the transcendent God.

29 Robert P. Scharlemann, *The Reason of Following: Christology and the Ecstatic I* (Chicago, 1991), p. 198.

30 Thomas J. J. Altizer (ed.), *Towards a New Christianity: Readings in the Death of God Theology* (New York, 1967), p. 315.

31 Lyotard, *The Postmodern Explained*, p. 76.

32 Altizer, *Towards a New Christianity*, p. 318.

33 Ibid, p. 12.

34 Ibid, p. 13.

35 See Manuel Castells, *The Information Age: Economy, Society and Culture, Vol. 2: The Power of Identity* (Oxford, 1997); Ernest Gellner, *Postmodernism, Reason and Religion* (London, 1992); Akbar S. Ahmed, *Postmodernism and Islam* (London, 1992).

36 This is Don Cupitt's term.

37 See Altizer, *Towards a New Christianity*, p. 315.

38 George Lindbeck, *The Nature of Doctrine: Religion and Theology in a Postliberal Age* (London, 1984).

39 This postmodern Augustinianism is evident in the final chapter of John Milbank's first major work, *Theology and Social Theory: Beyond Secular Reason* (Oxford, 1990). While the series *Radical Orthodoxy* has continued to develop this Augustinian emphasis – see my *Cities of God* (London, 2000), James K. A. Smith, *Speech and Theology: Language and the Logic of Incarnation* (London, 2002) and Michael Handby, *Augustine and Modernity* (London, 2003) – it has also undertaken a revision of Aquinas. See John Milbank and Catherine Pickstock, *Truth in Aquinas* (London, 2000) and Conor Cunningham, *Genealogy of Nihilism* (London, 2002).

40 See the final chapter of Rowan Williams, *Arius: Heresy and Spirituality* (London, 1987).

41 See Edith Wyschogrod, *Saints and Postmodernism: Revisioning Moral Philosophy* (Chicago, 1990) and, more recently, *An Ethics of Remembering: History, Heterology, and the Nameless Others* (Chicago, 1998).

42 See Graham Ward, *Barth, Derrida and the Language of Theology* (Cambridge, 1995).

43 By "authentic" here I am simply wishing to suggest that the work of Marion and de Certeau takes up and is situated within the theological horizons and philosophical methodologies of French poststructural thinking. Neither of these thinkers explicitly calls themselves postmodern.

44 Jean-Luc Marion, *Sur la théologie blanche de Descartes: analogie, création des vérités éternelles, fondement* (Paris, 1981), p. 23.

45 The distinction between the logic of philosophical thinking and Christo-logic is fundamental to the work of Hans Urs von Balthasar, whose influence on Marion's work is considerable.

46 Marion's phenomenological accounts of visibility and invisibility owe much to the work of the French philosopher Maurice Merleau-Ponty.

47 See Jean-Luc Marion, *Reduction et Donation* (Paris, 1989) and *Etant donne: essai d'une phenomenology de la donation* (Paris, 1997), both of which have now been translated.

48 Marion's understanding of Heidegger is a vexed one. See my essay "Theology and the Crisis of Representation," in Gregory Salyer and Robert Detweiler (eds.), *Literature and Theology at Century's End* (Atlanta, GA, 1995), pp. 131–58, and Laurence Hemming, "Reading Heidegger: Is God Without Being?" *New Blackfriars*, 76 (July/August 1995).

49 Jean-Luc Marion, *God Without Being*, trans. Thomas A. Carlson (Chicago, 1991), p. 138.

50 His attention to the nature of charity and love is developed further in *Prolegomena to Charity*, trans. Stephen Lewis and Jeffery L. Kosky (New York, 2002) and *Eros* (Paris, 2003).

51 Ibid, p. 63.

52 There has appeared an excellent book treating the theological nature of Certeau's

thinking: Daniel Bogner, *Gebrochene Geg-*
enwart: Mystik und Politik bei Michael de
Certeau (Mainz, 2002).

53 Michel de Certeau, *The Practice of Every-*
day Life, trans. Steven Rendall (Berkeley,
CA, 1984), p. 136.

54 Michel de Certeau, *The Mystic Fable*, trans.
Michael B. Smith (Chicago, 1992), p. 182.

55 De Certeau, *The Practice of Everyday Life*,
p. 137.

56 Ibid.

57 Ibid, p. 149.

58 De Certeau, *The Mystic Fable*, p. 293.

59 Ibid, p. 295.

60 Ibid, p. 16.

61 Ibid, p. 242.

62 Michel de Certeau, *The Writing of History*,
trans. Tom Conley (New York, 1988),
p. 129.

63 De Certeau, *The Mystic Fable*, p. 297.

64 Ibid.

65 Ibid, p. 157.

66 Ibid, p. 104.

67 Ibid, p. xiv.

68 Ibid, p. 178.

69 See note 17 for Lyotard's work on the experience of "presence" as the experience of
the sublime.

70 Jacques Derrida, *Aporias*, trans. Thomas
Dutoit (Stanford, CA, 1998), p. 15.

71 Michel de Certeau, "How is Christianity
Thinkable Today?" *Theology Digest*, 19
(1971), pp. 344–5.

72 De Certeau, *The Writing of History*, p. 43.

73 For a brief introduction to this movement
and what it stood for, see Toril Moi,
Sexual/Textual Politics: Feminist Literary
Theory (London, 1985), pp. 108–26.

74 Cixous, *"Coming to Writing" and Other*
Essays, p. 129.

Bibliography

Primary

Altizer, Thomas J. J. (ed.), *Towards a New Chris-*
tianity: Readings in the Death of God Theology
(New York, 1967).
—— *History as Apocalypse* (Albany, NY, 1985).
Certeau, Michel de, *The Mystic Fable*, trans.
Michael B. Smith (Chicago, 1992).
—— *The Certeau Reader*, ed. Graham Ward
(Oxford, 2000).
Cupitt, Don, *The Long-Legged Fly* (London,
1987).
—— *Last Philosophy* (London, 1995).
Griffin, David Ray, *God and Religion in the*
Postmodern World: Essays in Postmodern Theo-
logy (Albany, NY, 1989).
Marion, Jean-Luc, *God Without Being*, trans.
Thomas A. Carlson (Chicago, 1991).
Scharlemann, Robert P., *The Reason of Follow-*
ing: Christology and the Ecstatic (Chicago,
1991).
Taylor, Mark C., *Deconstructing Theology*
(Atlanta, GA, 1982).

—— *Erring: A Postmodern A/theology* (Chicago,
1984).
Ward, Graham, *The Blackwell Companion to*
Postmodern Theology (Oxford, 2001).
Winquist, Charles, *Epiphanies of Darkness:*
Deconstruction in Theology (Chicago, 1986).
—— *Desiring Theology* (Chicago, 1995).

Secondary

Berry, Philippa and Wernick, Andrew (eds.),
Shadow of Spirit: Postmodernism and Religion
(London, 1992).
Hoesterey, Ingeborg (ed.), *Zeitgeist in Babel:*
The Postmodernist Controversy (Bloomington,
IN, 1991).
Lyotard, Jean-François, *The Postmodern Ex-*
plained, trans. Don Barry et al. (Minneapolis,
MN, 1993).
Vattimo, Gianni, *The End of Modernity*, trans.
Jon R. Snyder (Cambridge, 1988).

Theology and the Sciences

"Theology and . . ." has become a rapidly expanding aspect of academic theology. The cultural and intellectual world has become more differentiated into a proliferation of disciplines and forms of cultural and religious expression; and at the same time modern education (especially a massive expansion of higher education worldwide) and communications have enabled more people to be aware of this diversity of intellectual and imaginative life. How might God be conceived as being in relation to that life? What are its consequences for understanding the created world, humanity, gender, institutions, evil and sin, scriptures, ethics, the future, and so on? How can Christian thought be responsibly engaged in the enrichment, critique, and transformation of that life? The complexity of this explosion of vitality is immense, and it is clear that generalizations, habits of response, and conclusions that had some validity in the past cannot be assumed to be adequate. For theology, there is no intellectually responsible alternative to full engagement with the particularities of each area.

Part III attempts this in relation to the physical, biological, and social sciences. These have engaged deeply with the realities and vitalities of the natural and social world. They focus energy, knowledge, and understanding in ways that have transformed modern civilization. Philip Clayton and Celia Deane-Drummond describe what has been happening in theology and the natural sciences, and offer pointers to what they consider fruitful ways forward. Richard Roberts lays out a typology of ways in which theology has related to the social sciences, then offers his own very different approach as an alternative to all of them.

Theology and the Physical Sciences

Philip Clayton

It is inconceivable that the Christian theologian would finally declare the natural world to lie outside the purview of her theology. Theology's task commences with the creation of "the heavens and the earth" by God; the creation of man and woman, and consequently all of theological anthropology has to be understood within the context of this initial act of creation.

From the Reformation until well into the twentieth century, theology was lamed by the modern turn to the human subject as the sole source of meaning and value, the sole arbiter of truth. Only in recent years have theologians begun to question the assumptions that for centuries artificially reduced the scope of theological reflection, knocked off balance the relationships among various individual doctrines, and threatened the completeness of systematic theology as a comprehensive endeavor. The recent renaissance of the theology of nature in dialogue with the physical sciences offers hope of restoring the traditional balance between key doctrines: God and world, creation and salvation, theological anthropology and *theologia naturalis*. In the process, theologians will be compelled to rethink the relation between humans and the rest of creation, as well as the nature of our responsibility toward self, other, and world.

Our task in these few pages is to explore the crisis in modern theology which led to the downgrading of the theology of nature, to understand what changes have made possible the recent rebirth of theological interest in the dialogue with the physical sciences, and to sketch, at least in outline, the sort of theology of nature which is genuinely responsive to recent breakthroughs in the natural sciences. Only against this broader backdrop can the emerging subfield of "theology and science" be understood.

The Downgrading of the Theology of Nature in Modern Thought

In Luther's mind the church's combination of Thomist theology, magisterial authority, and natural philosophy (*philosophia naturalis*) formed an impregnable fortress blocking his quest for reform. A truly Christian theology would need a new foundation. In turning to *sola scriptura, sola fides,* Luther placed the spotlight on the immediacy of the individual's relationship with God. Yet what he gained was bought with a price: the mediated hand of God, as expressed for example in the physical world and in the traditional teachings of the church, became obscured; its status as revelation became problematic. Calvin's Reformed theology likewise downgraded the "natural light" (*lumen naturalis*) to a minor supporting role. Without some revelation in nature, the vast majority of humankind could not be held responsible for their rejection of God; yet without the direct salvific influence of the Holy Spirit, the natural light could hardly be efficacious. The human intellect is too darkened by sin to respond positively to the knowledge available to it; thus Calvin writes early in the *Institutes*:

> When miserable men do seek after God, instead of ascending higher than themselves as they ought to do, they measure him by their own carnal stupidity, and neglecting solid inquiry, fly off to indulge their curiosity in vain speculation. Hence, they do not conceive of him in the character in which he is manifested, but imagine him to be whatever their own rashness has devised.

In Protestant scholasticism, in the sanctification movements associated with John Wesley and others, in the pietism of Jonathan Edwards, and in the moral theologies of the late nineteenth century, these same emphases were expressed again and again.

Another modern reformer is often blamed for the shift to human subjectivity as the main stage on which the divine is revealed. According to the standard account, René Descartes sought to ground all human knowledge in the certainty of the human subject, thereby elevating humankind into the ultimate metaphysical instance. This last claim is false: Descartes' metaphysics was clearly grounded in the notion of the infinitely perfect God (*infinita perfectio*), by whom humanity was created and on whom all reflection concerning human nature is to be modeled.[1] Nonetheless, it is true that Descartes thought he could correct for the excesses of scholasticism by turning to his new method of "clear and distinct ideas"; and it is true that, as a direct result of his work, the individual sense of subjective certainty came to play a greater role in modern theology than at any earlier point in its history.

The process of centering knowledge and metaphysics on the human subject culminated in the transcendental philosophy of Immanuel Kant. Since, for Kant, sentient beings create the world of experience by imposing a set of "categories of the understanding" upon their percepts or sense data, human knowers become the *de facto* locus of authority for defining knowledge and adjudicating between true and false (or justified and unjustified) beliefs. As long as anthropology *precedes* the theology of nature and sets its parameters in this way, no theology of nature can proceed without first analyzing the knower and his or her role in what is known. The massive influence of Kant on nineteenth- and early twentieth-century theology was multiplied further through the baptism of Kantian philosophy at the hands of Frederick Schleiermacher.

But theologians and philosophers do not deserve all the credit for the divorce between theology and science in the modern period. No less influential were the successes of the physical sciences during these years, combined with the self-understanding that fueled most of their work. The independence of natural science from any theological or metaphysical control, so powerfully expressed in Francis Bacon's criticisms of the four "idols" of medieval thought, was unfortunately inflated into the claim that science had usurped theology's place as a source of knowledge. The same methodology that produced the incredible advances in astronomy and fundamental physics thereby became the motivating force for a reductionist metaphysical position. All is "matter in motion," insisted Thomas Hobbes at the outset of *Leviathan*; the only remaining task for modern scholars is to spell out the details of how everything else can be derived from this core. For example, knowledge of abstract concepts must be traced back to physical sense data (cf. Locke's attack on innate ideas); explanations of complex organisms and systems must be reduced to the level of fundamental physical laws and dynamics; and everything non-physical – from angels to souls to morals to institutions – must either be discarded or reconstrued in physical terms.

Clearly, as long as these assumptions reigned, it was only prudent for theologians to cede the physical world to natural science as its rightful domain, limiting their own contributions to the realms of morality, beauty, and subjective feeling. But the move to limit theology in this manner – whether it marched under the banner of "sentiment" (Lord Shaftsbury and Hume) or "the moral law within" (Kant) or "the feeling of absolute dependence" (Schleiermacher) – represented a retreat from a robust theology of nature. Well into the twentieth century one still finds theologians accepting some form of reductionist physicalism as the proper context for theology. The only decision that remained for theologians, it seemed, was deciding whether to try to preserve *some other independent (non-scientific) realm of knowledge* as the rightful domain of theology, or to concede the epistemic ultimacy of physics and seek merely to show that theology, shorn of its own claims to knowledge, could remain consistent with the physical sciences.[2]

The Collapse of the Reductionist Program

It is widely agreed that by the end of the twentieth century the reductionist program had suffered a major, and possibly fatal, setback. What is crucial is that theologians understand this change, lest they go on battling the windmills of reductionism – or worse, assume that the windmills have won and retreat from the field.

What are the causes of this surprising shift? First and foremost, physics encountered what appeared to be permanent limits to the dream of a single explanatory system from which all the world's phenomena could be derived. The setbacks were multiple and decisive: relativity theory introduced the speed of light as the absolute limit for velocity, and thus as the temporal limit for communication and causation in the universe; Heisenberg's uncertainty principle placed mathematical limits on the knowability of both the location and momentum of a subatomic particle; the Copenhagen theorists came to the startling conclusion that quantum mechanical indeterminacy was not merely a temporary epistemic problem but reflected an *inherent* indeterminacy of the physical world itself; so-called chaos theory showed that future states of complex systems (like weather systems) quickly become uncomputable because of their sensitive dependence on initial conditions – a dependence so sensitive that a finite knower could *never* predict the evolution of the system (which is a staggering limitation in light of the percentage of natural systems that exhibit chaotic behaviors); Kurt Gödel showed in a well-known proof that mathematics cannot be complete . . . and the list can easily be extended.

The collapse of the reductionist program was the result not only of developments within the sciences themselves; it was also produced by an increased emphasis on holistic factors in the philosophy of science, by the birth of the history and sociology of science, by the waning influence of analytic philosophy, by the collapse of "foundationalism" in epistemology, by new data in support of emergence in the natural world (on which more below), and by an increasing awareness of the influence of metaphysical presuppositions on the actual practice of science. The *methods* of reduction – that is, the attempt to understand natural phenomena in terms of their constituent parts, their causes, and the laws that determine their behavior – still characterize the daily practice of science and will continue to do so into the future. But the *philosophy* of reductionism has started to lose its hold among students of science, allowing for a new awareness of the interrelationships between the natural sciences and other disciplines. Of course, the reductionist inferno has not yet fully subsided; large regions are still ablaze with its flames, and forests are still being reduced to the ashes of physical particles and physical causes. Scientists and science writers such as Steven Weinberg and Richard Dawkins represent flare-ups of the old philosophy that require dousing; and some of the attempts to formulate mediating positions – one thinks of E. O. Wilson's *Consilience* and Stephen J. Gould's *Rocks of Ages* – are actually less mediations than new forms of the same old philosophy. Still, a larger number of scientists and philosophers are working with a post-reductionist paradigm than has been true for generations.

The danger for theologians is thus not that they will lose the day to reductionist physicalism, but that they will fail to notice that the centuries-long battle with it has taken a major turn. The collection of changes, including in particular the collapse of foundationalism in epistemology, has produced a new climate now widely referred to (albeit misleadingly) as postmodernism. Taken together, these changes amount to an invitation for theologians, and metaphysicians in general, to take on anew the task of systematizing the various segments of human knowledge and belief. The terms of this new invitation rule out absolutist claims to knowledge; and there are other epistemic constraints that will have to be acknowledged. Still, the greatest tragedy would be for theologians to fail to notice the wind change and to continue trying to sail in the old direction.

Divine Action and the Theology of Nature

Permeating all science–theology debates is the question of divine action, which may represent science's single greatest challenge to theology. In retrospect, one realizes that many earlier accounts of God's intervention in the world were based upon the then-current gaps in human knowledge of the relevant natural processes. As science has learned to understand the laws that govern these processes and to predict outcomes with great precision, the conflict with theological accounts has steadily increased. Moreover, theologians have (rightly) become less willing to hold positions which, if true, would imply that valid scientific explanations are impossible in some domain.

Although the full debate concerning divine action cannot be summarized here, at least eight major positions can be identified.[3] I list them in order of increasing potential conflict with science:

1 Naturalist and physicalist theologies.
2 Deism of various types.
3 The view that all history represents a single divine act (Maurice Wiles).
4 "Double agency" views according to which both God and natural causes determine the outcome of every event (Austin Farrer and A. N. Whitehead).
5 "Top-down" accounts of divine action that leave the string of natural causes intact and inviolate (Arthur Peacocke).
6 Claims that divine interventions can be asserted only as salvation-historical or "transhistorical" or mystical truths, and hence do not conflict with science.
7 Claims that God normally respects the integrity of the natural order, but at least once transformed it (the resurrection).
8 Robust assertions of interventions of God and miraculous outcomes on a regular basis (C. S. Lewis, C. John Collins).

The so-called third quest for the historical Jesus, highlighted in the debates between Marcus Borg and N. T. Wright and packaged for the media at the meetings of the Jesus Seminar, can be seen as just one manifestation of how science–religion conflicts have affected theological claims to divine action.

How might the science-spawned debate on the nature and locus of divine action contribute to the task of a constructive theology of nature? An informative example comes from the Protestant, Catholic, and Orthodox theologians who contributed along with scientists to the recent *In Whom We Live and Move and Have Our Being: Panentheistic Reflections on God's Presence in a Scientific World.*[4] Most of the theologians grant that traditional theories of divine action are not compatible with current scientific explanations of the physical world. Yet, as Christian theists, they presuppose *some* influence of God on the world, and as theologians they are motivated to formulate it. How should theology conceive the God–world relation? Simply identifying God and world is problematic because theism requires that God serve as the source of the world. But if God's actions come from outside the natural world, they will conflict with natural laws and introduce new energies into closed physical systems, both of which set theology at loggerheads with the presuppositions, methods, and results of the natural sciences. If by contrast God is conceived as more closely connected with the world, the divine influences can be understood as a supplement to worldly events, utilizing their energies and causal structures. Many endorse this third option by utilizing the resources of panentheism – the theological view that the world exists within the divine, although God is also more than the world. Panentheists vary on what models they use for understanding the "within" relationship. Some affirm and others deny the "panentheistic analogy," the view that the relation between God and the world is partially analogous to the relationship between the mind and the body in human persons. If one employs this analogy, and if one understands mind as both encompassing physical processes and also going beyond them (as emergence theorists do), then an interesting possibility for construing divine action arises. God could utilize natural processes – physical laws, the form and structure of living things, individual motivations, and cultural evolution as a whole – as a means for divine action. As mind remains more than the physical processes of which it is composed, divine action contributes more than the sum total of physical processes in the universe.

Key Themes in the Theology–Science Debate

What resources does science offer theologians in this new era of intense post-reductionist dialogue between the two fields? What challenges does it continue to raise? Where is today's science consistent with traditional theology, and where are revisions and innovations necessary? Finally, how can the new discussion between theology and the natural sciences contribute to a renaissance of the theology of nature and, through it, to a reconception of theology as a whole? These questions can best be answered by considering the five major topics in contemporary debates between theologians and natural scientists.

Cosmology and creation

Developments in cosmology have always been heavy with theological significance, and the twentieth century was no exception. When, early in the century, Hubble's observations of a red shift in light coming from distant stars and galaxies lent support to the idea of a "big bang" from which all things in the universe originated, theologians were quick to point out that an origin of this sort was exactly what one would expect to find if the universe had been created by God. Opposition to the big bang theory has likewise been theologically motivated. When Fred Hoyle intro-duced the major alternative, the Steady State theory, he made it clear that a major motivation for his hypothesis was to remove the apparent support for creation provided by the big bang theory. The failure of Hoyle's theory, in turn, was heralded by theologians as a victory for the doctrine of creation.

In fact, matters are more complex. The big bang implies only that the universe had its origin in a singularity, a physical event not explainable in terms of the laws of physics. Since it is physically meaningless to speak of a cause of the big bang, some have taken recent cosmology to represent a defeat for natural theology, for no one can argue from the existence of the universe to God as its Creator if the big bang represents a final barrier to knowledge. Moreover, at least some cosmological theories deny that there was any initial moment, or "$t = 0$," at all, and hence no "moment" at which God could have created (the Hartle–Hawking hypothesis). In an oft-cited article, however, Robert Russell argues that, even without a moment $t = 0$, contemporary cosmology still supports the contingency of the actual universe, which is the core theological principle behind the doctrine of creation.[5]

A second form of natural theology focuses on the "fine-tuning" of the universe. A large number of physical constants and physical laws have precisely the right value for life to emerge. Had the mass of the proton or the strengths of the fundamental physical forces been different by even a minuscule amount, it would have been physically impossible for life to arise. Divide the number of such constants by the variance that would be sufficient to make life impossible, and you have a measure of the extreme improbability of life as we know it. Yet we exist. Many leading scientists and theologians see in this fact evidence of the providential hand of God and of the divine intent to create intelligent life. In a yet stronger version of the argument, known as the "intelligent design" argument, natural theologians such as William Dembski argue that the level of complexity needed to produce intelligent life *could* only have been created by an intelligent agent, where the "could" has the force of mathematical necessity.[6]

But such claims have also turned out to be controversial.[7] In a universe even slightly different from ours, science teaches, there would be no observers present in the first place; hence any universe that includes observers like us must obviously manifest whatever physical values are necessary for those observers to exist. This response, which has come to be called the weak anthropic principle, hardly offers a robust natural theology. Moreover, if there are multiple universes, perhaps even an infinite number of them, as some scientists think, then statistically it is not surprising that at least one would have the right combination of fundamental values to allow for life to emerge – and obviously observers could only find themselves in such a universe! Leading cosmologists such as André Linde, Martin Reeves, and Paul Davies argue that "multiverse" theories of this sort must be taken seriously.

Still, I suggest, it remains theologically significant that physicists would produce a cosmology that is consistent with divine creation. The evidence may not be sufficient to support a *natural theology* – a deductive, science-based argument for the existence of God – but it can be incorporated into a *theology of nature* in a compelling manner. This distinction, which has become central in the field, suggests a methodology for the theology–science debate that can help theologians to avoid, on the one hand, a disdain of physics and, on the other, overly optimistic assessments of new, physics-based proofs for the existence of God. Moreover, contemporary cosmology does raise explanatory questions to which theologians can contribute. For example, if there are laws that hold across the ensemble of universes posited by the multiverse theory, then there must be some explanation for these regularities; and God would provide such an explanation. One might also ask for an explanation for the existence of all these universes. Either all were independently created, which would massively expand the creative power of God over the greatness of creating a single universe, or all universes can be traced back to an Ur-universe, of which God might also be the Creator.

Quantum physics: Spirit, freedom, indeterminacy, and complementarity

Almost simultaneously with the revolutionary breakthroughs that transformed our understanding of the world of the very small in the opening decades of the twentieth century, scientists and philosophers were involved in debating their significance beyond physics, and theologians were not far behind. Although the ensuing discussion has been extensive and complex,[8] it is not difficult to summarize the relevance of its major themes for theology. First, theologians have leapt upon the discovery that the physical world is indeterminate at the quantum level. Heisenberg's uncertainty principle shows that the exact location and momentum of a subatomic particle cannot be known simultaneously. The Copenhagen interpretation of quantum mechanics, long the dominant interpretation, holds that this indeterminacy reflects not just a limit on our current knowledge, but a *fundamental ontological openness in the world itself.* If physics is therefore blocked from a complete, deterministic account of even the physical world, many argue, the hope for a reduction of all knowledge to fundamental physics must be dashed. The achievements of Laplace's imaginary demon, who (Laplace imagined) could predict all future objects and events in the universe given an exhaustive knowledge of its physical state in the present, are not possible even in principle.

Second, many (in my view, rightly) found the Copenhagen interpretation of quantum mechanics to be relevant to debates about free will and moral responsibility. Of course, it does not follow from quantum indeterminacy that human beings are free moral agents – to conclude thusly would be to commit yet another version of the reductionist fallacy that theologians have been attempting to avoid, since it would ground morality directly in physics. Nonetheless, it does seem accurate to conclude that indeterminacy in the physical world is a necessary condition for human (or other) free will. For consider the converse: if all events are *determined* at the physical level, then the world does not exhibit the sort of causal openness that would leave room for conscious agents, when they evolve, to affect the outcome of events. In this sense, the debate about indeterminacy and free will is paradigmatic for science–theology connections: the physics does not dictate the outcome of theological debates, but physical results do provide constraints on the debates, which increase or decrease the plausibility of specific theological proposals.

Third, the famous "complementarity thesis" advanced by von Weizsäcker quickly found application in Christology. Von Weizsäcker showed that light is sometimes best described as a wave and at other times as a stream of particles (photons); the two different descriptions, though they seem conceptually incompatible, are actually complementary, and both are required for a full understanding of the physical phenomena. Similarly, as theologians argued with regard to the Incarnation, the one person Jesus Christ can accurately be described as both "fully God" and "fully man." Although the two descriptions *seem* incompatible, both descriptions are required for a full understanding of the phenomenon.[9] As years went by, a large number of theological tensions were "resolved" by appeal to the principle of complementarity, including the God–world relation, the three persons of the Trinity, the nature of the church as simultaneously human and divine, and many others. In retrospect, it appears that rather a lot of mileage was credited to what could be at best a suggestive analogy. Moreover, the disanalogies were rarely acknowledged: quantum physics possesses a single mathematical account of light, about the adequacy of which there is no debate; it is only in the non-mathematical interpretation of the physical theories that complementary language is introduced.

Fourth, much has been made theologically of the role of the observer in quantum physics. Quantum mechanics is based upon the Schrödinger wave equation, which is a continuous function; yet what we observe when we make quantum measurements are discrete outcomes. This transformation is referred to in orthodox quantum mechanics as the collapse of the wave function, and the collapse is said to be caused by the observer's act of measurement. Thus, Erwin Schrödinger, in a famous thought-experiment, imagined a cat within an apparatus that was driven by a quantum event such as radioactive decay. On the standard view, the quantum event is observer-dependent: it could not occur if it had not been observed by the experimenter. Schrödinger suggested that if the radioactive decay were linked to the release of a poison, the cat would be suspended between dead and alive until the apparatus was opened up and observed. Many have held this result to imply that reality itself is in part a product of the observer's activity, and some have even suggested that only a conscious, intentional observer could bring about the transition from quantum indeterminacies to the determinateness of the macrophysical world. Obviously, this result would be of immense importance to theology, for it would anchor an ontology of conscious, rational, free human agency *within physics itself.* It also seems to support a quasi-idealist metaphysics, which would be congenial to theology. Unfortunately for its defenders, however, this argument has been undercut recently by growing support for "decoherence" theories, which hold that increases in scale by themselves are sufficient to cause the "collapse" into the one macrophysical world that we observe.

Fifth, it has frequently been argued that quantum theory points toward a metaphysics of a "deeper reality" that underlies the world of physical appearances. As the French physicist Bernard d'Espagnat argues, quantum fields are less like the Eiffel Tower than like qualities that we observe in the Eiffel Tower, such as its height, size, or shape. One must then ask, what are these qualities qualities *of*? According to d'Espagnat, the only possible answer is that the quantum mechanical properties are properties of some deeper underlying reality. Since we know how this reality manifests itself to us, but since the physics forbids us to speak about what it is "really like" when not measured, d'Espagnat speaks of it as a "veiled reality."[10] The-world-as-observed is a manifestation of the underlying Real. Intriguing parallels exist between this view and a theology of God as the ultimate reality (*esse subsistens*), wherein the world becomes a manifestation of divine being. This ontological argument based on quantum field theory may actually represent the strongest connection with theology that quantum physics can provide.

I have dealt with the quantum-physical cases in some detail because they beautifully illustrate the excitement, but also the dangers, of the science–theology dialogue. Consider these four features. First, in each example the scientific theories beg for philosophical interpretation and physicists are already enmeshed in debating the possibilities. Second, there are genuine entailments: the physical theories can actually support or undercut particular philosophical and theological positions. Third, scientific theories are never by themselves sufficient; they represent calls for new theological reflection, not substitutes for it. Fourth, physics–theology relations that are mediated by more general metaphysical arguments, as in the d'Espagnat example, stand up better to change than theologies that are built too directly on a particular scientific theory. In any event, it should be clear that theologians do not need to cede the entire field to physicalist or materialist metaphysics.

Nature and purpose

In discussing cosmology, we saw the appeal that some theologians have made to "intelligent design," claiming that it is the only possible explanation for the order that one finds in the universe. On the far side of the debate from the "ID move-ment" is the contention by Steven Weinberg that "the more the universe seems comprehensible, the more it also seems pointless." Sadly, the popular discussion has often treated the two most extreme views as the only two options: science presup-poses a meaningless and purposeless universe, whereas religion teaches the opposite. One sees this dichotomizing in popular religious caricatures of evolutionary theories. Scientific evolution is allegedly deterministic, mechanistic, reductionist, fatalistic, and opposed to all matters of value, faith, or religion. Blind mechanistic forces and chance together determine all outcomes in science, the religious critics contend, from the first self-replicating molecules to the compositions of Shakespeare; humans are demoted to the level of apes. In siding with God, by contrast, one sides with purpose, value, beauty, and the soul.

Sadly, many theologians have bought into this dichotomy – more in the US than in Britain, and on the Continent more among Catholic theologians than among Protestants. There are a few philosophers of science who support such radical antagonisms, such as Jacques Monod in *Chance and Necessity* and Richard Dawkins in his more radical writings. But more scientists today would presumably accept an *emergentist* understanding of cosmic evolution, one that is non-deterministic, non-reductionist, and open to the emergence of consciousness and culture (we return to emergence theory below). Moreover, a number of scientists and theologians have described the process of cosmic evolution in a way that reveals its fundamental compatibility with Christian theism. In his influential work *The Human Factor*, Philip Hefner describes human beings as "created co-creators" with God, who in their freedom and through their moral and religious decisions can choose to sup-port God's creative intent through the open-ended process of evolution. The recent Templeton prizewinner Holmes Rolston provides effective responses to anti-religious excesses among certain Darwinians in his *Genes, Genesis, and God*. Perhaps the most influential synthesizer of evolution and Christian theology is Arthur Peacocke. Peacocke emphasizes "the immanence of God as Creator, 'in, with and under' the natural processes of the world unveiled by the sciences."[11] On this view, "God is creating at every moment of the world's existence through the perpetually endowed creativity of the very stuff of the world . . . This means we do not have to look for any extra supposed gaps in which, or mechanisms whereby, God might be supposed to be acting as Creator in the living world."[12]

A new challenge to theology and to theological reflection comes from recent extensions of scientific explanation into the realms of human behavior, human morality, and human belief formation. The biological bases of human behavior were first explored in rough (and highly controversial) form by sociobiologists; recently, they have received more sophisticated treatment in the new field of evolutionary psychology. Given our close genetic parallels with the other higher primates and our common evolutionary heritage, it is not surprising that parts of our behavior should be explicable in biological terms. Not only sexual and aggressive behavior, but also social behaviors, the nature of long-term pairing (and tendencies to stray from it), reconciliation behaviors, and even altruistic behaviors have biological roots. Thus, in a recent collection on theology and evolutionary psychology, Michael Chapman argues "humans are [biologically] predisposed to misbehaviors codified as the Seven Deadly Sins – gluttony, greed, lust, vanity, envy, rage, and sloth."[13] More controversially, David Sloan Wilson maintains that the successes of Christian communities – his major example is Calvin's Geneva – can be largely explained in evolutionary terms through parallels with other cooperating communities in the animal world.[14] Still, it does not follow that human cooperation or altruism or belief in God is or "nothing more than" its biological foundations. In the furor which evolutionary psychology is creating and will continue to create, theologians can play a crucial role by challenging "nothing but" claims made by scientists, while acknowledging the strong parallels between humans and other animals.

Neuroscience and consciousness

The debate about mind or consciousness in light of contemporary neuroscience is one of the most fascinating, vital, and important areas in the entire science–theology debate. The signs of spirit in humankind – whether in the tripartite anthropology of the New Testament (*sarx, psyche, pneuma*) or in the more dualist accounts that have dominated much of Western thought (*res cogitans, res extensa*) – have long been taken as proof of God's existence and creative intent, as evidence of the *imago dei* in humanity, and as justification for sharply separating humankind from all other living things. In light of this history, the explosion of new knowledge of the brain in the twentieth century, due in large part to powerful new brain imaging techniques, has been seen as a frontal, and perhaps fatal, attack on theology.

It is important to understand what makes the challenge serious. If there were a "ghost in the machine," as Gilbert Ryle provocatively put it, then not only would the actions of this spirit in the brain be inaccessible to scientific study; its (from the standpoint of neuroscience) arbitrary and inexplicable actions would also imply the irrelevance of brain-based explanations of human thought and emotion. But the neurosciences have achieved more and more powerful explanations of human cognition, including detailed accounts of the mechanisms that underlie thought and increasing predictive abilities.[15] The degree to which the brain functions can be correlated with mentality will turn out to be much greater than we can currently imagine. Given the astonishing progress in understanding human thought in terms of the distributed systems of the brain, supported by an increasing ability to verify these theories with imaging techniques, must one conclude that in the end human cognitive functioning will be fully accounted for in neurophysiological terms?

There is a response that preserves what is most important to Christian theologians and to theological anthropology. But it comes with a price. Most scholars in the debate no longer believe that it is possible to preserve the strict Cartesian dichotomy between mind and body, understood as two separate but interacting substances. The question is, what is the alternative? The more radical theological responses are linked to the position developed by the famous neuroscientist Michael Arbib in conjunction with Mary Hesse in their 1984 Gifford lectures.[16] Arbib argues that ideas may remain theologically useful even after they have been fully correlated with physical processes in the brain, although one will no longer have reason to think they refer to any supernatural realities. Somewhat less radical is the suggestion by Nancey Murphy that the human person be understood in "non-reductive physicalist" terms, without abandoning the belief that we are the result of God's creative purposes and actions. Murphy and many of her co-authors in *Whatever Happened to the Soul?* argue that one can retain a Christian anthropology while abandoning all talk of soul or spirit and espousing a physicalist interpretation of the human person.[17]

Perhaps, however, such radical solutions are not necessary. We do not know in advance what the "final" theory of cognition will be, nor that it can be formulated in exclusively physical, neurophysiological terms. Not knowing, one is forced to *wager* on one outcome or the other. The thinkers just mentioned wager that the answer will be consistent with the core assumptions of physicalism. The theory of emergence provides grounds for a different wager.[18] It suggests that the explanatory principles and causes at each new level of reality are distinct and irreducible. Evidence for emergence is evidence that thought will never be fully explained in terms of lower-level processes. Neurophysiological processes, together with environmental influences, are part of the massively complex phenomenon known as mentality. Emergentists wager that mentality will contain elements unique to it and not explainable in terms of its contributing causes. Likewise, emergentists add, human religiosity will not be explained even by a full understanding of human mentality; it is "upwardly open" to forces and levels beyond the human. *What* that "beyond" may include is a topic on which Christian theologians have much to say.

I therefore suggest that theological anthropology can best be synthesized with science in the context of a theory of the emergence of consciousness or mind. Humans will never be fully understood without grasping the physical, biological, and neurophysiological constraints on thought, belief, and religious experience. Nonetheless, we are always more than these constraints, always open toward a *telos* that science alone cannot predict. For the Christian theologian, that *telos* is also implicit in the beginning: the One toward whom we strive is also the One from whom we spring; and to understand the One who created us is to understand our final culmination.

Eschatology and the fate of the physical universe

With a spate of recent publications, the theology–science discussion has begun to move into eschatology.[19] Clearly, their goal has been to establish parallels between biblical teachings and scientific forecasts about the end of the cosmos. Here, however, the chances of *rapprochement* seem slimmest of all. The future course of the universe can be predicted scientifically only by straight-line extrapolations from what we currently know, yielding the prediction of a final "heat death" of the universe, an eternal state a few degrees above absolute zero. Yet the biblical teaching is that, at some point, God will establish "a new heaven and a new earth" (Revelation 21: 1). In fact, the assumption that any Christian eschatology has to be based upon extrapolations from what we currently know about the cosmos is responsible for the "realized eschatology" positions of theologians such as Kathryn Tanner and Catherine Keller.[20] If the kernel of eschatology lies in the *difference* between what science would expect and what faith predicts, then science will be of little help in evaluating the content of Christian eschatology – beyond, perhaps, the observation that "it can't go on like this forever."

Achievement and Agenda

What is it that is shared in common among the theologians surveyed in this chapter? Above all, one perceives a commitment to doing theology in dialogue with all available knowledge. For some theologians, the result is a new form of natural theology, providing new grounds for an inference to the existence of the Christian God. For many others, however, the results of the sciences supply standards and touchstones for theological reflection but not necessarily evidence for its truth. Apart from the natural theologians, one cannot say that the current theology–science discussion is permeated by an Enlightenment optimism about the capacities of reason, nor that it seeks to use scientific knowledge as a *replacement* for biblical or special revelation. Few, if any, claim that what can be known about God through the study of nature provides an adequate basis for the religious life.

These theologians do agree, however, that whatever one learns from special revelation and whatever inferences one draws from it should be consistent with the results of disciplined study of the natural world. As a point of theological method, they argue that the rigorous standards for knowledge in the sciences do not need to be inconsistent with the life of faith. Indeed, many have suggested that the attitude of open, critical inquiry fostered in the sciences can and should serve as a model for theological inquiry – although the ways in which this commitment is spelled out run the gamut from T. F. Torrance's *Theological Science* to the hypothetical realism of Wolfhart Pannenberg's *Theology and the Philosophy of Science*.

Although the theological positions defended by the authors in this field are rather varied, certain standards for contributions to the field are now emerging. One finds standard textbooks, a canon of core literature, key distinctions, and widespread consensus concerning at least the inadequate positions – consensus on the best overall theological response being rather harder to achieve. As a sign of the growing influence of this subfield of theology, one notes the increasing references to scientific theories and data in recent works across the whole spectrum of theology. Most encouragingly, the field is beginning to make substantive contributions to constructive theology proper.

Notes

1 Philip Clayton, *The Problem of God in Modern Thought* (Grand Rapids, MI: Eerdmans, 2000), ch. 2.

2 In the latter category one thinks, among others, of Gordon Kaufman; see, for example, *In Face of Mystery: A Constructive Theology* (Cambridge, MA: Harvard University Press, 1993).

3 An excellent summary can be found in Thomas Tracy (ed.), *The God Who Acts* (University Park: Pennsylvania State University Press, 1994). By far the best single collection of scholarship on the problem is the "scientific perspectives on divine action" series (see bibliography).

4 Philip Clayton and Arthur Peacocke (eds.), *In Whom We Live and Move and Have Our Being: Panentheistic Reflections on God's Presence in a Scientific World* (Grand Rapids, MI: Eerdmans, 2004).

5 See Robert Russell's article in Russell et al. (eds.), *Quantum Cosmology and the Laws of Nature* (Vatican City: Vatican Observatory Press, 1993).

6 William Dembski, *The Design Inference: Eliminating Chance Through Small Prob-*

abilities (New York: Cambridge University Press, 1998); *Intelligent Design: The Bridge Between Science and Theology* (Downers Grove, IL: InterVarsity Press, 1999); *No Free Lunch: Why Specified Complexity Cannot be Purchased without Intelligence* (Lanham, MD: Rowan and Littlefield, 2002); and Dembski (ed.), *Signs of Intelligence: Understanding Intelligent Design* (Grand Rapids, MI: Brazos Press, 2001). The intelligent design argument is nicely summarized by Del Ratzsch, *Nature, Design and Science: The Status of Design in Natural Science* (Albany, NY: State University of New York Press, 2001).

7 Dembski's proposals, although they have sparked an entire movement, the "intelligent design" or "ID" school, have turned out to be highly controversial. See the sharp criticisms in Robert Pennock, *Tower of Babel: The Evidence Against the New Creationism* (Cambridge, MA: MIT Press, 1999).

8 For a good sample, see Robert J. Russell et al. (eds.), *Quantum Mechanics: Scientific Perspectives on Divine Action* (Vatican City: Vatican Observatory Press, 2002).

9 See the essay on complementarity by Christopher Kaiser, "Quantum Complexity and Christological Dialectic," in Wesley Wildman and W. Mark Richardson (eds.), *Science and Religion* (New York: Routledge, 1996).

10 Bernard d'Espagnat, *In Search of Reality* (New York: Springer-Verlag, 1983).

11 Arthur Peacocke, *Paths from Science Towards God: The End of All Our Exploring* (Oxford: One World, 2001), p. 136.

12 Ibid, p. 137.

13 Michael Chapman, "Hominid Failings: An Evolutionary Basis for Sin in Individuals and Corporations," in Philip Clayton and Jeffrey Schloss (eds.), *Evolution and Ethics: Human Morality in Biological and Religious Perspective* (Grand Rapids, MI: Eerdmans, 2005).

14 David Sloan Wilson, *Darwin's Cathedral: Evolution, Religion, and the Nature of Society* (Chicago: University of Chicago Press, 2002). For a variety of criticisms of Wilson's position, see the work cited in the previous note.

15 This is not the place to summarize the literature. For a first overview, see Robert Russell et al. (eds.), *The Neurosciences of the Person* (Vatican City: Vatican Observatory Press, 2000).

16 Mary Hesse and Michael Arbib, *The Construction of Reality* (New York: Cambridge University Press, 1986).

17 Nancey Murphy et al. (eds.), *Whatever Happened to the Soul? Scientific and Theological Portraits of Human Nature* (Minneapolis, MN: Fortress Press, 1998).

18 Philip Clayton, *Mind and Emergence* (Oxford: Oxford University Press, 2004).

19 John Polkinghorne and Michael Welker, *The End of the World and the Ends of God: Science and Theology on Eschatology* (Harrisburg, PA: Trinity Press, 2000); John Polkinghorne, *The God of Hope and the End of the World* (New Haven, CT: Yale University Press, 2002).

20 Kathryn Tanner, "Eschatology Without a Future?" in Polkinghorne and Welker (eds.), *The End of the World*; Catherine Keller, "Pneumatic Nudges: The Theology of Moltmann, Feminism, and the Future," in Miroslav Volf et al. (eds.), *The Future of Theology: Essays in Honor of Jürgen Moltmann* (Grand Rapids, MI: Eerdmans, 1996).

Bibliography

Barbour, Ian G. *Religion in an Age of Science.* Gifford lectures 1989–91. London: SCM Press, 1990.

Clayton, Philip. *Explanation from Physics to Theology: An Essay in Rationality and Religion.* New Haven, CT: Yale University Press, 1989.

—— *God and Contemporary Science.* Edinburgh: University of Edinburgh Press; Grand Rapids, MI: Eerdmans, 1997.

Davies, Paul. *The Mind of God: The Scientific Basis for a Rational World.* New York: Simon and Schuster, 1992.

Moltmann, Jürgen. *God in Creation: A New Theology of Creation and the Spirit of God.* San Francisco: Harper San Francisco, 1991.

—— *Science and Wisdom,* trans. Margaret Kohl. London: SCM Press, 2003.

Murphy, Nancey and George F. R. Ellis. *On the Moral Nature of the Universe: Theology, Cosmology, and Ethics.* Minneapolis, MN: Fortress Press, 1996.

Pannenberg, Wolfhart. *Toward a Theology of Nature: Essays on Science and Faith,* ed. Ted Peters. Louisville, KY: Westminster/John Knox Press, 1993.

Peacocke, Arthur. *Theology for a Scientific Age: Being and Becoming – Natural, Divine, and Human,* enlarged edn. Minneapolis, MN: Fortress Press, 1993.

Polkinghorne, John. *The Faith of a Physicist: Reflections of a Bottom-up Thinker.* Gifford lectures 1993–4. Princeton, NJ: Princeton University Press, 1994.

Russell, Robert J. (gen. ed.). *Scientific Perspectives on Divine Action* series (Vatican City: Vatican Observatory Press; Notre Dame, IN: Notre Dame University Press): Vol. 1: *Quantum Cosmology and the Laws of Nature,* ed. Russell, Nancey Murphy, C. J. Isham (1993); Vol. 2: *Chaos and Complexity,* ed. Russell, Nancey Murphy, Arthur Peacocke (1995); Vol. 3: *Evolutionary and Molecular Biology,* ed. Russell, William R. Stoeger, Francisco J. Ayala (1998); Vol. 4: *Neuroscience and the Person,* ed. Russell, Nancey Murphy, Theo C. Meyering, Michael A. Arbib (1999).

Russell, Robert J., William R. Stoeger, and George V. Coyne (eds.). *Physics, Philosophy, and Theology: A Common Quest for Understanding.* Vatican City: Vatican Observatory Press, 1988.

Russell, Robert J., Philip Clayton, Kirk Wegter-McNelly, and John Polkinghorne (eds.). *Quantum Mechanics: Scientific Perspectives on Divine Action.* Vatican City: Vatican Observatory Press, 2002.

Theology and the Biological Sciences

Celia Deane-Drummond

Introduction

Few might have predicted that one of the most popular areas of public debate in the third millennium would be both the promise and dangers of applied biological sciences. Half a century ago, there was a quiet revolution in the concept of biological life, following the discovery of the genetic code by James Watson and Francis Crick in 1953. From the 1970s there has been a growing awareness that the spread of human population and industrialization has contributed to environmental damage, threatening the survival of human and other species. Theologians concerned with pastoral and practical matters could no longer afford to ignore the relationship between theology and the biological sciences. Yet the way life and nature should be understood from a theological perspective has had a chequered history. Contemporary inquirers could well ask: what has theology to do with biology?

Envisioning the hand of God as in some sense operative in the natural world has a very long history. In the early patristic era the entire natural world was viewed as symbolic of the heavenly realm, pointing to theological truths. The Middle Ages fostered the concept that Nature was a book, to be read alongside the book of holy scripture. This opened the way for closer observation of the natural world, reinforced by the rediscovery of Aristotelian philosophy in writers such as Thomas Aquinas. However, it was only once experimental science became fashionable in the seventeenth century that a new kind of natural theology emerged, one that viewed the experimenter as discovering the design of God in creation. The botanist John Ray's *The Wisdom of God Manifest in the Works of Creation*, published in 1695, was popular for over a century, and went through ten editions by 1835. Unlike other authors who had interpreted their observations in the light of religious concepts, Ray was determined to establish natural history on an empirical basis. Yet the motivation for natural history was not just scientific curiosity; it became a religious duty to search for the empirical truth in the natural world so it could be used to serve humankind, and ultimately give glory to God. The seventeenth century also witnessed a collapse in the concept of the supernatural, so that in the most extreme case the resurrection was just another natural process. Instead of viewing nature as a threat, Francis Bacon, among others, believed that the natural world needed to be brought under the control of scientific reasoning. A number of questions surfaced that continue to engage those committed to a theistic understanding of the natural world. In what sense is God visible in the natural world? How does one explain the suffering apparent in natural processes? How does empirical science come to terms with the miraculous? What is the role of humanity in the natural world?

Yet a far more challenging scientific development was to await the religious community with the publication of Charles Darwin's *Origin of Species* (1865), which outlined his theory of evolution. This, in brief, states that variety exists in a population and that those individuals who are best suited to the environment will live longer, and hence have more offspring. This ensures that the characteristics of these individuals are passed down to the next generation through a process known as natural selection. Gradually, over long periods, new species emerge. His theory posed a significant challenge to natural theologies. For now new species were no longer fixed in a preconceived plan, but rather could emerge without necessarily involving the workings of a divine author. In addition, humanity no longer had a special place; rather, it was just one species from a branch of successful hominids. Of course, then, as now, theologians became adept at redesigning their theological explanations to take account of Darwin's theory. Theological justification could take a number of possible routes. One might be to reject Darwinism outright as being a scientific theory that is in opposition to Christian belief in a Creator. The rise of Creationist ideas, alongside a purported "scientific" explanation from the scriptural accounts, represents one form of popular accommodation that is rejected by theologians and scientists alike.[1] Alternatively, some form of theistic evolution is accepted, combining evolutionary ideas with belief in a Creator. In this scenario there are two alternatives. Either, according to the deist alternative, God simply started the process of evolution and then left nature to itself, or God is intricately involved in the process from the beginning, suffering in and with the processes of the natural world. The second alternative or variations on it are more influential in the twentieth century, which is the focus of this chapter.

The scientific community largely accepts Darwin's theory of evolution, although with some qualifications. The rediscovery of Gregory Mendel's plant breeding experiments highlighted the significance of discrete mutagenic changes. In the 1930s and 1940s most biologists came to accept neo-Darwinianism, combining the insights of Darwin with genetic theories about mutation. Darwin had no clear concept of how inherited variations were passed down between generations, or how such variations arose. Experimental research showed that the environment could influence the mutation rates. The balance of genes in a population would change if some individuals with a given mutant gene were able to survive better compared with other individuals in the same population. This is the genetic corollary to natural selection. There are other ways that gene pools may change, such as through more random processes (genetic drift). The evolutionary biologists John Eldredge and Stephen Gould have found punctuated equilibria, where rapid phases of evolutionary change are interspersed with much slower phases. Their results supplement evolution through natural selection.[2] New combinations of genes may lead to variations, and difference in physical appearance (phenotype) may appear even with the same genetic make up (genotype). In addition, changes in gene *regulation* are likely to affect the overall structure or morphology of an organism, and hence diversity. It is also somewhat misleading to speak of mutations as "chance" events, since microscopic events that seem random are a result of physical and chemical events, and lead to law-like properties at the macroscopic level. The full explanation as to the way genetic inheritance worked at the molecular level awaited the discovery of the structure of Deoxyribonucleic Acid (DNA) by James Watson and Francis Crick.[3]

Survey

It would be premature to think too harshly of those pioneers of the twentieth century who, on discovering the structure of DNA, claimed that they had found the "secret of life." The mushrooming of numerous branches of molecular biology and medical genetics, culminating in the multimillion dollar Human Genome Project with its aim to give a full chemical sequence of the human genome, speaks of the future potential of this technology. Similar arguments have been used in order to support human cloning.[4] Supporters normally highlight the medical advantages of the technologies and the possible alleviation of human suffering and pain. Yet its seeming dazzling scientific importance can cloud a number of social, political, theological, and ethical issues that are ongoing subjects of debate. At this juncture theology can no longer remain detached from ethical and pastoral concerns. If God is the author of creation, are there limits to the genetic manipulation of nature? What is the role of humanity in the process of evolution, are we becoming "fabricated" through our own inventions, or are we co-creators with God working for a better future? Who, for example, is to gain most from the technology? Does the desire for genetic change disguise a more sinister eugenics?

A key issue in human genetics concerns the extent to which humanity is determined by its genetic make up, reminiscent of the longstanding nature–nurture debate. A popular view is that we are simply genetically programmed, that the discovery of our genetic composition is all that is really required in order to define "self." A number of theologians challenge this so-called "gene myth," and they believe that such misconception leads to unwarranted fears about the dangers of genetic manipulation. Ted Peters, for example, is a strong advocate of human freedom; while we may be genetically constrained in our choices, this does not amount to genetic "programming." Hence, he argues that the use and application of genetics is more likely to be a gift of God to humanity, as long as it is used responsibly.[5]

The application of genetics to the non-human sphere raises a number of important issues, such as animal welfare, potential environmental damage, and more general questions such as how far and to what extent is humanity warranted in reordering the natural world. The question arises as to the relative value of humanity compared with non-humans. While in secular analysis the consequences are normally the measure which judges an action right or not, from a theological perspective other values come into play, including, from the Genesis account, the idea that all creation is good and belongs to God. The interpretation of the command to humanity to "have dominion" over the earth may lead to an emphasis on control, as in Francis Bacon, or, alternatively, on a greater sense of human care and responsible stewardship.

The philosophical tension between a stress on the value of either humans (anthropocentrism) or all biological species (biocentrism) is reflected in debates about how far it is right to use animals in experimental science, the relative weight given to protecting endangered species, and so on. Those who wish to extend human rights to animals are advocates of the animal rights movement. Peter Singer believes that animals deserve protection because they are sentient. Theologians have taken issue with Singer in that he seems to imply that humans lacking sentience are dispensable and have no moral worth. Tom Regan campaigns for animal rights and argues that animals are individual "subjects" of a life. The theologian Andrew Linzey justifies his theo-rights approach by suggesting that since God created animals vulnerable to human domestication, they deserve equivalent protection to children.[6] Should we use biological characteristics in order to define worth, or is human personhood beyond comparison with non-humans? Authors like Singer are nervous about any justification for giving a higher priority to humans, dubbing this "speciesism." Stephen Clark uses genetic science to support his case that humans are not significantly different from animals, though he is hesitant about the too facile endorsement of Darwin's theory. Such research presents a challenge to Christian anthropology: what does it mean to be human in a biological world where human genetic make up amounts to 98 percent of that of primates? Of course, at this juncture we need to remind ourselves that genetics alone is not responsible for human behavior, and that small genetic changes can lead to large changes in effects.

As evolutionary science continues to grow and develop, theologians working at the interface with biology have devoted considerable attention to meeting its particular challenges. The paleontologist and Jesuit priest Pierre Teilhard de Chardin (1881–1955) was one of the pioneers working in this field. He believed it was possible to create a synthesis between evolutionary ideas and Christian theology, culminating in a grand vision for the Christofication of the universe. Those theologians of the process theology school, such as Ian Barbour and John Haught, have had considerable influence, especially in the USA, adapting a process vision of reality drawn from the work of the philosopher Alfred North Whitehead. Other theologians are less convinced that scientific theories about nature can be incorporated into Christian theological frameworks without leading to distortion. Thomas F. Torrance argued for a Barthian approach to theology, but following the methodology of scientific empiricism. In other words, he develops a scientific theology. Alister McGrath also claims to aim at scientific and theological synthesis; however, it soon becomes clear that the vagaries of science are too precarious in their provisionality to give him any real confidence, so instead he opts for attachment to scientific empiricism as essential to theological insight.[7] How far such a methodology is universal in science is somewhat open to question; for example, the falsification hypothesis common in physical science is not used in ecological science at all.

Many theologians have responded to the particular challenge posed by the work of Richard Dawkins and his agenda not just to promote evolutionary ideas as the explanation for life, but also to dismiss religious experience in the name of scientific "realism." He is well known for his book *The Selfish Gene*. While he claimed that he was using the phrase in order to stress the particular tendency for genes to conserve themselves through each generation, the moral overtones were obvious. Mary Midgley was quick to point out the rhetoric in what Dawkins was attempting, by elevating "a humble piece of goo within cells to a malign and all-powerful agent."[8] She argues that attitudes will affect the form in which symbolism and imagination take shape. She suggests that Dawkins has a hidden religious agenda in his description of genes as the "primary policy makers" and characterizing altruism as still basically selfish behavior. Other sociobiologists, such as E. O. Wilson, have joined Dawkins' campaign to formulate a myth around genetics, though he is less nervous about using religious language in order to describe the achievements of evolutionary science. Midgley strongly objects to the egoism and fatalism in much of the language used by sociobioloigsts, believing that such language ultimately stems from "an unrealistic acceptance of competitiveness as central to human nature."[9]

Keith Ward has added to the debate by characterizing three areas of challenge posed by evolutionary theory. The first is that there is no ultimate purpose in the universe, the second is that life evolves simply through competitive ruthlessness, and the third is that mind happens as an "adjunct" to gene survival.[10] Like many contemporary biologists, he believes that natural selection on its own cannot *guarantee* the emergence of complex conscious life forms. He also shares with Stephen Clark the doubt as to why intelligent life emerged, as there is nothing to suggest that such a capacity would *inevitably* have greater survival rates compared with those with no rationality.[11] Of course, other "higher" human characteristics that go to make up cultures are not simply explicable through reproductive advantage.[12] One difficulty with Ward's argument is that if we accept that the natural probability of mind emerging is very low, and hence invoke divine purpose, then we are left with a God of the gaps, who fills in where science has failed to provide an explanation. Both Dawkins' confidence and Ward's rejoinder may account for the spectrum of possible debates, though it is important to face Dawkins on his own terms, namely through accepting the *possibility* that humanity did emerge through natural processes. In addition, there are other voices within evolutionary biology who argue that, given the conditions on earth, the evolution of something like humans is virtually inevitable. Simon Conway Morris is a good example of a biologist who is less hostile to religion compared with Richard Dawkins, but who still argues that convergence in evolution implies that human-like species are less the result of "chance" and more the result of an inevitable process.[13] At the same time he suggests that the particular conditions that arise in our solar system that give rise to life are rare; we live in a lonely universe where we are unlikely to encounter other hominoid-like species. Conway Morris speculates that if humans are "castaways" in the universe, then we might think of this as a biological gloss on the fall. Those with faith will inevitably see divine purpose in cosmological and evolutionary events. In fact the ultimate fate of the earth through science alone portrays a somewhat chilling eschatology, and one that Christian theologians would wish to reject. However, this does not mean that our limited understanding of evolutionary science needs to import God in order to arrive at a satisfactory position.

Theologians who are interested in the natural world include those who are concerned with environmental issues in general and ecology in particular. Many come to the debate as much concerned about the practical, political, ethical, and social issues as the scientific ones. Instead of the Darwinian images of competitiveness, biological processes such as symbiosis, cooperation, and integration of processes in ecological systems become inspirational models for human behavior. Feminists have been particularly influential through ecofeminism, including prominent feminist writers such as Rosemary Radford Ruether and Sallie McFague in the USA and Anne Primavesi, Ruth Page, and Mary Grey in the UK.[14] Page is concerned about the extent of suffering in evolution, so prefers God's immanence to be expressed as *with* creation, rather than *in* creation. Most ecofeminists believe that there is a link between oppression of the earth and oppression of women, though the possible advantage of identifying women with the earth is hotly debated. Carolyn Merchant has linked the Baconian urge to control nature with oppression of women, arguing instead for a relational approach to the natural world. As a corollary to the link between science and sexism, feminist authors have urged a new kind of science, one that focuses more on care, rather than control.[15] Ruether has included images of Gaia in her reconstruction of theology and nature (Gaia is the divine within nature that complements the God of law and covenant). Primavesi has taken up James Lovelock's model of the earth functioning as a single organism (Gaia) in order to argue for a reformulated theology along Gaian lines. While theologians who use the Gaia hypothesis stress aspects of cooperation that are implicit in this theory, closer attention to the details shows that in its most radical form it envisages resituating the place of humanity so that it is no longer the apex of creation, but a somewhat unwanted parasite on the planet. The tension implicit in Gaia reflects a more general issue characteristic of all aspects of ecotheology, namely the choice between individualism/anthropocentrism and holism/biocentrism. Liberation theologians such as Leonado Boff and Sean McDonagh have also been highly instrumental in raising the profile of the link between oppression of the poor and environmental issues.

The discussion so far might imply that ecotheologians are all radical in their approach to theology. This is far from the case. Concern for environmental issues is universal across the theological spectrum, from evangelical writers such as Stephen Bouma Prediger and Michael Northcott through to Orthodox theologians such as John Zizioulas. Reformed theologian Jürgen Moltmann has incorporated green thinking into his theology, stressing community relationships in the Trinity and ecology. In addition, Moltmann draws on ecological ideas to develop his Christology and eschatology. Christ becomes one who suffers with the earth, incorporating the natural world into the redemptive purpose. The main purpose of Moltmann's writings is to engender a theology that speaks to the pressing sense of environmental concern. He is less concerned to engage in detail with ecology as science. More recent work on scientific ecology has shown that the idea of ecology in terms of stable, interconnected systems is no longer accepted. Ecologists now are more likely to focus on flux, dynamic interchange, and the involvement of humans in ecological change. Theologians tempted to draw on models of ecology in terms of stable interrelationships need to be aware that this is an idealized philosophy, rather than ecological science.

Key Representatives

Pierre Teilhard de Chardin

Pierre Teilhard de Chardin was a brilliant scientist whose paleontological research challenged Darwin's assumption that cranial capacity in evolution emerged prior to toolmaking. He argued instead that evolution and toolmaking evolved together. Like the sociobiologists of a later generation, he believed that evolution was responsible not only for physical characteristics, but also for all sociocultural history. Yet it was the way he combined his scientific ideas with his theological vision that caused the most controversy.[16] He did not adhere to the materialism characteristic of Darwin's original thesis; instead, he suggested that matter was ever increasing in spiritualization. *The Human Phenomenon* (1940), possibly his most influential work, urged a unity of matter and spirit, thought and action, personalism and collectivism, plurality and unity. His earlier work, *The Divine Milieu* (1920), was more focused on his particular brand of Christian mysticism informed by an evolutionary account of creation. His commitment to ontological monism is very clear; God's imminent nature is interpreted in terms of the cosmic Christ. His law of complexity/consciousness attempted to explain the emergence of consciousness. Teilhard stressed the significance of human evolution, so that humans could not only influence, but also direct evolution; wars were simply growing pains of adolescent humanity that would ultimately grow up through the achievements of science and technology. Organic evolution functioned like a giant organism developing towards the goal of unity in matter and spirit. He understood each phase of evolution to represent distinct jumps over a critical threshold: first, the formation of elementary corpuscles of the cosmos; second, the formation of a biosphere; third, the formation of human species. At death an immortal center of consciousness in human beings united to form a planetary layer of super-consciousness around the earth, eventually to be united with God as Omega, the end of evolution.

Teilhard's grand synthesis was bold, optimistic, daring, and mystical, rather than systematic. It is not difficult to criticize his work from a scientific point of view, even though he was a well-respected paleontologist, and elected to the French Academy of Sciences in 1947. The place and significance he gave to humans is not evident in Darwin's theory, which posited a branching evolutionary path. There is no evidence for Teilhard's critical evolutionary thresholds, or for the concrete importance of mental activity in evolution.[17] Some scientists, nonetheless, warmed to his ideas, believing that the primacy he gave to science more than compensated for his lack of attention to detail. From a theological perspective it is also easy to find problems with his thesis: his vision is optimistic and anthropocentric in a way that finds fewer supporters today. In addition, his picture of resurrection amounts to imaginative speculation that is beyond the bounds of credibility. However, his vision is also prophetic in many of its elements. For example, his organic picture of the earth has been taken up and developed in Gaian theory, popular among many ecotheologians. His focus on process and final goodness is also characteristic of process theology and its current engagement with science. His attention to the importance of consciousness was misdirected in evolutionary terms, but has become an area of increasing debate. The unity of mind and brain, the relationship to the soul and the way in which consciousness emerges from our primate ancestors is still unresolved. In addition, importantly, Teilhard argued that just as theology needed science, so science needed theology if it is to have a "heart" as well as a "head."

Arthur Peacocke

Arthur Peacocke devoted the early part of his career to working on the chemical structure of DNA. As a biochemist turned theologian, he has helped to raise the public profile of issues in biology and theology, especially his reworking of theological ideas in light of current biological and evolutionary ideas. The influence of more liberal Anglican writers such as G. W. Lampe and David Jenkins is tangible in his discussion. Like Torrance, he envisages scientific method as being critical in its engagement with theology. However, he is more radical in his approach, in that he is prepared to take any article of faith as provisional, unless proved otherwise by scientific "evidence." He argues, in particular, that the experience of working as a scientist helps humanity understand God's interaction with the world. Understanding does not come through faith in the traditional way, but the other way round. Unlike Teilhard, who believed in rudimentary forms of consciousness in the world, Peacocke prefers the idea of emergence, that at increasing levels of complexity we find new properties emerging that are not predictable according to the lower levels of organization. Moreover, he suggests that, excluding behavior, the most successful species are not necessarily the most complex. However, he is wary of saying that humankind is just another animal; rather, there are unique characteristics of human species, just as in any other species. In other words, he argues for a holistic approach to life on earth, one that does not simply isolate the genes, but explores wider parameters of behavior, sociology, psychology, and religion.

Peacocke's Christology is liberal in its conception of Christ as a perfect human being, though he is also attracted to more abstract ideas such as the divine Logos incarnate in the world. God, for Peacocke, works through the interplay of chance and necessity in allowing the earth to evolve. However, he distances himself from those authors who wish to locate God's action in evolution at the microscopic level; rather, the action of God is through "top-down" or "whole–part" interaction, so that the influence is indirect, through a chain of levels acting in a "downward" way. Like process theologians, he argues for panentheism, though he retains the idea of a sacramental universe. He rejects classical ideas such as the fall of humanity, preferring reinterpretation in terms of failure to achieve potential given by God. Drawing on Moltmann, he is attracted to the idea of a suffering, pathetic, self-emptying God, one who shares in the suffering of all creatures, as well as humans. Humanity is co-creator, co-worker and co-explorer with God in creation.

Few scientists object to the way in which Peacocke has formulated his theology, though his sharp rebuttal of sociobiology may come as a surprise. His theological position is more controversial, in particular his claim that God can be envisaged through scientific exploration. Nicholas Lash, for example, believes that presuming that science is a mediator of the truth of theology through scientific observation is false, as it is based on the shift toward the spectator model of human engagement with reality that came to dominate the Western imagination along with the rise of modern experimental science.[18] His critique would also make him part company with more conservative theologians such as McGrath, who incorporates scientific empiricism into theological discourse. Lash, in particular, believes that diversity of approaches to God, with their fragmentary insights, is more characteristic of God compared with any grand order independent of self. However, while scientific theories may have the appearance of such independent reality, in practice science is more fluid and fuzzy at the edges, especially in its most creative and open aspects. Peacocke is drawn more to the latter, creative science, which has more in common with music or art than Lash implies. However, whether one is still committed to the way of achieving theological knowledge through scientific discourse is a matter of debate. The natural world is an ambiguous place in which to find God. It seems more likely, then, that only with the eye of faith can wonder in the natural world appear to be truly reflective of the glory of God.

John Zizioulas

John Zizioulas is an Eastern Orthodox theologian of some distinction who has devoted considerable energy to translating Orthodox ideas into a language that can be readily understood in the West. He is also characteristic of a larger movement within the Orthodox community that believes in the importance of caring for the earth as God's gift to humanity. The Orthodox perspective is one that sees "nature" as inclusive of human beings, and a radical distinction between God as "other" than creation. How can God and the world be linked without losing the radical distinction between the two? Zizioulas argues that the link between God and the world is possible through humanity. However, he rejects the emphasis on rationality as a basis for human superiority, as evolutionary research presents other animals having this capacity, and it can also be the basis for a rationalization of the world for selfish exploitation. He argues, instead, that freedom is the most important dimension of human beings. Freedom may be used in ways that are distorting, as is clear from the story of the fall. But, "By taking the world into his hands and creatively integrating and referring it to God, man liberates creation from its limitations and lets it truly be."[19] Christ acts as the model for the perfect relationship between humanity and the world, so that as the bread and wine is offered in the Eucharist, so the source of all creation as a gift from God becomes clear. It is through the liturgical act that God and creation are once again drawn into right relationship. Nature as sacred no longer is under the threat of death, but through the free choice of human beings enters life. This sacramental life, faithful to the teaching of the church, engenders an ethos, a way of life that counters the selfishness that Zizioulas believes is at the heart of the ecological crisis.

Zizioulas' writing is traditional in its biblical interpretation without ignoring the discoveries of modern evolutionary biology and science. He is prepared to listen to the insights of evolutionary ideas, without making these paradigmatic in his theology. He is also correct to believe that the problem facing humanity in practical issues such as the ecological crisis cannot be solved by theological endorsement of scientific empiricism. Rather, he calls for a specifically liturgical vision, one whose language and narrative is distinct from that of scientific reasoning with its modern tendency towards fragmentation and specialization. His stress on the importance of freedom would have resonance with other authors working at the interface between biology and theology, especially in areas such as genetics. The concept of humanity as priest of creation is more problematic, in that in environmental ethics there has been a shift away from anthropocentrism toward a greater sense of kinship with all creation. However, he is correct to place ecological concern at the door of a reenvisaged anthropology, for it is only inasmuch as humanity learns to change its behavior and attitudes that any hope of lasting ecological sustainability will come to fruition.

Theology and the Biological Sciences: A Tentative Agenda

One of the ongoing difficulties for any theologian working at the interface with the biological sciences is keeping abreast of scientific discoveries and trends. Theological concentration on history, rather than nature, is understandable in the wake of the plethora of knowledge and information in the sciences, including the biological sciences. It is also apparent that most of the key contributors to the field have had some training in natural science. Yet if biological science is to be taken as a serious issue for debate in theology as such, rather than just by an elite who happen to have combined both careers, then there is a need for more theologians to take biological issues seriously. Such a possibility may only come about if theology becomes a shared task, where mutual encounter and engagement can take place. In order to begin such a task theologians need more confidence in what they have to offer to debates about the place of science and technology. It is easy for theologians to be either timid when confronted by the enormous practical success of science, or dismiss science as bent on a philosophically naive empirical imperialism. Instead, respectful listening, a paying attention that needs to be at the heart of all theological enterprise, should serve to shape the way theologians approach biological discoveries. However, this need not lead to endorsement or appropriation of ideas emerging from scientific analysis. Rather, it is through careful reflection and discernment that the insights of science can be drawn upon in a creative process of exchange and interpretation. It is no longer possible to ignore the biological horizon of understanding, but the way biblical and theological interpretation intersect requires an ongoing effort. One way of achieving this task is through more corporate ways of working, so that exchange is facilitated between those with expertise in different fields. The humanities in general have been relatively slow to initiate such practices, while in the biological sciences team work is taken for granted as being essential in order to achieve its goals. The particular way in which such an exchange comes to fruition will depend on the particular interests of those aiming to engage in the dialogue. The first tentative goal can be summarized as a readiness for respectful attention between those of different disciplines in theology and the biological sciences.

In addition to this listening process, some readiness to contribute to practical issues that are of concern to citizens in general becomes part of a theologian's brief when working at this interface. Engaging in theological ethics is inherent in topics such as genetics, environmental issues, and the advances associated with new developments in medicine. There is always the temptation for those working at this interface to leave practical issues behind and just formulate theories of God and evolution that are remote from any pressing social concerns. Such theorization has little more impact than the theologies that it seeks to replace. In other words, it is a misplaced concreteness to claim that because scientific realism is operative in dealing with the world, a theology that takes account of such realism is practical in nature. A second goal can be summarized as a readiness to accept responsibility for working out the implications of such an exchange in practical decision making and ethics.

Thirdly, the various areas of systematic theology that encounter biological science are not simply restricted to a theology of creation, though of course this is significant. Rather, the full range of possibilities inherent in working through the implications of the biological sciences on theology in its broadest sense needs to be taken into account. Jürgen Moltmann, for example, includes his understanding of ecology in his discussions of a range of topics, such as creation, God, Christology, soteriology, eschatology, and anthropology. This is not to suggest that biological science is paradigmatic in shaping theological development. However, it is important to take into account the insights gained through biology and be able to give a reasonable response to such a challenge. The resurrection of Jesus, for example, would be impossible from a secular biologist's perspective, which would claim death is irreversible. This dilemma has taxed even the most able of theologians.[20] Yet this does not mean that faith in the resurrection is now no longer possible, or that Christ did not rise from the dead. The physical form in which he was raised is obscure from the gospel accounts; he could both eat, and pass through doors. It seems that we are dealing with a reality that is not normally predicated by science. This leads to a third goal: a readiness to accept the challenge of the biological sciences in all areas of theology, without necessarily simply accepting biological empiricism as the final arbiter of such theology.

Fourthly, there is a danger that once the biological sciences become companions to theology, the insights of theology for science and the practice of science are attenuated. Theologians who have been inducted into the sciences through long training or association need to be aware of the gift that theology can bring to the sciences, as well as the other way round. This is true in decision making, about which aspects of biological science need to be developed, as well as the application of biological science in biotechnology. Hence, discerning priorities for scientific research becomes the task of all citizens, including theologians. While theologians cannot change the content of science and it would be wrong for them to try and do so, they can influence funding policy. Consultation documents on cloning, use of genetic change to produce drugs, and the status of the embryo have all led to considerable debate on public policy in these areas. This leads to a fourth goal: a readiness to be engaged in policy making in the biological sciences, where such opportunities are available.

There are also wider social issues to consider in the wake of possible applications of the biological sciences in genetics and environmental science. While the former reflects the confident edge of biology, the latter is more aware of human limitations in our dealings with the planet as a whole. In both areas particular questions (such as that of social justice) are of interest to theologians. This goes further than simply arguing for ethical engagement as in the second goal outlined above. Rather, it suggests that particular areas call not just for theorization about the philosophical difficulty in application, but an engagement with those who are on the receiving end of injustices as an indirect result of the applications of biotechnology. This is not to suggest that all biotechnology is oppressive, but rather the task of the theologian is to recognize where this is the case, and work to alleviate the situation within his or her means to do so. A fifth goal might be: a readiness to recognize those situations where applications of biology have led to social injustices and work for its amelioration.

Other possible scenarios might be named, so the list is far from exhaustive. However, it shows the scope of the work to be done that is still very much an ongoing and expanding field of inquiry. By way of conclusion, it is clear that even though theology has expanded its horizons considerably through its engagement with the biological sciences, there is still the need to delve into the rich resources of its tradition, and to seek wisdom wherever it may be found, but a wisdom that is ultimately grounded in knowledge and love of God and God's creation.

Notes

1 This movement is influential in the USA, but it is exegetically and scientifically unwarranted.

2 Gould also suggests that the probability of complex life emerging is very low. Simon Conway Morris has challenged Gould's conclusions, arguing from the same fossil record that the probability of complex life emerging is high; see C. Southgate (ed.), *God, Humanity and the Cosmos* (Edinburgh: T. & T. Clark, 1999), pp. 150–1.

3 For an introduction to genetic science, see Southgate, *God, Humanity and the Cosmos*, pp. 143–50.

4 Christian theologians largely reject reproductive cloning, though opinions on "therapeutic" cloning to treat diseases are divided. Traditional Roman Catholic and Eastern Orthodox theologians reject all forms of cloning as showing insufficient respect for human dignity.

5 How to set such limits is more difficult. See C. Deane-Drummond, *Creation Through Wisdom: Theology and the New Biology* (Edinburgh: T. & T. Clark, 2000).

6 His attempt to argue for the presence of the Holy Spirit in animals from biblical sources is unconvincing. For discussion, see C. Deane-Drummond, *The Ethics of Nature* (Oxford: Blackwell, forthcoming).

7 See, for example, A. McGrath, *A Scientific Theology, Vol. 1: Nature* (Edinburgh: T. & T. Clark, 2001), pp. 45–9.

8 M. Midgley, *Evolution as a Religion* (New York: Methuen, 1985), p. 123.

9 Ibid, p. 140.

10 See K. Ward, *God, Chance and Necessity* (Oxford: Oneworld, 1996), p. 64.

11 For discussion in Stephen Clark see his *Biology and Christian Ethics* (Cambridge: Cambridge University Press, 2000).

12 Ward does not address the possibility that cultural constructs or memes are passed down through non-genetic means.

13 S. Conway Morris, "The Paradoxes of Evolution: Inevitable Humans in a Lonely Universe?" in N. A. Manson (ed.), *God and Design: The Teleological Argument and Modern Science* (London: Routledge, 2003).

14 For details of debates in ecofeminism, see C. Deane-Drummond, "Creation," in S. Parsons (ed.), *The Cambridge Companion to Feminist Theology* (Cambridge: Cambridge University Press, 2002).

15 Hilary Rose is a leading author in this respect. For discussion, see C. Deane-Drummond, *Biology and Theology Today* (London: SCM Press, 2001), pp. 184–207.

16 He developed Henri Bergson's ideas who, in *Creative Evolution* (1907), argued that all spirit in nature emerges as an *élan vital*.

17 Whether intelligent life is inevitable from an evolutionary perspective, or highly improbable, is a matter of ongoing debate.

18 N. Lash, *The Beginning and End of Religion* (Cambridge: Cambridge University Press, 1996), pp. 79–80.

19 J. D. Zizioulas, "Preserving God's Creation: Three Lectures on Theology and Ecology," *King's Theological Review* 13 (1), 1990, p. 5.

20 Wolfhart Pannenberg's theology shows this tension clearly.

Bibliography

Berry, R. J. *The Care of Creation: Focusing Concern and Action* (Leicester: Intervarsity Press, 2000).

Boff, L. *Cry of the Earth, Cry of the Poor* (Maryknoll, NY: Orbis Books, 1994).

Bouma-Prediger, S. *For the Beauty of the Earth: A Christian Vision for Creation Care* (Grand Rapids, MI: Baker Academic, 2001).

Clark, S. *Biology and Christian Ethics* (Cambridge: Cambridge University Press, 2000).

Clark, S. R. L. *How to Think About the Earth: Philosophical and Theological Models for Ecology* (London: Mowbray, 1993).

Conway Morris, S. *Life's Solution: Inevitable Humans in a Lonely Universe* (Cambridge: Cambridge University Press, 2003).

Deane-Drummond, C. *Creation Through Wisdom: Theology and the New Biology* (Edinburgh: T. & T. Clark, 2000).

—— *Biology and Theology Today: Exploring the Boundaries* (London: SCM Press, 2001).

—— *The Ethics of Nature* (Oxford: Blackwell, 2003).

Edwards, D. (ed.). *Earth Revealing, Earth Healing: Ecology and Christian Theology* (Collegeville: Liturgical Press, 2001).

Futuyama, D. *Evolutionary Biology*, 3rd edn. (Sunderland: Sinauer Associates, 1998).

Haught, J. F. *God After Darwin: A Theology of Evolution* (Boulder, CO: Westview Press, 2001).

Lash, N. *The Beginning and End of Religion* (Cambridge: Cambridge University Press, 1996).

Linzey, A. *Animal Theology* (London: SCM Press, 1994).

McDonagh, S. *To Care for the Earth: A Call to a New Theology* (London: Geoffrey Chapman, 1986).

McFague, S. *Supernatural Christians: How we Should Love Nature* (London: SCM Press, 1997).

McGrath, A. *A Scientific Theology, Vol. 1: Nature* (London: T. & T. Clark/Continuum, 2001).

Merchant, C. *The Death of Nature: Women, Ecology and the Scientific Revolution* (London: Wildwood House, 1982).

Midgley, M. *Evolution as a Religion* (New York: Methuen, 1985).

Moltmann, J. *God in Creation: An Ecological Doctrine of God* (London: SCM Press, 1985).

Northcott, M. *The Environment and Christian Ethics* (Cambridge: Cambridge University Press, 1996).

Page, R. *God and the Web of Creation* (London: SCM Press, 1996).

Pannenberg, W. *Towards a Theology of Nature: Essays on Science and Faith*, ed. T. Peters (Westminster: John Knox Press, 1993).

Parsons, S. (ed.). *The Cambridge Companion to Feminist Theology* (Cambridge: Cambridge University Press, 2002).

Peacocke, A. *Creation and the World of Science* (Oxford: Clarendon Press, 1979).

—— *Theology for a Scientific Age*, enlarged edn. (London: SCM Press, 1993).

—— *Paths from Science to God: The End of All Our Exploring* (Oxford: Oneworld, 2001).

Peters, T. *Playing God: Genetic Determinism and Human Freedom* (London: Routledge, 1997).

—— *Theology and the Natural Sciences* (Basingstoke: Ashgate, 2003).

Primavesi, A. *Sacred Gaia: Holistic Theology and Earth Systems Science* (London: Routledge, 2000).

Ruether, R. Radford, *Gaia and God: An Ecofeminist Theology of Earth Healing* (London: SCM Press, 1993).

Ruse, M. *Can a Darwinian be a Christian? The Relationship between Science and Religion* (Cambridge: Cambridge University Press, 2001).

Santmire, H. P. *Nature Reborn: The Ecological and Cosmic Promise of Christian Theology* (Minneapolis, MN: Fortress Press, 2000).

Southgate, C. (ed.), *God, Humanity and the Cosmos* (Edinburgh: T. & T. Clark, 1999).

Teilhard de Chardin, P. *The Human Phenomenon*, trans. S. Appleton-Weber (Brighton: Sussex University Press, 1999).

Torrance, T. F. *Theological Science* (Edinburgh: T. & T. Clark, 1996).

Ward, K. *God, Chance and Necessity* (Oxford: Oneworld, 1996).

Zizioulas, J. D. "Preserving God's Creation: Three Lectures on Theology and Ecology," *King's Theological Review* 13 (1) (1990), 1–5.

Theology and the Social Sciences

Richard H. Roberts

Introduction

At first sight, as observed from the standpoint of the social scientist, the relation of theology to the social sciences looks somewhat unpromising. The history of social science presents itself as a narrative of divergence from, and the surpassing of, both religion as such, and of the idea of there being a revealed core to Western culture. Modernity (*Neuzeit*) has witnessed the long and sometimes tortuous relinquishment of the central role of theology in culture and society. Indeed, sociology understood in terms of "grand theory" may plausibly be understood as an aspirant successor discipline to theology as "queen of the sciences." There is something of a natural progression from the *mentalité* of the once all-knowing theologian to that of the ambitious contemporary social scientist who aims not merely at comprehensive interpretation of human life-worlds, but also to promote the emancipatory role of social science as itself the agent of enlightened modernity. By contrast, the theologian would now seem to occupy a shrunken and marginalized residual territory confronted by a hostile secularized reality; such theology lives on in reduced circumstances. This is, of course, a gross simplification, not least because the theologies of mainline religion now face pluriform postmodern and New Age recompositions of the religious field.

From the early seventeenth century, as scholastic philosophy was confronted by early natural science and philosophy moved in Cartesian and empiricist directions, so the theological residuum was gradually whittled away. Correspondingly, from the early nineteenth century onward, disciplines in the social and human sciences differentiated themselves and this further usurped the territory of theological thought. Kant's magisterial attempt to stave off the nihilistic implications of an abstract juxtaposition of empiricism and idealism has now, some argue, reached the limit of its use. In an era of nihilism, the possibilities for theology seem both extreme and contradictory for, if we are to believe some commentators, there can be no common ground between theology and secular thought. Those who start out from such an uncompromising standpoint regard all mediating and liberal theologies as mistaken, even perverse, and have little regard for much of the theology examined in the present volume.

In the setting outlined above, it is possible to explore the relation of theology and the social sciences along two lines of approach. On the one hand, there are the efforts made by a number of theologians from Ernst Troeltsch and Dietrich Bonhoeffer onward, who have sought to take account of sociological insights in their work. On the other hand, however, there is the larger question as to how the divergence of and subsequent relation between two inherently complex and contrasting (and in many respects antagonistic) traditions of reflection should be understood once other factors are taken into account. We therefore adopt the following procedure. First, through a brief survey and typology, we outline five strategies of negotiation employed by representative theologians who have attempted to develop relationships between theology and the social sciences. Then, key issues are drawn out and related to current debates that provide the basis for a more general appraisal of the relation of theology to the social sciences in light of contrasting responses to modernity. In conclusion, an agenda for the reconstrual of the relation between theology and the social sciences is proposed. This involves both the formulation of a framework for the *episteme* of theology conceived as an emancipatory "human science" and suggestions for how this renewal might proceed.[1]

The engagement between theology and the social sciences has by and large been relatively one-sided. Some theologians have been committed to the use of socioscientific insights, whereas social scientists have characteristically resisted normative styles of thought and favored modes of rationality which valorize critical, interpretative, quantitative, and theoretical skills, as opposed to concerns with ultimate or transcendental questions. The sociological imagination as classically deployed undercuts religious and theological pretensions. Recently, however, the very extremity of twentieth-century history has provoked a number of sociologists into more explicit ethical and normative reflection.[2] Moreover, resurgent religion and religiosities, the ethnic revival, religiously justified terrorism, and the all-encompassing character of an "outer-directed" social order have provoked a revived socioscientific interest in religion that goes well beyond the limits of the subdiscipline of the sociology of religion. Other theoretical developments within poststructuralist cultural theory and associated sociological thought invite the posing of questions which, if they are not explicitly theological, certainly have a quasi-theological character. The representation of the human condition as susceptible to interpretation as premodern, modern, and postmodern also has considerable import for the construal of the relation of theology and the social sciences. Entrenched and doctrinaire oppositional stances may no longer be appropriate, but what alternative mode of intellectual cohabitation might now be more fitting is a contested question.

Theologians and the Social Sciences: Survey and Typology

From the side of the Christian church and academic theology, some theologians have long recognized that they cannot operate effectively without recourse to the social sciences. In "practical" or "pastoral" theology, eclectic appropriations of insights and methodology often take place, and pragmatic syntheses are arranged which enhance instrumental insight into the ministerial task and the ongoing life of the church. Moreover, in such areas as Old and New Testament studies, church history, and Christian social ethics, the use of material drawn from the social sciences has become increasingly common. Much more difficult issues arise, however, when we consider the role of social science in relation to systematic theology, for it is here that the immanent critique and relativism of sociological thought clashes with the reenactment (or even the re-creation) of tradition(s) in given sociocultural contexts. Under post-traditional or "detraditionalized"[3] social conditions the very idea of tradition is regarded as problematic, yet for others it remains indispensable.

The "turn to the subject" initiated by Martin Luther and furthered by later theologians, not least Friedrich Schleiermacher, intensified religious experience while loosening the hold of theological explanation upon the "outer" physical world. Such a development serves as a prelude to the growth of individualism and modern self-identity.[4] While Protestant theology thus willingly ceded sociocultural space in return for an intensification of religious consciousness, its battle with modernity was largely fought out elsewhere, notably in the long struggle with the implications of the historical–critical method and historicism. Having accepted an increasingly individualistic and subjective role in social reality (an option most consistently worked out in the history of Pietism), Protestant theology then had to suffer the virtual destruction of the scripture principle and its chosen textual foundations. Lacking the diachronic stability provided by the institutional hierarchy of Catholicism, German Protestant theologians were nonetheless culturally licensed to provide religious legitimation for a nascent and ascendant Germany. This theological and cultural role was based upon a transmutation of religious consciousness and the evolution of forms of enlightened religious inwardness (pioneered by Schleiermacher) which were compatible with the ethos of progress. In its turn, Protestant liberalism became a fundamental feature of the sociocultural compact between church and state (that as a consequence of Bismarck's *Kulturpolitik* also eventually came to include the Catholic Church), an arrangement which endured until the catastrophic collapse of Germany at the end of World War I.

The "first postmodernity" of the culture of the Weimar Republic[5] was the seedbed not only of twentieth-century Protestant theology but also of many other strands of thought (and notably of those conducted in dialogue with Marxism). For the intellectuals of Weimar, many of whom were Jews later to be scattered after Hitler's coming to power, it was Marxism which became the bearer of hope. Now, however, in the so-called "postmodern condition"[6] and after the collapse of communism (albeit recognized as an ideology long drained of authenticity), the present state of affairs in certain respects recalls the inner-European vacuum created by the implosion of Germany after the Armistice of 1919. In both contexts human beings confront rapid economic and technological change and sociocultural instability; now, under the conditions of "advanced" or "high" capitalism, they are seemingly obliged to shop for lifestyle options in competitive markets of human identity.[7]

As a consequence of the Reformation and the Enlightenment, both Catholic and Protestant theologies retrenched and retreated in distinctive ways. As regards the Catholic Church, the totalizing ambitions of scholastic theology were eventually reborn in reduced form in neoscholastic Thomism underpinned by the authority of Pope Leo XIII in response to the threat of immanentist thought. Speculative abstract theological reflection within Protestantism underwent a form of revival in German (above all Hegelian) idealism. The Western and Enlightenment aspiration toward the totalization of knowledge (paradigmatically represented in Goethe's *Faust* and its philosophical parallel, Hegel's *Phenomenology of Mind*) was transmitted to Marxism and to social science. In the battle for the *episteme* which took place (and continues) both between and within the disciplines of the emergent human and social sciences, which was mapped out with uncompromising clarity by Michel Foucault,[8] religion and theology have a problematic status. In the most general terms, "religion" and the "sacred" underwent marginalization and migration, and the history of aesthetics and the "sublime" is one point of entry into understanding this process. Significantly, as regards theology, not only did Wilhelm von Humboldt exclude the divinity faculty of the University of Berlin from the faculty of humanities, but this marginalization was also repeated in Wilhelm Dilthey's configuration of the human sciences (*Geisteswissenschaften*) in the early twentieth century.[9] Paradoxically (given its extraordinarily well-funded base in Germany), such has been the degree of cultural isolation of theology that the New Testament theologian Ernst Käsemann could write of the status of theological thought as a "nature reserve" in European culture. This is an apt but alarming image.

As noted earlier, the relationship between theology and the social sciences is problematic and as a first step we examine briefly, and in highly simplified terms, a typology of five possible strategies of appropriation enacted by theologians. First, the fundamentalist option involves the repudiation of modernity and concomitant forms of regression; second, theology can tend toward reductive absorption into the social scientific perspective (Ernst Troeltsch); third, the theologian may draw upon and use sociological categories as part of his or her essentially theological project (Dietrich Bonhoeffer, H. R. Niebuhr); fourth, theological and sociological categories can be regarded as co-inherent aspects of an integral "form of life," "life-world," or "phenomenology of tradition" (Edward Farley) which subsists at a remove from the question of modernity; fifth, the theologian may repudiate sociology as heretical secular thought and posit the persuasive option of commitment to the Christian cultural–linguistic practice (John Milbank). As we shall indicate in the sections that follow, the present writer considers that no one of these strategies should be considered adequate as it stands: further factors have to be taken into account.

Theology repels the social sciences: Fundamentalism

It is a mistake to confuse fundamentalism with premodern thinking as such. Fundamentalism involves in large part the rejection of modernity or its manipulation. Thus, in recent studies, Gilles Kepel and Martin Riesebrodt have depicted global fundamentalism as attempts at reconquering the world and patriarchal protest movements, respectively.[10] Scriptural literalism, the creation of consistent subcultures, the imposition of distinctive gender roles for men and women, and so on, are characteristic. It is, however, easier to discern the conflict between fundamentalism and modernity than that between active conservatism and so-called "postmodernity." Under postmodern conditions of fragmentation, rational choice gives way to "seduction" by the rhetorics of discourses which recognize no final hegemonies. Thus, curiously, the distinction between naive Protestant fundamentalism and the sophisticated quasi-fundamentalism of our fifth strategist is more a question of consciousness: the former is unaware of the full implications of modernity; the latter certainly is, but persists nevertheless in demanding decisions on the basis of an either–or choice between exclusive alternatives. If and when fundamentalism encounters social science it is most often where this makes instrumental use of social psychological or other techniques in order to facilitate conversion and other religious experience. The functional compatibility between instrumental reason as employed in technology and fundamentalist beliefs is well documented where (for example) the latter serve as means of social empowerment over against an invasive, Western-dominated modernity.[11] Postmodern or quasi-fundamentalism is, as argued below, altogether more problematic.

Ernst Troeltsch: Sociology overcomes theology

Ernst Troeltsch, the polymath sociologist and theologian–historian (and close associate of Max Weber), pioneered the application of sociological method to the study of Christian origins. Thus, the history of dogma (as paradigmatically represented by Harnack) became the model for a sociological interpretation of the interdependent relation between the transformed socioethical teachings of the church and the changing sociopolitical context of an organization that grew from its status as an obscure religious minority group with strong eschatological beliefs into the state religious monopoly of the late Roman Empire.[12]

Troeltsch's thought was dominated by a prolonged intellectual and personal struggle with historicism. This conception of history asserts the universality of cause and effect in the nexus of events and excludes *a priori* the "absolute truths" necessary to religious faith from objective historical study. In essence, Troeltsch argued that the modern idea of history depended on critical source analysis and psychological analogy and that history was of the development of peoples, cultures, and the components of cultures. According to this approach all dogmas dissolve into the flow of events, none of which is accorded a status of priority on the basis of extra-historical presuppositions. The historian works up from appropriate comparison through a combination of material drawn from evidence in order to work toward a comprehensive account.[13]

Troeltsch experienced a severe crisis of faith and then famously exchanged faculties. He was left with a residual and individualistic commitment to Christian values and with the scientific conviction that all historical truth was relative and conditioned. For Troeltsch, there was no escape (as with Karl Barth) from the rigorous constraints of *Historismus* into the dialectics of crisis, and the reappearance of the Word in the suprahistorical *Momente* existentially perceived in the interstices of the historical order. As a consequence, many twentieth-century Protestant theologians have faced a dilemma: should they opt for Troeltsch and the ascesis of historicism, or follow Barth on the dialectical path and renegotiate theologies of the Word?[14] In reality, this dilemma accords too dominant a role to historicism as the mediator of modernity, for, as is argued below, Christian theology has undergone an aborted and unsatisfactory encounter with modernity. This is the product, at least in part, of the institutional arrangements that have compounded the isolation of theology in the Anglo-Saxon world.

Ernst Troeltsch and his friend and colleague Max Weber were jointly responsible for the initiation and development of an organizational typology, the celebrated church–sect distinction, which related the social structure of religious organizations to belief and religious behavior. The dichotomies formulated by Weber and Troeltsch have been employed in systematic study of the whole Western Christian tradition. The further refinement of this theoretical approach proved particularly fruitful in the study of differentiated North American Protestantism, religious sects, and new religious movements. More recently, the church–sect typology and stratification theory have been applied to the study of the New Testament church.

H. R. Niebuhr[15] took up the Weberian church–sect typology and applied it to the analysis of the growth of denominations in a way typical of the pragmatic appropriations made by theologians. It is significant that Niebuhr's text is repeatedly cited within the theological literature, whereas, by contrast, the later sociological discussion of social movements has largely failed to make a transition to theology. Thus, while this latter discussion has considerable importance for understanding the dynamics of religious group behavior and is thus of relevance to contemporary theology, it has remained largely within the sphere of influence of the sociology of religion. In such particular contexts disciplinary differentiation and the corresponding protective, interest-driven strategies of disciplines (and subdisciplines like the sociology of religion) may distort and fragment what should ideally be a more comprehensive and integrated approach. Such failures of connection have had an impact not only upon the ongoing task of theology, but also on the informed study of religion. As a specific example, while the French sociologist Alain Touraine's studies of new social movements and of "post-industrial society" have had important implications for research conducted by, for example, the sociologist James Beckford into new religious movements in "advanced industrial society", the further step of applying such work in the field of theology has proved harder to achieve.[16]

The Weberian influence extends far beyond the much-cited "Protestant Ethic" thesis and the economic sociology of the first volume of *Economy and Society*. The theoretical work of the American sociologist Talcott Parsons (who did much to transmit Weber's ideas to the United States) and the structuration theory of the English sociologist Anthony Giddens, to take but two examples, both owe a considerable debt to Weber. The sociological tradition of grand theory has until relatively recently had minimal impact upon the practice of theology. Our fourth type, the mutual assimilation of theological and sociological categories, does express a greater measure of appropriation of Parsonian systems theory, but, as will become apparent, this is achieved at the cost of downplaying the substantive content of the theology in favor of phenomenological and systemic description. In reality, confrontation with modernity exacts a higher price, and this is perhaps nowhere more apparent than in Dietrich Bonhoeffer's attempt to relate a theology of the Word to convincing analysis of the social being of the Christian community.

Dietrich Bonhoeffer: Theology recruits sociology

Dietrich Bonhoeffer was raised in the elite center of German cultural life and he thus absorbed the major theological and cultural influences of his time. After early experience as a pastor he became convinced that there were profound flaws in a theology which seemingly failed to equip Christians to act effectively and in a distinctive way in a hostile social reality. Worse, this theology later proved incapable of resisting its political abuse by the German Christians. In his doctoral thesis, *Sanctorum Communio* (1930), Bonhoeffer engaged with the question as to whether Christianity has a sociologically definable essence. Taking up Ferdinand Toennies' famous categories of community (*Gemeinschaft*) and association (*Gesellschaft*), Bonhoeffer tried to understand how the church might enact itself in the context of a post-organic, associative modernity, and whether, furthermore, it had a sociologically definable essence which Bonhoeffer identified (in debate with K. L. Schmidt) as that of an agapeistic community. *Sanctorum Communio* is a pioneering work, but it was a relatively isolated example of the recruitment of specifically sociological conceptuality in the service of a theology of the Word. In terms of both substance and methodology this text remains an erratic and undeveloped element in Bonhoeffer's curtailed theological achievement. Besides the term "sanctorum communio," others such as "ethics as formation," "presence" in Christology, "religionless Christianity," and the "ultimate" and "penultimate" in theological ethics passed into post-World War II theological reflection in Europe and North America. Bonhoeffer's sensitivity to the all-pervasiveness of totalitarian social systems, which first became apparent in his observation of the German émigré community in Barcelona and was later developed in confrontation with National Socialism, is still of immense relevance. This was demonstrated not least in the struggle against apartheid in South Africa, but now in the post-communist era, when capitalism is without effective critique or constraint, Bonhoeffer's assertion of the penultimacy of all things over against the ultimacy of the divine has gained a new and urgent relevance.[17]

A second important aspect of Bonhoeffer's theological legacy consists in his confrontation with the progressive secularization of Western society and culture. This is an issue that not only provoked the so-called "secular theology" of the 1960s, but also provides within theological reflection the major parallel to an issue that dominated much postwar sociological study of religion. In much-quoted passages in the *Letters and Papers from Prison*, Bonhoeffer set out an agenda in which he accepted and ingested the implications of secularization, albeit with highly paradoxical consequences for theology. It was apparent to Bonhoeffer that the emergence of the world's autonomy, which had origins in science, religion, philosophy, politics, and natural law, was an inescapable reality. He concluded: "God as a working hypothesis in morals, politics or science, has been surmounted and abolished."[18] Thus any yearning for a lost golden past in the Middle Ages would be mere despair cloaked by infantile nostalgia. Bonhoeffer takes with absolute seriousness Kant's strictures on maturity as emergence from heteronomy and his injunction *Sapere aude* – dare to know – is incumbent not least upon Christians. Rather than side with either Barth (whose ontology Bonhoeffer had criticized in *Act and Being*) or Nietzsche (and relinquish theological language altogether), Bonhoeffer admits the reality of secularizing modernity and strives to interpret it theologically.

> And we cannot be honest unless we recognize that we have to live in the world *etsi deus non daretur*. And this is just what we do recognize – before God! God himself compels us to recognize it. So our coming of age leads us to a true recognition of our situation

before God. God would have us know that we must live as men who manage our lives without him. The God who is with us is the God who forsakes us (Mark 15: 34). The God who lets us live in the world without the working hypothesis of God is the God before whom we stand continually. Before God and with God we live without God. God lets himself be pushed out of the world on to the cross. He is weak and powerless in the world, and that is precisely the way, the only way, in which he is with us and helps us. Matthew 8: 17 makes it quite clear that Christ helps us, not by virtue of his omnipotence, but by virtue of his weakness and suffering.[19]

While it would be idle to pretend that Bonhoeffer's response to secularization was to play a large role in the postwar research or theoretical work of mainstream sociologists, his account did set an agenda worked out by theologians who sought further to explore the idea of a so-called non-religious gospel and a "secular city" in which thoroughgoing secularity could itself provide the basis of theological *jouissance*. Above all, and despite the relatively outdated character of the sociological theory he used, Dietrich Bonhoeffer provides an enduring theological prototype of critical and responsible reflexivity in the face of modernity. As will be argued further in the conclusion of this chapter, it is the development and reinforcement of such a reflexivity that has to be a central feature of a socioscientifically informed reconstitution of the theological task today. Whereas it is arguable that Troeltsch capitulates to modernity as he understood it and that Bonhoeffer sought to create a dialectical cohabitation which preserved the tensions in the confrontation, our next example, the work of Edward Farley, proposes a mutual absorption which blunts the substantive edges of both theology (as grounded in tradition and authority) and social science (as bearer of modernity).

Edward Farley: Theology and social science mutually merged?

It is not our present purpose to analyze or evaluate in detail the theological proposals of Edward Farley. What is of major concern here is how this representative thinker has assimilated socioscientific insights and made them mutual and intrinsic aspects of a method that seemingly overcomes any contested divergence between theology and the social sciences. Farley endorses theological proposals that reverse both the Barthian tendency to polarize "faith" and "religion" and the whole post-Enlightenment predilection for reconstructionist theologies which adhere to and amplify a single category of ethical or affective experience which then becomes the medium of theological construction. In this he is directly assisted by broadly phenomenological methods.

In *Ecclesial Man* (1975) Edward Farley tackled the problem of foundations, the ways in which realities are pregiven to theology, whereas *Ecclesial Reflection* (1982) concerns judgment, the ways in which those realities lay claim to truth. The task of foundations is, according to Farley, "that of describing faith, the faith world, the community of faith (ecclesial existence) as the matrix of reality-givenness."[20] The "criteriology" expounded in *Ecclesial Reflection* begins with an "archeology" of the "house of faith," which is analogous to Heidegger's critique of the history of ontology. Furthermore, Farley propounds a "phenomenology of tradition," that is, a phenomenology of "ecclesial process and its bearers."[21] The implications of this are spelt out clearly and pertain directly to our interpretation, for,

> the move from foundations and pregivenness to theological judgment is not simply a move into philosophy of religion nor from the determination of faith to the general level of ontology. Theological judgments are made from a historical faith-community which has a determinate corporate memory carried in a determinate network of symbols. The bearers of that determinacy, even written collections from the past, play some role in judgment. And the nature of that role is established not by authority but by the structure of the ecclesial process itself. This is why a phenomenology and even sociology of tradition plays such a central part in this prolegomenon.[22]

This sort of approach emancipates theology from the constraints of historicism and purports to overcome difficulties posed by alternative principles used by the ancestral "houses" of authority of Protestantism and Catholicism. More seriously, while this approach ostensibly liberates theology from the "house of authority," it thereby sidesteps the critique of power. Theology comes into existence at the point of correlation between the "meaning and proper function" of the literature of the ecclesial community and the "nature of ecclesiality and its duration over time."[23] Thus, theological reflection consists in "the depiction of ecclesiality (portraiture), the truth question, and reflective praxis."[24] In effect, the description and analysis of the means of "social duration" (Pitirim Sorokin) of ecclesial bodies replaces the prescriptive role of outdated, unacceptable tradition. It is an open question as to why such an approach should result in a distinctively Christian theology as opposed to the highly general, even reified description of "ecclesial being."

The intention here is not to test the adequacy of this sophisticated sociological and phenomenological synthesis as such, but to raise questions that stem from the broader context of the disjunction of theology and the social sciences. Thus the phenomenological approach exploited by Farley makes full and free use of apposite sociological conceptuality, but as *theology* is it more than a religiously nuanced "portraiture," and thus simply a phenomenology of religion? George Lindbeck's use of the idea of a "cultural linguistic practice" is similar in some ways to that of Farley; their American background of pragmatism enables both. There is a parallel between the phenomenological approach and recent reconstruals of Christian theology through the medium of theories of the origin and nature of language.[25] Both use theory as the basis for constructive proposals that appear to emancipate theological reflection from the Enlightenment critique. Yet can the Enlightenment principle be banished so easily? Is the descriptive phenomenological approach (or indeed the linguistic turn) not in some way an evasion? Our answer to these questions begins with an exploration of some of the wider issues affecting the relation of theology and the social sciences touched upon in the following section.

Postmodern quasi-fundamentalism (John Milbank)

One drastic and influential response to the whole problematic of the relation of theology and the social sciences is that advocated by the English theological thinker John Milbank in his monumental work *Theology and Social Theory*. Milbank provides an extended "archeology" of the "heresy" of secular (i.e., sociological) thought as it has diverged from Christian truth, and then poses an uncompromising either–or. Secular social theory and Christianity in effect stand in contradiction to each other. All the main components of secular social theory have a (usually genetic) relation with Christianity, and the main bulk of Milbank's work is dedicated to exposing these connections. Because there is no ultimate foundational basis in *rationality* for distinguishing between the claims of Christianity and those of secular reason, the project consists in an "exercise in skeptical relativism." Ultimacy is not a matter of rational choice; the Christian *perspective* is *persuasive* and not conveyed through "the apologetic mediation of human reason" (that is, put less ambitiously, through *argument* as such). Correspondingly, in a *Nietzschean* postmodernity the Christian perspective is offered to theologians for their positive appropriation.

Thus, according to Milbank, as metadiscourse and cultural–linguistic practice, "Christianity" relativizes modern (i.e., "liberal") theology, which is seen to be an immanent idolatry (the "oracular voice of some finite idol" stemming from history, psychology, or transcendental philosophy). Any "liberal" theology construed as an adjunct of secular reason faces a dilemma: it either fuses idolatrously with a particular immanent field of knowledge, or it is effectively alienated and "confined to intimations of a sublimity beyond representation."[26] Taken in the latter sense, theology as a "sublimity beyond representation" negatively affirms (from Milbank's point of view questionably) an autonomous secular realm open to rational understanding.

The situation is, however, further compounded by another complexity. While theology is not to be identified with secular reason it is nevertheless a wholly contingent historical construct embedded in "semiotic and figural codings" (in other words, its horizons are always those of cultural–linguistic practice). This state of affairs is conceded and endorsed: there can be no return to, or restoration of, the premodern position of Christianity. Christianity must neither accommodate nor adapt itself to the space apparently left to it within social reality. Any such involvement weakens Christianity as faith and as radical praxis by (mistakenly) searching for common ground.

It is at this juncture that Milbank notes a fundamental conjuncture: the postmodern necessity of myth. Nietzsche has shown that all cultural associations are traceable to the will-to-power. For Milbank, Nietzsche further indicates that the basis of *all* social and economic power is "religious" inasmuch as myth masks the will-to-power. Thus, social theory and theology subsist on the same ground: to pass *beyond* Nietzsche is to recognize "the necessity and yet the ungrounded character of some sort of metanarrative, some privileged transcendent factor, even when it comes disguised as the constant element in an immanent process."[27]

There can be no significant "sociological" representation of religion and theology precisely because *religion* is the ultimate transcendental. All forms of secular reason (and thus social science) can be traced archeologically to, and then deconstructed into, their *theological* progenitors. This can be understood as the *inversion* (not merely the reconstrual) of Hans Blumenberg's account of the "legitimacy" of modernity (as opposed to the perverse Christian obstruction of human *curiositas*).[28] Seen thus, secularity and secular discourse are *heresy* in relation to orthodox Christianity, and the archeological investigations will show that all "scientific" social theories are in fact "theologies or anti-theologies" in disguise.

We hear two "voices" in Western culture. The first is classical and medieval, the voice of an Alasdair MacIntyre speaking in Platonic–Aristotelian–Augustinian–Thomist terms.[29] The second is the nihilistic, Nietzschian voice which historicizes and seeks to show that "every supposedly objective reasoning simply promotes its own difference, and disguises the power which is its sole support."[30] In the final analysis the first, the voice of "Christian virtue," triumphs. In such a setting, a scenario implying a reading of the whole Western tradition, Christianity may reassert its total originality:

> Christianity, however, recognizes no original violence. It construes the infinite not as chaos, but as harmonic peace which is yet beyond the circumscribing power of any totalizing reason. Peace no longer depends upon the reduction to the self-identical, but is the *sociality* of harmonious difference . . . Christianity . . . is the coding of transcendental difference as peace.[31]

At the very last moment Christianity subverts and exposes the Nietzschian assertion that "difference, non-totalization and indeterminacy of being necessarily imply arbitrariness and violence."[32] In conclusion, Milbank posits a "third voice" which pursues the above "argument," which amounts in effect to a "choice," an effective *seduction* by one encoding as opposed to the other. This is what we might call the ecclesial supersession, a sublation in which a "historicist and pragmatist, yet *theologically* realist" position is advanced, in which no claim is made to "represent" an objective social reality; instead, the social knowledge advocated is but the continuation of ecclesial practice, the imagination in action of a peaceful, reconciled social order, beyond even the violence of legality.[33]

On the assumption that "truth is social," then a "lived narrative" projects and "represents" the triune God who is "transcendental peace through differential relation."[34] This is the ultimate "social science" and the sole offer that may establish theology, give content to the idea of "God," and impress itself upon the world through practice. The metadiscourse of theology is the "discourse of non-mastery" that may alone save us from nihilism. In the final analysis, this is a *theological* transvaluation of all "theology," myth, and "religion" (and the nihilistic human condition that they mask). Social science is at best a signpost to the root from which there has been catastrophic deviation; at worst it is a heretical perversion.

Milbank posits an abstract, quasi-manicheeistic (yet mutually involuted) opposition of false alternatives which entails abuses of both "theology" and "social theory." In effect, both "theology" and "social theory" (equivalent for present purposes to the social sciences) are reduced to the *rhetorics* embedded in and expressive of cultural practices in a way that universalizes Nietzschian perspectivism. But this procedure rules out through *a priori* occultation the wide variety of rationalities, epistemological strategies (not least induction), and epistemic resolutions that characterize both these areas of intellectual activity. Construed thus, theology becomes the imposition of stasis, a rearward-looking construal that has consequences that paralyze theology as embedded, grace-driven reflection entrenched in the real conflict and injustices of the human condition. Active theological thinking *from the future*, the anticipatory consciousness of the Spirit, is excluded. In somewhat extravagant but not altogether misleading terms, John Milbank may be said once more to enact the infinite cunning of reason that extinguishes itself and migrates in order to survive as "theology."

Sociology as a discipline should not be construed *reductively* and *exclusively* in terms of the perverse metanarrative of secular reason. Sociology and the social sciences may also be classically construed as the *critical representation* and *clarification* of the patterns of social organization necessary to the sustenance of humane societies, rather than (as Milbank would have it) the partner in the promotion of an allegedly necessary and totalitarian violence of order. The tasks of theology and sociology are mutual in at least as much as they address the human condition in exploratory and interpretative terms, and do not subsume (in however virtuoso a fashion) *everything* into the dance of death and totalitarian logic of Western secular reason. Moreover, sociology and theology which embody concerns for the other cannot afford to neglect or express contempt for ethnography, that is, the effective representation and interpretation of what is actually happening in human lives. Both theology and the social sciences should be concerned in their distinctive ways with life and with how things are.

On a scale of proximity and modes of negotiation and assimilation between social science and theology, fundamentalism tends to flee modernity (and thus the social sciences), but in so doing it may be tempted to exploit social scientific insights in instrumental ways to facilitate conversion experiences; Troeltsch tended to absorb theological questions into historicism and early social science; Bonhoeffer attempted (not least under the influence of Karl Barth) to maintain a dialectical cohabitation of theological and sociological categories; and Edward Farley has expressed theology in terms of a thoroughgoing appropriation of the phenomenology of ecclesial being. John Milbank drives a wedge between theology and the social sciences and demands that we resist all accommodations and decide upon one or the other in what amounts to a despairing postmodern quasi-fundamentalism of paradoxical sophistication. This depiction of possible ways of configuring the relation of theology and the social sciences is in no way exhaustive, but it is representative of a range of possible strategies in a fraught borderland.

Theology's use of social science: Some observations

The exceptionally high profile of Protestant theology in German thought and culture is unique in Europe, if not the world. Moreover, many of the subdisciplines within Christian theology either originated or were given vital impulse in Germany throughout the post-Enlightenment period. The contextual character of this widely disseminated and thereby universalized theological tradition cannot be left out of account.[35] It is only recently that a leading role appears to have passed to the United States and, in consequence, it is reasonable to anticipate the assimilation of distinctively American concerns and insights. The ascendancy of American theology is remarkable as regards both Protestant theology from the North and Catholic liberation theology from the Latin South, respectively. This growing, albeit differentiated hegemony is also evident in the proliferation of feminist and other special interest and communitarian theologies. These developments incorporate societal changes of profound significance. The shift of interest away from the archetypically "male" paradigm of all-embracing, hegemonic theologies of largely German inspiration, toward the contemporary pluralism of *theologies* of gender, race, ethnicity, sexual orientation, poverty, and so on, is contemporaneous with a major crisis in the ethnic "melting-pot" of the United States.[36] The responsible use of such theologies is, however, improbable apart from the just and intelligent deployment of social scientific insight that defines the constituencies to which each type of theological reflection primarily relates. In a "glocalized" (Roland Robertson) world, liberal values, conceptions of universal human rights, and theologies which imply catholicity are now prone to systemic crisis and readily attacked as postcolonial hegemony, cultural neo-imperialism or regressive patriarchy. Without effective means of representing human universals there is a danger that it will become impossible to represent any interests over and above those of special groups. It is at this juncture that religious and theological insights once more become an important resource.[37]

The brief typology presented in the foregoing section of this chapter and the differentiation and pluralism in contemporary theology alluded to above illuminate dimensions of the changing relationship between Christian theology and the social sciences. On a more abstract level what concerns us are the implications of what the English sociologist Anthony Giddens means when he asserts that modernity is intrinsically sociological.[38] In other words, if sociological (that is to say reflexive, as opposed to tradition-dominated) self-understanding is a defining feature of modernity, then theology is faced with the requirement that it engage in the comprehensive negotiation of its relationship with the social sciences. While some forms of liberation theology may have attempted this inasmuch as they sought to build contextual theological foundations influenced by Marxist insight (thereby invoking the consequences of a problematic alliance), the Western engagement has been fragmented and incomplete. The mediation of modernity and theology's response to it is, however, a matter of central importance around which cluster many aspects of the relation of theology and the social sciences.

Christian theology remains, and it should rightly so remain, church- or community-related theology. Despite its many ambiguous (and largely successful) attempts to gain and retain academic legitimacy, theological thought often subsists in social and economic contexts which distance it from any need to reckon, not merely with secularization, but also with the fuller impact of modernization and modernity. "Modernity," itself a much-disputed concept, has been opposed to "tradition." For some social scientists, the very idea of "tradition" is not merely seen as inherently problematic, but as a primary and defining characteristic of a superseded premodern condition.[39] Contemporary culture and society may thus be regarded as posttraditional.[40] Other sociologists have argued for the continuing force of the idea of tradition in ways that, for example, in part endorse Farley's formulations.[41] What greatly complicates the situation that we now encounter are two further factors. On the one hand, social reality has not remained static: the "sacred" has undergone ambiguous displacements and transmutations in reaching accommodations with modernity in what, for example, George Steiner has suggestively described as the twentieth-century "after-life of religion."[42] On the other hand, the Barthian critique of "religion" and the scission between theology and the academic study of religion has tended to disable the former's ability to come to terms with the resurgence of religion and its ambiguous "after-life."

A theology uninformed by engagement with the social sciences may well persist as a "radical," elaborate form of "false consciousness," but may well do so at a dangerous distance from what the German Reformed theologian Jürgen Moltmann once referred to as the "dialectic of the real."[43] This "real" now includes a range of new possibilities and challenges. For example, poststructuralist intimations of theology (or *a*theology),[44] New Age "self religion,"[45] globalized spiritualities,[46] goddess-centered neo-paganism,[47] varieties of fundamentalism,[48] and ecological religiosity all tend to outflank a wearied Christian theology often for the most part concerned with the internal politics of its own decline. Thus, Christian theology not only has to face up to its own partially aborted reception of modernity, but also its correlative fear and ignorance of new developments which meet human religious needs the world over. In addition, it must also confront and come to terms with acute and profound problems with regard to gender, power, and the status of nature that it will only begin adequately to comprehend if it successfully relocates itself at the conjuncture of premodernity (where its origins lie), modernity (where it underwent crippling damage), and the "postmodern condition" or, less contentiously, "high" or "late" modernity, in which new possibilities open up on a daily basis. The idea and the reality of "tradition"[49] have to comprehend and manage these dialectically cohabiting dimensions. If theology fails to achieve this then it may persist as *mauvaise foi* for as long as funding continues, but it will not be answering the challenge posed by the history and present state of the human and social sciences. To these challenges and opportunities we shall shortly return.

The argument pursued so far in this chapter does not imply that no effective collaborations between sociologists and theologians have taken place.[50] Our contention is, however, that such collaboration is not only marked more by discontinuity than coherence but also that underlying alliance and conflict there are major unresolved issues. These stem from the historic differentiation of disciplines and adjustments which relate to modernization, secularization, and the nature of the Enlightenment project. It will therefore require thoroughgoing methodological renewal within theology (rather than occasional intellectual transfers by unusually energetic theologians) before the disjunctions between theology, the sociology of religion, and mainline social theory are better understood and viable working relationships established.

Theology and the Social and Human Sciences: An Agenda

In my contribution to the second edition of *The Modern Theologians* I argued that much Christian theology had become isolated from major developments in the social sciences. This was not least as a result of the post-Enlightenment distribution of disciplines into faculties of humanities and theology masterminded by such figures as Wilhelm von Humboldt and Friedrich Schleiermacher in the course of the foundation of the University of Berlin. Nonetheless, some theologians have been aware of the damaging consequences of such alienation, and my purpose was to develop a representative typology of such responses. This modest project was, as it were, a limited historical outline of the "internal relations" of theological discourses subsisting at a distance from emergent sociological traditions. The latter were themselves self-consciously predicated upon the assumption that "theology," "faith," and "tradition" were localized aspects of a phenomenon that was in a strict sense a premodern residuum, the criticism or interpretation of which was, following the inspiration of Immanuel Kant, the *sine qua non* of human maturity.

Thus far, the present chapter has consisted in a lightly revised version of its predecessor: it has undergone little more than a tidying of loose ends and a sharpening of focus. The basic hypothesis of the chapter – that mainline modern Christian theology has for the most part been preoccupied with securing its own survival and evolved a range of internal strategies designed to achieve this perpetuation of identity in the face of the challenge of the social sciences – remains unchanged. Theology thus suffers from a fateful divorce from a context that is in reality no less fraught. On the one hand, there has been an ongoing "crisis" in the human sciences and the strategic *epoche*, or bracketing out of knowledges in the interests of a single set of scientific protocols, classically depicted in Edmund Husserl's *Die Krisis der europäischen Wissenschaften und die transcendentale Phänomenologie* (1935–7).[51] On the other hand, Michel Foucault's late twentieth-century account of the *episteme* and the "deaths" of "God" and "man" in his "archeology" of the human sciences likewise confronts and systematizes nihilism.[52] Husserl and Foucault thus frame some of the difficulties that surround the contemporary juxtaposition of the discourses of "theology" and "religious studies." The most pointed, indeed extreme, informed response to these multiple crises is represented by so-called "radical orthodoxy" and its depiction of the "other" of the "heretical discourses" of social theory. In 1996, when first completing this contribution, I argued as follows.

> We inhabit a wilderness, yet somewhere there are rocks that may be touched and from which sustenance will flow. Each person who is aware of such possibilities may seek out sources from within their own faith-tradition; ecumenism must now become an ecumenism of religions, not merely of belief systems within any given tradition. It is not the case that in premodernity the touching places were wholly obvious, nor is it true to think that reflexivity is the sole prerogative of modernity. Nor again should we believe that religion and theology die off on the margins in a secularized modernity; indeed, the resurgence of religion and religiosity precludes such naivety. The theological task of our day should not consist simply in attempts (however sophisticated) to recapture a lost past; yet "tradition" as a resource is as refunctionable in postmodernity (or "late modernity") as are all other cultural artifacts. How this reappropriation is responsibly to be conducted is a task we are only beginning to learn. The mechanical recapitulation of Christian doctrine merely as items in an inherited belief system, undertaken as though nothing had happened, is indefensible.
>
> The reconfiguration of the theological task requires immersion in the dialectics of identity as they emerge from the history and evolution of the social and human sciences in the transitions of modernity. Religion and the expression of its critical and responsible reflexivity, theology, can become methodologically equipped to address this enigma of identity. They will have to do so, however, while being willing to confront the absolute contrast of the individual and the collective, the relative and the absolute, and the immanent and the transcendent. These and other contingencies touched upon in this chapter are inherent in our condition as human beings. This means that all theology should be contextual and should relate to human needs, be it at the level of basic communities or the global condition. It should also be stirred by an articulate hope that things could be other than they are.[53] Anything less is a perversion. Understanding must be grounded in such correlations, but it is misleading to suppose that co-responsibility of this kind implies a contempt for the intellect. As Antonio Gramsci argued for

socialism, so for a theology informed by the social and human sciences, the theologian should be an organic intellectual, a risk-taker, a humane entrepreneur of the mind who is willing to withstand the systemic marginality that afflicts all those who are willing to cross boundaries in the borderland that is normative in the contemporary human condition.

In this passage the writer places himself above an empty present, cut off from the past, yet expressing the somewhat plaintive hope that new life might be somewhere found. By contrast, I now seek to argue for a contextual and somatic theology, a reflexive and mutual practice of committed embodiment, that may emerge in the course of an exposition of the "external relations" of theology as the latter seeks renewal in an increasingly globalized and fraught "new world order." By these means the global–local tension central to mainline contemporary social theory may be explored and recast in terms of the successive elective affinities, and thus the analogies, that surround and infuse the "ecologies" (physical, psychosocial, and human) in which humankind seeks to survive.

We have argued throughout this chapter that the current inner configurations of both mainline theology and the academic study of religion, besides the problematic disrelation between these fields of endeavor, ill-fit either party to engage with the complex situation we have adumbrated. If we apply David Harvey's insights into the "loss of the political" that takes place in the "condition of postmodernity" (a "condition" which has yet fully to be addressed) to the spheres of religion and theology, then it becomes apparent that a critique is required capable of finding its way behind this disciplinary dichotomy so as to articulate and interrogate the terms upon which "modernity" and the correlative "postmodern condition" have themselves been constituted. In other words, the transcendental critique of "modernity" should precede and then accompany the critique of modernity's representation of the religious factor.

Where, then, might we commence such a critique, and where, moreover, might we find a point of leverage? In the first instance my answer is that we invoke, radicalize, and enact the doctrine of incarnation, and reconstrue this as embodiment in the "far country" that is the recomposing religio-spiritual field today. In the absence of effective political or cultural critique of the "post-human condition" and the grotesque commodification of the production of the human in education, health, the social services, and the management of deviant behavior, we must first enter the backyard of our own somatic experience, bearing with us the hard questions that will bring no immediate comfort. This shift from "optic to haptic," from speculative theory to radical embodiment, might allow us to touch ground in the tension between global hegemony and the social and biological construction of the individual body, our own bodies. This will be a somatic theology, a mode of inquiry embedded in the specificities of place, yet simultaneously a practice that entails a theoretical striving for comprehension of enough of the whole for us to act in an informed way, and to promote a committed yet critical discourse that recovers normative judgment in an era of fragmentation, panic, and terror.

So contextualized, we may argue that Christian theology ought to seek reconnection with the primordial processes of deep socialization and with the globally distributed, but equally oppressed, dimensions of pre-traditional experience represented, for example, in the shamanic practice of the wounded healer, and thus with crucial factors in a fragmented religio-spiritual field in a state of recomposition. A "somatic" theology could thus be represented and enacted as the discourse of integration in newly reconstrued spheres of practice. In turn, the somatic turn implies corresponding and doubtless controversial changes in the nature of ecclesiology and the facilitative role of ministry in a transpersonal Christian community of a "priesthood of all believers." As I now construe the situation, a social scientifically informed reembedding of the gospel in a detraditionalized modernity might in this allow for fruitful reengagement with the "crisis" in the human sciences and with the "deaths" of "God" and "man." This could be conducted on a basis which recognized the deep, enduring, evolutionarily necessary and intercultural commonalities of the human condition; it would be a somatic, transpersonal, and transformatory theology.[54]

Notes

1   The term "human sciences" includes not only the social sciences but also other fields, notably discourse, law, history, literary theory and literature, and so forth. See the introduction to R. H. Roberts and J. M. M. Good, *The Recovery of Rhetoric* (Charlottesville, VA, 1993). As regards the future agenda, see Roberts, *A Critique of the Social-scientific Study of Religion* (Cambridge, 2005).

2   See Z. Bauman, *Modernity and the Holocaust* (London, 1989) and *Postmodern Ethics* (London, 1993).

3   See P. Heelas, S. Lash, and P. Morris, *Detraditionalization: Critical Reflections on Authority and Identity* (Oxford, 1995).

4   See C. Taylor, *The Sources of the Self* (Cambridge, 1989).

5   See R. H. Roberts, "Barth and the Eschatology of Weimar," in R. H. Roberts (ed.), *A Theology on its Way: Essays on Karl Barth* (Edinburgh, 1991), pp. 169–99.

6   See J.-F. Lyotard, *The Postmodern Condition* (Manchester, 1984).

7   See A. Giddens, *The Consequences of Modernity* (Cambridge, 1990).

8   M. Foucault, *The Order of Things* (London, 1970).

9   W. Dilthey, *An Introduction to the Human Sciences* (London, 1988).

10 G. Kepel, *The Revenge of God* (Cambridge, 1994); M. Riesebrodt, *Pious Passion: The Emergence of Modern Fundamentalism in the United States and Iran* (Berkeley, CA, 1993).

11 See Kepel, *The Revenge of God*.

12 E. Troeltsch, *The Social Teaching of the Christian Church* (London, 1931); M. Mann, *The Sources of Social Power*, Vol. 1 (Cambridge, 1986).

13 E. Troeltsch, *The Absoluteness of Christianity and the History of Religion* (London, 1972).

14 For an unmatched account of this crucially important era in the history of modern Protestant theology, see C. Gestrich, *Neuzeitliches Denken und die Spaltung der dialektischen Theologie* (Tübingen, 1977).

15 H. R. Niebuhr, *The Social Sources of Denominationalism* (New York, 1975; first published 1929).

16 See A. Touraine, *The Post-Industrial Society* (London, 1974); J. A. Beckford, *Religion and the Advanced Industrial Society* (London, 1989).

17 See R. H. Roberts, *Religion and the Resurgence of Capitalism* (London, forthcoming).

18 D. Bonhoeffer, *Letters and Papers from Prison*, 3rd edn. (London, 1967).

19 Ibid, pp. 360–1.

20 E. Farley, *Ecclesial Reflection* (Philadelphia, PA, 1982), p. xiv.

21 Ibid, p. xv.

22 Ibid.

23 Ibid, p. xvii.

24 Ibid, p. xviii.

25 See G. Ward, *Barth, Derrida and the Language of Theology* (Cambridge, 1995).

26 J. Milbank, *Theology and Social Theory* (Oxford, 1990), p. 1.

27   Ibid, p. 2.
28   See H. Blumenberg, *The Legitimacy of the Modern Age* (Cambridge, MA, 1985).
29   A. MacIntyre, *After Virtue* (London, 1981).
30   Milbank, *Theology and Social Theory*, p. 5.
31   Ibid, pp. 5–6.
32   Ibid, p. 5.
33   Ibid, p. 6.
34   Ibid.
35   See R. H. Roberts, "The Reception of the Theology of Karl Barth in the Anglo-Saxon World: History, Typology and Prospect," in Roberts, *A Theology on its Way*, pp. 95–168, for a cross-cultural account of the reception of one major strand of this tradition.
36   This has been represented in dramatic terms by Samuel P. Huntington in "The Clash of Civilizations" in *Foreign Affairs* (1993), pp. 22–49.
37   An important countervailing attempt to restate universal values in the context of growing pluralism is the global ethic coordinated by the Swiss–German theologian Hans Küng and promulgated at the Parliament of the World's Religions held in Chicago in 1993. See R. H. Roberts, "Globalized Religion? The Parliament of the World's Religions (Chicago, 1993) in Theoretical Perspective," *Journal of Contemporary Religion*, 10 (1995), pp. 121–37.
38   See Giddens, *The Consequences of Modernity*.
39   Ibid.
40   See Heelas, Lash, and Morris, *Detraditionalization*.
41   See E. Shils, *Tradition* (London, 1981).
42   G. Steiner, *In Bluebeard's Castle* (London, 1977).
43   J. Moltmann, *The Crucified God* (London, 1976).
44   See P. Berry and A. Wernick, *The Shadow of Spirit* (London, 1992).
45   See P. Heelas, *The Sacralization of the Self* (London, forthcoming).
46   See Roberts, "Globalized Religion?"
47   See M. Sjöö and B. Mor, *The Great Cosmic Mother* (San Francisco, 1991).
48   See Kepel, *The Revenge of God* and Riesebrodt, *Pious Passion*.
49   See Shils, *Tradition*.
50   See R. Gill, *The Social Context of Theology* (London, 1975); D. Martin, J. Orme-Mills, and W. S. F. Pickering, *Sociology and Theology* (Brighton, 1980).
51   See E. Husserl, *The Crisis of European Sciences and Transcendental Phenomenology: An Introduction to Phenomenological Philosophy* (Evanston, IL, 1970), pp. 135–7, 248, 256–7.
52   Foucault, *The Order of Things*, pp. 384ff.
53   See R. H. Roberts, *Hope and its Hieroglyph: A Critical Decipherment of Ernst Bloch's "Principle of Hope"* (Atlanta, GA, 1990).
54   The position briefly intimated in these concluding observations is indicative of a changed approach to Christian theology's engagement with the human and social sciences that was not, in its rewritten form, felt by the editors to be appropriate for the third edition of *The Modern Theologians*. While not demurring from this editorial decision, I wish nonetheless to register my ownership of a more fully developed perspective which will, I trust, in due course appear elsewhere.

Bibliography

Bauman, Z., *Modernity and the Holocaust* (London, 1989).
—— *Postmodern Ethics* (London, 1993).
Beckford, J. A., *Religion and Advanced Industrial Society* (London, 1989).
Berry, P. and Wernick, A., *The Shadow of Spirit: Postmodernism and Religion* (London, 1992).
Blumenberg, H., *The Legitimacy of the Modern Age* (Cambridge, MA, 1985).
Bly, R., *Iron John: A Book About Men* (Shaftesbury, 1991).
Bonhoeffer, D., *Act and Being* (London, 1962).
—— *Sanctorum Communio: A Dogmatic Enquiry into the Sociology of the Church* (London, 1963).
—— *Letters and Papers from Prison*, 3rd edn. (London, 1967).
Bourdieu, P. and Wacquant, L. J. D., *An Invitation to Reflexive Sociology* (Chicago, 1992).
Dilthey, W., *Introduction to the Human Sciences: An Attempt to Lay a Foundation for the Study of Society and History* (London, 1988).
Entemann, W. F., *Managerialism: The Emergence of a New Ideology* (Madison, WI, 1993).

Farley, E., *Ecclesial Man: A Social Phenomenology of Faith and Reality* (Philadelphia, PA, 1975).

—— *Ecclesial Reflection: An Anatomy of Theological Method* (Philadelphia, PA, 1982).

Foucault, M., *The Order of Things: An Archaeology of the Human Sciences* (London, 1970).

Giddens, A., *The Consequences of Modernity* (Cambridge, 1990).

Gill, R., *The Social Context of Theology: A Methodological Enquiry* (London, 1975).

Habermas, J., *The Philosophical Discourse of Modernity* (Cambridge, MA, 1987).

Harvey, V. A., *The Historian and the Believer* (London, 1968).

Heelas, P., *The New Age Movement* (Oxford, 1990).

Heelas, P., Lash, S., and Morris, P., *Detraditionalization: Critical Reflections on Authority and Identity* (Oxford, 1995).

Husserl, E., *The Crisis of European Sciences and Transcendental Phenomenology: An Introduction to Phenomenological Philosophy* (Evanston, IL, 1970).

Kepel, G., *The Revenge of God: The Resurgence of Islam, Christianity and Judaism in the Modern World* (Cambridge, 1994).

Lyotard, J.-F., *The Postmodern Condition: A Report on Knowledge* (Manchester, 1984).

MacIntyre, A., *After Virtue: A Study in Moral Theory* (London, 1981).

Maffesoli, M., *The Time of the Tribes: The Decline of Individualism in Mass Society* (London, 1995).

Mann, M., *The Sources of Social Power, Vol. 1: A History of Power from the Beginning to AD 1760* (Cambridge, 1986).

Martin, D., Orme-Mills, J., and Pickering, W. S. F., *Sociology and Theology: Alliance or Conflict* (Brighton, 1980).

Mestrović, S. G., *The Barbarian Temperament: Toward a Postmodern Critical Theory* (London, 1993).

Milbank, J., *Theology and Social Theory: Beyond Secular Reason* (Oxford, 1990).

Moltmann, J., *The Crucified God: The Cross of Christ as the Foundation and Criticism of Christian Theology* (London, 1976).

Niebuhr, H. R., *The Social Sources of Denominationalism* (New York, 1975).

Novak, M., *The Spirit of Democratic Capitalism* (London, 1991).

Riesebrodt, M., *Pious Passion: The Emergence of Modern Fundamentalism in the United States and Iran* (Berkeley, CA, 1993).

Ritzer, G., *The McDonaldization of Society: An Investigation into the Changing Character of Social Life* (London, 1993).

Roberts, R. H., *Hope and its Hieroglyph: A Critical Decipherment of Ernst Bloch's "Principle of Hope"* (Atlanta, GA, 1990).

—— "The Reception of the Theology of Karl Barth in the Anglo-Saxon World: History, Typology and Prospect." In R. H. Roberts (ed.), *A Theology on its Way: Essays on Karl Barth* (Edinburgh, 1991), pp. 95–168.

—— "Barth and the Eschatology of Weimar." In R. H. Roberts (ed.), *A Theology on its Way: Essays on Karl Barth* (Edinburgh, 1991), pp. 169–99.

—— "Globalized Religion? The Parliament of the World's Religions (Chicago, 1993), in Theoretical Perspective," *Journal of Contemporary Religion*, 10 (1995), pp. 121–37.

—— *Religion, Theology and the Human Sciences* (Cambridge, 2001).

—— (ed.), *Religion and the Transformations of Capitalism: Comparative Approaches* (London, 1995).

—— *A Critique of the Social-scientific Study of Religion* (Cambridge, 2005).

Roberts, R. H. and Good, J. M. M., *The Recovery of Rhetoric: Persuasive Discourse and Disciplinarity in the Human Sciences* (Charlottesville, VA, 1993).

Schutz, A., *The Phenomenology of the Social World* (London, 1972).

Shils, E., *Tradition* (London, 1981).

Sjöö, M. and Mor, B., *The Great Cosmic Mother* (San Francisco, 1991).

Steiner, G., *In Bluebeard's Castle* (London, 1971).

Taylor, C., *The Sources of the Self: The Making of Modern Identity* (Cambridge, 1989).

Touraine, A., *The Post-Industrial Society: Tomorrow's Social History, Classes, Conflicts and Culture in the Programmed Society* (London, 1974).

Troeltsch, E., *The Social Teaching of the Christian Church* (London, 1931).

—— *The Absoluteness of Christianity and the History of Religion* (London, 1972).

Ward, G., *Barth, Derrida and the Language of Theology* (Cambridge, 1995).

Theology, Prayer, and Practice

"The theologian is the one who prays," according to Evagrius Pontus; and, as Mark McIntosh points out in his contribution to Part IV, for much of Christian history it would have been assumed that the relationship between theology, prayer, and practice needed no separate attention in a volume of this kind. Not only would the connections between theological work and spiritual formation have seemed indissoluble to earlier generations, but also the need to attend to the practical implications of theological work within the Christian community has long been recognized. A study of any other part of this volume, indeed, will reveal many ways in which theological work in the twentieth century has been shaped by theologians' spirituality and practice of Christianity, including pastoral activities and concerns.

However, the interrelationship of theology with prayer and practice does raise important questions of its own, questions that give rise to distinctive theological reflection. Stephen Pattison and Gordon Lynch show how the developing discipline of pastoral theology has interacted with the human sciences and with the consequences of modern theology's "turn to the human." They show the importance of pastoral and practical theology's commitment to making theological sense of particular lived experience, and trace how this commitment is worked out in liberal, neo-traditional, and liberationist approaches. Mark McIntosh, by contrast, discovers in twentieth-century and subsequent developments a move *away* from some of the emphases of post-Enlightenment theology – away from understandings of the human that reduced "spirituality" to anthropology, and towards a new integration of theology and spirituality, as seen in the work of two such different thinkers as Simone Weil and Hans Urs von Balthasar.

Theology and Spirituality

Mark A. McIntosh

Introduction: Rediscovering a Relationship

We have to speak of the *relationship* between theology and spirituality today for a simple reason: for most of modernity they have in fact existed separately. In terms of the broad history of Christian thought, however, this separation is an anomaly. It has, moreover, given rise to expressions of theology and spirituality that would have been mightily puzzling to earlier eras. It would, for example, have been inconceivable to Bernard of Clairvaux that one could seek a deeper theological understanding of any subject apart from the practice of real encounter with the living object of theological inquiry, God. It would have been equally inconceivable to, say, Catherine of Siena that anyone would seek to grow towards spiritual maturity apart from the communal theological teaching of practiced believers. So we are on the edge of a historic rediscovery: a gradual reimagining of what theology might look like when its spiritual integrity is recovered. We may be able to grasp, at least partially, what this could eventually look like if we recall very briefly the roots of this unity between theology and spirituality (perhaps we could call it a holy wisdom) and how sight of this unity was eclipsed.

Early Christianity shows an awareness of God marked by a certain characteristic sense of God's startling vivacity. Jesus' teaching in the synoptic gospels frequently employs images of hidden abundance and unexpected reversal. The narratives of his healing and feeding likewise bespeak a transforming and liberating power that seems to climax with the stories of Jesus' own newly abundant resurrection life out of death. For St. Paul, this transforming and re-creating power of God's life works within the world through the death and resurrection of Jesus (see Romans 6) and is poured out within Christ's followers as the Holy Spirit works within them a share in Jesus' relationship with the one he calls Abba (Romans 8). In a classic formulation, Paul writes: "I have been crucified with Christ; and it is no longer I who live, but it is Christ who lives in me. And the life I now live in the flesh I live by faith in the Son of God, who loved me and gave himself for me" (Galatians 2: 19–20). We can see here the perfect integrity of theology and spirituality, for the *theological* vision of God's rescuing action (at work in Christ's self-giving love) is inseparable from the *spiritual* transformation of Paul's identity and its new life as springing continually from the hidden or mystical presence of Christ ("it is Christ who lives in me"). It is worth noting how reciprocal are these two aspects. It is precisely the transforming spiritual power of Christ's presence that permits a genuine theological understanding of what God has accomplished in Christ; and conversely, the communal theological reflection on God's action in Christ creates the environing matrix in which believers learn how to mature through the spiritual practices of discipleship.

This theme of a hidden and transforming divine abundance reaches powerful new clarity in the Johannine literature. Here it becomes even more evident that only a true sharing in the Spirit, in Jesus' relationship with the Father, can author the ever deepening unfolding of the truth in Christ. In John's Gospel, Jesus says to the disciples: "I still have many things to say to you, but you cannot bear them now. When the Spirit of truth comes, he will guide you into all the truth . . . He will glorify me, because he will take what is mine and declare it to you. All that the Father has is mine" (16: 12–15). The Spirit who comes to animate the new life of believers is precisely the theologian *par excellence*, who glorifies Christ by bringing to light the Father's love for him within the very life of the community. There is no room for separation here between the advancement of theological understanding and the transforming spiritual life of the community within which this deeper understanding comes to light.

In later writers such as Athanasius of Alexandria, Augustine of Hippo, or Bonaventure, this integrity of spiritual growth and theological understanding anchors the whole of their endeavor. Here is a typical perspective from Basil the Great of Ceasaria, commenting on a passage from John 14 in which Jesus remarks that the "world" will not know the Spirit:

> By "world" . . . [Christ] means those who are tied down by a material and carnal life, and restrict truth to what is seen by their eyes. They refuse to believe in the resurrection, and become unable to see the Lord with the eyes of their hearts . . . A carnal man's mind is not trained in contemplation, but remains buried in the mud of fleshly lusts, powerless to look up and see the spiritual light of truth. So the "world" – life enslaved by carnal passions – can no more receive the grace of the Spirit than a weak eye can look at the light of a sunbeam. First the Lord cleansed His disciples' lives through His teaching, and then He gave them the ability to both see and contemplate the Spirit.[1]

Once again, we can see the intrinsic connection between proper theological vision and spiritual healing and maturation. For Christians of this era, true theology is a sharing in God's own wisdom and knowledge of reality, which they refer to as "contemplation." Needless to say, the content of such knowledge can only be realized within the *lives* of those who, through an apprenticeship of spiritual formation and growth, are able, as Basil puts it, "to look up and see the spiritual light of truth."[2] At the risk of some over-simplification, perhaps we could simply note a significant but easily overlooked difference between method and formation: on the one hand, we have a modern confidence in *method* as a set of procedures designed to circumvent the apparently distorting role of persons in the quest for knowledge (think of the paradigmatic influence of the scientific method in modern thought, including theology); and on the other hand, when this method is adopted in modern theology, it hides from us how different it really is from the earlier notion of *formation*.[3] For whereas method is designed to remove the personal, formation intends to embrace and transform the personal by exposing the whole of human existence to God.

While one might conceivably argue today about whether authentically Christian theology can flourish when pursued apart from the spiritual transformation of the theological investigator, such a possibility would never even have occurred to earlier eras. The standard pedagogical scheme of the ancient Mediterranean world (which Christian teachers from the time adapted) recognized necessary stages of moral growth and spiritual practice before one attained to the maturity *capable* of contemplating wisdom.[4] Thus, for example, Aristotle observed (*Nicomachean Ethics* 6.8) that while children can become accomplished in mathematics, they are rarely truly wise because a deep understanding of the principles of life and their fitting application (wisdom) requires considerable experience and maturity. Such a view was entirely congruent with early Christian notions of theology as a holy wisdom. Christianity is both a discourse (or teaching) and a way of life, and these would *not* in the ancient view be at all separable in practice.

Perhaps the earliest signs of such a division emerge as the rising cathedral schools of European cities evolve gradually into universities. The academic mission of these new venues for learning was quite different from the monastic schools – where growth in Christian knowledge had taken place in the context of practicing Christianity as a way of life. In the new universities, Christian discourse migrated from exegetical contemplation of biblical texts into a rational argument about logical propositions. While this may seem a trifling example of more massive intellectual shifts, it points to the very heart of the distinction between theology and spirituality that we now take for granted. For on the monastic model (inherited from ancient Christianity), theological inquiry takes place precisely in the encounter between the mysteriously beautiful forms of biblical language and the patient, apprentice-like attention of the inquirer. The scholastic shift to logical argument as the singular means of theological inquiry did not of itself alone entail a cessation of spiritual transformation in the inquirer, but it did usher such transformation off into a separate and sometimes carefully segregated category of pious devotional thought.[5]

Paradoxically, the modern turn to the subject which might have been expected to restore some voice to personal spiritual transformation in theological endeavors has seldom done so – at least not in ways revealing of the authentically *theological* significance of spirituality. The reason for this is that the notion of the self – precisely as conceived by modernity – has leaned toward a kind of theological solipsism in which the voice of the divine interlocutor (central to classical Christian spirituality) has been reduced to various states of subjective self-consciousness.[6] Even for thinkers sympathetic to the role of spiritual conversion in theology, this privileging of the "interior" has made it difficult to recover an authentic sense of the genuinely divine Other when interpreting Christian spirituality. The development in late modernity, however, of various forms of liberation and feminist theology has given rise to an important recognition: namely, that personal transformation cannot be divorced from a dialogical encounter with a genuinely liberating divine Other. And this has reopened the modern self to a relational interpretation of its constitution that need *not* threaten to reduce every theological insight to an implication of anthropology.

Survey: Return to the Sources

In the first half of the twentieth century, several evolving streams of thought had most influence both in obscuring and in recovering the relationship between theology and spirituality. Somewhat apart from the other movements (considered below) were the efforts of such important British thinkers as William Ralph Inge, Evelyn Underhill, and Cuthbert Butler, each of whom, in a number of works, recalled for their readers the theological and philosophical significance of Christian spiritual traditions. They wrote, inevitably, in the long shadow of William James' highly influential *Varieties of Religious Experience* (1902), which argued that one can prescind from questions of belief and interpretation in studying religious experience. The enormous popularity of this approach, which seems to allow value-free analysis of comparable spiritual experiences conveniently abstracted from their native religious cultures, has obvious ramifications: by simply bracketing out the theological and philosophical elements from spiritual experience (as merely cultural or dogmatic accretions upon a putatively pre-thematic experience), James' approach tended very drastically to silence the *theological* witness of Christian spirituality, and to reinforce a modern predilection for "interiority."[7]

But writers like Underhill, particularly through her later work as a lecturer and retreat leader, consistently held before the public mind the very obviously *theological* ideas and imagery of Christian spiritual writers from many eras. Summarizing much of what her study of Christian mystics taught her, Underhill observed:

> Since the life of prayer consists in an ever-deepening communion with a Reality beyond ourselves, which is truly there, and touches, calls, attracts us, what we believe about that Reality will rule our relation to it ... We make the first and greatest of our mistakes in religion when we begin with ourselves, our petty feelings and needs, ideas and capacities. The Creed sweeps us up past all this to God.[8]

Underhill was suggesting that *what* Christians believe about God was not simply a matter of indifference or, worse, an impediment on the way to a more gratifyingly inward basking in one's "own" spirituality. Her portrayal of Christian spiritual writers suggested that far from getting in the way of their spiritual journeys, their theological commitments continually tested their "vague, dilute, self-occupied spirituality" and held them open to "this superb vision of Reality" – and, reciprocally, their spirituality led them ever more deeply into a personal encounter with the mysteries of faith they believed: "We pray first because we believe something; perhaps at that stage a very crude or vague something. And with the deepening of prayer, its patient cultivation, there comes ... the enrichment and enlargement of belief, as we enter into first-hand communion with the Reality who is the object of our faith."[9]

A strangely parallel dilemma was unfolding within what has been called the "internal evolution of Thomism" in continental European thought.[10] In various ways, the Kantian–Jamesian divorce between experience and interpretation remained dominant, even as it played out within the dramatic contrasts between rationalist neoscholastics like Réginald Garrigou-Lagrange and transcendental Thomists like Joseph Maréchal. The more studiously that theologians constructed their edifices through an analysis of human subjectivity or consciousness, the more difficult it continued to be to hear the genuinely *theological* voice of Christian spirituality.[11] This strange obscuring of theological implications was perhaps inevitable, no matter whether the analysis was of the neoscholastic "natural theology" sort that kept divine involvement pristinely separated from the natural functioning of the soul, *or* of the transcendental Thomist sort that attempted (like Schleiermacher) to accept and move beyond the Kantian critiques by grounding theology in an analysis of experience *beyond* the *a priori* conditions (declared by Kant) for thematized knowing. In the neoscholastic case, the theological implications of Christian spirituality are away off in a rarified realm of highly unusual psychological states; and in the transcendental Thomist case, spiritual experience is primarily of interest as a piece of evidence for the existence of transcendental experience behind Kant's categories – and whatever theological language such experiences might happen to be couched in would ultimately be secondary.[12] In neither case could the integrity of theology and spirituality become perceptible, let alone persuasive.

To make matters even more difficult for genuine spirituality–theology conversation, the situation was just as problematic on the side of the "spiritual theology" of the day. Part of the problem was that by the early twentieth century (especially in France) a voluminous and influential literature, highly neoscholastic in orientation, had focused attention within spirituality very narrowly on the progressive states of the individual soul.[13] "Mysticism" had come to be associated with a carefully circumscribed experiential state of immediacy to God. Such a view was very far from the understanding of the mystical in Christian antiquity and the Middle Ages (i.e., as the hidden and beckoning presence of God in creation, the church's common life and worship, and above all in scripture). Once again, the tension was over whether one is best advised to start from interior cognition and experience *or* from concrete existence and history, and the balance was once again in favor of the former. Given this narrow construal of the spiritual life and of "mysticism," it is not surprising that even such later giants as Karl Rahner and Bernard Lonergan, developing the transcendental Thomist approach, still centered their reflections on an analysis of human self-transcendence and cognitional intentionality. The upshot of this development was that their highly creative and influential theologies continued to be shaped quite deeply by the epistemological dynamism of the human *individual* – and this in ways that have made it rather difficult to hear the authentically theological insights of mystical writers who consider the hidden presence of God in creation, or in the biblical word, or in the dialogical structures of ecclesial life, or more generally in political, gendered, and relational dimensions of historical human existence.

However, another more positive stream emerged from the work of such figures as Henri de Lubac, Henri Bouillard, Jean Daniélou, Marie-Dominique Chenu, André Marie Dubarle, Yves Congar, and Louis Bouyer, and came to be termed the New Theology (*nouvelle théologie*). Working respectfully with the thought of Aquinas, but returning decisively to the Christian sources of antiquity and earlier Middle Ages, these thinkers renewed the possibility of a dialogue between theology and spirituality that would no longer be restricted to an analysis of inner individual states of experience or of self-transcendence. An early and important forerunner of this perspective, the Benedictine Anselm Stolz, had already made the argument (in a work published in 1936) that the mystical is *not* chiefly related to unusual psychological or cognitional states.[14] Drawing on the very sort of patristic studies that the *nouvelle théologie* was to highlight, Stolz argued that at least three crucial shifts had occurred, almost unnoticed, by the time systematic theology and spiritual theology had been divided from one another in early modernity.

First, the spiritual life had come to be analyzed (as just noted above) almost entirely within categories of scholastic faculty psychology (drawn from an Aristotelian analysis of the intellect), rather than in terms of the liturgical and communal life of believers. This led, second, to a loss of imagery and conceptualities attuned to the language of dialogue, of encounter between God and the community as the sign of God's cosmic plan of salvation. Ultimately, suggested Stolz, this meant a loss of the fundamentally trinitarian and relational structure of the Christian spiritual life: for earlier theologians,

> the perfection of the creature . . . is essentially an assimilation to a divine Person, to the Son, the first image containing within Himself the entire perfection of the Father. The office of the Holy Ghost as dispenser of the divine life to creatures is to seize hold of man and to mold within him the image of the Son. The basis of the assimilation to the Son is the incarnation.[15]

But this relational and trinitarian conception of spirituality – a conception notably well-suited to interaction with theology – becomes almost inconceivable once the whole mode of conceptuality is shifted into neoscholastic terms of a bare "assimilation of an intellectual soul or appetitive soul to the being of God."[16] Indeed, Stolz suggests, it would be more translucent to the actual divine economy of salvation to recall that "mystical union with God is seen in its entirety as essentially Trinitarian"; for the mystical life depends entirely on the concrete historical missions of the Son and Word and it aims for an incorporation precisely into the relations of the divine Persons: "true mysticism is always Trinitarian, that is, implies definite relations to the individual Persons. Union with God can be accomplished only as a union corresponding to what God is in reality."[17] In Stolz's view, then, the mystical life consists "in the fact that, incorporated in the Holy Ghost to the Son, we are conducted by the Son to the Father. This goes back to all that was said of the sacraments, especially the Eucharist, in connection with union with Christ as the ultimate basis of mysticism."[18] This means, of course, that spirituality is once again in conversation with the central theological themes of revelation and salvation and redemption, of liturgical prayer and trinitarian life.

All this points to the third (and in some ways the most difficult) point Stolz had to make (indeed, de Lubac was later harshly condemned for developing this view in much more depth). The effacement of trinitarian imagery and perspective went hand in hand, argued Stolz, with views that *separated* nature and grace, and that conceived of grace as simply actuated by God rather like an extraneous efficient cause. Once this extrinsic picture of nature and grace is adopted, theology completely loses touch with an older view of grace as a participation in the unfolding trinitarian art, shaping and transforming the whole of creation and history through its likening to the divine "ideas" of all things that have been known and loved eternally in the Word and Spirit. The problem, said Stolz, was that this older view of grace (in terms of a trinitarian dynamism) afforded precisely that inherently dialogical structure within which theology and spirituality could converse and illuminate each other;

but, by contrast, the early modern extrinsicist view of the nature–grace distinction had in Stolz's judgment almost entirely collapsed the conceptual framework within which the integrity of theology and spirituality could be conceived.[19] By reconceiving spirituality in terms of the journey toward likeness to Christ inaugurated in baptism, Stolz and the New Theology writers began to rediscover the trinitarian and dialogical ground upon which theology and spirituality could meet. The section that follows just below considers the explorations of two pioneers into this newly rediscovered landscape.

Two Key Figures

Simone Weil

While she was working in London for the liberation of her native France, Simone Weil (1909–43) entered the following in her notebook for the last year of her life: "There is something mysterious in the universe which is in complicity with those who love nothing but the good."[20] From the time of her early studies on Descartes and Kant, Weil was a probing analyst of modern thought, yet always with an openness to this mysterious attraction of the good. Her interests in a wide range of ancient and folkloric literatures led to a turning point during a Holy Week spent at the French Benedictine Abbey of Solesmes in 1938. During this time, in the midst of her own agonizing migraines, she was led to a new understanding of the death and resurrection of Jesus: "In the course of these services the thought of the Passion of Christ entered into my being once and for all."[21] As this experience began to bear spiritual and intellectual fruit for her she noted that it sometimes unfolded itself in new ways while she read through George Herbert's poem "Love" (the poem's theme, "Love bade me welcome, but my soul drew back," clearly addressed a deep dimension of self-doubt and painful reticence in Weil's own experience). During one of these moments, she sensed a profound intimacy with Christ:

> I used to think I was merely reciting it as a beautiful poem, but without my knowing it the recitation had the virtue of a prayer. It was during one of these recitations that . . . Christ himself came down and took possession of me . . . Neither my senses nor my imagination had any part; I only felt in the midst of my suffering the presence of a love, like that which one can read in the smile on a beloved face.[22]

In the contours of this mystical encounter one can see central features of Weil's theological contribution: hidden divine presence in the world, a theological epistemology grounded in spiritual ascesis, and a profound recognition of the trinitarian self-humbling at the heart of reality.

Her high-culture background as a fiercely dedicated scholar, teacher, and intellectual in solidarity with suffering persons (she attempted to work with field hands, factory laborers, and anti-Franco forces in Spain) had led her to a deeply critical perspective on social questions and the crushing limits of the human condition. And from 1938 and, later, her family's enforced departure from France (from an assimilated family of Jews, Weil's parents insisted on taking her with them to America, much against her wishes), she began to envision *in nuce* a theology of hidden divine presence to humanity in the midst of affliction. Weil's perspective is, throughout, marked by a sensitivity to costly divine self-giving and to its sheer gratuity as an invitation of love to the creation. Central to her conception is an approach to the Trinity that very remarkably foreshadows (and in some ways remains unsurpassed by) later developments in the thought of such magisterial figures as Barth, Rahner, and von Balthasar (and later still among liberation theologians, perhaps Leonardo Boff in particular). She models what might be considered the hidden spiritual vocation of theology as a movement of intelligence responding to the divine speaking both within and beyond words and all creatures. Given the frequency and significance of references in her later notebooks to figures such as Origen, the Desert Fathers, medieval women mystical writers (e.g., Marguerite Porete), and John of the Cross, one can only speculate regarding the further development of her theological insights had she not died at age 34.

The universe exists, in Weil's view, through a continual act of divine renunciation, that is, through a divine desire to make space for the genuinely *other* – not only the other in God (the Trinity), but a creaturely other. But just as the trinitarian life always exists through a free act of loving, making way for an other, this same mode of dialogical existence pulses as the deep structure of every creature. And, indeed, Weil argues that the moment when a creature recognizes and consents to this giving of attention to another (even sometimes at great cost to self) is the moment when creaturely life has begun to fulfill its calling to share in the divine self-giving life. In such moments the very same pattern of trinitarian self-giving that grounds creation may become mystically present in the act of a human person's loving attention to another creature (in the following passage she has just commented on the parable of the good Samaritan):

> God is longing to come down to those in affliction. As soon as a soul is disposed to consent, though it were the last, the most miserable, the most deformed of souls, God will precipitate himself into it in order, through it, to look at and listen to the afflicted. Only as time passes does the soul become aware that he is there.[23]

This same act of self-giving attention, rendering humanity transparent to its divine source, can be offered to God through the most mundane tasks, in sublime artistic and scientific work, and among many other patterns of life, above all through "pure friendship," which "is an image of the original and perfect friendship that belongs to the Trinity and is the very essence of God. It is impossible for two human beings to be one while scrupulously respecting the distance that separates them unless God is present in each of them."[24]

What these disparate acts have in common is a freedom and agency that knows how to use even the constraints of necessity to offer this gift of compassionate attention to the other (in emulation of Christ, who makes from distorted acts of human sin a way – upon the cross – to love the disciples and to offer himself to the Father). For human beings, this is especially difficult since the natural biological drives of human existence constrict the moral imagination to an egocentric perspective. But because Weil believes human personhood is inherently relational (grounded in the self-giving relationality of the Trinity), she argues that there is a hidden possibility for the self to grow, paradoxically, beyond what it thinks of as itself into a mysterious freedom and communion with God. The self will, however, experience this transformation as its undoing, and this is the case because God has given all creatures the freedom to exist according to their own natural laws – or, miraculously, through those very laws and *beyond* them towards a freely giving relationality rather than a naturally driven taking. We might say it is a matter of sustaining a difference and moving by means of it to dialogue, rather than allowing the difference to harden into a division.

What is required, therefore, is sufficient faith (and freedom from immature egocentrism) to endure the painful necessities of nature, not to be captivated by them, and to learn how to read in them the deep ordering love of the divine giver – difference as space for relationality, not alienation. An artist learns to sense with a non-possessive gaze the beauty capable of discovery by stone or wood or paint or sound. A scientist learns to read the deep logical structure within the matter of things. In such cases, the beholder has been set free from the need to shrink reality to the veneer perceptible and graspable by mere ego needs; instead, a contemplative attentiveness (closely akin to the compassionate and creative attention of moral imagination) has opened the mind to a hidden presence: "The object of science is the presence of Wisdom in the universe, Wisdom of which we are the brothers, the presence of Christ, expressed through matter which constitutes the world."[25] Just as the Word consents to speak the divine ordering within every particle of creation, and embodies that loving obedience in the Incarnation, so human beings can begin reciprocally to respond to that deep divine ordering within all things and to move through contemplation of it towards a participation in the divine self-sharing from which it springs. The "infinite distance between God and God" (the space-making of the trinitarian persons) makes room within itself to host the otherness of the universe, which has perversely turned its autonomy into bitter alienation:

> God created through love and for love. God did not create anything except love itself, and the means to love . . . He created beings capable of love from all possible distance, the infinite distance. This infinite distance between God and God, this supreme tearing apart, this agony beyond all others, this marvel of love, is the crucifixion . . . This tearing apart, over which supreme love places the bond of supreme union, echoes perpetually across the universe in the midst of the silence, like two notes, separate yet melting into one, like pure and heart-rending harmony. This is the Word of God. The whole creation is nothing but its vibration.[26]

While Weil's trinitarian thought merits further analysis in its own right, for the purposes of this chapter, two final points are crucial.

First, there is a very real sense for Weil in which all forms of reflection are motions of the creaturely intelligence discovering the divine self-expression within which all creation is embraced. It is not simply that all thought ultimately has God as its object (as Truth itself) but, in formal terms, God is also the pattern by *means* of which the mind can think: this is so because all creatures (minds included) are given their autonomous and distinct existence by the same act of free and loving divine self-othering by which the Word eternally expresses the love of the Father through the Spirit (or as Weil says in the passage just quoted, "the whole creation is nothing but its [the Word's] vibration"). Correlate with this is the inherently and necessarily transformational momentum of all acts of real intelligence and understanding; for the journey to truth is by nature a journey of sharing in the trinitarian life by means of which all truth exists. And this would, of course, certainly hold especially true for theology itself. Hence it would be a kind of nonsense, in Weil's view, to imagine an authentic theology apart from spirituality. This is confirmed by the second point we must observe here, namely that Weil explains this process of creaturely perception (of the divine source of reality) as an ascetical apprenticeship. Through an ascesis of renouncing (naturally) self-focused thought and behavior, one is freed for a deeper attentiveness to the other, and this in turn opens the mind to sense the deep resonance within all things, their echoing of the divine speaking that grounds them: "As one has to learn to read or to practice a trade, so one must learn to feel in all things, first and almost solely, the obedience of the universe to God. It is really an apprenticeship, it requires time and effort . . . Whoever has finished his apprenticeship recognizes things and events, everywhere and always, as vibrations of the same divine and infinitely sweet word."[27] Clearly, theological endeavor invites the inquirer towards a path of spiritual formation.

Hans Urs von Balthasar

With the Swiss Roman Catholic von Balthasar (1905–88) we find a parallel insight regarding the inherent spiritual momentum of an authentically theological life. (Because another chapter in this work deals directly with Balthasar, the present chapter focuses more narrowly on his views regarding the relationship of spirituality and theology.) Like Weil, Balthasar conceives the universe in terms of its creation by divine love. Yet his interpretation of how humanity comes to "read" the expressive form of love more overtly announces the would-be theologian's dramatic commitment to a transforming participation in the Word's self-expression. Whereas Weil's thought seems most akin to the ascending ascetical–contemplative journey described by Origen of Alexandria and his great student Evagrius, Balthasar's views are always charged by his many years as a Jesuit and guide along the Ignatian path of spiritual formation outlined in Loyola's *Spiritual Exercises*. From his long experience as a spiritual director and founder of a religious community for lay people, Balthasar was particularly attuned to the issue of personal calling or vocation, and to the discovery and responsive development of one's calling through a sharing in the reconciling mission of Christ. So we could say that Balthasar recontextualizes the classical Christian contemplative journey within the struggle of Jesus to hear and respond to the truth of the Father's call to him in every dimension of life.[28] This means, correlatively, that the *theological* task can only be drawn towards its own proper fulfillment as theologians respond to the grace of divine calling (analogously to Jesus).

As a result of Balthasar's doctoral studies in German literature and the cross-fertilization of those insights through his exposure to the *nouvelle théologie*'s return to patristic sources, Balthasar was adept at probing the theoretical depths within the aesthetic forms of ancient Christian spiritual texts. Throughout his important early studies of Origen, Gregory of Nyssa, and especially Maximus the Confessor, the Swiss thinker sought to depict the intrinsically theological insights of souls being drawn into divine encounter. This perspective was developed in later studies of a remarkable range of "spiritual" writers (from Pseudo-Dionysius, Bonaventure, Eckhart, Ruuysbroec, and John of the Cross, to Thérèse of Lisieux, to name only a few), in all of which Balthasar illuminated the interplay between spiritual vocation and theological vision.

For Balthasar, the correct response to modernity's turn to the subject was not simply to embrace this turn by searching for a transcendental (divine) condition for human subjectivity, but to learn how to discern the objective divine form impressing itself within the constraints of concrete, historical human existence. And for him, the clearest and most perceptible expressions of the divine "ideas" are not human cognitive states at all, but precisely the objective, historically enacted lives of holiness – the saintly teachers – within which the divine meaning can find embodied voice. "The saints are not given to us to admire for their heroic powers, but that we should be enlightened by them on the inner reality of Christ, both for our better understanding of the faith and for our living thereby in charity . . . The life of the saints is theology in practice."[29]

What Balthasar has in mind here is not a sort of algorithm by which theology could read off from various profiles in sanctity the deep meaning of the gospel; rather, he argues that as believers are drawn into the life of Christ, they develop a kind of contemporaneity with the gospel, in which they come to share in Jesus' "own vision and knowledge."[30] The tragedy for Christian theology has been that since the later medieval and early modern periods, its professional teachers have become captivated by a rationalism that continually attempts to *abstract* some truth from the various forms of revelation instead of living into those forms spiritually – and thereby discovering the theological truth by means of participation within its historical unfolding. This has had, in Balthasar's view, seriously deleterious effects in both theology and spirituality: " 'Scientific' theology became more and more divorced from prayer, and so lost the accent and tone with which one should speak of what is holy, while 'affective' theology [often called "spirituality" today], as it became increasingly empty, often degenerated into unctuous, platitudinous piety."[31] Balthasar envisions a theology that comes to know the truth of divine teaching as that truth shapes and conforms the life of the believing community to itself; this is, of course, very notably a *spiritual* process, for it renounces the idea that theological legitimacy depends upon the theologian's masterful grasp upon the subject matter (capable of demonstrating its perfect intelligibility to anyone), and instead seeks to hold the theological life of the community open to the transforming work of God.

Sometimes Balthasar conceptualizes this understanding of theology in "marian" terms, that is, as a human theological pondering that bears within itself a Word whose full meaning it can only realize through a devoted life of availability to the Word's unfolding mission in the world. In this sense, "spirituality" would not be so much about individual quests for self-transcendence as it would simply be the embodied unfolding of divine mystery within the communal life of believers, the transforming impression of the divine teaching as that becomes real in the life of faith, and hope, and love; and "theology" would then be the attempt to express (sometimes definitively, sometimes apologetically, sometimes speculatively) the "deep things of God" that animate and shape the Christian life. Balthasar traces the loss of this inner, transformational unity of theology and spirituality to a crucial shift:

[The classical unity of spirituality and theology] was known as *theologia mystica* by the Fathers and even by the medievals up to the twelfth century. It was only when the Spanish writers put much greater emphasis on the subjective experiencing of the mysteries that the word *mysticus* came to take on its modern meaning, and then, in order to comprise the whole of man's subjective relationship to Christian truth, it had to be supplemented by the idea of *askesis*. Consequently *theologia spiritualis*, by a rather doubtful process of simplification, came to be known, particularly in the nineteenth century, as ascetical–mystical theology, in which asceticism denoted the active work of the individual, and mysticism his increasingly passive experience of divine things. As a result of this pragmatic, psychological approach, the content of revelation was transposed into a subjective framework, and so the idea of the Word as Bridegroom, always present in the old *theologia spiritualis* or *mystica*, was almost completely lost. This produced a fatal cleavage between a "dogmatic theology" divorced from the subject and turned in on itself, and the psychological subject standing opposed to it; and, since there was no center in which they could meet, the separation persisted.[32]

The "center in which they could meet" is, for Balthasar, Christ. In his view, the deepest spiritual calling of every human being becomes most fully perspicuous when individuals come to share in the life of Christ; Christ's mission, then, becomes both the unfolding within history of the divine Word *and* the realm in which all find the consummation of their spiritual life. Drawing on Johannine perspectives, Balthasar sees both theology and spirituality, therefore, as the ongoing work of the Holy Spirit impressing within the heart of the believing community the truth of the Son.

The underlying trinitarian ground of Balthasar's conception becomes crucial here. In common once again with Simone Weil, the Swiss thinker understands the integrity of spirituality and theology to spring from the trinitarian pattern of divine life. This is so because the Divine Trinity both *expresses* the divine life (and so is the source of sacred teaching and theology) and also *constitutes and consummates* the divine life (and so is the source of the spiritual vocation of personhood) – and both acts are of course simply forms of the eternal trinitarian self-giving of the divine Persons. Or, to put it another way, God the Trinity shares forth the truth of the divine mystery by the very same means by which the divine Persons eternally "give way" one to another, eternally delighting in the mutual fruition thus made possible.

In a work written just after World War II, Balthasar worried over the destructive reduction and flattening of human life – to system, to ideology, to logical formulae, to the interests of power: "all of the perversions that human freedom can inflict upon being and its qualities always aim at one thing: the annihilation of the depth dimension of being, thanks to which being remains a mystery even, indeed, precisely in its unveiling."[33] This vulnerable yet enduring radiance and mystery inherent in all reality was for Balthasar the great sign of its miraculous source – as gift, as freely bestowed, as creation springing from the Creator. Theology can only be true insofar as it continually recollects this deep source of any sort of truth whatsoever. "The ultimate ground of the mysterious character inherent in the knowable is disclosed only when we recognize that every possible object of knowledge is creaturely, in other words, that its ultimate truth lies hidden in the mind of the Creator, who alone can speak the eternal name of things."[34] In this sense, theology's kind of knowing is no different than any other kind of knowing for Balthasar; for it is a knowing that must have God not only as its object, but also as its acting subject, as its teacher and its joy, its Word and its Spirit.

Debate and Agenda

We might gain some sense of the play of discussion presently by imagining two axes and using these to offer a very imprecise taxonomy of leading thinkers. Suppose the horizontal axis runs from a more practically oriented pole to a more theoretically oriented pole. At the more practical end there are very few writers who are much concerned with theological implications, but as we move toward the center of this axis there is the work of Diogenes Allen, Ellen Charry, Sandra Schneiders, and Philip Sheldrake, all of whom continue to contribute enormously to reflection on the concrete transformations entailed by the spiritual life, their theological under-pinnings, and to questions regarding how best academically to study and teach spirituality. Then suppose the vertical axis runs from a more historically oriented pole to a more constructively oriented pole. Moving, very roughly, from the former end towards the latter we would find such important scholars as Bernard McGinn, Andrew Louth, Denys Turner, Grace Jantzen, Rowan Williams, Oliver Davies, and Sarah Coakley, all of whom are signally contributing to the recovery of an integrity between spirituality and theology (and several of them have, interest-ingly, contributed to translations of Balthasar into English or worked carefully with his thought).

Coakley and Williams might be singled out at the present as offering particularly creative ways beyond a central impasse. In analyzing current debates, McGinn, Sheldrake, and more recently Edward Howells, have all helpfully identified what might be viewed as this central problematic: at one extreme would be a lingering Jamesian essentialism regarding the putative universality of religious experience, and at the other extreme would be an apparently reductionist constructivism in which all theological or philosophical teachings present in spiritual writings are analyzed down to a merely cultural idiom.[35] With either of these views the link between theology and spirituality is again severed. Coakley and Williams, however, consistently unveil a crucial reciprocity that overcomes the divide: Christian spirituality is portrayed as grounded in the self-giving freedom of the trinitarian Persons, and, on the other hand, Christian theology is seen evolving from the inherent spiritual pressure and questioning at the heart of the church's encounter with the reality of God. Coakley points out deftly that the cultural, political, racial, and gender particularities of spiritual writers can hardly be jettisoned in favor of some putatively more universal experience; for one thing, this supposedly universal experience often betrays its masculinist assumptions, and, for another, it is precisely by means of these particu-larities that the most creative and vital insights are often received – including, especially, in theology.[36] Furthermore, by focusing on the sometimes hidden inter-section between spiritual *practices*, spiritual writing, and theology, Coakley is able to portray not simply how certain doctrines in, say, Christology, developed within the praying life of the community, but also to provide a crucial conceptual matrix within which constructive theology itself might presently move to new levels of understanding.[37]

A similar theme is often illuminatingly present in Williams' thought, namely, the recovery of the idea that Christian theology not only has insights to gain from the spiritual journey, but also that theology is most authentic in being most available to the divine "investigation" it must undergo: "Language about God is kept honest in the degree to which it turns on itself in the name of God, and so surrenders itself to God: it is in this way that it becomes possible to see how it is still *God* that is being spoken of, that which makes the human world a moral unity."[38] Williams often reminds his readers that, for many Christian forebears, "theology" in the highest sense is not something accomplished primarily by the deft academic skills of the professional, but is rather a real knowledge *taught by God*. But while (as we saw above) early modern interpreters had tended to constrict this "supernatural" infusion of mystical theology to a series of highly unusual experiential states of consciousness, Williams keeps his readers attentive to the communal framework and the solidarity with Christ in which this sort of mystical theology comes to fruition. What is called for, Williams argues, involves

> subordinating the study of particular abnormal states of consciousness to the evaluation of the pattern of human reflection and behavior that is emerging through and beyond any such exceptional states. If the 'mystical' ultimately means the reception of a particular *pattern* of divine action (creative love, self-emptying incarnation), its test will be the presence or absence of something like that pattern in a human life seen as a whole.[39]

Several signs point to the integrity of spirituality and theology in the many writers we have considered, all too cursorily, in this chapter. Not all of these are often easily observed under the dual pressures of academy and church. Academic life sometimes seems to press towards the sort of universal standards of manipulable rationality that lures theology into a discomfort with lived spirituality, or else circumvents spirituality's authentic theological contributions by conveniently passing things along to a purely psychological or sociological analysis. But ecclesial life has its equivalent problematic pressures: propensities for devotional efficacy and a hurried (and often embarrassed) dismissal of significant Christian teaching in favor of pastoral utility. If the recovering theology–spirituality dialogue is to avoid these sorts of premature foreclosures of its possibilities, it will have to keep finding ways to hold itself accountable, indeed available, to divine teaching.

Notes

1   St. Basil the Great, *On the Holy Spirit*, trans. David Anderson (Crestwood, NY: St. Vladimir's Seminary Press, 1997), 95.

2   For a useful survey of the ancient Christian understanding of the spiritual matrix of theology, see Olivier Clément, *The Roots of Christian Mysticism: Text and Commentary*, trans. Theodore Berkeley (Hyde Park, NY: New City Press, 1995).

3   See Louis Dupré, *Passage to Modernity: An Essay in the Hermeneutics of Nature and Culture* (New Haven, CT: Yale University Press, 1993); Stephen Toulmin, *Cosmopolis: The Hidden Agenda of Modernity* (New York: Macmillan, 1990).

4   See the important studies of Pierre Hadot, including *What is Ancient Philosophy?*, trans. Michael Chase (Cambridge, MA: Belknap Press of Harvard University Press, 2002).

5   Important examinations of medieval shifts in the spirituality–theology relation can be found in the multi-volume history of

Western mysticism being written by Bernard McGinn under the title *The Presence of God: A History of Western Christian Mysticism* (New York: Crossroad/Herder, 1991–), and also Grace Jantzen, *Power, Gender, and Christian Mysticism* (Cambridge: Cambridge University Press, 1995), and Denys Turner, *The Darkness of God: Negativity in Christian Mysticism* (Cambridge: Cambridge University Press, 1995); also see ch. 2 of McIntosh, *Mystical Theology: The Integrity of Spirituality and Theology* (Oxford: Blackwell, 1998).

6 For a probing study of this tendency, see Fergus Kerr, *Theology after Wittgenstein* (Oxford: Blackwell, 1988).

7 For a perceptive and critical analysis of James' ideas and their aftermath, see the works of Nicholas Lash, especially *Easter in Ordinary: Reflections on Human Experience and the Knowledge of God* (Notre Dame, IN: University of Notre Dame Press, 1988) and *The Beginning and the End of Religion* (Cambridge: Cambridge University Press, 1996).

8 Evelyn Underhill, *The School of Charity* (orig. edn., 1934; Harrisburg, PA: Morehouse Publishing, 1991), 6.

9 Ibid, 6–7.

10 Gerald A. McCool, *From Unity to Pluralism: The Internal Evolution of Thomism* (New York: Fordham University Press, 1992).

11 See the excellent analysis in Fergus Kerr, *After Aquinas: Versions of Thomism* (Oxford: Blackwell, 2002).

12 Grace Jantzen examines this tendency within the Kantian/Jamesian line most tellingly in *Power, Gender, and Christian Mysticism* (Cambridge: Cambridge University Press, 1995).

13 For a brief and clear exposition of these writers and their debates, see Bernard McGinn, *The Foundations of Mysticism*, Vol. 1 of *The Presence of God*, Appendix, "Theoretical Foundations: The Modern Study of Mysticism," esp. pp. 277–80.

14 Anselm Stolz, *The Doctrine of Spiritual Perfection* [*Theologie der Mystik*], trans. Aidan Williams (1936; New York: Crossroad/Herder, 2001), ch. 9, "Mystical experience," throughout.

15 Ibid, 226.

16 Ibid, 227.

17 Ibid, 227–9.

18 Ibid, 228.

19 Ibid, 165–80.

20 Simone Weil, *First and Last Notebooks*, trans. Richard Rees (Oxford: Oxford University Press, 1970), 355.

21 Letter 4, "Spiritual Autobiography," in Simone Weil, *Waiting for God*, trans. Emma Craufurd (New York: Harper Collins, 2001), 26.

22 Ibid, 27.

23 Weil, "Forms of the Implicit Love of God," in *Waiting for God*, 93.

24 Ibid, 137.

25 Ibid, 108.

26 Weil, "The Love of God and Affliction," in *Waiting for God*, 72.

27 Ibid, 78.

28 Further on this see M. A. McIntosh, *Christology from Within: Spirituality and the Incarnation in Hans Urs von Balthasar* (Notre Dame, IN: University of Notre Dame Press, 2000).

29 Hans Urs von Balthasar, "Theology and Sanctity," in *The Word Made Flesh*, Vol. 1 of *Explorations in Theology*, trans. A. V. Littledale with A. Dru (San Francisco: Ignatius Press, 1989), 204.

30 Ibid, 203.

31 Ibid, 208.

32 Balthasar, "Spirituality," in *The Word Made Flesh*, 213.

33 Balthasar, *Truth of the World* (orig. published 1947), Vol. 1 of *Theo-Logic: Theological Logical Theory*, trans. Adrian J. Walker (San Francisco: Ignatius Press, 2000), 16.

34 Ibid, 17.

35 See particularly the appendix, "Theoretical Foundations," to McGinn's *Foundations of Mysticism*; Philip Sheldrake, *Spirituality and Theology: Christian Living and the Doctrine of God* (London: Darton, Longman and Todd, 1998); Edward Howells, "Mysticism and the Mystical: The Current Debate," *The Way* Supplement ("Christianity and the Mystical") 2002/102: 15–27.

36 Sarah Coakley, *Powers and Submissions: Spirituality, Philosophy and Gender* (Oxford: Blackwell, 2002), esp. 89–105.

37 Ibid, 1–39. See also Coakley, *God, Sexuality and the Self: An Essay "On the Trinity"* (Cambridge: Cambridge University Press: forthcoming).

38 Rowan Williams, "Theological Integrity," in *On Christian Theology* (Oxford: Blackwell, 2000), 8.

39 Williams, *Teresa of Avila* (London: Continuum, 1991), 145. See also the consist-ently integrated approach to spirituality and theology in Williams, *The Wound of Knowledge: Christian Spirituality from the New Testament to St. John of the Cross*, 2nd edn. (London: Darton, Longman and Todd, 1990).

Bibliography

Primary

Allen, Diogenes. *Spiritual Theology: The Theology of Yesterday for Spiritual Help Today*. Cambridge: Cowley Publications, 1997.

Balthasar, Hans Urs von. *Explorations in Theology, Vol. 1: The Word Made Flesh*. Translated by A. V. Littledale with A. Dru. San Francisco: Ignatius Press, 1989.

Basil the Great, St. *On the Holy Spirit*. Translated by David Anderson. Crestwood, NY: St. Vladimir's Seminary Press, 1997.

Charry, Ellen T. *By the Renewing of Your Minds: The Pastoral Function of Christian Doctrine*. Oxford: Oxford University Press, 1997.

Coakley, Sarah. *Powers and Submissions: Spirituality, Philosophy and Gender*. Oxford: Blackwell, 2002.

—— *God, Sexuality and the Self: An Essay "On the Trinity"*. Cambridge: Cambridge University Press, forthcoming.

Davies, Oliver. *A Theology of Compassion: The Metaphysics of Difference and the Renewal of Tradition*. London: SCM Press, 2001.

Jantzen, Grace. *Power, Gender, and Christian Mysticism*. Cambridge: Cambridge University Press, 1995.

Louth, Andrew. *Theology and Spirituality*. Oxford: SLG Press, 1978.

McIntosh, Mark A. *Mystical Theology: The Integrity of Spirituality and Theology*. Oxford: Blackwell, 1998.

Sheldrake, Philip. *Spirituality and Theology: Christian Living and the Doctrine of God*. London: Darton, Longman and Todd, 1998.

Stolz, Anselm. *The Doctrine of Spiritual Perfection* [*Theologie der Mystik*]. Translated by Aidan Williams. New York: Crossroad/Herder, 2001.

Turner, Denys. *The Darkness of God: Negativity in Christian Mysticism*. Cambridge: Cambridge University Press, 1995.

Underhill, Evelyn. *The School of Charity*. Harrisburg, PA: Morehouse Publishing, 1991.

Weil, Simone. *Waiting for God*. Translated by Emma Craufurd. New York: Harper Collins, 2001.

Williams, Rowan. *The Wound of Knowledge: Christian Spirituality from the New Testament to St. John of the Cross*, 2nd edn. London: Darton, Longman and Todd, 1990.

—— *Teresa of Avila*. London: Continuum, 1991.

—— *On Christian Theology*. Oxford: Blackwell, 2000.

Secondary

Clément, Olivier. *The Roots of Christian Mysticism: Text and Commentary*. Translated by Theodore Berkeley. Hyde Park, NY: New City Press, 1995.

Dupré, Louis. *Passage to Modernity: An Essay in the Hermeneutics of Nature and Culture*. New Haven, CT: Yale University Press, 1993.

Howells, Edward. "Mysticism and the Mystical: The Current Debate." *The Way* supplement ("Christianity and the Mystical") 2002/102: 15–27.

Kerr, Fergus. *After Aquinas: Versions of Thomism*. Oxford: Blackwell, 2002.

Louth, Andrew. *The Origins of the Christian Mystical Tradition: From Plato to Denys*. Oxford: Oxford University Press, 1981.

McCool, Gerald A. *From Unity to Pluralism: The Internal Evolution of Thomism*. New York: Fordham University Press, 1992.

McGinn, Bernard. *The Presence of God: A History of Western Christian Mysticism*. Multiple volumes. New York: Crossroad/Herder, 1991–.

Schneiders, Sandra. "Theology and Spirituality: Strangers, Rivals or Partners?" *Horizons* 13/2 (1989): 253–74.

Toulmin, Stephen. *Cosmopolis: The Hidden Agenda of Modernity*. New York: Macmillan, 1990.

Pastoral and Practical Theology

Stephen Pattison and Gordon Lynch

Introduction

Practical theology today

Practical theology's profile as a distinctive discipline within the broader field of theological studies has developed significantly since World War II. The decision to include this chapter in a major textbook reflects a growing recognition that pastoral and practical theology represent a serious field of study. The growing importance and autonomy of pastoral and practical theology is also reflected in the formation of professional academic bodies, like the International Academy of Practical Theology, the Society for Pastoral Theology (USA), and the British and Irish Association of Practical Theology, over the last two decades. Pastoral and practical theology are increasingly attractive to growing numbers of students. There are more than fifty courses offering specialized postgraduate study in this area in Britain alone.[1] Furthermore, some systematic theologians can now be seen emphasizing the practical or pastoral significance of their work.[2]

Pastoral and practical theology have reinvented and redefined themselves in the past fifty years.[3] Before World War II, these disciplines were understood as little more than passing on practical wisdom, based on experience, together with useful hints and tips for ministers and priests. Now pastoral and practical theology have developed a clearer, more autonomous, and more credible identity within the broader context of academic theology. To sloganize, they have moved from hints and tips to hermeneutics. They have also become both theoretically and practically much more sophisticated.

Across academic disciplines generally, the twentieth century saw an increasing interest in the theoretical and empirical study of everyday, lived experience.[4] Practical theology can thus be understood as part of a wider academic movement which treats contemporary human experience as worthy of sustained analysis and critical reflection. As a subdiscipline within theology, practical theology shares and focuses the general "turn to the human" in its aims, concerns, and methods. This anthropocentric movement has become a main feature of Western theologies in general over the last century or so.[5] While practical theologians generally remain deeply committed to engaging with Christian traditions, this engagement typically takes the form of a critical dialogue between those traditions and contemporary experience.

Some historical background

Pastoral and practical theology have a long and established history in the Jewish and Christian traditions. A concern for developing appropriate pastoral relationships in religious communities, and an interest in how such relationships reflect wider theological concepts, is evident in the Priestly, Prophetic and Wisdom traditions of the Hebrew scriptures.[6] Similarly, a number of studies have explored how theological concerns at different points in the church's history have been bound up with an understanding of what it means for clergy to offer sustaining, reconciling, healing, and guiding relationships to those within their care. Broadly conceived as theological reflection and guidance on issues of pastoral concern, pastoral theology has a history stretching back to the earliest centuries of the Christian church.[7]

It was not until the eighteenth century, however, that one of the first attempts was made by the Protestant theologian Friedrich Schleiermacher (1768–1834) to identify and theorize practical theology as a distinctive theological discipline. Practical theology, Schleiermacher argued, was the proper end-point of all theological study. It represented the outworking of Christian theology for the life and mission of the church. He characterized the relationship of practical theology to other major theological disciplines using the analogy of a tree. Theology properly begins at its "roots" with philosophical theology. This develops into the "trunk" of historical, exegetical, and dogmatic studies of the Christian tradition. The understanding gleaned from philosophical and historical theology finally finds concrete expression in application. The "branches" of practical theology are concerned with the leadership and governance of the church in relation both to individuals and to the whole community.[8]

Schleiermacher's understanding of practical theology gave it a clearer identity within the theological disciplines. From a contemporary perspective, however, it presents some problems.[9] Although Schleiermacher emphasized the importance of practical theology as the concrete outworking of theological knowledge, the content of this theological knowledge owed nothing to practical theology itself or to contemporary ecclesiastical experience; it was derived solely from philosophical and historical theology. Schleiermacher's model is an *applicationist* one. It moves in one direction only: from theory to practice. Thus understood, the role of practical theology is the fairly narrow deductive application of theological concepts derived from other theological sources and methods to organizing the church and caring for its members.

Much postwar liberal Protestant pastoral and practical theology has moved decisively away from this applicationist model and its deductive approach, toward an experiential–inductive method that we shall describe in more detail shortly. Through this process, the discipline has now begun to clarify its status and methods as an autonomous field of theological inquiry that is not as wholly dependent on other theological disciplines. The writings of US theologians Seward Hiltner and Don Browning have been crucial here.

In this chapter, we will look at the ways in which pastoral and practical theology has come to define itself as a discipline in recent decades. We will set out some of the tensions and ambiguities within this movement, and reflect on some of the prospects and challenges facing it in the future.

Survey: What is Pastoral and Practical Theology?

At this point it is important to offer some comments about what characterizes pastoral and practical theology as a form of theological study. Before discussing these core elements of the discipline, though, it will be helpful to say something about the terms "pastoral" and "practical."

For some writers, the terms "pastoral theology" and "practical theology" are virtually synonymous. However, there remain some significant underlying differences. Self-designated pastoral theologians tend to have a concern for theological reflection in relation to the life of the church, in particular with the work and experiences of those who practice some form of pastoral ministry within it.[10] Pastoral theology tends to focus on questions and concerns that emerge out of the practice of "pastoral care" (e.g., what theological concepts can provide a suitable framework for the practice of pastoral counseling, or what theological issues arise in relation to caring for people with HIV/AIDS).

Practical theology generally has a broader focus. Although still usually working within the framework of the life and mission of the church in the contemporary world, practical theology addresses a wider range of contemporary issues, many of which lie beyond the work of the individual pastoral carer (e.g., economic debt in the developing world, or new technologies in genetic science).

While there is some validity to the distinction between pastoral theology and practical theology, it should not be over-emphasized. There is, for example, a growing awareness in the literature on pastoral care that pastoral practice properly includes concern with wider social and political issues, as well as more narrowly interpersonal ones.[11] Thus, pastoral theology cannot be assumed to address only questions arising out of individual caring relationships.

There are also some regional variations in the meaning of practical theology. In the Netherlands, and some other parts of Europe, practical theology implies the use of social science research methods to generate findings that may be useful in pastoral settings.[12] In Germany, many practical theologians remain committed to Schleiermacher's understanding of practical theology as the science of church governance, leadership, and education. In an increasingly secularized Britain some writers use practical theology to describe a practice of normative analysis and critique of the action-guiding worldviews, assumptions, and behaviors prevalent in contemporary culture and experience that does not draw simply on the concepts, values, and beliefs of the Christian church.[13]

Despite these differences, there are characteristics that are shared by the vast majority of pastoral and practical theologians. These are (1) reflection upon lived contemporary experience; (2) the adoption of an interdisciplinary approach; (3) critical dialogue between theological norms and contemporary experience; (4) a preference for liberal or radical models of theology; (5) the need for theoretical and practical transformation.

Reflection upon lived contemporary experience

Pastoral and practical theology give methodological primacy to reflection upon lived contemporary experience. Whatever the focus of a particular pastoral or practical theological study, there is an assumption that its starting point is some kind of experience of that particular issue. This might be the theologian's own experience.[14] Or it may be experience that they have learned about through talking to other people (sometimes through structured empirical research projects) or through reading other accounts of people's experiences.[15] Experience, "the text of the present," provides the starting place for theological inquiry and against which its findings and value must be tested.

The primary importance of the theological study of lived experience was first highlighted by Anton Boisen (1876–1965), a key figure in the development of pastoral education in America, and the founder of the Clinical Pastoral Education movement.[16] From his experience of working as a hospital and mental health chaplain, as well as his personal experience of mental distress, Boisen developed a new approach to ministerial education in clinical settings like hospitals. Ministers were invited to reflect in depth about their own experiences of offering pastoral care to others. Such reflection helped ministers to become more aware of how to offer more effective pastoral support. More than this, Boisen argued that attention to patients' experiences could itself generate new understanding about the human condition and the nature of human relations to God, thus contributing to new theological insights. Boisen saw people as "living human documents"; they could be as profound a resource for theological learning as any written text from the historic Christian tradition.[17]

The adoption of an interdisciplinary approach

An interdisciplinary approach is adopted for the study of contemporary experience and as a preliminary to specifically theological analysis. The critical engagement with lived experience does not just require working with particular accounts or stories of contemporary experiences or issues and relating them to theological ideas and traditions. It also involves using non-theological academic disciplines that provide a wider theoretical context in which that experience can be understood. Particular use has been made of human sciences such as psychology, sociology, anthropology or political science, and increasingly, cultural studies, to offer wider perspectives.

Critical dialogue between theological norms and contemporary experience

Much pastoral and practical theology attempts to set up a critical dialogue between theological norms and contemporary experience. Following Boisen, and contrary to Schleiermacher's deductive, applicationist approach, it is assumed that attention to experience can provide significant data which can be used inductively and directly to inform theological understandings rather than just being the place upon which preexisting theological concepts are imposed. Pastoral and practical theologians are interested in what traditional theological norms can do to help in understanding a particular experience or issue. However, they are equally concerned to see whether there are ways in which contemporary experience might lead to the revision of theological concepts or other related practices in faith communities. Thus, a practical theological approach to thinking about marriage or sexual relationships in the contemporary world would require attention to what is known from contemporary human sciences and experiences as well as to the theological tradition.[18]

Given the interdisciplinary nature of its activity, pastoral and practical theology can therefore be characterized as a three-way critical conversation between contemporary lived experience, theological norms and traditions, and other academic disciplines that help us to make sense of that experience.[19]

This activity is typically described within the discipline as a process of theological reflection. There is not always clear consensus about how theological reflection should be conducted. However, a broad commitment to theological reflection is one of the shared defining features of many academic programs in pastoral and practical theology.[20]

A preference for liberal or radical models of theology

Because contemporary human experience is allowed to have a key role in shaping theological concepts, pastoral and practical theologians have a tendency toward adopting liberal or radical models of theology (e.g., liberation theology, black theology) rather than conservative ones.[21] People working in this discipline tend to be more interested in encouraging critical dialogue between contemporary experience and theological norms than in imposing preexisting concepts on to experience. This is one reason why relatively few conservative Evangelical theologians have had a significant impact on the field, as, like Schleiermacher, they prefer to give primacy to the theological tradition and its application rather than present experience. A main exception to this is Thomas Oden, whose work we shall return to later.[22]

The need for theoretical and practical transformation

Practical and pastoral theologians aim to make a difference in religious understanding and practice. Practical theology is not just a discipline concerned with the norms and practices of the academy, remote from the concerns and experiences of ordinary people. Nor is it study for its own sake. Ultimately, its practitioners, like the radical theologians referred to above, want to make an impact on the way things are understood and done in order to encourage more thoughtful, healthy, and authentic forms of living. Many of its adherents, while not necessarily being left wing in their political sympathies, would have sympathy for Karl Marx's eleventh thesis on Feuerbach: "The philosophers have only interpreted the world in different ways; the point is to change it."[23]

An example of practical theology in action

Each of the core characteristics mentioned above can be illustrated with reference to the growing literature within pastoral and practical theology that seeks to respond to the issue of the abuse of children.[24] Some of these studies are written by theologians and pastoral carers who have met and worked with survivors of physical and sexual abuse, and listened to their stories. Other studies have drawn more from written accounts of survivors' experiences that are in the public domain. In addition to hearing how these survivors interpret their experiences, these writers have often made use of resources from the human sciences that extend our understanding of issues surrounding the abuse of children. These include sociological studies on the prevalence of abuse, psychological studies on the nature and effects of abuse, and work within social work and psychotherapy on therapeutic practice with those who have been abused. In addition to the insights gained from listening to these experiences, and from the wider human science literature on abuse, these writers also engage with theological concepts and norms, and explore the relevance of these for the experience of abuse.

One consequence of taking the contemporary lived experience of abuse survivors seriously is that sharp, difficult questions can be raised about the nature of religious belief and practice. The existence of survivor support networks within the churches points to the fact that for some people, the religious community has been a primary place where they have experienced physical, psychological, or sexual abuse. In this context, one important issue often discussed is the theological notion of forgiveness, and a range of questions have been raised in relation to this. For example, if forgiveness is an important part of the spiritual life within the Christian tradition, what does this mean for survivors of sexual and physical abuse? Should they be encouraged to forgive those who have acted so damagingly towards them? To what extent is this forgiveness dependent upon repentance on the part of the abuser? Does lament or rage have an appropriate role in the life of the survivor? What do we learn about forgiveness from the experiences of survivors who have been damaged by being pressured by other people to forgive their abusers? To what extent have certain theologies of forgiveness had an ideological function in a church culture in which abuse has often been ignored, denied, or covered up by church authorities?

Questions such as these have led to a number of proposals for appropriate pastoral care for those who have been abused, for changing liturgical content and practices to make it more accessible for survivors of abuse, and for challenging patriarchal theological language and concepts that survivors experience as alienating and hurtful. The latter can reinforce hierarchical social relationships in which abuse becomes more possible.

The practical theology literature on child abuse demonstrates the main elements of practical theology in action. In this example, there is the privileging of contemporary experience, the use of interdisciplinary methods to understand that experience, critical dialogue between theology and experience, the adoption of liberal or radical theological models that highlight and question contemporary injustice, and the need to make a difference to understanding and practice.

Content and Debate: Three Styles of Pastoral and Practical Theology

Having given an initial overview of the discipline, we hoped that this chapter would then lead into a discussion of the two or three leading pastoral and practical theologians whose work has been most influential. In thinking about who we might focus on we informally polled about ten academics working in pastoral and practical theology in Britain and the United States to see who they would identify as the most significant. Respondents suggested the following names, with some names coming up more than once:

US   Anton Boisen, Don Browning, Howard Clinebell, Charles Gerkin, Seward
             Hiltner, Henri Nouwen, James Poling
UK   Alastair Campbell, Duncan Forrester, Elaine Graham, Emmanuel Lartey,
             Stephen Pattison, Ronald Preston
Elsewhere   Riet Bons Storm, Paulo Friere

Our small, unscientific sample generated the names of 16 people. Others could have been included who arguably have been just as influential (e.g., John Patton, Wayne Oates, Ed Wimberley, Thomas Oden, Bonnie Miller McLemore, Pam Couture, Rodney Hunter). The survey suggests two important points about pastoral and practical theology.

First, while tending to be organized around the core elements noted earlier, pastoral and practical theology does not have clear disciplinary boundaries. While most of those listed would define themselves as either pastoral or practical theologians (or indeed as both), Duncan Forrester and Ronald Preston are more often seen as social and political theologians. Paulo Freire was an educational theorist, not a theologian in any traditional sense at all. If pastoral and practical theology embraces a wide spectrum of theological reflection on contemporary experience, then potentially its boundaries can include people who would not regard themselves as working within this discipline, such as theological ethicists or social theologians.

Secondly, pastoral and practical theology is a diffuse discipline characterized by being all periphery with no center. This may well be a reflection of the fact that this is still a relatively small, new theological discipline still establishing its identity and concerns. Be that as it may, there is no single figure or small group that has dominated the center ground of the discipline. Hiltner and Browning have been influential writers, substantially clarifying the methods of pastoral and practical theology. They are more likely to be cited than others when this discipline is under discussion, as they were in our survey. But although pastoral and practical theologians tend to share some common methodological assumptions in their work, the majority of their energy is focused on the particular issues or themes that they are engaging with rather than with any common theoretical or theological agenda at the heart of the discipline.

A clearer picture of the diffuse nature of the discipline emerges when some of the areas considered in books recently published by a selection of British pastoral and practical theologians are listed:

- Shame (Stephen Pattison, *Shame: Theory, Therapy, Theology*).
- Feminist approaches to pastoral theology (Elaine Graham, *Transforming Practice*; Zoe Bennett-Moore, *Introducing Feminist Perspectives on Pastoral Theology*).
- Spirituality and mental health (John Swinton, *Resurrecting the Person*).
- "Generation X" spirituality and the religious significance of popular culture (Gordon Lynch, *After Religion*).
- "Post-human" technologies (Elaine Graham, *Representations of the Post/Human*).
- The beliefs and values of contemporary management theory and practice (Stephen Pattison, *The Faith of the Managers*).
- The theological distinctiveness of pastoral care (David Lyall, *The Integrity of Pastoral Care*).
- Pastoral ethics (Gordon Lynch, *Pastoral Care and Counselling*).
- Postmodern theory and pastoral theology (Graham, *Transforming Practice*; Paul Goodliff, *Care in a Confused Climate*).
- Justice and social policy (Duncan Forrester, *On Human Worth*).

There is some overlap between these topics. However, there is also a considerable range of areas being covered as well. The particular subjects that pastoral and practical theologians focus on may be influenced by their previous work experience (many have been ordained, some trained in health professions or as counselors or therapists), by their particular ideological and faith commitments, or by a broad range of other current interests and experiences. This is a discipline which concentrates on exploring particular topics that are interesting and important to those individuals working in it, rather than on any agenda, detailed methodology, or view of God common to all.

Given this complex diversity, it would oversimplify the picture if we now discussed just two or three individual pastoral and practical theologians. So we will further explore contemporary pastoral and practical theology by considering three different *styles* of working in this field. While certain writers clearly illustrate each of these styles, other writers in the field are less easy to classify; they may work within more than one of them. Distinguishing these three different styles will clarify some of the key emergent trends and tensions in this discipline.

Liberal–rational approaches

Liberal–rational approaches focus on developing clear, rational, academically justifiable and credible methodologies in pastoral and practical theology. Heavily influenced by the correlational method developed by Paul Tillich, they are best illustrated by the work of the American writers Seward Hiltner and Don Browning.

Seward Hiltner (1909–84) was an American Presbyterian minister and academic pastoral theologian. He held posts with various church agencies before going on to be professor of pastoral theology in the divinity schools of Chicago and Princeton.

Hiltner's thought was shaped by the theological method of Paul Tillich and by being a ministerial student under the supervision of Anton Boisen (whose emphasis on the value of the "living human document" we noted earlier). The possibility of learning theologically from human experience was a fundamental part of Hiltner's own approach. This was theologically legitimated by Tillich's notion of correlating contemporary experience with the theological tradition.

Hiltner wrote one of the first major books on the nature and methods of pastoral theology in the twentieth century. This set out basic principles for pastoral theology that remain deeply influential on the discipline to the present day. In *Preface to Pastoral Theology* (1958) Hiltner sought to clarify the relationship between pastoral theology and other branches of theology, and to offer a particular understanding of what it means to be a pastoral theologian.

Hiltner's work on pastoral theology proceeds on the basis of a broader understanding of the nature of theology. He saw theology as consisting of a wide range of subdisciplines, such as biblical theology, historical theology, doctrinal theology, ethics, pastoral theology, and educational theology. Rather than functioning in completely separate and autonomous ways, Hiltner believed that these subdisciplines should be interconnected and that work in each subdiscipline should have some effect on work done in the others. Within this broad range of subdisciplines, Hiltner made a further distinction between "logic-centered" and "operation-centered" disciplines. Logic-centered branches of theology included areas such as biblical or systematic theology which primarily had a textual or theoretical focus. By contrast, there are operation-centered disciplines (which included pastoral theology) whose "theological conclusions . . . emerge from reflection primarily on acts or events or functions from a particular perspective."[25]

Hiltner argued that pastoral theology represented a theological subdiscipline in its own right, generating theological insight from the practical vantage point of "the shepherding perspective." It did not simply consist of applying insights generated through theoretical discussions in biblical, historical, or doctrinal theology but, rather, following Tillich, correlating experience with theology. Pastoral theology is "that branch or field of theological knowledge and inquiry that brings the shepherding perspective to bear upon all the operations and functions of the church and the minister, and then draws conclusions of a theological order from reflection on these observations."[26]

"Shepherding" refers to the metaphor of pastoral care as that of the shepherd caring for their flock, a metaphor grounded in the life and caring practices of the church. Hiltner did not, however, simply equate shepherding with explicit acts of pastoral care such as visiting the sick, offering pastoral counseling, or comforting the bereaved. Rather, he saw shepherding as a more basic attitude that should inform all of the work of the minister and the church, but which at times would find appropriate expression in particular acts of caring. This attitude was one in which a minister or church would be fundamentally concerned for the healing, sustaining, and guiding of individuals who were anxious, deprived, suffering, confused, or facing difficult decisions. For Hiltner, pastoral theology is a process of reflecting on what happens when this shepherding perspective is brought to bear by ministers and churches on specific experiences of individual human suffering and uncertainty. By reflecting on particular experiences (in much the same way as Boisen advocated reflecting on pastoral experiences), new theological questions and insights could emerge that would be valuable for the wider work of theological reflection in the life of the church.

Hiltner's method has been developed and extended in the work of Don Browning. Until recently, Browning held a Chair within the Divinity School at the University of Chicago. He was a leading figure in the formation of the International Academy of Practical Theology. He has probably been the most influential figure within this discipline in the past forty years. Browning's *A Fundamental Practical Theology* (1991) is the most substantial attempt to define the nature and methods of practical theology written in recent decades.

Browning builds upon Hiltner's basic approach of encouraging a critical dialogue between experience and theology. While Hiltner saw pastoral theology as a sub-discipline within the wider structure of academic theology, Browning argued that theology as a whole should ultimately be practical in nature. Theology, for Browning, is a "fundamental practical theology." It consists of subdisciplines such as descriptive theology, historical theology, systematic theology, and strategic practical theology (by which he meant practical theology as it specifically relates to questions of pastoral ministry and church organization).

Browning significantly locates the understanding of practical theology within wider trends in cognate disciplines. He makes clear links between his work and the neo-Aristotelian moral philosophy of Alasdair MacIntyre, the neo-pragmatist thought of Richard Rorty and Richard Bernstein, and the hermeneutical theory of Hans-Georg Gadamer. The common link between each of these writers is the notion that "practical thinking is the center of human thinking."[27] This idea becomes the foundation for Browning's discussion of the methods of theology as a practical discipline. For Browning, then, the appropriate outcome of theological inquiry is "practical wisdom" (*phronesis*), rather than technical knowledge. Theological study can be evaluated by the extent to which it helps us live constructively and morally in our particular contemporary situation.

Browning characterizes his method for theological inquiry as a "revised correlational method." It has been particularly influenced by the work of Paul Tillich and David Tracy. This revised correlational theological inquiry can be undertaken in three stages.

The first stage is that of "descriptive theology." Here the task is to understand contemporary responses to a particular issue (whether from religious sources or not), and particularly to identify the basic assumptions and theories that influence these responses. This first stage is therefore one of trying to gain a better grasp of the "horizon" of contemporary living in a particular context or in relation to a particular issue.

The second stage of the process is that of "historical theology." This involves asking the question, "what do the normative texts that are already part of our effective history *really* imply for our praxis when they are confronted as honestly as possible?"[28] The "historical theology" stage is characterized by the process of gaining a clearer understanding of what normative Christian sources have to say in relation to the particular context or issue under consideration. It attempts to clarify the "horizon" of Christian norms.

The third stage is that of "systematic theology," "the fusion of horizons between the vision implicit in contemporary practices and the vision implied in the practices of the normative Christian texts."[29] By bringing the concerns, values, and beliefs evident in contemporary culture alongside the concerns, values, and beliefs of the Christian tradition it may be possible to generate new insights, both in relation to our contemporary lives and to our understanding of the Christian tradition itself.

The two fundamental questions that arise out of this third stage are, therefore, what new fusion of meaning is generated by bringing these two "horizons" together, and how can we demonstrate the validity of this new meaning, both within our religious communities and to the wider realm of public society?

The work of liberal practical theologians such as Hiltner and Browning is characterized by a commitment to the development of clear, rational methodologies for practical theological reflection and, particularly in the case of Browning, to the development of theological positions that are publicly intelligible and defensible in wider civic society. By contrast, another strand of pastoral and practical theology emphasizes the specifically *confessional* basis of this discipline and seeks to explore how the particular traditions and spirituality of the church can inform contemporary theological reflection.

Neo-traditional confessional approaches

Within recent confessional approaches to practical theology, a primary emphasis is placed on the importance of the theologian's personal spirituality or their pursuit of an authentic relationship with the truth as revealed within the Christian tradition. Two of the writers who have been most significant in the contemporary confessional approach to pastoral and practical theology are Henri Nouwen and Tom Oden.

Nouwen, a Catholic priest and theologian born in the Netherlands in 1932, produced a series of books on pastoral theology and Christian spirituality from the early 1970s until his death in 1996. Through this period there was an evident shift in Nouwen's interest and style of writing, from the academic and psychological approach of his papers published in 1969 in *Intimacy*, to his more popular texts on Christian spirituality such as *The Way of the Heart* (1981) and *The Return of the Prodigal Son* (1994). Nouwen's most influential book in pastoral theology was *The Wounded Healer*, first published in the US in 1979.

Nouwen moved from an engagement with the human sciences to placing greater emphasis on the relevance of the Christian tradition and specifically religious and spiritual experience for contemporary life. *The Way of the Heart* thus offers a series of reflections of the relevance of the Desert Fathers for contemporary spirituality. In *Letters to Marc about Jesus* (1988), Nouwen proffers his own particular readings of the relevance of the gospel narratives for today's world. Another striking development in Nouwen's style of writing was his increasing willingness to use his own autobiography as a basis for theological reflection. Some of his books are diaries in which Nouwen traces shifts in his understanding of himself and his spirituality, from time spent in a Trappist monastery, in a slum parish in Latin America, and ultimately his growing involvement with the L'Arche communities founded by Jean Vanier.

The contrast between the style of text produced by Nouwen and that produced, for example, by Browning, is striking. Browning has attempted to develop overarching methodologies for practical theological and moral reflection. Nouwen's work represents a more personal and fragmented attempt to relate his understanding of the Christian tradition to key themes and struggles of contemporary experience, such as loneliness, sexuality, violence, and social justice. Browning's work typically involves a theoretical engagement with other contemporary thinkers in theology, philosophy, hermeneutics, and ethics. Nouwen is more likely to cite the Desert Fathers, or reflect on stories from his own experience. It cannot be argued that Browning is simply a more academic, sophisticated thinker – Nouwen, after all, had doctorates in both theology and psychology and held chairs in pastoral theology at both Yale and Harvard divinity schools. Rather, it is better to characterize these as equally rigorous, yet quite different approaches to pastoral and practical theology. The one is academically based, analytic, systematic, and rationally oriented; the other is more an inhabited wisdom based on spiritual discipline, a contemplative and creative insight into the process of living within a sense of religious vocation.

The shift in Nouwen's writing from detailed engagement in pastoral psychology to a focus on the concepts and practices of the Christian tradition is also mirrored in the work of American pastoral theologian Thomas Oden. In the 1960s Oden was a leading writer in the attempt to integrate insights from Christian theology and counseling psychology. In *Kerygma and Counselling* (1966) Oden argued that underlying effective psychotherapy is a hidden assumption which is made explicit in the Christian gospel. The counselor's work in accepting, empathizing with, and being genuine with the client reflects the nature of God's prior acts of accepting love towards humanity, empathic engagement with humanity through the Incarnation, and congruent self-revelation of the divine nature. The counseling psychology of a secular humanist such as Carl Rogers could therefore be interpreted as implying the truth of God's relationship to creation that is proclaimed in the Christian tradition. While Oden's theological interests are evident, counseling psychology remained an important resource in his understanding of the nature of pastoral ministry.

Through the 1970s Oden underwent a form of conversion toward exploring the relevance of the historical Christian tradition for contemporary life and ministry. He came to reject the "turn to the human" and the privileging of contemporary experience as normative that characterizes much contemporary practical theology. Oden turned instead to a strong emphasis on the importance of divine truth as revealed through the Christian tradition. In other words, Oden moved from a correlational approach to theology focused on contemporary experience, and using the human sciences, to a much more applicationist approach focused on using the resources of Christian tradition.

In his seminal *The Care of Souls in the Classic Tradition* (1984), Oden observed that contemporary writers on pastoral care – such as Hiltner and Howard Clinebell – make frequent references to secular therapeutic theorists such as Sigmund Freud, Carl Rogers, or Eric Berne, but never refer to classical texts of pastoral care written by Cyprian, John Chysostom, Augustine, or Gregory the Great. This use of contemporary therapeutic theories to the exclusion of key historical Christian texts on pastoral care, Oden argued, was a dangerous loss of wisdom accumulated through centuries of pastoral theological reflection. Oden's work has therefore seen a significant move away from engaging with the human sciences toward exploring the relevance of Christian doctine, and patristic theology in particular, for contemporary ministry and theological reflection.[30]

For both Nouwen and Oden, there is a shift away from engaging with and hearing the voices of the human sciences (specifically, counseling psychology) toward giving primacy to insights and concepts from the historical Christian tradition for guiding pastoral theology and practice. While there are certainly significant differences between these two writers, both are committed to relating their under-standing of the historical Christian tradition to contemporary experience. Interest-ingly, there seems to be a greater readiness among such confessional practical theologians to write in ways that are accessible to non-academic audiences within the church. The work of Oden, and especially that of Nouwen, is much better known in non-academic contexts than that of Hiltner and Browning. This contrast of the liberal–rational and confessional approaches to practical theology thus raises the further questions of for whom such theology is being undertaken and what audiences and readers are intended to be drawn into and to benefit from it.

Radical–liberationist approaches

A third group of broad approaches to pastoral and practical theology can be described as radical–liberationist, insofar as they reflect the following three basic concerns that characterize contemporary theologies of liberation.

First, liberationist practical theology places a strong emphasis on social context, and in particular the relevance of social categories such as gender, ethnicity, sexual orientation, and dis/ability for experience in that context. Liberationist practical theology is therefore often written from a perspective consciously shaped by some form of social oppression or exclusion. Examples of this would include feminist practical theology,[31] black practical theology,[32] practical theology emerging out of the Korean experience of "han,"[33] or the experience of disability.[34] The liberal methodologies of Hiltner and Browning pay little attention to the social position-ing of those undertaking practical theological reflection. By contrast, liberationist approaches are born out of distinctive forms of social experience. Typically, they argue the need for forms of theology that are relevant to oppression and exclusion in that particular context.

Secondly, liberationist practical theology is typically conscious of structures and dynamics of power in particular social contexts. James Poling's study on the nature and abuse of power exemplifies a theological project that examines how power functions in particular contexts, sometimes to the detriment of people's psycholo-gical, physical, and spiritual well-being. We saw earlier that Browning characterized the initial task of practical theology as being to understand the questions, beliefs, and practices that are involved in some form of contemporary experience. From a liberationist perspective, this initial inquiry will be particularly sensitive to questions of how power functions in that context, how that power is maintained, what damag-ing consequences may relate to the exercise of that power, and what forms of resistance to that power can be identified.

Thirdly, liberationist practical theology is ultimately concerned with the promo-tion of human liberation and well-being. A liberationist practical theology can there-fore be judged effective in its own terms to the extent to which it stimulates thought and practice that lead to improvements in people's psychological, physical, and spiritual well-being in particular contexts. By contrast with Oden's confessional pastoral theology, which is concerned with maintaining the truth-claims of the historical Christian tradition, liberationist practical theology is primarily concerned with the practical and social implications of particular theological positions and discourses. Liberationist practical theologians are therefore open to exploring new theological languages and metaphors that may hold greater potential for human liberation than traditional discourses of God, creation, or Christian life.

The above descriptions of the three broad approaches to pastoral and practical theology are not exhaustive or mutually exclusive – Nouwen, for example, is considerably influenced by and committed to some liberationist ideas. They provide an understanding of some of the key parameters within which those within this discipline operate. Identifying these approaches adds to an understanding of pastoral and practical theology as a discipline that lacks a strong consensus as to its aims and methods beyond the broad principles identified at the beginning of this chapter.

Through naming these three different approaches to pastoral and practical theology, some of the key questions and debates that each of these approaches raises for the ongoing formation of pastoral and practical theology become visible.

The liberal–rational approach highlights the importance of identifying clear, intelligible, methodological procedures for conducting practical theological study. Writers like Browning have also argued strongly for the importance of being able to defend and justify practical theological conclusions to a wider public audience who may not share the same basic religious convictions. From the perspective of more confessional pastoral theologians this liberal commitment to public and academic styles of theology risks losing sight of the more basic question of the difference that personal devotion to God or commitment to a particular religious tradition might make to contemporary life and thought. In response, liberal practical theologians might raise questions about the degree of methodological clarity in some confessional approaches to the discipline.

From a liberationist perspective, by contrast, liberal attempts to find overarching methodologies for the discipline can appear suspect to the extent that they fail to acknowledge the importance of one's social positioning for the practice of pastoral and practical theology. Is it adequate, for example, for women, people of non-white ethnicities, gay men and lesbians, or people with disabilities to use exactly the same critical methods and tools that have been developed by white, male, heterosexual, able-bodied theologians?

Again, a confessional perspective can raise the question of whether it is sufficient for liberationist approaches to be concerned with human well-being, or whether pastoral and practical theology should be more concerned with defining itself in relation to some higher order of truth and relationship to the divine.

Thus, while there can be some borrowing of ideas and methods between these three approaches, there are certain tensions between them that continue to provide a focus for debate as to the proper nature of the discipline.

Influence, Achievement, and Agenda

In *Distinction* (1984) the French sociologist Pierre Bourdieu noted a significant shift within Western academic institutions in the latter part of the twentieth century. The easier access to these institutions for the new growing middle classes meant that universities and colleges had begun to revise their views on what constituted appropriate fields of academic study. Deference to the study of classic "canons" of art, literature, and other cultural activity began to be displaced by subjects closer to the day-to-day life of this new student population, such as popular culture and the media.[35]

The growth of practical theology as a discipline in recent decades can be seen as a comparable process of revision within the field of academic theology. There will be critics who lament the displacement of traditional theological disciplines. However, the growth of practical theology has allowed a new generation of theological students to bring their particular concerns and experiences into the arena of academic study. One of the greatest achievements of this discipline has been to provide space and a set of methods for those who want to reflect critically on their lived experience in relation to their faith tradition. This has been particularly important for those working in various forms of religious ministry who have struggled to find meaningful ways of relating theoretical concepts from, for example, doctrinal theology, to their practical experience of living and working alongside people.

At its best, practical theology enables people within faith communities to make creative and transformative connections between their experience and their particular tradition, in ways that produce both constructive forms of practice and renewed understandings of theological symbols and ideas. This is not something that has always been valued in what Hiltner referred to as the "logic-centered" disciplines of theology.

Practical theology's strength in making connections between theology and lived experience is associated with one of its most significant weaknesses as an academic discipline. Because those who undertake advanced study in practical theology are typically motivated by a desire to make sense theologically of their experience in a given context, the outcome of such study tends to be highly relevant to their personal development and practice. It is quite rare for this kind of study to generate books and articles that contribute significantly to the intellectual development of theoretical and methodological thinking in practical theology more generally. The current theoretical basis of practical theology is substantial. Browning, in particular, has articulated a significant and sophisticated theoretical framework for practical theological reflection (a process also continued in a more postmodern vein by Elaine Graham). But unless practical theology finds ways of continuing to generate theoretical work, it risks becoming detached from the wider activity of academic theology and its contribution to the construction of theological concepts, symbols, and narratives may be weakened. Thus it will fail to deliver on the hopes expressed by Hiltner and others that it can make a fundamental autonomous contribution to theology as such, as a theological discipline in its own right.

Practical theology faces a number of challenges in the future. One of these is to continue to develop as an academic discipline so that it does not remain the Cinderella of the theological world. Another is that of making fundamental, valued contributions to theology which are recognized as such by colleagues in the wider theological arena. As it is, the contemporary, practical emphasis of the discipline can make its findings seem ephemeral and quickly dated. A further challenge is for the discipline to continue to demonstrate that it actually can make a difference in practice and so is worth pursuing. These challenges can be summed up by saying that practical and pastoral theology needs to become more academically sophisticated and more theologically illuminative, at the same time as becoming more relevant, more practical, and more helpful to practitioners. This is a contradictory and demanding set of imperatives, to say the least. Looking outwards from the nature of the discipline itself, further challenges can be identified.

As with many other academic disciplines, practical theologians are being faced with questions of the implications of globalization for contemporary human experience. The events of September 11, 2001 provide a reminder that we are a global community in which the attitudes, perceptions, and beliefs of groups in one place can have a dramatic impact on people elsewhere. Everyday life is not a purely local affair. It is influenced by intricate networks of relationships, structures, multinational organizations, and practices that span the world. The focus of practical theological reflection cannot rest at the level of local experiences and concerns, but (in its liberative mode, for example) must ask how human liberation and well-being is promoted or hindered by these current international structures and relationships.

The growing recognition of the significance of the global dimension of human existence has led to a renewed understanding of the significance of local experiences and interests. While the presence of the symbols, structures, and institutions of global capitalism may be increasingly felt around the world, human life has not become homogenized across all contexts and cultures. Rather, human existence is better understood as now lived in the context of the "glocal": the complex and unique environment produced through the interrelationship between our local culture and the emerging global culture.[36]

This means that while practical theology will need to retain a global focus, the notion of universal theories and models of practical theology is inappropriate. Rather, we will need glocal practical theologies that recognize global issues and relationships, yet explore these in relation to the particular experiences, beliefs, symbols, and values of our own local cultures and traditions. Examples of such glocal practical theologies are already evident in the emergent contextual theologies of liberation in Africa, Asia, and Latin America. They can also be found in the growing literature on the nature of appropriate pastoral care within particular cultural contexts.[37] The notion of glocal practical theology might also draw our attention to the significance for practical theology of the cultural differences between the United States and Western Europe. What difference does it make for the theory and practice of practical theology, for example, when this discipline is practiced in the context of an American culture that remains overtly religious, in contrast to a British society that seems increasingly post-Christian or post-religious?

This latter question raises the final challenge to practical theology that we will consider here. While large parts of Western Europe show apparent signs of secularization, much of the world is witnessing a renaissance of religious belief and affiliation which often takes fundamentalist forms. Global trends in belief and religious adherence raise basic questions about how we value and engage with our religious traditions. Should practical theology be primarily concerned with communicating divine truth, as revealed through the Christian tradition, to the contemporary world? Or should it try to become the means by which religious tradition is renewed and reshaped in the light of contemporary experience? Does practical theology, as an academic discipline, have any useful role to contribute beyond the church within which it has almost entirely been confined up until now? The way in which these questions are addressed will have significant consequences, not only for practical theology as an academic discipline, but also for the shape of faith communities and wider societies as we enter a new and uncertain future.

Notes

1 See Paul Ballard, *Practical Theology: Proliferation and Performance* (Cardiff, 2001).

2 Examples are Al McFadyen, *Bound to Sin? Abuse, Holocaust and the Christian Doctrine of Sin* (Cambridge, 2001); Paul Fiddes, *Participating in God: A Pastoral Doctrine of the Trinity* (London, 2000).

3 See Paul Ballard, "The Emergence of Pastoral and Practical Theology in Britain," in James Woodward and Stephen Pattison (eds.), *The Blackwell Reader in Pastoral and Practical Theology* (Oxford, 2000), pp. 59–69; John Patton, *From Ministry to Theology* (Nashville, TN, 1990).

4 See Ben Highmore, *Everyday Life and Cultural Theory* (London, 2002).

5 See on this Alfredo Fierro, *The Militant Gospel* (London, 1977).

6 As discussed in Charles Gerkin, *An Introduction to Pastoral Care* (Nashville, TN, 1997).

7 See William Clebsch and Charles Jaekle, *Pastoral Care in Historical Perspective* (New York, 1967); Gillian Evans (ed.), *A History of Pastoral Care* (London, 2000); John McNeill, *A History of the Cure of Souls* (New York, 1977); Thomas Oden, *The Care of Souls in the Classic Tradition* (Philadelphia, PA, 1984).

8 Friedrich Schleiermacher, *Critical Caring: Selections from Practical Theology* (Philadelphia, PA, 1988).

9 See, for example, Emmanuel Lartey, "Practical Theology as a Theological Form" in Woodward and Pattison, *Blackwell Reader in Pastoral and Practical Theology*, pp. 128–34.

10 See, for example, Patton, *From Ministry to Theology*.

11 See Peter Selby, *Liberating God: Private Care and Public Struggle* (London, 1983); Stephen Pattison, *Pastoral Care and Liberation Theology* (Cambridge, 1994).

12 As in Johannes van der Ven, *Practical Theology: An Empirical Approach* (Kampen, 1993).

13 As in Elaine Graham, *Transforming Practice: Pastoral Theology in an Age of Uncertainty* (London, 1996); Gordon Lynch, *After Religion: "Generation X" and the Search for Meaning* (London, 2002).

14 Stephen Pattison, *Shame: Theory, Therapy, Theology* (Cambridge, 2000).

15 James Newton Poling, *The Abuse of Power: A Theological Problem* (Nashville, TN, 1991); Gordon Lynch, "Exploring the Client's View: An Agenda for Empirical Research in Pastoral Care and Counselling," *Contact: The Interdisciplinary Journal of Pastoral Studies*, 128 (1999), pp. 22–8.

16 See Gerkin, *Introduction to Pastoral Care*, pp. 60–3; John Patton, "Introduction to Modern Pastoral Theology in the United States," in Woodward and Pattison, *Blackwell Reader in Pastoral and Practical Theology*, pp. 49–59.

17 Compare Charles Gerkin, *The Living Human Document: Re-Visioning Pastoral Counseling in an Hermeneutical Mode* (Nashville, TN, 1984); Donald Capps, *Living Stories: Pastoral Counseling in a Congregational Context* (Minneapolis, MN, 1998).

18 See, for example, Jo Ind, *Memories of Bliss: God, Sex and Us* (London, 2003).

19 Laurie Green, *Let's Do Theology: A Pastoral Cycle Resource Book* (London, 1990); Stephen Pattison, "Some Straw for the Bricks: A Basic Introduction to Theological Reflection," in Woodward and Pattison, *Blackwell Reader in Pastoral and Practical Theology*, pp. 135–45.

20 See Ballard, *Practical Theology*.

21 See Pattison, *Pastoral Care and Liberation Theology*; Emmanuel Lartey, *In Living Colour: An Intercultural Approach to Pastoral Care and Counselling* (London, 2003).

22 But see also Derek Tidball, *Skillful Shepherds: An Introduction to Pastoral Theology* (London, 1986); Roger Hurding, *Pathways to Wholeness: Pastoral Care in a Postmodern Age* (London, 1998).

23 See Pattison, *Pastoral Care and Liberation Theology*, p. 32.
24 Poling, *The Abuse of Power*; McFadyen, *Bound to Sin?*; Hilary Cashman, *Christianity and Child Sex Abuse* (London, 1993).
25 Stewart Hiltner, *A Preface to Pastoral Theology* (New York, 1958), p. 20.
26 Ibid.
27 Don Browning, *A Fundamental Practical Theology: Descriptive and Strategic Proposals* (Minneapolis, MN, 1990), p. 8.
28 Ibid, p. 49.
29 Ibid, p. 51.
30 See Thomas Oden, *The Living God: Systematic Theology, Vol. 1* (New York, 1987); *Classical Pastoral Care* (Grand Rapids, MI, 2003).
31 See Elaine Graham, *Making the Difference: Gender, Personhood, Theology* (London, 1995); Zoe Bennett-Moore, *Introducing Feminist Perspectives on Pastoral Theology* (Sheffield, 2002); Bonnie Miller-McLemore

and Brita Gill-Austern (eds.), *Feminist and Womanist Pastoral Theology* (Nashville, TN, 1999).
32 See Edward P. Wimberley, *African American Pastoral Care* (Nashville, TN, 1991); Lartey, *In Living Colour*.
33 See Chung Hyun Kyung, *Struggle to be the Sun Again: Introducing Asian Women's Theology* (London, 1991).
34 Nancy Eiseland, *The Disabled God: Towards a Liberatory Theology of Disability* (Nashville, TN, 1994).
35 Pierre Bourdieu, *Distinction: A Social Critique of the Judgement of Taste* (London, 1984).
36 See Gargi Bhattacharyya, John Gabriel, and Stephen Small, *Race and Power: Global Racism in the Twenty-First Century* (London, 2002).
37 See, for example, Abraham Berinyuu, *Pastoral Care to the Sick in Africa* (Frankfurt, 1988); Lartey, *In Living Colour*.

Bibliography

Paul Ballard, *Practical Theology: Proliferation and Performance* (Cardiff, 2001).

Zoe Bennett-Moore, *Introducing Feminist Perspectives on Pastoral Theology* (London, 2002).

Don Browning, *A Fundamental Practical Theology: Descriptive and Strategic Proposal* (Minneapolis, MN, 1991).

Hilary Cashman, *Christianity and Child Sex Abuse* (London, 1993).

William Clebsch and Charles Jaekle, *Pastoral Care in Historical Perspective* (New York, 1967).

Nancy Eiesland, *The Disabled God: Towards a Liberatory Theology of Disability* (Nashville, TN, 1994).

Elaine Graham, *Transforming Practice: Pastoral Theology in an Age of Uncertainty* (London, 1996).

Laurie Green, *Let's Do Theology: A Pastoral Cycle Resource Book* (London, 1990).

Stewart Hiltner, *A Preface to Pastoral Theology* (New York, 1958).

Emmanuel Lartey, *In Living Colour: An Intercultural Approach to Pastoral Care and Counselling* (London, 2003).

Gordon Lynch, *After Religion: "Generation X" and the Search for Meaning* (London, 2003).

Bonnie Miller-McLemore and Brita Gill-Austern (eds.), *Feminist and Womanist Pastoral Theology* (Nashville, TN, 1999).

Henri Nouwen, *The Wounded Healer* (London, 1994).

Thomas Oden, *The Care of Souls in the Classic Tradition* (Philadelphia, PA, 1984).

Stephen Pattison, *Pastoral Care and Liberation Theology* (Cambridge, 1994).

—— *Shame: Theory, Therapy, Theology* (Cambridge, 2000).

John Patton, *From Ministry to Theology* (Nashville, TN, 1990).

James Newton Poling, *The Abuse of Power: A Theological Problem* (Nashville, TN, 1991).

Friedrich Schleiermacher, *Critical Caring: Selections from Practical Theology*, trans. James O. Duke (Philadelphia, PA, 1988).

Derek Tidball, *Skillful Shepherds: An Introduction to Pastoral Theology* (London, 1986).

Johannes van der Ven, *Practical Theology: An Empirical Approach* (Kampen, 1993).

Edward P. Wimberley, *African American Pastoral Care* (Nashville, TN, 1991).

James Woodward and Stephen Pattison (eds.), *The Blackwell Reader in Pastoral and Practical Theology* (Oxford, 2000).

Particularizing Theology

part 5

All theology is partial and particular, arising in and speaking to historical, social, and political contexts in which the theologians are interested parties. The twentieth century, however, saw the development of *self-consciously* partial and particular theologies, deliberately adopting standpoints previously marginalized or excluded in "mainstream" theology, and hence drawing attention to the limitations of the mainstream itself.

The particularizing theologies discussed in Part V should thus be read, not as the only "particular" theologies in the book, but as the theologies that bring every theologian's particularity – gendered, racial, cultural, economic – onto the agenda for the twentieth and twenty-first centuries. After all, today, the majority of Christians in the world live outside North America and Western Europe, white Christians are in a global minority, and, of course, at least half the Christians in the world are women. These points should be borne in mind by anyone who considers the theologies discussed in this section to be of only marginal or specialist interest.

Speaking of the partiality of theology, as well as its particularity, reminds us that the differences highlighted by these theologies are not innocent. They are often deeply conflictual and rooted in persisting global and local power imbalances. Political and social changes – decolonization, civil rights movements, changes in the position of women – are part of the context of these theologies, but the theologians are participants and not simply observers. The call to *liberation* theology, theology whose "partiality" places it on the side of the oppressed or the least powerful, arose in Latin America (see Rebecca Chopp and Ethna Regan's chapter). It is also profoundly significant for black theology in North America and South Africa (as Dwight Hopkins and Tinyiko Maluleke show), for theologies in Africa and Asia (as discussed by Tinyiko Maluleke, Felix Wilfred, and Archie Lee), and for feminist theology (Rachel Muers' chapter). The use of postcolonial theory (see in particular R. S. Sugirtharajah's chapter) enables theologians to develop a fuller account of how Christians can speak of "liberation" in contexts where theology, and Christianity, have been defined from the perspective of colonialism and imperialism.

A further vital issue for theologians who emphasize particularity is the relationship between theology and culture. What does it mean for Christian texts, practices, and claims to exist in a wide range of cultural contexts? Tinyiko Maluleke writes of the centrality of African culture and African Traditional Religions in the ongoing development of African theology; Archie Lee describes various ways of constructing the relationship between East Asian philosophies and literatures, on the one hand, and Christian theology on the other; and Felix Wilfred discusses the possibilities and limitations of "inculturation" against the religiously plural background of South Asia. Again, attention in this section to issues of theology and culture reminds readers of "mainstream" theology to be aware of its cultural and historical particularity.

Feminism, Gender, and Theology

Rachel Muers

Introduction

The emergence of women's voices, of feminist concerns, and of gender analysis was one of the most significant events in theology in the twentieth century. The point is not, of course, that no women thought theologically, or wrote theology, before the twentieth century – many did, and their influence on succeeding generations has been great. Nor is it that issues of sex and gender were insignificant in theological writing before the twentieth century – quite the reverse. The new event of the twentieth century was the explicit recognition, in the context of the feminist movement, of the ways in which earlier theology had tended systematically to silence women and to lend ideological support to their oppression.

Feminist theology arose and continues as the proclamation, in the voices of many different women, that the "good news" of the Christian gospel is good news for both women and men – and that the promise of liberation from sin refers also to the structural sin of sexism, as identified and challenged by feminist thought and action. The second half of the twentieth century saw the intensification of feminist campaigning and theorizing known as "second-wave feminism," and theologians have played a significant part in this movement from the beginning. In feminist theology of the "second wave," analysis of the social, political, and sexual oppression of women in particular contexts is set alongside critiques of earlier theology and attempts to construct theologies and spiritualities more conducive to the full flourishing of women. As the concepts of feminism, sex, and gender have become more problematic and complex, so also "feminist theology" has become more complex; but strong ethical and political commitment remains a key feature of theological engagement with these issues.

To do feminist theology, then, is often to make use of tools of analysis, developed in feminist theory that is not explicitly theological – that may, in fact, be explicitly anti-theological – to criticize and transform theological discourse. It is also, however, to reflect theologically on the limitations of "feminism" and feminist theory. Many Christian feminist theologians have brought their knowledge of theological discourses on gender symbolics, ethics, and eschatology – to name but a few areas – to bear on contemporary feminist debates.

In Europe and North America, women's greater access to higher education and to participation in public life created, in the twentieth century, the possibility of women's participation in the theological academy. At the same time, moves within many churches toward the admission of women to leadership roles and to ordained ministry became the focus for debate about the theologies that had excluded them previously. Alongside these developments in the North must be set the development of women's theology in Africa, Asia, and Latin America, both within and in critical conversation with postcolonial, liberation, and inculturated theologies. Women's voices have joined with those of men in the assertion that Christian theology could be done, not in the language of the Northern missionaries who had first brought and taught it, but in the language and out of the experience of the people who now practiced it. They have joined, also, in the calls for theology to promote liberation from colonial oppression, including the new colonialism of unjust global trade structures, and to stand in solidarity with the poor. These women's voices, however, sounded and continue to sound distinctive notes – recalling the multiple oppression suffered by women in patriarchal and colonial societies, analyzing the relationship between colonialism and sexism, and speaking women's distinctive experience of Christianity and of cultures. One of the strengths of feminist theology has been the promotion of global dialogues, on questions of common concern, among theologians from very different social and cultural contexts.

Survey

A survey of feminist theology must take account of the distinctiveness, not only of its content, but also of its approach, sources, and norms. One of the most important tasks of feminist theology, or any theology that takes seriously the question of gender, has been to think through the *doing* of theology as an ethical and political act. Within the theology that arises in this context of critical reflection, various key themes emerge – among them, the theological significance of difference and plurality; the revisioning of theological anthropology, particularly around issues of sin and human embodiment; and, perhaps as the central question, the naming of God.

Thinking the difference

In common with many of the movements described in this section on "Particularizing Theology," feminist theology has consciously recalled theologians to the ethical and political implications of what they say, who says it, and how it is said. For feminists, and feminist theologians among them, it is not simply that there is or can be no theoretical "view from nowhere"; it is that the claim to have the "view from nowhere" is ethically and politically problematic in that it works to suppress the voices and concerns of others. The plurality of voices, the multiplicity of perspectives, and the unavoidable reality of human difference emerges as a key theme in feminist theology.

Feminist theology, particularly in the North, has presented itself as a critique of the idolatries that have pervaded the churches and the theological academy as much as the wider society. Centrally, feminist theology attacks the idolatry of the *male* God that supports the ideology of patriarchy and, feminist theologians would argue, a multitude of other forms of oppression (although, as I will discuss further below, the interrelations of sexism and these other forms of oppression are contested within feminist theology). Thus, a critique of the exclusive use of masculine imagery for God – for example, in the work of Sallie McFague and others, of the "root metaphor" of *fatherhood* – may be placed alongside an analysis of the material and cultural subjugation of women and of the wider political problems with which Christian theology has failed to engage.[1] Rosemary Radford Ruether undertakes the extended analysis of Christian patriarchal "idolatry" as the precursor to her constructive theological project. This emphasis on anti-idolatry within the theological task is shared with other liberationist theological projects. It is important to note that it relies, within all such projects, on a theological (rather than simply a feminist/ pragmatic) claim – that the nature of God exceeds the possibility of comprehension through any set of names and images. There is an apparent affinity between feminist theology in this "iconoclastic" vein and negative or apophatic theology, in both its premodern and its postmodern guises.

The "anti-idolatrous" move with regard to God is paralleled by a deconstruction of the notion of "woman" operating in *both* mainstream/patriarchal *and* earlier feminist theologies. The attempt to put forward a singular understanding of "women's experience" had in fact, it was suggested, projected the characteristic experience of the white, middle-class, North American or European, heterosexual woman onto *all* women. Jacquelyn Grant, Katie Cannon, and others (drawing on the work of such theorists as bell hooks and Angela Davis) displayed the race-blindness of white feminist theology, while international dialogues of feminist theologians made the multiplicity of women's experience itself an unavoidable topic of theological thought.[2] It was suggested, explicitly or implicitly, that the universalized "woman" of early feminist theology in fact covertly depended on the retention of the sovereign "God" – even, or perhaps especially, where there was an emphasis on naming that "God" in terms more appropriate to "women's experience." The work of Mary McClintock Fulkerson and others, on the thought and practice of non-feminist Christian women, further complicates the picture, by asking how the academic feminist's voice relates to the voices of women who exercise religious and political agency within "patriarchal" frameworks.[3]

This critique of certain trends within early feminist theology carries with it the reminder that the doing of theology is political, not merely because the content of theological texts can be used to support or subvert political orders, but more importantly because the ways in which theological discourse is authorized, and access to it granted or denied, are embedded in structures of power. As suggested above, feminist theology begins by protesting about the ways in which women's theological speech has been systematically excluded or devalued. How can feminist theologians avoid repeating the same pattern, simply substituting their own voices and their own norms for those that have previously controlled theology?

Many feminist theologians choose to write in ways that make the limitations of their own perspectives explicit – acknowledging their own positions as members of particular groups. A more overtly political approach to this explicit adoption of a particular standpoint is to highlight the *accountability* of theologians to communities of the oppressed. Accountability is a central theme of postcolonial reflection on theological method, and of feminist postcolonial theology in particular; it is key, for example, to the work of Chung Hyun Kyung in Korea, as well as that of Ada Maria Isasi-Diaz among Latinas in the USA. The idea is to avoid taking the experiences of the poor or of women from them as theological "raw material" (repeating the imperialist move), without ongoing critical interrogation of their use by the communities from which they are derived. The theologian's "communities of accountability" are both the critics of her work and the sources of its norms – how does theology serve the flourishing of poor women in colonial or patriarchal societies? Linking theology to a particular community of accountability need not mean giving up on claims to that theology's truthfulness, but it does mean calling to account theological truth-claims that fail to acknowledge their own social and gender location.

This emphasis on particularity reminds us that feminist theology, like feminist thought more generally, emerges at the intersection between "modern" and "postmodern" frameworks of thought – arising from a "modern" emphasis on equality, rights and individual autonomy, but at the same time contributing to the moves that problematized "modernity." European and North American thought classed as "postmodern" has often included sustained attention to issues of gender, and has in turn been variously appropriated by feminist thinkers and theologians. The emphasis on difference and multiplicity, the exposure of the mechanisms of power operating within texts and discourses to suppress difference, and the questioning of any attempt to make universal claims about "humanity," are all aspects of postmodern philosophy that have been welcomed by feminist theologians.[4] While this appropriation of postmodern thought clearly helps to provide a theoretical basis for many of the methodological and substantive moves that feminist theologians want to make, it is also fraught with difficulty. Does the affirmation of "difference" actually risk losing or softening political commitment? Is it really helpful to women to call into question the categories of "subject" and "agency," just as women are beginning to be able to understand themselves as subjects and agents in theological and other contexts? These debates continue within feminist theory as a whole. Within feminist theology, their specific importance is perhaps to give feminist theologians a distinctive perspective on the multifarious debates over "where theology should go after modernity." Many feminist theologians, as I shall explore further below, find resources in premodern texts for their questioning of the Enlightenment "man of reason"; but at the same time they will, as feminists, acknowledge that patriarchy and androcentrism did not begin in modernity – whereas feminism did.

The critical re-reading of the texts of theological tradition, using the tools of feminist philosophy and criticism, has of course extended to the reading of the Bible. Modern feminist biblical scholarship can be said to have begun with the *Woman's Bible*, for which Elizabeth Cady Stanton drew together female biblical scholars to comment on all the biblical texts in which women appear or are mentioned.[5] The approach and content of the *Woman's Bible* can be seen to establish many of the concerns and debates that have shaped subsequent feminist biblical interpretation. If one only reads the texts that speak of women, does this collude with attempts to conceal or denigrate women's place in the communities that produced and preserved the texts? With this in mind, Elizabeth Schüssler Fiorenza's work on New Testament texts, for example, begins from the presupposition that women were important in early Christianity, and traces how the texts both reveal and conceal their religious lives. To focus on the texts in which women appear, as many feminist commentators still do, confronts one with the record of women's subordination, exclusion, and subjection to violence – realities that the texts not only record, but also repeat and enable to be repeated in the lives of people who read these texts. Phyllis Trible's work on the "texts of terror" in the Hebrew Bible brings this out, and puts to Christian feminist theologians the stark question: how can "texts of terror" be read as sacred text? Recognizing the biblical texts as products of patriarchal cultures – whatever else they are – gives rise to a range of reading strategies, from the call to discard or ignore texts that speak explicitly of women's subordination, to the reading of the Bible "against itself" to recover the suppressed voices or narratives of women. The very idea of biblical authority is a problematic area for feminist thinkers, appearing, as it is put forward in some contexts, simply a restatement of the demand that women allow themselves to be governed by a male God and his male representatives (the biblical writers and their – predominantly male – authorized interpreters). Models of biblical authority that stress the interaction between the text and the reader in an interpretive context, and that prioritize the ethical and political outworkings of biblical interpretation, have been important for feminist reclamations of the biblical text.

Gender analysis: Woman/body/nature[6]

Feminist critical re-readings of theological tradition make extensive use of the category of gender. What is gender, and what is its importance for theology? Most simply, the term denotes the set of structuring principles that distinguish males from females, or maleness from femaleness – and that make the comparable distinctions between persons in contexts where "male" and "female" are not the only two possibilities. The suggestion in earlier English-language literature that a clear division was possible between biological "sex" and culturally determined "gender" is now generally recognized as an oversimplification at best. It is, in fact, based on a "nature/culture" or "matter/spirit" division that is itself gendered – in that women and femaleness have been traditionally associated with nature and matter, as opposed to the masculine realms of culture and spirit. To recognize this is already to recognize the pervasiveness of gender – as an ordering principle that determines, not only relationships and hierarchies among persons, but also the shape of our cultural and "natural" world. To think about theology from the perspective of gender is to recognize this in theological texts and symbol-systems.

What do theologians find when they pursue such gender analyses of theological texts past and present? On the one hand, they find and expose the symbolic structures that support the material oppression of women. Early feminist analysis chronicles how these texts set up dualisms in which women and femaleness are associated with sinfulness and chaos – and with "the flesh" understood negatively, with matter rather than form, with chaotic emotion rather than divine reason. It notes the ways in which the naming of God as male is used to hold the structure of oppression in place. Mary Daly wrote, in a slogan that has been picked up by numerous others, "If God is male, then the male is God." If the highest value and source of value is only or mainly imagined in male terms – so runs the claim – the denigration of femaleness and the oppression of real women is inevitable.

The effects of gendered binaries – man/woman, spirit/matter, reason/emotion, soul/body – on theological thinking are not, however, as feminist theologians understand them, limited to the oppression of women. One of the key concerns of feminist theology has been for the theological revaluation of the body and of embodiment. It might have been assumed that a religion centered on the *incarnation* of divinity would not need such a revaluation. Numerous critical discussions in the twentieth century have, however, suggested that there is a persistent failure within Christian theology to take seriously the creation and redemption of the body, particularly the female body. Whether these discussions emphasize Pauline texts on "flesh" and "spirit," early asceticism, the ideal of celibacy, a Protestant focus on "inwardness," the Enlightenment rewriting of Christianity in terms of rational cognition – in short, at whatever points in the development of Christianity the problem is located – it is widely agreed that a renewed theology of the body is of central importance for contemporary Christianity. Analyses of the gendered binaries that have shaped philosophical and theological discourse reveals a complex of tendencies that would seem to make the revaluation of the body and of nature particularly important as a feminist concern. There is the pervasive identification of women with pre-cultural "nature" or with unformed matter, the gendering of nature as feminine ("mother nature," "mother earth," the "veiled goddess"), the focus on bodily difference as that which determines women's subordinate status. Women, as feminist readings of a succession of theological texts suggest, have been understood as to a greater extent than men defined by their bodiliness.

The theological revaluation of the body is important for feminists, not only because of the perceived denigration of *women's* bodies (especially) within Christian thought and theology, but because of the corresponding denigration of the body seen in early feminism. Theological challenges to the early "liberal" feminism, which sought to transcend women's bodily life through appeal to a sexless "reason," have in fact been able to draw on many traditional, often premodern, Christian resources. Contemporary theologians have rediscovered traditions of writing that see the sexed body as the location of God's redemptive activity.[7]

What does it mean in this context that Christian theology of the body is focused on the body of *Jesus*? The inescapability of this "male body" for Christian thought, especially seen in the context of the ways in which the maleness of Jesus' body has been used in debates around women's priesthood and ministry, has been a major factor in the rejection of Christianity by many of those who describe themselves as "post-Christian" feminists. Thus, for example, Daphne Hampson's objections to Christianity focus on the "scandal of particularity"; the particularity of Jesus, including his maleness, is inescapably central to Christianity, and for that reason, Hampson argues, there is no escaping male dominance within a Christian theological framework.[8] A wide range of responses to Hampson's challenge can be identified within feminist theology, all of which call into question in different ways the implied claim that the maleness of Jesus' body has a fixed and normative significance. It is important, and generally recognized as such by feminist theologians, to do this without denigrating the importance of Jesus' particular embodiment *per se*. Janet Martin Soskice's work on "turning the symbols," for example, points out the association of Jesus' body with "female" characteristics – life-giving blood, the birth of new life in the flow of blood and water. A very different example is Mercy Amba Oduyoye's work on African women's Christologies, which brings out the irrelevance of the question of Jesus' maleness in a context where the focus is his acts of physical healing, feeding, and restoring bodily well-being.

Feminist theology's commitment to "thinking the body" is not merely a shift in the subject matter of theology; it reflects a methodological move with significant political implications. The title of a well-known collection of feminist theological essays from the South, edited by Virginia Fabella and Mercy Oduyoye – *With Passion and Compassion* – suggests this move. Doing theology with "passion" means allowing theology to express the embodied location of the theologian, her desires and suffering – not detaching the activity of theological thought from the theologian's whole life. "Compassion" draws attention to the irreducible reality of suffering bodies, with which any theological attempt to proclaim "good news to the poor" is confronted. Speaking of "passion and compassion" in the doing of theology also draws attention to the association of Jesus Christ with "feminine" characteristics – and hence to the ways in which women expressing passion and compassion are bearers of the form of Christ.

Many Christian feminist theologians see a close connection between their work and the various movements termed "ecofeminist" – movements that link demands for the empowerment of women and the overthrow of patriarchy with a concern for the protection of the natural environment and an end to its unsustainable exploitation. In fact, feminist theologians, notably Rosemary Radford Ruether in *New Woman/New Earth*, were among the first to theorize the connections between the oppression of women and the degradation of nature. "Spiritual ecofeminism" has sought and devised rituals, myths, and images for the ecofeminist movement, to express and engender the sense of connection between women and the earth that shapes their political activity. In general, those describing themselves as "spiritual ecofeminists" have looked, not to the Christian tradition – regarded as irredeemably patriarchal and anti-nature – but to the religious traditions of indigenous peoples for inspiration in shaping such rituals. However, many theologians working within the Christian tradition share the ecofeminist claim that the reaffirmation of women's lives and experience, on the one hand, and the restoration of a right relationship between humanity and non-human nature, on the other, go together. As part of their feminist theological work, Christian theologians have reemphasized the resources within their own tradition for an ecologically aware theology and spirituality – one that does not separate humanity from nature as its ("masculine") overlord or possessor, but rather places humanity within nature, as embodied being existing in connection with and dependence on material reality. Feminist theologians from the South, speaking in solidarity with people whose lives have been most affected by the consequences of environmental degradation, and often drawing on traditions of religious thought to which the earth and nature are central, have been in the forefront of this Christian ecofeminism.

Alongside the focus on embodiment and nature, feminist theology has sought to prioritize characteristics that are felt to have been undervalued in male-dominated theology. A key example is the emphasis in much feminist theology on community and relationship. Over against the isolated and invulnerable self – modeled on the isolated and sovereign God? – feminist theologians have set a vision of the self formed in and through its relationships and the communities of which it is part, most itself when it is most open to relation. The critique of hierarchical relations, and the ways in which theologies and ecclesial structures reinforce hierarchies existing in wider society, is present both in feminist theological writings on community and in many aspects of feminist theological practice. The twentieth-century revival of interest in trinitarian theology, in the West, has been taken up by several feminist theologians as an indication of how this concern for community and relationality can be found at the heart of the theological tradition.[9] The feminist critique of the individualism – as they see it – of much (in particular) post-Enlightenment theology links closely to a wider concern to change the "subject" of theology – both the divine subject and the human subject.

What is "man" and what is God?

I have already referred to some of the concerns that lead feminist theological reflection to the question of how God is named and imagined – most importantly, the sense that the naming and imagining of God in male terms is idolatrous, leading to a misdirection of worship and a distortion of human relationships. Mary Daly's work, again in the forefront of the feminist critique of Christianity, describes the "Godfather" figure with which Christianity has often seemed to confront women – the apotheosis of male power backed up by violence. The further analysis and critique of this aspect of the naming of God has been a significant aspect of feminist theology. I have also, however, suggested that feminist theology has not been limited to the critical move of anti-idolatry. Feminist appropriations of trinitarian theology have offered a way of subverting the "Godfather" that can at the same time claim to be more true to the breadth of Christian theological tradition than the image of God against which it sets itself.

Also important for feminist theological work has been the reappropriation of the biblical figure of divine Wisdom (Proverbs 8 and 9) – a figure closely associated, not only with the act of creation, but also with the right ordering of human society and relationships, with divine presence in the human and natural order, and – as several feminist theologians have emphasized – in later Christian reflection with Jesus Christ. A parallel line of reflection takes up reflection on the *Shekinah*, the presence of God with God's people, also imaged as female.[10] In neither case is the female imaging of God intended to "replace" the male; the search, as feminist theologians understand it, is for a richer and more diverse language of divinity that would genuinely transcend an existing understanding of gender and gender relations – as, it is claimed, the Christian understanding of God should. In appropriating and reflecting on neglected biblical or traditional ways of naming God, feminist theologians also exercise critique, recognizing that they are still working within a patriarchal tradition. In reading texts on the naming of God, particular attention is paid to the moves by which female images of God have been either excluded or subordinated to the male.[11] An ongoing debate over the relation of Christian feminist theology to

"Goddess" religion, ancient and contemporary, arises in the context of the recognition that Christianity is partly premised on the *rejection* of a certain set of female images of God.

God is "supposed" on some level to be gender-neutral but has in practice been imagined as male; in the same way, feminist theologians have claimed, the human subject of theology has been thought as male. One of the most significant articles for "second-wave" Northern feminist theology has been Valerie Saiving Goldstein's "The Human Situation: A Feminine View." Goldstein was concerned, not so much with the problem of the masculine imaging of God, as with the unmarked maleness of the supposedly gender-neutral human subject of theology. She argued that theological accounts of sin had consistently emphasized the sin of pride – excessive self-assertion, the attempt to set oneself up as a rival to God – and that this failed to address the characteristic "sinfulness" of women in a patriarchal society, which could be better described as "sloth" – the failure to mature as selves, to take responsibility for their own actions, to overcome their reliance on others for validation. Saiving Goldstein's work, which has given rise to lively and ongoing debates, raises awareness of the many ways in which theology can reinforce the idea of the male norm – of which the assumption in liturgy, biblical translation, or theological writing that "he" or "man" can be made to stand for both sexes is merely one of the most pervasive examples.

Once the gender-neutrality of the human subject of theology is called into question, and normative humanity is no longer construed in male terms, maleness as well as femaleness becomes a possible topic for theological reflection. Theological accounts of masculinity developed in conscious response to feminism and feminist theology are, so far, few in number, but their existence is significant. They reflect the recognition that conflating the questions of "gender difference in theology" and "women's voices in theology" amounts to repeating the move that feminist theology criticizes – making men the "norm" and women the "different" or the "other." More developed, and in a more complex relation to feminist theology, is theological reflection on gay, lesbian, and "queer" identity.

Some Significant Figures

The anti-individualist emphasis of feminist theology extends, as I have suggested, to the critical analysis of theological method and theological style – so any listing of individual theologians as somehow central or representative is suspect from the start. I have attempted to show, in presenting these examples of feminist theological work, how each thinker is in conversation with a wider community both past and present.

Chung Hyun Kyung

Chung Hyun Kyung came to the attention of a wide global audience in 1991 when she addressed the World Council of Churches on the Assembly theme "Come Holy Spirit – Renew the Whole Creation." Her use of the image of *Kwan Yin*, the East Asian goddess of compassion and wisdom, to envision the Holy Spirit, with the suggestion that this was also a "feminine image of the Christ," caused enormous controversy. Several ongoing themes of Chung's theology can be seen in her use of *Kwan Yin*. Firstly, there is her commitment to the grounding of theology, not in dehistoricized "religious experience" but in the forms of religious practice and expression found among the people with whom the Christian theologian is called to show solidarity. She looks, then, to the lived experience of East Asian women – including the ways in which they imagine divinity – as both the inspiration for her theology and the source of its validation. Her address to the World Council of Churches, and her published writing, is explicitly a gathering of many theological voices, brought in as representatives of the communities to which she seeks to be accountable. One of the important and controversial aspects of her acts of "gathering" is the venture she makes, while being clear in identifying herself as a Christian theologian, into what she is happy to describe as syncretism – the interfaith exchange that she sees as basic to Asian spirituality in general and Asian women's spirituality in particular.

Secondly, *Kwan Yin* as symbol of the Holy Spirit is a feminine image of God – and the idea that women are created in God's image is central to Chung's thought. Particularly in Asia, as she understands it, the center of the feminist theological task is the affirmation of women as fully human and hence fully bearers of the divine image. The search is for a theology that both speaks the truth of Asian women's suffering – theology "from the broken body" in which women bear the image of God in being "crucified persons" – and speaks of the God who empowers them to overcome that suffering.

Thirdly, Chung speaks of *Kwan Yin* in the context of the transformation and purging of *han*. *Han* is a concept in her theology for understanding the meaning of liberation and salvation. It names the individual and collective accumulation of anger, resentment at unjust and unavenged suffering, hopelessness, and despair. Chung appeals to the tradition of *han-pu-ri*, the purging of *han*, wherein through the activity of shamans – most of whom are women – and other representative figures the histories that lead to *han* are told and social change is effected. She finds here a nexus, within the religious and cultural heritage of the people to whom she regards her theology as accountable, for speaking about an inclusive hope for spiritual and material liberation. This may not look like a particularly "feminist" move, but Chung suggests that women as victims of multiple oppressions who are given no means to voice those oppressions are paradigmatic bearers of *han*. Fourthly, the life-giving Spirit depicted in the figure of *Kwan Yin* relates not only to human life but also to the life of the whole of creation. Again drawing on the popular religiosity of the communities to which she refers her theology, Chung seeks to give voice to a spirituality centered on the earth and on the interconnectedness of nature.

Rosemary Radford Ruether

Rosemary Radford Ruether is perhaps the best-known feminist theologian in North Atlantic theological conversations. Her long career has been marked by the ongoing concern to uncover the connections between patriarchal social structures, militarism, and environmental degradation – and theologies that serve to maintain or conceal these connections. Alongside her feminist critiques of theological tradition, Ruether seeks to present accounts of Christian theology that draw on prophetic and wisdom traditions to advance the flourishing of humanity and nature. The interaction of prophetic and wisdom dimensions – and of two characteristic themes of feminist theology – in her thought is seen clearly in *Gaia and God*, in which "Gaia" as divinity immanent in the interconnectedness of humanity and nature is set alongside "God" as the divine demand that transcends the given connections. Both themes, Ruether recognizes, have the potential for misuse. She finds the liberative aspects of both themes reflected in the Bible and in Christian theological inheritance – but not only there, as the appeal to Gaia would suggest.

Ruether's Christology focuses on the prophetic tradition of the Hebrew Bible, within which she places Jesus – as one who, like the prophets who preceded him, calls the powerful to account for their acts of injustice through word and action, who practices solidarity with the poor and speaks of their priority within the Kingdom of God, and who consistently points not to himself but to the "Kingdom of God" and to the "one who sent him." Jesus' prophetic ministry calls forth the prophetic ministries of the communities that follow him, acting in the power of the same prophetic Spirit in which he acted – so that feminist theology and feminist reconstructions of Christian community are not "following Jesus' example" so much as "continuing Jesus' work." Thus, Ruether's response to the question "Can a male Saviour save women?" comes through a reconsideration, in line with liberation theologies, of what "salvation" means in this context and what aspects of Jesus' life are central to his "salvific" significance. Feminist theologians, Ruether and many others would claim, cannot simply appeal to Jesus' "normativity," as some other Christologies that emphasize his life and teaching might be inclined to do; even if Jesus can be called a "feminist," the appeal to a male norm will still tend to reinforce patterns of male authority.

Elisabeth Schüssler Fiorenza

Elizabeth Schüssler Fiorenza's seminal work *In Memory of Her* stands at the beginning of the "second wave" of feminist biblical criticism. Despite the numerous challenges to Fiorenza's approach – from feminists and others – she remains one of the most important articulators of the feminist application of the "hermeneutic of suspicion" in relation to biblical texts. Fiorenza takes up many of the tools of the historical–critical method, but (as Audre Lourde would put it) seeks to use them to demolish the "master's house." As noted above, her reconstruction of women's role in the early church is based explicitly on the presupposition of their significant presence, which has been partly concealed by the androcentric composition of the biblical texts and canon. Aligning her project with that of Joan Scott and other writers of "women's history," Fiorenza sets out (as her later writings make clear) to write history *for* the present struggle against injustice, and not simply to write the history *of* an irrecoverable or unalterable past. She rejects the claim of "historical objectivity" that has permitted the political and ecclesial effects of the dominant construction of church history to be ignored. She does want to assert that the biblical texts contain within them evidence of alternative ways of constructing society and human relations, which subsequent translation and interpretation have often minimized; but, at the same time, she makes this assertion with the explicit intention of empowering liberative action in the present. In so doing, she has opened herself to criticism from the the direction of "biblical studies" – while at the same time being too close, for some feminist theologians, both to the biblical canon and to the historian's quest for a "true picture of what happened."

In her later work, Fiorenza has preferred the term "kyriarchy" to "patriarchy" for the object of feminist critique, and the term "wo/men" for the group in the interests of whom feminist critique and reconstruction are performed. Kyriarchy refers to the system of lordship – the *kyrios* (lord) is the male head of the household, the leader of the church or the state, the colonial overlord, whose power over those subordinated to him is reinforced by religious, national, and other ideologies. In naming kyriarchy, Fiorenza seeks to take into account within feminist theology the fact that gender is not the only – and sometimes not the most important – factor in structuring inequalities of power. For example, white women have held power over black men and women for centuries, and even if the way in which they hold and exercise that power is itself restricted by their gender, "patriarchy" does not name the injustice by which their power is perpetuated. Speaking of kyriarchy, Fiorenza believes, helps to draw attention to the more fundamental problem of how systems of domination (another cognate word – *dominus*, lord) arise and are maintained, while acknowledging – because the *kyrios* is gendered as male – the important part played in this by gender.

Fiorenza's thought has been significant, alongside that of Ruether, in developing the idea of "women-church" – although the views of the two thinkers on this topic are subtly different. Fiorenza, drawing on her New Testament work, writes of "ekklesia" as the radically democratic space that arises outside existing structures of power as women and men are called to respond to the liberating action of God. She finds traces of ekklesia – which she often describes as the "ekklesia of wo/men" – in the New Testament writings, but is interested in it primarily as a possible space in the contemporary world – an imagined space in which new theologies and politics can emerge. She is, as the foregoing discussion of "kyriarchy" might suggest, not particularly interested in the establishment of "women-only" or even "women-led" communities, because a separation on the basis of gender alone could not ensure that all dimensions of oppressive practice were challenged. What the ekklesia of wo/men does enable Fiorenza to do is put forward a vision of church that can claim universal relevance in its prophetic mission.

Mercy Amba Oduyoye

Mercy Amba Oduyoye is a Ghanaian theologian whose work places the lives and theologies of African Christians in the context of the interactions between African traditional society, colonialism, and postcolonial national movements. There is, she writes, "a myth in Christian circles that the church brought liberation to the African woman"; her conviction that Christianity *can* mean liberation for the African woman is expressed alongside a critique of colonialist accounts that regard that liberation as already accomplished. Together with many feminist theologians of the South, she has called repeatedly for the voices of women from the South to be heard speaking their own words – represented neither by Northern feminists nor by Southern men. In her African context, this has meant the uncovering of African Christian women's theology, often preserved in oral rather than written form. Narrative is a key category for the presentation of this theology – a "ministry of storytelling" that encompasses both the honoring of the storytelling in which African women engage, and the telling of the stories of the women themselves. Her theological work has included the gathering of the "Circle of Concerned African Women Theologians" and an ongoing commitment to maintaining diverse communities of women theologians.

Oduyoye's critical appropriation of African traditional religion is significant for her theology. Her writing interweaves narratives and proverbs (the other key traditional genre she identifies as centrally significant for theology) from many African cultures with biblical texts and contemporary accounts of women's lives. Taking up the affirmation of God as source and sustainer of life, she hears and reflects on African women speaking of Jesus Christ as the giver of life and the healer of all afflictions – physical, social, and political. In common with many feminist theologians, she takes "life in all its fullness" as a central theological theme, and the "resurrection of the body" as the expression of the hope for comprehensive healing and liberation among African women. While retaining and developing the emphasis she finds within African traditional religion on the omnipresence of God and the unity of the cosmos, Oduyoye calls feminist theologians to a critique of the oppressive aspects of culture.

Luce Irigaray and her theological interlocutors

Calling Luce Irigaray a Christian theologian might be controversial; she is more easily characterized as a philosopher and psychoanalyst, a representative of twentieth-century "French feminism" – concerned with the symbolics of gender, with the thinking of "the feminine," and with the lessons to be learned from Freud, Lacan, and their feminist critics. However, theologians in Europe and North America (but not only there) concerned with the theological implications of sexual difference have over recent decades found Irigaray an extremely important dialogue partner, not least because of her extended and provocative engagement with the narratives and images of Christian theology. To the extent that Irigaray has been consistently concerned with how divinity can be thought and symbolized, she is unquestionably a "feminist theologian."

Irigaray's key theological concern, summed up in her article "Divine Women?," is for the female representation of God. The problem as she poses it is not so much that "if God is male, then the male is God," as that without female images of God, woman cannot be thought as anything other than the negation, the absence, or the unacknowledged ground of male subjectivity. Elsewhere, she has claimed that in patriarchal society there is only *one* sex – because women are always "the other of the same," the not-male or (which amounts to the same thing) the necessary complement of a predetermined maleness. The theological implications of this claim are worked out, in the first instance, in explicit relation to Feuerbach's thought. For Feuerbach, human beings needed images of God as the projection of the human possibilities they were to realize; for Irigaray, women (and men) need the female image of God in order for female subjectivity to be possible.

While this might seem to point to a reductive reading of theology – new theologies to be created in the service of a feminist project, using whatever images happen to suit women – Irigaray's thought as developed in and beyond this article is considerably more complex. Her idea of the "sensible transcendental," an attempt to think how embodied beings can transcend themselves in and through their embodied existence, is, as she herself realizes, profoundly connected with theologies of the incarnation. She returns frequently to the story of the Annunciation as a crucial point at which a decision concerning the meaning of incarnation is made. Is this the decisive suppression of woman's capacity to be anything other than a vessel for, and means of the reproduction of, a masculine self – the bearer of the Word of the Father? Or is it, Irigaray asks, the point at which the opening of women's embodied existence towards the transcendent becomes manifest through entering loving relation with the other? Irigaray is clear that the former has been the case in the history of Christian theology, but she is intrigued by the latter possibility – as are many of the theologians who have sought to use her thought to develop feminist readings of theological tradition.

Feminist theological conversations with Irigaray vary in emphasis. The features of her thought that have led many other feminists, particularly in North America, to regard her with suspicion – her insistence on the category of "woman" and "the feminine" and her preoccupation with the male/female couple – have often been important factors in theological appropriation of her work. Feminist philosopher/theologians who do not see themselves, as Irigaray does not see herself, as restricted to "Christian theology," have tended to stress her call for a feminine imaginary, and for the reimagining of God in ways that will empower women in *becoming* women. Within Christian theology, Catholic thinkers in particular – among them Janet Martin Soskice, Susan Frank Parsons, and Tina Beattie – have found her account of (what is in effect) the "graced nature" and eschatological orientation of sexually differentiated humanity very significant for theological conversations around Christology and the meaning of gender.

Gay, Lesbian, and Queer Theologies

The links between sexism and homophobia are well documented. The discourse of sexism, or patriarchy, relies on the maintenance of a clear division between male and female, and on the exclusion of "female" characteristics – including the erotic relation to men – from the male realm. While the patriarchal culture may, as Luce Irigaray suggests, be "hom(m)osexual" in that it allows women no identity that is not male-defined, the man or woman who fails to fit the expected patterns of relations between the sexes also represents a challenge to the gender-based ordering of social relations. The thinking through of the theological implications of non-heterosexual identities and relationships stands in a close relationship to feminist theology, but has followed its own distinctive trajectory. On the other hand, it is necessary to recognize that the victimization of gay men and lesbians in the churches and in theology raises distinctive issues and has a distinctive history.

Gay and lesbian theologies have extended the call for the theological revaluation of the body, towards a specific critique of the denigration of the erotic and the sexual in theology and ethics. Making the heterosexual or patriarchal assumption, thinkers such as Carter Heyward and Elizabeth Stuart have argued, allows sexual desire in general and women's sexual desire in particular to be excluded from theological texts. Carter Heyward's use of "eros" to designate the work of God in and through human relationships is a direct challenge to what she sees as the theological marginalization of eros, which is in turn linked to the marginalization – or far worse – of those whose expressions of erotic love contravene the established order.

The development of theology rooted in gay or lesbian "experience," especially in the USA, recalls the turn to "women's experience" in feminist theology – and comparable debates arise about the essentialization of such "experience," its relation to traditions and other norms of theology, and in particular its assumptions about the stability of gay or lesbian "identity." More recent developments in queer theology call this reliance on stable identities into question. Drawing on the queer theory of Judith Butler and others, which in turn draws on Foucault's account of sexuality, queer theology tracks how the use of gender binaries to structure texts and societies is also a way of suppressing "deviant" sexual desires that would endanger the stable categorization of persons. Queer theology brings, to a theological and ecclesial context that assumes the "naturalness" of heterosexual identities and relationships, the challenge to recognize that normative heterosexuality (as, indeed, the assignation of a single meaning to homosexuality) is potentially idolatrous. It calls for the diversity of desire and its expression to be acknowledged as potentially participating in the redemptive purposes of God. Some theologians in this developing trajectory, such as Eugene F. Rogers, see a close congruence between the insights of queer theology and older theological traditions of thinking about the body's "way into the Triune God" – so that queer theology becomes more "orthodox," and more sympathetically engaged with a wide range of theological thought, than the gay and lesbian theologies that preceded it. At the same time, Marcella Althaus-Reid's "queer" re-reading of Latin American liberation theology points to the possibility of using queer theory to destabilize a theological orthodoxy used oppressively.

Debate

The debates within and around feminist theology, and theology concerned with issues of gender, to some extent mirror debates in non-theological contexts. For example, one contentious question in feminist theology centers on the constructive response to the discovery of gender binaries – such as, for example, the association of femaleness with the body, over against maleness and the mind or spirit. Does one accept, temporarily or otherwise, the association of femaleness with the body and attempt the symbolic and material "emancipation" of both? Or does this merely reinforce the hierarchical ordering reflected in the original binary, giving added support to the implication that women are "more" essentially embodied than are men? Linked with this is the ongoing debate around the category of "women" – important, as I have suggested, for the political effectiveness of feminist movements (including feminist theology), but rendered problematic both by postcolonial feminist discourses and by queer theory. Is it possible or appropriate to speak of "women's experience" or "women's concerns" in theology? If not, is there even anything that holds "feminist theologians" together – and if not, is there a risk that the real achievements of feminist theology, including its ongoing challenge to sexist practices and structures within Christian communities, will be lost? Opponents of "feminist theology" are often only too anxious to generalize about it and the threats it (supposedly) poses to Christian faith. The need for solidarity among feminist theologians, a solidarity in which plurality can still be affirmed, seems more pressing in the context of such opposition. However, working out how such solidarity in difference can be thought and practiced, especially in the context of massive global imbalances of power and wealth, continues to be difficult.

Not all theology that takes issues of gender seriously can be labeled as "feminist theology"; but to speak of "gender and theology" rather than "feminist theology," as I have done at several points in this chapter, is already contentious. Where "feminist theology" named theology as a disruptive practice intended to advance feminist concerns, "gender and theology" appears to be reduced to one of many subtopics of study within a fundamentally unchanged theological academy. This is a real issue in contemporary theology. Will it be possible to make and carry forward the claim that gender pervades theological discourse, and that far from being a subtopic of theological ethics it is of central interest for all theological work? Or will such a claim merely make women's continuing material and cultural oppression in many parts of the world – including the Christian world – invisible once again? These questions become more important as engagement with issues of gender moves into the theological "mainstream." They are not merely questions of political strategy; they link into debates about the relationship between "women-church" and women's theological spaces, on the one hand, and traditionally male-dominated church and academic institutions, on the other. Is the relationship primarily one of internal critique, or of the prophetic creation of alternative forms of community?

As has already been shown, attitudes to tradition, canon, and authority have given rise to considerable debate within and around feminist theology from its earliest days. As the conversation between Christian feminist theologians and "post-Christian" or non-Christian feminists continues, the former have to explain the nature of their commitment to a canon of texts and a tradition of thought and practice that reflect androcentric origins. At the same time, the nature of feminist commitment is challenged – from the "other side" – by theologians who regard the introduction of feminist commitments to the reading of authoritative texts as a detraction from the authority of those texts. Approaches to reading that focus on conflictual interactions with texts – "reading against the grain" – stand in some tension with approaches that seek to "retrieve" inclusive and liberative readings.

This tension appears, not only in the reading of biblical and traditional texts, but in the appropriation or rejection of traditional symbols, particularly those that are derived from the Bible. Whether (and under what circumstances) a feminist can call God Father – as Janet Martin Soskice asks in the title of a well-known article – is still contentious. Is it really the case, as many Christian feminists have argued, that the naming of God as Father in fact serves to destabilize patriarchy? Is it important to find "female" images and symbols for God – and if so, where are these to be sought, and on what grounds can they be claimed as normative? Indeed, one of the central issues with which feminist theology began, and with which it is still struggling, is the question of religious language itself. Having called into question the traditional use of masculine language in theological texts – both to refer to God and to refer to humanity – on the grounds that it excluded women from the "image of God" and from full humanity, one must then ask what can justify the use of any particular language in speaking of God. Is the criterion a pragmatic one – what is the effect of this language on the lives of women and men, as they use it and inhabit the communities shaped by its use? That pragmatic criterion could itself, perhaps, be justified theologically – the language itself to be judged "by its fruits" as it is shaped by the divine movement toward the full well-being of humanity; but it would leave open the question of the critical limits on the re-naming of God.

Gay and lesbian theology, at least as it is received within church communities, often provokes "debate" scarcely worthy of the name; the bitterness of the disputes within numerous worldwide faith communities around the status of homosexual people and relationships shows little sign of changing. Here, the wider debates that come to the fore again concern the nature of biblical authority and the process of biblical interpretation, particularly in relation to "ethical issues" – and, linked with this, the nature of church community itself in relation to a wider cultural context. The call from queer theology for attention to a wider range of questions about how life in Christ transforms embodied identity has not yet been heard above the struggles focused on "the gay issue," but it does at least suggest that there are resources for this debate that have not yet been fully recognized.

Achievement and Agenda

It is no exaggeration to say that the encounter of theology with feminist movements and feminist tools of analysis has changed the face of theology. Feminists may question the extent to which this change is merely a change of "face" – a surface alteration of what remains basically the same theological structure – and whether a deeper change is either possible or desirable. At the very least, however, as a result of feminist theological work, the question of the implication of theology in gender-based patterns of domination has been made unavoidable. Discussions of the theology of atonement, to name one central and controversial example, have been significantly affected by the multiple challenges put by feminist theologies. These challenges arose from reflection on the ways in which atonement theology affects the lives of women through ecclesial practice and teaching, and through its failure to challenge injustice in the wider social context. Of course, feminist theologians are not the first or the only group to raise the question of the ethical and political implications of theology; but they have consistently drawn attention to a particularly pervasive aspect of the theological "scripting" of people's lives through the symbolics of gender. The importance in this of drawing new attention to the body and the erotic in theological anthropology should also not be underestimated.

As Rebecca Chopp has argued, the "achievements" of feminist theology, on its own terms, should be assessed not only through the texts produced and the ideas advanced but also through liberative changes in the lives of women and men.[12] Feminist theology has sought to make explicit the connections between theological thought, spirituality, and politics, and to raise theologians' awareness of the many communities to which they are accountable. In doing so, it has also broadened the criteria for theological "achievement." One indication of the state of the questions addressed by feminist theology were the final reports of the World Council of Churches' "Decade of Solidarity with Women" in 1997.[13] These reports gave a mixed picture of the lives of women in and in relation to Christian churches at the end of the twentieth century. On the one hand, there had been significant shifts in thought and attitudes, and a significant growth particularly in the awareness of Northern women of the need to enact solidarity with the women of the two-thirds world. (Neatly summing up some of the problems of marginalization that beset feminist theology, the report spoke of what had become a "decade of *women* in solidarity with women"). On the other hand, violence against women and women's poverty remained enormous and growing concerns to which responses – including theological responses – were urgently needed. Work in the Decade on the interconnections between theology, "women's issues," and other key global political concerns suggests that it would be counter-productive to lose the connections between feminist theory, feminist theology, and pastoral and political action.

I have suggested that the term "feminist theologian" implies already a double commitment, to some community of thinkers and activists working to advance feminist concerns and to some community and tradition (however contested) of thinking about God. Such a double commitment may, as Fiorenza has suggested, tend to produce the feminist theologian as a "resident alien" in either or both of her communities; and the perspective of the resident alien may be particularly fruitful precisely when we attempt to do theology, because it can lead one to call into question the self-evidence of statements about the divine that are made by both sides. This is not to romanticize the position of the resident alien – as any study of recent feminist theology will reveal, there are as many political struggles over cherished orthodoxies within "feminist theology" as outside it. However, at its best, feminist theology offers a space in which certain boundaries can be crossed more easily. "Interfaith" conversations are possible that are attentive both to the failures of the various faith traditions and to the indispensability of symbols and stories – that is to say, that reduce neither to an attempt to place others within one's own overarching narrative nor to a bland relativism that discounts religious particularity. Feminist theology has been forced to seek ways of speaking of God with people whose perspectives are radically different, without denying one's own particularity or falling back on the security of an unquestioned tradition. In doing this, feminist theology contributes significantly to a wider context of thinking and speaking about God.

Notes

1 Sallie McFague, *Models of God* (London, 1987).

2 For some important examples of theology deliberately presented "against the grain" of white Northern feminist theology, see Jacquelyn Grant, *White Woman's Christ and Black Woman's Jesus* (Atlanta, GA, 1996); Ursula King (ed.), *Feminist Theology from the Third World: A Reader* (London, 1994).

3 Mary McClintock Fulkerson, *Changing the Subject: Women's Discourses and Feminist Theology* (Minneapolis, MN, 1994).

4 Examples of feminist theology developed in extended dialogue with particular key philosophers of postmodernity are Sharon D. Welch, *A Feminist Ethic of Risk* (Minneapolis, MN, 1999), in dialogue with Foucault, and Ellen T. Armour, *Deconstruction, Feminist Theology and the Problem of Difference: Subverting the Race/Gender Divide* (Chicago, 1999), on Derrida.

5 Elizabeth Cady Stanton (ed.), *The Woman's Bible* (New York, 1898).

6 "Woman/body/nature" is used by Rosemary Radford Ruether in the postscript to *Sexism and God-Talk* (London, 1983).

7 For example, Sarah Coakley's rethinking of ascetic practices in *Powers and Submissions: Spirituality, Philosophy and Gender* (Oxford, 2002) and Caroline Walker Bynum's work on medieval women's piety in *Fragmentation and Redemption: Essays on Gender and the Human Body in Medieval Religion* (New York, 1994).

8 See Daphne Hampson, *Theology and Feminism* (Oxford, 1990), and the discussion of her position by a range of feminist theologians in Daphne Hampson (ed.), *Swallowing a Fishbone? Feminist Theologians Debate Christianity* (London, 1996).

9 See, for example, Elizabeth Johnson, *She Who Is* (New York, 1994); Janet Martin Soskice, "Trinity and the Feminine 'Other,'" *New Blackfriars* 75 (1994), 2–17.

10 On wisdom and Christology, see Elisabeth Schüssler Fiorenza, *Jesus: Miriam's Child, Sophia's Prophet* (New York, 1994).

11 For example, the Jewish feminist theologian Judith Plaskow, whose work has also been important for Christian feminist theologians, traces in *Standing Again at Sinai: Judaism from a Feminist Perspective* (San Francisco, 1990) how the *Shekinah* and other feminine imagery for God has been consistently rendered irrelevant and subordinated to masculine imagery.

12 Rebecca Chopp, "Feminist and Womanist Theologies" in D. F. Ford (ed.), *The Modern Theologians*, 2nd edn. (Oxford, 1997), pp. 389–404.

13 World Council of Churches, *Living Letters: A Report of Visits to the Churches during the Ecumenical Decade of Churches in Solidarity with Women* (Geneva, 1997).

Bibliography

Primary

Althaus-Reid, Marcella. *Indecent Theology* (London, 2000).

Chung Hyung Kyung. *Struggle to be the Sun Again: Introducing Asian Women's Theology* (Maryknoll, NY, 1990).

Daly, Mary. *Beyond God the Father: Towards a Philosophy of Women's Liberation* (Boston, MA, 1973).

Fabella, Virginia and Oduyoye, Mercy Amba (eds.), *With Passion and Compassion: Third World Women Doing Theology* (Maryknoll, NY, 1988).

Fiorenza, Elisabeth Schüssler. *Jesus: Miriam's Child, Sophia's Prophet* (New York, 1994).

—— *In Memory of Her: A Feminist Theological Reconstruction of Christian Origins* (London, 1995).

Hampson, Daphne. *Theology and Feminism* (Oxford, 1990).

Heyward, Carter. *Touching our Strength: The Erotic as Power and the Love of God* (San Francisco, 1989).

Isasi-Diaz, Ada Maria. *En la Lucha, Elaborating a Mujerista Theology: A Hispanic Woman's Liberation Theology* (Minneapolis, MN, 1993).

Johnson, Elizabeth. *She Who Is: The Mystery of God in Feminist Theological Discourse* (New York, 1994).

Joy, Morny, O'Grady, Kathleen, and Poxon, Judith L. (eds), *French Feminists on Religion: A Reader* (London, 2002).

King, Ursula (ed.). *Feminist Theology from the Third World: A Reader* (London, 1994).

McFague, Sallie. *Models of God: Theology for an Ecological Nuclear Age* (London, 1987).

Oduyoye, Mercy Amba. *Daughters of Anowa: African Women and Patriarchy* (Maryknoll, NY, 1995).

Rogers, Eugene F. *Sexuality and the Christian Body: Their Way into the Triune God* (Oxford, 1999).

Ruether, Rosemary Radford. *New Woman, New Earth: Sexist Ideologies and Human Liberation* (New York, 1983).

—— *Sexism and God-Talk: Towards a Feminist Theology* (London, 1983).

Soskice, Janet Martin. "Can a Feminist Call God 'Father?'" In T. Elwes (ed.), *Women's Voices: Essays in Contemporary Feminist Theology* (London, 1982).

—— "Trinity and the Feminine 'Other,'" *New Blackfriars* 75 (1994), 2–17.

Soskice, Janet Martin, and Lipton, Diana (eds). *Feminism and Theology* (Oxford, 2003).

Trible, Phyllis. *Texts of Terror: Literary-Feminist Readings of Biblical Narratives* (Minneapolis, MN, 1984).

Williams, Delores. *Sisters in the Wilderness: The Challenge of Womanist God-Talk* (Maryknoll, NY, 1993).

Secondary

Chopp, Rebecca. *The Power to Speak: Feminism, Language, God* (New York, 1989).

Grant, Jacquelyn. *White Woman's Christ and Black Woman's Jesus: Feminist Christology and Womanist Response* (Atlanta, GA, 1996).

Hampson, Daphne (ed.). *Swallowing a Fishbone: Feminist Theologians Debate Christianity* (London, 1996).

Jones, Serene. *Feminist Theory and Christian Theology: Cartographies of Grace* (Princeton, NJ, 2000).

Parsons, Susan. *Feminism and Christian Ethics* (Cambridge, 1996).

—— (ed.). *The Cambridge Companion to Feminist Theology* (Cambridge, 2002).

Stuart, Elizabeth. *Gay and Lesbian Theologies: Repetitions with Critical Difference* (Aldershot, 2003).

Black Theology of Liberation

Dwight N. Hopkins

Introduction

Black theology is a self-reflexive discipline questioning the intellectual consistency and practical accountability of African American people to the faith that they seek to believe in and practice. Methodologically, theological reflection is a second step. It presupposes the reality of black people in churches and community organizations involving themselves in advancing the particular affirming encounter between African Americans and God and reconstructing individual and systemic brokenness and woundedness. Black theology arises out of this ongoing dynamic and challenges people of faith to pause and think critically about whether what they are believing in and witnessing to is what they profess as their ultimate hope and final vision for all of humanity. Specifically, black theology investigates notions of racial and cultural identity in relation to faith.

The particularity of African American sources, out of which emerges black theology, determines the "black" dimension of this form of liberation theology. The claim is that people of African descent have undergone and continue to encounter rather clearly defined (if not certain unique) racial experiences revealed in a myriad of arenas. The first source of black theology, therefore, hinges on laying a genealogical foundation from Africa, especially the African west coast from which the majority of black Americans originate. Black theologians today differ on the extent of African influences on current US black citizens. The theological gamut ranges from Afrocentrists (i.e., scholars hoping to replace Europe with Africa as the center of black faith, thought, and ethics and positioning people of African descent as subjects and not objects of history), to those who remain open to possible universal lessons from European and European American theologians (i.e., relying on black history and culture while incorporating thought systems from Europe). The common denominator among advocates is the recognition that black folk are, to whatever degree, an African people, hence the 1990s increased popularity of the name "African American." In addition, all would agree that the African influence dictates a theological worldview of "I am because of the community's well-being," thereby fostering a corporate sense of blackness which unifies all of African descent.

The second source is likewise foundational, an underscoring of the (European Christian) slave trade in Africans and the 1619–1865 era of (white Christian) bondage of blacks in North America. Obviously, these momentous events likewise tie Africans and black Americans in connections that can never be broken. Yet the key to the slavery period, as a primal source for black theology of liberation, is its giving birth to a novel human creation called African Americans or black Americans. Prior to slavery, black folk did not exist. In this sense, slavery is a primordial marker for the intricate origins and formative intimacies of today's black people of faith. How were these new people born? And how did they maintain perpetual faith in the midst of one of human history's most brutal religious persecutions and intense exploitation of working people's labor power? Black theologians, in general terms, investigate this crucial period and discern that African Americans co-labored with God to forge themselves out of memories of African sacredness, a reinterpretation of slave master theology (that is, "slaves obey your masters" became "God is the highest authority"), and an accumulated commonsense folk wisdom surmised from daily survival. In a word, slavery indicates the coalescing of black people's race, culture, and faith identities.

A sense of a common heritage of struggle for the full humanity of black people underscores the third source. This suggests that a black theology of liberation takes seriously the power of God's grace of freedom reigning in and outside of Christianity and in and outside of churches. Wherever African Americans, especially poor and working-class folk, strive to be full human beings by asserting freely the racial cultural aspects of their total lives, black theology perceives God being with them. Hence, black theology draws on the rich and creative paradigms of Marcus Garvey and his six million black membership Universal Negro Improvement Association, the kaleidoscopic cultural contributions of African Americans – including the Harlem Renaissance, the 1960s black arts movement, musical expressions, material cultural forms, dance, sports, humor, and other types – the Nation of Islam (Malcolm X as the prime example), the National Association for the Advancement of Colored People, radical organizing to alter the US system, the press, workers' movements, the cyclical resurgence of Pan Africanism, intellectual and academic contributions, and much more. The plumb-line of struggle, hope, liberation, and eventual freedom forged by Yahweh in the Hebrew scriptures and that laid by Jesus in the Christian scriptures is complemented by the omnipresence of God's power for black humanity to be free wherever African Americans find themselves.

The fourth source of black theology of liberation is that of appreciating a healthy and holistic notion of gender. One possibility is to develop a black theology by relying mainly on African American women's sources, such as fiction, single leaders, or institutionalized movements. Immediately, Harriet Tubman, Fannie Lou Hamer, the women's club movement, women's roles in the Student Non-violent Coordinating Committee and the Black Panther Party, Zora Neale Hurston, black female slave labor, and ethnographic field work among today's working-class Christian women come to mind. Another avenue could be a dialogical encounter with current-day women's voices, heeding their critiques and offering constructive criticism, thereby forging a common stance. A third way might entail helping to provide equal opportunity of access and recognition; here, wherever black theology appears, womanist theology is cited and promoted. And fourth, black men could reconceptualize a new, progressive heterosexual and homosexual (from their respective sexual orientations) male gender. A turn in this latter direction more likely assures recognition of male structural power and the necessity of alleviating the oppression of women by equalizing systemic gender power asymmetry.

Yet one ascertains the fundamental source of a black theology in the centrality of the Bible for African American life. The power of Christian scriptures, for this theology, resides in an accepted thread of liberation permeating both the Hebrew and Christian parts of the text. The Exodus of slaves from bondage to freedom obviously becomes an overarching hermeneutical reference frame. Consequently, the Incarnation of Jesus accompanied by his proclamation to bring a new reality for the oppressed seals the cornerstone norm of liberation for black theology. Enslaved Africans and African Americans in North America viewed their predicament and resulting hope as parallel if not identical to the Hebrew slaves. In spite of white Christians tearing them from their African homeland and ritualizing a theologically justified slavery via homily, catechism, and lessons, enslaved black workers maintained hope in the many "miraculous" stories of Hebrew captivity and deliverance. This inchoate reading and production of a black theology feeds into current black theological developments. So too does a belief in Jesus as the ultimate freedom and healing for the materially poor and ill – freedom defines the very being of Jesus and Jesus offers freedom for people dwelling in structural poverty and for other working people.

Moreover, and closely related to the Bible, Christian churches become prime sites for relating to, leading, and sorting out a black theology of liberation. The black church endures as the oldest institution created by and owned by African Americans. It stands as one of the clearest examples of black power. More important than this sociological, political, and economic fact is black theology's vocation from the spirit of liberation to practice freedom. Clearly, institutionally, the black church is obligated by faith imperatives to act out a prophetic role in North American society and, indeed, the world. Biblical warrants of justice coupled with the black church's primary location wherever African Americans cluster (whether the inner city or the suburbs) suggest theological instructions and social location for black theology.

Survey 1: Origins

It is no accident that the leadership of the African American church's prophetic vectors (drawing on the Bible) and urban locations (existing in the heart of black America) gave rise to contemporary black theology of liberation. On July 31, 1966, northern African American clergy published their "black power" statement in the *New York Times* newspaper. In it they spoke to the leaders of the nation, white church members, black citizens, and the media. Most significantly, they corroborated the recent cry for black power enunciated by younger members of the faltering civil rights movement. And these pastors articulated persuasively that the challenge was to recognize how white men had inordinate power with no conscience and Negroes suffered from too much conscience without power. This one document signifies the commencement of contemporary black theology. Yet, like all irreversible turns in history, this theological affirmation of black power was preceded by major proliferations in the concrete struggles for African American freedom. In a word, black theology burst on to the national and international scenes out of racial and cultural movements.

In June 1966, the Student Non-violent Coordinating Committee (SNCC) (represented by Stokely Carmichael) broke with the non-violence by-any-means-necessary mantra of Martin Luther King, Jr. Carmichael and King, during the Meredith March Against Fear, headed the procession through the backwoods of Mississippi. On June 16, at a preappointed place in Greenwood, Mississippi, Carmichael, without King's knowledge, launched into a chant demanding black power. The crowd of civil rights workers and local rural blacks responded in Carmichael's favor. Due to the coverage by local, national, and international press, the militant call for black power was the shout heard around the world. The demand for black power spread like wildfire because it reflected the preexisting deeply held sentiments of the majority of poor and working-class blacks and a significant sector of middle and upper-income African Americans. Black power symbolized in the public theatre what the overwhelming majority of blacks had been thinking and saying to themselves behind closed doors. That is, every white ethnic group had used group power and the force of their financial, political, economic, and racial power to advance their group interests. Indeed, from a black power's perspective, white people as a whole, regardless of ethnic origin, coalesced as a solid racial block when it came to rallying against black folk and for white collective interests. In this sense, the black power program was an American phenomenon.

Moreover, black power argued against what it perceived as the spurious claims of the white community, that there were certain objective and normative means for achieving the civil and human rights for African Americans. On the contrary, the black power advocates stated that the key question remained who had the power to define and enforce definitions. For them, whites had used their power to define what was objective and normative for the liberation of poor and working-class blacks. The young organizers of SNCC asserted the socially and culturally determined and time-bound nature of all truth-claims and objective positions. For them, the decisive question was the possession or lack of possession of power. It was in reaction to the power issue that white Americans recoiled and struck out in very emotional and deadly ways. As long as Negroes in the civil rights movement accepted the framework posited by whites with authority, then Negroes were good Americans. However, when Negroes transformed themselves, independent of white definition, into black men and women and challenged the prerogative of naming, the monopolization of ownership of resources, and the redistribution of power, African Americans then became un-American.

The immediate reaction to black power was overwhelming condemnation by most white ministers. Still, such a reaction was not the first indication of the expendability of black rights in America. This visceral negative stance followed the increased waning of white liberal support for civil rights, President Lyndon B. Johnson's reversal of the War on Poverty, the ritual of summer urban rebellions or riots, beginning at least as early as 1964, the impatience of Northern inner-city blacks with the fruitless results of the Southern civil rights movements, the stepped-up attacks of right-wing Christian groups (such as the KKK), and the national white intransigence openly displayed and signified by Chicago's mayor Richard Daley's defeat of King's Northern civil rights campaign in 1966.

Likewise, theological schools, seminaries, and divinity schools in America reflected the conservative and growing liberal backlash of white churches. White academics, school administrators, and boards of trustees of these institutions represented a form of apartheid. Promoted as universal theological pedagogical curricula, in fact, these schools could have been particularly deemed "European" or "European American" graduate schools of religious higher education. Even the few black seminaries maintained European focused syllabuses and graduation requirements. In 1966, the number of tenured African Americans with PhD degrees on the faculty of accredited theological schools probably could have been counted on one hand. If an African American was invited to campus, it was usually to offer an invocation, a closing prayer, a sermon, or to speak on what was really happening to angry Negroes outside the walls of the school. But the teaching arm, the administrative staffs, and the trustee groups remained white. Like discourse in the broader civic realm, institutional theological knowledge was heavily laden with white interests and the force to define truth. It, too, was about the monopoly of white power.

Survey 2: Founding Generation

The *ad hoc* National Committee of Negro Churchmen, the signatories of the July 31, 1966 black power statement, announced that African Americans had the right to think theologically and that all God-talk inherently advanced notions of racial power. In March 1969, James H. Cone's *Black Theology and Black Power* was an inaugural book published on liberation theology. Using the lens of the African American experience, he argued that the core message of the Bible paradigmatically expressed by Jesus the Christ was liberation of the materially poor. Consequently, ecclesial formations, educational venues, and civic society were called by God to focus on the liberation of the least in society: the broken hearted, the wounded, working people, the outcast, the marginalized, the oppressed, and those surviving in structural poverty. Based on biblical theological criteria, Cone claimed, white churches and most African American churches had failed their vocational assignments regarding their faith and their witness. This text offered the first sustained theological argument relating to issues of liberation, racial cultural identity, and a new material kingdom on earth in the interests of society's majority. Due to this pioneering work along with his subsequent publications, Cone is generally cited, nationally and internationally, as the father of contemporary black theology of liberation.

Yet, despite filling the need for a coherent and persuasive theological articulation, Cone ushered in a sharp and pointed debate among the small first generation of black theologians. Now that the God-talk had been opened, diverse and multiple African American voices began to speak, not only against the provincial positions and discriminatory control of North American education by whites with power, but also in critique of Cone's line of argument. Albert Cleage offered a reinterpretation of the biblical witness from a black perspective. He cited the Bible as a drama played out between a literal phenotypical black Jesus and the occupying white, colonial presence from Rome (Europe). Jesus became a black-skinned zealot whose sole goal was to wage a national liberation struggle, by any means necessary, to free the oppressed black nation of Israel from the white European colonizers. Cone had stated that Jesus was black because the business of the messiah was to be where the oppressed were fighting for liberation. Jesus' being *is* liberation. The black poor organize for liberation. Thus to enter and dwell among that community, Jesus had to be black. In contrast, Cleage stated that regardless of Jesus' vocation and Jesus' social location, Jesus was black not simply due to a theological rationale, but due to his natural biological skin color. There never was a white Jesus and, therefore, to portray him as such a color in pictures and other iconography is blasphemy and the work of the Antichrist. Moreover, the challenge to the African American church is to become the hub of the earthly revolution for nation building. It's nation time. And the leadership for the community hinged on an African American ecclesiology.

J. Deotis Roberts approached black theology of liberation from a more pastoral position. He decried Cone's view as too strident. Hence, Roberts extended the peace offering of reconciliation to the white oppressor. In fact, he attempted to hold in equal tension liberation and reconciliation. For him, not only should an aggressive campaign for black rights be launched against white political systems (for Jesus' mandate and mission are liberation), but simultaneously a hand of reconciliation should go out to the white supremacist. The liberation–reconciliation dynamic, in addition, held implications for Christology. Roberts believed that black folk had the right to image Jesus as black primarily for psychological, medicinal reasons. Because African Americans had drunk so deeply from the well of self-hatred (that is, in the depth chambers of their black hearts, African Americans really do want to be white people), they required a profound and radical healing of self-love resulting in liberation. So they required a Jesus Christ imaged as biologically black for mental health rehabilitation and emotional restabilization. At the same time, according to Roberts, whites had the right to imagine and depict a white Jesus Christ. However, true reconciliation would result when both parties worshiped a colorless Christ.

Cecil Cone elaborated an entirely different trajectory in black theology. His unique stance begins with a description of profound theological crisis in black theology. This academic discipline suffered from too much reliance on the secular existentialism and politics of the black power movement (i.e., James H. Cone) and total mesmerization by white thought systems (i.e., J. Deotis Roberts). An authentic black theology, for C. Cone, draws from its primordial undercurrent the all-powerful African Almighty Sovereign God. When Africans and African Americans were enslaved in North America, they maintained their African sacred worldview and spiritual configurations and simply adopted Christian forms. If anything, black folk converted Christianity into sacred Africanity. Today's black theology, consequently, should issue from an Africanized Christianity different from white religion and the rebellious substance of black power.

In a similar vein, Gayraud S. Wilmore challenged James Cone's limited (for Wilmore) presentation of the African American religious experience. For Wilmore, prior to black theology, one has to peel back layers and discover the more all-encompassing notion of black religious thought. Black religious thought anchors itself in any manifestation in African history and today that expresses the ultimate vision and practical struggle for liberation. Wilmore pushes theologians beyond Christian proclamation, theological categories, and ecclesial formations. Wherever black folk (i.e., poor people, or illiterate people, or the masses) initiate efforts for freedom, one discerns the sacred reality of black religious thought out of which surfaces black theology. Black religious thought reflects on the liberative folk impulse that has powered every struggle of African people in North America.

Proceeding beyond Wilmore, Charles H. Long opts for an entirely different deconstructive–reconstructive enterprise. He feels that both Christianity and theology are imperialistic discourses that embody, in a highly overdetermined manner, hegemonic linguistic power. In other words, one who adopts their language usage and language categories has already acquiesced in a process whose very nature is to oppress people of color or Third World people. Prior to the arrival of Christianity and its justificatory arm (i.e., theology), Long asserts, there already existed very interesting and informative religious practices among indigenous communities. Thus, Christianity and its God-talk are by definition imperialistic; they are automatically over-against-others phenomena. So when one selects Christianity, one chooses voluntarily to be oppressed by the linguistic structures of the oppressors. James H. Cone employs both Christianity and theology and, thereby, his project suffers from the imitative game of mirroring white religious structures and systems of thinking. For Long, Cone's black theology is not black enough; it merely paints black existing white structures, which also shows the lack of doing black theology strictly from African American sources. Long, on the contrary, presents orientation to the ultimate as religious. Hence, whenever blacks pursue the ultimate, especially in non-Christian forms (for instance, jazz singers or black public spokespeople or other such sources), one experiences the conditions of possibility for particularized black, sacred linguistic and thought structures.

Survey 3: Later Generations

Since the late 1970s, other generations of black theologians have emerged. Jacqueline Grant's 1979 article "Black Theology and the Black Woman" heralded the eventual naming of African American women's religious experience as womanist theology and ethics. In her pioneering essay, Grant untangles the inconsistent internal logic of black theology as adjudicated by its own norm. If black theology is one of the initiators of liberation theology, based on the liberation of the oppressed, then how can it be authentic God-talk when the oppressed of the oppressed in the African American church and community are made imperceptible in – or assumed to be represented by – black male experiences? Restated, black women at best are invisible in black theology and, at worst, are intentionally exploited by African American men. Womanist theology and ethics, the progeny of an incipient black feminist theology, situates itself differently from (white) feminist theology – a discourse partially disabled by white supremacy – and (male) black theology – a discourse partially reeking of patriarchal hegemony. More affirmatively, it explores positive black women's sources in relation to God's siding with African American women and it highlights the multidimensionality and positionality of black women in church and society.

Perhaps the first book arguing for a reconfiguration of black theology is Delores S. Williams' *Sisters in the Wilderness: The Challenge of Womanist God-Talk* (1993). Williams investigates thoroughly the biblical character of the African slave woman Hagar, her son Ishmael, and their encounter with God. Instead of discerning liberation as the dominant theme within this divine response to the human conundrum, Williams uncovers a bi-focus theological dynamic: survival and quality of life. Similarly, God meets African American women in their dire predicaments and aids them in their daily survival. And God co-labors with black women to forge a quality of life appropriate to their situation and their heritage. Emblematic of God's relation to black women, the divine does not offer liberation to the African slave woman, Hagar. Obviously, Williams' paradigm shift challenges by reformulation the substantive concerns of black theology.

Furthermore, Williams poses new theological perspectives on black theology's doctrine of Christology. In some respects, the jugular vein of black theology has been "Jesus Christ liberator" – divinity with the centerpiece punctuated by the cross and resurrection. The faith assent and rational claim comprised the following. Satan with evil forces from his kingdom attempted to do away with Jesus the liberator. Yet the countermove in the crucifixion connotes Jesus' struggle against and defeat of oppression; and his subsequent rising at Easter portrays the final triumph and ascension into a new society. In radical contrast, Williams asserts that there is nothing salvific and liberative in the cross event. This wicked moment in Jesus' life literally shows the evil that men do against a Jesus whose power comes not from the crucifixion but through his ministerial vision of life when he walked this earth. Daily survival and a quality of life, therefore, accompany liberation. Womanists, by sustaining their integrated identities of gender, race, and class, carefully and critically compiled fundamental queries for the entire black (male) theological project.

The second generation of male black theologians, likewise, has forged common, yet separate, trails from the 1960s founding generation. And since its inception in 1970, the Society for the Study of Black Religion remains the premier organization for debates and developments. Pastoral theology has become a promising pathway that was left uncharted by the forefathers of the discipline, but now progresses in various directions. Black pastoral theology combines the liberation accent with attention to personal salvation and emotional and spiritual healing. In their groundbreaking text *Liberation and Human Wholeness: The Conversion Experiences of Black People in Slavery and Freedom* (1986), Edward P. Wimberly and Anne Streaty Wimberly deploy hermeneutic inquiry and sensitivity to postmodern constructs in a comprehensive investigation of autobiographies and interviews of formerly enslaved African Americans. The latter conjured images during religious conversion that intimated human wholeness and a relationality inclusive of minds, bodies, the environment, social institutions, other people, and, fundamentally, deep connections to the Christian God. What the slave heritage bequeaths to today's African Americans and, indeed, all Christians is the holistic reality of God's liberating activity: from personal guilt and sin, from political–economic–social–material oppression, from inner psychological turmoil, and from cultural debasement.

A senior pastor of a black church, James H. Harris explicitly depicts in *Pastoral Theology: A Black-Church Perspective* (1991) his pastoral theology as liberation theology. For him, authentic evangelical ministry yields concrete transformation and liberation. Consequently, the African American church has to extend itself beyond one-by-one soul-saving in Christ, and assume its ecclesiological vocation to forge social change and liberation. According to this normative criterion, the black church has been slacking in what Jesus has called it to be, preach, and do. As the institutional manifestation of the gospel message of freedom from injustice and oppression, a major task of the black church hinges on pursuing the end of racial discrimination and realizing equality. Christian freedom, regardless of color in the final analysis, means we are all unencumbered by the spiritual and material things of this world which turn us into what God has not created us to be.

Lee H. Butler, Jr.'s *A Loving Home: Caring for African American Marriage and Families* (2000) confronts us with the necessity of unifying spirituality and sexuality in our bodies as a precursor to healed and re-created relationships in the corporate body. Situating his argument within African American experiences, providing novel angles on liberation as transformation to freedom and power, and on healing as the cornerstone for renewed relationships, Butler works with notions of twoness, the metaphor of home, the substratum of African spirituality as communality, the Hagar biblical story on complicated family structure, the omnipresence of men and women classifying one another as evil, and a positive project indicating the unity of spirituality and sexuality in a salutary connection among the self, God, and the other.

Black theology has persistently perceived itself in solidarity with its "distant cousins" in Africa and with liberation movements and theologies in the Third World (i.e., Africa, Asia, the Caribbean, Latin America, and the Pacific Islands). This projection continues with the second generation. Noel Leo Erskine, in *Decolonizing Theology: A Caribbean Perspective* (1981), resources US black theology, Third World liberation theologians, and, with special insight, Jamaican–Caribbean social and religious evolutions. European Christian slavery in the Caribbean fostered a legacy of existential identity crisis. To be Christian meant (and still denotes) a European or white Caribbean person. The majority of black Caribbeans (of African descent) have suffered a faith, culture, and freedom paradox. On the one hand, they enjoy a rich reservoir of African and black-derived spirituality and culture. On the other hand, in order to be Christians, they must live as an extension of Europe and North America's provincial practices of Christianity. Restated, to experience God as imported by European and North American missionaries obscures the true identity and consciousness of the oppressed Jamaican and Caribbean peoples. Hence a deep commonality in a quest for black identity joins black theology in the USA and Caribbean theology. Furthermore, Erskine's voice targets the colonization of black folk's theology in the Caribbean: a reflection on the divine–human encounter marked by other-worldly salvation and the privatization of freedom. In his social and religious locations, Erskine surmises how such demonic individualism destroyed black family solidarity. Black religion, for him, initiated theological decolonization when God was recognized as freedom beyond liberation and combined this insight with indigenous manifestations of Afro-Caribbean culture and religion.

The present author's *Black Theology USA and South Africa* (1989) analyzes 16 black theologians, eight from each country. It discovers distinct differences overshadowed by more commonalities, especially in the theological areas of the culture of politics and the politics of culture. This interpenetrating dialectic is defined by historical–contemporary, theological, normative, and common resource parallels detected in both black theologies. Thus, this shared dialectic of culture and politics, elucidated by four parallels, serves as the condition for the possibility of unifying US and South African theologies.

George C. L. Cummings' *A Common Journey: Black Theology (USA) and Latin American Liberation Theology* (1993) entertains a similar methodological inquiry. For North American theologians, liberation manifests primarily in religio-cultural terms; whereas Latin Americans stress a socioeconomic significance. Both can undergo a common journey by jointly focusing more on the textures of the poor's situation, allowing this condition to evangelize the church, filling out the contours of a social analysis, and linking more tightly the liberating work of the Holy Spirit to our understanding of Jesus Christ. Josiah Ulysses Young's *A Pan-African Theology* (1992) explores a global theology for people of African descent. His work seeks insight from nineteenth-century black ancestors, the state of the black American underclass and African peasantry, African traditional and black religions, and black music. From these sources, he extrapolates that the providence of God (historically incarnated in the ancestors) is directly intertwined with the practicalities of liberation for the present-day African diaspora.

African American biblical scholars of the second generation of black theology have offered well-argued judgments and scholarly documented assessments that disrupt the dominant exegesis and accepted hermeneutics of the Hebrew and Christian scriptures. *Troubling Biblical Waters* (1989), by Cain Hope Felder, substantiates the claim of the pervasive presence of African people in the entire Bible. Furthermore, his book reveals scriptural areas denoting the interaction between class consciousness and freedom which, most pointedly, culminates in a biblical commission for justice. Most dominant biblical scholarship either ignores or denies that such a charge exists, according to Felder. Following a reinvestigation of race and class in the Bible, Felder takes on the instances of family. Biblical pictures display family statuses in a much wider realm than contemporary beliefs and practices. The biblical text, in fact, supports black women's ordination, portrays family life that denies the normativity of the nuclear family, and calls on the human family to link peacemaking inextricably to justice.

Felder's edited volume *Stony The Road We Trod* (1991) presses further along these lines by dismantling the Eurocentric politics of biblical analysis and interpretation. A group of 11 black Bible scholars portray and prove how biblical studies in formal schools of education and in churches certify the biased nature of European and European American cultures. In contrast, as a theoretical and practical antidote, *Stony The Road* reintroduces the ancient biblical worldview of racial and ethnic diversity. The most authoritative black biblical scholarship to date, this collaborative writing submits new insights on specific African American methods of scriptural interpretation and the particular biblical and extra-biblical sources (such as African American sermons, work songs, and even mottos) that modify hermeneutical and exegetical warrants. The unique acumen in black women's hearing and reading the Bible also finds a prominent role in this groundbreaking text. In addition, the book further clarifies race and ancient black Africa in the Bible, even crystallizing how ancient blacks were perceived, by the Hebrews and other peer groups, as objects of hope, wealth, and wisdom.

In his third book, *Then the Whisper Put on Flesh* (2001), Brian K. Blount continues a fresh, new voice in African American biblical discourse. Here he combines creatively black Christianity, biblical ethics, and New Testament cultural interpretations. He provides an entry point for the non-oppressed to read the Christian scriptures through the circumstances and conditions of the oppressed, mainly by drawing heavily on black folk's ethical engagement with the sacred text during US slavery. Methodologically speaking, Blount underscores the ways culture and context impact one's reading of the text, and he deduces convincingly that liberation exists as a decisive thematic unity for each of the writers in the New Testament.

African American ethicists, likewise, have written diverse interrogations of their discipline. Theodore Walker, Jr.'s *Empower the People* (1991) amalgamates African American political philosophers, sociologists, psychologists, musicologists, homileticians, black and womanist theologies, and ethicists into a black power manifesto of liberation struggle. More accurately, for Walker, neither liberal government nor philanthropy, but black church power is obligated to tackle fundamental negativities and proffer hope-inspiring possibilities for the African American community. The ethical agenda includes, but is not exhausted by, drugs, crime, premarital sex, black families, economics, education, music, black male–female connections, dance, African American church leadership, and governmental policy. In sum, Walker asserts a black theological social ethics (for the church) appropriated from what he terms black power philosophy or black theology.

In *Xodus* (1996), Garth Kasimu Baker-Fletcher moves a liberation ethics into a radical reconstruction of the African American male self – a self suffering from low self-esteem, low self-respect, and self-image crises with which the black church has failed to come to terms. Xodus conjures up a psychosocial space colored by an inclusive non-sexist, liberationist partnership with womanists, and a reassessment of myths of black bodies. Xodus' new reality, in the lineage of Malcolm X, urges black men to pursue defiant confrontation with white supremacy. While Martin Luther King, Jr.'s dream urges the realization of a multicultural society grounded on God's justice and unconditional love for all human beings, Xodus' space, ultimately, is cosmological and ecological, since all of creation emerges from the earth's dust which, for Baker-Fletcher, in West Africa attests to revelation and the divine. Along the journey to Xodus' male space, African American ecclesial formations need to transform into Xodus' black church that speaks holistically to the entire African American people, especially to poor women and young people.

What ethical implications can be drawn from the diversity of ways in which black people greet one another? Taking on seemingly mundane ritualized and stylized metaphors of recognition within the black community, Riggins R. Earl, Jr., in *Dark Salutations* (2001), explores salutations in Christian, Nation of Islam, and popular street cultures among male and female African Americans. In a word, such quotidian black greetings as "brotherman," "blackman," "sistergirl," and "soul sister" convey an ethical thoughtfulness about African American reflexivity on brotherhood and sisterhood as essential planks in their human dignity. Earl advances a black ethics of salutatory liberation that also has import for a more healthy interracial social witness.

Systematic and constructive theology rounds out this overarching survey of theological disciplines among second generation (male) black theologians. James H. Evans, Jr.'s *We Have Been Believers: An African-American Systematic Theology* (1992) reinterprets the major doctrines of the Christian church – revelation/liberation to eschatology – from the standpoint of black faith and freedom. His systematic work draws on the Bible, biblical commentary, first generation black theologians, African religious scholarship, pivotal black thinkers (W. E. B. Du Bois, Zora Neale Hurston, and Howard Thurman), white feminist writings, narrative theology, and seminal European thinkers (Karl Barth and Paul Tillich).

Tribal Talk: Black Theology, Hermeneutics, and African/American Ways of "Telling the Story" (2000) by Will Coleman, focuses on this frontier consideration: must black theology simply be Christian? *Tribal Talk* urges inter- and intra-generational black theological expansion so that all interlocutors of liberational black religiosity can talk among the tribe called the African diaspora. Coleman proves his case somewhat chronologically. Commencing with West African narrative cosmology (the departure point for most Africans), one enters African traditional faith beliefs and folklore, which lay a basis for African survivals after slavery's Middle Passage to the "New World." Initially, enslaved blacks (Coleman attends to slave narratives of the Carolinas, due to their location for continually receiving new boats of Africans) created hoodoo, a mixture of African survivals and African American religious novelty. Next, enslaved blacks nurtured their own folkloric spirituality, non-Christian spirituality, and then a reappropriated Holy Ghost pneumatology. Finally, *Tribal Talk* examines critically the consistent manifestation of a black Christianity lodged in African American churches. Arguing against Christian orthodox dogmatics and recognizing the multivocality of black life, Coleman advocates a plurality of African American narratives (West African, non-Christian, and Christian) for the decisive method of defining black theology.

Dwight N. Hopkins' *Down, Up, and Over: Slave Religion and Black Theology* (1999) constructs theology from enslaved African and African American religious experiences. Religious formations of race in Protestantism and American culture contextualize the contemporary Spirit of liberation among black folk. Black religion today can be understood better with historicity. That is to say, seeking religious freedom, Europeans brought their form of white supremacist Christianity and enslaved Africans brought their traditional religions to the so-called New World. Eventually, black folk developed faith in a Spirit of liberation expressed as God (the Spirit for us), Jesus (the Spirit with us), and human purpose (the Spirit in us). Concomitantly, this liberation spirit moved blacks to re-create their formerly enslaved selves on the levels of language, political economy, racial cultural identity, and daily rituals. The Spirit of liberation ultimately calls forth a metanoia: the birth of a new spiritual–emotional–psychological human being and the construction of a new commonwealth of collective ownership/stewardship of all of God's wealth on earth.

Yet not all in the second generation of black theologians have readily concurred with the black, liberation, and Christian presuppositions. Victor Anderson's *Beyond Ontological Blackness* (1995) wonders if blackness (in black theology) is merely (and tragically) an invention of whiteness. Moving us beyond the black heroic genius cult, Anderson grapples with and defends a non-essentialist notion of black identity, one better suited for naming and thereby freeing the multiple intra-communal identities among African Americans. Anthony B. Pinn's *Why Lord?* (1995) ponders why God has not ended (and, indeed, perhaps approved of) black suffering. Pinn states that there is nothing redemptive in black people's suffering. Hence, his alternative is to deny the existence of God and opt for a liberating, strong humanism – the catalyst needed for blacks to fight harder for their freedom.

Pursuing the theodicy doctrine from Jesus' crucifixion suffering and enslaved blacks' oppression, *Were You There: Godforsakenness in Slave Religion* (1996) by

David Emmanuel Goatley asks those who remain within the Christian camp to undergo a self-test about the efficacy of their God. He concludes that God, paradoxically, liberates the oppressed even in instances of God's hiddenness. With Mark L. Chapman's text *Christianity On Trial* (1996), the concern is not so much the idea of suffering and a just God, as the entire endeavor of Christianity itself. What does it mean for blacks to embrace a faith proselytized by white supremacist Christians? Does Christianity engender black liberation or oppression? From his study of major African American religious figures pre- and post-black power (1966), he surmizes that the survival and prophetic texture of black Christianity hinges on ongoing, trenchant critiques of white racist Christianity and an unrelenting critique internal to the black church.

Black theology writings have been predominantly Protestant, and this fact alone could obscure some of the more intellectually creative works hailing from black Roman Catholic theologians and womanists. African American members of the Roman Catholic Church endure a triple jeopardy: they undergo marginalization within black theology, in the African American community, and in the Catholic Church. Yet their voice has been ever-present in the scholarly terrain of contemporary black theological advancements. Lawrence Lucas published his *Black Priest White Church* in 1970 and provided an autobiographical statement, from his childhood days until his priesthood, of his journey within the Roman Catholic Church in New York City. A recurrent theme, from his vantage, is the rigid white supremacy of his church. In addition to structural, ecclesial racial injustice, Lucas cites the Roman Church's failure to accent the black poor and the existential dilemma that others wrestle with: is it possible to be black and Roman Catholic? Despite the searing pain and straightforward anger, he maintains hope, or else African Americans will desert the church. In a sense, to avoid such a desertion, all books since Lucas' have sought to resolve the black and Roman Catholic problematic.

Cyprian Davis' *The History of Black Catholics in the United States* (1990) offers a definitive testimony on the presence and contributions of African American Roman Catholics in the US. Indeed, he documents that the first group of Africans in the future US were Roman Catholics who spoke Spanish, thus preceding the 1619 Jamestown, Virginia arrival of 20 Africans in bondage brought to that English-speaking colony. These black Roman Catholics were under Spain's jurisdiction in 1565 in the colony of St. Augustine in northern Florida.

The 1995 publication of Diana L. Hayes' *Hagar's Daughters: Womanist Ways of Being in the World* provided the first Roman Catholic monograph to interpret womanist thought. Later, Jamie T. Phelps edited *Black And Catholic* (1997), the first book to bring together African American scholars writing on a black Catholic reevaluation of theology, biblical studies, ethics, history, religious pedagogy, and method and context. Its final essay, by M. Shawn Copeland, outlines foundational marks required for a Roman Catholic black theology. The scaffolding for an authentically black and truly Roman Catholic theology involves grounding in the black American religious experience and religious consciousness, affirming all dimensions of black being, comprehending God's word in black culture, confronting shortcomings in black religious experiences, apprehending and implementing today the tasks of Jesus' time, fostering interdisciplinarity, and integrating the aesthetic with ideational precision.

In 1998 Joseph A. Brown wrote *To Stand on the Rock: Meditations on Black Catholic Identity*, again ruminating on the "authentically black, truly Catholic" way of life. Brown summons what he calls the Black Catholic Church to recognize its coming of age in several respects. African American religious leadership must be trained and educated in the black cultural milieu, one characterized by the specificity of African American healing and transformation. Accompanying the cultural imperative is the obligation for leadership to receive economic support from the black Catholic community. African American priests and bishops, therefore, must perceive themselves as caretakers of the spirituality and cultural components of black people. A resulting dynamic is that leadership arises from the community, feels obligated to its point of origin, is accountable to the people, and approved by black Catholics. Brown ends with two additional counsels: an invitation for the laity to assume more leadership by institutionalizing itself within the Black Catholic Church and a plea for more unity among African American liturgists.

In *Taking Down Our Harps* (1998) Diana L. Hayes and Cyprian Davis amassed a collection of articles crucial to the emerging black Roman Catholic theology. Hayes' essay declares that black faith is the real Christianity and, therefore, the entire Roman Catholic Church is mandated to become ontologically black in its innermost being because Jesus dwells amid oppressed black Americans. Jamie T. Phelps' contribution proposes a reformed mission work to black Americans, manifesting rigorous church self-critique on the nature of its commitment to inclusivity, focused energy on psychological healing and viewing the full humanity of African Americans, and intense intra-church spiritual growth. And continuing her constructive method in black Catholic theology, M. Shawn Copeland's essay opts for a sober utilization of the method of correlation (i.e., the Christian gospel responds, though not in a naive fashion, to queries from today's human culture), linked closely to critique (of texts and traditions), retrieval (of marginalized blacks and black Catholic histories), scientific social analysis (i.e., social theories), and construction (i.e., advancing the particularities of a black Catholic theology).

In the midst of this plethora of black theological diversity and development since the 1980s, members of the founding generation continue to publish works crucial to the sustenance of the discipline of black theology. Charles Shelby Rooks has written a history of the Fund for Theological Education, a structure that recruited and/or funded the majority of African Americans holding PhD degrees in any field of religion from the early 1960s until the early 1990s. His work, *Revolution in Zion* (1990), merges a narrative of what-happened-to-blacks in American theological education with challenges for African American churches, and with the essential themes bursting forth from the volatile, racial drama in broader US society. This multi-level chronicle dissects the birth of a black theological community out of which surfaced a black theology of liberation. Without that broader community, black theology would not look like it does today. For that reason, Rook's account could be subtitled "the making of a unique American discipline."

Two additional senior scholars, Peter J. Paris and J. Deotis Roberts, have penned works linking African American theological scholarship with features of African studies or Afrocentricity (the notion of privileging African sensibilities over European). Paris' *The Spirituality of African Peoples* (1995) discerns a common spirituality disseminating from African traditional religions and pervading the religious and moral values of the African diaspora. As a senior black American ethicist, he substantiates African survivals through comparative religious studies and his years of travel and living in Africa, Canada and, of course, the United States. The first of its kind, Paris' scholarly move articulates a plausible argument that in the interdependence of God, community, family, and human being, a common moral discourse appears for Pan-African peoples. And this shared moral philosophy (whereby continental Africans and the diaspora holistically unite nature, spirit, and history) grows out of various elements from African traditional cosmologies: the paramount aim for African peoples is the preservation and promotion of various configurations of community; and the crucial moral attribute, among others, required to achieve this goal is good moral character.

J. Deotis Roberts produced the first full-length theological treatment of the Afrocentric renaissance reigning throughout significant segments of black America. The target audience for his *Africentric Christianity* (2000) is the black church. His research question centers on whether or not Africentricity ("Afri," for Roberts, etymologically adheres more faithfully to Africa than "Afro") comports with Christian notions. By way of comparing Africentric and Christian beliefs and rituals, Roberts first establishes a fundamental differentiation between culture (i.e., Africentricity) and faith (i.e., Christianity). The former uplifts the glorious African heritage of black Americans, hence facilitating black self-worth, while the latter's purpose is redemption, thereby ensuring entrance into heaven. With that distinct caveat, he anticipates a salutary interplay between the two phenomena. Rituals such as Kwanzaa, from the African side, and Christmas, for Christians, can complement one another to better enhance both the liberating racial–cultural dimensions of Africentricity and the linchpin faith in Jesus Christ Liberator – all for a more authentic witness and ministry of the black church.

We conclude this mapping of the intellectual terrain of black theology with the thinker with whom we started. James H. Cone's groundbreaking, ten-year study on Martin Luther King, Jr. and Malcolm X initiates comparative religious research on these two fountainheads in black Americans' perennial quest for faith, racial, and cultural meanings. Cone's thesis weaves the dream and nightmare metaphors of King and Malcolm, respectively, and sorts through the question: What does it mean to be a person and community of African descent in North America? His acclaimed *Martin & Malcolm & America* (1991) brings to bear a sympathetic but critical probing of each man's position on American society, their moves toward unique forms of socialism, black women, the poor, and the international arena, and the characteristics of black leadership. Despite popular misconceptions, both men, for Cone, displayed similar spiritualities of freedom for the oppressed. At the end of their lives, they were striding toward one another politically and culturally.

Agenda

The next phase of black theology necessitates heightened theoretical work based on the following practices. If liberation, in all of its variegated, multiple, ambiguous, and pluriform definitions, continues as a central internal criterion, then the rebuked and silenced segments in the discipline, the black family and church, and the larger

African American community, demand a scholarly hearing. More particularly, explorations into the young gay and lesbian voices in black theology portend pioneering work that could open up further the cognitive vistas for the academy and human living. Renee L. Hill and Horace Griffin have launched that scholarly expedition.

Similarly, black theology should take more affirming steps to cooperate closer with womanists. The collaborative writing of Karen and Garth Baker-Fletcher models one encouraging paradigm.

Interdisciplinary and multidisciplinary methodologies remain in order, connected to interaction with diverse departments within the university and other guilds. Black theology has always transcended provincial knowledge restrictions.

However, historical memory of the discipline informs us that epistemology and academic inquiry come from civic conversations outside of the gates of institutionalized higher education. Thus, religious studies and theology unite in their object of study (i.e., African Americans and global human interactions) and in their service beyond the formerly educated elites. So black theology's tradition embraces a profound sense that education serves the community beyond the Ivory Tower.

In this regard, how does black theology form partnerships with faith organizations, community groups, and local governmental initiatives? How does it speak to the national media? What value resides in interfaith projects centered on justice work? Who are the poor and how does one clarify the need for both material transformation and emotional healing among those marginalized and without voices? And what does black theology have to say about the poor and ecology? Finally, in this age of adverse globalization, black theology needs to establish an international network of black theologians, and solidarity with common interlocutors from Africa, Asia, the Caribbean, Latin America, and the Pacific Islands, most notably in the Ecumenical Association of Third World Theologians.

Through the particularity of the African American experience and a conscious reaching out beyond that social location, perhaps the contours of a new human being and new society will surface in our midst.

Bibliography

Anderson, Victor. *Beyond Ontological Blackness: An Essay on African American Religious and Cultural Criticism*. New York: Continuum, 1995.

Baker-Fletcher, Garth Kasimu. *Xodus: An African American Male Journey*. Minneapolis, MN: Fortress Press, 1996.

Baker-Fletcher, Karen and Garth Kasimu Baker-Fletcher. *My Sister, My Brother: Womanist and Xodus God-Talk*. Maryknoll, NY: Orbis Books, 1997.

Blount, Brian K. *Then the Whisper Put on Flesh: New Testament Ethics in an African American Context*. Nashville, TN: Abingdon Press, 2001.

Brown, Joseph A. *To Stand on the Rock: Meditations on Black Catholic Identity*. Maryknoll, NY: Orbis Books, 1998.

Butler, Lee H., Jr. *A Loving Home: Caring for African American Marriage and Families*. Cleveland, OH: Pilgrim Press, 2000.

Chapman, Mark L. *Christianity On Trial: African-American Religious Thought Before and After Black Power*. Maryknoll, NY: Orbis Books, 1996.

Cleage, Albert. *The Black Messiah*. New York: Sheed and Ward, 1968.

Coleman, Will. *Tribal Talk: Black Theology, Hermeneutics, and African/American Ways of "Telling the Story."* University Park: Pennsylvania State University Press, 2000.

Cone, Cecil Wayne. *The Identity Crisis in Black Theology*. Nashville, TN: African Methodist Episcopal Church, 1975.

Cone, James H. *Martin & Malcolm & America: A Dream or a Nightmare?* Maryknoll, NY: Orbis Books, 1991.

—— *Black Theology and Black Power*. Maryknoll, NY: Orbis Books, 1998.

Cummings, George C. L. *A Common Journey: Black Theology (USA) and Latin American Liberation Theology*. Maryknoll, NY: Orbis Books, 1993.

Davis, Cyprian. *The History of Black Catholics in the United States*. New York: Crossroad, 1990.

Earl, Riggins R., Jr. *Dark Salutations: Ritual, God, and Greetings in the African American Community*. Harrisburg, PA: Trinity Press International, 2001.

Erskine, Noel Leo. *Decolonizing Theology: A Caribbean Perspective*. Maryknoll, NY: Orbis Books, 1981.

Evans, James H., Jr. *We Have Been Believers: An African-American Systematic Theology*. Minneapolis, MN: Fortress Press, 1992.

Felder, Cain Hope. *Troubling Biblical Waters: Race, Class, and Family*. Maryknoll, NY: Orbis Books, 1989.

—— (ed.). *Stony The Road We Trod: African American Biblical Interpretation*. Minneapolis, MN: Fortress Press, 1991.

Goatley, David Emmanuel. *Were You There? Godforsakenness in Slave Religion*. Maryknoll, NY: Orbis Books, 1996.

Grant, Jacquelyn. "Black Theology and the Black Woman." In *Black Theology: A Documentary History, Vol. 1: 1966–1979*, pp. 323–38. Edited by James H. Cone and Gayraud S. Wilmore. Maryknoll, NY: Orbis Books, 1993.

Griffin, Horace. "Giving New Birth: Lesbians, Gays and the 'Family': A Pastoral Care Perspective." *Journal of Pastoral Theology* (summer 1993): 88–98.

—— "Revisioning Christian Ethical Discourse on Homosexuality: A Challenge for the 21st Century." *Journal of Pastoral Care* (summer 1999): 209–19.

—— "Their Own Received Them Not: African American Lesbians and Gays in Black Churches." *Journal of Theology and Sexuality* (spring 2000): 88–100.

Harris, James H. *Pastoral Theology: A Black-Church Perspective*. Minneapolis, MN: Fortress Press, 1991.

Hayes, Diana L. *Hagar's Daughters: Womanist Ways of Being in the World*. Mahwah, NJ: Paulist Press, 1995.

Hayes, Diana L. and Cyprian Davis (eds.). *Taking Down Our Harps: Black Catholics in the United States*. Maryknoll, NY: Orbis Books, 1998.

Hill, Renee L. "Who Are We for Each Other?: Sexism, Sexuality and Womanist Theology." In *Black Theology: A Documentary History, Vol. 2: 1980–1992*, pp. 345–51. Edited by James H. Cone and Gayraud S. Wilmore. Maryknoll, NY: Orbis Books, 1993.

—— "Disrupted/Disruptive Movements: Black Theology and Black Power 1969/1999." In *Black Faith and Public Talk: Critical Essays on James H. Cone's Black Theology and Black Power*, pp. 138–49. Edited by Dwight N. Hopkins. Maryknoll, NY: Orbis Books, 1999.

Hopkins, Dwight N. *Black Theology USA and South Africa: Politics, Culture, and Liberation*. Maryknoll, NY: Orbis Books, 1989.

—— *Down, Up and Over: Slave Religion and Black Theology*. Minneapolis, MN: Fortress Press, 1999.

Long, Charles H. *Significations*. Minneapolis, MN: Fortress Press, 1986.

Lucas, Lawrence. *Black Priest White Church: Catholics and Racism*. New York: Random House, 1970.

Paris, Peter J. *The Spirituality of African Peoples: The Search for a Common Moral Discourse*. Minneapolis, MN: Fortress Press, 1995.

Phelps, Jamie T. (ed.). *Black and Catholic: The Challenge and Gift of Black Folk. Contributions of African American Experience and Thought to Catholic Theology*. Milwaukee, WI: Marquette University Press, 1997.

Pinn, Anthony B. *Why Lord? Suffering and Evil in Black Theology*. New York: Continuum, 1995.

Roberts, J. Deotis. *Africentric Christianity: A Theological Appraisal for Ministry*. Valley Forge, PA: Judson Press, 2000.

Rooks, Charles Shelby. *Revolution in Zion: Reshaping African American Ministry, 1960–1974*. New York: Pilgrim Press, 1990.

Walker, Theodore, Jr. *Empower the People: Social Ethics for the African-American Church*. Maryknoll, NY: Orbis Books, 1991.

Wimberly, Edward P. and Anne Streaty Wimberly. *Liberation and Human Wholeness: The Conversion Experiences of Black People in*

Slavery and Freedom. Nashville, TN: Abingdon Press, 1986.

Williams, Delores S. *Sisters in the Wilderness: The Challenge of Womanist God-Talk*. Maryknoll, NY: Orbis Books, 1993.

Wilmore, Gayraud S. *Black Religion and Black Radicalism: An Interpretation of the Religious History of the African Americans*. Maryknoll, NY: Orbis Books, 1998.

Young, Josiah Ulysses, III. *A Pan-African Theology: Providence and the Legacies of the Ancestors*. Trenton, NJ: African World Press, 1992.

Latin American Liberation Theology

Rebecca S. Chopp and Ethna Regan

Introduction: Character, Origins, and Influences

Latin American liberation theology is a reflection on God's activity and transforming grace among those who are the victims of modern history. The reader who is not poor must approach this logos of the theos with an attitude of respectful care, so that it will not be received as an interpretation, a second-level reflection on common human experience, but rather as an interruption, an irruption of how God is active, life is lived, and Christianity is practiced among the poor. This chapter assumes that its readers are not the poor, the subjects of Latin American liberation theology, hereafter referred to as liberation theology; thus it attempts to let liberation theology speak in its voice, but to do so with interpreters who hold that this knowledge of God, while not directly commensurable with the modern theology of the First World, nonetheless has its own integrity and represents another strand of the ancient theological task of faith seeking understanding.

Liberation theology speaks of God as manifest in the poor of history, for it arises out of their experience of God, an experience that is dependent, as Gustavo Gutiérrez has insisted, upon God's choosing to reveal God's self in the poor.[1] It seeks to guide the transformation of all human beings into new ways of being human, ways not dependent upon structures of division between rich and poor, the persons and the non-persons of history.[2]

Many factors contribute to the distinctive voice of liberation theology in Latin America. The most important factor is its context in the situation of massive inequality and poverty; the poor often watch their children die from lack of adequate food, healthcare, and sanitation. They suffer frequent unemployment and, when they do find work, the wages are not enough to provide a decent standard of living. Many Latin American countries are emerging from decades of brutal dictatorships and civil conflicts, and while democracy has made great progress, it remains the region in the world with the greatest economic and social inequality.

This present context derives from the "modern" history of Latin America, a history which, since the "discovery of the New World," has been marked by oppression and colonization.[3] Spain and Portugal settled the New World through the devastation of native cultures in order to make slaves for the conquerors and to Christianize the "heathens." Even with the emergence of many Latin American nations in the early nineteenth century, neocolonialism, a system of economic dependency and exploitation, existed between these nations and First World countries, first with Great Britain and later with the United States. The 1950s and 1960s saw international commitments to develop dependent countries to be like First World nations such as the United States, but this movement only augmented dependent relations, this time through military oligarchies and multinational corporations.[4] The foreign debt of Latin America, at its worst in the 1980s, exemplified this dependency, and the burden of repayment was carried mainly by the poor.

A major factor in the development of liberation theology was the positions on justice and peace taken by Roman Catholicism and Protestantism in the 1950s and 1960s. Most important among these was the social teaching of Vatican II concerning human dignity and the need for structural change. Latin American bishops met in Medellín, Colombia, in 1968 to discuss the impact of Vatican II for Latin America; the papers adopted by the bishops became the founding documents of liberation theology.[5] At Medellín, the struggle for change that would guide liberation theology was invoked, a struggle against the institutionalized violence suffered by the poor as a result of an "international imperialism of money," represented by the upper classes and foreign monopolies.

A new vision of faith was articulated in the view of the poor as human subjects active in history. This vision was located in small grassroots communities where the poor could determine their own destiny and express their faith as they participated in conscientization or consciousness-raising.

Besides these historical events, three other influences must be noted: political theology, Marxism, and popular religion. Political theology arose in West Germany as a critique of modern Christianity's concern for the ahistorical authenticity of the bourgeois subject and a reformulation of Christian theology in light of events of massive suffering, such as the Holocaust. The works of political theologians such as Jürgen Moltmann and Johann Baptist Metz suggested new theological terms such as privatization, oppression, ideology, and liberation. Metz offered a new anthropology that was social and political, while Moltmann constructed an understanding of God in and through the reality of suffering. Both theologians spoke of Christianity as a critical witness in society.[6]

Marxism has influenced liberation theology as both a theoretical tool of social analysis and a philosophy of history.[7] As a tool of social analysis, Marxism has supplied a dialectical, rather than functional, analysis, which focuses on the relations of power and force in a society instead of cloaking such forces in an ideology of society as an organism needing balance. As a philosophy of history, Marxism has contributed, along with other philosophies, toward a view of the human subject as socially or historically constituted, history as open to change and transformation, and oppression and alienation structured through the productive relations of society. Liberation theologians, especially in the early years, critically adopted some of the language and insights from Marxism; but they did so only by transforming these insights and language into their own theological reflections.

A quite different, and more recent, influence is that of popular religion. As theologians focused increasingly on the "option for the poor" as a way of life, the importance of popular religion came to the fore. Popular religion takes seriously the cultural specificity of various Latin American peoples and requires a reflection on the particularities of Amerindians, blacks, women, and others who may have distinctive religious practices. It examines how the ideas and rituals of Christianity settled in among native religious practices. Liberation theologians, in general, came to a growing appreciation of how the people's religions included indigenous practices, Afro-American religions, animistic traditions, the practice of magic, and various synchristic blends of religious traditions. Finally, popular religion provides an understanding not only of survival practices among the poor, but also of potential resources for transformation. Devotion to Mary, for instance, includes prayer to the popular female figures Morentia of Guadalupe, the black Aparecida, Purisima, and the Virgin of Charity, to whom persons pray for survival. Theological reflection and praxis also make these manifestations of the mother of the redeemer a symbol of hope for all. As María Clara Bingemer has observed:

> What is new about this work is that it reveals a Mary no longer considered individualistically, in terms of a model of ascetic virtues to be imitated, but as a collective symbol, a type of the faithful people within which the holy Spirit of God finds fertile ground to raise up the new people, the seed of the kingdom, which will inaugurate the new creation.[8]

Survey

While there has been important systematization of liberation theology in recent years, it is not primarily academic discourse for academic debate; it is, rather, church theology in the context of basic Christian communities. These are grassroots communities in which Christians seek to form and live out their Christian witness in their historical situation. Thus the first locus of liberation theology is the church, not the academy, and it can be characterized as a reflection on and guide to praxis rather than a second-level hermeneutical reflection on the theoretical meaning of Christianity. This practical theological discourse on the reality of the poor is the first, or popular, level of three levels of liberation theology described by Leonardo and Clodovis Boff. The second level is the pastoral, meaning that engaged in by theologically trained bishops, pastors, and ministers whose primary focus is pastoral ministry. These are often a bridge between the popular level and the third level of the professional theologians.

Liberation theology is a critique of the structures and institutions that create the poor, including the primary identification of modern Christianity with the rich. In order to do this, liberation theology engages in dialogue not only with philosophy but also with the social sciences. As a theological discourse of critique and transformation in solidarity with the poor, liberation theology offers a theological anthropology that is political, an interpretation of Christianity that may be characterized through the term "liberation," and a vision of Christianity as a praxis of love and solidarity with the oppressed.

The image of human existence (and theological anthropology is always guided by an image) in liberation theology is the poor. The bishops of Latin America meeting at Puebla in 1979 identified the faces of the poor, the subjects of liberation theology:

> The faces of young children, struck down by poverty before they are born . . . the faces of indigenous peoples, and frequently that of the Afro-Americans as well, living marginalized lives in inhuman situations . . . the faces of the peasants; as a special group, they live in exile almost everywhere on our continent . . . the faces of marginalized and overcrowded urban dwellers, whose lack of material goods is matched by the ostentatious display of wealth by other segments of society; the faces of old people, who are growing more numerous every day, and who are frequently marginalized in a progress-oriented society that totally disregards people not engaged in production.[9]

This human reality, the reality of what it is to be the poor and despised of the earth, is understood, in liberation theology, through the term "praxis," which has three distinguishable meanings. First of all, praxis means that human beings are constituted through political–historical reality. Where one lives, the status of the socioeconomic class, what kind of power is available, must all be clear considerations for understanding human reality. Secondly, praxis means that human reality is intersubjective, that human beings are not ahistorical "I's" that express their unique essences in relations to others through language, but that all subjectivity arises out of intersubjective relations between human beings. Thirdly, praxis as the understanding of human reality means that humans must and can intentionally create history, transforming and shaping reality for the improvement of human flourishing.

This understanding of human reality through praxis is joined by an interpretation, a reformation, of Christian symbols through the central theme of liberation. The key term "liberation," like any key term functioning as a material norm in theology, is a tensive metaphor, naming the reign and nature of God, the normative vision of history, the work and person of Christ, the witness and mission of the church.[10] It is with the centrality of this term, and many rich readings of the Bible and Christian tradition, that liberation theology is most clearly understood as not merely a form of ethics or social witness, but as a systematic theology, a radically new interpretation and transformation of Christian faith itself. Sin, for example, in liberation theology is reflected on, not merely through individual moral acts or existential separation and despair, but primarily in terms of social structures. Sin results in suffering, whose burden is carried, time and time again, by the poor of history. Sin is radical distortion, not of some private relation with God, but of all reality, especially of the historical–political world that God gives us to live in. Redemption, correlatively, must relate to liberation, though, of course, it cannot be merely identified with any one liberating act; if redemption has to do with the reconciliation of humanity to God and salvation from sins, then it must be related to our present historical reality. Indeed, among the many readings of Christ in liberation theology – Christ as political rebel, Christ suffering as the scourged of the earth, Christ in solidarity with the poor and oppressed – it is Christ as liberator, as one who actually effects transformation, as one who brings new ways of being human, who is central.

Within the locus of this understanding of human reality and interpretation of Christian symbols, Christianity becomes a praxis of solidarity with and for the poor, working for liberation and transformation for all. Christianity represents the witness of freedom. It does not necessarily supply a new political ordering, nor offer a new theocratic state; rather, it testifies to freedom and liberation, taking sides where God takes sides with the poor and the despised of the earth. Christianity follows God, and as Gustavo Gutiérrez has suggested, "The love of God is a gratuitous gift . . . Loving by preference the poor, doing that, God reveals this gratuity. And by consequence as followers of Jesus Christ, we must also do this preferential option for the poor."[11] In this way, for Christians, faith and love are not separable, indeed may not be distinguishable from justice. Christianity must neither conform itself to culture nor be a radical separatist sect. Rather, Christianity must discern God's activity amid the poor and work for radical transformation of the structures of society in order that all persons may become new human subjects.

It is best, therefore, to think of liberation theology as a new genre of theology based on a specific praxis of faith. Though liberation theology shares some common resources with other theologies, its way of organizing, its criteria for reading scriptures and traditions, its tasks, purpose, and intent, are specific to Christian praxis amid the poor.

Liberation theologians write on issues such as Christology and ecclesiology, work on how to use the resources of the social sciences, investigate the relation of popular religion to liberation theology, or interpret biblical themes and narratives.

It is difficult to survey Latin American liberation theologians, since liberation theology is a relatively young enterprise, and many of the figures who have written in Spanish or Portuguese have yet to be translated into English. But a brief survey, by alphabetical order, of some of the major figures and their books that are available in English may indicate the range of issues and interests in liberation theology. The theologians mentioned below, like most Christians in Latin America, are mainly Roman Catholic. Liberation theology has arisen primarily in the context of the Roman Catholic Church in Latin America, though there has been a parallel movement in the Protestant churches. After this overview, we will consider an individual Roman Catholic theologian and then a Protestant theologian for a deeper interpretation.

Hugo Assmann has taught in his native Brazil, Germany, and Costa Rica. His *Theology for a Nomad Church* considers the practical and theoretical nature of theological method in a liberation context. Like other liberation theologians, Assmann's work draws on sociology as a major source for theological reflection and formulates the basis of theological method not through eternal absolutes but through a critical engagement with and interpretation of historical praxis. Also concerned with the nature and method of theological reflection is Clodovis Boff, a Brazilian theologian, whose *Theology and Praxis: Epistemological Foundations* is a thorough treatment of the epistemological presuppositions in liberation theology. Attentive to popular religion, he has also published *Feet-on the-Ground Theology: A Brazilian Journey*, a diary of his missionary work in northwestern Brazil. His brother, Leonardo Boff, is well known for his Christology, *Jesus Christ Liberator*. Boff's Christology is based on the situation of oppression in Latin America and stresses the priority of orthopraxis over orthodoxy and the anthropological over the ecclesiological element in Christology. In recent years, Boff's work has been directed to conversation, and controversy, with the institutional church. His book *Church: Charism and Power: Liberation Theology and the Institutional Church* seeks not only to address the concerns of the institutional church in relation to liberation theology, but also to offer a new model of the church. This new model is a pneumatic ecclesiology, recalling the primitive elements of community, cooperation, and charism in Christian life. In *Ecclesiogenesis: The Base Communities Reinvent the Church*, Boff offers a new vision of the church, based on the experience of basic Christian communities. José Comblin, in *The Church and the National Security State*, examined the doctrine of national security, which holds that Latin America needs military leadership to curb internal subversion and counteract Marxism. While the church often became captive to the state's need for security, the book also testifies to Christian fidelity to the gospel under the repression of these regimes. In his recent writings, the Belgian–Brazilian Comblin engages in a courageous critique of liberation theology and questions the adequacy of its responses to what he suggests is the main issue of the past generation, not revolution but urbanization.

Enrique Dussel's *A History of the Church in Latin America* has made a major contribution to a reinterpretation of the history of the church in Latin America, a history that has been neglected or interpreted only through the eyes of the victors. Dussel, an Argentinian Roman Catholic layman living in Mexico, is both a philosopher and a theologian, and he has developed philosophical categories for liberation theology. He considers the critique of the conquest of the New World by Antonio de Montesinos, Bartolomé de Las Casas, and Francisco de Vitoria as the first explicit liberation philosophy and the first counter-discourse of modernity. His recent work on a philosophy of liberation combines the critique of ontology born of Levinas with the Marxist critique of capitalism, engaging also in dialogue with other First World philosophers. He stresses the interrelatedness of politics and economics, and an ethics that gives centrality to the phenomenon of alterity, in which the "other" is the poor.

Along with ecclesiology, scripture has been a major concern for liberation theologians, both as they seek to interpret the concerns of poverty, oppression, and liberation in the Bible and as they reflect on the power of reading the scriptures as a liberating activity. Books such as José Miranda's *Marx and the Bible: A Critique of the Philosophy of Oppression* and his *Being and the Messiah* suggest a new way of reading the Bible, as well as a new biblical interpretation of topics such as sin and redemption.

Juan Luis Segundo of Uruguay is concerned with the use of scripture in theology. Segundo's *The Liberation of Theology* reinterprets the hermeneutic circle in theology, addressing how the Bible is to be interpreted in a manner that does not simply repeat past doctrines, but speaks to and transforms the present historical situation. Segundo, one of the most prolific writers on liberation theology, represents many theologians who, in the course of their careers, have "become" liberation theologians, moving from a form of theological reflection in a European style to reformulating theological reflection in the Latin American situation. In fact, Segundo's five-volume series entitled *A Theology for Artisans of a New Humanity*, written as liberation theology began to emerge, can be read as transitional pieces between the older European model of theology and the concerns and impulses that lie behind liberation theology. His series entitled *Jesus of Nazareth Yesterday and Today* continues the methodological work of *The Liberation of Theology* and develops a contemporary Christology. Segundo's work points to the richness and breadth of liberation theology. The work of Jon Sobrino of El Salvador indicates the radical reformation of Christianity and of theology that liberation theology represents.

Sobrino's *Christology at the Crossroads* offers a Christology that involves a re-reading of the historical Jesus (contending that Jesus was on the side of the oppressed) against the background of exploitation, injustice, and oppression in Latin America. Sobrino argues, in this widely read text, that we can come to know Jesus only by following Jesus, which means following Jesus into the struggle against oppression and for liberation. An equally radical treatment of ecclesiology is offered in Sobrino's *The True Church and the Poor*, which begins by tracing the differences between liberation theology and European theology and goes on to consider such ecclesiological issues as the practice of justice as essential to the gospel, the experience of God in the church of the poor, the theological significance of the persecution of the church, and evangelization as the mission of the church. In his *Principle of Mercy: Taking the Crucified People from the Cross*, Sobrino presents the existence of a "crucified people" and urges a theology of mercy. The theme of martyrdom frames Sobrino's work, from the early dedication of *Christology at the Crossroads* to two priests, "martyrs for the Kingdom of God in El Salvador," to *Jesus the Liberator*, dedicated to the martyrs of the University of Central America, and his abiding concern for the innocent and anonymous martyrs of Latin America.

Elsa Tamez, a Protestant, continues the reinterpretation of basic Christian doctrines within the context of the option for the poor in her *Amnesty of Grace: Justification by Faith from a Latin American Perspective*. Tamez reinterprets justification as displaying God's affirmation of life for all human beings and thus meaning, in contemporary reality, a humanization that stands in opposition to the condemnation of human beings through poverty, oppression, and marginalization. Tamez, Ivone Gebara, María Pilar Aquino, and others are part of a feminist movement within liberation theology. Prior to the late 1980s, there was little concern for the diversity of those who constituted "the poor" of Latin America. Since then, the theological voices of women, blacks, and Amerindians have begun to be heard in liberation theology, profoundly enriching its vision and critique.

Liberation theology has embarked on a bold, new interpretation of Christian witness in Latin America. Because of the breadth of issues considered, the many different approaches used, and the reformulation of theology itself, it is important to examine two specific theologians and trace the development of their particular concerns, resources, and methods. These are Gustavo Gutiérrez, a Roman Catholic from Peru, and José Miguez Bonino, a United Methodist from Argentina.

Two Liberation Theologians

Gustavo Gutiérrez

Gustavo Gutiérrez, perhaps the most influential of all liberation theologians, writes from the perspective of the poor; his translated books in English, such as *The Theology of Liberation, The Power of the Poor in History, We Drink From Our Own Wells*, and *On Job*, interpret the Bible, Christian faith, history, and subjectivity through the eyes of the oppressed, the victims of history. There are two distinguishable stages in Gutiérrez's articulation of theology as the language of God from the perspective of the poor. In the first stage, the poor were the center of theological reflection based on an argument about the irruption of the poor into history. In this stage, Gutiérrez offered a philosophy of history as the basis of theological reflection: modern history was characterized by historical praxis relying on individualism and rationalism to create the industrial, progressive First World. But this historical praxis was built upon massive social and economic contradictions, contradictions that rest on the backs of the poor. Gutiérrez argues that historical praxis is irrupted by the liberating praxis of the poor. This dialectical overturn of history, similar to Marx's reliance on the class revolution of the proletariat, occurs, in Gutiérrez's work, with a reliance on the symbols of Exodus and Promise, as well as an interpretation of history and politics in light of redemption and liberation.[12] He argues that liberation and redemption are related on three levels: particular acts, the project of history, and final redemption. This stage of Gutiérrez's theological reflection centers on present possibilities for radical transformation and understands "history" itself as carrying along this tide. Gutiérrez also offers a re-reading of the church and of poverty based on spirituality and an evangelical life. The church is a sacrament of God's grace, and as a sacrament it provides a prophetic witness in Latin America. But the church is also the locus of basic Christian communities, wherein, Gutiérrez suggests, a spirituality of gratuitousness flourishes: a spirituality based on the loving presence of God amid the scandalous condition of poverty.

It is this third theme, the gratuitous love of God, that comes to the fore in Gutiérrez's second stage. Displaced is the objectivization of liberating praxis as an autonomous force to change the world. Now, it seems that captivity, suffering, and exile are the more dominant themes. What Gutiérrez sees from the perspective of the poor is the love and presence of God in their long-suffering struggle to survive. God, faithfulness, and love among poor people now become the center of theological reflection instead of a particular philosophy of history.[13] The poor are the real subjects of theology, not because they express or bear a certain inevitable historical force, but because of God's presence. Gutiérrez's argument is worth underscoring at this point: the option for the poor depends not on an interpretation of history but on God's own choice. While the first stage could be interpreted as corrective of a modern philosophy of history, this second stage is more radical and constructive: more is called into question here about the constitution of modernity and Christianity, about what it is to be a human subject, about what it is to experience the love of God, about what it is to really hear the other of history speak. This stage is also marked by a more nuanced reading of Marx, and the acknowledgment of the inadequacy of the theory of dependency, which saw the underdevelopment of poorer countries as the historical by-product of the development of the richer countries, thus advocating liberation, not development, as the solution. Gutiérrez says that this theory does not take sufficient cognizance of the internal dynamics of countries.

This second stage also sees the development of the spirituality of liberation first mentioned in *A Theology of Liberation*. The emphasis on popular religion and spirituality is especially strong in Gutiérrez's works *The Power of the Poor in History*, *We Drink From Our Own Wells*, and *The Truth Shall Make You Free*.

Gutiérrez's insistence on doing theology, not simply *for* the poor, but from solidarity *with* the poor, and the correlative insistence on the particularities of the poor of popular religion in Latin America, has also resulted in a massive historical study of Bartolomé de Las Casas. Gutiérrez's *Las Casas: In Search of the Poor of Jesus*

Christ is a reading not only of the life of a heroic figure for liberation theology, but also an interpretation of history from and through solidarity with the poor. Las Casas' stress on evangelizing concern for the aboriginal populations, his linkage of salvation and justice, and his insistence on difference and otherness as a way to understand humanity, are all themes of Latin American history and its present reality. Las Casas worked against the systemic injustices and the oppressive cultural practices against the "others" of history. For Gutiérrez, to understand Las Casas is not only to claim a "tradition" behind liberation theology but to name the present reality: "Las Casas' witness is particularly important for the self-discovery that the peoples of Latin America must make today."[14] Gutiérrez, one of the primary interpreters of liberation theology, also acknowledges the serious and relevant critiques of liberation theology that have helped it to mature. His work moves in the direction of a radically new interpretation of Christianity; he has taken the basic symbols of Christianity and radically reworked them amid the experience of God's presence in the poor, but likewise, he has used these classical symbols of Christianity to give voice to the experience of the poor in history. In so doing, Gutiérrez has uncovered, for many of us, the presuppositions of power, dominance, and injustice in our basic theological beliefs. What does it mean for modern theology to be so concerned about the non-believers in history that it simply ignores the masses of poor? What does it mean for a progressive theology to be so committed to isolating an ahistorical religious dimension that it overlooks historical structures that divide human beings into rich and poor, keeping most of God's created subjects as non-persons in history? Both critically and constructively, Gutiérrez offers, by way of a continual journey, a new language of God that denounces sin and announces grace.

José Miguez Bonino

José Miguez Bonino's work, in books such as *Doing Theology in a Revolutionary Situation, Room to be People,* and *Toward a Christian Political Ethics,* exemplifies liberation theology's understanding of history as the arena of God's action. History has its locus neither in individual historicity nor in the worldly progressive realization of the bourgeoisie, but in the total sociopolitical–economic context in which humans live and in which God continually acts. His work illustrates that history has sociopolitical determinates based not only on sociological analysis, but also on theological and scriptural warrants that God acts in history. Indeed, he suggests that scripture be understood as a narrative of God's acts in history and be analogically applied to the present situation. Though God acts in history in different ways at different times, God always acts in love to transform history into the Kingdom of God.

The relation of history to the kingdom is central, according to Miguez Bonino, because in the scriptures this is how God is revealed. We do not relate kingdom to history for our own political ends, but because in the Bible God is constantly transforming history into the kingdom. This important and tensive relationship is, unfortunately, frequently misunderstood. There is a tendency to separate the kingdom and history, a position Miguez Bonino characterizes as dualism, which denies the basic biblical thrust of God in history. There is also a tendency merely to reduce the kingdom to history, or better yet a particular time and place in history, the monist solution, which denies the mission of Christianity and threatens to destroy the non-identity between Christianity and the world. Rather, the relation of history and the kingdom must be held to as a process of transformation, a process that might be compared to the resurrection of the body, which does not deny or negate but fulfills and perfects.[15] Miguez Bonino also relates history to the Kingdom of God eschatologically; like the Pauline doctrine of works, history takes on its fullness and meaning as it anticipates the Kingdom of God. History has a decidedly theological meaning, not merely philosophical or materialist. We act in history because God acts, or more precisely, God acts in history through love to bring the kingdom, and, in our obedience, we act through Christ's love to bring the kingdom.

It is this praxis of obedience which calls out for theology; praxis must continually interpret God's action in history based on biblical themes and understand the Bible in light of experiencing God's activity of history. This "hermeneutical" activity, that is, the activity of discerning, interpreting, and appropriating God's activity in history into the praxis of Christian obedience, begins by realizing its own concreteness; that is, it too is historically bound, and cannot reflect outside of the categories and conditions available in a particular historical situation. All theology is therefore situated and political: situated because it is done in a particular historical situation, and political because reflection, like all other aspects of life, grows out of the full sociopolitical reality. Yet theologians must not merely mirror the sociopolitical context; rather, they must position themselves in light of their obedience to Christian praxis, or, as Miguez Bonino says, "we are situated in reality to be sure – historically, geographically, culturally, and most of all groupwise and classwise – but we can also position ourselves differently in relation to the situation."[16] Thus theology must learn to dialogue carefully with the social sciences, in order to analyze, critique, and transform the historical situation in light of God's liberating activity.

Miguez Bonino's work demonstrates both the centrality of history in liberation theology, and the sociopolitical view of history. It is important to underscore that sociopolitical history is central to understanding not only because of sociological arguments, that is, that all knowledge is historically conditioned, but also because of scriptural arguments: history is the arena of God's action, action which is the transformation of history through love. Miguez Bonino's theology calls human beings to be responsible for history: responsible both in responding to God's love and responsible for their involvement in history. He also shows us that liberation theology has a decidedly sociopolitical cast: it advocates historical transformation, it discerns God's liberating activity, and it uses social sciences for analysis, interpretation, and appropriation.

Debate

Liberation theology has been received with a great deal of debate among First World theologians. Some have responded by rethinking the basic contours and commitments of their own theological and political positions, while others dismiss liberation theology as inadequate theological reflection or a form of politics using religion. The debate has been centered in three broad areas: liberation theology's equation of liberation and redemption, its turn to the political as the primary locus of human life, and its theoretical arguments in relation to ethics and social theory.

For many First World theologians, the equation of redemption and liberation tempts a kind of temporal messianism, a heralding of the reign of God on the side of one political cause.[17] This appears too reminiscent of totalitarian movements. It is also considered unbiblical, as it seems to place God on the side of the poor, in opposition to the rich.[18] Of course, other formulations are varied, some advocating an existentialist theology with implications to move into political realms, while others advocate a more realist power basis, noting that even Jesus said that the poor will always be with us. These arguments also touch upon a disagreement within liberation theology over how redemption and liberation are related, and upon the debate over the status of the option for the poor. As we have already seen, Miguez Bonino criticizes some liberation theologians for monist solutions, arguing for a position that distinguishes, while Gutiérrez advocates a three-level relation between redemption and liberation. The option for the poor is, as Gutiérrez suggested, a statement about God's gratuitousness and not a romanticization of the poor. This also relates to the debate among liberation theologians about the role of popular religion – whether or not it is a mystification of consciousness or authentic religious praxis.

Related to this criticism is the second, that liberation theology has reduced human life to the political realm.[19] For many years, Roman Catholic theologians distinguished between two realms that should be separated without interference: the political and the religious. The Second Vatican Council, with its new vision of the relationship between the church and the world, gave impetus to new theological reflection on social justice and politics. Liberation theologians hold a broad understanding of the political as the basis of life. Politics is not simply concerned with the managing of the state, but also with how our lives are organized and expressed, and how we fulfill our subjectivity. Politics is intrinsic to the definition of the human subject, not merely a secondary expression. The gospel, then, is not political in offering a particular theory of political management, but is political in terms of its promise and demand for the fulfillment of human life. Liberation theologians also respond that theology, like all other forms of thought, is always political, advocating a particular view of life and implying a vision of human flourishing.

But even if one grants that in some manner redemption and liberation are related, and that politics is a necessary dimension of understanding religion, questions can still be asked about liberation theology's theoretical formulations, more specifically, the relative adequacy of its ethical and social theories. Liberation theology lacks an adequate social theory of the relation between human consciousness and social structures.[20] In recent years, however, there have been significant developments in the area of ethics, although much of the literature is not available in English. Liberation theology has its origins in ethical indignation; thus, ethics is a constitutive dimension of this theology. It has placed the concerns of the poor and oppressed at the center of ethics. Developments in the area of philosophical ethics, exemplified in the writings of Enrique Dussel and Juan Carlos Scannone, are matched by a flourishing of Christian ethics in Latin America,[21] with a liberationist perspective integral to many theologians who may not necessarily identify themselves as liberation theologians. Liberation ethics embraces the concerns of human rights, feminism, bioethics, and ecology, but needs more development in areas like personal freedom and conscience. Solidarity is the key theme, a theme which forges a personalism from the perspective of the poor and oppressed, based on a communitarian vision of the human person that is broader and more inclusive than North American "communitarian" thought.

Achievement and Agenda: The Future of Liberation Theology

Any evaluation of the "achievements" of liberation theology must begin with the intent and promise of this theology to be a voice of the poor and to speak of God's presence and power among the victims of history. Concerns such as liberation theology's methodological rigor or its theoretical sophistication are important, but they are secondary to the rupturing presence of this theology. It has ruptured much of the discourse of modern theology, even as it has intensified and changed many of its concepts. Modern theology's turn to the subject tended to assume the bourgeois subject confronted with atheism, but the subject of liberation theology is the nonperson. Thus, the first accomplishment of liberation theology is to enable us to hear the voice of the poor and to allow that voice to challenge our values and beliefs, even as it highlights our participation in structures and systems that oppress others.

However, liberation theology's primary commitment is not to convert the rich, but to speak from the poor for the poor, giving voice to new understandings of God, love, sin, grace, and eschatology. This second accomplishment of new theological perspectives opens new ways of speaking about the human person, community, justice, the structures of the world in which we live, and hope for the future.

The third accomplishment concerns the methodological importance of liberation theology. Latin American liberation theologians, together with black and feminist liberation theologians, have made a convincing case for the situatedness of all knowledge. This achievement has three dimensions: (1) the situatedness of all knowledge; (2) the inclusion of ideology critique in theology; and (3) the argument for the positionality of theology, that is, the rhetorical commitments of knowledge. Liberation theologians, in a variety of ways, include ideology critique as intrinsic to the theological task, in order to reveal distortions of knowledge, interest, and power in social systems. Some years before poststructuralist claims about the relations of knowledge, interest, and power became popular in First World academic circles, Latin American theologians argued that reason itself is always a product of history. Liberation theologians pursue (in a way the poststructuralists often do not) a constructive vision, a world envisioned from the new subjectivity of the poor, a new relation between human consciousness and social structures.

Despite these accomplishments and its obvious maturation, there is general agreement that liberation theology is in crisis since the 1990s. Supporters of the movement lament its loss of direction and the weakening of its radical socioeconomic critique. Opponents suggest that the demise of socialism has rendered liberation theology passé or failed, and interpret the new emphases in liberation theology as a "retreat" into spirituality. It is erroneous to view the fall of the Berlin Wall as the destruction of the cornerstone of liberation theology. The preferential, but not exclusive, option for the poor – not Marxism – was always at the heart of liberation theology. However, this option for the poor faces different and complex challenges in the new global economy. While most liberation theologians, with varying degrees of skepticism, recognize the positive function of the market, they are concerned about the impact of neoliberalism. Neoliberalism, with its absolutist view of the market and its reductionist anthropology, sees the human person merely as an income-generating unit. While economic conditions have improved in Latin America, the masses of the poor have been joined by the newly impoverished of the middle classes. Future economic growth cannot occur at the expense of the poor and the destruction of natural resources. Liberation theology needs to seriously engage with this new economic and political reality through critique and constructive vision, maintaining the insistence on structural transformation and participatory democracy.

The diversity of voices that has emerged in liberation theology has unveiled both the complexity of the poor and the complexity of oppression. Capitalism is not the only form of oppression, but there is an interrelationship between it and racism, sexism, and other forms of oppression. It is suggested that this broadening of social analysis could blunt the socioeconomic critique that has been integral to liberation theology. Juan Carlos Scannone describes an "axial shift" from the socioeconomic to the sociocultural perspective, a shift which does not consist in substitution, but in a deepening of perspectives.[22]

Critics of liberation theology suggest that although it made an option for the poor, the poor later opted for Pentcostalism. The rapid growth of Pentecostalist Protestantism in Latin America since the 1980s is a phenomenon that has only recently been taken seriously by scholars. Some in the business sector perceive it as the arrival of the Protestant Reformation in Latin America, an arrival whose work ethic will overcome the cultural impediments to economic development. Many Catholics critique Pentecostalism as lacking in social concern, while others see the expansion of Protestant "sects" as a threat to the traditional role of the Catholic Church. The general perception is that Pentecostalism is a foreign import, which upholds an apolitical Christianity, while maintaining strong links to the Religious Right in North America. There were definite associations between Pentecostalism and some repressive regimes, unlike historical forms of Protestantism in Latin America that upheld the values of liberal democracy, but the reality is that "Pentecostalism" is an umbrella term, embracing a phenomenon which is marked by complexity both in terms of its composition and its relationship to politics. Its rapid growth, particularly among the urban poor, and its attraction, either in terms of conversion or affiliation, merits serious theological reflection and dialogue, particularly in the area of ecclesiology.

Whether or not one considers liberation theology to be the most significant theological movement to emerge in the twentieth century, it must be acknowledged that it has irretrievably changed the theological landscape. Even if the term "liberation theology" does not endure, its theological principles remain relevant for Christian theology and its radical challenges will continue to provoke church and academy to listen to the cry of the poor, and to speak of God and God's reign in solidarity with those who live on the underside of our times.

Notes

1 Gustavo Gutiérrez, "Theology and Spirituality in a Latin American Context," *Harvard Divinity Bulletin*, 14 (June–August 1984).

2 Though a common objection to liberation theology is that it will result in making the poor rich, simply exchanging one group of oppressors for another, liberation theologians, from their earliest works on, have advocated a transformation of social structures to rid the world of the massive disparities between the poor and the rich and have offered anthropologies of transformation stressing new ways of being human for all persons.

3 For good introductions to the history of Latin America, see George Pendle, *A History of Latin America* (New York, 1963); Hubert Herring, *A History of Latin America from the Beginnings to the Present* (New York, 1961); and Enrique D. Dussel, *A History of the Church in Latin America: Colonialism to Liberation (1492–1979)* (Grand Rapids, MI, 1981).

4 See José Comblín, *The Church and the National Security State* (Maryknoll, NY, 1979) and Robert Calvo, "The Church and the Doctrine of National Security," in Daniel H. Levine (ed.), *Churches and Politics in Latin America* (Beverly Hills, CA, 1979).

5 See Joseph Gremillion (ed.), *The Gospel of Peace and Justice: Catholic Social Teaching since Pope John* (Maryknoll, NY, 1976).

6 Representative works by these two theologians are: Jürgen Moltmann, *Theology of Hope: On the Grounds and Implications of a Christian Eschatology* (New York, 1967) and *The Crucified God: The Cross of Christ as the Foundation and Criticism of Christian Theology* (New York, 1973); Johann Baptist Metz, *Theology of the World* (New York, 1969) and *Faith in History and Society: Toward a Practical Fundamental Theology* (New York, 1980).

7 For examples of the critical uses of Marxism in liberation theology, see José Miguez Bonino, *Christians and Marxists: The Mutual Challenge to Revolution* (Grand Rapids, MI, 1976) and Juan Luis Segundo, *Faith and Ideologies* (Maryknoll, NY, 1984).

8 María Clara Bingemer, "Women in the Future of the Theology of Liberation," in Marc H. Ellis and Otto Maduro (eds.), *Expanding the View: Gustavo Gutiérrez and the Future of Liberation Theology* (Maryknoll, NY, 1990), p. 185.

9 John Eagleson and Philip Scharper (eds.), *Pueblo and Beyond: Documentation and Commentary* (Maryknoll, NY, 1979), paras. 32–9.

10 We use the term tensive metaphor to suggest the multiple meanings and yet systematic center of this theology in the term liberation. This is a metaphorical way of stating Tillich's notion of the material norm of theology. See Paul Tillich, *Systematic Theology* (Chicago, 1951), Vol. 1, pp. 47–50.

11 Gutiérrez, "Theology and Spirituality in a Latin American Context," p. 4.

12 This is developed in Gutiérrez, *A Theology of Liberation*.

13 This notion of two stages in Gutiérrez's writings should not be taken to mean a major break in Gutiérrez's theology; rather, it suggests a certain shifting of the center of his theological reflection from a philosophy of history to an argument about God.

14 Gustavo Gutiérrez, *Las Casas: In Search of the Poor of Jesus Christ*, trans. Robert R. Barr (Maryknoll, NY, 1993), p. 456.

15 José Miguez Bonino, *Doing Theology in a Revolutionary Situation* (Philadelphia, PA, 1975), pp. 136–43.

16 José Miguez Bonino, *Toward a Christian Political Ethics* (Philadelphia, PA, 1983), p. 44.

17 See, for instance, the charge by Dennis McCann that liberation theology "politicizes" the gospel: "Practical Theology and Social Action: or What can the 1980s Learn from the 1960s," in Don S. Browning (ed.), *Practical Theology: The Emerging Field in Theology, Church, and World* (San Francisco, 1983), pp. 105–25.

18 For instance, the 1984 "Instruction on Certain Aspects of the Theology of Liberation," issued by the Congregation for the Doctrine of the Faith, criticized "certain forms" of liberation theology for faulty biblical hermeneutics and uncritical use of

Marxism. The 1986 "Instruction on Christian Freedom and Liberation" was less critical and, although subordinating socio-political liberation to personal–spiritual freedom, it did endorse many of the key theological concepts of liberation theology.

19 Schubert Ogden, for example, has criticized liberation theologians for equating redemption and emancipation in his *Faith and Freedom: Toward a Theology of Liberation* (Nashville, TN, 1979).

20 See, for instance, Rebecca S. Chopp, *The Praxis of Suffering: An Interpretation of Liberation and Political Theologies* (Maryknoll, NY, 1986), pp. 144–8.

21 See Dean Brackley and Thomas L. Schubeck, "Moral Theology in Latin America," *Theological Studies* 63 (2002), pp. 123–60, an excellent survey of recent developments in the field.

22 "'Axial Shift' instead of 'Paradigm Shift'," in Georges De Schrijver (ed.), *Liberation Theologies on Shifting Grounds: A Clash of Socio-Economic and Cultural Paradigms* (Leuven, 1998), p. 91.

Bibliography

Primary

Alves, Ruben, *Tomorrow's Child: Imagination, Creativity, and the Rebirth of Culture* (New York, 1972).

Aquino, María Pilar, *Our Cry for Life: Feminist Theology from Latin America.* (Maryknoll, NY, 1993).

Assman, Hugo, *Theology for a Nomad Church* (Maryknoll, NY, 1976).

Boff, Clodovis, *Feet-on-the-Ground Theology: A Brazilian Journey*, trans. Phillip Berryman (Maryknoll, NY, 1987).

—— *Theology and Praxis: Epistemological Foundations* (Maryknoll, NY, 1987).

Boff, Leonardo, *Jesus Christ Liberator* (Maryknoll, NY, 1978).

—— *Church: Charism and Power: Liberation Theology and the Institutional Church* (New York, 1985).

—— *Ecclesiogenesis: The Base Communities Reinvent the Church* (Maryknoll, NY, 1986).

Comblin, Joseph, *The Church and the National Security State* (Maryknoll, NY, 1979).

—— *Called for Freedom: The Changing Context of Liberation Theology*, trans. Phillip Berryman (Maryknoll, NY, 1998).

Dussel, Enrique, D., *Ethics and the Theology of Liberation* (Maryknoll, NY, 1978).

—— *A History of the Church in Latin America: Colonialism to Liberation (1492–1979)* (Grand Rapids, MI, 1981).

—— *Philosophy of Liberation* (Maryknoll, NY, 1985).

—— *The Underside of Modernity: Apel, Ricoeur, Rorty, Taylor, and the Philosophy of Liberation*, trans. and ed. Eduardo Mendieta (New York, 1998).

Ellacuría, Ignacio and Sobrino, Jon (eds.), *Mysterium Liberationis: Fundamental Concepts of Liberation Theology* (Maryknoll, NY, 1993).

Gutiérrez, Gustavo, *A Theology of Liberation: History, Politics and Salvation* (Maryknoll, NY, 1973, 1988).

—— *The Power of the Poor in History: Selected Writings* (Maryknoll, NY, 1983).

—— *We Drink From Our Own Wells: The Spiritual Journey of a People* (Maryknoll, NY, 1984).

—— *On Job: God-talk and the Suffering of the Innocent* (Maryknoll, NY, 1987).

—— *The Truth Shall Make You Free: Confrontations*, trans. Matthew J. O'Connell (Maryknoll, NY, 1990).

—— *The God of Life* (Maryknoll, NY, 1991).

—— *Las Casas: In Search of the Poor of Jesus Christ*, trans. Robert R. Barr (Maryknoll, NY, 1993).

Miguez Bonino, José, *Doing Theology in a Revolutionary Situation* (Philadelphia, PA, 1975).

—— *Toward a Christian Political Ethics* (Philadelphia, PA, 1983).

—— *Faces of Jesus: Latin American Christologies* (Maryknoll, NY, 1984).

Miranda, José, *Marx and the Bible* (Maryknoll, NY, 1974).

Munoz, Ronaldo, *The God of Christians* (Maryknoll, NY, 1990).

Segundo, Juan Luis, *The Community Called Church* (Maryknoll, NY, 1973).

—— *Grace and the Human Condition* (Maryknoll, NY, 1973).

—— *Our Idea of God* (Maryknoll, NY, 1973).

—— *The Sacraments Today* (Maryknoll, NY, 1974).

—— *Evolution and Guilt* (Maryknoll, NY, 1974).

—— *The Liberation of Theology* (Maryknoll, NY, 1976).

—— *Jesus of Nazareth Yesterday and Today, Vol. 1: Faith and Ideologies* (Maryknoll, NY, 1982).

—— *Signs of the Times: Theological Reflections* (Maryknoll, NY, 1993).

Sobrino, Jon, *Christology at the Crossroads: A Latin American Approach* (Maryknoll, NY, 1978).

—— *The True Church and the Poor* (Maryknoll, NY, 1984).

—— *The Principle of Mercy: Taking the Crucified People from the Cross* (Maryknoll, NY, 1994).

Tamez, Elsa, *The Amnesty of Grace: Justification by Faith from a Latin American Perspective*, trans. Sharon H. Ringe (Nashville, TN, 1993).

Secondary

Alcoff, Linda Martín and Mendieta, Eduardo (eds.), *Thinking from the Underside of History: Enrique Dussel's Philosophy of Liberation* (Lanham, MD, 2000).

Berryman, Phillip, *Liberation Theology* (Oak Park, IL, 1987).

Brown, Robert McAfee, *Theology in a New Key: Responding to Liberation Themes* (Philadelphia, PA, 1978).

Candelaria, Michael. *Popular Religion and Liberation* (Albany, NY, 1990).

Chopp, Rebecca S., *The Praxis of Suffering: An Interpretation of Liberation and Political Theologies* (Maryknoll, NY, 1986).

De Schrijver, Georges (ed.), *Liberation Theologies on Shifting Grounds: A Clash of Socio-Economic and Cultural Paradigms* (Leuven, 1998).

Eagleson, Jon and Scharper, Philip (eds.), *Pueblo and Beyond* (Maryknoll, NY, 1979).

Ellis, Marc H. and Maduro, Otto (eds.), *Expanding the View: Gustavo Gutiérrez and the Future of Liberation Theology* (Maryknoll, NY, 1990).

Fabella, Virginia and Torres, Sergio (eds.), *Irruption of the Third World: Challenge to Theology* (Maryknoll, NY, 1983).

Freire, Paulo, *Pedagogy of the Oppressed* (New York, 1970).

Gibellini, Rosino (ed.), *Frontiers of Theology in Latin America* (Maryknoll, NY, 1974).

Gottwald, Norman (ed.), *The Bible and Liberation: Political and Social Hermeneutics* (Maryknoll, NY, 1983).

Lamb, Matthew, *Solidarity with Victims: Toward a Theology of Social Transformation* (New York, 1982).

Lernoux, Penny, *The Cry of the People: The Struggle for Human Rights in Latin America – the Catholic Church in Conflict with US Policy* (New York, 1980).

Metz, Johann Baptist, *Theology of the World* (New York, 1969).

—— *Faith in History and Society: Toward a Practical Fundamental Theology* (New York, 1980).

—— *The Emergent Church: The Future of Christianity in a Postbourgeois World* (New York, 1981).

Moltmann, Jürgen, *Theology of Hope: On the Grounds and Implications of a Christian Eschatology* (New York, 1967).

—— *The Crucified God: The Cross of Christ as the Foundation and Criticism of Christian Theology* (New York, 1969).

Sigmund, Paul E., *Liberation Theology at the Crossroads: Democracy or Revolution* (New York, 1990).

Stewart-Gambino, Hannah W. and Wilson, Everett (eds.), *Power, Politics and Pentecostals in Latin America* (Boulder, CO, 1997).

African Theology

Tinyiko Sam Maluleke

Introduction

> When we are looking for African theology we should go first to the fields, to the village church, to Christian homes to listen to those spontaneously uttered prayers before people go to bed. We should go to the schools, to the frontiers where traditional religions meet with Christianity. We must listen to the throbbing drumbeats and the clapping of hands accompanying the impromptu singing in the independent churches . . . Everywhere in Africa things are happening. Christians are talking, singing, preaching, writing, arguing, praying, discussing. Can it be that all this is an empty show? It is impossible. This then is African theology.[1]

For over fifty years, African Christian thinkers – theologians and non-theologians alike – have articulated their own brands of Christian theologies consciously and deliberately. Generally, this production has been ecumenical in nature, consultative, and in written form. Before the 1950s, African Christian theologies (henceforth referred to only as African theologies) had existed largely in *less* deliberate, less consultative, less ecumenical and hardly in written forms. One is not implying that only written theology is valid theology. Such a suggestion would fly in the face of advances made in liberation, feminist, and contextual theologies in the last twenty years or so. Most importantly, to suggest that theology is only theology once written would rob Africa of much theology. This is because in much of Africa, theology is danced, sung, performed, and lived rather than written. African theologians must therefore be good readers of books as well as good readers of their living contexts. In this chapter, our central focus will be on written African theology in as many of its varieties as we can muster. But this choice of proceeding is practical rather than inevitable.[2]

We could have chosen the oral theologies of African Instituted Churches and vibrant African Christianity, but there is a limit to the space and scope of our focus. Even this apparently well-delimited focus on written forms of African theology has become a vast and dynamic field, difficult to cover adequately in an essay. In keeping with the pragmatic nature of the approach used in this chapter, we will proceed thematically rather than chronologically; selectively rather than comprehensively.

Africa, African Theology, and Black Theology

Africa is vast, complex, and differentiated. We should never pretend to speak representatively and comprehensively about all of Africa. The tendency – prevalent both among some European observers of events in Africa and some Africans themselves – to speak of Africa as if Africa was a country is unhelpful. Firstly, it is important to be conscious of the vastness, divisions, affinities, and diversities of Africa. As Kwame Appiah points out in his *In My Father's House*, Africa is like a house in which there are many complex and different rooms, not just one simple room. Secondly, we must recognize the ideological and metaphorical side of the Africa construct. In this sense, Africa is an invention – and scholars such as Valentine Mudimbe have attempted to analyze aspects of the archeology and history of this invention. Africa is not just a geographical reality, it is an ideological reality with specific functions in the grammar of both colonial and postcolonial language. Therefore, talk of African theology must take cognizance of the baggage in the notion of Africa – both in terms of complex diversity and in terms of the ideological functioning of the notion. African theology is therefore a multiple and a multifaceted project.

Until about a decade ago, the theological terrain in Africa had been characterized in terms of African theology (mainly for Africa north of the Limpopo river) and South African black theology (mainly for South Africa and perhaps Zimbabwe and Botswana). The distinction has been a useful one because it points to differing theological methodologies and priorities. Generally speaking, we could say that in African theology, issues of cultural liberation are prominent, whereas South African black theology tends to foreground issues of political and economic liberation. In recent years and for various reasons, this distinction has come under increased strain. It has been found to be too reductionist in a continent in which there has been, for a long time, a lot more theological variety and innovation than the two types can adequately cover. The kind of theological ferment created by the African Initiated Churches was, for example, not adequately catered for by either of these two theological projects. Nor were the burgeoning feminist theologies of Africa. Another reason for discontent with the African theology/black theology divide has been that the differences between the two theologies have themselves been overstated. It is not so much that the two theologies had different agendas, but rather that they approach the same agenda, with broadly the same objective in mind, but with different sets of questions. Today, few keen observers of the African theological scene will take the familiar, artificial, and stereotypical "differences" between black and African theology seriously. Today, most scholars are agreed that both theologies are concerned with culture and both are concerned with politics and that in fact politics, economics, and culture are intricately intertwined.[3]

At an ideological level, we note that much discussion and debate has gone into the meaning and function of the notions of "Africa" and "black." It is noteworthy that until the 1970s, debate was still raging about the *bona fides* of an "African theology," with the adjective "African" being the major bone of contention. The major questions centered on the "risk" of suggesting that Christian theology could be African. John Mbiti expressed concern over the use of the term "African theology" as a big banner under which could be placed "all sorts of articles and references . . . the substance [of which] often turns out to be advice on how African theology should be done."[4] Indeed, it could be argued that until the mid-1970s, African theologians were still engaged in a multifaceted and spirited defense of the African theology project. This "defense" was characterized by several articles and books dealing with matters of definition of African theology. A basic argument in defense of African theology was that this project would honor the reality that African Christians had a cultural and religious "past" that has shaped their religiosity in particular ways. A relatively more recent and sophisticated statement of this defense of African theology is offered by Kwame Bediako.[5]

South African black theology has been equally (if not even more) preoccupied with issues of ideological orientation and definitional clarity. As a result there has been marked concern about definitions, the notion of black interlocutors as opposed to informants, the role of such interlocutors in black theological production, the question and place of blackness, blackness in relation to gender, the place and role of socioeconomic tools of analysis, and the ideological weight of the Bible, as well as the late but forceful emergence of gender analysis in African theology.[6] In this debate it has also emerged that black theology is not simply all theology done by black people. It is not merely a descriptive category, but one of theological and ideological orientation. Blackness, while including skin color, is construed as much more than that. It denotes a condition of mind and a specific choice of theological priorities.

In this chapter, the term African theology will be used as an encompassing notion within which the various emphases and types of African theologies, including black theology, are located. However, distinctions will be made where they are deemed essential for the clarity of argument.

The Agenda and Tasks of African Theology

One of the most jarring – for an outside observer – characteristics of African theology is its apparent utilitarian and particular nature. Here is a theological project put forth deliberately and unashamedly for the purpose of being at the service of a particular people and of a particular section of the Christian church. Not even Latin American liberation theology was this particular – eschewing as it did the temptation to overtly name itself in terms of a place or a people. Even the appellation "Latin American theology" has been more descriptive (often used by outside observers) than it has been ideological. But the "African" and the "black" in African theology and South African black theology are primarily ideological notions denoting orientation and approach rather than descriptions of the race or geographical location of the theologies in question. Of the many "internal" debates within African theology – broadly speaking – the issue of the need to serve a particular people of a particular place and time has seldom been in dispute. The critics of African theology have been prone to bring this up as a problem. That African Christian theology ought to be at the service of the church in Africa has seldom been in doubt. In other words, one of the chief tasks of African theology is to enable and inspire the church to develop its own theologies so that it may cease depending on "prefabricated theology, liturgies and traditions,"[7] and become "not an exotic but a plant . . . indigenous to the soil."[8]

Even more blunt has been South African black theology's insistence that theology should be constructed as a "weapon" with which to engage in the struggle of liberation for the black oppressed and marginalized masses. It was therefore in the crucible of real life struggles rather than in the realm of doctrinal and philosophical orthodoxy that the authenticity and efficacy of black theology was to be judged. Here, African theology's intention to enable the church was somewhat hampered, if not directly challenged. Indeed, there has been tension between African theology and the church in Africa. Service to the church and service to the people has not quite meant "giving the people and the church" what they want. There have been times when African theologians have felt called to disagree with the church. The South African Kairos Document of 1985 – which was a critique of both church and state – was one such moment. Such have been the tensions between African theology and the church establishment at times that Itumeleng Mosala – a leading South African black theologian – claimed black theology "has never been co-opted by the Establishment. No church has ever officially affirmed black theology as a legitimate and correct way of doing theology in South Africa. Not even the South African Council of Churches has given official recognition to black theology."[9]

Thus, while church and theological output have been connected in Africa, the relationship between the church and the theological community has not always been agreeable. Indeed, sometimes theological, ideological, and strategic differences – such as the controversy engendered by the moratorium debates in the 1970s – have threatened to divide the church community. The fact remains, however, that African theological output has emerged more from the womb of the church than that of the academy. Most African theologians – even the most radical – have maintained close connections with churches or with church groups. South African black theology itself originated and flourished in church caucuses, movements, and organizations.[10]

The bulk of Africa's ecumenical and theological consultations have been initiated by churches or church organizations and Christian councils.[11] However, the African church scene has been beset with an array of vexing challenges. Such challenges include "denominationalism and religious competitiveness,"[12] the reduction of Africa into a "dumping ground" for curious forms of North American charismatic and pentecostal groups, the rise of church Pentecostalism and Independentism and the concomitant decline in "historic mission church membership,"[13] and growing urbanization,[14] as well as the cultural, political, economic, sexual, and ecclesiastical oppression of African women.[15]

Such a set of challenges could not produce an easy-going and agreeable theological output. Recently, the particularity of African theology described above has deepened even more radically. This has been made possible by the forceful irruption of issues of gender and newer forms of oppression and other challenges in the age of globalization.

The Place of African Religion in African Theological Debate

African culture and African religion have long been acknowledged (albeit sometimes grudgingly) as the womb out of which African Christian theology must be and/or has been born. From various fronts, African Christians insisted that the church of

Africa and its theology must bear an African stamp. This has meant that African religion and culture have been put forward as an important interpretive framework for African Christian theology. However, references to both African traditional religions and to African culture remained a hazardous exercise in African theological construction. No other issue has generated the same amount of controversy as that of the relationship of African religion and Christian theology – both within and without African theology. Those who advocate the position that both African culture and African religion are a kind of preparation for the Christian message tend to take a largely positive but patronizing view of African religion and culture. The patronizing element comes when it is implied or even openly suggested that until the advent of Christianity, African religion and culture were somewhat incomplete. What has never been adequately explained is why the incomplete African culture and religion has not been totally eclipsed by Western Christian culture so that it surrenders totally to that which has come to fulfill it. In its bluntest theological and ideological form, the suggestion takes the guise of the statement that before the advent of Christianity – as mediated by the West – Africans had no knowledge of God and no conception of religion. The theological function of such a premise is seemingly an evangelistic one. But the ideological function is one of legitimizing conquest of Africans – for surely, a people with no conception of religion or God require every drastic measure imaginable, including violence, in order that they may be "saved." It seems to me that until African theology takes African religion and culture seriously, the discussion will continue to be artificial and patronizing. This means that African Christian theology cannot merely adopt classical Christian theological methodologies and motivations for the study of African religion and culture. It will be necessary for African theology to bracket judgment and the evangelistic motif if this endeavor is to be carried out meaningfully and constructively. The increasingly pluralistic context in Africa demands that we "listen" to other religions more carefully and more respectfully, without ceasing to be committed Christians ourselves and yet without a hidden evangelistic motive. We should, in the words of the late David Bosch,

> regard our involvement in dialogue and mission as an adventure [and be] prepared to take risks . . . anticipating surprises as the Spirit guides us into fuller understanding. This is not opting for agnosticism, but for humility. It is, however, a bold humility – or a humble boldness. We know only in part, but we do know. And we believe that the faith we profess is both true and just, and should be proclaimed. We do this, however, not as judges or lawyers, but as witnesses; not as soldiers, but as envoys of peace; not as high-pressure salespersons, but as ambassadors of the Servant Lord.[16]

Beyond Christian Theology

There is a deep sense in which African theology has never been just Christian theology. From its earliest times, written African theology has always sought not merely to dialogue with African religion and culture, but also to make sense of the complex world of African religion and culture.[17]

Strictly speaking, therefore, there has been up to now no such thing as a purely "African Christian theology" and the quest for such a theology has been a futile exercise. The majority of African theologians have not been highly concerned with a specifically "African Christian identity," either for themselves or for the church. Is this a weakness? African theology has been always interreligious, seeking to be more than a proselytizing theology. In other words, it is with good reason that African Christian theologians have had to ask themselves and be asked by others, "why do we continue to seek to convert to Christianity the devotees of African traditional religion?"[18] This is a crucial question for all African theologies in the twenty-first century. It seems to me that we will have to redefine the role of our theologies beyond seeking either to "convert" unreached Africans or support those who carry out such a task. Setiloane answered this question thus:

> I am like someone who has been bewitched, and I find it difficult to shake off the Christian witchcraft with which I have been captivated. I cannot say I necessarily like where I am. Second, I rationalize my position by taking the view that to be Christian I do not have to endorse every detail of Western theology.[19]

This may provide some leads for African theology to follow. Will it be possible to do exclusively Christian African theology, anymore than it was possible for the first generation of African theologians? I doubt it. If anything, the growing plural situation in Africa will demand an even broader and more rigorous interreligious approach. African Christian theologians and their churches will have to learn new ways of speaking to and relating to other religious people. We will have to listen anew to the critiques that have been leveled against African Christian theology by (apparently) non-Christian Africans such as P'Bitek and others.[20] This listening and dialogue must not be done on a basis of a rigid separation between "African Christian" theologians/intellectuals and "non-Christian African" intellectuals – as scholars like Kwame Bediako, in his *Christianity in Africa*, are sometimes apt to do.[21] In reality, such a distinction is difficult to sustain. We will have to take account of the entire spectrum and forms of African religious discourse as found in theological and other forms of literature.

The Bible

As with African religion and other aspects of African culture, the Bible has enjoyed a respected status and place in African theology. "Any viable theology must and should have a biblical basis," declared Mbiti, many years ago.[22] Similarly, Fashole-Luke claimed: "The Bible is the basic and primary source for the development of African Christian theology."[23] Mbiti continued:

> Nothing can substitute for the Bible. However much African cultural–religious background may be close to the biblical world, we have to guard against references like "the hitherto unwritten African Old Testament" or sentiments that see final revelation of God in the African religious heritage.[24]

What has been lacking is a vigorous debate on biblical hermeneutics akin to the vigorous debate that African (and non-African) theologians have had on culture, identity, and African religion. Indeed, the lack of "biblical foundations" is a charge that has been frequently leveled against various forms of African theology, almost as a means of control. Unfortunately, this has led to a situation in which "throughout Africa, the Bible has been and continues to be absolutized: it is one of the oracles that we consult for instant solutions and responses."[25] There could be other socio-religious reasons for the almost fanatical attachment to the Bible – especially in Protestant Africa. Bereft of rituals and symbols (a situation made worse by a mainly patronizing disposition toward African culture and African traditional religions), African Protestants have nothing but the Bible. Once their attachment to "the big black book" is attacked, they have nothing else to hold onto. However, on the whole, and in actual practice, African Christians are far more innovative and subversive in their appropriation of the Bible than they appear on the surface. Developments within South African black theology, Latin American-type liberation theologies, and African theology in the area of biblical hermeneutics since the early 1980s give us hope.[26] Several attempts are being made not only to develop creative biblical hermeneutic methods, but also to observe and analyze the manner in which African Christians "read" and view the Bible.

In an illuminating article, Zablon Nthamburi and Douglas Waruta propose a set of common themes that would characterize the biblical hermeneutics of African Christians: a quest for salvation/healing and wholeness; a keen awareness of human alienation; an appreciation of God's promise to "put things right"; a desire to know how to deal with the spirit world; attaching importance to initiation rites; an awareness of God's advocacy for the down-trodden; a sense of belonging in and to a visible community; commitment to social morality; and an intense concern for death and life beyond it.[27] The biblical hermeneutical principles of South African black theology could be summarized in this way: a suspicious and critical view of the status, contents, and use of the Bible; a commitment to reading "behind the text," inspired by a commitment to the cultural struggles of black workers and women; and finally a view of the Bible as (or a need for it to become) a "weapon of struggle" in the hands of blacks, workers, and women.

The Present and the Future: Rethinking Distinctions within African Theologies

We have already hinted that the conventional distinctions between "black" and "African" theologies as "siblings," "distant cousins," "old guard" or "new guard,"[28] "soulmates or antagonists,"[29] or theologies of "inculturation and liberation"[30] are no longer adequate. These distinctions no longer account sufficiently for either the supposed similarities or the differences between the various dynamic and emerging strands of African theologies. With the changing ideological map of the world and sweeping changes on the African continent itself, the agendas of what have been termed "African theologies of inculturation" as opposed to "African theologies of liberation," plus South African black theology, are moving closer together.[31] Having been cautious about speaking of "African culture" – due probably to the apartheid state's manipulation of African culture into the Bantustan system – South African black theologians have now begun to speak more freely about culture.[32] This is also illustrated by the increasing references made to the notion of *ubuntu* (African personhood) in numerous South African intellectual debates.

The coming together of agendas of African theologies does not, and should not, be interpreted to mean that any of the peculiar emphases in these theologies are becoming redundant and are about to be phased out.[33] This is a common, hasty conclusion often made in the zeal to construct newer and more definitive African theologies or theological paradigms. What the coming together of different agendas *does* mean is that we can no longer rigidly separate the various African theologies from one another. The established "cleavages" of African theologies are, furthermore, no longer an adequate indication of the variety and lively ferment that is taking place within African Christianity and between African Christian theologies. So we have to begin to "speak" and "do" African theology differently; in more dialogical, consultative, and open-ended ways.

We will now sketch a few emerging models of African theology. These merely illustrate some new currents, and are by no means comprehensive.

Theologies of the African Independent Churches (AICs)

A few scholars deserve special mention for their pioneering role in the irruption of AIC studies and the subsequent exposure of the significance of these churches for African Christianity and African theology: Bengt Sundkler (who wrote one of the earliest in-depth studies of AICs), Christian Baeta, David Barrett, Martinus Daneel, and Harold Turner.[34] Following the work of these scholars, a flood of theses and books on AICs has occurred.[35] The basic proposal of many AIC scholars is that the praxis of these churches must now be regarded not only as the best illustration of African Christianity, but also as "enacted," "oral," or "narrative" African theology – a type of theology which is no less valid than written African theologies. In this way, AICs are adding to and becoming a facet of African theology at one and the same time.

Furthermore, the numerical growth of these churches means that they have, in some parts of Africa, become *the* mainline churches. These churches, together with similar Christian movements among other primal societies, may be "seen as the fifth major Christian church type, after the Eastern Orthodox churches, the Roman Catholic Church, the Protestant Reformation, and the Pentecostal churches."[36] African theologies will no longer be able to ignore or dismiss the theological significance of the AICs in African Christianity. However, these churches must neither be romanticized nor studied in isolation from other African churches – including the so-called mainline churches. In the same way that an African theology based only on a reference to mainline churches is inadequate, so too is any African theology based exclusively on African independent churches.

The tendency to regard AICs as the most authentic (if not the *only* authentic) African churches has often created some unhealthy theological rivalry – notably between theologians rather than African Christians – wherein AIC praxis is supposed to be more African, more grassroots, more local, and more genuine than written academic African theologies. Such assertions have been unhelpful and tend to defeat the purpose for which they are made.[37] The issues are further complicated by the fact that, by and large, authoritative AIC scholars in the twentieth century have been overwhelmingly white (missionaries), with Africans themselves taking a back seat. But African silence on AICs may be a *loaded* and *eloquent* one, needing to be decoded and reflected upon. The white missionary domination of AIC studies may be attributable to the fact that the emergence of AICs almost without exception was initially viewed as a problem, and a reflection of the failure of missionary work. In many colonial African countries, AICs were initially viewed with suspicion because they were deemed either to be political movements in religious guise (Ethiopianism) or ecclesiastical movements with a political agenda. The call for a distinction between African Christianity and literature on African Christianity may be just what we need here,[38] so that reflection and research on AICs, however excellent and authoritative, must never be equated with the actual praxis of AICs. However, no serious African theology can ignore either the studies mentioned or the African Christianities displayed in AICs – for research and reality always mirror one another, albeit imperfectly.

African Charismatic/Evangelical Theology

Not only is African Christianity generally evangelical, if not pentecostalist in orientation, but there is also a sizeable body of literature and events which could be said to be representative of a theological strand of African theology. All over Africa, evangelicals exist in organized and confessional communities. They are, of course, no less heterogeneous in theological outlook than "ecumenical" African Christians. Within South Africa, one may think of Ray McCauley's Rhema Church and its affiliates, Michael Cassidy's Africa Enterprise, and a grouping which has until recently been called the Concerned Evangelicals. And these are only a drop in the ocean. There are also movements such as the Pan African Leadership Assembly (PACLA).[39] There have been tensions and probably justifiable suspicions between the largely evangelical PACLA and the more ecumenical All Africa Conference of Churches (AACC), and tensions remain between many sectors of evangelicalism and ecumenism all over Africa. The twenty-first century will not allow us either to ignore these tensions or smooth them over. One of the challenges we face is to seek out all expressions of African theology and Christianity, however inadequate and suspicious, so that we may expose them to serious and dialogical theological reflection. In as much as we have seen tensions between evangelicals and ecumenicals in Africa, there are also cases of solidarity in action and theological dialogue between these groups in many African countries. These may serve as a framework for further theological dialogue and partnership. African theology may be the richer for it.

Translation Theologies

Elsewhere, I have linked these theologies to the names of Lamin Sanneh and Kwame Bediako.[40] This, however, must not be taken to mean that Sanneh and Bediako present us with exactly the same agenda. Both of them are important, innovative voices whose thinking bears significant implications for African theology. In a series of works spanning a decade and culminating in his *Translating the Message*, Sanneh has argued passionately in defense of both African Christianity and the twentieth-century missionary enterprise.[41] The gist of his argument is that the clue to the tremendous growth of African Christianity during the twentieth century is the logic of the translatability of the Christian message or gospel into African vernacular languages. This is signified most potently in the historic necessity of translating the Bible into vernacular languages. It is this translatability of the gospel, rather than the agency of missionaries, that accounts for African Christianity. Therefore, our focus must shift from preoccupation with missionary omissions and the supposed link between Christianity and colonialism, to the "heart of the matter," namely gospel translatability.

Bediako shares with Sanneh the conviction that it is the translatability of the gospel more than anything else that made large parts of Africa so vastly Christian. He argues that African Christians and theologians alike must let the gospel speak to the African situation "in its own right." Bediako is highly critical of those African theologians who insist on assuming that Christianity is foreign to Africa, almost as the most basic premise of their theologizing. He argues instead that since the gospel is essentially translatable, and since the majority of Christians in the world are now in the Southern hemisphere, it no longer makes sense to speak of Christianity as "foreign" and Western, but we should view Christianity as a "non-Western" religion undergoing tremendous renewal.[42]

An equally essential task is to assist African Christians, theologians, and non-Christian intellectuals alike to exorcize the "phantom" foreignness of Christianity. The boldness and projectiveness of the proposals of Sanneh and Bediako are indisputable. However, I do think that they tend to work with a romanticized notion of translation. Translation is a much more precarious – even arbitrary – human endeavor than they care to admit.

African Feminist/Womanist Theologies

We have seen an explosion of African women's theological events, organizations, and publications since the mid-1980s. "Women's issues" have been on the agenda of the Ecumenical Association of Third World Theologians (EATWOT), the AACC, local Christian councils, and in para-church organizations since the early 1980s. However, it is a serious indictment of African male theologies that women's issues have not received immediate and unreserved acceptance.

Within South Africa, the first feminist conference which was predominantly black was held at Hamanskraal in 1984, immediately followed by a predominantly white feminist conference at the University of South Africa in the same year. The Hamanskraal conference noted that "whereas women form the majority of the oppressed, we note with regret that black theology has not taken women seriously, but has seen theology as a male domain."[43] Participants in a black theology conference held in Cape Town that same year concurred, albeit cautiously, in their final statement: "There are evidently structures oppressive of women inherent in both the black community and the church."[44]

From these tentative beginnings, feminist/womanist theology has been growing in Africa.[45] Continentally and internationally, one of the initial and significant catalysts for African feminist/womanist theology was EATWOT. From its inception, EATWOT has always had a strong contingent of women in its ranks. But the women felt that "our voices were not being heard, although we were visible enough . . . We demanded to be heard. The result was the creation within EATWOT of a Women's Commission."[46] Within the World Council of Churches, Oduyoye notes that "it took seven years from its founding for the WCC to establish a department to deal with the issue of cooperation of women and men in church and society."[47] Special mention must be made of the WCC's "Decade of Churches in Solidarity with Women," which officially ended in August 1998. Some of the "target areas [earmarked for special attention during the Decade] in 1987 were church teachings about women, women and poverty, women and racism, and violence against women."[48] These initiatives have resulted in chains of local consultations, events, and publications all over the world.

A significant consultation of Third World women took place under the auspices of EATWOT in 1986 at Oaxtepec, Mexico. One of the results of this event was the publication of *With Passion and Compassion*. On the African continent, the Circle of Concerned Women in Theology, with its Biennial Institute of African Women in Religion and Culture, was established in 1989 in Accra, Ghana.[49] Some of the papers read at the Accra meeting were published in the book *The Will to Arise*. Since then, a continent-wide multi-religious women's organization called the Circle of Concerned Women Theologians (CIRCLE) was formed – initially under the leadership of Mercy Oduyoye of Ghana, succeeded by Musimbi Kanyoro of Kenya, and more recently with Isabel Phiri of Malawi at the helm. One specific objective of the CIRCLE has been the production of African feminist/womanist literature and their output in this regard has been impressive. And it would be a mistake to limit the influence of the CIRCLE only to those publications linked directly to their consultations. What the CIRCLE has managed to do is to create space and inspiration for African women to dialogue and to publish.

Whereas black and African theologies have for the past half-century argued for the *validity* of African Christianities and the *legitimacy* of African culture, African feminist/womanist theology is charting a new way. This theology is mounting a critique of both African culture and African Christianity in ways that previous African theologies have not been able to do. From these theologies, we may learn how to be truly African and yet critical of aspects of African culture. African womanist theologians are teaching us how to criticize African culture without denigrating it. My prediction is that the twenty-first century will produce an even more gendered African theology. All theologians and African churches will be well advised to begin to take heed.

Theologies of Reconstruction

Leading the pack here are Kenya's Jesse Mugambi[50] and South Africa's Charles Villa-Vicencio – someone who no longer regards himself as a theologian. I have discussed their approaches in detail elsewhere and can only highlight here a few of the seminal points they make.[51] Although Villa-Vicencio's work was published first,[52] Mugambi had already been propagating the idea of a theology of reconstruction in the early 1990s in the context of AACC consultations.[53] It was, of course, *perestroika* (reconstruction) which inadvertently led to the break-up of the old USSR, which helped to popularize the notion of reconstruction. For Mugambi, both the inculturation and liberation paradigms within which African theologies had been undertaken are no longer adequate frameworks for doing African theology after the Cold War. Both inculturation and liberation responded to a situation of ecclesiastical and colonial bondage which no longer obtains. In place of the inculturation–liberation paradigm, which was mainly "reactive," we should install a "proactive" theology of reconstruction. Instead of calling for the ascendency of liberation over inculturation or vice versa – a "game" well-rehearsed in African theologies – Mugambi calls for an innovative transcendence of both.

Villa-Vicencio appeals for a post-Cold War (African) theology to engage in serious dialogue with democracy, human rights, lawmaking, nation-building, and economics in order to improve the quality of human life.

My main critique of both Mugambi and Villa-Vicencio is their apparent assumption that the end of the Cold War has immediate significance for ordinary Africans and that the so-called New World Order is truly "new" and truly "orderly" for Africans. But there are other problems. For all their concern about African theology's preoccupation with the Exodus motif, theologies of reconstruction appear to jump too quickly from Egypt to Canaan, from exile to post-exile – skipping the meandering and long sojourn in the wilderness (however mythical and legendary the historicity of the biblical account of this event might be). Many African countries have spent a long time in the wilderness after independence. Theologies that skip this experience in the rush to reconstruct and rebuild in the "newly found land" miss an essential contextual reality and a key methodological step.

Conclusion: Dynamism and Innovation

From the early 1980s, calls for African theologies and African churches either to recognize the paradigm shifts which were occurring before their own eyes, or to effect some paradigm shifts themselves, have increased.[54] This wave of creativity is a welcome sign that African theology and African Christianity are not about to die. On the contrary, African Christians are showing a remarkable knack for contextualization, dynamism, and innovation. The major works on African theology during the 1990s indicated that African Christian theology will not be allowed to degenerate into a museum piece. It is a dynamic, growing, multifaceted, and dialectical movement built diachronically and synchronically upon contextualization and constant introspection. In order for African theology to grow and effect meaningful paradigm shifts, careful note of the ground already captured must be made. This may prevent an unbridled manufacturing of an infinite number of supposedly "new" and "projective" African theologies which are not always thoroughly informed by what has been done before. Kwesi Dickson made the same point more than a decade ago, warning that "again and again contributions made at conferences have not been such as to build upon the insights which have already been gained into the subject."[55] Construction, innovation, and contextualization in African theology/Christianity should not be left entirely in the hands of each new generation of African theologians, as if

African theology was a frivolous and merely cerebral activity which is unconnected either to African Christian life or previous African theologies.[56]

Today, African theology faces new challenges in a fast-changing world. The HIV/AIDS pandemic and the adverse effects of globalization loom very large. It is my conviction that over the past fifty years African theology, in all its varieties, has laid a solid basis on which to tackle the challenges of the future.

Notes

1 Henry Okullu, *Church and Politics in East Africa* (Nairobi: Uzima Press, 1974), 54.

2 See Josiah U. Young, *African Theology: A Critical Analysis and Annotated Bibliography* (Westport, CT: Greenwood Press, 1993), 6ff., who identifies those whom he calls "the ancestors of African Theology," such as Clement of Alexandria, Origen, Athanasius, Tertullian, Cyprian, Augustine of Hippo, and Kimpa Vita or Dona Beatrice. See also John Parratt, *Reinventing Christianity: African Theology Today* (Grand Rapids, MI: Eerdmans, 1995); Marie-Louise Martin, *Kimbangu, an African Prophet and His Church* (Oxford: Oxford University Press, 1975); David J. Bosch, "Currents and Crosscurrents in South African black theology," in *Black Theology: A Documentary History, 1966–1979*, ed. Gayraud S. Wilmore and James H. Cone (Maryknoll, NY: Orbis Books, 1979); Kwame Bediako, *Theology and Identity: The Impact of Culture Upon Christian Thought in the Second Century and Modern Africa* (Oxford: Regnum Books, 1992).

3 See Tinyiko Sam Maluleke, "Black Theology Lives! On a Permanent Crisis," *Journal of Black Theology in South Africa*, 9: 1 (May 1995), 1–30.

4 John S. Mbiti, "The Biblical Basis for Present Trends in African Theology," in *African Theology en Route: Papers from the Pan-African Conference of Third World Theologians, Accra, December 17–23, 1977*, ed. Kofi Appiah-Kubi and Sergio Torres (Maryknoll, NY: Orbis Books, 1977), 90.

5 Kwame Bediako, *Theology and Identity* (London: Regnum, 1993).

6 Tinyiko Sam Maluleke, "African Ruths, Ruthless Africas: The Reflections of an African Mordecai." In *Other Ways of Reading*, ed. Musa Dube (Atlanta, GA: Society of Biblical Literature; Geneva: WCC, 2001), 237–51. See also Tinyiko Sam Maluleke, "The 'Smoke-Screens' Called Black and African Theologies – The Challenge of African Women's Theology," *Journal of Constructive Theology* 3: 2 (December 1997), 39–63.

7 Harry Sawyerr, *The Practice of Presence: Shorter Writings of Harry Sawyerr*, ed. John Parratt (Grand Rapids, MI: Eerdmans, 1996), 87.

8 James Johnson, quoted by Sawyerr, *The Practice of Presence*, 86.

9 Itumeleng J. Mosala, "Spirituality and Struggle: African and Black Theologies." In *Many Cultures, One Nation: Festschrift for Beyers Naud*, ed. Charles Villa-Vicencio and Carl Niehaus (Cape Town: Human and Rousseau, 1995), 81.

10 Tinyiko Sam Maluleke, "'A Morula Tree Between Two Fields': The Commentary of Selected Tsonga Writers on Missionary Christianity," D.Th. dissertation (University of South Africa, 1995).

11 See J. N. K. Mugambi, "The Ecumenical Movement and the Future of the Church in Africa." In *The Church in African Christianity: Innovative Essays in Ecclesiology*, ed. J. N. K. Mugambi and Laurenti Magesa (Nairobi: Initiatives, 1990), 14–20; *Claiming the Promise: African Churches Speak*, ed. Margaret S. Larom (New York: Friendship Press, 1994).

12 D. W. Waruta, "Towards an African Church: A Critical Assessment of Alternative Forms and Structures," in Mugambi and Magesa, *The Church in African Christianity*, 33.

13 David B. Barrett, *World Christian Encyclopedia: A Comparative Survey of Churches and Religions in the Modern World* AD

1900–2000 (Nairobi, 1962); Anderson and Otwang, *Tumelo*.

14   See Aylward Shorter, *The Church in the African City* (London: Geoffrey Chapman, 1991).

15   See *With Passion and Compassion*, ed. Virginia M. M. Fabella and Mercy Amba Oduyoye (Maryknoll, NY: Orbis Books, 1988); *Talitha, Qumi!: Proceedings of the Convocation of African Women Theologians 1989*, ed. Mercy Amba Oduyoye and Musimbi R. A. Kanyoro (Ibadan: Day-star Press, 1990); *The Will to Arise: Women, Tradition and the Church in Africa*, ed. Mercy Amba Oduyoye and Musimbi R. A. Kanyoro (Maryknoll, NY: Orbis Books, 1992); Oduyoye, "Christianity and African Culture," pp. 77–90; *Daughters of Anowa: African Women and Patriarchy; Women, Violence and Non-Violent Change*, ed. Aruna Gnanadason, Musimbi R. A. Kanyoro, and Lucia Ann McSpadden (Geneva: WCC, 1996); *Women Hold up Half the Sky: Women in the Church in Southern Africa*, ed. Denise Ackermann, Jonathan A. Draper, and Emma Mashinini (Pietermaritzburg: Cluster, 1991).

16   Quoted on the title page of *Mission in Bold Humility: David Bosch's Work Considered*, ed. Willem Saayman and Klippies Kritzinger (Maryknoll, NY: Orbis Books, 1996).

17   See Bolaji Idowu, *African Traditional Religion: A Definition* (London: SCM Press, 1973); Sawyerr, *The Practice of Presence*.

18   See Gabriel Setiloane, "Where Are We in African Theology?" In Appiah-Kubi and Torres, *African Theology en Route*, 64.

19   Ibid.

20   See J. N. K. Mugambi, *Critiques of Christianity in African Literature* (Nairobi: East African Educational Publishers, 1992).

21   Kwame Bediako, *Theology and Identity* (London: Regnum).

22   John S. Mbiti, *Concepts of God in Africa* (London: SPCK, 1979), 90.

23   Edward W. Fashole-Luke, "The Quest for African Christian Theologies." In *Mission Trends No. 3: Third World Theologies*, ed. G. H. Anderson and T. F. Stransky (New York: Paulist Press; Grand Rapids, MI: Eerdmans, 1976), 141.

24   Mbiti, *Concepts of God in Africa*, 90.

25   Oduyoye, *Daughters of Anowa*, 174.

26   See Simon S. Maimela, "Black Theology and the Quest for a God of Liberation," in *Theology at the End of Modernity: Essays in Honour of Gordon Kaufman*, ed. Sheila Greeve Devaney (Philadelphia, PA: Trinity Press, 1991), 141–59; Itumeleng J. Mosala, "The Use of the Bible in Black Theology," in *The Unquestionable Right to Be Free*, ed. Itumeleng J. Mosala and Buti Tlhagale (Johannesburg: Skotaville Press; Maryknoll, NY: Orbis Books, 1986); Itumeleng J. Mosala, *Biblical Hermeneutics and Black Theology in South Africa* (Grand Rapids, MI: Eerdmans, 1989); Takatso Mofokeng, "Black Christians, the Bible and Liberation," *Journal of Black Theology in South Africa* 2, No. 1 (May 1988): 34–42; Gerald O. West, *Biblical Hermeneutics of Liberation: Modes of Reading the Bible in the South African Context* (Pietermaritzburg: Cluster, 1991); Tinyiko Sam Maluleke, "Black and African Theologies in the New World Order: A Time to Drink From Our Own Wells," *Journal of Theology for Southern Africa*, No. 96 (November 1996): 3–19; Hannah W. Kinoti and John M. Waliggo (eds.), *The Bible in African Christianity: Essays in Biblical Theology* (Nairobi: Acton Publishers, 1997).

27   Zablon Nthamburi and Douglas Waruta, "Biblical Hermeneutics in African Instituted Churches." In Kinoti and Waliggo *The Bible in African Christianity*, 40.

28   See Josiah U. Young, *Black and African Theologies: Siblings or Distant Cousins?* (Maryknoll, NY: Orbis Books, 1986); Young, *African Theology*.

29   Desmond Tutu, "Black Theology and African Theology: Soulmates or Antagonists?" In *Third World Liberation Theologies: A Reader*, ed. Dean William Ferm (Maryknoll, NY: Orbis Books, 1986), 256–64.

30   Emmanuel Martey, *African Theology: Inculturation and Liberation* (Maryknoll, NY: Orbis Books, 1993).

31   See Mokgethi G. Motlhabi, "Black or African Theology? Toward an Integral African Theology," *Journal of Black Theology in South Africa* 8, No. 2 (November 1994): 113–41.

32   See Tinyiko Sam Maluleke, "African Culture, African Intellectuals and the White Academy in South Africa," *Religion and Theology* 3, No. 1, 1996: 19–42.

33 See Tinyiko Sam Maluleke, "Theology in (South) Africa: How the Future has Changed." In Macglory Speckman and Larry Kaufman (eds.), *Towards an Agenda for Contextual Theology: Essays in Honour of Albert Nolan* (Pietermaritzburg: Cluster, 2001), 364–89.

34 See Bengt G. M. Sundkler, *Bantu Prophets in South Africa* (Oxford: Oxford University Press, 1948); *The Christian Ministry in Africa* (Liverpool: Charles Birchal, 1962); *Zulu Zion* (Oxford: Oxford University Press, 1976); C. G. Babta, *Prophetism in Ghana* (London: SCM Press, 1962); David B. Barrett, *Schism and Renewal in Africa: An Analysis of Six Thousand Contemporary Religious Movements* (Nairobi: Oxford University Press, 1968); *World Christian Encyclopedia*; M. L. Daneel, *Old and New in Southern Shona Independent Churches* (New York: Mouton, 1971); *Quest for Belonging* (Gweru: Mambo Press, 1987); H. W. Turner, *History of an African Independent Church* (Oxford: Clarendon Press, 1967).

35 See Tinyiko Sam Maluleke, "Theological Interest in African Independent Churches and Other Grass-Root Communities in South Africa: A Review of Methodologies," *Journal of Black Theology in South Africa* 10, No. I (May 1996): 18–48.

36 Bosch in Daneel, *Quest for Belonging*, 9.

37 See Maluleke, "Theological Interest in African Independent Churches."

38 Bediako, "Five Theses on the Significance of Modern African Christianity," 21; *Christianity in Africa: The Renewal of a Non-Western Religion* (Maryknoll, NY, 1995), 264.

39 See Michael Cassidy and Gottfried Osei-Mensah, *Together in One Place: The Story of PACLA, December 9–19, 1976* (Nairobi: Evangel Publishing House, 1978).

40 See Maluleke, "Black and African Theologies in the New World Order"; Tinyiko Sam Maluleke, "Recent Developments in the Christian Theologies of Africa: Towards the 21st Century," *Journal of Constructive Theology* 2, No. 2 (December 1996), 33–60; Lamin Sanneh, *Translating the Message: The Missionary Impact on Culture* (Maryknoll, NY, 1989); Bediako, *Theology and Identity* and *Christianity in Africa*.

41 See Maluleke, "Black and African Theologies in the New World Order."

42 See Philip Jenkins, *The Next Christendom: The Coming of Global Christianity* (Oxford: Oxford University Press).

43 D. Ramodibe, "Women and Men Building Together the Church in Africa." In *With Passion and Compassion: Third World Women Doing Theology*, ed. Virginia M. M. Fabella and Mercy Amba Oduyoye (Maryknoll, NY: Orbis Books, 1988).

44 In Ramodibe, "Women and Men Building Together the Church in Africa," 20.

45 An issue of the *Bulletin for Contextual Theology in Southern Africa & Africa*, Vol. 4, No. 2 (July 1997) was devoted to feminist/womanist theology in South Africa. It also contains an annotated bibliography on South African feminist/womanist works.

46 Fabella and Oduyoye, *With Passion and Compassion*, x.

47 Mercy Amba Oduyoye, *Who Will Roll the Stone Away? The Ecumenical Decade of the Churches in Solidarity with Women* (Geneva: WCC, 1988), 3.

48 Oduyoye, *Daughters of Anowa*, 187.

49 See Oduyoye, "The Circle," in *Talitha Qumi!*

50 J. N. K. Mugambi, *From Liberation to Reconstruction: African Christian Theology After the Cold War* (Nairobi: East African Educational Publishers, 1995).

51 See Tinyiko Sam Maluleke, "Review of: Mugambi, J. N. K. 1995. *From Liberation to Reconstruction: African Christian Theology After the Cold War.* Nairobi: East African Educational Publishers," *Missionalia* 24, No. 3 (November 1996): 472–3.

52 Charles Villa-Vicencio, *A Theology of Reconstruction: Nation-Building and Human Rights* (Cape Town: David Philip Publishers; Cambridge: Cambridge University Press, 1992).

53 See A. Karamaga, *Problems and Promises of Africa: Towards and Beyond the Year 2000* (Nairobi: All Africa Conference of Churches, 1991); J. N. K. Mugambi, "The Future of the Church and the Church of the Future Africa," in *The Church of Africa: Toward a Theology of Reconstruction* (Nairobi: AACC, 1991); Tinyiko Sam Maluleke, "The Proposal for a Theology of Reconstruction: A Critical Appraisal," *Missionalia* 22, No. 3 (November 1994): 245–58.

54 David J. Bosch, *Transforming Mission: Paradigm Shifts in Mission Theology* (Maryknoll, NY: Orbis Books, 1991) uses the idea of paradigm shifts to explain the manner in which theologies of mission have changed over the centuries. It is an idea borrowed from the scientist Thomas Kuhn.

55 Kwesi A. Dickson, *Theology in Africa* (Maryknoll, NY: Orbis Books; London: Darton, Longman and Todd, 1984), 8.

56 See Maluleke, "Black and African Theologies in the New World Order"; "Recent Developments in the Christian Theologies of Africa."

Bibliography

Anderson, Allan and Samuel Otwang. *Tumelo: The Faith of African Pentecostals in South Africa* (Pretoria, 1993).

Baëta, C. G. *Prophetism in Ghana* (London, 1961).

Barret, David B. *World Christian Encyclopedia: A Comparative Survey of Churches and Religions in the Modern World AD 1900–2000* (Nairobi, 1962).

—— *Schism and Renewal in Africa: An Analysis of Six Thousand Contemporary Religious Movements* (Nairobi, 1968).

Bediako, Kwame. *Theology and Identity. The Impact of Culture Upon Christian Thought in the Second Century and Modern Africa* (London, 1995).

—— *Christianity in Africa: The Renewal of a Non-Western Religion* (Maryknoll, NY, 1995).

—— "Five Theses on the Significance of Modern African Christianity," *Transformation* 13: 1 (March 1996) 20–9.

P'Bitek, Okot. *Artist, the Ruler: Essays on Art, Culture and Values* (Nairobi, 1986).

Bujo, Bénezet. *African Theology in its Social Context* (Maryknoll, NY, 1986).

Chidester, David. *Savage Systems: Colonialism and Comparative Religion in Southern Africa* (Cape Town, 1996).

Comaroff, John and Comaroff, Jean. *Of Revelation and Revolution: Christianity, Colonialism and Consciousness in South Africa*, 2 vols. (Chicago, 1991).

Daneel, M. L. *Old and New in Southern Shona Independent Churches* (New York, 1971).

—— *Quest for Belonging* (Gweru, 1987).

Dickson, Kwesi. *Theology in Africa* (Maryknoll, NY, 1984).

Dube, Musa W. *Postcolonial Feminist Interpretation of the Bible* (St. Louis, MO, 2000).

Fashole-Luke, Edward W. "The Quest for African Christian Theologies." In *Mission Trends No. 3: Third World Theologies*, G. H. Anderson and T. F. Stransky (eds.) (Grand Rapids, MI, 1974).

Felder, Cain Hope (ed.). *Stoney The Road We Trod: African American Biblical Interpretation* (Minneapolis, MN, 1991).

Gifford, Paul. *African Christianity: Its Public Role* (Bloomington, IN, 1998).

—— (ed.). *Christian Churches and the Democratization of Africa* (Leiden, 1995).

Hastings, Adrian. *African Christianity: An Essay in Interpretation* (London, 1987).

—— *The Church in Africa 1450–1950* (Oxford, 1994).

Idowu, Bolaji. *Towards an Indigenous Church* (Oxford, 1965).

Isichei, Elizabeth. *A History of Christianity in Africa* (Grand Rapids, MI, 1995).

Maimela, Simon S. "Black Theology and the Quest for a God of Liberation." In *Theology at the End of Modernity: Essays in Honour of Gordon Kaufman*, Sheila Greeve Devaney (ed.) (Philadelphia, PA, 1991).

Mana, Kä. *Theologie africaine pour temps de crise. Christianisme et reconstruction de l'afrique* (Paris, 1993).

Maluleke, Tinyiko Sam. "Black and African Theologies in the New World Order: A Time to Drink From Our Own Wells." *Journal of Theology for Southern Africa*, No. 96 (November 1996): 3–19.

—— "The Rediscovery of the Agency of Africans." *Journal of Theology for Southern Africa*, No. 108 (November 2000): 19–37.

Mbembe, Achille. *L'Afriques indociles. Christianisme, pouvoir et etat en société postcoloniale* (Paris, 1988).

Mbiti, John S. *African Religions and Philosophy* (London, 1969).

—— *Concepts of God in Africa* (London, 1970).

—— *Bible and Theology in African Christianity* (Nairobi, 1986).

Mofokeng, Takatso. "Black Christians, the Bible and Liberation." *Journal of Black Theology in South Africa*, 2: 1 (May 1988): 34–42.

Molthabi, Mokgethi G. "Black or African Theology? Toward an Integral African Theology." *Journal of Black Theology in South Africa*, 8: 2 (November 1994): 113–41.

Mosala, Itumeleng J. *Biblical Hermeneutics and Black Theology in South Africa* (Grand Rapids, MI, 1989).

Mudimbe, V. Y. *The Invention of Africa: Gnosis, Philosophy and the Order of Knowledge* (Indianapolis, IN, 1988).

—— *The Idea of Africa* (London, 1994).

Mugambi, J. N. K. *From Liberation to Reconstruction: African Christian Theology After the Cold War* (Nairobi, 1995).

Oduyoye, Mercy Amba. *Daughters of Anowa: African Women and Patriarchy* (Maryknoll, NY, 1995).

Parrat, John. *Reinventing Christianity: African Theology Today* (Grand Rapids, MI, 1995).

Sanneh, Lamin. *Translating the Message: The Missionary Impact on Culture* (Maryknoll, NY, 1989).

Sundkler, Bengt G. M. *The Christian Ministry in Africa* (Liverpool, 1962).

Ukpong, Justin. "Developments in Biblical Interpretation in Africa: Historical and Hermeneutical Directions." *Journal of Theology in Southern Africa*, No. 108 (2000): 3–18.

West, Gerald. *Biblical Hermeneutics of Liberation: Modes of Reading the Bible in the South African Context* (Pietermaritzburg, 1991).

Young, Josiah U. *African Theology: A Critical Analysis and Annotated Bibliography* (Westport, CT, 1993).

Theologies of South Asia

Felix Wilfred

South Asia is increasingly drawing worldwide attention as one of the most fertile theological sites in contemporary times. South Asian theologians have developed theological insights and orientations by experiencing and exploring the uncharted terrains and paths to encounter the unfathomable mystery of God, and some of the deepest human experiences which open a window to the same mystery. They have been critical of theologies in terms of *systems*. There is, then, a *fragmentary* sense to all kinds of South Asian theologies. This fragmentary character has turned out to be also the creative moment of South Asian theologies, as they try to cope with ever new and challenging situations calling forth fresh responses.

It is well known that in modern times the category of history has assumed great importance in the Western development of theology. We could recall here the irruption of historical consciousness in the West through the historico-critical method in biblical interpretation and through such theologically significant philosophical work as that of Heidegger's *Sein und Zeit*. If temporality has found so much importance in the West, South Asian theology, for its part, has tried to place the accent on the other dimension of human existence – *spatiality*, which is so very crucial to the approach to truth, and consequently, also to theology. South Asian theologies are contextual in spirit, nature and orientation.[1]

Space or context can be described in various ways – most obviously, in terms of a specific culture, tradition, language, and so forth. This dimension has led South Asian theology to engage itself with the issue of so-called *inculturation*. But context is also characterized by the dominant issues and concerns of a particular people or society, which all shape its theological mood and orientation. Therefore, within South Asia in the last decades of the twentieth century, a variety of contextual theologies emerged; for example, *tribal theology* focusing on the issue of the marginalized peoples, and *dalit theology* derived from a reinterpretation of the gospel through the experience of suffering by the outcastes of South Asia.[2] The concerns addressed by these various contextual theologies have contributed to the shaping of the theology of religions, and to South Asian liberation theology, theology of mission, and so on. In such theologies there has come about also a deeper understanding of context: context is not simply the background against which the gospel is to be interpreted, but rather the culture and sociopolitical situation become new sources of theology and *loci theologici*.

To be able to understand South Asian theologies we need to take into account the multi-religious situation of the region, as well as its sociopolitical conditions. These two are intertwined in concrete life and are to be seen as the keys to South Asian Christian theology. This chapter will try to cover within the space available some of the important issues, and present very briefly four theologians from the region.[3]

Theology and South Asian Religious Traditions

South Asia is a region which shares a common Indic civilization and history. Indic is a civilizational concept, and not to be equated with the modern nation-state of India, which is one of its constituents, albeit a significant geographical portion of it. If when considering theology in India and Nepal it is important to understand Christianity's relationship to Hinduism, in Sri Lanka the same is the case for Buddhism, and in Pakistan and Bangladesh for Islam. Of course, there is the presence of a significant number of Hindus in Sri Lanka and a large number of Muslims in India, but I am referring here to the dominant religious traditions of the various countries. In the following paragraphs I shall inquire into the dynamics of the theological development that results from encounter with the different religious traditions.

Christian theology and Hinduism

In the development of Indian Christian theology, the relationship to Hinduism has been pivotal. The relationship has been a complex one, and the debate continues even today. We may distinguish three different paradigms in this relationship.

Christian theology through classical Hinduism

The struggle for national independence brought also an awareness of the indigenization of Christianity in the early decades of the twentieth century. Attempts were made to express Christian truths through Hindu categories, and, at a later stage, to interpret Christian doctrines and practices through Hinduism. The way for this kind of approach was paved by the Bengali convert Brahmabandhab Upadhyaya (1861–1907).[4] Later on, missionaries like P. Johanns (1882–1955) tried to carry forward the impulse of Upadhyaya through a series of writings known as "Christ through Vedanta." There have been many followers in this tradition ever since. The major concern here is to express Christian truths through Hindu categories, in which process the Christian truths in their formulations are taken for granted. There is no critical questioning about the formulations and their historical conditioning. For example, in the case of both the above mentioned authors the Christian truths taken for granted were those formulated in neoscholastic terms. A more thoroughgoing approach was initiated by the Protestant thinkers known as the "Rethinking Christianity in India" group, consisting of Vengala Chakkarai, Chenchiah and A. J. Appasamy, and others.[5] In more recent times, thinkers like Raimon Panikkar and Stanley Samartha have carried forward the ideal of dialogue with Hinduism with greater theological penetration and vigor.

There have been differences in the Christian approach depending upon the kind of Hindu school of thought taken as the point of reference. Some have related Christian theology to the *advaita* or non-dual doctrine represented by the medieval philosopher Sankara, whereas some others have thought that the *visishtadvaita* (qualified non-dualism), with its affirmation of a personal God, grace, and loving devotion, is closer to Christian theism. Still others have developed Indian Christian theology with *karma* or action as the point of reference.

The relationship has also taken a practical form, inasmuch as attempts have been made to integrate Hindu symbolism and rituals in Christian art, architecture, worship, and so on. This can also be seen in the Christian efforts to model *ashrams* according to Hindu patterns. The ideal of the *ashram* and the milieu it represents has given birth to a very refreshing kind of theology. To cite a few examples, we have the initiative of the French missionary Jules Monchanin, who started an *ashram* on the banks of the Cauvery at the outskirts of the city of Triuchirapalli in the southern Indian state of Tamilnadu; this tradition was continued by the mystic Abhishiktananda (Le Saux) and Swami Dayananda (Bede Griffiths). The latter was an Anglican convert to Catholicism, who joined the Benedictines at Prinkash Abbey, and then traveled to India and adopted the life of *sannyasi* (Hindu renouncer) and mystic for several decades. The writings of these and others associated with Christian *ashrams* remain an important source of South Asian theology.[6]

Theology and critique of Hinduism

The main focus here is not the type of critique exercised by many missionaries who spoke of Hinduism in the most derogatory terms – critique that has to be placed in the context of Christian apologetics and claims of Christianity to be the *vera religio*. Of more significance is the critique by the Christian dalits in South Asia who have challenged the type of Christian theology that feeds on classical Hinduism. The oppression and caste-discrimination they have undergone down the centuries has been, according to them, legitimized by Hinduism. How could they, then, find the Christian message of liberation in a theology couched in Hindu concepts and symbols? Further, the dalits point out that Hinduism itself is a modern construct and that it is made up of many and divergent streams of South Asian religious traditions. In this sense, they claim to have their own subaltern religious traditions which cannot and should not be equated with Hinduism. This kind of theological orientation is closely allied to the general political stand of the dalits *vis-à-vis* Hindu tradition, whose foremost representative has been the dalit leader Ambedkar.

Double-edged sword: Critique of Hinduism and critique of Christianity

There is a third paradigm, which can be characterized, for want of a better term, as secular in its character and approach. The protagonists of this approach view with suspicion any *rapprochement* between Christianity and Hinduism that is effected at the cost of liberation of the poor and the oppressed. We have, for example, theologians like Sebastian Kappen and Samuel Rayan, whose critique applies to Hinduism as much as to institutional Christianity when it comes to the issue of human liberation.[7] In this connection it needs to be pointed out that an important source of theologizing in South Asia is the involvement of committed individual Christians and groups at the grassroots. The immersion into the realities of the society and the experiences of daily life and struggles has led them to realize the negative role being played by religions in creating communal tension, conflict, and violence. They critically question Eurocentric theologies of the past and the present, and dispute the capability of these theologies to respond to current South Asian issues. In the same vein, people at the grassroots bring church structures and institutions under critical scrutiny.

Theology in relation to Buddhism and Islam

Similar positions can be identified in relation to Buddhism as were discussed above with reference to Hinduism. To be able to understand the theological development in a Buddhist country like Sri Lanka, we need to keep in mind an important common factor in South Asia. The seminaries and other institutions of formation for clergy and pastors may not be the most creative centers for theological pursuit. In fact, many of those institutions – with laudable exceptions – seem to repeat Western theological approaches, with some attempts at contextualization which remain rather at the surface level. Instead, deep insights and original orientations are coming out of various centers of study and dialogue. This is the case with regard to the relationship of Christian theology to Buddhism. In Sri Lanka we have many centers of Christian–Buddhist encounter like the Study Centre for Religion and Society with its first director Lynn A. de Silva, and the Tulana Research Centre directed by the well-known theologian Aloysius Pieris. There are other centers which try to combine a Christian–Buddhist interreligious approach with a liberational thrust.

For a long time, Buddhism was viewed by Christian missionaries as an atheistic system of philosophy, challenging Christian truths with a negative soteriology. Unfortunately, such views are persistent, and have given rise to heated controversy, especially in Sri Lanka, when John Paul II repeated such remarks in his book *Crossing the Threshold of Hope*.[8] There have also been polemics between Christians and Buddhists as to which of the two founders was supreme. The new development in the relationship is one of mutual discovery of the riches of these traditions, illumining in different ways the ultimate reality, the world and the universe. Furthermore, convulsions in society, especially the youth revolt of 1971 in Sri Lanka, have drawn together Christians and Buddhists in a common dialogue with Marxists for the cause of liberation.

An understanding of the relationship between Christianity and Islam in South Asia requires us first to recognize that Islam, like Christianity, is shaped in different ways by particular national histories, cultures, and traditions. Though the relationship of Christianity and Islam goes back to the seventeenth century at the time of the emperor Akbar in India,[9] in modern times there has not been a sustained dialogue with Islam in India comparable to that with Hinduism. However, we need to single out the important role played by the Henry Martin Institute originally founded in Lahore (present-day Pakistan) in 1930, and now functioning in Hyderabad, India. Unmistakably, in Pakistan and Bangladesh, the dialogue with Islam has been an important source of the development of contextual theologies.

In developing Christian theology in the Muslim environment, we need also to single out the contributions by Pakistani theologians like Louis Mascarenhas, Anwar M. Barkat, and Charles Amjad-Ali, centers like the Christian Study Centre in Rawalpindi and the Pastoral Institute in Multan, and journals like *Al-Mushir* and *Focus*. Similar efforts could be identified in Bangladesh, which is predominantly Muslim, and where the situation is similar to that in Pakistan. In addition, Bangladeshi theologians bring to bear upon their work the long Bengali tradition of Hindu *Bhakti* or loving devotion to God. The dialogue with Islam is not only a matter of doctrinal tenets; it also has – as has become too evident in recent years – a great deal to do with the political climate. In this regard, it may be pointed out how Pakistani Christians stood together with their Muslim neighbors in opposing the US-led war on Iraq in 2003, and Christian leaders brought out a joint pastoral letter expressing their solidarity with Muslims.[10] It is such concrete steps and decisions that contribute to greater understanding and dialogue among Muslims and Christians.

Theology of Religions

The interrelationship of Christianity with the various religious traditions and the continuing dialogue has also led to a development in the theology of religions. The South Asian theology of religions expresses some of the most insightful and far-reaching positions, which is unfortunately not sufficiently known outside Asia.[11] To understand the significance of this theology of religions it is enough to recall that Jacques Dupuis, who lived and taught for several decades in India, tried to voice in Rome the developing theology of religions in South Asia: it was found so disturbing that he became the eye of a theological storm around the turn of the twenty-first century.

At the beginning of the twentieth century, J. N. Farquhar and others tried to overcome the (until then) prevailing negative attitudes toward other religions by proposing the theory of fulfillment. This theory recognized positive values in other religions, with Christianity as the "crown" and fulfillment.[12] This theology of religions has had, and continues to have, numerous advocates. However, subsequent developments in South Asia have superseded such theories, and have opened up new horizons. The experience of interaction and dialogue with peoples of other faiths has led Christians to realize more deeply such basic truths as the single universal plan of God for the whole of humanity going beyond religious boundaries; the activity of the Spirit in the institutions, symbols, and expressions of other religions; and on the whole, a much broader understanding of the Kingdom of God. This has led to greater clarity in understanding and expressing the mystery of Christ, God, church, and the meaning of salvation.

All these realities of Christian belief are elucidated not in opposition to other religious traditions, but in relation to them. Such an approach naturally also involves a critique of traditional theology and its formulations. For example, several South Asian theologians believe that the mystery of Christ could be understood without the need to have recourse to such categories as uniqueness; nor would they think that the Chalcedonian formula best expresses the mystery of Christ. The ferment of new thinking in South Asia has found its way to the West through the adoption – not without hesitation – of its positions in official documents, such as those of the Vatican and the WCC, and the Federation of Asian Bishops' Conferences. It has also found its way to those Western theologians who have lived in or visited India and absorbed this theology and presented it to the West in their writings, couched often in a Western liberal spirit and terms. Unfortunately, there is no acknowledgement of what they owe to South Asia in their theology of religions.

The theology of religions is an important site of Christological interpretation in South Asia. Contrary to the dominant trend of interpreting Jesus Christ with regard to what distinguishes him from others and makes him unique, South Asians interpret Jesus with regard to what *relates* him with others. This is the crucial difference of perspective which shapes the nature and orientation of Christology, soteriology, and so forth. It is from this perspective that we can understand the significance of a statement like "Jesus is the Christ; Christ is not Jesus only."[13]

Christ is not the monopoly of the Christian community, and hence it is not surprising to see that peoples of other faiths have interpreted Jesus through their own religious experience, and from their particular backgrounds. In South Asia there is what could be described as the "Christology of non-Christians." We might recall here the interpretations and statements of significant figures like Mahatma Gandhi, Vivekananda, and others. The great Hindu mystic Ramakrishna Paramahamsa claimed to have had a mystical experience of Jesus Christ and the Virgin Mary. It is a fact that in the monastic order of Ramakrishna, founded by his disciple, Christmas is celebrated very solemnly and meaningfully every year. The approaches of neighbors of other faiths to Jesus Christ remain an untapped theological source in South Asia.

Similarly, the understanding of the church in South Asian theology is not limited to Christian communities or to issues like the local and universal church. Rather, the concern is for *universal community*, which cannot be realized without forging relationships with the larger community of peoples of other faiths and ideologies, to form truly "human communities" or "kingdom communities." If the understanding of salvation has often been conditioned by the category of causality and theory of satisfaction, South Asians think that salvation needs to be seen in terms of call, relationship, freedom, and response.[14] In this sense, salvation cannot be narrowed and confined exclusively to any one particular religious tradition; all religions as collective realities could serve as vehicle and medium of this relationship, and they do have a place in the universal plan of God's salvation.

Theology of Mission

South Asian theology of religions is intimately connected with new perspectives on mission. The situation of being a minority religious community of Christians, and developments in the political, social, and cultural spheres in the South Asian region, prompted Christians in this region thoroughly to rethink mission theology. The rather simplistic (and prevalent) view of mission as preaching, conversion, and baptism called for serious soul searching. The evangelical revival in England at the end of the eighteenth and beginning of the nineteenth centuries brought about a particular understanding of mission as the conquest and overcoming of the heathen religions of India and other countries of South Asia.

From understanding mission in terms of salvation or damnation, twentieth-century South Asian theology brought about a shift in understanding mission as in *relationship* and not in opposition to other religious traditions. In this connection, we should note also the debates in South Asia regarding the relationship between mission and dialogue. South Asian theologies have resisted dialogue as an instrument of mission – a position that had gained widespread acceptance in many theological circles in the West. Instead, they have sought to clarify that dialogue and mission have their own distinct characters and goals, and one should not be made subservient to the other. South Asian mission theology has experienced a widening of its scope through a fresh biblical hermeneutics. In this connection the contributions of scholars like George Soares-Prabhu, Pathrapankal, and others should be recalled. They have tried to relativize the great command of mission, and highlighted the importance of reading it in the light of many other commands and injunctions of Jesus.

Speaking of mission theology, we need to highlight also the singular contribution made by South Asia to ecumenism. For the first time, we saw the coming together of three churches to form a single ecclesial union. The formation of the Church of South India in 1947 is a landmark in ecumenical history.[15] This came about through the realization that confessional division was a hurdle to Christian witness. The coming into being of the Church of South India could be considered also as a theological response to the challenge of nationalism.

South Asian Liberation Theology

Anyone who thought that liberation theology in Asia is an extension of that theology in Latin America would be completely mistaken. The truth is that, even though the terminology of liberation theology was not used, it has been happening in South Asia since the last few decades of the twentieth century. The pioneers were people engaged at the grassroots, with workers' movements, student movements, and so on. The number of initiatives developed through such persons as Paul Casperz and Tissa Balasuriya would surprise those unfamiliar with non-Latin American liberation theology. Michael Rodrigo of Sri Lanka suffered a martyr's death for his commitment to liberation and for bringing together peoples of other faiths in common engagement for the liberation of society. Liberation theology was at once the fruit of such struggles associated with political movements, and inspiration for the same. There are many examples in India. Theologians like Sebastian Kappen, Samuel Rayan, M. M. Thomas, and others derived their inspiration by responding to the struggles of the people through their reading of the scriptures and interpreting them in context. It brought out also a new understanding of salvation and a new image of Jesus. Aloysius Pieris sees in Jesus God's defense pact with the poor.[16] Instead of placing the emphasis on those attributes and titles characterizing the divine nature of Jesus, these South Asian liberation theologians see the human dimension of the mystery of Jesus, his passion and death, and the hope he offers to the poorest of the poor. Simply reducing Jesus to his divine titles would make him but one more divinity among the millions of gods of Hinduism, for example. The humanity of Jesus is what South Asia badly needs.

A characteristic feature of South Asian liberation theology is that it has almost invariably related the issue of liberation to the question of religion and culture[17] – something which the Latin American theology tried to do in the second phase of its development, with a focus on such themes as popular religion and culture.[18] Furthermore, South Asian theology has had to confront not only the issues of economy and religion, but also a very specific social reality of caste stratification. In particular, the dalits' encounter with manifold social oppression led to a re-reading of the gospel; dalit Christians came to interpret the person and suffering of Jesus in close relationship to their own plight.[19] Marxist tools of analysis could not do justice to the social situation, so South Asian theology developed an analysis of society taking into account the caste structure, directing its critique against Brahminical hegemony.[20] The peculiar South Asian situation has provoked very incisive and original biblical contributions from George Soares-Prabhu and others.[21]

Some South Asian Theologians

Aloysius Pieris (1932–)

Pieris is a very creative theologian who draws upon many sources and weaves them into his theological vision. In particular, he brings to Christian theological thought and interpretation his accomplished scholarship of Buddhism. He proposes a theology of religions that distances itself from the oft-cited typology of exclusivism, inclusivism, and pluralism. His deep knowledge of Asian religious traditions leads him to break loose from this kind of framework, and to call for another paradigm, more consonant with Asian cultures and traditions. Nor does he advocate the kind of superficial comparison that produces little progress. Rather, he puts forward the necessity of a core-to-core dialogue between these religious traditions, a dialogue that will be mutually enriching. For example, he shows that, though Buddhism and Christianity give importance to wisdom and love, there is an inherent propensity to highlight wisdom in Buddhism, and love in Christianity.[22] The meeting of these idioms will bring out the best in both religious traditions and effect mutual transformation. Hence, Pieris argues for an intertextual reading of scriptures which will go beyond superficial comparison and lead the religious traditions to a symbiotic relationship. Pieris' reflections have resonated in many other parts of Asia where Buddhism has been a very influential force.

Pieris appeared on the international theological scene at the height of liberation theology in Latin America. He showed how that theology was still tied to the Western conceptual world, and pointed out the necessity of bringing intense conversation with the world of religion and culture into the liberation agenda. This, for him, is crucial, especially in Asia, which, according to him, is characterized by its deep religiosity and abysmal poverty. His theological effort has been to relate these two poles and in the process he has produced an Asian paradigm of liberation theology.[23] In this paradigm, voluntary poverty, the protest against selfishness and greed advocated strongly by the Indic religious traditions, is pressed into the service of overcoming material poverty through liberative engagement. Thus, the spiritual struggle and the engagement against material poverty meet and merge to become part of the same agenda of liberation.

Raimon Panikkar (1918–)

This seminal thinker, who made a highly significant contribution to the theology of religion in the twentieth century, is at home both in the Indian Hindu classical tradition and in the Western Greek and Latin traditions. His theological vision rests on certain philosophical premises. He is critical both of the cosmocentric worldview of the Indic tradition and of the anthropocentric worldview of the West, reinforced by modern science and technology. While underlining the importance and pitfalls of both, he suggests an inspiring *cosmotheandric* vision of reality, which is holistic in its nature and comprises the cosmic, divine, and human dimensions. This holistic outlook also leads him to affirm the radical relativity or relational character of all reality, which is not the same thing as an epistemological relativism.[24] This integral and relational reality comes to expression not simply through the instruments of *logos*, but more appropriately through the language of *mythos*.

This theoretical framework leads him to call for a cross-cultural enterprise, of which interreligious dialogue is an integral part. In this regard, his contribution has been remarkable. For him:

> the different religious traditions of mankind are like the almost infinite number of colors that appear once the divine or simply the white light of reality falls on the prism of human experience; it refracts into innumerable traditions, doctrines, and religious systems. Green is not yellow; Hinduism is not Buddhism, and yet at the fringe one cannot know, except by postulating it artificially, where yellow ends and green begins.[25]

In light of his cosmotheandric vision, Panikkar interprets the mystery of Christ as a point of convergence and unity of all reality, which is not exhausted in the historical Jesus. Out of his deep knowledge of Hinduism, Panikkar has also been able to produce a new perception and interpretation of the mystery of the Trinity.[26] No less significant have been his contributions to such current global issues as human rights, ecology, technology, peace, and "cultural disarmament," all of which proceed from his basic vision of reality.[27]

M. M. Thomas (1916–96)

M. M. Thomas was a leading lay theologian, whose influence extended throughout the continent, especially through his association with the Christians Conference of Asia (CCA). He was the embodiment of ecumenism, and was actively engaged in the WCC as the chairman of its Central Committee during some of the crucial years of its history (1968–75). He often disclaimed the title of "theologian." It was his concern to study the political and social processes in Asia and to bring the message of Christ meaningfully to bear upon them.[28] This led him to study the extent of the influence exerted by the person and message of Christ on some of the leaders and thinkers of the Indian Renaissance since the nineteenth century, and to discover the meaning of Jesus Christ in relation to the secular ideologies of India.[29] His theology was concerned with Christian involvement in politics, and, consequently, with political ethics from a Christian perspective. He gave expression to his views through the journal *Religion and Society*, in founding which he worked alongside the other great Indian theologian Paul Devanandan (1901–62). In all his theological enterprises Thomas remained Christocentric in his approach, though for his friends and critics alike it was enigmatic how he could reconcile his "rightist" Christology with his "leftist" social and political thought. He was moved and intellectually provoked by the unfolding of events in India and other parts of the world, to which he responded with great human and theological sensitivity.[30] His thrust and orientation were liberational, much before the advent of liberation theology. Even in those difficult times when the mainline churches were very much gripped by the fear of communism, M. M. Thomas was drawn to the concern for justice and emancipation he found in socialist thought and practice. Towards the end of his life, he was appointed as governor of Nagaland, a state at the northeastern borders of India with a large majority of tribal Christians – a recognition of his lifelong concern with social and political issues.

Pandita Ramabai (1858–1922)

Although she lived mainly in the nineteenth century, Ramabai is important for the Asian theological scene today, as a woman theologian who anticipated the concern of present-day South Asian feminist theologians in their struggle with South Asian society and its patriarchy. Here is a woman who was born into an orthodox Brahmin family, but rebelled against its conventions, learned Sanskrit (forbidden for women), and commenced her own independent spiritual and intellectual journey.[31]

Ramabai's journey led her to Christianity, which was for her not an end point. Though she converted to Christianity, she refused to conform to a Christianity cut out by missionaries and others, but reinterpreted it in unconventional ways on her continuous spiritual search. She was unsparing in her criticism of Christianity as she knew it from the Anglican tradition. Her devastating critique of church authorities and structures can be seen in her interaction and conflict with the community of sisters with whom she stayed in England for some time, and the correspondence with Sister Geraldine, her spiritual mother.[32]

Ramabai's theology was born out of her engagement and commitment to the cause of subjugated Indian women, whose plight she tried to improve through such acts as creating homes for young widows.[33] She also had a personal history of anguish and suffering: she lost her parents quite early in life, was widowed after a very short period of marriage, and saw her only daughter, Manoramabai, die on her lap. Ramabai may come across to many as a reactionary, but through her bold decisions she paved the way for the future shape of Indian/South Asian feminist theology. South Asian Christian women have to respond to the situation of a double oppression legitimized both by the religious traditions of the region and by Christianity. The present generation has a very inspiring forerunner in Pandita Ramabai.

Issues for Debate and Discussion

This overview raises a number of questions that have general significance for theology viewed from a global perspective.[34]

Continuity and discontinuity

How are we to interpret Christianity in South Asia? Is it an extension and continuation of Western Christianity, or is there room to speak of a caesura between South Asian Christianity and the Western Christian tradition? Even if we do not decide one way or the other, there is still room to debate to what extent there is continuity and to what extent discontinuity. Those who tend to give preponderance to continuity may resolve the issue by recourse to such categories as "inculturation" – as is being done in the Roman Catholic Church since Vatican II. But then the question is whether such categories are adequate to come to terms with the basic issue of continuity and discontinuity.

It appears to me that inculturation is basically an effort to make Christianity meaningful to postcolonial societies by incorporating into it the cultural elements of the context. I believe, by contrast, that it is important that we view South Asian Christianity as coming into being by a reappropriation of Christianity through the agency of South Asians themselves – which would include not only Christians, but also those who do not institutionally belong to Christianity, but share the same history, tradition, and culture and face similar opportunities and risks for life and survival. This introduces a new paradigm in the self-understanding of Christianity, and consequently a new paradigm as well in theology. The question of continuity and discontinuity also raises such questions as the role of tradition and the scriptures. Many traditional assumptions and presuppositions require to be reexamined.

The dialectics of incarnation and prophecy

Since the context defines the specificity of Christianity in a particular region, it is crucial that there be ever greater integration of Christian faith with the sociopolitical process of the locality. But the question that may immediately be raised is to what extent can Christianity really integrate itself with the context? There is not only the principle of incarnation, but also the challenge of prophecy.[35] Integration and immersion could turn out to be compromise. Hence the importance of the dimension of prophecy. When Christianity fails to root itself in the soil, given the colonial history of many so-called Third World societies, Christians will continue to be viewed and treated as aliens. If Christians exercise prophetic critique of culture, tradition, and the powers that be, without being rooted in the soil, their prophetic exercise will not have any cutting edge. The challenge is to bring into a dialectical relationship these two dimensions in such a way that the prophetic derives from "rootedness," and rootedness is not at the expense of prophecy. Theology in South Asia, as well as in other parts of the Third World, has the important task of contributing to consideration of this dialectic.

Church–society relationship

Over the centuries, the attitude of Christians to society and the political realm has conditioned theological orientations; and the converse is also true. The South Asian experience leads us to another set of problems and issues in this relationship. The reality on the ground is that South Asian Christianity finds itself in a minority *vis-à-vis* other religious groups (in Pakistan and Bangladesh, Muslims; in Sri Lanka, Buddhists; in India and Nepal, Hindus). Pakistan, for example, is officially an Islamic country, and the Christian community suffers a double oppression of being a minority religious group and for belonging to the lowest caste group. We need only recall here the protest suicide by Bishop John Joseph of Pakistan against the discriminatory laws in that country, particularly the laws regarding blasphemy.[36]

In such a context, Western models of pope and emperor, the two cities, sacred and secular, are not able to come to terms with the novelty of the situation and its complexity. For example, the war on Iraq in 2003, interpreted as a "Christian" enterprise of the West, led to the reprisal harassment and killing of Christians in Pakistan. Christianity is so deeply associated with the West that Pakistani and Bangladeshi Christians are targeted when there is a political clash between Western and Islamic countries. Then there are the questions surrounding religious freedom. While for many Westerners the possibility of conversion would be viewed as an integral part of religious freedom, many Hindus would seriously dispute it. For them, religious freedom would include professing one's faith, and propagating it, but not converting. The examples show that theology needs to evolve new paths and paradigms in the relationship of church and society.

Fundamental theology

Some of the questions and issues we have raised lead us to understand fundamental theology in a different light. Classical fundamental theology raises questions relating to faith and reason, but the experience in South Asia shows more and more that fundamental theology may have to do with other issues. Classical fundamental theology concerns itself with the *praeambula fidei*, and sets the stage and justification for systematic or dogmatic theological content. What South Asian theologies seem to indicate is that the questions we need to be concerned about are not primarily the *first principles* of theology, but rather *primordial features* of life. Even though theology is a *logos* – and hence there is the legitimate question of epistemology – theology needs to touch upon the reality of life, and serve its promotion and defense. Hence issues of food, water, shelter, equity, freedom, and solidarity become primary for theology in contexts like that of South Asia, where life is threatened by the denial of these basic human needs.

Paradigm shift: Theology of religions

Immersion in the South Asian situation and context tells us that theology of religions cannot be divorced from the *realpolitik* in the relationship among the various religious groups.[37] Undoubtedly, there have been many efforts to develop a theology of religions in Christianity, but much of this effort has been directed at waking Christianity from its slumbers, and engaging Christians in a dialogue among themselves about how to come to terms with religious diversity.

The South Asian theology of religions calls for a shift toward the concrete reality of everyday relationships among religious groups and the sociopolitical process in which these relationships express themselves. Here is the starting point for a theology of religions that takes place through dialogue. Hence the *dialogue of everyday life* becomes the starting point for a theology of religions; a different approach from the attempt to derive a theology of religions from Christian revelation and faith. Once again, we realize how the theology of religions cannot be reduced to such models as exclusivism, inclusivism, and pluralism. South Asian theology leads us in the direction of a theology of religions in constant dialogue with sociopolitical processes.

Conclusion

Ignorance and misunderstanding characterize the external image of South Asian theology. The theology being pursued in this region is in many respects little known in the West and in the rest of the world. The South Asian religious world, its culture and history, are so unfamiliar that many do not dare to enter that terrain. On the other hand, where it is known, it is often suspected and misunderstood, as the conflict of some of the South Asian theologians with the Vatican reveals. The general mood among South Asian theologians is one of relative indifference to the image their theologies project. They seem to be gripped by the questions they have to address – questions which do not have any precedents or models in Christian history to go by.[38] In their venture, they are less attracted by issues of orthodoxy and heterodoxy, than by a sense of fidelity to the gospel and the truth as revealed through the realities of their context.

A sincere dialogue with South Asian theology, on the part of theologians worldwide, is long overdue. Major shifts and new orientations are emerging, which have far-reaching consequences for the future of theology, and for Christianity as a whole. In these times of crisis of Christianity – in different continents, due to different factors[39] – we stand in need of radically new interpretations of Christianity to shape its future course. South Asia, with its great civilizational heritage, may have much to offer for this global project.

Notes

1   See Felix Wilfred, *On the Banks of Ganges: Doing Contextual Theology*, ISPCK, Delhi, 2002; "Die konturen kontextueller Theologie aus der Dritten Welt," in *Jahrbuch*

fuer Kontextuelle Theologien, Missions-wissenschaftliches Institut, Aachen, 1976, pp. 157–73; "Indian Theologies: Retrospect and Prospects. A Sociopolitical Perspective"; paper presented at the Annual Indian Theological Association Meeting held in Bangalore, April 24–29, 2003 (publication awaited).

2 A significant number of South Asian Christians are *dalits* (formerly known as "untouchables").

3 Cf. Robin Boyd, *An Introduction to Indian Christian Theology*, ISPCK, Delhi, 2000; Felix Wilfred, *Beyond Settled Foundations: The Journey of Indian Theology*, Department of Christian Studies, University of Madras, 1993. For a recent and very commendable work with a wealth of information on South Asian theologies, see John C. England, Jose Kuttianimattathil et al. (eds.), *Asian Christian Theologies: A Research Guide to Authors, Movements, Sources*, Vol. 1, Orbis Books, Maryknoll, NY, 2002.

4 Cf. Julius J. Lipner, *Brahmabandahab Upadhyay: The Life and Thought of a Revolutionary*, Oxford University Press, Delhi, 1999.

5 The name derives from a book published under the same name just before the International Missionary World Council's Conference in Tambaram (1938).

6 See Jules Monchanin, *Ermites du saccidananda*, Castermann, Tournai, 1956; Abhishiktananda, *La Montée au fond de coeur: Le journal intime moine chrétien-sannyasi hindou 1948–1973*, OEIL, Paris, 1986; Bede Griffiths, *The Cosmic Revelation: The Hindu Way to God*, Templegate, Springfield, 1983; Griffiths, *Return to the Centre*, Templegate, Springfield, 1976.

7 Cf. Sebastian Kappen, *Jesus and Cultural Revolution: An Asian Perspective*, BUILD, Bombay, 1983.

8 John Paul II, *Crossing the Threshold of Hope*, Alfred A. Knopf, New York, 1994, pp. 84–94.

9 See Arnulf Camps, *Jerome Xavier SJ and the Muslims of the Mogul Empire: Controversial Works and Missionary Activity*, Nouvelle Revue de Science Missionnaire, Fribourg, 1957.

10 The leaders noted: "As the calamity of war in Iraq looms on the horizon, we recognize that this war will have far-reaching and disastrous consequences for all our region. We share the concern of our Muslim brethren and all people of good will in expressing their total condemnation of this preemptive strike. See *Lahore Link Newsletter*, Lahore Archdiocese, January/February 2003, No. 37.

11 For a survey of the development, see Jose Kuttianimattathil, *Practice and Theology of Interreligious Dialogue*, Kristu Jyoti Publications, Bangalore, 1995.

12 J. N. Farquhar, *The Crown of Hinduism*, Oxford University Press, Oxford, 1913.

13 Raimon Panikkar, "Man and Religion: A Dialogue with Panikkar," *Jeevadhara* 11 (January–February 1981), p. 25.

14 See Michael Amaladoss, "The Multi-Religious Experience and Indian Theology." Paper presented at the Indian Theological Association meeting held in Bangalore, April 24–29, 2003.

15 See Bengt Sunkler, *Church of South India: The Movement towards Union 1900–1947*, United Society for Christian Literature, Lutterworth Press, London, 1965.

16 Aloysius Pieris, *God's Reign for God's Poor: A Return to Jesus-Formula*, Tulana, Kelaniya, 1999.

17 See Ignatius Jesudasan, *Gandhian Theology of Liberation*, Guajarat Sahitya Prakash, Anand, 1987.

18 See Juan Carlos Scannone, *Weisheit und Befreiung. Volkstheologie in Lateinamerika*, Patmos Verlag, Düsseldorf, 1992.

19 Here I would like to refer to a brilliant doctoral dissertation written by a dalit candidate under my guidance: A. Maria Arul Raja, *Dalit Encounter with their Sufferings: An Emancipatory Interpretation of Mark 15: 1–47 from a Dalit Perspective* (unpublished doctoral dissertation, University of Madras), Chennai, 2000.

20 See James Massey (ed.), *Indigenous People: Dalits. Dalit Issues in Today's Theological Debate*, ISPCK, Delhi, 1998; Arvind Nirmal (ed.), *A Reader in Dalit Theology*, Department of Dalit Theology, Madras, n.d; Paul Puthenangady (ed.), *Towards an Indian Theology of Liberation*, NBCLC, Bangalore, 1986.

21 See George Soares-Prabhu, *Biblical Themes for a Contextual Theology Today*, and *A Biblical Theology for India*, both in the Jnana-Deepa Vidayapeeth Theology Series, Pune,

1999 (the volumes containing the contributions of the author were edited and published posthumously).

22 Aloysius Pieris, *Love Meets Wisdom: A Christian Experience of Buddhism*, Orbis Books, Maryknoll, NY, 1988.

23 Aloysius Pieris, *An Asian Theology of Liberation*, Orbis Books, Maryknoll, NY, 1988.

24 Raimon Panikkar, *The Cosmotheandric Experience: Emerging Religious Consciousness*, Orbis Books, Maryknoll, NY, 1993.

25 Raimon Panikkar, *The Intrareligious Dialogue*, Paulist Press, New York, 1978.

26 Raimon Panikkar, *The Trinity and the Religious Experience of Man: Icon–Person–Mystery*, Orbis Books, Maryknoll, NY, 1973.

27 Raimon Panikkar, *Cultural Disarmament the Way to Peace*, John Knox Press, Philadelphia, PA, 1995.

28 M. M. Thomas, *The Secular Ideologies of India and the Secular Meaning of Christ*, CLS, Madras, 1976.

29 M. M. Thomas, *The Acknowledged Christ of Indian Renaissance*, SCM Press, London, 1969.

30 See Samuel Rayan, "M. M. Thomas – Response-ability," in K. C. Abraham (ed.), *Christian Witness in Society: A Tribute to M. M. Thomas*, Board of Theological Education – Senate of Serampore, Bangalore, 1998.

31 See Uma Chakravarti, *Rewriting History: The Life and Times of Pandita Ramabai*, Kali for Women, Delhi, 1998; Gauri Viswanathan, *Outside the Fold: Conversion, Modernity and Belief*, Oxford University Press, Delhi, 1998, pp. 118–52.

32 See A. B. Shah (ed.), *The Letters and Correspondence of Pandita Ramabai*, Maharashtra State Board for Literature and Culture, Bombay, 1977.

33 See Meera Kosambi, "Women, Emancipation, and Equality: Pandita Ramabai's Contribution to Women's Cause," *Economic and Political Weekly*, October 29, 1988: WS 38–49.

34 Cf. Felix Wilfred, "Asiatische Theologie an der Wende zum neuen Jahrhundert. Unbeantwortete Fragen und neue Horizonte," in *Informationen. Evangelisches Missionswerk in Deutschland*, No. 119, February 1999.

35 The Semitic tradition has developed a certain orientation to prophecy, which may not resonate with other peoples and cultures. There is the difference, for example, between "cultures of sin and guilt," and there are "cultures of shame" (Japan, China, Korea, etc.).

36 Anwar M. Barkat, "Church–State Relationships in an Ideological Islamic State," *Ecumenical Review* 29: 1 (1977); "The Islamization of Pakistani Law and Christian Theological Responsibility," *Al-Mushir* 3 (1978).

37 For example, the relationship between Muslims and Christians in a particular country in the West has much to do with the state's policy on immigration, asylum, and so on.

38 Felix Wilfred, *Asian Dreams and Christian Hope*, 2nd edn., ISPCK, Delhi, 2003.

39 On this theme a special issue of *Concilium* is in preparation, to be edited by Jon Sobrino, Teresa Okure, and Felix Wilfred.

Bibliography

Abeyasingha, N., *The Radical Tradition: The Changing Shape of Theological Reflection in Sri Lanka* (Colombo, 1985).

Adhikari, K. P., "New Hopes in Nepal," *Japan Mission Journal* 45: 1 (1991).

—— "300 Years of Christianity in Nepal," *Japan Mission Journal* 46: 1 (1992) and 46: 2 (1992).

Amaladoss, M. et al. (eds.), *Theologizing in India* (Bangalore, 1981).

Amalorpavadoss, D. S. (ed.), *The Indian Church in the Struggle for a New Society* (Bangalore, 1981).

Amjad-Ali, Christine (ed.), *Developing Christian Theology in the Context of Islam* (Rawalpindi, 1996).

Anwar, Gill Esther, "The Role of Women in Pakistan Theology," *Al-Mushir* 35: 2 (1993).

Asi, Emmanuel, "Liberation Theology: A Pakistani Perspective," *Logos* 28 (1989).

Balasuriya, Tissa, *The Eucharist and Human Liberation* (London, 1979).

—— *Mary and Human Liberation* (Colombo, 1990).

Barton, Mukti, *Scripture as Empowerment for Liberation and Justice: The Experience of Christian and Muslim Women in Bangladesh* (PhD dissertation, University of Bristol, 1998).

Boyd, Robin, *An Introduction to Indian Christian Theology* (Delhi, 2000).

Chakravarti, Uma, *Rewriting History: The Life and Times of Pandita Ramabai* (Delhi, 1998).

Channan, James, "Christian–Muslim Dialogue in Pakistan," in J. Paul Rajashekar and H. S. Wilson (eds.), *Islam in Asia: Perspectives for Christian–Muslim Encounter: Report of the Consultation Sponsored by the Lutheran World Federation and the World Alliance of Reformed Churches* (Geneva, 1991).

Clarke, Sathiananthan, *Dalits and Christianity: Subaltern Religion and Liberation Theology in India* (Delhi, 1998).

Dornberg, Ulrich, *Searching Through the Crisis: Christians, Contextual Theology and Social Change in Sri Lanka in the 1970s and 1980s* (Colombo, 1992).

England, John C., Jose Kuttianimattathil et al. (eds.), *Asian Christian Theologies: A Research Guide to Authors, Movements, Sources* (New York, 2002).

Lipner, Julius, *Brahmabandahab Upadhyay: The Life and Thought of a Revolutionary* (Delhi, 1999).

Kuttianimattathil, Jose, *Practice and Theology of Interreligious Dialogue* (Bangalore, 1995).

McCahill, Bob, *Dialogue of Life: A Christian Among Allah's Poor* (New York, 1996).

McVey, Chrys, "A Survey of Theological Developments in Pakistan," in *Jahrbuch für Kontextuelle Theologien* (Frankfurt, 1995), pp. 217–31.

Minderhoud, Jan, *Contemporary Nepalese Christianity: Churches Without Tradition?* (PhD dissertation, University of Utrecht, 1987).

Moghal, Dominic (ed.), *A Christian Church in Pakistan: A Vision for the 21st Century* (Rawalpindi, 1999).

Panikkar, R., *The Intrareligious Dialogue* (New York, 1978).

—— *The Unknown Christ of Hinduism: Towards an Ecumenical Christophany* (London, 1981).

—— *The Trinity and the Religious Experience of Man: Icon–Person–Mystery* (New York, 1973).

—— *Cultural Disarmament the Way to Peace* (Philadelphia, PA, 1995).

Parapally, Jacob (ed.), *Theologizing in Context: Statements of the Indian Theological Association* (Bangalore, 2002).

Pieris, Aloysius, *An Asian Theology of Liberation* (New York, 1988).

—— *Love Meets Wisdom: A Christian Experience of Buddhism* (New York, 1988).

—— *Fire and Water: Basic Issues in Asian Buddhism and Christianity* (New York, 1996).

—— *God's Reign for God's Poor: A Return to the Jesus-Formula* (Kelaniya, 1999).

Shah, A. B. (ed.), *The Letters and Correspondence of Pandita Ramabai* (Bombay, 1977).

Soares-Prabhu, George, *Biblical Themes for a Contextual Theology Today* (Pune, 1999).

—— *A Biblical Theology for India* (Pune, 1999).

Thomas, M. M., *The Secular Ideologies of India and the Secular Meaning of Christ* (Madras, 1976).

—— *The Acknowledged Christ of Indian Renaissance* (London, 1969).

Viswanathan, Gauri, *Outside the Fold: Conversion, Modernity and Belief* (Delhi, 1998).

Wilfred, Felix, *Beyond Settled Foundations: The Journey of Indian Theology* (Madras, 1993).

—— *On the Banks of Ganges: Doing Contextual Theology* (Delhi, 2002).

Contextual Theology in East Asia

Archie Chi Chung Lee

East Asian Theology: An Overview

The contextual theology of East Asia, like any other genuine theology that takes the reality of life of the people seriously, is historically and culturally conditioned. Such a theological construction is shaped by the religio-cultural traditions fundamental to the region. In East Asia, Confucianism and Buddhism constitute the cultural core, in addition to various indigenous religions, including syncretistic beliefs and shamanistic practices. The process of modernization also shaped the context into which Christianity was introduced and in which it has evolved. Catholic as well as Protestant missionary activities largely coincided with imperialistic conquest. The coming of Christianity is mostly entangled with the Western colonizers in the nineteenth century, except perhaps in the case of the early arrival of the Catholic faith in China and Japan in the sixteenth and seventeenth centuries.

Contextual theological thinking in East Asia is therefore colored by the interaction between Christianity and East Asian cultural traditions, against the sociopolitical background of the advance and imposition of the West. The door to these ancient cultures was forced open by the foreign invaders, be they adventurers, traders, diplomats, soldiers, or missionaries. The humiliation of the Opium Wars (1841–60) and the subsequent unequal treaties, though largely the bitter experience of the Chinese, is typical of the historical fate of East Asian peoples. Christianity came with the cannon balls and the military victory of Western powers.

It is, therefore, no wonder that the theological process in East Asia finds it hard to rid itself of the anti-West sentiment; and any deconstruction and reconstruction of Asian theology has to come to terms with this strong antagonistic mood. Going beyond historical confinement is the painful quest of the East Asian theological venture. Many are still caught up with this historical burden. There is an urgent call from the theologians of Hong Kong to reset the theological agenda in the face of the challenges of postcolonial criticism. The Hong Kong experience of being hybridized provides the space to reposition oneself in the East–West cultural dynamics and to negotiate for a theology that transcends the binary confrontational frame of mind. This postcolonial condition enriches and opens up a great possibility of embracing the diversity and plurality of the Asian reality.

Besides Western colonialism, East Asian countries have had to deal with imperialistic military force from within the region. Japan colonized Korea (1910–45) and Taiwan (1895–1945), and invaded China (1937–45) and Hong Kong (1942–5). The defeat of Japan (1945), the communist take-over of China (1949), the rule of Taiwan by the Nationalist Chinese Party (Kuomingtang KMT, 1945), the division of Korea into North and South (1953), the Cultural Revolution in China under Mao (1966–76), the British colonial rule of Hong Kong (1842–1997) and the handover of sovereignty to China in 1997 are some of the political events that have gone into the articulation of theologies in East Asia. In the midst of these historical incidents is yet another significant development in this region: the growth of nationalism and the rise of peoplehood. In the past twenty to thirty years, the economic advancement in countries in East Asia and the growth of globalization worldwide have had a tremendous impact on the societies and life of the people. Social injustice, economic exploitation, and political oppression have resulted in increased suffering among deprived and poor people in East Asian societies. One must not overlook the role played by the United States in the political scene and the market economy in East Asia.

Another characteristic of the East Asian theological effort is the appropriation of major cultural and religious traditions. How theology is to deal with Confucianism, Buddhism, and national as well as local religions is a pressing question. In the process of modernization, critique of tradition is inevitable. For example, feminist thinkers have criticized patriarchal structures and the traditional authoritarian mentality, uncovering the various discriminatory elements in East Asian societies, which are mostly derived from Confucian, Buddhist, Taoist, and Shinto thought.

Seen in terms of this process of reappropriation and reconfiguration of traditional cultural formulations, East Asian theology represents a critical appraisal of the Asian social set-up and a conscious effort to negotiate space for cultural resources in the context of concrete sociopolitical settings. "Doing theology with Asian resources," initiated by the Programme for Theology and Cultures in Asia (PTCA 1983–),[1] is a radical (and appropriate) approach to doing theology in East Asia.

One of the indispensable resources Asian theologies draw from for inspiration in their theological construction is the stories of the people. The stories may be taken from the cultural past, or they may be narrations from the present sociopolitical struggle for liberation and justice. *Minjung* theology (Korea) and homeland theology (Taiwan) share this common thrust of incorporating stories in the theological process.

Minjung theologians interpret stories as forming the social biography of the people, and in turn incorporate the lived experience of the people into the theology of *han* (the long-suppressed feeling of indignation and inner anger). This theology of the oppressed and the deprived does not aim at a systematic framework of abstract ideas, but liberative praxis for the renewal of the social order as a whole. Suh Nam Dong, Ahn Byung Mu, Kim Yong Bock, and David Suh, to cite just a few, follow this mode persistently.

The homeland theologians of Taiwan read both the historical narration of the Bible and that of the Taiwan people to construct their theological agenda. The biblical narratives are unpacked through deconstruction and critical assessment in the theological process of adoption and interpretation (for example, in the work of Wang Hsien Chih and Huang Po Ho).

The area of East Asia is extensive, and its vast geographical extent defies any attempt at comprehensive coverage. This chapter deals mainly with China, Taiwan, Japan, Korea, and Hong Kong, an area largely Confucian in its cultural milieu, in which theological critique of, and adaptation to, the traditional Confucian framework is part and parcel of the theological process. For the purposes of this volume, I have focused on theologians who produce works in English. Thus, many theologians in this region, who adopt the native language in writing, are not mentioned here. Due to constraints of space there is limited treatment of Catholic theology here. The gender imbalance among the theologians covered is apparent, and reflects the history and theological reality in Asia. It is only in recent years that women have begun to acquire wider literacy and become active players in the theological field, and feminist theology is gaining momentum in East Asian theological circles. Kwok Pui Lan's work on recovering the neglected women of the past century is significant here.

I begin with a discussion of two prominent East Asian theologians who have gone beyond their homeland contexts of Japan and Taiwan, and whose theology attempts to address theological issues from a wider Asian horizon.

Choan-Seng Song (1929–) and Kosuke Koyama (1929–)

The theological effort of both Song and Koyama is basically cultural in orientation. They teach in the US but travel a great deal to Asia in their theological journeys, making a personal commitment to the people and the Asian scene and crossing the cultural and sociopolitical frontiers between Asia and America. Song develops his "story theology" to make sense of the experiences of men, women, and children, which are embodied in narrative forms. To him, stories are usually taken to drive home theological themes, more or less analogically. Koyama adopts stories in an imaginative way. Stories stimulate the mind, open it up and stretch it. The agitated mind is then let loose, so to speak, to travel far afield to reach out for the divine in the midst of human reality. They present an alternative mode of doing theology to the conventional Greek and Western conceptual and discursive approach.

Song, the first Dean of the Programme for Theology and Cultures in Asia (PTCA), has a deep commitment to doing theology with Asian resources. He is a prolific writer who develops a theological method centered on giving Asian stories theological resonance.[2] A debatable, but nevertheless significant, theological position Song takes is his proposal for "a leap from Israel to Asia,"[3] intended to create a theological space for Asia and to open up a strategic theological frontier to Asian history. Asian theological construction does not need to be bound by Western theological formulations. Jesus' story, being the story of the reign of God and that of the suffering people, is the key to unlock the divine mystery and open up the theological space for both the stories of Asian people and the stories of the Hebrew scriptures. A theological feast of stories is served and these stories interpenetrate one another to give rise to Asian story theology.

The Incarnation is reinterpreted in terms of the embodiment of God's revelation in the culture, history, and life experience of people in Asia. Instead of a theological core centered on abstract formulations of Christology, Song shifts his attention to the Creator God and God's creation. His unfailing call for a positive assessment of Asian resources not only succeeds in establishing a new foundation, but also endeavors to raise the status of Asian cultural and historical resources in theology, to which revelatory potentiality is ascribed. The creation stories of Asia (Song's favorite resources) are read theologically. This critical commitment to Asian contexts and Asian resources is initially strategic, but future generations of Asian theologians have to go beyond an antagonistic posture to deepen the Asian theological endeavor.

Having worked in Chiangmai, Thailand as a theological teacher in the 1960s, Kosuke Koyama takes the context of the Thai farmer as the point of departure in his theological reflection. *Waterbuffalo Theology – A Thai Theological Notebook* depicts Koyama's theological journey by relating commonplace experience in the daily life of humanity in its specific sociopolitical and cultural environment. Koyama's theology focuses on the Cross, which has no handle for anyone to get hold of and control; the Cross becomes the criterion for appropriating the religious pluralistic tradition of Asia. His concept of "neighborology," however, makes room for the presence of God in human reality and guards against what he calls the "crusading mind" often manifested in Christian beliefs and practices. He lifts up the Christian "crucified mind" to nurture a genuine openness to God and to people of other cultures and faiths.

The theological agenda of Koyama is never pronounced and it is not his intention, nor that of Song, to set up a systematic and methodological framework. His imaginative and creative observation of the external world can be attributed to his extensive personal experience in Asia. The image of a God who walks leisurely at the human pace of 3 miles an hour is a good example of his imaginative theological horizon (*Three Mile an Hour God*). *No Handle on the Cross* is another pictorial and metaphorical theological work that is pregnant with great theological creativity. Like Song, Koyama is fond of biblical imageries and themes, especially those of the Old Testament, and has the literary as well as theological skills to bring them home to the cultural soil of Asia. *Mt. Fuji and Mt. Sinai: A Critique of Idols* serves as a pertinent example of contextual effort that speaks to the Asian scene and the biblical symbolism theologically.

Though known ecumenically in theological circles, Koyama has not been commonly acknowledged as contributing to theology in Japan, as he lives outside of Japan and is therefore assumed to address Japan as an object for non-Japanese Christians. It is clear, however, that Koyama's theological journey is not only characterized by his Japanese cultural roots but also, more significantly, by his specific claim to come to terms with his Japanese identity.

Japanese Theology

The defeat in war and surrender of Japan in 1945 gave rise to the breakdown of the old system constituted by imperialism, nationalism, and the divinity of the emperor in Shinto beliefs and practices. The challenges to Japanese tradition and to the interest in Western culture grew rapidly among intellectuals. Japanese theology has acquired a historical consciousness of the need for "an exodus" from "Germanic Captivity."[4]

Kazoh Kitamori's seminal book, *Theology of the Pain of God* (1946) (claimed to be the first Japanese book of theology introduced in the English-speaking world), attempts to engage the Christian God and the human situation in the context of the Japanese Buddhist milieu and social experience.[5] Despite his persistent denials, Kitamori's theology of the pain of God has always been accused of patripassianism.[6] The inability to make distinctions between the "concept of substance" and the "concept of relation" accounts for the critics' tendency to confuse Kitamori's "the pain of God" and patripassianism. The theology of the pain of God, according to him, does not regard that pain as existing in God as *substance*, but it underlines "the mediatory and intercessory love of God" in relating to humanity.[7]

In the prefaces to later editions of his book, Kitamori reflects on his experience of its reception and observes the changes in the theological scene as regards the perception of the "pain of God." He discusses whether or not his non-Western theology is "outside the gate, outside the city" of theology dominated by the tradition of orthodox (Western) dogma.[8] In the preface to the third edition (1951), Kitamori reports with joy that his book has stimulated great interest outside the churches, while productive conversations are also initiated within the church. Kitamori observes the great need for unity in the post-World War II situation of division, and argues that the cornerstone for unity lies in "God in pain" and "God embracing completely those who should not be embraced."[9]

The pain of God provides the key to the reconciliation of the seemingly contradictory themes of the love of God and the wrath of God. It also helps to enrich Kitamori's theology of the Cross, speaking of God's transcendental pain in coming to terms with the sinful world of humankind. The two resources for Kitamori's theological construction are his personal experience of suffering during the wartime period and his appropriation of the Japanese Buddhist tradition of suffering, especially the concept of redemptive voluntary pain initiated by love, *tsurasa*. God is perceived as having love that overcomes wrath toward sinners in inflicting pain upon God's own self.

Kitamori rejects the ontological divine being that does not suffer pain, and he criticizes the God of liberal theology, whose love is immediacy without pain. Human pain and divine pain are analogically understood, as they share something in common and in pain there is a mystic unity of the divine and the human. Though the Mu-Kyokai Christians accepted his thought,[10] he was unpopular in the postwar era when Japanese tradition was largely under attack and Barthian theology was favored. In such a historical moment Kitamori's appeal to Japanese Buddhism and his criticism of Barth went against the theological current.

Korean *Minjung* Theology

No account of the theological contribution of Korea to Christianity can be complete without due acknowledgment of the vibrant vitality of *minjung* theology. *Minjung* denotes an indispensable perspective in theological construction that engages with the plight and aspirations of oppressed and exploited people. In the agonizing experience of Korean theologians, the specific theological usage constitutes the core concern of *minjung* theology, in face of the raging brutality of postwar modernization and the economic growth of Korea.[11] Ahn Byung Mu and Suh Nam-dong are the major forerunners, and they are among the first generation of *minjung* theologians presented here, in addition to David Kwong Sun Suh and Kim Yong Bock, whose writings are readily found in English.

Suh Nam-dong (1918–84) insists on reinterpretation of the Bible in the context of the common people's struggle to survive and their fight for political liberation and economic justice. To him, the Exodus event, the prophetic word, and the event of the cross, are to be understood in materialistic terms for the salvation of the *minjung*, who are filled with *han*, a deep feeling of unresolved indignation.[12] The new Korean rendering of the request of the widow for vindication in Luke 18: 3–5 as resolving *han* is supported by Suh. He believes that "the very existence of the Korean nation has come to be understood as *han*" and "the existence of women was *han* itself."[13] Suh appeals to theologians in Korea to take *han* as a theological theme: "If one does not hear the signs of the *han* of the *minjung*, one cannot hear the voice of Christ knocking on our doors."[14]

Suh's theology is based on three points of reference, which he defends in preference to and in contrast with the traditional theological tenet expressed in the word "revelation." The two historical events of the Exodus and the crucifixion–resurrection, the history of the church, and the *minjung* movement in Korean history, are to be interpreted via the approach of the sociology of literature for the proper understanding and construction of the "social biography of the minjing," with the aim of promoting the identity of the *minjung* in their striving "to become the subjects of their own history and destiny."[15]

In the case of the Exodus, the revolution occurred only once at a particular historical point, while the event of the crucifixion–resurrection was aimed at permanent revolution. In the case of a one-time revolution, the *minjung* are the object of salvation (salvation from outside). In the case of permanent revolution, the *minjung* become the subjects of salvation (self-reliant salvation). Moses answered the cry (aspiration) of the people; but Jesus was the very cry (aspiration) of the people themselves. In this sense, Jesus was truly a *part* of the *minjung*, not just *for* the *minjung*. Jesus was the personification of the *minjung* and has become their symbol.[16]

Suh gives an interpretive *minjung* historical process and outlines the development of a historical consciousness of the *minjung* genealogy. He believes in the need to manifest and realize such a consciousness as "an appropriate political hermeneutics for today."[17] The subjected and victimized *minjung* have struggled in history for their liberation as a historical subject. To Suh, it is the infrastructure of revelation rather than the "suprastructure" (a term he uses to characterize C. S. Song's understanding of revelation), the social history of the *minjung* rather than the conceptual realm of ideas, that constitutes the centrality of the gospel or revelation.

Another prominent *minjung* theologian, Ahn Byung-mu (1921–97), a New Testament scholar, has contributed to establishing a basis in biblical interpretation for *minjung* theology. Through his intensive studies of the synoptic gospels, he identifies the *minjung* tradition in the Bible. He sees Jesus as a historical person who was surrounded by *minjung,* the *ochlos* (Greek "crowd") of his time. The *laos* (Greek "people"), the chosen people of God, on the other hand, have kept a distance from Jesus. Jesus' role with the *minjung* (*ochlos*) constitutes the focal point for understanding the *minjung* of Korea in their struggle for liberation and justice.[18] During the growth of the Korean military dictatorship in the 1960s, Ahn identified the oppressed in Korea with the *ochlos* in the Gospel of Mark, to whom Jesus relates closely. He argues that the gospel story is a *minjung*-centered account and is therefore a *minjung* event, which is transmitted as political rumors by the *minjung* of Jesus. The written text of the Bible and the social text of the *minjung* come alive and interact in such a way as to shed light on one another. This approach opens up spaces for Korean *minjung* theology to be connected to and grounded in the biblical tradition. The two stories of the Bible and of the *minjung* must come to a confluence to contribute to the liberation of the *minjung* of today.

Based on the idea of Chi-Ha Kim's play *The Gold-Crowned Jesus,* Ahn portrays the Christ as imprisoned by Christian dogma, and the liberated Jesus as at one with the poor, the miserable, and the persecuted. Ahn contrasts the Jesus event of the passion-history with the Christ-Kerygma developed in Paul and the church. Through the retelling of the passion-story, the people expose evil and unjust power and gain the strength and courage to resist it.

It is appropriate to take note of the contribution of Kim Yong Bock and David Kwong-sun Suh, who expound and further develop the basic themes of *minjung* theology. They also introduce it to ecumenical circles and to the international theological community. Kim Yong Bock takes up the portrayal of the social biography of the *minjung,* and David Kwong-sun Suh commits to the religious traditions of Korean *minjung.* Buddhist and Shamanist religious experiences are taken as embedded in the make-up of Korean *minjung* religious phenomena. Kim affirms the subjectivity of the *minjung* in history and proceeds to give the sociopolitical biography of the people.[19] David Suh believes that Korean Christianity has been shamanized, incorporating the deep-rooted spirituality of the poor, the oppressed, and the socially marginalized into theological reflection. The *han*-ridden *minjung* embodies a combat spirituality that cries out and longs for liberation. This is especially clear in the shaman ritual of the *gut,* which transforms and renews the life energy and vitality of the community by exorcizing all the evil and harmful spirits that threaten life.[20]

Chinese Theology

T. C. Chao (Zhao Zichen, 1888–1979) was one of the most prominent theologians and church leaders in twentieth-century China. His theological writings are prolific in both English and Chinese. As one of the presidents of the World Council of Churches elected in 1948, Chao resigned in protest against the WCC's statement on the Korean War in 1951. Gifted with poetic skills and drawn to the world of poetry through his excellent command of the Chinese language, Chao blends poetry and prose quite naturally in his theological writings.[21] Dialogue is his favorite literary form in his articulation of complicated theological ideas.[22]

Chao understands culture as being fluid, and in the encounter between Christianity and Chinese culture he believes that a new modern culture will emerge in the process of intensive interaction. Christianity has an indispensable role to play in the social transformation and national building of China, which were the major concerns of Christian scholars and other Chinese intellectuals of his time.

Confucianism and Buddhism have both played a part in transforming Chinese culture. The Buddhist translation of scriptures into Chinese, the long history of Buddhist interpretation, and the influence of Buddhist art on Chinese printing and artifacts are much appreciated by Chao. As a foreign religion, Buddhism has successfully grounded itself to become an inseparable and integrated part of Chinese civilization. It contributes to the religious and spiritual dimension of Chinese culture. In the midst of the Chinese quest for modernization and national regeneration, a new religious culture that is oriented towards ethical social participation is called for. Chao advocates a living Chinese Christianity that focuses on Jesus' "character and spirit" (*renge jingshen*). It is to the "Spiritual Christ" (*jinshen de Jidou*) that Chao looks.

To Chao, indigenization involves two levels: the discovery of the "innate Christ" of Chinese culture, and a process of critical appropriation of Christianity itself, eliminating the negative parts and selecting only the relevant and meaningful elements. In responding to the Anti-Christian Movement in China in the 1920s, Chao proposed building a Chinese church with its own native leadership, theology, liturgy, polity, organization, and architecture. He places great emphasis on attracting and developing intellectuals who will lead and shape the articulation of Chinese theological thought. He attributes the success of Buddhism in China mostly to the rise of a few dedicated Buddhist scholarly monks.[23] Establishing a sound and profound Chinese indigenous theology which speaks to the mind of Chinese intellectuals is a long-term endeavor that is badly needed in China, a theology that represents a confluence of different streams of Chinese culture and the Christian faith.

For Chao, Jesus and his ethical character constitute the foundation of the Chinese Christian theological articulation that should contribute to the transformation of Chinese society and the formation of a Chinese Christian character based on the personality of Jesus, the perfect person.[24] The traditional Chinese quest for an ideal personality and an inner self has great implications for Chao's theology in terms of the perception of the personhood of Jesus and his place in Christian life. Chinese intellectuals have recognized the significant theological contribution of the person Jesus to the Confucian teaching of cultivation of the heart and the self. Jesus' personality and character inspired not only Chinese Christian theologians (Wu Leichuan, T. C. Chao, and Y. T. Wu, to name just a few), but also Chen Duxiu, one of the earliest Chinese Marxists, who even initiated a call for the Chinese to internalize the great character/personality of Jesus and his profound concern for humanity.[25]

The Chinese thinking on the interrelatedness of humanity and nature is another cultural component Chao underlines in his theological reflection. Traditional Chinese thought perceives the way (*Dao/Tao*)[26] of humanity in the way of nature and in the heavenly way (*Tian Dao*). The oneness and unity of reality eliminate the division between self and other, subject and object. Personhood is traditionally not attributed to heaven and nature. The emphasis on the personal God and the personality and character incarnated in Jesus Christ naturally presents a great challenge to the Chinese mind.

While T. C. Chao frames his theological construction in the gradual transformation of society via formation of the person through cultivation and education, his contemporary, Y. T. Wu (Wu Yaozong, 1893–1979), advocates a social program of radical reconstruction of society in action. His humanistic presentation of Christianity contributes to the political, socialist, theological proposal for China. The realization of the Kingdom of God on earth can be achieved through the new humanity in Jesus Christ. Wu founded the Three-Self Reform Movement and drafted the Christian Manifests in 1950 to call for Christian commitment to fight against imperialism and foster patriotism. Wu responded to the new communist leadership in China with his initiative to seek ways to accommodate the Chinese church to socialism. To him, the liberation of the Chinese people achieved by communism has to be acknowledged by the church.

Following Wu's line, Bishop K. T. Ting (Ding Guangxun, 1915–), the single most influential church leader and theologian in the China Christian Council (CCC), the Three-Self Patriotic Movement (TSPM), and Nanjing Union Theological Seminary since China opened itself after the Cultural Revolution in 1978, attempts to come to terms with the socialist ideology and the communist reality of China. Ting especially advocates openness to non-Christians, for whose good deeds in the social context of communism he shows great appreciation. He tries to interpret Christianity to party leaders and officials and to negotiate for a larger space for practicing the Christian faith.

Ting's engagement with his context gives rise to his theology of love and his thinking on "the cosmic Christ."[27] The theological thrust of the concept is derived from his direct personal encounter with communist revolutionaries whose moral goodness and spirit of dedication are impressive. The manifestations of the true, the good, and the beautiful in the communist atheistic context testify to the various dimensions and embodiments of the cosmic Christ. The belief system provides no dividing line between Christians and non-Christians when it comes to living out love, which is the very essence of God's existence. Christ embraces the whole history, encompasses all human existence, and is present in a cosmic dimension. Therefore, Chinese Christians must ascertain the universal extent of Christ's domain. Redemption as a process of creation should not be understood as being restricted to the church alone. It is meant for the whole creation in its cosmic totality. Justification by faith must therefore be reconsidered in view of the indispensable concept of love in the Chinese context. Ting calls for "deemphasizing the doctrine of justification by faith."

Ting argues that love is the first and supreme attribute of God. Both Christians and non-Christians, being God's children, live and act in love. But Christians are called to bear witness to this very love of God, the Christ-like love with which God runs the universe. Reconciliation is an expression of love toward fellow Christians and non-Christians, which was urgently called for in the experiences of suffering and accusation in the aftermath of the Cultural Revolution. In Christ, God reconciles with the world as the greatest Lover. The emphasis on reconciliation has been a cause of concern for many of Ting's critics in view of the great sufferings experienced by the people. The prophetic tradition of the Hebrew Bible was not a focus for Chinese Christian thought in the first years after the reestablishment of the church in the 1980s. In the last decade, more prophetic voices have been raised, and there are now serious theological reflections on the bitter experiences during the Cultural Revolution.[28]

One of Ting's colleagues, Wang Weifan (1928–), develops a different approach to theology. He nurtures a Christian faith in its integration with Chinese literary tradition in the classical texts and the religiosity embedded in the mentality of Chinese people. He is especially fond of the mystical heritage in both Chinese and Western sources. His conviction is that God becomes flesh in cultures beyond Jewish and hellenistic confines. He follows Jesus' model of fulfilling the Jewish culture and argues for an affirmation of the sociopolitical context in which the church is situated. The major theological contribution Wang makes is the proposal to conceive God as "an ever-generating God" who is not only the source of life in creation, but also the constant generating and renewing life force. This notion of God he derives from the *Yijing* (*The Book of Change*).[29]

Wang reaffirms what had been formulated by Chinese Christians in the traditions of Nestorianism, which reached China in 635 CE, and the Chinese Mongolian "Teaching of the Blessed" (*Yelikewan*).[30] The central theological idea focuses on the word *sheng* ("life"). God is understood as a God of *sheng sheng*, "a Life-Birthing God" – the first *sheng* is used as a verb ("to give birth to") and the second as a noun ("life"). The unceasing generating God is a living and dynamic God who does not only give birth to life, but also sustains and protects it.[31] Wang skillfully interweaves the idea of a life-giving God and the Daoist concept of the vitality of the oscillating character of the *Dao*. The cyclical and reverting-back-and-forth *Dao* coincides with the constant reflexive nature of meditation and spirituality.[32] The unceasing life-giving God works through the constant oscillating *Dao* to strengthen the love of God within us. To Wang, the balance between faith and ethics constitutes the theological discussion in China and the key to a full life is the nurturing of personal character. He underlines the importance of a religious heart (*zhong jia xin*), a religiosity which embraces both this-worldly and other-worldly dimensions of life.

Wang Weifang affirms four components in building Chinese theology: revelation, tradition, culture, and praxis (or experience). The gospel is to be expressed in cultural forms, which to Wang are the embodiment of the faith of Christianity.

Talking about Chinese culture is not simple. It is not only that its long history has given rise to a complicated conglomeration which is characterized as pluralistic and diversified: the vehement May Fourth Movement (1919) and the iconoclastic Cultural Revolution (1966–77) shook the foundation of Chinese civilization and compel it to redefinition. The traditional form of Chinese culture cannot be grasped without taking seriously the violent impact of these two epoch-making historical occasions. Reflecting on the Cultural Revolution, which he personally experienced, Wang comments: "Its severity was not simply a matter of the damage done by Red Guards to countless priceless treasures, historical relics, and rare books. Much more serious was the sweeping critique and utter repudiation of the ethics and value system of Chinese culture in all its ramifications."[33]

The third challenge, alongside these two from the past, is the present policy of reform and modernization since 1978, which exposes Chinese spiritual poverty. Sober reflection on China's tradition and a quest for a refined Chinese culture are called for. It is the conviction of Wang that in addition to the classics as Chinese cultural sources, which still preserve something for a Chinese theology, "the cultural heart of the Chinese people" will also constitute the cultural sources. Theology from such a heart will have the color and rhythm of China.[34] Wang is still very hopeful of Chinese culture and he anticipates that a new refined Chinese cultural core will emerge to interact with Christianity.

Taiwanese Theology

Theology in Taiwan is mostly constructed in the mode of identification: God identifies with the people of Israel and through Jesus Christ with the suffering and hope of the oppressed Taiwanese people. The Presbyterian Church of Taiwan played an important role in the birth of contextual theology in Taiwan in its active and timely response to the Taiwanese sociopolitical reality and the plight of deprived aboriginal people. Its provocative statements in the 1970s provide a good theological platform for the continuous heated debates and consolidation of theological positions in churches and seminaries. Theological formulations were drawn up and practical steps taken to respond to the theological stimulation arising from the context. These epoch-making public statements are: "Statement on Our National Fate" (1971), "Our Appeal" (1975), and "The Human Rights Declaration" (1977). They embody the theological articulation in the process of the renewal of theology following the centennial celebration of the arrival of the Protestant Mission in Taiwan.

The identity of the Taiwanese people is the central issue in Taiwanese theology. It grows out of the historical experience of being dominated by colonization and dictatorial rule. The quest for the right to determine the future and the fate of the people is the core to "homeland theology" and the theology of *Chhut Thau Thin* ("a day to lift up one's head"). Wang Hsien Chi is acclaimed as the founder of homeland theology in Taiwan, which critically reappropriates the conquest and the royal traditions of the Hebrew Bible in conjunction with Taiwanese cultural resources and the historical experiences of the people of Taiwan. The political implication of this theological work is tremendous in the context of the sociopolitical reality of Taiwan. The theology of *Chhut Thau Thin* is proposed by Huang Po Ho, who defines its aim as "to raise one's head out of darkness to see the blue sky and breathe the spring air."[35] *Chhut Thau Thin*, referring to a traditional Taiwanese proverb, exhibits an appeal to the local culture and an effort to bring out the liberative power of the people's struggle for a bright future for Taiwan.

Feminist Theology in East Asia

In God's Image, founded by Sun Ai Lee Park, is the major journal through which Asian women express their theological concerns and thoughts. Women theologians from different Asian countries take their social reality and historical experience of domination and discrimination seriously in theological construction. The patriarchal and hierarchical social structures are under attack, together with the predominant male-centered cultural modes. In East Asia, the enslaving elements of Confucian tradition are identified and scrutinized. The same applies to the biblical and doctrinal traditions of the church. The patriarchal practices in the Bible and the church are to be deconstructed. Re-reading the Bible in the context of the experience of Asian women and in conjunction with the oral transmission of their stories is a major theological effort.[36] To Korean women theologians, native religiosity and spirituality are powerful resources to be appropriated. The shamanistic religious tradition can lend support to Korean women in their theological process. In such a reading, Jesus is seen as a priest of *han*, who helps to deal with the feeling of indignation and inner anger as a result of unjust suffering and oppression.[37]

Catholic women theologians also work hard to search their cultural resources and the Catholic tradition for liberating power. Goddesses are being reassessed critically and the role of Mary as co-redeemer is further discussed theologically and reclaimed for full human liberation.

Park Soon Kyung, pastor of the Women's Church in Korea and leading Asian feminist theologian in the Ecumenical Association of Third World Theologians (EATWOT), underlines the double or triple oppression women in Asia undergo. She names women as the *minjung* of the *minjung*, struggling to achieve liberation from harsh oppression.

In terms of a radical shift of approach to theology in Asian women's struggle for authentic womanhood and spirituality, Chung Hyun Kyung's proposal to "move away from Christocentrism toward life-centrism" is an attempt to address Asian women's reality of being oppressed by the male-dominated interpretation of Christianity both in the West and the East. Her suggestion to reverse the text–context paradigm is a significant step in addressing Asian women's predicament. Women's experiences and stories must take priority. The Bible and Christian tradition only become meaningful when they touch women's hearts. "We are the text" is strategically proclaimed by Chung.[38]

Asian feminist theology is the main concern of Kwok Pui-lan, a theologian from Hong Kong teaching in the USA, who has been doing theological deconstruction and construction with Asian sources and resources. The Bible should not be undermined in the non-biblical world of Asia, but it must be interpreted from the feminist theological consciousness of Asian women. Based on an extensive historical and theological analysis of Christian women's struggle in concrete situations, Kwok's *Chinese Women and Christianity, 1860–1927* has laid the foundation for her work in Asian feminist theology. Her *Introducing Asian Feminist Theology* offers a good summary of her own journey. Christology takes center stage in the debates of Asian feminist theology, in addition to the perception of the divine and the development of sexuality and spirituality from Asian women's perspective. Kwok's critique of Asian patriarchy in both the church and Asian religious traditions drives home the quest for liberating alternatives for Asian women.

Hisako Kinukawa, a New Testament scholar from Japan, reads the encounter between the women and Jesus in the Gospel of Mark from the rigidly gendered social structure of Jesus' time and the patriarchally oriented Japanese society. The hemorrhaging woman, the Syrophoenician woman, the poor widow, the anointing woman, and the women disciples of Jesus all risked severe social condemnation by initiating the crossings of sexual, ethnic, and ritual barriers to interact with Jesus. They dared to break out of their marginalized position in the patriarchal society. For example, the purity laws concerning women's blood were challenged by the hemorrhaging woman's move. Jesus, too, being a man in the patriarchal tradition, was greatly challenged by these women's initiating actions. He responded to the women's boundary-breaking acts of questing for contact and social integration by revealing his liberating and life-giving power. Kinukawa's unique contribution to the interpretation of the women and Jesus in Mark opens up a new contextual reading of the Bible in feminist theological construction, by drawing attention to the patriarchal bias of Asian society and that of Jesus' time.[39]

Conclusion

Theology in East Asia is surely theology in the making. The theological communities in the region are rapidly developing into an influential force in theological reflection and reconstruction, both inside and outside of East Asia. Many young and budding scholars are being trained in various local universities and theological seminaries, as well as in overseas institutions.

The quest for a theology radically rooted in the Asian context is shared by the various East Asian regions. The forms this theology takes are varied and pluralistic. The indigenization model, which aims at acculturating the gospel to the classical cultural soil of the land, often results in simple comparative studies of philosophical concepts and a static, fossilized, homogeneous and unitary form of culture. The native culture is either romanticized or polemicized in light of Christian faith.

On the other hand, the task of theology in East Asia is deeply hampered when the cultural and religious traditions of the people embodied in the classics, the stories of the people manifested in folktales and festivals, and the religiosity represented in the symbolic systems of a society are left alienated from the theological process. The derogatory and slanderous attitude of early missionary movements towards the so-called "heathen world" and its pagan practices in order to uphold the exclusive sacredness of the Christian claim inflicted significant damage to the religious world of Asia. Theological research in East Asia has critically taken a radical stance to affirm the religious–cultural forms of native resources.

The East Asian polytheistic consciousness is familiar with the variety of the divine in its various expressions and numerous names. The conceptual rendering of divinity in terms of "the one and the many" can best be comprehended as metaphorically meaningful, but never numerically accurate. The display of the rich syncretistic religious traditions in Asia no doubt demonstrates forcefully the sheer profundity of Asian religiosity.

East Asian theology is still at a crossroads, deciding on the future direction to be taken in order to bring its theology to a higher level of operation and a deeper level of existence. The conventional understanding of "theology in context" is no longer relevant, since Asia is not a mission field preoccupied only with making the foreign gospel comprehensible to Asians by merely having it translated into the language of the natives. Contextualization in terms of putting the text in literary, linguistic, and sociopolitical contexts is very limited and should be challenged.

The first step to moving beyond the communication mode to the construction stage of doing authentic theology is the recognition of divine activity in East Asian history. Song's willingness to grant revelatory status to East Asian culture is not only something to be desired, but must also be considered an essential step. The stories, histories, and present experiences of East Asian people are not merely context. They are texts to be read and interpreted theologically with the Christian text. The enriched encounter of the two texts in "cross-textual hermeneutics" can be adopted as a basic theological methodology. The East Asian cultural texts and sociopolitical texts should be taken seriously. They, too, may embody the prevailing but mysterious presence of the divine and contribute to the living theology of East Asian people. Cross-textual reading is a tool that recognizes the multi-scriptural and multicultural reality of East Asia. It intends to go a step further than comparative studies and drawing parallels, to engaging the two worlds of religious experience embedded both in the biblical text and in the rich Asian resources. Text A (the Asian text) and text B (the biblical text) must be brought together in genuine interaction and dialogue in order to facilitate the process of doing Asian theology. Methodologically, it is at the very center of the confluence of the Christian traditions and the Asian resources that theological meaning is to be generated.[40]

The West should no longer be the context of Asian theology. Simon Kwan, a young theologian from Hong Kong, sums up this very theological position from a postcolonial critique of binarism.[41] Kwan echoes a passionate call of another Hong Kong scholar, Angela Wai-Ching Wong.[42] Any counter-theology, taking Western theology as "its theological *others*" and embodying an anti-West sentiment, is in a way being dictated by an agenda arising from outside its own context. The pluralistic, syncretistic, and hybridized Asian reality is an asset for the construction of an enriching living theology for men and women of Asia.

Notes

1 A new name was introduced in 2001: Programme for Theologies and Cultures in Asia. Along with the change of the word "theology" to plural form came the new journal, the *Journal of Theologies and Cultures in Asia* (JTCA) and the commitment to do quality research on pluralistic theologies.

2 Choan-Seng Song's works include *Third-eye Theology* (1979), *The Compassionate God* (1982), *Tell Us Our Names* (1984), *Theology from the Womb of Asia* (1986), the trilogy in *The Cross in the Lotus World* (1: *Jesus, the Crucified People*, 1990; 2: *Jesus and the Reign of God*, 1993; 3: *Jesus in the Power of the Spirit*, 1994), and *The Believing Heart: An Invitation to Story Theology* (1999).

3 Choan-Seng Song, "From Israel to Asia – A Theological Leap," *Mission Trends* No. 3: *Third World Theologies*, ed. Gerald H. Anderson and Thomas F. Stransky, New York: Paulist Press; Grand Rapids, MI: Eerdmans, 1974, pp. 211–22.

4 Yasuo Furuya (ed.), *A History of Japanese Theology* (Grand Rapids, MI, 1997), p. 132.

5 Kazoh Kitamori, *Theology of the Pain of God* (Richmond, VA, John Knox Press, 1965), translated from the fifth revised edition in Japanese, *Kami No Itami No Shigaku* (Tokyo: Shinkyo Shuppansha, 1958), pp. 7–8.

6 Kitamori's preface to the fifth edition, and p. 115.

7 Preface to the fifth edition, and pp. 16–17.

8 Preface to the English edition," p. 8; preface to the second edition, p. 9.

9 Preface to the third edition, p. 11.

10 The Non-Church (*Mukyokai*) Movement was founded by Kanjo Uchimura at the beginning of the twentieth century. It advocates an assembly of Christians without the existing petrified form of the church and open to the creation of "the proper shape of the church." The Bible is held as the central and only source of Christian life when church edifices, clergy, sacraments, and institutions are all being done away

with. (Non-Church adherents are derisively referred to as "cross-legged" Christians because instead of sitting in Western-style pews, "they sit cross-legged on straw mats in homes, factories, schools, and anywhere – except churches – studying the Bible.") In the act of interpretation of the Bible, everyone is equal and no one has any more authority than anyone else. Though the Bible is the canon of the church, Non-Church Christians are committed to the Bible without being under the authority of the church. Christ is the only authority. Their answer to the danger of individualistic interpretation of the Bible is the emphasis on communal reading: "We read it as a group."

11   See Jin-ho Kun and Sookjin Lee, "A Retrospect and Prospect on Korean Modernity and *Minjung* Theology," *JTCA*, 1, 2002, pp. 156–75, which provides a splendid summary of the pretexts and critique of *Minjung* theology.

12   Suh Nam-dong, "Towards a Theology of Han," in *Minjung Theology: People as the Subject of History*, pp. 51–66. Examples of the suffering of factory workers and farmers are cited in this article. Suh also refers to artistic and literary works.

13   Ibid, p. 54.

14   Ibid, p. 65.

15   Ibid, p. 157.

16   Ibid, p. 159.

17   Ibid, p. 173.

18   Two of Ahn's articles are available in English in the *CTC Bulletin*: "The Transmitter of the Jesus Event" (Vol. 5–6, 1984–5) and "Jesus and People (*Minjung*)" (Vol. 7, 1987).

19   Kim Yong Bock, "Messiah and *Minjung*: Discerning Messianic Politics over against Political Messianism," in *Minjung Theology: People as the Subject of History*, pp. 185–96.

20   David Kwong-sun Suh, *The Korean Mingjung in Christ*, Hong Kong: Commission on Theological Concerns, CCA, 1991. See also "Shamanism and *Minjung* Liberation," in *Asian Christian Spirituality: Reclaiming Traditions*, ed. Virginia Fabella, Peter K. H. Lee, and David Kwong-sun Suh, Maryknoll, NY: Orbis Books, 1992, pp. 31–6.

21   This poetic gift is acknowledged and celebrated by Y. T. Wu in his preface to Chao's *My Experience in Prison*, Shanghai: Association Press of China, 1948, p. 2.

22   An outstanding example is his *Christian Philosophy*.

23   See T. C. Chao, "The Chinese People and Christianity," *Truth and Life*, 9/5–6, 1935, pp. 268–85.

24   T. C. Chao, "Christianity and Chinese Culture," *Truth and Life*, 2/9–10, 1927, pp. 247–60.

25   Wang Weifan provides a summary of the ideas of Chen Duxiu and the Chinese Christian intellectuals mentioned above in his paper in the Chinese original *Nanjing Theological Review* 3, 1999, pp. 42–6. The English translation appears in *Chinese Theological Review* 13, 1999, pp. 8–18. A note must be added to point out the discrepancies in the English translation. The Chinese concept of *renge* has been rendered as "characteristics" instead of the normal usage of "personality/character" (pp. 16–18).

26   The transliteration of the traditional rendering of *Tao* into *Dao* is adopted in this chapter.

27   K. T. Ting, "The Cosmic Christ," in Wickeri and Wickeri, *A Chinese Contribution to Ecumenical Theology*, p. 100.

28   See Francis Ching-wah Yip, *Chinese Theology in State–Church Context*, pp. 136–57.

29   Wang Weifan's *Chinese Theology and its Cultural Root* is his major theology book written in Chinese. A few of his articles have been translated and published in *Chinese Theological Review*. Being a biblical scholar, Wang has also produced commentaries on Corinthians, the pastoral letters, and Leviticus.

30   The Chinese name for the religion practiced by Yuan Dynasty Christians means "the blessed one."

31   Wang Weifan, "Chinese Traditional Culture and Its Influence on Chinese Theological Reflection," *Chinese Theological Review* 13, 1999, pp. 8–18.

32   Wang Weifan, "Reversion is the Movement of the Dao," *Nanjing Theological Review* 3, 1999, pp. 149–51.

33   Ibid, p. 80.

34   Ibid, p. 84.

35   Huang Po Ho, "Taiwanese Theologies," in *Dictionary of Third World Theologies*, ed. Virginia Fabella and R. S. Sugertharajah,

Maryknoll, NY: Orbis Books, 2000, pp. 195–6.

36 See Kwok Pui-lan, *Discovering the Bible in the Non-Biblical World*, Maryknoll, NY: Orbis Books, 1995.

37 See Chung Hyun Kyung, *Struggle to be the Sun Again: Introducing Asian Women's Theology*, Maryknoll, NY: Orbis Books, 1990.

38 Ibid, pp. 109–14.

39 Hisako Kinukawa, *Women and Jesus in Mark: A Japanese Feminist Perspective*, Maryknoll, NY: Orbis Books, 1994.

40 See Nam-Dong Suh, "De-theological Reflection on Folktales," in *The Search for Minjung Theology*, Seoul: Hangilsa, 1983, pp. 275–312.

41 Simon Shui-man Kwan, "A Discursive History of the Asian Theologial Movement – A Critique of its Binarism," *JTCA*, 1, 2002, pp. 93–133.

42 Angela Wai-Ching Wong, "Asian Theology in a Changing Asia: Towards an Asian Theological Agenda for the 21st Century," Proceeding of the Congress of Asian Theologians (CATS) May 25–June 1, 1997, Suwon, Korea, ed. Dhyanchand Carn and Philip Wickeri, pp. 30–9.

Bibliography

Abraham, Dulcie, et al. (eds.). *Asian Women Doing Theology*, Singapore: Asian Women's Resource Centre for Culture and Theology, 1987.

Chao, T. C. (Zhao Zichen). "The Appeal of Christianity to the Chinese Mind," *Chinese Recorder*, 49, 1918, 287–96.

—— "Christian Renaissance in China," *Chinese Recorder*, 51, 1920, 636–9.

—— "The Message of the Cross for China," *Chinese Recorder*, 67, 1936, 135–42.

—— "Christianity and the National Crisis," *Chinese Recorder*, 68, 1937, 5–12.

Chung, Hyun Kyung. *Struggle to be the Sun Again: Introducing Asian Women's Theology*, Maryknoll NY: Orbis Books, 1990.

Coe, Shoki. "Contextualizing Theology," in *Third World Theologies, Mission Trends* No. 3, ed. Gerald Anderson, New York: Paulist Press, 1976.

Fabella, Virginia and Sun Ai Lee Park (eds.). *We Dare to Dream: Doing Theology as Asian Women*, Hong Kong: AWRCCT; Manila: EATWOT, 1989.

Furuya, Yasuo (ed.). *A History of Japanese Theology*, Grand Rapids, MI: Eerdmans, 1997.

Germany, Charles H. *Protestant Theologies in Modern Japan: A History of Dominant Theological Currents from 1920–1960*, Tokyo: IISR Press, 1965.

Gluer, Winfried. *Christliche Theologie in China: T. C. Chao 1918–1956*, Gutersloh: Gutersloher Verlagshaus Gerd Mohn, 1979.

Kim, Heup Young. *Wang Yang-ming and Karl Barth: A Confucian–Christian Dialogue*, Lanham, MD: University Press of America, 1996.

Kitamori, Kazoh. *Theology of the Pain of God*, Richmond, VA: John Knox Press, 1965.

Koyama, Kosuke. *Waterbuffalo Theology*, London: SCM Press; Maryknoll, NY: Orbis Books, 1974. 25th anniversary revised and expanded edition, Orbis Books, 1999.

—— *No Handle on the Cross*, London: SCM Press; Maryknoll, NY: Orbis Books, 1976.

—— *Three Mile an Hour God*, Maryknoll, NY: Orbis Books, 1980.

—— *Mt Fuji and Mt Sinai: A Critique of Idols*, London: SCM Press; Maryknoll, NY: Orbis Books, 1985.

Kwan, Simon Shui-man. "A Discursive History of Asian Theological Movement: A Critique of its Binarism," *JTCA*, 1, 2002, 93–133.

Kwok, Pui Lan. *Introducing Asian Feminist Theology*, Cleveland, OH: Pilgrim Press, 2000.

Lee, Archie C. C. "Biblical Interpretation in Asian Perspective," *Asia Journal of Theology*, 7, 1993, 35–9.

Lee, Jung Young (ed.). *An Emerging Theology in World Perspective: Commentary on Korean Minjung Theology*, Mystic, CT: Twenty-Third Publications, 1988.

Lee, Oo-chung, et al. (eds.). *Women of Courage: Asian Women Reading the Bible*, Seoul: AWRC, 1988.

Michalson, Carl. *Japanese Contributions to Christian Theology*, Philadelphia, PA: Westminster Press, 1960.

Minjung Theology: People as the Subjects of History, ed. by the Commission of Theological Concerns of the Christian Conference of Asia (CTC-CCA), Maryknoll, NY: Orbis Books, 1983.

Mullins, Mark R. and Richard Fox Young. *Perspectives on Christianity in Korea and Japan: The Gospel and Culture in East Asia*, Lewiston, ID: Edward Mellen Press, 1995.

Song, C. S. "From Israel to Asia – A Theological Leap," in *Third World Theologies, Mission Trends* No. 3, ed. Gerald H. Anderson and Thomas F. Stransky, New York: Paulist Press, 1974.

—— *Third-eye Theology: Theology in Formation in Asian Setting*, Maryknoll, NY: Orbis Books, 1979.

—— *The Compassionate God*, London: SCM Press, 1982.

—— *Tell Us Our Names: Story Theology from an Asian Perspective*, Maryknoll, NY: Orbis Books, 1984.

—— *Theology from the Womb of Asia*, Maryknoll, NY: Orbis Books, 1986.

—— *Jesus, the Crucified People*, New York: Crossroad, 1990.

—— *Jesus and the Reign of God*, Minneapolis, MN: Fortress Press, 1993.

—— *Jesus in the Power of the Spirit*, Minneapolis, MN: Fortress Press, 1994.

Suh, David Kwong-sun. *The Korean Minjung in Christ*, Hong Kong: Commission on Theological Concerns, CCA, 1991.

Ting, K. H. (Ding Guangxun). *Christianity with a Chinese Face*, Cincinnati, OH: Forward Movement Publications, 1989.

—— *No Longer Strangers*, ed. Raymond L. Whitehead, Maryknoll, NY: Orbis Books, 1989.

—— *Love Never Ends* (English edition of *Ding Guangxun wenji*), ed. Janice Wickeri, Nanjing: Yilin Press, 2000.

—— "Fourteen Points," in *A New Beginning: An International Dialogue with the Chinese Church*, ed. Theresa Chu and Christopher Lind, Toronto: Canada China Program, 1983: 104–8.

Wang Hsien-Chih. *Tai-wan hsiang tu shen hsueh lunwen chi pien chu* (Homeland Theology in the Taiwanese Context), Taiwan Homeland Theology Research Papers, Vol. 1. Tainan: Tainan Theological College, 1988.

—— "Some Perspectives on Homeland Theology in the Taiwanese Context," in *Frontiers in Asian Christian Theology: Emerging Trends*, ed. R. S. Sugirtharajah, Maryknoll, NY: Orbis Books, 1994.

Wang, Weifan. "Changes in Theological Thinking in the Church in China," *Chinese Theological Review*, 1986.

—— "The Pattern and Pilgrimage of Chinese Theology," *Chinese Theological Review*, 1990.

—— *Chinese Theology and Its Chinese Cultural Root* (in Chinese), Nanjing: Nanjing Theological Seminary, 1997.

—— "Chinese Traditional Culture and Its Influence on Chinese Theological Reflection," *Chinese Theological Review*, 1999.

Wickeri, Philip L. *Seeking the Common Ground: Protestant Christianity, the Three-Self Movement, and China's United Front*, Maryknoll, NY: Orbis Books, 1988.

Wickeri, Philip L. and Janice Wickeri (eds.). *A Chinese Contribution to Ecumenical Theology: Selected Writings of Bishop K. H. Ting*, Geneva: WCC, 2002.

Wong, Angela Wai-Ching. "Asian Theology in a Changing Asia: Towards an Asian Theological Agenda for the 21st Century," *Proceedings of the Congress of Asian Theologians (CATS)*, 1997, 30–9.

—— *"The Poor Woman": A Critical Analysis of Asian Theology and Contemporary Chinese Fiction by Women*, New York: Peter Lang, 2002.

Wu, Y. T. (Wu Yaozong). *Meiyou ren kanjianguo shangdi* (No One Has Seen God), Shanghai: Association Press, 1943.

—— "Christianity and China's Reconstruction," *Chinese Recorder*, 67, 1936, 208–15.

—— "Whither the Chinese Church," *Chinese Recorder*, 67, 1936, 71–4.

—— *Talks on Christianity*, Shanghai: Association Press, 1950.

—— "The Contemporary Tragedy of Christianity," in *Documents of the Three-Self Movement*, ed. Wallace C. Merwin and Francis P. Jones, New York: NCCCUSA, 1963.

Yip, Francis Ching-wah. *Chinese Theology in State–Church Context: A Preliminary Study* (in Chinese), Hong Kong: Christian Study Centre on Chinese Religion and Culture, 1997.

Postcolonial Biblical Interpretation

R. S. Sugirtharajah

Introduction: Background, Influences

Extraneous theories have always been used to illuminate the Bible. The latest to be summoned into service is postcolonial criticism. Like most theories, postcolonial criticism did not originate within the field of biblical studies, but had its beginnings in other disciplines. Initially, it emerged as an arm of literary studies scrutinizing the literatures of Commonwealth countries which were part of the British empire. This critical practice was largely focused on the ways literatures of the former colonies were produced, marketed, and mediated in Western metropolitan centers. Now, however, postcolonial criticism finds itself located in a variety of fields, varying from medieval studies, to music and sociology, to sport – fields which do not lend themselves easily to postcolonial interests and concerns. These various disciplines acknowledge the severe impact of colonialism and recognize the force of the continuing neo-colonization in the form of globalization. In such a scenario, postcolonialism has become a profitable alternative theory to uncover colonial domination in all its forms.

So "when," "where," "who," and "what" is postcolonial? All these questions have simple and straightforward answers as well as sophisticated and complex ones.

First, the question of "when." When did the postcolonial start? Did it begin when the last Union Jack was lowered in a former colony, or when a newly independent country got its national flag, its anthem, and its airline? The simplest answer to the question is that, in its historical and temporal sense, postcolonial denotes the social, cultural, and political conditions after the historical demise of the empire. But the term as it is used in postcolonial discourse is more finely nuanced. What is manifestly clear is that postcolonial is not about chronological markers of "periods," "eras," or "aeons." It is about a series of anti-colonial resistances undertaken in order to instill a new sense of national pride and purpose, both before and after the formal end of territorial colonialism. It is as much about the pinch felt during the high noon of empire as about newer predicaments faced under neo-colonialism in the form of globalization.

The "where" of postcolonial raises questions regarding place or location. The obvious answer is the countries once controlled by former colonial powers, but now the space is opened up to include the very imperial centers, where the presence of blacks and Asians challenges the monolithic, unadulterated view of the former empires.

The question as to "who" can engage in postcolonialism is answered by some of the former colonized, who see their victimhood giving them a vantage point for employing postcolonialism as a redemptive theoretical tool. Some academics in metropolitan centers collude with such an idea and consign the application of the discourse to countries which were once colonized. In this way, they limit the potency of the theory and isolate its influence. The dismantling of the apparatus of colonialism is not something that is solely undertaken by those who were once colonized. Colonialism disturbs both the colonizer and the colonized and as such the decolonizing process involves both. The purpose of postcolonial discourse is not only to investigate how peoples and cultures were violated, but also to investigate the entanglement and entrenchment of European and American powers which sponsored, sanctioned, and sustained such atrocities. While the colonized liberate themselves from the oppressive structures, the colonizer has to confront the very structures which in the first place perpetuated such an unequal system. Since both the colonized and the colonizer have a heavy stake in unraveling past injustices and present imbalances, the postcolonial critical category is a serviceable tool for both.

Finally, "what" is postcolonial? Texts? Theoretical practices? Psychological conditions? Concrete historical process? Probably all of these. One has to admit that postcolonialism is a notoriously loose term covering a multitude of intellectual and textual practices. Each discipline has to come up with its own definition. Essentially, what unites these disparate disciplines are practices which

1   dislodge Western constructions of knowledge about the Other;
2   reclaim the histories of the subaltern and chronicle forms of overt and covert resistance;
3   resist and transcend binary models by which the West has categorized its Others;
4   expose the link between power and knowledge in the production of the colonial Other.

Postcolonial theory has emerged as a convenient marker for a range of critical perspectives on the social, cultural, and political process of decolonization and its aftermath. It is essentially an oppositional discourse which tries to "write back" and wreck any persisting colonial assumptions and ideologies. The scope and intention of the method are inevitably political, in a politics which is anti-establishment and progressive, varying from soft liberalism to radical socialism. Postcolonialism implies and imputes political and ideological commitment in the position of those interpreters who employ it as a theory. In other words, postcolonial critics engage in and carry on with anti-colonial praxis and theory.

One needs to distinguish between postcolonial theory and postcolonial criticism. What has now emerged and has a high premium in academic circles is the postcolonial theory which came to be identified with the work of Edward Said, Gayatri Spivak, and Homi Bhabha. It should be stressed that none of these scholars sets out to be postcolonial in their writings. It was only when theorizing became an attractive and an indispensable tool, and when these scholars recognized and addressed the central interests of the colonized other, that they came to be seen as originators and proponents of postcolonial theory. There were two precursors to the theory. One was the discourse of resistance in nationalist movements, and the other was creative literary production in the form of novels, poems, and art. There was a vigorous anticolonial liberationist discourse which emerged as a result of nationalistic struggle. These writings, both resistance discourse and liberative literature, in their own way highlighted the predatory nature of colonialism and the psychological and political havoc it caused. Among theoreticians, the leading figures were Frantz Fanon, C. L. R. James, Albert Memmi, and Aimé Césaire, and novelists such as Ngugi wa Thiongo, A. Madhavaiah, and Chinua Achebe, to name a few. These literary outputs are too complex to reduce into a single reading because they arise out of different colonial contexts and ideological needs. The point is, though, that postcolonial criticism had a longer antecedent history of criticism of colonialism before becoming a theory validated by metropolitan academic institutions.

Although the work of Said, Spivak, and Bhabha has relevance to biblical studies, the Bible as such plays only a marginal role in their writings. There are a few forays. Said himself has read the Exodus narrative from a Canaanite perspective, and Bhabha has theorized about the Bible as a colonial artifact. On the whole, nevertheless, their theoretical propositions are serviceable to biblical interpretation. The ideas in Said's *Orientalism* can be clearly applied to biblical studies. By Orientalism, Said means a Western discursive power to produce an "orient" (and, it could be added, other colonized regions) by "authorizing views of it, describing it by teaching it, speaking for it – in short, representing the colonized world in a style suitable for dominating, restructuring, and having authority over it."[1] Orientalism is a misrepresentation and falsification of other peoples by the West, which slots them into separate and distinct ethnic extractions or essences so that they become controllable and assessable. Bhabha's notions of hybridity and mimicry have clear biblical applications.[2] Hybridity is not syncretism – a much loathed concept in missiological circles. In syncretism a stronger culture, usually Western or Christian in modern times, swallows a weaker one. Hybridity, on the other hand, is a process where different cultures interact to create new transcultural forms. Spivak's concern with letting the subaltern speak (i.e., finding a voice for the colonized other) is a clear warning signal to those attempting to speak on behalf of the "other."[3]

Postcolonial biblical interpretation did not spring into the hermeneutical landscape instantaneously. For practitioners in the Third World, it is a natural progression through various stages: heritagist (seeking biblical ideas and concepts in the high culture of Hindu, Buddhist, and Confucian societies, and in the thought world of indigenous people), to liberationist (reading the Bible from a liberation perspective), to dissentient (reading which drew attention to internal dissent, the concerns and causes of minorities – Indian dalits (outcaste), Japanese Burakumins, tribals, and women), to the current postcolonialist phase.[4]

What does postcolonial biblical criticism aim to do?

1   It seeks to situate colonialism at the center of the Bible and biblical interpretation. The Bible emerged as a literary product of various colonial contexts – Egyptian, Assyrian, Persian, hellenistic, and Roman. Postcolonial criticism tries to look at

these narratives and investigate them for colonial assumptions, imperial impulses, power relations, hegemonic intentions, the treatment of subalterns, stigmatization of women and the marginalized, land appropriation, and the violation of minority cultures. In reading these texts, it endeavors to revive and reclaim silenced voices, sidelined issues, and lost causes.

2   It seeks to scrutinize biblical interpretation and expose the ideological content hidden behind its apparent claim to neutrality. What postcolonial biblical criticism does is focus on the whole issue of expansion, domination, and imperialism as central forces in defining both biblical narratives and biblical interpretation.

3   It seeks to re-read the Bible in the light of postcolonial concerns and conditions – plurality, hybridity, multiculturalism, nationalism, diaspora, refugees, and asylum seeking. The Bible is appropriated not because it has prescriptions for problems which arose in the wake of colonialism. Rather, it is to see whether it can lend itself and evolve as an appropriate Word of God in response to issues which were not the primary concern of these narratives.

Western biblical scholarship over the last four hundred years has been challenged and compromised by the impact of the values of the Protestant Reformation and by the effects of the Enlightenment in defining and shaping the discipline. Biblical scholars are largely trained in and influenced by the modernistic notion of using the rational as a key to open up texts. There has been a remarkable reluctance on the part of Western biblical scholars to address imperialism as an inherent component both in biblical narratives or biblical interpretation. Traditional biblical scholarship tends to lay much emphasis on the religious, theological, and socioeconomic background of biblical narratives and tends to ignore the presence of colonialism in them. What postcolonial biblical criticism seeks to do is to overturn this and place colonialism at the heart of biblical material and scholarship. The general perception is that biblical interpretation as it is practiced today has on the whole become ineffective because of its reluctance to address issues faced by people in their daily lives, and thus it has failed to be in the vanguard of social change. Postcolonialism, in conjunction with such allies as feminism and liberation hermeneutics, can rectify this enfeebled image.

Survey

Postcolonialism is a relative newcomer to the scene and only a few scholars are engaged in the practice. There are two kinds of users of postcolonial criticism with regard to the Bible: those working within biblical studies, and those outside the discipline. Those from the outside are from kindred disciplines such as systematic theology in the case of Kwok Pui Lan, and English literary study in the case of Laura Donaldson. Among those within the field, one can detect two further groups. There are biblical practitioners who unashamedly identify with postcoloniality, especially those from the former colonies who experienced its legacy and use it to interrogate colonial assumptions embedded both in the text and interpretation. These include Fernando Segovia, Musa Dube, Stephen Moore, and myself. There are also those who are heirs to the empire and those from the settler communities seeking to rectify past misdeeds and misrepresentations. They do not have the burden of guilt which plagued a previous generation, and do not have the inbuilt fear of criticizing the system, as they never participated in it. They make amends by exposing the colonial ideological and political positions found within Western scholarship. Among them are Roland Boer, Erin Runions, Richard Horsely, Sharon Ringe, Keith Whitelam, Michael Prior, and Havlor Moxnes. There are those such as the *Semeia* team, to be discussed below, outside the biblical fold, who use the tool profitably. The literary output of these above mentioned writers embodies the three aims set out earlier.

One can identify the following features in the literary output of these interpreters. First, their writings look at the colonial context of biblical narratives. Warren Carter's *Matthew and the Margins*, unlike the majority of Matthean studies, which focus on the first gospel's relation to Judaism, deals with Matthew's relation to the imperial power of the Roman empire. He raises issues of marginality and resistance, and re-reads the first gospel as a counter-narrative which speaks against the values, agendas, and commitments of the Roman imperial power and the ecclesiastical authorities. In particular, Carter's Matthew provides visions of the final establishment of God's empire.[5]

Richard Horsley has been successful in unearthing a wealth of subversive material and evidence of counter-hegemonic movements that remain buried or forgotten in the biblical texts. Recommending postcolonial reading as a way of going beyond the negative aspect of Euro-American biblical scholarship – its essentialist and apoliticized readings – Horsley sees his task as emancipating hitherto repressed and latent histories of Jesus movements that lie behind the New Testament writings. He goes on to explore these previously submerged histories of Jesus movements and Pauline communities, which became the victims of the grand narratives of Western Christianity. He rescues Mark and Paul from essentialist, individualist, and depoliticized Western readings, and reconfigures, not only how Mark and Paul explore and resist the dominant imperial culture in their writings, but also how they engage in building communities alternative to the imperial order.[6]

The Persian empire receives particular attention in the writings of Mosala and Berquist. While Itumeleng Mosala has shown the impact of the Persian empire in the Book of Esther, Jon Berquist has considered the early stages of the canonization of the Hebrew Bible as part of the imperial discourse of the Persian empire. He has illustrated how texts and movements located within the very canon go against the imperializing tendencies of the Persian empire. One such text is Isaiah 66: 1–5, a narrative from the Persian imperial period which spoke against the imperial administration.[7]

The second feature of postcolonial biblical interpretation has been to expose colonial intentions hidden behind Western biblical interpretation. Havlor Moxnes has shown how colonialism, national identity, ethnicity, and race have impinged upon and influenced the scholarly constructions of Galilee in nineteenth-century biblical scholarship in Europe. He has drawn attention to this especially in the writings of Schleiermacher, Strauss, and Renan. His contention is that these scholars have succeeded in constructing Galilee – the place of the historical Jesus – as an Aryan, non-Jewish territory, and Jesus as a non-Jewish person.[8] He also identifies remnants of this thinking in some twentieth-century constructions. This time, German nationalism was replaced by Israeli, which effectively erased the presence of Palestinians.

Similarly, he has shown how George Adam Smith's popular portrayal of Galilee, in contrast to the German and French construals which were seen through the prisms of nationality, race, and ethnicity, reflected two British class values: the Victorian home and family. The former provided a sheltered sphere of private life, a sealed-off zone against the vices of the city, and the latter inculcated a middle-class national character which was masculine, disciplined, and vigilant.

Similarly, Shawn Kelly has demonstrated how the disciplinary history of modern American biblical scholarship was influenced and compromised by the category of race.[9] Such an influence is at times refined, at times manipulative. In Kelly's view, the compromised position of current biblical scholarship, especially the New Hermeneutic movement in the USA, was due to its dependence on the philosophical and intellectual traditions of Hegel, Heidegger, and Romanticism. The practitioners of the New Hermeneutic movement appropriated the racial overtones entangled in German scholarship without questioning or moderating it.

Keith Whitelam uses Said's *Orientalism* as a way of critiquing biblical scholarship. For him, "biblical studies has been part of, and in many ways an extension of, Orientalist discourse."[10] Biblical scholars, under the influence of orthodox Christian theology and Zionism, and in their quest for Europe's past (and later in their search for the roots of modern Israel), have not only silenced all aspects of the history of Palestine from the Late Bronze Age to the Roman period, but have also presented Palestinians as lacking a cohesive national consciousness, order, and morality. All this is couched in the language of reasonableness and a claim to detachment. Whitelam's suggestion is that, if Palestinian history is to be freed from the tyranny of biblical scholarship, it has to be located elsewhere than in biblical or theological studies departments, and allowed to evolve its own theoretical framework akin to that of the Indian *Subaltern Studies*, which has been contesting and subverting the "master" and "official" historiographies.

For Michael Prior, the hermeneutical task involves coming to terms with the imperial past of the European expansion into Latin America, South Africa, and Palestine, and showing how the fabricated ethnocentric, xenophobic, and militaristic character of the Bible provided the legitimacy and inspiration for such a barbaric enterprise. For him, virtually all of the scholarship related to the question of land, which emerged after the founding of Israel in 1947 and after the 1967 war, has paid little attention to the plight of the indigenous inhabitants of these lands.

Thirdly, the essays in *Interpreting Beyond Borders* address one of the emerging postcolonial concerns of our time: the heavy migration and great movement of people across continents for reasons varying from political persecution to economic advancement. Such migration has produced a state of dislocation and displacement which has become a vantage point for reflection and interpretation. *Interpreting Beyond Borders* focuses on the emerging biblical interpreters from the former colonies, now residing and working in the West, who are examining their multiple identities, and exploring alienation and ethnicity and their longing for a home. Among the biblical stories, the story of Joseph has served to encapsulate many diasporas across many centuries, as a story of exile and alienation, loss and deception.[11]

Besides these writings, there are three anthologies which pursue postcolonial biblical interpretation. These are *John and Postcolonialism*, edited by Musa W. Dube and Jeffrey L. Staley, and two thematic *Semeia* issues: one edited by Laura Donaldson

(*Semeia* 75, 1996) and the other by Roland Boer (*Semeia* 88, 2001). All of these capture the mood, intention, and purpose of postcolonial biblical interpretation as outlined above. *John and Postcolonialism* addresses with critical skill and sensitivity questions of rapid globalization, increased travel, rising diasporic communities, and neo-colonialism. It explores topics such as the appropriation of John's Gospel in settler communities of the United States and Canada, and the use of John in the colonization of Africa, Asia, Latin America, and New Zealand. The essays show how the Johannine text was used to justify the invasion of others' lands, and how the same text can be read for decolonization and emancipation.

The *Semeia* 88 issue has largely to do with the settler and indigenous concerns of Australia, but includes issues related to the Pacific Islands and India. This anthology is an example of an outside intervention by scholars working in the fields of literary, historical, and cultural studies. The issues addressed include the complex ways in which the Bible was introduced to the indigenous people as a totem text of the colonialists' religion; the recovery of the Bible by the indigenous people whose voices were only registered partially in the imperial archives; the deconstruction of the Bible from its usual and safer habitat in English culture; the Bible's place in the rise of nationalism; the powerful indirect presence of the Bible in the public realm through literary works; the implication of the use of the Bible as a tool for education for conversion; the recognition of vernacular translation for nation formation; and the biblical monotheism as represented by both Moses and Jesus, and the reopening of cosmopolitan and many-layered polytheism over against monotheism.

Key Figures

Fernando Segovia

Fernando Segovia is a Cuban American who teaches at Vanderbilt University, Nashville. His chief contribution has been to introduce and work out a theoretical and methodological basis for postcolonial biblical criticism. This work grew out of various sources, both intellectual and experiential. He places postcolonial biblical criticism within the field of cultural studies, especially in terms of ideological criticism. He identifies three postcolonial "optics": shadows of the empire in the production of Judaism and early Christianity, colonial impulses that motor Western interpretation, and the emergence of Third World biblical critics who are trying to subvert both texts and dominant readings. For Segovia, biblical critics fall into two groupings: the vast majority of critics in the West, associated with the imperial tradition beginning with the phase of high imperialism and moving on to the present phase of neo-colonialism, and the minority critics from the former colonies who are raising their voices in the postcolonial phase of imperialism.

For Segovia, the postcolonial engagement in biblical studies is obviously a discourse of resistance and emancipation. The geopolitical relationship between the imperial and the colonial, the center and the margin, provides the interpretive reading lens and theoretical spectrum not only at the level of texts, but also at the level of interpretation, of readings and readers of texts. With decolonization and liberation in mind, what postcolonial biblical criticism does is to highlight the periphery over the center. For Segovia, such a venture is a "cosmopolitical" endeavor.[12] In other words, the postcolonial engagement of resistance and emancipation has to be undertaken with other oppositional discourses involved in similar liberative practices, such as Marxism and feminism. At the same time, Segovia cautions that such a collaborative task has to keep in mind the tainted track record of these discursive practices. The Stalinist-Leninist version of Marxism was as imperialist as any other Western empire, and its history is littered with violations of human rights. Western feminism has exhibited racism and marginalized women who were outside the Euro-American cultural loop.

Segovia's most innovative contribution has been in working out a hermeneutics of diaspora – a Hispanic American hermeneutics of otherness and engagement. The crucial marker of this discourse is the acknowledgment of the contextuality of text. Similarly, the reader is to be seen as culturally and socially conditioned. For Segovia, such a hermeneutics should reflect the diversity not only within Hispanic communities, but also within other diasporas, otherwise diasporic hermeneutics will end up replicating the very thing it repudiates by producing a master narrative with universalizing tendencies.[13]

R. S. Sugirtharajah

The present author, a Sri Lankan currently based at the University of Birmingham, was the first to introduce postcolonial criticism to biblical studies, in an article in *Asia Journal of Theology* in 1996. Both as a theorist and practitioner, my work has sought to identify, delineate, challenge, and expose those dominant and national and nativist interpretations which have become sedimented into "truth." My contention is that historians of biblical interpretation would like to attribute the current biblical discipline to the proud and happy outcome of the Enlightenment and to modernity, whereas the growth and development of the discipline can be traced to a contaminated aspect of modernity: colonialism. The task of tracing these connections is both historical and hermeneutical: historical in the sense of delving into the colonial archives and unearthing the imperial assumptions and intentions of biblical interpretation, as well as those who opposed them; hermeneutical in the sense of trying to re-read biblical narratives in light of such postcolonial concerns as hybridity, race, diaspora, and multiculturalism. My historical readings include a rehabilitation of John Colenso, a firm believer in the redemptive nature of the British empire who nonetheless took Zulu culture seriously in his interpretive efforts and challenged the racialist views of the time; the contestation between John Marshman and Rammohun Roy over the control of the meaning of the Bible; the forgotten biblical work of Olaudah Equiano, the freed slave who in turn was engaged in the abolition of slavery; and Pandita Ramabai's pioneering efforts in biblical translation.

The following five hermeneutical concerns are in my opinion most important. First, the postcolonial is an oppositional practice. It does not mean opposing simply for the sake of opposing, but raising questions and a process of stock-taking which tries to restore and recuperate memories, events, and texts which were suppressed or overlooked. It is a way of critiquing totalizing forms of Eurocentric and missionary thinking which have dominated biblical interpretation. For example, specific New

Testament texts were mobilized to sustain and collude with colonialism and colonial mission. A dormant text like Matthew 28: 19 was reactivated to bolster the missionary enterprise, and the fabrication of Paul's missionary tours in Acts coincided with the emergence of European missionary societies and Western mercantile companies in the eighteenth and nineteenth centuries.

Secondly, Orientalism is a Western misrepresentation of the Other, both in colonial and current biblical scholarship. For example, some of the exegetical conclusions found in a near-classic like Joachim Jeremias' *Parables of Jesus,* a text on which many generations of Third World theological students were raised, contain traces of Eurocentricism despite the claim to "objectivity." Jeremias' exegetical comments on the action of the servant who adjusted the accounts (Luke 16: 1–9) is more in keeping with tabloid journalism than the sober judgment of a dispassionate biblical scholar. (In Jeremias' view, this debt-fixing was because people in the East had no knowledge of accounting or book-keeping.)

Thirdly, there is a connection between colonialism and translation. In the missionary context in which Bible translations were undertaken, the asymmetry between the languages of the Bible, European languages, and vernacular tongues was exploited. All biblical translations were strangely influenced by the ecclesiastical and missionary traditions of parent and overseas churches and by the prevailing denominational theologies of the time. On the other hand, translated versions in the vernacular could enable "natives" to come up with their own unsupervised "counter-translations," which generated meanings unanticipated by the original biblical writers and destabilized the power of the missionaries to maneuver meanings.

Fourthly, contrapuntal reading should be promoted. Such an intertextual reading is a practical strategy to overcome the predominance and one-sided nature of literature which elevates and celebrates Western achievements and contributions. Building on and adapting the framework suggested by Edward Said, such a reading practice will encourage us to study simultaneously the experiences of the marginalized and of the mainstream, and illustrate convergences, absences, and imbalances. Contrapuntal reading is a serviceable strategy for recognizing the mutual theological and cultural strengths of the cosmopolitan *and* the vernacular, rather than permitting one to dominate the other.

Fifthly, there is the question of the prestige and position of the English Bible – the King James Version – the nearest to an epic that the English have had. Reappraising its Englishness highlights its association with English nationalism and its part in generating white mythologies, its pivotal role in the expansion of the empire, and its current position in the periphery of Western culture. In such a conceptualization of the "Englishman's book," we gravitate towards a notion of "book" which is both open and closed, with single and multiple signs, and which continues to preserve and revise the idea of what it means to be a "sacred" text in contemporary culture.

Musa Dube

Musa Dube, from Botswana, is a pioneer in devising postcolonial biblical criticism which integrates feminist concerns, especially those of African women. Her task has been twofold. She takes a closer look at the function of the literary construction of biblical texts so as to understand how, in their portrayals of characters, geography, travelers, and gender relations, they justified colonialism and legitimized the colonizer and colonized positions, thereby perpetuating dependency. She also investigates how mainstream white male and female interpreters, employing various critical practices ranging from historical–critical to literary–rhetorical and social–scientific, encourage readers to enter the world of the biblical writers and their rhetorical language of salvation history and universal mission. These writers, in Dube's view, do so without decolonizing their own positions or acknowledging the presence of empire and the imperial context in the biblical books. They do not problematize the power relations between themselves and their readers, or account for their gender, class, and race privileges. Her aim is to decolonize and depatriarchalize both biblical texts and their interpretations before the texts can be reclaimed for liberative purposes.

Among her many hermeneutical endeavors, Dube's most striking intervention has been to decolonize and depatriarchalize texts related to mission which are central to the New Testament and which feature women. She has demonstrated how female characters of dubious ethical standing and status feature predominantly in the propaganda stories which anticipate universal mission and intrusion into other people's lands and territories. The three key women characters are Rahab the prostitute, John's woman from Samaria (John 4), and Matthew's Canaanite woman (Matthew 15: 21–28). These women are characterized as either impure or feeble and unfit, and as such stand for the helplessness of their own people and thus warrant intervention and subjugation. Dube's concern is that these biblical women are monumentalized in mainstream white feminist discourse for their initiative, independence, and wit, which disregards the imperial impulses in the texts. There is an assumption among some feminist interpreters that the mission to the Gentiles is a liberative enterprise, but such an assumption, in Dube's view, overlooks the predatory nature of colonial expansion. For her, these paradigms are imperial constructions which serve to maintain colonial power.[14] What Dube advocates is a relation of liberating interdependence among races, cultures, and genders.

Dube's other preoccupation has been to subject colonial translation activity to a postcolonial scrutiny. Her particular interest has been to reexamine key colonial enterprises such as biblical translation and dictionary production, which propped up the colonial presence and power. For instance, she has narrated the fate of *Badimo* – ancestral spirits (sacred personalities) – who act as mediators between God and human beings, but are turned into demons, devils, and evil spirits in various dictionaries and versions of the Bible. These renditions show how the Setswana language, for example, was employed for colonial purposes. She has catalogued how in key gospel passages such as the Canaanite woman, Gadarene demoniac, and the commissioning of the disciples, various Setswana versions used *Badimo*, thus producing a negative picture. The Canaanite woman tells Jesus that her daughter is possessed with "High ones" or "Ancestors." In the Gadarene incident the sacred *Badimo* is presented as a tottering figure begging Jesus to leave him alone, and, much worse, Jesus casts *Badimo* out into the pigs. In the commissioning narrative, the disciples were instructed by Jesus to cast out *Badimo*. Instead of seeing *Badimo* as divine beings and as active collaborators with Jesus, they were equated with devils and demons. The intention of such mistranslations, according to Dube, is to warn

Christian believers to stay away from their own Setswana beliefs, which are portrayed as deadly and dangerous. To her surprise, Dube found out that the "natives" were not simply passive receivers of colonial translation, but had devised strategies of resistance to subvert translations which made *Badimo* into devils and demons. They reconfigured the Bible from their cultural perspective and saw it as a divining kit, thus replacing the traditional one, and as a means to get in touch with *Badimo*. Thus, the master's book, which was meant to wean converts from their Setswana culture, is now used as a vehicle to reconnect with that very culture and is seen as advancing and nurturing relationships. What is invoked here is the postcolonial recourse to nativism.[15] Dube's hermeneutical practice both stands within and also advocates Ngugi wa Thiongo's call for decolonizing minds and cultures.

Other significant figures

Roland Boer, from Australia, is one of the few biblical scholars advocating a profit-able Marxist intervention in biblical and postcolonial discourse. Untroubled by the current capitalist triumph, Boer asserts that Marxist theoretical categories are well suited to critique the ravages of the colonial past and the violence of the contemporary world. For him, the disruption of dominant reading practices and the realization of socialist promise in postcolonialism depend largely on the creative alliance between biblical studies and specifically Marxist literary theory and practice. Boer has introduced into colonial discourse analysis the concept of an explorer hermeneutic. This has its genesis in the way in which nineteenth-century white explorers of inland Australia made use of biblical and theological categories. The journals that these pioneering explorers kept were a testimony to their faith and Christian practice in a territory totally alien to them. These journals recount their belief in the Creator, the Almighty, their Maker who is their rock and refuge in times of trouble and tribulation, in the providential nature of their expedition, and their understanding of their own calling and vocation in the designs of colonial enterprise. Boer has also noted the preponderance of biblical imagery and allusion in their disjointed scribblings. These provided a convenient framework to explain some of the "strange" and "exotic" customs of the Aboriginals. The Israelite–Aboriginal links included mourning and burial customs, the use of smoke signals on mountain tops (Jeremiah 6: 1), reverence for elders, hunting methods – especially the use of axes, nets, and spears (Isaiah 24: 17), bodily ornaments such as the wearing of a bracelet of corded hair (2 Samuel 1: 10), the use of hard clay mounds instead of stones for cooking (Genesis 31: 46), magical stones, the method of carrying children on their shoulders (Isaiah 49: 22), and circumcision, which makes Aborigines the true children of Moses. In the view of these explorers, indigenous peoples became "implicit Israelites." Boer's particular interest is in seeing how these biblical and theological ideas play their part in the colonial "gaze," surveillance, and viewing of a previously unknown land. These explorers are in search of a vast canvas and a panoramic view.

The other issues which receive substantial attention in Boer's work are motifs of exodus, exile, and nomadism, and questions of identity and essentialism concerning the Israelites in the Hebrew Bible and Aboriginals and Europeans in the postcolonial Australian context.[16]

Laura Donaldson, who teaches English at Cornell University, is one of the few from outside the biblical discipline who has shown remarkable confidence in handling biblical narratives and applying postcolonial perspectives which highlight the concerns of Native American women. For her, postcolonial biblical hermeneutics should go beyond what she calls a monotheistic reading, a reading which is "so tightly structured by a single principle" that it rules out all other interpretive possibilities latent in the narratives. She advocates theoretically nuanced multiple and diverse strategies which will bring out suppressed or overlooked messages.

Among Donaldson's exegetical works, two exemplify such a stance. One is her reading of Ruth. Donaldson, as a Cherokee woman, tries to reconceptualize the role of Ruth in light of the specific cultural and historical predicament of a Native American woman. Faced with persistent calls for ethnic minorities to integrate and assimilate into mainstream white American culture, she unearths another often erased and under-interpreted indigenous figure, Orpah, the sister-in-law of Ruth, who, unlike Ruth, returns to her mother's house. In Orpah's decision, Donaldson sees a daring act of self- and communal assertion by an indigene who prefers to settle with the vernacular household of her mother rather than with an alien household with an Israelite father. It is Orpah who symbolizes hope and provides emancipatory potential for Cherokee women, because it is she who embraces her own indigeneity, clan, and culture. Seen in the light of Orpah's action, Ruth becomes a different figure.

Donaldson also re-reads Judges 19 and 20. She has shown how mainstream white feminists who highlight the heinous crime done to an unknown woman in Judges 19, fail to look at Judges 20, which provided biblical warrant for the war against the Pequot. Such an oversight, according to Donaldson, was due to the "disturbing myopia" displayed by feminist biblical scholars concerning colonialism and its entanglement within their own interpretive enterprise.

Debate

Among current theories, postcolonialism has been contested from within and from outside. Some of these debates do not have a direct relevance to biblical criticism. However, the emergence of postcolonial biblical criticism has raised questions regarding its relation to other emancipatory critical practices like liberation hermeneutics and feminist discourse, and its perhaps excessive dependence on theory.

Liberation hermeneutics and postcolonialism

Liberation hermeneutics and postcolonial criticism have certain common methodological alliances. Both still cherish certain modernist grand narratives such as liberation and communal harmony. They hold that these still have valid hermeneutical potency and purchase, since their potential has not been realized fully, as is evident in numerous communities and nations where people constantly encounter structural and personal oppression, and in communities torn by ethnic violence. Both liberation hermeneutics and postcolonial criticism take seriously the aspirations and elevation of the subaltern "other," be it women, the poor, dalits, burakumins, or tribals;

neither pretends to an impartial, objective, neutral, and universal reading of a text, but both are committed to an unashamedly biased interpretation which has two foci. One is to resist and liberate, and the other is to disrupt the dominant Western hermeneutical discourse by provincializing it and by the "reversing of the gaze." Neither hesitates to take a political stance and to offer ethical directions and moral vision, while admitting all the time the hazards of such prescriptions.

Although liberation hermeneutics and postcolonial biblical criticism are kindred spirits, they part company on a number of issues. The chief reason for this distancing is the deep-rooted allegiance of liberation hermeneutics to the ideals of modernism, which deters it from seizing on some of the strengths of postmodernism for its liberative cause. As one of the spin-offs of postmodernism, postcolonialism shares its opposition to master narratives and the determinacy of texts, but disassociates itself decisively from such aspects of postmodernism as its devaluation of history, playfulness with texts, and hesitancy to make any political commitment.

There are four areas where the arranged marriage between liberation hermeneutics and postcolonial biblical criticism feels the strain. First, the status and standing of the Bible. While liberation hermeneutics has successfully called into question some of the male-centered, ideologically biased, and anti-poor interpretations of Western biblical scholarship, it has been reluctant to question the authority of the biblical texts themselves. Postcolonial biblical criticism, on the other hand, challenges not only hegemonic biblical interpretations but also the position and prerogative given to the Bible itself. Postcolonial biblical criticism explores the gaps, silences, ambiguities, and complexities embedded within biblical narratives. The efficacy and meanings of the Bible are constantly questioned, whereas liberation hermeneutics is engaged in a re-reading exercise which reinforces the authority of the Bible. For liberation hermeneutics, the problem is not the Bible but the way it has been interpreted. Postcolonialism, on the other hand, sees the Bible as both a problem and a solution, and its message of liberation is seen as far more indeterminate and complicated. It is seen as a text of both emancipation and enervation. Postcolonial reading advocates the emancipation of the Bible from its implication in dominant ideologies at the level both of the text and of interpretation. For postcolonialism, the critical principle is not derived from the Bible alone, but is also determined by contextual needs and other warrants. It sees the Bible alone as one among many liberating texts. Liberation hermeneutics could usefully avail itself of some of the insights advocated by postcolonialism without abandoning or toning down its loyalty to the poor.

Secondly, the privileging of certain biblical motifs. A conspicuous case in point is the Exodus paradigm. In the initial euphoric days of liberation theology, the Exodus narrative became a foundational text, as Romans 1: 16 was for the Reformation. Reading from the oppressed point of view, liberation hermeneutics invested so much in this narrative that it overlooked the fate of the indigenous population which was at the receiving end of the emancipatory action, and the implications of such an interpretation for those who faced disruption and dispersion in their own lands, such as Palestinians, Australian Aborigines, New Zealand Maoris, Native Americans, and Indian tribals. Liberation hermeneutics also fails to raise the troubling question of what sort of God it is who sides with one set of people and neglects the rights of the other by such a liberative act. The God of the Exodus is the God who simultaneously liberates the Jews and enshackles Egyptians and Canaanites. Besides, focusing on liberation, liberation hermeneutics overlooks the elements of enslavement embedded in the very Exodus paradigm which it so fondly promoted. One of the immediate acts of the Israelites after their emancipation from Egypt was to regulate the buying and selling of slaves (Exodus 21: 1–11). Postcolonial biblical criticism, on the other hand, is mindful of the ambivalent nature of the Exodus narrative. Postcolonialism regards the Bible as endorsing both emancipation and enslavement. There has to be sensitivity to the displaced and uprooted people of both biblical and contemporary times.

Thirdly, the focus on the poor. Liberation hermeneutics' view of the poor is a restrictive one, and at times borders on idolization. Liberation hermeneutics is largely confined to the notion of the poor as economically disadvantaged. Where postcolonialism differs is that it recognizes a plurality of oppressions. Unlike liberation hermeneutics, postcolonialism does not perceive the "other" as a homogeneous category, but acknowledges multiple identities based upon class, sex, ethnicity, and gender. In their preferential option, there is a tendency in liberation hermeneutics to romanticize the poor. For example, liberation hermeneutics inclines to project the widow in Mark's Gospel as an exemplar of ideal piety (Mark 12: 41–44). Her piety and sacrifice are seen as standing apart from the futility of the scribal faith and the flaunting acts of the rich. In reading of the widow's mite, postcolonialism does not portray the widow as being applauded by Jesus as a model donor, but as a poor widow who was maneuvered and tricked by the system into giving up what little she possessed. The narrative is not about the endorsement of her action, but a condemnation of the abuse of power wielded by temple treasury authorities. If one sees it from the widow's angle, Jesus was not applauding her action but making an assault upon an institution which was exploitative. The gospels record a number of instances when Jesus pronounced the destruction of the temple system which spawned unequal social structures. Moreover, despite the methodological nuances and innovativeness of its language, the aim of liberation hermeneutics has been the same as in the colonial era – evangelizing the poor. Postcolonial biblical criticism, on the other hand, strives to go beyond the propagandistic tone and aims to locate biblical scholarship in a non-missionary and less apologetical context.

Fourthly, the Christian-centric nature of liberation hermeneutics. Since liberation hermeneutics emerged from Latin America, which is predominantly a Roman Catholic continent, its moral vision has been largely shaped by the Bible. Liberation hermeneutics' call for social change is based on the worldview provided by the Bible and thus overlooks sources other than Christianity. The moral vision expounded by liberation hermeneutics is almost exclusively informed by Christianity, whereas postcolonial biblical interpretation is informed by other major religious traditions as well as the Bible. Christian religion is not placed on a pedestal. It regards revelation as an ongoing process, which is not confined to Christianity. Liberation hermeneutics and postcolonialism share mutual agendas and goals, and hope for and work towards an alternative to the present arrangements. If liberation hermeneutics could abandon its homogenization of the poor, which sits uncomfortably with other constituencies, its unrelieved biblicism, and its lack of awareness of other religious traditions, which tend to dominate its interpretive agenda, it should be able to join forces with postcolonial thinking to work for a different world from the one we live in.

Feminist postcolonial biblical interpretation and feminist interpretation

Postcolonialism, unlike feminism in the West, did not emerge as a vehicle to express individual fulfillment or as a means of self-discovery, but wanted to resolve and rectify the injustice done to the colonized other. Though there is a shared intellectual and vocational mission between postcolonialism and feminist interpretation, Third World feminists distance themselves from the work of Western feminists in three ways:

1　For most First World feminists, patriarchy is at the heart of their interpretation and their aim is to address the devastation it has caused. For Third World feminists, colonialism and patriarchy are together at the center of interpretation.
2　Third World feminists have drawn attention to the fact that colonialism and patriarchy are not the same and that they have been at the receiving end of both. They point out that patriarchy is a phenomenon in which men oppress women, whereas in colonialism both men and women oppress men and women of other societies.
3　Postcolonial feminist biblical scholars like Dube and Donaldson, as noted above, point out that First World biblical scholars in their exegetical work and the reconstruction of the early church, often compromise and overlook the colonial context and content of these biblical materials.

Utilization of theory

There is at the moment a theory-fatigue in certain academic circles and there is even talk of a post-theory stage. There is a general aversion to employing theory because it kills the simple pleasure of reading and blots out the once taken-for-granted commonsensical approach to texts, their language and meaning. Theory can be pretentious and merely a passport to intellectual and academic respectability, its employment merely fashionable. But the lasting achievement of theory has been to inject an intoxicating brew of politics, culture, and ideology into academic discourse, despite its being resisted and loathed by mainstream interpreters. Theory has been useful in complicating and disrupting the unequal status of minority and mainstream scholarship, in elaborating on questions about identity, subjectivity, and sexual orientation, in revising and changing attitudes to empire and colonialism. More to the point, the employment of theory has shown clearly that reading and interpretation are not such harmless and safe pursuits as they are often made out to be.

Achievement and Future Agenda

It is too soon to celebrate the grand hermeneutical achievements of postcolonialism. It may not have moved mountains but, as a resistance category, postcolonial criticism in its own modest way has been able to subvert and embarrass, and to reverse and restore texts, cultures, and subalternities which have over the years accumulated misinterpretation and misrepresentation in Western and nationalistic writings. Postcolonial criticism has resisted the temptation to sanctify many fixed oppositions hitherto maintained – the colonizer as bad, the colonized as innocent; the West as greedy, the East as benevolent; Europe as intellectual, the Orient as spiritual. It has shied away from such a dual framework of "us" and "them." Such a categorization is too neat and fails to reflect the messy interconnections between the two. Postcolonialism has encouraged a more complex cross-cutting way of thinking. Instead of perceiving the West as demonic, it tries to establish a critical conversation which places the accent on mutual exchange and transformation. What is distinctive about the current enterprise is that it sees itself as an inevitable outcome of a complex contact between the former colonizer and the current decolonized. By thus moving beyond such absolutizing, postcolonialism can claim to be an advance. While resistance movements during the colonial period were influenced and constricted by parameters set by the colonialists, the current postcolonial discourse projects itself as a product of contentious reconfiguration of the two. It has crossed the barrier of binary exclusivity and owes its identity neither to the First World nor to the Third World. This new postcolonial space has released Third World interpreters from interpretive pigeon-holes – national, ethnic ghettos into which they were forced to retreat or from which they were told to speak. Postcolonial critics have proved capable of representing and mediating a variety of interests, identities, and constituencies, varying from local to global, vernacular to cosmopolitan. Postcolonial criticism encourages one to be creatively eclectic and to avail oneself of every discourse and methodology as long as they espouse and advance just and liberative causes. Put differently, one can engage in the interpretive task without the anxiety or nostalgia which bedevilled an earlier generation of Third World interpreters.

As for future tasks, firstly, biblical scholarship has not yet succeeded in producing a critique of its own involvement in assisting and reinforcing colonialism. Shawn Kelly and Halvor Moxnes are exceptions. This undertaking should be rooted in a vigorous problematization of some of the cherished achievements of biblical scholarship – historical criticism and the management of other peoples' texts. This reappraisal is long overdue. Much postcolonial work has centered on literary work and textual interpretation. An exclusive form of textual practice and an undue concentration on narratival form and content, important though they are, if done at the expense of social concerns, will take the gloss off postcolonialism's claim to be a liberative discourse. Mere literary resistance is not enough. A theory's credibility is judged by its capacity to shake societal structures that are complacent and arrogant about victimization and victims.

Secondly, much of postcolonialism's earlier appeal and attraction was its inventive fictional writing. It should recapture this genre and produce imaginative hermeneutics than wonder at the marvels of its own theoretical finesse.

Thirdly, postcolonialism has a role of vigilance as never before. Recently, there has been talk of a new imperium by politicians and political commentators in public discourse. The days of empire have not gone; America is seen as the new Rome.

After September 11, 2001 the West, especially the USA, has seized its chance to push through an imperialist agenda accompanied by a noble rhetoric of planting the seeds of democracy, liberty, and human rights in nations ruled by despots. This imperial intervention in public discourse is often redefined as humanitarian assistance and as a liberal enterprise serving both moral and strategic purposes. There is a thin line between humanitarian assistance and the imposition of one's values on other peoples. In light of this new threat, postcolonial hermeneutics has a continual role in reminding of the excesses of the past and dealing with a present which brims with a multitude of competing ideologies and religious claims. One of the enduring lessons of postcolonialism is that no one intervenes in other people's affairs unless there is something to gain from it materially, politically, or ideologically. As Aimé Césaire put it long ago: "No one colonizes innocently."[17]

Notes

1 Said, Edward W. *Orientalism* (London: Penguin Books, 1985).

2 Bhabha, Homi K. *The Location of Cultures* (London: Routledge, 1994).

3 Spivak, Gayatri Chakravorty. "Can the Subaltern Speak?" In Patrick Williams and Laura Chrisman (eds.), *Colonial Discourse and Postcolonial Theory* (New York: Harvester Wheatsheaf, 1993), pp. 66–111.

4 Sugirtharajah, R. S. *Postcolonial Criticism and Biblical Interpretation* (Oxford: Oxford University Press, 2002), pp. 43–73.

5 Carter, Warren. *Matthew and the Margins: A Sociopolitical and Religious Reading* (Maryknoll, NY: Orbis Books, 2000), p. 41.

6 Horsley, Richard A. "Submerged Biblical Histories and Imperial Biblical Studies." In R. S. Sugirtharajah (ed.), *The Postcolonial Bible: The Bible and Postcolonialism 1* (Sheffield: Sheffield Academic Press, 1998), pp. 152–73.

7 Berquist, Jon L. "Postcolonialism and Imperial Motives for Canonization," *Semeia* 75, 1996, pp. 15–35.

8 Moxnes, Halvor. "The Construction of Galilee as a Place for the Historical Jesus: Part I," *Biblical Theology Bulletin* 31 (1) 2001, pp. 26–37.

9 Kelly, Shawn. *Racializing Jesus: Race, Ideology and the Formation of Modern Biblical Scholarship* (London: Routledge, 2002), p. 5.

10 Whitelam, Keith. *The Invention of Ancient Israel: The Silencing of Palestine History* (London: Routledge, 1996), p. 234.

11 See García-Treto, Francisco. "Hyphenating Joseph: A View of Genesis 39–41 from the Cuban Diaspora." In Fernando F. Segovia (ed.), *Interpreting Beyond Borders: The Bible and Postcolonialism 3* (Sheffield: Sheffield Academic Press, 2000).

12 Segovia, Fernando F. *Decolonizing Biblical Studies: A View from the Margins* (Maryknoll, NY: Orbis Books, 2000), p. 141.

13 Segovia, Fernando, F. "Toward a Hermeneutics of the Diaspora: A Hermeneutics of Otherness and Engagement." In Fernando F. Segovia and Mary Ann Tolbert (eds.), *Reading from this Place, Vol. 1: Social Location and Biblical Interpretation in the United States* (Minneapolis, MN: Fortress Press, 1995), pp. 57–73.

14 Dube, Musa W. *Postcolonial Feminist Interpretation of the Bible* (St. Louis, MO: Chalice Press, 2000), pp. 157–84.

15 Dube, Musa W. "Consuming a Colonial Cultural Bomb: Translating *Badimo* into 'Demons' in the Setswana Bible (Matthew 8: 23–34; 15: 22; 10: 8)," *Journal for the Study of the New Testament* 73, 1999, pp. 33–59.

16 Boer, Roland. *Last Stop Before Antarctica: The Bible and Postcolonialism in Australia: The Bible and Postcolonialism 6* (Sheffield Academic Press, 2001), pp. 60–87.

17 Césaire, Aimé. *Discourse on Colonialism* (New York: Monthly Review Press, 1972).

Bibliography

Postcolonial biblical interpretation

Boer, Roland, *Last Stop Before Antarctica: The Bible and Postcolonialism in Australia: The Bible and Postcolonialism 6* (Sheffield: Sheffield Academic Press, 2001).

Dube, Musa W., *Postcolonial Feminist Interpretation of the Bible* (St. Louis, MO: Chalice Press, 2000).

Dube, Musa W. and Jeffrey L. Staley, *John and Postcolonialism: Travel, Space and Power: The Bible and Postcolonialism 7* (Sheffield: Sheffield Academic Press, 2002).

Carter, Warren, *Matthew and the Margins: A Sociopolitical and Religious Reading* (Maryknoll, NY: Orbis Books).

Horsley, Richard A. (ed.), *Paul and Empire: Religion and Power in Roman Imperial Society* (Harrisburg, PA: Trinity Press International, 1997).

—— *Jesus and Empire: The Kingdom of God and the New World Order* (Minneapolis, MN: Fortress Press, 2003).

Jian Dao: A Journal of Bible and Theology 8, "A Postcolonial Discourse" (1997).

Journal for the Study of the New Testament 73, "Postcolonial Perspectives on the New Testament and Its Interpretation, ed. R. S. Sugirtharajah (1999).

Kelly, Shawn, *Racializing Jesus: Race, Ideology and the Formation of Modern Biblical Scholarship* (London: Routleldge, 2002).

Prior, Michael, *The Bible and Colonialism: A Moral Critique* (Sheffield: Sheffield Academic Press, 1997).

Segovia, Fernando F., *Decolonizing Biblical Studies: A View from the Margins* (Maryknoll, NY: Orbis Books, 2000).

—— (ed.), *Interpreting Beyond Borders: The Bible and Postcolonialism 3* (Sheffield: Sheffield Academic Press, 2000).

Sugirtharajah, R. S. (ed.), *The Postcolonial Bible: The Bible and Postcolonialism 1* (Sheffield: Sheffield Academic Press, 1998).

—— *Asian Biblical Hermeneutics and Postcolonialism: Contesting the Interpretations* (Sheffield: Sheffield Academic Press, 1999).

—— *The Bible and the Third World: Precolonial, Colonial and Postcolonial Encounters* (Cambridge: Cambridge University Press, 2001).

—— *Postcolonial Criticism and Biblical Interpretation* (Oxford: Oxford University Press, 2002).

Whitelam, Keith, *The Invention of Ancient Israel: The Silencing of Palestine History* (London: Routledge, 1996).

Semeia 75, "Postcolonialism and Scriptural Reading," ed. Laura Donaldson (1996).

Semeia 88, "A Vanishing Mediator? The Presence/Absence of the Bible in Postcolonialism," ed. Roland Boer (2001).

Postcolonial theory

Adam, Ian and Helen Tiffin, *Past the Last Post: Theorizing Post-Colonialism and Post-Modernism* (Hemel Hempstead: Harvester Wheatsheaf, 1993).

Ashcroft, Bill, Gareth Griffiths, and Helen Tiffin, *Key Concepts in Post-Colonial Studies* (London: Routledge, 1998).

Goldberg, David Theo and Ato Quayson (eds.), *Relocating Postcolonialism* (Oxford: Blackwell, 2002).

Loomba, Ania, *Colonialism/Postcolonialism* (London: Routledge, 1998).

McLeod, John, *Beginning Postcolonialism* (Manchester: Manchester University Press, 2000).

Mongia, Padmini (ed.), *Contemporary Postcolonial Theory: A Reader* (London: Arnold, 1996).

Moore-Gilbert, Bart, *Postcolonial Theory: Contexts, Practices, Politics* (London: Verso, 1997).

Moore-Gilbert, Bart, Gareth Stanton, and Willy Maley, *Postcolonial Criticism* (London: Longman, 1997).

Quayson, Ato, *Postcolonialism: Theory, Practice or Process?* (Cambridge: Polity Press, 2000).

Said, Edward W., *Orientalism* (London: Penguin Books, 1985).

—— *Culture and Imperialism* (London: Chatto and Windus, 1993).

Schwarz, Henry and Ray Sangeeta (ed.), *A Companion to Postcolonial Studies* (Oxford: Blackwell, 2000).

Young, Robert J. C., *Postcolonialism: An Historical Introduction* (Oxford: Blackwell, 2001).

Global Engagements

In the twenty-first century, theology can as never before be conducted in, and as, global conversation. The theologies discussed in Part VI reflect internationally significant strands of Christian life and practice and are developed through global and intercultural engagement. All have often been marginalized in the study of theology in Western Europe and North America, but all are of great and ongoing significance for contemporary theology.

The ecumenical movement is perhaps one of the most obvious signs of the twentieth-century "globalizing" of theology's conversations. Mary Tanner traces the theological achievements of the ecumenical movement – with the distinctive issues and possibilities they raise, particularly in the areas of theological method and ecclesiology, which cannot be separated from wider questions about the identity of God and the vocation of humanity.

Rowan Williams' chapter on Orthodox theology, revised for this volume by A. M. Allchin and Peter C. Bouteneff, begins with a focus on Russia as the centre of Orthodox intellectual life for much of the twentieth century. S. N. Bulgakov, the Marxist economist turned philosopher and theologian, V. N. Lossky, the influential proponent of "negative theology," and G. V. Florovsky are discussed in detail. An extensive final survey of current Eastern Orthodox theology highlights points of growth in Western and Eastern Europe and worldwide.

Allan Anderson, in his chapter on Pentecostal theology, deals with an approach to theology that rose to global prominence in the twentieth century and that continues to grow rapidly in worldwide influence. Pentecostal and charismatic theology begins, as Anderson describes it, from the experience of "personal encounter with the Spirit of God," and this leads to distinctive theological accounts not only of pneumatology, but also of the Bible, of eschatology, and of the life of faith.

Finally, David F. Wells discusses the efforts of Evangelical theologians worldwide to maintain and render comprehensible in a postmodern age the central Reformation insights of *sola scriptura* and *solus Christus* – scripture as the "normative interpretive framework by which reality is to be understood," and the "indispensable centrality of Christ's Cross understood in terms of penal substitution."

Ecumenical Theology

Mary Tanner

Introduction

Ecumenical theology is the result of theological reflection oriented to the goal of unity: the unity of the church, the unity of humankind, and the unity of creation, in the perspective of the Kingdom of God. Ecumenical theology is done in a variety of contexts: local, national, regional, and international. An increasingly diverse group of men and women, from all continents and from many church traditions, during the last hundred years, have been drawn into the process of ecumenical theological reflection. The major currents of theological thought – biblical and historical theology, systematic theology, feminist theologies, liberation theologies – have influenced ecumenical theology. Leading theologians in these fields have been directly involved in the ecumenical enterprise, among them Karl Barth, Paul Tillich, Raymond Brown, Geoffrey Lampe, Yves Congar, Karl Rahner, Wolfhart Pannenburg, Jürgen Moltmann, John Zizioulas, Gustavo Gutierrez, Miguez Bonino, Letty Russell, Elisabeth Schüssler Fiorenza, and Phyllis Trible, to name a few. Churches of the Western tradition have brought a classical, rational, intellectual approach to the enterprise and churches of the Eastern tradition an experiential, non-intellectual, non-rational, sacramental, apophatic way of doing theology. Some of the most creative theological thought of the last century has emerged in this rich, diverse ecumenical movement with its primary concern for unity. It helps to understand the development of ecumenical theology to know a little of the history of the ecumenical movement.

Ecumenical Theology within the International Community of the World Council of Churches

The modern ecumenical movement had its origins in the missionary movements at the end of the nineteenth and beginning of the twentieth centuries, when the mainline Protestant churches began joining together in missionary endeavors. At first, denominational differences were relatively unimportant. What was important was cooperation rather than competition in missionary outreach. It was at the World

Mission Conference in Edinburgh, in 1910, often described as the beginning of the ecumenical movement, that an Episcopalian from the USA, Bishop Brent, pointed to the need for denominations to overcome their differences and to search for agreement in those areas which had once been the cause of division. This led to the First World Conference on Faith and Order in Lausanne, Switzerland, in 1927, which brought together Protestant, Anglican, Lutheran, and some Orthodox Christians in order to examine church-dividing issues. Two years before Lausanne another movement across the churches, the Life and Work movement, met in a World Conference in Stockholm, Sweden. The participants were convinced that the way for Christians to get together was to work together at social, industrial, and political issues, while agreeing to disagree on matters of faith and order.

These three streams of ecumenical activity became the founding movements of the World Council of Churches, inaugurated in 1948. First, Faith and Order and Life and Work came together. Then, in 1961, they were joined by the missionary movement. Although the WCC has changed considerably since its foundation in 1948, the three streams are still recognizable in its current programs and activities.

From the outset a tension was apparent between two types of ecumenism: the *reflective*, directed at finding agreement in faith, sufficient and required for the visible unity of the church, and the *practical*, which found unity in action, whether in mission or in responding to the needs of the world. Over the next sixty years that tension continued. The WCC has struggled, and still struggles, to articulate a coherent ecumenical theology which can hold together the diverse insights and activities of the different streams of ecumenical endeavor. This struggle goes on within an ecumenical community that has become increasingly diverse. What began as a largely European and North American community now embraces Christians from every cultural context. The number of member churches has also increased, each bringing with it its own characteristic tradition. After Vatican II the Roman Catholic Church joined the Faith and Order Commission of the WCC but remained outside the Council, while supporting a number of its programs and studies. What began as an almost exclusively white, male, academic, ordained group, now embraces women, laity, and younger representatives from different continents and ecclesial traditions. This increasingly diverse community provides an exciting forum in which to reflect theologically on unity. There is no doubt that, in spite of inevitable tensions in the ecumenical movement, the World Council of Churches is potentially the most creative forum in which to engage in ecumenical theology.

When it was first set up in 1948 the basis of the WCC was Christological: "The World Council is a fellowship of churches which accept our Lord Jesus Christ as God and Savior." But, partly as a result of increased participation of Orthodox churches with their emphasis on the work of the Holy Spirit, the New Delhi General Assembly in 1961 accepted an expanded basis incorporating reference to the Holy Spirit and placing the Christocentric basis in a trinitarian perspective: "The World Council of Churches is a fellowship of churches which confess the Lord Jesus Christ as God and Savior according to the scriptures and therefore seek to fulfill together their common calling to the glory of the One God, Father, Son, and Holy Spirit."

New Delhi was also the first Assembly to attempt a concise description of the conditions and expressions of the unity of the church, the goal of the ecumenical movement. The source of unity was affirmed in its report as "the love of the Father for the Son in the unity of the Holy Spirit." The church was understood as the way in which Christians already share in the divine trinitarian life. Within this trinitarian perspective the report holds together the unity of the church, the unity of human-kind, and the unity of creation, and looks to the consummation of all things in the perfect union of the Son, with the Father, through the power of the Holy Spirit. The report freely acknowledges that differences remained about the precise defini-tion of ecclesial unity and also the means of achieving it.

The move to an explicit trinitarian and Spirit-filled understanding of the purposes of God and the nature and vocation of the church marked a significant stage in ecumenical theology. It owed much to the influence of Orthodox theologians, among them Alexander Schmemann, John Meyendorf, Nikos Nissiotis, and John Zizioulas. Nevertheless, the WCC continued to struggle, and still does, to account theologically for the relationship of the church to the world in the perspective of the Kingdom of God. Those whose primary concern has been with the unity of the church have been accused of promoting a narrow agenda which looks back to a golden age of a united church, which in fact never existed, an agenda so concerned for unity that it appears to promote uniformity with little room for either diversity or for concern for the struggles for justice, peace, and the care of creation. On the other hand, those engaged in social, political, and economic struggles are sometimes accused of taking over the world's agenda and becoming simply another humanitar-ian organization, dismissing questions of the nature of the church, its unity, and graced life. Nevertheless, at times some programs emanating primarily from the Life and Work stream of the Council have produced crucial insights for enriching an understanding of the unity of the church. For example, the Program to Combat Racism in the 1970s, inspired by liberation theologians like James Cone, Tissa Ballisurya, and Desmond Tutu, showed clearly that if the church was to be a "prophetic sign" and an "effective instrument" in the struggles of this world, then churches had not only to overcome doctrinal differences, but also were required to overcome all forms of divisions and discrimination within their own lives.[1] Unity and renewal cannot be separated: they belong together. The same lesson came from the study, *The Community of Women and Men in the Church*.[2] What at first seemed to be a women's liberation struggle, taken over from the secular women's movement, was shown to be a profoundly theological study with implications for an under-standing of the doctrine of God, of men and women created and redeemed in the image of God, as well as for the life of the church, its liturgical language, its ways of doing theology, its sacraments and ministry. Many feminist theologians from academia contributed to this development in ecumenical theology: Letty Russell, Elisabeth Schüssler Fiorenza, Phyllis Trible, and Elisabeth Moltmann-Wendel. In a similar way, more recently, the program on Justice, Peace, and the Integrity of Creation resulted in new thinking on the church as "moral community" and unity came to be understood as "costly unity," and commitment together to the gospel, "costly commitment."[3]

The Canberra Assembly in 1998 was the first Assembly to have as its theme the third person of the Holy Trinity: "Come Holy Spirit, Renew the Whole Creation."[4] The two opening theological presentations could hardly have differed more. They served to highlight a growing tension in the theological stance of the ecumenical community. The Orthodox theologian Parthenios, Patriarch of Alexandria and All

Africa offered a profound reflection on the theme from deep within Orthodox tradition. His presentation placed pneumatology in a trinitarian perspective, emphasizing the need for the unity of the church, because without unity the Spirit's action is hindered within the church and thus its mission, its service to humanity, and its stewardship of creation are weakened. The Spirit's action in the church he related to the Spirit's action in the world outside the church. In this presentation the unity of the church as gift of the Spirit was placed at the center of ecumenical theology, while at the same time there was no separation of the church and its unity from the unity of the whole of humanity and of creation.

The second presentation from a Korean feminist theologian, Chung Hyan Kyung, interpreted the theme of the Assembly in music and drama, with feminist and Korean motifs, and appeared, to some, to identify the *Han*-ridden spirits of Korean culture with the Holy Spirit.

These two very different introductions to the theme of the Assembly highlighted a major difference between theological reflection done primarily from the perspectives of tradition and theological reflection, which begins from a particular cultural context. Sharp questions were implicitly raised about method in theological reflection, the role of tradition, and the role of contextual specificity. There were other questions, too. Is the Holy Spirit just one among many spirits? Does the Holy Spirit act in the world apart from the reality of the church? Does revelation come through other religions? Should all that is good and positive be attributed to the Christian God and are all cultures equally valid in helping to understand the Christian faith as the Greco-Roman culture? The theme of the Assembly thus opened up in a sharp way questions concerning the relation between gospel and culture. Can there ever be visible communion between churches which are incarnated in very different cultural contexts? Does the very diversity of cultural contexts militate against unity?

The two presentations had a further effect. Some Orthodox and some Evangelical participants were forced to ask themselves whether they could any longer belong to a fellowship of churches with such radical questioning of the tradition – of the trinitarian God, salvation, the good news of the gospel, and the church. Two Orthodox churches in time left the WCC and only after a seven year discussion between Orthodox and other member churches has the WCC endorsed the intention that member churches should reaffirm commitment to the trinitarian basis of the WCC and to ecclesiology as lying at the heart of the WCC's agenda.

Konrad Raiser, the General Secretary of the WCC from 1993 to 2003, has described the current ecumenical movement as ecumenism in transition.[5] He identifies a paradigm shift in the ecumenical movement, a shift with three main emphases: (1) a trinitarian understanding of the divine reality and of the relation between God, the world, and humankind; (2) life, understood as a web of reciprocal relationships, as a central point of reference (instead of history); and (3) an understanding of the one church in each place and in all places as a fellowship in the sense of a community of those who are different from one another. This shift entails beginning ecumenical theology with the *oikumene*, understood as the household of life, created and preserved by God, with its connections both between people and societies in infinite variety, and between the world of humankind and creation. This paradigm shift endorses the move from a Christocentric to a trinitarian view, emphasizing a social doctrine of the Trinity (following Moltmann and Boff), with a concept of perichoresis (mutual interpenetration of the persons), a communion of different persons. At the same time, it appears to emphasize the goal of the ecumenical movement as being a diversity of churches bound together in fellowship in the conciliar process of justice, peace, and the integrity of creation, rather than one church united in faith, sacraments, and ministry, manifesting its baptismal unity to the glory of the One God and for the sake of the world. The goal appears to be a fellowship of different ecclesial bodies that remain distinct. The vision of the church is one of reconciled diversity, where diversity rather than unity is the overriding characteristic. Whether this paradigm shift is one that will finally govern the ecumenical movement remains to be seen. Konrad Raiser has helped to raise some fundamental questions.

Ecumenical Theological Conversations

Achievements of the multilateral conversation

While ecumenical theological reflection is done within and between the varied programs of the WCC, the Faith and Order Commission holds a special responsibility for sustained ecumenical theological reflection. The fact that the Roman Catholic Church and some conservative evangelical churches have joined the Commission, but not the Council itself, makes Faith and Order the most comprehensive forum in which to do ecumenical theology.

The agenda for the Faith and Order theological conversation was largely set at the First World Conference in 1927. One of the strengths of the Commission has been its patient development of that agenda for more than 75 years. The agenda included issues of the confession of faith, the nature of the church, the sacraments and ministry, and the unity of Christendom. The formulation of the Chicago–Lambeth Quadrilateral by Anglican bishops at the 1888 Lambeth Conference had a considerable effect on the ecumenical agenda. The Quadrilateral emphasizes four characteristics for unity: the scriptures as the rule and ultimate standard of faith; the Apostles' and Nicene Creeds as sufficient for confession and teaching; baptism and the Lord's Supper as the two dominical sacraments; and the historic episcopate, locally adapted as a unifying ministry. Participants at the 1927 Faith and Order Conference explored their subjects using a comparative method, appropriate to a time when the churches were coming out of their isolation and getting to know their differences. They aimed at discovering what diversity is in fact essentially cohesive and consonant and what might remain church-dividing.

A major step forward for ecumenical theology came at the Fourth World Conference in Montreal in 1963, when a shift in ecumenical method opened up the way for a new period in ecumenical theology. Montreal helped the churches to overcome the polarization between those who appeared to affirm the principle of *sola scriptura* in doing theology and those who were guided by the tradition of the church. Montreal held that the one tradition is witnessed to in scripture and transmitted by the Holy Spirit through the church and finds its expression within the various traditions of individual churches. With this understanding, Montreal helped to overcome the divide between those who appealed only to scripture and those who appealed to the church's tradition by showing that the hermeneutical criteria referred to by different ecclesial traditions in fact properly belong together. Scripture is itself within the tradition of the church and tradition is passed on, with different emphases, within the traditions of all the churches. This opened the way for the ecumenical community to move from a comparative method in ecumenical theology to a consensus/convergence method. By returning together to the primary sources, the tradition of the gospel testified to in scripture, transmitted in and by the church, with a special emphasis on the patristic sources, theologians from different churches began to set down together a common understanding of the faith, the church, the sacraments, and the ministry, and, within the considerable agreement that they discovered in the ancient tradition, they were able to look at disagreements in a new way.

The most important result of this new methodology was published in 1982, *Baptism, Eucharist and Ministry* (BEM), probably the most widely distributed ecumenical document of the twentieth century.[6] BEM is a convergence text recording what theologians from widely different traditions – Catholic, Orthodox, Evangelical, Pentecostal – believed they could agree about baptism, Eucharist, and the ordained ministry. Accompanying commentaries record historic differences that have been overcome, or identify disputed issues needing reconciliation. BEM was widely studied and six volumes of official responses from the churches, as well as a response to the responses by the Faith and Order Commission, were published.[7]

Together, these reports are a valuable ecumenical theological resource. They show where breakthroughs in understanding have occurred as, for example, in the use of the biblical notion of *anamnesis* (memorial) to understand the way in which the Eucharist may be thought of as sacrifice, not as repetition of the once-for-all sacrifice of Christ on the cross, but as a memorial, not a "bare memorial," and one that ensures that the benefits of Christ's passion become a present, gifted reality for the eucharistic community.

Advance is made too on the understanding of the real presence of Christ in the Eucharist in the whole eucharistic celebration and in the bread and the wine. "While Christ's real presence in the Eucharist does not depend on the faith of the individual, all agree that to discern the body and blood of Christ, faith is required." Moreover, "It is in virtue of the living word of Christ and by the power of the Holy Spirit that the bread and wine become the sacramental signs of Christ's body and blood. They remain so for the purpose of communion."

The section on baptism goes a long way to reconciling those who baptize both infants and adults and those who baptize only adults. The section on the ministry makes progress in the understanding of the threefold ministry, suggesting that the threefold ministry may be both a sign of unity and the way to unity.

BEM is a remarkable result of ecumenical theology. Among questions raised by churches in response to the document was whether there lies behind the document a consistent and integrated doctrine of the church.

By the 1970s the Faith and Order discussion had identified three requirements for visible unity: a common confession of the apostolic faith, common sacraments and ministry, and ways of deciding together and teaching with authority. With substantial work already accomplished on sacraments and ministry, the Commission turned to the first item, the confession of faith. Taking the Nicene–Constantinopolitan

Creed as the most ancient and most widely used Creed, the Commission examined how the Creed encapsulates the faith of holy scriptures and also what are the major challenges to that faith today; challenges from the very existence, as well as the beliefs, of other faith communities, secularism, and modern scientific and technological advances.[8]

In *Confessing the One Faith* the Commission offers an ecumenical explication of the apostolic faith of the church, grounded in holy scripture and set forth in the Creed. The Commission hoped that this explication would help churches to recognize the one apostolic faith so that they could then confess it together. The report has important reflections on God as creator, the fatherhood of God, the Incarnation, and the procession of the Holy Spirit. On this latter issue the report sums up a lengthy ecumenical discussion on the procession of the Holy Spirit from the Father in the original form of the Creed and the implication of the addition, by the Western tradition, of the clause "and the Son" (the *filioque* clause). It suggests that despite the controversy created by the introduction of the term *filioque* by Western Christians to express the relation between the Father and the Son, both Western and Eastern Christians have wished to be faithful to the credal affirmation that the Spirit proceeds from the Father. They agree that the intimate relation between the Father and the Son and the Spirit is to be affirmed, without giving any impression that the Spirit is subordinate to the Son. Many leading biblical and systematic theologians contributed to this ambitious study in ecumenical theology, including Walter Kasper, Wolfhart Pannenburg, Jean Tillard, Nicholas Lossky, Geoffrey Wainwright, and Metropolitan Dr. Bartholomew of Chalcedon, now His All Holiness the Ecumenical Patriarch of Constantinople.

The Faith and Order Commission has not, as yet, produced a major study on the third requirement for unity – ways of deciding together and teaching with authority. The Commission passed from work on the three requirements for ecclesial unity to study ecclesiology. The theme of the Fifth World Conference on Faith and Order in Santiago de Compostela in 1993 – *Towards Koinonia in faith, life, and witness* – provided a theological framework for holding together an understanding of the nature of the church as koinonia, its faith, sacramental life, ministry, and its witness in the world.[9] The biblical concept of koinonia, variously translated as "communion," "participation," "sharing," and "community," proved to be the most promising theme for creative thinking about the church and its unity. Koinonia grounds the theology of the church in the life of the Triune God, who is koinonia. The conference explored what sort of church would reflect the participation that Christians have, through baptism, in the divine trinitarian life of communion. The insights of John Zizioulas influenced the discussion, as he argued that in a theology of communion all the life and structures of the church must be relational. The theme opened up new insights on the unity and diversity of the church, the relation of the local church to the universal church, the ministry of oversight exercised within the community and not above it, and the ministry of authority in the service of communion.

After the Conference the Commission continued to work on ecclesiology, publishing in 1998 the study document *The Nature and Purpose of the Church*.[10] Although the report begins with the church as *creatura verbi* (creation of the word) and *creatura spiritu* (creation of the Spirit), the understanding of the church as koinonia remains central in the text. Communion refers to the life of love of the three persons of the Trinity. God's intention in creation was to establish communion between God and humanity and the whole of creation. Communion is thus grounded in the order of creation itself, in the natural relations of family and kinship, of tribe and people, and in the good things of creation. The life of communion in the church builds upon and transforms, but never wholly replaces, the koinonia in the order of creation. The visible koinonia of the church is to demonstrate what God intends for the whole of humanity and creation – a foretaste of the kingdom. The report examines what maintains and nurtures the life of communion and hints at what is necessary for churches to move from partial communion to full communion. The report is a first attempt to state convergence in the area of ecclesiology, as BEM did for the sacraments and the ministry. It remains to be seen whether this work, when it is developed, will provide an ecclesiology which will be received by the churches.

Faith and Order has tried since the 1970s to hold its understanding of the church and its unity within a broader framework of the unity of humankind, though this has proved to be more difficult than might be expected. The report *Church and World* explores the essential link between the vocation of the church and the destiny of the world in the perspective of God's kingdom. *Church and World* lays much stress on the vocation of the church as "foretaste," "mystery," and "prophetic sign" of the Kingdom of God in and for the world. Without this wider perspective the task of overcoming theological differences that were the cause of church divisions is in danger of appearing inward looking, a luxury in the face of the brokenness and injustice of the world.

Bilateral theological conversations

It is hard to overestimate the effect that the Second Vatican Council, which ended in 1968, had on the development of ecumenical theology. Pius XI's encyclical *Mortalium animos* (1928) forbade Roman Catholics to participate in the developing ecumenical movement. But little more than forty years later, in his opening talk to the Council, Pope John XXIII emphasized the church's duty to work actively for "the full visible unity in truth" among all Christians. The Decree on Ecumenism, *Unitatis redintegratio*, acknowledged that other Christians are, by faith in Christ and baptism, in some measure of communion, albeit "imperfect communion" with the Roman Catholic Church.[11] Moreover, while the one church of Christ "subsists in" the Roman Catholic Church, other churches and ecclesial communities "are not without significance in the mystery of salvation." Following the Council, Roman Catholic theologians became major contributors to the development of ecumenical theology.

The entry of the Roman Catholic Church into the ecumenical movement led to a period of intense theological conversation in bilateral partnerships. The Roman Catholic Church began conversations with Orthodox, Methodist, Anglican, Lutheran, and Reformed partners, who in turn entered bilateral conversations with one another. The number of conversations has increased dramatically with Oriental Orthodox, Old Catholics, Baptist, Disciples, Pentecostals, Evangelicals, and Adventists forming a complex network of theological conversations. The reports of these conversations are published in two major volumes: *Growth in Agreement I and II.*[12] These volumes contain reports of conversations between 1970 and 2000 and are a rich resource of ecumenical theology.

The conversations differ according to whether their aim is the reestablishment of full communion, as in the case of the Roman Catholic–Eastern Orthodox dialogue, or simply to clarify differences in order to increase cooperation, as in the case of the Baptist–Lutheran conversations. The subjects covered in the dialogues are mostly dogmatic matters: the faith, ecclesiology, sacraments and ministry, tradition, and authority, though the Anglican–Roman Catholic conversation has tackled the subject of morals. The choice of subject is largely determined by the original cause of division. Many of the conversations show the influence of Montreal's breakthrough on scripture and tradition. They work with the method of going back to scripture and the ancient tradition of the church and seek to express the faith together in fresh language, which is not marked by the polemics of past division. However, some dialogues acknowledge a difference between the partners, both on theology and method. The Baptists in conversation with the Roman Catholics, for example, say that they rely on the Reformation principle of *sola scriptura*, interpreted under the guidance of the Holy Spirit, while Roman Catholics move from the scriptures interpreted in the light of the tradition under the leadership of the Magisterium in a communal process guided by the Holy Spirit.

In common with multilateral dialogue, the concept that links many of the reports is the biblical concept of koinonia, understood as the fundamental reality of the church. As the Methodist–Roman Catholic report insists, koinonia is not simply another model of the church.[13] It is the fundamental reality to which many biblical images point: "the Bride of Christ," "the household of God," "the vine," the Temple of the Lord." The emphasis on koinonia in the theological conversations opens up new avenues. First, it enables divided churches to recognize that they are already bound together in the communion of God's own life and love. So, Anglicans and Roman Catholics affirm that they are already in a "real though imperfect communion," they can recognize "the profound measure of communion" that exists, both within and between them. Methodists and Roman Catholics say that they already enjoy a "certain measure of ecclesial communion," and Pentecostals and Roman Catholics recognize "a certain though imperfect communion" binding them to one another, making a degree of common mission possible.

Secondly, the recognition of an already existing degree of communion opens the way for a step by step approach to unity. The most detailed working out of this journey by stages comes in the exciting Lutheran–Roman Catholic report *Facing Unity*, which sketches in some detail the different steps to be taken, the different stages to be reached, on the way from partial communion to full communion.[14] Thirdly, the emphasis on koinonia provides a theological framework in which to view remaining areas of difference.

While the theme of koinonia is common to many of the reports, there is a difference of opinion on what features of church life would properly belong to a fully, visible, ecclesial communion. The Anglican–Roman Catholic report, *Church as Communion*, suggests that the constitutive elements of communion are the common confession of the apostolic faith, revealed in scripture and set forth in the Catholic Creeds, with the acceptance of the same moral values, the same vision of humanity and hope in the final consummation of all things; a common baptism; celebration of one Eucharist; the leadership of the apostolic ministry with oversight entrusted to the episcopate, which holds the local church in communion with all the local churches; and a ministry of oversight having collegial and primatial expressions and open to the communities' participation in discovering God's will.[15] To these features of visible communion it adds the ministry of a universal primate as a visible focus of unity. These are not separable items but an interrelated package belonging to a fully visible ecclesial communion.

The Eastern Orthodox–Roman Catholic report, *Faith, Sacraments and the Unity of the Church*, emphasizes even more strongly the interrelation between the various constitutive elements.[16] So communion in faith is increased by sacramental communion, for every sacrament presupposes and expresses the faith of the church. The ministry maintains and guarantees the growth of communion in faith and sacraments. Thus, visible communion is only possible if churches have the faith, the sacraments, and the ministry in common. To this is added in a subsequent report the threefold ministry with apostolic succession, together with the possibility of taking council together and a ministry of primacy.

In contrast, reports from Reformation churches differ in what they agree are the necessary items for visible unity. For instance, the Reformed–Lutheran report, *Towards Church Fellowship*, affirms that full agreement in the right teaching/preaching of the gospel and the right administration of sacraments is both necessary and sufficient for the true unity of the church.[17] However, it goes on to suggest that there should be no separation between ministerial structure and church organization and the church-constituting elements of faith and sacraments. But there is no suggestion that a single ministry, episcopal succession, or collegial and primatial characteristics are constitutive of "full communion."

While there appear to be different understandings of what constitutes visible unity, there are convergences in understanding several of the characteristics of visible unity. In the area of faith there is agreement between the Eastern Orthodox and the Oriental Orthodox churches, as well as between the Roman Catholic and Oriental Orthodox churches, on Christology. In many conversations with the Orthodox the doctrine of the Trinity is brought back into the center of religious thought and life. As in the multilateral discussions, there is recognition that the *filioque* clause in the Western version of the Nicene Creed is no longer a dividing matter and some churches have, as a result, dropped the clause in liturgical celebrations. Reformed and Orthodox consider that their agreement on the Trinity cuts across the past mistaken polarized views of the doctrine of the Holy Trinity, according to which Latin theology moves from the oneness of God to the three persons of the Father, the Son, and the Holy Spirit, while Greek theology moves from the three persons of the Father, the Son, and the Holy Spirit to the oneness of God. Their current statement is preeminently a statement on the tri-unity of God as Trinity in unity and unity in Trinity.[18]

A third major breakthrough toward a common affirmation of the faith is in the area of the doctrine of justification. The most remarkable advance is found in the Lutheran–Roman Catholic dialogue. The results of lengthy studies are summed up in the *Joint Declaration on the Doctrine of Justification, 1999*,[19] which states that Lutherans and Roman Catholics:

are now able to articulate a common understanding of our justification by God's grace through faith in Christ. It does not cover all that either church teaches about justification; it does encompass a consensus on basic truths of the doctrine of justification and shows that the remaining differences in its explication are no longer the occasion for doctrinal condemnations.[20]

To have reached such agreement on an issue that lay at the heart of the Reformation divide is a remarkable achievement of ecumenical theology.

In their treatment of sacraments and ministry many of the bilateral reports affirm the agreements found in BEM. This helps to maintain a consistency between the conversations. Nevertheless, there remain areas of difference between some partners in each of these three areas. Baptists and Roman Catholics, for example, identify the difference between Baptists who baptize on personal testimony of faith and Roman Catholics (and others) who practice both adult and infant baptism. But even here the positions are not thought to be static and the report recognizes the need to reflect further together on whether faith is solely an individual response.[21]

Disciples and Roman Catholics believe "on the whole" they have great agreement on the understanding of the Eucharist, but they still need to discuss in more depth the nature of the presence of Christ in the Eucharist and the question of episcopacy as the institution necessary for an authentic celebration.[22]

The question of episcopacy remains an issue between those churches that have bishops and those that do not. But the focus of the discussion has shifted in helpful ways. There is agreement that the ministry of *episcope* (oversight) is exercised in different "modes" – personal, collegial, and communal – and that different churches emphasize one mode rather than another. The question for every church is how a right balance between the three dimensions can be restored so that they each serve the unity of the church.

The relation of episcopacy to the apostolicity and succession of the church is another issue discussed in a number of dialogues. There is a difference on the one hand between those churches (Eastern and Oriental Orthodox and Roman Catholic, in particular) who hold that bishops are a *sine qua non* for the visible unity of the church and who describe bishops as the successors of the apostles, the faithful "guarantors" of the catholicity and apostolicity of the church, and on the other hand, those who do not hold this. The treatment of apostolicity and succession in the Orthodox–Roman Catholic dialogue is promising. It moves away from viewing apostolic succession as tactile succession of hands on heads. Apostolic succession is described rather as being continuing fidelity to the apostles' teaching and mission, transmitted through local churches in which the bishop is located, rather than through a succession of isolated individuals. Apostolic succession is succession in a church that witnesses to the apostolic faith, in communion with the other churches, who are witnesses of the same apostolic faith.[23] The stress on the faithful continuity with apostolic teaching and mission, together with the refusal to separate the bishop from the community of faith, may open the way for fruitful discussion in future between churches that have bishops in the historic succession and those who do not.

Just as there are signs that future conversation on apostolicity and succession may make progress, so too there are similar signs of hope on the understanding of a ministry of universal primacy. Methodists, Anglicans, Orthodox, Old Catholics, Disciples, and Lutherans are among those who have approached the subject with Roman Catholic partners and have agreed the importance of the ministry of a person who can focus the unity of the church. What is, however, unacceptable to them is the automatic right of a primate to intervene arbitrarily in affairs of a diocese, or to claim universal jurisdiction, or to exercise primacy apart from collegiality, or to claim infallibility. Infallibility is regarded by many as applicable only to God. A more recent report from the Anglican–Roman Catholic Commission, *The Gift of Authority*, explores the ministry of the bishop of Rome within the context of the life of the whole church and within the collegiality of all the bishops from which the ministry of primacy is never to be divorced. Infallible teaching is the task of the whole church, though on occasions the bishop of Rome may, within the college, discern and declare the mind of the church and that teaching, in accordance with scripture, which will be received by the faithful.[24]

These reports mark the beginning of an important conversation on the ministry of universal primacy. Future discussions may well be helped by Pope John Paul's invitation to all churches, given in his encyclical *Ut unum sint*, to help him understand his ministry in the service of the unity of the church. As the Roman Catholic Church maintains that the ministry of the bishop of Rome is integral to the full visible unity of the church, this must be a crucial subject for both bilateral and multilateral theological conversations.

The motivating force behind these theological conversations continues to be the one that lay behind the calling of the First World Conference on Faith and Order in 1927, namely, the unity of the church for the sake of the mission of the church. Particularly interesting are the reflections on mission, evangelism, and proselytism in the two conversations between the Roman Catholic Church and the Evangelicals and the Pentecostals. Both show that when Christians get to know one another and come to respect one another, although their aim may not be visible unity and although there remain big differences in the area of doctrine, nevertheless, there is still a possibility to witness together on the basis of common faith in the gospel message.

Reception

The results of ecumenical theological conversations were never intended to remain as documents on library shelves. The aim is that they should act as instruments to bring churches closer to one another in a life of shared faith, sacraments, and mission. In recent years much attention has been given to how churches can receive the fruits of theological conversation in such a way that their internal lives are renewed and their relations with others are deepened. A helpful distinction has been made between the official response of the churches to a theological agreed statement and the absorbing of those agreements in renewed lives and changed relationships. Both properly belong to what has been called the process of reception.

When *Baptism, Eucharist and Ministry* was sent to the churches it was accompanied by carefully crafted questions. The first asked whether a church could recognize in the report "the faith of the church through the ages." No church was being asked in the first instance to compare it with its own confessional statements but, rather, with scripture and the tradition of the church. Churches were asked two further questions. First, they were invited to consider if they were able to recognize the faith of the church in the theological agreement and what changes they needed to make in their own internal life in order to live in conformity with that faith. Secondly, they were asked to consider what changes in relationships were appropriate with those who could also recognize the faith of the church in the report.

In a similar way, *The Final Report of the Anglican–Roman Catholic Commission* was sent to the two churches with two questions. The first invited the churches to consider whether the agreed statements were "consonant in substance with the faith of Anglicans/Roman Catholics" and if so what "concrete steps" might be taken on the basis of the agreements. In responding to BEM and ARCIC, churches devoted almost all their attention to the theological question and avoided replying to the far more demanding questions about the reception of the theological agreements in renewed lives and changed relationships.

However, in the 1990s, there were some significant developments in the area of reception. The celebration of the Joint Declaration on Justification in 1999 between the Lutheran World Federation and the Roman Catholic Church, the result of many years of theological conversation, has enabled these two communions to reconcile memories of mutual condemnation. New relationships have been established between Lutherans and Anglicans in Europe and in North America. The results of the theological conversations form the foundation for acknowledging the presence of the church of Jesus Christ in each other's lives and also the basis for making binding commitments to share a closer life of faith and mission. So, Anglicans with Lutherans, and Reformed and United churches in Germany, have entered the Meissen Agreement, marking a new stage on the way to visible unity. The remaining differences over episcopacy and succession preclude moving to visible unity, but discussions continue on this and other issues. The Anglican churches of Britain and Ireland have moved into communion, and the Porvoo Communion, with Nordic and Baltic Lutheran churches.

Both the Meissen and the Porvoo Agreements acknowledge their dependency on the multilateral and bilateral theological agreements. They show how theological agreements make possible the reception of each other in a closer communion in faith, life, and mission. Other partnerships between Methodists and Anglicans in the USA and Great Britain, for example, continue along a similar path of phased *rapprochement* made possible by the ecumenical theological agreements. This phased *rapprochement* on the basis of the theological agreements is a challenge to other churches to consider moving from theological conversation to changed relations. Unless there is continuing progress in the process of reception in changed lives and relationships, the theological conversations will remain the preserve of only a few and have little or no effect on the unity and mission of the churches.

Future Agenda

The twentieth century witnessed remarkable achievements in ecumenical theology, together with some practical moves to closer communion. The intricate web of theological conversations continues and it is possible to detect some of the issues that will need to be faced.

First, the matter of ecumenical method itself has come under question. Montreal was a turning point with its treatment of scripture, tradition, and traditions, enabling the conversations to turn from comparative theology to the production of convergence and consensus statements. Montreal's emphasis on the return to biblical and patristic sources inevitably raises the question of how those sources are themselves to be approached, whether through modern historical criticism, or a premodern method of typological or figurative reading, or through the experience of the reader. There has also been a challenge to do theology from context, whether cultural context, or liberationist context, or a particular issue of modernity like the ecological debate.

The counsel of a group of younger ecumenical theologians at the World Conference in Santiago, when faced with the question "how are we going to discover and develop a common framework of language and concept to carry the ecumenical discourse?" was to propose an extension of methodological approaches.[25] They looked to the future for a dialogue between contextual, convergence, and comparative approaches, explaining that these differing methodological approaches are not opposing, mutually exclusive options, but complementary. In response, the Faith and Order Commission began a study of ecumenical hermeneutics and has produced a first statement, *A Treasure in Earthen Vessels*.[26] A common understanding of the process of interpretation is crucial for the future of ecumenical theology.

A second issue relates to the overall frame of reference in which the ecumenical theological conversation takes place. The move to a trinitarian theology opened up many creative avenues, bringing East and West much closer together. But what has never been clear is the nature and interrelation of the unique activity of each person of the Trinity, nor what estimate should be given to the salvific work of the Son, not only in relation to the church, the Body of Christ, but in relation to the whole of humanity and of creation. The Canberra Assembly revealed the difficulty some have with claiming Christocentric universalism, preferring instead to emphasize the activity of the Spirit at work in the world outside the church. The redemption of humankind tends then to be overshadowed by the concern for the preservation of the created order, evangelization gives way to dialogue with other faiths, and the unity of the church becomes a luxury, the concern of only a few.

Thirdly, there are ecclesiological issues. The notion of koinonia, which has become so central in understanding the nature of the church and its unity, is called into question by some who say that it is made to bear more weight in the ecclesiological agenda than its biblical roots can sustain. If this were proved right then it would have serious consequences for agreements already reached, as well as for the hope that seemingly intractable issues, like the ordination of women and certain issues in the area of human sexuality, are most likely to be resolved within an ecclesiology of communion. There is also more work to be done on those things that sustain and nurture the communion of the church, not least of all how, in visible unity, Christians might take counsel, decide, and teach together. There are those who show little interest in this agenda, decrying what they call structural unity. Others maintain that some sort of structure, with personal, collegial, communal, and even primatial aspects, is absolutely required for the maintenance of unity and for effective mission. The challenge for the future is to show that to speak of structure does not imply either rigid uniformity or a hierarchical, coercive model in which there is no room for the voice of the laity or for the emergence of the *sensus fidelium*.

Perhaps the most tantalizing question is what is the goal of the unity that motivates ecumenical conversation? A number of models have been used to describe the goal: "organic union," "united not absorbed," "reconciled diversity," "full communion." It seems today that there is a major division between those who believe in a visible unity in which denominations cease to exist and those who think of reconciled diversity as the model in which communion is established between the denominations while they continue to remain recognizable and viable. It may be that the answer to this question has to be left to see what emerges as churches take steps and reach new stages in a complex network of phased *rapprochement* based on the firm foundation of the results of ecumenical theology. But as Lesslie Newbigin once suggested, it is impossible to be committed to unity without being able to give some account of the goal.

Notes

1 *Breaking Down the Walls: Statements and Actions on Racism, 1948–85*, A. van der Bent (ed.) (Geneva, 1986).

2 *The Community of Women and Men in the Church: The Sheffield Report*, C. Parvey (ed.) (Geneva, 1983).

3 *Ecclesiology and Ethics*, T. Best and M. Robra (eds.) (Geneva, 1997).

4 *Signs of the Spirit: Official Report of the Seventh Assembly of the WCC*, M. Kinnamon (ed.) (Geneva, 1991).

5 Konrad Raiser, *Ecumenism in Transition: A Paradigm Shift in the Ecumenical Movement?* (Geneva, 1989).

6 *Baptism, Eucharist and Ministry*, Faith and Order Paper 111 (Geneva, 1982).

7 *Churches Respond to BEM*, Vols. 1–6, M. Thurian (ed.), Faith and Order Papers 129, 132, 135, 137, 143, 144 (Geneva, 1986–8); *Baptism, Eucharist and Ministry 1982–1990*, Faith and Order Paper 149 (Geneva, 1994).

8 *Confessing the One Faith*, Faith and Order Paper 153 (Geneva, 1991).

9 *On the Way to Fuller Koinonia*, T. Best and G. Gassmann (eds.), Faith and Order Paper 166 (Geneva, 1994).

10 *The Nature and Purpose of the Church*, Faith and Order Paper 181 (Geneva, 1998).

11 *Unitatis redintegratio*, in *Decrees of the Ecumenical Councils*, N. P. Tanner (ed.) (Washington, 1990), pp. 908–20.

12 *Growth in Agreement: Reports and Agreed Statements of Ecumenical Conversations on a World Level*, H. Meyer and L. Vischer (eds.) (New York, 1984); *Growth in Agreement II: Reports and Agreed Statements of Ecumenical Conversations 1982–1998*, J. Gros, H. Meyer, and W. Rusch (eds.), Faith and Order Paper 187 (New York, 2000).

13 *Growth in Agreement II*, p. 587.

14 Ibid, pp. 443–84.

15 Ibid, pp. 324–43.

16 Ibid, pp. 660–8.

17 Ibid, pp. 233–47.

18 Ibid, p. 287.

19 Ibid, pp. 566–82.

20 Ibid, 566–7.

21 Ibid, p. 384.

22 Ibid, p. 397.

23 Ibid, pp. 677, 679.

24 *The Gift of Authority: Authority in the Church III* (New York, 1999).

25 *On the Way to Fuller Koinonia*, p. 162.

26 *A Treasure in Earthen Vessels*, Faith and Order Paper 182 (Geneva, 1998).

Bibliography

History and overviews of the ecumenical movement

Fey, H., *The Ecumenical Advance: A History of the Ecumenical Movement, 1948–68*, Vol. 2 (Geneva, 1993).

Lossky, N., Bonino, J. M., Pobee, J., Stransky, T. F., Wainwright, G., and Webb, P. (eds.), *Dictionary of the Ecumenical Movement*, 2nd edn. (Geneva, 2002).

Rouse, R. and Neil, S. C. (eds.), *History of the Ecumenical Movement 1517–1948*, Vol. 1, 3rd edn. (Geneva, 1986).

Ecumenical documents

A Treasure in Earthen Vessels, Faith and Order Paper 182 (Geneva, 1998).

Baptism, Eucharist and Ministry, Faith and Order Paper 111 (Geneva, 1982).

Best, T. and Robra, M. (eds.), *Ecclesiology and Ethics* (Geneva, 1997).

Church and World: The Unity of the Church and the Renewal of Human Community, Faith and Order Paper 151 (Geneva, 1990).

Confessing One Faith, Faith and Order Paper 153 (Geneva, 1991).

Decree on Ecumenism (Second Vatican Council) in Tanner, N. P. (ed.), *Decrees of the Ecumenical Councils* (Washington, DC, 1990).

Ehrenstrom, N. and Gassmann, G. (eds.), *Confessions in Dialogue* (Geneva, 1975).

Gassmann, G. (ed.), *Documentary History of Faith and Order 1963–1993*, Faith and Order Paper 159 (Geneva, 1993).

Gros, J., Meyer, H., and Rusch, W. (eds.), *Growth in Agreement II: Reports and Agreed Statements of Ecumenical Conversations on a World Level, 1982–1998* (Geneva, 2000).

Meyer, H. and Vischer, L. (eds.), *Growth in Agreement: Reports and Agreed Statements of Ecumenical Conversations on a World Level* (New York, 1984).

The Nature and Purpose of the Church, Faith and Order Paper 181 (Geneva, 1998).

Parvey, C. (ed.), *The Community of Women and Men in the Church: The Sheffield Conference* (Geneva, 1982).

Vischer, L. (ed.), *A Documentary History of the Ecumenical Movement 1927–1963* (St. Louis, MO, 1963).

Ut unum sint, Encyclical Letter of the Holy Father John Paul II, On Commitment to Ecumenism (Boston, MA, 1995).

Individual authors

Congar, Yves M. J., *Divided Christendom: A Catholic Study of the Problem of Reunion* (London, 1939).

Cullmann, O., *Unity Through Diversity: Its Foundation, and a Contribution to the Discussion Concerning the Possibilities of its Actualisation* (Philadelphia, PA, 1988).

Evans, G. R., *Method in Ecumenical Theology* (Cambridge, 1996).

Jenson, R., *Unbaptised God: The Basic Flaw in the Ecumenical Movement* (Minneapolis, MN, 1992).

Kinnamon, M., *The Vision of the Ecumenical Movement and How it has been Impoverished by its Friends* (Missouri, 2003).

Meyer, H., *That All May Be One: Perceptions and Models of Ecumenicity* (Cambridge, 1999).

Raiser, K., *Ecumenism in Transition* (Geneva, 1989).

Rusch, W., *Reception: An Ecumenical Opportunity* (Philadelphia, PA, 1988).

Eastern Orthodox Theology

Rowan Williams

Introduction: Background

For most of the twentieth century, the story of Orthodox theology is the story of Russian theology, both in Russia itself before 1917 and in the emigration afterwards (especially in Paris). The exceptional vitality of Russian intellectual life in the later nineteenth century was without parallel in any other historically Orthodox society – partly for the simple reason that no other such society had enjoyed real cultural independence for centuries. Even when Greece finally emerged as a nation after throwing off the Ottoman yoke, it was to be many years before it could begin to boast an intellectual ethos of its own. But Russia, accustomed to be the standard-bearer of the Orthodox world, was the setting for the first serious encounters between traditional Eastern theology and Enlightenment and post-Enlightenment thought; and it is as if three centuries of development in Western Christian thinking had to be telescoped in Russia into a few decades. If Russian religious thought appears at times bizarre, naïve, and extravagant to Western eyes, we should remember that it is a response to an unprecedented intensity of new impressions, with social and intellectual stimuli crowding in over a relatively brief period.

One crucial factor in understanding modern Russian religious thought is the role of Hegel and, even more, of Schelling in the formation of systems. Hegel's work became known in Russia first by way of the theological schools of the Ukraine; it has been very plausibly suggested that Hegel's interest in the late neoplatonism of Proclus resonated with a theology that accorded great authority to the Pseudo-Dionysius' writings, also deeply marked by the influence of Proclus. But two other factors should be borne in mind as well. German idealism arrived in Russia in close connection with German mysticism – both the Catholic mysticism of the medieval and post-medieval Rhineland and the quasi-hermetic Protestantism of Jakob Böhme. In the early decades of the nineteenth century, the new philosophical ideas coming from Germany appeared as simply another form of the new images of religious interiority offered by German hermetism and eclectic pietism. In other words, idealism was, from the first, received in Russia as a religious philosophy, which, though ambivalent from the point of view of Orthodoxy, might yet be put to work for the traditional faith. The combination of Böhme with Schelling and Hegel seemed to open the way toward a metaphysic of the world as organism, a participatory and intuitive account of knowledge, and a certain relativization of the ideas of an automomous and finite ego. It is fair to say that one problem that has *not* beset Russian religious thought is an excess of dualism.

In addition to this, however, it may be that Russian history itself helped to make Hegel attractive. It had been a history of violent alternations – from the Byzantine and European civilization of the Kievan period, to the increasing cultural isolation of the Mongol and Muscovite centuries, to the Francophile and Francophone culture of the governing class in the eighteenth century; and the war against Napoleon had involved a deep emotional retrieval of the Muscovite ideal of "Holy Russia." Culturally and politically, Russia was eager to find an identity that would resolve the contradictory heritage of the past and heal the injuries caused by the massive disruptions of that history. Thus, much of Russia's intellectual history up to 1917 (and since) has to do with the variety of conflicting "bids" to define the nation. Was its destiny to resolve its tensions by joining the history of the European "mainstream," or was there a quite different kind of polity and politics to which it could witness? Nehru or Gandhi? One of the most striking things about revolutionary Marxism in Russia is that it succeeded in blending these two opposing impulses. But for a society with this kind of agenda in the early decades of the nineteenth century, the appeal of a historically oriented metaphysic is obvious. Hegel confirmed the characteristic Russian tendency to fuse together the religious, the philosophical, and the political, and the whole of the enterprise of Russian religious philosophy reflects this fusion.

There were those, however, who, accepting this program, still believed that Hegel was to be left behind. Ivan Vasilievich Kireevsky (1806–56) published, in the year of his death, an essay on "The Need for New Foundations in Philosophy," which argued that Hegel represented the decisive end of one particular style of philosophy, that originating with Bacon and Descartes: a philosophy whose fundamental problematic was "What is it to *think*?" and which dealt with this in terms of analyzing the processes of observation and argumentation. Kireevsky turned instead to the alternative tradition represented by Pascal (and was also impressed by Schleiermacher), and to the anthropology of the Eastern Fathers, especially the monastic writers, searching for a perspective neither intellectualist nor voluntarist, for a doctrine of the formation of historical persons in action and relation, an integral view of the human. Reasoning, in such a perspective, is concrete and committed, not ahistorical, and we are delivered from the absolute dominance of a "tragic" vision of the relation between spirit and nature. Kireevsky's literary remains are fragmentary and slight, but the reader will catch startling glimpses of something like Kierkegaard as well as something like Heidegger, hermeneutics set against a logos metaphysic.

Vladimir Sergeevich Soloviev (1853–1900) represents most dramatically the opposite approach, a passion for metaphysical construction and systematization. His importance is chiefly in his elaboration of a quasi-mythological cosmology centered upon the figure of "Sophia," the divine Wisdom, the Eternal Feminine. For Soloviev, the Absolute exists both as being and as becoming, as a transcendent unity and as the totality of modes in which that unity can express itself and relate to itself; and this latter form of the Absolute, insofar as it always preserves a movement toward unity, is an organic whole. This is "Sophia" – fragmented in the empirical universe, but still at one in God. In this perspective, the incarnation of the divine Word is the central act of *reintegration* in the cosmos; in the church, in which the fruits of the incarnation are realized, human personality is united to the cosmic whole (*vseedinstvo*, "total unity"), and delivered from its finite limitations, its alienation from matter and from other subjects. The Orthodox Church does not operate by external and legalistic systems of authority, as does the Roman communion, nor does it countenance the individualism of the Protestant; it is therefore uniquely qualified to be the bearer of the promise of "sophianic" humanity, of *bogochelovechestvo*, "divine humanity" (or "Godmanhood," as it is often rendered). In Orthodox societies, the aim should be a "free theocracy," not legally imposed but organically evolving, which will draw other nations into a universal Christian communion, both church and state.

Soloviev develops some of the ideas of the earlier writer Alexei Stepanovich Khomyakov (1804–60), especially in the use of organic models for the church and in the elaboration of the concept of *sobornost'*, the Russian word for "catholicity," as a special designation for the supra-individual consciousness of the (Orthodox, especially Slavic) church. But the vision of Sophia is new, as is the passionate insistence on a universal perspective. Soloviev is without doubt the single most influential Russian religious writer of the age (his impact upon Dostoevsky is clear), and nearly all major Orthodox thinkers up to the Revolution are in one way or another in dialogue with him. However, his system gives very sharp focus to the problems hinted at by Kireevsky: what is the role of history in this, real, *contingent* history? And what can be said about individual identity and liberty in so comprehensive and near-deterministic a scheme? Soloviev's last works include a strange piece of apocalyptic fiction ("A Story of Antichrist") suggesting that he recognized the presence of irresoluble tensions in his metaphysics, and the possibility of tragic revolt and discontinuity. His legacy proved to be as controversial and many-sided as that of Origen; much of the work of his admirers is an attempt to restate a "sophiology" without the elements of pantheism and determinism that pervade a great deal of his writing.

The history of Russian theology in the twentieth century is largely one of debate between those who have, broadly speaking, felt comfortable with the legacy of Soloviev and those who have repudiated it in favor of a more consciously traditional and church-focused style, seeking to derive general principles for a theological anthropology from the interpretation of the fathers of the early centuries. Generally, the rejection of Soloviev has been accompanied by a suspicion of Khomyakov's theology as well. The appeal to a distinctive kind of corporate consciousness in the church, analogous to that typical of premodern, especially Slavic, societies has been seen as a naturalistic reduction of the supernatural reality of communion in the Holy Spirit. Twentieth-century Russian theology is thus, in its most creative period (ca. 1925–55), deeply marked by polemic. The rejection of Soloviev and others by a younger generation has some parallels with the rejection of liberal Protestant conventions by the new theologies of the Word in Germany. In both, there is an attempt to shed the legacy of idealism in philosophy, and to break free from what was seen as a psychologizing or moralizing or "naturalizing" of faith, so as to recover a sense of the givenness, the historical and punctiliar character, of a revelation that reconstructs the whole of human knowing and relating. What is different of course is the persistent Orthodox attempt to pursue a theology of the historical *mediation* of revelation, a theology of tradition. For many students of the field, this remains one of the most abidingly interesting and fruitful contributions of the Orthodox vision in contemporary theological discussion.

In what follows, three theologians, Bulgakov, Lossky, and Florovsky, will be discussed in some detail, before surveying and assessing the wider field of Orthodox theology today.

Three Orthodox Theologians

S. N. Bulgakov

Foremost among those who sought to rework Soloviev's themes in more acceptable form was Sergei Nikolaevich Bulgakov (1871–1944). Alienated from the Orthodox Church as a student, he had become a Marxist teacher of economics, with a considerable international reputation, before drifting away from dialectical materialism, first toward a Kantian moralism, then toward Hegel. He finally made his peace with the church in the early years of this century, and was ordained a priest in 1917; after expulsion from Russia in 1923, he spent most of his remaining years in Paris, as Dean of the newly formed Institut Saint-Serge, a seminary for *émigré* Russians – and also as a deeply loved pastor and director of souls. He was a prolific writer, whose dense and florid style conceals a surprising conceptual boldness which sets him apart from most of his fellow Orthodox theologians, and occasioned a minor ecclesiastical *cause célèbre* in the Russian emigration when, in 1935, he was denounced to the Patriarchate of Moscow as a heretic, and his theology was condemned by the Patriarchal *locum tenens*, Metropolitan Sergii. He was, however, supported by his own ecclesiastical superiors (whose relations with Moscow at this time were hostile anyway). His work attracted some interest outside the Orthodox world partly because he had become a well-known figure in the ecumenical movement, but a great deal of his writing remains available in Russian only.

Bulgakov's rejection of Marxism had a great deal to do with a theme that he explores in several essays between 1903 and 1911: the inadequacy of *homo economicus* as a basis for social and political ethics. An account of human needs in terms of economically determinable factors leads – paradoxically – to an alienation from the historical and the material, since it seeks a way out of *personal* struggle and growth, out of the risks of creativity. It sets up a mechanical opposition of economic interests, to be settled either by the logic of history (Marxism) or by the laws of the market (capitalism); but both resolutions sidestep the specifically human task of transfiguring the material world in and through the creation of community. Artistic and economic activity are equally indispensable in this – art as the gratuitous expression of an "eschatological" change in things, matter charged with meaning, economics as the functional harnessing of the world to human need. Either of these in isolation is destructive.

It is Bulgakov's interest in the *work* of humanizing the world that sets him apart from Soloviev, as well as from pure Hegelianism (he remarked once that no one who had ever taken Marxism seriously could accept abstract or passivist versions of idealist dialectic). Hence his assimilation of the Sophia myth represents a considerable qualification of Soloviev's version (and in this he was much influenced by the work of his spiritual mentor, Fr. Pavel Florensky, a brilliant and eccentric polymath who finally disappeared in the Gulag), and is continually being revised and refined throughout the whole of Bulgakov's work. Sophia *is* the divine nature, God's own life considered under the aspect of God's freedom to live the divine life in what is not God. God as Trinity is an eternal movement of "giving-away," displacement, so that God's very Godhead presupposes the possibility of there being an object of love and gift beyond itself. Bulgakov is careful to clarify (especially between 1917 and 1925) the point that Sophia is not a "hypostasis" (correcting both Florensky and his own earlier work), and to purge out any residual pantheism: divine Sophia is not an objectified World-Soul, but the impulse in things toward harmony and order, toward complex unity of organization. Bulgakov speaks of this impulse as the world's "eros"; and such language should remind us that Bulgakov's sophiology is far more a sustained metaphor than a theory.

Bulgakov rejects a matter–spirit dualism; but the nature–hypostasis dualism with which he often works introduces some of the dangers he wishes to avoid. When he says that the hypostasis of a human subject, the uncategorizable core of personal identity, is "uncreated" or "absolute," his concern is chiefly to deny that personal identity is an observable determinate *thing*; but the language is redolent of the Germanic hermetism which Bulgakov found both intensely attractive and theologically unsatisfactory. He constantly seems to be implying that there is in human psychology a level or dimension of direct *natural* participation in God – a view which Orthodox theological tradition has normally regarded with hostility. Thus, his account of human liberty oscillates between an impressive seriousness about freedom as constituted in historical relation and creativity, and a more monistic notion of a universal divine *Urgrund* of liberty, the image of God residing in a mysterious hinterland of transcendence common to all personal beings.

However, when he addresses the question of the divine image in his later and explicitly theological work, it is more often the *active* role of the human subject that is to the fore. Human being is the agent of meaning in the universe; when distorted self-love breaks the "sophianic" whole into mutually excluding fragments, the redemptive work of God as Word and Spirit is to enable us to be once again capable of revealing the wholeness of things, in work, art, and sacrament. This cannot be simply a matter of injunctions to be obeyed, programs to be followed: redemption actually effects a change in spiritual self-awareness, so that we know we can exist as selves *only* in communion with other selves. Here the nineteenth-century theme of "catholic" consciousness, *sobornost'*, reappears: the church, Bulgakov was fond of saying, is the fact of human "consubstantiality," not merely a society; it is "Sophia in the process of becoming." The language used about the church as ideal form of creation can, however, mislead. Bulgakov is quite clear that the empirical church is flawed, its work incomplete, its decisions provisional and risky, its existing limits "pragmatic not absolute" – which explains why he has little on the theology of ministerial or hierarchical authority, and was an enthusiastic advocate of intercommunion in certain circumstances. The church is essentially the fellowship of the

Spirit, held together by the ontological bond of God's love as figured in the Eucharist; the rest is a matter of conditioned historical decisions and policies.

Not surprisingly, perhaps, he is critical of certain kinds of Christocentrism in ecclesiology. If the identity of the church is made to reside solely in its relation to Christ rather than in the quality of its consubstantial and catholic life in the Spirit, the church will tend to look for Christ-substitutes – an infallible pope, an inerrant Bible – or to encourage people to concentrate on an *individual* relation to the Savior. But the work of the Trinity is fundamentally characterized by kenosis, a central theme in all Bulgakov's work, but especially in the theological writings of the 1920s and 1930s: Christ therefore acts in the church not as an omnipresent individual, focusing attention on himself, but through the Spirit's formation of the new consciousness – which in turn works "kenotically," directing us to the Father and working always with and never against created freedom. Thus Bulgakov's suspicion of Christocentrism does not mean that Christology does not have a central and normative place: here, in the life and death of Jesus, the kenotic pattern is spelled out. The divine self of the Word, unchanged as such, is the subject for which the human self of Jesus now becomes an object: the Word is the "I," the consciousness, for which the humanity of Jesus is the "me," the material of self-consciousness. This is a complex idea, which Bulgakov fails to work out in full detail, but which shows signs of rather more conceptual sophistication than some forms of English kenoticism. Here his doctrine of the "uncreated" hypostasis in all human beings serves him well: he can identify the ultimate subjectivity of Christ with the Word of God while avoiding downright Apollinarianism. But this whole area of his thinking is abstruse and unclear. His main concern in Christology, however, is to show how Christ is the place where uncreated and created Sophia are united: the divine life of unconditional self-forgetting generates a created, historical life of the same quality, in which the mutual isolation and refusal of fallen creation is overcome. The incarnate Word as incarnate selflessness is open to *universal* relation, universal accessibility: as that relation becomes ours in the Spirit, our isolation is ended, and the *sobornost'* of the new creation is established.

Bulgakov's achievement is remarkable. His work is sprawling, repetitive, unsystematic, and often appallingly obscure, but it is a rare attempt at a unified theological metaphysic. Many of his insights on the nature of the church became the common currency of the ecumenical movement, and were specially influential for Anglican writers of a certain generation. But other aspects of his work have remained almost unknown. He is one of the first theologians to use and develop the term "panentheism," to distinguish his doctrine of the world's ideality in God from pantheism; he is clearly fascinated by feminine imagery for the Godhead, although he works with an uncritical male/active, female/passive-or-receptive disjunction; he is certainly the only theologian of the century to use kenosis as a pivotal and normative concept for *all* language about God, in creation as in redemption; and in this as in other ways, his use of Jewish Cabbalistic imagery (the myth of *zimzum*, God's self-withdrawal in the creative act) is deeply suggestive. He has yet to be taken fully seriously by Western theology, although at the present moment, there are clear signs of renewed interest both in Europe and in the United States in Bulgakov's work. Of all the major Orthodox thinkers of the century, he is probably the one most consciously and extensively engaged with post-Enlightenment thought (and Western biblical scholarship). Among non-Orthodox writers, it is probably Hans Urs von Balthasar who stands closest to him – in the themes touched upon, but also in densely metaphorical idiom.

V. N. Lossky

The fierce debate over Bulgakov's work in 1935 and 1936 brought into prominence a young historian, Vladimir Nikolaevich Lossky (1903–58), son of a well-known (vaguely idealist) philosopher. Lossky had already begun work on Meister Eckhart (work which was to occupy him intermittently for the rest of his life), and had been instrumental in establishing the Brotherhood of Saint Photius in Paris, a group highly critical of Slavophil particularism and the mystique of Holy Russia, but also loyal to the canonical authority of the Patriarchate of Moscow, in contrast to the more aggressively anti-Soviet elements in the emigration and the liberal group (including philosophers like Nikolai Berdyaev and philosophical theologians like Bulgakov) gathered around Metropolitan Evlogii and linked to the Patriarch of Constantinople. The Brotherhood had been active in the denunciation of Bulgakov, and Lossky wrote a substantial (90-page) pamphlet on the whole issue in 1936. In this, he attacked Bulgakov's eclecticism and identified various errors and imbalances in his theology: he criticizes the crypto-Apollinarian strand in Bulgakov's Christology, his failure to get rid of the determinist or monist heritage of Soloviev, and above all his confusion of person, will, and nature. Kenosis cannot be "natural," cannot *be* the nature of God, since it is always a free act, in God and in us. If love is nature, it is not innovative or creative, it does not belong to the realm of the personal.

The distinction between person and nature is central in the whole of Lossky's work; but the important point to notice in the 1936 essay is Lossky's strong commitment to an "authentic," patristically based Orthodoxy, freed from the philosophical dilettantism, as he saw it, of the Russian tradition (he had a deep aversion for Dostoevsky). The rest of his sadly brief career as a theologian was devoted to the building-up of a patristic synthesis – classically expressed in his vastly influential little book of 1944, *Essai sur la théologie mystique de l'église d'Orient* (translated into English as *The Mystical Theology of the Eastern Church* in 1957). Digests of the lectures he gave in the last years of his life were published posthumously, edited by his pupil, Olivier Clément. Throughout his work, Lossky's major impulse is hermeneutical – in the tradition of Kireevsky rather than Soloviev. His project is to uncover in patristic tradition the kind of central and normative strand that can allow Orthodoxy to offer a resolution to the tensions of Western Christianity. This leads him into some slightly questionable historical judgments, and to what appears in his earlier work as a persistent unfairness to the Thomist approach (though his mature writing, especially the great book on Eckhart, goes far toward redressing this balance), and to many aspects of Western spirituality. Yet his unpublished wartime journal shows how deep was his affection for French Catholic culture, medieval and modern, and he was on friendly terms both with Thomist scholars like de Gandillac and Gilson and with the great names of the *nouvelle théologie*, de Lubac and Daniélou. His influence on Bouyer and Congar is manifest; and he also enjoyed warm relations with Anglican scholars of the day, notably E. L. Mascall. His polemical vigor was not exercised in the cause of Byzantine, let alone Slavophil, particularism, but in defense of deeply held convictions about what was authentically *Christian*.

His earliest theological work, prior to the controversy with Bulgakov, dealt with the theme of "negative theology" in Pseudo-Dionysius, and this forms the basis for much of the 1944 *Essai*. Negative theology is not, for Lossky, primarily a verbal technique, a dialectical move to qualify positive affirmations about God en route for a developed theory of analogy; it is the *primordial* theological moment, the moment of stripping and renunciation. Theology begins in a kind of shock to, a paralyzing of, the intellect – not by propositions that offend the intellect, but by an encounter with what cannot be mastered. The dialectical imagery of "light" and "darkness," as used by both Dionysius and his precursors, the Cappadocian Fathers, is designed to take us beyond both agnosticism (the being of God is ultimately inaccessible) and intellectualism (the being of God is akin to the finite mind and so its proper and natural object): the reality underpinning apophatic theology is "ecstasy" – not a particular brand of individual mystical experience, but the sober acknowledgment that we must let go of the control of conceptual analysis when we are touched by God and advance to a stage beyond the life of conscious "natural" individuality, closed upon itself. It is in this encounter, this recognition, that *personal* being is brought to birth. The life of an individual of a certain nature is not in itself the life of a person: individuality is a particular configuration of *repeatable* natural features. The person, on the other hand, emerges in and only in the act of spiritual creativity which is response to the self-gift of God – in *ekstasis* and kenosis, self-transcending and self-forgetting, the overcoming of the boundaries of mutual exclusion that define individuals over against each other.

It is in this context that Lossky claims that the doctrine of the Trinity is the cardinal point of "negative theology." It is a "cross for the intellect" not in merely providing a logical conundrum, but in presenting to us an image of the source of all reality that overturns our understanding of individuality as the most basic category. God is neither an individual nor three individuals: God is the supreme paradigm of the personal, a life wholly lived in *ekstasis* and kenosis, since the divine hypostases which are God are wholly defined by relations of love, gift, response. It is from the paradigm of the divine hypostases that we come to grasp our own vocation to personal being.

Thus Lossky attacks all theologies that concentrate on the level of "nature" – what can be grasped and objectified. His fierce criticisms of Western scholasticism are motivated by a conviction that the Western theological tradition separates the divine essence from the divine persons (and so elevates an abstract divinity over the living God), and operates a juridical and external morality based on an artificial concept of human nature, to which grace is added as an extra *thing*. His critique of the *filioque* in the Western Creed assumes that post-Augustinian trinitarian theology makes the source of the Spirit's life not the person of the Father but the abstract nature shared by Father and Son (in this critique, he goes further than most of his Orthodox predecessors, but has a special debt to the work of V. Bolotov on the *filioque* at the turn of the century, and to the patristic and medieval studies of L. P. Karsavin, one of his teachers). However, Lossky also insists that the reaction against scholastic Catholicism is just as unbalanced: here is "person" without "nature," voluntarism and subjectivism. The Protestant error is to turn away from the real ontological transformation effected by encounter with God. So, as Christian trinitarianism mediates between two misguided forms of monotheism, Hellenic abstract monism and Hebraic anthropomorphism and voluntarism, Orthodoxy mediates between Catholic essentialism and Protestant existentialism.

The critique of the West also draws in Lossky's interest in the speculations of the fourteenth-century theologian and mystic Gregory Palamas. Palamas had distinguished between the "essence" and the "energies" or "activities" of God, so as to insist that God was authentically known and "participated" through his activities while remaining incomprehensible in essence. Lossky believes that the absence of this distinction leads back to the unacceptable choice of intellectualism or agnosticism; either God is known in essence, in *definitions*, or he is not known at all. The doctrine of the "energies" allows both real and ultimate unknowing and a real share in the divine life. Lossky was not the first to revive interest in Palamas: Bulgakov had used him, and, in the 1930s, the Russian Basil Krivoshein and the Romanian Dumitru Staniloae had both published important scholarly studies. Lossky's work, however, established Palamas as a focal figure in Byzantine theology, and did much to stimulate the striking development of Palamas scholarship in Europe and the United States in the past thirty years.

There is a Kierkegaardian streak in Lossky (it is not surprising that he thought highly of the French Kierkegaardian scholar Jean Wahl), but it is balanced by a carefully worked out ecclesiology. The church exists at *both* "natural" and "personal" levels, human nature objectively restored in Christ, human persons each uniquely transformed by the Spirit. Thus, institutional and canonical regularities matter (Lossky's stubborn loyalty to the canonical authority of the weak and almost discredited Patriarchate of Moscow through many difficult decades expresses this eloquently); but they are not there to impose centralized despotism or unified models of spiritual growth. The institutional and the charismatic are bound together as inseparably as the Word and the Spirit in the Trinity. "Tradition" in the church is not just a process of narrowly doctrinal transmission, but the *whole* of the Spirit's ecclesial work, realizing in each, in a unique way, the heritage of all, by way of scripture, ministry, sacraments, iconography, and the disciplines of holiness. And catholicity is more than a sentimental *sobornost'*, a deep and emotional sense of solidarity; it is the capacity in each believer and each congregation to receive and live the fullness of God's gifts.

Lossky remains probably the best known and most influential of all modern Orthodox writers. His polemic can be wide of the mark at times, and he remains more firmly within the nineteenth-century Russian tradition than he might have cared to admit, but his originality and imagination in interpreting the Eastern Fathers should secure him a firm place among twentieth-century theologians, and practically all Eastern Orthodox ecclesiology in the past few decades has taken his scheme as a starting point.

G. V. Florovsky

Lossky was not alone in combating the influence of Slavophil mystique in Russian theology, and in trying to rescue the doctrine of the church's catholicity from edifying rhetoric about Slavic *sobornost'*. Georgii Vasilievich Florovsky (1893–1979) pursued the same course in search of a "neo-patristic synthesis," though he did so in more direct and conscious engagement with philosophical questions: his earliest essays (after he had abandoned studies in the natural sciences) addressed fundamental issues of metaphysics and epistemology. In these pieces, he repudiates absolute idealism, insists on the impossibility of affirming or denying anything about objects of cognition in themselves, since they enjoy an inaccessible presence to themselves, and argues on this basis for a radical causal under-determination in the universe, a kind of "free will" in the material order. He saw very clearly the connection between idealist epistemology (each particular proposition entailing and being entailed by the ensemble of true propositions) and a certain sort of determinism, and his later opposition to Bulgakov's sophiology has its roots in these essays of the prewar period and the early 1920s. In the 1920s, he was also involved in the "Eurasian" controversy among the Russian *émigrés*, a debate (once again) about where Russia was to be culturally "located"; his anti-Slavophil stance in this was pronounced and he was already looking to the ideal of a "Christian Hellenism," with patristic and Byzantine roots.

In the early 1930s, Florovsky worked for a while alongside Bulgakov in Paris (he was ordained in 1932), but his disagreements became sharper – and may have been further sharpened by contact with Barth in 1931. His theological papers in these years show both an aggressive insistence on the priority of revelation and a growing use of patristic categories and argument. In 1931 and 1933, he published his two magisterial surveys of Eastern theology up to the eighth century, and, in two important papers in 1936 and 1938, he castigated the bondage of Russian theology to post-Enlightenment philosophy and announced his program of "re-Hellenizing" the Christian faith, arguing that Christian theology could only recover itself by deepening its commitment to the baptized Hellenism of the Fathers and the Byzantine world. He never wavered in this loyalty to the Greek character of theology, in opposition both to Western religious and secular thought and to the ethnic religiosity of many Russians. In 1937 he published *Ways of Russian Theology*, a brilliant and encyclopedic history of Christian thought in Russia that elaborated a relentlessly hostile account of Slavophil Christianity and concluded with a clarion call to return to the fathers.

As much of his work shows, Florovsky's patristic enthusiasm was not as naive or as positivist as might appear (though one Russian reviewer in 1931 described an essay of Florovsky's on the atonement as "talmudic" in its use of the fathers). Florovsky's radical indeterminism disposed him to emphasize the central significance of *history* in knowledge – the encounter with a complex of contingent acts in which we encounter persons. In historical knowledge, above all, we must recognize the impossibility of "objective" mastery: historical inquiry brings a personal, a committed, agenda, and looks for personal records, unique points of view. There is no historical source that is not a point of view, and no historical research that is not done from a point of view. Historical "events" are acts, mediated by further acts of interpretation (Collingwood and Dilthey are invoked on this); and the meaning of history is an eschatological projection. As against preemptive efforts to settle the issue of meaning (Hegel, Marx, Nietzsche), Christianity takes seriously the unfinished and unfinishable character of historical activity, and thus the unique and unfathomable character of the acting *person*. But this also means that Christianity is irreversibly committed to what has as a matter of contingent fact been constructed in its history: we cannot pretend that we can free ourselves of "Hellenism," or that the kerygma is directed from and to a timeless interiority. Hence the priority of patristic methods and themes – though this does not mean that we can do no more than parrot slogans or imitate the style of a distant culture; simply that *these* are our starting point, *this* is how Christian language has concretely taken shape. If we wish to go on speaking a Christian language at all, we cannot ignore or try to dismantle this set of determinations.

As some Russian critics more sympathetic to Bulgakov noted, Florovsky did less than justice to the turbulently dialectical nature of patristic theology, and tended to treat as a finished whole what could only be part of a conversation (comparison with some recent theological uses of Gadamer is instructive). But Florovsky's sophisticated discussion of historical knowledge (most accessibly set out in an article for the 1959 Tillich *Festschrift*) is of great interest, the most detailed exposition of what we have been calling the "hermeneutical" alternative voice in Russian religious thought, suspicious of metaphysics divorced from doctrinal and ascetical tradition. The emphasis on historical creativity, history as a pattern of free acts, leads naturally to a critique of all theologies that undervalue the historical Jesus: for Florovsky, the category of *podvig* (roughly equivalent to "achievement," even "exploit," and common in speaking of ascetic saints) is central in understanding Christ, as in understanding all human action. Jesus' *whole* existence must be the triumph of freedom in the world if we are to be liberated for proper historical action. Thus his death must be, in some sense, his *act* – and not only contingently so. Florovsky startlingly revives the late patristic notion that Jesus, as possessing a sinless and unfallen humanity, did not *have* to die. And in that Jesus thus brings death itself within the scope of created freedom, the possibility of incorruptible life is implanted in humanity. Necessity, in the form of mortality and disintegration, is shown to be conquerable by freedom – the fusion of divine and human freedom in Christ. We shall die, but we know now that our human nature is still "free" beyond death, as it has been taken through death into resurrection by the man Jesus, whose glorified humanity is given to us in the Eucharist.

The Eucharist is thus also the foundation of true, ecclesial *sobornost'*. In it, we come to share fellowship not only with one another, but with the whole company of heaven and the entire cosmos; we do so because we here make contact with a humanity free from the limits of ordinary individuality, a humanity belonging to our history yet not sealed off in the past by death. And in the eucharistic fellowship, as "human impermeability and exclusivity" are overcome, human community becomes the image of the divine: the church (not the individual) is *imago Trinitatis*. Florovsky makes much in this context of the Farewell Discourses in the fourth gospel, though patristic evidence is harder to come by; following the lead of a very different kind of theologian, Antonii Khrapovitsky (Metropolitan of Kiev before the Revolution), author of treatises on the "moral idea" of various dogmas, he alludes to Cyril of Alexandria and Hilary of Poitiers. But the notion of the church as imaging the plurality-in-unity of the divine life owes more directly to the nineteenth-century Russian ethos than to the fathers. It may be a legitimate development of patristic themes, but Florovsky, as much as Lossky, cannot but read the fathers through spectacles faintly tinged with Slavophil interests.

Florovsky's range of skills and erudition is impressive, though the work overall is more uneven than Lossky's much slighter *oeuvre*. Considerable philosophical sophistication and originality stand side by side with what can sometimes be an archaizing and inflexible theological idiom. His insistence on freedom gives a rather voluntaristic flavor to some of his writings, and there is no clear category unifying the work of divine and human love to compare with the striking use of kenosis in both Bulgakov and Lossky. Methodologically, however, he is much the most lucid and systematic, and his work in this area deserves far more serious attention.

Survey and Assessment of Current Orthodox Theology

The Russian emigration produced many other significant figures, not least Nikolai Afanasiev, author of a major work on ecclesiology that developed many of the themes emerging in Lossky and Florovsky (the *imago Trinitatis*, the centrality of the Eucharist), and Pavel Evdokimov, a prolific and eloquent writer of books on the interrelation of liturgy, theology, and spirituality, indebted equally to Lossky and to Bulgakov, as well as to Jung and Eliade. A striking figure in the circles of Russian Paris in the years before and during World War II, was Mother Maria Skobtsova, writer, poet, monastic prophet, and activist. A friend of Nikolai Berdiaev, assisted and supported by Metropolitan Evlogi, she helped Jewish refugees during the Nazi occupation in France, and gave her life for another in Ravensbruck during the last days of the war.

As the first generation of *émigrés* died, the impact of the Russian theological revival spread beyond Slavic Orthodoxy. Greek-speaking theologians increasingly took up the challenge; until the 1950s, Greek theology had tended to be cast in a rather scholastic mode – doctrinal *capita* with patristic catenae added – but the impact of Lossky and Florovsky has transformed this situation in some areas at least of the Greek church. John Romanides developed a fiercely anti-Augustinian theology, tied in with a very personal view of church and political history. His profound patristic scholarship was brought to bear in a significant way on the theological conversations especially between Eastern Orthodox and Oriental (non-Chalcedonian) Orthodox churches.

Christos Yannaras studied Heidegger in Germany and produced a remarkable series of books uniting Lossky's theology with Heidegger's metaphysics. He must be counted as one of the most outstandingly creative voices in Orthodoxy today; his reworking of the essence–energies distinction in terms of *ousia* as *parousia*, "being" as "presence," and his elaboration of the category of *eros* as fundamental in understanding the personal, represent an important assimilation of major European philosophical concerns into a consciously but critically traditionalist theology. Yannaras has also made a considerable name as a writer on politics, ecology, and ethics. In his *The Freedom of Morality* and other works, he engages with a variety of sources to arrive at a renewed reflection on Christian ethics, which has stimulated thinkers such as John Breck and Stanley Harakas to produce thoughtful books on contemporary ethical issues.

(Metropolitan) John Zizioulas' work on ecclesiology links Afanasiev's themes (not without some criticism and refinement) to a whole metaphysic of relation, centered on the trinitarian image of being as *essentially* relational: the great philosophical error is to look for isolated ahistorical substances, since the source of all reality is not "a" substance but a relational system. Zizioulas' doctoral thesis, on Eucharist, episcopate, and unity, has been seminally important in ecumenical theology. In fact it is possible that he is the most widely read Orthodox theologian in the Western milieu. (Among others who have worked on the renewal of a theology more integrally related with both Orthodox spirituality and the contemporary culture, Panayotis Nellas deserves mention.)

In the United States, Alexander Schmemann and John Meyendorff transmitted the Russian *émigré* heritage to new generations, Schmemann with a number of works on liturgical and sacramental theology (above all that small classic, *The World as Sacrament* – revised and now better known as *For the Life of the World*), Meyendorff with several important books on Palamism, and Byzantine theology and history, and essays on ecclesiology. Schmemann in particular was at the forefront of a liturgical (and in particular eucharistic) revival in the Orthodox Church. This revival in many ways paralleled the eucharistic and liturgical movement in Western Christendom, and has brought the two worlds into a more evident harmony. Both the major Orthodox seminaries in the United States, St. Vladimir's and Holy Cross, produce substantial theological periodicals and publish a wide array of English-language books.

The Institut Saint-Serge continues in Paris, and several Orthodox groups there publish theological journals. Orthodoxy in France is now overwhelmingly Francophone, and its leading constructive theologian, Olivier Clément, is of French birth. A friend and pupil of Lossky, he has developed Lossky's critique of the abstract foundations of Western theism, and written of the dialectical necessity of European atheism as a step to recovering the vision of a living God. He has succeeded in constructing an Orthodox theology very deeply engaged with the mainstream of Western European culture, and free from either Byzantinist or Slavophil nostalgia. Another outstanding representative of St. Serge is Boris Bobrinskoy, who has continued to work on classical theological themes (e.g., the Trinity and the Holy Spirit) in a way which is rooted in patristic tradition but with great freedom and sensitivity to Western theological perspectives.

In Britain, (Bishop) Kallistos Ware has come to be an important interpreter of the Orthodox theological tradition to the English-speaking world. His primary activity has been as a teacher in Oxford, where many graduate students have come to work with him. At present, his numerous and substantial articles interpreting patristic theology and spirituality are being gathered together for publication in a series of volumes. He has also played an invaluable role in the translation of the Philokalia and liturgical texts into English. He has remained an active presence in ecumenical affairs, not least in the work of the Fellowship of St. Albans and St. Sergius.

Elisabeth Behr-Sigel is another whose theological work has constantly involved constructive dialogue with Western theological trends. She has written on Orthodox spirituality, and over very many years has produced important reflections on the nature of ministry, especially that of women, in the Orthodox Church. She, together with people like Bulgakov, Lossky, Lev Gillet, Anthony Bloom on the Orthodox side, and E. L. Mascall, Austin Farrer, L. S. Thornton on the Anglican side, was involved in the Fellowship of St. Alban and St. Sergius. The work of this body has resulted in unusually fruitful relations between Orthodox Christians and Christians of the West in Great Britain, most recently to be seen in the foundation of the Orthodox Christian Theological Institute in Cambridge, a part of the Theological Federation there.

Behr-Sigel has also been at the forefront of renewed thinking in the past twenty years on questions of gender. People such as Verna Harrison, Valerie Karras, and Wendy Robinson have begun to explore the way into a patristically based and practically expressed theology of gender. (The acknowledged fact of the position of lay theologians in the Orthodox Church makes possible promising developments in this and other fields.) Important and often challenging contributions in this area have also been made by Kallistos Ware, (Metropolitan) Anthony Bloom, and Thomas Hopko.

Up to 1969, theological work in the communist countries of Eastern Europe was largely limited to historical scholarship, with a few outstanding exceptions. Foremost among these was Fr. Dumitru Staniloae in Romania, a major interpreter of the patristic tradition (he wrote substantial studies of Gregory Palamas and Maximus the Confessor) and of classical monastic spirituality (he edited the Romanian edition of the Philokalia), as well as a constructive theologian of great stature. Staniloae's theological work was focused in three main areas. First, as we have seen, the renewal of the philokalic tradition. He incorporated into the Romanian Philokalia large sections of Maximus, Symeon the New Theologian, and Palamas, and provided the volumes with substantial theological and historical notes. Second, there was his major concern with the renewal of dogmatic theology. Here, he has much in common with Lossky and Florovsky – notably in his concern for an ecclesiology based on the living communion of persons; but he criticizes the over-schematic model he finds in Lossky, and has far more eagerness to engage with modern non-Orthodox thought than Florovsky. His most original contributions probably lie in his development of Maximus the Confessor's insights on the theology of creation, the world depending upon the "words" of God conceived as dynamic determinative actions of God, so that the world is a vehicle of divine agency, an agency brought to light and completion in the life of Christ and the church. Staniloae's *Dogmatic Theology* (which is now appearing in an English translation) discusses very fully many modern ideas about revelation, Christology, and so on, and has some penetrating observations on Barth.

A third element in the theological work of Staniloae was his constant interest in the conversation between theology and contemporary culture, in particular as present in the literary and poetic tradition of his country on the one side, and on the other, in his concern with the development of twentieth-century scientific speculation, made possible even in the years of communist dictatorship through his many contacts with the intellectual world of Romania.

In a striking but unplanned way, the theological concerns of a writer like Staniloae engaged with the deepest patterns in the thought of Maximus the Confessor have coincided with the rediscovery of this seventh-century thinker, who stood in his own time between the Christian East and West, on the part of a number of outstanding Western scholars, historians, and theologians, Hans Urs von Balthasar, Lars Thunberg, and Jaroslav Pelikan (who is now Orthodox) among them. Thus, a major figure in the theology of the first millennium, potentially of universal significance, has come to new life and new accessibility at the beginning of the third millennium. Something similar has occurred in the case of other major Byzantine theologians whose work has often been neglected in the West. Andrew Louth's magisterial study of St. John Damascene is a striking example of this. John Meyendorff's work on Gregory Palamas already in the 1950s aroused new interest in the West in the current relevance of this writer. Archbishop Basil Krivocheine, with his work on Symeon the New Theologian, and that of more recent writers, including Bishop Hilarion Alfeyev, provides another example of this trend. A more whole and balanced, as well as living and critical assessment of the interaction of East and West in Christian tradition, both in theology and spirituality, begins to become possible.

It is also significant in this connection to signal the revival, unexpected in the West, of monastic life on Mount Athos, and the beginnings of a new monastic theology to be seen in the writings of St. Silouan the Athonite and their exposition by his disciple (Staretz) Sophrony Sakharov. Similarly unexpected has been the revival in the non-Chalcedonian tradition of monastic life in the deserts of Egypt. Here the figure of Matta El Meskin and of Patriarch Shenouda III have both been of considerable and contrasting influence.

Since the great changes in Eastern Europe began, theological education has developed rapidly (if unevenly), and there is more vitality in some areas than there has been for centuries. In Russia, the extraordinary influence of Archpriest Alexander Men (murdered in 1989) has marked a whole generation of Russian intellectuals, especially those from a "dissident" background. His many books represent less a contribution to constructive theology than a program of orientation for theology, laying out basic principles for a critical but faithful reading of the Bible, for a theologically informed encounter with other faiths, and a vision for ecclesiology deeply indebted to the Russian speculative tradition of Soloviev and his disciples, but anchored in a robust sacramental doctrine. In the early 1990s, his influence was decisive in the formation of a number of study circles and "Institutes" for religion and theology in Russian cities. The Higher School of Religions and Philosophy in Saint Petersburg has been especially active, and has produced outstandingly interesting work in its journals. Here you will find essays on patristics alongside translations into Russian of Levinas and Voegelin and discussions of phenomenology and postmodernism, as well as literary-critical papers and studies in cultural history. The whole enterprise is a worthy successor to the work of the great Russian thinkers of the pre-Revolutionary period, whose significance for modern Russia has not been overlooked. Whether the leadership of the Russian church will be able to respond to this resurgence of intellectual creativity in a constructive way remains to be seen, but there are some signs of new life in the larger seminaries.

The constraints and tensions of modern ecumenical dialogue have not, on the whole, encouraged exploratory or creative theology in the Orthodox world in the past couple of decades (with some outstanding exceptions), but there are many encouraging signs, in the Third World as well as in Europe and the United States. Orthodox theology has lately had a considerable impact on Western theology (Congar on tradition and the Holy Spirit, Moltmann on the Trinity, various writers on the church), and is increasingly studied with academic seriousness. In the face of apparent tendencies toward ultra-conservatism in the aftermath of the fall of communism, there are also theological tendencies creating new possibilities for interchange. Many connections – historical and systematic – are coming to be made.

On the philosophical front, Zizioulas' recent work suggests the possibility of useful interaction between this kind of ecclesiology and various Western attempts at "postmodern" or "postliberal" schemes, in its critique of a metaphysic of unrelated substances and an epistemology based on the myth of a detached or neutral subjectivity. Orthodox theologians have shown willingness to engage with Heidegger, but it is perhaps time for a comparable engagement with Gadamer on the one hand and Wittgenstein on the other (the Romanian novelist Petru Dumitriu has testified eloquently to the importance of Wittgenstein in his own recovery of Christian commitment, but his is not a voice heard at all clearly within "mainstream" Orthodox theology).

For this sort of development to go forward, Orthodox theology at large has to overcome a certain suspicion of (at worst, contempt for) the world of Western philosophy, a suspicion that is part of the inheritance of the debates in the Russian emigration earlier in this century. The impressive examples of Clément and Yannaras, and (from the non-Chalcedonian world) Metropolitan Paulos Mar Gregorios of New Delhi, have shown what can be achieved by confronting the mainstream of European intellectual life, scientific and political as well as philosophical, with perspectives formed, but not restricted, by the Greek patristic vision. And it may be that, if this is to flourish, there needs also to be a new appreciation – however critical it may still be – of the contribution of the Russian religio-philosophical tradition, a reclaiming and reworking of some of the themes of Soloviev and Bulgakov. There are indeed distinct signs of a renewed interest in the work of Bulgakov himself, and of his friend Pavel Florensky, as more of their work becomes available in translation.

Particularly as a result of the Russian Revolution in 1917, and consequences that followed from it in other parts of Eastern Europe, the Orthodox churches passed through periods of extraordinary turbulence in the twentieth century. In many contexts theological education of a systematic academic kind was simply not viable. In these circumstances, Orthodox thought has shown remarkable resilience and self-renewing energy. This reinvigoration of theological activity in Eastern Europe, the continued productivity among Orthodox thinkers in the West, and the emerging interchange between them, are trends which carry great promise.

Acknowledgment

The third section of this chapter and the bibliography have been substantially revised and enlarged by A. M. Allchin and Peter C. Bouteneff.

Bibliography

Primary

Bulgakov, S. N., *The Wisdom of God* (London, 1937).
—— *Du verbe incarné* (Paris, 1943).
—— *Le Paraclet* (Paris, 1946).

—— *Philosophy of Economy: The World as Household*, trans., ed., and intr. Catherine Evtuhov (New Haven, CT, 2000).
—— *The Bride of the Lamb*, trans. Boris Jakim (Grand Rapids, MI, 2002).

Florensky, Pavel, *Iconostasis*, trans. Donald Sheehan and Olga Andrejev (Crestwood, NY, 1996).

—— *The Pillar and Ground of the Truth*, trans. Boris Jakim (Princeton, NJ, 1997).

Florovsky, Georges, *The Collected Works of Georges Florovsky* (Belmont, MA, 1972–9).

Lossky, V. N., *The Mystical Theology of the Eastern Church* (Cambridge, 1957).

—— *Orthodox Theology: An Introduction* (Clément's digest of Lossky's lectures) (Crestwood, NY, 1959).

Plekon, M. (ed.), *Tradition Alive: On the Church and the Christian Life in Our Time/Readings from the Eastern Church* (New York, 2003).

Staniloae, Dumitru, *Theology and the Church* (Crestwood, NY, 1980).

—— *The Experience of God (Orthodox Dogmatic Theology, Vol. 1: Revelation and Knowledge of the Triune God)* (Boston, MA, 1998).

—— *The Experience of God (Orthodox Dogmatic Theology, Vol. 2: The World, Creation, and Deification)* (Boston, MA, 2000).

Williams, Rowan (ed., trans., intr., and commentary), *Sergii Bulgakov: Towards a Russian Political Theology* (Edinburgh, 1999).

Secondary

Arjakovsky, Antoine, *La Génération des penseurs religieux de l'émigration Russe: La Revue 'La Voie' (Put'), 1925–1940* (Paris, 2002).

Blane, Andrew (ed.), *Georges Florovsky: Russian Intellectual and Orthodox Churchman* (Crestwood, NY, 1993).

Clément, O., *Questions sur l'homme* (Paris, 1972).

Dumitriu, P., *To the Unknown God* (London, 1982).

Evdokimov, P., *L'Orthodoxie* (Neuchâtel, 1965).

Gregorios, Paulos Mar, *The Human Presence* (Geneva, 1978).

Lelouvier, Y. N., *Perspectives russes sur l'église. Un théologien contemporain: Georges Florovsky* (Paris, 1968).

Nichols, Aidan, *Light From the East* (Edinburgh, 1995).

Read, C., *Religion, Revolution and the Russian Intelligentsia, 1900–1912* (London, 1979).

Roberts, E. and Shukman, A. (eds), *Christianity for the Twenty-First Century: The Life and Work of Alexander Men* (London, 1996).

Schmemann, A., *The World as Sacrament* (London, 1966), revised and expanded as *For the Life of the World: Sacraments and Orthodoxy* (Crestwood, NY, 1973).

Valliere, P., *Modern Russian Theology: Bukharev, Soloviev, Bulgakov: Orthodox Theology in a New Key* (Grand Rapids, MI, 2000).

Ware, K., *The Orthodox Way* (London, 1979).

—— *The Inner Kingdom: The Collected Works, Vol. 1* (Crestwood, NY, 2000); further volumes forthcoming.

Williams, G. H., "Georges Vasilievich Florovsky," *Greek Orthodox Theological Review* (1965), pp. 7–107.

Williams. R., "The Via Negativa and the Foundations of Theology: An Introduction to the Thought of V. N. Lossky," in *New Studies in Theology I*, ed. Stephen Sykes and Derek Holmes (London, 1980), pp. 95–117.

Yannaras, Christos, *The Freedom of Morality* (Crestwood, NY, 1984).

—— *Elements of Faith* (Edinburgh, 1991).

Zernov, N., *The Russian Religious Renaissance of the Twentieth Century* (London, 1963).

Zizioulas, J., *Being as Communion: Studies in Personhood and the Church* (Crestwood, NY, 1985).

Pentecostal and Charismatic Theology

Allan Anderson

Introduction

Pentecostalism emerged near the beginning of the twentieth century to become the fastest growing segment of Christianity found in almost every country in the world. There is a distinction between "classical" Pentecostal denominations (those which began in the first quarter of the twentieth century with roots in the Azusa Street Revival of 1906–8 in Los Angeles), the Charismatic movement within the "historic" churches (since around 1960), and the newer Charismatic and "Third Wave" independent churches (since around 1975). But these later movements were influenced by classical Pentecostalism and will be treated as essentially the same. The terms "Charismatic," "Pentecostal," and "Pentecostalism" refer to these different expressions, except when it is necessary to make the distinction.

At the beginning of the twentieth century various independent, evangelical, and "Holiness" groups existed in the Western world and on the Protestant mission fields with a particular expectation that the end of the world was to be accompanied by a worldwide outpouring of the Spirit. Premillennial dispensationalism, the revivalistic theology of popular nineteenth-century preachers like Charles Finney, Phoebe Palmer, and Dwight Moody, healing evangelists and the Keswick "higher life" movement in Britain fueled these ideas. The idea emerged that a crisis experience separate from conversion known as baptism in the Spirit should be received by every Christian as an "enduement with power." Charles Parham, a former Methodist preacher in Topeka, Kansas was responsible for formulating a new doctrine of Spirit baptism accompanied by speaking in tongues, and creating an "Apostolic Faith" movement in 1901. William Seymour, an African American preacher from Houston, went to Los Angeles with this message in 1906, and the Azusa Street Revival that he led for the following three years marked the birth of Pentecostalism and its transformation into an international movement.[1] In different parts of the world Pentecostalism was able to absorb various revivalistic movements that had occurred independently of events in North America, and within two years had already reached more than forty countries.

The second phase of Pentecostalism began in the late 1950s and 1960s, when ministers and members in the older Protestant churches began to seek the Pentecostal experience for themselves, the most notorious being that of Episcopalian vicar Dennis Bennett in 1960, reported in *Time* and *Newsweek*. In 1967 Pentecostalism entered the Catholic Church through contact with Pentecostals, influential Pentecostal publications like David Wilkerson's *The Cross and the Switchblade*, and healing evangelists like Oral Roberts. The Catholic Charismatic movement has since become the largest force within global Pentecostalism with its particularly sacramental form of Pentecostal theology, but as this is kept within the boundaries of Catholic theology it will not be dealt with here. In the mid-1970s a third phase of the movement arose in the form of independent churches that had only a tenuous relationship with denominational Pentecostalism and the Charismatic movement, but with the same distinctive emphasis on the gifts of the Holy Spirit that characterized the earlier movements. These "Neopentecostal" and Third Wave churches included some of the largest "megachurches" in the world by the end of the twentieth century and seemed the fastest growing sector within global Pentecostalism. These three phases of Pentecostalism are an oversimplification that strictly speaking only pertains to the Western world, and the emphases that we will consider belong to all the many different forms of Pentecostalism, including the distinctive African "churches of the Spirit" and Chinese grassroots Christianity. Pentecostalism today consists of literally thousands of movements, organizations, and denominations. As movements made up of ordinary people and (until recently) not having scholars trained in traditional theology, it is difficult to find prominent representative theologians within Pentecostalism, so this essay will attempt to collate from the many popular publications that have appeared and the writings of recent Pentecostal scholars. Most of these publications reflect the radical evangelical and "Holiness" theology out of which Pentecostalism emerged.

The Experience of the Spirit

The first Pentecostals believed that the Spirit had been poured out on them in order to engage in the end-time "harvest of souls" that would accompany the preaching of the "full gospel" throughout the world. Their efforts were grounded in the conviction that the Holy Spirit was the motivating power behind all such activity, and their Spirit baptism with the sign of speaking in tongues had given them different languages of the world. Pentecostals place primary emphasis on being "sent by the Spirit" and depend more on what is described as the Spirit's leading than on formal structures. People called "missionaries" did that job because the Spirit directed them to do it, often through some spiritual revelation like a prophecy, a dream, or a vision, and even through an audible voice perceived to be that of God. Pentecostal leader J. Roswell Flower wrote in 1908: "When the Holy Spirit comes into our hearts, the missionary spirit comes in with it; they are inseparable . . . Carrying the gospel to hungry souls in this and other lands is but a natural result."[2] Pentecostal missionaries got on with the job in a hurry, believing that the time was short. Declared *Apostolic Faith*: "This is a worldwide revival, the last Pentecostal revival to bring our Jesus. The church is taking her last march to meet her beloved."[3] Their mission activity was grounded in this premillennial eschatology and so their theology was a theology on the move.

The various expressions of Pentecostalism have one common experience and distinctive theme: a personal encounter with the Spirit of God enabling and empowering people for service, an experience often called the baptism in (or with) the Spirit. Pentecostals often declare that "signs and wonders" accompany this encounter, certain evidence of "God with us." Through their experience of the Spirit, Charismatics make the immanence of God tangible. Although different Charismatics do not always agree on the precise formulation of their theology of the Spirit, the emphasis on divine encounter and the resulting transformation of life is always there. This is what likens Charismatics to the mystical traditions, perhaps more than any other contemporary form of Christianity. Most early Pentecostals spoke of a longing for this experience, followed by extreme physical sensations and feelings of elation, and culminating in a release usually involving speaking in tongues, either at the same time as the "baptism" or soon afterwards. They spoke universally of this central experience and many believed that this Spirit baptism was normally accompanied by speaking in tongues. The first and subsequent issues of the Azusa Street newspaper *Apostolic Faith* declared their official position: "The Baptism with the Holy Ghost is a gift of power upon the sanctified life; so when we get it we have the same evidence as the Disciples received on the Day of Pentecost (Acts 2: 3, 4), in speaking in new tongues."[4] The "blessing" of Spirit baptism accompanied by tongues speaking was the doctrine that distinguished the early Pentecostals from other radical Holiness people. Undoubtedly, speaking in tongues was the most distinctive and central preoccupation of early Pentecostal experience.

William Seymour and most early Pentecostals believed that speaking in tongues was a gift of foreign languages (*xenolalia*) with which to preach the gospel to the ends of the earth in the "last days." Declared *Apostolic Faith*: "The baptism with the Holy Ghost makes you a witness unto the uttermost parts of the earth. It gives you power to speak in the languages of the nations."[5] Several issues of this newspaper claimed that foreign languages had been given to recipients of Spirit baptism at Azusa Street, by which their mission fields were identified. The belief in the restoration of tongues for missionary evangelism had been around in the Holiness and evangelical movements for at least two decades before the beginning of Pentecostalism, but this was seen as the fulfillment of that expectation. Many Pentecostal missionaries were later disillusioned when their hearers did not understand their tongues, but most adjusted their theology to a belief in "unknown" tongues, *glossolalia* instead of *xenolalia*.

Classical Pentecostals are usually taught to believe in the two distinct doctrines of "consequence" or "initial evidence" (that speaking in tongues is the consequence, or primary evidence, of Spirit baptism) and "subsequence" (that Spirit baptism is a definite and subsequent experience to conversion). The doctrine of consequence or initial evidence was probably first formulated in 1901 by Charles Parham, who made the theological link between tongues speaking and Spirit baptism. The doctrine was emphasized by the Azusa Street mission and has been a characteristic of North American Pentecostalism ever since, permeating its early publications and continuing to be a fundamental belief of most classical Pentecostal denominations in the Western world. The doctrine of subsequence had earlier origins in the nineteenth century Holiness movement. The Holiness interpretation of the teachings of John Wesley was that he was thought to have taught a "second work of grace" subsequent to conversion that came to be called "perfect love" or "sanctification." Pentecostals came to associate this experience with Spirit baptism.

Classical Pentecostals usually support the doctrines of consequence and subsequence by referring to the Book of Acts, especially the Day of Pentecost experience (Acts 2: 4), the experience of the Samaritans (Acts 8: 4–19), Cornelius (Acts 10: 44–8), and the disciples at Ephesus (Acts 19: 1–7) as normative models for all Christians. These passages, it is said, indicate that there is an experience of receiving the Spirit some time after conversion and that in each case, expressly or impliedly, those who received the Spirit spoke in tongues. Pentecostals point further to the experience of Paul, who wished that all the Corinthian believers spoke in tongues, but thanked God that he spoke in tongues "more than you all" (1 Corinthians 14: 5, 18). Classical Pentecostals have got around the implied statement of Paul that not all speak in tongues (1 Corinthians 12: 30) by distinguishing between tongues as a "sign" (as evidence of Spirit baptism) and tongues as a "gift" (not for all believers to use in church meetings). On the basis of these scriptures, they claim that the normative pattern of Spirit baptism is the "initial evidence" of speaking in tongues. The statement of faith of the interdenominational organization Pentecostal and Charismatic Churches of North America affirms: "We believe that the full gospel includes holiness of heart and life, healing for the body, and baptism in the Holy Spirit with the evidence of speaking in other tongues as the Spirit gives the utterance."[6] Some Charismatics, especially those from the early years of the movement, have followed this teaching, like J. Rodman Williams, a Presbyterian scholar, who says that speaking in tongues is the "primary activity consequent to the reception of the Holy Spirit."[7] With most Pentecostals, Spirit baptism is a distinct and separate experience that follows salvation; and it follows that for them, some Christians can be "saved" but not yet filled with the Spirit.

The doctrines of consequence and subsequence have been hotly debated, especially in recent years. James Dunn was one of the most influential evangelical scholars to enter into serious debate with Pentecostals on the subject of subsequence. His main argument is that the gift of the Spirit (or Spirit baptism) is primarily an experience linked to conversion and is not a distinctively subsequent experience that Christians should be encouraged to seek. In other words, in his view Spirit baptism is synonymous with conversion. He says that to "become a Christian, in short, is to receive the Spirit of Christ, the Holy Spirit. What the Pentecostal attempts to separate into two works of God is one single divine act." Several Pentecostal and Charismatic scholars have written long treatises in defense of the doctrine of subsequence in reply, the substance of which was that while they agreed with Dunn's contention that Paul's theology of the Spirit is primarily soteriological and initiatory (emphasizing the role of the Spirit in conversion), the theology of Luke is predominantly charismatic and prophetic, emphasizing empowering for mission. Dunn is therefore reading Pauline theology into the Lukan accounts, they maintain.[8]

The doctrine of consequence, another cornerstone of classical Pentecostal theology, has also been challenged, including from within classical Pentecostalism. As far back as the year the Azusa Street Revival began (1906), American missionary Minnie Abrams of Pandita Ramabai's Mukti Mission in India wrote that speaking in tongues would "usually" but "not necessarily" follow Spirit baptism. Seymour, some of the early European Pentecostal leaders, and Willis Hoover (founder of the Chilean

Pentecostal movement) also questioned the "initial evidence" doctrine. In 1918, healing evangelist and early Assemblies of God executive member F. F. Bosworth resigned from the denomination over the issue, saying that the gift of tongues was one of many possible evidences of Spirit baptism. One of the first classical Pentecostals in more recent years to challenge the assumptions of initial evidence was Gordon Fee, a well-known New Testament scholar and minister in the Assemblies of God, the largest Pentecostal denomination. He suggested that although Pentecostals could describe speaking in tongues as "repeatable" they could not claim it was "normative."[9] Assemblies of God New Testament scholar Robert Menzies defends the issue of "evidential tongues," saying that Pentecostals have been able to offer clear theological support for this position:

> The Pentecostal doctrine of evidential tongues is an appropriate inference drawn from the prophetic character of Luke's pneumatology (and more specifically the Pentecostal gift) and Paul's affirmation of the edifying and potentially universal character of the private manifestation of tongues. Therefore, when one receives the Pentecostal gift, one should *expect* to manifest tongues, and this manifestation of tongues is a uniquely demonstrative sign (evidence) that one has received the gift.[10]

The Assemblies of God in the USA reaffirmed their belief in classical Pentecostal doctrine in their General Council in 1991, declaring that Spirit baptism is an experience "distinct from and subsequent to conversion," and that speaking in tongues is the "initial physical evidence" of this.[11] In the same year, Fee published *Gospel and Spirit*, in which he argued that the doctrine of subsequence is not clearly taught in the New Testament and should not be seen as normative. He stated that the Pentecostal experience of the Spirit was a valid one, but his critique of Pentecostal theology created a strong reaction, perhaps particularly because he was coming from within classical Pentecostalism as one of its best-known scholars. Menzies, for example, charged that Fee's analysis meant that Pentecostals had nothing new to offer the broader Christian world theologically, it challenged Pentecostal understanding of Spirit baptism at its deepest level, and it undercut crucial aspects of Pentecostal theology.

Some Charismatics, while acknowledging a distinct experience of Spirit baptism, think that tongues may follow this experience but is not the necessary evidence of the baptism. Others see Spirit baptism as an initiatory experience that is part of (or the final stage of) the conversion process, and that gifts of the Spirit (including tongues) are given to all believers. Still others, especially Catholic Charismatics, see Spirit baptism in sacramental terms, as a release of the Spirit already given in baptism. This view seeks to be more accommodating to the theological positions of the older church traditions.

The experience of the fullness of the Spirit is the essence of Charismatic theology, but it is also necessary to distinguish between Western forms of Pentecostalism and that in other parts of the world. In Charismatic churches in Africa, Asia, the Pacific, and Latin America, the all-encompassing Spirit is involved in every aspect of both individual and community life. This is particularly evident in the person of the prophetic or charismatic leader, who is preeminently a man or woman of the Spirit. Theology is acted out rather than philosophized in the rituals, liturgies, and daily experiences of these Pentecostals. Pneumatology therefore becomes the most prominent part of an enacted theology in these churches. Charismatic pneumatology becomes a dynamic and contextualized manifestation of biblical revelation. The tendency to oppose or discount the emotional in Christian worship made some Western forms of Christianity unattractive, but the emphasis on the Spirit in Pentecostalism gave Christianity new vibrancy and relevance. Many have possibly misunderstood the seemingly strange and unnerving manifestations in Pentecostalism (especially in the Third World), but many have also missed the essential, dynamic nature of "spiritual" Christianity as portrayed in the Bible and have crowded it out with rationalistic theologizing. The Holy Spirit is the one to whom credit is given for everything that takes place in many Charismatic churches. The Spirit causes people to "receive" the Spirit, to prophesy, speak in tongues, heal, exorcize demons, have visions and dreams, live "holy" lives – and generally the Spirit directs the life and worship of these churches, the "leader" of all its activities.

Sometimes there may be play-acting and manipulation through spurious manifestations of the Spirit – but Christianity throughout the world has false prophets and people who use religious sanctions to enforce their will. And yet a criticism often justifiably leveled at Pentecostals is that sometimes a theology of success and power is expounded at the expense of a theology of the cross. When the Spirit is seen as a quick-fix solution to human distress and want, there is a tendency to disparage the role of suffering in the lives of those Christian believers whose needs seem to remain unanswered. People are not only convinced by the triumphs of Christianity but also by its perseverance in trials. The Spirit is also a gentle dove, a Spirit of humility, patience, and meekness, of love, joy, and peace. Overemphasizing the power of the Spirit often leads to bitter disappointment and disillusionment when that power is not evidently and immediately manifested. Pentecostal pneumatology must not only provide power when there is a lack of it, but must also be able to sustain people through life's tragedies and failures, and especially when there is no visible outward success.[12]

Pentecostal churches in the Third World have made a real and vital contribution to a dynamic and contextual pneumatology. The difficulty with some Western approaches to theology is a dualistic rationalizing that does not adequately understand a holistic worldview uniting physical and spiritual, and personal and social, for there is a presumed interpenetrating of both. The so-called "contextual theologies" are often articulated within the parameters of Western theology. The theological vacuum created as a result has often been filled by the grassroots theology of Third World Pentecostals, which is really a theology from the underside and a people's theology. The Pentecostal churches have made possible a dialogue between autochthonous worldviews, religions, and Christianity at an existential level. Both the Bible and human experience in most of the world often transcend and defy explanations and rationalizations. Africa is illustrative of this tension, where many people regarded Western missionaries with their logical presentations of "theology" as out of touch with the real, holistic world that Africans experienced. Their deepest felt needs were not addressed and their questions remained unanswered. In contrast, Charismatic churches were motivated by a desire to meet the physical, emotional, and spiritual needs of Africa, offering solutions to life's problems and ways to cope in a threatening and hostile world. Their pastors, prophets, bishops, and evangelists proclaimed that the same God who saves the "soul" also heals the body and is a "good God" interested in providing answers to human fears and insecurities, accepting people as having genuine problems and trying conscientiously to find solutions to them. The God who forgives sin is also concerned about poverty, sickness, barrenness, oppression by evil spirits, and liberation from all forms of human affliction and bondage. This message makes Pentecostalism attractive to people in these contexts. The insight of Africa and other Third World societies that life is a totality, that there can be no ultimate separation between sacred and secular, and that religion must be brought to bear on all human problems is their great contribution to the West, a belief and faith that the West now desperately needs in the face of the devastation brought by secularization.[13]

Pentecostals and the Bible

For most Pentecostals, theology is inseparable from the Bible in which they find their central message. Although identifying to a great extent with the "evangelical" position on biblical authority, Pentecostals are not usually preoccupied with polemical issues like the unity and inspiration of the Bible and other theological niceties. Their purpose in reading the Bible is to find there something that can be experienced as relevant to their felt needs. It is mainly in the West (particularly in the USA) where some Pentecostal academics have more closely identified themselves with a "conservative evangelical" approach to the Bible. There, a greater emphasis is placed on "correct" biblical hermeneutics (the "right" interpretation of the Bible) and on written theology. But most Pentecostals rely on an experiential rather than a literal understanding of the Bible, and it is therefore not very meaningful to discuss the interpretation of the text alone. Pentecostals believe in spiritual illumination, the experiential immediacy of the Holy Spirit who makes the Bible "alive" and therefore different from any other book. They assign multiple meanings to the biblical text, preachers often assigning it "deeper significance" that can only be perceived by the help of the Spirit. Much Pentecostal preaching throughout the world is illustrative of this principle, where narrative, illustration, and testimony dominate the sermon content rather than esoteric and theoretical principles.

All Christians enlarge and condition the meaning of the Bible for themselves out of their own life context and experiences with their own inherent presuppositions. Pentecostal literalism is quite consistent with its roots in the Holiness and healing movements, where there tended to be the same literalistic, legalistic approach. But Pentecostalism cannot simply be equated with fundamentalism, as preachers constantly interplay scripture with contemporary life and present the text as a reflection of common experience. Pentecostals take the Bible as it is and look for common ground in real life situations. On finding these correspondences, they believe that God is speaking to them and can do the same things for them. The Bible therefore has immediacy and relevance to life experiences. Pentecostals focus on divine intervention in these daily life situations by constantly emphasizing the miraculous and unusual happenings in the community of the local church.[14]

Pentecostals and Charismatics usually interpret the Bible in a way that primarily makes use of the normal or customary understanding of the literal words. "How does the Bible relate to our daily experiences?" is the implicit question behind Pentecostal hermeneutics. This is not slavish literalism – the Bible is not usually read in isolation from a real life community and concrete situation in the communities in which Pentecostals and Charismatics are found. Many, perhaps even the majority of Pentecostals, are underprivileged workers, subsistence farmers, or are unemployed, and many are functionally illiterate. In keeping with a strong sense of community, Pentecostals usually read (or rather, *hear*) the Bible in the community of the faithful, during celebrations of communal worship, where it is often directly related to the real problems encountered by that community. This experiential interpretation of the Bible as it is prayed, sung, danced, prophesied, and preached in the worship of Pentecostal churches implies an understanding of the Bible from the underside of society, where ordinary people can interpret the Bible from the perspective of their own experiences and struggles.

Probably above all other considerations, the Bible is believed to contain answers for "this worldly" needs like sickness, poverty, hunger, oppression, unemployment, loneliness, evil spirits, and sorcery. Throughout the world, Pentecostals will tell personal stories of healing, deliverance from evil powers, the restoration of broken marriages, success in work or in business ventures, and other needs which are met, usually through what is seen as the miraculous intervention of God through his Spirit. All of these experiences are often backed up, either implicitly or explicitly, by scriptural support, or something that God had revealed. The Bible therefore becomes the source book of miraculous answers to human need, as well as confirmation of the reality of "supernatural" experience. Pentecostals do not separate their understanding of the gospel from their personal experience of the events the Bible describes. In their liturgy, the telling of stories or "testimonies" is prominent, where people are able to relate their experiences of divine intervention and preachers pepper their sermons with real life illustrations in order that the congregation may further participate in the hermeneutical process and bring these experiences into daily life.

The characteristics of Pentecostal hermeneutics are diverse, because Pentecostals come to different conclusions on the meaning of scripture, despite their formal confessions of faith. They are usually unaware of their own biases and limitations and sometimes have an inadequate hermeneutic for the application of biblical principles to moral issues. They have a pragmatic hermeneutics that selectively decides what parts of the Bible to take literally and then spiritualize or allegorize the rest, and they tend to exegete their experience in their testimonies, preaching, and teaching. However, the strength of Pentecostal hermeneutics lies in the serious role it gives both the biblical text and the human experience.[15] Pentecostals use the Bible to explain the central emphasis on the experience of the working of the Spirit with "gifts of the Spirit," especially healing, exorcism, speaking in tongues, and prophesying. The *charismata* of the Spirit are the proof that the gospel is true.

However, we must remember that the Pentecostal "full gospel" is essentially a Christological construct where Christ is centrally Savior, Healer, Baptizer, and Coming King. Pentecostals understand this full gospel to contain good news for all life's problems, particularly relevant in the societies of the developing world where disease is rife and access to adequate healthcare is a luxury. "Salvation" (sometimes called "full salvation") is an all-embracing term, usually meaning a sense of well-being evidenced in freedom from sickness, poverty, and misfortune, as well as in deliverance from sin and evil. Healing from sickness and deliverance from evil powers are major themes in the lives of Pentecostals and are seen as part of the essence of the gospel. To support these practices they refer to Old Testament prophets, Christ himself, and New Testament apostles who practiced healing.[16] The "full" or "foursquare" gospel not only means that Jesus is Savior who saves people from sin, but also Healer from sickness and deliverer of people from the power of Satan. To this soteriological and Christological emphasis is added the pneumatological and missiological dimension: Jesus Christ is Baptizer in the Holy Spirit who empowers ordinary people to witness to the ends of the earth. To this is added a fourth, eschatological emphasis: Christ is the soon coming King preparing the church for his rule. The full gospel implies a reciprocal relationship between the Bible and the Spirit, for not only does the Bible explain the experience of the Spirit, but also perhaps more importantly, the experience of the Spirit enables people to better understand the Bible. The Holy Spirit is actually drawn in to the process.[17] Pentecostals believe that their message reveals an omnipotent and compassionate God concerned with all the troubles of humankind. Bishops, pastors, prophets, ministers, evangelists, and ordinary church members exercise the authority that they believe has been given them by the God of the Bible. Reinforced by the power of the Spirit, they announce the good news of deliverance from sin, sickness, and barrenness, and from every conceivable form of evil, including social oppression, unemployment, poverty, and sorcery.

Premillennial and "Realized" Eschatology

Early Pentecostals believed that their mission was part of the preparation for the soon return of Christ. The baptism in the Spirit and the tongues that they had received was above all a sign that the last days had come. Their eschatology was premillennial and dispensational, and it fueled the urgency of their evangelism from the beginning. Evangelistic sermons like those of Maria Woodworth-Etter and the early periodicals were filled with eschatological themes, probably the most prominent part of early Pentecostal preaching and teaching.[18] The belief in the soon coming of Christ overshadowed and motivated all missionary activities, tending to make Pentecostals poor strategists and little prepared for the rigors of living in a different continent and culture. When the end did not come as expected, Pentecostals adjusted to and adapted the mission strategies of evangelicals. The "eschatological hope" dominated the movement in its formative stage and the linking of the "full gospel" with the "last days" was a paradigm shift that set the Pentecostal movement apart from other evangelicals. *Apostolic Faith* was filled with this premillennial topic and reported many prophecies and visions to this effect. This was the motivation behind the emphasis on evangelism "before the end comes," and the more spectacular signs like speaking in tongues, prophecy, and healing were subordinate to and confirmed this emphasis. The signs and wonders that accompanied the preaching of the Pentecostal message were seen as evidence of the end time. It was believed that the new Pentecostal movement was the "Latter Rain" outpouring of the Spirit in the "Last Days" to precede the coming of Christ. It was the fulfillment of prophecy, especially that of Joel 2: 28–32.[19]

This was an "apocalyptic vision" that resulted in a particular type of spirituality. The church was, as Church of God theologian Steven Land puts it, "an eschatological community of universal mission in the power and demonstration of the Spirit."[20] The imminent return of Christ was the primary motivation for evangelism and world mission, which was seen essentially not as converting the world to Christ (evangelism), but as engaging in activity (evangelization) that would hasten the return of Christ in fulfillment of Matthew 24: 14. One of the first missionaries from Azusa Street, A. G. Garr, wrote in a letter from Hong Kong in 1909 that "His banner of love may float over all nations, and that His glorious Gospel may go forth, bringing out a people for His name's sake, that our King may come again."[21] Classical Pentecostal missions have therefore always been based on a particular eschatological view of salvation history.

The futurist premillennial framework that most early Pentecostals followed (and is still followed by many "classical" Pentecostals today) was that propagated by the founder of the Plymouth Brethren, John Nelson Darby. The *Scofield Reference Bible* (1909), the most popular Authorized (King James) version of the Bible in use by Pentecostals in the English-speaking world until the 1970s, further promoted this framework. These were the sources of the narrow premillennial dispensationalism that dominated North American Pentecostalism and Fundamentalism for much of the twentieth century and resulted in elaborate and often fanciful interpretations of both future and current world events in popular apocalyptic literature. US Pentecostal theology and political attitudes were profoundly affected by this eschatology, even though there were elements of dispensationalism at variance with Pentecostal practice.[22]

The Pentecostal belief in the "soon" coming of Christ with its impending doom for unbelievers lent urgency to the task of world evangelization. A detailed premillennial eschatology in the Pentecostal movement, however, would only arise years later when, with the increasing institutionalization of Pentecostal denominations, a more theological explanation of the imminence of the coming of Christ was felt necessary. Premillennialism has become so widespread in classical Pentecostalism that Steven J. Land considers it an essential part of its spirituality. Robert Anderson points out that because belief in *xenolalia* and Pentecostal expectations of the Second Coming began to fade, eschatology was replaced by speaking in tongues ("initial evidence") as the central feature of Pentecostal ideology in North America.[23] Furthermore, the millennial zeal of early Pentecostalism has been dampened among the more prosperous Pentecostals of today. Land points out that "upward social mobility is clearly affecting the apocalyptic fervor and urgency as the world looks a little better to contemporary, more affluent North American Pentecostals," and that the eschatological hope and enthusiasm to witness is found "more nearly in its pristine state among the burgeoning Third World Pentecostals."[24] The other consequence of the eschatological stress of Pentecostals has been that their belief in the imminence of the end has meant that there is little time for matters of social concern, as it is more important to get "souls saved."

However, the various emphases of Pentecostalism by their very nature tended to blur the distinction and tension in eschatology between the "already" and the "not yet." The promise of the Spirit was not only the fulfillment of prophecy and the sign of the last days, but it was also the tangible evidence that the last days had already come. Because the new age had already come through the power of the Spirit, its benefits of healing, deliverance, and prosperity were now available for the poor, the oppressed, and the dispossessed.

The Positive Confession or Word of Faith movement surfaced in US American independent Pentecostal ministries in the second half of the twentieth century and was an indirect development from Pentecostal "realized eschatology." Baptist pastor E. W. Kenyon taught "the positive confession of the Word of God," a "law of faith" working by predetermined divine principles, that healing is a completed work of Christ for everybody, to be received by faith no matter what the evidence, and that medicine is inconsistent with faith. The development of the movement was stimulated by the teachings of healing evangelists like William Branham and Oral Roberts, contemporary popular televangelists, and the Charismatic movement. It is now a prominent teaching of Pentecostal and Charismatic churches all over the world. Kenneth Hagin, widely regarded as father of the Faith movement, popularized Kenyon's teaching and said that every Christian believer should be physically healthy and materially prosperous and successful, a teaching supported by selective Bible quotations. Hagin said that it was not enough to believe what the Bible said; the Bible must also be confessed, and what a person says (confesses) is what will happen. A person should therefore confess healing even when the "symptoms" are still there. Thousands of Hagin's graduates have propagated his Word of Faith message all over the world and Hagin's books, videos, and tapes have been sold in their millions. This type of faith teaching, however, although in a less developed form, has been part of Pentecostalism at least since the time of the healing evangelists in the 1950s, especially Oral Roberts and T. L. Osborne, both of whom are often quoted by Hagin and his followers. Hagin's teachings are based on the books of Kenyon and emphasize the importance of the "word of faith," a positive confession of one's faith in healing, despite the circumstances or symptoms. Kenneth Copeland developed Hagin's teaching with a greater emphasis on financial prosperity and formulated "laws of prosperity" to be observed by those seeking health and wealth. Poverty is seen as a curse to be overcome through faith. Through "faith-force," believers regain their rightful divine authority over their circumstances.

The Word of Faith movement teaches physical healing and material prosperity usually through special revelation knowledge of a Bible passage (as distinct from "sense knowledge") – a "Rhema word" that is positively confessed as true. The teaching asserts that when Christians believe and confess this Rhema word it becomes energizing and effective, resulting in receiving it from God. When people do not receive what they have confessed, it is usually because of a negative confession, unbelief, or a failure to observe the divine laws. Some faith teachers reject the use of medicine as evidence of weak faith, and overlook or minimize the role of suffering, persecution, and poverty in the purposes of God. The Word of Faith has been one of the most popular movements in US Pentecostalism, not only propagated in Charismatic circles, but also influencing classical Pentecostals. Apart from the fact that this teaching encourages the American dream of capitalism and promotes the success ethic, among its even more questionable features is the possibility that human faith is placed above the sovereignty and grace of God. Faith becomes a condition for God's action and the strength of faith is measured by results. Material and financial prosperity and health are sometimes seen as evidence of spirituality and the positive and necessary role of persecution and suffering is often ignored. The Holy Spirit is relegated to a quasi-magical power by which success and prosperity are achieved and the effectiveness of the message is determined by the physical results.

Some critics have tried to link the Word of Faith teaching with Norman Vincent Peale's Positive Thinking, with dualistic materialism and even with nineteenth-century New Thought and Christian Science, but it is probably more helpful to see this movement within the context of Pentecostalism and its healing emphasis. Early Pentecostal preachers like Smith Wigglesworth emphasized faith and wrote words often quoted by Word of Faith preachers as long ago as 1924: "I am not moved by what I see. I am moved only by what I believe."[25]

Criticisms of the Word of Faith message have to reckon with the fact that the Bible is not entirely silent on the question of material need, that Christ's salvation is holistic, making provision for all human need and the enjoyment of God *and* his gifts. Salvation means the wholeness of human life, in which humanity has communion with God and enjoys the divine gifts. God desires to bless his children and this blessing seems to include provision for all their needs, but this is nowhere portrayed in the Bible as an irreversible law of cause and effect, as some "prosperity" teachers indicate. A "realized eschatology" which always sees the "not yet" as "already" is no worse than one that sees the "not yet" always as "not yet." One of the reasons for the emergence of independent and Pentecostal churches in the Third World was that many people there saw existing Christian missions as being exclusively concerned with the "not yet," the salvation of the soul in the life hereafter, and that little was done for the pressing needs of the present life, the "here and now" problems addressed by Pentecostalism.

Healing and Exorcism

Pentecostals understand that the preaching of the Word in evangelism should be accompanied by signs and wonders, and divine healing in particular is an indispensable part of their evangelistic strategy. Indeed, in many cultures of the world, where the religious specialist or "person of God" has power to heal the sick and ward-off evil spirits and sorcery, the offer of healing by Pentecostalism has been one of its major attractions. In these cultures, people see Pentecostalism as a "powerful" religion to meet human needs. The numerous healings reported by Pentecostal missionaries and evangelists confirmed that God's Word was true, God's power was evidently on their ministries, and the result was that many people were persuaded to leave their old beliefs and become Christians. Pentecostals believe that the miracle power of the New Testament has been restored in the present day to draw unbelievers to Christ. This is particularly effective in those parts of the world least affected by modernization, secularization, and scientific rationalism. The central role given to healing is probably no longer as prominent a feature for Western Pentecostalism, but in the rest of the world the problems of disease and evil affect the whole community and are not relegated to private and individual pastoral care or mere clinical treatment. These communities were health-oriented communities and in their traditional religions, rituals for healing and protection are prominent.

Pentecostals responded to what they experienced as a void left by rationalistic Western forms of Christianity that had unwittingly initiated what amounted to the destruction of ancient spiritual values. Pentecostals declared a message that reclaimed the biblical traditions of healing and protection from evil, they demonstrated the practical effects of these traditions, and by so doing became heralds of a Christianity that was really meaningful.[26] However, sadly, this message of power has become in many instances an occasion for the exploitation of those who are at their weakest.

The style of "freedom in the Spirit" that characterizes Pentecostalism all over the world has undoubtedly contributed to the appeal of these movements in many different contexts. A spontaneous liturgy, which unlike that of most older churches is mainly oral and narrative, carries an emphasis on a direct experience of God through the Spirit. It results in the possibility of ordinary people being lifted out of mundane daily chores into a new realm of ecstasy. This is aided by the emphases on speaking in tongues, loud and emotional simultaneous prayer and joyful singing, clapping, raising hands, and dancing in the presence of God – all common liturgical accoutrements. These practices made Pentecostal worship more easily assimilated into different cultural contexts, especially where a sense of divine immediacy was taken for granted; and these liturgies contrasted sharply with rationalistic and written liturgies presided over by a clergyman that was the main feature of most other forms of Christianity. Furthermore, this total participation was available for everyone and the involvement of women and the laity became the most important feature of Pentecostal worship, contrasting with the dominant role played by the male priest or minister in the older churches. Although many of the newer Charismatic churches have reinstated the traditional Protestant emphasis on the preaching of the Word by the minister as a central feature, it is still true to say that Pentecostalism allows for a much greater involvement in church services by ordinary members than is the case in older churches.

The Holy Spirit is the agent of healing and deliverance for Pentecostals and most believe in divine healing – they usually prefer this term to "faith healing" – a belief often bolstered by testimonies of people who have themselves experienced healing as a direct intervening act of God. Contemporary healing practices did not originate in early Pentecostalism, as the doctrines of "divine healing" and "healing in the atonement" were already widespread in the nineteenth-century Holiness movement and the ideas also existed in early Methodism.[27] Sickness, it was assumed, had its origins in the sin of humanity. At the beginning of the twentieth century, there was an expectation that signs and wonders would accompany an outpouring of the Spirit and a belief that healing was linked to the work of Christ on the cross. Healings demonstrated Christ's victory over all forms of affliction, a holistic salvation that encompassed all of life's problems. The presence of these signs and wonders was the realization of the coming of the Kingdom of God. For Pentecostals, the gifts of the Spirit, especially healing, exorcism, speaking in tongues, and prophesying, are proof that the gospel is true.

Early Pentecostals stressed that healing was part of the provision of Christ in his atonement, again following a theme that had emerged in the Holiness movement based on such texts as Isaiah 53: 4–5 and Matthew 8: 16–17. Dayton considers the "healing in the atonement" idea to have emerged "largely as a radicalization of the Holiness doctrine of instantaneous sanctification in which the consequences of sin (i.e., disease) as well as sin itself are overcome in the Atonement and vanquished during this life."[28] British Pentecostal Harold Horton represented the vast majority of early Pentecostals who rejected modern medicine. In his classic publication *The Gifts of the Spirit* (which first appeared in 1934) Horton speaks of "gifts" of healing "for the supernatural healing of diseases and infirmities without natural means of any sort." He says that "divine healing" is the "only way" of healing open to believers and "authorized by the scriptures."[29] Many Pentecostals have rejected the use of any medicine, traditional and modern, because its use is viewed as evidence of "weak" faith.

I am not convinced that the triumphs of medical science make alternative forms of healing redundant, as some would have us believe. For much of the world, this expertise is largely out of reach and unaffordable. As Claudia Währisch-Oblau has observed in China, the need for healings in Christian ministry there is in direct proportion to the unavailability of medical resources and the breakdown of the public health system. Prayer for healing is "an act of desperation in circumstances where they see few alternative options." She found that prayers for the sick and healing experiences were common to all the Chinese Protestant churches, and that healings were considered "normal" there. For people who believe themselves to be healed, the gospel is a potent remedy for their frequent experiences of affliction and is good news for suffering people.[30]

The pastor of the largest church in the world is David Yonggi Cho of Seoul, Korea. His teaching on sickness and healing is typically Pentecostal. Physical healing is seen as part of Christ's redemption, sickness is "from the devil" and a "curse," and God wants all people healed. Like most Pentecostal preachers, Cho makes extensive use of personal experience or "testimony" to illustrate his theology. This is particularly noticeable on the subject of healing, when Cho often refers to his own sicknesses and how he was healed, and gives testimonies of people healed during his ministry to them. Cho makes much of the experience of being "born again" and all his books have a strong soteriological and Christocentric tone. His holistic view of salvation is in common with Pentecostals all over the world, and one of the reasons why the Pentecostal message has spread rapidly among people in great need.[31]

Deliverance from demons, or exorcism, has always been a prominent part of Pentecostal praxis and exhibits a wide variety of procedures. Most Pentecostals believe in the biblical position of a personal devil (Satan) and his messengers known as demons or evil spirits. The reality of this dark spirit world and the need for there to be a Christian solution of liberation from it is particularly pertinent in those parts of the world where the unseen forces of evil are believed to be so prevalent. Exorcism, or as it is better known in Pentecostalism, "deliverance," is regarded as a continuation of the New Testament tradition and was a feature of the ministry of the healing evangelists and those regarded as having a special gift of "deliverance ministry." Although its incidence in Western Pentecostalism has probably declined, in some parts of the world it has become a very prominent activity, such as in Ghana and other parts of West Africa, where "prayer camps" have been set up specifically for the purpose of providing places for exorcism for victims of witchcraft. There are differences about what constitutes "demonization." Some believe that every mishap and illness is the work of Satan or his evil spirits, while others attribute only certain types of mental illness to Satan. Another commonly held practice related to exorcism is "spiritual warfare," an intense prayer activity where it is believed (on the basis of Ephesians 6: 12 and similar texts) that believers actively engage and resist the "spiritual forces of wickedness" that take control of individuals, communities, cities, and nations. During these times of intense prayer Pentecostals will sometimes fast for several days.

The widely differing Pentecostal and Charismatic movements have important common features. Far from being expressions of escapist behavior (as some have alleged), they proclaim and celebrate a salvation that encompasses all of life's experiences and afflictions, and they offer an empowerment providing a sense of dignity and a coping mechanism for life, and that motivates their messengers to share this good news with as many people as possible. Thousands of preachers have emphasized the manifestation of divine power through healing, deliverance, prophecy, speaking in tongues, and other Pentecostal phenomena. The message proclaimed by these charismatic preachers of receiving the power of the Spirit to meet human needs was welcome in societies where a lack of power was keenly felt on a daily basis. The main attraction of Pentecostalism in the Third World is still the emphasis on healing and deliverance from evil. Preaching a message that promises solutions for present felt needs, the "full gospel" of Pentecostal preachers, is readily accepted. Pentecostals confront old views by declaring what they are convinced is a more powerful protection against sorcery and a more effective healing from sickness than either the existing churches or the traditional rituals had offered.

Pentecostal Women

The Pentecostals, with their offer of full participation to all regardless of race, class, or gender, effected what amounted to a democratization of Christianity, a protest against the status quo. William Seymour's understanding of Spirit baptism included the dimension of racial, social, and gender equality in the family of God and a dimension of love for all people that transcended outward manifestations. Yet Pentecostalism has over the years not provided much theological justification for racial reconciliation, and the opposite has often been the case.

The use of women with charismatic gifts was widespread throughout Pentecostalism. This resulted in a much higher proportion of women in Pentecostal ministry than in any other form of Christianity at the time. This accorded well with the prominence of women in many traditional religious rituals in the Third World, contrasting with the prevailing practice of older churches, which barred women from entering the ministry or even from taking any part in public worship. Pentecostals, especially those most influenced by North American Evangelicalism, need to beware of limiting and quenching this most important ministry of women, who form the great majority of the church worldwide. Early Pentecostals declared that the same Spirit who anointed men also empowered women. One of the earliest women preachers in US Pentecostalism, Maria Woodworth-Etter, used biblical precedent to defend "women's rights in the gospel" to be "called and commissioned" as preachers. She declared in 1916: "It is high time for women to let their lights shine, to bring out their talents that have been hidden away rusting, and use them for the glory of God, and do with their might what their hands find to do, trusting God for strength, who has said, 'I will never leave you.'"[32]

However, the prominence (or otherwise) of women often depended on who told the stories. One female African American writer even suggested that it was Lucy Farrow, and not William Seymour, who was the main inspiration behind the Azusa Street Revival. But this liberty was grudgingly given in a male-dominated society. After its formation in 1914, a third of the Assemblies of God's ministers and two-thirds of its missionaries were women. However, women had no voting rights in their newly formed General Council, and they could be evangelists and missionaries, but not elders. Full ordination was granted to women in the denomination in 1935, but with so many limitations that few women sought ordination. Many of these limitations were only lifted in 2003. Nevertheless, as Harvey Cox observes, "women, far more than men, have become the principal bearers of the Pentecostal gospel to the four corners of the earth."[33] By 1936, two thirds of the members and half of the preachers and missionaries of US Pentecostal churches were women.[34] The prominence of women was certainly true in the Pentecostal movement in the USA, which earlier promoted the ministry of women whose exploits have been legendary. Florence Crawford left Seymour in 1908 to found the Apostolic Faith (Portland), Marie Brown (née Burgess) started the Glad Tidings Tabernacle in Manhattan, New York, and Carrie Judd Montgomery and Maria Woodworth-Etter held mass healing revivals all over the USA. Probably the most significant US American Pentecostal woman was Aimee Semple McPherson, who single-handedly built the largest Pentecostal meeting place in the world at the time and established a flourishing Pentecostal denomination in 1927, the International Church of the Foursquare Gospel. Many prominent early Pentecostal missionaries involved in the planting of Pentecostalism overseas were women. Kathryn Kuhlman astounded observers with her healing services in Pittsburgh and Los Angeles in the 1960s and 1970s, in which diseases were publicly identified and incidences of "falling under the power" or being "slain in the Spirit" regularly occurred. Women were effectively mobilized into service as ministers and founders during the early days of the Pentecostal movement both in North America and elsewhere, and the ministry of Pentecostal women continues today in many parts of the world.

The early emphasis on the ministry of women, however, formally disappeared later in classical Pentecostal missions and the importance of the experience of Spirit baptism in the lives of female ministers had "to take second place to the general patriarchal structure of church and society."[35] Cheryl Johns says "the Pentecostal story contains the story of the conscientization of women," a story "rich with symbols of freedom, partnership, and hope." She shows how the baptism in the Spirit in early Pentecostalism brought about a new dimension of freedom whereby women preached, spoke in tongues, gave interpretations, laid hands on the sick for healing, became missionaries, and led churches and even whole movements. Spirit baptism and the call of God were the only qualifications for the ministry, and this "preempted social norms and accepted patterns of ministry." Johns says the Pentecostal manifestations of the Spirit "served to liberate the people from dehumanizing cultural, economic, and social forces." Many Pentecostals, she continues, "have been co-opted out of our revolutionary mission and accommodated to culture." The

Pentecostal movement has failed to address social evils, at times choosing to perpetuate cultural oppression – especially in regard to gender, race, and caste. And so the order of the day (at least in the USA) is now "an abundance of 'priestly Pentecostalism' which is characterized by a hierarchical male clergy and a high degree of institutionalism."[36]

Achievement and Agenda

Pentecostal theology has come of age. It has to deal with its past as it reflects on the vision of its founders, who were women and men of faith and action rather than theoretical theologians of the ivory towers and the cloisters. This demonstrates that it is at least as important to practice theology as to theorize about it. In many parts of the world there are a myriad of needs that will seldom be met by old-fashioned, rational, and rather impotent, philosophical Christianity. The innovative Christianity of Pentecostalism takes seriously the popular worldview with its existential needs and makes a valuable contribution to a practical and contextual theology. Pentecostal theology may have to come to terms with its departure from the passions that ignited its early stalwarts to achieve "great things for God" in an age when Christian faith was passing through a crisis of confidence, especially in the Western world. It has to acknowledge its evangelical past, but must avoid the dangers of being drawn on the one hand into a fundamentalism at variance with its free and spontaneous spirituality, and on the other, into an institutionalism that stifles its former flexibility to change with changing contexts. The old "full gospel" message of "Jesus Christ the Savior, Healer, Baptizer, and Soon Coming King" still rings loud and clear in Pentecostal churches throughout the world. These theological emphases render them "conservative," as does their biblical literalism. Despite the similarities, however, this does not amount to a form of fundamentalism, because Pentecostalism emphasizes the intuitive and emotional through the revelations and freedom of the Spirit, rather than following a slavish biblical literalism.

As far as the future is concerned, Harvey Cox and others have shown how Pentecostal spirituality is reshaping the very nature of religion in the twenty-first century. The mushrooming growth of Pentecostal and Charismatic churches and the "Pentecostalization" of older churches both Protestant and Catholic, especially in the Majority World, is a fact of our time. There seems to be no stopping the relentless advance of Pentecostalism, in contrast to most other contemporary expressions of Christianity that seem to be in a state of permanent decline. Anyone wishing to measure the religious temperature of our world must take a hard look at Pentecostal theology. The future of Christianity itself and the encounter between Christianity and other faiths is deeply affected by it. Pentecostalism is continuing to expand and influence all types of Christianity throughout the world. Increasingly, these influences and interconnections have become both global and heterogeneous. In creative ways Pentecostals and Charismatics have promoted a globalized Christianity that has not lost touch with its local context. So at least for the foreseeable future, the continued vitality of Charismatic Christianity is probably assured. The whole Christian church may be thankful that this is the case, for it may mean the salvation of Christianity itself in the next century from decline and eventual oblivion.

Notes

1 See on this Allan Anderson, *An Introduction to Pentecostalism: Global Charismatic Christianity* (Cambridge, 2004).

2 *The Pentecost* 1: 1 (Indianapolis, IN, August 1908), p. 4.

3 *Apostolic Faith* 1: 1 (Los Angeles, September 1906), p. 4.

4 *Apostolic Faith* 1: 1 p. 2.

5 *Apostolic Faith* 1: 4 p. 1.

6 See J. Rodman Williams, "Baptism in the Holy Spirit," in S. M. Burgess and E. M. van der Maas (eds.), *New International Dictionary of Pentecostal and Charismatic Movements* (Grand Rapids, MI, 2002), pp. 354–5.

7 J. Rodman Williams, *Renewal Theology (2): Salvation, the Holy Spirit, and Christian Living* (Grand Rapids, MI, 1990), p. 211.

8 Howard Ervin, *Conversion-Initiation and the Baptism in the Holy Spirit: An Engaging Critique of James D. G. Dunn's Baptism in the Holy Spirit* (Peabody, MA, 1984); James B. Shelton, *Mighty in Word and Deed: The Role of the Holy Spirit in Luke–Acts* (Peabody, MA, 1991); Roger Stronstad, *The Charismatic Theology of St. Luke* (Peabody, MA, 1984); Robert P. Menzies, *Empowered for Witness: The Spirit in Luke–Acts* (Sheffield, 1994).

9 Gordon D. Fee, *Gospel and Spirit: Issues in New Testament Hermeneutics* (Peabody, MA, 1991), p. 98.

10 Menzies, *Empowered for Witness*, pp. 246, 254–5.

11 Ibid, p. 246.

12 See further Allan Anderson, *Moya: The Holy Spirit in an African Context* (Pretoria, 1991), pp. 41–6, 104–20; *Zion and Pentecost: The Spirituality and Experience of Pentecostal and Zionist/Apostolic Churches in South Africa* (Pretoria, 2000), pp. 239, 244–55.

13 See Anderson, *Moya*, pp. 100–4.

14 See Kenneth J. Archer, "Pentecostal Hermeneutics: Retrospect and Prospect," *Journal of Pentecostal Theology* 8 (1996), pp. 63–81.

15 See Walter Hollenweger, *Pentecostalism:Origins and Developments Worldwide* (Peabody, MA, 1997), pp. 307–21.

16 For more on this, see Anderson, *Zion and Pentecost*, pp. 137–41.

17 See Archer, "Pentecostal Hermeneutics: Retrospect and Prospect," pp. 63–81.

18 Maria Woodworth-Etter, *Signs and Wonders* (New Kensington, PA, 1916, reprinted 1997), pp. 483–4; *The Holy Spirit* (New Kensington, PA, ca. 1918, reprinted 1988), pp. 252–9.

19 For more on Pentecostal eschatology, see D. William Faupel, *The Everlasting Gospel: The Significance of Eschatology in the Development of Pentecostal Thought* (Sheffield, 1996).

20 Steven J. Land, *Pentecostal Spirituality: A Passion for the Kingdom* (Sheffield, 1993), pp. 59–63.

21 *Confidence* 2: 11 (Sunderland, 1909), p. 260.

22 See Faupel, *The Everlasting Gospel*.

23 Robert M. Anderson, *Vision of the Disinherited: The Making of American Pentecostalism* (Peabody, MA, 1979), p. 96.

24 Land, *Pentecostal Spirituality*, p. 76.

25 Smith Wigglesworth, *Ever Increasing Faith* (Springfield, MA, 1924, revised 1971) p. 30.

26 See Anderson, *Zion and Pentecost*, 120–4.

27 See Donald W. Dayton, *Theological Roots of Pentecostalism* (Metuchen, NJ, 1987), pp. 22, 115–41.

28 Dayton, *Theological Roots*, pp. 127–30, 174.

29 Harold Horton, *The Gifts of the Spirit* (Nottingham, 1976), pp. 99, 101.

30 Claudia Währisch-Oblau, "God Can Make Us Healthy Through and Through: On Prayers for the Sick and Healing Experiences in Christian Churches in China and African Immigrant Congregations in Germany," *International Review of Mission* 90: 356/357 (2001), pp. 87–102.

31 David Yonggi Cho, *Salvation, Health and Prosperity* (Altamonte Springs, FL, 1987), pp. 115–56; (with Harold Hostetler) *Successful Home Cell Groups* (Seoul, 1997), pp. 41–7; *How Can I be Healed?* (Seoul, 1999), pp. 15–20.

32 Woodworth-Etter, *Signs and Wonders*, p. 202.

33 Harvey Cox, *Fire from Heaven: The Rise of Pentecostal Spirituality and the Reshaping of Religion in the Twenty-first Century* (London, 1996), pp. 124–5.

34 Grant Wacker, *Heaven Below: Early Pentecostals and American Culture* (Cambridge, MA, 2001), pp. 159–61.

35 Willem A. Saayman, "Some Reflections on the Development of the Pentecostal Mission Model in South Africa," *Missionalia* 21: 1 (1993), pp. 40–56.

36 Cheryl B. Johns, "Pentecostal Spirituality and the Conscientization of Women," in H. D. Hunter and P. D. Hocken (eds.), *All Together in One Place: Theological Papers from the Brighton Conference on World Evangelization* (Sheffield, 1993), pp. 153–65.

Bibliography

Primary

Apostolic Faith 1: 1 (Los Angeles, September 1906).
Confidence 2: 11 (Sunderland, 1909).
The Pentecost 1: 1 (Indianapolis, IN, August 1908).

Secondary

Anderson, Allan, *An Introduction to Pentecostalism: Global Charismatic Christianity.* Cambridge: Cambridge University Press, 2004.

Anderson, Robert M., *Vision of the Disinherited: The Making of American Pentecostalism.* Peabody, MA: Hendrickson, 1979.

Burgess, S. M. and van der Maas, E. M. (eds.), *New International Dictionary of Pentecostal and Charismatic Movements.* Grand Rapids, MI: Zondervan, 2002.

Cox, Harvey, *Fire from Heaven: The Rise of Pentecostal Spirituality and the Reshaping of Religion in the Twenty-first Century.* London: Cassell, 1996.

Dayton, Donald W., *Theological Roots of Pentecostalism.* Metuchen, NJ: Scarecrow Press, 1987.

Faupel, D. William, *The Everlasting Gospel: The Significance of Eschatology in the Development of Pentecostal Thought.* Sheffield: Sheffield Academic Press, 1996.

Fee, Gordon D., *Gospel and Spirit: Issues in New Testament Hermeneutics.* Peabody, MA: Hendrickson, 1991.

Hollenweger, Walter, *Pentecostalism: Origins and Developments Worldwide.* Peabody, MA: Hendrickson, 1997.

Horton, Harold, *The Gifts of the Spirit.* Nottingham: Assemblies of God Publishing House, 1976.

Land, Steven J., *Pentecostal Spirituality: A Passion for the Kingdom.* Sheffield: Sheffield Academic Press, 1993.

Menzies, Robert P., *Empowered for Witness: The Spirit in Luke–Acts.* Sheffield: Sheffield Academic Press, 1994.

Wacker, Grant, *Heaven Below: Early Pentecostals and American Culture.* Cambridge, MA: Harvard University Press, 2001.

Evangelical Theology

David F. Wells

There are likely half a billion evangelical adherents worldwide, half as many as there are members in the Catholic Church but twice as many as in Greek Orthodoxy. They are a "multinational pluriform constituency," J. I. Packer writes, "a massive network of pulsating energies," and a religious world that is "constantly adjusting its cultural forms."[1] And it is also the latest burst of growth upon a tree whose roots go down very deeply into history. The difficulty in describing all of this theologically is, needless to say, considerable. I therefore need to limit my focus.

First, I will only be considering evangelical theology in the twentieth century and, in fact, I will be focusing mostly on the second half of that century. Evangelicalism undoubtedly thinks of itself as being in significant continuity with earlier traditions such as that begun by Wesley in the eighteenth century, or the Reformers in the sixteenth century or, before them, the fathers of the first five centuries. Yet, as we know it today, evangelicalism is the result of the burgeoning spiritual development that really began to gather momentum, in Europe and America, only after World War II. This has certainly been evident in the biblical and historical work that has flowed from evangelical pens in recent years, much of it finding its genesis in doctoral research in British universities,[2] and this in turn is now informing a new generation of theological work. Earlier, evangelical theology seemed to peak in individuals – James Denney, P. T. Forsyth, James Orr, B. B. Warfield, and, more recently, G. C. Berkouwer and Carl Henry – but this new work is looking more like a "school."[3] The towering peaks of earlier generations are now being complemented by ranges which, if they are sometimes smaller, are also more numerous and more diverse.

Evangelical theology builds upon scripture as the normative, interpretive framework by which reality is to be understood and at the heart of this revelation is the God who has given it. Early last century, James Denney said that theology is centrally about God and systematic theology is the systematic presentation of that understanding. However, he went on to say that the doctrine of God carries with it a worldview. Because theology "involves a general view of the world through God," as he put it, God "is related to everything that enters into our knowledge."[4] This worldview does not result merely from the appropriation of knowledge from fields outside of the biblical, but theology has something to say in its own right and that is what gives it its distinctive view of the world.[5]

To describe all of this, of course, is an enterprise too large for so brief an essay and so I need to delimit my focus, second, by looking only at the two core principles which are at the center of evangelical theology in its Wesleyan wing no less than in its Reformed wing, in its Anglicans as well as its Baptists. They are the Reformation's formal[6] and material principles, the twin convictions of the normative authority of the Bible as God's spoken revelation to the church and the indispensable centrality of Christ's cross understood in terms of penal substitution with its correlate of the need for personal conversion.

Sola Scriptura

The Reformation's principle of *sola scriptura* was its declaration that the written Word of God, because it is God's Word given to the church by the Holy Spirit's inspiration, is the authoritative source, the decisive criterion for Christian theology. The inspiration of scripture is understood to mean that God chose to unveil his nature, will, and intentions through the words of the biblical authors. Since he "has effected an identity between their words and his," Packer writes, "the way for us to get into his mind, if we may thus phrase it, is via theirs. Their thoughts and speech about God constitute God's self-testimony."[7] Because it is *God's* self-disclosure that we have in scripture, it follows that scripture must be antecedently true[8] and therefore, as David Tracy notes of this kind of approach, "the claims of modernity are not understood to have any inner-theological relevance."[9] Scripture is therefore to be interpreted on its own terms and not in terms of the cognitive norms of any subsequent culture. And despite its many literary forms and the cultural contexts in which its revelation was given, scripture is consistent with itself. Furthermore, it follows that the Holy Spirit, who worked within the biblical authors to produce this revelation and this consistency, is its privileged interpreter. No interpretation of scripture can be seen as tenable if it cannot be sustained by scripture itself. Therefore, "every other standard including, most particularly, the church as the single interpreter of the Bible and tradition as a 'second source' of revelation" is to be rejected, G. C. Berkouwer argues.[10]

The most expansive restatement of this general position in the recent period has been offered by Carl Henry. What stands out about his argument are first, the theocentricity of his understanding of biblical authority and second, the premium he places on reason as being the tool by which divine truth is grasped.

Revelation, he said, is "God's unmasking of himself, his voluntary act of disclosure," a disclosure that comes from "eternity, from beyond the absolute boundary that separates man from God." God himself thus breaks his own "eternal privacy."[11] In this startling and unexpected way, God stoops to make himself known. The Judeo-Christian religion, therefore, "centers supremely on the living God self-disclosed in his Word, and this biblically attested Word is communicated intelligibly in meaningful sentences."[12] Because knowledge of God is dependent upon God's own self-revelation, no more of him is known than what he has chosen to make known in this way. And what he has revealed comes in the form of personal address mediated through the language of scripture. The Holy Spirit's illumination, because of which the address is heard, is the illumination of the words of scripture and it is not some sort of parallel, extra-biblical revelation.[13] By this self-disclosure he makes himself known to his people. What is revealed in this way is therefore the presupposition of theology and theology is but the explication of what God has made known about himself.[14]

This conception therefore leads into a theological methodology which is deductive in nature.[15] Theology is the rational construction from this revelatory *a priori* because it is to reason that this revelation addresses itself in the first place,[16] though it would be incorrect to think that in the knowledge of God only the cognitive dimension is present. However, in the formulation of biblical truth,[17] logical consistency and inner, rational coherence are prerequisites for the validity of that work, since God is not a God of incoherence but of clarity, consistency, and order.

Henry's position, like that of evangelicals as a whole, must assume that the truth which God delivered through the words of scripture can actually be accessed by the reader.[18] In an earlier time this did not seem to be problematic, but clearly the Enlightenment raised questions on this point which have continued to gain force and, in the postmodern era, have taken a far more radical direction. They now rumble, somewhat ominously, through the academic world.

In 1957, Rudolf Bultmann wrote a brief essay that set the stage for much of what was to come in theology.[19] He argued that every contemporary exegete brings a modern "preunderstanding" to the text, that the text itself is "open," or fluid, and somewhat unfixed in its meaning, and that what it comes to mean happens in the moment of existential encounter. What the biblical text means was, for Bultmann, significantly decided by what was possible within the internal context of modern consciousness, for this is the only context within which that Word can be heard today. However, this preoccupation with the consciousness of the addressee of the Bible, Helmut Thielicke countered, typically reduces theology to anthropology. The issue, he argued, was whether "I draw the creative Word into my self-consciousness," in which case it ceases to be the creative Word, or "does the creative Word draw me into its sphere of influence," in which case I "am referred to something outside of myself."[20] Thielicke opted for the latter with qualifications and argued that this divine engagement, this cognitive liberation, is achieved as the Holy Spirit forms in the addressee a receptive consciousness, a new self-understanding. Yet it is not clear in Thielicke's work how exactly this consciousness is related to the revelatory Word or how the words of scripture are employed by the Spirit to create this new and different awareness. It illustrates the kind of difficulty of relating Word and Spirit which crops up periodically in evangelical theology.

This issue was brought to the fore at the time of the Reformation. Calvin not only argued for the authority of scripture but also for the necessity of the Holy Spirit's illuminatory role if the truth of scripture is to be received. But what, exactly, is the testimony of the Spirit which accomplishes this? Clearly, for Calvin, this illuminatory work of the Spirit should not be understood as a further revelation, authenticating the revelation already given in scripture, as if some further validation were necessary. Nor is it a revelation independent of that given through scripture. It is, instead, the Holy Spirit respeaking the words of scripture and opening minds to receive God's truth revealed in that biblical Word. Without "the illumination of the Holy Spirit," he declared, "the Word can do nothing."[21] With respect to the doctrine of scripture, he said, we must be persuaded beyond doubt "that God is its Author."[22] It is this persuading work that the Spirit does and the result is that faith is no longer beset by the doubts and vacillations natural to human experience.

It is this view of the Holy Spirit's work that became a part of the "Protestant principle." This is a principle, Bernard Ramm said, that is *external* in the functioning of the inspired scripture as authoritative and it is *internal* in the witness of the Holy Spirit who testifies to the authority which scripture has. "The *duality* of the Word and the Spirit must be maintained," he declared, "for it is in this *duality* that the Protestant and Christian principle of authority exists."[23] Yet maintaining both principles, and maintaining their working in relation to each other, has proved difficult.

On the more conservative end of the spectrum, it is the external, objective principle that is most commonly accentuated and reinforced. This probably has less to do with some kind of dependence on Enlightenment rationalism than with a healthy fear of what can happen in theology when this objective authority is supplanted by subjective intuition. In relation to the construction of theology, this has sometimes led to the Spirit's illumination being understated. Wayne Grudem's theology illustrates this propensity, for he has a substantial section in which he speaks first of scripture's authority but very little on the work of the Holy Spirit in relation to the biblical Word. By this authority he means "that all the words in scripture are God's words in such a way that to disbelieve or disobey any word of scripture is to disbelieve or disobey God."[24] He goes on to affirm scripture's perspicuity – that its main lines of teaching are clear – its necessity, and its sufficiency. The internal principle, the Holy Spirit's illumination, is not denied, but it is passed over in a paragraph and not really developed in its functional relation to the biblical Word at all.

On the other end of the theological spectrum, however, are the more overt expressions of the disengagement, in one way or another, of Spirit from Word. Donald Bloesch, for example, has refused "to posit an absolute equation between the letter of the Bible and divine revelation," but argues instead that the biblical words only point to "the self-revelation of Jesus Christ," which is where the locus of revelation lies.[25] Bloesch protects these revelatory insights which come, as it were, from above in much the same way as Barth did, by eliminating every other possible means of receiving any knowledge of God. God's acts in history are, Bloesch says, "superhistorical." They are "the work of God in history and not simply history itself."[26] The history Bloesch has in mind is not the network of earthly events, tied together by cause and effect, which can be investigated by reason but, rather, the plane of divine activity which is not subject to investigation and is grasped, not by reason, but by faith. And, like Barth, he has no place for natural revelation and thinks that the notion should be abandoned. After cutting away all scaffolding around faith, whether this comes from nature, history, or reason, Bloesch is then in a position to argue that "the decision of faith is as important as the fact of revelation in giving us certainty of the truth of faith."[27] Elsewhere, he distinguishes between the Bible being the Word of God functionally as opposed to being the Word of God intrinsically. He argues that "it is not divine revelation intrinsically, for its revelatory status does not reside in its wording as such but in the Spirit of God, who fills the words with meaning and power." It is the Word of God because "its authors were inspired by God; it becomes the revealed Word of God when God himself speaks through the prophetic and apostolic witness, sealing the truth of this witness in our hearts."[28] What Bloesch's kind of fideism means is that until the embrace of truth has happened, no truth has actually been given. Scripture is not, in and of itself, revelatory.[29] It is not intrinsically revelatory; it is only potentially revelatory and whether that potential is realized or not depends on whether Christ chooses to encounter someone through the words of scripture.

In the work of Stanley Grenz, the difficulty of relating Word and Spirit in the function of authority in the church becomes magnified still more. Like Bloesch (and for that matter, Barth), Grenz distinguishes between revelation and the Bible. "We cannot simply equate the revelation of God with the Bible," he asserts.[30] He thus makes a distinction between the word of God and the words of scripture. The former, he believes, is "the Holy Spirit announcing the good news about Jesus, which word the church speaks in the Spirit's power and by the Spirit's authority."[31] Elsewhere, he argues that the Spirit's speaking is not limited to the exegetical meaning of the text, but transcends it as he addresses the church today in its own particular context.[32]

Grenz has clearly shifted the locus of authority from Word to Spirit, which he does to avoid any kind of foundationalism. As a result, his discussion of special revelation is not placed at the beginning of his systematic theology, which would be customary, but is placed at the end. There, it is subsumed under the section in which he discusses the role of the Holy Spirit in the life of the church. It was, in fact, this kind of pietism that eventually led into Schleiermacherian liberalism, though this is something which Grenz rejects.

Furthermore, he shifts the hermeneutical locus from the Bible, in its capacity to interpret itself, to the community of faith created by the Holy Spirit. The Reformers viewed this kind of position as unacceptable because, they believed, it had led to the Word of God being taken captive by the teaching authority of the Catholic Church, with the result that its capacity to direct and reform the church had been rendered impossible without the consent of the Magisterium. What they rejected, Grenz has reappropriated, though the faith community he has in mind is one led, not by the Catholic Magisterium, but by local communities of faith.

It is rather clear, then, that in more recent evangelical theology the Protestant principle is being variously understood. However, it would probably be true to say that the debate over how the internal principle relates to the external is taking place, not so much in the traditional center of the evangelical world, but more on its edges. This bears out Fackre's observation that "the rubric *authority* is inseparable from its companion *interpretation*,"[33] because how an authority such as the Bible actually works all depends on what framework of theological understanding is established for it to discharge its authoritative function.

Solus Christus

The cutting edge of the Reformation slogans was the word "alone" or "only." The Reformers came to see that acceptance with God is found *only* through Christ, that it is found *only* because of God's grace, and that it is received *only* by faith. If acceptance with God through Christ's substitutionary work on the cross is solely because of God's grace, that means that the only contribution sinners make to their salvation is their own sin. If acceptance with God is found *in solo Christo*, then nothing can be added to what he did nor, indeed, does anything need to be added. They resisted every form of synergism in which God was thought to have contributed something to our salvation through Christ and we are left to complete what has been left undone by way of good works, church obedience, or penance.

It is this understanding which, in general, has flowed into evangelical theology, although there is a diversity of expression and emphasis that surrounds this unity. After all, the New Testament teaching on the death of Christ itself is expressed through multiple strands of thought. Its authors ransacked their vocabulary for words and images that might capture the meaning of Christ's death (words such as justification, reconciliation, propitiation, redemption, sacrifice, and atonement) and the result is a multifaceted understanding. In constructing New Testament doctrine, this language has to be worked out in its relations to the doctrines of God and to sin. It is this process that produces some differences in understanding. Speaking more generally, Berkouwer observed "there is hardly one aspect of the multilateral work of Christ which commands general agreement."[34] Yet there is a central core of understanding, which is in continuity with the Reformation, to which evangelical theology has been committed and on which it has been substantially agreed. So what does this consensus look like?

The central ideas can be summarized in a series of simple propositions. They are that Christ died for sinners, that he died to reconcile them to the Father, that he could not reconcile them without bearing their sin, and that he could not bear their sin without dying their death in their place.[35] These simple propositions grow out of an understanding of New Testament theology that sees Christ's death, not simply as a human tragedy, but as the provision of divine love as a result of which divine holiness is satisfied and sin's penalty is satisfied. When the apostles wrote about the Cross, therefore, they were writing about how Christ conquered what Luther would later call "the mighty powers" of sin, death, and the devil.

In this apostolic explication of the meaning of Christ's death, we also hear God's self-justification, the explanation as to how he remains just even as he justifies fallen sinners. It is at this point that the watershed lies between evangelical theology and the varieties of liberal thought that have continued into the contemporary period. The starting point of an evangelical conception is not in the benign good will of God but in his holy love, for the reconciliation of sinners is an impossibility if God's love has not provided the satisfaction for which his holiness calls. When that happened, his mercy was seen to have broken through his judgment.

This transaction occurred in space and time, in the fabric of history, as Christ bore our sins. To "say that Christ *bore* our sin is precisely the same thing as to say that he *died* for our sins,"[36] for he could not bear them without dying for them, Denney declared, and he added that the New Testament teaching admits of no other interpretation. P. T. Forsyth went on to explain that holiness "is not holiness till it go out in love, seek the sinner in grace, and react on his sin by judging it."[37] By the same token, love cannot but become sacrificial if that love leads to Christ's identification with sinners, for to be identified with them must mean that he stands with them in their fatal condemnation. It was thus because of love that he entered the wrath of holiness. Yet his act was God's because Father, Son, and Spirit are one in being. It was thus that the Godhead was joined in the common work of overthrowing sin, death, and the powers of darkness through the Son's work. In confessing the Father's holiness and in bearing its action, its judgment on sin, Christ did what only God could do. "In Jesus, then, we do not hear of God, we meet Him. He does not simply reveal God; he is God in revelation, the gracious God revealed."[38]

The death of Christ on the Cross, therefore, had its first effect within the Godhead itself. For when Christ died, he not only bore human enmity against God, but also the righteous wrath of God against that enmity. The biblical notion of propitiation should not be understood in a pagan sense, as if the Son had to placate and appease the Father who was unpredictable and capricious. Rather, it was the Father who himself provided the propitiation, so Christ's death was an offering made by God to God. As Bloesch puts it, "The holy God makes himself the object of his own wrath in the person of his Son Jesus Christ,"[39] thus enabling him to turn his righteous judgment away from sinners. In the Cross, therefore, is seen both God's love and his holiness, for it expresses both his judgment on sin and his love for sinners.

The consequence of this is explained in the New Testament by a number of images that reverberate through the pages of evangelical systematic theologies. Those who have been alienated from God, for example, are said to be reconciled through the gospel. This alienation has been twofold, for God is alienated from sinners by his righteous displeasure and they from him by their sin. In Christ, his wrath is turned aside and the penalty of sin is removed. Again, those who have been taken captive by sin and, behind that sin, by the powers of darkness, are redeemed and set free by Christ, who not only destroyed the hold of sin at the Cross but also broke the back of evil. And again, those whose sin has been imputed to Christ now have his righteousness imputed to them by grace alone through faith alone, and so may be said to be already justified.

At the time of the Reformation, the *solus Christus* tenet was advanced within an ecclesiastical context. It presented an alternative understanding to what prevailed in Roman Catholicism. Today, however, new questions have arisen about Christ's unique mediatorial role given the awareness which has steadily grown in the modern period of the other religions. Indeed, every religion which is built upon an authoritative source which claims to be uniquely true is confronted by the question as to how it is going to view the other religions. This is the case in Islam, as it is in Judaism, and it is even true of Hinduism. Is it true, then, that in Christ alone God meets us and in him alone salvation is found?

These are questions whose resolution has the power to transform the meaning of a person's theology, as we see in the case of John Hick. As a university student, he tells us, he had a personal conversion and became "a Christian of a strongly evangelical, and indeed fundamentalist kind."[40] However, some years later he had concluded that the dilemma he had to address was how he could reconcile the fact that there was only one true religion with his growing belief in the validity of other religions.[41] His conclusion, in the end, was that all religions are grounded in the same divine reality, that all are to some extent both true and false. The result was that he came to argue for a "theocentric" view of religions, one in which all religions are seen to be rooted in the same, non-trinitarian God. The consequence of this was that Christ was then seen to be no longer uniquely God incarnate. Divine language, Hick came to think, was used of him only in a metaphorical, not a metaphysical, way so Christ's participation in the divine differs from others in degree but not in kind. It was a recrudescence of classic Schleiermacherian liberalism. He then went on to declare with Paul Knitter, in the title of their 1987 book, *The Myth of Christian Uniqueness*. Clearly, Hick is now far from his evangelical point of origin as a university student.

This is not a road that evangelicals have shown too much desire to walk, though there are one or two exceptions. Notable among these is Clark Pinnock.[42] Pinnock's proposal was quite similar to what the Second Vatican Council had advanced. At its heart are two principles. First, he argued for the universal accessibility of salvation. This was based on biblical texts which state, for example, that Christ is the Savior "of all men" (1 Timothy 4: 10), that Christ is the light that lightens everyone (John 1: 9), and that God is not willing that any should perish (2 Peter 3: 9). These texts have most commonly been read as declaring the potential universal availability of salvation. Pinnock, however, understood these to speak of the universal *accessibility* of salvation. Second, Pinnock reaffirmed the traditional view concerning the indispensability of Christ to salvation, in contrast to what Hick has said. How, then, are these two principles to be made consistent with each other? What Pinnock did was to blur the distinction between general and special revelation, seeing in the disclosure God makes of his existence in nature and the reality of moral nature in all people (Romans 1: 18–20; 2: 14–15; Acts 17: 24–28) elements of saving grace which are mediated by the Holy Spirit. That being the case, the meaning of faith changes because it does not need to have Christ as its object. Furthermore, the Holy Spirit's work in salvation is also disengaged from any knowledge about Christ. For those who have not heard about Christ, or who are found in other religions, faith is defined simply as a trust in God. God accepts their faith, crediting to them the merits of Christ's death even though Christ remains unknown to them.

However, there are those who have wondered how different this solution really is from Hick's "theocentric" approach. Pinnock certainly holds a traditional view of the person of Christ as God incarnate which Hick does not, and yet at a functional level Christ has, as it were, been demoted in both proposals. For Pinnock, Christ remains unknown to those who turn to God outside of the hearing of the gospel, while for Hick, of course, he is simply unnecessary. Pinnock's suggestion that Christ can function savingly in this *incognito* way produces so many tensions and difficulties within the framework of evangelical thought that most evangelical theologians have decided that the historic stance of the church on this matter is less problematic than attempts at renovating it such as this.

What has bound evangelicals together, especially since World War II, have been the twin principles of *sola scriptura* and *solus Christus*. This certainly does not mean that these principles have always been held and expressed in exactly the same way, yet at the heart of the evangelical world there has been substantial agreement on these matters. And it has been this agreement which has generated its own form of ecumenicity. It is an ecumenicity which is not formally structured. There is no headquarters to direct its activities. Yet in loose and informal ways, it is an ecumenicity which has reached across the divides of ethnicity, culture, and denomination to enable evangelicals from around the world to communicate with each other, and to work together, as opportunity allows. It is one of the expressions of this ecumenicity to which I now turn.

Global Connections

The numerical center of gravity for evangelicals lies outside the West, but its theological center is still in the West, though a theological literature is now also emerging in Asia. The different contexts within which evangelical theology is now being done, and the different contexts into which it needs to speak, is what has generated a number of fruitful, cross-cultural exchanges.

The West, of course, is now highly modernized, its populations almost wholly compressed into cities, its capitalism advanced and flourishing, its technology brilliant and innovative, and its societies laced together by unprecedented lines of finance, transportation, and information. This social fabric, this modernized world, for a long time provided a comfortable home for Enlightenment ideology. These ideas, and the social context which has given them so much plausibility, is what promoted the rise of "modern consciousness." However, Enlightenment certainties have, in recent decades, become less certain and a considerable cognitive crisis within modernity has resulted. Today, in our postmodern condition, there are no longer any constructions that can be placed on reality that can be said to be true in any objective sense. The "metanarratives" have gone. The cognitive ceilings are falling.[43]

Evangelical theology done in this industrialized and urbanized West, if it is true to itself, must speak to this context. In doing so, however, its preoccupations become quite different from what would be typical in less developed parts of the world, though it is also clear that modernity is rapidly becoming a global phenomenon. In the West, theology is usually not driven to engage in sustained reflection on poverty, injustice, deprivation, disease, ideological and religious conflict, serious abuse of power, and systemic governmental corruption. Outside the West, these are often the realities that are far more pressing than the anxiety, the psychological homelessness, the loss of absolutes, the crumbling of meaning, and the obsessions with the self that are the hallmarks of modern consciousness. It is these very different experiences of life that cry out for cross-cultural dialogue for, without it, theology easily becomes lopsided, culture-bound, and impoverished. The question which arose was how evangelicals might unite across cultural and national boundaries in order to address some of these issues, recover the fullness of biblical faith, and so become more faithful in the propagation of the gospel.

Thus began a remarkable dialogue. In 1974, 2,700 evangelical church leaders and scholars assembled in Lausanne, Switzerland, for the International Congress on World Evangelization.[44] They came from 150 countries. Half were from the Third World and many from countries that, in the 1950s and 1960s, had emerged from under colonial rule at the end of four hundred years of European empire-building in the non-Western world. The participants came to reflect together on the nature of the gospel, as seen within its biblical context, and to understand afresh the consequent Christian obligations in the modern world.

This Congress was, in fact, continuing the earlier tradition of international missionary conferences that were notable in the second half of the nineteenth century and were the predecessors of the most important to that time, the Edinburgh Conference of 1910. What emerged from Edinburgh became, in due course, the

International Missionary Council which, in 1961, joined the World Council of Churches. From a structural point of view, then, the line of continuity ran from Edinburgh into the WCC. From a *theological* point of view, however, the line ran from Edinburgh into Lausanne. The evangelical impulse which had been present in Edinburgh has flourished far more easily in the context of Lausanne than in the WCC which, at Uppsala in 1968, even called for a moratorium on Western missions.

The Lausanne Covenant, which the Congress endorsed, reasserted classical evangelical theology. It grounded evangelism in the mandate given within an inspired, authoritative scripture. It defined the gospel in terms of God's forgiveness through Christ, rather than alternative notions such as the humanizing of society, and it framed all of this eschatalogically, thereby turning away from thoughts about the evolution of world history or the movement toward political utopias. It spoke instead of the inbreaking of God's kingdom which only he can bring about.[45]

Fifteen years after the Lausanne Congress, in 1989, over 3,000 gathered in Manila for a second Congress.[46] They came from 170 different countries which, at that time, was a larger number than was represented in the United Nations. These two Congresses helped forge links between evangelicals all over the world and provoked new thinking on a variety of biblical themes.

Following the 1974 Lausanne Congress, a number of smaller international gatherings were held to explore a variety of themes, only a few of which can be mentioned here. In 1982, for example, an international consultation was held in Grand Rapids in the US on the relation between evangelism and social responsibility. It was also a consultation about the relation between pragmatic American evangelism, fueled by American resources, and the way evangelism was being practiced in poorer parts of the world. Some Americans had, in fact, resisted linking evangelism and the exercise of social responsibility out of fear that a new Social Gospel movement might be born; many from the Third World insisted that the link must be forged because the gospel is discredited in the absence of compassion for those afflicted by disease, hunger, and injustice. The statement which emerged succeeded in addressing and resolving these competing perspectives.[47]

Two other consultations addressed the theme of Christianity and culture, the first being held in 1978 in Bermuda and the second in Uppsala, Sweden, in 1993.[48] The second of these considered the effects of modernity upon ideas of truth, authority, the doctrine of God, anthropology, morality, and eschatology. In its overall assessment, the second of these consultations was quite reserved about the prospects of Christian theology being able to sustain itself, at least in a traditional form, in the context of modernity, a reserve that now seems to be somewhat justified for, as the twenty-first century begins, Christian faith is growing everywhere but in the modernized West.

Finally, two consultations were held to consider the work of the Holy Spirit and conversion. The first was held in Oslo, Norway in 1985 and the second in Hong Kong in 1988. These consultations were jointly sponsored by Lausanne and the World Evangelical Fellowship. Despite the fact that the participants came from many different countries and cultural contexts, substantial agreement was reached on a variety of issues, such as understanding what is unique about Christian conversion, the role the Holy Spirit fulfills in bringing this about, and the interface between Christianity and the other religions.[49]

In looking back over the last half century, during which time this astonishing growth in evangelical faith occurred, and during which time it reached a new maturity, one fact seems to stand out above all others. It is that evangelical faith has grown and preserved its identity because it attempted to be doctrinal in its shape and biblical in its substance. It is this fact which explains how evangelicals have been able to work together so fruitfully across the divides of place, culture, and race. If evangelicals falter in the future, it will almost certainly be because they have been unable to stay this course. Evangelical theological identity is imperiled in many ways, but chief among them is the difficulty that attends maintaining a worldview that is markedly different from what prevails in the culture, be that the postmodern ethos of the West or the patterns of understanding that have grown up outside the West. In the West, those who inhabit a biblical worldview are those who have, for that reason, become a cognitive minority with all of the attendant pains that minority status brings. In this case, however, this status is entirely voluntary and therefore the temptations to yield to it are considerable. Preserving a biblical worldview is the greatest task evangelical theology faces, be it in the academy or in the wider society, and in working to do this it encounters its own greatest vulnerabilities.

Notes

1 J. I. Packer, "A Stunted Ecclesiology?" In *Ancient and Postmodern Christianity: Paleo-Orthodoxy in the 21st Century*, ed. Kenneth Tanner and Christopher A. Hall (Downers Grove, IL, 2002), 121.

2 See Mark A. Noll, *Between Faith and Criticism: Evangelicals, Scholarship, and the Bible in America* (San Francisco, 1986), 7–8, 122–41.

3 In addition to the works cited in this chapter, the following evangelical or conservative systematic theologies have appeared in the last half century and constitute this "school" of thought: James Oliver Buswell, *A Systematic Theology of the Christian Religion*, 2 Vols. (Grand Rapids, MI, 1962–3); Kenneth E. Geiger (ed.), *The Word and the Doctrine: Studies in Contemporary Wesleyan–Arminian Theology* (Kansas City, KS, 1965); Herman Hoeksema, *Reformed Dogmatics* (Grand Rapids, MI, 1966); John Murray, *Collected Writings of John Murray*, 2 Vols. (Edinburgh: Banner of Truth, 1977); Millard J. Erickson, *Christian Theology*, 3 Vols. (Grand Rapids, MI, 1983–5); Thomas N. Finger, *Christian Theology: An Eschatological Approach*, 2 Vols. (Scottdale, PA, 1989); James M. Boice, *Foundations of the Christian Faith* (Downers Grove, IL, 1986); Bruce Demarest and Gordon Lewis, *Integrative Theology*, 3 Vols. (Grand Rapids, MI, 1987–94); John M. Frame, *The Doctrine of the Knowledge of God: A Theology of Lordship* (Phillipsburg, KS, 1987); J. Rodman Williams, *Renewal Theology: Systematic Theology from a Charismatic Perspective* (Grand Rapids, MI, 1991); Alan F. Johnson and Robert E. Webber, *What Christians Believe: A Biblical and Historical Summary* (Grand Rapids, MI, 1989); Paul King Jewett, *God, Creation, and Revelation: A Neo-Evangelical Theology* (Grand Rapids, MI, 1991) and *Who We Are: Our Dignity as Human: A Neo-Evangelical Theology* (Grand Rapids, MI, 1996); Gordon J. Spykman, *Reformational Theology: A New Paradigm for Doing Dogmatics* (Grand Rapids, MI, 1992); Alister E. McGrath, *Christian Theology: An Introduction* (Oxford, 1994); Rousas John Rushdoony, *Systematic Theology*, 2 Vols. (Vallecito, CO, 1994); Morton H. Smith, *Systematic Theology*, 2 Vols. (Greenville, SC, 1994); Robert L. Reymond, *A New Systematic Theology of the Christian Faith* (Nashville, TN, 1998); J. I. Packer, *Concise Theology: A Guide to Historic Christian Beliefs* (Wheaton, IL, 1993). Omitted from this list, of course, are the many volumes

on particular theological themes or issues. Also omitted are the volumes in adjacent fields that bear on the doing of theology, such as Paul House's *Old Testament Theology* (Downers Grove, IL, 1998), George Eldon Ladd's *A Theology of the New Testament* (Grand Rapids, MI, 1974), and Donald Guthrie's *New Testament Theology* (Downers Grove, IL, 1984).

4 James Denney, *Studies in Theology* (London, 1907), 1. On the way in which worldviews have functioned in evangelical theology more recently, see David K. Naugle, *Worldview: History of a Concept* (Grand Rapids, MI, 2002), 5–32.

5 See Thomas Oden, *Systematic Theology*, 3 Vols. (San Francisco, 1989), Vol. 1, 329.

6 Oden's understanding of the formal principle is more complex in that he endorses the Wesleyan quadrilateral. However, he asserts that scripture is "the utterly reliable source and norm" of theology (ibid, 335) and that tradition, experience, and reason only have a legitimate function in the doing of theology as they are a faithful response to the truth of scripture. In this, Oden clearly is representative of other evangelicals who are outside Wesleyianism and who, in different ways, see a role for tradition and even experience in coming to an understanding of the meaning of scripture.

7 James I. Packer, "Biblical Authority, Hermeneutics, and Inerrancy." In *Jerusalem and Athens: Discussions on the Theology and Apologetics of Cornelius Van Til* (Nutley, NJ, 1971), 147.

8 In George Lindbeck's schematization, this approach is what he calls the "cognitive–propositional" position, one which sees biblical doctrine as providing accurate information about "objective realities" and the status of this doctrine is that of a truth-claim. See George Lindbeck, *The Nature of Doctrine: Religion and Theology in a Post-Liberal Age* (Philadelphia, PA, 1984), 129. However, it should be noted that Lindbeck's description of this position as one that is purely cognitive is inaccurate.

9 David Tracy, *Blessed Rage for Order: The New Pluralism in Theology* (San Francisco, 1988), 24.

10 G. C. Berkouwer, *A Half Century of Theology: Movements and Motives* (Grand Rapids, MI, 1977), 107. He has expanded on this understanding in his *Studies in Dogmatics: Holy Scripture*, trans. Jack B. Rogers (Grand Rapids, MI, 1975), 105–38.

11 Carl F. H. Henry, *God, Revelation and Authority*, 6 Vols. (Waco, TX: Word, 1979), II, 17.

12 Ibid, I, 27.

13 Ibid, IV, 256–315.

14 Ibid, I, 215.

15 See Peter Berger's description of this kind of theological methodology in his *The Heretical Imperative: Contemporary Possibilities of Religious Affirmation* (New York, 1979), 66–94.

16 Henry, *God, Revelation and Authority*, II, 225.

17 Ibid, II, 238–41.

18 Kevin Van Hoozer has defended this necessity against postmodern skepticism in his book *Is There A Meaning in This Text?: The Bible, the Reader, and the Morality of Literary Knowledge* (Grand Rapids, MI, 1999).

19 Rudolf Bultmann, *Existence and Faith: Shorter Writings of Rudolf Bultmann*, trans. Shubert M. Ogden (New York, 1960), 289–96.

20 Helmut Thielicke, *The Evangelical Faith*, 3 Vols., trans. Geoffrey W. Bromiley (Grand Rapids, MI, 1974–7), Vol. 1, 193–4.

21 Calvin, *Institutes*, I, vii, 4.

22 Ibid, III, ii, 15.

23 Bernard Ramm, *The Pattern of Authority* (Grand Rapids, MI, 1957), 30.

24 Wayne Grudem, *Systematic Theology: An Introduction to Biblical Doctrine* (Leicester, 1994), 27.

25 Donald G. Bloesch, *Essentials of Evangelical Theology*, 2 Vols. (San Francisco, 1978–9), Vol. 1, xi.

26 Donald G. Bloesch, *A Theology of Word and Spirit: Authority and Method in Theology* (Downers Grove, IL, 1992), 187.

27 Ibid, 21.

28 Donald G. Bloesch, *Holy Scripture: Revelation, Inspiration, and Interpretation* (Downers Grove, IL, 1994), 27.

29 Similar echoes of Barth are also heard in Gabriel Fackre. He begins by saying that scripture "is the *source* of authority" by which all theological affirmations must be judged. Yet it is Christ who is the norm for

the source of authority, which is the Bible. The Bible is read to see "how it bears witness to this One." See Gabriel Fackre, *The Christian Story: A Pastoral Systematics*, 2 Vols. (Grand Rapids, MI, 1978–87), Vol. 2, 52. What is left somewhat undeveloped is what the relation is between the Word living and the Word written, but clearly the fact that scripture is a "witness" to Christ suggests that he is the primary form of revelation, grasped in personal encounter, and the Bible is the secondary form of revelation. From a different angle, Dale Moody arrives at a similar point. It is pietism which leads him to say that special revelation "is an event in which God discloses himself to those who are ready to receive him," which suggests that if there is no reception, God can make no disclosure of himself and has not made any disclosure of himself, that the external principle of authority does not exist without the functioning of the internal. See Dale Moody, *The Word of Truth: A Summary of Christian Doctrine Based on Biblical Revelation* (Grand Rapids, MI, 1981), 38.

30 Stanley J. Grenz, *Theology for the Community of God* (Nashville, TN, 1994), 514.

31 Ibid.

32 Stanley J. Grenz and John R. Franke, *Beyond Foundationalism: Shaping Theology in a Postmodern Context* (Louisville, KY, 2001), 75.

33 Fackre, *The Christian Story*, Vol. 2, 63.

34 G. C. Berkouwer, *The Work of Christ* (Grand Rapids, MI, 1965), 9.

35 See John Stott, *The Cross of Christ* (Leicester, 1986), 63–7.

36 Denney, *Studies in Theology*, 104.

37 P. T. Forsyth, *Positive Preaching and the Modern Mind* (London, 1909), 254.

38 Ibid, 253.

39 Bloesch, *Essentials*, Vol. 1, 160.

40 John Hick, *God Has Many Names* (Philadelphia, PA, 1982), 14.

41 John Hick, *God and the Universe of Faiths* (Oxford, 1973), x.

42 Pinnock has explored this theme in *A Wideness in God's Mercy: The Finality of Jesus Christ in a World of Religions* (Eugene, OR, 1992). John Sanders has an almost identical proposal, offered in *No Other Name: An Investigation into the Destiny of the Unevangelized* (Grand Rapids, MI, 1992). Earlier, J. N. D. Anderson had offered some thoughts that were, by traditional standards, unusual on this subject, in *Christianity and World Religions: The Challenge of Pluralism* (Leicester, 1984).

43 See Peter L. Berger, *The Heretical Imperative: Contemporary Possibilities of Religious Affirmation* (New York, 1979), 1–31.

44 The presentations from the Congress are found in J. D. Douglas (ed.), *Let the Earth Hear His Voice: The Compendium of the International Congress on World Evangelization, Lausanne, Switzerland* (Minneapolis, MN, 1975). On the Lausanne Covenant itself, see John Stott (ed.), *Making Christ Known: Historic Mission Documents from the Lausanne Movement, 1974–89* (Grand Rapids, MI, 1996), 1–55. See also C. Rene Padilla (ed.), *The New Face of Evangelicalism: An International Symposium on the Lausanne Covenant* (Downers Grove, IL, 1976).

45 Peter Beyerhaus, "Evangelicals, Evangelism and Theology: A Missiological Assessment of the Lausanne Movement," *Evangelical Review of Theology*, 11: 2 (April, 1987), 169–74.

46 The presentations from the Congress may be found in J. D. Douglas (ed.), *Proclaim Christ Until He Comes: The Compendium of the Second International Congress on World Evangelization, Manila, Philippines* (Minneapolis, MN, 1990).

47 The document may be found in Stott, *Making Christ Known*, 165–213.

48 This consultation issued *The Willowbank Report* (see Stott, *Making Christ Known*, 73–113). The papers from the consultation were later published in John Stott and Robert Coote (eds.), *Down to Earth: Studies in Christianity and Culture* (London, 1981). The papers from Uppsala were published in Philip Sampson, Vinay Samuel, and Chris Sugden (eds.), *Faith and Modernity* (Oxford, 1994).

49 The results of these two consultations were later published. See David F. Wells, *God the Evangelist: How the Holy Spirit Works to Bring Men and Women to Faith* (Grand Rapids, MI, 1987); David F. Wells, *Turning to God: Biblical Conversion in the Modern World* (Grand Rapids, MI, 1989).

Bibliography

Bebbington, David. *Evangelicalism in Modern Britain: A History from the 1730s to the 1980s.* Grand Rapids, MI, 1992.

Bloesch, Donald. *The Evangelical Renaissance.* Grand Rapids, MI, 1973.

Blumhofer, Edith L. and Carpenter, Joel. *Twentieth-Century Evangelicalism: A Guide to the Sources.* New York, 1990.

Johnston, Robert K. (ed.). *The Use of the Bible in Theology: Evangelical Options.* Atlanta, GA, 1985.

Ramm, Bernard. *The Evangelical Heritage: A Study in Historical Theology.* Grand Rapids, MI, 1973.

Yates, Timothy. *Christian Mission in the Twentieth Century.* Cambridge, 1994.

Theology
Between Faiths

Christian theology is not undertaken without engagement, implicit or explicit, with non-Christian faiths. As Gavin D'Costa writes in chapter 36, existence in a religiously plural world has always been part of the reality with which Christian theologians have had to deal; and theological conversations occur "between faiths" as well as within and about them.

The twentieth century saw the development of various paradigms for understanding the relationship between Christianity and non-Christian faiths, as surveyed by D'Costa. Presenting his own influential typology of exclusivism, inclusivism, and pluralism, D'Costa also offers a way beyond it for the twenty-first century, calling for intensified "intra-Christian" work on theologies of religions alongside renewed attention to the particularities of "extra-Christian" theological and religious encounters.

The other three chapters in Part VII provide examples of the latter, by focusing on Christian theology's engagement with three major world faiths. (Further examples of attention to "extra-Christian" religious encounter can be found in chapters 28, 29, and 30 in Part V.) As Peter Ochs shows, Christian theological reflection on Judaism and Jewish–Christian relations developed rapidly in the latter half of the twentieth century, and continues to develop in many different directions. Ochs sees in postliberal theologies a "non-supersessionist return to scripture" that can be the basis for new, positive, Christian theologies of Judaism.

By comparison, the engagement of Christian theology with Islam is relatively undeveloped, although its importance at the beginning of the twenty-first century is apparent. Ataullah Siddiqui traces Christian understandings and misunderstandings of Islam, finding in the work of such theologians as Hans Küng the starting point for dialogue that has yet to engage fully with deep issues around the understanding of God, the Prophethood of Mohammad, and the interpretation of scripture.

Paul Ingram's chapter on Buddhism and Christian theology records a diverse international, intercultural, and interdisciplinary dialogue on many levels – conceptual, socially engaged, and "interior." Ingram draws particular attention to the practical and sociopolitical intentions and implications of interreligious dialogue.

Theology of Religions

Gavin D'Costa

Introduction

Christianity was born into a religiously pluralist world and has remained in one ever since. The mandate to go preach the gospel to the corners of the earth, as well as its own socioeconomic political position in society, has resulted in a complex range of relations and responses to other religions.[1] In the modern period, and especially in the West, it stands unsure of its own distinct nature and deeply aware of its implication in various imperialist exploits. Christians in the modern world cannot ignore the existence of other religions. Global communications, extensive travel, migration, colonialism, and international trade are all factors that have brought the religions closer to each other in both destructive and creative ways.

A brief look at some statistics may help, although their reliability is a problem, no less than their interpretation. Compare, for instance, a five hundred year gap: the difference between 1491 and 1991. In 1491 roughly 19 percent of the world's population was Christian and while 2 percent of the non-Christian world was in contact with Christianity, 79 percent remained entirely ignorant of its existence. Some 93 percent of all Christians were white Europeans. Compare these figures with 1991, when 33 percent of the global population were Christians, with 44 percent of the non-Christian world being aware of Christianity, while only 23 percent had no contact with Christians and the gospel. The numeric basis of Christianity has also radically shifted so that the largest Christian community is now to be found in Latin America, only then followed by Europe, with Africa third (and growing much faster than Europe), followed by North America and then South Asia.

To get a sense of the broader picture, it will be helpful to briefly survey the figures for 1991 regarding the numerical strengths of world religions. After Christians (roughly 1 billion), Muslims are the largest religious group (962 million), followed by Hindus (721 million), with Buddhists then forming less than half the number of Hindus (327 million). New religions, notoriously difficult to classify, number some 119 million, followed by another amorphous classification, tribal religions, which constitute roughly 99 million. Finally, but not unimportantly, Sikhs number nearly 19 million and Jews nearly 18 million.[2]

Christians cannot ignore the existence of other religions. Furthermore, with the awareness of their existence a host of theological, philosophical, methodological, and practical questions are raised. Should, for example, Buddhist meditation groups be allowed the use of church halls? How should religious education be taught? What kind of social and political cooperation or opposition is appropriate with people of other faiths? There are also fundamental theological issues at stake. If salvation is possible outside Christ/Christianity, is the uniqueness of Christ and the universal mission of the church called into question? Or if salvation is not possible outside Christ/Christianity, is it credible that a loving God would consign the majority of humankind to perdition, often through no fault of their own? Can Christians learn from other faiths? Can they be enriched rather than diluted or polluted from this encounter? Clearly, other religions in varying degrees have also undergone their own self-questioning in the light of religious pluralism and modernity, but that is another subject.[3]

There have been many different Christian responses to the world religions. To limit ourselves to the modern period may make things slightly easier. No set of categories is adequate to analyze and deal with the complexity of the topic, but it may help to label three types of theological response to other religions for heuristic purposes only. There are of course considerable differences between theologians belonging to the same "camp" and many features of overlap between different approaches. I shall call these approaches:

Pluralism: all religions are equal and valid paths to the one divine reality and Christ is one revelation among many equally important revelations.
Exclusivism: only those who hear the gospel proclaimed and explicitly confess Christ are saved.
Inclusivism: Christ is the normative revelation of God, although salvation is possible outside of the explicit Christian church, but this salvation is always from Christ.

Various presuppositions undergird each approach, often revolving around the doctrines of Christ, God, the church, and the human person.

Survey

Pluralism

Pluralism is almost entirely a recent phenomenon within Christianity and this kind of approach has many supporters within what is sometimes called "liberal Christianity." Although it has been prominent in Anglo-American circles, there are an increasing number of theologians in Asia supporting and developing this kind of position. However, the manner in which theologians arrive at this outcome is various and at times incompatible. Some argue that all religions have a common core or essence that can be historically codified, often within the mystical traditions of the world religions.[4] This emphasis on mysticism is also shared by what is termed the "perennial philosophy," which has followers in different religions. Here it is argued that a straightforward historical comparison of the religions will not show this common essence, which is only found among "esoteric" believers who have penetrated the mystical depths of their own tradition to discover the non-duality of God and the soul, a unity that transcends all formulations. "Exoteric" believers absolutize their symbols and creeds and fail to penetrate to the transcendent unity of religions. Hence, exoteric believers hold that submission to Christ and/or the church become the only way to salvation.[5]

Another form of pluralism begins from a consideration of historical relativity. Here it is argued that all traditions are relative and cannot claim superiority over other equally limited and relative ways to salvation.[6] Others argue that all religions have important and substantial historical differences and the view of a common essence is in danger of compromising the integrity of each particular tradition by emphasizing only one aspect of that tradition. The real unity of religions is found not in doctrine or trans-religious experience and esoteric doctrines but in the common experience of salvation or liberation, or in the common moral vision central to all religions.[7] This latter has been developed by Hans Küng, the Swiss Roman Catholic theologian, and the former by theologians influenced by liberation theology. Clearly, within this political perspective, one can see a similar role for a type of feminist theology of religions which focuses specifically on the question of the liberation of women within the world religions.[8] Others, such as the English Christian philosopher of religion John Hick, have developed a position mainly in dialogue with traditional Western philosophy and the world religions. It will be instructive to look in detail at Hick, who combines many of the emphases in the above approaches.

John Hick's pluralism

Initially, Hick argued that the *solus Christus* assumption (that salvation is only through Christ) held by exclusivists is incompatible with the Christian teaching of a God who desires to save all people. There are many millions who have never heard of Christ through no fault of their own, before and after the New Testament period – the *invincibly ignorant*. It is therefore un-Christian to think that God would have "ordained that men must be saved in such a way that only a small minority can in fact receive this salvation."[9] Hick argued that it was God, and not Christianity or Christ, toward whom all religions move, and from whom they gain their salvific efficacy. Hick therefore proposed a *theocentric* revolution away from a *Christocentric* or *ecclesiocentric* position that has dominated Christian history. But what then of Christ? Hick argued that the doctrine of the incarnation should be understood mythically. That is, as an expression of devotion and commitment by Christians, not as an ontological claim that here in first-century Palestine and in this particular man, Jesus, God has chosen to reveal himself uniquely and definitively, in what was later called the "God-man."[10] Hick stressed the doctrine of an all-loving God over that of the *solus Christus* principle.

An important later development in Hick's position came in response to the criticism that his theological revolution was still *theocentric* and thereby excluded non-theistic religions. Pluralist positions, typically, must account for problems such as this if their claims are to be taken seriously. Hick developed a Kantian-type distinction between a divine noumenal reality "that exists independently and outside man's perception of it" which he calls the "Eternal One," and the phenomenal world, "which is that world as it appears to our human consciousness," in effect the various human responses to the Eternal One.[11] These responses are then seen as both theistic (e.g., the Trinity in Christianity, Yahweh in Judaism, or Allah in Islam) and non-theistic, (e.g., Nirvana in Buddhism or Nirguna Brahman in Hinduism). In this way Hick tries to overcome any underlying theistic essentialism.

The above arguments cumulatively suggest that Christians can fruitfully view the history of religions as a history of the Eternal One's activity without making any special claims for Christianity. Christian attitudes to other religions need not be characterized by a desire to convert, or claims to superiority, but a will to learn and grow together toward the truth. Mission should be jointly carried out to the secular world by the religions, rather than towards each other. Hick suggests that exclusivism and inclusivism cannot provide such fruitful conditions for interreligious dialogue.

Hick's philosophical approach to religious pluralism could be contrasted with the very pragmatic approach taken by those deeply influenced by liberation theology, such as Paul Knitter or the Asian Roman Catholic theologian Aloysius Pieris. Pieris emphasizes the overcoming of the theocentric, Christocentric, and ecclesiocentric problems that bedevil this debate by emphasizing the liberative sociopolitical power of religion as the only criterion for authenticity. For example, he finds that Buddhist monasticism (with its voluntary, rather than imposed, poverty) and its commitment to the cessation of suffering through gnosis allows "an engagement in a positive and practical program of psychic–social restructuring of human existence here on earth in accordance with the path leading to nirvanic freedom."[12] Hence, the religions must work together in this common cause and Pieris renounces claims for Christianity's uniqueness and his own church's fulfillment theology as forms of Western imperialism.[13]

The pluralist approach to the theology of religions is attractive for many reasons. To those tired of religions being the cause of wars and injustice, arrogance and imperialism, self-importance and pomp, this approach suggests an alternative. Pluralism also attracts the increasing number of secularized non-churched agnostics or "religious" in Western society. Further, to those whose philosophical background suggests the importance of a weaning from either/or clarity, from relentless ontological exactness about every characteristic of the mystery of the divine, pluralism is an intellectual way out of a long historical impasse.

Exclusivism

Some argue that the rape of cultures and civilizations has often been justified in the name of Christianity armed with an exclusivist missionary theology.[14] Furthermore, racism and colonial imperialism are often closely identified with Christian mission. This checkered history cannot be denied, although it is a complex and ambiguous one. Hence, we should also note the persuasive arguments that much missionary work was not in fact pursued in tandem with empire-building, but actually resisted it.[15] Others have defended the rich cultural contributions made by missionaries in terms of the issue of "translation" and criticized the Western "guilt complex" in relation to mission work.[16]

I have highlighted these issues to show the ways in which theological attitudes are so closely related to practice. Nevertheless, there are serious theological issues underlying exclusivism that cannot simply be equated with racism and colonialism. No major systematic theologian holds a rigorist exclusivism, so in this section I will outline a position without close reference to a single named theologian. The exclusivist position (most often found in Lutheran and Calvinist circles) is fundamentally concerned to affirm two central insights. The first is that God has sent his Son, Jesus Christ, to bring salvation into the world and that this salvation is both judgment and mercy to all human beings who are deeply estranged from God. Salvation therefore comes from faith in Christ alone – *solus Christus*. In this respect, many inclusivists, as we shall see shortly, share this affirmation. Secondly, this salvation won by Christ is only available through *explicit* faith in Christ, which comes from hearing the gospel preached (*fides ex auditu*), requiring repentance, baptism, and the embracing of a new life in Christ. It is in the context of this second axiom that inclusivists usually differ from exclusivists.

Concerning the first principle, most exclusivists regard human nature as fallen and sinful. Hence, men and women are only capable of idolatry, for all their attempts to reach God are precisely that: human attempts at capturing the living God. This was the position of the great Swiss Reform theologian, Karl Barth.[17] (While I cite Barth, he admittedly also overturns these categories by being an exclusivist, inclusivist, and universalist all at once!) Herein lies the judgment of God upon all acts of idolatry, for all human actions ultimately (in subtle and not so subtle ways) usurp God's power in creating gods of their own making. However inspiring, intelligent, and humane a religion may be, such religions are never more than the products of fallen persons, who in their very attempt to reach out and upwards, compound their own situation. They blind themselves to the way in which God has reached down and inward to humanity in the person of Christ. In fact, the extent of sinfulness is such that human beings are incapable of truly recognizing their own situation of radical fallenness and it is only in the light of Christ that sin is seen most clearly and fully for what it really is: human pride and hubris.[18]

Given the predicament of humankind, the logic of this theology requires that salvation is an utterly gratuitous gift, entirely unmerited by us. Rather than be indignant at the particularity of God's action (as are pluralists), the exclusivist is awed and grateful at God's gratuity. God's mercy and redemption are not something merited by us, and this gift's particularity is nevertheless universal in import and offer, so that the exclusivist can only humbly proclaim this truth rather than question it. Hence, mission and evangelism are more appropriate than dialogue. Doctrinally, the *solus Christus* and *fides ex auditu* principles are paramount, for anything less compromises the incarnation and atonement and God's salvific action toward his creatures.[19]

No exclusivist would usually wish non-Christians any ill, or that they be lost. Instead, they would emphasize the urgency and necessity of worldwide evangelization, other than spend time and energy on improper speculation about the possibility of salvation occurring in the non-Christian religions. However, some state baldly the apparent consequences of this approach, as found in the proclamation of the Chicago

Congress on World Mission in 1960: "In the years since the war, more than one billion souls have passed into eternity and more than half of these went to the torment of hell fire without even hearing of Jesus Christ, who He was, or why He died on the cross of Calvary."[20]

Others, it must be said, refuse to speculate on the outcome and destiny of the non-Christian for a variety of reasons. The first is to suggest that we cannot know the fate of non-Christians and must simply trust in the mercy and justice of God.[21] Hence, such exclusivists are willing to acknowledge that salvation may be offered to the invincibly ignorant, although they refuse to speculate further about how this will happen. On the other hand, the American Lutheran George Lindbeck, who emphasizes that becoming a Christian is a process of being formed by cultural–linguistic practices, argues that if Christianity is a learned form of life then it follows that "there is no damnation – just as there is no salvation – outside the church. One must, in other words, learn the language of faith before one can know enough about its message knowingly to reject it and thus be lost."[22] Lindbeck (and this recalls my earlier comment on Barth's breaking of the typologies) in fact holds out on theological grounds a hope for the salvation of all and suggests a post-mortem confrontation with Christ (thereby satisfying the *fides ex auditu* principle) to account for the fate of non-Christians.[23] A Roman Catholic Dominican pupil of Lindbeck's, Joseph DiNoia, has given this possibility a developed formulation in terms of employing the doctrine of purgatory (a process of cleansing also undergone by the Christian) as a means whereby the non-Christian who has already responded positively to God in their lives will be purified in anticipation of the trinitarian beatific vision.[24] A third and somewhat novel strategy (some might say heretical) has been suggested whereby reincarnation is posited to solve the problem of the invincibly ignorant who will therefore have a chance to hear the gospel at least once before they "properly" die.[25] It is clear, then, that the boundary lines between these latter forms of exclusivism and some forms of inclusivism are thin and grey.

Exclusivism has often attracted those rigorously concerned about ontological and epistemological claims generated through Christian discourse and practice, refusing to "abandon" (as they see it) such claims to suit non-Christian discourses, be they secular modernity, liberal Judaism, or Hinduism. In an age when uncertainty and change trouble many, it has also attracted those who wish to see Christianity as a bastion against modern times.

Inclusivism

Inclusivism has a long lineage in the Christian tradition, at least in so much as grace has been acknowledged to operate outside the confines of the visible church. Quite a number of Roman Catholics, Orthodox, and Protestants share this approach, with varying differences. The main differences revolve around the question as to whether non-Christian religions can be said to have salvific structures; and whether, finally, a person can come to salvation apart from explicitly confessing Christ.[26] Regarding the latter, inclusivists often seem to allow for salvation without explicit confession in Jesus Christ, although when pressed, the theological necessity of requiring some sort of explicit trinitarian knowledge and practice, as a condition of final salvation, renders them "exclusivist." Inclusivist logic means that it has been rightly associated with theologies of fulfillment, drawing on the ancient tradition of a *preparatio evangelica*. That is, the acknowledgment that pagans were inspired by God – even though this ancient tradition was developed in relation to philosophers such as Aristotle and Plato, and not to religions and cults. In what follows, I will focus on the major twentieth-century inclusivist, Karl Rahner, a German Jesuit.

Karl Rahner's inclusivism

Rahner's theological anthropology shapes his brand of inclusivism, although he argues his case from Catholic doctrine. Rahner argues that the precondition of finite (categorical) knowledge is an unconditional openness to being (*Vorgriff*), which is an unthematic, prereflective awareness of God – who is infinite being. Our transcendental openness to being constitutes both the hiddenness of grace and its prethematic presence at the heart of our existence. Men and women therefore search in history for a categorical disclosure of this hidden grace. In Jesus' total abandonment to God, his total "Yes" through his life, death, and resurrection, he is established as the alpha and omega, the cause, culmination, and prime mediator of grace. Therefore, Christian revelation is the explicit expression of grace which men and women experience implicitly in the depths of their being when, for example, they reach out through the power of grace in trusting love and self-sacrifice, or in acts of hope and charity.

Rahner attempts to balance the *solus Christus* principle with the doctrine of the *universal salvific will of God*, so as to maintain that Christ is the sole cause of salvation in the world, but that this salvific grace may be mediated within history without explicit knowledge of Christ.[27] Such is the case in the history of Israel which Rahner calls a "lawful religion" prior to the time of Christ. Rahner maintains that Israel remains a lawful religion for those who have never been confronted historically and existentially with the gospel. By this he means that although a person might hear the gospel being preached historically (by a pastor whose life is dissolute and dishonest), that person may not have existentially been addressed for all sorts of reasons (the difficulty of making sense of the pastor's message given his scandalous life). Hence, it may be that the addressee cannot really count as having "heard" the gospel and rejected it. To return to the argument: if Israel in a certain context had a "lawful religion," may it not in principle be the case with other religions of the world?

Rahner argues that if salvific grace exists outside the visible church, as he believes it does in the history of Israel, and in creation and through conscience, then this grace is both causally related to Christ (always and everywhere – as prime mediator) and his church (as the social-historical vehicle of this grace). Rahner argues that Christology and the doctrine of God cannot be separated from the church, as Christ is historically mediated through the church. This means that Rahner must reconcile membership of the church as a means of salvation and the possibility that salvific grace is mediated outside the historically tangible borders of the church. He does this along the lines of the traditional Catholic teachings regarding the *votum ecclesia* (a wish to belong to the church), and the related notion of implicit desire. (See the beginnings of Rahner's thought on this matter in relation to Pius XII's *Mystici Corporis Christi.*)[28] Hence, if and when non-Christians respond to grace, then this grace must be mediated through the non-Christian's religion, however imperfectly. Therefore, non-Christian religions may in principle be "lawful religions" with the same qualifications registered regarding Israel. Rahner thus coins the term "anonymous Christian" (this refers to the source of saving grace that is responded to: Christ), and "anonymous Christianity" (this refers to grace's dynamic orientation toward its definitive historical and social expression in the church).[29]

Because God has already been active within the non-Christian religions, the Christian can be open to learning about God through her non-Christian partner. Furthermore, the Christian is also free to engage in active social and political cooperation when appropriate. Hence, the inclusivist has a firm theological basis for fruitful dialogue. Given Rahner's notion that grace must seek to objectivize itself, mission is clearly important. Hence, Rahner is able to affirm that Christianity is the one true religion, while at the same time holding that other religions may have a provisional salvific status.

Inclusivism is often attractive to those who wish to retain the ontological and epistemological tenets of traditional faith, while developing them and relating them positively to the modern world in an open and inclusive form. Further, given the positive experience of the presence of non-Christian religion in the world, it is a theological approach that seems to do justice to newer experiences and more ancient traditions.

Debate

Objections to pluralism

There have been a number of objections specifically to Hick's thesis, some of which indicate more general problems with pluralism.[30] First, there are objections to the way in which the centrality of Christ seems to be bypassed. It is argued that Hick's initial theocentric revolution is based on a shaky premise. He rejects the *sola Christus*, for he thinks it leads to the *a priori* damnation of non-Christians. We have seen above that it need not, and often does not. Furthermore, when Hick proposes to emphasize God rather than Christ, he is in danger of severing Christology from ontology and introducing a free-floating "God" divorced from any particular revelation. In fact Judaism, Christianity, and Islam have all tended to center on revelatory paradigms for their discourse and practice. Hick's theocentricism pays little attention to the importance of historical particularity and the grounding of theistic discourse. In fact, the theological basis of his proposal (that of an all-loving God) is undermined if Hick cannot give normative ontological status to the revelatory event upon which this axiom is grounded – originally for Hick, that of the revelation of God in Christ. And even if he responds, as he has done, that "an all-loving God" is to be found in Judaism and Islam, it is certainly not so easily found in Buddhism or Confucianism.

A related objection follows from Hick's response to precisely this seeming prioritization of theism. Critics maintain that if the meaning of "God" lacked specificity in Hick's theocentricism, it seems further relativized in his more recent works as the personal, loving, creator "God" is viewed as one aspect of the "Eternal One" that apparently can also be characterized by non-personal, non-creator, non-theistic predicates. As all such predicates are from the human side, Hick argues, they are thereby not properly applicable to the Eternal One in any literal way. Critics reply that if this is so, "God" cannot be said to be personal or loving in any proper ontological sense. The Kantian noumenon encountered a similar problem in not providing for a correspondence between phenomena and things-in-themselves. Hick seems to be identical to transcendental agnosticism (i.e., affirming a transcendence without any qualities).[31] Despite Hick's stress on soteriocentricism in terms of ethics, can he properly address the question of the nature of God (or the Eternal One) who actually saves and liberates people, or is his doctrine of "God" in danger of avoiding all particularities so as to accommodate every particularity? Again, Hick's response is along the lines that we can never properly describe the Eternal One "in himself, herself, or itself," only in "relation to us." Clearly, the outcome of these debates remains unresolved, but highlights the theological centrality of Christology, the doctrine of God, and the relation of practice and theory in the discussion about other faiths.

Pieris' liberationist attempt to bypass problems of Christocentricism, theocentricism, and ecclesiocentricism is admirably motivated by a desire for justice and righteousness in Asian society – and not least, peace between the Asian religions. However, critics have argued that Pieris cannot really address the question of liberation without the categories of Christ, God, and the church.[32] It is precisely in Christ and the trinitarian revelation therein that the decisive meaning of liberation is to be found. The further Pieris tries to get away from such specification, the closer he gets to other but unstated sets of assumptions. From where does he derive the meaning of "liberation"? Why should such a meaning be privileged and exalted above all religions and used as a judge of them? Is this not a new form of imperialism? Fundamental to this debate is the understanding of *action*. The critique cited above derives from the argument that all action is always employed within a narrative form which both shapes and informs it, so that one cannot simply parallel similar actions (feeding the poor), as if they did not occupy different narrative spaces. Stanley Hauerwas raises this pointed criticism at Gutiérrez's liberation theology.[33]

The debate will clearly continue and one can see the complex interrelations of a number of issues.

Objections to exclusivism

The type of exclusivism I outlined faces a number of difficulties. Hick has criticized this position for being incompatible with the God of love disclosed at the heart of Christianity. Citing the 1960 statement of the Congress on World Mission regarding the billions of souls in the torments of hell (see above), Hick argues that such an outcome is theologically unacceptable, especially when one considers the invincibly ignorant.[34]

There are two important points in the exclusivist response. First, for some exclusivists, Hick presumes too much in questioning the ways of God as being unjust! Rather, given human sinfulness, we should start from being amazed that God saves anyone at all. The issue at stake here concerns human nature. Secondly, a number of exclusivists have taken seriously the problem of the person who through no fault of his or her own has never heard the gospel. And these developments have been outlined above.

Another criticism aimed at exclusivists is that grace, within the Christian tradition, is not limited purely to an explicit confrontation with Christ.[35] This contention is based on a number of arguments. In traditional Christian theology, Judaism up to the time of Christ was certainly accorded revelatory status. Hence, a Christian exclusivist who denied any revelation outside Christ would be hard-pressed to explain the use of the Old Testament as part of Christian scripture. Might a strict exclusivism end up as Marcionite – that is, denying the validity of Jewish (Christian) revelation? Besides the history of Israel testifying to salvific grace outside the particular event of the historical Jesus, there are also a number of passages within the New Testament that highlight the importance of right living. If, for instance, a person's courageous self-sacrificing love is due to certain demands within their religion, can these acts of *responding to grace* be divorced from the mediations of such grace? Is Gandhi or Dalai Lama's holiness to be explained despite their religious traditions? And can the humanist's self-sacrificial love for another, so powerfully portrayed in Camus' *The Plague*, have nothing to do with Jesus' implied teaching that "as you did it to one of the least of my brethren, you did it to me" (Matthew 25: 40)?

The exclusivist may respond in a number of ways.[36] First, exclusivists point out that the revelation Israel received was always directed toward Christ and was not properly salvific in itself; except by virtue of its teleological completion in Christ. Hence, the real question here is whether implicit faith in Christ is alone sufficient for salvation, or whether it requires at some later stage, explicit faith. It is interesting to note that the major inclusivist theologian, Rahner, also held in his writings on death that a post-mortem meeting with Christ was essential for the completion of our lives and in preparation for the beatific vision.[37] Furthermore, to return to exclusivist responses, if salvific grace is available through creation and history, apart from explicit faith, does this not call into question the necessity of Jesus Christ for salvation? Exclusivists also respond that any resort to arguments from virtuous actions is to depart from the *sola fide/Christus* principle, and concedes to Pelagianism. Clearly, the arguments will rage on, but again we find the central questions revolving around Christology, God, church, theory and practice, and human nature.

Objections to inclusivism

Rahner is criticized by both pluralists and exclusivists. Pluralists argue that the term "anonymous Christian" is deeply offensive to non-Christians and creates a stalemate in dialogue with each side calling the other names (anonymous Hindus, anonymous Muslims, and so on).[38] Hans Küng has accused Rahner of creating a terminological distinction to sweep a resistant non-Christian humanity into the Christian church through the back door.[39] Rahner has made it very clear that his theory is for internal Christian consumption only (i.e., it is a question within dogmatic theology and not a reflection meant for interfaith dialogue). He is simply reflecting on the possibility that the non-Christian may already have encountered God and, if this is so, then

"God" must be the same God as disclosed by Christ. Of course, pluralists respond that this is still an imperialist assertion, always claiming to know more about God than anyone else, and it also sees "others" purely in terms of their reflection of Christianity, not as genuinely "other." The latter criticism is also advanced by postmodernists.[40] Pluralists also criticize the way in which Rahner wants to secure all grace as Christologically *mediated* when he in fact acknowledges that it is mediated within other religions where Christ is not *known*. This, they want to argue, amounts to a theoretical ownership of God, with contrary practical consequences. Rahner would no doubt respond that his argument is one regarding ontological causality, not particular historical mediation.

Rahner also faces severe criticism from those who oppose pluralism and see in his theology certain pluralist tendencies.[41] For instance, it is argued that Rahner compromises the *solus Christus* principle in a fundamental manner. Salvation is made possible without surrender to Christ and this inevitably renders Christ unnecessary in the economy of salvation. If salvation requires no explicit faith at all then this dangerously obscures the way in which the church claims to form and nourish genuine faith within a historical–social community. From his cultural–linguistic perspective, Lindbeck accuses Rahner of operating with a very defective view of the relationship between experience and interpretation. Experience is apparently seen as prior to all interpretation, which leads to what Lindbeck calls "experiential expressivism," the notion that expression must follow experience. This is contrasted with the cultural–linguistic model, where it is argued that experience is in large part shaped by the interpretive tradition that generates the experience. Hence, in Rahner's experiential expressivism, Christianity is wrongly seen as just a better interpretation of the same experience of grace in different religions. But surely Christian faith is more than this? Rather, it is being shaped in a specific Christoformic fashion by involvement within the specific community of the church. Hence, the question posed to Rahner: what would the difference be between an anonymous and an explicit Christian in terms of faith? Further, Rahner's invisible church, it is claimed, is unbiblical and also detracts from the importance of explicit confession as a criterion for membership.[42] The very foundations of Rahner's theology which undergird his theology of the anonymous Christian have also been called into question by the Roman Catholic Hans Urs von Balthasar, who has seen in Rahner's transcendental anthropology the danger of the conflation of nature and grace and the reduction of revelation to a predetermined anthropological system.[43] Balthasar is concerned that by viewing supernatural grace as being part of the very nature of men and women, Rahner minimizes both the transforming power of the glory of the Lord that shines forth in Christ and the character of sin and of tragedy, which also explains Rahner's impoverished theology of the cross.

Rahner has responded to these criticisms and I cannot follow the complex debate here, except to note that he has maintained against his more conservative critics that there is no compromise on the basic tenet (shared with exclusivists) that salvation comes exclusively through faith in Christ; and that Christ's life, death, and resurrection have ontologically (not chronologically) brought salvation irrevocably into the world. Rahner claims he is simply offering one explanation of a teaching maintained by the church that salvation is available to invincibly ignorant non-Christians and he is not unconditionally endorsing the value of non-Christian religions *per se*.

Objections to the threefold typology

There are some who have claimed a fourth option or there are those who are unhappy with this threefold classification altogether (and therefore, also with any fourth option). Regarding those who propose a fourth option,[44] DiNoia defines exclusivists as those who hold that only those who explicitly confess Christ *in this life* will be saved. Hence, his purgatorial option allegedly constitutes a fourth option. I have seen this move as a version of exclusivism. In Heim's case, he suggests that each religion be acknowledged in its difference, but that these differences be related and grounded in the Christian doctrine of the Trinity. It might be argued that this is only a development of inclusivism, rather than a fourth option. Ogden's fourth option rests on the distinction that pluralists claim that other religions *are* salvific means, while he wishes to claim that they *may* be salvific means. This perhaps questionably presumes that all pluralists are committed to an *a priori* affirmation of other religions as salvific means, which is not the case. Clearly, the way one defines pluralism, inclusivism, and exclusivism determines the number of alternative options. However, there are those who are unhappy with the basic typology, including myself.

Challenges to the whole enterprise have been put forward by many. I will briefly examine Kenneth Surin, John Milbank, and Gavin D'Costa, all primarily reacting against pluralism but finding problems with the entire typological project.[45] Surin's criticism is essentially political and genealogical (deriving from Michel Foucault), suggesting that rather than serve up theologies about religious unity in an abstract, ahistorical, and apolitical fashion, real attention should be paid to the social, political, and power relationships between religions in their particular locality. Theological talk has usually served to obscure rather than identify the real terrain in which the exercise of power in the materialist order operates. Such materialist hermeneutics are the key to understanding the generation of various legitimating theologies – and pluralist theologies legitimate late modernity and capitalism. While Surin's criticisms are powerful and incisive, there is a danger that theology is reductively encoded by Surin's materialism.

Milbank, while sharing much in common with Surin, proposes quite a different role for theology. Milbank is deeply suspicious of the notion of "religion," as well as the belief that dialogue provides a privileged access to truth. Rather, he urges that Christianity must simply proclaim its vision through its particular form of practice within the church. The church can do no other than this, nor ought it to try. What both Surin and Milbank do so clearly is alert us to the fact that all theology is a political and social practice. Milbank advances the case, in claiming a heavenly practice for Christians, a practice with a difference.

My own position has changed over the years. Once a convinced Rahnerian, I now find myself both troubled by the threefold paradigm and the theological construal of the problems. I have strong reservations about the threefold paradigm, despite my having employed it heuristically in this chapter. We have already seen the thin dividing lines between strong forms of inclusivism and weak forms of exclusivism, and likewise with weak forms of inclusivism and certain forms of pluralism. The typology is constantly inadequate. Furthermore, typologies easily harden into

Procrustean beds, forcing diverse materials into uncomfortably controlled locations. All this should keep us on our guard. However, and more significantly, I think it is the case that in using the depictions (pluralism, inclusivism, and exclusivism) we disguise the fact that what we are really dealing with are different forms of *exclusivism*. Pluralism often claims the high ground in being more tolerant, more liberal, more affirmative of truth in other religions, etc. The threefold typology rhetorically reaffirms this false self-description. Pluralism, as I argue elsewhere, has its own intolerant, illiberal, exclusivist logic. It is a form of secular agnosticism, reducing all religion to private confession, controlling the public sphere with its own implicit ideology. In this sense Hick's pluralism is an exclusivist secular agnosticism, ruling out of court all truth-claims other than his own, allowing for the truth of only one "religion," his own mythological modernity. Pluralism must operate with criteria to discern "truth," "God," and "salvation."[46] And in so doing, it will naturally exclude all that is not in keeping with these criteria. Hence, in this respect, it is no different from exclusivism. (I have extended this analysis to Jewish, Hindu, and Buddhist types of pluralism, arguing that once stripped of "rhetoric" – nice attitude – ontologically and epistemologically, pluralism is no different from exclusivism).

I would also suggest that inclusivism has the same logic – most clearly in Rahner's work. Rahner is happy to acknowledge God's grace operative outside the visible boundaries of the church. However, when pressed as to the final destiny of men and women, Rahner cannot depart from the necessity of the beatific vision, the trinitarian glory of God, which thereby requires that all non-Christians will only be finally and fully saved through participation in the beatific vision. This may well exclude the mediation of the church in heaven, but it does finally require what exclusivists require, explicit confession to the triune God. In this sense, inclusivists are ontologically no different from exclusivists, although they sometimes have different epistemological assumptions. The difficult *criteriological* questions that underlie this debate are therefore not always highlighted via this typology, although, as has been seen above, it is the choice and use of such criteria that dictate the differences within this schema.

Theologically, I suggest that Christians use the resources of trinitarian theology to reflect on the particular engagement with differing religions, eschewing overall theologies of religions which fix the "other." Both difference and discontinuity, as well as fragmentary commonality and continuities, must be held in tension, allowing theology and practice to grow through this critical engagement.

Achievement and Agenda

The achievement of the modern debate is that the question of other religions is here to stay with Christian theology into the twenty-first century. This can be regarded as an achievement in the sense that the credibility of Christianity will partly depend on the way in which it can respond to the bewildering plurality that characterizes the modern world. This works in at least two ways. If Christianity is not able to see itself as distinct and unique in any sense at all, it will probably be assimilated and absorbed by traditions that do feel they have a special vision for the world. People are not particularly interested and challenged by nothing at all! On the other hand, if

Christian theology denigrates the rich heritage of millions of women and men it will fail to respect the goodness of creation affirmed within its own creed and foolishly turn its back on the many riches and glories found within other religions. By facing up to the difficult theological issues raised by the presence of other religions, one can only hope that various churches will be able to deal more constructively with the complex reality facing them.

The modern debate has raised an agenda, which will expand and be reshaped as time progresses, ranging over questions regarding the nature of religion, the socio-political context of religious encounters, the person of Jesus Christ, the nature of God, and the character of the church and its mission. It would be fair to say that at the heart of the matter lies the question: "Who do you say that I am?" The way in which Christians relate to other religions is deeply shaped by the way in which they relate to Jesus Christ, thereby showing that the future agenda is both intra-Christian and extra-Christian. By intra-Christian I mean that the various developments in theology will substantially affect the questions of other religions. This relates both to questions of method and theological context. For example, within "liberal" Christian circles, especially where there is a strong emphasis on "God" and sociopolitical liberation, we are likely to find a certain pattern in responding to other religions which is predictable prior to interreligious encounter. On the other hand, theologies that are strongly Christocentric, utilizing categories such as story or narrative, are more likely to emphasize the particularity of the Christian message and its power to shape people in terms of a specific narrative. Such theologies are likely to be more suspicious of liberal approaches, although they will not necessarily result in negative assessments of other religions. Furthermore, the recent recovery of trinitarian theologies is also likely to give the debate a new injection of life, for it gives a richness to Christology that is often neglected.[47] We have seen to some extent the way in which liberation theology has affected the debate, and in the future feminist, ecological, postmodern, Asian, Latin American, African, and very many other types of theology will all bring their own distinctive insights to bear more fully on the matters of Christology, God, the church, and other religions. It is difficult to predict the outcome of such theologies, but it is also difficult to see how Christ, God, and the church can be bypassed in any serious attempt to grapple theologically with the question of other religions.

By extra-Christian I want to register an issue, among many others, that could not be dealt with in such a short chapter. I have had no time to deal with the dynamics of specific encounters where the theology of religions may take on all sorts of encounter-specific characteristics. For example, in the Jewish–Christian dialogue, the anti-Semitism within traditional Christology comes to the fore in a most painful and disturbing manner; as well as the nature of God's promises regarding his "covenant."[48] Also, and less aired, is the question regarding Messianic Jews and Hebrew Christians, who have often been shunned and rejected by both Jews and Christians. Clearly, the issues in this latter arena are quite different to ones raised when Christianity encounters a profoundly non-theistic tradition like Buddhism, where it has not had the same fratricidal relationship, although here the context of colonialism is deeply relevant and often painful. Hence, the debates with Buddhism have ranged over very different issues, such as the relation of apophatic theology to the apparent non-theism of Buddhism; the meditative techniques within Buddhism that bring about a freedom to act in charity and love; and the question of the portrayal of Buddhism in the West, for example, the Victorian construction of Buddhism.[49] Hence, extra-Christian presence in the debate is likely to create all sorts of unforeseen developments. Furthermore, these specific encounters also raise the question of the relationship between a theology *of* religions and a theology arising out of specific encounters. Some argue that the latter should have priority over the former, and some would go further to suggest that the latter even invalidates the exercise of the former altogether.[50]

We have also not touched on the question of inculturation, which is closely linked with our theme, as the culture for so many churches, especially in Asia and Africa, is formed by various non-Christian religions. Hence, as we saw with Pieris above, the question of a truly Asian church may call for an entirely different attitude to Buddhism and Hinduism than has been traditional in Western theologies. There are already churches in Asia where readings from the sacred scriptures of the Hindus such as the *Bhagavad Gita* or *Upanishads* are incorporated into the liturgy (usually prior to the Old Testament and sometimes instead of the Old Testament – thereby reflecting a fulfillment theology of inclusivism). And in such churches one can often find a liturgy and lifestyle which Western Christians may find hard to recognize due to its deeply Indian roots. There are also individuals such as Brahmabandhab Upadhyay who considered themselves Hindu-Christians, which raises all sorts of new and interesting questions. When I mentioned that the different developments in theology are likely to shape the way this question is approached, it is clear that theologians from churches often faced with this dramatic religious plurality are likely to be the main practitioners of future theology of religions. There are also issues of the relationship of theology of religions to systematic theology and the study of religions within the church and within the academy. While some see this area as integral to systematic theology with institutional repercussions,[51] others have argued for a more ambitious non-denominational global or world theology which has radical and far-reaching implications.[52] This whole issue raises the question which has remained implicit throughout this exploration: does our theological method significantly determine our answer to the question concerning other religions? Might it be the case that a theology of religions must ultimately pay as much attention to the "other," as it does to the manner in which we deal with the gracious and holy "Other," who is made known in Father, Son, and Spirit?

Notes

1 See F. Sullivan, *Salvation Outside the Church?* (London, 1992).

2 D. Barrett, "The Status of the Christian World Mission in the 1990s," in G. Anderson, *Mission in the Nineteen Nineties* (Grand Rapids, MI, 1991), pp. 72–3.

3 See, for example, P. Griffiths (ed.), *Christianity Through Non-Christian Eyes* (New York, 1991); H. Coward, *Pluralism: Challenge to World Religions* (New York, 1985).

4 W. James, *The Varieties of Religious Experience* (London, 1902).

5 A. Huxley, *The Perennial Philosophy* (New York, 1945); H. Smith, *Essays on World Religions*, ed. D. Bryant (New York, 1992); and S. H. Nasr, *Knowledge and the Sacred* (New York, 1981).

6 E. Troeltsch, *The Absoluteness of Christianity and the History of Religions* (London, 1972).

7   For the first, see P. Knitter, *One Earth Many Religions* (New York, 1995) and *Jesus and the Other Names* (New York, 1996). For the second, see H. Küng, *A Global Ethic for Global Politics and Economics* (London, 1997) (which is in some sense a return to the Kantian position on ethics in religions) and A. Pieris, *An Asian Theology of Liberation* (New York, 1988).

8   M. O'Neill, *Women Speaking, Women Listening* (New York, 1990); R. Ruether, "Feminism and Jewish–Christian Dialogue," in J. Hick and P. Knitter (eds.), *The Myth of Christian Uniqueness* (New York, 1987), pp. 137–48; P. Cooey, W. Eakin, and J. McDaniel (eds.), *After Patriarchy: Feminist Transformations of the World Religions* (New York, 1993).

9   J. Hick, *God and the Universe of Faiths* (London, 1977), p. 122.

10 Ibid, pp. 165–79.

11 J. Hick, *An Interpretation of Religion* (Basingstoke, 1988), pp. 233–52.

12 A. Pieris, "Black Flags for the Pope," cited by R. Cruz, *The Tablet*, January 14, 1995, pp. 36–7.

13 Pieris, *Asian Theology*, pp. 35–40, 47, 60.

14 J. Morris, *Heaven's Command: An Imperial Progress* (London, 1973).

15 B. Stanley, *The Bible and the Flag* (Leicester, 1990).

16 L. Sanneh, *Encountering the West* (London, 1993); "Christian Mission and the Western Guilt Complex," *Christian Century*, April 8, 1987, pp. 330–4, respectively.

17 K. Barth, *Church Dogmatics* (Edinburgh, 1970), Vol. 1.2, p. 17. See also chapter 1 in the present volume.

18 K. Barth, *Church Dogmatics* (Edinburgh, 1956), Vol. 4.1, p. 60.

19 H. Lindsell, *A Christian Philosophy of Religion* (Wheaton, PA, 1987); D. Strange, *The Possibility of Salvation Among the Unevangelised* (Carlisle, 2002); D. Carson, *The Gagging of God* (Leicester, 1996).

20 J. Percy (ed.), *Facing the Unfinished Task* (Grand Rapids, MI, 1961), p. 9.

21 L. Newbigin, "The Basis, Purpose, and Manner of Inter-Faith Dialogue," in R. Rousseau (ed.), *Interreligious Dialogue* (Montrose, 1981).

22 G. Lindbeck, *The Nature of Doctrine: Religion and Theology in a Postliberal Age* (Philadelphia, PA, 1984), p. 59.

23 G. Lindbeck, *The Church in a Postliberal Age*, ed. J. Buckley (London, 2002), chs. 6, 14.

24 J. DiNoia, *The Diversity of Religions: A Christian Perspective* (Washington, DC, 1992).

25 O. Jathanna, *The Decisiveness of the Christ Event and the Universality of Christianity in a World of Religious Plurality* (Berne, 1981).

26 For a defense and development of inclusivism, with reference to different denominational responses, see the Belgian Jesuit, J. Dupuis, *Towards a Christian Theology of Religious Pluralism* (New York, 1997).

27 K. Rahner, "Christianity and the Non-Christian Religions," in *Theological Investigations* (London, 1966), Vol. 5, pp. 115–34.

28 Rahner, *Theological Investigations* (1963), Vol. 1, pp. 1–89.

29 Rahner, *Theological Investigations*, Vol. 5, ch. 5; Vol. 6, (1969), chs. 16, 23; Vol. 12, (1974), ch. 9; Vol. 14 (1976), ch. 17; Vol. 16 (1979), chs. 4. 13; Vol. 17 (1980), ch. 5.

30 For a good bibliography of critical debate on Hick (pre-1994) and his own response, see *The Rainbow of Faiths* (London, 1995); and further, Chris Sinkinson, "The Nature of Christian Apologetics in Response to Religious Pluralism: An Analysis of the Contribution of John Hick" (PhD thesis, University of Bristol, 1997).

31 G. D'Costa, "John Hick and Religious Pluralism: Yet Another Revolution," in H. Hewitt (ed.), *Problems in the Philosophy of John Hick* (London, 1991), pp. 102–16, and Hick's response follows.

32 G. D'Costa, "Nostra Aetate – Telling God's Story in Asia: Problems and Pitfalls," in L. Kenis and M. Lamberigts (eds.), *Vatican II and Its Legacy* (Leuven, 2002), pp. 229–350; on Knitter, see G. D'Costa, *The Meeting of Religions and the Trinity* (Edinburgh, 2000), pp. 30–47; J. Milbank, "The End of Dialogue," in G. D'Costa (ed.), *Christian Uniqueness Reconsidered* (New York, 1990), pp. 174–91.

33 S. Hauerwas, "Some Theological Reflections on Gutiérrez's use of Liberation Theology," *Modern Theology*, 3, 1986, pp. 67–76. I have developed this approach to reflect on Küng: "Postmodernity and

Religious Pluralism: Is a Common Global Ethic Possible or Desirable?" in G. Ward (ed.), *The Blackwell Companion to Postmodern Theology* (Oxford, 2001), pp. 131–43.

34 Hick, *Universe of Faiths*, pp. 121–2.

35 Rahner, *Theological Investigations* (1966), Vol. 4, pp. 165–89.

36 Strange, *The Possibility Of Salvation*, offers a very robust response.

37 K. Rahner, *Theology of Death* (London, 1965).

38 Hick, *Universe of Faiths*, pp. 131–2; A. Race, *Christians and Religious Pluralism* (London, 1983), pp. 45–62; A. Pieris, *Love Meets Wisdom* (New York, 1988), pp. 3–4, 131.

39 H. Küng, *On Being a Christian* (London, 1976), pp. 77–8.

40 G. D'Costa, "Trinitarian *différance* and World Religions: Postmodernity and the 'Other,' " in U. King (ed.), *Faith and Praxis in a Modern Age* (London, 1998), pp. 28–46.

41 M. Ruokanen, *The Catholic Doctrine of Non-Christian Religions* (Leiden, 1992); H. van Straelen, *The Catholic Encounter with World Religions* (London, 1966); DiNoia, *Diversity of Religions*; Lindbeck, *Nature of Doctrine*.

42 Lindbeck, *Church in a Postliberal Age*, ch. 6.

43 H. U. von Balthasar, *The Moment of Christian Witness* (New York, 1969); R. Williams, "Balthasar and Rahner," in J. Riches (ed.), *The Analogy of Beauty* (Edinburgh, 1986), pp. 11–34.

44 DiNoia, *Diversity*; S. M. Heim, *The Depth of the Riches: A Trinitarian Theology of Religious Ends* (Grand Rapids, MI, 2001); S. Ogden, *Is There Only One True Religion or Are There Many?* (Dallas, TX, 1992).

45 K. Surin, "A Politics Of Speech: Religious Pluralism in the Age of the Macdonald's Hamburger," in G. D'Costa (ed.), *Christian Uniqueness Reconsidered* (New York, 1990), pp. 192–212; Milbank, "The End of Dialogue"; D'Costa, *The Meeting of Religions*.

46 D'Costa, *Meeting of Religions*, pp. 19–52.

47 See, for example, D'Costa, *Meeting of Religions*; N. Smart and S. Konstantine, *Christian Systematic Theology in a World Context* (Minneapolis, MN, 1991); R. Panikkar, *The Trinity and the Religious Experience of Man* (London, 1973).

48 J. Pawlikowski, *What are They Saying about Jewish–Christian Relations?* (New York, 1980); and see the three other chapters in Part VII of the present volume.

49 Pieris, *Love Meets Wisdom*; R. Panikkar, *The Silence of God* (New York, 1989); W. Lai and M. von Brück, *Christianity and Buddhism* (New York, 2001); P. Almond, *The British Discovery of Buddhism* (Cambridge, 1988).

50 M. Barnes, *Theology and the Dialogue of Religions* (Cambridge, 2002).

51 G. D'Costa, *Theology and Education: The Virtue of Theology in a Secular World* (Cambridge, 2005); and Smart and Konstantine, *Christian Systematic Theology*.

52 W. C. Smith, *Towards a World Theology* (Philadelphia, PA, 1981); L. Swidler and P. Mojzes, *The Study of Religion in an Age of Global Dialogue* (Philadelphia, PA, 2000).

Bibliography

Almond, P., *The British Discovery of Buddhism* (Cambridge, 1988).

Balthasar, H. U. von, *The Moment of Christian Witness* (New York, 1969).

Barnes, M., *Theology and the Dialogue of Religions* (Cambridge, 2002).

Barrett, D., "The Status of the Christian World Mission in the 1990s," in G. Anderson, *Mission in the Nineteen Nineties* (Grand Rapids, MI, 1991).

Barth, K., *Church Dogmatics* (Edinburgh, 1956–70), Vols. I.2 (1970) and IV.1 (1956).

Carson, D., *The Gagging of God* (Leicester, 1996).

Cooey, P., Eakin, W., and McDaniel, J. (eds.), *After Patriarchy: Feminist Transformations of the World Religions* (New York, 1993).

Coward, H., *Pluralism: Challenge to World Religions* (New York, 1985).

D'Costa, G., *Theology and Religious Pluralism* (Oxford, 1986).

—— "Christ, the Trinity, and Religious Plurality," in G. D'Costa (ed.), *Christian Uniqueness Reconsidered: The Myth of a Pluralistic Theology of Religions* (New York, 1990), pp. 16–29.

—— "John Hick and Religious Pluralism: Yet Another Revolution," in H. Hewitt (ed.), *Problems in the Philosophy of John Hick: Critical Studies of the Work of John Hick* (Basingstoke, 1991), pp. 102–16.

—— "Trinitarian *différance* and World Religions: Postmodernity and the 'Other,'" in U. King (ed.), *Faith and Praxis in a Modern Age* (London, 1998), pp. 28–46.

—— *The Meeting of Religions and the Trinity* (New York, 2000).

—— "Postmodernity and Religious Pluralism: Is a Common Global Ethic Possible or Desirable?" in G. Ward (ed.), *The Blackwell Companion to Postmodern Theology* (Oxford, 2001), pp. 131–43.

—— "Nostra aetate – Telling God's Story in Asia: Problems and Pitfalls," in M. Lamberigts and L. Kenis (eds.), *Vatican II and Its Legacy* (Leuven, 2002), pp. 229–350.

—— *Theology and Education: The Virtue of Theology in a Secular World* (Cambridge, 2005).

DiNoia, J. A., *The Diversity of Religions: A Christian Perspective* (Washington, DC, 1992).

Dupuis, J., *Towards a Christian Theology of Religious Pluralism* (New York, 1997).

Griffiths, P. (ed.), *Christianity through Non-Christian Eyes* (New York, 1991).

Hauerwas, S., "Some Theological Reflections on Gutiérrez's Use of Liberation as a Theological Concept," *Modern Theology*, 3 (1986), pp. 67–76.

Heim, S. M., *The Depth of the Riches: A Trinitarian Theology of Religious Ends* (Grand Rapids, MI, 2001).

Hick, J., *God and the Universe of Faiths* (London, 1977).

—— *An Interpretation of Religion* (Basingstoke, 1988).

—— "Straightening the Record: Some Responses to Criticism," *Modern Theology* 6 (1990), pp. 187–95.

—— "Responses," in H. Hewitt (ed.), *Problems in the Philosophy of John Hick: Critical Studies of the Work of John Hick* (Basingstoke, 1991).

—— *The Rainbow of Faiths* (London, 1995).

Huxley, A., *The Perennial Philosophy* (New York, 1945).

James, W., *The Varieties of Religious Experience* (London, 1960).

Jathanna, O., *The Decisiveness of the Christ Event and the Universality of Christianity in a World of Religious Plurality* (Berne, 1981).

Knitter, P., *One Earth Many Religions* (New York, 1995).

—— *Jesus and the Other Names* (New York, 1996).

Küng, H., *On Being a Christian* (London, 1976).

—— *A Global Ethic for Global Politics and Economics* (London, 1997).

Lai, W. and von Brück, M., *Christianity and Buddhism* (New York, 2001).

Lausanne Statement, *Christian Witness to the Jewish People* (1980).

Lindbeck, G., *The Nature of Doctrine: Religion and Theology in a Postliberal Age* (London, 1984).

—— *The Church in a Postliberal Age*, ed. M. Buckley (London, 2002).

Lindsell, H., *A Christian Philosophy of Religion* (Wheaton, IL, 1949).

Milbank, J., "The End of Dialogue," in G. D'Costa (ed.), *Christian Uniqueness Reconsidered* (New York, 1990), pp. 174–91.

Morris, J., *Heaven's Command: An Imperial Progress* (London, 1973).

Newbigin, L., "The Basis, Purpose and Manner of Inter-Faith Dialogue," in R. Rousseau (ed.), *Interreligious Dialogue* (Montrose, 1981), pp. 13–31.

Ogden, S., *Is There Only One True Religion or Are There Many?* (Dallas, TX, 1992).

O'Neill, M., *Women Speaking, Women Listening: Women in Interreligious Dialogue* (New York, 1990).

Pannikar, R., *The Trinity and the Religious Experience of Man* (London, 1973).

—— *The Silence of God: The Answer of the Buddha* (New York, 1989).

Pawlikowski, J., *What are They Saying about Jewish–Christian Relations?* (New York, 1980).

Percy, J. (ed.), *Facing the Unfinished Task: Messages Delivered at the Congress on World Mission* (Grand Rapids, MI, 1961).

Pieris, A., *An Asian Theology of Liberation* (New York, 1988).

—— *Love Meets Wisdom* (New York, 1988).

—— "Black Flags for the Pope" (Robert Crusz citing Pieris), *The Tablet*, January 14, 1988, pp. 36–7.

Race, A., *Christians and Religious Pluralism* (London, 1983).

Rahner, K., *Theological Investigations* (London, 1963–80), Vols. 1, 5, 6, 12, 14, 16, 17.

—— *Theology of Death* (London, 1965).

Ruether, R. R., *Faith and Fratricide: The Theological Roots of Anti-Semitism* (New York, 1974).

—— "Feminism and Jewish–Christian Dialogue," in J. Hick and P. Knitter (eds.), *The Myth of Christian Uniqueness* (London, 1987), pp. 137–48.

Ruokanen, M., *The Catholic Doctrine of Non-Christian Religions According to the Second Vatican Council* (Leiden, 1992).

Sanneh, L., "Christian Mission and the Western Guilt Complex," *Christian Century*, April 8, 1987, pp. 330–4.

—— *Encountering the West: Christianity and the Global Cultural Process: The African Dimension* (London, 1993).

Sinkinson, C., "The Nature of Christian Apologetics in Response to Religious Plural-ism: An Analysis of the Contribution of John Hick," PhD dissertation, Bristol, 1997.

Smart, N. and Konstantine, S., *Christian Systematic Theology in a World Context* (Minneapolis, MN, 1991).

Smith, W. C., *Towards a World Theology* (Philadelphia, PA, 1981).

Stanley, B., *The Bible and the Flag* (Leicester, 1990).

Strange, D., *The Possibility of Salvation Among the Unevangelised: An Analysis of Inclusivism in Recent Evangelical Theology* (Carlisle, 2002).

Surin, K., "A Politics Of Speech: Religious Pluralism in the Age of the Macdonald's Hamburger," in G. D'Costa (ed.), *Christian Uniqueness Reconsidered* (New York, 1990), pp. 192–212.

Swidler, L. and Mojzes, P., *The Study of Religion in an Age of Global Dialogue* (Philadelphia, PA, 1990).

Troeltsch, E., *The Absoluteness of Christianity and the History of Religions* (London, 1972).

Van Straelen, H., *The Catholic Encounter with World Religions* (London, 1966).

Judaism and Christian Theology

Peter Ochs

Introduction

The most significant Christian theologies of Judaism in the past decade promote four theses: (1) a return to scripture as the foundation of Christian theology; (2) non-supersessionism as a condition for *Christian* renewal; (3) Jewish–Christian theological dialogue as a practice of Christian theology *per se*; and (4) a scripture-based practice of Abrahamic (Jewish–Christian–Muslim) theological inquiry. These theses are most fully developed and integrated by the movement of what some label "postliberal Christian theologians": academically trained scholars whose goals include "faithful yet creative retrieval of the Christian tradition, ecumenically open renewal of the church, and compassionate healing and repair of the world."[1] While "modern" or "liberal" theologians laid the foundation for Jewish–Christian dialogue after the Shoah, and while they continue to foster major grassroots efforts to remove anti-Judaism from the churches, recent liberal theologies of Judaism tend to replay the constructions of a previous generation. Postliberal theologians believe these constructions are too human centered to guide Jews and Christians to a deeper level of dialogue: recovering the scriptural roots of their shared devotion to God's Word.

The past decade has also been marked by renewed openings to supersessionism in the "Radical Orthodoxy" movement and by tendencies to anti-Judaism in the new "post-postmodern" Christian theologies. (As used here, "supersessionism" refers to the Christian belief that, with the Incarnation of God in Jesus Christ, Israel's Covenant with God was superseded and replaced by God's presence in the church as the Body of Christ: in other words, that God's love for the church replaced His love for the people Israel.) Outside the boundaries of academic theology, this decade has also seen the reemergence of nationalist–Christian anti-Judaisms in areas of the former Soviet Union; strong supersessionism among new conservative Christian movements, both in the United States and in developing nations; and what might be termed a theo-political anti-Judaism among some Christian critics of the State of Israel.

Survey

Beginning in the 1950 and 1960s, the first major contributions to Jewish–Christian dialogue were made by liberal Protestant and Catholic theologians, whose primary concern was repentance for centuries of Christian anti-Semitism. Theologians like Roy and Alice Eckardt, Edward Flannery, Franklin Littell, John Pawlikowski, Rose Thering, and many others worked strenuously on behalf of Jewish civil rights in the United States and Europe and called Christians, after the Shoah, to renounce all forms of anti-Judaism as well as supersessionism.[2] Some of the more radical theologians among this group read the long history of Christian mistreatment of the Jews as a mark of irremediable errors in the heart of classic Christian doctrine. For Roy Eckardt, "The Christian crime of today is that of an ongoing anti-Semitism and anti-Judaism that refused to end when the Holocaust took place."[3] He concluded that the only solution is to reidentify Christianity "as essential Judaism for the Gentiles."[4] In *Faith and Fratricide*, Rosemary Ruether argued "that the anti-Judaic myth is neither a superficial nor a secondary element in Christian thought. The foundations of anti-Judaic thought were laid in the New Testament. They were developed in the classical age of Christian theology in a way that laid the basis for attitudes and practices that continually produced terrible results."[5] The cure, she argued, is to demythologize classic Christology so as to remove its potential for supersessionism. In more recent work, Ruether expressed her concern that Israel, too – the state and the people – now needs to adopt a comparably prophetic self-criticism, in particular of its errant mythology of Zionism.

Liberation theologians of the 1970s and 1980s offered comparable criticisms of Judaism's relation to land and law. Leonardo Boff, for example, wrote that liberation theology adopts "the Exodus as a paradigm of all liberation . . . But the agency of liberation has now been given to a new Israel: 'God is no longer the old God of the Torah,' but 'a God of infinite goodness' . . . He draws near in grace, going far beyond anything prescribed or ordained by the law."[6] Rejecting these radical criticisms of scriptural religion, Pawlikowski, Van Buren, Krister Stendahl, and others offered non-supersessionist theologies that now appear as mediating forms of liberal/postliberal theology. Pawlikowski, for example, offered a Catholic critique of

> Pannenberg, Moltmann, Küng, Gutiérrez, Sobrino, Boff, and Bonino for succumbing to the traditional Christian temptation to render the identity of Jesus – and hence the distinctiveness of Christianity – by employing stereotypical, negative contrasts with Judaism . . . He rejects those theologians who have gone to the other extreme by surrendering too much of the distinctiveness of Jesus. These include Ruether, van Buren, Eckardt, Schoenveld, and Hellwig.[7]

Van Buren offered a comparable, Protestant critique of the twin dangers of anti-Jewish and anti-Christological theologies. Drawing, in part, on the New Testament scholarship of E. P. Sanders, he characterized Jesus as the one who, "sent only to save the lost sheep of Israel . . . became the One who gathers Gentiles to the God of Israel." Unlike Eckardt, van Buren identified this One as the Christ, Son of God, who was crucified and resurrected. This resurrected Christ is no impediment to philo-semitism; rather, the very "mystery of the Trinity is the mystery of a historical event – the gathering of a Gentile church into the worship of Israel's God."[8]

As will be described in detail below, the postliberal theologians took one additional stride away from the liberal model of theology, which they criticized as an effort to substitute conceptual constructions for the authority of scripture and doctrinal tradition. They argued that the words of scripture and of doctrine command behavior in ways that cannot be formulated *a priori*, but only in the immediate contexts of ecclesial life and its crises. In their view, the purpose of theology is to help the church repair its tendencies to disunity. Theologians offer this help by identifying how these tendencies appear in a given epoch and by recommending context-specific ways of reforming them. These recommendations emerge from theologians' study of scripture and of doctrine as sources of guidelines for this reformation. According to the postliberal theologians, supersessionism is one of the tendencies that threaten church unity today. It does so in three ways: (1) it represents a misreading of church doctrine that engenders potentially heretical behaviors in the world; (2) it is the product of a misguided scriptural hermeneutic that engenders potentially heretical readings of scripture; and (3) it reinforces the primordial church schism, which is between the church and the people Israel. While the stated goal of postliberal reform is to heal divisions in the church, the effort also appears to hold surprising promise for Jewish–Christian theological dialogue. The surprise is that, dedicated to unifying the church and reaffirming its Christological mission and trinitarian doctrine, postliberal theology also appears, through this very effort, to reaffirm the religion of Israel in a manner unparalleled in any other Christian movement.

Some of the more well-known postliberal theologians are: in the United States, Scott Bader-Saye, Michael Cartwright, James Buckley, James Fodor, Douglas Harink, Stanley Hauerwas, Kevin Hughes, Robert Jenson, Stacey Johnson, Gregory Jones, George Lindbeck, Bruce Marshall, Ephraim Radner, Rusty Reno, Eugene Rogers, Kendell Soulen, Robert Wilken, and David Yeago; in the UK, Nicholas Adams, Oliver Davies, David Ford, Daniel Hardy, Ben Quash; in Germany, Johan Goud, Bertold Klappert, Friedrich Marquardt, Gerhard Sauter, Martin Stöhr, and Peter von der Osten-Sacken.

There are, however, other critics of modern theology who believe that postliberal theology goes too far in its critique of supersessionism: theologians in the Radical Orthodoxy movement and a more variegated movement of Christian socialists self-described as post-postmodern. Both movements criticize modern efforts to unify Christianity under certain conceptual rubrics (such as love, or justice, or compassion), as well as postmodern efforts to reduce Christology to kenosis understood as an ethic of surrender to the needs of the other. Their remedy is to remove conceptual intermediaries to the noetic presence of Christ. By way of ecclesial practices, liturgy in particular, Christ is to become the direct subject of intellectual intuition and, thus, a direct guide to the disciplines of reason as well as to personal, societal, and ecclesial practices. While Christ is introduced to the world by way of the New Testament witness, scripture can also function as an offending intermediary if its language-specific textuality obscures the unalloyed truth of Christ. The biblical people Israel has its place in the story of Jesus Christ, but the particulars of Israel's language, practice, and history belong only to the material textuality of the gospel, rather than to its noetic witness. The noesis of Christ speaks universally, moreover, and thus knows no difference between Jew and Gentile, or Jew and Greek. Rabbinic Judaism therefore lacks any privileged place in Christian theological inquiry: as a people like any other people, Jews should be treated with justice and compassion, but their religious claims are true – according to the one, universal standard of truth – only in the degree to which they anticipate or correspond with aspects of the truth of Christ. Rabbinic law, moreover, offends if it purports to represent more than local custom: its particularity and materiality preclude its serving as a vessel of divine self-disclosure. Among theologians associated with Radical Orthodoxy, generalizations like these are more evident in the writings of John Milbank and are suggested only piecemeal in writings of others, such as Frederick Bauerschmidt, Phillip Blond, William Cavanaugh, Michael Handy, David Hart, Catherine Pickstock, and Graham Ward. Among what we are labeling "Christian–socialist post-postmodernists" are Alain Badiou, Slavoj Žižek, and Philippe Lacoue-Labarthe.

Named Theologians

Barth, Marquardt, and Osten Sacken: The transition to postliberal non-supersessionism

On first appearance, Barth's uncompromising Christocentrism is not a source of encouragement for Christian non-supersessionism. For Barth, the law is fulfilled in Christ and Israel's persistence in it remains a mark of sinfulness. In the *Church Dogmatics*, Barth thus refers to the synagogue as "the disobedient, idolatrous Israel of every age," "with no part now in the fulfillment of the promise given."[9] Nonetheless, this same Barth has proved to be the single most significant contributor to postliberal Christianity's reaffirmation of Israel's enduring Covenant. Wyschogrod offers an explanation: "Because he reads scripture obediently, [Barth] becomes aware of the centrality of Israel in God's relation with humanity and with the very message that Christianity proclaims to the world."[10] Because he does not substitute humanity's word for the word of God, Barth learns of Israel's role in sacred history the way the traditional Jew learns it, thus acknowledging the enduring election of Israel. "Without any doubt, the Jews are to this very day the chosen people of God in the same sense as they have been from the beginning, according to the Old and New Testaments."[11] "A church that becomes anti-Semitic or even only asemitic sooner or later suffers the loss of its faith by losing the object of it";[12] even so, the chosen people remains irremediably sinful without Christ.

Barth, in sum, provides a basis both for reaffirming Israel's Covenant and also denigrating it. Barth's students find a way, however, to overcome the denigration and thus reaffirm both Barthian Christology and a Barthian-yet-post-Barthian doctrine of non-supersessionism. In Germany, two of the most visible proponents of this move were Friedrich Marquardt and Peter von der Osten Sacken. Marquardt attempted to break the link between Christianity and anti-Judaism. Offering a close study of Jesus' life as *part* of Jewish history, he describes Jesus' uninterrupted loyalty to Torah. According to Wyschogrod, Marquardt's greatest contribution is his understanding of Israel, in von Balthasar's terms, as "formal Christology."[13] This is to display the continuities of Christian theology with the biblical history of Israel:

showing, for example, how incarnation is itself a Jewish notion, displayed in God's indwelling in the people Israel. Marquardt argues that, by saying no to Jesus, Israel draws attention to the fact that the world is not yet redeemed and that there is a waiting in creation to which Israel witnesses. Von der Osten Sacken reclaimed Israel's "no" in a comparable way, claiming that "God adheres to his election of Israel . . . even if it says no to Jesus Christ."[14] With their "no" to the gospel, the Jewish people exhibit, not rebellion, but an obedience "which is determined by their zeal for God (Romans 10: 2)."[15] This "no" thereby "results in the extension of salvation to the Gentiles and in no way implies the rejection of the Jewish people."[16] Guided both by historical–critical study and a pragmatic concern to obviate anti-Jewish readings of the New Testament, von der Osten Sacken concludes that Jesus' uniqueness does not lie in his piety, which is Jewish, but in his mediatory role. Jesus is Messiah as the one who reconciles Jews and Gentiles: bringing Gentiles into fellowship with God and thereby bringing Jews into fellowship with Gentiles – but "*without* becoming Christians."[17] More recently, von der Osten Sacken's work has acquired more of a "postliberal" tenor: focusing on liturgical and scriptural reading practices as sources of a Barthian-post-Barthian Christology and promoting comparative studies of liturgy and scripture as sources of Christian non-supersessionism.

Lindbeck, Soulen, and Marshall: Scriptural and trinitarian non-supersessionism

The prototypical, postliberal argument against supersessionism was introduced by George Lindbeck in conversation with Hans Frei.[18] Lindbeck introduced his postliberalism to a broad public in *The Nature of Doctrine* (1980). His more recent writings have made explicit how this postliberalism requires non-supersessionism as well. The argument may be schematized as follows.

1 Postliberalism is a reformational movement, calling modern theologians to repair tendencies to disunity in the church.
2 The method of reform is to re-read scripture as a set of instructions about how not to misinterpret the Reformation doctrine of *sola scriptura*.
3 These include instructions about how *not* to overlook the enduring place of the people Israel in the gospel narrative. It is, in fact, *heretical* to overlook Israel's enduring Covenant with God.
4 When freed from this heresy, Christians will read the gospel as both a narrative of the life of Christ and a reading of the history of Israel. This means that to read one text of scripture is also to re-read some other text of scripture. Figural reading is indigenous to the gospel narrative.
5 Reading this way, Christians will discover that their practices of reading scripture are themselves close to the reading practices of classical rabbinic Judaism. For the rabbinic sages, every text of scripture possesses both a "plain sense" and another, "interpreted sense." The plain sense should be apparent to every knowledgeable reader, but it never tells the whole story. At a given time and place, the plain sense will also display additional levels of interpreted meaning; for example, about how to enact the commands of Torah in the context of life in fifth-century

Babylonia or twelfth-century Spain. Christian readers will discover, similarly, that the plain sense of the gospel narrative discloses ever new meanings; about how, for example, to imitate the life of Christ in fourth-century Rome or sixteenth-century Germany.

6 Reading this way, Christians will read their scriptures as a source of instruction about how both to study and imitate the life of Christ. They will find that this instruction challenges several modern patterns of life and study. As Frei argued in *The Eclipse of Biblical Narrative*, and Lindbeck in *The Nature of Doctrine*, this instruction challenges modern tendencies to read scriptural texts as *expressing* certain values and *denoting* certain beliefs that could also be taught independently of the scriptural narratives. To read this way is to revere certain symbols (that name values) and propositions (that name beliefs) as if the biblical narratives were derivative of them and as if, therefore, Christian life could be practiced on their authority alone – independently of the detailed narratives of the life of Christ *and* of the life of Israel that these narratives re-read. For Lindbeck, these modern tendencies are doubly heretical: first, because they lend divine authority to symbols and propositions purportedly *about* the life of Christ that are not themselves revealed as scripture; and second, because they thereby occlude the narrative setting of the life of Christ in the life of Israel. Whether they are self-described as liberal or orthodox, such tendencies eventually occlude the place of Israel in salvation history.

7 As a corrective to these modern tendencies, Lindbeck proposes a doctrinal reform: the Reformation doctrine of *sola scriptura* must entail non-supersessionism. This leads to the most surprising claim of Lindbeck's postliberalism: in order to repair the Catholic–Protestant schism, postliberal reformers need first to repair a Jewish–Christian schism. Within the present time between the times, this does not yet mean unifying the Gentile church and the people Israel but, rather, recovering the hermeneutic through which the gospel story of Jesus Christ is read *also* as a re-reading and continuation of the scriptural narrative of the Covenant of Israel. *This* is the hermeneutic through which Catholics and Protestants will rediscover their shared means of participating in the body of Christ. Through this hermeneutic, Christians may also see how rabbinic Judaism offers a comparable, if different, re-reading and continuation of Israel's scriptural narrative.

In *The God of Israel and Christian Theology*, Kendall Soulen introduced his argument for postliberal non-supersessionism: the plain sense of the entire scripture teaches that God's identity as the God of Israel is inconceivable apart from the election of the Jewish people. Nevertheless, according to Soulen, Christian theology has traditionally assigned to God's interaction with Israel a propaedeutic function within the economy of sin and redemption, serving only to foreshadow God's redemptive work in Christ. This has a doubly unfortunate result. On the one hand, Christians have understood the distinction between Jew and Gentile as a means to the end of Christ's redemption, after which Jewish existence would lack any meaning in God's plan. On the other hand, Christians have tended to make the biblical theme of "creation and consummation" subservient to the biblical theme of "redemption from sin" – rendering Israel's story as one of incomplete redemption from sin. The cumulative result of this misreading is a semi-gnostic distortion of Christian thought that "rejects gnosticism at the level of ontology but not at the level of covenant history. [Gnosticism] . . . nullifies the intrinsic goodness of creation and misinterprets redemption in Christ as deliverance from the created order. [Christian supersessionism misreads] . . . redemption in Christ as deliverance from God's history with Israel and the nations."[19] Against this reading, Soulen recontextualizes the economy of sin and redemption within the larger economy of creation and consummation, described now in terms of the canon-spanning story of God's election of Israel as a blessing for the nations. The end and fulfillment of God's consummating work is not to annul the difference between Israel and the nations, but to bring both into the "mutual relatedness" and interdependence that is called *shalom* (after Job 5: 22–24; Psalms 29: 11; 128).[20] Within this context, Soulen depicts Christ as the climactic recapitulation of God's earlier works of redemption on Israel's behalf, for the sake not only of Israel, but also of the mutual blessing between Jew and Gentile. In sum, "Christians should acknowledge that God's history with Israel and the nations is the . . . enduring medium of God's work as the Consummator of human creation, and therein it is also the . . . enduring context of the gospel about Jesus."[21]

In more recent writings, Soulen extends his argument for the "economy of consummation" by exploring the consequences of a non-supersessionist doctrine of the Trinity.[22] Consistent with both Lindbeck and Jenson's recent work, Soulen suggests that the Tetragrammaton, YHVH, remains the name of the God to whom Jesus prayed. He says that, while Christians have always affirmed in some fashion that "YHWH is the Triune God," they have interpreted the two parts of this affirmation according to the scheme of Old Testament/New Testament, with the result that God's identity as YHWH is left in the past. In place of this, he proposes that Christians interpret the confession "YHWH is the Triune God" according to the logic of "Jesus is the Christ," with the result that both parts of the affirmation speak to past, present, and future.[23]

In *Trinity and Truth* and related essays, Bruce Marshall summons the tools of analytic philosophy to clarify and defend the postliberal argument for non-supersessionism. With Soulen, he "agree[s] on the need for a Trinitarian theology that avoids supersessionism," while offering a somewhat different means of achieving this.[24] In Marshall's terms, Soulen argues that "the God of Israel *is* the Trinity," in the sense that the two identities – "the God of Israel" and "the Triune God" – are one and the same. Drawing on the philosophic theory of reference, Marshall argues that these identities have a different "sense," even if we come to believe that they *refer* to the "same entity." While agreeing that the church worships the God of Israel and the Triune God, Marshall agues that this implies *neither* that when Israel worships the God of Israel, it is worshiping the Triune God, *nor* that, when Israel fails to recognize the Triune God *as* the God of Israel, it then fails fully to worship the God of Israel. In both cases, worship is directed to different *identities* that we, as theologians, recognize as referring to the One God.[25] More recently, in fact, Soulen has proposed a similar approach: suggesting that, for example, in the Lord's Prayer, the words "Our Father" and "Thy name" (YHWH) "point to two mutually interpreting and indispensable poles of Jesus' identification of God."[26]

Jenson and Bader-Saye: The embodied church and ecclesiological non-supersessionism

For Robert Jenson, the perennial work of theology is to help the church restore ecclesial unity. Modern theology has, however, lost its capacity to do this work because it has abstracted itself from the actual body of Christ, which means from all of the concrete life of the church – from gospel study and liturgical practice to everyday acts of sin as well as of piety. For Jenson, modern theology has turned its attention to concepts and theories in place of all these embodied realities. In this warning, he displays the Christological roots of his attention to the history, scripture, and Covenant of Israel. When Christian theology remembers the body of Christ, it also remembers Israel: because the body of Christ is also Jesus' Jewish body ("the risen Jew, Jesus of Nazareth");[27] because the Word that is made flesh is also the Word of Torah ("that flesh which Torah became and is");[28] because the Torah made flesh is the God of Israel incarnate; and because the gospel of Christ is thus also a reading of the story of Israel.

For Jenson, the modern Christian turn to concepts occludes the life of Israel because it occludes the embodied life of Christ. While praising recent efforts to repair modern theology from out of premodern ecclesial traditions, he warns that antecedents to modern conceptualism can be found there, too, in some patristic and medieval tendencies to accommodate trinitarian theology to hellenic ontologies of timelessness and perfection. These, he argues, are ontologies of the spirit without the body, and Christian theology loses its capacity to help repair the body of Christ when it forgets the body. Trinitarian belief is not, therefore, about some *number* of divine persons. It is fundamentally the Christian belief that God is incarnate in Jesus Christ, which is fundamentally the Christian belief that God has no qualities that we know apart from what both the Old and New Testaments say God does. "The doctrine of Trinity only explicates Israel's faith in a situation in which it is believed that the God [who "raised Israel from Egypt"] has prior to the general resurrection raised one of his servants from the dead."[29]

In sum, theology is not about some timeless truths of being, but about the lived relations that bind God and church in this world. Except in prophetic or mystical vision, such relations are visible to us only in their lived effects in this world. For Jenson, the relation of church to God is, indeed, an eternal relation, but it is not a timeless one, since the eternity of the God of Israel is an eternity that has entered historical time. It enters by way of God's Covenant with Israel, among whose fruits is God's redeeming Israel from bondage and thus from death; and it enters by way of God's incarnation in Jesus of Nazareth, among whose fruits is Jesus' resurrection on the third day.

In *The Church and Israel After Christendom*, Scott Bader-Saye explores the consequences of non-supersessionism for the ecclesiology and politics of the church itself. What doctrines, he asks, have Christians distorted in their efforts to occlude the place of Israel's Covenant in the economy of salvation? What difference will it make for the life of the church if Christians begin to re-member Christ's embodiment in Jewish flesh? Bader-Saye's most striking conclusions concern the place of election and community in the church. He argues that, strictly as a reaction against Judaism's material and communal theology of election, the church fathers nurtured an "individualized and spiritualized" doctrine of the church as the "soul" of society, as distinct from its body. But, when it no longer rebels in this way against its "Jewish flesh," the church should now recognize the communal and material dimensions of its own election, reclaiming its own identity as a political body.[30] This will, of course, be a political body unlike the politics of the nations. Bader-Saye contrasts the voluntarism and violence of the modern nation – where freedom means choice and violence is associated with the necessary ways of the world – with the political witness of the church, characterized by the freedom of the chosen and by non-violence. He reads Ephesians 2 as

> a stunning witness to the unity of church and Israel in God's covenant: "Remember that at one time you Gentiles by birth . . . were . . . without Christ, being aliens from the commonwealth of Israel, and strangers to the covenant of promise, having no hope and without God in the world. But now in Christ Jesus you who once were far off have been brought near by the blood of Christ."[31]

Bader-Saye concludes that "the church, as God's chosen people with Israel, is called to embody a politics of election . . . [witnessing] to God's election of Israel as the founding act of all true politics."[32]

Yoder, Cartwright, and Hauerwas: How will the non-violent church relate to the Jews?

In the latter years of his life, the Mennonite theologian John Howard Yoder composed a study of Jewish–Christian relations that illustrates both the extent and the limits of postliberal non-supersessionism. Published posthumously, *The Jewish–Christian Schism Revisited* advances this claim against supersessionism: that the Jewish–Christian schism "did not have to be," since classical Christianity is epitomized by the theology of Israel in Babylonian exile. For Yoder, this theology is captured by Jeremiah's injunction to "seek the peace of the city where they had been sent" (Jeremiah 29: 4–7): the city you inhabit in exile. The schism did not have to be, on the one hand, since, until it was misdirected by its own Constantinism and anti-Judaism, Christianity found its model in exilic Judaism. After Jeremiah, this Judaism was epitomized by what Yoder considers early rabbinic Judaism's pacifist pursuit of religion without land, king, Temple, and priesthood. It did not have to be, on the other hand, since, with this exilic ethic, early rabbinic Judaism was fully consistent with Christianity until, reacting against Christian anti-Judaism, the rabbis retracted their practice of universal proselytism and redefined Judaism as an ethnic-specific religion. In the process, the rabbinic sages undermined their deeper, exilic predilections and adopted a utopian model of Judaism situated in the Land and governed by a Jewish theocracy. In other words, classical Christianity and classic Judaism had the *potential* to share an exilic theology that anticipated the goals of both radical Anabaptist Christianity and non-Zionist, exilic Judaism.

Michael Cartwright, who edited the Yoder collection, also appended to it a commentary on the strengths and weaknesses of Yoder's alternative to Christian supersessionism. The greatest strength is that Yoder rethought Jewish–Christian relations *not* in reaction to the Shoah, but because Christians lost their ability to read the scriptures when they sought to make Christianity intelligible without Israel. For Yoder, the radical Reformation has already offered Christians a tried-and-true model for recovering this ability, since "the Anabaptists of the sixteenth century 'were alone among the reformers in their insistence that the New Testament be read as a continuation and development of the Old.'"[33] Yoder's argument also displays a great weakness, however. For Cartwright, this is a tendency to over-determine the meaning of scripture: claiming that it is possible to identify, in clear terms, the meaning of Israel's entire narrative history. For Yoder, this meaning is displayed in Jeremiah 29, read as a prototype of Israel's "Jeremianic turn," from a land-centered people to one defined by exile, pacifism, and universal service. While acknowledging the place of this "turn" as one element of Second Temple and rabbinic Judaism, Cartwright questions Yoder's effort to generalize this one part into the whole, thereby erasing all the other dimensions of Judaism. Such erasure is a classic mark of supersessionist readings. Cartwright's concern is that "the hermeneutical logic that [Yoder] deploys contradicts his own goal of fostering Jewish–Christian dialogue" and overcoming supersessionism.[34]

While emulating Yoder's Anabaptist reform, Stanley Hauerwas argues against what he considers two false models of Christian universalism: the Constantinian model that accommodates the church to the conditions of worldly power, and the modern, liberal model that identifies the imitation of Christ with obedience to a discrete set of universalizable moral principles. Against the Constantinian model, he argues, with Yoder, that Christianity is a witness to Jesus' preaching "against the nations" and against the pursuit of worldly power through the instrument of worldly power. Against the modern model, he argues, again with Yoder, that the person of Jesus Christ, alone, is the paradigm for what it means to follow Christ. To learn who Jesus is means to study the gospel witness and to share in the sacramental and societal practices of the body of Christ. With Yoder, Hauerwas reads scripture as a source of directives to act, but he tests these directives according to their capacities to mold lives of virtue (in *imitatio Christi*) rather than in their coherence with any discrete series of principles (moral or Christian). Someone, to be sure, needs to judge the success or failure of exemplary Christian lives, but Hauerwas relies for such judgments on living communities of the church as they receive its traditions and test them against the challenges of the day. In this way, he argues against the need to rely – as Yoder relies – on the rational coherence of a single discipline of judgment, informed, as it must be, by discrete principles of rationality and virtue. Hauerwas thereby appears to take Yoder's critique of liberal theology one step further: returning to scripture not only as referent of ecclesial authority, but also as prototype for the practice of Christian theological reasoning. Where Yoder named scripture the authoritative source for his various reformatory *principles* (such as "the Jeremianic turn"), Hauerwas has nurtured a generation of students who study scriptural (and liturgical) practices as generative sources of more unpredictable and context-specific judgments.

Hauerwas' practice generates two paths to non-supersessionism, one direct, one indirect. The indirect path is opened by his critique of conceptualism. There is no need, he argues, to press as brilliantly as Yoder pressed to isolate the "essential" virtues of being Jewish and being Christian, since those virtues are displayed only in the lives lived by Christian saints and tested through the judgments of the church as a community of disciples. When the "essence" of Christianity is defined through a set of universal principles, the relation between Christian and Jewish identity will be governed by the predictable, philosophic law of excluded middle, rather than by the unpredictable demands of scripture. Jewish identity will either be assimilated to Christian identity or pre-defined as non-Christian and therefore *against* the universal principles of humankind. These are the options posed by classical supersessionism. Hauerwas' indirect path to non-supersessionism is opened by the gospel narrative. With the other postliberals, Hauerwas finds nothing in the practice of *imitatio Christi* that supplants Israel's Covenant. Since the life of Israel is always part of the life of Christ, theologians need to isolate that fact only where and when it is forgotten.[35]

Hardy and Ford: Anglican postliberalism as a pneumatological route to non-supersessionism

In the way that dialogue between Lindbeck and Frei helped articulate "Yale school" postliberalism, dialogue between Daniel Hardy and David Ford has helped articulate an Anglican variety of postliberalism that takes a different but complementary path to non-supersessionism. While Lutheran postliberals tend to reform *sola scriptura* as the condition for repairing modern Christian theology, and Free Church postliberals add a more pointed focus on Christocentric practices, Anglican postliberals draw their primary direction from pneumatology. They share in the "return to scripture," but read scripture always "with the Spirit."

For both Hardy and Ford, liberal conceptualism errs by abstracting the church out of its pneumatological life. To recover pneumatology is to recognize that, when offered independently of direct encounters with God, theological claims are mere conceptual constructions. Hardy and Ford caution, however, that such encounters must be disciplined in two ways. On the one hand, direct references to God's presence must be strictly demonstrative; a claim *that* "God is here" must be empty of any iconic representation of *what* is encountered. On the other hand, such "pointing" cannot be treated as adequate; theologians must also state something informative about God. Putting these two disciplines together means that theological claims may be offered *only* as the products of temporally extended processes of reasoning that interpret such encounters within the context of a received tradition of belief and practice. This "received tradition" includes the accumulated record of Christian scriptural interpretation, doctrinal deliberation, liturgical practice, and salvation history in all its sociopolitical detail. To "interpret" such encounters means to read them in relation to a particular ecclesial communion and historical moment.

Guided by these pneumatological disciplines, theological claims should, according to Hardy and Ford, preclude relativism, since they are *themselves* marks of some actual relation between the divine presence and a specific Christian community. These claims should also preclude dogmatism, since they make positive claims about God only in relation to fallible processes of interpretation. While there is, therefore, an apophatic dimension to Anglican postliberalism, it is not a radical apophasis. The way we come to know God is not, in form, different from the way we come to know *any* "other out there." One knows any other only through an *encounter* that engages all of one's senses and relations. In this sense, Hardy and Ford subscribe to a "sapiental pneumatology": a path to wisdom about God in relation to our lives in the world.

Sapiental pneumatology generates two correlative paths to non-supersessionism: relational and epistemological. The relational path is to be led, by the Triune God, to anticipate that every two-part relation will open to a third: that the Word that leads one to the Father will also open one to the Spirit; that the community one loves will also open one to yet other communities; that no theological concept is an end in itself, but an opening to yet another. The epistemological path is to be led, by the Spirit, to the mystery that accompanies every encounter with God and to the endless activity of discovery that is opened by each mystery. In relational terms, this "endlessness" is not mere formlessness, but an unending iteration of three-part relations, where every discovery ("that X is Y") opens to its relational third: "that 'X is Y' is (in relation to) Z; but 'Q is Z,' and so on." Sapiental pneumatology thereby engenders epistemological generosity: Christian theologians discover God's triune identity, but they do not perceive that identity with the clarity and finality that precludes their learning something more from other witnesses to other encounters. For Hardy and Ford, there are criteria, but no clear and distinct formulae, for defining when and how these witnesses will appear. The criteria are formed at the "blurry edges" of each account of the identity of God, so that each characteristic of God's identity remains both *closed* to possibilities that would contradict what has already been seen (or what is thus doctrinal) and *open* to new dimensions that are yet to be seen.

Hardy and Ford's engagement with Judaism reflects both pneumatological paths. According to one path, the Word that is Christ is embodied in Christ's Jewish body, which lives in relation to the Word that is Torah, which is exhibited in the life of the people Israel. Christians will therefore come to know more of Christ incarnate if they come to know the Jews and their Torah. The other path leads to more unpredictable results. These Anglicans *might happen* to meet Jews whose accounts of the divine presence overlap in some ways with their own accounts. If so, then it would not be surprising if these Jews and Christians seek some form of theological dialogue. If the dialogue includes scriptural study, then it would not be surprising if the Christians discovered ways that their scriptural tradition honored the enduring Covenant of the Jews and, moreover, if the Jews discovered ways that their scriptural tradition honored Christianity's witness to the God of Israel. These paths have led Hardy and Ford to extend theological dialogue beyond the Jewish community, as well. They are co-founders of the Society for Scriptural Reasoning, which promotes theological dialogue among Muslim as well as Jewish and Christian scholars of scripture and hermeneutics.[36]

Milbank and radical orthodoxy: Challenges to postliberal non-supersessionism

John Milbank, founder of the Radical Orthodoxy movement, offers a critique of modern conceptualism that overlaps in many ways with the postliberal critique. He does not, however, share postliberalism's thoroughgoing critique of supersessionism, and the two movements' disagreements about supersessionism may also signal less obvious disagreements about the authority of scriptural discourse. Milbank's recent theology of the gift offers one illustration of these points of disagreement.

For Milbank, only a Christocentric understanding of divine gift corrects weaknesses in both modern and postmodern accounts of divine–human exchange. He argues that both accounts are misled by the same purist assumption that, if "God" names the one who donates the gift of being itself, then God's perfect giving must be incompatible with reciprocity and, thus, with actual relation to human *beings*. The modern account is, he says, typified by anthropological studies of gift-exchanges in folk societies. Here, a gift is offered with the tacit assumption that, after appropriate delay, the donor will also receive a gift in return. The modernist concludes that, because gift giving is unavoidably reciprocal, it must be a strictly human affair; we know only our own being. Postmodernists argue, however, that even this knowing is non-knowing. Derrida argues, for example, that the modern account discloses the deception present in all gift giving. On the one hand, any gift comes with some form of self-interest; on the other hand, we cannot do without gifts, since the desire to give is "the ethical impulse itself," and there is no way for human society to function without it.[37] For Derrida, the result is that human society must live its contradiction and its deception: to give is also not to give.

In Milbank's reading, postmodern theologians like Levinas enact the implications of Derrida's reasoning: God, alone, is gift-giver, but since we cannot know God's gift of being *as* given *or* as *being*, we encounter it only in the non-being of our relation to others.[38] But, Milbank argues, what Levinas calls the "other" can, in the end, only represent the object of my projected "I" and cannot, therefore, truly interrupt egoism.[39] Only that which arrives as pure gift can be said to accomplish this.[40] And pure gift has been disclosed only in Christ, in whom God's gift of love is pure *and* reciprocal. The eucharistic "gift given to us of God himself in the flesh" is the "gift of an always preceding gift-exchange," which is the exchange of love between Father and Son, between Being and beings and between Christ and his church.[41] By participating in Christ, humanity thereby receives the gift of giving as well as of receiving.

Milbank credits both "Israel's law" and Greek political philosophy with having uncovered the capacity of giving that transcends egoism. Israel understood that God gives to Israel without limit, so that Israel could give herself to God without limit too and, in that giving, release "sheer forgiveness" to others. But, Milbank argues, Israel extended this forgiveness only to those within Israel, including only other Jews in their Mosaic "blood-covenant." Paul showed that, in Christ, this blood-covenant and its attendant forgiveness are extended to all humanity: "an infinite exchange between peoples and . . . the full realization of the covenanted fiction of 'one blood.' "[42] For this reason, perhaps, Milbank writes, in an informal essay, of "an unfortunate tendency within contemporary theology to play down the Christian 'going beyond the law,' which incoherently and anachronistically seeks a kind of alignment with post-biblical rabbinic law."[43] This refers, most likely, to the tendency of Christian postliberalism to unite non-supersessionism with its critique of the liberal church. Milbank appears to conclude that Israel's law made a step toward the understanding of gift that is fully disclosed in Christ, but that, in light of this disclosure, rabbinic law appears as an effort to particularize God's gift of love and particularize what is universal. He thereby appears to conclude that, by valorizing rabbinic Judaism as an expression of Israel's enduring Covenant, postliberal theology has rendered its Christology "incoherent and anachronistic." If so, then postliberalism and Radical Orthodoxy may differ in their approaches to scripture as well as to Judaism.

Debate

Three questions capture the central debates now in the Christian theology of Judaism.

A question from the past decade: Barthian or liberationist/ liberal approaches to Judaism?

This question still animates theological debates, particularly in the academy. On the one hand, a surprising number of liberal theologians still associate "Barthianism" with "dogmatic" and supersessionist uses of scripture. The postliberal theologians mentioned in this chapter argue, to the contrary, that their "return to scripture" is this generation's means of removing supersessionism and undermining conceptual dogmatisms, modern or anti-modern. While liberal theologians remain among the most active reformers of Christian supersessionism, the next phase of Jewish–Christian dialogue may call them, as well, to deeper engagement with the text-based reasoning that typifies Jewish religiosity.

A question for the present decade: Postliberal or "radically Orthodox" approaches to Jewish–Christian theological dialogue?

Postliberal theology's "return to scripture" has engendered a renaissance of Jewish–Christian theological dialogue. For theologians of Radical Orthodoxy, aspects of this dialogue may represent, to the contrary, a fall from the clarity of God's self-disclosure in Christ. As illustrated in Milbank's theology of the gift, the difference may reflect divergent approaches to scripture. For postliberals, the gospel is authoritative *both* as a witness to the fact of Christ's death and resurrection *and* to a particular practice of reading the narrative of Christ as a reading of the salvation narrative of Israel. This reading is therefore always tripartite: linking any theological doctrine with a reading of Old Testament with a reading of gospel. Israel's Covenant thereby enters Christian theology in two ways. This Covenant is an explicit subject of at least the Old Testament reading. And the tripartite form of reading is one face of the Covenant itself: as a Word (1) through which God's will (2) is *spoken* to God's people (3) in the material context of their lives at given times. For this reason, Lindbeck depicts the Church *as* Israel: not to replace the Jewish identity of Israel, but to adopt that identity as also the type of the Christian community to whom that Word is addressed.

Theologians of Radical Orthodoxy do not appear to share this tripartite practice of reading gospel. First, they may not regard a reading of the Old Testament as *necessary* to a reading of the gospel. Second, they may thereby allow a two- rather than three-part reading of the gospel: where the narrative of Christ (1) may be said to *disclose* (2) a theological truth (such as "Christ alone displays the free gift of God's love"), rather than speaking God's Word (2) *to* his people or his church (3) in a given time and place. Radical Orthodox theologians may defend this two-part reading as a corrective to postliberal relativism.[44] Postliberal theologians may identify this two-part reading as another form of conceptualism.[45]

A question for the next decade: Is the study of scripture a basis for inter-Abrahamic relations?

The next decade may generate three different answers to this question. Liberal theologians may argue that Christians, Jews, and Muslims must reinterpret their scriptures in the interest of universal principles of human rights, justice, and peace. Radical Orthodox theologians may argue that universal peace can be guaranteed only through the truths disclosed in Christ, who *is* peace. Postliberal theologians may argue that the inter-Abrahamic study of scripture should both strengthen each of the three Abrahamic traditions of faith and disclose scripture's rules for cooperative reasoning among the three traditions.[46]

Influence, Achievement, and Agenda

In 2001, five Jewish theologians published *Dabru Emet: A Jewish Statement on Christians and Christianity* as a full-page ad in the *New York Times*, signed by over two hundred rabbis. The theologians also co-edited a scholarly book on the topic, *Christianity in Jewish Terms*, with commentaries by twenty Jewish and ten Christian theologians. The project was sponsored by the Institute for Christian and Jewish Studies in Baltimore, Maryland, which also published an accompanying resource book for discussion groups. *Dabru Emet* offered a Jewish theology of Christianity, including claims that Jews and Christians worship the same God and draw on common scriptural sources of faith and ethics. The authors wrote that their work was inspired by the efforts of liberal and postliberal Christian theologians, in the decades after the Shoah, to remove anti-Judaism from Christian practices. They were also inspired by Christian colleagues who encouraged their studies of Judaism and who joined with them in defending scriptural religion against the twin challenges of modern secularism and anti-modern religious triumphalism. For these authors, Jewish–Christian theological dialogue strengthens Jewish faith after the Shoah, as much as it strengthens God's work in the world beyond the precincts of Jewish practice.

Does this dialogue strengthen Christian faith as well? How Christians answer this question may signal how they will seek to reform Christianity in the next decade. Christians who reform the modern church through a "return to scripture" will also, it appears, engage themselves in theological dialogue with Judaism. Christians who object to that dialogue will also, it appears, object to too "literal" a return to scripture: grounding theology on scripturally based *truths* rather than in the ongoing practice of scriptural study. Christians whose theologies draw primarily on extra-scriptural sources may care for the rights of Jews, but may have limited interest in biblical or rabbinic Judaism.

Acknowledgments

My thanks to several scholars who reviewed earlier drafts of this chapter and offered very important guidance: Michael Cartwright, David Ford, Stanley Hauerwas, Bruce Marshall; with my thanks for particularly detailed assistance from Scott Bader-Saye and Kendall Soulen.

Notes

1 James Fodor, chapter 14, this volume.
2 Many worked together in the Christian Scholar's Group, formerly in Baltimore, and now in Boston.
3 Eckardt, 1993, p. 55.
4 Cited in Pawlikowski, 1982, p. 57.
5 Ruether, 1974, p. 226.
6 Boff, 1978, p. 284; cited in Pawlikowski, 1982, p. 72.
7 Hawk, 1992, pp. 130–1.
8 Van Buren, 1980, p. 92.
9 Barth, 1936–69, II.2, p. 234.
10 Wyschogrod, 1972, p. 111.
11 Barth, 1954, p. 200.
12 Barth, 1936–69, II.2, p. 234.
13 Wyschogrod, 1992.
14 Von der Osten Sacken, 1986, p. 163.
15 Ibid, p. 165.
16 Ibid, p. 166.
17 Ibid, p. 58.
18 As is well known, Lindbeck's primary interlocutor was Hans Frei, who is another of the founding fathers of postliberalism as well as of its non-supersessionist character. For economy of reporting, we focus here on the more recent work of Lindbeck and Jenson. See also chapter 14, this volume.
19 Soulen, 1996, p. 110.
20 Ibid, p. 131.
21 Ibid, p. 110.
22 Soulen, 2003.
23 Ibid, p. 52.
24 Marshall, 2001, p. 236, n. 3.
25 Ibid, pp. 262–3.
26 Soulen, 2003, p. 31.
27 Jenson, 1982, p. 13.
28 Ibid, p. 12.
29 Jenson, 1997, p. 63.
30 Bader-Saye draws his understanding of Jewish election from the writings of David Novak and Michael Wyschogrod and then extends this understanding to the election of the church as well.
31 Bader-Saye, 1999, p. 112.
32 Ibid, p. 148.
33 Yoder, 2003, p. 109.
34 Cartwright, 2003, p. 218.
35 As response to the forgetting, for example, Hauerwas devotes his book series, *Radical Traditions: Theology in a Postcritical Key*, to publishing unapologetic Jewish and Muslim, as well as Christian, theologies.
36 See the *Journal of Scriptural Reasoning*, www.etext.lib.virginia.edu/journals/ssr/.
37 Milbank, 1995, p. 30.
38 Jean-Luc Marion criticizes Levinas' radical apophaticism at this point. But, as Milbank reports with displeasure, even Marion concludes that the gift, while given, must be offered "indifferent to reception": a gift beyond being.
39 Milbank, 1997, p. 38.
40 Ibid, p. 39.
41 Milbank, 1995, pp. 150–2.
42 Ibid, p. 149.
43 Milbank, 2002, p. 313.
44 See Milbank, Pickstock, and Ward (1999).
45 See Harink (2003), Radner (1998), and Reno (2002).
46 See the Children of Abraham Institute website, www.childrenofabrahaminstitute.org.

Bibliography

Bader-Saye, Scott, *Church and Israel after Christendom: The Politics of Election* (Boulder, CO, 1999).

Barth, Karl, *Church Dogmatics*, trans. G. W. Bromily, T. F. Torrance et al. (Edinburgh, 1936–69).

—— "The Jewish Problem and the Christian Answer," in *Against the Stream* (London, 1954).

Boff, Leonardo, *Jesus Christ Liberator* (Maryknoll, NY, 1978).

Brooks, Roger, *Unanswered Questions: Theological Views of Jewish–Catholic Relations* (Notre Dame, IN, 1988).

Cartwright, Michael, Introduction and afterword, in John Howard Yoder, *The Jewish–Christian Schism Revisited* (Grand Rapids, MI, 2003), pp. 6–29, 205–40.

Eckardt, A. Roy, *Christianity and the Children of Israel* (New York, 1948).

—— *Reclaiming the Jesus of History: Christology Today* (Minneapolis, MN, 1992).

—— *Collecting Myself: A Writer's Perspective* (Atlanta, GA, 1993).

Fisher, Eugene (ed.), *Visions of the Other: Jewish and Christian Theologians Assess the Dialogue* (Mahwah, NJ, 1994).

Ford, David F., *Self and Salvation* (Cambridge, 1999).

Frei, Hans, *The Eclipse of Biblical Narrative* (New Haven, CT, 1974).

—— "The 'Literal Reading' of the Biblical Narrative in the Christian Tradition: Does it Stretch or Will it Break?" in Frank McConnell (ed.), *The Bible and the Narrative Tradition* (New York, 1986), pp. 36–69.

Frymer-Kensky, T., D. Novak, P. Ochs, D. Sandmel, and M. Signer (eds.), *Christianity in Jewish Terms* (Boulder, CO, 2000).

Gunton, Colin E., *Trinity, Time, and Church: A Response to the Theology of Robert W. Jenson* (Grand Rapids, MI, 2000).

Hardy, Daniel W., *Finding the Church* (London, 2001).

Harink, Douglas, *Paul Among the Postliberals* (Grand Rapids, MI, 2003).

Hauerwas, Stanley, *With the Grain of the Universe* (Grand Rapids, MI, 2001).

—— *The Hauerwas Reader*, ed. J. Berkman and M. Cartwright (Durham, 2001).

Hawk, Matthew Comer, "Root, Branch, and Rhetoric: Judaism and Christian Self-Understanding After the Holocaust" (PhD dissertation, Yale University, 1992).

Jenson, Robert W., *The Triune Identity: God According to the Gospel* (Philadelphia, PA, 1982).

—— *Systematic Theology, Vol. 1: The Triune God; Vol. 2: The Works of God* (New York, 1997, 1999).

—— "Toward a Christian Theology of Israel," *Pro Ecclesia* 9, 1 (1999), pp. 43–59.

Klein, Charlotte, *Anti-Judaism in Christian Theology* (Philadelphia, PA, 1978).

Levinas, Emmanuel, *Otherwise Than Being or Beyond Essence*, trans. A. Lingis (The Hague, 1981).

Lindbeck, George, *The Nature of Doctrine, Religion and Theology in a Postliberal Age* (Philadelphia, PA, 1984).

—— "Postmodern Hermeneutics and Jewish–Christian Dialogue: A Case Study," and "What of the Future? A Christian Response," in *Christianity in Jewish Terms*, ed. T. Frymer-Kensky et. al. (Boulder, CO), pp. 106–113, 357–366.

—— *The Church in a Postliberal Age*, ed. J. Buckley (Grand Rapids, MI, 2003).

Littell, Franklin, *The Crucifixion of the Jews* (New York, 1975).

Manuel, Frank, E., *The Broken Staff: Judaism through Christian Eyes* (Cambridge, MA, 1992).

Marquardt, Friedrich-Wilhelm, *Die Entdeckung des Judentums fur die Christliche Theologie, Israel in Denkens Karl Barths* (Munich, 1967).

—— *Das christliche Bekenntnis zu Jesus, dem Juden: Eine Chistologie*, 2 vols. (Munich, 1990–1).

Marshall, Bruce, "Israel," in *Knowing the Triune God: The Work of the Spirit in the Practices of the Church*, ed. J. Buckley and D. Yeago (Grand Rapids, MI, 2001), pp. 231–64.

—— "Do Christians Worship the God of Israel?" in *Knowing the Triune God*, ed. James J. Buckley and David S. Yeago (Grand Rapids, MI, 2001), p. 236, n. 3.

—— *Trinity and Truth* (Cambridge, 2000).

Milbank, John, "Can a Gift be Given? Prolegomena to a Future Trinitarian Metaphysic,"

Modern Theology 11, 1 (January 1995), pp. 119–61.

—— *The Word Made Strange* (Cambridge, MA, 1997).

—— "Sovereignty, Empire, Capital, and Terror," in *Dissent from the Homeland: Essays after September 11*, ed. S. Hauerwas and F. Lentricchia, *South Atlantic Quarterly* 101, 2 (spring 2002), pp. 305–23.

Milbank, John, Catherine Pickstock, and Graham Ward (eds.), *Radical Orthodoxy, A New Theology* (New York, 1999).

Mussner, Franz, *Tractate on the Jews: The Significance of Judaism for Christian Faith*, trans. Leonard Swidler (Philadelphia, PA, 1979).

Novak, David, *Jewish–Christian Dialogue: A Jewish Justification* (New York, 1989).

—— *The Election of Israel: The Idea of the Chosen People* (Cambridge, 1995).

Ochs, Peter (ed.), *The Return to Scripture in Judaism and Christianity* (Mahwah, NJ, 1993).

—— "Recovering the God of History: Scriptural Life after Death in Judaism and Christianity," in *Jews and Christians, People of God*, ed. C. Braaten and R. Wilken (Grand Rapids, MI, 2003), pp. 114–37.

—— "Trinity," in *The Cambridge Dictionary of Jewish–Christian Relations*, ed. E. Kessler (Cambridge, 2004).

Pawlikowski, John, *Christ in the Light of the Christian–Jewish Dialogue* (New York, 1982).

Radner, Ephraim, *The End of the Church: A Pneumatology of Christian Division in the West* (Grand Rapids, MI, 1998).

Reno, R. R., *In the Ruins of the Church: Sustaining Faith in an Age of Diminished Christianity* (Grand Rapids, MI, 2002).

Rothschild, Fritz A. (ed.), *Jewish Perspectives on Christianity* (New York, 1990).

Ruether, Rosemary R., *Faith and Fratricide: The Theological Roots of Antisemitism* (New York, 1974).

Ruether, Rosemary R. and Herman J. Ruether, *The Wrath of Jonah: Religion and Nationalism in the Israeli–Palestinian Conflict* (San Francisco, 1989).

Sanders, E. P., *Jesus and Judaism* (Philadelphia, PA, 1985).

Sonderegger, Katherine, *That Jesus Christ was Born a Jew: Karl Barth's "Doctrine of Israel"* (University Park, PA, 1992).

Soulen, R. Kendall, *The God of Israel and Christian Theology* (Minneapolis, MN, 1996).

—— "Hallowed Be Thy Name! The Tetragrammaton and the Name of the Trinity," in *Jews and Christians: People of God*, ed. C. Braaten and R. Wilken (Grand Rapids, MI, 2003).

Thoma, Clemens, *A Christian Theology of Judaism*, trans. Helga Croner (New York, 1980).

Van Buren, Paul M., *A Theology of the Jewish–Christian Reality*, Parts 1–3 (San Francisco, 1980, 1983, 1988).

Von der Osten Sacken, Peter, *Christian–Jewish Dialogue: Theological Foundations*, trans. M. Kohl (Philadelphia, PA, 1986).

—— *Martin Luther und die Juden* (Stuttgart, 2002).

Ward, Graham, *Barth, Derrida and the Language of Theology* (Cambridge, 1995).

World Council of Churches, with Allan Brockway et al., *The Theology of the Churches and the Jewish People: Statements by the World Council of Churches* (Geneva, 1988).

Wyschogrod, Michael, "Why, Was and Is the Theology of Karl Barth of Interest to a Jewish Theologian?" in *Footnotes to a Theology: The Karl Barth Colloquium of 1972*, ed. M. Rumscheidt, *SR Supplements* (1972), pp. 95–111.

—— "A Jewish Perspective on Karl Barth," in *How Karl Barth Changed My Mind*, ed. Donald K. McKim (Grand Rapids, MI, 1986), pp. 156–61.

—— *The Body of Faith: God in the People Israel* (San Francisco, 1989).

—— "Review of Friedrich-Wilhelm Marquardt, *Das Christliche Bekenntnis zu Jesus, dem Juden. Eine Christologie*," *Journal of Ecumenical Studies* 29, 2 (1992), pp. 275–6.

Yoder, John Howard, *The Jewish–Christian Schism Revisited*, ed. M. Cartwright and P. Ochs (Grand Rapids, MI, 2003).

Islam and Christian Theology

Ataullah Siddiqui

The lines between theologians' explanation and analysis of Islam and missiologists' selection and interpretation of it overlap considerably.[1] The motive and orientation of inquiry are largely overtaken by past relations and perceptions of Islam, so that theology is penetrated and overlaid by history. This is equally true of the approach of those missiologists who rely principally upon anthropological methods. Whenever theologians and missiologists examined Islam, they measured it against their own convictions and culture, more or less remaking it as the historical "common enemy" of Christendom. There are always exceptions, which we will examine later, but their imaginative reexamination of theology has only just begun. The task of constructing a new theology that is adequate to the new sociopolitical realities (plural communities in close neighborhood within and between nations) is a daunting task. In this chapter I examine some of the major questions for Christians in relation to Islamic beliefs and practices:

- What to make of Islamic monotheism, the Muslim understanding of the oneness of God?
- What to make of the post-biblical Prophet, the center and horizon of Islamic ethics?
- What to make of Islam's Revelation (i.e., the Quran) and the role of secular–historical scholarship in shaping its meanings in the future?
- What to do with dialogue so that it can address these issues in future interfaith relations?

Since how we fashion dialogue for and about interfaith relations depends on the quality of encounter with the core issues of theological concern represented by the first three questions, it is best to begin with a brief overview of those issues, namely God, his Messenger, and his Book.

Islam declares itself in conformity with, consummating and to some extent correcting, all previous revelations. It particularly affirms the divine origin of Christianity (as also of Judaism), but keeps its distance from, indeed criticizes, the central doctrine of Christianity. The divide between Islam and Christianity that most needs bridging derives from their different understandings of God and relationship with him.

In the Islamic perspective, God's "care" for humankind, his "concern" for their "salvation," is expressed in the paired miracles of creation and revelation, together enabling human beings to realize their potential for good and to defeat their potential for sin and wrongdoing. God *commands*, and human beings *obey*, but they obey through free will by interiorizing those commands. Since the commands are to be and to do good, they are inherently appealing. Also, they are readily interiorized because they correspond to an innate disposition (the "signs in their selves"), and because they are supported by the intelligibility, harmony, and utility of the external world (the "signs on the horizons"). Then, as faithful practice matures, obedience is rewarded with grace, the consciousness of being always under God's supervision. This in turn reinforces the disciplines (the faithful practice) that stabilize character and deepen submission to God. In mainstream Islam this consciousness of God never presumes to "fellowship" or "intimacy" in any form analogous to interpersonal relationships between human beings. Such presumption, for Muslims, violates *tawhid* (the oneness, transcendence, and otherness of God) and risks his wrath – manifested in this world as a forgetfulness such that humans either think of themselves as vulnerably dependent on natural forces and events, or as powerfully independent, avid for more power and aggressively self-centered in accruing it. Therefore, in the Islamic perspective, the transcendent oneness of God is uncompromising and uncompromised.

The Christian approach to Islamic monotheism has sought, for the most part, to judge it against the doctrine of the Trinity. Christians stress the "personhood" of God so that his care and concern for human salvation are celebrated without the cautious inverted commas Muslims use around such terms. That caution has been caricatured to the extent that *tawhid* has been dismissed as no better than "a glorification of the number one."[2] Such caricature is an obstacle to constructive relationship; just as is the oversimplified understanding of Christian doctrine that too directly identifies Christ with God the Creator and Judge.

God's will is directly communicated, in the Islamic perspective, only through revelation to a succession of prophets and messengers, culminating and ending with the Prophet Muhammad. That which was revealed to him over the last 23 years of his life was meticulously preserved in the Book of God called the Quran (literally, "recitation"), a solidly reliable, stable text, unchanged despite shifts and schisms within the House of Islam that can be dated back to its first half century. To know how to understand and apply the Book, the Book commands the Muslims to depend on the *Sunnah* (the precept and practice) of the Prophet, whose personality and character are revered as "embodying" the Book.

The faithful practice of Islam, its rites, its spirituality, its ethics, its law, its dynamic for individual or collective life, are focused on the Quran and *Sunnah*. Self-referral to the Prophet is central for Muslims, for identity as well as for action, since their faith and worldview are anchored to his testimony. It should therefore be a priority (as well as an objective) of constructive dialogue to overcome the misrepresentations of his life and person that for so many centuries permeated Christian approaches to Islam and the Islamic world.

Christians have been striving to rethink their relationship with people of other faiths, Muslims included, since the first decade of the twentieth century. The effort began with intra-Christian debate about mission and ecumenical concerns. Interrupted by war, this effort was resumed soon after World War II. Churches in the non-Western world faced the challenge of being perceived in the newly independent states as a legacy of Western colonialism. They became more innovative, dynamic, and sensitive to local cultural contexts. Christians in the non-Western world (in many areas of which Muslims were the majority) sought a local niche for themselves, dissociated from Western Christianity, and associated, as far back as possible, with local history.

Christians in the West began reassessing and repenting the modes and attitudes of their past relationship with the Islamic world. They offered, and appealed for, dialogue. They did so as the Western world settled into a period of political stability, and attained new heights of cultural and economic power and new means of projecting it. The Islamic world at that time did not enjoy a comparable self-confidence. The euphoria of being rid of colonial rule quickly passed. The rifts between state and society aggravated by colonial rule were not healed by independence. Political boundaries and economic and administrative structures inherited by the new nation-states retained their orientation to the history, culture, and economies of the former colonial powers. Nationalism or socialism or near-feudal monarchy alike failed to make constructive contact with their Islamic traditions, and the distance between regimes in power and general population settled into mutual distrust. Islamic scholarship and curricula had been too long excluded from the domain of public service to establish themselves otherwise than as a resistance phenomenon: genuinely but narrowly pious, and oriented to maintaining religious–cultural identity. Large sectors of the populations of the Muslim states were, in any case, too preoccupied with day-to-day survival (so many were and are still refugees from war or oppression or destitution) to reconnect constructively with their past heritage.

In sum, not the most propitious juncture to hear the call for a new relationship with Christians at Bahamdoun in Lebanon in 1954 to open up to them, to explore hopes of making common cause against the expulsion of religion from human affairs. Even among those who were willing to enter into dialogue, their expectations and priorities were different from their Christian partners in dialogue.

Survey

Islam as theological concern

We will begin with Karl Rahner (1904–84), who viewed Islam, Judaism, and Christianity as the religions of Israel and acknowledged that they all professed monotheism, except that Judaism and Islam had "failed to achieve" that monotheism "which finds expression precisely in the doctrine of [the] Trinity." He took pains to explain this difficult so-near-yet-so-far relationship with Islam to his fellow Christians. He also clearly and firmly held the view that the "Christian proposition of God's oneness refers to a concrete absolute." Admitting frankly that he was no expert on Islamic theology and should not be regarded as such, he described its core doctrine with eloquence and placed it as a concrete monotheism. He imaginatively explored the Trinity *vis-à-vis* the monotheism of Islam as the "three-foldness" of One. He believed that the crucial difficulty between the two faiths lay in the Christian understanding of the concept of "person." He called this concept the "radicalization" of monotheism, but did not explain what this radicalization was. In Rahner's writings there is an implicit but firm dismissal of God's communication through human agency. "The mediation itself," he argued, "must be God and cannot amount to a creaturely mediation."[3]

Rahner's concept of "anonymous Christians" is perhaps also helpful in this context. He was in no sense "liberal." Rather, he understood Christianity "as the absolute religion, intended for all men." To him, other religions were religions instituted by man and ineffectual for salvation. However, he addressed this issue in a unique fashion. He asked: when does the "absolute religion" begin in a person's life? Does it begin at christening or only when one becomes aware and deliberate about the "absolute religion"? Now, as this question *cannot* be answered for others, it *need* not be: Christians may confront others not as non-Christians but (perhaps more kindly) as "anonymous Christians." This anonymity could be considered a sort of progress in relationships with Muslims and Islam.

The *Church Dogmatics* of Karl Barth (1886–1968) do not provide any opportunity for a fair hearing for the Prophet of Islam. The Prophet's message and monotheism, Barth believes, is "no different than 'paganism,'" a paganism all the more dangerous because Islam was able to instil in its followers the "esoteric essence" which Barth equates with monotheism.[4]

In relation to Islam, Barth was a theologian preoccupied with history, locked in the past, resisting the future. Among others of a like temper, we may include Emile Brunner (1889–1966), who held firm positions with regard to other faiths. As Jesus is the "'fulfillment of the Law': as Mediator, Revealer, Reconciler . . . He does not wish to have any more hearers, but *disciples* who do His Will."[5] Any option for dialogue with Islam is precluded. Paul Tillich (1886–1965) puts the blame for Islam's success in the region where Christianity was born squarely on the shoulders of Eastern Christianity, which he describes as largely a "sacramental superstitious form." Once it lost its puritan temper, it was inevitably overcome and subdued by Islam.[6] Tillich believes that the historical approach to scripture is a "great event in the history of Christianity," one of which he believes Protestantism can be proud. He points out that Islam, like Orthodox Judaism, had no experience of historical criticism and thus fell into a "narrow spiritual" world of its own, so missing out on the creative development of spiritual life.[7]

Islam as a missionary and missiological concern

Mission among Muslims has undoubtedly been the most difficult issue of relationship between the faiths, particularly over the last hundred years. During the early part of the twentieth century the Christian approach intended conversion, concentrated and coordinated as never before (largely by Protestant and Anglican missionaries) to win the minds and souls of Muslims. The Cairo Conference of 1906 for Muslim evangelism set the tone and temper. Its reports and its literature made available to those involved identified a clear purpose and unifying theme: the opportunity that awaited Christians in this context. The approach that followed was a twin-track policy: preparation of the necessary manpower to achieve the objective of mission, and Westernization or secularization of Muslim society through education and relief programs.

Duncan Macdonald (1863–1943) was a Scottish missionary with an academic orientation but little experience of living among Muslims. He was aware of and concerned about the presentation of the Prophet in Western and Christian scholarship. He was convinced that Christians who hope "to enter into relations with Muslims should know how Muslims think and feel about Muhammad."[8] He imagined the sociological and psychological environment that might explain his account of the Prophet as a traumatized and unsettled personality. For example, he conjectured that Muhammad's upbringing as an orphan led to his seeing devils, angels, and *jinns*. He also partly blamed such things on the monks and hermits that Muhammad met in their caves and cells during caravan journeys through the Syrian desert. The Prophet, in Macdonald's mind, was a product of social conditions and psychological anxiety. He also believed that Muhammad succumbed to worldly temptations in Madinah. He did believe that Muhammad was part of the line of Old Testament prophets, but not of the caliber of an Isaiah or Amos.

Hendrik Kramer (1888–1965), like many of his predecessors, also believed that the Prophet surrendered to the temptations of power after his migration from Makkah. He saw Islam as "a superficial religion that has almost no questions and no answers," and therefore incapable of dealing with human problems. He attributed Muslims' strong resistance to conversion, which he experienced during his stay in Indonesia, to a mind-set fixed particularly by the Quran, in "an enormous amount of stubborn, ingenuine, theological thinking."[9] Islam is dismissed out of hand because it did not address what Christianity regards as the central issue of faith: sin and salvation. Kramer's judgment of Islam is in the end shallow and superficial in respect of all major aspects of faith and religious practice. In his missiological commitment he was confrontational and "aggressive" towards Islam. However, his preferred method was to follow a "sympathetic" approach whereby he could lead non-Christians to fulfillment of their religious quest.

The anthropological approach to Muslim society, which Zwemer (see below) so ardently championed, left a legacy that was picked up by later generations of missionaries. One such approach is widely known as the contextual approach to Islam.[10] Among Roman Catholic circles the practice of this approach may be compared with an "inculturation" process. The primary focus of effort shifts from Muslim faith to Muslim culture, also known as "folk Islam." This missionary *adaptation* and *accommodation* technique has become a unique vehicle for communicating the Christian message in an overwhelmingly Muslim society. Under the banner of contextualization, a whole host of activities are undertaken, at both local and international levels. The objective is "to maximize the impact of the gospel upon the receptor community." At international level, a series of conferences to reach the Muslim community were hosted during the mid-1970s and are now known as the Lausanne Covenant. In 1978 the "Gospel and Islam" conference brought people of similar tendency to consider the approach collectively. Today, the intellectual underpinnings for such ventures are provided by missionary training centers such as the Samuel Zwemer Institute in Pasadena, USA.

Islam as mystical and spiritual

The central figure in this effort of relationship and appraisal is undoubtedly Louis Massignon (1883–1962). A diplomat and academic, he served in Palestine in 1917–19 as an assistant to the French High Commissioner before taking a post as lecturer in Islamic philosophy in the University of Cairo. Massignon viewed Islam as a challenge. It was Christians' duty to meet this challenge by placing themselves at the very center of Muslim beliefs. The Prophet appealed to Massignon as one who yearned to be in a God-centered world where Jews and Christians are part of a wider family. This attitude to Islam's central personality was a bold and visionary one. Massignon defended the Prophet from the charge of being a false prophet, while maintaining the safe Christian distance that sees prophethood in Islam as lacking the intercessory function. For "false" and "true," Massignon preferred the terms "positive" and "negative" to distinguish "two attributes of authentic prophecy." One "challenges and reverses the human values," and the other is much more eschatological, where the Prophet bears witness to the "final separation of the good from evil."

Unlike others (e.g., Zwemer or Cragg), Massignon vigorously approved of the Prophet's Madinan period. He saw the Prophet's involvement in political reconciliation as an "entire politics [which] succinctly reflected his contrasting the concrete problem to be resolved with that which his faith dictated to his heart."[11] Massignon strongly believed that the Holy Spirit was at work and would bring Islam closer to the Christian faith. His strong sense of Christian responsibility is demonstrated in his concept of a *badliya* ("substitution") movement. He was instrumental in inspiring groups of Christians to take the sins of Muslim souls on themselves. He believed that, by doing so, they were offering their lives to God for their fellow Muslims, who could then attain salvation in union with Christ. Such a radical departure that contradicted the prevailing attitude of proselytizing Muslims was bound to face opposition. But largely his sympathetic approach to Muslims generated a great deal of respect for Massignon. It also inculcated a group of people who shared a similar vision and who were instrumental in bringing a host of other scholars within the Roman Catholic Church to this view. Among others, we should count in this group Father Ginlio Basettisani, Charles Ledit, and Jea-Muhammad Abd-el-Jalil.

Islam as an ecumenical concern

The World Council of Churches (WCC) as an ecumenical effort has its origin in early missionary movements such as at Edinburgh (1910), Jerusalem (1928), and Tambaram (1938). It eventually came into existence in 1948. It provided a forum for lively debate among Christians about their relationship with other faiths and in-depth discussions about unity and cooperation among the churches.

As well as the Protestant churches the WCC also included Eastern Orthodox churches in its membership. The debates about relations with other faiths generated various discourses in the early phase of the WCC's work. The contributions of Stanley J. Samartha from India and George Khodr from Lebanon – both with direct experience of living in pluralistic societies – provided a practical component in the WCC's guidelines for relations with other faiths. Khodr argued that Christ is not exclusively bound to the church, but is also to be found outside the church; nor is the saving work of the Holy Spirit confined to the church alone. Samartha argued that the biblical understanding of truth is not "propositional but relational, and is to be sought, not in the isolation of lonely meditation, but in the living, personal confrontation between God and man, and man and man."[12] This common concern for humanity and relations based upon human and humanitarian concerns provided a much needed space where Islam and Christianity could engage in something like equality and openness.

More recently, the WCC has moved its emphasis to contemporary relations between the two communities against the background of political events and movements – the fall of the Soviet Union, the Gulf War, religious/political terrorism, and the growing demand for cultural (as well as political and economic) independence expressed as a demand for a return to tradition and shariah.

Islam as historical and phenomenological concern

Montgomery Watt's (1909–) approach to Islam is largely based upon "historical scholarship." His two-volume biography of the Prophet largely seeks explanatory efficacy in the socioeconomic and political factors that gave rise to a person like Muhammad among the Arabs.[13] Although he adopts a "scientific" approach, his work is also intended to enable theological judgment of the Prophet. He construes the Prophet's religious ideas as a projection of socioeconomic aspirations, ignoring any function for revelation and connection with God. In his later writings Watt moved more explicitly to theological concerns. He described Muhammad as "a genuine prophet in the sense that God used him to communicate truth about himself to human beings."

On the opening page of *Muhammad's Mecca: History in the Quran*, Watts states his personal opinion:

> I am convinced that Muhammad was sincere in believing that what came to him as revelation (*wahy*) was not the product of conscious thought on his part. I consider Muhammad was truly a prophet, and think that we Christians should admit this on the basis of the Christian principle that "by their fruits you will know them," since through the centuries Islam has produced many upright and saintly people. If he is a prophet, too, then in accordance with the Christian doctrine that the Holy Spirit spoke by the prophets, the Quran may be accepted as of divine origin.[14]

Watt's approach remained skeptical of the Muslim position in that he argued for influences from Judeo-Christian traditions, particularly "from the books of Genesis and Exodus" and "extra-biblical Jewish sources."

Cantwell Smith (1916–2000) draws attention to the change in attitude, particularly in the Western world, to revelation and scripture. The Old and New Testaments need no longer be seen, in the possessive partisan way, as the only texts worthy of being called Revelation. The term may now be applied to various kinds of texts which other communities regard as sacred, even if they are rejected by Christians.

Smith invites Christians – Western Christians in particular – to understand how Muslims see the centrality of their scripture. "Muslims do not read the Quran and conclude that it is divine, rather, they believe that it is divine, and then they read it. This makes a great deal of difference, and I urge upon Christians or secular students of the Quran that if they wish to understand it as a religious document, they must approach it in this spirit."[15] Smith is cautious in his approach to the Prophet: "The personality of Muhammad is essentially irrelevant," he argues, because to "accept that he is a prophet is to accept the Quran as binding."[16] In Smith's account, the Prophet's inspiration came from outside the Arab cultured milieu, beginning with a firm conviction that Judaism and Christianity needed reform but ending up giving the Arabs a monotheistic faith. Smith remarks that "the Islamic seems to be the only religious movement in the world that arose historically not primarily out of a reform of the indigenous religious tradition of the people to whom it was presented." And "the Prophet's message was delivered to the Arabs as reformulation not primarily of their own, idolatrous, religious tradition but of the tradition of Christians and Jews."[17]

More Detailed Study

Zwemer

Samuel Zwemer (1876–1952) was a member of the Reformed Church in America and trained at the seminary in New Brunswick. His vocation was to work among Muslims in the heartland of Islam. Islam, in his Christian understanding, was a religion born to destroy the faith of Christ and therefore an anti-Christian religion. He studied Islamic faith in order to know the Muslim people, who needed to be rescued from the curse of Islam. He referred to Muslims as "the millions still under the yoke of the false prophet."[18] His approach was largely anthropological, given that he wanted Christians to be able to connect to popular Muslim beliefs, rituals, and cults – if they could do that, they should have no difficulty in communicating the message of the gospels – in a Muslim cultural setting. In his writings he emphasized the significance of law, the centrality of the Prophet in Muslims' lives, and the Quran as the book of guidance for Muslims. He condemned in the strongest terms anything that did not fit the Christian description of faith, truth, and revelation. *The Moslem Doctrine of God* (1905), *Mohammed or Christ* (1916), *Christianity the Final Religion* (1920), *The Glory of the Cross* (1928), *The Cross Above the Crescent* (1941), and *The Law of Apostasy in Islam* (1923) are just a few titles that reflect his desire to see the Christian understanding prevail and Muslim beliefs perish. He was also keen to describe Islam within a popular Arab cultural context, one that had "influenced" the shape of Islam. *The Influence of Animism on Islam* (1920) and *Studies of Popular Islam* (1939) reflect his determination to persuade us to regard Islam as a religion that should not be taken seriously, and certainly not on a par with Christianity.

Working at the height of the colonization period, Zwemer was convinced that Western–Christian values were here to stay, particularly among the peoples he worked with. This imperialistic vision of mission saw Muslims in terms of an opportunity for the expansion of Christianity by establishing churches among them. He took very little note or care of the local churches that had existed for centuries and contributed in various ways to the cultural milieu of local society. Instead, he was enthusiastic for the church, particularly his Reformed Church of America, to strike roots in the heartlands of Islam. He looked down from an imperialistic height upon the Islamic world and saw "unoccupied field." He exhorted the participants at the Edinburgh Missionary Conference of 1910 that, for the followers of Christ, "there should not be unoccupied fields." The economic situation, the subjugation of Muslim intellectual life, the imbalance of political power, all contributed to his writing of *The Disintegration of Islam* (1916). This inevitable disintegration would be, in his view, "a divine preparation" for the evangelization of Muslim lands.

Zwemer recognized the centrality of the Prophet Muhammad for the Muslims. He distinguished the Muhammad of history from the Muhammad of popular Muslim devotion. He attacked the former vehemently and used the other as a means to appeal and approach. Though aware of Carlyle's writing on Muhammad and Arnold's on Islam, he generally chose to rely on Hugh Broughton's description of the Prophet.[19] Like Karl Barth, he was not prepared to recognize that the God of the Muslims and Christians is the same God. Indeed, he insisted that such a view is preposterous, that "nothing could be further from the truth." The God of Islam is a "negative" God, "the Pantheism of Force."[20] He nursed the hope that the spread of secularization and a growing Western-educated elite would be allies of Christian churches, that "educated Muslims" would speak the language of "Christian missionaries,"[21] a hope that resonated with subsequent missionaries like John Mott. For Zwemer, Islam was a *Challenge to Faith* (1907), a challenge that preoccupied his entire life. He was so focused on Islam and Muslims that he neglected entirely the challenge of modernity and its impact on Christianity itself. He left a strong legacy and influenced a generation of missionaries after him, working under various banners such as the Lausanne Covenant, the Contextual Mission (Phil Parshall), the Samuel Zwemer Institute in Pasadena, and the proponents of the study of "folk Islam" (Bill Musk).

Cragg

Kenneth Cragg (1913–) holds that what Islam is, is "what Muslims hold it to be." After Zwemer, Cragg is like a breath of fresh air. Cragg's speciality is to see Islam from *within* and to make sense of it for Christians. He is an eloquent interpreter. Core to his interpretive effort is the notion of *retrieval*. He means by it to enable Christians and Muslims to rise above historic misunderstandings between the two faiths and make sense of Christian beliefs, applying ("retrieving") Quranic and Islamic ideas to provide Islamic reasons for being Christian. Cragg is very much concerned with Islam's opposition to key Christian concepts: there is "still too much in [the] Islamic disqualification of Christianity which has mistaken both the Christian thing and its own Quranic documents." As far as Islamic "documents" are concerned, he argues, there are "positive implications for the faith of the Christian within Islamic theology" and they "are significant and must, at all costs, be imaginatively and loyally retrieved."[22] Cragg remains "imaginative" in his exploration of Islam, while retaining his "loyalty" to his Christian faith and mission.

A number of recurring themes in Cragg's approach lead us to suggest that he moved forward in his exploration of Islam, but remained deeply rooted within Western historical scholarship. That scholarship either measured Islam against the criteria of anthropological and critical–historical scholarship, or as a missionary field. Cragg seems to venture along both directions. He suggests that the Prophet's mind is a product of two elements: (1) the inner struggle that kept him away from the city of Makkah and led him frequently to visit the cave of Hira where he meditated; his orphaned upbringing, his wondering reflections on nature and procreation and the prevailing injustices that he so helplessly observed; (2) his awareness of Makkah's prosperity and the prestige and power it brought to the Makkans, and the centrality of the Kabah that attracted so many pilgrims each year. These two elements gave rise to *Rasuliyyah* (the messengership). While the first led him in a mystical and spiritual direction, the second found an urge and "yearning for a source of unity" for the Arabs and the "idea and the ideal of scripture, and of being scripturarist."[23] It is the power and prestige of Makkah and its economy, Cragg remarks, "which may well have obsessed his mind."

The image of the Prophet that we get from Cragg's writings is of a man whose heart is preoccupied with the spirituality and mystical experience of the pre-prophetic period, and which he applied during his prophetic ministry in Makkah. As for the idea of "the Warner," as the Quran describes him, and his becoming a Prophet, Cragg suggests, these were largely contributed by Old and New Testament teachings, through the Jews and Christians. Muhammad in Makkah was a Muhammad like Jesus, persecuted, maligned, and a bleeding "suffering servant" Prophet. Hijrah is the turning point for the Prophet and for Islam. Migration to Madinah changed the Muslims from "a group into an army, from a community of faith to an order of authority."[24] Cragg links the event of Hijrah to the concept of Jihad and questions the nature of the Prophet's motivation: "Where Islam is potentially universalized in *Hijrah* it is inherently politicized in *Jihad*. The move *out* of Mecca *with* the faith presages the move *against* Mecca *for* the faith. In that transition, not only is the *Hijrah* implemented in its prospective relevance, but Islam is defined in its essential character." He asks: "What is the relevance of power to truth?"[25]

This question is the consistent theme of all Cragg's writings on Islam, varied for different contexts. Most recently he has highlighted the situation of Muslims living as a minority in relative comfort and security, entitled to observe all the basic Islamic requirements without interference. He asks: "Are Muslims then not back in the Meccan situation without the persecution they first had there? Is not the priority of Mecca over Medina, of faith and piety over power and arms, indisputable on every ground of Islam's definition?"[26] The separation of Madinah from Makkah remains for Cragg the "extraneous material" which he wishes Muslims to address.

Cragg's criteria for judging Muhammad are what he frankly calls "Christ-criteria." The central obstacle to a positive Christian response lies in the "military dimensions of original Islam" and "its uninhibited embrace of the political arm are certainly crucial factors in deterring the Christians from a positive response to Muhammad."[27] In this sense, Cragg has moved far from the traditional Christian view of Islam as an obsession with law and politics, the peace of the sword, with a consequently weakened understanding of peace of the soul, the individual's private victory over his own sinfulness. This is not a view that is likely to inspire, still less satisfy, a Muslim understanding of the Prophet's character and achievement, or of the character and achievements of Islamic civilization. However, it has been very influential among a generation of Christians across all denominations. Despite differences in approach to Islam, both in their theology and their missiological concerns, they all meet at Cragg's "corner" to compare, consult, and assess their own understanding of Muslims.

Küng

Hans Küng (1928–) is one of the most influential contemporary theologians who has left his mark on Christianity and Christian understanding of other faiths. Expressed in shorthand, Küng is a Roman Catholic theologian with a Protestant tendency. He has long been a controversial figure, with troubled relations with the Vatican, particularly after the publication of his doctoral dissertation *Justification*.[28] His doctoral thesis was on Karl Barth and this may have influenced him in his view of his church. However, he remained free of the influence of Barthian doctrine on other faiths, particularly Islam.

Küng is a theologian who took Islam and Muslim thought very seriously. He is aware that any Christian understanding of Islam will always be against the background of past encounters and contemporary relations between Islam and the West. He states: "Let us admit the fact: Islam continues to strike us as essentially foreign, as more threatening, politically and economically, than either Hinduism or Buddhism, a phenomenon, in any case, that we have a hard time understanding." Then he emphasizes that this is precisely the task of ecumenical Christian theology: "to face the challenge of Islam and work for mutual understanding."[29] Unlike Zwemer, Küng accepts that both Christians and Muslims believe in the same creator and sustainer God, and he approaches Islam accordingly.

Küng locates Islam within a wider Christian theological perspective. He approaches the nature of the Prophet Muhammad and rehabilitates him to a Christian theological setting through the prism of the Old Testament. He situates him geographically in Arabia, and theologically where the tribes of Arabia encountered Judaism and Christianity. Therein lie the sources from which the idea of God and forms of piety in Islam sprang. While Küng's assessment of the Prophet is not free of anthropological judgment, he does clearly hold that to say "the Prophet lacked originality . . . is a serious misunderstanding."[30] But is this originality due to what he received from God, as the Muslims believe, or because of some ambition for authority and power? That question is left unexplored in Küng's work. He is, however, keen to place the Prophet alongside the Old Testament prophets. He provides seven parallels, which it is instructive to recall fully, as this is perhaps the first time in modern Christian theological assessment that the Prophet Muhammad featured so prominently.

> Like the prophets of Israel, Muhammad based his work not on any office given him by the community (or its authorities) but on a special, personal relationship with God.
>
> Like the prophets of Israel, Muhammad was a strong-willed character, who saw himself as wholly penetrated by his divine vocation, totally taken up by God's claim on him, exclusively absorbed by his mission.

Like the prophets of Israel, Muhammad spoke out amid a religious and social crisis. With his passionate piety and his revolutionary preaching, he stood up against the wealthy ruling class and the tradition of which it was the guardian.

Like the prophets of Israel, Muhammad, who usually calls himself a "warner," wished to be nothing but God's mouthpiece and to proclaim God's word, not his own.

Like the prophets of Israel, Muhammad tirelessly glorified the one God, who tolerates no other gods before him and who is, at the same time, the kindly Creator and merciful Judge.

Like the prophets of Israel, Muhammad insisted upon unconditional obedience, devotion, and "submission" (the literal meaning of "Islam") to this one God. He called for every kind of gratitude toward God and of generosity toward human beings.

Like the prophets of Israel, Muhammad linked his monotheism to a humanism, connecting faith in the one God and his judgment to the demand for social justice: judgment and redemption, threats against the unjust, who go to hell, and promises to the just, who are gathered into God's Paradise.[31]

From these seven parallels and in the context of Muslims living by the faith given through Muhammad, Küng concludes that for "the men and women of Arabia and, in the end, far beyond, Muhammad truly was and is *the* religious reformer, lawgiver, and leader: *the* prophet, pure and simple."[32]

Strictly speaking, the nature of prophethood in Islam and the account of the prophets in the Old Testament are incompatible. Prophets are shown in the latter as fallible and weak in moral character. Islam, though acknowledging their humanity and hence their weakness, sees their weakness as corrected, their humanity perfected, under the guidance of God. This is the character of the Prophet that the Quran commands his followers to emulate. Another issue is that the Prophet is a messenger for the whole of humanity, so to attach his mission and ministry exclusively to "the men and women of Arabia" is contrary to the Muslim view. In assessing Küng's contribution to the debate on the Prophet's rehabilitation to a Christian theological understanding of Islam, Muslims will appreciate his strong and bold steps, but will remain skeptical insofar as he does not go far enough.

Another difficulty is Küng's assessment of the Quran. For Muslims, it is the Word of God revealed to Muhammad verbatim. Küng suggests that this "must be taken seriously," if only because generations of Muslims "have drawn strength, courage, and comfort from it in their public and private lives."[33] So far so good, but then he states: "There was no Arabic translation of the Bible in existence; if there had been, the passages in the Quran relating to the Bible would have been clearer, more precise and less fragmentary." What is implied here is human authorship of the Quran. Küng goes on at great length to explain borrowings from the Judeo-Christian traditions. He urges both Muslims and Christians to continue discussion on this issue, reminding Muslims that what Christians have gone through (textual criticism and deconstruction), they too will have to experience and come to terms with. The assumption is that the Islamic world has much catching up to do with the Western world, and in the process will follow the same pattern as their Christian and Jewish counterparts. In particular, he hopes that the "historicocritical study of the holy book will eventually be allowed to become a reality."[34] Following that, Küng perhaps expects that a "reformed Islam" will emerge, able not only to deal with the strongly orthodox temperament of Muslims, but also to countenance compromise with the doctrine of an Enlightened Christianity. That in turn is the basis of Küng's hopes for a "global ethics."

Nostra Aetate, Lumen Gentium, and Islam

Nostra Aetate (1965) is a watershed in the Roman Catholic Church's understanding of Islam and its relations to Muslims. The document placed the church center stage in the challenge to other faiths. The document was also in some ways an admission of the past record of the church's unjust treatment of Islam, which has been a major obstacle to better relations between the two communities. The document high-lighted common areas of faith like the "worship of One God," itself a major step forward. It also pointed out other commonalities such as "Abraham, Jesus, Mary," and that the Muslims await "the Day of Judgment and [the] reward of God." An important section of the document contains a plea for both Christians and Muslims "to forget the past" and it urges that "sincere efforts be made to achieve mutual understanding for the benefit of all men," with the aim of promoting "peace, lib-erty, social justice and moral values."

These noble ideals are not at all in conflict either with Islam or any other faith, nor should they be. It is noticeable, however, that the document's selection of commonalities, derived from their Christian emphases, picked out prayer and alms-giving, but not pilgrimage or fasting, though these practices do also figure in Christianity. More significantly, the document "shied away" (to use Küng's remark on *Nostra Aetate*) from naming and recognizing the central figure of Islam: Muhammad. It also avoided using the name of "Islam," so crucial for Muslims. Despite these weaknesses, the document does indicate the church's willingness to engage with Muslims at various levels on various issues.

An even more positive church statement, issued during the same period as *Nostra Aetate*, was called *Lumen Gentium*.[35] It perhaps touched a raw nerve in various quarters by openly embracing the idea that "the plan of salvation also includes those who acknowledge the Creator, in the first place among whom are the Moslems." Of course, this does not mean that the church has now accepted Islam as on a par with Christianity. The document refers to God as one who does not exclude Muslims from the *plan* of his salvation, and that *plan* remains intact within the church. Even this position, despite being so carefully constructed, could not satisfy many within the church. This may have been the core contention among those church members who raised the issues of salvation and mission *vis-à-vis* the purpose of dialogue. In order to clarify the church's position, the Vatican's Secretariat on Interreligious Dialogue occasionally issued its reflections under the title *The Attitude of the Church Towards the Followers of Other Religions* (1984). In 1991 Pope John Paul II issued an encyclical, as a direct result of which a further explanation was published jointly by the Secretariats of Interreligous Dialogue and the Congregation for the Evangel-ization of Peoples under the title *Dialogue and Proclamation* (1991).

Nostra Aetate inspired and challenged other churches, too. It brought about new ways of understanding Muslims and Islam, particularly in the context of large numbers of Muslims living in European cities. The Catholic initiative of a "Commis-sion on Islam" resulted in guidelines for *Dialogue Between Muslims and Christians,* published in 1969. The Council of European Churches (CES) established a Consultative Committee on "Islam in Europe" in order to help churches with their "human pastoral and theological" concerns. By 1987 the Protestant and Catholic Churches pooled their human and financial resources and jointly created the "Islam in Europe Committee." Theological reflections on the presence of Islam in Europe were consistently addressed, but increasingly the Committee has been drawn into the state of Christian–Muslim relations in Muslim countries.

New theological approach to Islam

The increasing interaction between Muslims and Christians in Europe, in South and Southeast Asia, and in Africa, is inspiring Christian theologians to look at Islam in a postcolonial, pluralist setting. John Macquarrie, Maurice Wiles, John Hick, and Keith Ward are addressing such challenges.[36] Here I mention, very briefly, the approach of Keith Ward as an example of this new theology.

Ward proposes an "open theology" to engage with other faiths. He suggests that there "are forms of revelation one's own tradition does not express." He sees Islam as a "unique witness to the nature and purpose of God." He emphasizes (as Cantwell Smith and others did) that each tradition needs to be seen within its own context, and its formulation and expression of faith should be affirmed. Christian theology has traveled some distance from the attitude of Barth and Brunner, but it needs to, and can, some closer still to other faiths. Ward strives to bring Christianity to a "common position" in line with other faiths, and not necessarily to set up a "common structure" for the different faiths. The "common position" assumes a general connectedness with others.[37] He cautions against unnecessary dispute with others' perception of their faith, and is at ease with a "lowest common denominators" approach provided it carries one to the higher goal of connectedness.

Ward places Islam within the Judaic tradition. "Islam universalizes Judaism," he argues, but because "there is very little interest in God's self-revelation," Islam is at odds with Christianity. Regarding the Quran, he suggests it could be a "divinely inspired" book similar to the idea of an inspired *theopneustos*, "breathed out by God" as applied to the Hebrew Bible. The "breathed out by God" creates the human absence in the Hebrew scripture and in the Quran. If the former is acceptable as a divinely inspired work then why, he asks, can the Quran not be called divinely inspired?

Assessment

Christians – theologians and missiologists – make their own history; that is, they shape their own thought, both deliberately and without conscious intention, in response to the environment and the challenges they face. The last hundred years of theological development show many conflicting responses to Islam and Muslims. Each response, in the end, reflects the past but also appeals to a specific model of how Christians want to relate, and of what there is (in the other) to relate to. In the process each response has encountered, in part or in passing, the series of questions listed at the beginning of this chapter.

Understanding of God

Theologians such as Küng and Ward, and also a growing generation of missiologists, are recognizing the fact that the Islamic concept of God is not something other than their own. However, the old perception of Allah as a Muslim deity is still expressed by polemicists. Perhaps the difficulty arises when the nature of God in Christianity and Islam is compared and perceived. The Muslims' God is a transcendent, whose care for his creatures is mediated through revelations and the promise of mercy and justice. The Christians' God is revealed as man suffering for humanity.

Prophet Muhammad

Muslim belief about the Prophet Muhammad and the Christian understanding of his Prophethood will remain a contentious issue. Christian understanding of the role of prophets (in Cragg, for example) is shaped by the Old Testament, and expects Muslims to "reconsider" and "rethink." While that difficult issue is unresolved there is certainly a growing Christian realization that they have to see the Prophet of Islam in a new and more positive light. Short biographies of Muhammad by Martin Forward and by Karen Armstrong are indicative of this new direction.[38]

Scripture and secular–historical scholarship

Almost all theologians or missiologists look forward to a self-critical assessment of the Quran and Islamic Revelation generally, though for different reasons. One reason is the desire to see Islam emerge from its "medieval closet" and discover attitudes such that the modern world would be comfortable with them and they with it. In this respect, Muslim aspirations for life under the shariah are seen as regressive. Of course, Muslims have the mechanism of *ijtihad* to enable adaption to changed or new circumstances, and they are using it. However, pressures, the pace of change in the contemporary world, the aggressiveness of contemporary culture and its extraordinary invasiveness, alongside political and economic realities too brutally obvious to mention, make it very difficult to countenance and effect change while maintaining a loyal and dignified relationship with tradition.

The role of dialogue

Dialogue between the two faith communities has, so far, largely focused on social, communal, and general religious issues. Difficult theological issues have been post-poned for the sake of good manners. Plainly, dialogue must generate enough mutual respect and trust before it can risk trespassing on the boundaries of sensitivity. However, the two communities must at some stage confront these issues in a sincere and serious manner if a positive tolerance is to be realized between Christians and Muslims. In light of the historical legacy and the sociopolitical realities of the present time, it may already seem difficult enough to achieve non-conflict, a sort of well-meaning indifference.

Achievement and Agenda

Throughout the twentieth century, Christians (in the West in particular) have changed considerably their approach to other faiths, including Islam. The Islamic world is no longer regarded as an "unoccupied" missionary field awaiting conquest, but as a testing ground for the virtues of "neighborliness" and "hospitality." This shift has entailed a corresponding change in theological and social outlook. Without losing the centrality of witness to the Muslims, the balance of emphasis has moved toward service and dialogue.

Through its *Nostra Aetate* document, the Roman Catholic Church provided much needed encouragement to positive understanding of Muslims. The Pontifical Council for Interreligious Dialogue initiated and sustained the effort to educate its members to engage, actively and continually, with Muslims and their organizations in various areas of common concern, such as "Migrants and Refugees," "*Dawah* and Mission," and "Environment." The effort to work together is well illustrated by the exchange agreement between the Gregorian University and the University of Ankara's Ilahiyat (Divinity) Faculty to teach, respectively, Christianity and Islam, in each other's faculties. Though only for a semester a year, such entry into the other's curriculum represents a significant breakthrough for both sides.

The World Council of Churches, through its Office on Interreligious Dialogue, has sponsored several occasions for dialogue, often working with Muslims in their planning and realization. There has been a perceptible shift by the WCC from a primary concern with mission and Christian witness to a more demanding concern with such issues as law and society, religious freedom, individual and community rights, and Christian–Muslim tensions in the world. A series of dialogues held through the 1990s and into this century demonstrate the maturing of relations between Muslims and Christians.

Efforts on the Muslim side to establish dialogue were initiated by institutions such as the World Islamic Call Society in the 1970s and 1980s. These have been followed up since by other institutions, such as the Al al-Bait Foundation, which set up the Royal Institute of Interfaith Studies in 1994, and more recently the World Council of Muslims for Interfaith Relations (WCMIR), based in Chicago.

The WCMIR suggests that the subject of dialogue is no longer taboo among the generality of Muslims. However, significant and necessary as dialogue has been, and though it has striven neither to diminish nor evade the difficult issues, it has so far been largely confined to academics, clerics, and religious leaders: it has yet to become rooted in the general religious conscience of Muslims or Christians. The latter by and large have made much better progress in this regard than the former. Granted the situation is still somewhat fragile, the Christians have begun to make what may be called structural changes in theological discourse and in seminary curricula that include exposure to other faiths and a sympathetic understanding of them. Muslims, by contrast, both in the East and in the West, have only noticed that they have not yet done the same, recognized the need to do it, but not yet started to do it. Muslims' seminaries (and the schooling of Muslims generally) need to incorporate understanding of other faiths into their curricula.

The European perception of what religion is, and what it is or can be for, has been shaped by Christianity. The role of religion – where it enters into the life of society and the reach of its authority – is judged according to the historical and cultural experiences of Christianity in Europe. The same historical and cultural experiences have shaped Christian evaluation of the Muslim perception of what religion is, and what it is or can be for. Equally, Muslim judgments about Christianity have been informed by their experience of European presence in their countries. Entering into meaningful dialogue offers to both Muslims and Christians the possibility of seeing with different eyes, of experiencing their own and the other's tradition, from fresh perspectives, with an opportunity perhaps (certainly the responsibility) to clear away the debris of history.

Nostra Aetate certainly generated and enabled a great deal of good will between the two communities. But it is still rather muted in respect of recognizing Islam and its Prophet. Of course, Muslims do not expect from those who are not Muslims an affirmation of the Prophet and the faith of Islam. But what they do ask for is a formal negation, a rejection, of the unjustifiable statements against the Prophet Muhammad and Islam in general that have, over the centuries, been knowingly or unknowingly sanctioned by church authorities. Dialogue should labor to first distance, and then annul, such statements. One need not wait for another Vatican Council to address the issue; it is urgent enough to be addressed in an encyclical and to be addressed without equivocation.

Despite continuing dialogue, we still carry images of the other, only some of which we are able to share with our partners in dialogue and discuss openly; others are either kept to ourselves or aired, if at all, only in the presence of co-religionists. Also, there are a range of issues – about scripture, about the devices and strategies deployed in mission, about historical narratives, about the role of religion in social life, its relations with the state and with economic structures and systems that seem to invest only material well-being with value – that need to be discussed with more openness and clarity than they have been. They cannot be discussed effectively unless, alongside interfaith dialogue, intrafaith dialogue is more vigorous and honest in recognizing the worth and dignity of the other faith and the integrity and good intentions of its adherents. Intrafaith dialogue that explores the "otherness" of the other with greater breadth and sympathy is a necessary preparation for interfaith dialogue, enabling the reciprocated trust on which its success depends.

Notes

1 I use "missiological" in the sense that its approach to Islam, and for that matter to other faiths, was largely motivated by the practice of Christian missions that make use of disciplines such as cross-cultural communication, anthropology, and theology.

2 Karl Barth, *Church Dogmatics*, Vol. 4 (Edinburgh: T. & T. Clark, 1964), p. 183.

3 Karl Rahner, *Theological Investigations*, Vol. 18 (London: Darton, Longman and Todd, 1984), p. 116.

4 He also persistently claimed that Islamic monotheism "could be constructed without God." God in Islam, in his view, was a strategic device that the Prophet adopted and adapted, an "invented way" that could

not, therefore, be considered as given and revealed. See Karl Barth, *Church Dogmatics*, Vol. 2.1 (Edinburgh: T. & T. Clark, 1964), p. 448. Barth also found it very useful for his polemic to liken Hitler's National Socialism and its ruthless enforcement of its political agenda to Islam: "At the point where it [National Socialism] meets with resistance, it can only crush and kill – with the might and right which belongs to Divinity!" He saw in Hitler's National Socialism *new Islam*, its myth as a new Allah, and Hitler as this new Allah's Prophet. See Karl Barth, *Church and the Political Problem of Our Day* (London: Hodder and Stoughton, 1939), p. 43.

5 Emile Brunner, *The Mediator: A Study of the Central Doctrine of the Christian Faith* (London: Lutterworth Press, 1952), p. 591.

6 Paul Tillich, *A History of Christian Thought* (New York: Simon and Shuster, 1967), p. 87.

7 Paul Tillich, *Systematic Theology*, Vol. 2 (London: James Nisbet, 1957), pp. 124–5.

8 Duncan Black Macdonald, *Aspects of Islam* (New York: Macmillan, 1911), pp. 89ff.

9 Hendrik Kramer, *The Christian Message in a Non-Christian World* (London: Edinburgh House Press, 1938), pp. 216–17.

10 See Phil Parshall, *New Paths of Muslim Evangelism: Evangelical Approaches to Contextualization* (Grand Rapids, MI: Baker Book House, 1980).

11 David Kerr, "'He Walked in the Path of the Prophets': Toward Christian Theological Recognition of the Prophethood of Muhammad," in Y. Y. Haddad and W. Z. Haddad (eds.), *Christian–Muslim Encounters* (Gainesville: University of Florida), p. 429.

12 Stanley J. Samartha (ed.), *Living Faiths and the Ecumenical Movement* (Geneva: WCC, 1971), p. 154. See also George Khodr, "Christianity in a Pluralist World – the Economy of the Holy Spirit", in Stanley J. Samartha, (ed.), Living Faiths and the Ecumenical Movement (Geneva: World Council of Churches, 1971), pp. 131–42.

13 Montgomery Watt, *Muhammad at Mecca* (Oxford: Clarendon Press, 1953) and *Muhammad at Medina* (Oxford: Clarendon Press, 1956).

14 Montgomery Watt, *Muhammad's Mecca: History in the Quran* (Edinburgh: Edinburgh University Press, 1988), p. 1.

15 Cantwell Smith, *Questions of Religious Truth* (London: Victor Gollancz, 1967), p. 49.

16 Cantwell Smith, *Islam in Modern History* (New York: New American Library, 1957), p. 27; see footnote 18.

17 Cantwell Smith, *Meaning and End of Religion* (New York: New American Library, 1964), pp. 98, 99.

18 Samuel Zwemer, *The Moslem World* (Young People's Missionary Movement of the United States and Canada, 1908), p. 9.

19 See *The Muslim World*, Vol. 4, January 1914, pp. 64–8.

20 See Samuel Zwemer, *The Cradle of Islam* (Edinburgh: Oliphant Anderson and Ferrier, 1900), pp. 171, 173.

21 See Samuel Zwemer, *The Disintegration of Islam* (New York: Fleming H. Revell, 1916), p. 197.

22 Christopher Lamb, "Kenneth Cragg's Understanding of Christian Mission to Islam," in David Thomas and Clare Amos (eds.), *A Faithful Presence: Essays for Kenneth Cragg* (London: Melsende, 2003), p. 130.

23 Kenneth Cragg, *The House of Islam* (Belmount, CA: Dickenson Publishing, 1969), p. 23.

24 Kenneth Cragg, *The Event of the Quran* (London: George Allen and Unwin, 1971), p. 129.

25 Ibid, p. 134.

26 Kenneth Cragg, *Am I Not Your Lord?* (London: Melisende, 2002), pp. 12–13.

27 Kenneth Cragg, *Muhammad and the Christians* (London: Darton, Longman and Todd, 1984), pp. 31, 145.

28 Hans Küng, *Rechtfertigung: die Lehre Karl Barths und eine katholische Besinnung* ["Justification: The Doctrine of Karl Barth and a Catholic Reflection"] (Einsiedeln: Johannes Verlag, 1957).

29 Hans Küng, *Christianity and World Religion* (London: SCM Press, 1986), p. 19.

30 Ibid, p. 25.

31 Ibid, pp. 25–6.

32 Ibid, p. 27.

33 Ibid, p. 33.

34 Ibid, p. 35.

35 For both *Nostra Aetate* and *Lumen Gentium*, see Austin Flannery, *Vatican Council II: The Conciliar Documents* (New York: Costello Publishing, 1988).

36 See John Macquarrie, *The Mediators: Nine Stars in the Human Sky* (London: SCM

Press, 1995); Maurice Wiles, *Christian Theology and Inter-religious Dialogue* (London: SCM Press, 1992); John Hick, *The Metaphor of God Incarnate* (London: SCM Press, 1993). See also (for Hick's view on Islam) Adnan Aslan, *Religious Pluralism in Christian and Islamic Philosophy: The Thought of John Hick and Seyyed Hossein Nasr* (London: Curzon Press, 1998).

37 Keith Ward, *Religion and Revelation* (Oxford: Clarendon Press, 1994), p. 337.
38 Martin Forward, *Muhammad: A Short Biography* (Oxford: One World Publications, 1997) and Karen Armstrong, *Muhammad: A Biography of the Prophet* (London: Victor Gollancz, 1991).

Bibliography

Cragg, Kenneth, *The House of Islam* (Belmont, CA, 1969).
—— *The Event of the Quran* (London, 1971).
—— *Christian and Other Religions: The Measure of Christ* (Oxford, 1977).
—— *Muhammad and the Christians* (London, 1984).
—— *The Call of Minaret* (Oxford, 2000).
—— *Am I Not Your Lord?* (London, 2002).
Flannery, Austin (ed.), *Vatican II*, Vol. 1 (New York, 1998).
Gaudeul, Jean-Marie, *Encounters and Clashes: Islam and Christianity in History* [Vol. 1 Survey and Vol. 2 Texts] (Rome, 1990).
Goddard, Hugh, *Christians and Muslims: From Double Standard to Mutual Understanding* (London, 1995).
—— *A History of Christian–Muslim Relations* (Edinburgh, 2000).
Kerr, David, "'He Walked in the Path of the Prophets': Toward Christian Theological Recognition of the Prophethood of Muhammad," in Y. Y. Haddad and W. Z. Haddad (eds.) *Christian–Muslim Encounters* (Gainesville, FL, 1995).
Kramer, Hendrik, *The Christian Message in a Non-Christian World* (London, 1938).
Küng, Hans, *Christianity and World Religion* (London, 1986).
Macdonald, Duncan Black, *Aspects of Islam* (New York, 1911).
Mitri, Tarek (ed.), *Religion Law and Society: A Muslim–Christian Discussion* (Geneva, 1995).

Neill, Stephen, *Christian Faith and Other Faiths: The Christian Dialogue with Other Religions* (Oxford, 1970).
Race, Alan, *Christians and Religious Pluralism: Patterns in the Christian Theology of Religions* (London, 1993).
Rahner, Karl, *Theological Investigations*, Vol. 18 (London, 1984).
Samartha, Stanley J. (ed.), *Living Faiths and the Ecumenical Movement* (Geneva, 1971).
Siddiqui, Ataullah, "Fifty Years of Christian–Muslim Relations: Exploring and Engaging in A New Relationship," *Islamochristiana* (Vol. 26, 2000).
Smith, Cantwell, *Islam in Modern History* (New York, 1957).
—— *Meaning and End of Religion* (New York, 1964).
—— *Questions of Religious Truth* (London, 1967).
Ward, Keith, *Religion and Revelation* (Oxford, 1994).
Watt, Montgomery, *Muhammad at Mecca* (Oxford, 1953).
—— *Muhammad at Medina* (Oxford, 1956).
—— *Islam and Christianity Today: A Contribution to Dialogue* (London, 1983).
—— *Muhammad's Mecca: History in the Quran* (Edinburgh, 1988).
—— *Muslim–Christian Encounters – Perceptions and Misperceptions* (London, 1991).

Buddhism and
Christian Theology

Paul O. Ingram

Introduction

Christians have encountered Buddhists since the first century CE.[1] Yet from this time until Francis Xavier's Jesuit mission to Japan in the sixteenth century, Christians were little informed about Buddhist traditions and practices. As knowledge of Buddhism gradually made its way into the West, Christian encounter with Buddhism was more monological than dialogical, for cultural and historical reasons peculiar to both traditions. Serious Western attempts to understand Buddhism in its own terms did not begin until the emergence of scholarly research in the field of history of religions (*religionswissenschaft*) in the nineteenth century, which provided the foundation for Christian encounter with the world religions in general, and with Buddhism in particular.

Until recently, the agenda of most Christian theological reflection on Buddhism was demonstrating the superiority of Christian faith and practice as the sole vehicle of humanity's salvation. However, since the first East–West Religions in Encounter conference, organized by David Chappell in the summer of 1980 at the University of Hawaii, the structure of Christian theological reflection on Buddhism has slowly changed from theological monologue to dialogical encounter, at least in liberal circles of contemporary Catholic and Protestant thought. The initial East–West Religions in Encounter group is now permanently organized as the Society for Buddhist–Christian Studies (SBCS). This society and its journal, *Buddhist–Christian Studies*, has evolved into an important international forum for worldwide support of the continuing dialogue now occurring between Christians and Buddhists.

Survey

Contemporary Christian encounter with Buddhism reflects the diversity of post-modern and, some would argue, post-Christian cultural and religious diversity, in that Christian encounter with Buddhism is itself pluralistic. This pluralism is rooted in the history of Christian encounter with the world religions since the first century, a history in which there have existed a limited number of theological options for considering other religious traditions. They could be rejected as idolatrous, with the result that Christians would seek to replace them through the conversion of their followers. Hellenistic paganism was seen in this way. Or the Greek and Roman philosophers could be seen as possessing limited goodness and truth which is fulfilled and perfected in Christianity. Christian response to neoplatonism illustrates this possibility, so that Christians sought to convert neoplatonists to Christianity while at the same time preserving this tradition's attainments. Sometimes the other tradition was viewed as non-religious, in which case it could be allowed to continue alongside Christianity. In the seventeenth century, Jesuit missionaries in China treated Confucianism in this way.

By the second half of the twentieth century Christian theology of religions within some liberal circles took a new direction when many theologians recognized non-Christian religious traditions as valid in their own right. Much energy in Christian scholarship on non-Christian religions went into the effort to develop a neutral methodology for the comparative study of religions. Tolerance became a central theological virtue. Partly as a negative reaction to this trend, neo-orthodox thought proposed that Christian faith is not one religion among others, but in fact is not a religion at all. Thus Karl Barth, Emile Brunner, and Dietrich Bonhoeffer defined "religion," including "Christian religion," as a human activity, whereas what is crucial in Christian faith is God's decisive action and response to the world through Jesus Christ. Responding to God's act in Christ is "faith," not "religion." Because of the influence of Protestant neo-orthodox theology following World War II, theology and history of religions developed independently of one another as specialized academic disciplines with little interdisciplinary contact.

In Protestant theology, "no salvation outside the church" has generally meant no salvation apart from explicit Christian faith and commitment to doctrinal propositions. When Barth wrote that Christian faith is not "religion" because "religion is unbelief," meaning "man's attempt to justify and sanctify himself before a capricious and arbitrary picture of God,"[2] he set the essentials of Protestant neo-orthodoxy's approach to Buddhism in particular and non-Christian religious traditions in general: no "religion," including Christianity understood as a "religion," has any truth that can lead persons to salvation because all "religions" are inventions by sinful human beings seeking to establish a saving relationship with God by means of their own contrivances. The opposite of "religion" is Christian faith, which is not a "religion" but a "witness" to a different reality, namely, "God's condescension to us." Christian faith always rests on God's prior action of breaking into the conditions of existence through the life, death, and resurrection of the historical Jesus as the Christ. In regard to Buddhism, Barth once took note of the similarity between the doctrines of faith and grace in Christian and Japanese Pure Land Buddhist traditions. But he dismissed this aspect of Buddhist doctrine as an inferior expression of what Christians experience through faith in Christ.[3]

While it is clear that most Christians have understood that participation in Christian faith and practice are the only means of salvation, this has not always implied the absence of God's saving action for non-Christians or the inability or unwillingness to incorporate truth perceived in non-Christian traditions into Christian self-understanding. But from the time of Constantine the Great, when the church began transforming itself into a sacred institution claiming both religious and secular authority over the lives of Christians and non-Christians, what is today called "theology of religions" took on a hardline exclusivism: all human beings must become Christian in order to be in a saving relationship with God. This idea, later promulgated by the Council of Florence (1438) as the doctrine of no salvation outside the church (*extra ecclesiam nulla salus*), is the classical form of Christian theological exclusivism. In pre-Vatican II Roman Catholic theology of religions, "no salvation outside the church" meant no salvation apart from participation in Catholic sacraments and ethical teachings. When the Second Vatican Council published the *Dogmatic Constitution of the Church* and the *Declaration of the Relationship of the Church to Non-Christian Religions* in 1964 and 1965, respectively, Roman Catholic theology of religions and its conversation with Buddhism took on a more inclusive character.

Barth's exclusivist theology of religions in particular, and Protestant new-orthodox theology in general, did not take the world's religions seriously as objects of theological reflection. But after World War II, voices arose within Protestant and Catholic circles that gave more critical attention to the world's religions. Two important transitional Protestant figures in this regard are Paul Tillich and Jürgen Moltmann, both of whom set important precedents for the development of theological encounter with Buddhism and other religious traditions.

After Tillich's encounter with important Buddhist philosophers in Japan and the publication of his *Christianity and the Encounter with the World's Religions*, he concluded that his "method of correlation" was inadequate for judging the truth of non-Christian traditions. Tillich's method of correlation, deeply influenced by Søren Kierkegaard's existentialist philosophy, asserted that the universal questions all human beings have about the meaning of existence are most completely answered by the Christian revelation. He did not seriously entertain the possibility that there might be more adequate Buddhist or Hindu or Islamic answers to these universal questions. But his experience in Japan taught him that there might be some questions and answers in Buddhist tradition that might correlate more adequately to the structures of existence than Christian answers to these same questions. Consequently, Tillich began reflecting on how Christian encounter with religious pluralism might deepen both Christian theology and Christian experience. Unfortunately, Tillich died before he could develop his evolving insights into a systematic theology of religions.[4]

Similarly, Moltmann wrote of the need for Christian encounter with the world's religions as a means of not only Christian renewal, but the renewal of non-Christian religions as well. But before Christians can enter dialogue with non-Christians, two historic prejudices governing Christian interaction with the world's religions must be explicitly renounced: the absolutism of the church and the absolutism of Christianity. Moltmann's theology of religions is intentionally inclusivist. For him, faith as trust in God's actions for humanity and the entirety of existence, past, present, and future – not faith in theological systems or institutions – makes dialogue with non-Christians not only possible, but also theologically necessary. Moltmann's understanding of religious pluralism is significant because he returned to the New Testament's understanding of Christian interaction with non-Christians. Thus his theology is inclusive because he affirms that the reality Christians encounter in the life, death, and resurrection of the historical Jesus as the Christ has also encountered human beings through non-Christian experience and practice.[5] Since conservative and fundamentalist Protestant theologians have taken an essentially exclusive stance toward the non-Christian religions, including Buddhism, the Protestant theologians cited in this chapter represent, in various ways, the liberal end of the theological spectrum that has followed the precedents set by Tillich and Moltmann's encounter with the world religions.

Post-Vatican II Roman Catholic theology of religions is marked by an inclusivist approach that gives Roman Catholic encounter with Buddhism more theological unity than that generally found in liberal Protestant circles. The two most important voices of current Catholic theological reflection on religious pluralism are Karl Rahner and Hans Küng, whose theologies of religions provide the foundations for most contemporary Catholic theological encounter with Buddhism. Rahner's theology of religion centers on his notion of "anonymous Christianity," according to which devout Buddhists, Muslims, Hindus, or Sikhs encounter the same reality that Christians encounter through faith in Christ, only do not realize it. They are "anonymous Christians," meaning Christians without realizing it. Accordingly, the missionary task of the church is to make anonymous Christians explicitly Christian through conversion to the church's teachings and participation in its sacraments.[6]

Accordingly, Küng concludes that the world's religious traditions, by which he means all religious traditions other than Roman Catholicism, should be understood as "extraordinary ways of human salvation." The Catholic Church, however, is the "ordinary way." Therefore, persons may attain salvation through the particular religious traditions available to them in their historical and cultural circumstances, since God – whose fullest self-revelation is through Christ – is also at work in the extraordinary ways of non-Christian teachings and practices. But compared with the extraordinary ways of salvation, the salvation offered by the church seems, in Küng's view, the fullest expression of God's self-revelation through Christ. Since neither Küng nor Rahner evaluates non-Christian religious traditions as valid avenues to saving truth in their own right, but rather as "preparations for the gospel," the church should undertake missionary efforts to non-Christians while simultaneously recognizing the truths of non-Christian traditions.[7]

Because Buddhists and Christians often engage in dialogue for different reasons, it is useful to describe three major forms of dialogue that have evolved in Buddhist–Christian encounter over the past twenty years: "conceptual dialogue," "socially engaged dialogue," and "interior dialogue." The boundaries separating these three forms of dialogue are not always clear. While most theologians stress conceptual dialogue in their encounter with Buddhism, a growing number emphasize socially engaged dialogue, while Christians interested in such spiritual disciplines as contemplation and meditation focus on interior dialogue. Because each form of dialogue is, in fact, interdependent, Christians experienced in dialogue generally seek to integrate conceptual, socially engaged, and inner dialogue even if they usually emphasize one particular form of dialogue in their conversation with Buddhist tradition.

Conceptual dialogue

The focus of conceptual dialogue is doctrinal, theological, and philosophical. It concerns a religious tradition's self-understanding and worldview. In conceptual dialogue, Buddhists and Christians compare theological and philosophical formulations on such questions as ultimate reality, human nature, suffering and evil, the role of Jesus in Christian faith and the role of the Buddha in Buddhist practice, and what Christians and Buddhists can learn from one another. Three Western theologians, two Protestant and one Roman Catholic, one historian of religions, and three Asian theologians will serve as examples of Christian conceptual dialogue with Buddhism.

Few Protestant theologians have conceptually engaged Buddhism more systematically and incorporated Buddhist thought into their theologies more intentionally than process theologian John B. Cobb, Jr. In fact, Cobb is one of the first major Protestant theologians to appropriate the scholarship of history of religions, particularly in regard to Buddhism, as an object of his theological reflection. His conversation with Buddhism is grounded on the notion that interreligious dialogue is a conceptual process of passing "beyond dialogue."[8] Passing beyond dialogue does not mean the practice of dialogue needs to stop, since theological reflection is itself a dialogical process. Rather, "passing beyond dialogue" names the process of continual theological engagement *in* dialogue as a contributive element of one's continued growth in Christian faith. Cobb assumes the same process occurs for Buddhists as well who, faithful to Buddhist tradition, go beyond dialogue with Christian tradition.

For Cobb, dialogue is itself a theological practice that involves two interdependent movements: (1) in dialogue with Buddhists, Christians should intentionally leave the conventional boundaries of Christian tradition and enter into Buddhist thought and experience, (2) followed by a return to the home of Christian faith enriched, renewed, and "creatively transformed," which is part of what Cobb means by "passing beyond dialogue." The goal of interreligious dialogue for Christians is "creative transformation," defined as a process of critically appropriating whatever one has learned from dialogue into one's own faith and practice, whereby one's faith is challenged, enriched, and renewed. For Christians, the image of creative transformation is Christ, who explicitly provides a focal point of unity within which the many centers of meaning that characterize the present age of religious pluralism are harmonized. Since Cobb thinks that no truth can be foreign to the truth Christians experience engendered by faith in Christ, Christians can and should be open to the "structures of existence" of the other "religious ways" of humanity.[9] However, appropriating Buddhist doctrines into one's theological reflection does not entail imposing Christian meanings foreign to Buddhist experience. Conceptual dialogue that leads to the creative transformation of Christian faith should falsify neither Christian nor Buddhist experience.

The specific forms of creative transformation that Cobb seeks in his dialogue with Buddhism are interrelated with his commitment to the process metaphysics of Alfred North Whitehead. For example, dialogue with Buddhism, he believes, can help Christians understand how inadequately theology has reflected on the non-substantial character of God. To make this point, he incorporates the Mahayana Buddhist doctrines of "emptying" (Skt., *sunyata*) and "non-self" (Skt., *anatman*) into his doctrine of God. What does Buddhist philosophy mean when it teaches that an event (e.g., a moment of human experience) is "empty?" As Cobb correctly interprets this Buddhist teaching, it means (1) that the experience is empty of substance, so that the moments of a person's experience are not unified by an enduring "I" remaining self-identical through time; (2) the experience lacks all possession, since whatever constitutes it does not belong to it; (3) the experience does not possess a form that it imposes on its constituent elements; and (4) the experience is empty of permanent being. Because all events are constituted by "non-self" because they are "empty" of "self-existence" (*svabhava*), there are no permanent "things."

Cobb contends that there are remarkable affinities between these Buddhist notions, Whitehead's doctrine of the "consequent nature of God," and biblical (especially Pauline) images of God and human selfhood. God's "consequent nature" names God's relation to temporal processes in their entirety. It is God's aim at the concrete realization of all possibilities in their proper season.[10] For Cobb, this means that God is "empty" of "self" insofar as "self" is understood as an essence that can be preserved by excluding "other" things and events.[11] In his view, theology should reject notions of God as an unchanging substance and the immortality of the human soul, notions rooted in Greek philosophy, by reappropriating biblical (especially Pauline) teaching. In other words, dialogue with Buddhism, mediated through Whiteheadian process philosophy, brings theological reflection into closer alignment with biblical tradition, given the fact that traditional Christian teachings of God as an unchanging substantial essence along with the doctrine of an immortal soul are in harmony neither with biblical tradition nor the "structure" of Christian experience.

It is not only Christian tradition that can be creatively transformed through dialogue with Buddhism. Since Buddhism and Christianity are different "structures of existence," the process of creative transformation for Buddhists in conceptual dialogue with Christians will be experienced differently by Buddhists. While the specific character of this process is up to Buddhists to decide for themselves, Cobb suggests that there are areas where Buddhists could learn from Christianity. For example, in Japanese Pure Land Buddhism (*jodo shinshu* or "True Pure Land School"), Amida Buddha is ultimate reality personified as compassionate wisdom, who brings all sentient beings into the Pure Land through his "other-power" without regard to a being's "self-power." Cobb suggests that dialogue with Pauline–Augustinian–Lutheran traditions of "justification by faith through grace alone" can deepen Buddhist understanding of this form of religious experience, thereby deepening the personal dimension of its own traditions. Here, the experience of "faith through grace" and the experience of Amida Buddha's compassionate "other-power" provide a common experiential entry point for Buddhist–Christian dialogue.[12] Furthermore, Buddhists can learn much from the Christian doctrine of the Incarnation: in the life, death, and resurrection of a human being living two thousand years on the fringes of the Roman empire, human beings encountered God incarnated within the rough and tumble of historical existence. For Christians, this means that the experience of faith and its doctrinal interpretations are historically contextualized.

Buddhists, particularly in Japan, are beginning to incorporate historical research into Buddhist thought. Yet Cobb claims that Jodo Shinshu Buddhists have not yet worked through the problem of the relation of history to faith. In Cobb's words, Buddhists can "indeed find in Gautama himself and in the history of Buddhism much to support it . . . However, there is nothing about Buddhist self-understanding that leads to the necessity of finding the requisite history solely in India and East Asia."[13] Like Christianity, Buddhism intends universality and like Christianity, Buddhism too needs an inclusive view of all things. Today, such a view must include world history. World history includes the history of Israel and Jesus. Therefore, including the history that supports Christian claims about the graciousness of God in its own particular history supports as it universalizes Jodo Shinshu claims of the universal compassion and wisdom that characterize ultimate reality personified as Amida Buddha.

Perhaps the most radical attempt to reinterpret Christian theology through the categories of Buddhist thought is John P. Keenan's reading of Christian tradition through the lenses of Mahayana Buddhist philosophy, particularly the idealist metaphysics of Yogacara ("Way of Yoga") philosophy and Madhyamika ("Middle Way") epistemology, as a means of clarifying New Testament understandings of Christ. Keenan sees this as a means of developing new forms of Christological thought capable of expressing faith in ways relevant to postmodern experience of the relativity of all normative claims about reality. Consequently, the goal of Keenan's work is the creation and defense of a "Mahayana Christology" focused on demonstrating how the Christ that was incarnate in the historical Jesus is also the "heart of wisdom" attested to in the Gospel of John, the synoptic gospels, the Pauline Epistles, and the Epistle of James. By "heart of wisdom," Keenan means an apprehension of the structures of existence as interdependent, which he believes is the core of both Buddhist and biblical traditions. The explicit goal of Keenan's Mahayana Christology is to regain contact with biblical meanings as a means of reinterpreting orthodox Christological traditions in a manner spiritually relevant to a postmodern, post-Christian age characterized by religious pluralism.

The thesis of Keenan's Mahayana Christology is that Christ is the Wisdom of God, the textual roots of which lie in the wisdom traditions of the Hebrew Bible and Christian experience of Christ as the wisdom of God incarnate (John 1: 1–14). The Mahayana Buddhist name for this Wisdom is "Emptying" or *sunyata*, which in Buddhist tradition has no theistic connotations whatsoever. Nevertheless, Keenan's thesis is that what Mahayana philosophy describes as "wisdom," meaning the apprehension of the interdependence of all things and events as empty of independent and permanent self-existence or "own-being" (*svabhava*), is philosophically and experientially similar to Christian mystical teaching regarding Christ as the Wisdom through which God creates and sustains the universe. In this sense, "wisdom" or *logos* is incarnated not only in Jesus, but also in all things and events in the universe at every moment of space-time. In other words, Buddhist teachings about interdependence and non-self clarify Christian experience of interdependence and the "emptiness" of all things and events of permanent "own-being."

An example of how Keenan applies Mahayana philosophy to the service of Christian theological reflection is his account of how the historical Jesus incarnates the Logos. According to his Mahayana interpretation of the historical Jesus, Jesus – like all phenomenal things and events – is empty of any unchanging essence that might identify Jesus and serve as an unchanging definition of his being, a "Jesus-self" that remains self-identical through time. This does not mean that we cannot form any notion of what Jesus was like, for the gospel traditions and the writings of St. Paul point to a clearly identifiable human being. Yet the historical Jesus possesses no clearly identifiable selfhood beyond Jesus' dependently co-arising words and actions recorded in the biblical texts. There is no permanent selfhood for Jesus at all, since all things and events – including human beings – according to Mahayana philosophy *and* biblical tradition, are empty of permanent selfhood.

Rather than seeking an understanding of Jesus as the Christ in terms of identifiable metaphysical essences, for example as was done in the Nicene and Chalcedonian Creeds, Keenan thinks it best to shed essentialist metaphysics in Christological reflection by concentrating on the themes of emptying and non-self. Nowhere did Jesus as portrayed in the gospels cling to permanent selfhood. The Gospel of John and the synoptic gospels, the Pauline Epistles, and the Epistle of James specifically identify Jesus with wisdom, understanding wisdom to mean an immediate awareness of God as Father (Abba). Matthew identifies receptivity to wisdom with a childlike disposition unspoiled by learning coupled with non-clinging to permanent selfhood (Matthew 18: 1–10). Or as understood through the lens of Mahayana Buddhist thought, the primary motif of the gospels, the Pauline Epistles, and the Epistle of James is a call for conversion away from a sign-clinging mind that would equate faith with a single doctrinal position to a mind that is receptive of the Spirit and thereby aware of God as Abba, which Keenan believes is the heart of "Christian Wisdom." "Jesus disappears in the reality he proclaims. In Ch'an (Zen) Buddhist terms, he is a finger pointing at the moon."[14]

Unlike Cobb and Keenan, Hans Küng's conceptual dialogue with Buddhism does not lead him to incorporate Buddhist doctrines into his theology as a means of creatively transforming Christian tradition. This is because Küng's theological interpretation of Buddhism presupposes Vatican II's theology of religion. Specifically, Küng employs a comparative methodology in his theological engagement with Buddhist traditions, noting that post-Vatican II Catholicism has irrevocably committed itself to dialogue with the world's religions. Relying on scholarship in Buddhist studies as well as his personal participation in Buddhist–Christian dialogue, Küng's method is concerned with pointing out what he perceives are the similarities between Christian and Buddhist doctrines and practices, as well as the incommensurable differences. His purpose is mainly the clarification of differences in order to help Christians gain better comprehension of Christian faith, while simultaneously helping Buddhists obtain clearer understanding of Christianity.

The starting point of his conversation with Buddhism is his comparison of the historical Jesus and the historical Buddha, and the roles of Jesus and the Buddha in Christian and Buddhist tradition. Küng first notes "a fundamental similarity not only in their (Jesus' and Gautama the Buddha's) conduct, but also in their message":[15] both were teachers whose authority lay in their experience of an ultimate reality; both had urgent messages, although the content of each differed, which demanded of people fundamental changes of attitude and conduct; neither intended to give philosophical explanations of the world, nor did they aim to change existing legal and social structures; both worked from the assumption that the world is transient; both taught that all human beings are in need of redemption and transformation; both saw the root of humanity's unredeemed state in human egoism, self-seeking, and self-centeredness; and both taught ways of redemption.

Yet in spite of the similarities Küng perceives between Jesus and the Buddha as historical figures in the history of religions, what he characterizes as the "smiling Buddha" and the "suffering Christ" reveal not only incommensurable difference between Christianity and Buddhism, but also several "tensions" inherent within

Buddhism itself that Buddhists might address through dialogue with Christian teaching. As Küng interprets the history of early Buddhism, after Gautama achieved his Awakening, he spent the next forty years of his life teaching and gathering an inner circle of disciples to form the first monastic community in the history of the world's religions. This monastic community (*samgha*) grew and was supported by a larger lay community of unordained men and women. The Buddha taught detachment from the rough-and-tumble of political and social existence, counseling his monks to seek Awakening by withdrawing into the practice of meditation, and his lay followers to live in society as non-violently as possible in order to acquire positive karmic merit in the hope of achieving a better rebirth in a future life. The Buddha was quite successful in his lifetime, and he died peacefully after forty years of teaching and forming his monastic community.

Jesus was altogether different. His public life lasted at most for three years and ended in violence. His whole life was a life of suffering, without a trace of success in his lifetime. When he died, he was alone, deserted by even his closest disciples, the image of the sufferer pure and simple, which the earliest Christian community interpreted as an act of supreme self-sacrifice that demonstrates God's love for humanity. Jesus was not a teacher of monasticism, and demanded that his followers take up a life of social engagement with the forces of injustice and oppression in the world based on love for neighbors and compassion for the poor and the oppressed. Jesus was not a monk and he did not create a monastic community as the central path for his followers. Monasticism, although still practiced in several different forms of Christian tradition, is not central to Jesus' teaching of the Kingdom of God, nor is it central for Christian faith, nor a necessary means for salvation. Salvation is eternal life in the Kingdom of God, into which all are welcomed who follow Jesus' way of selfless love directed toward all. For Jesus the sufferer not only exudes compassion, but also demands it as the defining expression of the community that follows his way.

Gautama also knew suffering, which was his first Noble Truth: all existence is suffering (*duhkha*). The key to release from suffering, he taught, lies within human beings. Self-discipline in the practice of non-violence toward any living thing and the practice of meditation are the sole requirements for the achievement of Awakening, the attainment of which leads to no further rebirth in the realm of samsaric suffering. Awakened ones, that is, Buddhas, are eventually "extinct," no longer involved in the cycles of rebirth that constitute existence. Accordingly, the Buddha is a paradigm, a model against which his followers are taught to test and measure their own progress toward Awakening. The emphasis of Buddhist practice is self-effort, not reliance on a power outside of one's self-efforts: in following the Buddha's example, one becomes *like* the Buddha. For Buddhists, the Buddha is the shower of the way to Awakening.

But the historical Jesus as the Christ, for Christians, *is* the way. That is, Jesus *became* the way of salvation, meaning eternal life in the Kingdom of God made manifest in Jesus' life, death, and resurrection. Salvation comes through trust in Jesus as the Christ expressed through active and loving social engagement with the world in the struggle to create a human community based on love and justice, rather than through meditation. The model of this community is the Kingdom of God, partly realized in the community of faith called the church and completed in the future when God finally achieves God's intentions in creation. Thus "salvation" in Christian tradition and "Awakening" in Buddhist tradition are not identical concepts or experiences, even though Christians can learn much from the practice of meditation. Accordingly, while Küng believes Buddhists indeed experience "salvation," it is through Christ's "extraordinary" working through the practice and traditions of faithful Buddhists, some of whom have attained Awakening. While Christians can and should be open to Buddhist experience and can learn much from Buddhist insights regarding interdependence, suffering, and its causes, the ordinary way of salvation is through faith in Jesus as the Christ.

Winston L. King was a historian of religions whose scholarship in this academic field became the foundation of his theological encounter with Buddhism. Drawing on years of scholarly engagement in Buddhist studies and his participation in Buddhist–Christian dialogue, his primary theological interest was the clarification of the purpose of genuine interreligious dialogue. For him, the purpose of dialogue was not "dialogical action" – his designation for what Buddhists now call "social engagement" – meaning humanistic cooperation among faith traditions in resolving social issues. Nor is dialogue the sharing of spiritual techniques in the practice of "interior dialogue." While recognizing the importance of both forms of dialogue, the essential purpose of Buddhist–Christian dialogue, indeed of Christian dialogue with the world religions in general, is addressing the doctrinal "sticking points" between religious traditions. Accordingly, King wrote that Buddhist–Christian conceptual dialogue does not involve incorporating Buddhist concepts into Christian theological reflection.

Genuine interreligious dialogue requires that participants be committed to their own religious tradition while simultaneously remaining open to the possibility of conversion to the religious tradition of one's dialogical partner. Such a dialogue is more than mere friendship and toleration of differing points of view. Dialogue requires openness to deep change, which for King implied willingness to face one's own incompleteness. For this reason, he thought few persons ever seriously engage in interreligious dialogue. Therefore, since doctrinal issues are at the heart of interreligious dialogue, King pointed to three doctrinal matters at the center of Buddhist–Christian dialogue which generate "non-negotiable" differences, meaning core teachings so necessary to both traditions that they are not open to challenge.

First, King doubted that Christian theism will ever have much to contribute to most Buddhists, while Buddhist non-theistic teachings about ultimate reality will not have much appeal for Christians. Second, Christian and Buddhist conceptions of human selfhood are likewise incommensurable. Regarding the third area, "religiously inspired social action," King thought that Christian tradition is much more socially engaged in the struggle against human and environmental injustice than Buddhist tradition, and therefore Christians do not have much to learn from Buddhists. Thus he argued that because Christian faith and practice focus attention onto the world in a way that Buddhist teaching and practice do not – because of Buddhism's teaching that Awakening is experienced by means of meditation as a timeless moment that transcends the flux of historical space-time realities – Buddhists in dialogue with Christians might deepen their sense of history and help Buddhists become better prepared for social engagement.[16]

A number of East Asian and South Asian theologians have engaged in theological dialogue with Buddhism as a means of reinterpreting Christian faith in the thought forms of their cultures. Among the most articulate are Seiichi Yagi, Masaaki Honda, and Lynn A. de Silva. Yagi and Honda are Japanese theologians who live in a culture permeated with Buddhist images and ideals and whose theological reflections are in large measure a response to the creative presence of Buddhism in a culture in which Christian faith and practice are foreign. As do Cobb and Keenan, Yagi and Honda – though in different ways – intentionally expose their Christian experience to interpretation through the lenses of Buddhism, much as the church fathers and mothers filtered Christian experience through the lenses of hellenistic philosophy. Thus, both are committed Japanese Christians who focus on translating the deepest levels of faith through the categories of Buddhist thought and practice in an effort to integrate Christian faith and practice more coherently with cultural traditions that are non-Western.

Yagi is a biblical scholar who is known for using the techniques of literary and historical criticism to compare the religious consciousness of Paul with that of Shinran (the thirteenth-century "founder" of Jodo Shinshu or the True Pure Land School of Buddhism), and the consciousness of the historical Jesus with that of Zen masters. By specifying three kinds of religious experience (the communal, the individual, and the interpersonal), he develops an interpretation of Christian experience of the transcendent whereby the levels of range of experience in Paul are correlated with those of Shinran, while Jesus' awareness and articulation of God parallel those of Zen statements in which there is no longer a dualistic awareness nor a focus on concerns pertaining to the usual self. He concludes that the structures of Christian and Buddhist experience are similar, which he asserts establishes a foundation for Asian theological reflection that transcends the usual categories of Western philosophy.[17]

Whereas Yagi uses biblical studies and comparative methodologies for theological reflection on Buddhism, Honda grounds his theology on his interpretation of foundational Christian doctrines, especially the doctrines of the two natures of Christ, the Trinity, and creation *ex nihilo*. Rejecting the epistemological assumptions of Greek philosophy and Cartesian epistemology, he rethinks these key Christian doctrines through the categories of the Japanese Zen Buddhist philosopher Kitaro Nishida, especially Nishida's "topological logic," or what Honda calls "the Buddhist logic of *soku*" or "not same, not different." He thus claims that the structure of the Buddhist and Christian "spiritual fact" – the simultaneously irreversible and reversible relation of the Dharma and God to the world – are identical. For this reason, in expressing the deepest awareness of God, the origins of the universe, and the self, Christian truth-claims should be expressed in the awareness of *soku*, and therefore beyond the capacity of doctrines to completely capture or articulate. The result is a transformed vision of Christian theology which remains committed to Christ, yet appropriates the insights of Buddhist experience and doctrine.[18]

The Theravada (Elder's School) Buddhist tradition of Sri Lanka provided the cultural context of de Silva's theology. In similarity with Honda and Yagi, the question that guided his theological reflection is how Christian faith can be articulated in forms meaningful to South Asian Christians apart from the categories of Western philosophy. Since Theravada Buddhism underlies the culture of not only Sri Lanka, but also all of South Asia – with the exception of Vietnam, where Mahayana forms of Buddhism predominate – de Silva interpreted Christian experience through the lenses of the Buddhist tradition of his culture. In so doing, he believed he was not falsifying Christian tradition. In his view, it is the importation of Western cultural norms and thought forms as a means of interpreting Christian faith to South Asian Christians that constitutes a falsification of Christian tradition for South Asians.

De Silva's engagement with Buddhism focused on the "problem of the self." According to him, the Buddhist doctrine of "non-self" (Pali, *anatta*, Sanskrit, *anatman*) enshrines the truth about human existence which is in accord with not only contemporary science, but also the Hebrew Bible and the New Testament. While the idea of an immortal soul is an established belief for most Christians, it cannot be supported by biblical texts. Furthermore, biblical images of selfhood are corroborated by the Buddhist doctrine of non-self. In other words, the Buddhist doctrine of non-self reveals the meaning of selfhood in the biblical texts – meanings that are lost when biblical texts are read through the filter of Greek philosophical notions about the soul. In the biblical tradition, the self is an interdependent psycho-physical unity of "soul" (*psyche*), "flesh" (*sarx*), and "spirit" (*penuma*) that bears close resemblance to the Buddhist analysis of the self. Consequently, Buddhist *and* biblical views of the self agree that there exists no immortal soul that remains self-identically permanent through time.

Not only does the Buddhist notion of non-self clarify biblical notions of selfhood, it also clarifies the doctrine of the resurrection. If persons are constituted by non-self, the question remains: what continues after death? In contrast to the Buddhist doctrine of reincarnation, the biblical answer is the doctrine of resurrection. Resurrection does not mean the survival of an immortal soul or a reconstituted corpse. For if the doctrine of non-self corresponds to reality, transience and mortality are cosmic facts and death is the end of existence. There cannot be survival after death unless and only if God re-creates a new being. This, according to de Silva, is the truth of the biblical teaching of resurrection interpreted through the lenses of the doctrine of non-self. Resurrection is an act of God by which he creates what St. Paul called a "spiritual body."

To explain the meaning of spiritual body, de Silva employed a "replica theory," according to which at the moment of death, God creates an "exact psycho-physical replica of the deceased person." It is a new creation. But because it is a re-creation, the spiritual body is not identical with the self that existed in an earthly body. It is an exact psycho-physical replica. The doctrine of the resurrection as a "replication" is, he believed, a way of meaningfully reconceiving "the hereafter while accepting the fact of *anatta*."[19]

Socially Engaged Dialogue

Although Buddhists have emphasized socially engaged dialogue with Christians more than conceptual dialogue, Christian conceptual dialogue with Buddhists has also generated interest in the relevance of Buddhist thought and practice to issues of social, environmental, economic, and gender justice. Since these issues are systemic, global, interconnected, and interdependent, they are not religion or culture specific. Participants in all religious traditions have experienced these forms of oppression. Accordingly, Christians and Buddhists have apprehended common experiences and resources for working together to liberate human beings and nature from global forces of systemic oppression.

The term "social engagement" was first coined in 1963 by the Vietnamese Zen Buddhist monk Thich Nhat Hahn as a description of the Buddhist anti-war movement in Vietnam and is now the most common term describing Buddhist social activism.[20] Some Christian liberation theologians have also appropriated this term in their theological reflection. The heart of Buddhist traditions of social engagement are the doctrines of interdependence and non-violence. "Interdependence" (*pratitya-samuptpada* or "dependent co-arising") is the doctrine that all things and events at every moment of space-time are constituted by their interrelationships with all other things and events, so that nothing exists in separation from other things and events. All things and events are mutually co-created by this web of interrelationships. Since these relationships are always in a state of change and process, all things and events are in a constant state of change and becoming. Impermanence is therefore an ingredient in the structure of existence itself. This means that no thing or event is ever separate from any other thing and event; all things and events become joined in a mutual web of interrelationships.

Part of the meaning of "Awakening" (*nirvana*) is experiential awareness of dependent co-arising, which in turn engenders "compassion" (*karuna*) for all sentient beings. Compassion is awareness that in a mutually interdependent universe, the suffering of others is the suffering of all, which in turn energizes action to relieve sentient beings from suffering. In turn, compassion engenders non-violence as the ethical core of Buddhist social activism.

Socially engaged Buddhists are uncompromising in the practice of non-violence and this has raised for Christians questions about justice. Justice is a central theological category for Christians, but notions of justice have not played an equivalent role in Buddhism. Christian tradition gives priority to loving engagement with the world as the foundation for establishing justice. So, for Christians, the question is to what extent does non-violent compassion toward all sentient beings, even to aggressors doing harm to whole communities of persons, itself become an occasion for injustice?[21] While justice is not identical with revenge, Christian traditions of social justice demand that those who do harm "not get away with it," which means that the establishment of justice may necessitate the use of violent means. Consequently, while the practice of non-violent compassion as the ethical norm for Buddhist social engagement has forced Christians to reexamine the relationship between love, justice, and violence in social activism, love as involvement with the world in the struggle for justice has energized Buddhists to examine the relation between the practice of non-violent compassion and justice. Yet both Christians and Buddhists seem agreed that working together to resolve justice issues is not only possible but also necessary, even though the foundations of Buddhist social engagement and Christian social activist traditions are not identical.

Although a number of theologians are in dialogue with Buddhist traditions of social activism, Paul F. Knitter is perhaps the best-known Christian thinker currently socially engaged in dialogue with Buddhists. Knitter posits the existence of a "common context" from which religious persons of different religious traditions, in this case Christianity and Buddhism, can and should enter into dialogue. Drawing on Christian liberation theology, he identifies this common context as "the *preferential option for the poor and non-person*, meaning the option to work with and for the victims of this world."[22] Consequently, apart from commitment to and identification with the poor and the oppressed in the global struggle for justice, conceptual dialogue between Christians and Buddhists remains an elitist enterprise with little relevance to the lives of oppressed persons. Furthermore, Christians and Buddhists have recognized poverty and oppression as common problems from which human beings need liberation. It is necessary, therefore, that Buddhist–Christian dialogue evolve into a shared commitment to the liberation of human beings from all forms of oppression. In the common struggle for liberation, Christians and Buddhists share a "common ground" that enables them to hear one another and be mutually transformed in the process. Thus, while it is important for Christians and Buddhists to engage conceptually, such dialogue is elitist and irrelevant apart from socially engaged dialogue grounded in the preferential option for the poor and the non-person.[23]

Interior Dialogue

In the work of most Christians in dialogue with Buddhism, conceptual dialogue engenders interest in socially engaged dialogue, and both forms of dialogue have led a few Christians and Buddhists to "interior dialogue." Interior dialogue concentrates on participating in Christian and Buddhist spiritual practices and techniques and reflecting on the resulting experiences. The main concerns of interior dialogue arise directly out of the practice traditions of both traditions.

Since spiritual and monastic disciplines continue to energize Catholic experience, while monasticism and disciplines such as contemplative prayer have, since Luther's time, been viewed as forms of "works righteousness" and consequently deemphasized in Protestant tradition, Roman Catholics have been most open to interior dialogue with Buddhists. While a number of Catholic monks, nuns, and laity are interested in this form of encounter with Buddhism, Thomas Merton's encounter with the Dalai Lama and other Tibetan monks, Thai Buddhist monks, and Zen teachings and practices served as a paradigm for other Catholic thinkers. Merton's specific interest in Buddhism evolved out of his frustration with the state of Catholic monasticism as he had experienced it as a Trappist. Toward the end of his life, he had reached the conclusion that Christian monastic traditions should be reformed by means of dialogue with Buddhist monks and nuns through mutual participation and sharing of Christian–Buddhist meditative techniques and experiences.[24] The purpose of "contemplative dialogue," as he referred to what is now called "interior dialogue," is to discover whether there exist similarities and analogies in Christian and Buddhist experience in spite of the doctrinal differences in Christian and Buddhist thought. He came to the conclusion that while doctrinal differences will always differentiate Christian and Buddhist traditions, doctrinal differences do not invalidate the existential similarities of the experiences engendered by Christian and Buddhist monastic disciplines like contemplative prayer and meditation. For the truth discovered by both Christians and Buddhists is beyond the power of doctrine to delimit and specify in any complete way.[25]

Merton's sudden death on December 10, 1968 while attending a conference on monasticism in Bangkok prevented him developing his insights into a systematic theology of monastic experience. However, other Catholic theologians have followed Merton's lead, among them Raimundo Panikkar. Having come to Buddhism through his studies of Hinduism, the depth of Panikkar's understanding of Buddhism is rarely found among Christian theologians. His deep knowledge and respect for Indian religious history effectively allowed him to analyze issues of Buddhist–Christian dialogue from *both* the Christian and the Buddhist sides.

In *The Silence of God, The Answer of the Buddha*, Panikkar explored the radical incommensurability between Christian theism and Buddhist "non-theism" as a means of helping Christians search for new meanings of God beyond the limits of the traditional categories of Euro-American theological tradition. Unlike Cobb's primarily conceptual dialogue with Buddhism, the stress of Panikkar's encounter with Buddhism combines "interior dialogue" with conceptual dialogue. This interest reflects Pannikar's training as a Jesuit. As a Jesuit rooted in the traditions of Catholic monastic and mystical theology, his intention is to help Christians experience, as well as rationally understand, that the object of Christian faith is a reality that is beyond the boundaries of theological thought, including Christian doctrines.

Accordingly, Christians need to hear the "answer of the Buddha" – the ultimate reality to which the Buddha awoke as non-personal and beyond language and symbol, as well as the Buddha's teaching about non-self, impermanence, clinging to permanence, especially to religious doctrines, as the cause of suffering – as a means of entering the "silence that is the reality of God" beyond the limitations of doctrinal description, even those of Christian theology.[26] "Entering this silence," as Merton phrased it, has always been the goal of Catholic monastic practice and is the heart of Christian mystical theology, according to which doctrines are symbolic pointers, not literal descriptions. Cling to a doctrine *about* God, one only has a doctrine *about* God; comprehend that doctrines are symbolic pointers to a reality beyond the definitions of doctrine, one has a means for entering the Silence that is God beyond anything theological reflection can imagine God to be or not to be. The non-theism of the Buddha's "answer" can thereby remind Christians of the non-personal dimensions of Christian theism experienced as the "silence of God" through the practice of Christian contemplative prayer.

Among Catholic Christians theologically engaged with Buddhism, Ruben Habito is unique in that (1) he trained in Zen meditation under Yamada Koun Roshi (1907–89) and received Yamada Roshi's "seal of approval" (*inko*) as his "Dharma heir" during his years in Japan as a Jesuit, and (2) he is interested in both interior and conceptual dialogue with Buddhism. Accordingly, the focus of Habito's theological encounter with Buddhism is his interior dialogue with Zen Buddhist traditions of practice, which he has incorporated into his particular form of contemplative prayer, along with the reformulation of Christian theological categories in light of this interior dialogue. In this, he is rooted in Roman Catholic traditions of interior dialogue with Buddhism that include Philip Johnston, Thomas Merton, and Thomas Keating.[27]

The central theological question Habito brings to dialogue with Buddhism centers on the question of liberation. Since both Christian and Buddhist practices are methods of experiencing liberation, Habito is interested in the core of Buddhist and Christian identity, symbolized by the Buddha's Awakening experience under the Tree of Awakening and Jesus as the Christ hanging from the Cross.

For example, in an essay entitled "The Resurrection of the Dead and Life Ever-lasting: From a Futuristic to a Realized Christianity," Habito points to two articles in the Apostle's Creed – "I believe in . . . the resurrection of the body and the life everlasting" – as the sources for what he perceives is the interplay between the "future outlook" and, borrowing a phrase from Zen Buddhist teaching, the "real-ized outlook" of Christian experience. While both outlooks are interdependent and presuppose faith as trust in the promise of eternal life made manifest in Jesus' life, death, and resurrection (the future aspect), he argues that the resurrection of the body and life everlasting are simultaneously a present reality open to anyone who accepts Christ here-and-now (the realized aspect). Hence, Christian faith's realized aspect entails the experience of eternal life and resurrection in the here-and-now moment of the experience of faith. Zen's stress on experiencing the liberating insight of Awakening in the here-and-now moment of experience can help Christians appreciate the realized aspect of Christian experience of liberation more fully. Habito's biblical support for this conclusion is the last judgment scene in Matthew 23: 31–46, which proclaims that faith in Jesus as the Christ entails a way of life open to the needs of one's neighbors, and that acting accordingly is the gate to a future eternal life experienced in a realized moment of awakened experience here-and-now.[28]

Assessment

The theologians cited in this chapter, as well as others not cited for reasons of space, testify that Christian theology is deeply affected by its encounter with Buddhism. Furthermore, theologians in dialogue with Buddhism have deep respect and admira-tion for Buddhist faith and practice. None treat Buddhism as an error to be eradic-ated, although some, like Karl Rahner and Hans Küng, see distinctive Buddhist doctrines as incomplete truths that are fulfilled in Christianity. Nor is there a hidden missionary agenda in most Christian dialogue with Buddhism. Yet the very openness of Christians and Buddhists to the possibilities of mutual creative transformation through dialogue has brought to light issues and questions that are now setting the agenda for continuing Buddhist–Christian encounter. Four issues and an emerging consensus merit special comment.

First, Christians have tended to be more open to creative transformation through conceptual dialogue with Buddhism than have Buddhists in conceptual dialogue with Christianity. In fact, Buddhist conceptual engagement with Christian theology has had little positive or negative impact on the development of contemporary Buddhist thought. The reason is that Buddhism is much more worldview-specific that Christian tradition. That is, one can appropriate the worldviews of Marx, exist-entialism, Plato, Aristotle, or neoplatonism; one can be a Thomist or neothomist, a scientist, or even a Buddhist, according to Cobb,[29] and still be a Christian. But the doctrines of impermanence, non-self, and dependent co-arising are so necessary to the structure of Buddhist faith and practice that Buddhism is not open to creative transformation through conceptual dialogue with Christianity. Accordingly, it does not seem appropriate to think of creative transformation of these defining Buddhist doctrines because they have been indispensable to Buddhist faith and practice for twenty-five hundred years. Without these defining doctrines, Buddhism ceases to be

"Buddhist." Thus, theology as "faith seeking understanding" does not have a correlate in Buddhist experience. This fact should not be interpreted as evidence of Christian superiority and Buddhist inferiority. According to Buddhist self-understanding, doctrines are "vehicles" or "pointers" that guide the practice of meditation in the hope of awakening to an ultimate reality, called "Emptying" or *sunyata* in Mahayana Buddhism, that is absolutely beyond all conceptualities and symbols.

This fact has pushed current Christian–Buddhist conceptual dialogue to evolve beyond its earlier search for common doctrines and experiences to focus more on the "hard" issues of what appear to be incommensurable differences between Christian and Buddhist doctrines: Buddhist non-theism and Christian theism, the role of Jesus in Christianity and the role of the Buddha in Buddhism; Christian emphasis on faith and grace and Buddhist focus on the practice of meditation; the place of contemplative prayer in Christianity compared with the role of meditation in Buddhism. The main question behind this form of current conceptual dialogue is whether the doctrinal differences between Christianity and Buddhism are contradictory or complementary concepts that point to an ultimate reality underlying Christian and Buddhist experience. So far, a consensus has not emerged among Christians and Buddhists interested in this question.

The second issue concerns how to prevent Christian–Buddhist encounter from remaining an elitist intellectual enterprise of interest only to professional academic theologians, philosophers, ministers, priests, monks, and nuns. The solution is expanding the dialogue to include interested Christian and Buddhist persons active in their religious communities into the discussion, both as listeners and teachers of intellectuals who may not have adequate perceptions of the actual religious experiences of ordinary Christians and Buddhists. For Christians, the goal is the church's creative transformation. For Buddhists, the question is what "creative transformation" means given the specific doctrinal content that defines Buddhism's worldview. But the Christian community as a whole (the church) and the Buddhist community as a whole (the *samgha*) needs to be brought into this discussion. Exactly how to do so is a matter of ongoing conversation between Christian theologians and Buddhist teachers.

Third, interior dialogue has brought a number of difficult and unresolved questions to consciousness that are now energizing much Christian–Buddhist discussion. What is the connection between theological and philosophical conceptualities to the specific experiences engendered by Christian contemplative prayer or Buddhist meditative discipline? How does theological expectation influence the experiences gained through contemplative prayer or Buddhist meditation? Carmelite nuns do not ordinarily interpret their experience through the practice of contemplative prayer as oneness with the Buddha Nature that constitutes all existence at every moment of space-time. Nor do Zen Buddhist nuns practicing meditation normally interpret their experiences as union with Christ the Bridegroom. Do Christians practicing a Buddhist discipline of meditation guided by Christian theological assumptions obtain experiences a Buddhist could recognize as Buddhist? Do Buddhists practicing Christian contemplative prayer guided by the Buddhist worldview obtain Christian experiences? Is conceptual theological reflection and Buddhist doctrine inherently part of Christian and Buddhist spiritual disciplines? Does one not receive from a religious discipline what one's tradition conceptually trains one to expect to receive? What are the connections between conceptual dialogue and interior dialogue?

Fourth, some Christians and Buddhists are now reflecting on the possibility of including the natural sciences and the social sciences as a "third partner" in their conceptual dialogue. What the natural sciences are revealing about the physical processes at play in the universe certainly have a bearing on Christian and Buddhist self-understanding and practice. All of the natural sciences and the social sciences – from the implications of big bang cosmology, relativity theory, and quantum physics for the central doctrines of Christian and Buddhist tradition, particularly Christian theism and Buddhist non-theism, to the implications of the biological and ecological sciences for Christian–Buddhist social engagement with environmental issues, to the implication of the psychological sciences for the practice of Christian and Buddhist contemplative–meditative disciplines, to the need to bring the social sciences, partiularly economics, into Christian–Buddhist social engagement with issues of poverty and economic injustice – have contributions yet to be made to contemporary Buddhist–Christian dialogue.

Finally, an important consensus seems to have emerged from contemporary Christian–Buddhist encounter. Conceptual, socially engaged, and interior dialogue are interdependent. Or to paraphrase the Epistle of James, "conceptual dialogue and interior dialogue apart from socially engaged dialogue is dead" for the same reasons that "faith without works is dead." That is, the central point of the practice of Christian or Buddhist faith, in separation or in dialogue, is the liberation of human beings and all creatures in nature from forces of oppression and injustice and the mutual creative transformation of persons in community with nature. Both the wisdom that Buddhists affirm is engendered by awakening, and the Christian doctrines of creation and incarnation, point to the utter interdependency of all things and events at every moment of space-time – a notion also affirmed by contemporary physics and biology in distinctively scientific terms.[30] Awareness of interdependency, in turn, engenders social engagement, because awareness of interdependence and social engagement are themselves interdependent. Thus we experience the suffering of others as our suffering, the oppression of others as our oppression, the oppression of nature as our oppression, and the liberation of others as our liberation – and thereby we become empowered for social engagement.

Consequently, Buddhist–Christian dialogue in all three of its forms needs to include focus on practical issues that are not religion-specific or culture-specific, meaning issues that confront all human beings regardless of what religious or secular label persons wear. This has become the major principle of Buddhist–Christian dialogue and is in agreement with Christians like Martin Luther, Martin Luther King, and Mother Theresa; the Vietnamese Buddhist monk Thich Nhat Hahn and the Thai Buddhist layman Sulak Siveraksa; the Hindu sage and activist Mahatma Gandhi; as well as Jewish and Islamic calls that we struggle for justice in obedience to Torah or surrender to Allah guided by the Quran: namely, that religious faith and practice do not separate us from the world; Christian–Buddhist dialogue throws Christians and Buddhists *into* the world's rough-and-tumble struggle for peace and justice. Buddhist–Christian dialogue is now guided by a concern for the liberation of all sentient beings, for as both Christian and Buddhist teaching affirm in common, we are all in this together. Distinctively Christian practices and distinctively Buddhist practices cannot have it any other way, because in an interdependently becoming universe, there is no other way.

Notes

1 The first textual reference to Buddhism in Christian sources appears around the year 200 in the *Miscellany* (*Stromateis*) of Clement of Alexandria, who wished to show that Christian *gnosis* was superior to every other form of wisdom: "And there are in India those who follow the commandments of the Buddha, whom they revere as a God because of his immense holiness." Cited in Hans Küng, *Christianity and the World Religions* (Garden City, NY: Doubleday, 1986), 307.

2 Karl Barth, "The Revelation of God and the Absolutism of Religion," in *Church Dogmatics* (Edinburgh: T. and T. Clark, 1956), Vol. 1, part 2, section 17.

3 Ibid, 340–4.

4 Paul Tillich, *Christianity and the Encounter With the World's Religions* (New York: Columbia University Press, 1963) and *Systematic Theology I* (Chicago: University of Chicago Press, 1951), 3–68.

5 Jürgen Moltmann, *The Church and the Power of the Spirit* (New York: Harper and Row, 1971), 151ff. Also see Richard J. De Martino (ed.), "Dialogue East and West: Paul Tillich and Hisamatsu Shin'ichi," *Eastern Buddhist* 4 (October 1971): 39–107 and *Eastern Buddhist* 5 (October 1972): 107–28.

6 Karl Rahner, *Theological Investigations, Vol. 5* (Baltimore, MD: Helicon Press, 1966), 131. Also see essays in other volumes of *Theological Investigations*, especially volumes 6, 9, 12, and 14.

7 Hans Küng, *On Being a Christian* (New York: Pocket Books, 1978), 89–116.

8 John B. Cobb, Jr., *Beyond Dialogue: Toward the Mutual Transformation of Christianity and Buddhism* (Philadelphia, PA: Fortress Press, 1982), ch. 2.

9 John B. Cobb, Jr., *Christ in a Pluralistic Age* (Philadelphia, PA: Westminster Press, 1975), 21, 58.

10 Alfred North Whitehead, *Process and Reality* (New York: Macmillan, 1967), 31.

11 See John B. Cobb, Jr. and David Ray Griffin, *Process Theology: An Introductory Exposition* (Philadelphia, PA: Westminster Press, 1976), 136–42.

12 John B. Cobb, Jr., *Beyond Dialogue: Toward a Mutual Transformation of Christianity and Buddhism* (Philadelphia, PA: Fortress Press, 1982), 128–43.

13 Ibid, 139.

14 John P. Keenan, *The Meaning of Christ: A Mahayana Theology* (Maryknoll, NY: Orbis Books, 1989), 228.

15 Hans Küng, *Christianity and the World Religions* (New York: Doubleday, 1986), 322.

16 Winston L. King, "Interreligious Dialogue," in *The Sound of Liberating Truth: Buddhist–Christian Dialogues in Honor of Frederick J. Streng*, ed. Sallie B. King and Paul O. Ingram (London: Curzon Press, 1999), 41–56 and *Buddhism and Christianity: Some Bridges of Understanding* (Philadelphia, PA: Westminster Press, 1972).

17 See Seiichi Yagi, "Paul and Shinran, Jesus and Zen: What Lies at the Ground of Human Existence?" In *Buddhist–Christian Dialogue: Mutual Renewal and Transformation*, ed. Paul O. Ingram and Frederick J. Streng (Honolulu: University of Hawaii Press, 1986), 197–215 and (with Leonard Swindler) *A Bridge to Buddhist–Christian Dialogue* (New York: Paulist Press, 1988), chs. 1–4. Also see Seiichi Yagi, "Buddhist–Christian Dialogue in Japan: Varieties of Immediate Experience," *Buddhist–Christian Studies* 14 (1994): 11–22.

18 Mahaaki Honda, "The Encounter of Christianity with the Buddhist Logic of *Soku*: An Essay in Topological Theology," in Ingram and Streng *Buddhist–Christian Dialogue*, 217–30.

19 Lynn de Silva, *The Problem of the Self in Buddhism and Christianity* (New York: Barnes and Noble, 1979), 7.

20 According to Kenneth Kraft, *Inner Peace, World Peace: Essays on Buddhism and Nonviolence* (Albany, NY: State University of New York Press, 1992), 18, Thich Nhat Hahn published a book by this title in 1963. While I have not seen this text or any other scholarly reference to it, Christopher S. Queen notes that the French term *engagé*, meaning "politically outspoken" or "politically involved," was common among activist

intellectuals in French Indochina long before the 1960s. See Queen, "Introduction," *Engaged Buddhism: Buddhist Liberation Movements in Asia*, ed. Christopher S. Queen and Sallie B. King (Albany, NY: State University of New York Press, 1996), 1–44.

21 Cf. Cobb, *Beyond Dialogue*, chs. 4–5 and John P. Keenan, "Some Questions About the World" and "The Mind of Wisdom and Justice in the Letter of James," in King and Ingram, *The Sound of Liberating Truth*, 181–99, as two important examples of contemporary Christian dialogue with Buddhists on the relation between non-violent compassion and love as the center of Christian traditions of social justice.

22 Paul F. Knitter, "Towards a Liberation Theology of Religions," in *The Myth of Christian Uniqueness: Toward a Pluralistic Theology of Religions*, ed. John Hick Maryknoll, NY: Orbis Books, 185.

23 Ibid, 185–6.

24 Thomas Merton, "Monastic Experience and East–West Dialogue," in *The Asian Journal of Thomas Merton*, ed. Naomi Burton et al. (New York: New Directions Books, 1968), 309–25.

25 Thomas Merton, "Marxism and Monastic Disciplines," in Burton, *The Asian Journal of Thomas Merton*, 332–42. Also see Lawrence S. Cunningham, *Thomas Merton and the Monastic Vision* (Grand Rapids, MI: Eerdmans, 1999), 155.82.

26 Jonathan Montaldo (ed.), *Entering the Silence: The Journals of Thomas Merton, Vol. 2: 1941–1952* (San Francisco: Harper San Francisco, 1996) and Raimundo Panikkar, *The Silence of God, The Answer of the Buddha* (Maryknoll, NY: Orbis Books, 1989), ch. 10.

27 See Philip Johnston, *Silent Music: The Science of Meditation* (New York: Harper and Row, 1974); Thomas Keating, *Open Mind, Open Heart: The Contemplative Dimension of the Gospel* (New York: Continuum, 1997) and *Invitation to Love: The Way of Christian Contemplation* (New York: Continuum, 1997); and Thomas Merton, *Mystics and Zen Masters* (New York: Dell Publishing, 1967) and Burton, *The Asian Journal of Thomas Merton* (New York: New Directions, 1973), 211–56, 297–304, 309–17.

28 See Ruben L. F. Habito, *Zen Breath, Healing Breath: Zen Spirituality for a Wounded Earth* (Maryknoll, NY: Orbis Books, 1993) and "The Resurrection of the Dead, and Life Everlasting: From a Futuristic to a Realized Christianity," in King and Ingram *The Sound of Liberating Truth*, ch. 19.

29 John B. Cobb, Jr., "Can a Christian be a Buddhist, Too?" *Japanese Religions* 10 (December 1978): 1–20.

30 See Arthur Peacocke, *Theology For a Scientific Age* (Minneapolis, MN: Fortress Press, 1993), 39–43 for a wonderful summary of the current consensus among scientists regarding the interdependent and interconnected structure of the physical universe.

Bibliography

Primary

Barth, Karl. "The Revelation of God and the Absolutism of Religion," *Church Dogmatics*, Vol. 1, part 2, section 17 (Edinburgh, 1956).

Cobb., John B., Jr. *The Structure of Christian Existence* (Philadelphia, PA, 1967).

—— *Christ in a Pluralistic Age* (Philadelphia, PA, 1975).

—— "Buddhist Emptiness and the Christian God," *Journal of the American Academy of Religion* 45 (1977): 11–24.

—— "Can a Christian Be a Buddhist, Too?" *Japanese Religions* 10 (December 1978): 1–20.

—— *Beyond Dialogue* (Philadelphia, PA, 1982).

de Silva, Lynn A. *The Problem of the Self In Buddhism and Christianity* (New York, 1979).

Dumoulin, Heinrich. *Christianity Meets Buddhism* (La Salle, IL, 1974).

Habito, Rubin L. F. *Healing Breath: Zen Spirituality for a Wounded Earth* (Maryknoll, NY, 1993).

Keenan, John P. *The Meaning of Christ: A Mahayana Theology.* (Maryknoll, NY, 1989).

—— *The Gospel of Mark: A Mahayana Reading.* (Maryknoll, NY, 1995).

King, Sallie B. and Paul O. Ingram (eds.) *The Sound of Liberating Truth: Buddhist–Christian*

Dialogues in Honor of Frederick J. Streng (London, 1999).

King, Winston L. *Buddhism and Christianity: Some Bridges of Understanding* (Philadelphia, PA, 1962).

—— *In Hope of Nibbana* (La Salle, IL, 1964).

Küng, Hans. *Christianity and the World Religions* (Garden City, NY, 1986).

Merton, Thomas. *Mystics and Zen Masters* (New York, 1967).

—— *The Asian Journal of Thomas Merton* (New York, 1973).

Panikkar, Raimundo. *The Silence of God, The Answer of the Buddha* (Maryknoll, NY, 1990).

Tillich, Paul. *Christianity and the Encounter With the World's Religions* (New York, 1963).

Yagi, Seiichi. "Buddhist–Christian Dialogue in Japan," *Buddhist–Christian Studies* 14 (1994): 11–22.

Yagi, Seiichi and Leonard Swidler. *A Bridge to Buddhist–Christian Understanding* (New York: Paulist Press, 1988).

Secondary

Adeny, Francis. "How I, A Christian, Have Learned from Buddhist Practice, or 'The Frog and the Lily Pad . . . Not Waiting,'" *Buddhist–Christian Studies* 21 (2001): 33–6.

Amore, Roy C. *Two Masters, One Message: The Lives and Teachings of Gautama the Buddha* (Nashville, TN, 1978).

Corless, Roger and Paul F. Knitter. *Buddhist Emptiness and the Christian Trinity: Essays and Explorations* (New York, 1990).

De Martino, Richard J. (ed.) "Dialogue East and West: Paul Tillich and Hisamatsu Shin'ichi," *Eastern Buddhist* 4 (October 1971): 39–107.

—— "Dialogue East and West: Paul Tillich and Shin'ichi Hisamatsu," *Eastern Buddhist* 5 (October 1972): 107–28.

Fonner, Michael. "Toward a Theravadin Christology," *Buddhist–Christian Studies* 13 (1993): 3–14.

Gross, Rita M. and Terry C. Muck (eds.) *Buddhists Talk About Jesus, Christians Talk About the Buddha* (New York, 2000).

—— *Christians Talk About Meditation, Buddhists Talk About Christian Prayer* (New York, 2003).

Ingram, Paul O. *The Modern Buddhist–Christian Dialogue* (Lewiston, IL, 1988).

—— "Buddhist–Christian Dialogue and the Liberation of Women," *Buddhist–Christian Studies* 17 (1997).

—— *Wrestling With the Ox: A Theology of Religious Experience* (New York, 1997).

—— "On the Practice of Faith: A Lutheran's Interior Dialogue with Buddhism," *Buddhist–Christian Studies* 21 (2001): 43–52.

—— "A Christian Theological Reflection on the Buddha," *Studia Missionalia* 51 (2002): 379–95.

Ingram, Paul O. and Frederick J. Streng (eds.) *Buddhist–Christian Dialogue: Essays in Mutual Transformation* (Honolulu, 1986).

Keating, Thomas. *Invitation to Love: The Way of Christian Contemplation* (New York, 1997).

—— *Open Mind, Open Heart: The Contemplative Dimension of the Gospel* (New York, 1997).

Lefebure, Leo. *The Buddha and the Christ* (Maryknoll, NY, 1993).

Lopez, Donald S., Jr. and Steven C. Rockefeller (eds.) *The Christ and the Buddha* (Albany, NY, 1987).

Mitchell, Donald W. and James Wieseman (eds.) *The Gethsemani Encounter* (New York, 1998).

Muck, Terry C. *Spirituality and Emptiness* (Mawah, NJ, 1992).

—— "Readiness: Preparing for the Path," *Buddhist–Christian Studies* 21 (2001): 51–6.

Prabhu, Joseph (ed.) *The Intercultural Challenge of Raimundo Panikkar* (Maryknoll, NY, 1996).

Pye, Michael. "Skillful Means and the Interpretation of Christianity," *Buddhist–Christian Studies* 10 (1990): 17–21.

Streng, Frederick J. *Emptiness: A Study of Religious Meaning* (Nashville, TN, 1967).

Theology in Many Media

Theology, as *reasoning* about God, is self-evidently not confined to the production of written texts, however easy it is to forget the numerous other media of theological thought. Theology done in non-verbal media may have very different contexts of production and reception, but, as the chapters in Part VIII show, the theologian who works mainly with texts is impoverished if she neglects it. The twentieth century saw the rapid development of new media, such as film, but also enormous change and experimentation in music and the visual arts.

The chapters that follow trace, on the one hand, how theology is *done* in many media – how music, art, and film can be vehicles for distinctive and creative theological reflection. Thus, John de Gruchy reflects on the themes of embodiment, representation, and beauty as central to both theology and the visual arts. Jeremy Begbie discusses music's "way of perceiving the world" as a way of thinking through trinitarian theology, Christology, and pneumatology. Jolyon Mitchell, similarly, explores the theological visions conveyed in the films of Ingmar Bergman, Francis Ford Coppola, and (most controversially) Mel Gibson.

On the other hand, these chapters also record the engagement of theologians in criticism of, and comment on, the media discussed. All record the "hesitation and suspicion" (Begbie) reflected in many theological reactions to art, music, and film, but all also trace the recognition at various points throughout the twentieth century of the ways in which theologians can learn from and converse with the arts. De Gruchy shows, through engagement with the work of John Dillenberger and others, how artists have enabled twentieth-century theologians to "see things with new eyes," while Begbie examines the importance of music for the work of Karl Barth and Dietrich Bonhoeffer. Mitchell examines the achievements and possibilities of a growing body of "theological film criticism" that goes beyond arguments about the morally improving or corrupting character of films.

Theology and the Visual Arts

John W. de Gruchy

Introduction

Through the centuries the visual arts have powerfully stirred the human spirit, but of all the arts they have been most neglected by theologians. Yet, as Karl Rahner argued, "theology cannot be complete until it appropriates" the non-verbal "arts as an integral moment of itself and its own life, until the arts become an intrinsic moment of theology itself."[1] If we reduce theology to "verbal theology," Rahner continued, we unjustifiably limit "the capacity of the arts to be used by God in his revelation." Fortunately, the situation changed significantly during the latter half of the twentieth century, with an increasing number of theologians recognizing the importance of the visual arts in doing theology and, alongside this, a renewed interest in theological aesthetics.

Irrespective of whether theologians have engaged the visual arts in their work, the visual arts have played a significant albeit contested role in the history of Christianity. At various times this has led to theological reflection on what is liturgically and pedagogically appropriate art. Such theological reflection is not, however, the same as doing theology in dialogue with the visual arts. Nor is it engaging in theological aesthetics, the particular theological discipline that seeks to explore the meaning and significance of the arts in relation to Christian faith. Theological aesthetics is not a substitute for studying the visual arts as such, but it can help place them within an interpretive framework in terms of the Christian tradition, other theological disciplines, and the history and theory of art.

Most contemporary theologians engaged with the visual arts comment both on their role within the life of the church and their broader cultural significance. For them, the visual arts, whether as products of faith or despair, the work of believers or non-believers, or whether intended for the sanctuary, the gallery, or the public square, have the potential to awaken sensibility to reality in all its tragic ugliness and transforming beauty. They can enhance life by providing pleasure, a major purpose of the arts, but more especially they can help us see in fresh and often startling ways what would otherwise be hidden from sight. In such ways they help define and renew our humanity.

The term "visual arts" may be understood to include architecture, film, and related media, as well as installations, sculpture, and painting. Our focus is on the graphic arts, though much of what we shall discuss has wider relevance. There are further distinctions that are often made with regard to the visual arts, such as those between "fine," "high," "popular," "naïve," "folk," and "primitive" art. Terms such as "fine" or "high" are often used to define the "classics" of a particular art tradition, but they should not be used to denigrate one form in favor of another. There has been a tendency for those theologians interested in the visual arts in the West to focus their attention primarily on "fine" or "high" art. Yet it is often "popular" art that expresses the faith and doubts, hopes and fears of people. Perhaps a more useful distinction is between good art, that is art that has integrity, and kitsch (itself a slippery term), which is banal and mediocre. Another distinction often drawn is between "religious," "spiritual," and "secular" art. This, too, has some value, but it is also problematic. In speaking of theology and the visual arts we do not only have in mind those works of art that have an obviously religious theme, though many great works of art, as in the Sistine Chapel or the paintings of Rembrandt, certainly do. We also have in mind the many works of art which may be classified "secular" but which enable us to perceive reality in ways that challenge and inform faith and praxis.

This chapter is divided into three parts. The first provides a brief survey of the historical role of the visual arts within the Christian tradition, concentrating on the Iconoclastic Controversy and its significance for our subject. The second part suggests how some theologians in the twentieth century responded to the visual arts in doing theology. The third part sets out some issues that are of particular importance in setting the agenda for the ongoing theological task.

Historical Survey

Despite the strictures against idolatry in the Hebrew scriptures, descriptions regarding the building and furnishing of the Temple in Jerusalem indicate considerable aesthetic interest. Of course, representations of God were forbidden, but there was plenty within the Temple to attest to the liturgical importance of the visual. Likewise, examples of visual art, some of it influenced by Greco-Roman culture, have been discovered in synagogues of post-exilic Judaism, demonstrating that such art was not deemed to break the first commandment but was considered appropriate adornment.

There are examples of pre-Constantinan Christian visual art, notably in the Roman catacombs, but Christian art only began to flourish once Christianity became the official religion of the Roman empire. Just as Christianity interacted with and appropriated the thought-forms of hellenistic culture, so it borrowed from the art of classical Rome and Greece in visually depicting its faith. The dangers in doing so were evident to theologians and bishops, who regularly warned against idolatry. But this did not prevent Christians from expressing their faith in visual symbols, or in painting images of biblical stories and themes, of Jesus, Mary, the martyrs and saints. As the church became more established there was a proliferation of iconography that informed and sustained a largely illiterate popular piety. Icons became a "fifth gospel," communicating the gospel narrative and inspiring devotion. The proliferation of icons was such that by the eighth century theological, ecclesiastical, and political forces converged in a controversy about them that threatened to tear apart the church in the Eastern empire.

The Iconoclastic Controversy was a defining moment in the history of Christianity and, as it happened, in the development of visual art in the Western world. All sides agreed that there should be no visual representations of God as such, for that would be idolatry. But the iconoclasts, generally associated with the emperor's court, rejected the use of any image (*ikon*) in the sanctuary. On the other side, the iconophiles, largely centered in the monasteries, insisted that while much visual art was inappropriate, icons of Christ, the Virgin Mary, and the saints were essential to the life and worship of the church. The iconophiles won the day, hence the fundamental role which icons play in the liturgical and spiritual life of the Eastern and Oriental Orthodox churches.

The Iconoclastic Controversy highlights two conflicting theologies in the history of the relationship between Christianity and the visual arts. The iconoclasts represent a tradition that has strong roots in the Hebrew scriptures, and one that was also powerfully expressed within Islam, the rapidly expanding new religious movement of the time that was threatening the borders of Byzantium. Iconoclasts, whether Christian, Jewish, or Muslim, insist that any attempt to visually represent God distorts the truth and dishonors God. Indeed, while not necessarily against the use of symbols, they reject visual images as such because of their idolatrous potential, and emphasize almost exclusively the importance of the Word. The counter-argument of iconophiles is premised on the Incarnation. In Jesus Christ, God has accommodated the divine nature within the constraints of the human for the sake of the redemption of the world. The Word, which became flesh, was seen, touched, and handled (I John 1: 1), and it remains appropriate to experience the Incarnate Word through all the senses. Hence, icons prayerfully and faithfully produced have the capacity to communicate the truth and become means of grace.

Although the outcome of the Iconoclastic Controversy settled matters in the East, it was different in the Western church, where the issues continued to surface within the Roman Catholic Church and later the churches of the Protestant Reformation. Martin Luther and John Calvin set the pattern for their respective traditions. Luther was more interested in music than in visual art, about which he was largely indifferent. Calvin recognized the value of the visual arts as a source of pleasure, but would not permit such art in the sanctuary. Protestants have therefore tended to be much more cautious with regard to the visual arts than Roman Catholics, and sometimes severely iconoclastic. But the Council of Trent (1545–63) was also sensitive to the dangers of visual art, laying down rules for what was appropriate. Contrary to Protestant iconoclasm, Trent sought to encourage the arts in the life of the church, but at the same time felt the need to keep in check developments that had led to the proliferation of art in churches during the Renaissance when many of the patrons of the visual arts were popes, cardinals, and bishops. Partly as a result of both Protestant and Catholic attitudes to artists and the visual arts, artists increasingly felt alienated from the church in post-Reformation Europe, resulting in a humanist emphasis on "art for art's sake" typified by the Bohemian aesthetic movement in the nineteenth century.

Nonetheless, there were several important historical junctures in the relationship between Christianity and the visual arts subsequent to the Protestant Reformation, such as during the Baroque period and nineteenth-century Romanticism. The relationship was also affected by the global expansion of Christianity into new contexts, leading to visual expressions of Christian faith reflecting other than European cultures. The ecumenical and liturgical movements in the twentieth century likewise stimulated renewed interest in the role of the arts in the life of the church. As a result there was a fresh flourishing of the use of visual arts in the churches, demonstrating the irrepressible desire of many Christians to express their faith in art and a partial overcoming of the alienation of artists more generally. Concomitant with these developments was a renewed theological interest in the visual arts.

Contemporary Theology and the Visual Arts

Few English-speaking theologians, especially Protestants, were interested or engaged in our subject at the turn of the twentieth century. One exception was P. T. Forsyth (1848–1921), a Scottish Congregationalist, who early on in his career as a theological professor in London recognized the theological and religious significance of the visual arts. In a series of lectures entitled *Religion in Recent Art*, first published in 1887, Forsyth discussed the pre-Raphaelite movement in England, and later dealt more broadly with the arts in *Christ on Parnassus* (1911). As a Calvinist, Forsyth's interest was not visual art in the sanctuary, but its necessity for religion and life, insisting that no "religion can be true religion if it does not encourage art."[2] Forsyth demonstrated an intimate knowledge of Romanticism and the pre-Raphaelites, and an ability to reflect theologically on their significance for religion and culture. With his acute sense of the tragic dimension of life amid natural beauty, which he discerned both in great art and the Bible, he emphasized the morally transforming power of the gospel as the ground of hope.

Paul Tillich (1886–1965), a German Lutheran chaplain during World War I, had first-hand experience of its horror in the trenches on the Western Front, but found respite from its bludgeonings "by devoting his leisure to the study of art."[3] As a result, art not only became a passion but also a source of divine disclosure, revealing the nature of the human condition and providing intimations of ultimate reality. But whereas Forsyth discovered this in the pre-Raphaelites, for Tillich it was the work of the Expressionists that provided a prophetic critique of bourgeois society, revealing its emptiness, ugliness, and guilt, and at the same time breaking open the possibility of redemption and hope.

Tillich's emphasis on the prophetic role of the artist was at the expense of the role of the artist as an agent of grace and healing. This role of the artists was, however, strongly asserted by George Bell, Anglican bishop of Chichester, whose contribution to relating theology and the church to culture and the visual arts in England during the 1940s and 1950s was immense. With the Incarnation as his point of departure, Bell emphasized the material character of Christianity, and called the churches to enter into a partnership with artists, recognizing their potential ministry and God-given vocation.[4] Bell knew that he was taking a risk, given both the fact that so many artists were non-believers and his conviction that no art in the sanctuary should contradict the gospel. Yet, for Bell, all true art had its own integrity and functioned in a sacramental way. There is, he insisted, a common bond between all who believe "in justice and truth, mercy and love, in art and poetry and music," for these are indestructible.[5] Bell's interest in the arts has had a lasting influence in the Church of England, and his sacramental understanding of their role has become a particular contribution of Anglican theologians to the discussion on our subject.[6] Many parish churches and especially cathedrals, Durham being an excellent example, carry on this legacy in emphasizing the importance of visual arts, encouraging artists to contribute to the life of the church.

However, it was in the United States that the dialogue between theology and the visual arts made most headway within the academy, and it did so not least because of the presence and influence of Paul Tillich, who had fled Nazism in 1939 and immigrated to New York. Indicative of this development was the symposium of essays on *Christian Faith and the Contemporary Arts* published in 1957, and republished three times within the next five years. In the opening essay, Nathan Scott, Jr., of the University of Chicago, commented that the current cultural experience required theologians "to enter into a new and hitherto largely untried collaboration with the whole community of the modern arts."[7]

One of those influenced by Tillich was John Dillenberger, who later testified that it was Tillich alone, of all the major theologians to whom he was introduced as a student, who "seemed to . . . involve the full range of humanity's sensibilities in his theology."[8] Dillenberger went on to make a major contribution to the dialogue between theology and the visual arts and to enabling the churches to recover this sensibility. The establishment of the Jane and John Dillenberger Endowment for the Visual Arts at the Graduate Theological Union, Berkeley, California, in 1981 was the first of many programs for theology and the arts that now exist in theological seminaries in the United States. In Britain, the "Theology through the Arts" program at the universities in Cambridge and St. Andrews, directed by Jeremy Begbie, has similar goals.

Dillenberger's seminal study *A Theology of Artistic Sensibilities: The Visual Arts and the Church* (1986) remains a significant contribution to our subject. Although by the 1980s the situation had improved, it was still Dillenberger's contention that theologians "by and large do not yet know the extent to which their own disciplines may be enriched, if not transformed, by a deeper exposure to the arts, including the visual arts."[9] In many ways this remains the case. Dillenberger identified four main approaches to the subject and his typology provides a useful framework for our discussion.

The first approach is associated most of all with Karl Barth, whose theology of the Word of God breathed new life into the Reformed tradition and beyond. Barth upheld Calvin's resistance to the use of the visual arts in the life of the church, even though he had a particular love for the music of Mozart and an appreciation of the visual arts. But the fact that Barth and others for whom the dangers of idolatry and the preeminence of "the Word" generally preclude the role of the visual in doing theology, does not mean that they provide no resources that can meaningfully be appropriated for that task. Quite the contrary is often true, as I have tried to show elsewhere with reference to both Barth and Dietrich Bonhoeffer.[10]

The second approach Dillenberger identified is associated with Tillich and others who have affirmed the relationship between art and theology, even regarding culture as a source for doing theology. But ironically, as Dillenberger notes, Tillich's "dazzling theological interpretations" of modern art, which inspired many, were "grounded in theological seeing without faithfulness to the artworks themselves" and therefore remained "unconvincing to critics and art historians."[11] There is always a danger in theology imposing itself on the arts and thereby misreading their character, but we cannot escape our own presuppositions and experience. What is necessary is not so much satisfying art historians in doing theology, though their role is obviously important in helping us understand, but being responsive to the challenge presented by the visual arts as they existentially address us within our own contexts. A more serious criticism of Tillich and others who have done theology in dialogue with the visual arts is that their interest is almost totally confined to the "fine" and "high" arts.

The third approach regards the arts as models for theological work. Among those whom Dillenberger identifies in this category are the Catholic theologians Hans Urs von Balthasar, Karl Rahner, and David Tracy. For Dillenberger, neither Balthasar nor Rahner, despite their commitment to the task, provide much help in actually relating theology and the visual arts, a view I do not fully share. But Tracy's recognition of visual art as "affirming and stretching our sensibilities" in doing theology certainly provides a helpful model[12] and, I suggest, indicates how we may engage the visual arts beyond the paradigms of Western theology and art.

Of all the theologians of the twentieth century, von Balthasar put theological aesthetics firmly on the agenda, especially with his magisterial multi-volumed *The Glory of the Lord*. Moreover, he has brought back the notion of beauty into theological discourse, something that has been seriously neglected in theology, philosophical aesthetics, and art criticism since the nineteenth century. There is point to the criticism that his approach is less to allow works of art to speak for themselves, and more to fit them into his overarching theological framework. This serves his apologetic purpose that art finds its true meaning and goal within the framework of Christian faith and, more specifically, the Roman Catholic Church. But in serving this end, von Balthasar provides us with a wealth of insight derived from his immense knowledge of European history and culture, as well as his theological acumen so firmly rooted in the incarnational theology of the patristic period. In short, his reflections on art, whether the work of believers or not, Catholics or Protestants, provide us with a *tour de force* of the terrain, but also demands of us an independent judgment based on our own theological convictions and knowledge of visual art.

If von Balthasar's intent was apologetic, so too was that of the neo-Calvinist Dutch scholar H. R. Rookmaaker, whose book *Modern Art and the Death of a Culture* (1970), not mentioned by Dillenberger, has become a classic within more conservative evangelical circles. A professor of the history of art at the Free University Amsterdam, Rookmaaker maintained that developments within the visual arts in the early decades of the twentieth century inaugurated a "new era in cultural history."[13] But while modern art perceived and portrayed the death of Western culture, it failed in its analysis of human nature and its destiny from a Christian perspective. A convert to Christianity during World War II, Rookmaaker used his extensive knowledge of modern art to interpret the meaning of the gospel, and to suggest how art could be renewed and become a source of renewal through its encounter with evangelical Christianity.

Rookmaaker's influence has been widespread within evangelical circles where, during the latter decades of the twentieth century, there has been a remarkable interest in the arts. His legacy is reflected within a circle of neo-Calvinist artists and scholars in the United States. Preeminent among them are two philosophers, Nicholas Wolterstorff (formerly of Yale University) and the Canadian Calvin G. Seerveld. Both recognize the need to overcome the gap between "high" and "popular" art, and to recover the role of art as integral to what it means to be human and to live life fully as a Christian. Hence, for Wolterstorff, to understand art it is necessary to understand life, and to recognize works of art "as instruments and objects of action."[14] There is a need, both Wolterstorff and Seerveld argue, to recover a Christian aesthetic and appreciation for the arts, not just for enjoyment, contemplation, and delight (something of great importance), but also as a source of glorifying God and for the sake of the just transformation of society. Thus art, aesthetic sensibility, doxology, and creativity are essential elements within the everyday life of the Christian.

We return to Dillenberger's typology, and specifically to his fourth set of theological models that he labels "alternative," within which he includes liberation and feminist theologies. Although he only makes a passing reference to them, this serves as a reminder that the dominant models of twentieth-century theology in the West are not the only ones. For this reason the description "alternative" is not helpful, for it conveys a Eurocentric set of assumptions about both art and theology, as well as their relationship. If we are to do justice to our theme we have to take into account the plurality of theological approaches that proliferated as the century reached its climax, many of them located beyond the boundaries of Western theology and art and their respective canons. With this in mind, we may venture to suggest that the story of theology and the visual arts during the course of the twenty-first century will be significantly different to the one that we have told thus far. So let us consider some of the contours that have emerged and are most likely to shape the next phase in the engagement of theology and the visual arts.

Issues and an Agenda

The engagement

There are encouraging signs that theologians are heeding the call to make the visual arts intrinsic to their task and becoming aware of the importance of aesthetics. Yet there is a long way to go before this becomes as integral to doing theology as, let us say, engagement with philosophy or the social sciences. So some comments on how this engagement may develop, on several complementary levels, is necessary. One level is that of theologians developing an informed knowledge of the visual arts in the same way as they usually do of other disciplines and fields of inquiry and praxis. This requires, at least, that the subject become an integral part of theological education. Another level is engaging in dialogue with artists around their work, exploring issues of mutual concern for themselves and for the wider society. In doing so, theologians and artists may well recognize that their roles are not dissimilar and often mutually reinforcing, especially as agents of prophetic critique and healing.[15] Yet a further level is that of encouraging and participating in the development of creativity and aesthetic sensitivity in the life of the church. The need is not simply that of awakening a sense of the visual or an appreciation for art, but for theologians to discern how engagement with the visual arts challenges, informs, and enriches the doing of theology as both public and ecclesial discourse. In order for this to happen it is important to recognize that this is not an elitist escape into theological aestheticism, but a way of engaging reality from a different perspective – a perspective that is broken open by the visual as well as other arts.

Artists enable theologians to see things with new eyes, to see things differently. But the engagement is not one sided. If theologians only repeat what the art historians and critics say about the visual they have failed to make the unique contribution to the discussion that derives from Christian faith. In dialogue with the visual arts, theologians bring to the discussion, for example, an understanding of human nature in all its perversity and potential that can critically inform the conversation. Without prescription or presumption, theologians need to engage artists in dialogue around those issues that threaten contemporary society. This task has a particular urgency in an age in which there has been an explosion of image-production not least through the power of advertising in a consumerist global economy.

The fact that theologians do not explicitly engage the visual arts in their work does not necessarily mean that their contribution to the discussion lacks potential for this task. Liberation and feminist theologians, for example, have not been directly involved in dialogue with the visual arts, not because they have no appreciation for the arts, but because of the way in which they have perceived their own agenda. However, once connections are made between art and the struggle for justice, between ugliness and poverty, beauty and redemption, between awakening creativity, renewal, and transformation, between embodiment, representation, and identity, such theologies inject a new dynamic into our subject. Let us briefly focus on some of these themes to illustrate how the engagement may be mutually helpful.

Embodiment

Embodiment is a key category for both theology and the visual arts and, as such, a point of connection between them and therefore between theologians, painters, architects, and sculptors. We experience the vision of the artist through its embodiment, through its incarnation as material reality, for that is the medium through which the visual artist communicates. Likewise, we experience the reality of God through God's embodiment in Christ, through our experience of "the body of Christ," the body of "the other," through whom Christ encounters us, and therefore through our own bodies, our senses. Exploring what this means for theology and the church today in dialogue with the visual arts provides new perspectives and insights concerning the meaning and significance of the Incarnation and the sacramental character of reality, as well as the agonies and ecstasies of human life.

But embodiment is not simply about the material; it is about the creative spirit that shapes and gives life and form to the material, as is evident in all great sculpture. Theologically speaking, we celebrate the body against a false dualism of soul versus body; but Christianity also refuses to make the body a fetish, as in much contemporary culture, which denies the creative and redemptive Spirit that gives life to the body. Embodiment is ambiguous for this very reason, and nowhere is this more evident than in our recognition of the body's limitations and inevitable decay. This ambiguity raises significant questions that need to be addressed. For example, how do we pursue the importance of the visual or of any other sense in a world where so many people have lost the use of their sensual faculties?[16] What do we mean by beauty, given the extent to which beauty is so often associated with the "body beautiful" rather than with that which is evident in weakness and suffering, thereby transcending the body? Or, how and by whom is "the other" to be represented in doing theology or in the visual arts? Let us begin by reflecting on this last question.

Representation

The question of representation is equally critical for visual artists and theologians. Consider, for example, the way in which images are abused in the media in representing "the other" or "the good," whether in the service of consumerism or national and sectarian interests. Or consider the way in which "the other" has generally been represented in colonial literature and art, in theological treatises and polemics. False representation, as in propaganda, is an abuse of the visual, the use of the visual to dehumanize and subjugate. False representation is idolatry, an idolatry that distorts not only the reality of God but also the image of God in humanity and creation. The prohibition of the production of false images of God in the Decalogue is the premise for not abusing "the other" and the creation. How, then, is "the Other," the "Wholly Other," to be represented without distortion, and therefore in a way that does not subjugate the divine to our own purposes?

Theological positions adopted during the Iconoclastic Controversy or in subsequent polemics between Catholics and Protestants were invariably related to cultural issues and social forces of the day, reflecting the current power relations and ideologies. This has always been of concern to iconoclasts who argue that bringing the visual arts into the church and especially images of Christ can so easily confine the church to a particular cultural interpretation of the gospel. Orthodox icons, for example, reflect a particular Byzantine cultural tradition. Some cultural expressions, such as anti-Semitic representations of Jesus, certainly undermine and seriously distort the Christian gospel. But the rejection of visual representation does not necessarily overcome ideological distortions and misrepresentation, for iconoclasts are as prone to that danger as iconophiles. Rhetoric and visual art are equally dangerous in the hands of the ideologue and propagandist.

All art, like all theology, is located within a particular cultural setting, and paradoxically its universal significance derives as much from that fact as from anything else. The gospel is universal in its significance, but it can only be significant for us when it is related to our particular context and culture. The visual arts are important in enabling this process to take place within the church and society precisely because of their power to embody and represent. This presupposes on the part of the artists a concern for truth and integrity. The iconophiles insisted that the Incarnation gave legitimacy to the production of images of Christ and the saints provided that they represented the truth perceived by faith and tradition. Our canvas must necessarily be broader than the Byzantine, but the problem of relating image production to truth remains. How do we represent Christ today amid the clash of competing images that seek to claim our allegiance? How do we represent Christ today in relation to the "religious" or "secular" "other"? But even more, how is Christ represented to us by "the other," and by the artist who expresses the anguish and hope of those who are oppressed? Theologians who engage the visual arts should do so in ways that enable us to see reality from the perspective of those who suffer, are oppressed, or are different in other ways from us.

The visual arts serve as antennae of culture, enabling us to come to a greater appreciation of the many cultures around the world that increasingly interact with each other. Western theologians would do well to remember that some of the great advances in both theology and the arts have come about as a result of the interaction of cultures. One significant side effect of the missionary expansion of Christianity into many different cultural contexts has been a flowering of good religious art that expresses the biblical narrative as well as the meaning of faith, reconciliation, and hope in the idiom of those cultures. This is an important resource for theological reflection in its attempt to relate to cultural and religious pluralism today, providing as it does a window of opportunity for theologians to explore the riches of other cultural and religious traditions through their art works. In doing so, theologians along with artists should reconsider what is meant by taste and beauty, that is, they need to learn how to exercise aesthetic judgment.

Taste and beauty

Awakened sensibility assumes the development of good taste. This is not a subject that is normally talked about by theologians, nor do preachers recognize that bad taste, as Frank Burch Brown has reminded us, is sinful.[17] Such a notion might appear outlandish and elitist, and yet on reflection bad taste is a moral liability whereas good taste, properly understood, generates human community and helps us express the glory of God.[18] Bad taste, as Brown helps us to understand it, is akin to sloth, pride, intolerance, and idolatry, whereas good taste is analogous to our experience of holiness and healing. So the formation of good taste does not mean simply developing an appreciation for "fine" art in the Western tradition, but an appreciation for good art rather than the banal and mediocre.

This brings us to the importance of developing an adequate theological aesthetics as an integral element in doing theology in dialogue with the visual arts. As we have noted previously, the two tasks are distinct yet, as Edward Farley reminds us in *Faith and Beauty*, it would be rather strange if theological aesthetics ignored the arts.[19] Farley's own contribution to the discussion is particularly important in highlighting the connection between beauty and ethical self-transcendence, and doing so in a way that helps rescue the arts from simply functioning as pedagogical devices in the interests of the church.

The importance of beauty as the key category in aesthetic theory was recovered during the twentieth century and, largely through the influence of von Balthasar, it has reentered theological discourse. This has helped us discern the true character of beauty as distinct from its parodies that are so evident in contemporary culture. True beauty attracts us in ways that transform and humanize, providing intimations of transcendence within the material and mundane. False beauty seduces us in ways that dehumanize and destroy. True beauty is inseparably connected to both good-ness and truth, and each of these transcendentals, as Plato called them, needs the others. Without beauty, truth and goodness lose their power to attract and therefore redeem, but without ethical self-transcendence, without goodness and truth, beauty becomes seductive and destructive. Beauty as conveyed through the arts can become a way of encountering God.[20]

If the crucified Christ, an image without beauty and one associated with criminality and death, is at the center of Christian theology, and if for the eyes of faith this event has become redemptive and therefore beautiful, then our understanding of beauty has to be radically revised. Much modern art has been a protest against seductive beauty and for this reason has employed the ugly as a way to shock us into recognition of its banality and danger. But ugliness in itself has no power to redeem and renew life and humanity; it may be good as a tool for protest but it is not helpful for healing. Central to Christian theological aesthetics is a theology of the cross that enables us to discern the relationship between ugliness as indicative of sinfulness, and therefore a focus of protest, and beauty as redemptive, and therefore integral to the gospel and the witness of the church in the world. For while beauty gives pleasure, and must always be understood to do so, it is not pleasure oblivious to the plight and suffering of others, but rather a pleasure that evokes passion.

Creativity, art, and transformation

There are many people in all societies whose poverty keeps them in bondage to ugly environments that crush their creativity just as they crush their bodies, and whose lack of resources and education prevents them from developing an appreciation for art. At the same time, through discovering their creative abilities, people are enabled to rise above their circumstances and contribute not only to their own well-being but also to the healing of their communities. In this and other ways art can con-tribute to social liberation and transformation, something demonstrated in the struggle against apartheid in South Africa and now in enabling people to respond to the HIV/AIDS pandemic. In like manner, the development of aesthetic awareness and creativity in the life of the church is an essential element in its life, witness, and renewal.

The renewal of the church is always the work of the Holy Spirit. The Spirit is the Spirit of creativity, calling forth gifts within the life of the people of God and enabling their use. From that perspective, creativity and the awakening of aesthetic sensibility begin to emerge in times when the church is open to the Spirit and to the renewal that the Spirit brings. This is not the same as an awakening of interest in the arts. Rather, it is the awakening of creativity and aesthetic awareness in such a way that the various art forms are appreciated and allowed to develop organically within the life of the church. In this way the visual arts become an integral part of the worship and mission of the church, having a liturgical coherency and theological significance that is otherwise not possible. But the awakening of aesthetic awareness and creativity is about more than producing art for the church's own benefit. It is about producing Christian artists whose work will contribute to the well-being of society.[21] Such considerations have considerable implications for theologians engaged with the visual arts, and for the theological formation of ministers, priests, and the church as a whole.

The most obvious form of visual art that relates to the church is architecture, for it is through its embodiment in brick and mortar, concrete, steel, and glass, amid the other structures of village, town, and city, that the church gives visible evidence of its presence. The church building is, in this sense, a mediating structure between the liturgy and the public square. Of course, the church as the "people of God" is visibly present in many other ways in society, for the church as such is not the building in which the church as "people of God" worship. Yet there is a connection between the two, for the building within which the liturgy occurs provides both the internal space for that event and the external face as representation of what is taking place and what it means. *How* the building *represents* the church as a living, witnessing community to the world outside is part of what the church is attempting to say to the world about its reason for existence.

Equally important is the creation of the space within which the liturgy takes place and in which, to go one step further, other appropriate works of art may be situated. This is a critical issue for discussion between the church's theologians and artists. Art works do not have to be imported into the life of the congregation, nor do they have to be produced by distinguished professional artists. Appropriate art in the life of the church arises out of its own life of faith and witness. The church building is not meant to be an art gallery or museum, but a place of worship, and therefore one that should enable praise and the preaching of the gospel. Yet, within these boundaries of appropriateness, there is an important place for art produced by the great artists of our time and therefore a need to overcome the alienation from the church that so many artists experience. Helping to overcome this alienation is a task in which theologians can and should play a key role.

Notes

1 Karl Rahner, "Theology and the Arts," *Thought* 57, No. 224 (March 1982): 24.
2 P. T. Forsyth, *Religion in Recent Art* (London: Hodder and Stoughton, 1905), 145.
3 See James Luther Adams, *Paul Tillich's Philosophy of Culture, Science and Religion* (New York: Schocken Books, 1965), 66.
4 G. K. A. Bell, *Christianity and World Order* (London: Penguin Books, 1940), 57.
5 Ibid, 146ff.
6 See David Brown and Ann Loades (eds.) *The Sense of the Sacramental: Movement and Measure in Art and Music, Place and Time* (London: SPCK, 1995).
7 Nathan Scott, Jr., "Art and the Renewal of Human Sensibility in Mass Culture," in Finley Eversole (ed.), *Christian Faith and the Contemporary Arts* (New York: Abingdon, 1957), 21–9.

8 John Dillenberger, *A Theology of Artistic Sensibilities: The Visual Arts and the Church* (London: SCM Press, 1986), x.
9 Ibid, 248.
10 John W. de Gruchy, *Christianity and the Modernization of South Africa*, Christianity and the Social History of South Africa, Vol. 2 (Cape Town: David Philip, 2000), 111–21.
11 Dillenberger, *A Theology of Artistic Sensibilities*, 221.
12 Ibid, 226–7.
13 H. R. Rookmaaker, *Modern Art and the Death of a Culture* (Wheaton, IL: Crossway Books, 1994), 131.
14 Nicholas Wolterstorff, *Art in Action* (Grand Rapids, MI: Eerdmans, 1980), 69.
15 See Deborah J. Haynes, *The Vocation of the Artist* (Cambridge: Cambridge University Press, 1997).

16 See T. J. Gorringe, *The Education of Desire* (London: SCM Press, 2001).

17 Frank Burch Brown, *Religious Aesthetics: A Theological Study of Making and Meaning* (Princeton, NJ: Princeton University Press, 1989), 136.

18 Ibid, 146.

19 Edward Farley, *Faith and Beauty: A Theological Aesthetic* (Aldershot: Ashgate, 2001), 110.

20 See Richard Viladesau, *Theology and the Arts: Encountering God Through Music, Art and Rhetoric* (New York: Paulist Press, 2000).

21 See Hilary Brand and Adrienne Chaplin (eds.) *Art and Soul: Signposts for Christians in the Arts* (Carlisle: Paternoster Press, 1999).

Bibliography

Apostolos-Cappadona, D. (ed.) *Art, Creativity, and the Sacred* (New York: Crossroad, 1995).

Begbie, J. S. *Voicing Creation's Praise: Towards a Theology of the Arts* (Edinburgh: T. & T. Clark, 1991).

Brown, F. B. *Religious Aesthetics* (Princeton, NJ: Princeton University Press, 1989).

De Gruchy, John W. *Christianity, Art and Transformation* (Cambridge: Cambridge University Press, 2001).

Dillenberger, J. *A Theology of Artistic Sensibilities* (London: SCM Press, 1986).

—— *Style and Content in Christian Art* (New York: Crossroad, 1988).

Finney, P. C. (ed.) *Seeing Beyond the Word: Visual Arts and the Calvinist Tradition* (Grand Rapids, MI: Eerdmans, 1995).

García-Rivera, A. *The Community of the Beautiful: A Theological Aesthetics* (Collegeville, MN: Liturgical Press, 1999).

Hammond, P. *Liturgy and Architecture* (London: Barrie and Rockcliff, 1960).

Haynes, D. J. *The Vocation of the Artist* (Cambridge: Cambridge University Press, 1997).

Morgan, D. *Visual Piety* (Berkeley: University of California Press, 1998).

Ouspensky, L. *Theology of the Icon* (Crestwood, NY: St. Vladimir's Seminary Press, 1978).

Rookmaker, H. *Modern Art and the Death of a Culture* (Leicester: Intervarsity Fellowship, 1970).

Schloeder, S. J. *Architecture in Communion* (San Francisco: Ignatius Press, 1988).

Seerveld, C. *Rainbows for a Fallen World* (Toronto: Tuppence Press, 1980).

Viladesau, R. *Theology and the Arts* (New York: Paulist Press, 2000).

Von Balthasar, H. U. *The Glory of the Lord*, 3 Vols. (Edinburgh: T. & T. Clark, 1982–6).

Walker, K. *Images or Idols?* (Norwich: Canterbury Press, 1996).

Wolterstorff, N. *Art in Action* (Grand Rapids, MI: Eerdmans, 1980).

Zuidervaart, L. and Luttikhuizen, H. (eds.) *Pledges of Jubilee: Essays on the Arts and Culture, in Honor of Calvin G. Seerveld* (Grand Rapids, MI: Eerdmans, 1995).

Theology and Music

Jeremy S. Begbie

Introduction: A Notable Silence

In modern theology, music is conspicuous by its absence. The theology and literature interface is well served and the same increasingly applies to other art forms, not least the visual arts. But music has attracted little attention. Although a number of musicologists have made courageous forays into theology,[1] few theologians have repaid the compliment.[2]

In some respects this is puzzling, given the supposedly limitless interests of theology, the universality of music in all cultures, the unprecedented availability and ubiquity of music in the West, the persistence of music in the worship of the church, the intense interest shown in music by many philosophers, the growing literature on the politics, sociology, and psychology of music, the recent emergence of ethnomusicology, and the deployment of musical metaphors by natural scientists. Moreover, the theological tradition has reared those with strong musical interests – Augustine, Luther, and Calvin are three outstanding examples. Nevertheless, more often than not, and certainly in modern times, the theologian's stance toward music has been characterized by hesitation and suspicion, with the result that what theological attention music has been given has habitually gravitated toward ethics, and the moral propriety of this or that form of music.

Doubtless, there are factors at work here that apply to virtually all the arts: the church's fear of idolatry, an anxiety about the arts' materiality, the seeming triviality of the arts compared to more pressing life-and-death issues, the fact that the church is no longer a major agent of artistic renewal, the wane of explicitly religious symbolism in the arts, and a cast of mind which tends to isolate the arts and marginalize them in favor of other spheres of human endeavor. With regard to music in particular, its powerful emotional appeal is still often the cause of much fear, not least among Christians. Music's notorious inability to "refer" with precision and stability to extra-musical objects and states of affairs makes many dubious about its ability to be "truth-bearing." Moreover, music's transience would also seem to be theologically problematic (where is the symphony when the last chord ceases?), especially insofar as theology is thought to deal with matters which are enduring and abiding.

Added to all this, there is the sheer difficulty of speaking about music in ways that do justice to its appeal and that genuinely shed new light upon it. The long but uneasy marriage between music and language in history reveals at once the affinity between the two and language's limitations. Given Christianity's commitment to words, music presents an irksome challenge to theology, for it can be an impressive means of Christian communication yet at the same time stubbornly resistant to being captured linguistically. As George Steiner observes: "In the face of music, the wonders of language are also its frustrations."[3]

Two Recent Contributions

Whatever the reasons, a modern "theology of music" – that is, a sustained attempt to situate music within a Christian theological framework – is still to be written. Recently, however, some moves in this direction have been made.

Albert Blackwell, Professor of Religion at Furman University, South Carolina, in his wide-ranging and substantial book *The Sacred in Music*, has sought to demonstrate the "sacramental potential" of music.[4] "Sacramental" can be applied to "any finite reality through which the divine is perceived to be disclosed and communicated, and through which our human response to the divine assumes some measure of shape, form, and structure."[5] Blackwell cites Luther as summing up his book's thesis: "in music we may taste with wonder, though never comprehend, the wisdom of God."[6] Two wide sacramental traditions in Christianity are delineated: the "Pythagorean" and the "Incarnational." The former stresses intellectual appreciation, finding the grace of God through contemplating invisible objects of our understanding as well as the subjects of our own thought. The ancient Pythagorean musical vision was at root mathematical and intellectual: music serves the mind's apprehension of the harmony of the universe, a harmony that can be expressed in ratios or proportions. For Blackwell, insofar as music is grounded in sonic principles embedded in the world, music can elicit a basic "trust in cosmic order" which in Christian terms "contributes to trust in the second Person of the Trinity," the Logos of the world. In this way, music can mediate and disclose the divine. The second, "incarnational" tradition stresses the sensed materiality of divine disclosure. It grows out of encounters with the divine in the physical world perceived through the senses: the perceptible sounds of music, as sensed realities, can act as vehicles of divine encounter. Blackwell believes this tradition is an essential "counterpoise" to the silent, abstract, and cerebral contemplation characteristic of the first tradition.

Aware that his broad sacramental outlook might overlook the darker dimensions of life, in a series of extended reflections on the fall, Blackwell argues that music is not only caught up in the ambiguities that sin generates, but that it also has at its disposal distinctive resources to give expression to life's "terrible beauty": tonal tension, harmonic dissonance, acoustical interference, and minor modes. Moreover, he believes that the beauty of music "can help to save a fallen world."[7] This is claimed while acknowledging the danger of drawing simple and easy connections between music and goodness, truth and beauty. Music is to be celebrated as a gift of God's general grace (as an outgrowth of natural acoustical phenomena), a gift of special grace (as a medium of human creativity), and as a gift of saving grace (an aid to human salvation). As saving, music can be a vehicle of healing and harmony (individual, social, and cosmic). The final chapter of Blackwell's book reveals his deep legacy to Christian traditions of mystical experience (as well as his debt to Schleiermacher): he testifies to the importance of music's power to outstrip verbal language and act as a "sacramental vessel" for worship.

In a number of writings, Jeremy Begbie (the present author) attempts to outline a vision somewhat more theologically focused than Blackwell, but with a similarly broad cosmic scope.[8] I seek to set music in a Christological and trinitarian context, believing that this is sorely needed in the current (post)modern climate. Crucial for me is the doctrine of creation out of nothing, and with it a stress on the liberty of the creation in its contingent but ordered (and beautiful) otherness. Creation flows from the free love of God, in which I posit another reality with its own distinctive integrity, which is neither God (and therefore not to be worshiped) nor chaotic matter (and therefore to be respected in its own dynamic orderliness). God's unconditional commitment to the created physical world is radically reaffirmed through the Incarnation, when the Son, through whom all things were made, assumes human flesh. In this very physical life, matter is assumed, judged, and, on the third day, raised to a new mode of being, prefiguring "the new heaven and new earth." This divine creating and vindication of the physical world carries an immense encouragement for the musician to treat it as a proper, meaningful environment to enjoy and explore, worthy of attention, cultivation, and adornment.

In this environment, making music can be seen as part of the human vocation, as God's image-bearers in the world, to "voice creation's praise," to extend and elaborate the praise which creation already sings to God. Sin is a refusal to praise God, an honoring of the creation rather than Creator. True praise is restored and raised to a new level through the incarnate Son: as one of us, he offers a life of unbroken praise, even to the point of death on a cross where the consequences of humanity's refusal of God are fully borne and taken away. Our original vocation as God's image-bearers can advance again, now with a redeeming dimension. Through the risen Christ, in the Spirit, humanity is freed to interact with the created world to the glory of the Father: physical reality is neither ignored nor overridden, but enabled to take on new, hopefully richer, meaningful forms, anticipating the final re-creation of all things.

Music, then, in my view, is first and foremost a distinctive way of returning praise to God. I offer a number of practical outworkings of such a vision.[9] At the very least, it entails respecting the world's "sonic order," the physical integrities of sounds and their dynamic interrelatedness, calling forth an attitude of perceptive trust. It encourages us to take seriously the mediation of music through our own bodies. It is vigilant about the dangers of deifying music (a perennial temptation in modernity, not least in worship): music is not the sound of God, but the sound of the created order praising God.[10] Because it is a vision pivoting around the cross and resurrection, it entails taking radical evil with great seriousness – avoiding musical sentimentality, kitsch, and any attempt to diminish the horror of the tragic by reducing it to an appearance or subsuming it too quickly into a harmonious whole – and at the same time viewing music as (potentially) a way of sharing in the renewal of the spoiled creation, and thus as a foretaste of its ultimate transformation.[11]

Two Musical Theologians

Although theologies of music may be scarce, there have been theologians who, without treating music at length, have nevertheless found themselves drawing naturally and extensively upon music to further and enrich their pursuits. This can go far beyond embellishing some theological truth that is already known and clearly delineated. Musical practices, together with their second-order discourses, can act as unique and powerful media of theological discovery and articulation.[12] In modern times, the two figures who stand out most strikingly in this respect are Karl Barth and Dietrich Bonhoeffer.

Karl Barth

"I even have to confess that if I ever get to heaven, I would first seek out Mozart, and only then inquire after Augustine, St. Thomas, Luther, Calvin, and Schleiermacher."[13]

Barth's extravagant devotion to Mozart, amounting almost to an obsession, is legendary. Records of Mozart accompanied his daily meditations before he set to work on whatever issue was occupying him in the steady accumulation of the *Church Dogmatics*. Why did he believe this composer deserved a central place in theology, "especially in the doctrine of creation and also in eschatology"?[14] Why was he so certain that when the angels praise God they play only Bach, but that together *en famille* they play Mozart and God listens with special pleasure?[15]

Barth's treatment of Mozart in *Church Dogmatics* III: 3 offers the best way in. Here he contends that Mozart's music embodies and gives voice to the authentic praise of creation, and creation precisely *as* created – limited and finite. A fulsome eulogy on Mozart appears in the midst of a discussion of the "shadowside (*Schattenseite*)" or negative aspect of the universe.[16] He is not entirely precise here as to what this "shadowside" is, but comparison with a later passage makes it probable that he is thinking of finitude and all its effects (including death), the quality of having been created out of nothing and therefore always being on the verge of collapsing back into non-existence.[17]

Barth is especially keen to distinguish the shadowside from evil (*Das Nichtige*). Failure to do this both masks the destructive nature of evil and might suggest that finitude is intrinsically fallen. The shadowside is the expression of God's "positive will, election and activity."[18] In this context, Mozart's music is presented as singing the praise of the cosmos in its "total goodness," *including* its shadowside. The music does indeed contain its "No," but this is the "No" of the shadowside, not evil.[19] What does it matter if Mozart died in misery like an "unknown soldier," Barth asks, "when a life is permitted simply and unpretentiously, and therefore serenely, authentically and impressively, to express the good creation of God, *which also includes the limitation and end of man*?"[20] Mozart heard the harmony of creation in which "the shadow is not darkness, deficiency is not defeat, sadness cannot become despair, trouble cannot degenerate into tragedy and infinite melancholy is not ultimately forced to claim undisputed sway."[21] Mozart even acknowledges the limit of death. But he heard the negative only in and with the positive: the overriding impression and impact of the music, for Barth, is God's almighty "Yes" to creation. Here creation praises God *in its very finitude* and thus demonstrates what authentic praise truly is.

Confirming this, later Barth speaks of the difference between the shadowside and *Das Nichtige* – when the creature "crosses the frontier" of finitude, "nothingness achieves its actuality in the created world."[22] This is just what Mozart's music does not do. It does not try to be divine. Nor does Mozart: he does not obtrude himself in some "mania for self-expression,"[23] or try to force a "message" on the listener.[24] He does not "*will* to proclaim the praise of God. He just does it – precisely in that humility in which he himself is, so to speak, only the instrument with which he allows us to hear what he hears: what surges at him from God's creation, what rises in him, and must proceed from him."[25] "He simply offered himself as the agent by which little bits of horn, metal and catgut could serve as the voices of creation."[26] This, for Barth, is what gives Mozart's music its "freedom," its effortless and light quality.[27]

These reflections can be grasped more fully and seen to have wider significance if we turn to the much disputed passages on "parables of the kingdom" and the "lights" of creation in *Church Dogmatics* IV: 3.[28] Here Barth claims that Jesus Christ, as the one true Word of God, bears testimony to himself and to his work of reconciliation by calling forth "parables" that witness to his glory – not only in the Bible and the church, but also in spheres where God is not explicitly acknowledged. Such "signs" and "attestations" are provisional, secondary, and eschatological, pointing to the unique and paradigmatic primacy of revelation and reconciliation in Christ. David Moseley has convincingly argued that the unmentioned figure haunting these discussions is Mozart, and that these sections of the *Dogmatics* and Barth's perspective on Mozart are mutually illuminating.[29] Barth was writing the material on "parables" at roughly the same time as he was working on his Mozart Bicentenary pieces, which use the phrase "parables of the kingdom" to describe the theological status of Mozart's music. Further, reading Barth's comments on Mozart along with his treatment of "parables of the kingdom" helps us to see that there is no U-turn on "natural theology" in the later sections of the *Dogmatics* (as is sometimes supposed) – for in Barth's world, no music (not even Mozart's) in and of itself could ever have become an independent, let alone normative, source of revelation. Although Barth could speak of Mozart's music as "theology," a "miraculous" phenomenon akin to "revelation," "mediating" the constant praise of the cosmos, he understood this to be possible only in conformity with scripture and the proclaimed gospel. The methodological primacy given to God's reconciling self-disclosure in Christ is just as strong as in his earlier work. In addition, Moseley suggests that Barth's musical experience shaped his thought in wider fronts: his understanding of freedom, play, creaturely reality, and time.[30]

There is evidence, then, to suggest that music was "woven in" to Barth's theology in quite profound ways. To spend too long arguing about whether or not Barth is actually *right* about Mozart is to risk missing this more important matter. Without any lessening of his passion for methodological rigor, music (especially Mozart's) is being allowed to provide its own particular kind of theological witness to the grace of God in Jesus Christ.

Dietrich Bonhoeffer

Unlike Barth, Bonhoeffer was an accomplished musician, and though he left us with no essay or book on music, there are scattered references to music throughout his works.[31] But it is in his last writings that music arises most frequently. Imprisoned for his part in a plot to assassinate Hitler, he struggles among other things with the question of who Jesus Christ is for us today, and what shape concrete obedience to Christ should take in the complexities of his time. Music emerges repeatedly in the discussion.

He has no radio or gramophone. Apart from music heard very distantly in and beyond the prison, he is conscious only of the music embedded in his memory: "the music we hear inwardly can almost surpass, if we really concentrate on it, what we hear physically."[32] A letter to his parents shows the impact and importance of his musical memory:

> For years now I've associated [the *Mass in B Minor*] with this particular day [Repentance Day, November 17], like the St. Matthew Passion with Good Friday. I remember the evening when I first heard it. I was eighteen, and had just come from Harnack's seminar, in which he had discussed my first seminar essay very kindly, and had expressed hope that some day I should specialize in church history. I was full of this when I went into the Philharmonic Hall; the great *Kyrie Eleison* was just beginning, and as it did so, I forgot everything else – the effect was indescribable. Today I'm going through it, bit by bit, in my mind, and I'm glad the Schleichers can hear it, as it's my favorite work of Bach.[33]

However, music does more than provide memories to sustain him in his meager existence. It exemplifies a dimension of living Bonhoeffer believed the church needed to recover. In his earlier work, Bonhoeffer had spoken of Christ's relation to the world in terms of four divine "mandates" or commands – labor, marriage, government, and the church[34] – and music is counted under the mandate of labor. In *Letters and Papers from Prison* he locates music in "the broad area of freedom," which embraces art, culture, friendship, and play. He writes:

> I wonder whether it is possible . . . to regain the idea of the church as providing an understanding of the area of freedom (art, education, friendship, play), so that Kierkegaard's "aesthetic existence" would not be banished from the church's sphere, but would be reestablished within it.[35]

Bonhoeffer, it seems, wanted to rehabilitate the aesthetic in the church, and its sheer gratuitousness is what impresses him most. The things belonging to the realm of "freedom" we do, not in order to achieve a particular end or goal, or because they are necessary, but just for the joy of doing them.

This, of course, could be read as a form of aesthetic escapism. That Bonhoeffer has nothing of the sort in mind is clear if we go on to consider his deepest engagement with music in *Letters and Papers*, when he allows music to stimulate particular types of theological discourse: indeed, he often appears to be *thinking musically*.[36] Now removed from the political maelstrom, this key dimension of his life, internalized through memory, is being allowed to play a quite distinctive role in mediating and shaping his theology. This is especially clear in the use he makes of the musical metaphor of polyphony. He ponders the fragmentary character of wartime Germany and the fierce struggle to live responsibly as a Christian: "The longer we are uprooted from our professional activities and our private lives, the more we feel how fragmentary our lives are, compared with those of our parents."[37] But this very fragmentariness

> may, in fact, point towards a fulfillment beyond the limits of human achievement; I have to keep that in mind, particularly in view of the death of so many of the best of my former pupils. Even if the pressure of outward events may split our lives into fragments, like bombs falling on houses, we must do our best to keep in view how the whole was planned and thought out.[38]

Speaking of the individual as a fragment, he writes: "The important thing today is that we should be able to discern from the fragment of our life how the whole was arranged and planned, and what material it consists of. For really, there are some fragments that are only worth throwing into the dustbin." But there are others "whose importance lasts for centuries, because their completion can only be a matter for God, and so they are fragments that must be fragments – I'm thinking, e.g., of the *Art of Fugue*."[39] Bach died before completing this polyphonic *tour de force*. It weaves a musical tapestry of fierce intricacy, but eventually dissipates on an empty page.

This links with comments Bonhoeffer makes in earlier letters. Many of the allusions to music in *Letters and Papers from Prison* concern Heinrich Schütz (1585–1672), whose music Bonhoeffer came to know well. Writing of Schütz's setting of the hymn "O bone Jesu" (a hymn so important to Bonhoeffer that he asked for it at his funeral), he sketches out some of the musical notes in his letter, and asks: "Doesn't this passage, in its ecstatic longing combined with pure devotion, suggest the 'bringing again' of all earthly desire?" The allusion is to the gathering up, the recapitulation of all things in Christ envisaged in Ephesians 1: 10 – "a magnificent conception, full of comfort."[40] Nothing of value on that day will be lost; all things – including our earthly desires, our longings and yearnings – will somehow find their proper transformation. Bonhoeffer's own adult life, now heading toward death, and the "broken up" quality of his prison writings resonate with this poignantly. There is a sense that a completion, and thus some kind of "making sense," will be granted by God, easing the anxiety about the unfinished character of his life now. Like the *Art of Fugue*,

> if we accumulate, at least for a short time, a wealth of themes and weld them into a harmony in which the great counterpoint is maintained from start to finish, so that at last, when it breaks off abruptly, we can sing no more than the chorale, "I come before thy throne," we will not bemoan the fragmentariness of our life, but rather rejoice in it.[41]

Elsewhere, he coins the term "polyphony of life," centering around a *cantus firmus* (the principal or central theme that winds its way through a piece of medieval polyphony, providing coherence and enabling the other parts to flourish):

God wants us to love him eternally with our whole hearts – not in such a way as to weaken our earthly love, but to provide a kind of *cantus firmus* to which the other melodies of life provide their counterpoint. One of these contrapuntal themes . . . is earthly affection. Even in the Bible we have the Song of Songs; and really one can imagine no more ardent, passionate, sensual love than is portrayed there (see 7: 6). It's a good thing that the book is in the Bible, in face of all those who believe that the restraint of passion is Christian.

If the *cantus firmus* is secure, we need not fear the other voices: "Where the *cantus firmus* is clear and plain, the counterpoint can be developed to its limits." Bonhoeffer reads the relation between the *cantus firmus* – love of God – and the surrounding counterpoint – earthly affection – in terms of the divine and human in Christ: "The two are 'undivided and yet distinct,' in the words of the Chalcedonian Definition, like Christ in his divine and human natures." He asks: "May not the attraction and importance of polyphony in music consist in its being a musical reflection of this Christological fact and therefore of our *vita christiana*?" A diversity of loves and desires can flourish around a firm *cantus firmus*, everything depending upon having the *cantus firmus* in place:

I wanted to tell you to have a good, clear, *cantus firmus*, that is the only way to a full and perfect sound, when the counterpoint has a firm support and can't come adrift or get out of tune, while remaining a distinct whole in its own right. Only a polyphony of this kind can give life a wholeness and at the same time assure us that nothing calamitous can happen as long as the *cantus firmus* is kept going.

In a letter of the next day he speaks of pain and joy as two elements in life's polyphony. And to Bethge, who is enjoying a good deal more freedom and opportunity, he writes: "I do want you to be *glad* about what you have; it really *is* the polyphony of life."[42] The same circle of ideas emerges in later letters: he notices how some of his fellow prisoners find it hard to harbor conflicting emotions at the same time:

When bombers come, they are all fear; when there is something nice to eat, they are all despair; when they are successful, they can think of nothing else. *They miss the fulness of life* . . . everything objective and subjective is dissolved for them into fragments. By contrast, *Christianity puts us into many different dimensions of life at the same time* . . . life isn't pushed back into a single dimension, but is kept multi-dimensional and polyphonous.[43]

It is hard not to think of Bonhoeffer's own life at this time as richly polyphonic – his engagement to Maria, his contact with friends and family, staff and inmates. In addition to theology he is also writing fiction, drama, and poetry, and reading history, poetry, science, novels, philosophy, and much else besides. And throughout he is writing theology.

In sum, Bonhoeffer's experience of music seems to have a large part in generating and articulating that vision of the Christian life which so concerned him in the prison years – an intensely Christological vision of a "this-worldly" life, which refuses any evasion of the concrete and practical, a confident, joyful, multi-dimensional kind of living where a huge diversity of interests, concerns, passions, and activities can flourish around the *cantus firmus* – the love of God.

Musical Theology

Barth and Bonhoeffer clearly show that music can contribute to theology as much as benefit from it. In both cases, music provoked and provided fertile conceptual resources. The economist Jacques Attali declares: "Music is more than an object of study: it is a way of perceiving the world."[44] Arguably, a substantial agenda opens up for theologians when music is treated in this way (far more extensive than Barth and Bonhoeffer realized) – when music is approached as a set of practices enabling *perception* and *disclosure*, in addition to expression and communication. Space forbids more than a brief glance at three areas meriting further exploration, concentrating mainly on the "tonal" tradition, which has dominated Western music for the past three hundred years.

Musical time and salvation

In the West, especially since the seventeenth century, music of all sorts has generally operated according to teleological principles. That is, it typically possesses a dynamic order which is sensed or perceived as directional, leading to some kind of goal or goals. We sense it is "going somewhere." It makes us *want* future sounds, or at least, expect them. This teleological dynamic is engendered mainly through the twin elements of tension and resolution. Tensions are set up which demand some form of resolution (even if the resolution is extended or delayed). Configurations of tension and resolution work in many different ways and levels, often engaging every parameter of music – melody, metre, pitch, timbre, etc. One of the commonest is harmonic tension and resolution, when certain chords (such as the dominant seventh) are used to arouse a sense of incompleteness and anticipation, this tension being resolved by more stable chords.

The theological resonances of these patterns are striking and instructive, and might go at least part of the way towards explaining why music has been so pervasively employed by the church in its celebration of God's saving work. For example, because music operates by making us wait for resolutions, it can school us in a concentrated way in the biblical art of *patience*. One of the crucial skills of any composer is ordering the dynamic "space" between tension and resolution, deferring gratification but in such a way that hope in the assured resolution is sustained. Israel's faith might be characterized as one enormous upbeat spanning the centuries, in a continual, though varied state of patient tension. In the New Testament the tension is resolved in Christ but also heightened, for through the Spirit we know the final completion and are yet made to wait for its full climax: "For the creation waits with eager longing . . . if we hope for what we do not see, we wait for it with patience" (Romans 8: 19, 25). This waiting, because it lives "in between" promise and fulfillment, in a "meantime" charged with hope, need not be empty or void. Music grants us a "meantime" which is not a bland, homogeneous and inert state, nor a period of stoical resigned fortitude, but one which is fulsome and enriching. At its best – and there is much church music which singularly fails to do this – music invites us to discover a kind of patience which enlarges and deepens us in the very waiting. In effect, music says to us: "There are things you will learn only by passing through this process, by being caught up in this series of relations and transformations."[45] In the New Testament, patience is often associated with growth in steadfastness and faith through perseverance in the midst of opposition (see, for example, Hebrews 11). In the patience proper to salvation something new is learned that cannot be learned in any other way.

Music can also be highly instructive in offering the experience of hope being intensified through multiple fulfillments. As in scripture, so in a piece of music, not every resolution is delayed, otherwise we would simply lose patience and interest. We are given partial resolutions of varying degrees of settledness. These provisional realizations, far from diminishing expectation and longing, serve to intensify them. The pattern is most clearly seen in musical metre (the patterns of beats underlying music). Metre operates at different levels, creating a hierarchy of waves of tension and resolution. A move towards resolution at one level will increase the tension on a higher wave at a higher level. However strong the sense of resolution may be at any particular level, there will always be a higher level (or levels) in relation to which every resolution process generates a heightening of tension, giving rise to a stronger reaching out for further resolution. This is how music makes us "want more" of itself. The correspondences between this and the character of Jewish and Christian hope are remarkable and hardly need to be pointed out. Fulfillments *both* ease tension *and* intensify it. The coming of Christ is a *resolution* on the level of the collective hopes of Israel; at other levels, supremely in the overarching purposes of God, it functions as a spur towards *yet more fervent longing* for a final resolution of the promise originally given to Abraham. Arguably, numerous problems in eschatology have arisen through too great a reliance on linear models, and a failure to think in terms of a multi-leveled temporal process. (The widespread belief that a "fulfillment" can only properly take place in one singular event is a good example.) In music's metrical structure, the multi-leveled character of Christian hope is enacted, embodied in sound, and rendered lucid; in turn, this can encourage patterns of thinking far more true to the shape of biblical hope than in the over-linear models so often employed.[46]

Musical space: Trinitarian Christology

Another basic characteristic of most of the music we hear is that it combines two or more notes. Certainly, much music in history has not mixed its notes – Gregorian plainsong, for example. Nevertheless, the majority of music we encounter in the West today involves at least two notes being played or sung at once. An obvious feature of the perception of two sounds is that they do not occupy bounded zones in our aural field. Unlike two colors, which cannot be visible in the same space *as* two colors, sounds can be heard in and through each other while remaining perceptually distinct. Two notes fill the same heard "space," yet we can hear them *as* two notes. They need not hide each other, nor merge.

This simultaneity in the perception of sound can offer a powerful challenge to some of the habitual modes of thinking that have come to dominate much theology, especially those that rely excessively on the eye. The Council of Chalcedon's Christo-logical statement (451 CE) is a case in point. Whatever its strengths, a common criticism of Chalcedon is that it is too "static," presenting a picture of two "natures" – divine and human – sitting alongside each other, juxtaposed uneasily in a single individual, Jesus Christ. Whatever its strengths, and whatever the qualifications that are quite properly made about Chalcedon, the question of how an infinite, omni-present, omniscient God can co-habit with a limited human being does seem to be heightened rather than eased, especially if the statement is interpreted largely through visual ways of conceiving space. It seems to result in a precarious orthodoxy – humanity and deity "balanced" in perfect equilibrium like a double-weighted bar, poised high above heresy, as if humanity and deity are working against each other: the more of one, the less of the other. Attempts to ease things by holding that Christ's deity was diminished in some way (that he was a sort of "scaled down" version of God), or that Jesus' humanity, though real, was substantially adjusted to cope with God's overwhelming presence, only seem to distort the New Testament's testimony.

The broader matter at stake here is, of course, the way we imagine God's presence in the world. If space is construed visually as a kind of container "in" which two things cannot be in the same space at the same time, and a thing cannot be in two places at the same time, then it is hard to conceive of God as fully God, upholding the universe of space and time, while at the same time being active in the world. And if the notion of God's interaction in the world *is* to be maintained, it is hard to resist the conclusion that the more active God is in the world, the more restricted the world is going to be, the less "room" it will have to be itself. The perennial tendency of modernity – to assume that the more God is active in the world the less "room" the world has to be itself, and the less humanity will be able to flourish – is of a piece with this, and the common slippage into some form of divine–human "merger" hardly surprising.[47] Such "zero-sum" theology is, however, more likely avoided if we begin to think in terms of two notes heard together: here we confront not two realities vying for the same space, but co-presence without mutual exclusion and without merger, both in the same heard "space." Moreover, in the case of one note resonating with and "setting off" the other, a conception can open up of God interacting with the world intimately, not stifling its particularity but liberating it, "setting it off" to be more fully the world God created it to be.

The same musical conceptuality can be pressed in trinitarian directions. It may be that a large part of our chronic tendency to treat the Trinity as essentially problem-atic, an intellectual and fundamentally mathematical conundrum, has been fueled by an excessive reliance on visual conceptions of space, according to which "three in one" will always be deeply problematic. The disarming simplicity of a three-note chord facilitates conceptions of Father, Son, and Spirit "in" and "through" each other (perichoresis) far more naturally.

And so to Christology. Need we view the humanity of Christ sitting awkwardly alongside the divine eternal Son, coexisting (competing?) within the one "space"? Would it not be truer to the New Testament to conceive of the "overlapping" of divine and human spaces, without loss of either, within a dynamic of trinitarian overlapping spaces? In Jesus Christ, the divine Son who is eternally in communion with the Father engages with our world so closely so as to assume humanity, flesh and blood; and far from being compromised, in him humanity reaches its intended destiny: life with the Father through the agency of the Spirit. Here we can begin to think of the closest interaction of divine space and human space ("without division, without separation") without compromise ("without confusion, without change"), all within a matrix of trinitarian persons-in-relation. The common charges brought against Chalcedonian Christology – that it is too static, that it is fixated with "natures" rather than persons, and that it cannot do justice to the trinitarian setting of Christology – now all seem much weaker. And this is even more so if we begin to think in terms of simultaneous melodies rather than notes, a drama of interpenetration between the triune God and humanity.

Of course, if we were to expand on this, we would need to make many qualifications. The intra-trinitarian relations are not identical to those between the Son and the humanity of Christ. And we would need to insist that we are not attacking visual modes of thinking in themselves – a chronic and much discussed Protestant tendency – or ignoring the fact that there have been some magnificent visual renderings of the Incarnation and the Trinity. The main point here is to suggest that serious difficulties arise if we rely too heavily or exclusively on one sense at the expense of others, and that the world of simultaneously sounding notes offers a wealth of underdeveloped resources for Christology.[48]

Musical improvisation: Church, spirit, and body

Improvisation, "the simultaneous conception and production of sound in performance,"[49] despite the flurry of interest in it in recent years by musicologists, is treated by many musicians with suspicion, even disdain. Yet the evidence is that not only is there an element of improvisation in virtually all music of all cultures, but that there is scarcely a musical technique or form of composition that did not originate in improvisation or was not essentially influenced by it. This suggests that instead of regarding music which is strictly notated and largely planned as the norm and improvisation as an unfortunate distortion or epiphenomenon, it might be more illuminating to invert that and ask whether improvisation reveals to us fundamental aspects of musical creativity easily forgotten in traditions bound predominantly to the practices of rigorous rehearsal and notation. If it does, any conversation between theology and music must take improvisation very seriously. Moreover, we quickly discover that striking theological overtones emerge in any study of improvisation.[50] We can highlight this by referring to just two fields of doctrine: the church and the Holy Spirit.[51]

Much of the recent literature on improvisation has highlighted the implicit social and even political provocations it presents. In particular, it disrupts conventional barriers between "composer," "performer," and "audience," since an improviser is normally all three concurrently. Improvisation seems to offer uncommon opportunities for profitable "dialogical interrelations" between musicians.[52] In more formalized concert music-making, communication is interposed by an external agency, the score. By shifting attention to social process rather than the resulting text, improvisation encourages a particular kind of immediacy of personal exchange which is undoubtedly one of its most attractive features.

In this way, improvisation can embody to a significant extent what Alistair McFadyen has described as "undistorted communication."[53] In "monologue" the individual manipulates or is manipulated: one person treats the other as a means to an end, such that the other becomes self-confirmatory. The other's otherness becomes "a repetition of a previously privately coordinated understanding."[54] In "dialogue" (undistorted communication), the other's particularity is acknowledged such that one allows for the possibility of one's own expectations and intentions to be resisted: "To recognize and intend the freedom of the other in response is to recognize that the form and content of that response cannot be overdetermined by the address."[55] There is "a readiness to allow the calls of others to transform us in response."[56] This does not mean that we assume the superiority of the other, nor quantitative equality between dialogue partners.

Commenting on McFadyen's work, Francis Watson writes: "Something similar is suggested by the Pauline image of the church as body, where the allocation of varying gifts and roles by the same Spirit establishes a formal [not quantitative] equality . . . within a diversity of roles which allows for hierarchical elements so long as these are understood in strictly reciprocal rather than monological terms."[57] Very much the same could be said of improvisation, in which there can be growth of personal particularity through musical dialogue. All the skills which promote reciprocal "undistorted communication" – which should characterize the church as persons-in-communion – are present in a very heightened form; for example, giving "space" to the other through alert attentiveness, listening in patient silence, contributing to the growth of others by "making the best" of what is received from them such that they are encouraged to continue participating, sensitive decision making, flexibility of response, initiating change, role-changing, and generating and benefiting from conflict. Without the mediation of a verbal text and conventional verbal communication, these skills have to be learned in musical modes and thus in a sense *re*-thought and *re*-learned. This may well contribute to freer communication in other fields. There is much to draw upon here if we want to develop a properly theological account of ecclesial freedom which sees it as mediated by and through the other in a process of concentrated dialogical action, where the constraint of others is not experienced as essentially oppressive but as conferring and confirming an inalienable particularity and uniqueness. Not only are modernist conceptions of self-determined and self-constituted individuals questioned, but so also is the dissolution of self-identity implicit in some postmodernism.[58] Significantly, homogeneity of sound has little place in jazz. "Sound in jazz is . . . the slow, expressive vibrato of Sidney Bechet's soprano sax; the voluminous, erotic tenor sax sound of Coleman Hawkins, the earthy cornet of King Oliver; the 'jungle' sound of Bubber Miley."[59]

We move to a second area: the Holy Spirit. Improvisation, to a very large extent, entails what the poet Peter Riley has called "the exploration of occasion."[60] Much depends on the particularities of the specific context of performance; for example, the acoustic of the building, the time of day, the number of people present, their expectations and experience, their audible responses as the performance proceeds, and, not least, the music produced by fellow improvisers. These elements are not accidental to the outcome but constitutive of it. A skillful improviser, in bringing alive the "given" material – whether chord sequence, the agreed shape of a piece, or whatever – attempts not only to be sensitive to such contextual factors but also to incorporate them into the improvisation, in order that the improvisation is "true" and authentic to this time and place. Moreover, with its large measure of openness, this particularizing process, it is commonly acknowledged, generates an intense sense of anticipation and hopefulness, a sense of "wanting more."

At a time of renewed interest in the doctrine of the Holy Spirit, this dimension of improvisation may have much to contribute in the search for new conceptualities in pneumatology. The Spirit is the Spirit of faithfulness, of fidelity to the givenness of God's self-declaration in Jesus Christ. But, far from merely replicating this "given," the Spirit constantly actualizes it in a way which engages with and brings to fruition the particularities of each time and place. As is often now said – and here much recent pneumatology is attempting to obviate problematic and even harmful aspects of the Western tradition – although it is the work of the Spirit to unify, to bind people and things together, this activity includes in and with it the recognition and promotion of particularity and distinctiveness. On the day of Pentecost, the Spirit did not create one uniform language but liberated people to hear each other "in their own tongues" (Acts 2: 6, 11). Pentecost was a divine "exploration of occasion" if ever there was one. Furthermore, this particularizing activity is a function of the Spirit's eschatological ministry: to anticipate here and now in ever fresh ways the Father's final, eschatological desire, already realized in Christ (2 Corinthians 1: 22; Ephesians 1: 14; Romans 8: 23). Particularizing engenders hope. Life in the Spirit, therefore, involves a combination of faithfulness to the past, particularizing what is received in the present as an anticipation of the future. This is the dynamic of musical improvisation. If it is true, as many urge, that we require models of the Spirit's work which, in hermeneutics, take full account of the particularities of the present as well as faithfulness to the apostolic witness of scripture,[61] and which in theologies of mission and ministry avoid over-stressing backward orientation to the career of Jesus and the apostolic church, then improvisation has much to offer, given the way in which its disciplined fidelity to a shared tradition and its concern for singularity of circumstance are interwoven within a dynamic of hopefulness.

Coda

> A beat poised, a crossgrained rhythm,
> interplays, imbrications of voice over voice,
> mutinies of living are rocking the steady
> state of a theme; these riffs and overlappings
> a love of deviance, our genesis in noise.[62]

It remains to be seen how far theologians avail themselves of the opportunities afforded by music, opportunities which we have only hinted at above. But it may well be that the discovery this poet has made about the potential of music to evoke the dynamics of the creation of the cosmos – and he is writing of improvisation – will be repeated in all sorts of ways that will astonish us and make us wonder how it is that so much theology this past century has managed to do with so little music.

Notes

1 For example, Wilfrid Mellers, *Bach and the Dance of God* (New York, 1981); *Beethoven and the Voice of God* (London, 1983).

2 Barth and Bonhoeffer are the two most notable exceptions (discussed below), and we shall touch upon some of the others.

3 George Steiner, *Errata: An Examined Life* (London, 1997), p. 65.

4 Albert Blackwell, *The Sacred in Music* (Cambridge, 1999).

5 Ibid, p. 28.

6 Ibid, p. 165.

7 Ibid, p. 159.

8 See Jeremy S. Begbie, *Music in God's Purposes* (Edinburgh, 1988); *Voicing Creation's Praise* (Edinburgh, 1991); *Theology, Music and Time* (Cambridge, 2000).

9 See Jeremy S. Begbie, *Resounding Truth* (Grand Rapids, MI, forthcoming).

10 Begbie, *Theology, Music and Time*, p. 277.

11 Begbie, *Voicing Creation's Praise*, pp. 204–32.

12 In addition to Barth and Bonhoeffer, mention should be made, for example, of David Cunningham's discussion of polyphony in relation to trinitarian theology in *These Three Are One: The Practice of Trinitarian Theology* (Oxford, 1998), pp. 127ff.; Jon Michael Spencer's "theomusicology" in *Theological Music: Introduction to Theomusicology* (New York, 1991), *Theomusicology* (Durham, NC, 1994); Frances Young's hermeneutical study *The Art of Performance: Towards a Theology of Holy Scripture* (London, 1990); Nicholas Lash and Stephen Barton's development of the notion of "performance" in Nicholas Lash, "Performing the Scriptures," in *Theology on the Way to Emmaus* (London, 1986), pp. 37–46, and Stephen C. Barton, "New Testament Interpretation as Performance," *Scottish Journal of Theology*, 52/2, 1999, pp. 179–208.

13 Karl Barth, *Wolfgang Amadeus Mozart*, trans. Clarence K. Pott (Grand Rapids, MI, 1986), p. 16.

14 Karl Barth, *Church Dogmatics*, trans. and ed. G. W. Bromiley and T. F. Torrance, Vol. III: 3 (Edinburgh, 1960), p. 298.

15 Barth, *Wolfgang Amadeus Mozart*, p. 23.

16 Barth, *Church Dogmatics*, III: 3, pp. 297ff.

17 Ibid, pp. 349ff.

18 Ibid, p. 350.

19 Ibid, pp. 297ff.

20 Ibid, pp. 298ff.; my italics.

21 Ibid, p. 298.

22 Ibid, p. 350.

23 Ibid, p. 298.

24 Barth, *Wolfgang Amadeus Mozart*, p. 37.

25 Ibid, p. 38.

26 Barth, *Church Dogmatics*, III: 3, p. 298.

27 Barth, *Wolfgang Amadeus Mozart*, pp. 47ff.

28 See Karl Barth, *Church Dogmatics*, trans. and ed. G. W. Bromiley and T. F. Torrance, Vol. IV: 3 (Edinburgh, 1961), 69.2.

29 I am greatly indebted to Dr. Moseley, a former Cambridge graduate student, for his very fine thesis " 'Parables of the Kingdom': Music and Theology in Karl Barth" (unpublished doctoral dissertation, University of Cambridge, 2001).

30 Ibid, ch. 7.

31 For fine treatments of Bonhoeffer on music, see Andreas Pangritz, *Polyphonie des Lebens: zu Dietrich Bonhoeffers "Theologie der Musik"* (Berlin, 1994), and "Point and Counterpoint – Resistance and Submission: Dietrich Bonhoeffer on Theology and Music in Times of War and Social Crisis," in Lyn Holness and Ralf K. Wüstenberg (eds.), *Theology in Dialogue: The Impact of the Arts, Humanities, and Science on Contemporary Religious Thought* (Grand Rapids, MI, 2002), pp. 28–42; John De Gruchy, *Christianity, Art and Transformation: Theological Aesthetics and the Struggle for Justice* (Cambridge, 2001), ch. 4.

32 Dietrich Bonhoeffer, *Letters and Papers from Prison*, ed. Eberhard Bethge (New York, 1972), p. 240.

33 Ibid, pp. 126ff.

34 Dietrich Bonhoeffer, *Ethics* (London, 1965), p. 179.

35 Bonhoeffer, *Letters and Papers*, p. 193.

36 Andreas Pangritz believes that Bonhoeffer's experience of music played a crucial part in preparing the way for his final and best-known theological reflections. See Pangritz, "Point and Counterpoint."

37 Bonhoeffer, *Letters and Papers*, p. 219.

38 Ibid, p. 215.

39 Ibid, p. 219.

40 Ibid, pp. 170ff.

41 Ibid, p. 219. The *Art of Fugue* was handed down with the chorale "I come before thy throne" as a conclusion.

42 Ibid, p. 305.

43 Ibid, pp. 310, 311; my italics.

44 Jacques Attali, *Noise*, trans. Brian Massumi (Manchester, 1985), p. 4.

45 Rowan Williams, *Open to Judgement: Sermons and Addresses* (London, 1994), p. 247.

46 See Begbie, *Theology, Music and Time*, ch. 4.

47 See Colin Gunton, *Yesterday and Today: A Study of Continuities in Christology* (London, 1997), ch. 6.

48 See Jeremy S. Begbie, "Through Music: Sound Mix," in Jeremy S. Begbie (ed.), *Beholding the Glory* (London, 2000), pp. 138–54.

49 Roger Dean, *Creative Improvisation* (Milton Keynes, 1989), p. ix.

50 For example, writers such as Arthur Peacocke have made effective use of the model of improvisation in relation to the doctrine of creation, to illuminate God's free interaction with the world. See Arthur Peacocke, *Theology for a Scientific Age* (Oxford, 1993), pp. 175ff.

51 For much fuller discussion, see Begbie, *Theology, Music and Time*, chs. 7–9.

52 E. Prévost, "Improvisation: Music for an Occasion," *British Journal of Music Education*, 2/2 (1985), pp. 177–86.

53 Alistair McFadyen, *The Call to Personhood* (Cambridge, 1990), ch. 4.

54 Ibid, p. 26.

55 Ibid, p. 119.

56 Ibid, p. 121.

57 Francis Watson, *Church and World: Biblical Interpretation in Theological Perspective* (Edinburgh, 1994), p. 112.

58 Ibid, ch. 6.

59 Joachim E. Berendt, *The Jazz Book: From New Orleans to Jazz Rock and Beyond* (London, 1983), 144. The ethical implications of jazz for modeling "desirable social relations" are explored vividly by Kathleen Marie Higgins, with particular reference to "progressive" jazz and race relations. See Kathleen Marie Higgins, *The Music of our Lives* (Philadelphia, PA, 1991), 170–80.

60 As cited in Dean, *Creative Improvisation*, p. xvi.

61 For an expansion of the improvisatory model in biblical hermeneutics, see N. T. Wright, *The New Testament and the People of God* (London, 1992), pp. 139ff.

62 From "Cosmos," in Micheal O'Siadhail, *Hail! Madam Jazz: New and Selected Poems* (Newcastle, 1992), p. 149.

Bibliography

Augustine, *Confessions*, ed. Henry Chadwick (Oxford, 1991).

Bailey, D., *Improvisation: Its Nature and Practice in Music* (London, 1992).

Barth, Karl, *Church Dogmatics*, III: 3, trans. and ed. G. W. Bromiley and T. F. Torrance (Edinburgh, 1960).

—— *Wolfgang Amadeus Mozart*, trans. Clarence K. Pott, (Grand Rapids, MI, 1986).

Begbie, Jeremy S. (ed.), *Voicing Creation's Praise: Towards a Theology of the Arts* (Edinburgh, 1991).

—— *Beholding the Glory* (London, 2000).

—— *Theology, Music and Time* (Cambridge, 2000).

—— (ed.) *Sounding the Depths: Theology Through the Arts* (London, 2002).

—— "Unexplored Eloquencies: Music, Religion and Culture," in Sophia Marriage and Jolyon Mitchell (eds.), *Mediating Religion* (Edinburgh, 2003), pp. 93–106.

Blackwell, Albert L., *The Sacred in Music* (Cambridge, 1999).

Bonhoeffer, Dietrich, *Letters and Papers from Prison*, ed. Eberhard Bethge (New York, 1972).

Campling, Christopher R., *The Food of Love: Reflections on Music and Faith* (London, 1997).

Chafe, Eric, *Tonal Allegory in the Vocal Music of J. S. Bach* (Berkeley, CA, 1991).

Cunningham, David S., *These Three Are One: The Practice of Trinitarian Theology* (Oxford, 1998).

De Gruchy, John W., *Christianity, Art and Transformation: Theological Aesthetics in the Struggle for Justice* (Cambridge, 2001).

Dean, Roger, *Creative Improvisation* (Milton Keynes, 1989).

James, Jamie, *The Music of the Spheres: Music, Science and the Natural Order of the Universe* (New York, 1993).

Jones, Ivor H., *Music: A Joy for Ever* (London, 1989).

Juslin, Patrick N. and Sloboda, John A., *Music and Emotion: Theory and Research* (Oxford, 2001).

McFadyen, Alistair E., *The Call To Personhood: A Christian Theory of the Individual in Social Relationships* (Cambridge, 1990).

Mellers, Wilfrid, *Bach and the Dance of God* (New York, 1981).

—— *Beethoven and the Voice of God* (New York, 1983).

Moseley, David, " 'Parables of the Kingdom': Music and Theology in Karl Barth" (unpublished PhD dissertation, University of Cambridge, 2001).

Nattiez, Jean-Jacques, *Music and Discourse: Toward a Semiology of Music*, trans. Carolyn Abbate (Princeton, NJ, 1990).

O'Siadhail, Micheal, *Hail! Madam Jazz: New and Selected Poems* (Newcastle, 1992).

Peacocke, Arthur, *Theology for a Scientific Age* (Oxford, 1993).

Pelikan, J., *Bach Among the Theologians* (Philadelphia, PA, 1986).

Pike, Alfred John, *A Theology of Music* (Toledo, OH, 1953).

Sloboda, John, *The Musical Mind* (Oxford, 1983).

Steiner, George, *Real Presences: Is There Anything in What We Say?* (London, 1989).

Sudnow, D., *Ways of the Hand: The Organisation of Improvised Conduct* (London, 1978).

Watson, Francis, "Theology and Music," *Scottish Journal of Theology* 51 (1998), pp. 435–63.

Williams, Rowan, *Open to Judgement: Sermons and Addresses* (London, 1994).

Young, Frances, *The Art of Performance: Towards a Theology of Holy Scripture* (London, 1990).

Zuckerkandl, Victor, *Sound and Symbol: Music and the External World* (London, 1956).

—— *Man the Musician* (Princeton, NJ, 1973).

Theology and Film

Jolyon Mitchell

Introduction

Is the church in conflict with the cinema? There is a well-known, and often quoted,[1] scene in *Cinema Paradiso* (1988) in which a middle-aged priest sits alone in the picture house of a small Italian town. He is watching a film and every time a couple embrace, he angrily rings a small bell. The projectionist then marks the offending frames on the reel and later edits out these cinematic kisses. Later in *Cinema Paradiso* the small boy who witnesses this censoring returns as a middle-aged film director, and is given an old reel of film to watch. To his amusement, he finds that it is all the excised material spliced together into a chain of kisses.

Theologians currently engaged in film criticism often look back at Catholic and Protestant attempts at censorship with a mixture of bemusement and fascination. While ecclesiastical protests against the cinema have become much more sporadic, the image of Christians morally outraged by a particular film remains a recurring news story. Demonstrations against films such as *Monty Python's Life of Brian* (1979) or *The Last Temptation of Christ* (1988) reinforce the popular perception that many Protestants and Catholics remain deeply uneasy about film's perceived capacity to corrupt viewers.[2] Protests against motion pictures are not a new phenomenon. As early as 1907, in the New England city of Worcester, the *Catholic Messenger* denounced films as "the Devil's Lieutenants," while Swedish evangelical church ministers in the same city condemned attendance at the movie theatre as a serious sin. So strong was their anti-cinema rhetoric that "some youngsters developed a morbid fear just walking by a movie theatre."[3]

To suggest that the churches have always been in conflict with the cinema is to ignore the full history of their interactions. There have certainly been moments of intense opposition, such as in 1910 when Pope Pius X prohibited the showing of films in Catholic churches or when the Legion of Decency "totally condemned" particular movies.[4] By contrast, there have been periods of mutual involvement, which go back to the very start of moving pictures. From the first decade of film, far from being in conflict with the industry, some Christians creatively used or indeed helped to create movies. For instance, dramatized passion plays took on a cinematic lease of life following the advent of motion pictures in the late nineteenth century.

A French religious publishing house, La Bonne Presse, financed one of the first ever films to focus on the life of Jesus. *La Passion* was made in Paris in the summer of 1897. This silent, black and white motion picture lasted five minutes, but was popular enough to allow La Bonne Presse to become a film production company. Sadly, like many films from the earliest days of cinema, it has not survived.

There are numerous other early examples of cinematic passion plays.[5] For instance, Rich Hollaman and Albert Eaves produced *The Mystery of the Passion Play of Oberammergau* (1898). Misleadingly, it was also titled *The Original Oberammergau Passion Play*. This was one of the first North American attempts to film episodes from the life of Jesus, and was filmed not in Oberammergau but on the roof-terrace of the Grand Central Palace Hotel in New York. Hollaman's version lasted 19 minutes and had 23 scenes, starting with the shepherds at Bethlehem and concluding with the ascension. Filmed in the late autumn, this is one of the only Jesus movies to have snow in the background of many of the scenes. The revelation by the local press, a week after its opening, that this was not actually the Oberammergau play but was filmed in Manhattan does not appear to have deterred audiences. One itinerant evangelist even purchased a print and traveled the country using it at revival meetings. This became an increasingly common practice, with gatherings in revival tents combining preaching with showing a film. Other short films based on scenes from the life and death of Christ were actually made by evangelists to attract audiences and illuminate their message. For instance, at the start of the twentieth century in Australia, Herbert Booth, son of the founders of the Salvation Army, used specially filmed scenes of martyrdoms and Christ in agony on the cross as part of his "multimedia" presentation *Soldiers of the Cross*. The event received commendations from both the secular and the religious press.[6]

During the first twenty years of cinema many became absorbed by the potential of the evolving medium of film. One of the most prolific Christian advocates for film was the Reverend Herbert Jump, a Congregationalist minister, whose pamphlet *The Religious Possibilities of the Motion Picture* (1910) is one of the earliest theological apologia for film. He uses the parable of the Good Samaritan for the foundation of his argument. This exciting "robber-story" rooted in experience and realistic representation of violent crime, provides a precedent for using film didactically. Jump playfully suggests that the only thing needed to transform this parable into a successful motion picture is a new title: "The Adventure of the Jerusalem Merchant." Films can make the gospel vivid, like the word-pictures of great preachers, illustrated slide lectures, and cathedral art. The motion picture is "the most wonderful invention that has come into existence since the invention of the printing press in the fifteenth century." While he recognizes some dangers in the medium, overall Jump perceives it as an ally of the church, which can help as an entertainment device, a tool of religious instruction at Sunday school, an informer about missionary work both at home and abroad, a teacher to socially educate the needy, and a powerful illustration for the preacher.[7] During these first decades of the "seventh art," film may not have received sustained theological analysis, but Jump is a leading representative of those who outlined pastoral rationales for the uses of film.

At this early stage, as so obviously in film's later history, it was economic necessity that played a highly significant role in how films were made and marketed. Film producers became increasingly sensitive to their potential audiences' different desires. Several of the earliest film catalogues provide purchasers with a choice of the number of scenes from cinematic passion plays. Some went further, ensuring that Catholic exhibitors were offered versions of passion plays which had more scenes centering on Mary.[8] The episodic nature of the gospel narratives particularly suited early styles of filmmaking, which offered audiences short scenes. In later silent films these were connected by title cards. The audience's knowledge of the biblical stories allowed producers to cut directly from scene to scene without having to provide over-explicit narrative links.

Significantly, portraying biblical stories (like filming versions of Dickens or Shakespeare) provided a ready means of respectability in a period when many filmmakers were eager to shed film's more sordid associations. The aim was to demonstrate that film could be edifying rather than merely titillating. Another factor was the desire to experiment with the new medium, and create unexpected spectacles. An early film based on the Bible that did not rely on the passion play model was made by Georges Méliès, one of the fathers of French cinema and a groundbreaking director in terms of his development and use of special effects. *Le Christ Marchant Sur Les Flots* (1899/1900) may only last 35 seconds, but Méliès used trick photography (a simple double exposure) to astonish audiences by showing a miracle occur in front of their own eyes: Jesus walking across the Sea of Galilee (see Figure 1). As just one in a whole series of magical "effects" from the Méliès stable, some viewers believed that such showing debased a divine miracle. The vast majority of Méliès' work does not treat religious themes explicitly, but the responses to his work demonstrate how audiences could be mesmerized by what they saw on the silver screen. The sheer novelty of the spectacle engaged, delighted, and surprised. In this chapter I first outline three significant interpretative practices, investigating how Christians have responded to film over the last century. Through this framework I provide a historical survey which offers a point of entry into a rapidly expanding literature.

Survey: Theological Criticism of Film

Over the last hundred years, no mutually agreed pattern of theological engagement with films has emerged. The landscape is marked by fragmentation and a diversity of approaches. This is not surprising given the multiplicity of theological beliefs, methods, and practices reflected through much of this volume of *The Modern Theologians*. Mainstream film studies has largely ignored theological and religious film criticism.[9] Nevertheless, there already exist several useful taxonomies setting out the different ways in which theology and film can interact.[10] John May, for example, believes that over the last forty years there has been a shift in how theologians have engaged with film. This has moved through five stages: first, discrimination, which concentrates on the morality of specific portrayals; second, visibility, which focuses on how religious figures or themes are represented; third, dialogue, which promotes theological conversations with particular films; fourth, humanism, which examines how film can promote human progress and flourishing; and, fifth, aesthetics, which ultimately explores how the transcendent may be manifested at the cinema.[11] As May concedes, there is inevitably blurring between these categories.

Rob Johnston's matrix, set out with clarity in *Reel Spirituality*, intentionally offers a complementary framework. Recognizing the parallels with May's work, he also provides five basic categories to reflect the theological responses by the church to

Figure 1 *Le Christ Marchant Sur Les Flots* (1899/1900). Director George Méliès.

movie-going: avoidance, caution, dialogue, appropriation, and divine encounter.[12] These groupings highlight the range of perspectives offered by various theologians. This includes the whole spectrum of writers, from those who espouse withdrawal from the cinema to those who advocate that watching a film may actually be an occasion of divine encounter. Johnston observes that many theologians who promote a highly critical response to film begin the dialogue from the womb of theology and often judge films on the ethical presuppositions that they bring to the movie. By contrast, those who celebrate the revelatory potential of movies tend to immerse themselves in the world of the film and its aesthetic qualities before drawing upon theological resources for interpreting the film. Johnston's own approach to the cinema is made clear in the text and through the book's subtitle: *Theology and Film in Dialogue*.

The presuppositions behind several of the approaches described by both May and Johnston are inevitably diverse. Some critics have shunned the cinema as a medium that can corrupt morally, socially and doctrinally, while others have embraced it as a catalyst for theological exploration or even an art form with transcendent potential. Corruption, exploration, and illumination provide the structure for the following discussion. This leads on to a consideration of different film directors' visions and the variety of responses by audiences to film.

Film corrupts?

Suspicion of film grew in the 1920s, heightened by a series of scandals in Hollywood, confirming fears that the industry was inherently decadent. In 1923 the evangelist Jack Linn asserted the movies are the "devil's incubator," which are not "conducive to morality or spirituality." For Linn, "a Christian cannot even darken a movie theatre, and at the same time fellowship with Christ'(*sic*).[13] Linn's was by no means a lone voice. John Rice's *What is Wrong with the Movies?* (1938) remains one of the most outspoken Protestant polemics against cinema. He attempted to demonstrate that the "commercial cinema is an unmitigated curse" and like Linn he believes "it is so vile in its influence that no Christian should ever set foot in a movie theatre." He believes "the movie is the rival of schools and churches, the feeder of lust, the perverter of morals, the tool of greed, the school of crime, the betrayer of innocence."[14] *What's Wrong with the Cinema?* (1948), written by British Baptist minister Morgan Derham, similarly reveals the depth of disquiet about films felt in many Protestant Churches in the middle of the twentieth century. Derham believed that cinema has the power to strike at the very core of the viewer, combining "every psychological device for the swaying of human emotion and reason." For Derham, the cinema industry "is an evil system" and film producers "are hedonistic money-makers." Derham exhorts Christians to "leave the commercial Cinema organization where it belongs – as part of the satanic system for the blinding of men's eyes, and the hardening of hearts."[15] Unlike some of the earliest Protestant enthusiasts for film, such as Herbert Jump, this masculine trio of Lynn, Rice, and Derham provides examples of those who saw the cinema in direct conflict with the church.

Anxiety about the power of film to corrupt viewers is also expressed in Burnett and Martell's *The Devil's Camera* (1932) (see Figure 2), which is dedicated to the "ultimate sanity of the white races" and betrays anti-semitic sentiments. They assert that the "cinema, taken as a whole, is the greatest lie of our time because it is grossly misrepresenting life."[16] As with many other early critical accounts of film they highlight what they perceive to be satanic influence, "the devil is in full, spiritual control of modern film production." They also see idolatry portrayed on the screen, "the golden calf is god of the cinema."[17] The dominant motif of *The Devil's Camera* is that "film-poison" is doing "unimaginable harm," feeding the worst passions and seducing the "imaginations of the peoples of the world." Burnett and Martell are critical of Church leaders who ignored or dismissed the cinema. In contrast to some of the most vitriolic accounts of movies they nevertheless, in their final chapter, celebrate film technology as "a marvelous instrument," which has the potential to educate, to entertain, and to build up the churches.[18]

The belief that film corrupts morals and perverts theological vision is also particularly prevalent in the earlier Catholic documents considering film. For instance, the first papal encyclical letter on film, Pope Pius XI's *Vigilanti Cura* (June 29, 1936), reflects a deep anxiety that the motion picture could be a "school of corruption," that "destroys the moral fiber of the nation."[19] The encyclical assumes that films have considerable power in changing people's behavior and beliefs: "There does not exist today a means of influencing the masses more potent than the cinema." This can be for good or for evil. There is a celebratory and hopeful tone in some of the statements about film's potential for good. While bad motion pictures can damage the soul and be "occasions of sin," "good motion pictures are capable of exercising a profoundly moral influence upon those who see them." For this reason "the motion picture should not be simply a means of diversion, a light relaxation to occupy an idle hour; with its magnificent power, it can and must be a bearer of light

Figure 2 Front Cover of *The Devil's Camera: Menace of a Film-ridden World* (London: Epworth Press, 1932)

and a positive guide to what is good." Addressed in the first instance to the Catholic hierarchy in the USA and then to other bishops around the world, it celebrates the success of the Legion of Decency, which encouraged Catholics to sign a pledge "binding themselves not to attend any motion picture which was offensive to Catholic moral principles or proper standards of living."

Over twenty years later Pope Pius XII's encyclical letter on motion pictures, radio, and television, *Miranda Prorsus* (September 8, 1957), develops several of the themes in *Vigilanti Cura*. For instance, it outlines the significant role of Catholic film critics for setting out the moral issues and instructing their readers in terms of the moral position to be adopted. Alongside reviewers, spectators themselves have a "duty of conscience," similar to when casting a vote, each time they "buy a ticket of admission." Both documents contain within them what might be described as a Christian rigorist response to film, which assumes that motion pictures have considerable power to shape the moral and theological horizons of their viewers. The practical aim was to encourage Christians to be vigilant about films, to view suspect films cautiously, and to avoid some films entirely.

At the height of the Legion's influence, if a film broke the production code's guidelines, it could find itself receiving much worse than negative reviews: thousands of Legion members would stay away from its screenings. In pre-World War II America, virulent anti-Semitism heightened the perception that Hollywood was dominated by Jews, lay well beyond the control of the Christian churches, and therefore needed to be resisted.[20] Deep-rooted suspicion towards film as potentially an evil influence, Hollywood as the new Babylon, and filmmakers as the corrupters of children, continues to this day, with some religious leaders encouraging their constituencies to avoid suspect films. For example, in Kerala, South India, going to the cinema is still viewed with suspicion by many older Marthomite Christians. In parts of North America, a single example of nudity, bad language, sexual innuendo, or unnecessary violence can ensure that a film receives a warning notice, communicated by email or websites strongly advising against viewing. In many cases the force of the cinematic narrative is eclipsed by an unacceptable scene: a moment deemed to be ethically unacceptable such as the "unnecessary nudity" in *Schindler's List*.[21]

Film explores?

Some theologians came to recognize that while film has the potential to amuse, to entertain, and to distract, it also has great potential to explore profound theological questions and moral dilemmas. The result of this understanding was that, particularly in the second half of the twentieth century, a number of less negative Christian responses to film developed. The applause that Pasolini's *The Gospel According to Saint Matthew* (1964) received from the 800 bishops gathered in Rome for Vatican II is symptomatic of the growing enthusiasm for the theological uses of film. Even in some of the most critical Catholic writings discussed above there is an understated ambivalence about film.[22] Some more recent official Catholic documents reflect a less suspicious attitude toward film in general. For instance, the pastoral instruction *Communio et Progressio* (May 23, 1971) celebrates films as works of art that can compellingly treat subjects that concern "human progress or spiritual values."

Moreover, certain institutions within the Catholic Church became involved in both the production and the funding of films, which sometimes included scenes that the Legion of Decency would have found deeply problematic (e.g., *Romero*, 1989). The Office [later, Organization] Catholique International du Cinéma (OCIC) was founded in 1928 at an international Catholic congress on cinema in the Hague. Its founding was supported by Pope Pius XI, and initially it was intended to promote "moral films" and support Christians working in the film industry. After World War II it set up an international film prize. Here was a Catholic body which had moved beyond censoring cinema and was now keen to celebrate some films, particularly those "most capable of contributing to the moral and spiritual elevation of humanity."[23] The OCIC award has been conferred on directors such as John Ford and Francis Ford Coppola. OCIC (now SIGNIS) not only supports the awarding of prizes and the development of national film offices, but it also organizes Catholic film juries, which continue to serve alongside ecumenical juries at the world's major film festivals. There are no restrictions on the kind of films that can receive awards. This has sometimes led to conflict between juries and the Catholic hierarchy. The most celebrated case was Pasolini's *Teorema* (*Theorem*), which was offered the grand prize at the 1968 Venice film festival, only for the film and the jury to be later condemned by the Vatican. In spite of such disagreements, film juries remain autonomous, and are allowed to bestow their prizes upon whomsoever they deem fit. Numerous other religious prizes were awarded to films by Bergman, Bresson, and Fellini.[24] Pasolini may have been an atheist Marxist, but *The Gospel According to Saint Matthew* was named best religious film of the year in 1964 by OCIC, who admitted that while Pasolini "did not share our faith," he had produced a "Christian film that produces a profound impression."[25] There is now an increased recognition, by some, that films can explore with great depth, power, and artistry moral dilemmas and theological questions.

Peter Malone, an Australian Jesuit, has devoted much of his writing and teaching career to the enterprise of showing how films are often redolent with theological and moral meaning. Malone's *Film and Values* (1984) is "based on the assumption that contemporary films, the vast majority of them, are not corrupting"; in fact, through storytelling, films often explore and express the heart of the human condition. He suggests that films can function as transformative parables and as such have the potential to "challenge the stands we take, test the values we profess to act by."[26] Malone's work tends towards careful analysis of films and the characterizations they present. This can be seen clearly in *Movie Christs and Antichrists* (1990), which is one of the first books to make the distinction between the Jesus-figure and the Christ-figure in films. The former was the representation of Jesus himself on screen, such as in *The King of Kings* (1927) or *The Greatest Story Ever Told* (1965) and the latter was the portrayal of characters whose depictions resonate with the life or death of Christ, such as the protagonist in *Cool Hand Luke* (1967) or *Pale Rider* (1985). Several other writers have made extensive use of this distinction between *Jesus*-figures and *Christ*-figures in films, such as Lloyd Baugh in *Imaging the Divine* (1997). As Baugh and other critics acknowledge, identifying a film's protagonist as a Christ-figure may reveal more about the interpreter than illuminate the actual narrative.[27]

Malone is an exception in the early days of theological film criticism, as the majority of exploratory work in the 1960s and 1970s was by North American scholars. Writers such as Neil Hurley, John May, and James Wall led this exploration.[28]

Hurley's three books on film demonstrate a fascination with both the specific content of numerous movies and the directorial influence on what is shown. In *Theology Through Film* (1970) Hurley sets out a "cinematic theology." He famously begins by asserting that "movies are for the masses what theology is for an elite." He attempts, for example, to trace transcendence through a number of contemporary films, suggesting that it is possible to identify signs of grace on the screen. Like Hurley, Wall's method of reading films theologically has evolved over a number of years, in particular while he worked as editor of the *Christian Century*, writing reviews and editorials. In *Church and Cinema* (1971) Wall concentrates on the director's vision of the world as a channel of revelation. May, like Hurley and Wall, emphasizes the role of the director in shaping each film's distinctive perspective. For example, in his later discussion of *The Godfather* trilogy he uses director Coppola's intentions as the touchstone for his interpretation of these classic films. By putting considerable emphasis upon the director's vision, Hurley, May, and Wall show themselves to be sympathetic to elements of the *auteur* theory. This roughly refers to the approach in film criticism which privileges the perspective of the director as the "author" or the organizing genius behind the film.

Film illuminates?

Film may have the potential to provoke theological and ethical questioning, but do movies have an inherent capacity to illuminate scriptural texts? Recently, a number of biblical scholars have answered this question affirmatively. Adele Reinhartz uses *Scripture on the Silver Screen* (2003) to assist in the development of "biblical literacy," while the diverse essays in *Screening Scripture* (2002) demonstrate how "intertextual connections between scripture and film" are possible. These books have earlier precedents. For example, while Larry Kreitzer is by training a biblical scholar, he has made his name through exploring the ways film and fiction can illuminate biblical texts. To date, Kreitzer has produced four books which aim to enable "a dialogue to take place between the biblical text, great works of literature, and that most persuasive of modern art forms, the cinema." He describes this process as "reversing the hermeneutical flow." In essence, this triadic approach means using classic works of literature and their cinematic interpretations as a way of shedding fresh light on biblical passages. For instance, Kreitzer provides a careful reading of different versions of *Bram Stoker's Dracula*, both the novel (1897) and the Coppola film (1992), to illuminate the blood motif in Paul's first letter to the church at Corinth. Kreitzer's case studies usually concentrate upon classic novels and films such as *Dr. Jekyll and Mr. Hyde*, *Spartacus*, and *Ben Hur*. He brings the skills of a New Testament scholar to bear upon such texts. Kreitzer's three-way or triadic approach is becoming increasingly well known, though it has been criticized for its preoccupation with authorial intent.[29] Nevertheless, Kreitzer's books have made a significant contribution to the rapidly evolving research areas related to theology and film.

Robert Jewett is another biblical scholar who has immersed himself in the world of film criticism. His stated motivation and method are different from Kreitzer's. In his first two books on film he uses St. Paul as a conversation partner with specific movies, claiming that, given Paul's missionary desire to be all things to all people, if there had been film in his day, Paul would also have engaged with film criticism.

Instead of Kreitzer's triadic approach Jewett uses a two-way "interpretive arch," which intends to treat both biblical and cinematic texts with exegetical respect. He often moves the reader from the world of the film text to the world of the biblical text and back again.[30] One concern raised about both Jewett and Kreitzer's approach is the perceived tendency to rely upon literary models of film criticism, rather than embracing the rich resources of film theory, such as various psychoanalytic-based or spectator-led approaches.[31] The danger is that the attempt to "read" a film turns it into something that it is not: a written text. Films cannot be reduced to mere words to be analyzed.[32] Other skills, such as visual sensitivity, are required to analyze a film.

Several writers on theology and film go even further than Kreitzer and Jewett, suggesting that movies can act sacramentally. In *Images of the Passion* (1998) Peter Fraser examines the films which in his opinion best portray Christ's passion, describing them as sacramental films. For Fraser, "the sacramental film allows for the appropriation of spiritual presence sought by the devotional writers, but in a public experience."[33] Each chapter offers an interpretation of a specific film, such as *Gallipoli* (1981), *The Mission* (1986), and *Black Robe* (1991), and Fraser suggests that if the *Diary of a Country Priest* (1950) is embraced as the director Bresson intends, then viewers "will be brought into a sacramental experience with the living God."[34] This is a hard claim to verify, but it does exemplify a belief that film can illuminate the viewer. For Fraser, the sacramental film can become an object of "mystical contemplation," and he predicts that in the future films may well become "more prominent in popular practices of Christian piety."[35]

This prediction does not appear so far fetched with the production of *A Movie Lectionary* entitled *Lights Camera . . . Faith!* (2001, 2002, and 2003) by Peter Malone, with Rose Pacatte. These three books bring specific films into dialogue with the Catholic Lectionary Gospel readings. Part of the vision behind this trilogy is to encourage church leaders to use film in the context of worship, as part of the homily or post-communion meditation. Referring to over 70 films in each book they bring an individual movie to contrast or illustrate an element of Jesus' teaching and actions as represented in Matthew, Mark, Luke, and John. A whole range of film genres are drawn upon: from family films such as *E.T.* and *The Lion King* to horror movies like *The Exorcist* and *Bram Stoker's Dracula*; from prison stories such as *The Shawshank Redemption* and *Dead Man Walking* to war movies like *Saving Private Ryan* and intimate dramas like *Truly Madly Deeply*; from the commonly discussed *Babette's Feast* to the more haunting *The Sixth Sense* (for All Souls Day). The diversity of selection is intended to have a wide appeal, stretching both theological and cinematic horizons. The encouragement to integrate films into worship is reminiscent of the use of motion pictures in church meetings during the early part of the twentieth century. These books further reflect how film is now perceived by some as a potential catalyst for prayer, a place of devotion, and a source of revelation.

Catholic author and film critic Andrew Greeley supports such a view, claiming that film as part of "popular culture" is a *locus theologicus*, a theological place – "the locale in which one may encounter God."[36] For Greeley, God "lurks in the places in which the 'stories' of popular culture occur."[37] He developed these points more explicitly in *God in the Movies*, where he claims that cinema is a place where viewers can encounter the divine.[38]

While other recent writers claim to look for and even find "God in the movies," they invariably admit that this is an arduous task, similar to trying to catch light.[39]

Director and screenwriter Paul Schrader provides a sophisticated account of the revelatory function of film. On the basis of a study of three non-Hollywood directors (Ozu, Bresson, and Dreyer), Schrader suggests that through their realistic and sparse filmic style it is possible to encounter the sacred.[40]

Cinematic Figures: Directorial Theology

Films can offer alternative views of reality. George Lucas, creator of the *Star Wars* films, made it clear that he does not want to invent a religion or offer answers through his films, but he does want to make young people think about mystery, and to ask: "Is there a God? What does God look like? What does God sound like? What does God feel like? How do we relate to God?" He claims to have put the Force into the *Star Wars* movies in order to "try to awaken a certain kind of spirituality in young people," so that they might begin to ask questions about what he describes as "the mystery."[41] Lucas hopes that his *Star Wars* films will lead audiences to ask questions about the existence and nature of God.

Few directors have studied theology in depth and few consciously attempt to articulate theological themes through their work. Their intention is rarely, if ever, explicitly theological. By attending to specific scenes, films, or directorial statements it is possible, however, to discern how even directors can express themselves like creative theologians. Directors can be seen as visual storytellers grappling with theological issues in new and original ways. Their craft is neither primarily text-based nor rooted in logical arguments, but rather partly dependent upon the skillful juxtaposition of images, sounds, and dialogue to create a narrative. "I've turned from an image maker into a storyteller," German director Wim Wenders claims. "Only a story can give meaning and a moral to an image."[42]

Directors work not in a closed study or quiet library, but among a large group of industry professionals. For example, the team that Krzsztof Kieślowski used to create *The Decalogue* (1988), a series of short films made initially for Polish television and loosely based upon the Ten Commandments, reflects his belief that filmmaking is essentially a collaborative practice. By concentrating upon the work of directors I am not suggesting that the role of other members of the team, such as the screenwriter, producer, director of photography, film editor, composer, casting director, or actor, can be ignored. To focus upon the director's work, writings, and background is not to ignore the inherently communal nature of their profession, nor the economic constraints or social pressures faced by filmmakers, but it is one valuable approach to reflecting critically upon the theological significance of film production and content.

Ingmar Bergman

The Swede Ingmar Bergman (see Figure 3) is widely recognized as a cinematic master-craftsman, one of the leading film directors of the twentieth century. He appears to have been intrigued by the legend of Chartres, which told how the cathedral was burnt down, then rebuilt by thousands of anonymous craftsmen. In his introduction to the script of *The Seventh Seal* (*Det Sjunde Inseglet*, 1956) he identifies himself with those nameless builders:

If I am asked what I would like the general purpose of my films to be, I would reply that I want to be one of the artists in the cathedral on the great plain. I want to make a dragon's head, an angel, a devil – or perhaps a saint – out of stone. It does not matter which; it is the sense of satisfaction that counts. Regardless of whether I believe or not, whether I am a Christian or not, I would play my part in the collective building of the cathedral.[43]

As the son of a Swedish Lutheran pastor, Bergman was brought up in a pious home, which shaped his self-understanding and theological questioning, which in turn influenced his filmmaking.

Bergman "contributed vividly to the cinema of alienation, the cinema of the dispossessed individual, the post-Christian fallen world" of the second half of the twentieth century.[44] Films such as his bleak trilogy about people living in search of comfort and guidance in the absence of God, *Through a Glass Darkly* (1961), *Winter Light* (1962), and *The Silence* (1963), and his Passion film *Cries and Whispers* (1973), explore several of these themes. In *Winter Light*, for example, a Swedish pastor continues to worship even though he has lost his own faith and is faced by the death of God all around him. On the one hand, Bergman saw himself as someone like this pastor who had lost his faith and now confesses that the artist "considers his isolation, his subjectivity, his individualism almost holy."[45] The artist is trapped in his own loneliness, walking in circles, unable to recognize the existence of the other. On the other hand, it appears that during the 1950s and early 1960s Bergman could not easily dis-

Figure 3 Director Ingmar Bergman with camera and Bengt Ekerot (Death) from the outdoor location of *The Seventh Seal* 1957. Photograph British Film Institute.

pense with his understanding of God's place in the creative process. Earlier, in the introduction to *The Seventh Seal,* he not only bemoans the individualism of the artist, but also claims that "art lost its basic creative drive the moment it was separated from worship." Given his own wrestling with the apparent disappearance of God, it is surprising that he believes that this separation was like the severing of an umbilical cord:

> In former days the artist remained unknown and his work was to the glory of God. He lived and died without being more or less important than other artisans; "eternal values," "immortality," and "masterpiece" were terms not applicable in his case. The ability to create was a gift. In such a world flourished invulnerable assurance and natural humility.[46]

Bergman was far from unknown when he wrote this introduction. *The Seventh Seal* was the seventeenth film that he had directed and remains one of the most commonly cited. At several moments the star of this film is not the knight (Block) or his squire (Jöns), but death personified. The backdrop to the film is the plague. The film is permeated by the theme of death, exploring how different characters respond to their own impending death. Returning from the Crusades the knight may try to escape death by playing it at chess, but he will never win nor escape. Bergman admitted that this cinematic exploration was cathartic, in that after making this film, while he still thought about death it was no longer an obsession. Bergman is a director who repeatedly expresses his theological angst on screen, especially during the first two decades of his filmmaking. Block's journey in *The Seventh Seal* resonates with Bergman's own experience: a search for a silent God in the face of both death and human love.[47] While he may not have explicitly dedicated his work to the "glory of God," his ability to create and to explore through the screen was clearly a gift that provokes profound theological questions.

Francis Ford Coppola and The Godfather

Several specific scenes from Coppola's films provoke a different kind of theological questioning. They reflect Coppola's Italian heritage and Catholic upbringing. The original *Godfather* (1972) movie (see Figure 4) contains what is widely regarded as one of the classic moments in filmmaking: the baptism sequence.[48] The sequence builds to a crescendo: as Michael Corleone becomes a godfather in church, three other interlacing narratives accelerate toward their violent denouements. The language of repentance, the threefold renunciation of Satan, and the confession of faith are shattered in the light of the violence that Corleone precipitates. Stylistically echoing but going much further than the Odessa steps montage in Sergei Eisenstein's *Battleship Potemkin* (1925), Coppola creates a series of powerful dramatic ironies. Intercutting between the scenes creates a series of ironic visual resonances; for example, a priest's hand crosses the baby with water, which cuts to a barber anointing his gangster customer with shaving cream, preparing him to go out and murder. Particularly skillful is the juxtaposition of Corleone becoming a godfather to his sister's child in church with the cold-blooded killings he ordered, simultaneously making him a mafia godfather through the blood he has spilt. The idealistic Michael of the early part of the film has vanished, replaced by Corleone the new godfather.

Figure 4   Director Francis Ford Coppola directs Marlon Brando (Don Vito Corleone) and Al Pacino (Don Michael Corleone) in *The Godfather* (1972). Photograph British Film Institute. *The Godfather* © Paramount Pictures. All rights reserved.

The editing between the baptism in church and the series of mafia murders has been mimicked in numerous films ever since it was first released in 1972.

Nonetheless, director Coppola was disappointed by audience responses to the protagonist Michael Corleone: "I felt I was making a harsh statement about the Mafia and power at the end of *The Godfather I*, when Michael murders all those people, then lies to his wife and closes the door. But obviously many people did not get the point I was making."[49] Instead of finding him a morally repugnant figure, many were attracted to Al Pacino's strong portrayal and his exertion of ruthless power through violence.

The subsequent two Godfather films can be interpreted as Coppola's attempt to correct this misapprehension. Consider, for example, the closing scenes of *The Godfather, Part III* (1990), reminiscent of *The Godfather*'s baptism sequence, which intercuts the Easter production of *Cavalleria* with a series of assassinations, moving toward the climax of an attempt on Michael's life. The assassin misses and shoots Michael's daughter instead. "In a poignant inversion of the *Pietà*, Michael embraces Mary's lifeless body on the steps of Palermo's Opera Massima." Some suggest that Coppola was identifying with Michael, as Coppola's own son Gian-Carlo ("Gio") was killed in a speedboat accident aged 22, and it was his daughter Sofia who played Mary in the film. Michael's "silent scream of anguish is one of the most moving moments in the history of cinema."[50] Far from endorsing the myth of redemptive violence, the protagonist Michael Corleone falls into the twilight world of suffering alone in his old age.

Mel Gibson and The Passion of the Christ

Even before its release Mel Gibson's cinematic rendition of the final 12 hours of Jesus' life had provoked controversy. The Anti-Defamation League (ADL), originally founded in the early twentieth century partly to challenge the stereotyping of Jews in films, had joined forces with an *ad hoc* group of Jewish and Catholic scholars to request that the film avoid any anti-Semitic representations. Their concern was heightened by an awareness of the history of passion plays.[51] Some of the most extreme anti-Jewish violence in medieval Europe came after Holy Week dramas, which sometimes portrayed the Jews as being collectively responsible for "deicide." Following pre-release viewings, the ADL declared: "We are deeply concerned that the film, if released in its present form, could fuel the hatred, bigotry, and anti-Semitism that many responsible churches have worked hard to repudiate."[52] In response to such concerns Mel Gibson asserted: "*The Passion of the Christ* is not anti-Semitic" and is instead about "faith, hope, love, and forgiveness."[53]

From many other public statements it is clear that Gibson had no intention of stirring up anti-Semitic feelings. Unlike Cecil B. DeMille, who made several changes to *The King of Kings* (1927) in response to complaints, Gibson made very few changes to *The Passion* in light of the criticisms.[54] Gibson had no way of controlling the responses of a vast global audience, which paid over 620 million dollars to see his film. *The Passion* became the "highest-grossing historical epic of all time at the worldwide box office".[55] In addition, within a week of its release *The Passion* DVD sold nearly 9 million copies, outstripping even *The Lord of the Rings*. While some viewers did not find the film anti-Semitic, others found the portrayal of many of the Jewish characters to be deeply problematic, believing that the film trampled over guidelines set out by the American Catholic bishops on dramatizing the passion.[56] These diverse responses illustrate the gap between directorial intention and audience reception. Powerful cinematic signs will be interpreted by viewers in a myriad of ways irrespective of what the director and production team have hoped to create. The mise-en-scène of the trial and scourging had the Jewish leaders wearing imposing costumes and stern countenances, showing an indifference toward the suffering that indirectly they were responsible for. Like most films, *The Passion* was able to sidestep textual debates, such as how far elements or readings of the New Testament are themselves anti-Semitic. Partly because film can offer rich visual details to audiences, *The Passion* had the potential to portray the first-century Jewish people as more heterogeneous than "the Jews" of John's Gospel. According to several critics, the film failed to take this opportunity, and resorted instead to cinematic stereotypes which showed many of the Jews to be without compassion and sadistic. Admittedly, a few within the Jewish hierarchy and crowd were portrayed as deeply uneasy by the weight of violence thrown against Jesus, but the film does little more than gesture

toward the divergence of beliefs to be found within second temple Judaism. Which-
ever way that Gibson's work is interpreted, *The Passion* has provoked considerable
debate around anti-Semitic representations, contributing to a resurgence of awareness of this deeply problematic practice.[57]

The second significant area of controversy emerged after the release of the film.
The violence was unforgiving and in particular the scourging scene leaves nothing to
the imagination. Partly created by CGI (computer generated imagery) it showed
layers of Jesus' skin being ripped off by a brutal and sadistic flaying by several
Roman soldiers. Some viewers saw this depiction as "pornographic,"[58] while others
commended a de-sanitized truthful representation of the passion. Even though
Gibson and the director of cinematography, Caleb Deschanel, carefully studied the
paintings of Caravaggio, the depiction of Jesus' brutalized body is closer to Matthias
Grünewald's 1515 *Isenheim Altarpiece* than to Caravaggio's *Flagellation of Christ*
(1607), which leaves Jesus comparatively unscathed. There is little mercy shown to
the viewer, as the film takes us along a cinematic Via Dolorosa, showing a bloodied
Jesus stumble, fall, and then for over 20 minutes die an excruciating death on the
cross. One irony is that the film found a loyal and large following from many
conservative Christians, who are often among the loudest critics of the violence
to be found in Hollywood movies. In contrast to Quentin Tarantino's *Kill Bill:
Volume 1* (2003), Gibson avoided any hints of comic-book violence, offering his
audience instead a cinematic depiction of "how it was." Even Gibson himself
acknowledged the "intensity and brutality" of the film when he released *The Passion
– Recut* at Easter 2005, which had six minutes of the most violent scenes removed.

Why so much graphic violence? Was it to make a drama with Aramaic and Latin-
speaking characters more understandable to audiences raised on *Mad Max* (1979)
and *Lethal Weapon* (1987) movies, and ever more explicit war films? The realism of
the violence in *The Passion* is not only a claim to authenticity, but also an expression
of how both audiences and directors have become increasingly used to gazing upon
dismembered limbs and blood-spattered wounds. "I wanted it to be shocking,"
Gibson explained. "And I also wanted it to be extreme. I wanted it to push the
viewer over the edge . . . so that they see the enormity – the enormity of that
sacrifice – to see that someone could endure that and still come back with love and
forgiveness, even through extreme pain and suffering and ridicule."[59] The execution
scene of William Wallace in Gibson's *Braveheart* (1995) intimates this desire to
shock and to display sacrificial martyrdom.

Several theologians have objected both to the extreme violence of *The Passion* and
to the closely related representation of a theology of substitutionary atonement. This
highlights a third area of controversy: Gibson's theology as expressed cinematically.
The Passion represents a forceful cinematic account of Gibson's beliefs, which puts
significant emphasis upon the sacrificial nature of Jesus' death. As it stands this
cinematic attempt to recreate first century Judea mixes together elements from the
four gospels, strands of post-medieval Roman Catholic European theology, and the
writings of an Augustinian German nun and mystic, Sister Anne Emmerich (1774–
1824).[60] As with so many other Jesus films, *The Passion* also draws upon the long
tradition of Christian art to express theology visually. Many, if not all, of the 14
stations of the cross, so frequently artistically represented, find cinematic expression
in Gibson's film.[61] This film resonates with the individualistic piety that draws the

believer to focus intently upon the suffering, the wounds, and the death of Christ. This sacrificial death is for the individual viewer's sins as much as it is for the sins of the world. The fact that the film gives such sparse attention to the resurrection echoes those Christian pieties and theologies which tend to drive a wedge between crucifixion and resurrection. A further irony is that the film was embraced so whole-heartedly not only by many fundamentalist but also by evangelical Christians,[62] with many churches pre-booking entire cinemas, when these very groups often also believe the Catholic theology as represented by Gibson is deeply flawed. This idiosyncratic alliance helped put *The Passion* at the top of the global film charts. Around the world several newspapers described it as "The Greatest Story ever Sold."[63] The marketing was skillfully done, with the emphasis upon its "veracity" and the severe criticism, even the "torment" and "persecution," that its director faced were used to good effect in heightening support for the film.

Any account of directorial theology is inevitably selective. There is not space here to consider the theologically rich work of directors such as Carl Theodor Dreyer, Robert Bresson or Andrei Tarkovsky. Bergman, Coppola, and Gibson are only three out of a whole pantheon of film directors who have expressed theological narratives and themes cinematically. For example, DeMille's religious epics, *The Ten Command-ments* (1923), *The King of Kings* (1927), and his "talkie" *The Sign of the Cross* (1932), draw viewers into the narrative in a very different way from Gibson's *The Passion*. His work may have a didactic preaching tone, but viewers are also offered alluring images, such as a scantily clad Mary Magdalene surrounded by male admirers in *King of Kings* or Empress Poppea bathing in milk in *The Sign of the Cross*. DeMille's combi-nation of sexual comedy and religious themes brought him huge success at the box office, but also opposition from both the Catholic and Protestant churches. Study-ing his *oeuvre* of over seventy films highlights how complex it is to discern precisely how a director's own beliefs and background actually shape the final production.[64]

This is also the case with Martin Scorsese, whose training at a seminary school, spending a year when aged 14 at Cathedral college in New York, is sometimes used as a key to interpret his films. He was in earnest from the age of eight about becoming a priest, and his Catholic upbringing in Italian New York appears to have had a significant influence upon his filmmaking. He may no longer be a practicing Catholic, but the themes of sin, violence, and redemption are never far from the surface of his films, such as *Taxi Driver* (1976), *Raging Bull* (1980), and *Cape Fear* (1991). His earlier *Mean Streets* (1973) shows the main character struggling with conflict between what he hears and does in church and what he finds on the streets where the gun rules. Standing in sharp contrast to the theology expressed through *The Passion*, the controversial *Last Temptation of Christ* (1988), based on Kazantzakis' novel, reflects Scorsese's own wrestling with the nature of Christ as a doubting person fully tempted and fully human.[65]

Scorsese, Bergman, and even Gibson are examples of directors who acknowledge some basis in theological thinking, Coppola and DeMille more rarely, while the majority of directors tend to express theological themes without formally naming them as such. The theme emerges from the narrative because it is expressive of primal fears, aspirations, and predispositions, not because it has been consciously planted there. My contention in this section is that to speak of directorial theology does not exclude the possibility of acknowledging the wider role of both the production team and the audience in creating theological meaning around specific films.

Influence, Debate, and Agenda

There has been a marked increase of literature published on theology and film over the last decade. Nevertheless, compared to many lines of theological inquiry, theological film criticism is still in its early days. One significant change of emphasis over the last ninety years is a shift from pastoral concern about the impacts or benefits of film, to more sustained critical analysis by theologians who are often writing for a narrower readership. Increasingly, theologians are using film as a source to illustrate rich theological themes or debates. Recent examples of this practice include L. Gregory Jones' extended use of *Unforgiven* (1992) in *Embodying Forgiveness* (1995), David Brown's brief analysis of Jesus films in *Tradition and Imagination* (1999), Graham Ward's discussions of *The Matrix* in *Cities of God* (2000), David Cunningham's use of film to illuminate the Apostles' Creed in *Reading is Believing* (2002), Gerard Loughlin's analysis of the *Alien* films in *Alien Sex* (2003), and David Jasper's consideration of films of the desert in *The Sacred Desert* (2004). In these books film is used to illustrate and to support a broader thesis. The cinema is now often portrayed not as a problem to be negotiated, but more as a resource to be mined. These theologians are going far beyond moral criticism to engage with the theological issues provoked by different films. They demonstrate how some of the most theologically interesting films are not necessarily explicitly religious in content.

The fact that many Christians regularly now go to the cinema, watch videos or DVDs, and read and write film reviews, has ensured that in several accounts the censorious role of the churches has taken on the air of a distant half-forgotten memory. There is a sense in which iconoclastic approaches to the cinema are acknowledged, but ultimately ignored. Theological exploration of films has taken on a far more confident role both in the academy and in the church. Theological film criticism has moved beyond defending the appropriateness of going to the cinema or watching particular films, and now analyses in some detail how films actually explore moral issues and theological themes. The return to the cinema raises a number of significant questions for Christian theologians. For example, is there a distinctively theological way of analysing films or do Christians simply draw upon elements of film criticism for their own theological purposes? Many theologians appear to be immersed in either textual analytical discussions or authorial approaches to film. "It is somewhat disappointing to find that writing on film which does take religion seriously has largely ignored the broader social, cultural, and historical contexts within which films are made and consumed."[66] Films such as *It's a Wonderful Life* (1946), *On the Waterfront* (1954), *Dead Man Walking* (1995), and *Dogma* (1999) are not only useful for provoking theological questions, they can also be valuable as thermometers of a culture's *Zeitgeist* at a particular moment in time. What, for example, does the delight in cinematic fantasy as found in the *Lord of the Rings* trilogy and the *Harry Potter* films show about this current age?

Many theological responses to the cinema are founded on the belief that movies work like the moment from Edwin Porter's *The Great Train Robbery* (1903), where

Barnes, leader of the outlaw band, points his gun out towards the audience and fires point blank into their faces. Film legend has it that the result was extreme: some viewers are believed to have screamed, ducked, or put their fingers in their ears, and others supposedly even ran out of the cinema. This is probably a romanticized retrospective view of early cinema: there may have been flinching at the Lumière brothers' showing in 1895, but audiences were already becoming canny and skeptical spectators by 1903. Nonetheless, the unstated assumption in several of the approaches discussed in earlier sections is that through films the bullet of narrative content fires out at the viewers, and has a powerful impact on audiences. This "magic bullet theory" of communication is now rarely explicitly defended, but the idea of a passive audience soaking in the messages that are fired at them remains surprisingly tenacious in many Christian documents and theological reflections about film. One way of enriching the evolving theology and film debate would be to leave behind a passive receptor paradigm and replace it with a more sophisticated understanding of audiences as active spectators. In other words, to investigate not only what films do to the audience, but also what audiences do with films.[67]

Up to this point theological film criticism has largely emerged from the West and tended to assume a Western audience.[68] This ignores a significant element of current film consumption. For example, a packed cinema or video house in Accra, with a full house watching a locally produced Ghanaian or Nigerian film rich in religious symbolism, brings new meaning to the term "active audience." The viewers are rarely silent, and often they actively cheer, boo, or pray out loud for the characters.[69] This experience stands in sharp contrast with sitting in a Western multiplex watching a Hollywood film, where the audience tends to be far quieter. Except for the occasional cough, rustle of sweet wrappers or munching on popcorn, any talking is normally "shushed" and exclamations are rare, the exceptions being laughter or gasps or screams of surprise in horror movies and thrillers. The silencing of the Western audience is a fascinating story well told elsewhere.[70] Appearances can be deceptive. This silence does not mean that audiences are entirely passive. For well over twenty years researchers have explored how viewers actively weave complex patterns of meaning on the basis of the films, and other media, that they consume. This could go further: how precisely do audiences in different cultural contexts make theological meaning from what they see? How important a factor is their local church, practice of prayer, or understanding of theology in helping them make sense of a specific film? To what extent does this network of experiences shape and color the way they process what they view? Few scholars have actually tested the claim that films have replaced the institutional church as the provider of religious symbols and theological meaning. There is clearly a need for both empirical investigation and greater conceptual clarity around the claim that films can act as points of transcendence or even channels of revelation.

Cultural resistance in the face of films that exploit, stereotype, or damage comes in many forms. For example, Cheryl Exum's consideration of cultural representations of biblical women in *Plotted, Shot and Painted* (1996) proposes a strategy of resistance, which self-consciously "takes seriously the gender politics of both representation and interpretation."[71] Approaches such as this emphasise how the male gaze tends still to dominate both the production and reception of many films. Other writers look for the building up of Christian communities, distinct linguistic and interpretive communities, in the face of the perceived onslaught of the global culture industries which produce films.[72] But this may simply be another form of cultural withdrawal that draws a sharp divide between secular, profane films and holy, sacred believers. It ignores the possibility that films such as *All Quiet on the Western Front* (1930) can themselves articulate a sharp cultural critique. Films can interrogate theology. The church has much to learn from specific prophetic films.

Nevertheless, there remains a need for nuanced critiques of the film industry itself. How far has it become an agent of capitalism and consumerism? How far has the film industry become an alternative kind of church, with its own sacred times and spaces, its own viewing rituals and canonization ceremonies? How far does it promote the accumulation of wealth and individual celebrity over the formation of character and caring communities? How far does the industry create cinematic distractions from the real and endemic violence in the world? These questions are complicated by the fact that while many films celebrate the myths of heroic individualism or romantic love or redemptive violence, others function counter-culturally, challenging the status quo in a way reminiscent of some of Jesus' most provocative teaching. The global increase in the viewing of films, as well as the crossover of movies to television, videos, and DVDs, heightens the significance of these questions. Seeing with the help of film can be encouraged not through the endless censoring enacted in *Cinema Paradiso*, but through communal worship, caring practices, and reflective education.

Notes

1   See, for example, F. Walsh, *Sin and Censorship* (New Haven, CT, 1996), p. 1. For further discussions of censorship, see G. Black, *Hollywood Censored* (New York, 1994) and M. Bernstein (ed.), *Controlling Hollywood* (London, 2000).

2   For contrasting accounts of the protests against *The Last Temptation of Christ*, see M. Medved, *Hollywood vs. America* (New York, 1992), pp. 38–49 and M. Miles, *Seeing and Believing* (Boston, MA, 1996), pp. 33–40. For both films, see L. Baugh, *Imaging the Divine* (Kansas City, KS, 1997), pp. 48–71.

3   R. Rosenzweig, "From Rum Shop to Rialto: Workers and Movies" in G. A. Waller (ed.), *Moviegoing in America* (Oxford, 2002), pp. 36–7.

4   See Ronald Holloway, *Beyond the Image* (New York, 1977), p. 26 and James M. Skinner, *The Cross and the Cinema* (Westport, CT, 1993), Figs. 10 and 11, and pp. 193–4.

5   See Charles Musser, "Passions and the Passion Play: Theatre, Film, and Religion

in America, 1800–1900," *Film History* 5 (1993): 419–56.

6   See R. Johnston, *Reel Spirituality* (Grand Rapids, MI, 2000), p. 32.

7   H. Jump, "The Religious Possibilities of the Motion Picture" in T. Lindvall (ed.), *The Silents of God* (Lanham, MD, 2001), pp. 55–78. See also *Film History* 14: 2 (2002).

8   See L. Baugh, *Imaging the Divine* (Kansas City, KS, 1997), pp. 7–8.

9   For an exception, see Krzysztof Jozajtis, *Religion and Film in American Culture: The Birth of a Nation* (unpublished PhD thesis, Stirling, 2001), p. 98.

10 For a typography influenced by R. Niebuhr's *Christ and Culture* categories see the introduction by Clive Marsh in C. Marsh and G. Ortiz (eds.), *Explorations in Theology and Film* (Oxford, 1997).

11 John R. May, "Religion and Film: Recent Contributions to the Continuing Dialogue," *Critical Review of Books* in *Religion* 9 (1996), pp. 105–21.

12 Johnston, *Reel Spirituality*, pp. 41–62.

13 C. H. J. Linn, "The Movies – the Devil's Incubator" in T. Lindvall (ed.), *The Silents of God* (Lanham, MD, 2001), p. 279.

14 John Rice, *What is Wrong with the Movies?* (Wheaton, IL, 1938), p. 14.

15 Morgan Derham, *What's Wrong with the Cinema?* (London, 1948), pp. 17–18.

16 R. G. Burnett and E. D. Martell, *The Devil's Camera* (London: 1932), p. 71.

17 Ibid, pp. 108–9.

18 Ibid, pp. 116–17.

19 For *Vigilanti Cura* and other Catholic documents cited in this section, see either the Vatican website or Franz-Josef Eilers (ed.), *Church and Social Communication: Basic Documents*, 2nd edn. (Manila, 1997).

20 See Steven Carr, *Hollywood and Anti-Semitism* (Cambridge, UK, 2001).

21 See US Federal Communications Commission's final judgment (January 11, 2000), rejecting Thomas B. North's complaint that the pre-10.00 p.m. nudity contained in the network presentation of *Schindler's List*, February 23, 1997, was actionably indecent.

22 See, for example, Pius XI, *Vigilanti Cura* (1936), II.

23 See Gaye Ortiz, "The Catholic Church and Its Attitude to Film as an Arbiter of Cultural Meaning," in Jolyon Mitchell and Sophia Marriage (eds.), *Mediating Religion* (London, 2003), pp. 179–88.

24 Ronald Holloway, *Beyond the Image* (New York, 1977), p. 29.

25 L. Baugh, *Imaging the Divine* (Kansas City, KS, 1997), p. 97.

26 Peter Malone, *Film and Values* (New York, 1984), pp. 3, 43.

27 See Paul Coates, *Cinema, Religion and the Romantic Legacy* (Aldershot, 2003), pp. 79–82.

28 For a fuller critical exposition of these and several other approaches, see Steve Nolan, "Towards a New Religious Film Criticism: Using Film to Understand Religious Identity Rather than Locate Cinematic Analogue," in Mitchell and Marriage, *Mediating Religion*, pp. 169–78.

29 Ibid, pp. 173–4.

30 See also Bernard Brandon Scott, *Hollywood Dreams and Biblical Stories* (Minneapolis, MN, 1994).

31 See Nolan, "Towards a New Religious Film Criticism," pp. 169–78.

32 See T. M. Martin, *Images and the Imageless: A Study in Religious Consciousness and Film* (Lewisburg, PA, 1981), p. 122.

33 Peter Fraser, *Images of the Passion: The Sacramental Mode in Film* (Trowbridge, 1998), p. 5.

34 Ibid, p. 11.

35 Ibid, p. 6.

36 Andrew M. Greeley, *God in Popular Culture* (Chicago, 1988), p. 9.

37 Ibid, p. 121.

38 Albert Bergesen and Andrew M. Greeley, *God in the Movies* (New Brunswick, NJ, 2000).

39 See Roy M. Anker, *Catching Light: Looking for God in the Movies* (Cambridge, UK, 2004), and Catherine M. Barsotti and Robert K. Johnston, *Finding God in the Movies* (Grand Rapids, MI, 2004).

40 Paul Schrader, *Transcendental Style in Film: Ozu, Bresson, Dreyer* (Berkeley, CA, 1972). For a definition of his terms, see pp. 3–13.

41 George Lucas interview with Bill Moyers in *Time*, April 26, 1999.

42 Geoffrey Nowell-Smith (ed.), *The Oxford History of World Cinema* (Oxford, 1996), p. 625.

43 Ingmar Bergman, introduction to *The Seventh Seal* script (London, 1968, revised 1984).

44 Melvyn Bragg, *The Seventh Seal*, BFI Classics (London, 1993), p. 11.

45 Bergman, introduction to *The Seventh Seal*.

46 Ibid.

47 See J. Kalin, *The Films of Ingmar Bergman* (Cambridge, 2003), pp. 57–67.

48 See Naomi Greene, "Family Ceremonies," in Nick Browne (ed.), *Francis Ford Coppola's The Godfather Trilogy* (Cambridge, 2000), p. 144; and John R. May, "The Godfather Films: Birth of a Don, Death of a Family," in John R. May (ed.), *Image and Likeness: Religious Visions in American Film Classics* (Mahwah, NJ, 1992). In this section, I am particularly indebted to May's discussion.

49 Cited in May, "The Godfather Films," p. 65.

50 Ibid, p. 75.

51 This concern continued after its release. See also Marvin Perry and Frederick M. Schweitzer, "The Medieval Passion Play Revisited," in S. Brent Plate, *Re-Viewing the Passion* (New York, 2004), pp. 3–19;

and Karen Jo Torjesen, "The Journey of the Passion Play from Medieval Piety to Contemporary Spirituality," in J. Shawn Landres and Michael Berenbaum (eds.), *After the Passion is Gone* (Walnut Creek, 2004), pp. 93–104.

52 ADL press release, August 11, 2003.

53 Gibson interviewed by Diane Sawyer for ABC's *Primetime*, February 14, 2004.

54 The most significant change was the line based upon Matthew 27: 25, where the crowd says "His blood be upon us and upon our children." The original line was kept in the film, spoken in the "original" language, but the subtitle was removed.

55 See, for example, John Dominic Crossan's review "Hymn to a Savage God," at www.beliefnet.com and now published in Kathleen E. Corley and Robert L. Webb (eds.), *Jesus and Mel Gibson's The Passion of the Christ* (London, 2004). See also National Conference of Catholic Bishops, *Criteria for the Evaluation of Dramatizations of the Passion* (1988).

56 Leonard Klady, "The Passion and the Profits" in *Screen International*, December 3, 2004, p. 56.

57 See Terry Goble, "When Lightning Strikes Twice: Signal Graces, Mel Gibson and *The Passion of the Christ*," *Borderlands: A Journal of Theology and Education*, Issue 3 (summer 2004), pp. 46–9.

58 James Caroll, "An Obscene Portrayal of Christ's Passion," *Boston Globe*, February 24, 2004.

59 Gibson interviewed by Diane Sawyer for ABC's *Primetime*, February 14, 2004.

60 See *The Dolorous Passion of Our Lord Jesus Christ from the Meditations of Anne Catherine Emmerich* (Rockford, IL, 1994).

61 See David Morgan, "Catholic Visual Piety and the Vision of the Christ," in S. Brent Plate (ed.), *Re-Viewing the Passion* (New York, 2004), pp. 85–96.

62 See Leslie E. Smith, ". . . Understanding Evangelical Support for *The Passion of the Christ*," in J. Shawn Landres and Michael Berenbaum (eds.), *After the Passion is Gone* (Walnut Creek, 2004).

63 See, for example, *The Age*, (Melbourne, Australia, February 25, 2004).

64 Despite several attempts, it is even more difficult to identify the precise extent that Hitchcock's Catholicism shaped his representation of guilt and innocence in his "wrong man" films, where a wrongly accused attempts to clear his name. See Eric Rohmer and Claude Chabrol, *Hitchcock: The First Forty-four Films* (New York, 1978).

65 For a fuller discussion, see Jeffrey Mahan, "Celluloid Savior: Jesus in the Movies," *Journal of Religion and Film*, 6: 1, April 2002.

66 Jozajtis, *Religion and Film in American Culture*, p. 98.

67 See Clive Marsh, *Cinema and Sentiment: Film's Challenge to Theology* (Carlisle, 2004).

68 For an exception, see S. B. Plate (ed.), *Representing Religion in World Cinema* (New York, 2003).

69 See Jolyon Mitchell, "From Morality Tales to Horror Movies," in P. Horsfield et al., (eds.) *Belief in Media* (Aldershot, 2004), pp. 107–20.

70 See Lawrence W. Levine, *Highbrow/Lowbrow: The Emergence of Cultural Hierarchy in America* (Cambridge, MA, 1988).

71 J. Cheryl Exum, *Plotted, Shot and Painted: Cultural Representations of Biblical Women* (Sheffield, 1996), p. 53.

72 See M. Budde, *The (Magic) Kingdom of God: Christianity and Global Culture Industries* (Boulder, CO, 1997).

Bibliography

G. Aichele and R. Walsh (eds.), *Screening Scripture: Intertextual Connections Between Scripture and Film* (Harrisburg, PA, 2002).

R. M. Anker, *Catching the Light: Looking for God in the Movies* (Grand Rapids, MI, 2004).

B. Babington and P. W. Evans, *Biblical Epics: Sacred Narrative in the Hollywood Cinema* (Manchester, 1993).

M. L. Bandy and A. Monda, *The Hidden God: Film and Faith* (New York, 2003).

C. M. Barsotti and R. K. Johnston, *Finding God in the Movies* (Grand Rapids, MI, 2004).

L. Baugh, *Imaging the Divine: Jesus and Christ-Figures in Film* (Kansas City, KS, 1997).

K. L. Billingsley, *The Seductive Image: A Christian Critique of the World of Film* (Westchester, IL, 1989).

R. A. Blake, *After Image: The Indelible Catholic Imagination of Six American Filmmakers* (Chicago, 2000).

W. Blizek (ed.), "Special Issue on *The Passion of the Christ*," *The Journal of Religion and Film*, www.unomaha.edu/jrf/previous.htm#Passion, Vol. 8, No. 1 (Nebraska, April 2004).

R. G. Burnett and E. D. Martell, *The Devil's Camera: Menace of a Film-Ridden World* (London: 1932).

I. Butler, *Religion in the Cinema* (London: 1969).

T. Cawkwell, *The Filmgoer's Guide to God* (London, 2004).

A. Clarke and P. Fiddes (eds.), *Flickering Images: Theology and Film in Dialogue* (Macon, GA, 2005).

P. Coates, *Cinema, Religion and the Romantic Legacy* (Aldershot, 2003).

K. E. Corley and R. L. Webb (eds.), *Jesus and Mel Gibson's The Passion of the Christ: the Film, the Gospels and the Claims of History* (London, 2004).

D. S. Cunningham, *Reading is Believing: The Christian Faith through Literature and Film* (Grand Rapids, MI, 2002).

J. Cunneen, *Robert Bresson: A Spiritual Style in Film* (New York, 2003).

E. Christianson, P. Francis, W. Telford (eds.) *Cinéma Divinité: Religion, Theology and the Bible in Film* (London, 2005).

C. Deacy, *Screen Christologies: Redemption and the Medium of Film* (Cardiff, 2001).

—— *Faith in Film: Religious Themes in Contemporary Cinema* (Aldershot, 2005).

S. Faux, *Finding Meaning at the Movies* (Nashville, TN, 1999).

E. Ferlita and J. May, *Film Odyssey: The Art of Film as Search for Meaning* (New York, 1976).

P. Fraser, *Images of the Passion: The Sacramental Mode in Film* (Trowbridge, 1998).

A. Gibson, *The Silence of God: Creative Response to the Films of Ingmar Bergman* (New York, 1969).

B. Godwa, *Hollywood Worldviews: Watching Films With Wisdom and Discernment* (Downers Grove, NY, 2002).

E. L. Graham, *Representations of the Post/Human: Monsters, Aliens and Others in Popular Culture* (Manchester, 2002).

A. Greeley, *God in Popular Culture* (Chicago, 1988).

G. Higgins, *How Movies Helped Save My Soul* (Lake Mary, FL, 2003).

R. Holloway, *Beyond the Image: Approaches to the Religious Dimension in the Cinema* (New York, 1977).

N. P. Hurley, *Theology Through Film* (New York, 1970); reprinted as *Toward a Film Humanism* (New York, 1975).

—— *The Reel Revolution: A Film Primer on Liberation* (New York, 1978).

—— *Soul in Suspense: Hitchcock's Fright and Delight* (London, 1993).

D. Jasper, *The Sacred Desert: Religion, Literature, Art, and Culture* (Oxford, 2004).

R. Jewett, *St. Paul at the Movies: The Apostle's Dialogue with American Culture* (Louisville, KY, 1993).

—— *Saint Paul Returns to the Movies: Triumph over Shame* (Grand Rapids, MI, 1999).

R. K. Johnston, *Reel Spirituality: Theology and Film in Dialogue* (Grand Rapids, MI, 2000).

—— *Useless Beauty: Ecclesiastes through the Lens of Contemporary Film* (Grand Rapids, MI, 2000).

H. A. Jump, *The Religious Possibilities of the Motion Picture* (New Britain, CT, 1910).

R. Kinnard and T. Davis, *Divine Images: A History of Jesus on the Screen* (New York, 1992).

L. and B. Keyser, *Hollywood and the Catholic Church: the Images of Roman Catholicism in American Movies* (Chicago, 1984).

L. J. Kreitzer, *The New Testament in Fiction and Film* (Sheffield, 1993).

—— *The Old Testament in Fiction and Film* (Sheffield, 1994).

—— *Pauline Images in Fiction and Film* (Sheffield, 1999).

—— *Gospel Images in Fiction and Film: On Reversing the Hermeneutical Flow* (Sheffield, 2002).

J. S. Landres and M. Berenbaum (eds.), *After the Passion is Gone: American Religious Consequences* (Walnut Creek, CA, 2004).

T. Lane, *What's Wrong With the Movies?* (Los Angeles, CA, 1923).

D. J. Leab (ed.), "Film and Religion" issue of *Film History: An International Journal*, Vol. 14, No. 2 (London, 2002).

T. Lindvall, *The Silents of God: Selected Issues and Documents in Silent American Film and Religion, 1908–1925* (Lanham, MD, 2001).

G. Loughlin, *Alien Sex: The Body and Desire in Cinema and Theology* (Oxford, 2004).

J. Lyden, *Film as Religion: Myths, Morals, and Rituals* (New York, 2003).

P. Malone, *Movie Christs and Antichrists* (New York, 1990).

C. Marsh, *Cinema and Sentiment: Film's Challenge to Theology* (Carlisle, 2004).

C. Marsh and G. Ortiz (eds.), *Explorations in Theology and Film: Movies and Meaning* (Oxford, 1997).

J. W. Martin and C. E. Ostwalt, Jr. (eds.), *Screening the Sacred: Religion, Myth and Ideology in Popular American Film* (Boulder, CO, 1995).

T. M. Martin, *Images and the Imageless: A Study in Religious Consciousness and Film* (Lewisburg, PA, 1981).

J. R. May (ed.), *Images and Likeness: Religious Visions in American Film Classics* (Mahwah, NJ, 1991).

—— (ed.), *New Image of Religious Film* (Kansas City, KS, 1997).

—— *Nourishing Faith Through Fiction: Reflections of the Apostles' Creed in Literature and Film* (Franklin, MA, 2001).

J. R. May and M. Bird (eds.), *Religion in Film* (Knoxville, TN, 1982).

E. McNulty, *Praying the Movies I and II: Daily Meditations from Classic Films* (Louisville, KY, 2001 and 2004).

M. R. Miles, *Seeing and Believing: Religion and Values in the Movies* (Boston, MA, 1996).

J. P. Mitchell, *Media and Christian Ethics* (Cambridge, forthcoming 2006).

J. P. Mitchell, "From Morality Tales to Horror Movies: Towards an Understanding of the Popularity of West African Video Film," in P. Horsfield, M. E. Hess, and A. M. Medrano

(eds.) *Belief in Media: Cultural Perspectives on Media and Christianity* (Aldershot, 2004).

J. P. Mitchell and S. Marriage (eds.), *Mediating Religion: Conversations in Media, Religion and Culture* (London, 2003).

S. B. Plate (ed.), *Representing Religion in World Cinema: Filmmaking, Mythmaking, Culture Making* (New York, 2003).

—— (ed.), *Re-viewing the Passion: Mel Gibson's Film and its Critics* (New York, 2004).

S. B. Plate and D. Jasper (eds.), *Imag(in)ing Otherness: Filmic Visions of Living Together* (Atlanta, GA, 1999).

J. Pungente and M. Williams, *Finding God in the Dark: Taking the Spiritual Exercises of St. Ignatius to the Movies* (Ottawa, Ontario, 2004).

A. Reinhartz, *Scripture on the Silver Screen* (Louisville, KY, 2003).

J. R. Rice, *What is Wrong with the Movies?* (Murfreesboro, TN, 1938).

R. Riley, *Film, Faith and Cultural Conflict: The Case of Martin Scorsese's The Last Temptation of Christ* (London, 2003).

W. D. Romanowski, *Eyes Wide Open: Looking for God in Popular Culture* (Grand Rapids, MI, 2001).

E. Runions, *How Hysterical: Identification and Resistance in the Bible and Film* (New York, 2003).

T. Sanders, *Celluloid Saints: Images of Sanctity in Film* (Macon, GA, 2002).

P. Schrader, *Transcendental Style in Film: Ozu, Bresson, Dreyer* (Berkeley, CA, 1972).

R. Stern, C. Jefford, and G. Debona, *Savior on the Silver Screen* (New York, 1999).

B. P. Stone, *Faith and Film: Theological Themes at the Cinema* (St. Louis, 2000).

W. B. Tatum, *Jesus at the Movies: A Guide to the First Hundred Years* (Santa Rosa, CA, 1997).

J. M. Wall, *Church and Cinema: A Way of Viewing Film* (Grand Rapids, MI, 1971).

R. Walsh, *Reading the Gospels in the Dark: Portrayals of Jesus in Film* (Harrisburg, PA, 2003).

G. Ward (ed.), "Film and Religion" issue of *Literature and Theology*, Vol. 12, No. 1 (Oxford, 1998).

M. Wright, *Religion and Film: An Introduction* (London, 2005).

Epilogue:
Twelve Theses for Christian Theology in the Twenty-first Century

David F. Ford

The Epilogue to the second edition of *The Modern Theologians* faced the turn of the millennium with a celebration of the abundance of God indicated by the contents of that volume: "The global upsurge of Christian theologies, as one community or group after another has found its voice, can be read as testimony to the polyphonic abundance of God."[1] It went on to ask a series of questions about the health of the discipline of theology. These were:

- How to attest in truth to God and to all else in relation to God?
- How can theology distribute its efforts so as to be thoughtfully responsible in many spheres?
- Will the academy be a place of genuine theology?
- Will churches be communities genuinely informed by theology?
- Who does theology?
- How to celebrate the millennium?

In the years since then the global polyphony has intensified and those questions have continued to be relevant. This Epilogue offers, to complement the questions, twelve theses (or slogans, or maxims) as a personal postscript. They are distilled from the experience of editing the three editions and of having had nearly twenty years of conversation and correspondence around this project of trying to give an account of the past century of Christian theology. That has not only been a significant element in my theological education; it has also helped form some ideas about the future of theology.

The theses are offered without commentary, in the hope that they might act as a stimulus provoking readers in the twenty-first century to think, talk, and write Christian theology worthy of the best in this volume – even if they disagree with the theses.

1   God is the One who blesses and loves in wisdom.
2   Theology is done for the sake of God and the Kingdom of God.
3   The cry of prayer is the beginning, accompaniment, and end of theology: Come, Holy Spirit! Hallelujah! and Maranatha!
4   Study of scripture is at the heart of theology.
5   Describing reality in the light of God is a basic theological discipline.
6   Theology hopes in and seeks God's purposes while immersed in the contingencies, complexities, and ambiguities of creation and history.
7   Theological wisdom seeks to do justice to many contexts, levels, voices, moods, genres, systems, and responsibilities.
8   Theology is practiced collegially, in conversation and, best of all, in friendship; and, through the communion of saints, it is simultaneously premodern, modern, and postmodern.
9   Theology is a broker of the arts, humanities, sciences, and common sense for the sake of a wisdom that affirms, critiques, and transforms each of them.
10 Our religious and secular world needs theology with religious studies in its schools and universities.
11 Conversation around scriptures is at the heart of interfaith relations.
12 Theology is for all who desire to think about God and about reality in relation to God.

Note

1   David F. Ford (ed.), *The Modern Theologians: An Introduction to Christian Theology in the Twentieth Century* (Oxford, 1997), p. 721.

Glossary

All dates CE *unless otherwise stated*

a priori Latin phrase used to characterize reasoning from causes to effects, from abstract notions to their consequences, and from assumed principles; of or pertaining to knowledge known independent of any evidence or warrant (e.g., mathematical truths).

Abrahamic Of or pertaining to the biblical patriarch Abraham, or those religious traditions which claim continuity with him or his faith – Judaism, Christianity, and Islam.

absolute *Geist* The notion of unconditioned reality understood either as the spiritual ground of all being or the whole of things viewed as a spiritual unity, and associated with the philosophers Schelling (1775–1854) and Hegel (1770–1831).

absolutism Position which makes one element, text, person, ideology, or reality supreme or absolute in relation to everything; or an understanding of the absolute (ultimate reality) as existing independently or unconditionally.

abstract Ideal; separated from matter, practice, and particulars.

actuality Reality; the state of existing in reality.

Ad hoc Latin expression meaning "to this end," used of arguments, strategies, or practices undertaken only for the particular purpose in view and on no other general criteria.

Adventists Various Christian groups which all hold that the second coming of Jesus Christ is to be expected immediately.

aesthetic existence In Søren Kierkegaard's *Enten-Eller* (Either-Or), this denotes an attitude that orientates life to the enjoyment of the beautiful; the opposite of ethical existence.

aesthetics The philosophy of the beautiful; the study of the feelings, concepts, and judgments related to perception of the beautiful. Theological aesthetics are specifically the aesthetic dimensions of a religious tradition's own thought, worship, and practice.

agapic, agapeic, agapaic Having the quality of *agape*, a Greek word for "love" used in the New Testament to describe the love of God expressed in Jesus Christ and commended among human beings.

agential   Of or pertaining to an agent (one who acts) or agency (action or capacity to act of an agent).

agnosticism   Belief that it is not possible to know the truth value of a certain proposition or propositions; often referring to the belief that no one truly knows, or can know whether or not God exists.

Allah   In Islam, the Supreme Name of the Absolute, or divinity; the proper and true name of God, through which humanity calls upon him personally.

altruism   Benefiting others for their own sake alone; the opposite of egoism (action for one's own sake alone); more generally used of regard for the good of others as a principle of action.

analogy   The relationship between two or more different uses of a word such that the use is neither equivocal (the meanings on each occasion are utterly diverse and unrelated) nor univocal (the meanings are the same).

analogy of being   Doctrine associated with Thomas Aquinas (1225–74), and attacked by Karl Barth (1886–1968), that, in virtue of the ontological dependence of creatures upon God, "being" is predicated analogously of God and creatures, first because God is the cause of being in creatures, and second because of the similarity in greater dissimilarity between the relationship between God and his existence and that of creatures with theirs.

analogy of faith   Doctrine associated with Karl Barth (1886–1968) that although God is unknowable to us, God nevertheless grants the believer a share in God's own self-knowledge through faith, whereby the language of scripture is rendered by grace an adequate witness to God.

analytic philosophy   School which practices philosophy as a method of inquiry which involves assessing statements or complex systems of thought by breaking them down (analyzing them) into their simpler components, whose normative relations that are the justification of the system or statement may then be examined.

Anglican   Of or pertaining to the churches and the members of the churches stemming from Henry VIII's schism from the Roman Catholic Church in 1534 and now members of the Anglican Communion.

Anglo-catholic   Strand within the **Anglican** Communion that stresses a high doctrine of the **sacraments**, an episcopacy deriving from the apostles, continuity with the church of the early centuries, and ultimate independence from the state.

animism   Cultural and religious systems which associate spiritual life with inanimate objects and natural phenomena and involve a pantheon of such spiritual beings.

annunciation   Announcement by the Angel Gabriel to the Blessed Virgin Mary that she would bear Jesus, and Mary's response of consent.

anthropocentric   Centered upon humanity or an understanding of human nature.

anthropology   Theory or study of the nature of human being or of humankind.

anthropological turn   The move in modern thought to focus on anthropological questions.

anthropomorphism   Conceiving of some being or beings, especially God, in terms of human attributes and characteristics.

anti-foundationalism   Rejection of the supposition that certain universal or normative criteria exist and provide the basis for all philosophical and/or theological truth-claims.

anti-realism Rejection of the idea that there are mind-independent knowable facts, objects, or properties, either in relation to a particular form of inquiry or in general.

anti-Semitism Prejudice against and hostility toward Semites, usually meaning Jews.

apocalyptic Literally, the unveiling of what is covered or hidden; a genre of literature concerning the last things and the end of the world, often containing dreams, allegories, and elaborate symbolism.

Apollinarianism Denial of a human soul in Christ on the basis that the divine **Logos** performed that function, as articulated by Apollinarius (ca. 310–90); this view was condemned at the Council of Constantinople in 381.

apologetics Branch of theology concerned with defense of **orthodox** Christian doctrine in the face of criticism and alternative points of view, usually attempting to meet critics' questions and objections by looking for shared grounds or criteria for what is reasonable or true.

apophatic Of or pertaining to what is beyond speech; in particular, relating to the method of **negative theology** which stresses the transcendence of God over all human language and categories, and prefers forms of reference which say what God is not.

aporia Greek word meaning "difficulty" which denotes an irresolvable inconsistency in a position or system.

Apostles' Creed Ancient statement of beliefs used widely in the Western church from the seventh or eighth century, but not of apostolic origin.

apostolic succession The means whereby the ministry of the Christian church is believed to be derived from the apostles, usually by a continuous succession of bishops.

apostolicity State or quality of being in continuity with the church of the apostles by succession of bishops and continuity of doctrine, or in continuity with the faith of the apostles.

apotheosis The assimilation of a human being to a god; the assumption of extraordinary or divine powers or virtue; glorification or exaltation, associated with the **canonization** of saints.

archetype The original pattern or mold from which copies are made.

Aristotelian Relating to the philosopher Aristotle (384–322 BC), his thought, or that of his followers.

ascesis The practice of self-discipline.

asceticism Principles or practices of self-discipline, employed to combat vices or encourage virtues, often for religious reasons.

ashram Secluded residence of a religious community, often with a guru; more generally, popular term for the hermitage of a holy person.

a/theology Religious discourse predicated on the radical absence of God or divine meaning in the world or in language, which absence is signified, seen, or effected in the complete self-evacuation of the divine in the crucified Christ.

atheism The belief that God does not exist, that there is no God.

atonement Literally, at-one-ment; the work of Jesus Christ on the cross reconciling the world to God; the doctrine of the salvific work of Christ.

Augustinian Relating to Augustine of Hippo (354–430), bishop, theologian, and saint, his thought and that of those influenced by him.

autonomy Self-directing, independent.

Bacchanalian Relating to *Bacchanalia*, a Roman festival in honor of the god Bacchus, which was marked by riotous drinking and drunken revelry in general.

Baconian Relating to the thought of Francis Bacon (1561–1626), who advocated a new empirical method of scientific inquiry based on induction from evidence in order to gain a certain structure of knowledge that could be used to manipulate nature through technology.

Baptist One who baptizes; more commonly, a member of the Baptist churches, Christian groups which are separate from state churches, and which only baptize believing adults, by full immersion.

Barthian Relating to the thought of the **Protestant** theologian Karl Barth (1886–1968), most often associated with a rigorous **Christocentrism** and opposition to **natural theology**.

beatific vision Vision of the Trinity that, according to Christian theology, is the final destiny of the redeemed and the principal joy of heaven.

being Existence *per se*; all existence considered in the abstract.

Benedictine Relating to the Rule of St. Benedict of Nursia (ca. 480–547) for the monastic life, and those monastic orders which observe it, especially the Benedictine Order – a confederation of religious houses that follow the Rule.

biblical theology Theology conceived from and with constant reference to the Bible; a movement among twentieth-century scholars producing theology derived from biblical history and concepts, the former considered as the medium of revelation and generally reliable, the latter distinctive of the Bible, sufficient for theology, and coherent in relation to one another.

big bang theory Model for the history of the universe according to which it began in an infinitely compact state, then expanded rapidly and has been expanding ever since.

binarism Division of a domain into two discrete categories or polarities (e.g., the division of meat into "raw" and "cooked"); sometimes a pejorative term for structuralist scholarship that analyzes all aspects of all cultures in terms of such polarities.

binitarianism Doctrine that there are just two divine persons in God.

bourgeois French word denoting a member of the middle classes, a capitalist, an exploiter of the proletariat (the lowest class in a society, the wage-earners); also a socially and aesthetically conventional person.

Brahmin Or Brahman: member of the Brahmana – the priestly caste in Hindu tradition.

Byzantine Relating to Byzantium – the Eastern Roman empire – its politics and culture; of the Eastern Orthodox Church and its theology; sometimes used pejoratively of excessive bureaucracy, from which Byzantium is said to have suffered.

Cabbalistic Referring to Cabbalism, or the Kabbalah, the name for various streams of Jewish mysticism and spirituality; having a private or mystical sense.

canon law Body of church rules or laws.

canonical Of, prescribed by, or in conformity with, a rule or canon, in particular to the church's **canon law**, and to a list of accepted books in the Bible.

canonization   The act of formal admission to the canon or list of the saints of the church; to regard as a saint.

cantena   Latin word for "chain" denoting in theology a form of commentary on the Bible that lists extracts from older commentaries for each verse.

capita   Latin word meaning a subject heading (e.g., at the start of a chapter).

capitalism   Economic system in industrialized societies in which the concentration and control of the means of production (capital) is in the hands of private (i.e., non-governmental) owners; resources and wealth are acquired through the operation of a free market; and the maximization of profit is the key stimulus of economic growth.

Cappadocian Fathers   Three bishop–theologians from Cappadocia (in modern Turkey): Gregory of Nazianzus (329–89), Basil of Caeserea (330–79), and Gregory of Nyssa (330–95). Their theology, especially concerning Jesus Christ, the Holy Spirit, and the **Trinity**, was supported by the first Council of Constantinople (381).

Cartesian   Referring to the philosophy of René Descartes (1596–1650), often indicating the separation of subject from object, knower from known, and affirming that the individual thinking self is the best starting point for philosophy (c.f. **cogito**).

Cartesianism   The set of philosophical principles set out in the work of René Descartes (1596–1650).

categoreal, categorial   Working with or in the terms of a fixed number of basic categories; relating to or involving categories.

catholic   Universal, comprehensive; often used to refer to those churches which affirm continuity of faith with the Christian creeds of the first five centuries.

Catholic Creeds   Statements of faith drawn up by the ecumenical councils of the church, namely those of Nicaea I (325) (the **Nicene Creed**) and Constantinople I (381) (the **Nicene–Constantinopolitan Creed**).

catholicity   Universality; the quality of being universal, of affirming continuity with the faith of the whole undivided church of the first five centuries as expressed in the **Catholic Creeds**.

causality   Relation or operation of cause and effect.

Chalcedonian   Relating to the Council of Chalcedon (451) and especially the confession which it attached to the Creeds of Nicaea I (325) and Constantinople I (381), and which affirmed Christ's full humanity and divinity and the union of those two distinct natures in his one divine person, without confusion, change, division, or separation.

Ch'an Buddhism   From the Chinese pronunciation of Dhyana or Jhann: a school of Buddhism focused on direct experience in meditation and simple activity, and opposed to discursive thinking, which is considered an impediment to awakening – the sudden recognition of the Buddha nature within.

chaos theory   Scientific inquiry into mathematically simple systems that exhibit complex and unpredictable behavior.

charismatic   Of or pertaining to the ecclesial work of the Holy Spirit in general, or the Spirit's gifts in particular, especially prophecy, healing, the words of wisdom, discernment of spirits, speaking in tongues, interpretation of tongues; also refers to a Christian movement (sometimes called Neopentecostalism) beginning in the 1960s, which encourages the exercise of the gifts of the Holy Spirit.

Chicago–Lambeth Quadrilateral Also called the Lambeth Quadrilateral: a statement first formulated by a General Conference of the Episcopal Church in Chicago in 1886 and revised and approved by the Lambeth Conference of 1888, that states in four articles the essentials for a reunited Christian church, from the perspective of the Anglican Communion.

Christocentrism Characteristic of theological systems whereby God is only held to reveal himself in Jesus Christ; any set of religious beliefs or theology focused on the person of Christ.

Christology Branch of theology concerned with the doctrine of the person and work of Jesus Christ.

Christomonism Generally used pejoratively, to describe a theological system which uses Jesus Christ as an overriding regulative principle, to the relative exclusion of other doctrines.

Church of England The English branch of the Western church, especially after its secession from communion with the bishop of Rome; the Anglican Church in England.

classical Relating to the standard accepted formulation of something, or to what became the paradigm for what followed; more specifically, referring to the period, civilization, and thought of ancient Greece and Rome.

classical theism Understanding of God as absolute, unchanging, and transcending the world, which reached its classic expression in the Middle Ages.

cogito (the) Short for *cogito ergo sum*, Latin phrase meaning "I am thinking, therefore I exist." The *cogito* is the starting point of René Descartes' (1596–1650) system of knowledge, as an indubitable premise for reliable knowledge (c.f. **Cartesian**).

collectivism Belief that land and the means of production should be held collectively, that is, in common; practice or principle prioritizing the group over the individual.

communion Sharing or holding in common; fellowship; an organic union of persons.

communism Belief that all productive property should be held in common and society ordered without private property; thought stressing cooperation rather than competition, for the sake of a common or transcendent good or for its own sake.

communitarianism Characteristic of philosophical positions that emphasize the psycho-social and ethical importance of belonging to a community, and hold that ethical judgments are justified only within reasoning proceeding from a community's traditions.

concelebration The joint celebration of the **Eucharist** by a number of priests; an ancient practice restored by Vatican II.

concupiscence Inordinate desire for created or finite goods proceeding from sense perception.

confessional Referring to a theological position (sometimes called confessionalism) based on a particular confession or statement of faith (usually one of the **Reformation** statements); or, more widely, referring to a stance or position adopted from the inside as distinct from **phenomenology** or observation from the outside.

Confucianism Western name for a complex body of Chinese tradition including ethical, religious, and political teachings in which the influence of Confucius (sixth–fifth centuries BC) is central, characterized by a common ethical ideal including an affective concern for all living things, a reverential attitude toward others manifested in observance of formal rules of conduct, and judicious development of proper conduct in changing circumstances.

consequentialism The philosophical doctrine that all actions are right or wrong solely in virtue of their consequences, and that a good action is one which maximizes certain valued consequences.

constructivism View which holds that norms, beliefs, or knowledge in one or several fields is produced by a community (e.g., of scientists) rather than *determined* by an objective reality.

consubstantial With or of the same substance or being; from a Latin translation of the Greek word *homoousios*, which was incorporated into the creed at the Council of Nicaea (325) in order to designate the relationship of Jesus Christ to God.

consumerism Sociality or view of society centered around the desires and needs of the individual as the paying consumer of limited goods in an open market.

contemplative In Christianity, of or pertaining to contemplation; the graced state of intense and immediate apprehension of God beyond the powers of the rational mind in the context of liturgy and solitary prayer.

contextualization Viewing, placing, or considering in a particular setting; the practice of theology with responsibility to, and in dialogue with, the particular forms of life, religious thought and symbolism, and sociocultural and economic situation of a community.

contingency Fortuitous character of non-necessity of an event or being.

continuous function In mathematics, a relation between variables which, when plotted on a graph, is represented by a continuous curve.

correspondence theory (of truth) Theory that proposes that statements are true provided there exists a reality corresponding to it; the truth of statements is thus the quality of proportion whereby they accord with reality.

cosmic Christ According to Pierre Teilhard de Chardin (1881–1955), Christ is not only the origin and principle of the existence and evolution of the universe and its contents, but also his incarnation has begun a process of "Christification" in which God purifies and fulfills the cosmos by uniting it to himself organically.

cosmology Study of, and speculative theory about, the cosmos or universe.

counterpoint In reference to early music: music consisting of two or more melodic lines that sound simultaneously; melody added as accompaniment to a given melody or plainsong.

Counter-Reformation The revival and reform of the Roman Catholic Church from the mid-sixteenth century to the mid-seventeenth century, which dealt with abuses by strengthening papal power, founding new religious orders, and applying more rigorous church discipline, and defined doctrine over against those of the **Protestant Reformation**.

creation *ex nihilo* Literally, creation out of nothing; see **creationism**.

creationism Doctrine that God creates a soul out of nothing for each human individual at conception; more commonly, doctrine that the world was created by God without any preexisting materials, thus out of nothing (*ex nihilo*); a version of this doctrine that takes a literal reading of the biblical accounts of creation to depict accurately the origins of the cosmos, life, and the human species.

creed A concise, formal, and authorized statement of essential points of Christian doctrine; a system of religious beliefs or a set of principles on any subject.

Darwinian Of or pertaining to the thought of Charles Darwin (1809–82) or his followers, especially his theory of evolution.

death of God In modern theology, the surrender or dispersal of transcendence on the part of the deity in order to enter the finite realm of history, signified or effected by Christ on the cross; the abolishment of religion by humanity in order to become fully responsible for their actions (Nietzsche); a name for theologies which attempt to articulate Christianity without, or which question, belief in the existence of a transcendent God.

deconstruction A destabilizing method of analysis and description which exposes by means of internal critique the arbitrariness, manipulation, or bias in both the composing of texts and the construction of modes of thinking, speech, or behavior, and demonstrates how their logic invites its own refutation.

deification Act or process whereby participation in the life of the Trinity to a degree inherently impossible for created nature is graciously granted to the believer by God as the fulfillment of human nature.

deism Understanding of God as creator, but denying continuing divine participation or intervention in the created order.

demythologization Process of interpreting traditional texts considered mythological (in the sense that they express their meaning in terms of an outmoded or mythological worldview), with the aim of showing that their continuing **existential** or practical relevance can be grasped despite their mythological expression.

denomination Self-governing and doctrinally autonomous religious bodies or denominations within Christianity.

determinism The doctrine that all historical events can be understood wholly in terms of some antecedent cause or causes, and are the necessary effects of such causes; theologically, it is sometimes held to be a consequence of the doctrine of the sovereignty of God.

Deus absconditus God hidden from human perception.

Deus mortuus God as dead.

Dharma In Hinduism, cosmic rule giving things their natures; at the human level, social customs necessary for social order and righteousness – one of the four fundamental pursuits of life; in Buddhism, universal truth or law, especially as proclaimed by Buddha.

diaconate The office of deacon in the church; the period of office of a deacon; a body of deacons.

dialectic Method of reasoning (sometimes called dialectical method) in which the conclusion emerges from the tension between two opposing positions; or a force seen as operating in history, moving it through conflict toward some form of culmination. The radical tension between cross and resurrection is often treated in dialectical terms (by Jürgen Moltmann, for example).

dialectical theology Theology of the period after World War I (initiated mainly by Karl Barth's *Epistle to the Romans*), which radically negated (above all by reference to the crucifixion) all human ways of knowing and relating to God, and stressed the corresponding need for God's initiative in **revelation**; also known as crisis theology because of its stress on God's judgment (Greek *krisis*) on church and world.

dialogical Of or pertaining to the nature of dialogue, especially of dialogue as the existential condition of humankind where the self exists to communicate dialogically with the other without beginning or end (as in the dialogism of Mikhail Bakhtin (1895–1975)).

diaspora Dispersion of the Jews among the Gentiles; Jews living outside the land of Israel; by extension, dispersion of any body of people living outside their homeland; any body of people who live, or have been forced to live, outside their homeland.

diastasis Greek word meaning separation; used by Hans Urs von Balthasar (1905–88) to talk of the distance in the **Trinity** between the Father and Son in the generation of the latter, which is spanned by the Spirit, who is their common love.

différance French neologism coined by Jacques Derrida (1930–2004) to denote the prime condition of language whereby (1) the differentiation of signs from each other makes it possible to distinguish things and (2) signs refer, or defer, to each other, never capturing the transcendent meaning or presence toward which they point.

docetism Belief that the humanity and death of Jesus were not properly real, but were just an appearance taken on by the **Logos**; it was condemned as a heresy in the early church (from a Greek verb, *dokeo*, one of whose meanings is "to seem or pretend").

dogmatic Of or pertaining to doctrines and their expositions.

dogmatics The study and articulation of Christian doctrine, sometimes distinguished from a more systematic approach to theology.

doktorvater In German theology, an academic mentor-figure.

Dominican Member of, or relating to, the Roman Catholic religious order of preaching friars founded by St. Dominic (1170–1221).

donative Of or pertaining to the free bestowal of a gift.

dualism View of the world which holds that there are two ultimately distinct principles or spheres, such as good and evil, matter and spirit, or nature and grace.

ecclesial Of or pertaining to the church (from the Greek *ecclesia* or assembly).

ecclesiology Understanding or doctrine of the church.

eclectic Embracing diverse and varied sources or genres.

ecumenical Relating to **ecumenism**; of or pertaining to the church as a whole, beyond or before its divisions.

ecumenism From a Greek word for the whole inhabited world; in Christianity it is a movement for worldwide unity among Christian churches; sometimes used of cooperation between religions.

egalitarianism Belief that all human beings are equal and should be treated equally.

election Doctrine that God chooses people for salvation (and, within some traditions, for damnation); divine choice, especially in regard to salvation or damnation.

empiricism Theory of knowledge where sensory experience is the source and test of all knowledge.

encyclical In modern Roman Catholicism, a circular letter sent across the world by the pope to all Roman Catholics.

Enlightenment Movement of European thought (at its height in the eighteenth century) which typically emphasized human reason and experience and the autonomy of the individual, rather than traditional (religious or other) authority.

Enlightenment rationalism Belief of thinkers associated with the **Enlightenment** that there is a universal human rationality, which is the ground of our rights and whose exercise is the condition of our freedom in any action, and which is capable of discovering the true form of all things.

epiphenomenal Accompanying some process or state of affairs in a merely incidental way, and having no effects of its own.

episcopacy System of church government by bishops.

episcopalian Of or pertaining to episcopalism or episcopalianism, a form of church government in which ultimate authority resides with a body of bishops rather than with one leader or with the general membership; more specifically, a term for Anglicans and the Anglican Church in Scotland, the USA, and some other countries.

epistemic Referring to the structure of knowledge.

epistemology Theory or study of human knowing, regarding its bases, forms, and criteria.

epochal Characterizing, formative of, or definitive of, an epoch: a period of time.

eros A Greek word meaning love or desire.

eschatology Understanding or doctrine of the eschaton, or ultimate destiny of the world.

essence The primary or basic element in the being or nature of a thing; that without which it could not be what it is.

essentialism Understanding of objects in terms of their **essence**, which distinguishes between properties that are essential to it being what it is and those that are not (accidents).

eternal recurrence Endless cycles in which the universe returns to reenact exactly the same course of events; a theme of much Greek thought and embraced by Friedrich Nietzsche (1844–1900) in *The Will to Power* as the joyful affirmation of the recurrence of our actions.

eternity Mode of existence that is fundamentally different from time – without beginning, end, or separation of moments, for example. In classical Christian theology it is a mode of existence proper only to God and understood as "illimitable life" (Boëthius, ca. 480–525).

ethical naturalism Ethical position grounded in natural or biological principles.

ethnography Study of human society and culture, also called cultural anthropology.

Eucharist Sacrament or celebration of the Lord's Supper (from a Greek word for thanksgiving) involving the blessing and distribution of bread and wine as signs of the body and blood of Jesus Christ.

eucharistic devotion Devotion to or reverence of Jesus Christ as bodily present in and with the bread and wine of the **Eucharist**.

evangelical Relating to the New Testament gospel or a concern for preaching it; also, a term for **Protestants** in Germany and Switzerland; also, a term for a diverse movement, spanning many Protestant churches and groups, with special concern for the final authority of scripture, the centrality of the atonement effected by Christ on the cross, evangelism, and personal salvation and holiness.

evangelical revival Movement – **evangelical** in the last sense above – in Britain and America, involving growth in church attendance, the inculcation of an evangelical spirituality, the promotion of certain political and social–economic concerns (e.g., the abolition of slavery in the British empire), and expansion of missionary work overseas, in the eighteenth and early nineteenth centuries.

evolutionary theory Explanation of the origins and diversity of forms of life on earth as the product of descent with modification from the earliest forms of life, by way of natural selection upon the products of genetic variation and mutation within and between species in particular environments.

exclusivism Belief that God will not grant salvation to those outside the Christian church, or outside faith in Christ.

exegesis Act of explaining a text – in theology, usually a biblical text (from a Greek word meaning "to explain").

existential Of or pertaining to individual existence and subjectivity, describing the way of being that is distinctive of human life, action, and orientation toward the world.

existentialism Movement of thought focusing on individual existence and subjectivity, which affirms that existence precedes essence (especially in the sense that a person's decisions and responses to contingent events, rather than his or her supposed essential nature, constitute who that person essentially is), thus upholding the freedom of the will and its irreducibility to anything else. It wrestles with aspects of the human predicament such as anxiety, dread, inauthenticity, meaninglessness, alienation, guilt, anticipation of death, and despair.

extrincism Understanding that the truth of religious dogma can only be received, not demonstrated.

falsification hypothesis Idea propounded by Karl Popper that the merit of science consists in its putting forward hypotheses that are capable of being refuted by evidence.

fascism Political ideology stressing the need for social cohesion, strong leadership, and the revival of national culture; political movements and regimes espousing this ideology; also used as a pejorative term for highly authoritarian ideas, individuals, institutions, or practices.

feminism Movement concerned with the dignity, rights, and liberation of women and the implications of this for humanity.

feminist theology Theology sharing the concerns of **feminism**; in Christianity, especially focusing on the critique of the tradition as **patriarchal** and on reconceiving it in non-patriarchal terms.

finite Limited, especially to the natural order; unable to transcend certain boundaries.

finitude Condition of being **finite**.

formal Abstracting and attending to the form of a phenomenon. For example, formal logic abstracts and analyzes the logical form of an argument.

formalist Understanding that holds that form is what is important in anything.

foundationalism Thesis that valid philosophical or theological truth-claims are founded on self-evident propositions or on truths of experience (or a combination of the two).

Freudian Relating to the thought of Sigmund Freud (1856–1939), founder of psychoanalysis, and his followers.

fundamentalism In Christianity, a varied movement usually affirming a set of basic beliefs by reference to the authority of a literally interpreted, inerrant Bible.

genealogy Account of the origins and development of an idea or way of thinking about the world (a discourse); account of the ancestral roots of an individual, people, or culture.

German Idealism Movement in German philosophy which began with the attempt to complete Kant's project of deriving the principles of knowledge and ethics from the spontaneity and autonomy of the human mind or spirit, as represented by J. G. Fichte (1762–1814) or G. W. F. Hegel (1770–1831), for example (c.f. **idealism**).

globalization Process whereby the diverse regions and peoples of the world and their polities, economies, and cultures become increasingly closely interrelated, chiefly through trade facilitated by technological advances, sometimes established by military conquest or colonial **hegemony**, and not necessarily to the advantage of all parties concerned.

gnosis Greek word meaning knowledge. In a diverse group of religious movements in Late Antiquity gnosis denotes special, secret knowledge concerning the cosmological origins of the material human condition and the way in which freedom from that condition may be obtained for an elite. Some Christian groups espoused similar views and were condemned as heretical. The word also had orthodox Christian uses (e.g., in Clement of Alexandria's theology).

gradualism View that change accretes slowly in a steady series of small steps.

Gregorian plainsong Unaccompanied music for voice, sung in the medieval modes (scale or sequence of notes basic to the music) and in free rhythm, according to the accentuation of the words.

habitus Latin word meaning the condition or state of a thing; in sociology, the geographical, socioeconomic, and cultural environment conditioning thought and practice.

harmonic dissonance The discordant sounding together of two or more notes, which are perceived to have "roughness" or to be in tension; the opposite of consonance – the sympathetic vibration of sound-waves of different frequencies related in simple ratios of small whole numbers.

Hebraic Of or pertaining to the thought-forms, language, religion, and culture of the Hebrew people.

hegemony Leadership or domination; often referring to the domination of one person, class, culture, or idea over others.

hellenism Greek culture and ideas influential in non-Greek areas in the period after Alexander the Great.

henotheism Worship of one god in preference to or to the exclusion of other deities.

heresy Formal denial or doubt of official doctrines or practices of a religious community – in this case of the church – the character, extent, and official teachings of which are a subject of controversy between Christian **denominations**.

hermeneutics Study of interpretation and meaning.

Hermetism Tradition of thought associated with the mysterious figure Hermes Trismegistos, and especially with a collection of texts of a generally gnostic character attributed to him and produced in Alexandria between the first and third centuries, whose rediscovery in the Renaissance was influential in relation to later esoteric philosophy, magic, and various types of **cosmology** and mystical spirituality.

heterodoxy Deviation from what is considered **orthodox**; an erroneous opinion; the quality of being deviant from orthodox (i.e., of being "heterodox").

Hijrah Arabic word meaning emigration, which in Islam denotes the emigration or flight of Muhammad from Mecca to Medina in July 622 CE.

Hinduism Varied body of religious practices and philosophical beliefs native to India, centered on the sacred texts of the Vedas, and characterized by belief in reincarnation and in a supreme divine being of many natures and forms, and by the search for liberation from earthly suffering.

historical criticism Approach to a text which seeks to determine its meaning in light of what it would have meant in its earliest form and context, and to understand beliefs, institutions, and practices in terms of how they were produced by historical conditions and events.

historical Jesus Understanding of Jesus of Nazareth through critical evaluation of the sources and hypothetical reconstructions of his life and teaching against criteria of historical plausibility in the context of first-century Palestinian Jewish society and religion.

historical theology Study of theology before the modern era, variously defined, often seeking to locate its expression in historical context, and to understand the course of its development through such contexts.

historicism Approach that affirms the radical segregation of human from natural history, and emphasizes strongly the historicity of all human activity and knowledge (i.e., its contingency in particular historical circumstances).

historiography The writing of history; historical accounts in general.

homily A religious discourse or sermon; in particular, a discourse intended for spiritual edification.

hominid **Primate** of the *Hominidae* family, to which human beings and several fossil forms belong; characteristic of that family.

hominoid Of human form, resembling humans; an animal resembling humans; a primate of the *Hominoidea super* family, to which humans and anthropoid apes belong.

homo economicus Economic humanity; human beings engaged in economies of goods exchange.

humanism Movement, originating in the Renaissance, to understand human life without recourse to higher (divine) authority; more widely, a worldview cultivating respect for humanity and confidence in its possibilities.

hybridization Term in postcolonial theory denoting the production of new forms of migrant or minority discourses that flourish in the **diasporas** of the modern and **postmodern** periods, and which destabilize identities and differences constructed around binary oppositions.

hypostasis Greek word originally having a range of meanings, including "substance"; in Christian theology since the Cappadocian Fathers it has come to mean, in relation to Jesus Christ and the **Trinity**, the individual subject in which the concrete reality of a nature inheres, the subject of attributes; also denoted in the West by the word persona, or person.

icon Flat picture representing Christ, the Blessed Virgin Mary or the saints, or occasionally biblical scenes, which are, in some Christian traditions, held to mediate symbolically the presence of the one depicted. Icons are reverenced because of the role played by those depicted in God's economy of salvation. In the case of Christ, it is his humanity that is reverenced, since divinity cannot be depicted.

iconoclasm Literally, the breaking of images; in Christianity, opposition to religious images and **icons**, which can involve destroying such images; more widely, disrespect for or attack on established beliefs, ideas, or practices.

iconography Illustration or depiction through visual images and symbols (as distinct from iconology: the study and interpretation of images and symbols).

idealism Philosophical tradition originating with Plato, which understands the mind, ideas, or spirit as fundamental to reality. The forms of idealism most influential on modern Christian theology have been Kant's transcendental idealism and the absolute idealism of J. G. Fichte (1762–1814), F. W. Schelling (1775–1854), and especially G. W. F. Hegel (1770–1831).

ideology Structure of concepts and beliefs governing the action and understanding of a group of people; often used pejoratively to describe beliefs and ideas which are rationalizations justifying vested interests or an oppressive system or practice.

idol Attempted representation of God as such, who cannot be represented, thus false. Also, by extension, the literal attribution of creaturely properties and predicates to the divine nature, in contravention of the difference between God and creatures; the attribution to creatures of the position and honor due only to God.

idolatry Literally, worship of **idols**, which is by definition misdirected, hence false worship; the worship of, or treating as ultimate, anything less than or (what amounts to the same thing) other than, God.

Ignatian Of or pertaining to the thought, life, or spiritual disciplines taught by St. Ignatius of Loyola (ca. 1491–1556), founder of the Society of Jesus (the Jesuits).

Ijtihad In Islam, an independent judgment concerning a legal or theological question and based upon the interpretation and application of Islamic law (from an Arabic word meaning exertion).

image of God Quality of humanity bestowed in creation and in some accounts held to be marred in the fall in virtue of which humans have aptitude for an intimate relationship with the Trinity; classically understood to consist in the soul's attributes of free will and rationality.

imago dei Latin for the **image of God**.

imago trinitatis Latin for the image of the Trinity; understanding (found first in Augustine) of the soul as faintly reflecting the unity in distinction of the Trinity in the interaction and mutual dependence of memory, understanding, and will; Augustine holds that the soul is most truly the image of the Trinity when it participates most fully in the Trinity in the **beatific vision**.

immanence (divine) Presence of God within the world, including everyday events and situations.

immanentism The view that any events or phenomena within the world are explicable in terms of other events or phenomena within the world, thus excluding any direct agency of God or other supernatural powers; or a view of God which stresses his **immanence** or indwelling in the world rather than his **transcendence**.

in nuce Latin expression meaning in a nutshell; in condensed or embryonic form.

Incarnation Literally, becoming flesh; the event of God the Son assuming human nature in Jesus Christ.

incarnational theology Theology which stresses the central importance of the **Incarnation** and understands other issues in the light of that doctrine.

inclusivism Position which holds that a particular religion offers salvific truth by including rather than denying the truths of other religions.

incommensurable Of two or more cultures, religions, systems, or ideas that do not share any common basis for evaluating one another or for agreement.

inculturation Process of negotiation internal to the reception of a religion in any culture between the culturally conditioned form of a religion as it is introduced and the forms of the culture into which it is introduced.

indeterminism The view that some events (often specifically **quantum** events) have no causes; they just happen, and nothing in the previous state of the world explains them.

indic Of or pertaining to India, its peoples and cultures; of or pertaining to the Indo-European family of languages.

indigenization Making indigenous; adoption by the people of an area as their own.

individualism Attitude or position favoring the rights, value, or salvation primarily of persons, understood as autonomous and not essentially social.

indulgences Remission granted by the church on God's behalf of the temporal penalty due to sin, where that sin has been forgiven, in virtue of the merits of Christ and the saints.

infallibility Inerrancy, being incapable of making a mistake; more specifically, the Roman Catholic dogma that pronouncements of the pope made *ex cathedra* are without error.

intellectualism Privileging of the role of the intellect, especially in an account of salvation or sanctification; a contrary emphasis to voluntarism, which privileges the will.

intersubjectivity Mode of relating between persons, understood as human subjects with interiority.

intuitive Of or pertaining to the act of intuition – the apprehension of truth by the mind without prior reasoning from first principles or empirical evidence.

ironization Making something ironical; using something ironically.

Jesuit A member of the Roman Catholic Society of Jesus, founded by St. Ignatius of Loyola in 1534.

Jihad "Holy War"; in Islam, divinely instituted warfare to extend Islam into non-Islamic territories (the *dar al-harb* or abode of struggle) or defend Islam from danger.

jinns In Islam, inhabitants of the subtle and immaterial, or subtly material, world into which our material world is plunged as into a liquid. Some *jinns* have free will and rationality, and some do not.

Johannine Of or pertaining to the fourth gospel of the New Testament and its theology, which are traditionally attributed to St. John.

jouissance Notion developed by Jacques Lacan (1901–81) to describe a going beyond oneself in relation to the fullness of Being: an ecstasy that does not end in equilibrium.

justification Being pronounced or made righteous; the act of God through the death and resurrection of Jesus Christ, bringing about reconciliation between himself and human beings.

justification by faith Reformation doctrine that righteousness is a status before God imputed to the one who has faith in Jesus Christ to save him or her, apart from the merit of any good works he or she may have performed, which are ineffective to make him or her righteous.

karmic Relating to *karma*, a Sanskrit word meaning action; in Hinduism and Buddhism, karma is the metaphysical residue of self-regarding action, expendable through the experiences of repeated birth.

kenosis Greek word for "self-emptying," used in theology to describe Jesus Christ's laying down of certain divine attributes (e.g., glory, omnipotence) in order to become fully human. Sometimes used more generally of all analogous self-emptying.

kenotic Christology Understanding of the **Incarnation** of Jesus as involving **kenosis**.

kerygma Greek word meaning proclamation; the message preached by Jesus; the proclamation of the early church about Jesus Christ; the existential message of Christianity.

Kierkegaardian Relating to the philosophy of Søren Kierkegaard (1813–55).

Kingdom of God Manifestation of God's justice and loving purposes for creation anticipated in the Old Testament, announced and instantiated in the teaching and ministry of Jesus Christ, and to some degree realized in the life of the church in anticipation of its full realization in the ultimate destiny of the world, or eschaton.

koinonia Greek word meaning communion or fellowship; in ecumenical theology, the communion of Christian persons with the persons of the Trinity and with one another in the life and liturgy of the body of Christ, the church, especially as constituted by the **Eucharist**.

laity The members of a church (from the Greek *laos*, meaning the people); sometimes distinguished from the clergy.

lectionary Cycle of readings for public worship in a denomination prescribed for each service of each day of the year, and reflecting the liturgical seasons of the church's calendar.

Leibnizian Relating to the thought of Gottfried Wilhelm Leibniz (1646–1716), German rationalist philosopher, and his followers.

liberalism Moral or political ethos concerned to guarantee the freedom of each individual to do as he or she pleases (so long as it does not violate the equally legitimate freedom of others) and which celebrates **pluralism** and respect for personal **autonomy**. In theology, a movement attempting to open theology to modern experience, worldviews, and criteria, and especially to the contributions of other academic disciplines; more specifically, nineteenth-century liberal theology tended to stress religious experience, historical consciousness, and the need for freedom from traditional dogma and frameworks in recovering Christianity.

liberation theology School of theology originating in Latin America in the 1960s in contexts of political and economic oppression, which seeks to apply the Christian faith from the standpoint of the needs of the poor and exploited.

linguistic idealism **Idealist** thought that takes seriously the mediation of all subjectivity in language.

linguistic turn Movement in modern philosophy and other disciplines that stresses the inescapably linguistic character of thought and experience – that we "live, move, and have our being" in language.

liturgy Communal worship of God (from a Greek word meaning action of the people); more narrowly, a terms for the various aspects of prescribed public worship.

loci theologici Areas of theological inquiry or doctrinal definition.

locum tenens Someone who takes on the professional duties of another in their absence; a person who holds office on a temporary basis.

logical positivism, logical empiricism Philosophy holding that only assertions verifiable from sensory experience or deducible from such assertions are meaningful, or weaker versions of this position.

Logos Greek word with wide semantic range (word, reason, story, argument, account); in ancient philosophy, especially Stoic philosophy, the rational or ordering principle in something or in reality as a whole; in **Christology**, it denotes God's eternal and **hypostatic** self-expression, or Word, often understood to be the ultimate principle of creation, who became incarnate in Jesus Christ. See **Logos Christology**.

Logos Christology **Christology** whose key concept is Jesus understood as the historical expression of the eternal, divine **Logos** through which everything was created.

Lord's Supper The ritual meal instituted by Jesus Christ at the Last Supper before his death. See also **Eucharist**.

Lutheran Of or pertaining to churches, traditions, or theologies stemming from the **Reformation** tradition begun by Martin Luther.

Magisterium The Roman Catholic Church's official teaching authority, exercised ordinarily in the instruction of the faithful, and occasionally in solemn declarations of the pope or councils of bishops approved by the pope.

Mahayana Buddhism Form of Buddhism, prevalent in the Far East, which is distinguished by its teaching of Great Compassion: the practitioner should have compassion for all sentient beings to the extent that he or she should delay his or her own nirvana until all other beings shall have been blessed.

Marxism Thought or movement stemming from Karl Marx (1818–83).

materialism Position which asserts the sole and/or ultimate reality of matter.

Mennonite Of or pertaining to the Christian denomination founded by Menno Simons (1496–1561), which opposes infant baptism, the taking of oaths, military service, and the holding of civic offices by Christians.

messiah Promised deliverer of the Jewish nation; Jesus as the fulfillment of that promise and savior of humankind; any liberator figure; from a Hebrew word meaning "anointed" and connoting one set apart for a divine purpose.

metanarrative Overarching narrative or account which attempts to comprehend, include, or explain other narratives.

metaphysics Philosophical investigation of the nature, constitution, and structure of reality (c.f. **ontology**).

Methodist Member of, or relating to, the **Protestant** denomination founded by John Wesley (1703–91).

methodology Reflection on the systematic approach to a topic or field.

modernism In arts and culture a movement in the first half of the twentieth century which rejected many of the established assumptions and practices in the arts (e.g., melody and harmony in music; pictorial representation and perspective in the visual arts; traditional realism in literature). In philosophy, thought that is

foundationalist, essentialist, and **realist**. In theology, the movement to update traditional beliefs in the light of modern knowledge.

modernity   Condition or quality of being modern, distinguished by a sense of separation and distance from the past, emphasized by advances in all fields of human endeavor.

modes   In music, a mode is a way of ordering a scale (sequence of notes ascending or descending which start and finish on the same note) that is the tonal basis for a section of music and which helps to define its character.

monasticism   Practice of **ascetical** communal living under religious rules, motivated by the desire to seek God; often a permanent vocation.

monism   Position that one regulative principle governs the universe; also, a position that all reality is one, or is to be explained in terms of one fundamental constituent.

monotheism   Belief in only one God as ultimate reality.

moralism   Practice of a natural system of morality; religion consisting of, or reduced to, moral practice.

mystery   Reality that must be revealed and that is beyond human comprehension, and which perhaps must be shielded from profanation (e.g., the deeds of God depicted in scripture, or the **Eucharist** or baptism).

mystical theology   Theological reflection made possible by divine illumination, in which the mind is drawn beyond all conceptions to union with the **Trinity**; theology concerned to defend or set forth the conditions of possibility of such a union; theology that grounds or interprets a particular strand of **mysticism**.

mystical tradition   Body of writings in the Christian tradition concerned with **mysticism** or **mystical theology**.

mysticism   Strand in many religions stressing the knowledge of God or the **transcendent** through experience, often in the form of immediate intuition or other direct communication or sense of union, and often denying the possibility of adequate linguistic communication of such experience; sometimes contrasted with the knowledge of God through indirect means such as reasoning, scripture, or tradition.

myth, mythos   In theology, usually an expression of religious meaning through story or symbol, often using a premodern worldview.

mythology   Study of, or a collection of, myths.

narrativism   Understanding that sees Christian theology as grounded in the narrative of the Bible, especially the story of Jesus; some narrativists ground this approach by claiming that human experience and self-understanding are irreducibly narrative in character.

Nation of Islam   Former name of a sect popularly known as the Black Muslims of America, which taught black racial superiority and advocated a separate state for blacks in the United States; it gained international prominence under Malcolm X. After the death of its founder Elijah Muhammed in 1975, and following the example of Malcolm X, Muhammed's son Wallace led the majority of the sect to orthodox Islam. A dissident faction led by Louis Farrakhan retains the name and original anti-white and separatist doctrines of the group.

nationalism   Understanding and practice articulating identification with and commitment to a nation: a political community based around a common language, culture, and sometimes ethnic origin and identity.

National Socialism German form of **fascism** espousing the racial and cultural superiority of the so-called Aryan race, their triumphant destiny and right to living space, advocated by Adolf Hitler and practiced by the infamous regime he led in Germany between 1933 and 1945.

natural philosophy Name for the several lines of inquiry into the natural world and cosmos now grouped under science.

natural selection Natural process whereby the life forms best adapted to survive and feed in particular circumstances – especially where competition for resources is fierce – survive at the expense of the less optimally adapted, and pass their genes on to future generations; one of the mechanisms of biological evolution.

natural theology Theology attempting to know God and God's relationship to the world through nature and human reasoning without divine **revelation**.

naturalism Position affirming that the world can be understood (especially through the natural sciences) without reference to any explanatory factor beyond the natural order, which is usually understood in a **materialist** way.

Naturwissenschaften German word meaning the natural sciences.

negative or apophatic theology Theology that denies that any of our concepts can be properly predicated of God as we understand them, which therefore qualifies assertions about God with negations of those assertions, understands the knowledge of God as lying beyond human comprehension or speech and thus gained by divine illumination of the mind, and prefers the negative language of silence and darkness to talk about it.

neo-empiricism Movement of new or revived interest in **empiricism**, which is the strand in philosophy which attempts to tie knowledge to what can be observed to be true by sensory experience.

neo-Kantianism A movement of revived interest in the philosophy of Kant, after the decline of Hegelian **idealism**; in theology it especially emphasized Kant's distinction between pure and practical reason as a means to meet the scientific challenges to the validity of religion and theology.

neo-orthodox Term applied to the Protestant theological movement associated with Barth, Emil Brunner, and Reinhold Niebuhr, referring to their attempt to counter the "unorthodox" **liberal** nineteenth-century theology by regrounding theology on the principles of **Reformation Protestantism**.

neoplatonism Religious philosophy of Plotinus (ca. 205–69) and his followers, which owed most to Plato and offered a rational spirituality aimed at union with the One or the absolute which unites all reality.

neoscholasticism, neothomism Nineteenth- and twentieth-century Roman Catholic movement which revived the theology and philosophy of Thomas Aquinas and made it the norm against which all other theology and philosophy are judged.

Nestorianism Heresy condemned at **Chalcedon**, understood to hold that there are two persons in Jesus Christ – the divine and the human – thus effectively dividing his two natures. Nestorianism is named after Nestorius (ca. 381–ca. 452), for a time bishop of Constantinople, who was thought (probably erroneously) to be the author of this view.

Newtonian Of or pertaining to the thought of Sir Isaac Newton (1642–1727), scientist, alchemist, mathematician, and theologian, author of the theory of universal gravity and inventor of calculus.

Nicene Creed Properly the **Creed** formulated at the first Council of Nicaea (325), noted especially for its affirmation that Jesus Christ is of one substance, essence, or being (Greek *homoousios*) with God the Father. Also used of the **Nicene–Constantinopolitan Creed**.

Nicene–Constantinopolitan Creed Creed promulgated by the first Council of Constantinople (381), which affirmed the **Nicene Creed**, and while omitting the Nicene explanation of *homoousios*, added material on the person of Christ, the status and work of the Spirit, the church, baptism, the resurrection, and eternal life.

nihilism Philosophy of the negation, rejection, or denial of some or all aspects of life (e.g., moral judgments) or of its significance as a whole; belief that all reduces ultimately to nothing; from the Latin for "nothing."

noetic Of or pertaining to the mind or intellect, or the process of thinking or perceiving; that which has a purely intellectual basis (from the Greek *nous*, "mind").

Non-Church Movement Or *Mukyokou* movement, founded by Japanese Christians in opposition to the dominance of Western culture in Japanese Christianity and the high value placed on specific ecclesiologies by Western denominations, preferring a relatively unorganized Christian assembly.

nouvelle théologie French term meaning new theology, applied to a loosely associated movement in modern Roman Catholic theology that sought to renew Roman Catholic teaching and practice and ecumenical dialogue through a return through critical study to Christianity's sources in the early Christian centuries and medieval period.

novitiate Status of being a novice (probationary member of a religious community); the period of time in which one is in that state; a group of novices.

objectivism The theory that the world exists in itself independently of our comprehension of it; or that knowledge is based on factual evidence that describes things as they are and is discovered by objective methods of science and reasoning; or that the only true knowledge is that derived from and/or confirmed by sensory experience. In relation to values, the theory that values are independent of our comprehension of them, but can be found and known, and should be used as principles for human judgment and conduct.

obscurantism Opposition to reform and enlightenment.

ochlos Greek word for crowd, used in the New Testament.

Old Catholics Group of small national churches, consisting of Christians who have at various time become separated from communion with the bishop of Rome since the **Reformation** (but not **Protestants**); sometimes Roman Catholics in England are called Old Catholics.

omniscience Possession of complete knowledge of all things.

ontology Branch of philosophy concerned with the study of being, or reality in its most fundamental and comprehensive forms (c.f. **metaphysics**).

onto-theology Usually a pejorative term, applied to theology that identifies questions about God with questions about being.

orders Various kinds of ministry in the church as understood by the Roman Catholic, the Eastern Orthodox, and Anglican Churches: usually, bishops, priests, deacons, and monks and nuns.

ordination Rite by which one enters an **order** of the Christian church.

Oriental Orthodox   Modern designation for those Eastern churches who rejected the **Chalcedonian** definition and in particular the phrase "in two natures."

Orthodox, Eastern   Family of churches constituting by their full communion a single church and claiming direct descent from the church of the apostles and the seven **ecumenical** councils.

orthodoxy   Right belief in and adherence to the essential "orthodox" doctrines of a faith as officially defined; or conventional or traditional belief.

overdetermined   Causally determined in more than one way – more than is necessary.

paganism   Beliefs and practices of "pagans"; a term principally used of those who worship one or more gods but are not strictly monotheists.

Palamism   Teaching associated with Gregory Palamas (ca. 1269–1359), especially concerning the defense of the form of **mystical** prayer called hesychasm and the distinction drawn in that defense between the unknowable divine **essence** and the divine operations or energies, which may be directly experienced as deifying grace.

paleontology   Study of fossil remains.

Pan Africanism   Idea or advocacy of the political union of all indigenous inhabitants of Africa.

panentheism   Understanding of the world as existing in God yet without negating the **transcendence** of God (God is both in and beyond the world); often also holding that the world and God are mutually dependent upon each other for their fulfillment.

pantheism   Understanding that identifies God and the world as one, either without qualification, or with the world as a divine emanation, body, development, appearance, or modality.

papacy   Office of the bishop of Rome, or pope, the leader of the Roman Catholic Church; in Roman Catholic understanding, the system of centralized government of the Roman Catholic Church headed by the pope; the claim that by divine appointment he has universal authority over all Christendom.

parabolic   Term used in the synoptic gospels to denote a wide range of sayings of Jesus of Nazareth, including proverbs, metaphors, allegories, and stories, concerning the **Kingdom of God**; any short story used to advance an argument.

paradigm   A pattern; a set of assumptions or habits that shapes thought, inquiry and/or practice.

paradigm shift   Term coined by Thomas Kuhn to denote a revolution in the framework of assumptions governing inquiry in a particular field.

particularism   The privileging of the particular in accounts of what and how we know over, or to the exclusion of, universals.

particularity   What is specific, definite, and distinctive; often implying the primacy of reference to **contingent**, historical reality over general or abstract statements.

passion play   Vernacular religious drama, which flourished in the Middle Ages, depicting the passion and resurrection of Jesus Christ.

passivist   Emphasizing the passivity or minimal role of the subject in an event or process, especially of the believer in sanctification.

patriarchy   Social organization wherein families and communities are headed by men; in feminism, patriarchy denotes more generally the hegemony of men over women in society.

patripassianism Doctrine that God the Father suffered in the passion of Jesus Christ; hence by implication, in some cases, that the persons of the **Trinity** are the various modes of presentation or activity of the one divine identity (otherwise known as modalism).

patristic Referring to the "fathers" of the church – church leaders and theologians who shaped the basic character of mainstream Christianity in East and West – and the period in which they wrote, from the second century to the end of the seventh century CE.

Pauline Relating to St. Paul, his writings, thought, and practice.

Pentecostal Relating to Pentecost (Greek name for the Jewish festival of Weeks, and the occasion on which the Holy Spirit came upon the earliest church in Jerusalem); **Pentecostalism** is a Christian movement stressing the powerful and unrestrained work of the Holy Spirit in the church, and the importance of receiving the same gifts of the Spirit as were given to the apostolic generation.

perfectionism Belief that Christians may achieve perfection in this life and should strive to do so.

perichoresis Greek term for the mutual indwelling or co-inherence of the three members of the **Trinity** (the Latin equivalent is *circumincessio*).

personalism Philosophical movement, beginning in the nineteenth century, which holds to the ultimate ontological and moral importance of self-conscious agents (persons), their states and characteristics in society, and the immortality of the soul, usually underwritten by dependence on the Supreme Person, God.

Petrine Of or relating to St. Peter, especially to the authority said to have been invested in him as chief of the apostles by Christ, and transmitted to all his successors as bishop of Rome.

phenomenal Relating to appearances, or to what appears to the human observer.

phenomenology Philosophical movement aiming to ground philosophy in a descriptive and scientific method, which understands religious and other phenomena in non-**reductionist** terms as they reveal themselves to consciousness, and seeks the distinctive laws of human consciousness, especially emphasizing its intentional character.

phenomenology, existential Descriptive philosophy of consciousness, focusing especially on the individual's immediate experience of his or her situation and self, as a thinking, believing, hoping, fearing, desiring being with a need to find purpose and a will that determines action.

phenotypical Of or pertaining to phenotypes: organisms as distinguishable from others by observable features, or the sum of the attributes of an individual resulting from the interaction of its genotype and its environment.

Philokalia Title of two different works: one an anthology of Origen's (ca. 185–254) writings compiled by Basil the Great and Gregory Nazianzen in 358–9 (the Philokalia of Origen), the other a collection of ascetic and mystical writings from the fourth to the fifteenth centuries and focused on the teachings of hesychasm (silent prayer) (the Philokalia of Sts. Macaris Notaren and Nicodemus of the Holy Mountain); from a Greek word meaning love of the beautiful.

physicalism Position which holds that all reality is really physical.

pietism Originally, a seventeenth- and eighteenth-century Protestant movement reacting against the **rationalism** and rigidity of traditional **Lutheran orthodoxy**

with an emphasis on the personal, devotional, and practical aspects of Christianity; more widely, a type of faith combining deep feeling, stress on personal salvation and holiness, and lack of concern for theological education.

Platonic Of or pertaining to the Greek philosopher Plato (ca. 429–347 BCE), his doctrines or those influenced by his thought.

pluralism Situation or understanding which embraces a diversity of contrasting cultures, values, ideas, religions, or other major elements seen as independently valid.

pneumatology Branch of theology dealing with the doctrine of the Holy Spirit.

polity Organized community or state; a form of government; the civil order or administration of a state.

polyphony The juxtaposition of several melodic lines sounding at the same time (*see also* **counterpoint**).

polytheism Belief in several gods.

positivism In the nineteenth century, a movement associated with Auguste Comte (1798–1857) which saw history in terms of inevitable progress culminating in the "positive" stage of scientific knowledge, technology, and an **atheist** religion of reason and humanity; in the twentieth century, logical positivism has been a philosophical movement stressing **empirical** verification, natural scientific method, and the rejection of **metaphysics**.

post-Kantian Of or pertaining to philosophy and theology that attempts to move beyond schools of thought indebted to the thought of Immanuel Kant (1724–1804).

postcolonial Of or pertaining to the period beginning with colonialization and the cultures of those colonized; relating to the study of such cultures, especially their literature.

postliberalism In theology, a movement especially associated with Yale Divinity School and Duke University since the 1980s, which characteristically affirms Christian **orthodoxy**, criticizes the **liberal** reliance on human experience, and reclaims the notion of community tradition as controlling influence on theology, in particular the constitutive role of the overarching biblical narrative in the Christian community's self-understanding.

postmodernism Position which regards much of the present intellectual and cultural situation, especially in advanced **capitalist** societies, as in discontinuity with modernity, springing from a decline in confidence about the possibility of universal, rational principles, and manifesting itself in skepticism about progress, objective or scientific truth, or fixed meanings. It is often characterized by eclecticism and self-conscious parody.

postmodernity The sum complex of reactions to and developments of the condition of **modernity**, including socioeconomic and technological changes, like the emergence of the Internet, the consumer society, the preponderance of mass media and its enormous influence and susceptibility to politically motivated manipulation, and the continued growth of **capitalism**, but also characterized by skepticism about grand explanatory schemas, suspicion of authorities, playfulness with regard to traditions and the use of signs, and vibrant and highly eclectic pluralism, for example.

poststructuralism The view that all perceptions, concepts, and claims to truth are constructed in language, as structuralism argued, but that they are transient and are the products of contexts (social and psychological) which do not obey structural laws.

potentia obedientialis   Latin phrase meaning the "obediential potency" of human nature: its potency for divine grace which is "obediential," since dependent on God's good pleasure for its realization.

praeambuli fidei   Presuppositions or preliminaries of faith; the conditions for God's self-communication making itself understood and accepted by human beings.

pragmatic   Practical, aiming at usefulness and effectiveness; in philosophy, relating to **pragmatism**.

pragmatism   A position stressing knowledge derived from experience and experiment for the sake of practical ends determined by interests and values; truth-claims are justifiable as the fulfillment of the end for which the experiment was conducted (i.e., by practical utility and consequences).

praxis   Greek term for action, practical ability, or practice, used in **Marxism** and adopted by Latin American **liberation theology** to denote a combination of action and reflection aimed at transforming an oppressive situation.

prefigure   To represent or indicate beforehand; used of Old Testament persons and events as they point forward to and are answered by persons and events in the New Testament, for example.

premodern   Of or pertaining to premodernity and patterns of thought, beliefs, culture, practices, and systems prior to the advent of modern thought in the sixteenth and seventeenth centuries.

Presbyterian   Of or pertaining to Presbyterianism, a **Reformed** church tradition, particularly influenced by Calvinism, in which authority is centered upon elders.

pre-thematic   Of or pertaining to subjective states and experiences before they are interpreted in categories; the opposite of **categoreal**.

primate   Member of the mammalian order, primates, including humans, apes, monkeys, and prosimians.

primatial   Relating to the role of leader or primate among the bishops of a church or communion of churches.

process philosophy   Understanding founded by Alfred North Whitehead (1861–1947) which attempts to avoid epistemological skepticism by replacing the **Cartesian** category of substance with the category of actual occasion, which denotes the process of becoming or the weaving together of the inheritances of the past. An actual entity is in the process of becoming a unified perspective on its past.

process theology   Theological movement, following **process philosophy**, which emphasizes notions of movement and becoming (process), rather than being or substance, and which stresses God's dipolarity, capacity to be affected by creation, and persuasive rather than absolute power, and affirms divine participation in process.

procession   In the Christian doctrine of the **Trinity**, derivation (proceeding, procession) of the Son and the Holy Spirit from the Father.

Procleanism   Philosophy of Proclus, **neoplatonist** philosopher of the fifth century CE, and his followers.

procrustean   Resembling, in argument or practice, the mythological character Procrustes ("the Stretcher"), who had two beds, one short and one long, and boasted that they would fit everybody. Procrustes made good his boast by stretching those too short for the short bed (even to death), and severing the feet or legs of those too tall for the long bed. Someone is procrustean if they try to distort evidence to fit a theory, for example.

programmatic   Setting out the future course of a program of inquiry or the elaboration of a position.

prolegomena   Work of a preliminary, introductory nature, preparing for fuller treatment.

Protestant   Name for those Christians and churches which separated from the Roman Catholic Church at the **Reformation**, and for other churches and groups descended from them; of or pertaining to such Christians and churches and to Protestantism.

Protestant scholasticism   The approach and theology of post-**Reformation** Protestant theologians who were concerned to systematize and elaborate the theology of the reformers in a manner resembling the method of the medieval schools.

providential   Of or pertaining to providence, the divine governance of the world and human affairs.

psychoanalysis   Approach to the diagnosis of psychological problems of a subject, involving the interpretation of dreams, literature, and everyday life. **Freudian** psychoanalysis explains neuroses in terms of a conflict between love and hate caused by disparate, fantastic images, themselves derived from a parental figure and projected onto the self or others.

psychotherapy   Treatment of disorders of personality or emotion by psychological methods.

Pure Land Buddhism   Devotional form of Buddhism centered on the Buddha Amitabha, who founded a Buddha-land, of which he became the ruler. Appeal to Amida, as he is known, at the moment of death, concentration on Amida for ten moments, or faith in the efficacy of a vow of commitment to Buddha are held to cancel the karmic consequences of evil deeds and lead to rebirth in the Pure Land, in which everything is conducive to Buddhist enlightenment.

quantum mechanics   Describe the behavior of quanta – discrete subatomic quantities of energy in the form of waves or particles (e.g., light); associated with Max Planck (1858–1947), Nils Bohr (1885–1967), Ernest Schrödinger (1887–1961), and Werner Heisenberg (1901–76), among others.

Quran   Or Koran: holy book of Islam, understood to be God's Word revealed to Mohammad in a form of Arabic, written down by him and arranged after his death.

radical   Of action, change, or an idea: going to the origin or root, relating to or impacting upon what is fundamental, far-reaching in scope.

radical evil   Account of the origins and nature of evil which stresses its reality as such, over against attempts to explain evil actions or events in terms of other principles.

rationality   That which is characterized by conformity with reason, adhering to qualities of thought such as intelligibility, consistency, coherence, order, logical structure, completeness, testability, and simplicity.

realism   A philosophical position (in opposition to nominalism) affirming that a universal category (e.g., animal) may have a reality outside its individual manifestations (e.g., lion, cow) and independently of human consciousness; or a philosophical position (in opposition to **idealism**) affirming that reality exists independently of the human knower.

reason Deliberative faculty of the mind capable of argument or demonstrative inference and used in making judgments in matters of conduct and action (practical reason); faculty of the mind concerned with ascertaining truth, and which, above and beyond the faculty of understanding, grasps first principles intuitively, and regulates the activity of the understanding; the faculty of reason may be considered the unity or hybrid of these two kinds of reason.

recapitulation Summing up and fulfillment of past events in salvation history in the life, death, and resurrection of Jesus Christ; the bringing together of all things under Christ as their head.

redemption Literally, buying back; a financial metaphor (relating originally to ransom payments and slave-buying) for **atonement**, reconciliation, or salvation; the act or process by which liberation from bondage (described variously in Christian theology as sin, death, the law, the devil, the world) takes place.

reductionism Explanation of complex data in inappropriately simple terms; in theology, often referring to the attempt to explain beliefs (e.g., referring to God) in terms that do not assume the reality of God (e.g., in psychological, sociological, philosophical, or other terms).

reference Relation pertaining between instances of language-use and the world; for example, the relation between a name and the thing named.

Reformation Movement for the reform of the Roman Catholic Church, beginning in the sixteenth century, resulting in the formation of independent **Protestant** churches.

Reformed Of or pertaining to churches stemming from the "second Reformation" and privileging the theology of John Calvin and those who developed his work (Calvinists); of or pertaining to theology and practice in the tradition of Calvin and Calvinism.

relativism A position holding the impossibility of obtaining final, eternal truth or values, and stressing diversity among individuals, groups, cultures, and periods; sometimes also ruling out the comparison of truth-claims and values.

relativity theory Comprises Albert Einstein's (1879–1955) theory of special relativity, according to which uniformly moving observers with different velocities measure the same speed of light, from which Einstein deduced that the length of a system shrinks, and its clocks slow at speeds approaching that of light; and his theory of general relativity, according to which the geometry of space-time may vary from place to place – a variation or curvature associated with the presence of gravitational fields which, acting through the curvature, can slow clocks and bend light rays.

religiosity Religious feeling or belief, especially when affected.

representation, crisis of Collapse of confidence in the possibility of true representation of reality in the arts, associated with **modernism**.

repression In Freudian **psychoanalysis**, a defensive mechanism whereby memories, perceptions, or feelings that would arouse the forbidden are banished from the conscious to the unconscious mind.

revelation Disclosure of what was previously unknown; in theology, usually the disclosure to human beings by God of his nature, salvation, or will. Special revelation is the disclosure by extraordinary means of truths about God otherwise hidden from humanity in its sinful condition.

Romantic idealism See German **idealism**.

sacralize Make sacred.

sacrament Action, ceremony, or celebration in which created things become channels and symbols of God's activity and promises (in Roman Catholicism: baptism, **Eucharist**, confirmation, matrimony, holy orders, penance, and extreme unction; in **Protestantism**, usually baptism and Eucharist); more widely used to refer to the ways in which the presence of God and salvation are communicated through action and material reality; Jesus Christ as the supreme instantiation of this activity.

sacramental Of or pertaining to a **sacrament** or the nature of a sacrament; a sacrament-like sign not recognized as a sacrament proper (e.g., the sign of the cross, or saying grace at meal times).

sacraments, dominical The sacraments instituted by Jesus Christ (the Lord – hence "dominical," from the Latin *dominus*, "Lord"), namely baptism and the **Eucharist**.

sacramentum mundi Literally, "the sacrament of the world," the whole created order seen as a sign of divine blessing and grace.

Sacred Heart of Jesus The physical heart of Jesus Christ as a symbol of his redemptive love in the Roman Catholic tradition of devotion to the Sacred Heart; the tradition emphasizes "reparation" for outrages committed against this love. Often the subject of popular devotional art.

samsaric Of or pertaining to *samsara*, the cycle of birth and death as a consequence of action (the causal principle of which is karma) in Asian religions; from the **Sanskrit** for "wandering."

sanctification Process of being brought into a state of holiness.

Sanctification movement Movement in Protestant pietistic evangelicalism promoting the pursuit of holiness.

Sanskrit Ancient Indo-European language, in which are written religious texts in the Hindu and Buddhist traditions.

satisfaction, theory of Theory of the **atonement**, first propounded by Anselm of Canterbury (1033–1109), wherein the death of Christ as God and man is understood as a sacrifice of infinite merit that alone offers full satisfaction for the infinite offense of human sin against an infinite God.

scholasticism Education, methods, and theology of the thirteenth-century Christian thinkers often called the Medieval Schoolmen, and of their followers in later times, notable especially for their application of logic to theology to reveal the underlying agreement between contradictory statements in philosophical, medical, legal, and theological texts and so to attain the core inner truth to which those texts bore witness. Scholasticism underwent a revival in Roman Catholicism in 1850–1960; see **neoscholasticism**.

scientism Usually a pejorative term, describing the view that the methods and objects of inquiry recognized by science are the only proper elements of any philosophical or other inquiry.

second order Of or pertaining to discourse that describes the grammar, structure, or logic of first-order discourse – that is, the ordinary language of a linguistic community (e.g., the language of the church, in which Christians pray, praise, and make claims about Jesus Christ).

Second Vatican Council See **Vatican II**.

secularism Position advocating the elimination of religious influence in the state, social institutions, and the understanding of reality as a whole.

secularization Process whereby religious influence is progressively eliminated from the state, social institutions, and accounts of reality.

semiotic Of or pertaining to signs.

semi-Pelagianism Usually a pejorative term to describe positions close to Pelagianism – the belief that humans are required to, and thus are capable of, earning some merit before God by their own effort.

seminary Ecclesiastical establishment for the study of theology and for the training of those intending the Christian ministry or priesthood.

sensus fidelium Latin for the sense of the faithful – the intuitive grasp that Christian believers as a whole have for those affirmations and practices that are in accord with the Christian faith.

sentient Capable of sensory perception.

shamanism Form of magico-religious life of society found in Siberia and Inner Asia, which centers on the person of the Shaman as the master of ecstasy. Shamanism is a technique of ecstasy, usually coexisting with other forms of magic and religion but not defined by them. The Shaman specializes in a trance state in which his soul is believed to leave his body and ascend to the sky or descend to the underworld.

Shariah Revealed law of Islam as set forth in the **Quran** and Hadith and elaborated by analytical principles by various schools of jurists.

Shinto Complex of religious myths and rituals indigenous to Japan and centered on tutelary deities; later reinterpreted and to some extent combined with Buddhism; the two were officially separated in 1868 but in practice continue to combine in new Japanese religions.

simulacrum Material representation of a person or thing; a thing having the appearance but not the substances or proper qualities of what it represents; a deceptive imitation.

slavophil Of or pertaining to love for Slavic people and culture.

social theology Theological reflection on human experiences and problems in a social context.

socialism Political and economic theory which advocates the communal ownership and control of the means of production, capital, land, and property; in **Marxist** theory, a transitional state between the overthrow of **capitalism** and the realization of **communism**.

sociality State or quality of being social; social interaction; disposition or actualization of society formation.

sociobiology Study of the biological, ecological, and evolutionary aspects of social behavior, which explains the structures and phenomena of human society in terms of biological factors and mechanisms.

sola fide Abbreviation of the **Reformation** watchword, *sola fide Christi* – "by faith in Christ alone."

sola scriptura   Latin for "scripture alone": another principle of the Reformers, meaning that only scripture, and not tradition, was the authority for the church.

Sophia   Greek for wisdom; the personification of wisdom; the **hypostasis** of the wisdom of God, often identified in Christian theology with the **Logos**, **Word**, or Son.

soteriology   Branch of theology concerned with the doctrine of salvation (or reconciliation, **atonement**, or **redemption**).

spatialization   Substitution of an abstract and purely immanent ordering of reality for the dimension of time and its participation in eternity; the privileging of the abstract over the temporal and eternal.

speculative theology   Theology that seeks greater understanding of orthodox Christian beliefs by offering possible explanations that go beyond what is explicitly claimed in established theological warrants.

statism   Subservience in religious matters to political expediency; government by the state, especially centralized state administration and government.

steady-state theory   Theory of the universe that proposes that the universe is isotropic (has the same physical properties in all directions), and essentially unchanging when viewed on a large scale, since matter is continuously generated to counteract the universe's expansion.

stoicism   School of philosophy founded and taught in the Stoa (or "porch" – a lecture hall) in Athens by Zeno (335–263 BCE); form of **materialist pantheism** which sees God as the energy pervading and sustaining the natural world and as the rationality or **Logos** which orders it, and which emphasizes living in conformity with this natural order; best known for teaching detachment from desires and passions in the interests of self-sufficiency and imperturbability.

subjectivism   Approach to knowledge focusing on the knowing subject rather than the object to be known, emphasizing the contribution to knowledge of the knower's mental constitution and states and denying the possibility of affirming truth objectively; or, an approach to aesthetics and ethics emphasizing values as reflections of the feelings, attitudes, and responses of the individual and as having no independent or objective validity.

subjectivity   State of being a self-conscious, thinking agent; or, state of being personally involved so that one's perceptions and understanding are relative to one's individual experience or characteristics.

sublime   A concept deeply embedded in eighteenth-century **aesthetics**, describing that which exceeds our perceptual and imaginative grasp, which is vast, exhilarating, majestic, and which arouses pride, awe, and sometimes terror. Linked by Immanuel Kant (1724–1804) with the realization of moral freedom.

substance   Permanent nature of a thing in which properties or attributes inhere; a particular kind of matter.

supernatural   Relating to that which is conceived to be beyond the natural order, or beyond nature unaided by grace.

supernaturalism   Thought dealing with that which is conceived to be beyond the natural order.

symbiosis   Interaction between two dissimilar organisms living in close physical association, especially where mutually beneficial.

symbol Thing which represents or recalls something else, either by possessing analogous attributes or by association.

symbolic Of or pertaining to a **symbol**; in **poststructuralism**, the world constituted by linguistic signs in which subjectivity is realized and expressed.

symbolism Use of symbols; the meaning of a thing used as a **symbol**.

syncretism Attempted fusion or reconciliation of different religious or philosophical traditions, tenets, or practices.

synoptic Referring to the Gospels of Matthew, Mark, and Luke; more generally, describing a combined or comprehensive view or presentation of something.

systematic theology Type of theology seeking to give a rationally ordered, comprehensive account of the doctrines of a religion and their interrelationships.

Talmud Body of detailed commentary and elaboration on parts of the Mishnah (the Jewish legal and theological system completed ca. 200), often in the form of debates and dialogues between rabbis.

teleology Theory that certain phenomena or acts are to be explained in terms of their end (*telos*), purpose, or intention; explanation in such terms.

telos See **teleology**.

temporality State of being in time.

textual reasoning Reasoning concerning issues of practice that is shaped by close interaction with the authoritative texts of a tradition in accordance with the way they are read in that tradition (their "plain sense"), especially a religious tradition; in particular, as practiced by contemporary Jewish scholars and philosophers in relation to the texts of the **Talmud**.

textuality Distinctive quality of a particular text or discourse; the identifying qualities of a text.

theism Belief in, or set of beliefs about, God.

thematized Brought to explicit reflection and understanding in terms of a theme or subject (c.f. **categoreal**).

theocracy Literally, rule by God; an institution or society which is governed by its religious institutions.

theologia crucis Latin for "theology of the cross"; a theology that judges all affirmations about God and humanity by the paradoxical revelation of the crucified God – Jesus Christ crucified.

theopaschite Understanding that the divine nature of Jesus Christ suffered on the cross, originally held by a sixth-century group who held that Jesus had one nature after the union of his divine and human natures in the **Incarnation**; by extension, of any theology which asserts the suffering of God.

Thomism Term for the theology of, and the schools of thought stemming from the thought of, Thomas Aquinas (1226–74).

threefold ministry Ordained ministry of the church structured in three orders, after the model of the early church, the orders being bishops, priests, and deacons.

Titanism Name coined by Hans Urs von Balthasar (1905–88) to denote the attribution of the rich fulfillment, understood in Christianity to be offered in Jesus Christ, to human nature as an inherent possibility.

Torah In Judaism, the will of God as revealed in Mosaic Law.

tradition Socially embodied argument about correct doctrine and or best practice extended over time; the handing on of received doctrines or practices.

traditionalism Position appealing to past forms of a religion, culture, or other form of belief, understanding, or behavior; more specifically, a reaction to **modernism** and the **Enlightenment**, holding that religious knowledge cannot be derived from human reason or experience but only through faith in divine **revelation** communicated through tradition.

transcendence Existing, going, or leading beyond; of God, referring to his being beyond all created reality; of self, going beyond one's present state, often by knowing, willing, or some other mode of consciousness.

transcendental condition Something transcending subjective experience that is the necessary condition of the possibility of that experience.

transcendental method Philosophical approach that begins with an understanding of experience and interpretation as made possible by transcendental conditions.

transcendental philosophy Usually referring to the philosophy of Immanuel Kant (1724–1804) and his followers.

transcendental theology Theology influenced by Immanuel Kant (1724–1804), which understands God as the ultimate horizon and term of the subject's self-transcending movement in experience.

transcendental Thomism Theology that seeks to express **Thomism** in terms of **transcendental conditions**.

transfiguration Change in appearance or form – often into a more glorious or elevated state. In particular, the glorious change in appearance of Jesus on Mount Tabor as narrated in the synoptic gospels.

triduum mortis Three days between Maundy Thursday evening and the end of Holy Saturday, in which churches remember the passion, death, and descent of Christ to the dead in the liturgy.

Trinity In Christian understanding, the three divine persons – Father, Son, and Holy Spirit – sharing one undivided divine nature subsisting wholly in each person. The **immanent Trinity** is the Trinity considered in itself in the interrelationship of the three persons. A social doctrine of the **Trinity** conceives the Trinity in interpersonal terms as a society of three.

triptych Set of three writing tablets hinged together; picture(s), carving(s), or relief(s) set on three hinged panels and often used as an altarpiece; a set of three pieces of art connected thematically or intended to be performed together or in sequence.

Triune Of or pertaining to God as **Trinity**.

tropic Of or pertaining to a trope: a figure of speech consisting of the use of a word or phrase in a different sense to its normal use.

typology Construal of historical or textual relations between two events or persons separated in the stream of a narrative, especially in the Bible considered as an overarching story, whereby an earlier event or person (the "type") is seen to resemble the later event or person (the "antitype") to a limited degree in form or the divine action seen in both, which is realized more fully in the later person or event; classification in categories or "types."

underdetermination Bringing into being of a system or state of affairs where not every outcome is the necessary consequence of the conditions existing at the outset, thus allowing a measure of freedom or choice.

Unitarian Of or pertaining to Unitarianism: an understanding and religious movement associated with rejection of the doctrine of the **Trinity**, denying a differentiated understanding of the persons in God, and denying the divinity of Jesus Christ and of the Holy Spirit.

universalism Understanding of the all-encompassing nature of salvation, including the belief that ultimately all will be saved.

Urgrund Primal basis of a reality.

Vatican II The Second Vatican Council of the Roman Catholic Church (1962–5), held in the Vatican and characteristically associated with an attitude of renewed openness to the church's cultural and ecumenical environment, and with a desire to adapt its laws and institutions to the times.

velleity Least or low degree of volition for something without any effort or action towards its realization.

vera religio Latin for true religion: the notion that of all the varied religious cults of the world, Christianity is the one wherein God has clearly revealed himself and offers salvation.

vita Christiana Latin for the Christian life.

voluntarism Understanding of human action focusing on the role of the will in determining action and behavior and stressing human freedom; theology which stresses the role of the human will in salvation, or the overwhelming and unqualified significance of the divine will in creation and redemption.

wisdom theology Conception of theology as concerned with meaning, interpretation, and truth in relation to life and community pursued in conformity with the identity and purposes of God and oriented to the future; a theology which seeks, exhaustively and collaboratively, to engage with apparently separate and opposed modes of thought, interpretation, and practice in pursuit of the wisdom of God available for our transformation.

womanist theology Reflection on religion and religious experience from the perspective of Black women.

Word The divine **Logos**, or second person of the **Trinity**, who became incarnate in Jesus Christ; in **Reformed** theology, the presence of God speaking through the reading and preaching of the Bible; the Bible as the communication of God to humanity or vehicle of that communication.

Yahweh The Hebrew Tetragrammaton (the name of God given to Moses in Exodus 3: 14) with vowels added that are thought most likely to represent its vocalization.

Zeitgeist German word meaning the spirit of the age: the mood, ethos, or aesthetic, moral, political, and intellectual instincts of a people in a particular period.

Index

Printed and bound by CPI Group (UK) Ltd, Croydon, CR0 4YY